C000008805

A good master teaches that it is a privilege to be taught by him and that what he has to teach is itself an exaltation.

Charles Morgan, *Liberties of the Mind*

Just as I am – Thy LOVE unknown
Has broken every barrier down –
Now to be Thine, yea Thine alone,

*To Robert Ewins, Don Gibb, Denis Grundy and Joe Rich—
four good masters, because it was indeed a privilege and I was exalted.*

O Lamb of GOD, I come!

*My biggest (and incalculable) debt as always with my books is to my family,
especially Barbara, whose support has been constant.*

JUST
AS I
AM

Published
2017.

A life of

J.R. Darling

CONTENTS

ILLUSTRATIONS

PREFACE

It is actually much harder to write well about someone you admire: dismissing Althusser, ridiculing Martin Amis, diminishing Lucien Goldman—child's work. But while it is easy enough to assert that Camus was a great writer, Kolakowski a brilliant philosopher, Primo Levi our greatest Holocaust memoirist and so on, if you wish to explain precisely why these men matter so much, and what influence they exerted, then you have to think a little harder.

Tony Judt (with Timothy Snyder), *Thinking the Twentieth Century*

The subject of this book was admired (or even loved) by numerous people. In Tony Judt's terms, he was a man who mattered much and was very influential. This book explains how and why that was. He first came across my radar in late 1969 during my Diploma of Education at the University of Melbourne. At the conclusion of a lecture in the Redmond Barry building, Faculty of Education staff distributed copies of *Melbourne Studies in Education, 1968–1969*. I recall bundles of the books being unpacked and passed back up the rows. As we teacher trainees thumbed through our copies, the title of the first essay caught my eye: 'Educational recollections of the thirties', by Sir James Darling. What particularly attracted me was not so much the surname as the date. Twelve or so months earlier my arts honours thesis had encompassed part of this decade and, after fifteen months or so poring over newspapers and documents, and conducting interviews, here was yet another memoir of that period. The thesis and my final-year study of the European interwar dictatorships had left me with an abiding fascination for the 1930s—which seemed then to be a decade of wasted opportunity and dashed hopes (although not, as I was to discover, in Darling's life). With my student years shortly to end, a teaching appointment (and income) beckoned. I put aside Darling's recollections until later. Fast forward to 1983, and I was a lecturer in the Faculty of Education at Monash University in the area of educational administration—now renamed educational leadership, thanks to the currency accorded the second of those two words. I was trying to push the boundaries in this scholarly field and, one morning when I buttonholed my colleague Alan Gregory with a lament about the dearth of real people in the field's literature, I must have muttered something about biography as a way of breathing life into dry bones. Alan cut me short by mentioning Darling and his memoirs, *Richly Rewarding*, and that if a biography was a genuinely serious interest, then he would sound out the man himself (whom he knew). Tentatively, I replied affirmatively. Shortly afterwards, the subject of this book agreed to meet me and the long march to this publication commenced.

Life's trajectories rarely unfold uneventfully. Sadness and hope were intermingled while writing this book, with hope eventually triumphing—next to his autograph on my copy of *Richly Rewarding*, Darling penned 'In hope'. On the sad side of the equation, Darling died before seeing the fruits of my labour. My research and writing had been squeezed in and around the normal work imperatives of a faculty. Periodic breaks from the routine in the guise of sabbatical (or Outside Studies Program) leave granted by Monash University were invaluable. So also was the generosity of the Australian Research Council (and its predecessor the Australian Research Grants Committee) in providing financial assistance to defray archival travel costs. Some months after Darling's death, a second traumatic death occurred: my youngest daughter. The fog of the pain of her passing took an age to lift. The strain of concentrating on anything, let alone researching and writing, was unendurable. Oddly, appointments to senior faculty administrative responsibilities eventually helped me to reconnect. Incumbency of a succession of such posts, however, put completion of the second half of this book on hold for more than a decade. After relocating to Cambridge in 2008, I resumed the information gathering and writing while simultaneously being head of faculty for three-and-a-half years.

The question that this book tries to answer is: how did it happen that the son of the proprietor of an unprepossessing, struggling and insignificant turn-of-the-twentieth-century English preparatory school in Kent ended up 19,000 kilometres away in a foreign country where, in his ninth decade, he was feted at its bicentenary as one of 200 nation-building Australians? The short story is as follows. Like many members of his social class and background, Darling was a product of English public schooling, in which he followed the conventional route from preparatory school to boarding school and university, except that his undergraduate course was delayed by army service in the final year of World War I and shortened by his need as an ex-serviceman to support himself financially in employment. Thanks to a chance event after eight years as a schoolmaster, his vocation took him to the southern hemisphere. If his English education pathway was conventional, part of his experience of it was unconventional: he participated in a program in political education just prior to heading off to the war that marked him for life. Once in Australia, he became an innovative headmaster. His 1930s reforming zeal revitalised the rather sleepy and isolated school to which he had been appointed and enabled it to outstrip its rivals in the esteem stakes to become an object of national envy. Frustrated by the impact of war and postwar shortages, he then marked time for most of the 1940s. Consolation for his thwarted ambitions during this low period came as state and federal avenues of influence opened up. Then followed a second wind: renewed innovation in three substantial ventures in the 1950s when the Commonwealth government's call on his expertise and time increased significantly. Progressively over four decades or so (1940s–1980s), Darling developed an extensive public profile, an impressive reputation and a range of capabilities encompassing in addition to schooling, higher education, broadcasting, immigration, road safety, ecumenical and social outreach, international education and the performing arts. While he moved in antipodean elite and ruling circles, he managed to retain a well-honed liberal outlook and conscience-driven integrity in his exercise of a humanising influence on public policies and decisions.

The other part of the story is about how two worlds meet in the life of this man: the UK and Australia. The first of these countries at the time of his birth (1899) was at the pinnacle of imperial grandeur; the second was within the imperial fold, just about to federate but yet to forge a national identity. Fast-forward 96 years and the first, divested of empire, was still seeking a post-imperial role; the second was about five years shy of a referendum on whether or not to become a republic. Darling lived just under a third of his life in the land of his birth and the remainder in his adopted country. What began as a self-chosen temporary sojourn in Australia ended up as a permanent relocation. During six-and-a-half decades in Australia, he returned home to the English and Scottish sides of his family on eight occasions (1934, 1939, 1948, 1955, 1962, 1968, 1977 and 1987). Between the year of his arrival (1930) and the year of his death (1995), he drew on the best of the attributes offered by both worlds. Each time that he returned to Australia he brought back memories of ways of doing things at Home, while each time he departed Australia he carried a deepening reservoir of experiences and commitments that tempered his understanding of what he encountered in the UK. 'Home' as a constant point of cultural reference began to fade and in the end Australia was home. If the continuity of an individual's identity comprises a shifting balance of inherited and acquired characteristics, the former surrender space progressively throughout a life to the latter. With Darling, the acquisition side of that continuity was sourced from a society and culture separate from what he had inherited. But there was a larger scale changing balance of continuity occurring simultaneously. Through his eyes one detects evidence of a larger drama playing out: the changing relations between two independent nations, as the younger and brasher of the two divests more and more of its British-ness. Darling's own struggle to come to terms with his Australian-ness, then, parallels his adopted country's emergence from the chrysalis of nationhood to acquire a sense of its distinctiveness. Moreover, he was an important contributor to his adopted country's growing awareness of itself, directly through his own responsibilities as a public man and indirectly through his educational influence on numerous Australians who became leaders in their fields—as the realisation dawned that for every decision that Australia's citizens made they did not have to turn to the Mother Country as their default reference point.

The title of this book is taken from the opening line of Darling's favourite hymn, written by Charlotte Elliott, the first stanza of which reads:

> Just as I am, without one plea
> but that thy blood was shed for me,
> and that thou bidst me come to thee,
> O Lamb of God, I come.

In a religious sense, 'Just as I am' captures the idea of a Christian soul exposed to the judgement of his or her Lord free of all pretension, pride, hypocrisy, vainglory and fantasy. To be naked before one's maker also betokens authenticity, as if the believer says: Take me as you find me; I cannot be other than what I know that I am. As such, 'Just as I am' goes to the heart of another, parallel struggle in the theatre of Darling's mind throughout his life: his attempt to stay true to self, which was expressed in his family's motto: *Esto quod esse videris* (be what you seem to be). In this internal conversation, Darling lived in thrall to his conscience, with thraldom being understood positively as a compass rather than as a shackle. Necessarily, all biographers develop distinctive understandings of their subjects and they adopt particular approaches to representing the life and work of those individuals. The form taken by such representations is shaped in significant measure by the media for self-expression available to, and utilised by, their biographical subjects. As far as sense of selfhood is concerned, the orthodox avenue of access has been the diary or journal. And yet apart from a few sporadic attempts (in 1929, and in the 1960s–1980s), Darling mostly didn't maintain a diary—which reflects the fact he was (and saw himself as) a man of action. His main means of reflecting on his actions and his feelings about those actions (his way of thinking aloud, if you like) was the voluminous correspondence that he maintained. Although his numerous letters served all kinds of instrumental purposes, depending on the particular trigger for putting pen to paper and the addressees, these (particularly his letters to intimates from the early 1930s onwards) provided the means for him to work through his action-related ideas and beliefs, and to verbalise the internal conflicts that these created for him. Not surprisingly, then, one catches him thinking aloud in so many of his letters and striving (by reasoning step by step through the possibilities that he perceived) to convince himself, as much as his interlocutor, of what was right, good or proper. What is genuinely surprising about his letter-writing, however, are two things: the extraordinary sense of candour that he adopts with his correspondents, and the vast range of them with whom he chooses to be frank, because many of them were people whom he had never met and was unlikely ever to meet. With such frankness, Darling was trusting almost to the point of naivety.

The approach adopted in the book is to elucidate the range of contexts (educational and non-educational) in which Darling lived his life, and pursued his plans and activities. The reason for this decision is to communicate accurately how particular sets of circumstances imposed limits on what he was able to do, while also opening up possibilities and giving him achievable options. I have then conveyed what he saw himself as trying to do and why, and also how others perceived him. I am also interested in what caused him to be the person that he was, bearing in mind the broad trajectory of his life and the point made earlier about shifting continuity. Clearly, his upbringing and his educational experiences shaped him, but numerous subsequent influences also moulded him. In respect of what he did and achieved, I have been mindful about particular contributions that he made to Australian society in key spheres of his life, and where possible have communicated a sense of their impact and significance, both immediate and lasting. On this point, a number of his schemes took off, while others were lead balloons that fell to earth. But if an assessment of a life's work is to be properly appraised, then failures have to be considered as well as successes. Needless to say, a biographer's decisions about all of these matters are complicated by the fact that individuals do not act alone: a number of the schemes and ideas documented were of Darling's own making, while in others he worked jointly with colleagues to bring them to fruition, and in still others he inaugurated them and then bowed out and left someone else to follow through. These considerations have influenced my partitioning of the material into chapters. First, Darling's life has been divided into three parts, each proportionately about a third of his life: Part I is about his years in England before making Australia his permanent home; Part II covers the period of his headmastership at Geelong Grammar School— the centrepiece of his working life; and Part III is about his career switch to the Australian Broadcasting Commission and other public engagements until his death. Within these divisions, the chapters are mostly chronologically sequenced, although from Part II Darling's life is grouped thematically into his school and non-school commitments or I have split discussion of a time period into two parts in adjacent chapters. Finally, within the overall chronological arrangement, occasional chapters are devoted to critical episodes or events.

A number of people have helped shape my thinking about this book. Thanks are extended to the friends, colleagues and Darling family members who have commented at some stage of the writing on all or some of the draft. They include Geoffrey Blainey, David Conolly, John Darling, Colin Evers, Don Gibb, Jane Gray, John Gray, Peter Gray, Robert Gray, Alan Gregory, Barbara Gronn, Cameron Hazlehurst, Ken Inglis, Lawrence Ingvarson, Graeme Johanson, Morris le Fleming, Andrew Lemon, Tony Melville, Michael Collins Persse, Tony Ryan, Dick Selleck, Geoff Serle, Ben Shearer, Caroline Shearer, Ivan Sutherland, Liza Sutherland, Ged White, Marie White and Richard Wilson. I am very grateful to Helen Clements for her secretarial help. I also wish to thank Geelong Grammar School, the Monash University Faculty of Education, the University of Melbourne and members of the Darling family for their generous financial support, without which this publication would not have been possible.

My thanks are also extended to the following organisations that kindly provided me with access to archival material (summarised in full, with collections of private paper holdings accessed, in the bibliography): Australian College of Education (Adelaide); Australian Council of Churches (Melbourne); Australian

Council for Educational Research (Melbourne); Bodleian Library (Oxford); Charterhouse School (Godalming, Surrey); Christ's Hospital (Horsham, Sussex); Geelong Grammar School (Corio and Timbertop); Godalming Corporation (Godalming, Surrey); Headmasters' Conference (London); Highfield School (Liphook, Hampshire); Lambeth Palace Library (London); La Trobe Library (Melbourne); Melbourne City Council (Melbourne); Melbourne Grammar School (Melbourne); Merchant Taylors' School (Crosby, Lancashire); National Archives (London); National Archives of Australia (Canberra, Melbourne and Sydney); National Library of Australia (Canberra); National Newspaper Museum (London); Newington College (Sydney); Oriel College (Oxford); Repton School (Repton, Derby); Scotch College (Melbourne); State Library of Victoria (Melbourne); Toc H (Melbourne); University of Birmingham (Birmingham); University of Cambridge Library (Cambridge); University of Melbourne (Melbourne); Victorian Public Record Office (Melbourne); Wesley College (Melbourne).

Three people were especially helpful during the production of this book. The publisher, Sandy Grant, who believed in the project from the get-go, provided strong support throughout, exercised patience in answering my numerous queries, calmed my anxieties and retained his sense of humour. Lachean Humphreys, my managing editor, was equally patient, enthusiastic, delighted to be steering the project and was always helpful. Susan Keogh, who copy-edited the text, brought a depth of experience and firmness to the task, was always prompt and was diplomatic when I took issue with her judgement. She saved me from numerous grammatical infelicities, smoothed my (occasional) crudities of expression and made the text more accessible to the reader. I owe her a big debt.

ACRONYMS AND ABBREVIATIONS

A list of acronyms and abbreviations used solely in the notes appears at the start of the Notes section.

ABC   Australian Broadcasting Commission (later Corporation)
ABCB   Australian Broadcasting Control Board
ACER   Australian Council for Educational Research
APS   Associated Public Schools
ARSC   Australian Road Safety Council
ATS   Amalgamated Television Services
CPS   Commonwealth Public Service
GGS   Geelong Grammar School
GTC   General Television Corporation
HWT   Herald & Weekly Times
IARTV   Incorporated Association of Registered Teachers of Victoria
OGG   Old Geelong Grammarian
OSC   Oversea Settlement Committee
OTC   Officer Training Corps
PNG   Papua and New Guinea
RSL   Returned Services League (later Returned & Services League)
SOA   Senior Officers' Association
SSO   Sydney Symphony Orchestra
TC   Television Corporation
UAP   United Australia Party

I

ONLY ENGLAND
1899–1930

Only England could have produced him.

Oscar Wilde, *The Picture of Dorian Grey*

1

VICTORIAN FAMILY, EDWARDIAN BOYHOOD

1899–1912

These days we think of Edwardian Britain as the time of the lotus eaters, the decade or more of prosperity and pleasure before the Armageddon of 1914. Happy cockneys spent Bank Holiday Mondays in Margate or at the funfair on Hampstead Heath. The metropolitan middle classes 'dressed' for dinner. In the provinces, clerks and shopkeepers worked hard and lived well. The aristocracy and the very rich hunted in winter, shot during the autumn and played tennis under the endless blue skies of spring and summer. All that happened. But Edward's reign began in a mood of national uncertainty. Victoria's death had disturbed the confidence that comes with continuity.

Roy Hattersley, *The Edwardians*

On the afternoon of Thursday, 6 February 1896, Augustine (or Austen) Major Darling of Blairlodge, Polmont, Scotland, was married to Jane Baird Nimmo of Falkirk at Westbank, her father's residence (Jane was referred to by the Nimmos as Jeannie). The ceremony was conducted in the drawing room. He was thirty-eight and she was twenty-five. The happy event (which was also her birthday) was headlined 'Fashionable Marriage in Falkirk'. A 'large gathering of friends of both families' was present as the Reverend James Aitken, West UP Church, Falkirk, and Canon Watson of Sharnford Rectory, Leicestershire, officiated. Mr E.H. Lacon Watson was groomsman and the bridesmaids were Misses M.R. Nimmo, M.H. Aitken and Flora Sheriff (niece of Jane). There were over 100 'handsome and costly' wedding presents. After the ceremony, the newlyweds departed for London and Oxford. Six weeks later, Jane's father remarked to Emily Darling, Austen's mother, on the occasion of her daughter Ruth's marriage in England to Mr Lacon Watson, how 'happy … our recently married couple appear to be'. On 10 February 1897, the Darlings' first child, Margaret Robertson, was born. Shortly afterwards, the family moved south to Tonbridge, Kent. James Ralph was born next on 18 June 1899 (Waterloo Day), followed by Janet (who lived for only fifteen weeks) in 1902, Mabel in 1903, Jean in 1906 and Austen Eaton in 1908. James was the second child and elder son.[1]

The Edwardian era in which the Darlings' boy was to grow up may have commenced uncertainly, as claimed by Roy Hattersley, and was poised for the changes that he documents, yet its Victorian inheritance was one of continued stratification and hierarchy. Great Britain, *au fin de siècle*, was probably the world's greatest political and military power and certainly one of the wealthiest. Notwithstanding its wealth, about a quarter of Britain's population was destitute. The Darlings were not rich, but part of that 'solid middle class' that comprised about 6 per cent of the population at the end of King Edward VII's reign. On the other hand, 'there were so many kinds of middle class domestic life in Edwardian England', one historian noted, 'that no general picture can serve'. Annual earnings of £150 incurred income tax and about 300,000 households brought in £700 or more—'the level necessary for really comfortable middle class living'. Austen Darling was recalled as a frugal man: he did not own a motor car and only installed a telephone in retirement. The fee income from his small preparatory school was probably sufficient to cover the school's costs, but to feed, clothe and educate his family, and to pay the wages and keep of up to six domestic servants, he must have relied on his wife's income from her marriage trust. At £23,000, Jane's trust fund was substantial. It derived largely from income from Candie, a Robertson–Nimmo property on the Firth of Forth (near the refinery complex now at Grangemouth), a fund that came to Jane about a year after her marriage. (Austen's mother left him an estate valued at £4516 when she died in 1913.) Whatever the couple's exact combined income, when they resided in Tonbridge they could afford to send the weekly family washing to the washerwoman, Mrs Hunt, in Suffolk. Sir James Darling recalled his father saying that in a good year the total family income was £1600. If so, then the Darlings were well beyond the £700 cut-off.[2]

Not only was James born into reasonably comfortable social circumstances, but he also grew up in an era that privileged males. It was not simply that well-educated women (such as James' mother) were yet to be enfranchised politically but, as Virginia Woolf said: 'all the weapons with which an educated man can enforce his opinions' were beyond or nearly beyond the grasp of women, so that 'even if we used them we could scarcely inflict one scratch'. For young males, the formative agencies and institutions that shaped their identities were overwhelmingly paternal: in respect of family, school, university, church, army and empire there were taken-for-granted prototypes and standards of gentlemanly conduct to which young men were expected to conform. And yet despite the submission (or even subjugation) of women, their nurturance (as mothers, sisters and nannies) was equally decisive in determining how young Edwardian middle-class males learnt to be men. On their journey to manhood, boys attained with varying degrees of success the roles expected of them, such as husband, father, officer, schoolmaster and clergyman. In James' case, when striving to live up to the expectations of his parents, particularly those of his father, he struggled; not with paternalism or with gentlemanly ideals as such, but with himself, and he believed that he let down his father.[3]

Within these broad social and cultural assumptions, there are missing pieces in the mosaic of James' childhood. Details of diet and household expenditure patterns, for example, have not survived, and knowledge of family members' health is meagre. For other aspects of their lives there exist only isolated scraps of information. But allowing for this patchiness, the weight of the available evidence suggests that, in an extended family in which everyone knew and accepted their places, there was a breadth and depth of parental love for the five children. Any temptation to dismiss as rose-coloured Sir James Darling's recollection that 'my father and mother were wonderful parents and we all had the happiest of home lives' is belied by the evidence. James' good fortune stemmed from three main features of his family's life. First and foremost, the Darlings were strongly Christian. Second, as a school proprietor's son, James was educated at home, mostly by his father. To the extent that Austen Darling was a model for what his son later became, he was successful; James was not the kind of quisling, for example, that his contemporary, the novelist Graham Greene, confessed to being. As the headmaster's son at Berkhamsted (Hertford), Greene invented stories about cruel beatings at his father's hands to try to curry favour with his friends. Most importantly, for James to be educated in his father's school meant that the potential scarring rigours of boarding schooling were delayed until he was thirteen (and more psychologically robust) instead of having to be confronted from the conventional age of eight. Third, James' family life comprised a large extended 'tribe' (as his mother once described it to her mother-in-law) of siblings, aunts and uncles, cousins, pupils, teachers, friends and domestic servants, the effect of which was to offer the children all manner of adult models and diverse sources of influence. Although knowledge is sketchy about this tribe of Darling and Nimmo forebears, and its impact on James' navigation through the evolving Edwardian world, an invaluable source is *The Darlings of Eyke and the Nimmos of Falkirk*, the outcome of exhaustive research by Morris le Fleming (nephew of Sir James Darling)—who notes that 'hard evidence of the origins of our branch of the family has not been easy to find'.[4]

Confidence about the Darling lineage firms from the late eighteenth century in the persons of James Darling (d. 1809?), possibly a shepherd, and his wife Margaret (née Wilkinson?, 1741?–1800) of Ford Westfield, Northumberland. Their son was Ralph (1786–1866)—except that with James Darling's wife being aged about forty-four or forty-five at Ralph's birth le Fleming comments that, 'although not impossible', this age 'casts doubt on her being his mother'. As a young man, Ralph Darling enlisted in the 11th Light Dragoons (known as the Cherrypickers and later renamed the 11th Hussars), and served in the Peninsula War and at Waterloo. Ralph probably enjoyed 'a certain celebrity status' as a

Waterloo veteran. On the strength of this and while possibly also he was seen as being in need of support, arrangements were likely to have been made by Lady Stanley (of Hooton Hall, Eastham) for Ralph to move to one of her husband's properties. Subsequently Ralph Darling became a tenant farmer on another Stanley property at Winwick. About 1814, he married Jane Ellen Evans (1786–1853) of unknown provenance. Their third child, James George (James Darling's grandfather), was born in 1825. Ralph Darling styled himself as a gentleman (on his son's 1848 baptism certificate) and, after Jane Ellen's death, he described her as 'My Dearest departed wife—One of the best Christians'. His son James George studied at Trinity College, Dublin, and until his death in 1891 he 'held a succession of curacies and livings', including Bethersden, Kent, where he married Louisa Susannah Burnett (1818–1853), daughter of the rector, and Stanton-by-Dale, Derby, where he established a school. After Louisa's death, he married Mary Emily (or Milly) Johnson (1825–1913), of Southport, in September 1854. The following year, James George received his first preferment from the Earl of Derby (Lord Stanley)—sometime Conservative prime minister (1852, 1858–59, 1866–68)—when he succeeded Mr Whittington as rector of St Luke's parish church, Lowton, Lancashire, a living 'much divided formerly by party spirit'. Despite the good wishes of correspondents, the couple's life did not prosper. Emily's first child, Mary Jane (b. 1855), died after six weeks and, even though James George had raised sufficient funds to enlarge the chancel and rebuild the church, her 'delicacy of health' forced them to leave in late 1856. James George had come to Lowton with a glowing testimonial. The rector of Stanton-by-Dale said that he 'evinced theological learning which makes him respected among his own body: possessing talents which would fit him for a polite and educated congregation & which can accommodate themselves with much felicity to a country and illiterate one'. The Earl of Derby regretted 'the loss of your services to the Parish', but he consented to an exchange with the incumbent of a tripartite-endowed living in Eyke, Suffolk, where James George remained for thirty-five years as rector.[5]

Few details survive about Emily Darling's family, other than that it was large and extended, and located in Cheshire and Lancashire. Her daughter Roberta, sister of Austen Darling, recorded that Emily was one of four children, two of whom died of scarlet fever. Emily's father, James Johnson, died in 1826 (aged thirty-five) followed by her sister, in which case at sixteen she was an only child. Portraits of both parents capture them as physically handsome and attractive. Emily's mother, Mrs Margaret Johnson (née Carter, 1799–1870), was believed to have been a friend of the novelist, Mrs Gaskell, and Emily's aunt, Mary Major, after whom she was apparently named (and hence Major as her son's second name), 'took her travelling'. She 'went to operas and concerts—she had many beaux—some because of her well to do uncle and aunt'. Diary entries show Emily to have been a meticulous observer and devoted to her husband, James George. A contemporary described her letters as 'so full of sound piety and good sense'. Six children were born at Eyke: Austen, James Darling's father, was the eldest (b. 1857), followed by Henry Eaton Hodgkinson (b. 1859)—christened after Professor Eaton Hodgkinson, the famous materials engineer, and known to his nephews and nieces as 'Uncle Harry'—Blanche Emily Roberta (b. 1861), or 'Aunt Roberta'; Georgina Margaret (b. 1862); Ruth Emma (b. 1864), 'Aunt Ruth'; and James George Reginald (b. 1867), known as 'Uncle Reggie'. For his part, James George's diary discloses an earnest, even zealous and possibly guilt-ridden, man who experienced difficulties with his father, Ralph. The rector of Winwick had reassured James George in 1855 that:

> so far from entertaining a doubt of your intercourse with Hulme [his father's farm] being prejudicial against [you], we have evident proof that the duties of a son and brother which you have hitherto discharged so faithfully will never operate but in your favour.

While the precise nature of James George's relationship with his father is unclear, he was beside Ralph Darling's deathbed at Tarporley in 1866. 'Father very ill' (12 February), he recorded in his diary. Then, with death imminent, he noted (17 February): 'The last sad look'.[6]

When James George and Emily arrived at Eyke in December 1856 the conditions were primitive. Mary Emily recalled that:

> There were poles in the churchyard & the women dried their clothes there. The churchyard was the village playground & consequently had scarcely any grass in it. We had no house. No school. My late husband built the school first, then we partially restored the Church and built the Rectory.

The new school opened in June 1857. Whereas James George had declared the forerunner of the Eyke Primary School to be 'the mere shadow of a school', his new venture offered at one penny weekly 'in addition to a sound scriptural education such other instruction as will fit [the children] for their respective stations in life'. A sound social order was ensured by his offering of sound morality and bodily conduct. Even though the harshness of 'instant dismissal' awaited children who infringed the school's rules, James George Darling was revered by the children of Eyke. They 'sympathetically led the singing' at his funeral and 'claimed the Rector as their friend'. Their grief, it was said, was 'evident and genuine'. He was 'always ready to come forward as the champion of the poor', a newspaper reporter eulogised, 'but valued their independence as highly as their prosperity'. Intriguingly, some 'very brave letters' written by James George (while he was dying) to his son Austen gave his granddaughter Margaret (James Darling's elder sister) 'a rather different [even more sympathetic?] picture of him' when these were discovered later in the family papers.[7]

If the Darlings were a quintessentially English family, then the Nimmo diaspora was imperial in its reach with, in addition to its home base in Scotland, members scattered in England, Australia, New Zealand and Canada. *The Red Book*, an extensive set of notes compiled by Alexander Nimmo (1782–1859)—the first of four successive Alexander Nimmos—and augmented by his son Alexander (1824–1898), James' maternal grandfather, provides useful information. The early Nimmos were tanners in Falkirk. Each of the Nimmo boys wrote reverently of their father. The first Alexander Nimmo described his father, James Nimmo (1745–1824), as 'of full habit of body till his declining years but never inclined to corpulence' and enjoying 'almost uniform good health'. His father was also 'free from the ambition of making money or rising in the world'. Of his mother, Mary Nimmo (née Russell, b. 1753), Alexander Senior said that she was 'endowed with a little more refinement and taste than was possessed by my Father'. Alexander Senior married Mary Crawford (1787–1866) in December 1817. His writing is sprinkled with such self-improvement virtues as the need to 'impress upon my children that next to habits of serious piety and strict virtue those of sobriety and industry contribute most to comfort and happiness'. He wanted his offspring to refrain from 'self-indulgent propensities' and to practise instead 'the self-denying principles of a virtuous life'. The same tragic spectre of death visited on the Darlings and the Johnsons befell Alexander Senior and Mary Nimmo, only more so: the sole survivor of seven offspring was the second Alexander. In the face of 'inexpressible grief', the Nimmos displayed a similar stoic acceptance of the divine will as had James George Darling: 'Such has been the dispensation of an all wise Providence and it becomes us in humble submission to seek to realize the sanctified effects of its visitations'. Alexander Junior, a lawyer, married twice, first to Helen Russell (1828–1865) in June 1857. They had four children: the third Alexander, James, Catherine and Mary. In 1926, the son of the third Alexander—also christened Alexander (1907–1970), but known as Sandy, James Darling's cousin—emigrated to New Zealand where he farmed, initially on the North Island and later on the South, firstly near Otago and then Canterbury Plain. Earlier in 1882, the third Alexander's brother James Nimmo (1859–1905) had emigrated to Australia, initially to join his uncle John Robertson (general manager of the Scottish Australian Investment Company) on a cattle station about 500 kilometres west of Brisbane, at Mount Abundance near Roma, Queensland. In 1886, he married Mary Lethbridge (1866–1936), great-granddaughter of the early New South Wales Governor Philip Gidley King.[8]

After the death of Helen, the second Alexander Nimmo had married John Robertson's sister, Margaret (1830–1886), in April 1869. They had three children: Jane Baird (James Darling's mother), William (d. 1871) and Margaret Robertson, known as Aunt Peg. When James Darling came to Australia in 1930, he stayed with his Aunt Mary during term holidays, and her third son, another cousin, Harold (or Putt) Nimmo who—after a military career, was a member of the multi-national UN Mission patrolling the India–Pakistan border near Kashmir—became James' close companion. Little is known of

James Darling's maternal grandfather (the second Alexander), except that he too esteemed his own father, believing that 'no man could leave behind him a higher character for truthfulness and uprightness—there was no guile in him—he could not even understand a dishonourable transaction far less do one'. As for the upbringing of his daughter, Jane Baird Nimmo, there is scant knowledge other than that she and her sister Margaret attended a private girls' boarding school (Coed-Bel, in Chislehurst, Kent) and that as a young woman she wanted to be a missionary. Nor is it clear how she met Austen Darling. He had been an assistant master for some years at Clevedon, Somerset, and had then moved north to Blairlodge, a public school in Polmont where, presumably, they were introduced. They were engaged in July 1895. In the eyes of all concerned it was thought to be a good match. John Robertson is said to have recorded in his diary: 'Jeannie says that she wishes to marry Mr. Darling. Such is life!' Miss Nimmo was assured by Emily Darling that Austen 'has never once in the whole course of his career caused us a moment's discomfort'. To be sure, he was 'a splendid fellow', asserted another contemporary, 'absolutely trustworthy & honourable, & most chivalrous, kind & considerate'. In fact, he continued, 'I don't think it is easy to find a better specimen of the best type of English gentleman'.[9]

Austen and Jane Darling probably came to Tonbridge in 1898 where he purchased the goodwill of the Castle School that, until April of that year, had operated in a dwelling in the grounds of Tonbridge Castle, an ancient Norman keep acquired by Tonbridge District Council in 1897. As a rather nondescript preparatory school it was an odd choice, although it had been listed as a 'very successful' school for boys. Some months after James' birth at Kirklands in Dry Hill Park Road at the north end of Tonbridge, his family moved into Clare House, on the London Road, overlooking the grounds of Tonbridge School, where the Castle School commenced in 1900. Not only was he frugal, but Austen Darling was also unambitious and, as Margaret (who had been reading their father's correspondence) later relayed to her brother James during World War II, so too were those in his social circle:

> It struck me so that Daddy's men friends never seemed to write anything, but shooting, games & their difficulties in securing pupils for their more or less moribund schools. They all seemed to have exiguous incomes & considerable financial strain—they never mention politics or principles of education, hardly ever a book or a theatre. Granny always wrote in a fever of anxiety about Daddy's health & Uncle Reggie always abt investments or administration of the family property.

Her brother recalled their father as 'a gentleman in the old sense, always polite and considerate to women, except his sisters, and especially so to servants'. Furthermore:

he was never jealous, or even covetous, he bore no grudges and he thought
the best of other people. He could be and was friends with everyone and was
about the least self-conscious man on earth.

Known to his grandchildren as Bumper, Austen was a tall thin man with a ruddy
facial complexion. He had large hands and feet. He always wore large heavy
boots and walked with a slight stoop. After being educated at Ipswich Grammar
School and Winchester College, Austen read Mods and Greats at Oriel College,
Oxford, where he obtained a third, the basis for his son's claim that his father 'was
more of an athlete than a scholar'.[10]

There is a suggestion that as a boy Austen may have tried for Eton. Such
an ambition for him is perhaps consistent with the aspirations and character of
his father, James George, who not only appears to have had himself baptised
a second time (and whose decision it was to style himself George) but, in the
words of his great-grandson, evinced 'an apparent desire to re-invent himself'.
James George's rather cryptic and equivocal pencilled diary entry for what looks
like 1870 reads: '21 & 22 Eton Examn Austen there', beneath which is the
word 'Failure' written in ink. Austen wanted to be a soldier but was discouraged
by his father. As late as June 1897 he was a lieutenant in the Public School
Volunteers at Blairlodge and later a sergeant major in the 'Olds & Bolds'. Shortly
after his marriage to Jane Nimmo, a school governor asked the Reverend L.R.
Phelps, the Provost of Oriel, how on earth it was that 'with such really wonderful
testimonials' Phelps' erstwhile pupil had not yet got a headmastership and
how, in particular, as a Suffolk man, he could possibly have failed to secure an
appointment at Woodbridge School the year before. Austen's apparent lack of
enterprise accounts in part for the Castle School's rather poor status in the eyes of
its competitors, particularly the more up-market Yardley Court School. Not only
did Austen lack drive but his sense of timing was astray as well. Yardley Court
had opened in September 1898, a year after the Council's purchase of the Castle,
'at the instance' of the Reverend Joseph Wood, the Head of Tonbridge School.
'It has the candid approval of the Governors of Tonbridge School though it does
not form part of Sir Andrew Judd's foundation', proclaimed *Kelly's Directory* for
1909. (Such public school patronage was crucial to the success of preparatory
ventures.) The Castle School had some visibility until about 1906, because the
other directory, *Mate's*, listed both preparatory schools as preparing boys for
Tonbridge and as a 'boon to parents'. The Castle School and its competitor,
therefore, probably began on approximately equal terms, although their fortunes
were to change dramatically, with the former, due mainly to Austen Darling's
parsimony, becoming 'a very badly-off school'.[11]

English preparatory schools increased in number in the last quarter of the
nineteenth century, particularly in seaside resorts, the south-east, London and
the Home Counties, with 'the most representative kind of preparatory school'

located along the south coast, especially in Kent, Sussex and Hampshire. Tonbridge sat astride the River Medway, which flows north-east into the Thames estuary from its source in the Weald, a long and wide stretch of clay and marshland. Historically, Tonbridge had been the principal crossing point of the Medway, a river that was frequently in flood. In 1842 the South Eastern Railway linked Tonbridge with London. The 1890s was a decade of civic zeal and reform, and the town was 'impatient to be free of the stifling restriction of government by Parish Vestry'. After it became an Urban District in 1894, Tonbridge's streets were widened, hovels cleared and drainage installed. The population was 12,736 in 1901, about 3500 of whom were aged ten years and under, with a further 2800 aged twenty-one to thirty. The major employment avenues for men were in the delivery and conveyance of goods, building and construction, agriculture and foods, with domestic service being the main occupation for women (as was also the case nationally). Tonbridge's two other claims to fame were the manufacture of the famous Ives cricket balls and the printing of the influential journal *Punch*. A neighbour of the Darlings recalled Edwardian life in Tonbridge as 'very pleasant'. Despite the availability of all the pre-conditions for a flourishing school, the Castle School's success was only middling. It is not mentioned in an authoritative history of English preparatory schools—although there is mention of a defunct preparatory school founded in the nineteenth century, 'Tonbridge Castle, Tonbridge'. Tom Darling recalled Clare House as a 'most ghastly' dwelling. A photograph taken in about 1913 shows twenty-six pupils (including three Darling children and a cousin)—numbers not too far below the Board of Education's preparatory school average size of thirty-six in 1900. And, while Austen Darling may well have simply preferred shooting and growing prize-winning roses to the neglect of schoolmastering, as his son James has claimed, his spartan regime was not the exception: austerity ruled everywhere, including at the famed Temple Grove, Surrey, where it was claimed that 'in the dormitories snow frequently piled upon the blankets and ice formed on the water jugs: the lavatories ... would have been condemned in a slum tenement'.[12]

The Castle School 'was not a bad school and what we learned we learned thoroughly', Sir James Darling recalled. The school room itself was 'a fairly primitive establishment'—at one end Austen taught the top form while at the other end Mr Ford was in charge of the intermediate group. In the basement of the main house Miss Howes taught the youngest children. The building looked 'like a Wesley chapel'. Its dimensions were 15 metres by 6 metres and it was constructed of tin. There was a workshop attached in which the boarders learnt carpentry but it was poorly heated by oil stoves. The quality of the school's teaching has been recalled as 'undistinguished'. As a schoolmaster, Austen Darling was not unreasonable in his treatment of his pupils. He never beat them, as his nephew Tom Darling recalled:

He used to, and I know now it was simulated, lose his temper with the boy. He could be very frightening looking because he had very bright eyes and a moustache.

Tom Darling thought that Miss Howes was a 'fairly good teacher', which contrasts with Sir James Darling's recollection of her employing a ruler, 'sharp side forward, on our knuckles' and kicking 'less effectively with her little feet'. She lived on the first floor of Clare House and Mr Ford, or 'Pick' (a sobriquet derived from Pickford), lived on the second. Ford's particular weapon was a blow from a hexagonal blue pencil on the knuckles or even 'an outsized ruler on the bottom'. James was in Miss Howes' charge for two years until the end of 1906. Up to the beginning of that year, when a report on his progress first appeared for French, his studies comprised 'English Subjects' (divinity, English grammar, English history, geography, dictation and composition) and 'Mathematics' (arithmetic, Euclid and algebra). His academic accomplishments were patchy. He was well below the average age of his classmates in these two years and it was not until 1906 that he performed anywhere near the top half of the form. 'Very satisfactory', which was the description of his early advancement penned by his father, suddenly became 'capital progress' after a 'very good examination' in December 1905.[13]

Miss Howes' assessments of James were bland. By age seven, he was learning Latin and French and progressed well in each. 'He finds little difficulty with his Latin', his father wrote. An early surviving piece of his school work, written when he was six, was dated '1905' on the rear side by his mother:

Dictation	Darhing

You may have <u>heird</u> people sayy say
that every-one in England is free. That
<u>meens</u> that every one can do as th he <u>lieks</u>
if only he <u>dose</u> not <u>heirt eney</u> one <u>elss</u>;
and h <u>lords</u> are made to keep one man from
harming another. The <u>lords</u> tiell us what
it is for the good of all that all should do.
9 faults

Who or what in the mind of a small boy provides protection: laws or lords (which he seemed to think)? Once free of Miss Howes' clutches, there was a regular pattern in James' studies, a predictability evident in the monotony of Mr Ford's and his father's remarks: 'Writing is still bad, but is improving' and 'he is making satisfactory progress' (English subjects and French, September–November 1907). James performed unevenly and unspectacularly. Illness appears not to have affected his attendance or performance: apart from four weeks early absence in June–July 1905, there were only one or two weeks missed until three weeks absence in 1911. Nonetheless, he lapsed frequently into inconsistency of effort and seemed ill organised in his approach. 'Works intelligently but is rather untidy' (mathematics, September–November 1907) and 'his [examination] papers are so carelessly written that he hardly makes the most of his knowledge' (November–December 1907), his father opined. Both Austen and Mr Ford constantly exhorted James to improve his 'bad' handwriting. James was easily dispirited, and chafed when pressure was applied. Thus, his father wrote in late 1909 that 'he does not tackle the uninteresting part of his subject with sufficient determination'.[14]

James' conduct was normally recorded as 'good', except that 'inattentive in class' occasionally crept in. In January 1908 he commenced the study of Greek. It was his fourth language and he was eight years old. Mr Ford's remark that 'he has made a very good start' augured well but he had slipped to only 'fair' by June. The high watermarks in his achievement came in the first half of 1909 and again in 1911. In between times he had clearly not been performing to his father's standards, particularly in Latin and Greek: 'He is easily disheartened and shirks the drudgery of learning Grammar or of subjects which are distasteful to him'. Even so, James was sixteen months younger than his twelve classmates for that year (1910) and was ranked fourth. His father's comment indicates the rigour demanded of a young Edwardian boy. Even when his son seemed to be doing very well, there would always be an air of restraint in Austen Darling's assessment. In early 1912 he commented: 'He has made excellent progress this term & has much more confidence in his powers. His unseen translations are rather variable but show some knowledge of English.' Only in his son's last report did the verdict that 'he has done good work and an excellent examination' amount to unconditional praise.[15]

In addition to classroom instruction, Mr Ford taught the children to swim at a branch of the Medway. There were team competitions against other schools, and once a week a man came to teach gymnastics. There were also performances of *Alice in Wonderland*, in which James once played a guinea pig, and Shakespeare's *Julius Caesar* in which he was a Roman tribune. The children would also be taken out into the hop fields where they saw the East End London hop pickers. These Sunday afternoon walks often turned out to be 16-kilometre round trips, but there were offers of tea on the way home whenever Austen Darling knew the farmers. Sunday mornings were spent at church. Initially, the Darlings worshipped at St Saviours, and then later at the parish church where Austen became a warden. As Tonbridge was a strongly evangelical town, the service was matins at 11 am, with Holy Communion offered only once a month. Austen Darling regularly wore a frock coat and top hat. 'He always read the lessons and he read them very well indeed.' On communion Sundays, the parents stayed behind after matins while their children returned home. 'We often wondered what awful things happened at communion because it was so secret.' Sometimes there were embarrassing mishaps in church:

When father forgot his spectacles and noticed it when he got there, I used to
have to rush home panting to get his spectacles back in time for him to read
the lesson.

On other occasions there were comic incidents: 'We used to put a penny in the
bag. Father dropped the bag once and I had to collect the collection off the floor.'
There was no regular Sunday school to attend, but instead a children's service.[16]

While later acknowledging that 'it is almost impossible for a man to write
sanely about his mother', James Darling described his mother as 'the undisputed
centre' of his childhood. Her father, the second Alexander Nimmo, said to Emily
Darling in 1896 that 'the happiness of our families must be thought of before our
own', a maxim strongly adhered to by his daughter. One Tonbridge neighbour's
recollection of her was 'the most marvellous person, she was very upright, very
Scottish', which accords closely with her nephew's memory of her as 'extremely
moral, extremely nice'. Her grandson's much later recollection of her at Trimley,
Suffolk, squares with these perceptions: 'A particularly vivid memory was morning
prayers in the morning room, kneeling beside her and all the household gathered
round, sitting, having their prayers said each morning'. While she was recalled
by her grandson as never saying 'anything nasty about anybody', at the same time
she would 'put you in your place if you stepped out of it at all'. 'I suppose the Free
Church Scottish rather Puritan background [instilled] a very stern sense of duty.'
Jane's description of dancing, in one letter to her mother, as indulging in 'a burst
of frivolity', followed by what she called 'muddleheadedness' the next morning,
indicates that she was by no means a killjoy.[17]

For upper- and middle-class Edwardian infants, nannies were the women
with whom they had most contact. For James, this was Nanny Murray, 'the
vaguest possible creature', who 'never usurped the function of mother'. 'It was
sitting on mother's knee that sensuously I remember.' Nanny Murray came for
Mabel about 1904 when James was four. Mabel had been a sickly child but soon
her mother was able to say that she 'grows sensibly & is not a bit weedy with it
all'. There had been an earlier nurse named Jessie, disliked by James' elder sister
Margaret. Nanny Murray was from the far north of Scotland. Her brother was
the butler to the Marquis of Bute, a fact of which the Darlings were extremely
proud. Nanny Murray slept in the second-floor night nursery with the children,
and woke and dressed them each morning:

> We would have breakfast in the nursery, the day nursery. On wet days and cold
> days in winter we would play in the nursery. In the summer and warmer days
> we had a special corner in the garden where we used to play. We had a garden
> of our own and a sandpit. This is as children, as young children. From there we
> graduated to having meals with the grown-ups. At least you had breakfast and
> there were prayers before breakfast. Then again we would go down and do the
> shopping in the town. It was a treat to do it with mother; normally I think it

would be with nanny. Certainly we would go down into the drawing room at
five o'clock and play with the games box. On Sundays we sang hymns around
the piano and then we were sent off to bed. And I expect mother came to kiss
us in bed, I don't remember that.

A clear line demarcated Nanny Murray's daily discipline and Jane's occasional
punishment, which would be inflicted for 'deliberate disobedience or being
rude'.[18]

The other influential women at Clare House were the servants, all of them
Christian by inclination. The sewing lady, Miss Hadaway (or Way-Way), who
came twice a week, was a 'desperately poor' woman who sat in the nursery and
told the children stories. When the number of children increased an under-nurse,
Nellie (a niece of Miss Hadaway's), was employed. Eventually, she became a
missionary. Then there was a cook, Bessie, a parlour maid, Fanny, a housemaid,
and a 'tweenie' (or between-maid). Finally, there was a gardener. Except for the
gardener, they all lived at Clare House where they were given board, lodgings and
uniforms. The maids 'stayed forever, they were absolutely constant'. Amidst these
numerous people, both family and non-family members, the Darling offspring
'were subjected to the strongest and most beautiful aspects of Christianity'. The
tone of the morality was one of sweet reasonableness rather than puritanical
high-mindedness. In addition, the children had the free run of over nearly half a
hectare of ground, with all of its interesting nooks and crannies. They befriended
their neighbours, one of whom later refreshed James' memory of their happy
times together: 'It only seems yesterday that you woke all the courtiers in the
Hall at Judde House [in Tonbridge School] by a sound kick to Joan [Whitby]'s
golliwog!' The children also enjoyed Tonbridge's annual and seasonal festivities,
such as Cricket Week: 'the most terrific orgy of entertainment' that included
a Venetian fete and a military tattoo. An especially prized event was 'the great
family pilgrimage' every summer to Emily Darling's cottage at Eyke, Suffolk, and
occasionally at Easter to the Nimmos in Falkirk.[19]

The quality of family life can also be glimpsed in the children's letters.
These expressed happiness, contentment and the joy of constant stimulation. In
1901, Margaret said of James (in large upper-case letters):

> Dear Mother, Jim does not cry at all when he has his bath now. Grannie has
> gone home now and Uncle Reggie. We are going to church today. From your
> loving Margaret.

Mabel, the middle child, who found pairing off with one of the others difficult
('if anyone gets left out usually, it is she', her mother once wrote), enthused
in October 1914: 'I am getting on very well in lessons this term for I have
been top twice running'. Jean and Eaton who, like Margaret and James, were
playmates, wrote mostly to Margaret (then at Cambray House, Cheltenham

Ladies' College). Jean recounted all manner of interests and adventures: frogs in the garden, a rose bower, playing conkers, sightings of Allied aircraft, trips with Nanny and Miss Howes to see wounded Belgian soldiers, and attempts to converse with them, sometimes in French for, after the outbreak of hostilities in 1914, Nanny and Miss Howes nursed the wounded. Eaton, a particularly imaginative little boy, proclaimed to his big sister in 1914: 'I am writing a [sic] autobiography of my life'. 'We go to cricket now and I nearly always get no runs except on Wednesday and Saturday because we play with small boys.' He ended with the boast 'I can go on the tall stilts'. There was also 'a ripping dip' at a waifs and strays bazaar. Eaton and James, however, were not close. James was ten years older and, apart from playing stump cricket in the garden during term holidays, they had little in common. Eaton's hair stood up on end 'just like a toothbrush'. 'Most extraordinary. It would never lie down and we used to laugh: "Poor old Eaton!"' At Repton in the 1920s, Eaton fagged for Christopher Isherwood, later the famous English writer. Apart from his distinctive hair and a squeaky voice, Isherwood recalled him as 'one of the smallest boys in the whole school' but also as very intelligent. As a boy, Eaton 'was a most delightful companion, full of fun and energy, witty in a slightly caustic way, but resentful of any attempt to help him'. His elder brother remembered that he 'seemed to have a firm determination to remain an "under-dog" even, though perhaps this isn't fair, to cling to his grievances against a wicked world, a rather Kingsley Amis type, perhaps'.[20]

The totality of these ingredients of a paternal family and social order structured James Darling's childhood. To contemporary eyes Edwardian paternalism is another world. Fathers, the icons of this order, have often been characterised by historians as psychologically or emotionally absent because their practice was to keep themselves at arm's length from their children's upbringing. This made them difficult for sons and daughters to come to know, and invariably difficult to please. Even when James was no longer a boy but an emerging young man, it was easy for him to think of himself as inadequate in a father's eyes:

> In the holidays after my first term at Repton my father insisted on me going to church in a straw hat which still had on it the prep school colours. And this was to me an utterly appalling insult, absolutely devastating. There were terrible floods of tears at the age of 13.

James was particularly irritated by his father's hobby of shooting. He loathed slogging through wooded country to entice pheasants out into the open. Moreover, as an Edwardian paterfamilias, Austen Darling was not easy to get to know. His brother, James George Reginald, was much the same, as Norah Darling (James' cousin) recalled:

> How could we get on with our father? We looked up to him. But they [James George Reginald and Austen] were the most undemonstrative couple of men

that you could possibly imagine, completely and utterly undemonstrative. I had one letter in my life from my father and that was only because my mother was in hospital, and he had to write that letter because I was at school. And in my day you only got home at half term and nobody came near you so you had to have a letter from your home. And I couldn't read it. I had to get somebody else to read it because I couldn't understand his writing.

At the same time, there was another imperative at work in this big family, as James himself recognised: a coexisting sense of mutual awareness, responsibility and support. Perhaps it was this childhood combination of paternalism and fraternalism, the one vertical and hierarchical, the other lateral and community-like, that sowed the seeds of a model of social and organisational relations on which he would later draw.[21]

Calm, constant, warm, secure, ordered, predictable and well defined but also sheltered: these contours of the microcosm of James' boyhood world make it easy to see why the persistent myth of the Edwardian era, as Roy Hattersley says, is to view it as 'a long and leisurely afternoon'. The three main geographical points of reference in James' childhood comprised two at opposite ends of the country and the third towards the middle: the centre at Clare House, Falkirk at the periphery and an outlier at Eyke in Suffolk. The two key people in the sprawling tribe of family and school relationships were his father and his mother, the one English, the other Scottish, and the two principal religious and moral influences were Anglican and Presbyterian. These dualities yielded two enduring parental images for James. First, there was a father, austere almost to the point of parsimony, an adept sportsman in his youth, and a lover of the garden who was 'so much more concerned with his own interests' and content to leave 'the care of his children to his wife while retaining his position as head of the family'. Second, there was the cameo of a mother who was 'intensely religious', and imbued with a strong sense of duty and public spiritedness, such that after World War I she stood for, and was elected to, the Tonbridge Council. Her example is a perfect illustration of how the public and the private worlds which Virginia Woolf described as being 'inseparably connected' came together, although in this instance without 'the tyrannies and servilities of the one' that she described becoming 'the tyrannies and servilities of the other'. In respect of public and private worlds, the extent of the penetration of the wider Edwardian world into everyone's consciousness in Tonbridge, particularly that of the children, cannot be known. As James would discover in the future, there was much in the world that was antipathetic to his upbringing. At one extreme, above him and his family, for example, was an aristocratic stratum, the world in which the Prince of Wales moved (as he continued to do when he became King) that at its worst 'took serial promiscuity for granted'. At the other extreme, beneath James' family and social class, 'poverty was rife in cities'. His limited awareness came during visits to Westbank and the comparatively much better-off Nimmos, because to pass through Camelon,

which housed many industrial workers, was to be exposed to a contrast between
'the poverty which could be seen there and our own affluence' and 'made some
mark even on my young mind'. A key childhood maxim that stayed with him was
that 'from those to whom much has been given, much shall be demanded'. For
all that he had been given, his self-description many years later was of a boy with
an inferiority complex and a 'very nasty little boy' at that; 'clever and advanced'
for his years in school, but 'very noticeably lacking in any of the qualities which
make for either success or popularity'. Shortly, in the autumn of 1912, just as he
was about to add one further significant geographic point of reference to his life,
in the guise of another preparatory school, he would be able to test the truth of
this description and to discover how well he had been prepared for life beyond
the cocoon of his family.[22]

HIGHFIELD AND REPTON

1912–1916

If a boy can't have a good teacher, give him a psychological cripple or an exotic failure to cope with; don't just give him a bad, dull teacher. This is where the private schools score over state-run schools; they can accommodate a few cultured madmen on the staff without having to offer explanations.

Robertson Davies, *Fifth Business*

In September 1912, for reasons that are unclear, Austen enrolled James in the Highfield School, Liphook, Hampshire. After a final scholarly grooming by Tonbridge School's senior classics master, James had been taken by his much-loved Uncle Wattie (Lacon Watson) to sit for the Winchester scholarship examination. When he was unsuccessful he came to Highfield, founded by E.A. Wells as a day preparatory school at Southampton in 1887. In 1904 it numbered thirty-eight pupils. Two years later, the Reverend Wilbur Riches Mills (1876–1953) purchased the school and, by 1914, the year after James departed, there were more than sixty pupils enrolled. Mills expended considerable effort in finding a new site for his investment and chose well, paying a mere £300 for 120 glorious hectares in an area near where Hampshire adjoins Surrey and Sussex. Highfield moved to Liphook in 1907. By the time that James arrived, there were new buildings, large grounds and a chapel of which the school was 'very proud'. It was a well-endowed and generally happy institution with pleasant walks nearby in lovely countryside. Only one or two masters had 'some kind of pretence of scholarship', James told his mother, and 'our French master [Mr Sandberg] is a most awful spec'. C.B. Fry's son was a fellow pupil and one day the famous cricketer came down to play 'and made 98 and got himself out'. James entered the upper IVth, the scholarship form. His year there rid him of any precocity brought from the Castle School. Here, his mathematics master did him 'a great deal of good'.[1]

Highfield was still being constructed while James attended it and, in early 1913, it was afflicted by sickness, the bane of every preparatory school proprietor's life. The 'vagaries of the English climate' were bad enough, the drill master lamented, but on one occasion the affliction had been measles. Every school activity was temporarily halted. In his final term, James was appointed a prefect. As if to contradict his father's low opinion of his sporting ability, he was also a member of the school's gymnastics VIII and was selected twice in the 1st XI cricket team. Here he scored 11 and a miserable 1 run. He did win a Blues swim, the equivalent for poor swimmers of one length of Highfield's pool, but at the sports could only manage second in a consolation race. A surviving photograph captures him standing at the ready in a Rugby line-out. He performed at least moderately well scholastically for he won a prize for 'Tennyson' and a special prize for Greek. The single most important event while James was at Highfield was his chance meeting in early 1913 with William Temple, then the headmaster of Repton (and later Archbishop of Canterbury). Despite Austen's encouraging final report on his son, it was decided after two terms not to resit the Winchester scholarship examination and to enter a lesser-ranked school. He won the top scholarship to Repton. During the scholarship examination, James had stayed with Temple and his mother. Temple expressed his delight at the young lad's 'success in coming out top' and looked forward to 'seeing you here next term'— welcoming words that began a friendship lasting three decades until Temple's death in 1944. Mills had been partly responsible for this sudden turn of events and kept 'a very happy memory' of James' year (although James had not warmed to him). Once Austen preached in the Highfield chapel but never visited James at Repton.[2]

    In Church of England folklore there are three types of archbishops: saints, administrators or theologians. Temple was widely regarded as saintly, an attribute in which the 'spiritual emotions are the habitual center of the personal energy', whereas Geoffrey Fisher, who succeeded him at Repton (and at Canterbury), typified the administrator. The pattern of headmaster-bishops emerged in the nineteenth century and Temple followed the example of his liberal father, Frederick. The elder Temple had preceded the luckless Henry Hayman as head of Rugby (1857–68) until Gladstone, the prime minister, had him appointed to the bishopric of Exeter. Frederick Temple was a member of the Taunton Commission, became Bishop of London in 1885 and then finally Archbishop of Canterbury from 1897 until his death in 1902. His son, a close friend and contemporary at Rugby of the economic historian, R.H. Tawney, was an associate of Albert Mansbridge and president of the Workers' Education Association from 1908 to 1924. It was said of William Temple that 'his deliverance from a life of metaphysical swimming and cultural ease came through his inherited sense of duty towards the peoples' education'. He was ordained in 1909 and during a tour of Australian universities in 1910 he accepted the Repton headmastership. He had vague ideas about reforming the English public schools, but shortly after his arrival doubted whether headmastering 'is really in my line'. In fact, Repton was 'a false move' and, in the summer of 1914, 'after a week of reflection', he resigned after only four years to accept the living of St James, Piccadilly, London. 'By nature a man of new plans and ideas' and ill suited to overseeing the kind of reorganisation of the school that had taken place under his predecessor, the *Reptonian* (the school magazine) thanked Temple for his 'stimulating companionableness'.[3]

Asked when he returned home whether he liked Temple, James replied: 'very much but he seems a bit old-fashioned'. Unaccompanied by his parents and feeling some qualms he set off by train on his first day. He had been awarded an entrance scholarship (worth £80 annually) and in 1915 he won a foundation scholarship. He and three other scholarship winners, R.L. Holdsworth, D. McLeod Innes and A.T.O. Lees, went straight into the Lower Vth on the classical side, where he did work 'which I had done before and with very little interest'. His form master was M. Morgan-Owen, the famous Welsh international centre-half and Repton football coach. Repton itself, on the River Trent, had very ancient links. In pre-Christian times it was the chief town in the kingdom of Mercia. Christianity came to Repton with the conversion of Peada in 653 and it was an episcopal seat until this moved to Lichfield in 669. In the twelfth century an Augustinian priory was built but, after the dissolution of the monasteries in 1536, monasticism ended and the priory was demolished. Repton School owed its origin to the executors of the will of Sir John Port, a wealthy landowner from Etwall, who purchased the ruined buildings in 1559. The school commenced in 1557, the year of Port's death, when he expressed his wish to be the benefactor of a 'Grammar School in Etwalle or Reptone'. Until the nineteenth century, Repton admitted three categories of pupil: grammar boys, who paid a small fee for masters and their own board; town boys, who paid for their board but received endowment-funded free education; and poor scholars, who were paid an allowance. Despite its founder's intentions, by mid-century Repton was no longer a charity school and had become a fee-paying boarding school catering to a burgeoning English middle class.[4]

It was under Repton's reforming equivalent of Rugby's Thomas Arnold, Dr Steuart Adolphus Pears (headmaster from 1854), that its transformation into a full-blown English public school was completed. Pears had been an assistant master at Harrow for seven years during the incumbency of the Reverend C.J. Vaughan (one of a number of masters and boys under Arnold at Rugby who became headmasters). Harrow was an 'inspiring setting' for Pears and the Rugbeian inspiration was duly transported to Repton. By 1857, enrolments had risen from 48 to 107. One of the first acts of the strongly evangelically inclined Pears was to build a chapel, the centrepiece of his educational endeavours. He also had new classrooms constructed and boarding houses outside the school's famous arch. Repton's stocks rose with mid-Victorian economic prosperity and as Pears' reputation spread. Finally, to complete the high-minded Victorian balance—*mens sana in corpore sano* (a sound mind in a sound body)—Pears reorganised the games infrastructure. He introduced the usual status differentials and the complete schoolboy paraphernalia: colours, blazers, ribbons, coats and caps. He tightened discipline. The curriculum was 'overwhelmingly classical', although he encouraged an extra-curricular interest in science and the founding of a science society. Full public school status was achieved in the 1860s and in 1874 Repton was acknowledged by Parliament as a 'First Grade Boarding School'. Pears retired due to ill health in 1874 and he died the following year aged only sixty. In 1910, the enrolment was 368. Temple was the fifth headmaster to succeed Pears. He arrived, complete with his 'infectious laugh' and accompanied by his aged mother as his hostess at the Hall. 'He was Oxford come to Repton.'[5]

James' previous Castle School pattern of indifferent scholastic performance repeated itself at Repton. In Lent term 1914 he was promoted to the Middle Vth under J.S. Shearme (previously 'a first-rate athlete' at Westminster), and after two terms spent a year with the Reverend A. Cattley in the Upper Vth. In the summer of 1915, he reached the Lower VIth, where he remained for a year, and then the Upper VIth, where he spent four terms. Until he came under Cattley's tutelage, he coasted. In June 1914, Shearme said that his classical work had been 'very fair, but his exercises often show signs of carelessness'. 'In form he is attentive & keen' but he seldom did 'quite as well as I expect him to do'. After only a term in the Upper Vth, James' housemaster, Stratton, intoned:

> Merry and bright, in spite of his troubles with his form-master, always entertaining & full of conversation. But at the same time he <u>must cure his carelessness</u> if he is going to make a scholar.

Fisher (by now headmaster) advised that 'the quicker he does it, the better for his mental growth'. 'Troubles' was Stratton's oblique allusion to the legendary Cattley (known as 'the Cossack') of whom James had run foul. Basil Rathbone, the English actor, who had been at Repton some years earlier, many years afterwards told Darling why he wasn't a Cattley favourite. At a study tea, Rathbone had thrown butter in the direction of the door, but with disastrous results: Cattley entered the room as Rathbone launched his projectile. Cattley was James' nemesis. In a letter to his mother he erupted:

> I have been having a stormy week this week; I don't think I can stand doing verses alone for much longer, it is absolutely terribly [sic] and from what he says I seem to get worse and worse. I also seem to have struck a mine over a certain Greek Prose which according to him is 'peculiarly careless and vile', so altogether I am rather dreading Monday when I get the things back.

Cattley's temper was fearsome and he was extraordinarily liberal with impositions when boys misconstrued their Latin.[6]

James was head boy of Cattley's form. Unlike Holdsworth and Innes who had been promoted to the Upper Vth after only one term, he was held back (despite Cattley ranking him first of thirteen or fourteen boys in two consecutive terms in 1915). Three times Cattley used the exemplary phrase 'has a bright mind', but he seemed bent on punishing him. 'Slipshod' for French and 'always scratchy and untidy' for his classics and general work degenerated into 'nearly all his written work is untidy & careless' and 'spoiled by slovenliness and inaccuracy'. 'If he wd only take more trouble', Cattley despaired. Stratton warned Austen to adjust his expectations:

> Going on very well out of school & not badly in school really. He will have a hard time in the Upper fifth but it will be very valuable to him. But you must not expect very good reports. Mr. Cattley doesn't give them.

James did his best to make light of the unpleasantness. There were occasional compensations. Once he told his mother how:

> yesterday and today we had too [sic] most collossal [sic] exhibitions of [Cattley's] temper, which were most fearfully funny, he really is a babe, the way he loses his temper over nothing, and he is most amusing when he stamps about and foams.

He gave her a blow-by-blow rendition:

> Feb 8th Had a terrible time in verses.
>
> 9th Stumped on con[strual]. Did 35 lines perfectly right only not in the language he liked. Only had 35 minutes to prepare 50 lines and the old lesson for which I was absent. Gross oil.
>
> 10th Went on for the whole lesson again. Am getting fed up with Cossack.
>
> 11th Foam in Greek History. McL[ean] got 80 [lines] J. sent to the bottom.
>
> 12th Terrific foam in the morning. Personally got through all right.
>
> 13th Absolute climax. Terrific foam. Best there has ever been since I have been in the form. Expect another field day on Monday!!

When a terrified lad fainted, Cattley spat dismissively: 'Take him out!'[7]

One day (Wednesday, the field day for Repton's officer training corps—OTC), Cattley punished James by making him run about wearing a heavy overcoat and carrying a Lee–Enfield rifle. He fainted and had to be carried off, and there was a row between Stratton and Cattley—such rows between masters were thought by young schoolboys to be 'a very good thing' to try to engineer. In September 1915, there was a respite when James slipped out of the Cossack's clutches and into the safety of the Lower VIth and its classics master, E.A. Scutt. Stratton continued to reassure Austen about his son's progress—'going on very well indeed in every way'—while observing wryly that 'he seems to appreciate being in the Lower Sixth'. Scutt's very first report was glowing: 'Has done extremely good work in Proses, Prepared Translation and Unseens, and writes excellent essays. Has made very satisfactory progress.' A month or so later, however, 'very erratic' appeared, followed by 'he has steadied himself latterly'. Assessments of James' English essays from another master, Crommelin-Brown, included 'apt to be incoherent', and Fisher described him as 'at times incoherent' and an 'intelligent if rather undeveloped confirmand'. During his two years in the Vth, James had so far studied Latin, Greek and divinity, French, history, English and science. Few English public schools accorded science the status that Repton gave it: in addition to the science society, the curriculum included chemistry, light, heat, mechanics, hydrostatics and electricity. Finally, on reaching the VIth, James studied the works of Livy, Catullus, Virgil, Cicero, Juvenal, Lucretius and Horace in Latin. In Greek the diet included Homer, Plato, Thucydides, Demosthenes and Aristophanes.[8]

English public schools distinguished between subject sides, with the classical side pre-eminent. Next in the pecking order came the modern side (dismissed by one commentator as a refuge 'for the second rate') and then the army side to cater for boys going to Woolwich (as engineers or gunners) or Sandhurst (for the infantry or cavalry). Repton was one of the last schools to have early morning (or First) school which began at 7.15 am:

> I remember because the bell, the first bell, rang at seven minutes past seven and the next bell rang for two minutes between 7.13 and 7.15. I found that I could get up at the first bell, 7.07, have a cold bath, dress, take a cup of coffee, collect my books which had been arranged the night before, and run down and get into school on time.

Chapel commenced at 8 am, after which boys then walked back to their houses for breakfast. At 9.15, forty-five minutes preparatory work (or prep) was completed in houses and then three classroom periods before lunch. In summer there were games, followed by more prep and then two periods of school till 4 pm, games again until 6, then tea, and one-and-a-half hours study before bed. Higher form boys went to bed an hour later again. In winter, games were normally played immediately after lunch. There were three half-holidays per week (Tuesday, Thursday and Saturday) for which extra periods were substituted in the mornings. There were Saturday morning classes and a period of divinity before chapel at 11 am on Sunday. The afternoons were free for activities such as walks before another chapel service at 6.30 pm. All boys boarded in one of eight houses, each of which (apart from Hall) accommodated about forty boys. Boys slept in dormitories, with about ten boys of all ages to a dormitory, including a dormitory head, seconds and fags. Studies comprised six to eight boys to a room, including the study holder (usually one of the VIth), two or three seconds who shared a table, and two or three fags.[9]

At some schools a senior boy could shout 'fag' and every little boy was expected to respond, but at Repton only house prefects could fag the lower school. To be a decent study-holder's fag promised beneficent paternalism, in which services performed by a younger boy—for example, dusting, laying the study fire, making toast for the study-holder's tea, posting letters and running odd errands—earned the protection of an elder one, because 'you felt he was there to look after you and he seemed very large and very important'. But fagging was not all sweetness and light, as Eaton discovered. Once at Repton, when he mislaid Christopher Isherwood's football boots, Isherwood caned him, with the result that 'a certain confidence had been broken between us' so that 'our relations could never be the same again'. In addition, similar to other quasi-monastic sets of living arrangements that segregated one sex off from the other, school board-ing houses were open to abuse, either through bullying or same-sex attraction. James was bullied—although never as grossly as Brown in *Tom Brown's Schooldays* (who was held over a fire). As at most schools, Repton had its share of 'bloods' or philistine sporting heroes whom H.A. Vachell, a school novelist, described as 'tremendous swells, grown men with a titillating flavour of the world about their persons' and whom Alec Waugh's *The Loom of Youth* depicted swaggering around as if they 'had taken a mortgage on the place'. For the most part, Repton's bloods irritated the juniors with petty taunting, such as knocking books out from under their arms (when school ritual dictated that hands be kept in pockets). As a scholarship boy, James had to endure gibes such as 'you are paid to come here', and duck out of the way of footballs kicked at him when he crossed the yard.[10]

As for same-sex attachments, these assumed a number of guises between boys or between masters and boys. In the former instance, C.S. Lewis provides in *Surprised by Joy* an account of his experiences at Wyvern (which Sir James Darling later affirmed mirrored most closely the Repton situation). Lewis' reconstructed dialogue records a boarding house tart (as such boys were known) lasciviously eyeing off some new arrivals: 'Ho-ho! I know what *you're* looking for.' As to relations between boys and masters, a genuine strength of feeling could develop. One Repton master wrote in his memoirs how:

> I had become very quickly aware, at Repton, that I not only liked boys in general, but felt a very special strong and emotional affection for certain boys ... They were mostly sixth form boys, and mostly boys of marked character and ability who, if they were not killed in the 1914 war, have since done very well; so it was not just a case of the lusts of the flesh.

Same-sex attraction in boarding schools occurred when young men were ripening physically and emotionally; as a consequence they were potentially vulnerable. Lewis disclaimed 'the vice in question [as] one to which I had never been tempted'. Later as a headmaster, Darling had to contend with the intermittent problem of such boarding house vice. There was a foretaste of what was in store in late 1917, when he extricated two boys in Stratton's house from an ugly set of circumstances.[11]

When James reached the VIth form, life became interesting for him under the sway of two intellectually formidable and inspiring masters, D.C. Somervell and Victor Gollancz. Their impact on the school would principally be felt in the classroom but also, importantly, in the Repton School Debating Society. The influence of school debating on James and his friends began in late 1915. The convention was that speakers argued for the case that they supported to ensure that 'you meant what you were saying'. James gave his maiden speech to the Debating Society on 4 November, and thereby became a member, when he opposed James Harford's motion: 'That this House considers that corporal punishment causes more evil than it cures'. Reports of the twelve Debating Society meetings from then until James departed indicate that it was a robust forum, with the tone not always restrained and gentlemanly. Usually, about forty people assembled by 6.30 pm to hear masters and boys weigh in on current topics. Gollancz and his adversary, a master named Snape, 'used to use the Debating Society to come and be rude to each other'. Every now and then the big guns appeared. In December 1916, for example, Fisher and Snape led the affirmative on the motion that 'in the opinion of this House, the dismemberment of Germany is absolutely essential to the future peace of Europe', while Somervell and Gollancz led the negative. Over 140 people crammed into Pears Hall and voted for the motion by a huge margin. Wartime Hun-hatred at Repton was evident in Captain Sharp's vitriol when the *Reptonian* recorded him as pointing out that 'his object was the dismemberment of [German] individuals' and when another Old Reptonian advocated 'the annihilation of the Germans on the analogy that if Cromwell had annihilated all the Irish there would have been none to trouble us now'. Some speakers resorted to snobbery—as in a motion proposed by James' friend Sam Richardson on the effects of 'magazines and inferior literature': only the latter (read by the 'lower classes' and comprising love stories and adventure tales) had detrimental effects, said Richardson, whereas magazines were read by 'more educated people'. And when James proposed to establish a dramatic society, one boy claimed that 'the *elite* of Repton are people whose time is more than filled already. They have their hobbies', and yet these were the very people 'most capable of running' such a society.[12]

The topics debated ranged from war-related (dismemberment of Germany, Allied reprisals), through topical (corporal punishment, the purpose of punishment, elevation of the physical sciences, votes for women, state-provided employment, the value of classics) and innocuous (abolition of tails and Eton collars, a drama society) to trivial (popular literature, ghosts). James led the debate on four occasions and spoke from the floor five times. His remarks supporting corporal punishment revealed a rather dispiriting view of human nature. 'A man devoid of self-respect could only be touched bodily', he asserted, and could not be reformed properly after imprisonment. Indeed, 'had not a brief, if unpleasant flogging, something of the noble Spartan strain?' And, because James 'was certain that a man who had been flogged smarted with moral pain no more than did a convict', then clearly there was little point in appealing to anything like a conscience. Punishment rather than redemption was paramount, but for a young man devoid of such severity in his own life to be arguing that 'the object of punishment was prevention of crime by fear' was a hard line to take. Perhaps he was signalling the need for order and obedience. Later, in February 1917, when seconding the motion that 'a criminal is punished, not to fulfil the idea of justice, but to safeguard the community', James' defence of society's collective interest was less primitive: laws, which justify the administering of punishment, do not stand for retribution but are devised (as the motion said) 'to safeguard the community and allow the State to develop'.[13]

In October 1916, when stoutly defending the humanities, glimmers of James' idealism shone through. Speaking on this same topic, Gollancz hinted at what he and Somervell were about to unleash on the VIth: 'Here too there must be a reformation in the teaching of classics'. James also spoke on the role of women and on state-provided employment, where the crux of the issue for him boiled down to strikes, with his attitude again betraying a concern for obedience:

> Mr. SOMERVELL was induced to protest against Mr. Darling. It was *not* a question of strikes. The unemployed poor are not slackers; you don't slack and starve for fun. The idle rich, it is true, do exist, but they are only a small class. Reform would make the unemployed more contented, and add to the labour of the community; guild socialism would turn the business oligarchies into democracies.

James' two other areas of involvement before he entered the Upper VIth were sport and the Literary Society. Until late 1914, when military reports from France began trickling in, football and cricket mostly filled the pages of the *Reptonian*. Cricket was Repton's genuine claim to fame. (In 1908, when five lads played for county teams during vacation time, Cambridge sent what was virtually a university-strength side and Repton defeated it.) James was an occasional bowler in Stratton's 2nd XI and in June 1915 his was the best of seventeen 'conspicuous performances' listed: 9 wickets for 15 runs against Latham House, his name and the mention of him as one of the three most successful bowlers was underlined with thick blue ink in the copy of the *Reptonian* that he sent home to his mother. In 1916, James trundled down 37 overs and claimed 23 victims at an average of 5.8, which ranked him nineteenth overall in the house 2nd XI averages. Once he bagged 5 for 31 against Priory House. A year later he was fourth in the house 2nd XI bowling averages (19 wickets at 4.1) just behind James Harford (21 at 3.9). Twice he took more than five wickets, including 6 for 20 in his sole listed appearance in the house 1st XI, but his incompetence with the willow always forestalled mention of his batting.[14]

James' motion at the Repton School Debating Society in 1916 to form a dramatic society in peacetime was carried, but artistic productivity languished. Prompted largely by Crommelin-Brown, the Repton School Literary Society met intermittently for play readings and to hear papers. James' literary activities were few. He played a spirit in Yeats' *The Countess Cathleen* in December 1915 and Mrs Sorby in Ibsen's *Wild Duck* the following March. Some of his friends presented papers to the Literary Society, mostly on the English romantic poets. James himself was fond of Robert Browning and read a paper on him in November 1916, for which he earned himself a flimsy twelve-line summary in the *Reptonian*. Until Gollancz came to replace Scutt in March 1916, Somervell was the only master who had tried to stir Repton out of its numbing conventionality. But for the reality of war beginning to seep into everyone's consciousness, Repton was a closed and inward-looking small world. Letters to the *Reptonian* deplored the moribund state of the Debating Society in 1914. When an exceedingly poor attendance prompted the abandonment of a debate, an exasperated Somervell wrote a lengthy, stinging, although elegantly worded, letter:

> Now I don't want to be rude: I don't want to appear ungrateful for the rapt and awful attention with which that audience listened to me last term. But this attitude of patient and demure attention is all wrong, all alien to the Debating spirit, and depressing and awe-inspiring to the speakers. The audience must try and remember it is not in Chapel: also that it is not there to be instructed (it surely gets enough of that elsewhere). It is there to debate, to argue and disagree with speakers, approve or disapprove of them and show them so, to win or lose votes by its hearty 'hear! hear's!' and its telling interruptions, as much as the speakers by their speeches. Of course the President must rule and moderate: but he should be given something to do, and if he is wise he will know that it is best to have too little order rather than too much.

'I don't want to preach but—I'm just going to', Somervell continued, this time with athleticism in his sights. He claimed that no-one had any more right to label debates 'a bore' than to make similar accusations about cricket practice, because that would endorse the 'most damaging criticism' of the public schools: 'that their boasted training in *esprit de corps* never gets beyond the sphere of sporting interests'.[15]

Not even Somervell's rhetoric, however, could stem the tide of lassitude. A year later and still limping, the Debating Society debated a motion deploring its own existence, with the proceedings punctuated by oppressive periods of 'silence'. Nor did school music escape Somervell's wrath. He was met with howls of outrage in the *Reptonian* when he fumed at 'third rate tosh' served up by a visiting musical company: 'this is what they have to offer!' He argued for the simultaneous provision of goodness as well as pleasure in entertainment. 'Should not music be part of a liberal education, too', he pleaded. Philistinism was entrenched at Repton and James was aware of it. When asked to become a member of Repton School Literary Society, for instance, early in 1915, he told his mother, a little bumptiously: 'in its own studious way [it] is a bit of an honour I suppose; it is nothing thought of, however'. Fisher had had to adjust to the sudden loss of masters to the services and a school cramped by wartime restrictions. Compared with Temple, a 'veritable oratorical Niagara', Fisher personified the public school headmaster stereotype. 'I could still remember his voice in Pears Hall', recalled a former pupil:

> where the whole school assembled and were making a frightful noise. And his voice, which was a wonderful voice, cut across it and silenced them all in about half a minute.

He behaved similarly in chapel, when all the boys were crocodiling in and taking their places. Fisher would be there in his seat:

> He probably wouldn't be taking chapel, some master would. But he would sit at the front, there in his place, and he would look down, and you would see this scowling headmaster looking down, probably trying to browbeat some boy who was talking or laughing in the background.[16]

By the time James reached the Lower VIth, he was showing signs of maturing. Despite his earlier uneven scholastic work he had won a couple of prizes, including two in mathematics in 1914 and prize money for distinctions gained with which he purchased a book. There was a high point in April 1916 when he topped the Lower VIth. 'The G[eorge] D[enman] examiner was quite favourably impressed with some of his work', wrote Fisher on James' report. Then, inexplicably, James lapsed in late 1916. Perhaps this was because of illness— for he was afflicted by terrible hay fever—or because he succumbed to bouts of adolescent torpor. His acting up made Stratton uneasy:

> I have not been altogether pleased with him this term. As a prefect he has had no trouble, I think, in keeping order, but he is quite extraordinarily juvenile in other ways. I have never before had to complain constantly of a boy at the top table for coming in to meals with his clothes or nails dirty. And he has developed a quite dreadful habit of never saying anything without a silly nervous little laugh. I do hope he will learn to be natural again, & not think it necessary to try to be clever or funny every time he opens his mouth. I am afraid that the experiment of making so young a boy a house prefect has not quite had the effect that I hoped & expected.

At the same time, external events were beginning to register. L.A. Burd's history lectures helped (attested by James' surviving meticulous notes of Burd's classes on

the Bavarian invasions, in Christmas term 1915). Increasingly, the war intruded
into James' life, especially when he returned to Tonbridge in term vacations.
Interspersed with the pleasantness of cycling over to Rotherfield to see a school
friend (Charles Sidey) and his family was James' awareness of distant rumbling.
Not only was listening to the troop trains one of his 'most vivid recollections' but
he could also 'hear the guns from France in Tonbridge'. Moreover, soldiers, often
Belgians, were 'billeted on us'. Miss Howes and Mr Ford went off to serve, and,
when Nanny Murray learnt bandaging, James was used as a dummy patient. At
Repton, where 'everybody was terribly on edge', a long-serving, loyal, German-
born master had been accused of being a spy, and something similar happened
in Tonbridge where a German missionary had been living. But in 'those days
of frenzy and idiocy', the people turned on him, accusing him of spying and of
planning to blow up the bridge across the Medway. The poor man was hounded
out of town as a traitor.[17]

Games success may have been acme of a boy's horizons at Repton. In this
vein, Hopeful asked the *Reptonian* whether 'it might be possible to provide
members of the School who are in [two of the] teams with a special hat band?'
If this kind of thinking was the sum of what counted as reward for endeavour
then cherished public school ideals were looking somewhat tarnished. Somervell
thought so and he suggested this litmus test of tolerance of unorthodoxy:

> It strikes me that some energetic person might make a classified list of the
> suggestions that have appeared in the *Reptonian* correspondence columns in
> the last year, let us say with notes attached stating whether the suggestion has
> borne fruit. Such a list published annually would constitute an interesting
> review of one aspect of School politics.

Other voices echoed Somervell. To anyone believing that boys were sent to
Repton to become gentlemen and that a gentleman's supreme duty was to be
considerate of others' feelings, Every Man For Himself wrote:

> To these I would reply three things—firstly, that of course masters have no
> feelings; secondly, that you cannot expect a boy of only sixteen or eighteen
> to consider anyone else's feelings but his own. Thirdly, I would say that they
> have defined the term 'gentleman' wrong. Everyone knows that a gentleman is
> a man who knows how to eat peas correctly, doesn't wear a made-up tie, and
> calls a serviette a 'table-napkin'.

Next, in a facetiously worded attack on the sacred cow of cricket, Cheer-oh said
that 'the time has come when at least 5 per cent. of the School almost enjoy it'.
Could not an extension of time for playing it be permitted? 'Who can gainsay
that this would fill to the brim our cup of happiness?' he asked, tongue in cheek.

The correspondent was probably a disgruntled house 2nd XI player, Harford (the editor) protested in his reply.[18]

This seemingly innocuous letter touched a nerve and epistles appeared out of the blue. W.G. slammed Cheer-oh for 'withering satire'. Then, Argos (an Old Reptonian) replied in a lather of indignation about a spirit of 'unquenchable enquiry' animating the school:

> It is now nearly three years since some of us last sat on 'the Bank' on a perfect summer's day, when the war cloud was yet no bigger than a man's hand: it is three times as long since we last all wore that livery which—poor old-world sentimentalists that we are—it is still our pleasure to pull out of the well-worn bag on those fleeting and priceless days that from time to time we still can spend in England.

Cheer-oh was lambasted as a hot-blood and a zealot. Cricket to a Reptonian had been 'the measure of his life', not merely some incidental happening, and the game was all that mattered, yet Cheer-oh wanted to debase it. The most optimistic response came from 2nd Lieut who bubbled with pride in the fact that it was Repton, his old school, which he believed was the first to try to elevate education for average boys:

> The greatest complaint against the Public School boy used to be that he had no 'public spirit'; he was a perfect gentleman, but, as regards everythings [sic] of interest in contemporary matters, whether social, political or imperial, a perfect ignoramus, neither knowing nor desiring to know.

But, at long last, with the launch of a new and vigorous school publication, *A Public School Looks at the World*, and the formation of a new society, the Civics Class, 2nd Lieut thought that he was witnessing an opportunity to change that situation once and for all. With James in mid-1916 now being a member of Upper VIth, he was poised to participate in this ferment on which 2nd Lieut was pinning his hopes.[19]

SOME SYSTEMATIC TEACHING ON QUESTIONS OF THE DAY

1916–1917

... when a boy reaches his public school he finds himself in a world where actions are regulated not by conscience, but by caprice.

Alec Waugh, *The Loom of Youth*

There were five issues of *A Public School Looks at the World* between June 1917 and March 1918. To later generations habituated to criticisms of social distinction, stratification and authority, the furore generated by this schoolboy paper within and beyond Repton might be scarcely worthy of note. But with England and Germany locked in mortal combat, public school apologists—reeling from the publication in July 1917 of Waugh's *The Loom of Youth*—regarded the paper as bordering on treachery. Gollancz and Somervell at Repton, and Waugh in his autobiographical novel, aimed to shake public schoolboys out of their complacency. The Repton VIth read Waugh's book and three reviews appeared in *A Public School Looks at the World* in December 1917. Such was 'the fuss' created by *The Loom* that Holdsworth (in Oxford) reported to James in November that 'Phelpy [Phelps, Provost of Oriel College] was very disturbed' about it and 'questioned me rather innocently on the subject of language and filth which I answered as tactfully as possible under the circs'. So significant was the impact on James of Repton's own fuss that it transformed him. When wrestling with controversy later during his Geelong Grammar School (GGS) headmastership and broadcasting work, the Gollancz and Somervell experiment was his reference point.[1]

A Public School Looks at the World, known in Repton argot as the Pubber (to rhyme with Grubber for the tuckshop and Reptogger for *Reptonian*), emerged from a voluntary politics (or civics) class that was part of an experiment in political education inaugurated by Gollancz and Somervell with Fisher's blessing in January 1917. In Gollancz' reminiscences of two years at Repton, *More for*

Timothy (in which James is Cherry Aynsworth), he says that the inspiration for political education came to him following tea with the VIth at his house, when one boy, D.A. (Amyas) Ross, infuriated him by criticising the Irish—the Dublin Easter rebellion having taken place earlier that year:

> I told him not to talk like a prejudiced fool: I asked him what the hell *he* could know about? Had he studied the question? Had it ever occurred to him that to stigmatise people as incapable of anything at all till you'd given them the chance of doing it was quite half-witted? ... Had he ever considered what it'd feel like to be unable, no matter how much you wanted, to run your own bloody show in your own bloody way? Had he taken any stock of the fact that oppression, even if imaginary, embittered people?

Ross wilted under this barrage. When the rest of the group chimed in, including Cherry—who 'twittered about patriotism and the duty of all good Englishmen to stand by their country' but then attacked the poor—Gollancz was dumbfounded:

> Here was a set of boys, nearly all of whom I knew to be decent and generous, even perhaps great-hearted; and yet not one of them, to judge from their talk, had the smallest degree of sympathy with people less well-off than themselves, or any stomach for an argument that ran counter to their prejudices. They had simply accepted like a flock of sheep what had been fed to them; and what had been fed to them was poison.

Was Cherry:

> whom I knew to be sensitive, indeed exceptionally so, if nothing remarkable for brains or force of character, to grow up with such a notion [that poverty was the fault of the poor] irremovably fixed in his head[?]

Immediately, Gollancz resolved to teach politics during classics classes with the VIth.[2]

Poverty was one of the essay topics that he set and he was aghast at what the boys wrote. After about four weeks the 'quavery minor and affectionate' Cherry was showing promise. Gollancz sought to disarm his charges' prejudices:

> 'You [Cuddyfoot] talk the most awful drivel. You keep saying that poverty is the fault of the poor, but make no effort to prove it. Can you prove it? ...
> 'I wrote what I thought. And I still think it's true.'
> Here Ross came tearing in, like a bloodhound that's scented its quarry: 'But you've just admitted,' he cried—and there hung about him the overpowering excitement people exhibit at football matches—'that you don't know anything about it.'

'I meant I didn't know anything special. What do you know about it? Do you know anything special?'

'That's got nothing on earth to do with it. We're discussing now whether you're entitled to make the statements you make ... in your essay. I agree with V.G. that you're not.'

'Still,' said Aynsworth tremulously, 'I don't believe in socialism. Men weren't intended to be equal.'

'And who told you that that's what socialism means?' I asked him. 'Not that we were talking about socialism, anyhow.'

'What does socialism mean?' drawled Holdsworth ... Within minutes of Holdsworth's question ... the whole place was in an uproar.

The 'movement', as Gollancz dubbed it, now began in earnest with classroom discussions. Then, in that 'pre-ludial autumn', he and Somervell planned the civics class. Commencing just before Christmas, membership was voluntary, except that once accepted as a member a boy had to attend for an entire term. Civics would be held weekly on a half-holiday. The *Reptonian* wished this new venture well, proclaiming it a worthy adjunct to the public school's gentlemanly ideal and appealing to everyone to take 'the long view'. After these preliminaries, 'some systematic teaching on questions of the day' commenced. There were 29 lectures in 1917: introductory (two lectures), parliamentary reform (two), the position of women (three), the future of empire (three), trade unions (one), individualism and cooperation in industry (four), the organisation of peace and a League of Nations (three), conservatism (two), liberalism (one), modern Ireland (three), Alsace-Lorraine (one) and the Russian Revolution (four). Most began historically and ended 'on the verge of the future with a note of interrogation', with each weekly evening lecture lasting an hour.[3]

'We have not heard much useful criticism of the class', Gollancz and Somervell wrote when justifying their innovation in *Political Education at a Public School*. Initially, thirty-eight boys applied to take part. A few were rejected as too young and the membership settled down to over forty, at the core were those in the VIth, including James—a group, Somervell later remarked, who 'combined enthusiasm with "respectability"'. At twenty-two, Victor Gollancz was barely older than boys in the VIth. He had taken a first in classical moderations at Oxford and had been on home service as a 2nd lieutenant in the Northumberland Fusiliers. When rejected for military service due to poor eyesight, Fisher seconded him to Repton in early 1916. The boys referred to him as VG. James' notebook sketch depicted him with spectacles perched on the end of an elongated nose, with a black mustachio smudge above his lips. Harford recalled Gollancz as having 'the most restless and alert intelligence' expressed in his eyes, and as speaking in a 'very clear animated voice, with a range of tone which included an excited bantering falsetto which was quite irresistibly comic'. He 'fascinated us, and held us by the sheer brilliance and magnetism of his mind and personality'. James thought that Gollancz was 'electric' in the classroom:

> He would sweep into the room, usually late, with a disreputable gown under his arm and plunge straight into a fluent outpouring of whatever had been latest in his mind. No matter if this had little to do with the nominated subject of the period ... There was an exciting freshness about everything which he taught and he treated us more like undergraduates in a tutorial than as schoolboys in a class ... It was impossible not to be carried away by him but he welcomed argument and disagreement. The tremendous range of his intellect may have been his greatest quality, but it was the enthusiasm which carried all before it.

Gollancz opened the boys' eyes to a range of intellectual and artistic endeavours, including literature, poetry, art and music. He helped them to write Latin prose 'as though we thought in Latin'.[4]

David Somervell, whose sobriquet was Slimy (alliteratively abbreviated from Somervell—Slimy Bill), discharged less enthusiasm than his colleague, but for James Harford (whose sister Thea later married him) he was an equally remarkable master. His pithy recollection is of a mind both 'capacious and stimulating', always 'in one gear' and of a stern man with a forbidding presence:

> In appearance he was very tall and thin, with a scholarly stoop and a vast head, intellectual looking, with strong glasses and an air of authority. His voice had a wide range of inflection, his speech was a kind of caricature of the Oxford accent and manner. He voiced opinions on every subject, trivial or weighty, with Johnsonian deliberation and didacticism, extraordinary aptness and a wealth of epigram. He was completely without self-consciousness or inhibition ... He was intensely musical and by another twist of the road might have been a musical critic of note.

From the moment of his arrival at Repton Gollancz was ecstatic. 'I am having a far happier time here than ever I dreamed of or hoped', he told his friend Harold Rubinstein. The '[Lower] Sixth, who, if not very clever, are a charming lot of men, & one or two of them already very close friends of mine'. Ominously, Fisher noticed that friendship and warned Gollancz that it was ill advised. When offered a permanent job at the Ministry of Munitions in the summer of 1916, Gollancz rejected it and returned to Repton, whereupon Fisher put him in charge of the Upper VIth. By Christmas, he and Somervell were pedagogical bedfellows. Being 'a friendly soul with an expansive temperament', recalled Somervell, it was 'inevitable that I should go into partnership with Victor'—a formidable alliance between the young, vibrant and mercurial Gollancz, and the more measured, sober and circumspect Somervell.[5]

Gollancz' Repton opponents categorised him as dangerous. *Political Education at a Public School* (co-authored with Somervell) provides little support for such an assessment and there were even less grounds subsequently in the sentimentality of *More for Timothy*. Both men were reformers. Neither wanted to abolish the public schools (at least not immediately), although to throw them open to boys from all social backgrounds was folly. Rather, the public schools were 'supremely worth preserving'. Instead of seeking an end to class war, their priority was the spiritual resuscitation of what they regarded as venerable, although stuffy and ossifying, institutions—a self-evidently liberal standpoint:

> the supreme object of the genuine educationalist must be to bring out and reinforce that love of beauty, that passion for truth, and that disinterested desire to do what is right and good simply for its own sake, which are latent, in however slight a degree, in most young minds, but which are so commonly neglected and overlooked that men learn to hate and dishonour these things, instead of finding in them their greatest joy.

Crude philosophies of 'practical' education and 'vulgar efficiency', popularly known as 'Prussianism', were the authors' targets as much as class prejudices about refinement and the right to rule. They criticised the fact that, alongside such materialism, 'the life of the intellect, the life of the spirit and the true culture that is fostered by the love of great literature, art, and music' counted for little. Gollancz and Somervell blamed the curriculum, in particular classics (the system's 'staple diet'), for the public schools' failure to realise their ideals. For some boys the classics were a source of 'intellectual pleasure' but for others (perhaps most) they entailed 'the boredom of irregular verbs'. The 'one great reform' needed for curriculum revitalisation, in their view, was to substitute a political education for a classical one. The idea that the classics were doomed was the source of their radicalism:

> It is an appalling thought that the best educated members of the most powerful Empire in the world should leave school without ever having been trained to consider seriously the realities of the world about them, and the true nature of the responsibility which they bear.

The world was desperate for men of vision equipped with knowledge and imagination, they believed, and 'able to build a new national and international order of which the foundation is reverence for personality and the keystone brotherhood'. As consummate schoolmasters, the success of what they were proposing, of course, would rely heavily on their own charisma and intellectual acuity.[6]

As well as being a separate subject, politics was infused into classics classes. James' notebooks record four topics: 'The Meaning of the Study of Politics', 'The Chief Broad Characteristics of Greek Political Thought', 'The Pre-Socratics,

Socrates and the Minor Socratics' and 'Plato, His Life, Methods and Early Dialogues'. His notes on the first topic begin with the claim that sociology is the science of society and 'contains all the others'. Society is divided industrially and individually; political economy studies the former and ethics is the science of individual morals. 'Even a man on a desert island, even an atheist, has need of rules', he noted. Political science, once 'interchangeable' with ethics, according to the Greeks, but now connected to economics, is the study of men grouped under a common government or in a common state. All these sciences are 'interlaced and interconnected'. Politics was both a science and an art—a science when it investigated the combination of men of 'a certain view', and an art when these same men asked 'how can we make an Ideal State?' Political science could be studied either by observing a currently existing system, or 'you may take the nature of man and lay down [?] from that' what ought to be. Ethics was to be approached in exactly the same way. After sketchy annotations about tyranny, evil, rights and nature, James recorded the injunction that political science 'must give principles of co-ordination etc *not* rules to be enforced'. The ethical side of politics derived from metaphysics, with the abolition of slavery cited as one application of such a principle. 'A few evangelicals and puritans brought it about by working on the assumption of Englishmen that all men are equal.'[7]

In the summer of 1917, political education was 'at its zenith', according to Gollancz. Harford suggested something akin to the *Spectator* or the *Nation* so as to 'canalise the political waters that were swirling into spate'. The Pubber was born and Harford was its first editor. Its five editions yielded twenty-five articles, ten book reviews, nine poems, five 'Notes on Current Events', a letters column, two editorials and two sermons. The authors mostly signed themselves with their initials. Each edition carried about three pages of advertisements. For nine months the Pubber provided evidence of the liberal climate that Fisher tolerated, although he censored letters both critical and supportive of the paper because 'no one will suppose that I agree with all your views: with some I violently disagree'. Despite his censorship, as two reviewers of Waugh's *Loom* noted, Repton was at last beginning to free itself of philistine 'blood' dominance, so that intellectual and aesthetic idealism could come into their own. James' sole contribution was 'Patriotism', an essay in which he discussed different types of patriotism and their contribution to humanity (the highest good) and proposed 'true patriotism' which 'should look within', instead of the patriotism of competitive national and imperial struggle:

> [Patriotism] should be, first, a love of all the individuals who are our com-patriots. True patriotism would abolish poverty. It would spend less time watching the dockyards of its neighbours, and more time in investigating its own slums. It would spend less time abusing Lord Haldane because he admires the German schools where he was educated, and more time seeking to improve its own educational system. It would spend less time in making

England invincible in arms, and more time in seeking the true principles of
universal peace.

James' essay was an apologia for a hierarchically ordered society, except that his
model was not working: Gollancz noted that 'Cherry was getting uncomfortable'
and 'distressed' by the thought of poverty. On the other hand, 'he didn't like
equality either'. In fact, 'he hated the very thought of it: squire and villager, master
and man, with benevolence at the top and deferential courtesy at the bottom—
this is what he found irresistible'. Cherry's great fear, Gollancz thought, was that
'unless we were careful, equality might be the outcome of our meddlesomeness'.
Less obviously, James' essay also indirectly highlighted the importance of
group or tribal loyalty that was distinct from, and of higher importance than,
individualism. In a similar way, a man's 'true self' could be found only by 'merging
himself in his nation' because, just as individuals served their nation, nations
served humanity.[8]

James' progress in the Upper VIth was uneven. In the summer of 1916,
Gollancz observed that he had 'worked very well and keenly' in classics, despite
work that was 'often disfigured by elementary mistakes'. Stratton noted that he
was 'developing rapidly'. Fisher penned 'good' and suggested 'a trial fling' at a
scholarship. By November, however, James had stumbled. Again Gollancz pulled
no punches: 'His pure classics ... are poor' and showed 'little improvement',
although indications of 'a capacity to think' and 'a tendency towards some
independence of mind' were positive signs. Stratton, on the other hand, after
witnessing further evidence of James' earlier embarrassing behaviour, had
spotted maturity:

> At the top table he was really rather terribly self-conscious and juvenile
> to start with. He never said anything without a little laugh. No doubt you
> [Austen Darling] understand without further elaboration. However, I talked
> to him about it and he is now quite natural. As a very junior house prefect he
> has been quite a success. As far as I know he has had no difficulties in keeping
> order etc. On the whole I will write his report Good: I am pleased with him.

But his progress was not sufficient to win a scholarship. After James had sat for
the Oxford college scholarship examination, Phelps wrote: 'We couldn't select
you for this year'. His general paper had been first class and his essay, which
was 'not so badly thought of as you feared', was awarded B++. For his Latin
and Greek prose, however, James was advised to 'not ask too much'. Gollancz
had been vindicated, although Phelps had detected 'plenty of promise'. By early
1917 (with the civics class well under way) James was performing better: classics
displayed 'a distinct improvement' and his essay writing was at a 'high level'.
Stratton no longer had 'complaints to make' and in July affirmed James as 'a very

delightful person' who had 'developed amazingly'. Even Gollancz saw 'definite improvement' despite his 'still weak classics'. Indeed, there was 'a growing strength and certainty of touch'. Yet, just as he was beginning to blossom, James took on additional responsibilities. Austen was concerned that he had 'a good many irons in the fire', whereas a scholarship would enable him to be 'ticketed as a scholar of Oriel'. In his final Repton term (when the number of school societies was 'absolutely bewildering'), James was a school prefect, librarian, head of school, *Reptonian* editor, Repton School Debating Society chairman and founder of a theological society.[9]

James' last sighting of Holdsworth, Harford, Zevan Manoukian and the others was at a holiday harvest camp at Brampton, Cumberland, in August 1917 where, camped under canvas for several weeks, they had worked as farm labourers as part of Repton's contribution to the war effort. The weather was mostly inclement and little of note was accomplished, despite the local newspaper's appreciative words. 'The less said the better', James' *Reptonian* editorial noted. It was 'ridiculous to have come so far to drive grouse, mow lawns or move hen houses', and hardly stuff of 'National importance'. Nonsense, 'I enjoyed it', chirped Holdsworth: 'you must try and make your soul adaptable'. With Harford in the army at Newmarket, Holdsworth and Manoukian at Oxford, and McLeod Innes at Cambridge, Darling and Ross were the remaining members of the 'old firm'. And because the others were wary of what they regarded as Ross' conceit and precocity, James was deputed to apprise them of developments. 'I can't say how glad I am that you have really taken the place in all branches of Repton life that was really due to you', McLeod Innes told him. He craved to be back in the civics class and insisted on more news from James than the 'sundry hints in your letter which leave me in delightful mystification'. James' new theological society evoked the most favourable comments. He had broached the possibility of it with his father in September. Austen saw merit in it, provided that it was not merely an opportunity to mouth opinions. Balmforth (Balmers), the chaplain, gave it his blessing. Holdsworth had always found God 'very indispensable' and wished that he could have been a member; so too did McLeod Innes, although his Christianity was a trifle wobbly. Harford called it 'admirable' as, after having just lunched with Temple, his religious convictions felt stronger. James' friends were also intrigued by an upcoming mock trial, 'Rex *v.* Holmes', staged in October 1917. Holdsworth hoped that it would not end 'in complete frivolity' and that 'V.G.' would come up to 'scratch'. James was the judge in front of over 300 boys:

> Last of all Mr. (Justice) Darling, encased in a wealthy wig and an unique creation in collars, succeeded in dragging with him a large mass of red robe on to a dizzy height in the neighbourhood of the organ. He was assisted by a figure in sundry and gaudy garments, surmounted by an old top hat, and carrying a large book for reference in matter of precedent.

As Sherlock Holmes dressed in a gown and smoking a pipe, Gollancz stole the show:

> The judge assumed the black cap, or rather had it thrust upon his head by his obsequious secretary [Amyas Ross], but he had been taken by surprise—for he had himself made up the case—and had been expecting the verdict 'not guilty'. He, therefore, murmured the soothing news that the deceased Sergt.-Major had been revived by artificial respiration, so that he could not administer the death sentence.

James, his robes falling all around him, descended from his judge's 'perch', and led a confused judicial procession out 'amidst the shouts of the populace'.[10]

All the while, James' friends were giving him a foretaste of the fate in store for young idealists. From Magdalen, Holdsworth noted that his roommates were 'curious people'. Two of them talked 'filth for half an hour', and then suddenly switched and discussed poetry 'in quite an elevated way'. But he still believed in principles, he reassured James, and 'it will take more than this bloody system to beat them out of me'. Whenever he was having a good drink, was in a humorous mood or saw someone like John Masefield, the poet, at Boar's Hill, then life felt 'distinctly good'. Overall, the good outweighed the bad, 'so cheer up', Holdsworth enjoined him. Manoukian, the self-styled 'arch Athenian', graphically described the collapse of adolescent yearnings. He was desperate for the war to end and for a saner world:

> I have completely mastered my depression, although I had not deceived myself as to its causes. The causes were there are there for you and me and us all, so long as the war continues and even after. But I had not yet formulated my philosophy. I had only then 2nd hand views in which I didn't really believe such as Jingoism, church Christianity and a little too many common places [Gollancz' blackboard phrases] on trust.

The army had nearly destroyed Manoukian's faith. Instead, 'in intense work, in joie de vivre and in hope', but 'above all in building up some conception of the world and one's function in it', he had found independence and happiness. In 'Idealism and Education', in the November Pubber, he accused the army of destroying the altruism of school days with 'ignorance, shallowness, and vice', so that one was always disillusioned. While conceding all of the shortcomings of the army, Harford was more optimistic and held out the prospect of 'universal companionship, generosity, tolerance, cheerfulness, in fact complete brotherhood'. These attractions were better than anything similar at a public school, and there were far 'worse places than the army!' Even though James' stocks had risen, in the absence of the others, Gollancz pitched all his hopes for the future of political education onto Amyas Ross. Regardless of what James' friends thought about him, Ross was 'in a position of undisputed moral leadership', so much so that Gollancz dubbed Christmas term 1917 'the Amyas era'.[11]

By late 1917, the original political experiment was having a wider impact. One correspondent expressed 'a much-felt want' to be part of it and complained to the *Reptonian* that much of the school was excluded from the civics class. In addition to that class and the Pubber, Fisher had also authorised timetable changes in September 1917. 'Surely a place ought to be found in the regular curriculum for subjects that concerned every single human being as such', both Gollancz and Somervell had argued. After Brampton, all VIth boys would have two hours per week of modern history, one of outlines of world history, one of general principles of science, and three of political science and economics. James thought that the new arrangements were 'great'. After the publication of 'Patriotism', Fisher (claimed Gollancz) had said that 'Cherry's pieties could very properly have been delivered from the Repton pulpit'. Moreover, Cherry was 'coming on now … with remarkable rapidity'. But Darling's article and another by Ross triggered a wholesale 'row'. A hearty among the masters (the Ox) complained to the *Reptonian*, but his letter was withheld. Another letter referred to 'the movement for turning Repton into a collection of little prigs'. Somervell (the *Reptonian* censor) convened a conference between himself, Gollancz, Ross, Pruke (i.e., Snape), the Ox and the head prefect. It was agreed that the words: 'Nothing that appears in this paper is to be taken as expressing the opinion of the school as a whole' would be printed on subsequent Pubbers. Despite these developments, Fisher was still supportive as 1917 drew to a close. He even praised Ross' December editorial 'The paper and its critics', in which Ross had said that 'when we think the Government is making mistakes, we criticize those mistakes'. Fisher had censored only three letters, two of which were severely critical and another that was highly commendatory, because Ross' words had removed any need for controversy. In fact, an impartial reader of his editorial, said Fisher, 'will not fail to note how closely you anticipate the spirit and even some of the details of President Wilson's speech to Congress on December 4th last'.[12]

Despite a long-serving master's claim that political education was 'the best thing that's happened since I came here', a conservative reaction was building. It was led by Snape, who was not to be taken lightly. What finally forced Fisher's hand, however, was the insertion by Ross of a seemingly innocuous London address, 'and Henderson & Sons, 44 Charing Cross Road, S.W.1', after the usual authorisation ('Published by the Repton School Ltd.') in the final edition of the Pubber. Ross had tried to widen circulation by advertising the Pubber with Henderson's, a London bookshop known as the Bomb Shop and far too pink in its leanings for critics. To compound Ross' indiscretion, Henderson (the proprietor) bore a close physical resemblance to V.I. Lenin, and his sole criterion for the selection of books was that 'they must be rebel'. A Debating Society debate in February 1918 hastened the Pubber's demise when the motion that 'in the opinion of this house it is disgraceful that Conscientious Objectors, whether genuine or not, should be disenfranchised', was carried by twelve votes in the upper house and lost by twenty in the lower. About 170 staff and boys attended. Masters had sided against masters, and boys against boys. Snape was vehement and unrelenting in his Hun-hatred. 'The man who refuses to fight against Prussia', he barked, 'that obscene horror, the enemy of God and Man, is without a creed, without moral fibre, and without tenacity, an accomplice of Prussia'. Gollancz had spoken but Somervell, who 'deplored the whole business', had abstained. The Rev A.J. Agard-Butler, 'a Prukite master, a dimmish clergyman of a few months standing' (according to Gollancz) had suggested that, in his day, Ross and his seconder would have been ducked in the horse pond. The very next morning, an army class boy, P.G. Agnew (later Sir Peter Agnew, a Conservative MP) was thrown into 'the Stinker' (the Steinyard, a tributary of the Trent) and 'some of the little rebels were grossly bullied'.[13]

Denied a renewed appointment by Fisher for the following summer, Gollancz pleaded for his disciples' help. In France, Harford received 'a brief distraught letter' informing him that Fisher had decreed 'no more liberalism at Repton ... and sacked me without notice. I'm of course utterly forlorn—life for the time has lost every bit of meaning'. He also appealed to James (at Weedon, Northamptonshire, and absorbed in the minutiae of artillery manuals):

> Fisher has decided to suppress the Civics, Pubber, and Pol.Sci, and has asked me not to return on the ground that as long as I am there there is bound to be a strong liberal movement, which latter is undesirable. So there it is. I am of course utterly desolate.

'Now perhaps', he implored him, 'you will break your lengthy silence and give me a word of solidarity'. Letters of support for Gollancz 'poured in', but to no avail: the War Office had left Fisher with no alternative when it threatened to shut down the Repton OTC. For Gollancz who resigned, and for Somervell who accepted a position at Tonbridge, the 'struggle against Persia' was over.[14]

During these events in late 1917, James prepared for his scholarship examination. Family and friends had offered moral support. When he had last sat for the scholarship, Phelps confidently predicted that 'if you go on as you are going you will "romp in" next year'. McLeod Innes had also flattered him by saying that 'the Schol is assured' and Cattley hoped that James' final term at school would 'prove a very successful one in every way'. Even the *Highfield School Magazine* said that he was 'scholarship hunting at Oxford'. Despite this support, little help reached James apart from an excited letter from Holdsworth and some earnest advice from Gollancz. Holdsworth had undertaken some espionage:

> Your first two exams are (1) the General paper (2) Greek Unseen. The General Paper is corrected by the Viscount _____ (some [?] name like Schiller) the Warden of Wadham. That is all I remember. I called casually on Phelpy

and noticed a complete list of the exams on the table, searched <u>feverously</u> for a pencil and paper to copy them down and unfortunately found none, or I could tell you more.

Gollancz advised him to read Cicero, the symposium of Plato, Aeschylus and Catullus, all of which 'should keep you going pretty well', and then Blake's 'Songs of Innocence' for good measure. Prior to the examination (December 1917), James and some other candidates stayed for a weekend with a Rugby master, Philip Martin, in his house near Oxford. While there, James (in what was possibly his first attempt at smoking) suffered a ghastly bout of nicotine poisoning. Austen's worst fears were realised: James failed to win a scholarship. Martin was supportive and made a deep, albeit fleeting, impression on James who poured out his sorrows to him. Martin replied:

> You need not be ashamed, whatever happens, to write or talk about things. You have come to that conclusion on your own account though. And, as you say 'if we fail' it is well to remember that ''Tis not in <u>mortals</u> to command success' and perhaps go onto say with [the poet] Henley 'my head is bloody, but unbow'd'. The tragedy of failure is not in the lack of success—it only becomes a tragedy when it becomes defeat—admitted and accepted as inevitable—when, in fact, the struggle ceases …

The situation 'hasn't, nor shall it, come to a mere wreck', Martin insisted: 'and I am not excusing failure'.[15]

Phelps put on a brave face: James had obviously been distracted by the prospect of military service:

> so that probably you did not do yourself justice in yr. papers, and in your work—but, I must add, that you impressed us all by your account of Reptonian activities, in wh[ich] your modesty prevented you from saying <u>quorum pars magna fui</u> [of whom I was a great part]—& I felt that the subjects wh[ich] are just now so much in the minds of us all meant more to you than to the others, and what was to them only a part, so to say, of life, was to you life itself.

If James felt that he had sacrificed everything, then he had done so 'in the best of causes'. He could never look back in vain on his school life because he had lived it 'on the side of right' and had helped make things better than he had found them. James then wrote to Gollancz and thanked him for everything. Gollancz urged him to 'keep jolly about things and don't get depressed', but James was so disconsolate that when he subsequently met Holdsworth, the latter found it 'a great task to cheer you up that day'. From James' 'brazen narrative of 4–7 pm debaucheries', Holdsworth's efforts were evidently aided by some dissipation, as a result of which, he predicted, 'conscience will, no doubt, drag you down to the valley of penitence'. Austen hoped that his son would not be disappointed. He discounted the result by saying that it did not matter 'so much as if you had to go up immediately', but there was a sting in the tail:

> Perhaps when the war ends we may be able to move into a small house and save some money if anyone has any money by that time. It would mean however that you would have to do things very economically which I am afraid you would not like.

Manoukian told James to forget classics and Oxford that in the end counted for little:

> You will have done far more by formulating for yourself some philosophy of life or rather feeling the need of such, by purifying your soul of British and insular prejudice and looking out on Europe, nay a world composed of potential genii like ourselves, by training your body to work and your mind to know and your eyes to see etc than by gaining £0000 of Oriel scholarship.

Manoukian had won a scholarship. He saw it as a ladder to increased knowledge of the classics and greater wisdom, but he never climbed it as he died in battle.[16]

However distasteful the prospect, James might have to return to Repton, which, as he told Martin, he dreaded. Martin soothed him by discounting scholarship as 'over-rated' and proposing a 'doctrine of arrangement' to rationalise what had befallen his young friend:

> Let's see. You have worked for this, and really wanted it, prayed for it, and failed. Now the 'unlit lamp, and the ungirt loin' cannot be imputed—& there seemed a good chance of your getting it, I take it. Why this failure then? Now, I cannot answer that, any more than you can—but that is not to say that it has no answer! I have been butting blindly about the world myself, for enough grass to discourage anyone, without finding the thing to do … At times I have been frightfully down, for I can with justice reproach myself for years wasted at Oxford and else-where—when the lamp was, if not unlit, in grave danger of extinction!

Martin had failed a medical course, the war had come and he was invalidated out. After that, a 'curious combination of circumstances, unsought of by the way', landed him at Rugby. Hope sprang eternal and 'I dream dreams once more!' And because being a schoolmaster was as far from his original goal as was imaginable, James should feel nowhere near as discouraged as he had.[17]

If it was not to be the life of the mind, then, where did James' talents lie? Phelps' advice had been:

[to] take as your motto for 1918 'Covet earnestly the best gifts'—and remember
that the men who do the most good in the World are the men whose presence
makes evil unprofitable.

James had been doing considerable good at Repton and at least three boys were
in his debt. The first, McLeod Innes (recalled by Gollancz as 'an ugly little poet'),
had been suspected of theft:

one night [his housemates] got hold of him, and pulled out his moustache
hair by hair; and then several of them beat him in turn, while others held him
over a table. I know about this because I saw what he looked like next morning
when he came into class, and made enquiries.

The public humiliation of this allegedly 'unprepossessing little chap' took place
in front of his boarding house, following which he was 'completely isolated by
society'—shortly afterwards Somervell removed his work from the *Reptonian*.
One day at football, James spoke to McLeod Innes and ended his pariah
status. Afterwards he wrote regularly to him. Mortified by what he had done
and bewildered by his motives, McLeod Innes confessed to being thoroughly
chuffed when James wrote. 'It is very noble of you', he said. Somervell was 'so
glad' and commended James on his moral courage. The second boy was Harold
Abrahams—the future English Olympic sprinter. Abrahams was a wretchedly
lonely young boy, by no means 'academically sound' (as described later by the
Master of Gonville and Caius College in the film *Chariots of Fire*) but 'arrogant
and defensive to the point of pugnacity'. Abrahams had reported a fellow
Strattonite to McLean (the head of Stratton) for reading during Balmforth's
sermon. For his sins, the offender 'received 6 in pyjamas!' and called Abrahams a
'swine'. James' friendship resulted in an invitation to Abrahams' home. 'I do hope
you can come', he implored James:

I feel more than delighted whenever I think that I got to 'know' you at the
[Brampton] camp. I had always wanted to and hoped vaguely that a chance
would come one day. I was fearfully bucked when I knew you were coming
to the camp.

After an enjoyable evening's company with James, Abrahams once again felt
'bucked with life'. 'Will you believe it', Abrahams wrote, 'I woke up in the middle
of the night saying to myself "I'm so glad, I've got to know Darling"'.[18]

James' third good deed was to rescue the Stratton house 2nd XI wicket-
keeper from a sexual encounter with an older boy. The culprit had offended at
least twice, once with the junior and once with a friend of James. 'He is a fool',
McLean said about the offender: 'a nice lad but lamentably lacking in intellect!

But how did they meet during prep-time?' James' young friend was beaten and
the guilty boy expelled. The night before the latter left James tried to console
him. 'What a fool I have been', he wailed, overwhelmed by concern that his
misdemeanour may have cost him an army commission. 'I shall be stranded if it
does'. The younger lad confessed what he had done and, after Brampton, invited
James to his home. James sought Austen's advice, which was that 'if you think you
can do any good I should go by all means'. With James' connivance McLean tried
to have the lad made one of his fags. 'Thank you for telling me', said McLean.
'Unless house prefects work together, and not secretly, it is absolute rot'. As dispirited about the scholarship failure as James was, these incidents point to strengths
of character that were obvious to his friends. 'Take care of yourself as good people
are very scarce!', a Brampton acquaintance wrote. He was extraordinarily lucky
to have been taught by Gollancz and Somervell, and if Aldous Huxley (later
the famous novelist) had not transferred to Eton after one term as a temporary
Repton master, he might have been even luckier. The recent political education
experiment had quickened the pulse of an essentially minor, provincial English
public school. 'There happened as between Victor and these boys, what I have
never seen happen anywhere else, education not by mimetic drill but by direct
communication or inspiration', Somervell wrote later. James was stimulated by
exciting ideas, his horizons were broadened and he acquired intellectual curiosity. A model of the Renaissance man had been held up as an ideal to the VIth.
For this reason if for no other, as the war ground on into 1918, James had much
for which to be thankful. The prospect of VIth dinners in London in January
lay in front of him, and later on the possibility of even more 'colossal dinners' in
Brussels, such as Harford had been indulging in with Holdsworth. Beyond that,
the future looked grim for them. The words of gentle Alan Gorringe, Gollancz'
'best' friend on the Repton staff—shortly to die of pneumonia (and to whom he
and Somervell dedicated their second book *The School and the World*)—so poi-
gnantly encapsulated the fearsome tragedy that lay in wait for James' generation.
"Sworth is here this weekend', he told him:

> and is in great form—full of health & vitality and looking beautiful in its best
> sense. It is altogether horrible to think of him so soon to go off to run the risk
> of being killed in the attempt to kill others.

Gorringe prayed earnestly for peace, so that 'many of those I know so well—you
for instance—may be spared this appalling ordeal'. He wished James every good
luck and all the necessary health and strength.[19]

4

BAPTISM OF FIRE

1918–1919

We were eighteen and had begun to love life and the world; and we had to shoot it to pieces.

Erich Maria Remarque, *All Quiet on the Western Front*

The military preparedness of English schoolboys was mostly undertaken by school OTCs. Officer cadet training was introduced in 1908. It replaced the older school corps attached to volunteer militia to rectify a dearth of regular officers and to 'improve and standardize military training'. The OTC was intended as the preparation for a commission that would 'appeal to the intelligence and patriotism' of its members. Schools received an annual training grant of £3000 and could determine their own form of corps organisation. They reported directly to the War Office, which regarded the OTC as 'an integral part of the military machine of the Empire'. In 1914, Repton's cadet corps comprised all eligible boys divided according to War Office instructions into A and B companies (known as the efficients and the inefficients). The houses were split into four platoons per company, usually headed by masters holding a cadet corps commission. By early 1916, those platoons comprised four sections of eighteen boys each. Two years' service was considered sufficient to qualify a boy as an efficient cadet. The number of boys who thought of the Repton OTC as playing at being soldiers or who became militarily predisposed as a result of their experiences is guesswork. Sir James Darling thought that the OTC was a joke and recalled very few contemporaries who were keen on it. The outline of the new corps arrangements in the May 1914 *Reptonian* (on which James scribbled for his father 'this part of the Reptogger may interest you') expressed scepticism. Of the newly intended company set-up it noted merely that the line between some 'weaker members and the better specimens of the inefficients is very slender indeed', and that borderline cases would need 'continual re-sorting'.[1]

When war was declared, the OTC's call on boys' time increased and there were frequent complaints in the *Reptonian*. From 1915 there were two weekly afternoon parades on Mondays and Fridays, and an afternoon uniform parade each Wednesday, including field operations, and evening lectures on Tuesdays and Saturdays. In March, the Friday parade switched to Saturday afternoon, which meant the loss of a half-holiday. In March 1916, James was a lance-corporal and by May 1917 he was No. 12 Section Commander, 3rd platoon, A Company. In June he was promoted to corporal and to sergeant in November. Certificate A boys were proficient at 2nd lieutenant level and exempted from additional training. They were posted when they were eighteen-and-a-half years old, when there were cadet unit vacancies. Apart from regular drill, bugling, drumming, competitions and participation by the shooting VIII in the prestigious Ashburton Shield at Bisley, the Repton OTC's major activities were the annual camp and periodic interschool field days.[2]

As for his knowledge of war, an English schoolboy relied on what he was told or read mainly in newspapers. At school, addresses, sermons, school magazines and debating societies were the main information sources. (If, like James, he lived in the south-east, he might also hear distant cannon fire and notice repatriated wounded men.) One historian claims that these media predisposed a generation of young men to patriotism and 'moral' preparation for war; another criticises deleterious school magazines because old boys' letters from France bred a 'blithe, almost carefree heroism'. If not militarism at Repton, then patriotism probably, although the *Reptonian* was not a propaganda mouthpiece. Rather than indoctrinating boys, it brought home the reality of the war in four main ways: cumulative lists of dead and wounded Reptonians; mentions in dispatches for gallantry; letters; and verse expressing battle themes. In the chapel each week the names of casualties were read aloud. About 250 Old Reptonians on active service had died when James left school—the equivalent of two-thirds of the total enrolment. 'Capella' complained (in May 1917) about the absence of the national anthem in chapel at the end of services: 'this is universally done in our Churches and why not in School Chapel?' While thirty-six Old Reptonians' letters from the front described grim events for youthful minds, details were usually recounted baldly or mechanically (to circumvent censorship): the picture conveyed was combat tedium and drudgery. Occasionally there were grisly tragedies, such as on a troop train journey when a soldier stood on top of a carriage 'and a bridge knocked his head in' and another 'got his throat cut by telegraph wires crossing the line'. The emotion evoked was as likely to be revulsion as heroism.[3]

Likewise, the 222 *Reptonian* obituary notices (before James departed) manifested little colour or sentimentality. The scholastic achievements and sporting accomplishments of the fallen were acknowledged, but only when John Howell (rated in his final year as the best-ever batsman to attend Repton—C.B. Fry included) was killed in France in September 1915 did the school indulge in anything approaching veneration.

To us his memory remains as that of our ideal of a clean-minded, fearless schoolboy, wonderfully good at games but quite unspoiled by success, certain to make his corner of the world the better for his presence, as shown by the good influence which he exercised on us all.

And when Lieutenant J.G. Smyth became the first Old Reptonian Victoria Cross winner, the *Reptonian* bent over backwards to avoid exultation. Mentions in dispatches and military honours obtained comprised bluntly worded single-line notices. References to Germany used restrained wording: 'Hun' was seldom used; mostly the *Reptonian* said 'the enemy', 'Germans' or 'the Boche'. A letter describing the fabled 1914 sharing of Christmas even said that 'an informal truce was made and we spent the day talking to our friends the Germans ... Fancy talking to a real live Iron Cross and not shooting the owner!' Likewise, the Turks were commended by a correspondent as behaving 'very well': indeed, 'stopped shelling ambulances as soon as the Red Cross flag was hoisted in a conspicuous place—let go captured Red Cross doctors and orderlies, and returned our wounded'. Finally, only three poems made an explicit connection between games and war.[4]

The real effect of the war, as the *Reptonian* said (in 1915), was to return to school to find 'our ranks' depleted:

It is as if these boys, whom we have known so well here, begin to go out in response to the call they feel made upon them that the real significance of the present situation is brought home even to those who have no relatives fighting. The number of empty seats in Chapel, besides the many vacant spaces in our own Houses, remind us of it continually.

If James read the obituaries, then until about Christmas 1915 many may have meant very little to him; in only a few cases could he have put faces to the names. But when senior boys departed, the real significance of what was happening hit home:

I can well remember boys who had been ... arbitrarily called up at any stage of the school term, coming round the bedders on their last night at Repton and shaking hands with everyone, knowing, as we also knew, that in the following term, at the voluntary intercession services in Chapel on Friday evenings, we might hear their names read out by the boss in the O.R. casualty list for that week.

With the average life expectancy of a Western Front subaltern estimated at three weeks (during the winter of 1916–17) this likelihood was very real.[5]

In May 1917, James had enlisted at Derby as a gunner in the Royal Field Artillery. In January 1918 he was ordered to attend the Royal Field Artillery

Cadet School at Weedon, Northamptonshire. A little over four years beforehand
he had arrived at Repton as a timid fourteen-year-old, easily bruised emotionally
and lacking in confidence, yet here he was at eighteen about to become an officer
who would command men (senior in age and lower in social rank). He was not
alone: right around the country similarly aged schoolboys were being entrusted
with the defence of the realm. As gentlemen, English officers were supposed to
have 'an effortless and uncontrived capacity for radiating self-assurance, good
manners and a courteous if paternalistic mien towards those of inferior station'.
James had to acquire this quality, but learning it did not come naturally and
his inexperience showed. A recruit's daily routine comprised early morning
stablework followed by riding school, parade, gun drill and physical training
before lunch, and the learning of battery procedures from artillery manuals
after lunch. In two reports soon after his nineteenth birthday (June 1918), the
colonel commanding 1A Reserve Brigade described him as 'very young', but
'will improve with experience, a nice boy'. His education, gunnery, map reading
and signalling skills were all rated as 'V.F.' (very fair) in his first (cadet school)
report, but for riding and command he obtained only an 'F' (fair). In his second
(school of instruction) report, education and gunnery had risen to 'G' (good), his
map reading and command were rated 'V.F.' but his riding was stuck on 'F'. The
second time around, his overall assessment looked much better, for it said 'fit for
service [in] Bty. Young, clever but not very quick. Has fair Command & should
make a useful Officer with more age'.[6]

       As confirmation of his youthful naivety, James was laughed at when kneeling
beside his barrack bed to pray, until a voice ordered the barrack room to let him
be, and he embarrassed himself trying to ride a horse—he had no desire to be a
foot-slogging infantryman. There were weeks of frustration until, when having to
mount a hardened and cunning nag named Dirty Dick, he succeeded after being
thrown off on the initial attempt. He learnt that a soldier's life was an endless
round of polishing, grooming, riding, drilling and physical training. 'I do pity
you', Charles Sidey, a friend, had consoled him the night before he had departed
for Weedon: the next day (21 January) Sidey supposed would 'seem like being
a new boy at a school'. By April, James was boasting to Harford: 'I have as you
will see from my address reached the dizzy heights of the senior troop here'. The
fine detail of his notebooks recorded the grinding slog of learning to be a battery
leader, as he wrestled with obtaining clear sightings, finding correct elevations,
calculating the right range and securing the accurate fire of an 18-pounder. The
next month was spent firing guns on Salisbury Plain at the Lark Hill School of
Gunnery, which, he had told Harford, was bound to be 'unadulterated Hell'. On
8 July 1918, he was commissioned as a 2nd lieutenant, having been described as
5 feet 10 inches (178 cm) tall, and 'underdeveloped in maturity and physically
weak'. James' final duty prior was attendance at a gunners' defence course in
September at Whitley Bay, Newcastle, where there was yet another rearing
horse. At the end of that month, he departed for France, in time for the final

stages of the war, although the next few weeks were of 'tremendous personal importance'. Pre-embarkation, Margaret came to London to farewell him. His first night in the field was encampment at Boulogne and the next morning he reported to brigade HQ, 78th Brigade Royal Field Artillery, minus his suitcase, which had been stolen from the train, leaving him bereft of his field glasses and personal effects.[7]

James complained to Margaret that he had to wait before reporting to his battery. He was in the 'most godforsaken place in this country, miles away from the front line, and with absolutely nothing to do'. He wished that he had brought some very long books to help pass the time. Eventually, he reached C. Battery—apprehensive, given that his predecessor had survived a mere three days. Supported by a gas offensive, the 78th Brigade's batteries were assisting an infantry advance on Gouzeaucourt, just south of Cambrai in northern France. The Germans had counterattacked and on 27 September drove back the 78th. Stuck in a cubby-hole dug into the side of a road covered only by a tarpaulin, James lay awake in a cold sweat:

> every shell which landed within a square mile of us seemed to be going to land on me; I could not distinguish between the roar of an old 9.2 as it rolled over to the wagon lines behind and that other roar which any shell makes when it is indeed likely to land close to you.

His precarious shelter served as an officers' mess. Having to stumble over dead bodies in the dark amid unrelenting German shelling had made his arrival unpleasant. The pounding went on for days. Every morning, he would crawl out to inspect the shell holes made in the night, and remembered vividly reassuring himself that only a direct hit was lethal and that he would be unaware of it.[8]

James' arrival coincided with the final Allied offensive on the Hindenburg Line. The Germans were retreating rapidly. By 8 August, the British sector of the front ran almost in a straight line on a north–south axis from Arras to just below Villers-Bretonneux. By 26 September the line had moved east through to St Quentin in the south, although it was still west of Cambrai in the north. As the official war historian observed, these were extraordinarily quick gains made with far fewer losses than two years earlier:

> The ground, besides being traversed by the south–north course of the Somme and the Canal du Nord, and affording a multitude of small features and localities suitable for concealment of men and guns, was seamed with the trenches and wire of former positions, which furnished a succession of lines admirably suited to an enemy carrying out a series of delaying tactics.

Such topography was not conducive to full-frontal assaults and the use of tanks. Consequently, the artillery 'had to be called upon for a prolonged work of devastating fury'. During these delaying tactics on poor terrain James took his first active command. After eight hours continuous enemy bombardment, the Third Army was within 5 kilometres of Cambrai. The Germans held on for nearly another fortnight. On 5 October, C. Battery crossed the Canal du Nord. After further fighting the next day in the Vaucelles Wood, there was a day-long pause before all batteries covered an infantry attack on Inchy at 1 am on 8 October. That day, C. Battery's 18-pounders were commended for 'good work in chasing over 100 bosch out of WALLINCOURT [sic] TRENCH LINE back into WALLINCOURT VILLAGE'. To press home their advantage, GOC 17th Division ordered the 51st Brigade to act as an advance guard with a number of artillery units (including the 78th) at 5 am on 9 October. The advance comprised five 'bounds' to capture 6 kilometres of territory, including Walincourt and high ground to the north, and Selvigny and the road running north of it, on a 'bright autumn day', with a touch of cold in the early twilight advance and then pleasant warm sunshine soon after sunrise'. Because the Germans had been retreating during the night for a determined last stand at the River Selle, the British now moved forward 'with prudent caution' past Walincourt and by 9 am had accomplished three of their five objectives.[9]

The British Army next reached Beaumont and Inchy, the first places at which James' battery encountered civilians. He and his men were billeted by the local winemaker. They were now beyond the Hindenburg Line. For the next ten days, the Germans stubbornly repulsed the British advance until 20 October when Neuvilly fell. James spent part of this period at Solesmes. 'We are in a village', he told Margaret, 'luckily in a cellar and he shells the place to [the] full off and on night and day'. On 22 October the British crossed the Selle and pressed on through Vendiges au Bois, Ovillers to Poix du Nord. Once more C. Battery was commended, this time for 'good shooting at MGS [machine guns] and during the barrage at 16.00 hrs. sniped the enemy as they retired'. The British then pushed due east through the village of Locquignol and La Forêt de Mormal—an oak and birch wood about 14 kilometres by five to six in size and traversed by narrow unmetalled tracks that marked off the forest into 'large diamond-shaped blocks'. Here James tried foolishly to circuit a huge landmine crater and succeeded in getting a wagon and six mules stuck in mud. After a short lull, 78th Brigade moved on through Futoy, and La Tête Noire to Limont-Fontaine, in early November, when the British suffered casualties from enemy fire and, tragically, from 'short shooting of some of our own batteries' (a not uncommon occurrence, as fledgling subalterns found the precise execution of three or four rounds grossly difficult). After the selection of suitable ground and cover, the accurate trajectory of a shell over 2750 metres was affected by barometric pressure, air temperature, and wind velocity and direction. In what was called the rectangle of error (about 90 metres in length on its long sides), 75 per cent of shells fired would land in a central area 50 metres wide and the remainder on either side of that zone. After each barrage the angle of elevation was lifted a further 25 metres as the infantry moved in. Once, James badly misjudged the angle: to calculate the range he used the map, except that his calculation was too short. Another potential hazard was caused by the slow rate at which messages travelled back to the artillery, so that the infantry could already be in possession of a target whenever a bombardment began. On one occasion when James felt 'very diffident'—because he had 'worked it out several times and still lacked confidence'—he ordered only a token response and 'then switched over to something else'.[10]

When James' men died, he relied on Margaret to do what she could to make things easier for the soldier's family. 'You might go and see her [the widow of one of his men]', he urged his sister, 'and see if you can do anything to help her or put her on the right track for getting help if she is in financial trouble'. In his own close brushes with death, he had his share of luck. With six guns normally in a line, each about 6 metres apart, a shell once landed between the first and second guns, 10 metres to the rear:

> Not only did it not go off but it bounced on something. It went into the ground and bounced out again and lay there, a bloody great thick sausage thing, which caused us considerable alarm … we were none of us game to touch it. Then we had to sit and watch it until somebody capable, an engineer or somebody, came and removed it.

In early November, the 17th Division moved on to Berlaimont. Still located on the left bank of the Sambre River, the British headed north to Bavay and then to a village on the Belgian border near Charleroi, where James first heard news of the Armistice on 11 November. Some Allied Army units went on to the Rhine, but James was ordered to return to Allery, a village halfway between Paris and Calais near Abbeville, and so missed out on a representative parade of the 78th in the presence of the king at Neuvilly on 4 December. Once, prior to the Armistice, he went down with fever, soaking wet from falling into water up to his neck. Then, in the bitter winter cold during the march back to Allery, he fainted on parade. Compared to the experiences of others around him, dying of the influenza that was devastating the army, these were minor inconveniences. With the cessation of hostilities, his sole recreation was playing poker. He was 'horribly bored' and wanted to go to Oxford, he told Phelps, except that he wasn't really sure. Because he had no idea about a suitable future line of work, could Phelps suggest anything?

> To be perfectly honest I have seen so little of the war that it has had no effect on me, and I feel almost the same as I did this time last year when I had just failed to get a scholarship. So you see my present state of mind is a trifle decayed.

To make matters worse, following their liberation, Allery's inhabitants had not rushed to embrace the British whereas in previously liberated villages and towns they had acclaimed them with *'les ons qui nous délivrent!'* ('our liberators!'). 'They are altogether too fond of the Australians who were here before us and had too much money to spend.'[11]

James thought that the countryside was lovely, although it was always raining and that, as the men (with demobilisation in mind) still had to attend to their horses and vehicles, they were discontented. To add to his annoyance (because of his limited facility with French) he was made liaison officer for the 17th Division, with the unhappy result that he had to adjudicate frustrating arguments with French peasants about reparations for items such as damaged trees. Their speech, he told Phelps, was 'a most horrible mixture of the remnants of the grammar book, some patois and a few words of English thrown in'. On the other hand, there were a few compensations, as he told Margaret:

> we are all kicking our heels [up] and wasting time doing absolutely nothing ...
> We were having a fair number of Race meetings, at which I was very unlucky, but the frost has stopped them. And now we are hoping for some toboganning tomorrow.

He had received news of Mabel and Jean, he continued but, having nothing significant to report, 'they are getting the wind up at home'. There was one item of interest: after taking leave in February 1919 he would be part of the Allied Army of Occupation. 'I am quite looking forward to going to Germany; it will be interesting', he wrote, and '24/6 a week extra pay, is not to be scoffed at by any means'. After two days protracted travel from Boulogne, James joined the educational training scheme as a replacement teacher in Cologne. There had been instruction of reservists in France since early 1917. The scheme followed the recommendations to the Ministry of Reconstruction of a committee on adult education (chaired by the Master of Balliol—with the membership including Temple's two close friends, Mansbridge and Tawney). Colonel Lord Gorell (Deputy Director of Staff Duties, Education, War Office) estimated that there were upwards of three million potential students for whom to provide classes. The scheme commenced in January, when 'some of the movement consequent upon the signing of the Armistice had ceased and before the sun of demobilization had begun effectively to melt away the masses'. Shortly afterwards, James was posted to Northern Divisional Ammunition Column at a village called Widdersdorf.[12]

At the Handels-real-schule in Cologne, the British Army established the Headquarters General and Commercial College. Here there were subjects for Bachelor of Arts and Bachelor of Science degrees. There were commercial, art and music streams and even provision for ordinands. James told Margaret that he was studying Pitman's shorthand. Serving teachers and students were permitted to 'claim priority of release' and were very quickly demobilised. As James had

had a good education and had suffered little during the war, he felt obliged to become an education officer. In May 1919, he undertook a short course at the VIth Corps School of Education. Earlier in January, Phelps had suggested an application for the Egyptian Civil Service. James spotted an opportunity 'for doing well and doing good', but nothing came of it. He said to Phelps that his overriding concern was to find work so as not to be 'dependent on my people again if it can be helped'. His choice of education signalled that he was sensing a possible vocation: 'I am going to go on a course of teaching and am going to teach elementary reading, writing and arithmetic to the troops whether the[y] want it or not'. A month later he told his mother that he was 'really teaching people':

> They certainly do not go to sleep and I don't think they are bored, but whether they learn anything or not, I am afraid I cannot say. At least, I think, we make their minds begin to work and that is the aim of Education in the army as I see it.

The futility of occupation life had little to commend it. He liked Cologne, he said to Margaret, and the Rhine was 'lovely' except that much of his life was spent in idleness and dissipation. Although some of his peers seized the opportunity to sow their oats, James' main indulgence was mild drinking. 'There are five girls in my billet at present; there is safety in numbers', he reassured his sister, 'and one of them is teaching me German, which is a thoroughly objectionable language'. Still, being interrupted by one of them was 'quite a new way of ending a letter. Cheerioh', he quipped cheekily. Occasionally he went to nightclubs and played billiards in a village farmhouse requisitioned as an officers' mess. He also went to the opera: mostly for performances of Wagner, Gollancz' favourite composer.[13]

In August 1919, James was recalled to the War Office School of Education in Newmarket, which he attended until mid-September. As part of the army's educational training scheme, War Office schools originally had offered month-long intensive courses. Their duration was now doubled so that officers might 'receive instruction in the scope and object of educational training and in the theory and practice of teaching'. Besides this practical element, seven academic options were offered. James chose 'Social Science and Modern Industrial History'. He loved it. As a potential instructor he was assessed as 'distinguished'. One man at Newmarket who endeared himself was Major James (later Sir James) Shelley (Professor of Education, University College, Southampton), the school's chief instructor. After his course, James returned to Germany and, after applying for demobilisation, was discharged at the Crystal Palace Dispersal Unit on 31 October 1919. In December he relinquished his temporary commission but retained his rank. Two years in the army had changed him: demanding exercises, constant activity, order and discipline, had physically developed and toughened him. When demobilised his health was rated as 'A1' although, due to his own carelessness, his teeth had given him wretched trouble, and over the summer in Germany his hay fever had played havoc. He now knew firsthand the ever-present danger, the ubiquitous noise, the unpleasantness, the inhumanity, the ennui (which, to try to alleviate, he had constantly urged Margaret to send him books) and the sheer horror of war. 'The actual experience re-assured me', he reflected years later, 'that I wasn't as miserable a little creature as I thought I was and that I had come through, without disgracing myself, a certain amount of pressure'.[14]

Amid all the horror and destruction, he had also encountered straightforward human decency and honesty. Apart from Shelley, there was the simple respect engendered by Edmunds, his groom in Cologne, and the quiet, unquestioning dedication of Wishart, his battery sergeant-major who, during James' early uncertainty as an officer, had let him down gently. Tragically, Wishart had died in the brickfields of the Poix du Nord shortly before the Armistice. Supreme among these newly influential people, however, had been Major C.F.K. Marshall, to whom James owed 'a very considerable debt':

> He knew every man in the Battery and the horses as well. He demanded efficiency and had a fierce and effective temper which was terrifying while it lasted, but he had the one essential quality of a commander, the capacity to command respect, on the basis of the recognition that he really cared for those for whom he was responsible.

Marshall taught James never to spare himself when in command, and the importance of securing the safety and comfort of one's subordinates, along with devotion to duty. Marshall endeared himself by suggesting that James remain an army officer. Commanding men had not been easy for him as they were mostly Durham miners who, rather than automatically obeying, tended to 'do what they were told if it was explained to them what the point of doing it was'. In going beyond the field dressings, diseases, diet and sanitation of his Weedon notes by having Margaret visit the widow of one of his men, James was appreciated:

> I received your parcel all right and was very grateful for it, it came at a very good time for the children were all down with the measles and they enjoyed the biscuits and sweets, and I need not say that I am enjoying the cigaretts [sic] all right.

He learnt other lessons about the responsibilities that were bestowed on those in command roles, such as occasional free licence with the truth, especially when drafting commendations for gallantry:

> Just before the end of the war the Major said: 'Oh Lord, you can write better than I can. Put in two sergeants for a Military Medal'. I said: 'Well what shall

I say?' He said: 'Oh, make up any story you like'. So I made up two stories and
put them in. One man got a D.C.M. and the other got nothing.

The most important thing that James learnt was to not show fear, especially
when it would unnerve rank-and-file soldiers: 'Normally you were more frightened of making a fool of yourself I think', such as 'diving for cover when it was
unnecessary'.[15]

By early 1919, James' mind had turned to Oxford. In January, the secretary
of the Oxford Appointments Committee enquired of him whether or not he
had matriculated. Phelps ascertained James' eligibility to enter Oriel: as he had
passed the Oxford and Cambridge Higher Certificate Examination three years
earlier, he was qualified for admission. Later that year, he made up his mind. As
Austen would pay the necessary £180 annually to support him, James could fulfil
Phelps' fond hope 'that some means may yet be found to send you to Oxford—
when peace comes'. Because of his reluctance to impose further financial burdens
on his family, James took a shortened two-year course over five terms. If he felt
inclined to teach, then this program would equip him to be the schoolmaster
that McLeod Innes had taken for granted both of them would become. 'We
shall merely have to carry on the Gollancz traditions—a noble & inspiring
prospect! Tho' not fraught with the possibilities of danger that beset the actual
reformer.' For the moment, however, James joined the swelling ranks of English
ex-servicemen about to descend upon the ancient and venerable university beside
the Isis.[16]

A PLEASANT OASIS

1920–1921

I want to be at work in the world, and not dawdling away three years at Oxford.

Thomas Hughes, *Tom Brown's Schooldays*

In 1920, when James went up to Oriel, the famous college was almost 600 years old. When founded in 1324 by Adam de Brome (almoner to Edward II), Oriel comprised a provost and ten fellows. It was rebuilt in 1619 and completed in 1642 just prior to the English Civil War. The College had a long and proud tradition of intellectual pre-eminence until the mid-nineteenth century, prior to which 'an Oriel Fellowship became the blue ribbon of academic life'. Many well-known Victorian names were Oriel men: the Arnolds and Froudes, Wilberforce, Keble and Newman. Its intellectual ascendancy was eclipsed, however, during Balliol's rise under the mastership (1870–93) of Benjamin Jowett who was acknowledged as 'a great kind of pot-hunter'. Such was Balliol's turn-of-the-century status that the Liberal prime minister, H.H. Asquith, characterised its men as exuding a 'tranquil consciousness of effortless superiority'. Indeed:

> no other University had a College such as Balliol between 1870 and 1914, devoted to selecting and preparing young men for high office and then, through the network of old Balliol men, ensuring that they secured it.[1]

Margaret's last few letters to James at Repton gave him an idea of the idyllic undergraduate life that lay in store. 'I have been here for nearly three weeks and have done disgracefully little work', she wrote from Newnham, Cambridge. Shortly after she said:

> I seem to be quite incapable of working hard at all, I suppose it is because it is two years till Trip[os] and I feel I can take things easy this year.

She painted a picture of an endless whirl of societies, committees, study circles, tea parties, theatre and languid summer days spent on the river:

> It is really awful dissipation, isn't it ... next week there is going to be a regatta in punts and canoes which ought to be great sport. We must try and go on the river a lot at Tonbridge this time for I want to learn to punt very much and I also think it would be quite good to go on the Medway in a canoe.

A joy of being an undergraduate was encountering eminent people. Presumptuously, Holdsworth had already bragged to James about meeting John Masefield:

> I went to have tea with him at his house at Boar's Hill. He is delightful. You know what he looks like: tall & gaunt, with sparse hair & a very humane face & the gentlest of voices. His wife too is very intellectual, and very nice, though a little less reserved than Jan. They are both awfully nice. Both frightfully keen at present on the latest idea of an Oxford Repertory Theatre. There is to be a great meeting next week of the greatest sons of enlightenment at his house the viscounts Galsworthy, Granville Barker & some others.

Holdsworth recounted how Masefield, 'with feverish excitement', was awaiting the fall of the Lloyd George ministry and how he was 'very very sympathetic with the Russian Revolution'. Kerensky (the head of the provisional Russian government in 1917), Masefield had told him, had 'married a flashy Russian actress whom the Soviets put in the prison of St. Peter & St. Paul, and insisted on sleeping in the Czar's bed-chamber', allegedly the cause of his unpopularity with the Bolsheviks.[2]

At Oxford, James entered a 'training ground or privileged nursery for the upper classes'. He took rooms at 6 Ship Street, above those occupied by another Old Reptonian, the young actor, Maurice Colbourne, just in time for the commencement of term on 18 January. He boarded there for two terms before coming into college, thereby reversing the normal Oxford custom of entering college in first year and only then going 'into digs' for one's final year. It was not until his second year that he moved into the second quad, when his accommodation then comprised a sitting room and a bedroom, and looked out over Oriel Street where his father had taken rooms years before him, and which adjoined Phelps' own lodgings. The Phelper, as the grand old man was known, with his peculiarly repetitive way of speaking, was an inveterate correspondent, a great raconteur and much loved by students. 'Never worry after 5 o'clock, my dear Darling', he would say, 'after 5 o'clock I mean, after 5 o'clock'. The attraction of college life for Phelps derived mainly from the fact that the young students were mostly from the same social stratum, so that 'a body of men brought up under similar conditions and the same ideas, educated at schools of the same type, develops a corporate life, intimate, wholesome and moderately industrious'.[3]

James' reversal of the usual order of accommodation coincided with a host of other modifications to traditional Oxonian customs. Indeed, a 'new ardour' was engulfing Oxford as the university did its best 'to catch up and be worthy of the men who had died'. A columnist in the *Oxford Magazine* at the commencement of term, for example, took stock of the three preceding terms in which the university had been full of students once again:

> There can be little doubt that the leaven of men who have spent all or part of their undergraduate years in responsible posts in the army is working among the other undergraduates, and while, of course, there are brilliant exceptions, it is no exaggeration to say that the present generation is yielding the best series of pupils any living tutor can remember.

This same columnist noted the huge increase in student numbers and a rise in the average age of the undergraduates. Accordingly, tutors were bound to see a dramatic improvement in the quality of work. There was evidence of a changed outlook. Athletic success was suddenly played down and undergraduate talk concentrated more on 'shop'. The new generation was used to exercising responsibility, was quieter overall than its predecessors and the value of the university experience had never been so appreciated by the young. In particular, the beauty of Oxford was firmly impressed upon the men who had recently returned from 'the drudgery of military service in uninteresting countries'. On the other hand, the increased numbers of students added to the accommodation pressures—more of them had to live further away from their colleges and then mostly in lodgings unaccustomed to taking in undergraduates. One result was that hard-pressed landladies short of servants provided only one meal a day, so that every available place in college was taken at dinner. Tuition fees had also risen along with the cost of meals. In some colleges, something approaching a revolution in management had taken place: with this generation newly matured by its experiences of responsibility, there was a sudden increase in consultation over internal college affairs.[4]

Another important feature of postwar Oxford was as significant as James' formal studies in shaping his youthful outlook. In the summer of 1921, the *Isis*, a major organ of student opinion, drew attention to the politicisation of Oxford, a development about which it was deeply ambivalent. There were now four political clubs: the Tory Carlton Club, the Liberal Club, the Labour Club and the New Reform Club, each with its own premises and an estimated combined membership of 1000. In normal times when 'men have gone from Oxford into the world', as the *Isis* put it, political clubs were no more than mere discussion societies. Now, however, when 'men have come from the world to Oxford' after the war, student politics was 'at once more vigorous, more firm and more practical'. Politicians descended on Oxford in droves and 'no street corner is free from some huge poster announcing the visit of a political notoriety'. Because these public figures spoke at club meetings, the *Isis* feared that the Oxford Union had ceased to be the political centre of gravity. Why go to hear an undergraduate speaking on the coal strike when a Cabinet minister or Labour politician could be heard elsewhere? The paper hoped that the political education provided by the clubs would continue when the ex-servicemen went down, although it regretted how political groups were waxing fat 'on the malted milk of outside speakers'.[5]

A feature of university life impervious to the postwar changes and that was the quintessence of the Oxford undergraduate experience, was the creation of enduring friendships. James had had numerous friends at Repton, and what had cut deepest with McLeod Innes after his expulsion was that, by disgracing himself, he had dishonoured his friends:

> Friendship was always a very precious thing to me: I did not make many friends, and always valued those who were my friends the more: and of course they are a thousand times more precious at this time.

He lamented to James, '—"Donec eris felix [your friends remain so long as you are happy] ..." as you probably remember'. To Aristotle, friendship was as important as justice among the virtues, to the extent that 'between friends there is no need for justice'. Indeed, 'friendliness is considered to be justice in the fullest sense'. Genuine friendship was entirely without calculus or utility because a true friend was well disposed towards, and purely desirous of, the good of the other person. From the bond of friendship flowed such simple qualities as goodwill, wit, affection and conviviality. And yet paradoxically, because of the depth of loyalty and the small number of people with whom one could reasonably hope to be truly intimate, friendship entailed exclusiveness, as well as equality. An image that captured masculine friendships in the cloistered, monastic world of Oxford is C.S. Lewis' description of 'golden sessions', those blissful occasions upon which:

> four or five of us after a hard day's walking have come to our inn; when our slippers are on, our feet spread out towards the blaze and our drinks at our elbows; when the whole world, and something beyond the world, opens itself to our minds as we talk; and no one has any claim on or any responsibility for another, but all are freemen and equals as if we had first met an hour ago, while at the same time an Affection mellowed by the years enfolds us.

Let a friend 'be to me a spirit', said Ralph Waldo Emerson, 'a message, a thought, a sincerity, a glance from him, I want, but not news, nor pottage', that is all.[6]

James read history along with some political science and economics subjects. Since the late nineteenth century, the study and writing of history in England had slowly begun to professionalise with the founding of learned societies and journals, although amateur traditions of scholarship were still alive and well at Oxford and Cambridge. The extent to which Oxford's historians manifested 'a conservative, priestly temperament' and saw their subject as 'a complex morality play', locked into a substantially reverential Whiggish view of the country's progress to great power status, remains a matter of historiographical argument. However the postwar Oxford study of history might be most accurately characterised, the teaching comprised a system of lectures and tutorials. Lecturers introduced a subject and 'prevented the student from becoming lost in his reading'. The information that they provided enabled students in conjunction with their tutors 'to build on an intelligible narrative structure'. Despite the prominence accorded lecturers, undergraduates mostly had contact with their tutors. This was Oriel's great strength. The famous historian of the seventeenth century, G.N. (Nobby) Clark (later the provost and then Regius Professor), was James' tutor. Clark would outline a modern history syllabus to him and, in addition to attending perhaps six or eight lectures at various locations around the university, each week James would read him an essay. Two lecturers who captured James' interest were Lewis (later Sir Lewis) Namier (Balliol) and W.W.G. Adams (All Souls) who lectured on representative government.[7]

James' daily college routine commenced with his scout waking him, fetching him hot water to wash himself, lighting his study fire and then bringing him breakfast. Having dressed by 9 am, he was then free to do as he wished: to go to lectures, to study or even to play golf if that took his fancy. At tea-time, a 'fairly social occasion', anchovy toast and chocolate biscuits were available in the junior common room. *Patchwork*, Beverley Nichols' novel of postwar Oxford, described tea as 'the time when the Oxford politicians held forth in front of the fire, while the aesthetes looked on with bored toleration and the athletes tumbled over chairs in the background'. James' routine was to work intently for two hours after tea between 5 and 7 pm, a period that he thought many other students wasted. After dinner in hall, his evenings consisted of working on essays, talking, attending Union debates, or going to concerts or clubs. There were very few rules, apart from being forbidden to enter college after midnight, and very few taboos, save one: to arrive at morning chapel in slippers was an offence that drove Phelps 'dead nuts'. The penalty was an irritating invitation to walk with the Phelper until such time as the offender's feet were blistered or his slippers were soaked by wet grass. Apart from that it was near-to-a-perfect existence, 'utterly free from compulsion, utterly free from responsibility, associating with people you liked, not associating with people you didn't like'.[8]

In his second year James cemented his friendship network. He remained a friend of Sam Richardson from Repton who put him in touch with Temple after a seven-year break. Richardson suffered severe head wounds during the war, was supposed to have recovered but had relapsed:

> He was in his rooms and two or three of us went and shared the watching over him. We sat up all night with him during which time he was awake there was the most dramatic and exciting talk about heaven and all kinds of things.

Tragically, Richardson died in early 1921. Shortly after, Temple wrote to James, saying that his talk with the two of them during the previous term 'makes me want to send you a line just now'. James' numerous friends at Oxford included Cedric Willway (president of the Oxford Carlton Club); Kenneth Lindsay (chairman and founder of the Oxford Labour Club); the bespectacled and slightly built, Malcolm MacDonald (son of the first Labour prime minister, Ramsay MacDonald, and secretary of the Oxford Labour Club); A.E. (Fritz) Cornwall, and W.C. Sellar and R.J. Yeatman—who later achieved fame as the authors of *1066 and All That*. But most of all he met an extraordinary man, Louis Wharton, for whom he maintained an undying admiration as his 'most lasting friend'. Every now and then the *Isis* would nominate as an Isis Idol an Oxford undergraduate who had won a Blue or was thought to be destined for sporting fame, and it would publish a brief article on him, accompanied by a large photograph. Holdsworth, a highly accomplished cricketer and association footballer, was an Idol in November 1920, and the Idol for June 1921 was James' fellow Oriel man, Wharton. One of eleven children, the son of a Trinidad lawyer and his French wife from Martinique, Wharton came to Oxford as a journalist with the *Morning Post*. He was short in stature and described by the *Isis* as 'swarthy, thick-set, grotesque and frankly forbidding; but not without a certain majesty'. Not only was he an outstanding footballer and cricketer, but Wharton was also recognised as the most eloquent, witty and spell-binding Union orator. The *Isis* depicted him as Louis d'Oriel, 'so potent and so ascendant a deity'.[9]

James did not speak at the Union ('I couldn't be bothered waiting for my turn', he later claimed), but in debate after debate his friend's speeches were described rapturously. The highpoint of Wharton's Oxford fame came in March 1921 when, before a packed house of more than 800 people, and with Asquith himself speaking against the motion ('That in the opinion of this House the Government has failed to secure a Peace worthy of the sacrifices, or adequate to the purposes of the War'), he attacked the coalition government. He was a candidate for the presidency of the Union and, even though on this occasion he gave 'what must have been among the most able and masterly speeches ever delivered by anyone in the Union Society', said the *Isis*, his forthright approach may have cost him the presidency, which he lost narrowly to Beverley Nichols. Kenneth Lindsay, by contrast, 'one of the best and most pleasing speakers', was a solid, earnest performer with the occasional light touch, whereas Cedric Willway, who had very few pretensions to being an orator, spoke usually in a halting manner and then generally only on 'those rare occasions when the life of his party demands his protection'.[10]

Postwar Oxford was believed to be inclining more and more leftward in political temperament, the same direction towards which James was leaning, for he joined the Oxford Labour Club and became a committee member. He was also the chairman of its literary group, which, along with an educational group, had been formed in early 1921. Their meetings were 'much appreciated', according to the *Oxford Magazine*, and by the summer both groups were flourishing. When the poet Robert Graves addressed the group on writing poetry, James, as the chairman, was somewhat embarrassed by having to contend with a woman's criticism of Siegfried Sassoon's poetry during a question directed to Graves, with Sassoon sitting in front of her. On one occasion, Hilaire Belloc addressed the group on prose, and on another G.K. Chesterton spoke. Although Phelps referred to James' 'keen interest in modern movements' and said that 'if his views are in some points a little crude, he has come by them independently, & they mean much to him', the precise nature of his political beliefs at Oxford can only be inferred. Clearly he held strong opinions on Anglo-German relations, for he led the negative side in an Arnold Society debate at Oriel on Wharton's motion 'That this House condemns the action of certain Senior Members of the University in advocating the resumption of friendly relations with Germany'. As this motion was lost by a mere six votes, he is likely to have argued persuasively against his influential friend. At the next meeting of the Arnold Society he was not so successful and his motion—'That this House condemns the present policy of the Government with regard to reparations from Germany'—was lost twelve to seven. In his last Arnold debate before he went down, James seconded the motion 'that this House favours the discontinuance of the Anglo-Japanese Alliance'. There is no indication of his views in relation to the Labour Club's motion in March 1921 which, after long and heated discussion, was lost by just one vote: 'That this House believes that the Socialist Commonwealth can sooner be achieved by a violent break in the present system than by a gradual conversion'.[11]

While up at Oriel, James founded a society known as the Hypocrites Club that convened for occasional eating and entertaining in a medieval house near the Folly Bridge. His father warned him about the likelihood of friends overstaying their welcome—should he ever decide to keep a supply of alcohol in his study (because on a meagre allowance he could ill afford to carry others' bad debts)—and perhaps this possibility stimulated the initiative or the club's motto, *ariston men hudor* (water is best). The Hypocrites lingered for a time at St Aldate's after James went down: two surviving photographs of 1924 and 1925 fancy-dress parties show E. Evans-Pritchard (later a renowned anthropologist) dressed as a sheik, and a youthful Anthony Powell, the novelist, adorned by a fireman's outfit. Unlikely as it might seem (given his previous track record) the remainder of James' leisure time was devoted to sport. He chanced his arm at rowing, but found it painful and abandoned it. He played fives and cricket, this time village cricket with a team known as the Oxford Outcasts, as well as hockey, and he also experienced the enjoyment of sculling. The fellowship of good friends manifested itself in one other particularly delightful way. With luck, students might obtain invitations to reading parties during vacations, when about a dozen young men accompanied dons to a village where they would read and work. As James read voraciously, such parties were very appealing—his cumulative record from 1917 listed over 340 titles and twenty-one of Shakespeare's plays as read at some stage up to 1920. He attended two such parties while he was at Oxford. The first, in August 1920, was at the Wilton Rectory, Wiltshire. On this occasion, the group was religiously inclined and under the tutelage of the college dean, the Reverend E. Graham. The second, in March 1921, was at Market Cross Inn, Alfriston, Sussex. James' photographs of both occasions evoke Lewis' image of 'golden sessions'. At reading parties, 'one worked quite hard and you talked a great deal'.[12]

James also turned his hand to writing. With Alan Ayling (a Repton contemporary) he penned a mirthful sonnet on indigestion in March 1920. Then came 'The great circus at Olympia', a short story about Hubert, a scion returning from a British imperial settlement, with an embarrassing compulsion to shoot lions, and a poem called 'German counter-revolution. March 1920'. 'Grovely Wood' was written in August at Wilton. It tells how, on a walk through the wood to Salisbury Cathedral, James witnessed three acts of medieval heroism in which good eventually triumphed over evil, and it ended, reassuringly, with 'God's in his heaven all's right with the world'. There were a couple of other scrappy plays—one about a political conspiracy—but these were prematurely abandoned. Indeed, several early efforts were aborted, presumably as his inspiration waned, including one fifteen-page fictional narrative of a walking tour across the Sussex Weald to the south of Guildford. In this piece, set in midsummer 1920, he drew liberally on his own experiences. One delightful sentence described his battle with an old foe, hay fever:

> Walking through great fields of hay, I became sore afflicted so that my nose ran and my eyes itched and watered, and my mouth uttered blasphemy and profanation enough to warrant immediate and eternal damnation.

He even wrote a tidy and inventive item called 'The art of swearing'.[13]

Eighteen months soon passed. 'Perhaps', Kenneth Lindsay later pondered of his postwar generation at Oxford, 'we took ourselves seriously, if that is a debit mark'. But with three years at Oxbridge regarded as the summit of one's aspirations, public schoolboys subsequently scarred by years in battle could not really have behaved otherwise. For James, however, three years was definitely a luxury, for 'the circumstances demanded that I should get a degree as quickly as possible and start earning'. He took out a BA in history with distinction—although only just, he reflected later. But what was he going to do? Nobby Clark thought that he was 'well fitted' to tutor schoolboys and university candidates. As school-mastering seemed to be an option, he applied for a London County Council teaching post. Fisher described his ability as 'good' and pointed to his 'competent scholarship and sound ability'. Interestingly, the one attribute that each testimonial author emphasised, just as Phelps had done, was James' concern for current issues. 'Coming to the College from military service', said Clark:

> he soon attracted my attention as having a greater width of interests and a better grasp of contemporary political and social problems than the majority of those who came up with him.

Rather than a life spent in detached scholastic contemplation, then, James opted to be a man of action. Thanks to the war, he had witnessed human suffering and misery firsthand. As an undergraduate, his awareness of life's tragedies had been heightened by visits to the Bermondsey and the Oxford and Bermondsey boys' clubs. And while the war may not have destroyed his Christian faith—for he attended chapel and listened to visiting clergy such as Temple (who preached at St Mary's in February 1920)—by periodically attending different churches and in ceasing to be a regular communicant, he was going through the motions of his faith. After his Final Schools in June, he left his application for a teaching post with an Oxford employment agency and headed off on a walking tour to north Devon and Cornwall. While still contemplating the possibility of a London County Council position, a letter arrived from H. Cradock-Watson, formerly of Tonbridge School, a friend of his father's, and now the headmaster of the Merchant Taylors' School, Crosby, Lancashire. There was a vacancy for a master. 'I may say it is my full intention—from what I hear of you—to offer you the post', Cradock-Watson wrote, as 'I think you would like the work here'. James was twenty-two. On his elder sister's birthday in 1919, he quipped that '22 is quite an old woman isn't it?' At that age, there was no doubt about his transformation. There were the physical features and habits of manhood: the boyishness evident in photographs had disappeared and he was much thinner. He smoked a pipe, partly out of pleasure and partly out of self-consciousness (to disguise a receding chin). He accepted Cradock-Watson's offer and that summer he headed north to Liverpool, where Fisher's confidence that he 'will make a strong, virile and effective teacher' would be put to the test.[14]

6

PUBLIC-SPIRITED PEDAGOGUE

1921–1928

... he, or they—it comes to the same thing—have the fiend's own knack of discovering a man's weak place.

Rudyard Kipling, *Stalky and Co.*

The original Merchant Taylors' School was founded in Great Crosby in 1620. The imposing set of buildings that Darling entered had been built as a new school in 1878 on the Liverpool Road when it had been 'refounded, re-established, and rehoused as a public school' on standard Victorian lines. The Merchant Taylors' School had a strong reputation for scholarship and, on Cradock-Watson's arrival in 1903, it was admitted to the Headmasters' Conference. From 1905 it was an endowed school receiving state and Lancashire County Council grants. It was inspected by the Board of Education and about a sixth of its enrolment received county and municipal scholarships, and exhibitions, and were educated free of charge. It managed like most direct grant schools to achieve 'a social admixture which it is impossible to find in any other type of school'. In 1921, the enrolment was 541, the highest ever. Except for a boarding house of about thirty boys, Merchant Taylors' School was a day school organised for games into six sets based on the geographic areas from which the boys commuted daily.[1]

Imbued with idealism, Darling had headed north in a similar way to Holdsworth, who went to Harrow, Harford to Eton and Ross to the Workers' Educational Association. Like many contemporaries who had survived the recent carnage, awareness of a lost generation weighed heavily on him. 'We cannot but think of them this evening', said Frank Fletcher (headmaster, Charterhouse) on the Sunday after Armistice:

> remembering them with pride and with the renewed resolve to make ourselves more worthy, with a sense that henceforward we and all the nation are no longer our own: we have been bought with a price.

Darling's appointment was probationary and subject to the new county Burnham salary scale. The governors tried (unsuccessfully) to have Darling paid an increased allowance for war service. He was form master of IIIC, a class of 28 twelve-year-old boys. He taught them most of their subjects and immediately got into difficulties. For the first three days when the boys were without any books or timetable 'they ran rings around me'. Despite his troubles, he resorted only once in 1921 to the discipline register (the Black Book)—one R.B. Brown received four cuts on the hand for being 'troublesome'. Darling did not let on to Phelps and told him just after Christmas that he 'was alarmed to find myself thoroughly happy. I always like the boys and the masters and now, I think, I like the work'.[2]

These early experiences were not without pain, and as an antidote he turned again to creative writing. He penned 'The pedagogue's pedestal' and 'To those about to teach':

> 'Discipline is only a question of personality', I was told, and glorying in my possession of it and remembering the ease of control as a prefect at school and as an officer in the army, I faced my first form with something approaching confidence.

His confidence was ill founded:

> Some time in my first term my form had purposely or by mistake produced the wrong books for the lesson; their other books were in lockers in the room; lamb-like I told the boys to get them out. They did so and the Headmaster, who was in the corridor, entered upon a sea of pandemonium as unpleasant to me as it was enjoyable to the form.

Such incidents were embarrassing. Cradock-Watson 'had shown a desire to obtain me, and had treated me in a flattering manner as a "catch"'. In these two reflective pieces, Darling made light of his lack of ability with stern admonitions: single out a scapegoat, be strict and rely on sheer brutality, among other possible solutions. Despite coming down hard on himself, he admitted that 'I personally can never keep [strictness] up for long'. Indeed:

> I can well remember the first time when I saw the light of terror in a boy's eyes and I was so unnerved at the thought of anyone being frightened of me that I ceased immediately from my harangue.[3]

Any loss of social face evaporated when he read 'The appreciation of poetry' to the Merchant Taylors' School Literary Society in December. This cogently argued paper displayed a competent grasp of technique and an unpretentious style, although an attempted portrayal of his capability (or even superiority) is detectable in his reliance upon numerous Latin and Greek quotations. Indeed, he confessed to Phelps, an *Anglice Reddenda* (extracts for unseen translation) lent by his landlady's daughter had helped earn him the epithet 'scholarly' for what, in his own eyes, was 'a rather bad paper'. 'The Headmaster has been suitably informed', he told Phelps. Darling had emphasised the musical quality of poetry, and had ranged from the Freudian explanation of creative force (libido) through to the Romans and Athenians, the devices of rhythm and metre, and thence to Shakespeare and Robert Browning. His literary outlook manifested intellectual dualisms between body and soul, and matter and mind, as well as essentialism with such passages as 'the poet and the artist have the gift of seeing the beautiful more often'. Always, he asserted, the appeal of literature was to the soul and, at its heart, was spiritual. Poetry would simply be a 'collection of words' to the materialist. In 'The dramatic art and modern playwrights' he expressed awareness of the dramatist's need for order and unity within the constraints of space, time and setting. Drama worked by illusion, he wrote, but by the sheer power of its presentation, the cinema could depict real objects and destroy imagination. Louis Wharton chided him for using 'script', however, when he really meant writing and insisted in jest: 'please be more precise, exact and meticulous in your use of words. And you a schoolmaster!' Having disavowed scholarly pretensions since leaving Repton, there was an inescapable sense in what Darling said and how he said it that he was trying to prove something, and to put distance between himself and his new colleagues. These features also characterised his subsequent authorship, and are a sign of a young master cultivating an image and constructing his public persona.[4]

Early on, Darling also made his mark at the Debating Society. At a meeting in October 1921, devoted to unfinished stories, his story was voted as the best of a dozen attempts to give a half-finished tale a happy ending. In November, he led for the negative on the motion 'That the League of Nations is, at present, an impracticable ideal' yet, despite his 'brilliant piece of rhetoric' outlining the League's achievements, the motion was soundly beaten. He presided at a Debating Society meeting in December and in April 1922 he gave an amusing speech on the cinema's negative public influence. A fortnight later, after seeing Wharton, Yeatman and another Oriel friend, George Lawrence, at an Alfriston reading party, he told Phelps that he would remain at Merchant Taylors' School for another year before moving on: 'I enjoyed last term for the most part very much and have a free hand to undertake practically any experiment which seems advisable to me at the moment'. Another reason to be satisfied was that he founded a club for boys at Christ Church, Everton. Allen Whitmore—an Oriel friend (who had arrived in late 1921 and shared rooms with him in Mrs Hudson's lodgings in Galloway Road, Waterloo)—persuaded him to assist in starting the club in 1923 and soon after Darling had sole charge. The club met on Monday and Wednesday nights in a cellar in Howe Street and later in a large hall at St Polycarp's Church. For two years or so, Darling ran the club with the assistance of an older boy and original member W.R. (Bill) Milmow. It made a shaky start but, with Whitmore's assistance, Darling ensured its survival over the summer. Several masters and the boys from his form and the boarding house also helped out. Football matches were organised against other clubs, and there were occasional cricket matches between the club and his third form boys. Darling's fear that the Merchant Taylors' School boys 'may try to patronize the others' proved groundless. At weekends he would take the lads on rambles through the countryside. Club nights began at 6 pm. Darling would arrive at 7. The club offered boxing (for which, to his amazement, he provided the instruction), bagatelle, gymnastics and other rough-and-tumble games. The club's unofficial link with Merchant Taylors' School had Cradock-Watson's blessing. Despite its location in a deeply divided part of Liverpool (with loyalists of both Orange Day and St Patrick's Day), the boys were mostly docile and from a depressed social stratum. The mere mention of policemen sufficed to send them scurrying. Darling insisted on prayers before the evening's conclusion because he wanted the boys to associate their enjoyment with religion.[5]

While in the north, Darling kept regular contact with his friends. After his first summer term (July 1922), he had begun learning Italian with the determination to master it at Wilton later in the year. In August he and Margaret went on a nine-day bicycle tour through Shropshire, Herefordshire, Monmouth, Gloucestershire, Wiltshire, Hampshire and across to Tonbridge. A solicitor's plate at Bridgnorth, which read 'Messrs Dolittle and Dally' provided a source of much mirth, but memories of hay fever and the army put paid to any enthusiasm for Salisbury Plain. He also stayed with Louis Wharton who, like Willway, had been admitted to the Bar. Wharton had been gravely ill although his symptoms were difficult to diagnose. He was constantly fatigued and awaited a verdict from a nervous disorders specialist. When hospitalised, he was approached to be a Conservative Party candidate, but he demurred. During the new school year Darling's confidence as a teacher grew. His new third form with its scholarship boys was a clever one and he had considerable success with Latin. He described himself as 'well pleased with my present post in all but the financial side' and began sounding out Phelps about a resident mastership elsewhere. Cradock-Watson praised Darling's 'good work' with the junior boys and in history, and his 'sound work' in economics:

> He has, of course, still a good deal to learn, both in the handling of boys
> and in the management of his work, but he has all the necessary keenness
> and goodwill, and with patience and the perseverance he has already shown,
> should prove a really good Master.

Darling's contribution to the Debating Society early in his second year was 'an unfailing source of inspiration to the younger members' and, at the end of 1922, Cradock-Watson appointed him as assistant housemaster in Harrison House. He regarded his salary increase as 'a great improvement on the former estate'.[6]

Ambition was starting to rear its head, then, and in only his second year as a master Darling was already planning his future. Moreover, the network of connections that he had been consolidating was working for him. Since coming down from Oxford he had kept in regular contact with Geoffrey Fisher and occasionally had visited Repton. Once a term he also spent a weekend with Temple who, two years beforehand, had been appointed to the nearby Diocese of Manchester. Darling was also cultivating Phelps. Both Fisher and Temple, he informed the provost, were urging him to seek another appointment. As he was known to J.F. Roxburgh (a housemaster at Lancing), he had his eye on Stowe (about to open in May 1923 with Roxburgh as its headmaster), although an older public school would suffice.

> It may seem a falling off of my ideals but the trouble about this sort of place is that it is hidebound by examinations and nothing short of a great headmaster can break the ties.

On his way back from Scotland in early 1923 Austen visited his son and remarked to Phelps that two years in Liverpool was enough. It 'has been a useful experience & I think he has made good'. Phelps, an Old Carthusian and a member of Charterhouse's governing body, arranged for Darling to see Fletcher. Darling had no idea whether he had made a good impression, but the visit further stoked his ambition, including running his own school:

> I am quite determined in my own mind to get a headmastership of some school like the one at which I am, before I die but my desire to do a proper public school now, is chiefly due to the fear that I may not get a headmastership at all and should be stranded in some horrible spot to the end of my life.

Darling had found a suitable vocation and was setting his sights high. A number of his university contemporaries had read history, which might make landing a job in this field difficult and obtaining a public school headmastership might be easier.[7]

Meanwhile, the boys' club was making progress, with the program varied over the summer of 1923 to provide swimming and cricket on three evenings. Occasional Merchant Taylors' School financial collections were used to purchase gymnastic equipment. Darling hoped that he might formalise the connection between the school and the club. After two years there was very little in the school's day-to-day routine in which Darling was not involved with the result that, as he impressed upon Phelps, 'I work almost invariably from 8 am to 1 pm and do not read'. In addition to the club, school societies and house, he coached the 2nd and 3rd XI cricket teams and, in December 1923, he became adjutant to the captain of the corps, his housemaster, colleague and friend, Ivan Butler-Wright. His biggest victory was to persuade Cradock-Watson to agree to reconstitute the six sets into four houses (North, Crosby, Waterloo and South) and even to recommend the new housemasters. 'It is pleasing at my early age to be able to experiment like a Headmaster upon a school', he crowed loftily to Phelps, while also bragging that 'the Headmaster "really feeds out of my hand now" and it is not very good for my moral character'. In his spare time, Darling enjoyed Liverpool's social life. Here, family connections proved useful, because the Rector of Childwall had been Austen's friend and Darling partnered his daughters at balls, tennis parties and philharmonic concerts. He and Whitmore also went to an occasional Sunday lunch with the Fisher family. (Fisher was an Old Reptonian, although no relation to the headmaster, and a London and North Western Railway senior executive.) Darling also went to lavish Sunday luncheons with his mother's friend from Coed-Bel days, Miss Hobbs (or Aunt Hattie) and her three bachelor brothers, all of whom lived in a big house near his lodgings. During vacations he went home to his family in Tonbridge, where they were joined by Louis Wharton and his friend, Hilda Davis, and Margaret and her Cambridge friends.[8]

Despite his earlier disavowal to Phelps, Darling continued to read widely and fifty-eight books for the first nine months of 1922 augmented his list. Moreover, he produced additional literary pieces. On the lighter side, Mrs Hudson's ivory collection was probably the stimulus for 'Elephant tusks', which disdained the 'taste of a large proportion of the inhabitants of this island', and a calamitous tale about 'The bashful elephant'. He also provided a well-sustained and evocative description of the Hohenzollern monarch's humiliation in 'The abdication of the Kaiser. Nov 1918' and wrote 'The economical field marshal', which relied on such alliterative phraseology as: 'so because of a caterpillar, a cauliflower, a conductor, a brass candlestick and a cow ...' Other untitled bits and pieces included one about a cynic ('Robert Lucas'), another about a fugitive seventeenth-century Dutch Christian ('Hans') and one about Charlemagne being crowned king by the pope—in contrast to Napoleon's crowning of himself. On a more serious note, in 1923 Darling wrote about spiritual growth in 'Education' in which he proclaimed that education should be 'a never-ending striving towards an unattainable ideal'. 'At school and in the world', he continued, 'the soul is brought up to be capable of appreciating the light'. Appreciation of poems, pictures and music was a sign that 'progress is taking place, for they are the manifestation on earth of the light'. For a similar reason, in a piece entitled 'The novel', he deplored the way in which circulating libraries purveyed cheap pap and pandered to mass desires for indolent relaxation.[9]

Darling's most intriguing effort was the outline and first act of a play that manifests personal preoccupations and unresolved conflicts. Three of the eight characters had Darling family names (Jane, Ruth and Mabel) and he was John, just down from Oxford. The mother criticises her son for letting her down and two sought-after but abandoned hopes of Darling's are revealed: a scholarship and a first-class Oxford degree. The dialogue was fantasy, but the special pleading in this family parlour game was uncannily close to home:

R[uth, John's aunt]: ... Where is John?

J[ane, John's mother]: Oh I expect he's up in his room with the gas-fire on, working with the typewriter and imagining that he is composing a masterpiece. He always manages to receive an inspiration about five minutes before meal-times in order to let no-one forget that he is a genius.

R: That wasn't very kind, dear. I don't think you realise how clever John is and in a way, what a privilege it is for us to have had the responsibility of his upbringing.

J: If he's such a genius as you think, it's rather odd that he always got bad reports and a fourth class in his final examination at Oxford.

John is consumed by guilt for imposing an intolerable debt on his family while supporting him at Oxford, especially when he had performed below expectations. Ruth agrees that John simply has to support himself:

R: Yes he must do that of course. I do hope we have had the last of his bills from Oxford. It is very difficult to pay them now especially when we borrowed so much in order to send him to Oxford. I don't know when we shall get it all paid back ...

J: We musn't [sic] hide from ourselves that it's going to be difficult. He is still under the impression that we are quite well off; we have never told him otherwise and he only thinks us rather mean.

In this ménage à trois, Jane has substituted for Darling's father and Ruth his mother.[10]

The young schoolmaster's hopes of realising his aspirations bore fruit in May 1924. Thus far Phelps had been unable to secure for him a Charterhouse vacancy, but now Fletcher offered him an appointment to commence the following summer. 'I shall be a credit to your support', Darling reassured Phelps:

The grounds are lovely, and I was most impressed. I felt strangely small in chapel this morning and I know I shall find it difficult to work my way into the scheme of things there. In some ways the place in Liverpool was easy work; I got on very quickly there and must not expect to do the same at Charterhouse.

He was convinced that the move was the right one 'from the point of view—at least of my future'. So too was Austen. If his son sought the headship of a county school, then that could be more easily achieved as a public schoolmaster. Temple was delighted at Fletcher's offer:

> To be Head of a school like your present one may be a bigger job than to be Head of a well-established 'Public School', because you have a chance of finding the right solution of the chief of educational problems. But as a member of staff you can do nothing permanent. Your influence at Charterhouse will in fact go further, & your being there increases the chance of a Headship & all its openings later.

Darling's Merchant Taylors' School colleagues, especially those connected with the boys' club, were sorry to see him go. The club itself was stronger than ever. After a highly successful Christmas party in 1923, the membership doubled to sixty early in the New Year. Milmow had been a godsend. At this point, however, it ran into trouble. When the largely unsympathetic vicar realised that Catholics were members, he wanted them expelled. A furious and disgusted Darling located new premises at the Victoria Settlement, and the club formally became the Merchant Taylors' School Boys' Club. After Darling's departure, R.G. McKinlay (the new secretary) said that: 'it is difficult to over-estimate the loss which the club will sustain by his leaving the School', and yet 'it must be gratifying to him to know that the adoption of a boys' club by the school has at length materialised, and thus crowned his energetic pioneer work'. Darling became vice-president. He visited the club again in January 1925 and then later that year a portrait of him, 'framed in accordance with the taste, and at the expense, of members of his original club', was secured for the new premises. (In 1930, the club moved again. Its building was bombed in 1940, reopened in 1950 and was still going strong in the 1960s.)[11]

After an end of term camp, followed by a delightful walking tour in the Cotswolds with two Merchant Taylors' School boys, Capper and Irving (taking a route suggested by Phelps which culminated in Oxford), and a brief holiday near St Andrews, Darling commenced at Charterhouse in mid-September. Established in 1611, it was slightly older than the Merchant Taylors' School and, in company with Eton, Harrow, Winchester, Westminster, Shrewsbury, Rugby, St Paul's and Merchant Taylors' (London), it was one of the prestigious Clarendon nine. In 1872, Charterhouse moved out of London to Godalming, Surrey, where:

> the new buildings and many of the rooms were given the names of the London school: Crown Hall, Long Room, and the Writing School. They even took great chunks of masonry with them, like the Gown-boy Arch, and stuffed them into the new school.

Soon after Darling's arrival, the *Carthusian* listed many postwar changes and improvements, with the reconstitution of the Games Committee as the most important. The significance of the change originated with Fletcher's arrival from Marlborough in 1911 when he found that 'the industry and discipline of the school had suffered' during the fourteen years of his predecessor, Dr G.H. Rendall. Such was the ascendancy of the bloods that Fletcher recalled the captain of football steaming into his room on a wet afternoon after an OTC parade and saying: 'I've come to show you, sir, in what state Major S. has brought us in'. Scarcely a decade before Darling's arrival, then, athleticism had been quelled.[12]

Charterhouse was a significant step up from the Merchant Taylors' School. After barely a fortnight, Darling confessed to Phelps that it was 'a little overwhelming', so extraordinarily good and efficiently run that there was not much for him to do apart from his daily responsibilities:

> No doubt that should furnish all we ought to ask, but I confess to more violent ambitions. I must, I think, feel what I read called 'the burning shame of sin which consumes the reformer's soul'.

Darling was form master of the under IVth B, twenty-three boys to whom he taught Latin and English. 'They have succeeded in trapping me already in four points of elementary Latin grammar', he quipped to Phelps. He also taught modern English and some history to the Vth form, and English and divinity to the science and biology specialists. Masters and boys alike had been friendly so far, and his rooms were very comfortable. It was not long, however, before he was chafing under the school's Toryism. When he complained, Temple said:

> Probably on the whole most boys there will seem far less enthusiastic, even less interested. The specially vile idolatry of Good Form requires the suppression of any impulse to show keenness about anything that matters, and the only way to be sure of avoiding the manifestation is to crush the feeling. But you will, by degrees, get through that crust. And then you will have more good material to work on than at Liverpool; and there can be no doubt that the experience of a place like Charterhouse is worth a lot.

Darling said nothing to Phelps, but he was having difficulty reconciling his recent experiences with his emerging liberal outlook.[13]

In his talks about religion and politics with Darling at Bishopscourt, Manchester, Temple (a Labour Party member since 1918) had reinforced Gollancz' influence. Louis Wharton was forever teasing his friend with 'O you Socialists!' and 'When the Socialist State arrives will it give us our tobacco and beer free?' Despite their differences in political outlook, shortly after leaving Oxford Darling and Wharton were part of a small circle of friends who met or dined at a flat in Earl's Court owned by Lawrence and Jean Neal. Lawrence Neal had been a fellow pupil with Kenneth Lindsay at St Olave's, a London grammar school, and had married Jean Guthrie-Smith, a Scottish friend of

Lindsay's and a poet of minor distinction who had taken a social science degree at the London School of Economics. It was also through Lindsay that Wharton had met another member of this little circle, his future wife, Hilda Davis. As the daughter of Émil Davis, a financial journalist from Welwyn Garden City (and a London County councillor, honorary treasurer of the Fabian Society and first editor of the *New Statesman*), Hilda had grown up in the circle of Sidney and Beatrice Webb. She too had studied social science, at the University of London. Neal—later a founder with Lindsay in 1931 of Political and Economic Planning (or PEP)—whose family was in retailing, also grew up in a progressive liberal environment and his wife Jean had been a self-confessed socialist at eighteen. Wharton lodged with the Neals. In the intimacy of this circle, the magnetism of Wharton's personality attracted Darling (recalled at this time as a youthful enthusiast) and Cedric Willway. All of them were idealistic and enjoyed conversation:

> We believed the world was a better place. The war had been finished and there would never be another war. We were serious-minded, you know. We believed we had privileges and we ought to help people who didn't have privileges. You see, it wasn't a welfare state.

The group's exhilaration was shortlived because a specialist's diagnosis revealed that Louis had contracted disseminated (or multiple) sclerosis. His promising sporting career was aborted and, as he became progressively more immobile, work at the Bar proved impossible. He and Hilda returned to Trinidad in 1924 to undertake legal work with his father.[14]

When he heard that his friend had gone to Charterhouse, Wharton told Phelps that he hoped that the school would not be 'too unimpressionably cast iron for him'. Happily for Darling, he soon made his presence felt. Shortly after Ramsay MacDonald's government lost office (November 1924) Darling defended socialism at the debating society where the motion was: 'That this House deplores the temporary defeat of the Labour Government'. The *Carthusian* reported that:

> He [Darling] said that the present distress was real, and that the dissatisfaction of the people must be removed. The one remedy was increased production: that Socialism would bring this about, he left people to infer. He compared the Socialist party to the other two parties, and seemed fairer than he was which is very good speaking.

At a later meeting, Darling attacked 'the intolerance of public schools'. He was also highly critical of the hegemony of classics. Having tried to find new ways of constructing English essays, and building up the literary style of the biology and science specialists, he criticised the public schools' neglect of the English language:

the writing of a correct English sentence is at least as good a training and probably a more difficult achievement than the writing of a Latin one ... I spend six hours a week teaching [Latin] to boys who will never read Virgil with pleasure or write L.I. prose in other style than that of Jones mi[nor]: and I feel that there must be some fallacy in a system in which it is insisted that only by elementary Latin can a boy be taught to use his brain and to think clearly.

Later, he and a colleague, G.C.W. (Gerry) Dicker, persuaded Fletcher to allow them to try to improve English teaching, but their report and recommendations came to nothing. The boys were aware that Darling did not fit the schoolmasterly mould. R.L. Arrowsmith, for example, a VIth-form boy in Darling's first year, could not remember a serious conversation with a master (apart from his housemaster and tutor) as there was very little boy–master out-of-class contact, a practice that Darling reversed:

He just perfectly naturally from the word go started walking about, talking to anybody as if they'd known him all their lives in the most friendly fashion. And before long he had us coming and going... and talking very frankly about all sorts of problems, and about the school.

Patrick Wilkinson recalled Darling as the only master whom he ever asked to tea in his study:

I think such an invitation was quite a rarity in the school. I only remember that we got into serious conversation about life, and that he suddenly asked me: 'Do you ever feel like Keats—'now more than ever seems it rich to die?" I had never felt any such thing, and being very immature was quite out of my depth.

Neither Arrowsmith nor Wilkinson was taught by Darling, but J.H.C. Morris and Patrick Law whom he did teach each remembered him as an 'inspiring teacher'.[15]

As at Merchant Taylors' School, Darling immersed himself in school societies. In early 1926 he joined the Library Committee, took a leading role in school drama and was 'a valuable recruit' to the new Shakespeare Society, about which the editor of the *Carthusian* was enthusiastic as he helped elevate the standard of the society's readers. He was recalled as 'a first class producer of plays' performed by colleagues, wives and friends. In 1926, he played Robert Gilmour 'with great success' in the masters' production of *The Man from Toronto* and the next year he acted in an Old Carthusian production of *Hamlet*. Later, after a leading role in *The Importance of Being Earnest*, 'Mr. Darling', along with another master, Ivor Gibson, 'struck out a new line at Charterhouse' by producing Shakespeare's *The Tempest*, performed by the Vth, 'on a stage as nearly representing the Elizabethan stage as possible'. But his productions did not always go without a hitch:

> I remember a Shakespeare Society reading of the *Wild Duck*, no doubt at your [i.e., Darling's] instigation. For some reason this took place in Pageites and not at Northbrook. The Uncle [A.L. Irvine] giggled offensively throughout and you got crosser and crosser.

Irvine was a classics master, and a prickly individual who had founded the society and delighted in catching out young masters, usually by testing their knowledge of quotations. He later acknowledged that, while he and Darling did not always agree, he had 'the greatest admiration' for his work. In one production, Darling played opposite the wife of a colleague for whom the script required her to exclaim 'Oh! Archie, darling!' To boys in the audience helpless with laughter Darling was forever after known as 'Archie'.[16]

In 1927 Darling established the Literary and Political Society. Among the speakers was a noted Carthusian, the author Richard Hughes. Then, with Gibson and another master (Hodge), Darling founded an under-sixteen debating society. Just prior to leaving Charterhouse, he was remembered as having bequeathed to a colleague (W.O. Dickins) a revitalised debating society in the guise of a Charterhouse parliament. 'For this he was most generous with time and invaluable documentation.' Darling also played cricket on Bramley Green with the Maniacs, a team of masters and boys and, in the annual Brooke Hall–Maniacs match, he occasionally sparkled with the willow (one top score of 38), although his rather 'round arm' medium-pace bowling let him down. In late 1924, he had joined the corps in which, with G.R. Renwick, he eventually had charge of D. Company. Darling was recalled as an 'efficient but not, I think, an inspired leader of boys in this field', for he was 'much too intelligent' a man to swallow the advisability of outmoded field day manoeuvres. Naturally enough, 'we enjoyed teasing him about this, and he took it very good-naturedly'. Finally, he became a house tutor in Saunderites where, on one evening, another former pupil remembered, Darling 'let a sudden light into my infant mind, explaining that in economic life no transaction took place unless each party to it considered it to be to his advantage'. Hitherto, this particular lad had imagined that 'one party always got the best part of the bargain and that the other party "lost"'.[17]

The event that put Darling offside with Charterhouse's conservatism, particularly in Brooke Hall, was the general strike of 1926. Erected as the result of a legacy of £5000 in 1910, Brooke Hall was described by Fletcher as 'a happy mixture of a common room and a club', but for a young and inexperienced master it could be 'awe-inspiring'. Gerry Dicker remembered Darling commenting on how he (Dicker) had been invited immediately to Brooke Hall dinners, but that he had had to wait. 'I was told', W.O. Dickins recalled:

and can well believe—that in 1926 he [Darling] roused the anger of some conservative colleagues by voicing support for the generally unpopular side of the strikers in the general strike of that year.

The *Carthusian* called the strike 'deplorable'. Many Englishmen and women were worried by the spectre of Bolshevism and the strike (3–9 May), called by the Trades Union Congress to support the Miners' Federation of Great Britain, divided national opinion. There was a palpable feeling of conspiracy:

> I remember Holdsworth coming down with a team from Harrow and looking nervously around and saying: 'Is there anywhere we can go where we can talk?' as though one was in a secret society and that it wasn't safe to talk publicly.

For Darling's friend, Robert Bernays, the strike stretched family relations to breaking point and he left home during it, 'otherwise he would have come to blows with his father'. With Hilda Davis, Bernays had once been a member of the 1917 Club (a group commemorating the Bolshevik Revolution) and then a master at Charterhouse. In July 1925, the mine owners decided to end the 1924 agreement by which MacDonald's Labour government had helped the miners win increased wages. A dispute was only avoided when, at the eleventh hour Baldwin (the new Conservative prime minister) agreed to a nine-month industry subsidy until May 1926. On the morning of Tuesday, 4 May, more than three million workers went on strike. Special constables were to assist with maintaining law and order. Only one passenger train arrived in Godalming from London and workers on the new Charterhouse school chapel downed tools. Darling sympathised with the miners, although he signed on as a special constable (he was not called out). While he believed that the general strike was a 'grave error', he thought that Tory hotheads were exploiting it for their own purposes.[18]

Six months later, Darling was elected to the Godalming Borough Council. He followed a family precedent: in 1919 his mother had been elected as the Women's Citizens Association candidate to the Tonbridge Urban Council. 'Congratulations on doing so well in the poll', he had written from Germany. At Charterhouse, there were close links between town and gown even though Godalming had once coveted the school site. A noted Charterhouse classics master, T.E. Page, had been a councillor (and joked about the school's and the town's 'deep and dear attachment of a common sewer') and P.C. Fletcher, a senior master (and Frank Fletcher's cousin), had once been mayor. As the borough was responsible for sewerage, electricity, schooling, Poor Law relief, housing and roads, Darling gained some valuable administrative experience. From 1927, in addition to monthly council meetings, he attended the council's committees for highways, lighting and transport, water, and drainage, farm and recreation grounds. These bodies dealt with such matters as extensions to the town's pumping station, the provision of new bridges, applications by schools for the use of amenities, the surfacing of thoroughfares, minor works tenders, and proposals for the improvement or acquisition of public land.[19]

Darling was elected as a Labour councillor, and he chaired the party's Godalming branch. A series of talks to branch members and the Guildford Trades and Labour Council in 1925 indicates his lukewarm view of state socialism. When speaking to a Charterhouse Debating Society motion 'That this House believes that the present European civilisation is on the decline and will shortly be replaced by another', he said that 'a change was certainly coming but it would not come through Russia'. Instead, 'it would be internal'. The representation of interests achieved by Mussolini's corporate Italian state had attracted his attention, he admitted, because 'one can imagine great advantages in a highly centralised and efficient state such as Italy'. As a believer in the sacredness and sanctity of British institutions (with their need for reform), however, he did not advocate revolution. His views on political commitments were an extension of his views at Oxford in a paper entitled 'The reform of parliament'. And when in another item ('The meaning of democracy') he wrote that 'the future of democracy in England lies in the hands of Labour', his view of democratic political evolution was Whiggish. He pinned his faith in representative institutions and also, significantly—given his rejection of direct democracy (such as the referendum and the recall, as they showed 'the inability really of the electorate to judge on technical matters and their liability to be led off the track and to be swayed by irrelevant matters')—a system directed from above. He didn't think that England was socially, educationally and industrially, let alone politically, democratic but political reform was still the proper path to 'real' democracy. Darling was not a guild socialist, because guildsmen rejected state encroachment as being inimical to freedom and thought that representative government was equivalent to the privilege of choosing rulers, which was close to what Darling implied was its principal virtue, whereas guild socialists espoused representation through maximised and decentralised self-government. Their democratic model was economic and comprised decentralised producers' guilds in all spheres of life (akin to the consumer cooperative movement), and based on what they assumed to be humanity's natural instinct for association. Having once written that it would be easier to achieve socialist boroughs than a socialist state in England, Darling was probably not at odds with this conception. In 'The completion of democracy', he focused on the reform of work. He refused to side with capital or labour, and sought a way of reconciling both groups' interests. As everyone needed to be provided for, commodities had to be available at a marketable price 'and' also at a price sufficient to ensure a reasonable standard of life for their producers.[20]

A concern for the welfare of all social sectors, then, was contending in Darling's thinking with an adherence to representative, albeit protective and slightly dirigiste, democratic institutional arrangements. He said little about liberty in his talks and—except in a discussion of local rating where the words 'equality really [means] progressive taxation' appeared—not much about equality.

As for credit reform, which Darling thought would be a herculean task for Labour, he argued that, despite cyclical monetary fluctuation and its attendant misery, the state should play only a limited role because ultimate credit control lay with the Bank of England. Ought the state seek control of the Bank and become the country's banker, then? 'I think not', he told the Godalming branch. Once more, he put his faith in institutions and in the inherent reasonableness of those who administered them:

> working as it does with the state [the Bank of England] still has the reputation for financial sagacity so that people will expect from it business sense rather than political necessity.

Government support of the bank made it sufficiently 'bulwarked against panic' and, with more expertise than Treasury, it could stand up to the government if it had to. Bill Locke (a bricklayer at Charterhouse for more than fifty years)—who stopped work during the general strike—remembered Darling as having 'a good judgment of justice'. Darling's words to a meeting of liberals—'many of us find it difficult to justify our claim to the title of Labour and none like to be wrongly termed Conservative'—suggest that, with his social background, he stood out as different. Even though Darling was virtually the sole middle-class member of the Godalming branch, Bill Locke said that his presence gave it important respectability at a time when many working men were loath to admit their allegiance publicly for fear of accusations of Bolshevism. (It was not uncommon in locations where the party's clandestine status could not be disavowed for meeting halls to be deserted and for workers to hide outside rather than be seen to be waiting for a speaker.) Darling, Locke recalled, wanted to end the automatic, slavish genuflection of working people to their social betters. He remembered that Darling succeeded in having added to Charterhouse's library order, as well as *The Times* and the *Daily Express*, the *Daily Herald*—the newspaper sympathetic to the cause of the workers. Locke thought that he also persuaded Fletcher to allow a school carpenter and local party branch member to address the boys, when both the Conservative and Liberal parties had sent their own speakers.[21]

In late 1925 Austen lamented to Phelps that his son was still critical of the public schools and that 'he will always be agin the government as they say in Ireland'. Yet the sense of service and duty that propelled many young public school men into public service applied equally in his son's case. A range of responsibilities gave vent to Darling's social conscience, including his interest in boys' clubs: he stayed with Harold Napier (of the Oxford and Bermondsey Mission) over Easter of that year to learn more about club work. And, once a week, in the second half of 1925, he gave weekly lectures on Wednesdays at Pentonville Prison, often accompanied by Gerry Dicker. On arrival, they were escorted to a cell by a chaplain and left alone with about twenty prisoners. The joke in Brooke Hall was that Pentonville's prisoner escape rate rose sharply every

Tuesday to avoid subjection to an educational ordeal. On this same Wednesday each week, Darling also lectured at Toynbee Hall. As part of the fruit of Balliol's zeal for university extension and social reform, Toynbee Hall was founded in Whitechapel in 1884. Numerous reformers, including Milner, Tawney, William Beveridge, Clement Attlee and Cosmo Lang (then Archbishop of York) had been inspired there by the prospect of educating the working classes. Darling met Kenneth Lindsay who was then in residence as Barnett Research Fellow and writing a book on education and social reform under Tawney's supervision. Darling was pleased with the 88 pages of notes that he delivered over about six months on 'The masters of English literature' and Dicker recalled him preparing late at night—although a class of thirty shrank to a handful towards the end and then just 'one faithful female' in January 1926. To meet this demanding commitment, Darling cycled to Godalming straight after school to catch the London train. From Pentonville he went to Toynbee Hall for a meal. He returned home by bus to Bank and the underground to Waterloo in time to board the last train to Godalming, cycle up the hill, and snatch some sleep before waking again at 7.15 am.[22]

Perhaps Darling's most important work was for the League of Nations Union. It was something of an ordeal, as speakers were sandwiched between dances and songs of the nations, with the audience comprising the parents and the singers, and the results 'discouraging'. His surviving lectures (written in uncharacteristically bland, dreary prose) once again display his idealism. His concentration on the detailed League machinery for the maintenance of collective security highlights his reliance on factual material in the union's pamphlets. This detail is also symptomatic of the effort needed to convince critics of the virtues of Wilsonian ideals. Darling's exaggerated assertions were unconvincing. Two were that '[the League] is the one thing which stands between Europe and the collapse of European civilisation' and that 'we are making a revolution in international relations and are building a world in which war will eventually seem only a memory of barbarism'. The prospect of another war repelled League enthusiasts who traded on the discredit into which the old power balance of alliances and treaties had fallen, but who were often naively utopian, particularly when so patently great a power as the USA refused to join the League. Darling's optimism was evident in such passages as 'this guarantee, if entered into honestly …', and especially in the injunction to 'remember always that the presumption is that the nations are acting in good faith and that other people do not want war any more than we do'. Indeed, hope hinged on an about-face in attitudes to power or what Darling kept referring to as a 'new psychology'. Disarmament, he believed, would help instil that attitude by lessening the desire for war.[23]

After three years with under IVB, Darling became form master of the under VIth history specialists and the Vth modern (i) non-specialists. While he was still intent on reforming the teaching of English, and had told Phelps that Oxford and Cambridge ought to require proficiency in the native tongue as a condition of entry, he was devoting much more energy to history. He taught by resorting to 'wide sweeps', with his notes displaying a reliance on intricate maps of European discovery voyages, lists of parliaments and legislation, time lines of battles and events, diagrams and tables. Darling also drew on his notes of Namier's tutorials at Oxford and postwar printed material from Newmarket. He taught mainly European, British and economic history, and some medieval. Phelps wished him luck in obtaining more history scholarships for Charterhouse but Darling did not like his chances, as the best boys were always reserved for classics and other schools gave boys a head start by requiring earlier specialisation in history. Furthermore, boys were unwilling to devote long hours to the required reading or were prevented by numerous house duties. Provided that they were from privileged backgrounds, they could also afford to enter Oxford and Cambridge as commoners rather than relying on scholarships. Confronted by such obstacles, Darling thought that most history teachers simply gave up on scholarships. Darling was recalled as unconventional in his approach. Patrick Law remembered that he got the boys to talk, rather than simply talking himself, and that he was interested in 'the social side of history'. John Bowen recalled his intriguing essay questions, such as asking boys to write about Browning's remark: 'Ah, but a man's reach should exceed his grasp, / Or what's a heaven for?' Another specialist, John Keith, told Darling that he owed him a tremendous amount of gratitude, not because he had taught him a lot of knowledge (he questioned the value of Darling's maps, time charts and colour schemes), but because 'you did educate me' and 'you broadened my outlook tremendously'. Keith loved economics, particularly whenever 'you got a good argument going'.[24]

Darling ensured that his network of connections worked to his pupils' advantage. As he had with promising Merchant Taylors' School boys, he put in a good word to Phelps about Carthusians, provided that they were prospective Oriel material. Bowen and Law were two specialists about whom he felt highly. He impressed upon Phelps how he had tried to broaden boys' outlooks, and that both Bowen and Law were a sign of the quality to come:

> I really believe that the standard of this academy has gone up [for] the top of
> the Modern Side is certainly both younger and better than it was when first
> I came here.

With an exercise entitled 'The diary of John Bull from the wars of the roses until today', Darling also discovered an intriguing way of making the heroes of history come alive for the boys. They were required to imagine themselves as ageing by a decade for every actual century of civilisation, so that they would witness numerous epochal events. Another idea was to take a topic such as blindness and ask: 'what did the man who was born blind mean when he said that scarlet was as the blare of the bugle?' A former science specialist said that Darling 'revelled in that and [he] went as far as to show my piece to Frank [Fletcher], but I don't think it was quite his cup of tea'. The most impressive acclaim received by Darling was an anonymous nine-page eulogy:

> Here [at Charterhouse], I have been fortunate to have been during my last year under two masters with ideas differing from the traditional school master. Both these men have 'B's in their bonnet' the one Pacifism [the German master, Tresslar], the other socialism [Darling]. Both these men are in dead earnest and being clever are able to influence those under them very strongly.

Sadly, this lad continued, other members of Brooke Hall were very conventional and did not bring their political views into their classes.[25]

Darling's Charterhouse years had a remarkable civilising effect on him, an influence reinforced by his friendship with Aubrey Scott, his neighbour, colleague and fellow bachelor from whom, particularly, he learnt what it meant to be refined. With his typical wit Temple recommended Scott as someone whom Darling should get to know. 'He [Scott] used to behave like a friend of mine and might resume the habit', he wrote shortly after his friend's arrival at Charterhouse. Although Scott lacked a university degree, Fletcher appointed him after the war (during which he had won a Military Cross). An older man, Scott broadened his young colleague's tastes in music, painting and literature. Every Saturday evening they played in a bridge four with two other masters (Lake and Thomson), and travelled together on the continent in their holidays, sometimes accompanied by Darling's future brother-in-law, Ralph le Fleming, or Bernays, and occasionally by Eaton and his friend Desmond Lee (later a classical scholar and fellow of Corpus Christi, Cambridge). Scott's example may have influenced Darling's paper 'On reading', with its signs of growing cultural sophistication:

> [Readers] have this in common with friends that we each see in a book something which perhaps is apparent only to us; and our appreciation of them depends on our own qualities as well as the qualities of the book in question.

Books could not replace friends, but they could enhance friendships.[26]

Gibson was another influential Charterhouse master. In their correspondence since Merchant Taylors' School, or their meetings at Old Reptonian dinners and at the Lollards Tower, Lambeth Palace, Temple had tried to still Darling's religious restlessness. 'You are such a capital Christian that it is a real pity you should not find it out!', he said in late 1924. Three years later, Temple wrote: 'I have never had any doubt that all of you is Christian except your mind!' But it was Gibson, a poet, and often an ill man who, on an occasion when Darling admitted to feeling 'unusually depressed and frustrated', took him aside and helped assuage his doubts by challenging him to take Holy Communion regularly, to pray and to read his Bible for three years and only then decide whether or not he was a believer. Gibson's recipe worked. Despite Darling's religious torment, God had a place in his writings. In his discourse on reading, for instance, he esteemed beauty as a spiritual quality and claimed that in great literature there was always 'something of the creative genius of God'. And, in his most accomplished literary effort, a sonnet about how the stonemason for the Charterhouse Memorial Chapel had captured the Creator's presence, Darling wrote:

> Above the highest oaks, slender but firmly set,
> Your strong ribbed back and western arch magnificent
> Rise in their lasting stone, a golden monument
> To men who died for boys impatient to forget.
> Sternness but just relieved by dainty parapet
> The buttress shadows are its own choice ornament.
> Work of ephemeral man, superbly permanent,
> The Chapel gives God's truth to man's regret.
> Poet or prophet momentarily knows
> The passing inspiration of his soul
> And writes for few while revelation flows;
> Who builds in stone, hardly in time's control
> To all who see illimitably shows
> His glimpse of the impenetrable whole.

Years later when Gibson died, Darling affirmed his spiritual influence as 'decisive' and drew from his example the lesson that 'almost all the good one can do in this world is by personal influence on other persons'.[27]

Since first meeting Frank Fletcher, Darling had been eager to work under him. With Cyril Norwood, who had just departed from Marlborough for Harrow, Fletcher was the doyen of the English public school headmasters. The son of a Lancashire colliery owner, he had a first in classics from Oxford and was a liberal by temperament. 'The academic successes and the general vigour of the school life were greatly increased' during his twenty-four years at Charterhouse, and he tolerated the masters developing 'on their own lines'. 'A splendid delegator' was how one former pupil and master summed him up. Fletcher held high ideals. His chapel sermons and addresses (*Brethren and Companions*) emphasise the need for honourable clean living, self-discipline, restraint, purity of heart, generosity and associated virtues that (for his generation) were the hallmarks of the Christian gentleman. The other headmaster with whom Darling became friendly was W. Hamilton (later Sir William) Fyfe, head of Christ's Hospital, Horsham (about 30 kilometres from Godalming) from 1919 to 1930. They had met during the general strike. Before the war, with his close friends, Temple and Tawney, Fyfe was part of a leftish reform group at Oxford known as the Catiline Club that agitated for the admission of increased numbers of working-class students. A Christian and a liberal, the scholarly, witty and urbane Fyfe had sympathised with the miners during the strike and his brother, H. Hamilton

Fyfe, a noted journalist, edited the Labour *Daily Herald* and the *British Worker* (the trades unions' strike paper). Darling's point of connection with Fyfe was probably Kenneth Lindsay, because the latter met Fyfe at Toynbee Hall and then visited Christ's Hospital for long talks while researching a book. Darling and Fyfe conversed about educational and social issues. Fyfe appealed to Lindsay and Darling as an unconventional headmaster—an innovator 'ready to experiment and encourage sensible children' in an unconventional public school.[28]

After four years at Charterhouse, Darling had accomplished much more than his self-representation as the pathetic linoleum salesman John Rowland in the family drama with Ruth and Jane. Late in 1928, however, these halcyon days were about to be interrupted. The year before, there were two *Carthusian* articles about the settlement of English public schoolboys in South Africa and agricultural training in Ontario, Canada. Each highlighted opportunity, pioneering and adventure, and pompously referred to 'boys of the Public School type'. 'In these times of economic pressure', said the first, 'it is surprising that more young men do not turn to the Dominions as a field for settlement'. If Darling had read them, then he probably hadn't given them a second thought. But one Friday morning, Fletcher beckoned to him through the Brooke Hall window and asked him to read a letter. A faint bell of recollection may have chimed, for he had an offer to lead a party of English schoolboys to New Zealand. Darling told Phelps that it seemed 'too good an opportunity to miss' and that, 'it occupies my mind to the exclusion of all other things'. After thinking about it over the weekend he decided to accept. Nearly three months later, on New Year's Day, 1929, shortly before he and the boys set sail, the full import of what he might be letting himself in for began to sink in. The thought of such a trip, he confessed to Phelps, was 'awe-inspiring'. The significance of Darling's decision cannot be overstated: travel might broaden the mind but the forthcoming impact of being tour leader would be much more far-reaching. If seven to eight weeks' combat in north-western Europe, along with the training and readiness for it and its post-Armistice consequences, had matured him physically, then about a decade later the eighteen or so weeks of this tour (with two-thirds of it spent on ships) remoulded him in an equally fundamental although different manner. The tour would introduce him to an entirely new circle of people with a way of thinking that was foreign to him but which he had to assimilate. In contemporary idiom, Darling's southern hemisphere sojourn was to be a game-changer and produced an outcome that he could not have foreseen.[29]

7

DOMINIONIST?

1929

This land of such dear souls, this dear dear land,
Dear for her reputation through the world—

William Shakespeare, *King Richard II*

The personal reassessment that Darling experienced as a result of the tour coincided with a recasting of British imperial policy and a resurgence of visionary idealism among British conservatives, in particular Leopold (or Leo or L.S.) Amery, Secretary of State for the Colonies (1924–29). After World War I, imperial enthusiasm had cooled in the face of pressing domestic economic problems. At the same time it was deemed important to retain the dominions' loyalty and imperial membership. With regard to the white dominions, as they were called (Australia, Canada, New Zealand and South Africa), the idea of the Commonwealth superseded the terminology of empire, a new notion of kinship expressed in the Balfour Declaration adopted at the Imperial Conference of 1926. Dominions were:

> autonomous communities within the British Empire, equal in status, in no way subordinate to one another in any aspect of their domestic or external affairs, though united by a common allegiance the Crown, and freely associated as members of the British Commonwealth of Nations.

What united these nations was 'the cultural and racial sympathy that was supposed to exist between Britain and the dominions and which derived from the "British" character of their populations'. Migration during the 1920s was a way of solidifying this affinity because, as settler societies almost wholly dependent upon primary production for their wealth, the dominions sought population for their underdeveloped territories.[1]

British thinking on settlement and migration was shaped by the *Empire Settlement Act* of 1922. The key government policy agency was the Oversea Settlement Committee (OSC), an advisory body on which successive secretaries of state relied (and dominated), which was serviced by the Oversea Settlement Office, at first a branch of the Colonial Office and after 1925 part of the newly created Dominions Office. Overseas settlement entailed population movement within what was construed as an imperial family. Indeed, one of Amery's predecessors as secretary of state, Viscount Milner (1919–21), asserted that overseas settlement 'shall be regarded from the standpoint of the unity of Empire'. Only 'more direct responsibility' by the British government would guarantee that 'settlers of the right type', 'directed' to the dominions, could maintain that unity. At its barest essentials, settlement was a vehicle for redistributing excess British population, with distribution meaning movement of 'the white population to the best advantage of the Empire as a whole', or 'in the most efficient manner as between all its parts'. On this reckoning, the dominions were merely distant extensions of Britain: 'British by birth and tradition and therefore British in sympathy'. Not all economic and industrial interests accepted this cosy imperialism, however, and the OSC conceded that 'incidentally and accidentally the actual movement of migration may help to relieve the labour market in times of industrial depression and many who emigrate may actually be unemployed'. The stark economic division of labour clothed by these imperial apologetics was that in return for Britain's import of their primary products capital, manufactured goods and manpower resources were exported to the dominions, with this reciprocity guaranteeing export markets for all concerned.[2]

The *Empire Settlement Act* empowered the secretary of state to formulate or cooperate in 'agreed schemes' for providing assistance to 'suitable persons' in the UK who intended to settle in the dominions. Such schemes were either 'a development or land settlement scheme' or 'assistance with passages, initial allowances, training or otherwise'. As early as 1920, the Secondary School Headmasters Employment Committee requested the OSC's assistance in locating training in farm work and suitable openings for eighteen-year-olds, a suggestion taken up by the OSC as highly desirable, and something particularly urged upon it by Darling's friend Fyfe at Christ's Hospital. In October 1923, the overseas settlement of schoolboys was 'thoroughly discussed' at the Imperial Economic Conference and its desirability was 'generally recognized', although Lieutenant-Colonel Buckley (Secretary, Overseas Trade) placed public schoolboys after youth, families and women in the preferred settler pecking order. He detected no dominion demand for schoolboys, but merely reduced employment in the army, the navy, the civil service and particularly the Indian Civil Service for 'young fellows of this class'. Because 'they are now looking further afield', Buckley urged, 'this is an opportunity you in the Dominions might well wish to take into account'. In 1925, more than 300 schoolboys immigrated to New Zealand as part of the cadetship scheme agreed to between the New Zealand Farmers' Union and the dominion government.[3]

The public schools' intimate connection with imperial policy was consolidated by Amery's membership of the Public Schools' Employment Bureau—an agency chaired by Fyfe and set up by the Headmasters' Conference to promote schoolboy migration—but especially by the School Empire-Tour Committee. The former headmaster of Winchester, Dr M.J. Rendall, 'an ardent imperialist who believed unambiguously in the superiority of the Anglo-Saxon race', had retired in 1924 and, while touring the empire for the Rhodes Trustees, had conceived of the idea of schoolboy tours. Amery established a provisional committee in the summer of 1926, with Rendall as acting chairman, for the first tour of forty boys to Australia (led by the Reverend G.H. Woolley). The next year Amery reconstituted this body as the School Empire-Tour Committee with Rendall as chairman, the Hon. Miss Margaret Best ('everybody's favourite aunt ... an enlightened imperialist') as full-time secretary, and Fletcher and Norwood as Headmasters' Conference representatives. The committee met at the Imperial Institute in London. There was a tour that year to South Africa followed by another to Canada in 1928. The tour organisation machinery comprised a director assisted by two or three co-directors (one of whom was usually a young army officer), and an agent who arranged the tour program in the host country and met the party with a complete timetable when it disembarked. A tour group would normally visit farms, settlements, industrial works, development projects, agricultural and pastoral shows, and schools.[4]

Rendall wanted an Eton master to lead the 1929 tour, but when he informed the School Empire-Tour Committee in October 1929 that this 'had proved impracticable', Fletcher 'especially commended' to the meeting 'a Charterhouse master [who] should be written to, to undertake the work'. The brief discussion on the lawn outside Brooke Hall had followed the next morning. The final number of applications was forty-five. The group was due to sail (second class) from Southampton on the Shaw Savill and Albion liner, *Ionic*, on 4 January 1929 and return in mid-May. The tour cost per boy was £115. Bill Lamaison, a Charterhouse under-VIth non-specialist, remembered Darling in class one day recruiting Carthusians by saying: 'come on boys you must support me against all these Etonians and Harrovians'. Among the forty-five boys, the strongly represented schools were Charterhouse (nine), Stowe (seven), Eton and Harrow (four each) and Repton (three). Another boy, John Weston, recalled that prior to departure Fletcher invited the Charterhouse boys to lunch with him, which was considered a special treat. As the tour leader, Darling was to be assisted by Lieutenant G.W.G. Smith-Dorrien (of the King's Royal Rifle Corps, a Harrovian and eldest son of General Sir Horace Smith-Dorrien), the advance agent, Francis Portal (a Wykehamist, son of a landed family and later a baronet), and Michael Scott, a student at New College, Oxford, and a musician.[5]

Darling's diary (compiled on his return) indicates that the tour unleashed a latent enthusiasm for empire. His reporting style was self-mocking, with incidents and activities liberally embellished melodramatically. He conveyed (to himself) a feeling of triumphant satisfaction that he had measured up to others' expectations. His account of meeting the boys and their parents at the Grosvenor Hotel in London on 3 January plays down his youthfulness, his responsibilities and the fact that he was about to be thrust into the limelight After extricating himself from the milling parents and boys, he dined with Aubrey Scott and then met Rendall and his co-directors:

> It was an anxious but amusing meeting. Dr Rendall was magnificent, urbane and indefinite, Miss Best kind, re-assuring and efficient, the boys nervous and anxious to escape, the parents doubtful of the age of the directors and inclined to make little requests for their sons, which inevitably were forgotten when we started. The directors, myself[,] Smith-Dorrien and [Michael] Scott were alternately weighed down with the heaviness of our responsibilities and inflicted with mirth when we realised how ridiculous it all was.

The next morning, the party departed from Waterloo station at 8 am after a formal farewell ceremony in the staff dining room:

> The porters at the Grosvenor, although heavily tipped were very slow at getting the luggage off and it was ten minutes later when I discovered the room full of parents and boys. Dr Rendall rather agitated by my non-arrival, Miss Best as usual calm and re-assuring. Sir James Parr [the New Zealand High Commissioner] was fortunately a little late, and Smith-Dorrien, true to form, a little later still. More parents regarded me askance, the Carthusian boys winked at me and then Dr Rendall got up to speak.

Rendall emphasised the imperial nature of the tour, enthused about the youthful directors and urged everyone to be grateful for the forthcoming hospitality. 'Never forget', he said:

> that you have done nothing to deserve it. Do not only feel gratitude but express it. Do not let any stupid English reluctance prevent you from telling your hosts that you have enjoyed your entertainment as you have never enjoyed anything else before.

Parr hoped that some boys might one day return to New Zealand. 'Two or three years under an experienced farmer' and '£500 or £1000 to ensure success' were essential in such a venture. At Southampton, a Pathé man photographed the boys as they boarded, then the mayor (M.H. Pugh) wished them 'godspeed, and a very happy time', reported *The Times* (or 'Bon Voyage' with 'execrable pronunciation' as Darling noted facetiously). To the 'last cheers' of Miss Best and Dr Rendall on the quay, they set sail.[6]

From Southampton, the *Ionic* headed south-west for eighteen days towards the Panama Canal. With so many boys in such confined space for such an extended period, the voyage tested Darling's organising mettle. His first problem was that everyone felt cramped. The *Ionic* was built soundly enough 'but not with much intelligence', he thought, although it moved rather slowly and provided 'a fairly steady passage for elderly ladies who wished merely to sit still'. Of 400 passengers, 18 travelled first class, about 100 second class and the rest third. In his second-class cabin, Darling envied those travelling in first:

> The first class few reigned majestically upon the promenade deck and boat deck the envy of the other two classes. If there is anything calculated to make me a socialist it is to travel second or third class for six weeks and watch the first class passengers; if there is anything certain to make one belief [sic] in the intrinsic rightness of class distinction it is to travel [on the return journey] for six weeks on a one class boat. We have done both.

Lack of space was alleviated when the purser arranged for the boys to use the first-class decks in the afternoons, although there was very little room elsewhere. The daily meal routine was regimented: 'Our food was taken in the 2nd class dining-saloon very comfortably but at ridiculous hours: breakfast at 7.30, lunch at 12, tea at 4.30, and dinner at 6'. Even though Darling said the meals were 'astonishingly good', he thought that the boys soon tired of ship food. Generally, the time dragged and, inevitably, ennui resulted from the voyage's monotony. John Weston wrote home that while life was enjoyable and slack he had 'read a good lot'. Most debilitating of all was the capricious weather. When crossing the Bay of Biscay a heavy swell caused the *Ionic* to roll 'quite unpleasantly' and virtually everyone was seasick. The false dawn of a beautiful day and calm sea that followed ended with the unleashing of nature's awesome fury. With the ship lurching precipitously, Darling dispatched the boys to bed. On his estimate, the *Ionic* was rolling about 30 degrees to either side. Terrified, he lay in a cold sweat listening to the vessel's groaning while memories of German artillery fire in France flooded back:

> It was useless to tell oneself this was a mild thing or that the Ionic had often been in worse and that ships do not sink in storms. The ill-fated Vestris [the Lamport and Holt liner that sank in the Atlantic with over 100 lives lost on 12 November 1928] was too fresh in my mind and will-power too weak to force the mind into saner channels.

He tried to comfort the boys while struggling to retain his composure. After another day of rage there was calm and everyone sunbaked in 'perfect' weather until on 22 January they reached Colon, Panama.[7]

Here Darling's imperial prejudices surfaced. Colon was 'as nasty a place as one is likely to find': a bric-a-brac town of wooden houses with shaky, dirty and insecure verandahs, and tawdry decorations that gave it the appearance of a Mexican frontier location in an American western movie. The jumble of races included Jamaicans who were 'immensely proud of the fact that they were British and not American', and whose patriotism stirred his own. An unanticipated disruption to the tour party's arrangements reinforced these sentiments. In his concentration on the presence in the harbour of the cruiser HMS *Caradoc*, the British consul had not made the transport arrangements agreed earlier with Portal. Belatedly, three 'inferior', 'rickety' buses were procured, but in the meantime the boys, all decked out in their duck suits and topis, had boarded three other vehicles ordered by the ship's agents. Everyone now had to disembark 'for fear of injuring [the Consul's] prestige'. Already delayed by losing a day waiting for American naval vessels to pass through the Canal, there was further irritation at American hands:

> A heated argument followed, in the centre of which I found myself awkwardly placed. The drivers were all niggers [sic], but the proprietor of the first three busses [sic] was also present, one of those really objectionable Americans with a grating voice[,] foul language and an unjustified contempt for the rest of the world.

To Darling's chagrin, the consul was doubly disappointing when the party visited him because, instead of offering 'consideration and assistance' when Darling introduced himself, he had 'very little idea of who we were' and had forgotten Portal's visit. From their buses the boys watched American submarines, fascinated by their strange curvilinear hull markings and the sailors in their distinctive gob hats as the vessels negotiated the three tiers of locks that lifted them nearly 30 metres up to the lake formed by the damming of the River Chagres at Gatun. During their twenty-minute wait, they observed the fine detail of American engineering ingenuity, including the crisp operating precision of the gates, chains and mules. The boys returned laden with hawkers' bananas and spent the afternoon on the *Caradoc*. Here, Darling met a Carthusian boy's father who was:

> a most pleasant example of the British naval officer, as indeed were all the crew of the Caradoc, so that our souls filled with the glories of our naval race as we sailed away from the Cruiser.

At the rather high-class Washington Hotel, everyone swam in the pool, had a meal and then spent an evening in town until 11 pm. Next morning, the *Ionic* passed through the locks, across the lake and down the Culebra Cut, with its cliffs as high as 60 metres. They then descended the Pedro Miguel Locks and sailed on to the Miraflores. To the sound of the 'difficult to live up to' backchat of the American soldiers, they cleared the Miraflores Locks and entered the Pacific as the sun was setting.[8]

When news of the journey to Colon reached England, Rendall reported to the School Empire-Tour Committee's New Zealand sub-committee in late February that the tour was progressing well. A cable from the Prince of Wales greeted the boys at Colon. Darling 'reported favourably on the party as a whole', said Rendall, and had singled out nine boys as 'excellent members'. The boys had been issued with notebooks with carbon copy pages to be used either as diaries to record various 'doings' or for letters home to their parents. On this second leg of the journey, the monotony was broken only by the occasional excitement of seeing smoke on the horizon, a bird, a shoal of porpoises or a whale, although Darling did his best to dispel it with a strict daily routine. For five minutes or so after breakfast there were prayers, followed by lectures on the British empire, with the boys in deck-chairs 'sleeping in the most obvious way and watching flying fish, if they were sufficiently awake to do so'. In the afternoon, the purser and a sports committee arranged 'innumerable decksports'. The passengers and his co-directors were attentive to Darling's lectures, but he 'could get no signs of interest at all' from the boys, even though they listened intently to one passenger's two 'extremely interesting' talks. Smith-Dorrien, with 'the absorbing thoroughness which he gives to everything he undertakes', had more success. He arranged deck tennis, quoits, boxing, obstacle races, mock horseracing, greasy pole fighting, pyramids, horse and riders in the bath, assorted ball games and 'all the other fatuous games, by which people on board ship try to make out that they are enjoying a necessary exercise'. Disdaining what he saw as evidence of the contrived sincerity with which people make out that they are enjoying themselves, Darling asked himself (somewhat airily) of one passenger why 'no woman can play Bridge at once well and with decency?' And as for the purser, Darling wondered: why were some men 'never so happy as when dressing up—like children'?[9]

In the evenings, Darling moralised, there was an endless stream of dances to the sounds of 'a glaring panatrope' at which there were many 'incurable ladies men'. There was also what he dismissed as an act of convivial folly, a fancy-dress ball, in which everyone tried to be someone else and overplayed their roles. To cap it all, there followed what he considered was the ultimate act of human frivolity: admission to Neptune's Court for those passengers crossing the Equator for the first time. Such humiliating 'horse play', he complained was not his idea of fun (on 'a really cold and gloomy day'). 'With as good a grace as I could muster' he steeled himself for the embarrassment of being ducked:

> Nothing is more difficult to pretend to enjoy a joke which does not seem in the least amusing. Of dignity I have no ambition, but the most miserable of men cannot but feel a fool when he stands in the middle of a crowd, intent on laughing at him and submits to be messed about by people whom he does not like. It is worse if one is a school-master surrounded by jubilant charges.

Humiliated, he retreated, sulkily, to find peace and quiet by himself in the deserted smoking room. On a positive note, a success of the outbound voyage was Michael Scott's 'This tour of grace'—a parody of Noel Coward's play *This Year of Grace*. There were also two other productions, 'The monkey's paw' and 'A night at the inn'. Rendall's astuteness paid off, because Scott 'did more in drawing [the boys] together into a common effort' with this revue 'than any school master could have done by months of pious endeavour'. Two other events relieved the tour group of the tedium of sea travel. These were the Pitcairn Islanders' visit to the *Ionic* and what Darling dubbed 'l'affaire Rosie'. After about a month out to sea, the first distraction provided Darling with steadily accumulating evidence of British munificence, this time as a result of the graciousness of Queen Victoria in permitting the HMAS *Bounty* mutineers and their descendants to remain as Islanders. Darling wrote a detailed diary account of the people, their origins, their society and their dependence on the passing ship trade. The boys took numerous photographs of the Islanders and their wares, including the characteristic three-boat formation ritual with which they approached ocean liners. Darling noted, patronisingly, that they were: 'pleasant looking people, simple and only mildly daft'. When the Islanders eventually disembarked, singing their farewell hymns, Darling consoled himself that they were 'intensely loyal and British'.[10]

The second little saga exasperated Darling and required delicate handling. 'Rosie …' was the cryptic caption under Michael Scott's photograph of a female passenger whom Darling considered rather venal. He labelled her the 'tigress'. Portentously, Scott's camera had captured this young woman reclining languidly by the Washington Hotel pool complete with teasing smile. When the weather calmed, and having apparently tried unsuccessfully to ensnare some of the first-class passengers she turned on Darling's young men (he claimed). He was diffident about having to contend with quite so worldly and sophisticated a woman in an episode that (if he is to be believed) nearly got out of hand. 'Natural modesty and loyal scruple prevents me from absolute sincerity in describing her character', his later affected comment read, as 'she was something new to my experience'. Rosie claimed that she was about to divorce her husband in New Zealand. Darling tried to segregate her from the boys and took the precaution of writing to Fletcher. She then complained about his 'frequent animadversions' on her character while he (supposedly 'quaking at the knees') removed two boys from drinking with her on deck, as a result of which she protested to the commander who refused to support her. Then, fast becoming an embarrassment to herself, she lashed out and threatened to complain to the shipping line. During the last few days of the voyage her attention was diverted by an older passenger. Clearly, because of protracted confinement, new and unanticipated (and unusual) demands in the art of boy management had arisen for Darling. John Weston wrote home that:

> I think Darling is doing very well on the whole, this certainly is a very difficult
> position, everyone I think respects him & no-one tries to 'mob' him, he

manages to keep everyone in very good order without being dictatorial or school masterly! although people do give him a certain amount of worry, for instance some people emptied some fire buckets! & the Captain got rather annoyed with Darling about it.

When approaching Auckland, Darling took ill for a couple of days and was confined to bed. Shortly after, when the pilot came aboard with mail, everyone knew that their destination, *Aotearoa*, the land of the long white cloud, was at last in sight.[11]

The tour proper now began (two days late), although the party probably wasn't aware of the parlous state of New Zealand's economy. A long boom from the mid-1890s had ended abruptly in 1920, followed by an alternating pattern of recession, recovery and further recession amid optimism about inevitable improvement. Political instability, disillusionment and economic insecurity marked the 1920s. The country's economic order rested on the shifting sands of world commodity prices (in wool, butter, cheese and frozen meat): for about four decades until World War I, Britain had absorbed 80 per cent of New Zealand's exports, with the percentage slipping from a 1921 high of 86 per cent to 72 per cent in 1928. Three years earlier an economic crunch had come when wool prices plummeted 40 per cent and butter fat 15–20 per cent, and yet production kept rising due to greater farm efficiency and innovations (milking machines, regular herd testing and pasture improvement). There was a higher export value due to an increased volume of trade, but a huge loss of £10 million in 1926 on 1925 prices—'eloquent', observed the government statistician, 'of what falling prices mean for the Dominion'. The country's economic plight was worsened by a 'steep rise' in unemployment in 1926 and an escalating foreign debt.[12]

At 268,000 square kilometres, New Zealand was slightly larger in area than Britain but dwarfed by it in population—1.47 million in April 1929, of whom about 65,000 were Maoris. In 1929, six of every ten New Zealanders lived on the North Island, with about a third of the population concentrated in Auckland, Wellington, Christchurch and Dunedin. With 210,000 inhabitants, Auckland was the largest city. 'Urban drift' had accelerated since the turn of the century. An important adjunct to natural population increase was immigration from Home: it accounted for more than 30 per cent of the dominion's population growth in the previous three decades. Assisted immigration fell dramatically from more than 10,000 in 1926 to about 2000 in 1929. Trade deficits impacted directly on immigration because, unlike Canada and Australia—which, consistent with OSC thinking, relied on voluntary migration societies (for example, the Salvation Army as part of its outreach and similarly a charity, Dr Barnardo's Homes) to sponsor immigrants—New Zealand depended uniquely on 'nomination'. In 1923, the British Oversea Settlement Delegation to New Zealand commented that nomination had had 'very satisfactory results', although given that the nominator (a New Zealand permanent resident) had to 'make provision for maintenance and employment for the nominee upon arrival' and then 'guarantee that the nominee will reside in the Dominion for at least five years', such results were unlikely during economic downturns. With the numbers seeking assistance to find work rising sharply from 3000 in 1926 to more than 10,000 in 1927, there were calls for cutbacks in assisted immigration. While the OSC acknowledged the dominion's increasing difficulties in settler absorption, it saw this as purely temporary and likened New Zealand to the USA fifty years earlier: possession of 'limitless natural resources and industrial possibilities which seem only to require population for rapid development'.[13]

From 14 February to 28 March Darling's touring party traversed New Zealand. On the first morning in the ship's smoking room, the business-like Portal, armed with a map of New Zealand, pins and tape, outlined the travel route. The trip comprised a long loop down the two islands and back to Auckland. After a day in Auckland they went south to New Plymouth for three days, stopping at the Waitomo Caves south of Hamilton, and then on to Wellington. Next, they crossed the Marlborough Sounds to Picton and Blenheim. There were five days in Christchurch and a further five in the Mount Cook alpine area from where Darling went to Queenstown. After the others had gone further south to Invercargill, Darling rejoined them, and the party wound its way circuitously northwards to Dunedin, Oamaru and Waitaki, then by the *Maori* to Wellington, on to Palmerston North, Wanganui, Wairarapa and Hawke's Bay, Rotorua, Hamilton and Auckland. Occasionally the country's worsening economic factors registered in the boys' consciousness. At their first luncheon at the Farmers' Trading Coy in Auckland, hosted by the Rotary Club, a businessman 'pointed out that New Zealand was undergoing a period of depression'. Darling noted that 'this caused a minor crisis[.] Mr Attmore [Minister of Education] snorted the Mayor wobbled while the rest shuddered. The offender was rebuked by the next speaker.' Here Darling learnt an important lesson. Whatever he might confide to the privacy of his diary would make little difference, but what he said publicly at a particular moment mattered greatly, because almost every word uttered stared back at him in the next day's newspapers, and by those words he and the tour party were judged. On this occasion he was reported as noting only 'a slight difference of opinion as to the economic condition of the country' and adding that 'neither side can influence us. That is just one of the things we have come to see for ourselves'. Although this was 'a very good speech', as John Weston noted in his diary, Darling had to be doubly careful. Rather than their hosts treating the boys as temporarily released from their school commitments, they were predisposed to see them as the cream of the English public schools and as possible settlers with the requisite financial capital. Seven of Woolley's 1926 group, for example, had settled permanently in Australia, so that these 'young scions of England's finest stock', as the *New Zealand Herald* labelled Darling's group, were seen as well worth cultivating.[14]

The tour was changing Darling's outlook in unanticipated ways, a metamorphosis that obliged him to confront his own Englishness. For a start, New

Zealand was a social democracy whereas England wasn't, and his firsthand experience of it made him ambivalent. On the way to the Masterton show, for example, he chatted to an Old Carthusian, Jim Vogel (grandson of a noted New Zealand politician, Sir Julius Vogel) about Aubrey Scott and Charterhouse, and later reflected that:

> They seemed a long way off and interests no longer so important as they once had been. I found that all the time this tour occupied my mind so fully that it was impossible to keep up connection with anything at home and when I did eventually return it was to a world almost new and though everyone else had gone on without a break my mind had to make a new start in everything.

Warmth and friendliness, like that of the 'simple and unpretentious' New Plymouth settlers, were encountered everywhere. Not only was the country free of rigid class barriers, but for Britishers it was a self-made society in which they could advance economically and socially by their own efforts. At Featherstone, he had stayed with the brother of the English composer, Sir Edward Elgar, who said that:

> there were a hundred people on the ship [on which he came to New Zealand] and I kept a record of all of them and only ten per cent have got anywhere near where I got.

The effect of this new world absence of class distinction in Christchurch was that:

> everyone was conscious of his own dignity as a man with the least desire to insist upon it or to despise anyone else. It was actually true that every man regarded himself as being as good as his fellow but not as being any better and there was the proper absence of class consciousness because classes were not divisions of which anyone was conscious.

This new state of affairs provided an unsettling contrast with what he was used to.[15]

New Zealand had a double-barrelled effect on Darling. He mentally positioned England and its culture as better than anything that the new young country had to offer, while being disdainful of New Zealanders who sheepishly imitated English ways and then paraded themselves as superior. Juxtaposed with the recognition in his diary of the countryside's spectacular beauty are asides about boring distances, sparse settlement, dust and burnt-off bush. Next, until thousands of hanging glow-worms reflected themselves in the water and prompted him to quote a Wordsworth poem, he dismissed the Waitomo Caves as no better than those at Cheddar Gorge. Then, on the way back to Wellington from Masterton, accompanied by the mayor, the elderly and bearded Mr Troup, he was condescending about the man's well-meaning art gallery plans:

> I feared from his conversation that the Wellington Art Gallery would be like the others, a sort of second rate Birmingham full of the imitations of Burne Jones and Lord Leighton and decorated with the culminating glory of the Monarch of the Glen.

At a dance that evening, he was bored by a New Zealander who tried to convince him of the dominions' virtues over England. 'Seldom', he reflected, 'have I heard it so blatantly and stupidly expressed'. But when the tour party crossed the Cook Strait to Marlborough on the *Tamahine* New Zealand's provincialism and England's superiority hit him. From Picton they had sailed in motor launches for a picnic at Ship's Cove where the navigator James Cook had landed. As they passed an old three-masted sailing ship 'resting high and dry', Darling speculated on the hardships of the earlier settlers. It was as well to remember their resourcefulness, 'when one gets a little tired of the ancestor worship of the modern New Zealander', he noted, and then eulogised Cook as 'the great discoverer' because he reasoned that the explorer had not received in English history 'the recognition which is his due'.[16]

The group's arrival in Christchurch yielded Darling's most explicit statement of his English superiority. The city itself was an 'idealised imitation of an English Cathedral town' with its 'not very large' cathedral, 'built at the worst time of Victorian neo-Gothic enthusiasm' and its square reminiscent of 'those squares in second rate French towns to which one invariably drifts after one's arrival at the station'. There was genius in the city's river park named after the Avon River because it was 'a very good imitation'. He conceded to Christchurch 'the individuality of which the city is so proud' except that this feature still only made it the most English-like town in the country. But what was really unpalatable was the social mimicking of England, especially by the self-styled aristocrats whom he thought were snobs:

> They live in fashionable English houses in the fashionable part of the town and in the manner of the English 'County' despise the ordinary inhabitants of the town and take no share in its municipal life.

The attitudes of this stratum derived from having entertained visiting dignitaries (such as the Duke of York) or having played tennis with them on their private courts—as was true of the particular family with whom John Weston stayed. As far as Darling was concerned, these people lacked the necessary intellectual leavening that made London society bearable, and they performed none of the social and charitable semi-feudal duties of English county families. Despite the local hospitality, he kept himself to himself in a hotel from which he 'could more plainly see their faults'.[17]

Despite this patronising dismissal of their hosts, Darling insisted that the boys meet their expectations. These were high, so that from the day of their arrival newspaper editorials lionised them. Cringing adulation spewed forth:

> 'What are you going to do when you get back?' a gentlemanly youth of 17 was asked. 'I shall go into Parliament; at least, that is the intention of my Pater', replied the lad with the utmost composure. It is typical of the tremendously earnest outlook adopted by these young men towards life that each has his career plainly set out before him. Fate decrees that they should lead men and that they accept the responsibility with perfect confidence and equanimity.

Other manifestations of journalistic obsequiousness included 'model English gentlemen', 'profound men' and 'a Solomon of 17'. A *Dominion* report surpassed the others in quoting with alacrity a New Zealander returning on the *Ionic* who described the boys as:

> men in the making, and who would stop at nothing in an emergency. They appear to have been born to command, be it on the playing fields, in the navy, or the fields of battle, or in commercial life. Above all they are most cheerful companions.

Public consumption of fawning imagery was one thing, but the reality was something else, so much so that Darling thought that his hosts were being taken for a ride. Portal, for instance, persisted with deliberately contrived unpunctuality and affected a 'carefully assumed nonchalance', Darling said, while Smith-Dorrien was equally lax. Not only were they upper-class by background but their political convictions and their attitudes to empire were deeply conservative. Well versed in official formalities, their cavalier behaviour taunted him:

> I was never really free from nervousness at Government House, in spite of the kindness of [the Governor General] Sir Charles and Lady Alice [Fergusson]. I was always stupidly afraid that something would go wrong or that somehow I or another of us would upset sensibilities or trespass against an etiquette of which I was ignorant.

Darling often wondered whether Mr Ardell, the hospitality officer accompanying them from the New Zealand Ministry of Internal Affairs 'was seeing a little too much behind the scenes'.[18]

From time to time the boys let the side down. Smith-Dorrien was in charge of most of their day-to-day supervision but Darling's 'awful thundering of Jove' was

the final word. On two or three occasions he was critical of the boys' exalted sense
of self-importance and claimed to be relentless in having to drive them so hard.
Thus, he 'brutally' denied them rests while they were descending Mount Egmont.
He was appalled by the way that they 'disgraced themselves' at a Government
House reception and embarrassed at 'the devastation' caused by their voracity.
Again, at Wellington, he railed at 'tired and rather blasé boys' for not wanting to
dance at a function, and said: 'I passed on my anger as my way is'. Next morning:

> although we were already late I had collected as many of the party as I could in
> a room at the Town Hall and cursed them for their bad manners at last night's
> dance, for their unpunctuality of the morning and, the general tendency to
> blaséness which was becoming apparent to me.

He doubted whether his words had any laudable effect, but at the time 'they
were the only weapon which I had with which to exercise any influence'; for
days on end 'I had no chance of any influence on them at all'. Darling was constantly wary of publicity. When two tour groups were badly beaten by Wellington
College's 1st and 2nd XI cricket teams, he took this as 'disastrous to our prestige'
because the results would be 'freely reported' in the newspapers. From then on,
touring boys combined with New Zealanders in scratch matches. The composing of speeches that were intended to strengthen the imperial connection (a key
purpose of the tour) and then delivering them wrought a change in his beliefs.
(At Blenheim, on 23 February, he gave his fourth speech that day and his twentieth in nine days.) With the reprinting of his utterances whenever he spoke, he
came to accept at face value what he was saying, so that by the end of the tour the
empire was making sense to him. New Plymouth was where the penny dropped
and the significance of what he was being required to do hit home. Portal had
insisted on wreaths being placed at town cenotaphs, which meant that Darling
would have to speak. He 'strongly objected':

> There was going to be quite enough insincerity in speech-making anyhow,
> and the boys were going to become more and more bored by the sound of my
> voice, and I was determined that I should not spoil by wearisome iteration a
> feeling that, if only demanded once, might be sincere.

For this reason he decided on only such one address and worked extremely hard
at it: he wrote it out in full and tried to learn it by heart.[19]

Two newspapers reprinted Darling's New Plymouth address. The *Otago
Daily Times*' editorial called it 'a graceful tribute' to New Zealand servicemen,
with his words achieving the requisite solemnity:

> He said he thought it was right that they should stop at that spot and that
> he should speak to them in order that at least once while in New Zealand

they should recognize the sacrifice New Zealanders had made for the Empire in the war. He could not estimate just how much the war might mean to those boys, but to those who had lived through the war years it would always remain the most important thing in their lives. The people of this country, as those of England had done, had sent armies to the war. The need for sending men may have seemed less in New Zealand than at Home, but New Zealand had responded generously, and he wanted the boys to think what the sacrifice made meant to the people of this country. It meant that if the men lived through the war many would come back to start life over again, as they had had to leave their work in the best part of their lives. If they died their bodies would be thousands of miles from their homes and their people would have only empty tombs to look upon.

As they were standing before a cenotaph that replicated one at Home, Darling emphasised the shared ideals of the two countries and their two peoples' common attributes. While a boy laid the wreath, he hoped that in silence they would think about these commonalities. Later, he surprised himself at what he had done:

> The speech itself was another ordeal. Quite a number of citizens were present and when we had all assumed the expression usual on such occasions, I made my utterance. The boys seemed fairly good and I myself was, I think, the only person whom it struck as odd that I, Jim Darling, should be standing in so pompous a fashion, uttering a funeral oration. Often in the tour, I have wanted to laugh at myself, but never more than then, when I should have so completely collapsed to see my brother or my friends amongst the audience. Could Tommy [Thompson, Charterhouse] have been there, how he would have laughed! or Scott, or Hilda and Louis. Yet I was quite sincere in what I said. The model of the English Cenotaph standing there by the sea in the Antipodes, and standing for the memorial to those who had died so far from home, for the place that they called Home, did touch me and nothing which I said do I in any way depreciate. It was only very odd that I should be the central figure doing this serious thing.

He experienced this same affinity of sentiment and spirit between the two nations the next morning in church when reading aloud the English prayerbook.[20]

Darling constructed his diary of the tour as though trying to convince himself of being able to withstand the strains of leadership. Attending to such mundane chores as composing letters of thanks may have kept him up late at night, but constant reiteration of the fact made it sound like special pleading. So too did his assertion that he had coped better than anyone else with the tour's demands. Awareness of the importance of the august company that he was keeping and his inner battle to gear himself to deliver speeches meant that Darling was mentally repositioning himself socially. In this respect, he projected himself as being assessed or on trial. He described his very first speech (for the initial Auckland lunch), for example, as a 'timorous bark' amid the 'troubled sea' of economic controversy:

> Portal was by my side, suffering considerably and Mr Ardell opposite me had his eye on me and was ready to criticize, forty-five boys were, I suppose, expecting me to make a fool of myself, the fate that boys seem always to desire for their masters, and at the same time more or less conscious that their reputation would be a little compromised by my failure. The speech was got through somehow, with no bones badly broken.

In fairness, the official civic and government welcome at Wellington Town Hall on 19 February was likely to have intimidated anyone, for the huge *Dominion* photograph has Darling engulfed by a phalanx of dignitaries that included the mayor, the prime minister (the ageing and nearly blind Sir Joseph Ward), at least two other Cabinet members, parliamentarians and councillors. 'I had no idea what was in store for me', Darling confided. After some effusive speeches of welcome, he claimed that he was 'wiping sweaty palms with a dripping handkerchief' and was ready 'to get up and run'. When he spoke, he tried to tell a joke or two and confessed to being nervous:

> Mr J. Darling (Charterhouse) said that if in the course of his speech he was found stammering for words, it should be understood that he was not accustomed to speak in such eminent society, for he did so in fear and trembling.

The *Dominion* report continued:

> Everywhere he went he appeared to be speaking in eulogistic terms, but he hoped that people would not think he was doing so because perhaps he felt that such was expected. He could assure all those in New Zealand that he was absolutely genuine and sincere. But the public was making such a fuss of the party that he was beginning to believe that they were really glad to see them (Hear, hear, and applause).

This particular speech, Darling noted, went down 'comparatively well'.[21]

Portal claimed in Hamilton in March that the tour succeeded because of 'teamwork and co-operation', even though in Christchurch relations had disintegrated during a tension-ridden period. The boys arrived 'tired and dejected' from Marlborough very late one Sunday evening after being delayed by two vehicles breaking down. The government had arranged for the party to be the official guests of the City Council, with its Labour mayor, a Baptist minister, the Reverend J.K. Archer. In most major centres, local entertainment committees comprising public school and old boys' association representatives planned itineraries and arranged billets, but in Christchurch the town clerk took over a half-completed program from the committee secretary, a member of the self-styled aristocracy: 'From this swapping of horses a certain amount of bad feeling remained and almost at once I realised that I had to move very cautiously'. That night Darling felt very fatigued and 'badly off form' which did not augur well. Next morning, the boys went to the Cashmere Hills for a lecture on Canterbury province and then a visit to the city's Bridge of Remembrance. Aware of the local aristocracy's antipathy to the mayor (a vocal champion of Christchurch's unemployed) Darling braced himself for the noon reception.[22]

Archer rose to speak. The *Dominion* quoted him later (as Labour Party organisation chairman) as saying that 'the only remedy for the existing condition of things was the absolute destruction of capitalism ... the root evil of the world', but on this occasion Darling thought that he was 'a well-meaning and very stupid sentimentalist rather than a fierce Bolshevist':

> He reminded us we were privileged guests and that we were not seeing New Zealand as it really was, that we must keep our eyes open to the existence of slums in Christchurch far different from the houses in which we were privileged to stay, and that if we thought of emigrating we must realize that New Zealand expected emigrants to work and that there was no easy road to success.

Groping for a little levity, Archer then diverged:

> The only headmaster he'd ever met used to go to sleep with a bottle of whisky or a glass of whisky by his side till he got up.

He was followed by a 'brilliant' speech by Darling's former Newmarket instructor, James Shelley (who, having departed England, was Professor of Education at Canterbury College). To retrieve the situation with his own light touch, Shelley assured the mayor 'that his recollection was that no English public schoolmaster would go to sleep with a *full* glass of whisky by his side'. Darling then tried to appease both sides of this 'unedifying display of local politics'. 'I wasn't prepared to spit in the eye of the Labour mayor', he recalled, but his co-directors believed that he went too far in placating him:

> I began by a reminder to his worship that this was not the usual speech of welcome and that its strangeness had spoilt the speech which I had prepared and that he had provoked me to reply to some of his implied criticisms. I then proceeded quite tactfully, but I think effectively, for those that had ears, to defeat him.

After the reception, the touring party broke into four groups to visit schools. Darling spent the afternoon at the Boys' High School and enjoyed it 'very much'.[23]

Not only had Shelley unexpectedly crossed his path, but by an even odder coincidence he met an acquaintance of James Harford—his Reptonian friend—the Countess Thelma Metaxa, lady-in-waiting to Lady Alice Fergusson. As he felt stifled by the pretentiousness of the leading Christchurch families, she was an admirable confidante. On the evening after the reception, Darling dined with John Studholme, a Canterbury farmer active in municipal government. Later, Darling confessed that, having goaded his hosts about their smugness, he misbehaved by announcing boldly: 'I am a socialist'. The countess was 'amused' but Portal and Smith-Dorrien were scandalised. The next day, following 'a rather boring visit' to the Lake Coleridge hydroelectric scheme, Christchurch's pride and joy, Darling and the countess chatted briefly. Shortly afterwards, she wrote to Harford and reported that Darling said 'he thought people thought him a prig'. On the contrary, she thought that he was 'a nice sort of man and I admire his carrying out of an extraordinary difficult job. He speaks publicly awfully well and tactfully'. The previous evening Darling and Michael Scott had extricated themselves 'by most ill-timed disorder' from Studholme's dinner and, with two of the boys, went to a Toc H meeting. In his diary, Darling expatiated at length on the humility and self-effacing dedication of the Toc H members. The placement of this episode in the middle of a description of the gentrified inertia and complacency engulfing him suggested that he was trying to purge himself of suppressed hostility. In England, Darling was a Toc H member in Godalming and he thought that the organisation expressed genuine Christianity:

> I shall never forget the scene of that Toc H meeting when it broke up into little groups of men, cheerful though some were unsuccessful, a mixture of all classes, and professions yet all agreeing in spirit though not in words in the eagerness of their discussion of the most real of the problems of life, the problem of how to find a right standard of values and when found to make one's life, the demand of economic necessity, and the standards of the world agree in any way with it.

That evening's meeting gave him the solace that he needed, but most pleasing of all was the contrast between Toc H's meeting and Christchurch's municipal jealousies.[24]

The next night the party visited Christ's College. Darling could not take to the headmaster, and saw him as weak and ineffective, and intent on aping 'fatuous traditions' that were impeding a decent education in England. Darling thought that he made a bad speech which:

> was not enthusiastic either on behalf of the Empire or of the public schools and it may have been mildly pinkish though no-one seems to have noticed it except Portal and Smith-Dorrien.

After attending a cinema, he and Scott returned to their hotel. Disgruntled, tired and (on his own admission) spoiling for a fight, a blazing row then ensued in the hotel office:

> Almost at once Portal and Smith-Dorrien came in and the fat was in fire. Of the ensuing quarrel I am really ashamed partly because I enjoyed it, and partly because I allowed myself to be beaten and was careful afterwards to give no cause for offence. The matter was patched up afterwards largely as a result of the loyalty of the other two and is no credit to me, and actually I never really forgave them and have not yet done so, not for their political opinions to which they are entitled, nor for their criticism of myself which was intelligible, but for their incredible imbecility in producing their criticism that night and the pompous vacuity and self importance with which they delivered their strictures.

His diary entry then said: 'I let Portal talk for some ten minutes and then really let myself go as I rarely allow myself to do'. Fortuitously, a medical crisis (a boy's appendicitis) helped heal the rift. After a 'delightful time' at the Hermitage Chalet on Mount Cook and a walk on the Franz Josef glacier, Darling had gone on alone to Lake Wanaka and Queenstown. Portal and Smith-Dorrien returned with the sick boy. Quick thinking in this isolated area was called for. With the local doctor's calibre questionable and the other 60 kilometres away rumoured to have a drink problem, Darling took the latter option. After a harrowing drive on poorly surfaced roads and the boy in great pain, an operation was performed at Cromwell. With everyone else by now in Invercargill, Darling maintained a hospital vigil for three or four days until rejoining the others in Dunedin.[25]

Shortly afterwards, to Darling's relief, the tour was out of the public gaze for a week while the boys were billeted on farms. He stayed with the Elgars, where he had to deal with another round of dominion gentility and met local dignitaries active in the cause of boy migration—including R.S. Abraham (President, New Zealand Association of English Public Schools) and D.H.S. (Dan) Riddiford at Feilding, with whom he formed a 'lasting though intermittent friendship'. Darling also visited Abraham's former school, Wanganui, although he thought that it slavishly aped English public school practices as well. Five absorbing days were then spent exploring the geological wonders of Rotorua where there were more 'incidents' when some of the boys at a dance were unduly attracted to Maori girls. Their behaviour provoked another harangue from Chief (their sobriquet for Darling) who had sat up 'half the night' waiting for his 'wandering sheep to return'. Finally, at Hamilton, on 27 March, Darling made his very last New Zealand speech. In front of a large crowd of tour organisers, borough council-lors, members of Parliament, the bishop and hundreds of secondary school boys, the mayor said that 'no visitors could be more welcome'. In his reply, Darling thanked the mayor's fellow countrymen for their cordiality, Sir Joseph Ward for his help as their host (as they had been official guests of the government of New Zealand), and the various local committees for an 'immensely successful tour' in which 'the divergent views and tastes of the party had been amply catered for'. The educational and social sides had been 'nicely balanced', while 'Never had they seen people who seemed to be so happy and contented as the people of New Zealand'. He asked his hearers 'to believe that everything done for the visitors was greatly appreciated', as they had had a marvellous time. The next day (Maundy Thursday), Darling and Portal paid their last respects to Sir Charles Fergusson and, after a farewell lunch, the party boarded their boat. As a large crowd watched their steamer break the billowing streamers, the boys 'gave three cheers' for their hosts and they were off to Sydney, travelling second saloon class.[26]

On Easter Saturday, an Auckland newspaper described the boys' delight with New Zealand:

> We were struck with the entire absence of class distinction … everyone speaks
> to everyone else whether you are fighting for a sandwich at a railway station or
> in a tramcar. This was a most delightful revelation.

While the group was crossing the Tasman Sea over Easter, there were services on Good Friday and Easter Day, with the captain, by his choice of hymns, betraying his ignorance of the significance of the days. In Sydney, the party was welcomed by the governor, Sir Dudley de Chair, who 'had the greatest difficulty thinking of the names of any schools except Eton'. The boys went to the Royal Show and Taronga Park Zoo. They then spent three days in Hobart where, to everyone's disappointment, 'it rained incessantly'. In Melbourne on 8 April there was yet another civic welcome for them. On this occasion, the lord mayor was mildly critical of British car manufacturers for allowing Australia to be flooded with American vehicles. In his reply, Darling said that complaints about British cars were 'a source of annoyance to us', but for boys who might go into business these conversations and impressions of the dominions could only ensure 'a closer economic union'. After lunch at the Menzies Hotel, Darling and some boys went to Melbourne Grammar School while others visited Scotch College. The next day they ventured into the Australian bush at Healesville and Marysville where, John Weston told his parents, the scenery was truly 'magnificent'. The second last Australian port of call was Adelaide. Here, at one of the three schools that they visited, Darling met an English clergyman, the Reverend K.J.F. Bickersteth, headmaster, since 1919, of St Peter's Collegiate School. Although Bickersteth was a fairly rigid Anglo-Catholic Christian, Darling was impressed by 'a rather fascinating sort of electrical man'.[27]

Life's events can often turn on what, in retrospect, are momentary encounters. And so it was after having met Bickersteth, because Darling let drop that if a vacancy arose in Australia then he might care to alert him. Shortly afterwards Bickersteth commended the boys to Rendall and also said to Darling that:

I need hardly say that your all too brief visit here was a great delight to me. It was so pleasant to meet people with whom one has not got to begin at zero before starting interesting conversation.

In Adelaide, Darling met the second of the two vice-regal representatives whom, after the Fergussons, he most admired on the tour, the governor and his wife, Sir Alexander and Lady Hore-Ruthven. At Perth, the party farewelled Portal who remained behind to look after yet another appendicitis victim. Cabled requests for permission to operate were bluntly swept aside by the boy's parents with 'disapprove of operation except to save life'. As the four medical opinions that Darling obtained all agreed that under no circumstances should the boy be permitted to travel, the lad's condition had its humorous side: unless his parents relented (which they did), he would have had to remain in Australia indefinitely. The party headed for Colombo on the *Moreton Bay* (a one-class, £40 per berth boat) full of complaining British emigrants returning home. (John Weston remembered that nine boys were jammed into his cabin.) At Colombo, an Old Carthusian entertained them. Back on board, Darling lectured on Egypt in anticipation of visits to the pyramids, the Sphinx and the relics of Tutankhamen. Instead of passing through the Suez Canal, the party travelled overland to Cairo, where the boys were the guests of Lord Lloyd, the High Commissioner for Egypt and the Sudan. The party's last stop was 'that heroic and entrancing place', Malta, after which the *Moreton Bay* rounded Gibraltar and steamed into Southampton on 18 May.[28]

Reflecting on the tour, Darling expressed personal misgivings. From the outset there had been a political headache, due to his lack of 'firm belief' in the empire and the public schools. As for imperialism:

I had always maintained that the Empire was purely a society of nations bound together by ties of mutual interest, and that if these ceased to exist then dissolution was inevitable. I had even maintained that in some cases this dissolution was imminent or would seem, in the eyes of the future historian, actually to have taken place.

The tour had mellowed his opinions, but he hadn't jettisoned all his previous views:

my imperialism, still lacks something of the enthusiasm of a Joseph Chamberlain or any New Zealander. The truth is that the sentimental aspect of the British Empire has no appeal for me and yet that it is a very important thing. A socialist by politics, as I still am, I was doubtful as to the propriety of associating myself with a venture in which conservatives primarily were interested and it was only because I underestimated the political nature of the tour that I even consented to take it.

As to how much of his soul he was 'forced to sell', he had no idea.[29]

Darling's other concern was that the tour still left him ambivalent about the public schools. For four months his bottled-up emotions had been throttling his conscience:

> I hate their intolerance of other people, their slowness in moving to a new idea, their over-emphasis on games, the dirtiness of their ideas, and above all their narrowness of outlook. I know that the boys who go to them are for the most part too well-provided with money and not sufficiently with ambition, that they are too much inclined to want only pleasure out of life and shun seriousness as much as they do religion. I abominate the contemptuous ignorance with which as boys they spoil any new idea and the stupidity with which as men they habitually are even unacquainted with the movements of the time.

Despite these shortcomings, he had had to be an apologist for the public schools in a country recently settled by Europeans in which others had delivered, and had heard him deliver, eulogy after eulogy in homage to them, 'which no public school man would have had the face to utter':

> It required a rather dishonest subtlety to speak with decency and not to let the tour down. It was more difficult for me because of a distressing incapacity to tell downright lies or to speak absolutely dishonestly. It was fortunate perhaps for the tour, that when I of intention omitted eulogy, my hearers took it for granted and counted it merely as my modesty which kept me silent.

Darling regretted having agreed to go. Everyone had congratulated him on being chosen and had urged him to enjoy it. Self-pityingly, he claimed that 'no one seemed to sympathise with my view of the situation and no one really does so yet'. On the other hand, in July 1929 when Louis Wharton returned from Trinidad he noticed the change in Darling and remarked to Phelps that the tour had obviously done him good in 'making him surer of and in himself'. 'It has, too, considerably broadened his outlook, and not merely, as R.H. Tawney would say, elongated his conversation. He is now An Imperialist.' Regardless of what he had thought and said about the public schools, if Darling still harboured ambitions to be in charge of one, then New Zealand (and Australia) had set him up nicely: he had observed headmasters in action and acquired a feel for what was required. Significantly, therefore, less than a fortnight after returning from his antipodean 'sound sentence', he had already sounded out his friend, the newly enthroned Primate of England, about whether or not to apply for a headship.[30]

8

TRANSITION

1929–1930

> *… Round the decay*
> *Of that colossal Wreck, boundless and bare*
> *The lone and level sands stretch far away.*
>
> Percy Bysshe Shelley, *Ozymandias*

In the week after his return home, Darling attended a School Empire-Tour Committee meeting. There was backslapping all round. Rendall expressed the committee's 'cordial gratitude' to Darling. The two appendicitis cases, 'one most serious', had been dealt with 'most carefully and tactfully'. He then quoted Darling's assessment of Smith-Dorrien as the hardest working of the four leaders and Portal as 'a miracle of efficiency'. Michael Scott had helped with the musical and general culture of the tour, and had been 'invaluable in connection with the pocket money'. Scott had remained in Egypt for ten days with two of the boys—an arrangement to which Darling 'rather reluctantly' agreed and cabled to obtain authorisation. Portal (in Adelaide) wrote that the party had been a happy group and had made an 'excellent' impression. Darling had 'performed a miracle', he said, by rising to the occasion in his speeches and moulding the boys (who varied greatly in type) into a workable unit by their arrival in Auckland. The 'Public School-Empire Tour Society New Zealand 1929' had been formed to entertain New Zealanders visiting England and nearly all the boys had joined. Smith-Dorrien highlighted Darling's lectures on the history of the empire as much appreciated. Privately, he told Darling that he had taught him a great deal. Their disagreements had crystallised his ideas: 'what fun they were (disagreements I mean)'. Darling described the boys as 'good stuff', although because of its generous hospitality, New Zealand really deserved to see the best that England had to offer, namely its potential leaders.[1]

Darling's full report was discussed in February. In it he summarised the mechanics of the tour, while disclosing none of his anxieties about public schooling and the tour's imperial justification. He highlighted the dominion's intense loyalty and the English boys' possession of that indefinable something 'which the New Zealand boys have not got and which their parents would like to see in them'. Future chief directors had to be 'politically sound' due to the prominence given by newspapers to speeches on the tour's objects. Although New Zealanders had expected to see the 'real future leaders of the country', the normal sense of school prefect responsibility was insufficiently evident in the tour group, although with no genuine privileges to grant would have been of little use anyway. Smith-Dorrien highlighted Darling's effective division of responsibilities between the directors that left each 'to see his own job through' and Portal described Darling's speeches as 'one of the most fortunate aspects of the whole tour'. With the exception of tours to India and East Africa, the committee rejected Darling's recommendation that a doctor should be one of the leaders, although it deemed his report to be of 'special value' to future antipodean tour leaders.[2]

In the summer of 1929, Darling returned to Charterhouse. He joined Fyfe as a Public Schools' Employment Bureau member and was active with him on its New Zealand sub-committee, so much so that R.S. Abraham described Darling as a veritable 'sheet anchor' (although New Zealand's economic climate was less conducive to immigration). The bureau was cumbersome and frustrated Fyfe, Darling and Lindsay (then Director of Voluntary Migration Societies, Dominions Office) in their efforts for the dominions. Back on the other side of the world, about when the *Moreton Bay* entered the Mediterranean, the headmaster of GGS, the Reverend Dr F.E. Brown, resigned with effect from July and the headmastership was vacant from the end of December. In June, Australian and New Zealand newspaper advertisements invited applications until 15 August. The school council chairman, Donald Mackinnon, was in England and had engaged officials of the Board of Education, Rendall and the headmaster's brother, the Reverend W.J. Brown (head of Norwich School) to locate English candidates.[3]

Darling's moment of truth was fast approaching. Earlier he had contacted Temple about a headship vacancy at Framlingham, a small Suffolk grammar school. Having been advised by his uncle Reggie to pursue it, he was 'to some extent interested'. Temple had been moderately encouraging but Darling declined to proceed. Shortly afterwards Bickersteth cabled: 'Geelong Grammar School vacant great opportunity suggest you apply'. The Framlingham decision had probably been right, Temple said, but:

> I don't know what to say about the question of your going to Geelong. I believe you would do it extremely well, and it is a most important job, but I have of course always pictured you in England. I am afraid it is not a point where friends can be of much use to you. I can only say that I should feel very strong reasons for either decision.

Darling then consulted Fletcher who referred him to Rendall, but for the time being he put thoughts about headships aside and holidayed in Majorca with his former Carthusian pupil, Hugh Derry. Meanwhile, Mackinnon had cabled the GGS council to say that the summer vacation was creating difficulties in locating candidates, and that he would delay his choice of successor until October. When Darling returned from Europe, Rendall confirmed that there were very few good English applicants. Neither knew that eight Australasian applicants had been reduced to two, along with an English clergyman (the Reverend E.A. Berrisford) with whose testimonials, Mackinnon was informed, the council was impressed. Darling sought support from Fisher and Phelps:

> I am, I fear, presumptuously and at any rate reluctantly, applying for the headmastership of Geelong School in Australia. Would you be so kind as to write me a testimonial and let me have it here as soon as you can. Actually I very much hope that nothing comes of this but it has to be done I am afraid.

What Darling intended by the final cryptic sentence is unclear. His application was late. On 16 September he and two clergymen (Berrisford and the Reverend Christopher Storrs) were interviewed at the Board of Education Office of Special Inquiries and Reports by Mackinnon, Rendall, Brown and two Board officials—one of whom (Ainsworth) was also a member of the School Empire-Tour Committee. The council's advertisement had specified a communicant member of the Church of England, although not necessarily a clergyman. Rendall insisted that Darling would be unacceptable in exclusive and conservative Melbourne Club circles and Fletcher believed that GGS wanted a married clergyman of forty. The likelihood of Darling's unacceptability was compounded when Brown asked him whether he was in holy orders or contemplating holy orders, and Darling had to say no.[4]

Rendall was convinced that Dr Brown 'had his own man' in mind and even 'partly cherish[ed] the exploded view that a HM should nominate his successor'. When pressed further by Brown's brother about whether he was married, and if not was he contemplating matrimony, Darling's reply (he claimed later)—'Well, not specifically'—turned out to be his trump card with Mackinnon. Indeed, Ainsworth confirmed the next day that he was the preferred candidate. When he requested a testimonial from Temple, Darling was assured that he was right to apply. He also contacted Phelps and (again enigmatically) confessed: 'you will understand that I am sure that I want to take this job very little but have done it rather priggishly because it seems worth doing'. What was more: 'I cannot see what happens after it but nor did I see any way out of what seemed a demand upon me'. This was an awkwardly disguised attempt to rationalise ambition as a call to serve—a ploy that would come in handy again. The thought of leaving Charterhouse appalled him because, all things considered, it had given him so much:

They have I am sorry to say decided to send my name first and another man second to Australia where the appointment will be finally made so that in terms of the race-course the betting is on my having to go. I feel curiously more resigned than I would have expected. It is a job to do, if I can do it, and apparently nobody good enough would apply for it—the lazy blighters.

Oh, and by the way, he quipped to Phelps, 'I shall want an M.A.'[5]

With Darling's desire for a headship likely to be fulfilled, he was unsure whether he had made the right decision. 'The other bloke's name is really a sop to Australia so that she appears to make a choice', his future brother-in-law Ralph le Fleming reassured him (Ralph and Mabel married in August 1930). 'For God's sake do your whack at the damned place quickly and then get an English school', he urged. To quell his doubts, Ainsworth said:

> I hope you did not misunderstand anything I said at the interview. I did not imply at all that you ought to wait until your mind was more settled. What I wanted to find out was whether you yourself were conscious of any kind of stress because your thoughts were still in some directions unsettled.

Fyfe made light of the news by threatening to cable Corio that his friend had been convicted or suspected of the Reading shop murder, although 'that might be a recommendation in N.S.W!' Darling had been convinced to apply by his father, bursting with 'paternal pride' although sorrowful that he might have to go so far away. Austen's doubts about the wisdom of his advice were put aside: 'I do think I was right; the thing was absolutely thrown at you'. Then followed a remarkable fatherly compliment:

> I feel that you may now live in this house some day and carry on the name in this Country. I shall also feel that if I go, your mother will have someone of substance behind her on whom she can rely. God bless you.[6]

Mackinnon sailed for Australia in late September. The next month he reported to the GGS sub-committee. His son Kenneth hoped that:

> your Mr Darling does not withdraw from the lists before the final selection is made. It would indeed be a tragedy for Geelong if he is as fine a man as you told me.

If Amery's praise for a successful tour and Temple's judgement that Darling 'has the making of a very remarkable schoolmaster' were insufficient to persuade the council, then Fletcher's testimonial would have clinched it:

> Darling is keen, vigorous, conscientious, and very attractive; a man who has grown and will keep on growing. He is spiritually earnest and thoughtful,

with a full realisation of the importance of the religious side of school life. He has an unusual gift for getting into touch with boys individually. His work on the New Zealand tour showed that he could take responsibilities, organise, and speak; a good man when he started on tours, he came back in every way developed and improved by his experience.

On 11 November, the GGS council agreed unanimously to appoint him. The next day Mackinnon cabled Rendall who informed Darling of the offer and advised immediate acceptance. 'I do most earnestly & sincerely pray', he wrote ponderously:

> that you will rise to its scope and be able, after not a few but not too many years of service, to feel thankful for this strange & unsought opportunity & what it has brought you.

Austen Darling made an extraordinary confession. Not only was his son's prospective appointment bigger than anything that he had done, but also that he had lacked ambition:

> my general view of life … has been, I am afraid, to avoid responsibility where it could be avoided without cowardice. Therefore I have not been as useful in my life as I might have been. My excuse is that I had no great opinion of my own intellectual capacity which is [a] good deal below yours.

About a week later in Corio, Rod Andrew (captain of Perry House and a GGS prefect) noted in his diary:

> The new head master was disclosed in this morning's paper. He is only 30 and so it is very brave of the Council. However for them to appoint so young a man seems to point to his outstanding ability.

Finally, at the December meeting of the council, Darling's acceptance of its offer was reported. He was due to arrive on 11 February.[7]

The stars had aligned for Darling. Congratulations flooded in. He was Repton's second recent gift to Australia, Fletcher said—the other was the new Anglican Archbishop of Melbourne, Frederick Waldegrave Head. Phelps was very glad and said that Charterhouse's debt to Darling's generosity was incalculable. Fyfe was ecstatic. So too was Bickersteth. He had been at Corio two days before the appointment decision and had said that 'if they appointed a layman, they would be lucky to get you'. Darling's mind was already in gear, and he sounded out Fyfe and George Turner (Norwood's successor at Marlborough) about possible exchanges of masters. Fyfe was supportive and Turner said that E.C. (Cecil) Marchant was now at GGS, and due to return in the autumn. Also, if Darling wanted the services of P. Fletcher, a master seeking an Australian exchange, then he would release him. In the final two or three hectic months before he departed Charterhouse, Darling was in charge of the VIth history specialists and continued his wider involvement in the school. *The Testament of Beauty*, a long idealistic work by the Poet Laureate, Robert Bridges, had just been published, and it so influenced Darling that he taught from it. His class performed *Two Gentlemen of Verona*, he gave a lecture on the New Zealand tour in October, another with over 100 lantern slides to the Godalming branch of the League of Nations Union in late November, and then one more to the Guildford Rotary Club—this time emphasising the importance of empire and the unity of the English race. In the wider world, the economic signs were not good. There had been months of stock exchange speculation mania in New York. Despite lifting its lending rate, the Bank of England could not stem the tide of funds sweeping across the Atlantic. Record amounts of stocks changed hands and confidence peaked in late September only to quickly dissipate. Panic followed. On 'Black Thursday', 24 October, 13 million shares changed hands at prices that shattered dreams and hopes. The New York stock market finally bottomed out in November. In Australia, the Bruce–Page ministry lost office and the Labor party swept to power on 12 October. With unemployment rising to 13 per cent, declining business profitability, a yawning trade imbalance, falling export commodity prices and shrinking capital inflow from London, the new government faced big problems.[8]

Brooke Hall farewelled Darling at a dinner on 11 December. From Crosby, Butler-Wright congratulated 'that young man, I knew, who saw visions' and reassured him that the house system that he had devised was flourishing. In what his sister Margaret described as final nightmarish days, Louis Wharton's letter to Jane Darling was the most apposite farewell. He had just said goodbye to Darling at the station, after having spent an enjoyable evening together with their friends. Her son, he said, was in good spirits:

> I am firm in the belief that he has done right in going—not because of his career, but because his work so far away from the things and people he loves will tend to allow him full development. He never thought enough of himself. Circumstances will force him to appreciate himself more fully, and when you next see him you will see in actuality the James you have always imagined!

Allow yourself to be conceited, he encouraged her, and 'do nothing but pride yourself on the lovely thing you have sent to Australia for her good'. The final picture that everyone was left with, as a New Zealand tour boy recalled, was of Darling wearing his new overcoat and carrying armfuls of *Home Chat* as he said goodbye. For the second time in twelve months he headed for the other side of the world. This time, Austen informed Phelps, he was travelling first class, which reminded him how as a small boy he used to travel with his father, James George, who believed that first 'was the only class by which a gentleman can travel'.[9]

Three days out to sea, in his first letter to the Old Rectory, Trimley, Suffolk (where the family now lived), Darling pledged that he would 'try to live up to you Mother Dear, but it won't be so easy when you are so far away'. In the next letter he was astonished at 'how very lazy one can become' so quickly, except that this time, without schoolboys to supervise or lectures to deliver, he had adapted swiftly to shipboard life and was determined not to succumb to its tempting indolence. His routine was to read a couple of books daily and observe the passengers—the giddy young things were 'most decorous'. He went ashore at stopover points for occasional sightseeing, but otherwise slept, conversed and played bridge. He resolved to stop speculating about his future responsibilities: 'I haven't really settled down to think yet and I think it is best so'. Released from his normal surroundings and routines he became introspective. Once again, his new world prejudices surfaced. His brief experience of Australians some eight months earlier suggested that they differed from New Zealanders—both he and Portal in their respective tour reports contrasted the two countries' newspaper journalism styles: New Zealand's was adulatory and Australia's more critical. He had a bit of information about his new school, because Aubrey Scott's father had introduced him to an enthusiastic Old Geelong Grammarian (OGG) named Radford then teaching at Wellington, and a Labour crony put him in touch with Nervynia Masterman, a cousin of K.C. (Kay) Masterman (an Old Carthusian recently appointed as GGS's Brice Mackinnon classics master). Then, a former master under Dr Brown, an Englishman, Harold Scott, had written from the Edinburgh Academy to say that GGS was a 'capital place'. Scott had married the daughter of a former GGS council chairman (H.P. Douglass), and attested to the hospitality and kindliness that he had received in Australia. He also warned Darling (for what must have seemed an obscure reason) about Corio's hot northerly winds, but the most useful advice was from his doctor cousin at Southport, Queensland, John Nimmo, who said that, apart from the run-of-the-mill schoolboy, Darling could expect to deal mainly with the sons of graziers who were intent on returning to the land and who had 'little ambition to achieve scholarly fame'. Clothes were more expensive in Australia and the climate uncertain, but the biggest shock in store for his English cousin would be the publicity given to Melbourne interschool sport. In fact, Nimmo said, the public schools' boat race was 'about the biggest event of the year' except for the Melbourne Cup, the nation's most famous horse race.[10]

As in New Zealand, Darling's sense of English cultural superiority could not be restrained as he typecast the ship's passengers. Of two kinds of Australians, he told his mother, the 'really nice' ones buoyed him up and made him impatient to reach his destination. Of those on board, he judged one rather breezily as the *Otranto* neared Fremantle as comparing 'very favourably with anyone I've met before'. But there were also a good many 'perfectly ghastly Australians' who boarded at Colombo although 'they are no more acceptable to the nice Australians than they would be to us':

On the other hand I rather think that Australia will be much more snobbish than England and that it will be very difficult not to feel the same way oneself. When they are horrid they are more awful than you can imagine because they feel so keenly that they are as good as anybody else and have a right to stamp about the place.

Schools attracted much more interest in Australia than in England and being the head of one would give him 'a good kick-off'. A few OGGs had met him in Fremantle and he had 'a lovely day there'. He said that he felt quite happy to be in Australia: 'Your welcome in Western Australia cheered me up a lot'. Nearing Adelaide he mused that 'the more I see of the products of the school the more I like them':

> People speak most enthusiastically about the place and boys come to it from all over Australia. On the other hand, I doubt whether the masters will be a very good lot. The standard will be pretty low, and there will be a snobbishness about the place which I shall not like. This seems the general impression.

By Australian standards the appointment was a big one in which case it would provide a good opportunity for much interesting work and, if GGS had as much money as he imagined, then it might become 'a really good school'.[11]

On Saturday, 8 February, he disembarked at Adelaide to be met by Mackinnon. They travelled to Melbourne by train and Darling remembered being 'thrilled by the sight of my first bushfire and surprised at the nonchalance with which he regarded it'. The next day, at a lunch at Mackinnon's house, Darling was welcomed by L.A. (Dicky) Adamson (headmaster of Wesley College), R.P. (Lofty) Franklin (headmaster of Melbourne Grammar School), Frank Tate (the recently retired Director of Education in Victoria), Sir Archibald Strong (Professor of English, University of Adelaide) and members of the GGS council. Nobody 'could have been less than twenty years older than I and most of them were more'. That afternoon he was driven to Corio where he spent time with Dr Brown before farewelling him the next day. 'Well, here we are!' he announced cheerily to his mother. At thirty, Darling was three years younger than Fletcher when he had been appointed to Marlborough, a year older than Temple at Repton and three years older than Fisher who had been appointed headmaster at twenty-seven. He was only the fifth headmaster in GGS's 75-year history. In 1913, shortly after Dr Brown's arrival, GGS had moved about 10 kilometres north of Geelong to its current location on broad flat land at Corio. It was one of six fee-paying denominational schools comprising the Associated Public Schools of Victoria (APS), with Melbourne Grammar School (Church of England), Geelong College and Scotch College (Presbyterian), Wesley College (Methodist) and Xavier College (Catholic). Melbourne Grammar and GGS had cachet. According to the novelist, Graham McInnes, a Scotch boy in the 1920s, 'we recognized uneasily that Melbourne Grammar and Geelong Grammar had the edge on us in terms of social status', and the Australian war historian Dr Bean noted how few people could think of GGS 'without the mind flashing over to Eton'. Rod Andrew's summing up of the school when he left was that it turned out a man of 'sound character, honest loyal—rather stupid but very lovable'. On the other side of the world, Sellar wondered to Phelps 'how Darling will fare in Australia'. No doubt 'he will get on'.[12]

In fact, Sellar's friend was on a fast learning curve. He had to come to terms with the way of life of the new country, get to grips with his new job and what was expected of him, and to decide what it took to be a headmaster and whether he had it in him. The attitudes that stirred at sea surfaced again and, after barely a month in the country, Darling sounded off to his mother. His nice Australians were Anglophiles or Austral-Britons and included Miss Margaret Macarthur Onslow (from Camden Park near Sydney) whom he had met on the *Otranto*. It was this group, associated with landed wealth, city clubs, empire loyalty and conservative politics, with which he soon fell in. His visit to Camden Park in May prompted him to exclaim that 'the whole district is more or less feudal'. Despite Rendall's concern about the Melbourne Club, Darling was nominated for membership early in 1930. On the other hand, one of the first conclusions that Darling drew was that (in his reckoning) the wrong people were running Australia and were running it very badly. The worst offender was the new federal Labor government, in particular the prime minister, James Scullin:

> No-one seems to understand the most elementary economic principles, and the government simply runs round in circles taxing frantically and killing what it taxes as in the worst period of the decadence of past nations in history.

And yet the decent people, he complained, who were in so many ways nice and respectable refused to take responsibility for governing the country. Moreover, they were so terrified of investing their money that the economic situation was becoming grim. His disdain had solidified by the end of the first school term (May) and, while holidaying with Bickersteth at the nearby resort town of Barwon Heads, he lashed out in a hyperbolic vein reminiscent of D.H. Lawrence (after his brief Australian sojourn a decade earlier) in *Kangaroo*:

> The country really is democratic and everyone is afraid to rise above the ruck in morals, in tastes or in behaviour. The result is really deplorable. If ever there was a place that needed leading, it is this country and if we don't do something in the next ten years it will be too late.

In a volley of rash and superficial judgements he lambasted the country's key institutions. It was irreligious (aside from a very active Catholic Church), the Labor Party was riddled with Irish Catholics ('there is only one Protestant member of the Federal Govt!'), the police forces were monopolised by Catholics and corrupt, and the quality of the newspapers was even poorer than at home. No-one cared two hoots. The public schools had to give a lead in 'work, conscience and public taste' and the country's so-called aristocracy or plutocracy simply had to take religion seriously.[13]

As for the better Australians, they had even more polish 'if they have been home'. While liking them and being thankful for their goodness to him, Darling dismissed most of them as philistines:

> All the theatres are second rate and the bookshops completely out of date. That will correct itself when I am as out-of-date as the shops but at the moment they are just about getting the books which I read with a thrill two years ago. Everyone is asking each other whether they have read the <u>High Wind in Jamaica</u> or <u>The Good Companions</u>.

Leonard Hammond, a young Godalming man who came as Darling's valet, shared his sense of cultural oppression:

> If it wasn't for the lovely books Mr Darling lends me, I think I should become bored to death with these 'little Australians' who imagine that Australia is [the] leading country in the world.

Lacking familiar scenery, seasons, friends and family, Darling was detached and ill-at-ease in his new surroundings until well into his first year. Apart from Camden Park, which he considered lovely and English, he mostly abhorred the Australian countryside. Marvelling at Mrs Brown's gardening and the 'wonderfully kept grass', he highlighted the greenness of the school's cricket oval in February, something which 'sounds silly to you [mother] but it is a great thing out here'. Corio, when he first saw it, was 'a sort of cross between Salisbury Plain and Romsey Marsh'. The weather was 'abominably oppressive', and rain was 'the sole topic of conversation'. By May, the grass was a 'beastly brown' and the effect of heavy rainfall on the national outlook dumbfounded him: it was regarded as a sign of Providence and people seemed to know of its arrival up to two days in advance: 'It is odd to be in a place where rain is gold dropping from heaven. The whole mentality of the country is changed by two inches [50 mm] of rain.' His first southern hemisphere winter was his lowest ebb. Bitterly bemoaning the howling wind outside and the refusal of his study fire to burn, he wrote: 'It really is a vile place altogether and why anyone ever wanted to populate it heaven alone knows'.[14]

In regard to his new responsibilities, Darling was wearied by the demands of being in charge while simultaneously tempted by the possibilities. Hugh Derry imagined him having to wear a mask and removing it every now and then, rather than being 'Headmaster to the core'. On his first night, Darling had gone to bed musing that 'there is a good deal to think of' and feeling slightly anxious following his initial meeting with the masters. He liked them 'fairly well though without being so much impressed by their superiority to myself as perhaps a more modest man should have been' and was reassured that they 'professed themselves full of loyalty'. Once again (as at Merchant Taylors' School) he was trying to prove himself to himself while keeping his new colleagues at arm's length, with the only difference that then he was a master whereas now he had to think as the headmaster. An early indication that he was making a good fist of things came from R.G. Jennings. (Dr Brown had described Jennings as 'invaluable' and said that he knew of 'no more capable housemaster of a Junior House anywhere'.) He reported to Jane Darling in April 1930 that her son:

> has won the confidence and goodwill of us all. A new life and vigour has already come into the school, and he is going to do really great work. We are all impressed by his clear vision and the wonderful understanding he has of the problems which naturally come his way. I hear on all sides most happy expressions of confidence in him, as well as personal regard. I only hope he will become really fond of the new work and of the school, so that he may find some real compensation for the loss of so many home ties and interests … I feel that I already owe a great deal to him personally. He is so delightfully encouraging and sympathetic … We realize how fortunate we are in having such a man to lead us.

Jane forwarded Jennings' letter to Aubrey Scott, and told her son that 'it confirmed him in the opinion that you really are making good over your job though sometimes you don't know it yourself'. The young headmaster's need for reassurance was evident from the outset. After barely a week he wailed that the job was 'a little overwhelming':

> I have had about ten days of thinking how wonderful it was to have the chance of making something of a really remarkable place but I found out so much and so much from day to day that I am beginning to feel incapable of dealing with the situation and I can't bear the strain of being the headmaster all the time.

The expectation that the boys had to stand up out of 'extravagant respect' whenever he appeared was odious, but what particularly rankled was 'the attempt to preserve the totally unnecessary amount of dignity which my predecessor attained to naturally'. Thanks to the 'father was always right' convention instilled by Brown, the masters called him 'Sir', he felt 'stuck up as a disciplinary head all the time' in chapel and most of his day was spent interviewing people, all of which went against the grain.[15]

As for his age, the new headmaster was scarcely a decade older than some of the boys and a number of the masters were older than him. To be on intimate terms with such people while endeavouring simultaneously to maintain an authoritative aloofness was an acquired art. A senior boy, H.D. (Blue) Steward, remembered his 'long, gaunt, ungainly figure' and another, Michael Thwaites, recalled that he was a 'tall and rather formidable looking figure with a beaky nose and piercing eyes'. To H.B. (Jo) Gullett, Darling was 'a very nice looking fellow'. But youthfulness did not always work to his advantage. Bishop Baker was completely deceived by it, as his son Selwyn recalled:

> I do remember shortly after Sir James' appointment as a young lad I was visiting the school with Father who mistook Sir James for one of the senior boys! That was how young he looked at the time that he took over his headmastership.

One result of projecting himself constantly as the headmaster was that Darling felt desperately lonely, a feeling compounded by the fact that he was at everyone else's beck and call. Also, as an object of curiosity, he was conscious of himself being inspected by people's gazes and 'overwhelmed by parents who come in absolute shoals just to look at me'. As a result he felt highly self-conscious and unable to take small mishaps in his stride:

> We are in the middle of Holy Week and I have just come back from conduct-ing the Tuesday night service. I did it very badly and I feel annoyed with myself. It is hateful to do these things and remember oneself in doing them all the time but I don't seem to have got beyond that stage yet somehow.

All day he had dealt with a procession of boys, save for an hour salvaged to prepare what he was going to say, whereupon he promptly forgot it and got into a muddle.[16]

In the face of self-imposed stringency, Darling was likely to flounder. The wish to be 'off duty sometimes' was understandable, as were such self-pitying remarks as 'I'm not good enough to carry the strain continuously' and 'this job is a little outside my capacities':

> One needs to be able to hold a huge number of different things in one's mind, realizing how they will affect each other and somehow being able to be enthusiastic about them from Science to Music or Rowing.

The incessant demands and the 'unremitting pressure' were such that he could rarely ease off: no matter how tired he felt, he had to 'keep the machine moving'. It was hard to find anything that didn't need altering and the more that he looked the worse the situation was. The root of the problem was his predecessor's repressiveness. This had slackened during the previous year and 'the devils seem to have come in with a vengeance'. Darling's most pressing concern was the masters.

They were 'quite nice but rather second class and none of them in the least possible to talk to'. Somehow he had to entice capable men and prune the dead wood. They had been handled like 'mere ushers and simply do not understand being treated as equals'. But another part of this 'scandalous inadequacy' was that there were few capable Australian masters. And, as for luring the Englishmen whom he had already sounded out, the Council of Public Education 'make a great deal of difficulty'. Darling wanted to employ fresh English graduates, but when he tried to ignore the council's rules, he hit a brick wall and, in an ensuing battle of wills, he became tangled up in a clash of cultural values.[17]

Registration as a teacher in Victoria was required by the Council of Public Education pursuant to section 103 of the *Education Act*, 1915. The difficulty for Englishmen was that registration required completion of a one-year Diploma of Education, which denied Darling access to them for twelve months. Even in his own case, Merchant Taylors' and Charterhouse teaching had not been sufficient evidence of 'fitness to teach', so that the Chief Inspector of Secondary Schools, J.A. (Arnie) Seitz, had had to inspect him. (He was registered in late April.) To break this logjam he dealt personally with P.N. Hansen (the president of the Council of Public Education and Tate's successor as Director of Education) to find a way to circumvent the requirement. They met in late March. He believed that Hansen sympathised with him in attracting young Englishmen and, while not considering teacher training 'valueless' but 'a very useful experience', Darling had no wish to flout the rules. Instead, to capitalise on the misaligned English and Australian school calendars, Darling suggested a 'compromise'. The department could have an English graduate whom he appointed from September for third term and perhaps for a week in the succeeding year for 'intensive work in Melbourne', during which, Darling reasoned, he would 'not expect to be bothered with the necessity of putting a man to watch him'. Then, as courteously as possible while standing his ground, he played the English superiority card:

> Although this man would not possibly gain as full instruction in methods of teaching as a man doing the full year, I would submit that, he being a Graduate from Home and very different methods of education, might possibly be as good or better a man than a man wholly educated out here, and that also in the interests of education out here and in the broader interests of co-operation between Australia and England the work of an Englishman at an Australian school is valuable.

This subterfuge didn't wash. When R.H. Croll (the council's registrar) spied the word 'compromise', he claimed that the proposal was unprecedented, and that while Darling's other scheme of English and Australian exchanges would not require Englishmen to be registered, it would still require the sanction of the council's registration committee.[18]

Hansen then sought the opinion of L.J. Wrigley (Professor of Education, University of Melbourne) who said that the only recognised basis for Diploma of Education teaching practice exemption was five years' teaching experience. An intensive course in third term was 'quite impractical'. In mid-April Hansen dispatched both Croll's and Wrigley's opinions to Darling and sought a response. A fortnight later an exasperated Darling replied, 'confidential between ourselves':

> That is to say, it is not going to be put tactfully, to avoid hurting the feelings of people who might be over-sensitive, in the matter. It is rather a personal explanation to you yourself, who will recognise the truth of what I say.

Wrigley's and Croll's responses were quite unsatisfactory, he said bluntly, because they denied his premise's validity—that making it easier for English graduates to teach would be for the good of Australian education—and 'unless we start with that idea, any proposals of co-operation are bound to fail'. The plausibility of Darling's English superiority argument required acceptance of a distinction between education and training, and a difference in quality between Australian and English (that is, Oxbridge) universities. The absurdity (for him) of Victoria's requirements was due to the lack of virtue in elevating a trained man above an educated one:

> It is not reasonable to pretend that the whole English Public School system is at fault, when it takes men with Oxford and Cambridge Honours Degrees and makes them School Masters straight away. Though it may be true that they would be better if they were trained, it is not true that they would be better if trained and without the Honours Degree. In this country a man can be qualified to teach because he knows how to teach, without really knowing anything which he could teach. You have, therefore, got the opposite failing, and in my mind, it is a failing more serious than the English one.

It was impossible for English masters to take an extra year to obtain a diploma. In any case, Oxbridge honours degrees guaranteed something that a Melbourne degree couldn't: that 'the man is an educated man', meaning that he was already to some extent qualified to teach, and 'certainly quite as much qualified to teach as a man without a Degree who has yet trained as a teacher'. Despite this difference, Victoria registered 'a trained man of this sort' but not an English graduate.[19]

Appealing personally was getting him nowhere. The bitter lesson was that Australians would not fall meekly into line with English assumptions. On a hiding to nothing, Darling went down fighting:

> There is no great attraction to an Englishman who can get a job in an English School, to come out to Australia instead. The pay is worse in most cases. The country is far from Home. The possibilities of promotion are less, and the

work, in all probability, of a lower standard, and the status of the Profession definitely lower socially than it is at Home. If one adds to that the necessity to a man either of spending three hundred pounds at least on an extra year at the University taking a Diploma Course or the training of him when he comes out here, you are very effectually preventing any infusion of English blood into the profession out here.

Maybe that was the registration system's purpose, in which case there was no better guarantee of the outcome. But if the argument for new-blood appointments was acceptable, then a resolution might be possible. Failing that, then nothing could be done. The registration requirement was a bad law and needed to be altered. 'I am sure that that is better than the evasion of the law, into which one is otherwise driven.' The state's regulations were utterly inefficacious, he concluded, especially when he wanted passionately to raise the quality and status of Australian masters:

It is the most valuable work that any man could do for this country, and one way of doing it is to introduce the English type of School Master into the Country, because he automatically does not consider himself an usher and has the proper high opinion of his own importance. I, of course, here have an added difficulty in finding men of character, capable of being House Masters. I agree that that is the difficulty peculiar to this School, but it is a very real one, and it is, I am afraid, true, that the Englishmen are much more capable of taking on that job than the type of Australian who goes into the teaching profession.

Training would be helpful when a man already had a well-trained mind. Hansen affirmed the value of training, even for 'honours men', agreed with the proposed masters exchange, saw virtue in Englishmen teaching in Australia, but refused point blank to countenance outsiders being put 'in a more favourable position with regard to registration than our own people here'. The council's regulation was in no way bad and he was astounded that Darling had even countenanced possible evasion. He brushed aside the new chum's dismissal of trained Australians as teachers not knowing what they professed to know, because 'our whole aim is to obviate this and I think our present system does secure that our teachers must know their subjects before they are allowed to teach them'. In the face of Hansen's adamantine refusal, Darling backed off and conceded that English masters in Australia for two years might profit from a diploma.[20]

An unproductive argument going round and round in circles offered a valuable insight into the limitations of different cultural assumptions, and constraints on Darling's discretion. There was a similar episode in a difference of opinion with an OGG over a boy's future education. 'You will naturally feel inclined to advise boys with any prospects to complete their education at an English University', his correspondent had written, but what about Australian

universities: 'Ought we to send too many of our best young men elsewhere[?]'
Moreover, there was 'a very real advantage' in an Australian university education
for prospective professional men because 'one gets to know and be known of by
a number of fellow practitioners' who were also Australian graduates. Darling's
sole concession was that a year at the University of Melbourne and then two
years spent at Cambridge (a path that GGS parents were pursuing) was a system
'possible to develop', although:

> it would be idle to maintain that Universities here provide as good an education
> as Oxford and Cambridge, and for a boy who was capable, I think that Oxford
> or Cambridge is most valuable.

While conceding that he had not really delved very far into the matter, this
had not prevented him from insisting that Australian university courses were
nowhere near broad enough.[21]

Another worry was the calibre of the boys. To this same correspondent
Darling said that he was 'particularly anxious that the boys in this school should
regard it as their duty to take a lead in the Nation' because 'the best men in
Australia do not lead it'. Most of the boys, he told his mother, were nice enough,
and that while some were quite able the majority were 'unintellectual oafs':
whenever he taught a class their behaviour was 'unnaturally good, and the real
response quite terribly slow'. Furthermore, the standard of their work was 'absolutely appalling'. Some of the charming and friendly boys were in Junior House,
their quality being due entirely to Jennings who was a real genius: 'notoriously
good with mothers [and] a great standby altogether'. John Jermyn remembered
how on Darling's first day at Corio he came to the Junior House dormitory and
spoke to every individual boy as they were preparing for bed. Sam McCulloch
recalled an occasion in which Darling came:

> & told David Hay, Alan Hamer & the rest of us how [he was] counting on
> us to help make GGS the type of school [he] had in mind that it should be.

Despite Jennings' best efforts, his work was destined to come to nothing when
the boys entered the senior school:

> I am pretty sure that it is chiefly due to bad work in school and a habit which
> they get there of complete mental vacuity. They really are unbelievably stupid
> and quite unblushingly uneducated. I don't know that one will ever be able to
> alter that much. They come from homes in which books are unknown. For the
> most part they are not educated at all until they come to us at 10, even later
> and some of them can hardly read or write.

But all was not lost, because every now and then when the dry bones stirred these Australian boys took the initiative much more readily than their English counterparts. One day when Darling accompanied the famous English organist, Sir Hugh Allen, on a tour of the school, he found boys gardening, which English lads would never do. Almost any kind of activity was 'an advance on the aimless empty-headed wandering' in which they used to indulge.[22]

Darling's incremental improvements did not compensate for his loneliness. In the small world of Corio he missed his immediate family and his close friends. 'No-one could have been so fortunate in his friends as I have been', he admitted to his mother. Aubrey Scott sent him two books a fortnight after having read them himself, but Darling's packing cases did not arrive until late February. 'Empty bookcases are rotten things to live with.' He tried to keep up with English events but was thwarted by Charterhouse's bookshop, which mailed his newspapers monthly rather than weekly. 'I wish I was back at Home', he lamented to the proprietor. Despite Darling's gloom, Scott reassured him that 'your cares haven't quite blighted your humour', so 'cheer up'. He was annoyed that his time demands prevented him replying to letters arriving from England every Monday: 'I can't keep up with the answers so that I suppose they will stop'. Eaton teased him unmercifully about his tardiness. Darling's first year at Corio coincided with a high watermark for his circle of friends as they were scattering around the world. After their wedding in August, Mabel and Ralph went north to Durham, Eaton was tutoring an industrialist's son in Westfalen, Germany, and Hilda and Louis returned to Trinidad. 'I can't exist at all without my ties', Hilda wrote from Port-of-Spain, 'yet I abominate this island entirely and utterly, the heat, the people and the food, will resignation come with age[?]', she wondered. That 'enthusiastic Dominionist' Fyfe went to Canada to be President of Queen's University, and the 'elusive pimpernel' Bernays was a journalist with the *News-Chronicle* and a Liberal member of Parliament.[23]

To replace this English group, Darling was eased into three Australian networks. The first comprised the Western District graziers who were well represented among the OGGs and on the school council. With their Scottish upbringing and as heirs of an erstwhile squatter class, these men valued 'worldly success as the reward of moral rectitude'. Their hearts and minds were 'turned towards the Old Country'. Darling dined with them, spent weekends at their properties and was admitted to their club. He devised plans for the school with them and began to assimilate their world view. The second group, facilitated by Margaret Best, who had introduced him to her 'most cultured' friend that 'great imperialist', Miss Rosa Sibella Macarthur Onslow, or Aunt Sib (the great-granddaughter of the pioneers, John and Elizabeth Macarthur), was Sydney society. The third group, through Penelope and Henry Gullett (MHR for Henty), the parents of his pupil Jo Gullett, comprised the politicians whom he befriended, such as Charles Hawker (an OGG and MHR for Wakefield). There was always mirth and frivolity with couples like the Gulletts. Letters to him would be addressed 'Dear Friend D' and signed 'a true Nationalist' or 'Yours right royally "Lady Gullett"'. It was at their property near Canberra, Hill Station, that Darling first met the man who would become a very close friend, R.G. (Dick) Casey, after he had returned from London in 1931 (as the liaison officer to the British Cabinet and the Foreign Office). Jo Gullett recalled a picnic with the Caseys and Keith Officer (External Affairs Branch, Prime Minister's department) during which people let their hair down and Officer took a shine to Darling—a 'tremendous do': the children built a dam in a stream, and 'Dick and Jim both took off their socks and rolled up their jolly trousers' to paddle and to poke fun about the shape of their legs.[24]

Invitations to dine with GGS masters' families, particularly E.L. Nall (housemaster of Cuthbertson), W.N. Jaffray (a mathematics and science master), Masterman and Jennings, helped divert Darling from periodic bouts of feeling down. He became especially close to his fellow countryman Marchant, prior to the latter's return to England in September 1930. 'My dear "J"', Marchant would write impishly, '—so be ye christened, if it savours not too much of lack of respect for the noble office which ye bear'. He provided moral support in Darling's first two terms: 'I felt I could talk to him because he was leaving anyhow. I could commit myself to him about my troubles.' Solace for his loneliness was also afforded by guests whom he entertained especially if they were English:

> Do you know, it is the first time that I have ever felt welcome at the school? And what a feast of conversation for starved souls. It really was a most delightful time. As we passed along the Geelong road next day, we pictured you as happier—the rain, and perhaps the grass a shade nearer green.

A newly arrived Englishman was bound to feel downcast, this particular correspondent said, 'but you have such a wonderful bit of work to do: I wish you the courage and the optimism necessary for it with all my heart'. Finally, being able to spend time reasonably regularly with the various Nimmo relatives also helped to buoy him up, especially Harold (Putt) Nimmo (who had had the headmaster's house furnished for his arrival in February), and a cousin by marriage, Jack Cunningham (manager of the Cheetham salt works, Geelong), and his wife who looked after him over Easter.[25]

Shifts in Darling's outlook soon became obvious. In September 1930, he flew from Sydney to Brisbane to stay with John Nimmo after stopping over at Camden where he met Sir Otto Niemeyer—the head of the four-member Bank of England mission advising Scullin's government on credit restoration. The Camden set reinforced Darling's growing disdain for Labor. Niemeyer was impressed by the youthful headmaster, but Darling was downcast after meeting 'our deus ex machine [sic]', although he departed Camden full of enthusiasm for a fellow guest, T.R. Bavin, the New South Wales Nationalist premier. Darling impressed on Phelps that:

RIGHT James and his sister Margaret
BELOW Mabel (in tree), Jean and
Eaton Darling

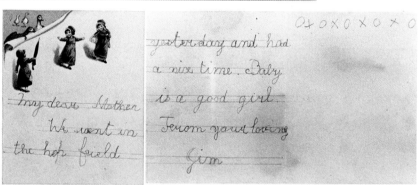

My dear Mother
We went in
the hop field
yesterday and had
a nice time. Baby
is a good girl.
From your loving
Jim

TOP Nurse Murray
ABOVE An early letter

TOP Castle School, c. 1913. 2nd row, L to R: Eaton (in hat with doll), Mabel, father, Jean, mother. Back row, 2nd left: Tom Darling (cousin)

ABOVE Arms raised for the ball at Highfield

TOP LEFT Happy at Highfield
TOP RIGHT In Stratton's Yard, Repton
ABOVE LEFT David Somervell
ABOVE RIGHT Victor Gollancz

TOP LEFT 2nd Lieutenant, July 1919
TOP RIGHT Punting with Margaret at Oxford
ABOVE Merchant Taylors' cadets: Darling (2nd row centre) with Butler-Wright (on his left)

TOP New Zealand tour group: Darling,
4th from bottom right
ABOVE Portal and Smith-Dorrien
RIGHT Neptune ceremony, *Ionic*

TOP *Otranto* group
ABOVE Camden Park

TOP LEFT Every inch the headmaster
TOP RIGHT John Manifold
ABOVE With John Nimmo, Southport, September 1930

If he [Bavin] gets knocked out by Labor in the coming elections we shall really
be in a bad way. Labor here is hopeless, corrupt I think as well as out of date
but anyhow deplorably old-fashioned and ignorant of the meaning or purpose
of socialism.

Coincidentally, Bernays arrived a few days later en route to India (to write a book
about Gandhi) and remarked that, while Niemeyer was rigid and doctrinaire,
although good for Australia, Bavin struck him as 'vain, pompous and jealous'.
Despite the erosion of their friend's political allegiances, others in England still
thought that he was a Labourite. Aubrey Scott was nonplussed about Darling's
change of heart. 'I am appalled to hear that you are reactionary', he wrote, 'or should
be if I believed it for a moment: and your reasons are so odd'. Scott could imagine
himself turning Blue in a hot Labour area, but 'at Charterhouse, and equally in
your surroundings I should have thought, the thing is impossible'. The likelihood
of the second part of the prediction of a friend (probably Louis Wharton) to
Phelps that Darling would 'marry and become a conservative', was firming.[26]
    As for the first part of the forecast, matrimonial prospects until recently
had seemed as far off as ever. Darling longed to be married and hankered after a
young woman from the *Otranto*. Most people who knew him thought that he was
reading too much into a friendship. When Bernays met her in Sydney he advised
strongly against matrimony and Scott, who had been hearing vague rumours
about nuptials, said bluntly that in regard to holy wedlock there was only one
criterion: 'does she compare favourably with Hilda?' Scott was unimpressed by
Darling's suggestion that 'you'll have to get used to such and such' and took this
to be a bad sign. Jane Darling was also unpersuaded by his sketchy details about
the young woman, particularly when Margaret insisted on coming to Australia
to keep house—to provide companionship but also to sort out the constant
bickering between his valet and the kitchen staff. Partly because of this romance,
his mother deduced, he was fobbing off his sister. Nothing came of his fleeting
matrimonial fantasies, but procrastination over Margaret's offer got under his
mother's skin. 'You say you "instinctively fear being watched doing your job"', she
wrote incredulously. 'I'm afraid I'm feeling rather hot and sore over the want of
appreciation of my Margaret' because she has 'never settled down since you left'.[27]
    Despite these strictures, Jane Darling's three- or four-page letters written
regularly every Wednesday were a great comfort. They disclosed the usual
personal and family details, for which she constantly apologised, as well as her
longing for his future return, expressions of her great hopes for him, and simple
homespun homilies. The vast distance between them precluded any direct help.
It was 'not much use answering moods that have been affecting you five weeks
ago', she complained, because the weeks of waiting for reply letters meant that
'I can't help you in your ups and downs, my dear'. Nevertheless, her words
proved invaluable in other ways. First, she helped him believe in himself with
the reassurance that he was capable, up to the job and doing worthwhile work in

his speeches and sermons, the high quality of the school magazine (the *Corian*) and his early publications. Second, apart from her suggestions about taking more exercise and smoking fewer cigarettes, she provided commonsense advice. He had not yet learnt to 'take no thought for tomorrow':

> That doesn't mean carelessly letting things slide but the older I get the more I realise the truth of the importance of just plugging along 'doing the next thing which I know to be a duty' and finding invariably that when that's done 'the second is already clearer to me'. It isn't easy to hold oneself in sometimes when there seems to be hosts of duties treading on each other[']s heels in front of you but I am sure if we go steadily along doing the best we can we do always find that God is there to give us the strength according to our day.

On another occasion she quoted a friend who had said that '"if you do what you can you'll do more than you think"!!—and you musn't worry yourself into fiddlestrings if you can help it'. Third, she compiled a 'Jim portfolio' of items on her 'beautiful son!' and told him how proud he had made her feel: 'It is very few couples who can look at the career of all their children with the satisfaction we can'. All five were doing worthwhile things, not just because they provided money but because they were useful, and that was pleasing.[28]

The most important thing that Jane Darling did was to convey what firsthand witnesses of her son's work had been saying. Aubrey Scott was 'awfully pleased' to see Jennings' letter. Darling's cousin Helen Nimmo had met a Miss Black from Mount Noorat in Victoria who was 'very enthusiastic about the way you are "pulling the school together"! See that now!' Most important, however, Marchant had visited her after returning to England:

> It was very nice hearing from someone who had worked under you and saw what a difference your drastic changes were going to make in the school. What a nice man he is; I expect you are very sorry to part with him.

Hammond's letters also offered 'interesting sidelights on your life' and the GGS English master who went to Charterhouse for a year in 1930, C.R. Bull (Margaret described him as a 'trifle pedagogic but interesting', although 'peculiarly pedantic and stilted at first'), provided 'a lot of inside information' when he came to Trimley in early September 1930. Phelps disclosed that he had met the Bishop of Ballarat in London who had told him that GGS was 'a gleam of hope in his Diocese', and even Dr Brown mentioned to him that he had heard only good reports about his successor's efforts. Such feedback provided strong grounds for confidence in himself.[29]

Darling reflected later that he established himself in others' eyes and bolstered his authority early on by exuding 'self-confidence and dogmatic certainty', and by 'recourse to the negative'. Of one early miscreant he wrote:

> I feel very little hope about him, but was quite sure that if I expelled him there
> was no hope at all. In my argument with him on the first occasion … I could
> discover no moral sense and nothing to which I could appeal. On the second
> occasion after beating him rather mercilessly (which incidentally he took very
> well) he seemed to show some signs of realising the seriousness of his position.

Another early victim recalled an announcement that boys should not throw
things out of classroom windows. This lad ignored the warning:

> The chapel bell went and as I walked towards the door of the chapel I saw the
> headmaster with his eye fixed upon me so I hoped to slip by unnoticed, but
> he called me over and said: 'What is your name? Then come and see me after
> chapel'. So he called me into his study and said: 'What were you doing?' and
> I said 'Oh, I was throwing stones through the window'. He said: 'You know
> there had been warnings against this? Well I do not regard this as a serious
> moral offence, but I do regard it as a serious breach of discipline. Bend over
> that chair'. And he gave me four. I didn't feel any animosity because I'd never
> thought of that interesting distinction before and I thought this man must
> have an interesting mind.

Darling also cracked down on the practice of public drinking by boys and young
OGGs. Embarrassing incidents when boys returned by train from sporting
fixtures against St Peter's, he told Bickersteth, made him 'question the advisability
of letting boys off the string ever'. Temptations had to be removed:

> I have heard it is the custom of the parents of some boys in this school to allow
> their sons while they are here to have accounts at your hotel [the Menzies]. I
> do not wish you to break any professional etiquette in the matter but would be
> grateful if you could inform me of the names of such boys.

He didn't approve of the practice and his action was 'a matter of principle' and a
'precaution for the future'.[30]

Darling clamped down on anything likely to inflate a boy's sense of self-
importance, particularly publicity about their activities. At a Government House
function he prevailed on Keith Murdoch (editor of the *Herald*) to help him in
regard to the public's interest in school sport. The presence of photographers
and reporters at the house athletics sports was undesirable, Darling insisted,
'for many reasons which you'll understand and [I] should like the practice to
be discontinued'. He went on: 'I do not feel that it is good for boys to have
their photographs in the papers with the frequency with which they do appear
now'. He was also willing to incur the wrath of critics when expected to publicly
conform to practices with little to commend them. When the English air ace
Amy Johnson was scheduled to land at the Geelong racecourse, he refused

(unlike the state schools) to declare a half-day holiday. An appeal from Senator Guthrie that 'it is not what Miss Johnson has done for aviation, but what she has done, and is doing, for Empire prestige' fell on deaf ears.[31]

In other matters Darling miscalculated, a sign that he was allowing his high-and-mighty sensitivities to get the better of him. In November 1930, Melbourne Grammar's 1st XI resoundingly defeated GGS one Saturday afternoon at Corio and Darling thought that the visiting boys behaved badly after the match by clambering all over a school bus: 'Our driver ... remonstrated with them and one of them in the course of further argument asked him "What it had to do with him, you bloody bastard!"' As a 'fatherly act' rather than in anger, he told Franklin, the driver had hit the boy 'because of the danger that might at some future date come to anyone, who had made a habit of using the word "bastard"'. Darling accused Melbourne Grammar's teams of even more bad behaviour, particularly at lunch, that was quite inappropriate for public schoolboy guests. The GGS masters were all talking about the incident, he said, and then in a convoluted way he said that:

> personally I should always be glad to know or think I should be glad to know (or think I should) of any unusual falls from grace of my own boys and I expect that you feel the same.

But for the bus driver incident, which required an explanation, he would not have bothered Franklin. One of the offending Melbourne Grammar boys was Manning Clark (the Australian historian) who remembered later that he and his peers had devoured their food at lunch. Franklin made light of the incident by reading them his purported reply to Darling: 'they all insist there is no truth in what you say, to the best of my knowledge as headmaster anyway. This correspondence is now closed.' In his actual reply Franklin drew attention to the inexcusable 'epithet', and the discrepancies in the accounts of the driver and the boys, and left the matter there.[32]

Shortly after this incident Darling's first school year in Australia drew to a close. At one point Gerry Dicker had characterised the challenge confronting his friend as a 'rather grim and very difficult job' in which he must have been finding 'the Australian self-complacency extraordinarily alienating'. Lack of personal contact with Englishmen and English ways of thinking was bound to leave a gap. Darling's only antidote for combating his homesickness and his complaints about Australian shortcomings was to throw himself into his work, thereby stifling regrets about where he was and how far he was from where he wanted to be. Eaton had dismissed one of his letters home late in the year as gloomy 'enough to depress a herd of insensitive cows', but in his last one for the year Darling left the strong impression that he felt that he was getting somewhere. Austen had urged him to be patient, to hasten slowly and to trust that things would improve, whereas his son confessed that 'I have probably done it too quickly but I never was very good at waiting'. Slowly but surely he revealed himself as more willing to take part in the life of his new country and his mother detected signs of feeling more established: 'I notice a distinct difference since you got to the end of your first year'. As newly appointed headmaster, the events in the school calendar had been challenging but sources of valuable lessons. At lunchtime on the day of Darling's arrival at Corio, Blue Steward recalled, he had tried to break the ice with the senior boys by asking for a relevant quotation. Someone shot back: 'A little knowledge is a dangerous thing ...' At his first council meeting in March, he was appreciative of the honour bestowed in appointing him 'at so tender an age'. At his first address to the OGGs in April, he gave 'a most difficult speech', but Mackinnon said that he 'got through it splendidly ... and they were properly impressed'. In that same month he dismissed his first member of staff. Then came his brushes with parents, some of them indignant about his disarmingly honest reports on their sons. 'Let me know who the parents are', Mackinnon said, 'and perhaps some of us might change their outlook'. Finally, there was his first speech-day address. Again Mackinnon said that 'there is no doubt people like straight talk. They welcomed an unconventional presentment.' Thus, 'without any undue misfortunes', Darling informed Rendall, but with 'rows of every kind known to a schoolmaster', his first year was behind him and had given him twelve months' valuable experience on which to build.[33]

II

NATURALLY FITTED
1930–1961

... there are some who are naturally fitted for philosophy and political leadership, while the rest should follow their lead and let philosophy alone.

Plato, *The Republic*

RENAISSANCE

1930–1934

Mr. Flaggon had come to Chiltern with a determination to do great things for education.

G.F. Bradby, *The Lanchester Tradition*

Donald Mackinnon, Darling's strongest supporter, died on Anzac Day, 1932. In a long public career, Mackinnon had been a Victorian parliamentarian and minister of the Crown, a public servant and a diplomat. 'Indisputably the best School in Australia in every way' was how Darling summarised Mackinnon's hopes for GGS in his speech-day report that year. By the end of the 1930s, Mackinnon's faith would be vindicated. An extensive building program commenced at Darling's instigation in 1932–33 and there was a major curriculum reorganisation in 1935. These and other initiatives gave the school national yardstick status in boys' education, with Darling's handiwork the envy of his fellow headmasters. Recognition came in the mid-1930s, by which time Darling had fostered two interlocking educational networks that were key to his success. The first centred on the University of Melbourne and included the vice-chancellor, R.E. Priestley, and professors S.M. Wadham (agriculture), L.F. Giblin (economics), G.S. Browne (education) and D.B. Copland (commerce). Wadham joined the school council in 1932. Giblin, the self-styled 'protector' of a small contingent of Tasmanian GGS boys, stayed at Corio occasionally and then trumpeted Darling's liberalism wherever he went. Priestley made ten weekend visits during the period 1935–38 and wrote glowing diary entries, while Browne's enthusiasm for Darling's plans was boundless. Priestley said that Browne described GGS as 'the perfect school'. Darling's work impacted on teacher training through Browne's lectures and the annual groups of trainees that he brought to Corio. Darling also addressed school speech nights, talked to teacher unions and insisted that all schools, regardless of sector, were part of one indivisible system. These activities also paid dividends. While only 13 per cent of GGS admissions in 1930 were from government schools, the decade average rose to 20 per cent (23 per cent for 1933–37) despite two substantial fee increases.[1]

Darling's other network was both national and international. It centred upon the newly created Australian Council for Educational Research (ACER) and it included the chief executive, Dr K.S. Cunningham, and president of the council, the eminent Frank Tate. It was nearly five years after Darling's arrival that Tate came to Corio, whereupon Darling told Browne that he was 'so glad' that he had arranged the visit. Darling's link with Cunningham was invaluable, because in addition to four articles for the *Australian Quarterly*, and reports of his speeches in the *Age* and *Argus* newspapers, Darling's reforms became known through the ACER Research Series. Cunningham also publicised Darling's work in progressive educational circles, principally the New Education Fellowship, and connected him with two influential Americans, Dr F.P. Keppel of the Carnegie Corporation and Dr I.L. Kandel of Teachers' College, Columbia. Despite Darling's early disavowal, Cunningham wrote of GGS that it was 'regarded by competent judges as perhaps the most progressive school which Australia possesses'. And, after he visited Corio, Kandel said that GGS was an 'outstanding institution' that 'stands out alone' as a departure from the Australian norm.[2]

Darling was also assiduous in generating favourable press coverage. An important contact here was his friend R.L. Curthoys (*Argus* editor until 1935) in his capacity as chief correspondent of *The Times* of London. When members of the Headmasters' Conference of Australia ceased paying for the printing of speech-day reports in the metropolitan newspapers in 1936, school publicity began drying up. Early in 1937, Darling told Curthoys that the *Argus* had 'apparently deliberately, cut out anything to do with the school'. He said that 'I could get it altered by talking to [Staniforth] Ricketson [chairman of the *Argus & Australasian Ltd* and a GGS parent]' although 'I do not want to do this'. Consequently, councillors were concerned 'that I should seize every opportunity to get decent publicity where it is possible'. In 1937 alone, forty-nine letters passed between Darling and his friend. These dealt with a host of educational and other matters, including Curthoys' new draft of GGS's prospectus, articles on education that he helped Darling compose, front-page coverage in *The Times Educational Supplement* that he had secured for the school and his procurement of a reconditioned printing press for Corio from Sir Keith Murdoch. It was through Curthoys that Darling wrote the leading article on education for the 'Australia 150th Anniversary Number' of *The Times* in January 1938 (to which Wadham and Copland also contributed).[3]

Darling's final public relations masterstroke was to throw open the school to external scrutiny. Other headmasters, such as Franklin, were reluctant. While admitting that Darling had 'done wonders' at Corio, Franklin's view of a school was 'a place where in semi-seclusion boys can develop from quiet study a mind capable of real independent thought'. By contrast, Darling 'would rather bring the world into the school & the schoolboy into the world'. Droves of visitors made a pilgrimage to Corio. In addition to welcoming Sir John Monash (the Australian Corps commander and feted war hero), Florence Austral (the singer), and those in the recently formed United Australia Party (UAP) with close ties to the school, including J.V. Fairbairn (an OGG and councillor), Hawker, Gullett and Casey, Darling also invited English dignitaries visiting Australia. These included celebrities such as Lewis Casson and Sybil Thorndike in 1932 (of whom Jo Gullett said she was 'very good but a trifle trying I should think' and went on 'with a bit of nonsense'), H.V. Hodson (editor of *Round Table*) in 1933, and John Masefield (the Poet Laureate) and his wife in late 1934. They were captivated. Darling's claim in November 1936 to the British High Commissioner, Sir Geoffrey Whiskard (Lindsay's former Dominions Office boss) that he 'always found it difficult to consider myself justified' in inviting such people was false modesty. After all, he wanted their approval and for them to spread the word. When Sir Percy Buck (Professor of Music, University of London) was due in Melbourne in 1937, William McKie (GGS director of music and Melbourne Town Hall organist) was insistent: 'we must get him down to the school'. Buck wrote of the new music program: 'Honestly I think everything is so firmly on the right lines that I don't see how the most fertile brain could make any serious objection'.[4]

After his first year of settling in, when 'it has been our duty more to observe and prepare rather than to alter', Darling laid out his reform credentials. There was 'too much talk of tradition', he informed the OGGs, and 'slavish imitation' that had retarded growth in England was to be avoided. Instinctively, he was a prudent innovator rather than a wild iconoclast, and the way forward was to adapt GGS's strengths: 'I feel that Dr. Brown has left here a foundation upon which any man ought to be proud to build'. In going with the grain, Darling's approach differed from that of the Reverend C.T. Parkinson (from 1933, headmaster of the King's School, Parramatta), for example, who was condemned as 'out of step with his time and his colleagues'. An Australian, Parkinson had been at Christ's Hospital under Fyfe—he 'seems somewhat dull', Margaret confided to their mother after she met him for the first time—although Dr Brown's view was that King's might prosper under his tutelage. 'Sydney and N.S.W. are keen to make it the school of the state', he warned Darling, '& nothing would give them greater pleasure that it should be known as the best, as well as the oldest school in Australia'. After reading Darling's essay 'Education to meet the need of the modern state', Parkinson dashed off a four-page note in which he endorsed his fellow head's views and complained bitterly about the circumstances at King's. 'Nothing but purely materialistic acquirement of irrelevant facts for putrid examinations'—an even more graphic description than Fyfe's characterisation of Canadian schooling as 'simply a sausage machine for exam: fodder'. When resistance solidified against his reforms, Parkinson complained to Darling, who said:

> The whole problem with which you are faced seems to me very similar indeed
> to mine except that I think yours is more difficult owing to the fact that your

place is less obviously bad. I had row after row and was able to point [to?] the moral from the rows.

King's people had been doing their job reasonably well 'according to their lights' and probably resented anyone trying to set them right.[5]

Dr Brown's approach at Corio had been Arnoldian: first religion, next character and then intellect. As often as not, as Margaret Masterman (wife of K.C. Masterman) recalled, such ingredients produced a young Geelong Grammarian who was 'quite charming but bone from the neck up'. Darling stuck with Brown's priorities while releasing the potential that Rod Andrew had identified:

> If the new head will carry on the tradition of character and discipline in the
> school and add to it a greater intellectual power and a deeper appreciation of
> beauty—if he can breathe the new spirit that sparkles in modern literature—
> the spirit of adventure in modern art and the more liberalised spirit of modern
> theology into the school, then every Geelong Grammarian will have reason to
> be proud of one of the finest schools in the Empire.

In a number of respects, GGS's self-image as the Eton of the Antipodes was dubious. Very few of the (eighty or so) masters during Brown's incumbency had been educated in English public schools and only a handful had taught in them. Moreover, as a city boy and the son of a Bristol small businessman, Brown was an odd choice to head an isolated semi-rural boarding school with Etonian aspirations. He was also a creature of the English industrial midlands with no experience of boarding schools, and a mathematics master not a classicist. When the council appointed him it expected 'a grammar school master to establish a public school structure'. He had arrived in January 1912 with his wife Ada and five children. He was fastidious, parsimonious and obsessive about detail. To most people in the Corio bubble, he came across as stiff, taciturn, remote and aloof, yet he was liked. Brian Jones (the acting Brice Mackinnon classics master in 1928) recalled Brown as a 'resolute, sombre, rather lonely figure ... leaning against the wind'. After winning the under-fifteen sprint in his first year, Michael Thwaites was called to Brown's study and told: '"Thwaites, lead a hard life. Lead a hard life, Thwaites". It was like a Victorian admonition which I remember to this day.' There was no motor car, no entertaining and no affluence or easy living during Brown's period. His succeeded in consolidating the school's religious infrastructure. The Chapel of All Saints (endowed by the Falkiner family) was consecrated, and Brown acted as chaplain, took senior scripture classes, prepared candidates for confirmation and preached. He emphasised the orthodoxy of received religion and the need for strong faith and morals.[6]

But Brown was unable to attract and retain capable masters. Compared to Scotch College and Melbourne Grammar, GGS stipends were appallingly low and many masters were poorly trained. They were cut off from the social life of

Melbourne, and if they were married they usually saw their families only once a week in Geelong: small wonder, then, that about 70 per cent of his masters resigned for more lucrative and congenial appointments. G.C.T. Giles, for example, a brilliant scholar (and the first Brice Mackinnon master), stuck it out for just three years before he left. After only his first year at Corio, Masterman had resolved to leave, along with Bull, but hesitated to see who Brown's successor would be. Brown's austerity was also discouraging. As a student, John Gorton (future Liberal Party leader and Coalition prime minister), for instance, could not warm to him and Brown was unable to get his measure. But there was another side to Brown. Rod Andrew drew attention to his 'very keen although refined' sense of humour and Brian Jones, when he was a prefect, could even recall Dr Brown wearing a light jacket during summer or a Panama hat in the holidays rather than his regulation clerical garb. 'When he talked easily with you and smiled he was irresistible.' One particular delight was to be invited to Sunday evening supper, although the art mistress, Mary Finnin, thought that Ada Brown's afternoon teas were 'rather formal and staid'. She was quintessentially English, but he 'didn't put on any dog at all'. When Brown returned to England as parish priest in Henley-in-Arden, Warwick, Darling shrewdly informed him of his plans, and welcomed his encouragement and advice. Brown invariably sympathised and confessed timidity in respect of what was proposed.[7]

Staffing was Darling's first priority. At his first school council meeting he tabled his recommended salary increases for the existing masters and the need for new blood. Accommodation was 'seriously overcrowded' and he requested a secretary. In respect of curriculum, he reorganised the timetable from the beginning of 1931. Not only had he noticed an objectionable amount of slackness (in the amassing of spare periods by boys), but he could not detect any logical progression through the year levels. He made two changes. First, able Leaving Certificate examination candidates would complete more subjects over two years rather than a minimum number in one year and then a few more the year after. He wanted boys to have a stronger subject grounding prior to examination as well as wider and delayed choices for those seeking a university education. These latter boys would benefit from a 'proper VIth form' fully endowed with privileges and the honour of membership, and taught by the headmaster. From Charterhouse, Bull expressed delight. Here was the chance of an education rather than subjects on demand. John Gorton thought that, with less time for practice and the boys' minds off sport, the new timetable might indirectly improve performance. Darling's change worked well. G.K. Smith took nine Leaving subjects in 1931–32 when only five were necessary: wide reading with no set books in English literature in the first year, and going beyond the maths and sciences subject requirements. 'It was a marvellous innovation. Then we did Leaving. Well, Leaving was a walkover.'[8]

Second, for boys planning to return to the land there was an intermediate form. In addition to English, arithmetic, history and geography, they studied agricultural chemistry and biology as part of science. After protracted consultations with Wadham, Darling had chemistry, biology and physics laboratories installed in the newly extended science block. Amid 'hammerings and the noise of falling bricks' in the quadrangle, Perry House was also renovated. Council spent nearly £8500 on building works in 1930 but the £30,000 or more required for all the new amenities and accommodation that Darling wanted was deemed prohibitive. These initiatives were a rehearsal for the large-scale overhaul required if GGS was to become, in John Manifold's words, 'the great public school of Australia'. Manifold's aspiration was fuelled by the antipathy that he and some councillors felt about the word Grammar in the school's name. In the late 1920s, the council had sought a title change to Corio School. Humiliatingly, in September 1929, in the face of stiff OGG opposition, it back-pedalled on its request to the Melbourne diocesan synod to approve the rewording. When Darling arrived some four months later, the council had only just resolved to defer a name change. Grammar aside, by the end of first term 1930 it was clear that Darling would provide an English public school structure and style. Similarities with Charterhouse were becoming clear: a fortnightly Shakespeare society met in the headmaster's house, there was a library committee, an out-of-school committee and, for the first time the *Corian* was produced by an editorial sub-committee of boys. In second term, the Corio Ornithologists' Society and the Camera Club commenced, and the Literary, Debating and Musical Society divided into two. In 'emulation of Canberra' the senior society had its own parliament in which John Gorton, 'the very type of vigorous, full-blooded, go-getting, up-and-coming, he-man', was cutting his political teeth.[9]

Darling's job was made easier when Margaret arrived in October 1931. She stayed nearly two years. James also invited Eaton who came late in the following year. Earlier, Eaton had written from Westfalen, Germany, to say that he was consumed by personal inadequacy, and an inability to impress favourably his elders and betters, and anyone with whom he had had 'any official connection'. He was resigned to never being successful. After Westfalen, he worked at Borstal where, according to Austen, he had been deeply depressed. With few future prospects and very little money, Eaton was on his way to teach at Trinity College, a missionary school in Kandy, Ceylon (now Sri Lanka). Margaret told their mother that Eaton was uncomfortable at Corio, although Colin Gordon, a former Carthusian appointed by his brother in September 1931, was one person with whom he got on. They were 'very funny together with "the Headmaster"', she teased, although James was still apprehensive in his job and concerned about Eaton taking a rise out of him in front of the younger masters. Family members had a way of shattering boys' illusions about their headmaster, as the senior prefect for 1933, Bill Lloyd, found out when he visited Trimley:

> It is very dangerous for you to send boys to your parents['] house. It will make all the boys think of you as a boy also! Your name is mentioned almost with

levity, respectful levity of course, but never with the awe, perplexity or hatred one was accustomed to at Geelong. The cap and gown carries a little nonsense, necessary nonsense, with it—doesn't it?

By mid-February, Eaton had headed off to Sandy Nimmo in New Zealand until late April and then to the Trinity job in June for which, said Margaret, 'he really has only the very vaguest of information'.[10]

All the while, Eaton's brother was preoccupied with growing the school. But such expansion would modify GGS's existing practices, particularly its administrative apparatus and leisurely pattern of arm's-length governance. On a day-to-day basis Darling relied on a low-key arrangement of delegated authority to housemasters and masters, periodic help from the council secretary E.A. (Ned) Austin, domestic and outside staff supervision by the bursar, Milton Thewlis, and his own secretary, Vi Moden. Because of the distance separating the headmaster and councillors residing in the Western District, a lot of out-of-council business was conducted by letter. Increased enrolments would impact on the school's character and necessitate substantial construction. Darling had promised the council an expansion plan by April 1931, but another year passed before its finalisation and then a further eighteen months before it was financially underwritten. His first thought was that Junior House was the key to expansion. Despite the worsening economic Depression, admissions were holding up and, he told council in July 1931, all fifty-three boys enrolled for 1932 were destined for Junior House even though there were only forty-five available places. At that point he was convinced of two things: the need to separate Junior House from the senior school and that with three overcrowded senior houses it was 'not wise to send the younger boys into them'. What, therefore, was GGS's preferred enrolment target? This had to be clarified for future applications and the school's internal organisation. There was no point to Junior House growth without a subsequent senior school increase. His initial stab was 515 (about the size of Winchester): 350 senior boys and 165 juniors. Whatever the eventual numbers cap, Junior House was the main source of supply and 'incidentally our main advertisement at the moment'. But predicting numbers was not a learned science: a fortnight after the meeting he told Phelps, gloomily, that the possible loss of fifty boys in third term would mean drastic economies. 'It isn't much fun when one has just re-organised the school in one way to be forced to re-organise it again completely'.[11]

By 'our main advertisement' Darling was alluding to the parental pulling power of Jennings and his little fiefdom. Born in Adelaide in 1879, and educated at St Peter's, Reginald Gellibrand Jennings (or Jenno to the boys) had come from Melbourne Grammar to Corio in 1914. Renowned for his three successive pairs of spaniels (Ping and Pong, then Gnip and Gnop, and then Ping and Pong again), Jennings was serious, dignified and had a gift for teaching small boys. He was a highly talented cricketer although a severe asthmatic. Chivalrous, fussy and punctilious, Jennings instilled old-fashioned gentlemanly Christian

virtues in Junior House boys. A stock phrase was: 'Boy! Stand to attention!
Salute!' He tended to lack a sense of humour although there were occasional
funny moments:

> In the morning, in Junior House, there was an inspection. All the boys were
> lined up, right down the long passage, both sides, and Jenno went along
> inspecting boys: hands, thumbs, fingers and he'd look them over. He came
> to one boy and his shirt was rather a different shade from the others. 'Where
> did you get that shirt, boy'? 'Myer's, Sir'. 'Well you get onto Buckley's straight
> away'. That boy happened to be Ken Myer!

Jennings prided himself on preparing boys successfully for navy entrance examinations. He was famous for an outdoor exercise, the 'great push', and an industrial
scheme in which boys were trained in business principles and their civic duties to
the poor. Jennings was also an accomplished minor author. His most well-known
book was *The Human Pedagogue* (1924). Russel Ward (a GGS master and later
a historian) claimed that every line of it 'dripped with the most excruciatingly
refined and bogus sentiment', but Brian Coulter (a Junior House master) recalled
that if returning boys were 'at all tactful', they carried a copy of Jennings' book
at the top of their suitcases. Sir Rupert Hamer (a future premier of Victoria)
read the *Pedagogue* before entering Junior House and his parents were favourably
impressed.[12]

At the next council meeting, Darling switched tack: Junior House accommodation in late 1931 was unlikely to be quite as tight. No more than 300 boarders were expected for 1932 and he would now defer splitting the two sections
of the school. With the wider economic circumstances working against him as
the Depression deepened, he revised his thinking down. A possible substantial
financial loss loomed. In August the teaching staff agreed unanimously to a 5 per
cent salary reduction from January 1932 (following which Darling's salary was
£1425, and Masterman's and Jennings' at £760). During the summer vacation,
Darling was hatching a 'big scheme', but fluctuating estimates of pupil admission
numbers played havoc with boarding house calculations. Risks to the wellbeing
of Junior House boys promoted at thirteen and a half or younger to houses chock
full of senior boys concerned him. Both Cuthbertson and Manifold houses were
built to accommodate fifty, but each contained eighty-four boarders and had to be
reduced. Class sizes were too large—thirty-two against a desired twenty-eight—
and there was a classroom shortage. Then he reversed course again: in Junior
House there were to be 123 boys, 'an impossible number for anyone but Jennings
to handle' and yet Jennings (recuperating from illness at Mount Macedon in
mid-1932) was no longer 'quite the man he once was'. Only thirty boys were
likely to be ready for the senior school in 1933 and yet fifty names were down for
entry to Junior House. 'What am I to do with them and where are they to go[?]'
Darling wailed to Mackinnon. Surely it was 'bad policy to turn boys away'.[13]

Darling's other wish-list priorities were a music school ('almost immediately necessary'), a hall, a new library, a pavilion, and carpentry and engineering shops. Moreover, even with the eventual restoration of the salary cut, the masters' stipends were way too low:

> The problem put shortly then is this, that this school, if run as I think it ought to be run, and in the only way which can produce good results, will not pay unless it is over-full.

In early 1932 there were only three options: first, persist with recent economies and live within the school's means (and deny or forgo betterment); second, increase tuition fees (and facilitate higher salaries and reduced house sizes); third, 'take the risk and start now on a forward policy'. Darling preferred the third. He proposed three steps: additional Junior House classrooms and accommodation, next the construction of a fourth senior house, and then a fifth house in the senior school or relocation of Perry. His pitch to Mackinnon was:

> I admit that if I see all this done in my lifetime I shall be surprised and yet I hardly see how we are to carry on without it. We want to be good, not merely to be making the best of a bad job. I have done my best under the present circumstances but there is much that under the present circumstances cannot be done. I should think that psychologically and financially this is a good time in which to be bold, and I suppose that I am not very patient by nature.

A slight admission increase in early 1932 ('disgustingly full by some miracle', he told Archbishop Head) might persist if he could bring his plans to fruition. On the other hand, the danger was 'new headmasters elsewhere (e.g. at King's, Parramatta) who will be fashionable in their turns. It would be well to take our opportunity while it presents itself.'[14]

Mackinnon was encouraging. So long as the enrolments held up, the depressed economic circumstances were conducive to expansion: building costs were reducing, contractors were tendering low to obtain work and borrowing was cheap due to falling interest rates: 'My present impression is that we shd face the situation & begin a programme. It seems inevitable that we must have a second junior house.' There were further grounds for hope:

> [Your letter] puts the position very clearly & I agree with your views. The present time when the popularity of the school is established & money goes a long way encourages one to hope that a strenuous effort might give great results.

The day after the March 1932 council meeting Darling replied that, although the councillors were 'a little alarmed and slightly inclined to say that it was quite impossible to find the money', they had agreed to the preparation of estimates. The three unknowns were: the number of boys needed for the school to pay its way, whether the additional boys could be found and whether the council could procure the money. On the second point Darling was adamant: 'we shall be able to get as many boys as we want'. Mackinnon sympathised and said that the council's 'trepidation' was not surprising:

> 'This is rather sudden' to some, & of course upsetting to others to whom 'safety first' is a guiding star. Nevertheless the Scheme must be seriously considered. As to finance by means of debentures or gifts from friends of the School: we are all getting rotten balance-sheets the last year or two. Most landowners are living on their capital & 'rates & taxes' alone are more than their own living expenses.

Mackinnon was confident of obtaining finance from the Australian Mutual Provident Society (AMP) 'or some other money-lender' but—having lived through the 1893 bank crash—he cautioned '(not a bank)'. In April, council reviewed Darling's calculations. It decided on an enrolment of 500 boys (425 boarders and 75 day boys), a maximum of 56 boys per house, a Junior House target of 150 and an AMP loan for £60,000 to pay for extensions and additions. It was also agreed to obtain legal advice as to possible realisable assets in the A.H. Whittingham estate (which Darling had deliberately not included).[15]

Arthur Herbert Whittingham had died in June 1927. While his will provided an annuity for his widow, GGS also stood to benefit substantially from his estate, because there was provision for the payment of a 'school fund' sufficient to return by way of investment in government stock an annual income of £200. The fund amounted to £4000 at 5 per cent interest. More importantly, however, clause 11 also bequeathed to the school the residue of Whittingham's 'trust fund' consequent upon the sale of all real and personal estate, which was valued by the Union Trustee Company at nearly £93,000. It mostly comprised a pastoral leasehold in Queensland and was unconverted because the trustees claimed an entitlement to 5 per cent commission on all estate income, including Mrs Whittingham's annuity fund. The dispute over this latter matter prevented GGS from benefiting from the estate money. Eventually, in July 1933, the Queensland Supreme Court found against the plaintiff regarding commission arising out of estate income. At the same time the Court found for the defendant (Mrs Whittingham) on whether her annuity was charged against the whole of the estate or the residue as claimed by the school. In September, the school council appealed to the High Court. A year later (when Darling was on leave in England), the High Court found for the school. Whittingham's property (Alice Downs) was finally auctioned in late 1936 and, in February 1937, almost a decade after Whittingham's death, nearly £80,000 in estate money eventually came to GGS.[16]

Meanwhile, everyone's hopes took a beating in May 1932 when AMP rejected the requested £60,000 and suggested another enquiry in twelve months. John Manifold continued the negotiations but was exasperated by the AMP board's intransigence. Another councillor, Max Bell, said to Darling that the Bank of Australasia advised waiting for twelve months before expansion. Although Bell and Manifold agreed to hold fire, an undeterred Darling pressed on with a number of smaller demands. The new chairman after Mackinnon's death was Manifold. His and Darling's letters outbound and inbound soon adopted the more familiar salutation of given names, and their mutual confidence grew as they got each other's measure. To soften up Manifold before the June council meeting, Darling complained that he was desperately short of teaching space, and again emphasised the library, Junior House classrooms, and carpentry and engineering shops. What was more annoying, he inquired: to have to turn boys away or to have them wait? Buchan, Laird & Buchan (the school's architects) were instructed to prepare plans for Darling's requests, which were discussed in July, with Max Bell to report on the council's financial position in August. Meanwhile, Darling, assisted by Thewlis, devised yet another big scheme outline. In the first of two letters, he told Manifold:

> The more one thinks of it the more clear it seems to become that there is no choice except between doing nothing and doing the whole thing, and some-times I feel that to press for the big scheme is a heavier responsibility than I like to take.

If Manifold was slightly unnerved by the last part of that sentence, then there might have been a sharp intake of breath on reading this next passage:

> I rather think it would be a good thing if I propose the whole scheme, put it to the Council and then leave them to decide without me, for when all is said and done the success or failure of it must depend upon me, and really the Council would probably have to decide between me and the scheme. I do not mean that I have any intention of resigning immediately but I do not think that I could carry on indefinitely without the prospect of getting the place as I want it.

As with Hansen and the Council of Public Education, Darling's insistence on having his own way was getting the better of him: putting his own future on the line amounted to holding a gun at the council's head—a high-wire tactic that he would call on again.[17]

After an incessant barrage of correspondence, and persuasive talk at Corio and the Melbourne Club, Darling finally got his way. The council had been bullied into submission: to not have fallen into line with his plans was (effectively) a vote of no confidence in him and in their earlier decision to appoint him. Little wonder, then, that Manifold let Darling know in disarmingly frank terms that he knew what he was up to—which, in effect, was: I'm your man if you are after the best school in Australia, but deny me what I want and I'll be on the next boat back home. Manifold put down a marker: he would not be hostage to idle threats of resignation, nor would he block Darling's avenue of exit:

> You do not really want my assurance that the job is worth while. I realize—& sympathize very fully indeed—that the real sting in your problem is involved in the necessarily deliberate decision to cut off your possible retreat on England. Well I think that no one could, & in any case should not try to influence your decision on that point—it has to be your own. In the light of your present knowledge, I imagine that you would have been seriously dissatisfied with yourself if your machinations to avoid appointment had proved successful. If that comes as near the truth as I think, it will prove a difficult thought to put under now.

With that he adroitly redirected the gun towards the headmaster's foot. Darling snapped out of his trough of despond and his note accompanying the figures in his second letter to Manifold bubbled with enthusiasm. He had had a long talk the previous evening with a businessman (and GGS parent) whom he had befriended, G.S. Colman (of Australian Estates), and he was convinced that two other businessmen, Sir George Fairbairn (an OGG) and Sidney Myer (the retailer and a GGS parent), would each lend the school £10,000 at 4 per cent interest. Colman had assured him of an economic improvement in 1933. Although there were doubts about securing the necessary admissions, Darling thought that 'it would be wise to risk doing the whole thing', and was convinced that the time was right. Putting everything else to one side, Darling told Manifold that 'the school is booming in spite of the depression and at the expense of other schools'. Next year, he thought, would 'really show some results which ought to have a good effect as advertisement'.[18]

Apart from outlining the headmaster–chairman terms of engagement, these exchanges highlight the interplay of supply and demand in the fee-paying independent schools market, and the extent to which either factor could be manipulated. From the point of view of admissions, a school's preferred situation was to avoid a fall in numbers that might spark a downward spiral or vicious circle. Darling soon twigged that the supply side was his priority and that he needed to improve the school's appeal. Provided that fee increases could be minimised or avoided, applications converted into acceptances of offers and admissions sustained, then there was a sound financial basis for extensive capital investment in plant and amenities to cater for the projected increased demand. Not surprisingly, then, nearly all his council reports began with estimates or actual enrolments, projections of departing boys and admission inquiry numbers. From the perspective of 1932, government tuition fee subsidies to middle-class parents that might augment demand (and reduce the risks of borrowing) were still three decades or so away, but the cheapened price of money made the prospect of GGS's long-term debt less intimidating. Manifold knew the delicate balancing act entailed when deciding on fees and, after mulling over the advisability of Darling's proposed big financial outlay, replied:

> Yes, I think we would get the boys (boarders)—I am not so sure about the day boy side. I have always had a very strong idea that the available boys vary in numbers from year to year & in groups of years ... But our good will & status has increased & continues to increase so rapidly & solidly that you cannot set a limit to our drawing power. Therefore I think there is no real danger on that score.

The persistent unknown in the equation, given the possibility of increased tuition fees, was the effect on demand of lifting these to a level sufficient to underwrite expansion. Fee increases were counterproductive if they made the school even more socially selective, for which reason Manifold confessed to being 'a little more concerned on the point'; were they to be increased then 'we may be dubbed again "that rich and expensive school"'.[19]

At about this time, Margaret returned from visiting the Nimmos in Queensland and told their mother that while James looked well he was 'mentally tired' from thrashing out his various schemes. 'Excellent!' exclaimed Gerry Dicker when he heard about Darling's progress from Marchant and the Junior House master F.N.B. Newman (then in England). By the end of 1932 the 'signs of recovery were unmistakable', although the building industry's recovery still 'lagged well behind' other sectors. Despite the more propitious circumstances, Darling suddenly got cold feet and switched tack yet again. He now concentrated on the senior school and debentures as his preferred means of finance. Prior to Jennings' return from recuperation, Darling broke the news that there would be no work on Junior House: 'The trouble is that such building would involve us necessarily in the whole big scheme and the money required seems alarming'. He apologised and explained that the aim was 'to make the position in Junior House intolerable so that we can do what we want'. Correcting himself he said that 'it is necessary to make the transition stage from 120 to 150 less abrupt' and finding thirty extra boys in one year was difficult. Darling wanted £18,000 and, in his letter of explanation to Jim Fairbairn he invoked the logic of a virtuous circle:

> First of all, we have got to a stage in the school in which the numbers of the forms are too big and reorganisation there becomes necessary. This implies more classrooms and more masters and more masters implies more accommodation for masters. Besides the actual numbers in the form, there is a need to provide a greater choice of subjects in the higher forms and this is

accentuated by the fact that the standard of work in the school has improved considerably so that it is the upper forms that are unusually full.

Furthermore, as new accommodation produced no financial return and was still to be paid for, without a fee increase extra boys had to be admitted. In November 1932, when Margaret noted that her brother was totally preoccupied with confirmation candidates and plans for the buildings and had 'no thoughts for anything else', six men, including Sidney Myer, one Manifold and three Fairbairns lent the school the money in the form of debentures at 4 per cent interest. The commitment so worried Manifold that he vowed never to do it again. Once more, Laird drew up plans for alterations and additions. From Henley-in-Arden Dr Brown gave his blessing and in Winchester Dicker said that Darling's plans were exciting.[20]

Two things had convinced Darling to retreat to plan B. He suspected that John Turnbull (a councillor) opposed his big scheme. With Manifold's concurrence, Darling had deliberately increased the pressure on accommodation in September by admitting more boys to 'bring things to a head'. He would now settle for new classrooms, extensions to the dining hall and alterations to two houses. He was also mindful of the impact of the council's decision to absorb the Geelong Church of England Preparatory School (GCEPS) in January 1933 (after soundings from the latter). A number of OGGs' sons attended GCEPS— described rather neatly by its head, the Reverend P.H. Dicker, as 'preparatory in a detached way' to GGS. There were twenty boarders and fifty-five day boys in Dicker's charge in 1932. 'The day boys are very good since Dicker has been there', Darling told Manifold, and the new arrangement was advantageous, as GCEPS enhanced GGS's link with the provincial city through the day-boy intake. Slightly fewer than 20 per cent of boys coming to Corio in the 1930s entered from Bostock House (as GCEPS became known in early 1933). Indeed, when Darling introduced Dicker to the February 1933 council meeting he referred to GCEPS as 'in reality a Junior House'. An important takeover condition was that while GCEPS increased its fees GGS incurred a capital liability of £5000.[21]

By 1933, the prospects for expansion were looking up. Following a profit of nearly £3000, the 5 per cent reduction in masters' salaries was restored. 'Rather epoch making' was how Darling described to John Manifold the new living arrangements in the houses, the Junior House reorganisation, the dining hall and his other plans, although he was a bit ahead of himself in suggesting that GGS could now claim to be 'providing the best education possible in this country'. Nonetheless, the word was spreading. 'You must have heard of the great things James Darling is doing at Geelong', Louis Wharton told Phelps. Margaret had been the conduit of news to Louis and Hilda and she also reported to Trimley on the new buildings that were 'rising rapidly all round us'. Except for the dining-hall extensions, most would be ready for the beginning of first term. Her brother was pleased with their appearance, even though 'there is still a great deal of debris about'. While she felt that they were 'quite hopelessly ugly, I am afraid & so incredibly commonplace', he took a different view: 'Jim was very elated after Monday's Council meeting when he displayed everything to the Council & they were thrilled to think what a good advertisement it was for the School'. Vic Tunbridge recalled when he arrived at Corio as a master in 1933 that the alterations to the houses were a vast improvement for homework and weekend living. Brown had had living rooms built on to the houses, but Darling provided individual study areas (known as cabins in Perry and cubicles elsewhere). Opinions about the buildings differed. Bill Landale (a prefect in 1932) read the *Corian* in Germany and thought that the photographs suggested that the study rooms 'must be a wonderful success', whereas Bill Lloyd (in England in 1934) was told (tongue-in-cheek) that the Junior House plans 'offended the aesthetic sensibilities'.[22]

Jennings, Margaret said to their mother, was disgruntled because his school 'which was always the showpiece', had been 'rather neglected & he is clamouring to have his building done'. With the economy on the mend and enrolments topping 400 for the first time in March 1933, the council's energies were focused on underwriting the big scheme. This was not going to be easy and Manifold was despondent: 'I feel ashamed (almost) to be so wretchedly negative'. 'Are you any nearer a solution?' Darling inquired plaintively of Turnbull on Anzac Day. In May, the latter informed council that he had applied to AMP for a £40,000 loan. The next month (in advance of AMP's assent to its request) council accepted in principle the terms of the loan and the necessary security. And yet still Darling equivocated about the finer points of his plan, thanks to Jennings. Again Margaret noted how tired he looked towards the end of term, just prior to a week in Sydney at the Headmasters' Conference. 'Now they are embarking on this new building scheme for Junior House', she remarked, 'so I don't see much prospect of work slackening off'. Acutely aware of the need for the financially prudent Turnbull to be on side, Darling wrote him a four-page letter in late June in which he pleaded for sympathy and understanding. Sensing that Jennings' best years might be behind him, he toyed with two versions of an intermediate house to be run by Newman or, if necessary, by himself. On the eve of her return to England, Margaret was thrown by the effect of these 'vague ideas' on her own plans, and yet the prospect of 'discussing and superintending all the building' and coming into closer contact with boys before they moved to senior school had its own appeal. Darling then jettisoned the intermediate idea as 'a mistake'—an offence to Jennings and an unsatisfactory solution to senior school overcrowding. There was still the problem of pressure of numbers at the bottom end of the school, with immediate accommodation required there and later at the upper end as a consequence of the enrolment flow-on. The estimates may not have convinced Turnbull. The headmaster's arguments for a school divided at age thirteen (for cheapness and reduced Junior House overcrowding within the already agreed-upon estimates) were full of holes (in anticipation of appeasing

Jennings). Jennings would be outraged by transition at thirteen and, regardless of what Darling had in mind by saying 'it will also be easy to move over to the Newman regime when Jennings goes', was unlikely to be 'pacified'.[23]

Confronted by Darling's 'several conflicting schemes' ('none of which quite pleased him', Margaret observed), Turnbull was undecided. 'The whole position is very difficult and I cannot even yet make up my own mind on the scheme.' A week later, Darling tried again, this time in a five-page report to council, in the first four of which he apologised for chopping and changing, and suggested that he had 'returned to the original full scheme [of early 1932] as the only possible one to advocate'. Assuming that council was committed to a £40,000 loan and that there would be a net addition of forty-seven boarders in 1934–35, he estimated that, after loan repayments and the use of insurance premium payments as collateral, for those two years the deficit would be about £4000. An increase of fifty-seven boys would reduce that figure to zero. He conceded that the figures made 'very alarming reading' but that, if council didn't proceed, the alternatives were to forgo sizeable potential income, either by containing future Junior House numbers or turning away boys aged over fourteen (due to continued overcrowding) by not building a new senior school house. The council agreed to Darling's amendments and requested the Bank of Australasia to increase its overdraft by £15,000 to £25,000. Two special council sub-committee meetings followed. As a result of the first (17 July) being informed that the bank could give 'no undertaking' on the overdraft, council decided to approach AMP for £55,000. A tightly worded three-page letter laid out the school's case. In return for this loan, council would hand over security on every portion of school property and take out a further endowment policy of £10,000. The justification for the loan's size was that 'it will free the school from [the] danger of such interference from the bank as might materially affect the efficient running of the school' and that it would 'create a school in the matter of buildings and equipment much in advance of other schools'. Success hinged on the recruitment of extra boys; the grounds for confidence were that boarding numbers had been steadily rising since 1930. This increase was not attributable to the recent improvements in facilities and these were still to have 'a far greater advertisement value'. Moreover, the enrolment of very young boys ensured increased numbers for many years—as had happened during an earlier expansion period (1914–20). The council had committed to 'a progressive policy' and to taking advantage of 'a rising tide'.[24]

Sadly, its efforts were in vain. A second special meeting on 24 July was informed that AMP had rejected the additional £15,000. Only on the condition that the overdraft would not exceed £5000 without its consent would the request be forwarded to Sydney for approval. Manifold had anticipated this contingency when lobbying the AMP board and was uneasy about the board's limits on GGS's freedom. As Turnbull had also failed to dissuade the AMP directors, council was advised to reject the conditions. Eventually, after a meeting between Turnbull, Manifold, Darling, Thewlis and AMP agreement was reached. The loan figure was reduced to £45,000, with £30,000 to be advanced initially—on the same terms of security—with a further £15,000 forthcoming 'if and when required within the next two years'. This outcome put the headmaster on notice to ensure that anticipated admissions materialised, so that a new senior house 'will then be both necessary and justifiable from the financial point of view'. Council endorsed the new arrangement. Darling informed the parents by saying that the new buildings were part of a general council plan 'to have fewer boys in each House': five houses of sixty-two, a day house of sixty and a junior school comprising three houses of fifty, for a total of 520. Darling was proud of his achievements. Randall Deasey remembered how his headmaster used to joke with the prefects about the wonderful businessman that he would have made. Relieved that the hard work was over, he told Bickersteth (about to return to Felsted in England) that he had 'got the first part of the scheme through but not the new Senior House as yet'. Bickersteth flattered him:

> I am really appalled at the wonderful work you have done at Corio. It makes my fourteen years at St. Peters seem effortless and unenterprising when compared with your successful onslaught on your manifold problems in 3½ years—any how all Australia is talking about it & your fame has gone far and wide.

Already GGS stood 'head and shoulders above any other Australian school' and could not fail to prosper.[25]

Darling's changes were a far cry from the school's recent primitive conditions. Enticed from the Gordon Technical College by Brown in 1928 to teach art, Mary Finnin had been aghast at what she discovered. The art room was no bigger than a sitting room, with nothing but a blackboard, desks and some T-squares. Unfortunately, Darling told his mother, after all the hard work there was a minor hitch due to a cost underestimate of £6000. By comparison with GGS, expansion by rival schools seemed effortless:

> Wesley have been given carte-blanche by Mr. Nicholas [a businessman and benefactor] to build a new school spending as much as they like. It is going to cost them £145,000 the lucky brutes.

But Dr Brown suspected that, even with this huge endowment, Wesley was more likely to gain at the expense of Scotch rather than GGS. There was a close parallel between what Darling was trying to do and Edward Thring at Uppingham in England about eighty years beforehand. When each headmaster took over their respective schools they were about the same age (Darling thirty, Thring thirty-one) and, within five years, the infrastructure of both schools had been transformed. Uppingham was much smaller than GGS (and Thring's governors had been determined to thwart him). Both men shared two educational beliefs:

the importance of the headmaster knowing every individual boy, and attending to his needs, and the provision of adequate 'machinery' with which to facilitate boys' learning. For Thring 'every brick put in place in a school, every plot of ground laid out, should be so disposed as to assist in making it easy to do right and hard to do wrong'. Only with his 'almighty wall' in place could Thring devote attention to the development of each boy.[26]

While attending to Corio's equivalent of Thring's wall, Darling began a curriculum overhaul. 'To encourage every boy in the direction to which his inclinations would lead him, while preventing him from becoming mentally lopsided' was his first enunciation of a set of principles. He devised a timetable embodying a broad education and a set of specialised directions, while refusing to be hostage to the traditional attraction of the land to GGS boys. He even told the parents that such an employment option would diminish. By late 1932, his own analysis of the composition of the school's admissions convinced him that the curriculum alternatives open to their offspring boiled down to three: professional, commercial and agricultural courses, with each beginning in the IVth form, followed by two years spent at the Leaving Certificate level and then university preparation at Leaving Honours in the VIth. As well as meeting the needs of individuals, these initiatives tackled what he believed were the prevailing low intellectual standards. Although he loathed examination-dominated learning, and after having assured the council of improvements in results in 1932, Darling began arguing that his reforms were paying off in improved examination performance. Some figures that he gave Franklin pinpointed dreadful GGS Intermediate Certificate results: over five years from 1928, less than one-third of GGS candidates for each year had secured the certificate outright in the December examination without having to sit the following February supplementaries. Franklin's Melbourne Grammar figures for the same period were only marginally better. In 1932, however, most GGS boys passed their Leaving. Not normally given to public displays of enthusiasm, the second master C.A. Cameron could scarcely contain himself: sixty boys passed Intermediate with four subjects or better and 75 per cent of those who sat for the Leaving passed it with an average of over seven subjects.[27]

Like Thring, it was imperative for Darling to know every boy. He was an affectionate and friendly headmaster with boys and they found him approachable. When Bernays departed Corio he told his friend that the boys 'are extraordinarily companionable and their admiration even adoration for you must be very satisfying'. J.S. Guest remembered Darling coming down to cricket practice to bowl in the nets. (Blue Steward had encouraged him to when he discovered that he loved cricket.) That was all very well, said John Keith and Ronald Hughes from faraway Charterhouse, but had he bowled anyone out yet and did he play with the same dexterity as when fielding in the deep for the Maniacs on Bramley Green? Since his Merchant Taylors' School days, a mark of Darling's approach had been to take a personal interest in his promising young charges. He made

Steward a school prefect only a few days before he left in 1931. Steward spotted the announcement on a noticeboard in the quad on the day of his very last cricket match. He had just made 87 runs against Xavier and Darling called him in:

'What are you going to do when you leave here?' I said: 'Well, I was thinking of doing Law, Sir'. 'Ha! My boy, let me give you some advice'. He said: 'You haven't got the capacity to concentrate long enough to do a university course'. For the previous two years I had really done nothing. Nothing, I didn't have to. And I said: 'Oh well, do you have any alternative suggestions?' He said: 'Yes. I think you ought to go to Fiji and grow bananas!' I said: 'Oh, thank you very much, Sir'.

Darling was wrong: Steward made a last-minute switch to medicine and finished fourth in the University of Melbourne class list. Meanwhile, Steward continued with cricket and in 1938 played at Corio:

I was captain of the old boys team and Darling saw me. I don't know how far away he was but I could see his long legs accelerating as he came towards me. He put out his arms, embraced me almost and said: 'Steward, I'm delighted'. And I think I had tears in my eyes.

Looking back on the earlier incident, Steward conjectured that Darling was probably thinking: 'he's got ability but he doesn't try. I'll put him to the test, tell him he's a loafer.'[28]

OGGs soon acknowledged the impact of Darling's changes. Leslie Parker was glad that he had returned for another year at school, and Francis Stuart (cramming for a Latin 'small' before entering Brasenose College, Oxford) confessed that finally he understood what his headmaster had been driving at. Only when aboard ship had 'your idea of a full life and a profitable one become clearer'. If the letters to Darling from pupils and former pupils were to be believed, then the new regime was 'amazingly successful'. Indeed, 'the place seems quite a phenomenon now: a school expanding and conscious of itself'. After his unpromising beginning with stone-throwing, Michael Thwaites was displaying his poetic talents and grateful for his enriched experiences:

This last year [1933] has been about all that I could have desired, and I honestly feel that I owe the school (vile phrase!) something too great to be measured. And I don't think you're really so stupid as to think that you personally have quite failed either to influence my way of thinking or to win my true affection.

There were creative activities in and out of class. Thwaites was one of four boys whom Bull bundled into his old Chevrolet one day and drove to the Dandenong Ranges to read Milton's *Samson Agonistes*. Notwithstanding these glowing endorsements, Darling could not appeal to every boy all of the time. Jo Gullett, for one, was pugnaciously ambivalent. His letters home provide a vivid picture of Junior House and Manifold, and then as a house prefect, of life closer to the throne. The blunt and no-nonsense Gullett (hot-tempered like his father Henry) was small in physique, and survived on his wits. He fought back with fisticuffs whenever, thanks to his swarthy visage, he was dubbed 'dago' and 'chink' by his fellow students. A fierce defender of the underdog, Gullett loathed snobbery, bunging on side and the 'footling idea' of some of the prefects:

> A fellow here called Beurepaire [sic] whose father owns a pub (not that anybody thinks about that) had the nerve to say all sorts of nasty things about you [H.S. Gullett]. He shut up when I started on his own noble profession.

Gullett admired Bull and Cameron whereas other masters found him cheeky and impertinent. Knowing the headmaster from within the privacy of his own family when Darling stayed at Hill Station, he had difficulties coping with Darling's headmasterly behaviour.[29]

As a middle-class larrikin, Gullet would stand up to Darling in the VIth form. If the headmaster launched into his pet theme and criticised Australians for their pursuit of money and material wellbeing 'Jo said he totally disagreed'. He thought that the headmaster was 'quite wrong. It was a false picture of the values of most Australians'. J.S. Guest recalled Darling's English classes as mostly comprising discussion. Michael Thwaites found Darling's teaching to be 'inspirational rather than systematic' and recalled his 'surprising frankness'. But Gullett objected to Darling's obscurely worded essay topics, such as 'Deep in unfathomable mines', for which he told his parents that goldmines and El Dorado 'will not be a success I fear'. Bill Lloyd, on the other hand, playfully admitted later how he used to rehearse vengeance fantasies: 'I often felt, sitting gloomily & resentfully in the VIth form room, "He shall have his reward—yea verily"'. Gullett also deplored pessimism, so that when Giblin lectured on the fourth year of the Depression, Gullett jested that 'depression is a very popular theme here'. While Darling was gearing up for his final assault on the big scheme, Gullett wrote a long reflection to his father. The head, he thought, was 'a gloomy wretch'. A headmaster could always snub a boy if the boy was to ever get the better of him and so, he said, because he was not confident enough to chip Darling, 'I keep quiet':

> The Head when discussing the shortcomings of the human race always takes a very tolerant and condescending attitude which is only outdone by Lloyd & the book-liking Manifold. To contrast his behaviour to you and Mum with that of his Cesarean [sic] air to the boys is extraordinary. He says things he does not believe and must be an awful hippocrite [sic]. Nevertheless I do like him as do we all after talking with him though I could never be awfully fond

of a chap who did not have something of the same feeling for me and I do know I rank very low on his list.

The implication was that Darling played favourites. If so, then the attention that Darling lavished on boys like Lloyd (whom Gullett described as 'a splendid leader', 'honest and loyal with his prefects who return his decency'), for whom he held high hopes, is accounted for by his enthusiasm for them and the importance that he attached to being a prefect.[30]

Darling fully expected his school prefects to exercise moral authority. Gerry Dicker spent 1933–34 at Corio and he recalled the early prefects as 'by any standards an outstanding group of boys, noticeably more adult and responsible than their counterparts in [England]'. They were constantly in the head's company. He lunched with them each day at the prefects' table and they met with him over supper in the second half of evening prep. 'I remember feeling very important', recalled Michael Thwaites, 'he gave you the feeling that your opinion was worth hearing'. There was also Sunday lunch with him followed by a game of croquet, and then an annual camp or retreat at Easter at which there was lots of discussion which Dicker thought was 'an opportunity to get to know these boys better'. His confidence in prefects for 1933 was one reason that Darling gave for choosing the following year as his first period of leave. Occasionally, they were disloyal or let him down. Once, when a house prefect and a school prefect absconded instead of going on a Saturday party (a dawn-to-darkness outing undertaken by a party of three boys), he complained bitterly to Manifold about their lack of honour, 'too much sentimental shading off of black and white' and 'Melbourne's attempt at Society', although in fairness, he admitted, the other prefects had not protected the defaulter. Dr Brown sympathised and said that his battles were with prefects who smoked. Despite Gullett's vote of confidence, Lloyd thought that he failed as a leader:

> Your standards are so high they nearly dumbfound me. All your decent ideas on personal behaviour, drink and women I can see all too clearly and hope I can always regulate my life on those ideals. But your tremendous care for the rest of the human race baffles me. If you were self centred and personally ambitious in the lowest sense perhaps you would find it hard to convince yourself that the goats really mattered. That is my big struggle. I know I should help the weak and I try to (although you don't think so).

The powerlessness of the position of senior prefect depressed him:

> You fill people to saturation point with ideals and then you give them a job in which they do nothing. You do all the work and it is only your presence which is reviving the school. This is not a complaint, rather a hymn of praise. I am looking forward to next term. My only sorrow is that you regard me as a

complete worm on numerous occasions. If you knew how hard I try to please you you would understand why I seem petulant when rebuked.

There were times when Darling felt that he would never accomplish anything. In his bleakest moments he invoked genetic explanations about errant streaks running through particular families or he despaired about the poor Australian 'material' on which he had to work.[31]

Darling persisted with attracting masters from England to assist in uplifting the school. Temple warned him that choosing the right man was 'the most important part of an HM's job' and Darling asked Bickersteth to seek out men 'prepared to throw in their lot with the country'. His impassioned plea to Dicker in early 1932 to come out to GGS appealed to a sense of civilising mission:

> Does Australia matter in the scheme of things? I don't know: it is terribly isolated and rather foolish. When you see it floundering you will want to help it go right and when you understand the tremendous though rather sentimental loyalty you will want to use it in the right direction. And moreover they are boys like other boys and in many ways extremely attractive. They are beginning to look up and want to be fed.

Three Englishmen came: Colin Gordon, Dicker and P. Fletcher. They were successful and much liked. 'Pinky' Fletcher was a well-known eccentric. Bull found out what he could about him and said that he was 'a splendid man & amazingly energetic'. Sir Rupert Hamer remembered meeting Fletcher one day during a school vacation in Collins Street, Melbourne:

> Thrusting through the crowd was this red-headed master I knew so well, thrusting his way through and walking as fast as he could, swinging his arms. I greeted him. He said: 'Come down to the corner'. So I trailed after him as he dashed his way through the crowd to the corner of Collins and Swanston streets. When I got there he was looking at his watch. 'A record!' he said.

The masters felt as positively as the boys about the changes in the school. William McKie, the music master who replaced McKinnell (a less successful English appointee), considered GGS to be 'an uncommonly good school, the best I have ever known'. In early 1934 Bull complained of exhaustion at all the hard work but complimented Darling on his inspiration and organisation. For Dicker, returning home was heart-rending. En route to Marlborough, and eventually to Cheltenham, Fletcher wrote that at Corio in 1932–33 he had found 'a perpetual inspiration'. Later on he said that by comparison Marlborough 'seemed staid & backward' and Cheltenham was 'in a mid-Victorian state of unenlightenment'. (On learning of this admiration for GGS's headmaster, Marchant said that it proved what a 'queer fish' Fletcher was.)[32]

Two pageants united masters and boys and symbolised the school's rejuvenation: the Latin Play (*The Aeneid*) of October 1931 and Thomas Hardy's *The Dynasts* in October 1933. The dramatic presentation of the fifth book of *The Aeneid* on the shores of the nearby lagoon occurred because Masterman drew Darling's attention to the approaching bi-millenary of Virgil's birth. 'Excellent', said Francis Keenlyside, and 'a brain wave', wrote John Keith, from Charterhouse. Old boys in England concurred. The OGG Alan Brown reported that Elliot Grant was most enthusiastic and that Michael Thwaites was busy writing Latin verse. At Trinity College, Melbourne, Leslie Parker said that everyone there was 'intrigued': 'I believe', he teased, 'that you are to have Fox Movietone on the spot'. Mary Finnin's compact *Corian* account of the Latin Play highlighted its educative value and worth as the 'essential co-ordination of thought and activity between individuals in a community'. Darling said as much to council. The lessons that he drew from these and subsequent large-scale productions (particularly during World War II) concerned what could be achieved if and when everyone pulled together in the interests of all. *The Times Educational Supplement* noted how the production brought together the practically inclined masters (such as Cameron) and the scholars (such as Masterman). Michael Thwaites recalled the weather on the day as perfect. Dr Brown was ecstatic. The pageant was a brilliant idea. In Gerry Dicker's view, *The Dynasts* was successful as 'a whole school effort, in which every boy and master had a share':

> Philip Fletcher and I were responsible for various token armies, and the uniforms and other dresses seemed to have been imported for the 150th [sic] anniversary of the founding of Melbourne. I suppose that 200 boys took part, and there had to be some pretty rapid changes of uniform, e.g. from French to Austrian armies—and there were Russians in the retreat from Moscow and naval scenes from the Battle of Trafalgar, as well as military episodes like Waterloo. There were some country scenes from England, too, representing the life of rustic folk along the coasts, half expecting an invasion across the channel.

Dicker recalled the bonfires lit behind Manifold House to represent the burning of Moscow before the retreat began, and being unable to induce a boy sitting on a wall overlooking bonfires to speak his lines until the smoke was well up in the sky.[33]

Prior to *The Dynasts*, during the toing and froing with AMP, Darling read a paper entitled 'Renaissance' to the University of Melbourne Literature Club. 'Invigorating, like a flute sounding a note of hope in the distance. Here is the way to speak to the young: continuity, evolution, faith', Senator Duncan Hughes told the *Australian Quarterly* editor when he read it. Darling had defined renaissance as 'a second birth', a 'new kind of birth', which summed up the four years since his arrival. Disclaiming literary competence and ignoring for the most part

the intellectual outpourings of the Elizabethan age, Darling looked back with
a historian's eye. He proposed a cyclical view of history: creativity followed by
stagnation and decay, with dissatisfaction triggering renewed bursts of energy.
But beneath his mention of the innovating Elizabethans as 'all about twenty-one'
years old, clear and unmistakeable allusions to himself were discernible. Typical
of twenty-one, 'that most trying age', was a blend of arrogance and indifference,
when a man was keen to do good, to set the world right and to accomplish great
things. By twenty-one, 'the worst of those abominable inhibitions which made
life intolerable at seventeen' were finally shed. Furthermore, beyond twenty-one,
indeed until thirty-five (and Darling was now in his thirty-fifth year), a man
could 'no longer play with his beliefs':

> he must fight for them and for stability, the age during which a man finds his
> level in the world, sheds the illusions of his daydreams and recognises the limit
> of his capacities, the extent of his weaknesses, and discovers how far and with
> what aid he can face life.

His own middle age—'the beginning of a period of formalism, the prelude to
decay and discontent and the beginning again of the cycle'—was still some years
in the future. For the moment, however, despite the social ills of unemployment,
economic chaos and political uncertainties in Europe, Darling detected signs of
hope or even vigour in developments everywhere in science, the arts and music.
There were similar signs at Corio. 'I think all of us who left last year felt that we
were leaving just as the school was beginning to come into her own', wrote Alan
Brown, and 'it really does amount to a sort of resurrection of the dead', said Brian
Jones. Darling was also conscious that what the public schools should be doing
was exactly what he had been accomplishing: adapting old traditions to a new
environment. This was a period that later he looked back on nostalgically and, in
a subsequent bout of pessimism, told Bill Lloyd (then teaching in a preparatory
school in Dorset) that GGS in 1936 had suddenly become 'feebly mediocre' by
comparison. Be that as it may, by 1934 the infrastructure of Corio's renaissance
was in place. After six months respite in England, then, Darling could return to
tackle his next challenge: the restructuring of the curriculum.[34]

PATERFAMILIAS OF CORIO

1934–1939

'Look at these Australians—they're awfully nice, but they've got no inside to them. They're hollow. How are you going to build on such hollow stalks?'

D.H. Lawrence, *Kangaroo*

In the summer of 1933–34, Darling returned briefly to New Zealand. With Dicker, Gordon and Tunbridge he arrived in Wellington on 2 January with a dozen GGS boys. Old Christ's Collegians had organised a cricket tour. During some memorable matches, one of his GGS protégés, David Hay, averaged 67 runs for eight innings. After everyone else headed home, Darling and Dicker stayed with Dan Riddiford before returning to Corio at the end of January. One of the boys noted how Darling was 'one of us' out of school, and 'Headmaster and a bit more' in school. Shortly afterwards, the year's sweet start was soured by an automobile accident that killed a young woman. Darling was blameless, but the tragedy disturbed him. After watching cricket at Scotch College he had returned to Corio in his new Morris Isis with Dicker, Aunt Sib and her companion Hilda Lomax. At dusk a car coming from the opposite direction pulled out to pass the vehicle in front of it, into the path of Darling's oncoming car, and then headed for the verge on the passenger side of Darling's car. Darling steered between the two vehicles, whereupon the swerving driver veered directly into his path. Darling hurt his thumb, and the other three were thrown about badly and experienced delayed shock. Gerry Dicker recalled that his friend was 'much upset by the whole affair and the consequent coroner's inquest' which brought down a verdict of death by misadventure. Shamefaced, he confessed to his mother that his priorities had been wrong:

> I felt definitely horrid at the beginning of this term when I came back from New Zealand, quite resentful in my innermost heart at not having been made enough fuss of. Now something has happened which has been a bit of a lesson

to me, if taken in the right way and I only want to get away and hide myself.
Not that I expect the wholesome humility to last for long, but it has made me
think again this time and see something of how unpleasant I had become.

Aunt Sib reassured Jane Darling that he had not been at fault (about a year later
Darling was in another car accident, this time in Prahran, Melbourne, although
there were no fatalities).[1]

After the school council meeting on 9 April, Darling departed for England.
He was accompanied throughout the Middle East by his friend and fellow headmaster from Geelong College, the Reverend Frank Rolland. When he arrived
home he intended to see his friends and then the family at Trimley in August.
'Your sister said that you were looking splendid when you landed', wrote Michael
Thwaites. Manifold had been in England since March and the two of them
visited Charterhouse, where they dined in Brooke Hall and later inspected
the Oundle School's boarding houses. 'A nice kettle of fish' with the chairman
and headmaster absent simultaneously, Manifold jested. Darling then went to
Winchester where, after an 'unbelievably beautiful day', he wondered aloud to
Dicker (at Corio) whether:

> it is really wise to come home and stir myself up as I have been stirred up …
> There is so much here that we cannot even imitate, and from a distance
> Geelong seems so entirely unattractive that one cannot imagine how one got
> to like it when one was there.

He had 'long and interesting discussions' with Dr Brown; his friends had the
distinct impression that he had become his own man. In his absence the prefects
kept him up to speed with developments, gossip and trivia—Ned Austin's 'champion split infinitive' in chapel, 'which Mr Gordon pounced on'—and occasional
boarding house misdemeanours and the execution of 'swift and painful' summary
justice. They also reported on their fellow prefects and the masters:

> Poor Hay gets very worried at times, but we endeavour to cheer him up;
> George Lindon is excellent, and he and Hay are terribly funny, they walk
> round like a couple of guilty conspirators; I always spoil everything by saying
> in a loud voice: 'Found out anything?'

If the road death hadn't brought Darling back to earth, then school tragedies may
have done: a boarder died from peritonitis and another electrocuted himself.[2]
John Leach was severe on fellow prefects who put friendship ahead of their
responsibilities. Stories of visiting St Peter's and King's boys' exploits were regaled:
orgies of smoking and drinking by the former and, in the case of the latter, tales
of 'regular Orsinos'. Occasionally, Darling chided Leach for indiscretions, but
Bill Lloyd distinguished between pimping and pointing out avoidable mistakes.

C.A. Cameron (or Cacum, because he ended sentences with 'um') was relishing his temporary authority. He 'looks well, & I believe is filling the post of Acting Headmaster with calmness and wisdom', Thwaites noted from Trinity College, Melbourne, and in his first 'Kronikle' Leach reported that:

> Mr Cameron has taken the reins of government, and from what I can see, he intends to hold them tightly, He sits in your 'box' in Chapel, and is very dignified, he also signs himself A—Headmaster ... Lunch at present is rather a strain. On Tuesday Hay became mute, [Elliot] Grant talked volubly to Mr Austin, Sam [McCulloch] retired behind his fern, [Rupert] Hamer and Lindon chatted confidentially, so it was left to me to converse with A Headmaster.

McKie thought that things were going along nicely but towards the end of term detected 'a little creaking in the machinery'. Dicker also kept Darling updated and in anticipation of his friend's reluctant return flattered him about what he would discover.[3]

Dicker was right: his friend was sad to leave England. Manifold sympathised but said the mood would pass 'once you have made the break'. 'I feel very much inclined to make this spell my last spell in Australia', Darling wrote to his mother as the RM. *Berengaria* left Southampton, 'but I don't know that I should be much good in England and I am some sort of use out there'. With tears in his eyes, Austen (now seventy-seven) kissed his son goodbye, never to see him again. Then, as Louis Wharton had done in 1929, Bickersteth consoled Jane Darling with her son's 'unique' and 'splendid' work, his increasing influence and the hope that eventually he would be 'brought home' to a bigger English school. Darling departed in late August. En route to the United States he met Sybil Thorndike again, for whom it was a 'jolly voyage together' with cocktails on the palm court promenade deck and 'a yarn'. In New York, Keppel's assistant at the Carnegie Corporation assured him that his boss would come to GGS in the following year. In Toronto Darling met Bickersteth's brother, Burgon, then Hamilton Fyfe and his wife Dorothea at Kingston, and finally Hugh Derry at Winnipeg. He read a lot and (surprisingly) was secretary of the ship's sports committee.[4]

An enigmatically worded letter reached Trimley. It said that 'other and more important reasons for it having been a good trip' home would be revealed in late October. This was an oblique reference to the fact that he had fallen 'very much in love' with a young Melbourne woman. The first hint of romance came to Trimley from the RMS *Aorangi* as it approached Auckland. Darling's state of mind was a far cry from earlier in the year when, resigned to being single, he complained of being starved of 'the ordinary affections of mankind'. He had tried to make light of bachelorhood. 'I do really feel the lack of anyone to be really fond of', he had moaned to his mother:

and I don't see any chance of falling in love, at least not now that I have
seen the divine Marlene Dietrich in 'The Shanghai Express', the most perfect
creature ever made, with a voice like silver moonshine. I suppose Eaton loves
her too.

E.D.C. Lake, from Charterhouse, recalled his wife saying that Darling's sensible
justification for marriage had been that 'it would be so nice to have some one
in the room to whom you need not talk all the time'. Manifold's antidote to his
friend's bleak moods and complaints about indigestion was that he 'get married':

> I have hesitated a long time about adding this—not because I have any doubt
> about my advice being good, but because she will have to be a very special girl.
> I think you are much too good at other things to be very good at this. Indeed,
> you have admitted as much.[5]

Darling's elder sister was not averse to matchmaking and had she had her
way he might have married Joan Brett, whom she befriended on her way out
to Corio. Brett (almoner at the Royal Melbourne Hospital) shared a common
interest with Margaret's brother in the resolution of social problems. Occasionally
she spent a weekend at Corio with Margaret who reported to Trimley that he
and Brett 'have the most profound discussions on religion & social problems &
thoroughly enjoy themselves'. Margaret had intended to return with him in 1934
provided that 'he had not picked up a wife on the way'. Returning home the year
before she wrote:

> I should be sorry to think I was not going to see Corio again as I have a
> great affection for the school and am now getting to know more of the boys.
> Anyhow I seem to be rather committed now to having my affections torn
> between two continents which is certain to be difficult especially as they are
> such widely separate ones.

Darling revealed how much he had depended on her and suggested that she
return in January, although his new romantic attachment altered matters. The
young woman was Margaret Dunlop Campbell, the elder daughter of John
Dewar Campbell (who had died in 1931) and Margaret Henrietta Campbell
(neé Dunlop). She was nineteen years old. They had been introduced soon after
the *Aorangi* left Vancouver. Now more than ever Darling needed his mother's
counsel. In October he wrote twice to ask that she break his news 'gently' to his
sister. That same month Miss Campbell agreed to marry him. Early in November,
when Melbourne gossip was 'beyond all hope', he contacted his sister again to
thank her and asked her to return to Corio. His friends were delighted with the
engagement. J.D.G. Medley (head, Tudor House, Moss Vale)—whom Darling
had met in 1932 and with whom he stayed regularly when returning from

Camden—jested about an aunt, 'possibly Dunlop', who had telephoned about his friend: 'I gave such replies as my fancy dictated to me and hope that I have not blasted your bliss by over-emphasis on your good qualities'. Penny Gullett exclaimed: 'what a slump there will be in widows:—Ha Ha' and Dorothea Fyfe congratulated him on his 'unknown Goddess', teasing him with the salutation 'Darling Darling'. Finally, Temple trusted that the young lady 'will be firm with you' and, in his inimitable way said: 'may the joys of matrimony strengthen your swishing arm—and even improve your service at tennis'.[6]

The wedding was scheduled for August 1935. Meanwhile Darling tackled the reorganisation of the curriculum, having told Dicker when at Winchester:

> I think that we'll do it and risk it. It implies cutting out the Intermediate and risking a good deal with the Leaving, but it also implies much less marked and competitive schoolwork. It is like all that I do, a compromise.

His antagonism towards the Intermediate stemmed from his belief that education ought to be geared to the capacities of young people. In his chapter in P.R. Cole's book, *The Education of the Adolescent in Australia*, he claimed that, sandwiched between primary and university education, there were conflicting views about secondary education's purpose. University requirements were overriding and he was determined to sever the link. Secondary education was a 'continuation' of the primary stage, not a vehicle for university preparation, and had to lead a boy:

> through adolescence, continuing the disciplined training of the mind which was begun when he learned to add and to multiply, to develop any natural aptitudes which he may possess, in such a way that he can use and enjoy them all his life, to teach him independence, to think honestly and to have a right judgement, to give him a thirst for wisdom and understanding, to make him a knowledgeable citizen of a complicated world and an honourable and unselfish member of a democratic community, to help him towards usefulness in a society which pays only for services rendered, but above all to make him capable of arriving at a standard of values and of having the moral courage to abide by them.

Secondary education should begin no later than age thirteen. It ought to further develop the knowledge acquisition under way at the primary level in arithmetic and English grammar (rather than knowledge acquisition *per se*), comprise half of the desired ingredients of a liberal education (advanced mathematics, Latin and general science) with the other half of the curriculum focused on 'actual living' (the social sciences, literature, religion, the arts and physical training), and free of the tyranny of examinations.[7]

Darling attacked the Intermediate as anachronistic in the *Sydney Mail Schools' Number*. Because it served no useful purpose for boys capable of taking the

Leaving and was not required by businesses, it should be abolished. Completion of the Leaving and subsequent specialised work was sufficient to satisfy university matriculation requirements. Darling confirmed the Intermediate's abandonment on speech day in 1934, with his new scheme:

> ... designed to insist upon the minimum basis of a secondary education, and to allow the individual a facility which he has not previously possessed of developing his peculiar capacities according to his peculiar tastes. It ought to prevent any boy from feeling that he is a failure, because he finds academic work difficult.

From 1935 the four stages at GGS would be: primary (until age eleven and a half), post-primary (eleven-and-a-half to fifteen-and-a-half years), Leaving Certificate (fifteen-and-a-half to sixteen-and-a-half years) and senior school. After primary, the subject groupings were to be: 'training' (Latin, with German later and mathematics); 'compulsory' (general science and English); and, 'interest' (history, geography, French, music, art, manual work and English literature). Beyond post-primary, boys could complete a preparatory Leaving year or the Leaving, followed by either honours work in the VIth specialist form or a non-specialist public affairs form for boys not intending to go to university, the purpose of which was 'preparation for citizenship in a democratic country'. The net effect was to create three separate schools (or pathways): normal, agriculture and business.[8]

Acclamation followed. R.K. Whately (Director, Victorian Vocational and Child Guidance Centre) was 'delighted' by the emphasis on individual differences. Theodore Fink (chairman of directors of the *Herald* and the earlier Royal Commission on Technical Education—which laid the foundations of Victorian secondary education) praised him for emphasising individuality and assisting boys to resist potent and 'deadening herd influences'. For Frank Shann (head, Trinity Grammar School), Australia now had in GGS a school that was 'comparable with the best of the English public schools', while R.B. Coutts (head, Huntingtower School) said that GGS was fast becoming 'an educational mecca'. Parkinson was ecstatic. Darling's timetable was 'almost everything that a timetable ought to be and I regard it with the utmost envy'. Finally, James McRae (Hansen's successor as Director of Education) said that he stood 'solidly behind you in the reforms which you have outlined'. He had quoted Darling's address at several recent speech nights. Unsolicited praise persisted into the new year and a former pupil, Bill Landale (New College, Oxford), reported that Oxonian OGGs were interested and thought that the scheme would prepare businessmen 'possessing a sound practical education'. In early February, after a weekend at GGS, Browne asked Darling to deliver the eighth John Smyth Memorial Lecture:

> I am perfectly sure that your scheme of reorganisation is the most important experiment being carried out in Australia at present. I am worried that you

are a little despondent about it—Australian education is at the cross-roads, &
your school will have a great deal to do with determining future directions.

Cunningham included two pages devoted entirely to the new GGS scheme in
his Australian education chapter for the 1936 *Year Book of Education*, and how
it 'recognises the primary function of the school as that of equipping pupils for
intelligent citizenship'. Finally, Kandel congratulated him on a 'masterly analysis'
in his book chapter for Cole. He regretted the training and content dualism in
the 'traditional' psychological justification for Darling's new curriculum, but saw
merit in education being less academically remote.[9]

The euphoria of this highly favourable reception quickly dissipated as there
was a £5000 loss in 1934, £1000 more than anticipated. When Dicker departed
for Winchester before speech day, he thought that councillors were 'getting pan-
icky' but Darling told Manifold that there was no reason for disquiet. The fee
increase from £141 to £165 in 1936 would cover the £1000 and the anticipated
1935 loss, even with a possible attrition of thirty boarders. And because the new
scheme had undoubtedly 'hit the popular nail on the head', financial cheeseparing would detract from its impact, whereas properly handled it would be 'a
better advertisement than anything which we have done'. It was important to
capitalise on it. The imperative was not to convey outward distress about the
deficit, regardless of inward feelings of alarm. The Reverend W.P.F. Morris
(head, Brisbane Grammar School and a former GGS master) thought that the
fee increase would isolate GGS even further from the mainstream. 'The average
Australian' would query the return to the country given by church schools and
Labor politicians would ask: 'why should Manifold and Fairbairn pay £200 a year
for their boys' education? Tax the b—s more!' Darling's reply transposed exclusivity (Manifold's concern) into virtuous service: GGS's increased fees would
provide high-end market cover for other independent schools. If there was no
alternative to investing capital to raise schoolmasters' status and get the best educationally, then 'lesser' Melbourne schools could follow suit and 'still compete
with us'. GGS's difficulty was that to be built to the scale 'as we eventually hope
to have it', small specialist senior classes and high overheads constrained it. He
knew that he was 'extravagant in what I want to provide for the money' but in
wealthy Victoria such fee increases were sustainable. He was mindful of exclusiveness and GGS's plutocratic connections, and whether such a school ought to
exist in Australia, but all that could be done about the existing social system was
for favourably positioned boys to accept their wider responsibilities. He loathed
GGS being the rich man's school, but he had a duty 'to provide more in the way
of educational experiment and practice than less fortunately placed schools can
manage'. Morris was floored: 'You have the mind of a great leader and statesman'.
There was no way in a state 'practically socialised already' that he could replicate
Darling's plans. Church-provided schooling post-dated forty years of state-sub-
sidised secondary education and Queensland was nowhere near as prosperous.[10]

There was no denying GGS's exclusiveness. The 1934 fee increase to £141 had already made it more expensive for boarders than eight other Victorian Church of England boys' schools and way beyond the reach of most Australian parents. Capital city average weekly earnings in 1933 were £3 5s and two of every three Australian male breadwinners earned £155 annually or less. Three-quarters of GGS admissions for 1930–39 were Anglicans and 20 per cent Presbyterian. About 40 per cent of Australians were Anglicans, but only 9 per cent attended fee-paying schools. Furthermore, 90 per cent of GGS boys were boarders, 60 per cent came to Corio for between four and seven years and, four out of every five of those enrolling came from fee-paying preparatory schools or were educated privately or by governesses. Virtually all GGS fathers were professionals (35 per cent), businessmen (33 per cent) or landed (31 per cent). Indeed, one in every three boys admitted in Darling's first decade was the son of a grazier or a doctor. Even though Australian wealth was more evenly spread in the 1930s (compared with fifty years earlier), GGS boys were from families at the upper income levels of three occupational strata that comprised less than half the national workforce. So comparatively well-off were most GGS parents that, after a confirmation service in 1932, Margaret told her mother that the parents' appearance 'did not make one think that the depression was affecting them very seriously as they all had large cars & much jewellery'. She supposed that she had 'never met wealthy people before', but certainly she had 'never seen so much & such beautiful jewellery as I do out here'.[11]

One denominational feature of this exclusiveness galled Darling. The council's policy towards non-Protestant boys (a handful of Jews and Catholics) required parents to sign a form denying special treatment for worship. This barrier deterred the parents and the rabbi of one Jewish boy, Zelman (later Sir Zelman) Cowen, who enrolled instead at Scotch: 'you knew just how much I wanted to come to Geelong Grammar'. In 1935, the Sydney mother of a Catholic boy signed the form and was horrified when he was unable to attend a weekly mass in Geelong. 'I strongly disapprove of the policy of making it difficult for R.C.s to come to the school', Darling told Manifold, as it was unwise and unchristian. If the boy could attend mass and confession once a month, then mother and son would be content. Manifold was sympathetic but annoyed that a matter of principle had been foisted on the school in a manner not of its own choosing. Darling talked to Archbishop Head, who thought that the monthly proposal was fine. Manifold agreed that the suggestion might allay the Presbyterian councillors' fears and dissuade them from seeing this case as 'a matter of life and death'. He was correct. In future Darling exercised discretion in enrolling Catholics and arranging monthly mass attendance.[12]

Despite the acclaim of Browne, who thought that if Melbourne Grammar could appoint someone like his friend after Franklin's retirement then Victorian education would really go places, and Frensham's headmistress, Winifred West, who thought that GGS had been 'pulled together' since her last visit, Darling wanted tangible evidence of his reforms' impact. In 1935, he detected improved results at the universities of Melbourne and Cambridge, and in the scholarship results for Trinity and Queen's colleges (Melbourne). More able boys had been accelerated through to Leaving, but badly prepared boys coming to GGS and those aged ten to thirteen 'with whom we ourselves have failed to deal' remained a headache. Perhaps the ground lost prior to the age of thirteen could not be made up or parents had inflated expectations of their sons' capacity to cope with the Leaving. A major success was the new public affairs form under J.C. Nield. In 1936 Darling split it in two, with both classes taking non-examinable general and vocational subjects, and the second working at an advanced level. In that year more than fifty boys had already passed the Leaving Certificate and would continue for one or two more years. For the first time, hardly any boys remained who were admitted prior to his arrival and not educated exclusively on his preferred lines. Following Jim Mann's success in 1932, Michael Thwaites had just been named Rhodes Scholar for Victoria—GGS's second ever—and other boys won university exhibitions. In future, there would be an upper and a lower VIth form, with a more generalised curriculum that was expected to generate even stronger university results. Furthermore, Geelong House day boys over the past seven years had done remarkably well, both scholastically and on leaving school, so that the arrangements to facilitate their travel and that of Bostock House boys had been worthwhile.[13]

External opinion endorsed Darling's redirection of the school. Giblin, for example, told his wife how he had stopped over at Corio and discovered how 'boys being encouraged to think for themselves are doing so and the results are sometimes embarrassing', although this was 'all right I think'. Two of Browne's Diploma of Education trainees provided comprehensive observations of GGS after three weeks in residence (when Darling was in England). Both 'looked very frightened the first day', Leach confided, but they were 'rather nice, although rather professional in school'. A.J.M. Davies was astounded by GGS's thoroughness in pursuing its aims and struck by how the substitution of tables for classroom desks transformed 'a well drilled audience focussed on a master into a co-operating community'. The entire range of a boy's needs seemed to be adequately catered for, and the workshops provided practical activities for those for whom intensive bookwork was drudgery. He had never seen a school in which music, art, military work, debating and acting were so naturally absorbed into the daily routine. Sport was no longer merely competition between experts as elsewhere, but also genuine exercise and games. GGS was a community 'which really means business'. C.J. Horne concurred. The school's tone denoted 'a willing and happy co-operation between boys and masters, with the prefect body working as a most efficient link'. The school definitely wanted boys to think for themselves. He had 'nothing but praise' for English teaching in the VIth, 'pianos are numerous' and every conceivable interest was catered for. Horne had 'never trained and played with finer or cleaner fellows' in sport, and GGS was developing 'the all-round man who will not fail to make his way'.[14]

Darling had left little to chance. In 1930 he had introduced assessment of intelligence and vocational aptitude to guide curriculum decisions, mainly as a 'check upon ourselves'. (Fintona Girls' School did likewise in 1935 and so too did Littlejohn's successor—Gilray—at Scotch.):

> They sometimes help one to decide whether a boy is industrious but imbecile when one has put him down as intelligent but idle. It is a very real danger that we may fall into, and I.Q's are useful though with a more limited usefulness than the real enthusiasts claim.

Boys aged ten to thirteen admitted to the junior or senior schools were tested. Darling took comfort from the close correlation between the 1930 testing of thirty-three GGS boys with IQs above 100 and thirty-eight eighteen-year-olds five years later who had reached Intermediate standard (nine boys), Leaving (nineteen boys) or were qualified to enter a university (ten boys). In 1938, Whately was contracted to test the capacity to reason, the extent of a boy's vocabulary, speed of reading, aptitude for accountancy and for draughtsmanship, capacity to calculate arithmetically and manual dexterity. Henceforward boys' results were reported to parents. Whately's assessments were made without consulting the masters' records and 'in the majority of cases his report will co-incide with our ideas'. Prior to recording Whately's results, boys' cards contained purely personal information and health details, along with a comment by Darling (for example, 'A person of considerable interest with a brain above the ordinary and a will of his own. Often perverse and very difficult to convince but might do quite well').[15]

Every so often, Darling wondered whether the tone and condition of the school were actually improving. In 1935, he uncovered instances of boarding house immorality. A Tudor House boy sent by Medley, already dreading the prospect of boarding house life, was distressed about alleged 'vice' and had started absconding. It was unclear who alarmed him: some Grammarians on an earlier trip down, one of Medley's masters or the boy's father. Darling was aware of 'a row' about bad influences in Cuthbertson while he was away in England. Five years earlier, Rod Andrew was incredulous after being woken for a hasty late-night conference with Masterman and a senior Perry boy when they found out about goings-on in Cuthbertson. Darling conceded that there were still pockets of vice in the houses but that the prefects and housemasters had mostly contained them, and was adamant that 'more muck comes into this school than goes out of it'. 'It's a glorious life, isn't it?', he quipped to Medley, when dismissing the Tudor House master's possible rumour-mongering as 'rather an overdose of New South Wales patriotism'. The master concerned admitted to having heard 'a good deal of common room gossip in Sydney about Geelong as an abode of vice', but denied passing it on to boys heading to Corio. Was GGS a 'hotbed of vice', the boy's father had asked Medley:

> I said that at any big school you could get into a hotbed, if you wanted to, that my own son was there and was not as far as I could see, a frequenter of hotbeds, that I knew you well enough to assure him that no serious hotbed would exist for long while you were headmaster ... It is, of course, quite incredible that a boy like [—] could get into even a small hotbed within 2 or 3 days of his arrival at a new school, unless the school was of such a kind that it consisted entirely of hotbeds!

The incident made Darling despondent. Excessive vigilance was perhaps calling forth 'a bag of victims and the stench of corruption' as 'these matters do tend to come in waves'.[16]

The school 'never seems to have been worse and I discover one crime after another', Darling complained to his mother. He appealed to Manifold for a long talk about the school's 'rotten state'. No stone had been left unturned in trying to improve it, and yet 'the moral standard remains much worse than it should be'. He had just that minute punished two boys 'caught in the same business':

> I don't believe that more restrictions on liberty would make things any better, but am tempted to impose them. The only real hope lies in greater keenness in everything and the diminution of the feeling of failure which so many boys have. They lose faith in themselves, then they lose their self-respect and then the trouble begins.

His new scheme of work would engage boys in interesting activities, but it implied less supervision and more opportunity for wrongdoing by those disinclined to respond. Should one endorse the necessary freedom or play safe? If any factor was to blame it was the size of the houses. This latest incident was a tragedy because he believed that he had been making headway, whereas he was 'forced back on to the belief that there is something radically wrong with the way I run things'. Manifold urged him to stick to his guns and not restrict liberties. He could not understand boys' feelings of failure. 'Are we pushing them too hard in work, & does it arise from getting lost[?]' he wondered. And how did they have the time to be so introspective? McKie told Leach about Darling's woes and Leach wondered whether the fault was his from the previous year. In the end the visit of the Japanese Christian social reformer, Toyohiko Kagawa, helped alleviate Darling's distress. Kagawa addressed huge crowds with his 'testimonies for Christ': 115,000 people at 178 meetings in sixty-seven days in Australia, and over 80,000 in New Zealand and Hawaii. He was at Corio when Darling was experiencing periodic anguish in 'reconciling my position here in a school which depends for its existence on a social system of which I cannot approve'. Listening to Kagawa was the perfect antidote, with his 'astonishingly versatile and deep mind' and 'immense calm', with the power of God working in him to such an extent, Darling told his mother, that he could do the work of ten men without getting weaker. Priestley chaired a public lecture and was equally impressed, but thought that Kagawa's social science was a bit suspect.[17]

If the boarding houses were to blame for vice and filth, rectification of overcrowding was impossible unless council would allocate more money. In August 1935, the *Corian* published Darling's three-page building plan. A new boarding house was Darling's first priority because it would facilitate increased senior school enrolments and relieve the pressure on Manifold and Cuthbertson. An appeal had raised about £1100. Next, he wanted more accommodation for married masters, better provision for concerts and gymnastics, proper music facilities, workshop extensions, improved art and library facilities, completion of the chapel, and additional general classrooms and laboratories. The estimated cost was £40,000. He submitted his plans to council in February 1936. With Turnbull and Thewlis, he approached AMP for another loan, but was now in an awkward position. By procuring the loan, he told his mother, 'we shall make it impossible to do any more for many years to come', and if he departed GGS then his successor would have little to spend. Councillors were aware of this possibility and he speculated that they might want a guarantee of his willingness to remain for a specified period. Appointment to a similar job at home was unlikely if he was much older than forty-two, he thought, but for the time being he wanted to complete what he had started. His worries were groundless: AMP agreed to a further loan of £20,000, sufficient to fund a new boarding house, and in July council endorsed Darling's suggestion to name it Francis Brown House.[18]

At the July council meeting, he also tabled a report from McKie that showed 'how utterly inadequate' the facilities were for teaching music, whereupon it was agreed to launch an appeal to build an art and a music school. Darling estimated that a building for art would cost about £3000, with a further £8000 needed for a music school. By the following March (1937), council had approved the construction of the art school (costing nearer £5000) paid for by Whittingham estate money. Curthoys secured maximum publicity in the *Argus*. The two-storey building's shell would be erected by the contractors, with the interior furnished and equipped by boys under art staff supervision. The new facility would provide, in addition to painting and drawing, leatherwork, pottery, weaving, forge work, photography, printing and smithing. Next, thanks to a £10,000 donation by Max Bell's family, the music school could also be constructed and equipped. To the singing of massed house choirs and brass band accompaniment, the English conductor Dr Malcolm Sargent opened it in August 1938. In accepting this gift on behalf of the school, Manifold thanked the four donors and confessed that 'never, in our wildest dreams, have we conjured anything so near perfection as this wonderful reality—a complete unit, perfect in its minutest detail; beautiful, and so exactly suited to our every need'.[19]

Darling's expansion plans were now accomplished. Despite the battle for money, the comparatively easy acceptance of his reforms surprised him. Apart from the recent generation of old boys, whom 'you will never satisfy', he said to a beleaguered V.L. Johnstone (head, Southport School), he had had pretty much everything in his favour, whereas Johnstone could not win over his old boys; he had not been forgiven for trying to get rid of the cadet corps and the Brisbane general public was being sticky. Darling recounted the loyalty of old boys aged over forty-five and yet, like Parkinson at King's and Bickersteth at St Peter's, he felt mostly 'distrusted and disliked' by those from the last twenty years. A 'first-class and thoroughly loyal second master [Cameron]', who knew how people would react to proposals, was also important:

> It is sometimes necessary to damn the consequences, but I think it is most important to choose the ground on which one is going to fight, and only fight about what is really important.

Timing and connections with other schools had also worked to Darling's advantage in strengthening GGS's marketability. Within four years of his appointment two senior APS headmasters, Adamson (Wesley) and Littlejohn (Scotch), died after very long incumbencies. After the death of Father Frost (rector of Xavier) in 1932 and Franklin's retirement from Melbourne Grammar in late 1936, only Rolland was senior in experience. But at just thirty-seven, Darling was more influential educationally. After Bickersteth's departure and with Parkinson in hot water at King's—he threw in the towel in 1938—Darling's only serious rival for public pre-eminence in boys' education was probably L.C. Robson (head, Sydney Church of England Grammar School—or Shore). Not only had Priestley been struck by Browne's high regard for Darling, but also by the latter's influence on Gilray's plans for Scotch. Darling's curriculum changes were also a topic of conversation at Government House, Priestley discovered, and they were the object of envy elsewhere. When he mentioned GGS to P.M. Hammond, of Brisbane Boys' College in 1937, Priestley was 'surprised to come again up against the rather bitter jealousy and envy that Darling's show engenders in the breast of his rivals'. Hammond scoffed that 'anyone could do what Darling had done if he had the money that was forthcoming at Geelong', but Priestley begged to differ.[20]

As well as being in the right place at the right time, Darling had also strengthened Geelong and Melbourne connections. He knew that day-boy admissions from the provincial city were a powerful public relations weapon: 'The School cannot but suffer from the criticism that it is snobbish and the exclusion of Day Boys would inevitably be construed as such'. Until 1936, £48 purchased a day boy's tuition, membership of clubs, homework supervision and two meals daily for a year. For another £4 10s a boy was collected at Corio railway station in the morning and returned home by 9 pm. But nothing could be taken for granted. (Charles Hawker warned him about a 'fashion for local schooling'

in Adelaide and that several Geelong families 'have slipped to St Peter's'.) In
Melbourne, Darling cemented links with fee-paying preparatory schools. The
numbers admitted from Miss McComas' Glamorgan in Toorak were decreasing
by the mid-1930s, but during the years 1933–39 twenty-two boys came from
Miss Adderley's Adwalton in East Malvern. His big success was the attraction
of Melbourne Grammar boys. About a third of GGS admissions in the 1930s
were from the metropolitan area and sixty-one (six per year) left GGS's bigger
Melbourne rival for Corio. So strong was GGS's encroachment into Melbourne
Grammar's territory, especially during the instability after Franklin's departure,
that for six of ten years in the 1930s over half GGS's Melbourne admissions came
from just seven Yarraside suburbs, particularly Toorak and South Yarra. The fact
that Franklin's replacement, Stacey Colman (Archbishop Head's thirty-year-
old nephew from Shrewsbury), was not a raging success also helped. Despite
Bickersteth's assurance that he was very good academically and Giblin's view
that he was boyishly irresponsible, the word from Fletcher in England was that
Colman was 'too finely touched' and lacked 'the toughness of fibre needed'. After
presenting the speech-day prizes at Melbourne Grammar in 1937, Priestley
thought Colman was in for a 'sticky time'. By April he had resigned due to
ill health—and was sequestered in a remote seaside cottage out of Melbourne
society's gaze. Beyond the state capital, GGS's market was mostly Victorian, but
Darling's other triumph was his understanding with Medley, who sent twenty-
eight boys down to Corio. Medley kept his pupils until thirteen and prepared
them with 'our ideas of what is necessary'.[21]

Not only did GGS's growth occur at the expense of prestigious APS schools,
but also the 'lesser' ones that Darling had claimed would benefit from the mul-
tiplier effect of his fee increase. Alistair Crombie (later, History and Philosophy
of Science, Oxford University) was the first Whittingham scholar admitted to
GGS in 1930 and the Reverend Morris (his former headmaster) protested that
'the rich man is taking one of my ewe-lambs'. The estate's vast sum for a well-
endowed school 1600 kilometres away was intended to lure a boy from his home
state and a Queensland school to boot, as though neither were good enough for
him. When Darling quibbled about the lad's capacity, Morris was stung: 'For six
years I have taught, nursed and cared for this boy', and yet '"the rich man" not
only takes him but wants me to examine his wool and flesh to see if it is up to the
standard of the rich man's table!' Likewise, the Reverend S.R. Dickinson (head,
Haileybury College) had felt aggrieved when he lost a boy to GGS in the third
term of 1935, his parents having been advised (like another Haileybury family
two years previously) that a place could not necessarily be guaranteed for their
boy at GGS in February:

> One does not enjoy being fined ten or twelve guineas for having done very
> well by a desirable boy, especially when it would be so much better for him to
> start off scratch in a new school at the opening of a year.

Able boys who left in September also forfeited the chance of winning prizes. In this instance, Darling justified himself by arguing that early enrolment ensured that incoming boys got used to doing things in the GGS way, which was 'rather different from that of other schools', before beginning their first year in the senior school with 'a clear year after they have become acclimatized'.[22]

In March 1938, Darling explained to readers of the New Education Fellowship's *New Era* that he had succeeded in encouraging more and more boys into the professions. (For 1930–39, about 40 per cent annually of GGS leavers entered the professions or universities.) In addition to maintaining GGS's Christian tradition, ensuring that boys were prepared for their examinations and developing their natural aptitudes, he also felt obliged 'to train boys to take part in a democratic community which still badly needs constructive statesmanship'. He championed this theme of service and *noblesse oblige* on speech day after speech day. To rebut the claim that GGS reproduced privilege, Darling believed that he had to send out men 'who will be of value to Australia'. That was 1931. A year later he said: 'If we, with all our chances, cannot do what is right, we are failing in our duty'. Having located a vocation that was not already overcrowded 'for the boy with brains and the anxiety to be of use in the world', he promoted the Commonwealth Public Service (CPS) to parents:

> The Civil Service is one of the noblest of professions, if it is properly regarded and our best boys should be able to aim at leading in it. At the moment, owing to the recruiting age and various conditions, the Civil Service seems closed ... This is a dangerous state of affairs for it is just by filling those services that the English Public Schools have contributed something to England.

Unlike at Home, where Oxbridge graduates populated the upper levels of the civil service, the chief stumbling block was the preference accorded ex-servicemen in post–World War I CPS recruitment. Indeed, 'the pre-1934 situation on the whole was depressing': only 49 out of nearly 1800 junior clerks appointed after 1918 were school-leavers possessing the Leaving Certificate. During the Depression the CPS was increasingly attractive to 'able school-leavers and their parents', but only in 1935 did the Public Service Board try to attract boys by restoring competitive examinations held in conjunction with the Leaving Certificate. So sluggish was the infusion of school-leavers, however, that by 1939 they comprised fewer than 17 per cent of the CPS.[23]

To be a realistic vocational option, then, there had to be provision for graduate entry as administrative and clerical officers. Pressure on the Public Service Board for such admission had mounted in the 1920s, especially from the universities. Dismissively, Darling told his mother that the public service was 'recruited almost entirely from the High Schools and the Roman Catholic Schools and as a result is not a very well-educated or stable body'. And yet (to his credit), if the social composition was as imbalanced as he asserted then he refused to rectify it by capitulating to sectarian pressures. In 1936, when the Diocese of Melbourne was concerned about the number of Catholic CPS recruits and the archbishop's attention was drawn to the desirability of increasing the proportion of Church of England entrants, Darling saw no merit in the idea. 'It is rather a serious matter I think', he told Head:

> not so much that other people get into the Civil Service, as that our boys do not seem ready to make the sacrifice of personal prospects and comfort entailed by offering themselves for the Services.

The real problem, Darling thought, was that the desire for personal gain prevented young men from entering, rather than 'lack of knowledge, opportunity, or need'. Earlier (1932), with the backing of the Headmasters' Conference of Australia and the support of Hawker (Minister of Commerce), Darling tried to have the conditions of entry to the CPS altered. After a deputation with Littlejohn to the prime minister (J.A. Lyons) and further pressure on Hawker, legislation was passed in December 1933 permitting up to 10 per cent of annual CPS positions to be filled by university graduates after a successful entrance examination to the third division.[24]

A related cause championed by Darling was national service. Over dinner one night in 1936 a state politician from the UAP, W.S. Kent Hughes, had tried kindling his enthusiasm for an Australian youth movement:

> I asked the VIth. form and the P.A. forms this morning whether they would like to be drafted for three months into a Labour Camp in between school and university, or school and business, the idea being that they would be mixed up irrespective of class and put on to manual work of some value to the country, e.g. Gippsland. The voting was 36 in favour and 16 against, most of the No's admitting that it would be good for them even if they did not like it.

Shortly afterwards, Browne tried to interest him in a teacher-exchange scheme for young Germans. Although he saw value in Kent Hughes' idea, Darling was sceptical and told Browne that he didn't know how to make it work. He also said that 'I hate the Nazi movement so much myself that I feel I might offend [a German on exchange] myself with every word I uttered'. With the international situation worsening, however, by 1938 he accepted the need for national military preparedness or mobilisation and Australia could be a model for what a country should be. Giblin and Copland (who had been pressing the Commonwealth to formulate a national defence program) concurred. Darling's major concern was manpower preparation and leadership, especially among schoolboys. 'I agree with Jim Fairbairn's remarks in the Argus this morning (Friday)', he told Copland, 'about the necessity for consecutive periods of training', whether voluntary or compulsory, with the new National Fitness movement possibly playing a role in preparing leaders and recruits. He and Copland then urged delegates at the Australian and New Zealand Association for the Advancement of Science (ANZAAS) conference in Canberra in January 1939 to take seriously the European military build-up, but they were howled down. Even so, recalled the English Fabian socialist H.G. Wells (who attended ANZAAS), the conference deliberations had moved quickly from the ubiquitous bushfires then raging to the very real possibility of incendiary bombing attacks on Australia and the problems of coastal defence.[25]

Immediately after ANZAAS, Darling inaugurated national service in the belief that if the nation was invaded then its resourcefulness and untapped capacities would be called on. In addition to one afternoon of cadets, another was devoted to training boys in first aid, fire-fighting, drainage construction and prevention of soil erosion, surveying and map-making and construction of a miniature rifle range. With instruction provided by the school's tradesmen, the boys' skill training was extended to include signalling, lifesaving, physical training, carpentry, mechanics, bricklaying, forge work, painting and electrical work, riding, camping, cooking, stump grubbing, driving and, later, air-raid precautions. Idealistic talk of service became 'the much more exacting task of doing that service', with the boys bettering themselves and contributing to the wider community:

> Thus, if a boys' club in Melbourne or Geelong wants to be fitted out as a gymnasium or to have any carpentry work done, or if a youth hostel requires a swimming pool or a camp site prepared, a party of boys more or less capable is sent away to do the work for them. In addition, we run regular holiday camps, particularly in connection with forestry work which is much needed in this State and would not otherwise be done owing to the scarcity of money and labour.

Thus, national service at GGS was justified as a practical way of developing citizenship and of coordinating efforts for the common good. In 1939, Giblin thought that Darling's scheme was 'doing very well & making pretty strong roots' and that Bull (the master in charge) 'had done a first rate job'. 'I should say his patience and tolerance were just the qualities required for the tender young plant.'[26]

This initiative was grist to Darling's mill in publicising GGS as a showpiece, for which Curthoys was an important publicist. So taken was he with Darling's reforms that, after resigning from the *Argus*, he became an unpaid agent: 'If at any time you want help in discreet publicity for the school, you only have to ask for it'. Instead of simply reacting to uninvited negative publicity, proactive promotion of the school was a tactical switch by Darling. When the *Sydney Mail* approached him in 1934 he replied that the policy was 'not to advertise' the school. In 1937, however, he acceded willingly to Curthoys' advice that 'we must feed the papers gently':

The general procedure, I think,—if you approve—shd be that you will send
me rough notes of the subject matter you have decided is suitable to [sic]
publicity, I will then prepare a draft of publicity matter and submit it to you,
you will approve, reject or amend it as you think fit, and when it is approved,
I will circulate it to the newspapers on your behalf.

Curthoys sought simultaneous publicity in all the dailies, but this was unworkable
as not all produced school columns on the same day and the afternoon *Herald*
refused to publish material already appearing elsewhere in the morning. Darling
appreciated the lengths to which Curthoys went on GGS's behalf, and when
he saw what a splendid job his friend had done in one report he confessed that
journalism was clearly not as easy as it looked. Thanks to Curthoys a detailed
report on GGS's third pageant play, *Alpha and Omega*, appeared in *The Times
Educational Supplement* (as earlier with *The Aeneid* and *The Dynasts*). *Alpha and
Omega* was prepared in just five weeks and performed in October 1936, to the
north of the chapel. Every junior and senior boy took part in this biblical drama
written by two staff members and a boy, for which all the costumes and sets
were made at Corio after a year's study in divinity classes of the prophet Isaiah
and the apostle Paul. It was presented as an act of worship, and was yet another
object lesson for Darling in a school working together and boys making willing
sacrifices. Two years later, GGS mobilised itself for the fourth and final time
during the 1930s when, before an audience of more than 500 people, the boys
performed Dickens' *Pickwick Papers*.[27]

Another interesting variation from the norm generated considerable publicity when Darling scheduled an exhibition and inspection in May 1938 to
replace the usual speech day. Again he conferred with Curthoys about doing
something a little different. The exhibition was 'what I call first-class publicity', Curthoys said: 'I hope that won't shock you'. Darling invited Frank Tate to
open it. The aim was to allow visitors to see the school in operation. There were
twenty-six sections in the displays in locations such as the chapel, the library and
the public affairs form. He introduced Tate by praising him for having done more
for education in Victoria than anyone else and thanked him for being a friend of
GGS. Every school society, club and group took part. Cunningham, Curthoys
and Priestley all came down over the weekend. Priestley thought that Tate made
'just the right sort of speech' but Darling's chapel sermon on the topic of the body
and its members bothered him:

> As a result I fancy that the term 'orange-suckers' will be replaced by the term
> 'appendix' as a title for the useless members of the Community at the school.
> My brain works queerly. I was quite interested in following his argument,
> but he used as an analogy the crippling effect of the loss of a leg even to a
> centipede. One half of my brain for the remainder of the service was puzzling
> itself with the exact effect on the gait of a centipede of the loss of a pair of legs.

By contrast, Curthoys thought that Darling 'touched a high-water mark' with his sermon. From a publicity point of view, the entire weekend was a triumph, he said, but best of all was the old-world courtesy that he experienced whenever he came to Corio. It was disappearing nearly everywhere else and yet the best thing of all was 'that the boys don't know they have such a grace'.[28]

Priestley's orange-sucking was a euphemism for Darling's obsession with loafing boys. On Priestley's first visit in May 1935, Darling convinced him that if they both toured the school on a Sunday afternoon there would be clutches of boys idly doing nothing. Thereafter, searching for orange-suckers was a regular weekend ritual. Invariably, their forays unearthed a result that approximated Giblin's description of GGS whenever he visited: that it was a hive of industry. Yet so accustomed was Darling to picking holes in his own handiwork in the presence of his guests that, after one visit, Giblin made a point of highlighting a contrasting mood to his wife: 'Darling in good form, and feeling pretty happy about the school. No gloom this time.' Orange-sucking aside, the boys responded positively to Priestley's lectures on his experiences as a member of Antarctic expeditions led by Scott and Shackleton. Apart from the relaxation afforded by a weekend visit, Priestley's affection for GGS arose from simple enjoyment of a social game of cricket or a hit in the nets, and talking with senior boys who were more forthcoming than their English counterparts.[29]

Had the totality of Darling's reforms and initiatives realised Donald Mackinnon's hope for GGS to be Australia's best school? The word best is in the eye of the beholder but, with much depending on recognition of Darling, the evidence suggests that they may have done. Professor H.S. Carslaw (mathematics, University of Sydney) told Darling that he was 'the Leader in Secondary Education in Victoria (& Australia)' and what is clear is that those who visited Corio liked what they saw and went away invigorated for the reform of their own schools. The Reverend Canon A.G.G.C. (Guy) Pentreath (Bickersteth's successor) said that St Peter's council was insular in its outlook and got the shock of its life at Corio in 1936 when it inspected the new buildings. Equally, the quality of the GGS cadets put his boys to shame. 'I only know that when the boys are evading games & bringing trumped up excuses & the spirit of boredom descends upon the games', Pentreath confessed, 'I get frightened, and feel that there are bad forces beating us down into slackness'. When F.H. Archer and the Caulfield Grammar School council had visited Corio in 1935, the experience was 'bracing'. N.W. Roff from Launceston Grammar School (and a former GGS master) said there was no way that he could keep quiet about Darling's work, and even girls' school headmistresses, such as Nora Collinson of Lowther Hall, and M.A. Bailey from Ascham, in Sydney, said that what he was doing was a great stimulus to their own efforts. But for all those who visited Corio to see firsthand or heard of what he was trying to do, there may still have been as many others looking elsewhere for inspiration.[30]

After all, as Darling said of himself in the Smyth lecture (which Priestley recorded as 'really first class') he was not at heart an educational theorist.

The process of producing public schoolboys in England and Corio relied on 'the painful processes of trial and error'. He drew on the best of the English tradition (as he understood it) to revitalise a school. For this reason he was an orthodox educational reformer—orthodox like Gollancz and Somervell before him in exploiting the potential of an existing model, rather than devising an alternative. There were three elements in his approach to reform. First, there was the Thringian impulse to create conditions for the benefit of every pupil:

> the function of the school is to develop individuals, having in mind their
> different capacities and their different ambitions. It is also its function to create
> a mechanism and an atmosphere in which everyone can develop himself fully
> on all sides of physical and mental character.

This idea entailed getting the measure of and knowing well every boy, but despite his best efforts to provide for everyone, he knew that he was crying for the moon. This aim was only attainable in a school of moderate size. This same aim also accounts for his reluctance to admit boys older than fifteen, because by then they were too fixed in their ways to be remoulded. Second, he wanted every boy to be able to think for himself rather than parrot received ideas. This aim entailed fostering a liberal climate of opinion, as evidenced by the number of invitations to social reformers—including occasional Communists (such as Ralph Gibson and Dr G. O'Day)—who addressed the public affairs form or society. Later, his liberalism nearly brought him undone, but Russel Ward, a leftward-inclined scholar who taught at GGS between 1936 and 1939, afterwards assessed Darling as 'incomparably the most humane, liberal and best employer I ever had'.[31]

The third thing Darling wanted was for GGS boys to make useful contributions after leaving school. If this meant producing an elite of Christian leaders (for which Archbishop Head was grateful) and an aristocracy of talent and taste, then so be it. An *Argus* editorial quoted Darling on the importance of religion in education, and every now and then his public statements on such a matter drew him into prolonged debates with members of the general public with whom at times he was almost naively frank. In one instance he conceded the point that the business world did not really want thoughtful young men guided by Christian values, in which case GGS boys may have been unfit for the world:

> We must, I think, also admit that it may be the function of a school like this
> to teach people to destroy the better system which alone makes a school such
> as this possible, and that again involves my paradox and doubt, but these are
> doubts, I think, which concern me in my own conscience rather than doubts
> which should necessarily be passed on to the boys.

This reluctance to make his doubts their doubts stemmed from a high-minded idealism. He did not see it as his job to prejudge issues that he wanted boys to decide on for themselves. This liberalism was evident in his most succinct summary (so far) of the nature of education, the Smyth lecture, where he maintained that it was essentially a preparation for civic virtue, the production of good men and women for the good life in a free community. His own undoubted success in creating 'a real community in miniature' at GGS was confirmed by W.F. Connell who was in residence at Corio (in 1938) as one of Browne's Diploma of Education students (and later a Professor of Education who reviewed the school for Darling), and who had already witnessed it among OGGs as a fellow student at Trinity College.[32]

In pursuit of his aims, Darling relied on a boundless supply of energy, and a straightforward inspirational administrative style entailing leading by example and trusting others to whom he granted the freedom to act responsibly. Although he thought that he was known for his 'notorious aggressiveness on committees', his relationship with the school council was marked by implicit faith and under-standing—notwithstanding his muted threat of resignation in 1932. As school council chairman, Manifold kept a respectable distance, because he did not want to 'queer your pitch' by over-enthusiastic support of the headmaster. Forever rest-less, Darling was a man on a mission: witness the characteristic urgency with which he impressed on one OGG the idea that democracy and religion 'have got to be saved by us' and that 'there isn't much time left for us to do the saving'. Even though the European dictators by then were malign influences, taken literally his claim was nonsense. Darling was said to possess a 'marked tenacity of purpose' and, Henry Gullett once told him, a 'capacity to get things done & plenty of personality'. And yet while he was impatient to effect change, he remained per-sonable and friendly. Despite what he had said to V.L. Johnstone, he was revered by his more recent old boys who recounted their recent doings. In England, Bill Landale struggled with English history but enjoyed hearing Sir Oswald Mosley, Bertrand Russell and Harold Laski speak at Oxford. Bill Lloyd, who always wrote 'Dear Headmaster', poured out intensely personal confessions about lapsed spirituality, blighted idealism and wasted introspection. Sam Wood was eternally grateful for Darling's arrangements for him at Brasenose College, while Alan Hamer (at Magdalen College) reported on 'Organist William [McKie]' and Jack McKinnell 'bursting with energy' and how he had breakfasted in the early hours at Worcester with two OGGs, Alan Brown and Mick Richardson. Such was Darling's generosity to these young men that when they were in England, the Old Rectory at Trimley became a boarding house and his English friends (espe-cially Dicker and Bernays) also became their friends and maintained a watchful eye. He introduced them to key people and, when short of money, he dug into his own pocket and gave them his own (or had others dig deep). Occasionally he heard what he would rather not have heard—such as Lloyd's insistence that London was a real eye-opener because an English gentleman was simply 'a parcel of petty prejudices' and lonely Englishmen abroad like the headmaster merely stressed the pretty side of English culture.[33]

Miss Margaret Campbell, herself much younger than her fiancé, knew that in marrying him she was betrothing herself to a job or an institution and a way of life. She had to come to terms quickly with what Bernays called 'the frequent domestic crises when all "conversing" ceased in the kitchen for indefinite periods—and generals and arch-bishops were threatened at any moment with possible fasts'. Darling put the delicacy of her position gently to his mother: 'she feels conscious of her deficiencies'. Personal details about their headmaster always risked being the plaything of boys, particularly his sensitivities about matrimony. Darling was embarrassed (and slightly piqued) at lunch one day in 1934 when telling the prefects about his trip home and either George Lindon or David Hay had asked him about 'this young lady on board': 'I hear, Sir, that you have been seen with a red-headed girl in Sydney'. And when John Leach visited his old school he reported to Darling how Colin Gordon, amid contented sighs from Cameron, had given everyone 'a graphic description of your last few hours as a bachelor'. (In fact, Darling spent the morning visiting Newman, recovering from tuberculosis, along with a pupil who, after falling out of a tree, had cut his leg and was in a Melbourne hospital.) And because he did not want schoolboys ogling on his wedding day, Darling had deliberately arranged a mid-week ceremony just before the end of term. After a lengthy engagement, the happy couple was married at the Toorak Presbyterian Church on the afternoon of Wednesday, 21 August 1935, followed by a reception at Kintyre, the house that the Campbells had built at 9 Heyington Place. Fifty years later, on their golden wedding anniversary, Darling remembered how the wedding party 'was conducted as a matter of principle without the benefit of alcohol'. Margaret's friends had not been surprised, although his guests were slightly bemused and he regretted, looking back, that he had been churlish in stipulating 'no alcohol, no speeches'. The wedding was not without its humour: Margaret's sister Alison, a small girl of about fourteen, was bridesmaid and walked down the aisle with Darling's best man Colin Gordon who was 6 feet 4 inches (1.93 m) tall. The other humorous item was the *Star* newspaper's report. There was a full-page picture of Margaret 'under the heading Abyssinian princess weds, with a much smaller picture inside with another lady headed Headmaster's bride'.[34]

A couple of years afterwards, with her husband's educational reform stature rising, Margaret told her mother-in-law how 'terribly proud of him' she was. In August 1937, his credentials were tested when the New Education Fellowship Conference—a gathering of world-renowned educators organised by ACER—convened in Melbourne. Darling attended only a few of the sessions, although he chaired one on religion and education, but he brought the delegates to Corio. He congratulated Cunningham on a conference that had so successfully awakened public opinion. Kandel was one of the delegates and after the conference he reported on his visit to GGS. He was impressed by what he saw and, in *Impressions of Australian Education*, he said that the school was a notable example of an experiment that would impact on the centralised Australian state systems.

His nine-page report found much to praise: the favourable aesthetic environment for learning created by the buildings, the fine start made in ascertaining pupils' needs with the record-card system and Whately's efforts at measuring abilities, and the classrooms in which he had not come across one dull lesson or an inert group of pupils. GGS's significant feature, he thought, was 'the courage displayed in attacking the problems of what to teach and how to teach in a fresh and vigorous manner'. Kandel endorsed the ends for which Darling justified education and his recent reorganisation of the curriculum, except on one point: Darling's retention of certain general subjects as providing 'training for the brain', because Kandel did not believe such a distinction was psychologically justifiable. He praised the public affairs form, the provision of music and art, and the recognition given to manual subjects and, like Curthoys, he was impressed by the boys' naturalness, both in and out of class. The headmaster's disavowal of the Intermediate was entirely justified, although adherence to the Leaving examination as somehow guaranteeing GGS comparability of standards with other schools was questionable, because exactly the same criticisms levelled at the Intermediate applied to the Leaving. The demands of that examination inevitably disturbed an otherwise fine program, but this interruption could be eradicated were GGS to become a class A school (under the Schools Board system). In the meantime, GGS was meeting 'soundly and with courage' the problems being confronted everywhere as a result of the constraining effects on secondary schooling of an academic tradition and that, but for Darling's clear vision of what education might do for boys, it might not have achieved. When he read what Kandel had written, Archbishop Head saw strong vindication for just about everything Darling had done to produce intelligent and capable Christian citizens.[35]

CONSCIENCE OF THE COMFORTABLE CLASSES

1931–1939

Of all the dreams of those Europeans of what Australia might be—the south land of the Holy Spirit, or the land where the great dream of the Enlightenment would be fulfilled, or where the blood would never stain the wattle, or a New Britannia in another world—all that seemed to survive was the idea of Australia as a place of 'uncommonly large profit'.

C.M.H. Clark, *A History of Australia*, vol. VI

While he was busy revitalising GGS, Darling was publicly engaged beyond his little oyster at Corio. His commitments varied in their demands on him and their significance, but they extended his influence (and that of the school) into education and social policy in Geelong, Melbourne and nationally. In December 1931, he attended the initial meeting of the Headmasters' Conference of Australia. Then in March 1932 he became a member of the Schools Board and, when Littlejohn died in late 1933, Darling replaced him as a member of the council of the University of Melbourne. He was also a member of Toc H, and in Geelong (with Bull) he organised the University's Extension Board lectures and established the Unemployed Boys' Centre. Other provincial city engagements included membership of the Geelong Girls' Grammar School (the Hermitage) council, the Geelong Citizens' Relief Committee, and work (again with Bull) for the Geelong Free Library and Children's Library (as a result of which he was active in the Free Library Movement). While he did not found the service club, Apex—it began in Geelong in 1930 as the Young Businessman's Club at the instigation of two OGGs, John Buchan and Ewan Laird, and an Old Geelong Collegian, Langham Proud—Darling encouraged Apex with talks about service, and he secured its involvement in the Unemployed Boys' Centre. He was a member of an ACER consultative committee on secondary education reform and the Council of the Diocese of Melbourne; he founded the St John's Fellowship and tried to establish an APS-sponsored social settlement in Port Melbourne.[1]

These affiliations provided him with additional networks and strong interconnected memberships. The importance of the Headmasters' Conference was that it yielded firsthand knowledge of his fellow heads and their thinking, and was a reference point before launching new schemes. The inaugural meeting at Corio in December 1931, for example, helped him gauge the strength of feeling about public service careers for boys (mentioned to parents a week earlier on speech day). In 1928 there had been a meeting of the heads of twelve Church of England boys' schools and five other schools' representatives convened on Bickersteth's initiative at St John's College, Morpeth, to discuss the religious function of church schools. Conference itself emerged in subsequent discussions between Bickersteth, Robson and Darling. Another meeting at Corio of eight Australian heads (already members of the English Headmasters' Conference) devised the Headmasters' Conference of Australia's initial composition, membership criteria and machinery. Darling was honorary secretary. The inaugural gathering's agenda included resolutions deploring his pet aversion: public attention accorded interschool sport. It also considered Commonwealth government recognition of school cadets, school and chamber of commerce cooperation, the League of Nations, schoolboy empire tours and relations with the press. Darling took a lead on the importance of sex instruction in schools (when 'standards seemed to be falling and restraints to be loosening') and the educational value of the arts. Until the creation in 1936 of the ministerial peak body, the Australian Education Council, the Headmasters' Conference along with ACER and the Australian Vice-Chancellors' Committee was one of the country's few national education forums. Its muscle in concert with the vice-chancellors was evident in its strong stand on public service graduate entry. Probably at Darling's instigation, a Headmasters' Conference deputation met with Bruce (assistant treasurer and former prime minister) and then the heads submitted a series of resolutions to the prime minister and state premiers. The universities and schools turned out fine young men of character and ability ('among the best this country produces') who were not attracted to civil service employment. A 'special class' was needed from which to recruit for administrative posts in Australia, Papua or League of Nations–mandated territories. Entry would be by competitive examination and access would require Leaving honours or university honours. After coordinating with the universities, Littlejohn and Darling met the prime minister.[2]

Toc H, by contrast, might have lacked the conference's prestige and power but offered fellowship and inspiration to serve others. Specifically, through its meetings and outreach activities, Toc H sought to preserve and further the fellowship and service that were initially manifest in active service during World War I. It was barely five years old in Australia when Darling arrived. Originating at Poperinghe, Belgium, Toc H was signallers' language for TH—initials for

Talbot House (a rest-and-recreation house named after a young British soldier, Gilbert Talbot, killed at Hooge in July 1915). It was founded by the Queensland-born Reverend P.T.B. (Tubby) Clayton. Lord Forster (governor-general) suggested an Australian Toc H and, when Clayton visited from England in 1925, he established branches, with Geelong's formed in 1926. Darling joined the Toc H council in 1930 but complained that he was 'a rotten member'. In 1934 a link between GGS and Toc H was established with the appointment of Hubert Rutter (an OGG) as schools' secretary. The Headmasters' Conference viewed the schools section as a way, said J.F. Ward (head, Prince Alfred College, and father of GGS's assistant master, Russel), of acquainting boys with 'the claims of social service in the community' so that they might 'do something in the community when they leave school'. Awareness of the Depression's impact had prompted Toc H in May 1930 to work for distressed Melbourne and Geelong families. In 1930, the Reverend P.W. Baldwin (national padre of Toc H) preached on poverty and Toc H's attempts to alleviate it. GGS boys were 'very moved' and collected items such as clothes and footwear for distribution to local charities. The following year, the Boys' Employment Movement was formed at a meeting convened by the lord mayor of Melbourne at the request of the Central Council of Victorian Benevolent Societies. Darling learnt of it from G.R. Giles, a vocational guidance officer with the Education Department. Toc H's efforts and the Boys' Employment Movement were the prompts for Darling's schemes for boys' employment and the social settlement.[3]

In early 1932, a Geelong mercer John Tweeddale (a socially commit-ted Presbyterian) had tried unsuccessfully to persuade Geelong City Council to assist unemployed youths. Eventually, a committee including Tweeddale was formed (at Darling's instigation) to locate premises for an unemployment centre. McPhillimy Brothers made available a confectionery factory in Spring Street, West Geelong, at a weekly rental of £1. The scheme, his sister Margaret told their mother, was an attempt 'to stir up some people in Geelong to look into the question'. 'Thank heavens', Darling exclaimed to Manifold when the Unemployed Boys' Centre opened on 29 September, for it would demand of him only one weekly meeting. Known as the Centre, its creation coincided with the trough of Victoria's Depression unemployment. Fourteen was the official school leaving age and the introduction of post-fourteen state secondary school fees in 1932 meant that boys from families unable to afford such schooling remained in primary schools. Wages for fourteen- and fifteen-year-olds were kept low by employers, although by 1933 the proportion of fourteen-year-olds in the popu-lation had declined. Toc H's West Geelong house-to-house survey of juvenile unemployment (undertaken at Darling's prompting) revealed that 38 per cent of 343 boys aged from fourteen to eighteen were unemployed and 16 per cent were at school for only part of the day. Initially, the Centre's three aims were to find employment for boys aged from fourteen to twenty, fit them for that employ-ment, and keep them 'interested and occupied in the interim'. Maurice Nathan

(GGS prefect and future lord mayor of Melbourne) led the fund-raising charge at Corio, said Darling's sister Margaret, with sports day stalls followed by four one-act plays in the evening. By December, GGS had raised about £275 for the Centre. The *Corian* editor, Bill Lloyd, called juvenile unemployment the world's 'greatest tragedy'. He rejected the idea that as 'a privileged moneyed class' GGS boys were especially obliged to help the needy, when their obligation was the same as anyone else's: to act out of 'elemental decency and natural instinct'. GGS boys had denied themselves 'a few shillings self-indulgence and some of us have actually scrubbed floors (to the amazement of a metropolitan newspaper)'.[4]

The Centre's renovated building consisted of two floors of activity rooms: a gymnasium to the right of the entrance and then an ablutions room, engineering and carpentry rooms, with a storeroom, offices and a committee room on the left. Outside were a forge, a playground and provision for bricklaying. Upstairs on the left was a small hall, kitchen and cafeteria, while on the right there were a library, games room, hobby room, an office and club rooms. The Centre opened daily from 9 am to 5 pm when about sixty-five boys attended. After six months, 260 unemployed boys were enrolled and more than thirty found employment. Enrolled boys reported to the Centre at least monthly. Initially, the Centre relied on the generosity of individuals and business houses for finance and donations (furniture, fittings, equipment and machinery)—the Ford Motor Company gave timber and the Education Department provided tools. Instruction was offered in motor mechanics, carpentry, ticket writing and accounting. Tours of factories were arranged. Films were screened. There were cricket and basketball matches against local teams. There were also a wireless, gymnasium equipment, a library of 300 books, free newspapers (provided by their proprietors) and some rent-free land was available for farming. Darling, his friend Casey and J.O. McEwan (of Dalgety's) were trustees. An eighteen-member committee of management included Darling, Newman and Pinner, the district inspector for schools (A.J. Law), two state school headmasters, Apex and Rotary representatives, a Methodist clergyman, two or three businessmen, a retired teacher and a Young Farmers' Club representative. The daily work of the Centre and its volunteer assistants was supervised by a full-time manager and an assistant manager (an engineer released from his employment by Kent Hughes, Minister of Sustenance and Labour) on salary with the Victorian railways.[5]

After twelve months the Centre broadened its approach. It helped boys become 'useful citizens' and ascertained their work intentions with vocational guidance (for which the Boys' Employment Movement was shouldering the burden in Victoria). By channelling boys into activities based on their aptitudes, employers saved themselves 'time, worry and money' in applying to the Centre, and an abrupt change from unemployment to employment was also minimised. The Centre proudly boasted that it could supply a boy for temporary, permanent or occasional jobs 'within half an hour in Geelong and suburbs'. James McRae (Director of Education and architect of the department's vocational guidance) visited the Centre in August 1933. In December, following a request from Giles (now the secretary of the Boys' Employment Movement), the Centre changed its name to the 'Boys' Employment Movement, Geelong', and affiliated itself with the Boys' Employment Movement in Melbourne, Ballarat and Bendigo, with Darling and Law 'quite willing that this should be done'. There were also personnel changes: appointment of a new business manager and superintendent (R.W. Curtis). Darling thought that Curtis was 'extremely good' at handling boys 'with firmness and tact'. Curtis exercised considerable personal influence and was adept at finding boys with special aptitudes. Darling could not speak 'too highly' of his work, for he had the essential qualities of sympathy, patience and strength of character as well as the imagination to see his way out of difficulties.[6]

With the Merchant Taylors' School club experiences behind him, Darling had been well attuned to the problem of juvenile unemployment. He saw merit in Kent Hughes' frequent allusions in his second reading speech on the Unemployment Relief (Administration) Bill to the need for local administration of relief, for accurate statistics, social science and a social science diploma at the university, and he marked such passages in his copy of the speech. *Unemployment among Boys*, a book authored by two Englishmen (Eagar and Secretan) had also helped shape his thinking. Youth unemployment was an individual and a social scourge because it destroyed hope and made boys 'premature cynics'. Today's 'Can't Works' degenerated into the 'Won't Works' and 'Don't Works' of tomorrow. Out-of-work boys were not junior wage earners but workmen and citizens in training. These authors' solution to enforced idleness was day continuation (the official term for continuing) schooling for fourteen- to eighteen-year-old youths—although to their dismay the London County Council's provision of compulsory day continuation schools was aborted in 1921 after only a year. Voluntary classes were offered in 1922, followed by unemployment centres for boys and girls conducted by local educational authorities, and controlled (and mostly funded) by the Ministry of Labour. Eagar and Secretan dismissed these facilities as well-intentioned palliatives, housed for the most part in 'dingy and unattractive buildings', exuding 'the stale atmosphere of the elementary school' and riddled by confusion of purpose. The passage that caught Darling's eye read:

> The ideal Centre would consist of a permanent building, with a permanent nucleus of staff devoting themselves to the work as a life problem, and forming, in effect, a kind of club to which juveniles could come when unemployed, and with which they could retain connection even when employed. In it would be provided workrooms and classrooms, facilities for bathing, washing and boot-cleaning, a canteen, and some rooms for recreation purposes.

Here was a ready model for the Centre.[7]

Darling's involvement in the Centre was regular from 1932 until his return to England in 1934. Thereafter he pulled back and in 1935–36 had attended only a handful of meetings. GGS's links were maintained when the public affairs form joined the committee in 1936 and Milton Thewlis was the Centre's honorary auditor. Casey maintained his interest and was 'rather impressed' with Curtis, while lamenting that as a trustee he had 'not been able to do very much'. The Centre's biggest problem was a shortage of funds and it was substantially dependent on GGS's largesse. Darling and the pupils were often singled out by the committee for praise: the school had raised £304 in the Centre's first eighteen months and donated library books, sporting goods, boots, shoes and materials. GGS's major fundraising effort on the Centre's behalf was 'The School Exhibition' in July 1935—a series of displays and activities illustrative of Hamlet's 'What a piece of work is man'. For an entire weekend visitors were enlightened about human endeavour throughout history by presentations in song, dance and drama, for which, in characteristic GGS-style, 'each investigation and every piece of work [arose] out of a need and [was] directed towards an end'. Giblin was sceptical about the frantic last-minute preparations, but when he viewed the finished product entailing 'an extraordinary amount of individual work by boys', and mostly on their own initiative, he told his wife that 'it was really very good'. McPhillimys' factory was renovated in 1936 largely as a result of GGS's efforts. Of £1641 raised by the committee by 1941, the school provided about £1000. Even after affiliating with the Melbourne Boys' Employment Movement and receipt of a grant of £125, the financial situation was 'grave'. Businesses were not especially helpful with placements: they had unrealistic expectations in wanting to cherry-pick boys from groups supplied by the Centre while others did not meet their needs. That said, the Centre's business manager noted in 1934 that 'during the past six months we have not made an error of judgement' with placement. Such was the Centre's level of expertise by 1937 (when the state government assumed full financial responsibility for its placement and training work) that the committee believed that 'the Movement has established itself as a permanent part of the Social Service Structure of the State'. The achievements were substantial: more than 1000 boys had been placed in full-time employment. Even so, inability to meet the needs of older boys (who were 'losing their interest in life') made GGS's headmaster 'completely despondent'.[8]

Darling's ameliorative approach to boys' unemployment typified that of 'reasonable' men (as historian Stephen Alomes called them). He believed in local initiatives and the organic growth of projects to attack social misery and distress—a self-help temperament typifying Anglo-Australian, middle-class, Christian reformers. As he later told Robert Menzies, the Centre was a simple and inexpensive measure that produced 'incalculably good results':

> Our solution preserves, in the English way, government finance with local and voluntary administration, it secures the possibility of the employment of individuals by individuals instead of numbers in a card index and it creates a natural nucleus for youth and Community centres.

While tolerating some government support for local initiatives, Darling was suspicious of state interference in social reform. Early in the World War II, when many boys who would otherwise have been at the Centre were in munitions work, and manpower controls reduced its operations to part-time in the evenings, he told Judge Stretton (of the Workers Compensation Board) that 'this sort of effort ought to be local though fitting into a general framework'. Experience with the government had not been particularly happy as state enterprises 'seem to be inevitably tied up with third rate civil servants, and you are liable to arbitrary action such as the closing of the centre without any warning'. The Centre's committee, which scrupulously maintained its social acceptability in the public gaze of political and industrial interests, thought similarly. It refused to compete with industry in the making of items and would not advertise for small jobs, even though the Centre received excellent publicity through detailed weekly, and later bi-weekly, reports in the *Geelong Advertiser* and 3GL radio broadcasts. The committee also refused to attend a public meeting convened in 1935 by the Geelong Unemployed Organisation to discuss methods of solving unemployment and tried (without luck) to persuade the Trades Hall Council that its work for boys was 'non-political and non-sectarian'. The Trades Hall's representative (from 1934) rarely, if ever, attended meetings.[9]

The concern of reformers with clubs, boy unemployment, settlements, community centres and youth policy formed a coherent strand within progressive English (and to some extent Australian) social thought. After the political and economic crisis of 1931, 'middle opinion' in England coalesced around a belief in the social order's essential soundness but its need for reform (as typified by Political and Economic Planning—PEP). By 1937, Darling's friends Lindsay (who visited Corio in January), Bernays and MacDonald (ministers in Chamberlain's National government) typified such thinking, while left-wing opinion was identified with Gollancz' Left Book Club (founded in March 1936). What later became known as postwar 'Butskellism' originated from this centre ground. Darling's views on settlements took shape in discussions with Joan Brett. There were existing Melbourne and Sydney university settlements but (in apparent ignorance of them) his sister had bemoaned to their mother the lack of social service training in Australia and a dearth of settlements. Initially, Darling wanted the OGGs to be responsible for a social settlement but by 1933 he turned to the APS headmasters. He and Brett planned a location in either Fitzroy or Richmond, in inner Melbourne, but his idea languished until after his return from England. In July 1937 he revived it after consulting J.S. Hyslop (Director of Training, Victorian Council of Social Training) although he was still uncertain about what he wanted. Frustrated in her efforts to convince parsimonious state departments of the worth of employing social workers, Hyslop welcomed Darling's interest in social work and support for the idea.[10]

The Centre succeeded because its aims were clear and the requisite infrastructure was in place (and a version of it was still going strong at the 1982 jubilee).

But Darling's settlement idea struggled to get to first base. 'At the moment', he told Curthoys, 'we are held up for want of a man'. His difficulty was that, apart from Rolland (and perhaps Stewart, Adamson's successor at Wesley), the idea of an APS settlement did not capture his fellow heads' imagination. He took their inertia as evidence of an Australian character flaw. To the Right Reverend E.H. Burgmann (Bishop of Goulburn) he bemoaned Australians' 'lack of moral and mental integrity' and an 'unblushing lack of conscience in this connection, which gets me down':

> And the other thing which shocks all Englishmen is the sloppiness of their public conscience, which looks to us like the deification of the good fellow without principles. I am convinced that the gambling and the desire to get rich quickly has a lot to do with it, and is the other thing which we cannot understand.

He tried 'very hard not to apply English standards all the time', he told Burgmann, even though he took them for granted as 'absolute standards, and that comes to the same thing'. Whenever he complained about a visiting Englishman's sense of superiority or whenever England's 'hopeless misfits' were inflicted on Australia—such as one of his former Repton fags who wrote from Sydney in 1933 pleading for money—there were signs that Darling was beginning to identify with his adopted homeland. And yet settlements worked in Australia, as the Reverend R.G.C. (Brother Bill) Nichols (vicar of St Mark's, Fitzroy) demonstrated. Lord Somers (the governor) had opened the University of Melbourne Social Settlement (for which Nichols took the initiative) at St Mark's in 1927, as Darling knew through Joan Brett.[11]

Darling also grizzled about his fellow heads' foot-dragging and Australia more generally to Colman: 'It is very difficult in this country to get anything started, and much more difficult to keep people up to their promises when you think that you have secured them'. As he often did in his letters, he set out his options on paper and worked through them one by one, pro and con. The best settlement model, he believed, was to appoint 'a boys' club man out here' as a salaried warden and send him to England for experience and training. Meanwhile, a University of Melbourne graduate should undertake a 'scientific economic' survey to define 'the function' to be served by a settlement. He wrote similarly to Stacey Colman at Melbourne Grammar who, as he had just arrived in Melbourne, said that he could be of little use, although he saw merit in the proposed survey. Like his friend, Curthoys saw little hope of enlightened social thinking, especially on the conservative side of politics 'while the old gentlemen of the National Union remain in possession'. Younger conservatives, such as the GGS council chairman, Jim Fairbairn, endorsed social reform but looked to Darling to give a lead. 'People want life to be a game of heads the individual wins[,] tails the state pays the individual[']s losses', wrote a bewildered Fairbairn.

In a well-received speech to the Victorian Council of Social Training in 1937, Darling drew attention to the 'illimitable field' for social work in Australia, but for which there would not be 'illimitable resources' until the community 'shakes itself out of its damnable complacency and realises that work needs to be done', the *Argus* reported him saying. Darling was high-handedly scornful of a lack of social machinery to mitigate the Depression's impact. The only way forward, he asserted, was 'co-ordinated and scientific social work' to avoid 'overlapping, pamperization and indiscriminate charity' rather than teaching people to help themselves and giving them the facilities that they needed to do so.[12]

By early 1938 a start was finally made with the appointment of a warden to the Port Melbourne Settlement, located in Boy Scout premises in Nott Street about 3 kilometres south-west of the city centre. Port Melbourne was a working-class suburb of large factories and a mostly unskilled workforce (a high proportion of whom were unemployed). The suburb was attracting attention. In 1927, at the request of the Port Melbourne City Council, the State Savings Bank of Victoria had commenced a housing estate known as Garden City. In 1936, more low-cost public houses were erected at Fisherman's Bend, following surveys by the Housing Investigation and Slum Abolition Board—an agency originating from the indefatigable efforts of F.O. (Ossie) Barnett, an accountant and leading Methodist layman. Barnett regarded Darling's Victorian Council of Social Training speech as 'a tremendous inspiration' and his own address to GGS's Public Affairs Society prompted a housing survey in Geelong and a report to the government. Almost single-handedly, Barnett had shamed a parsimonious government headed by A.A. Dunstan (the premier) into belated action on slum clearance.[13]

Cause for celebration following the appointment of the warden was short lived. The first problem was that the warden's experience was confined to boys' clubs and he was unqualified for social work. Despite a 'complete lack of academic background', he was admitted to the Diploma of Social Studies in February 1938. So keen was Hyslop to assist the headmasters that he completed one year of training, rather than the customary two, and a year abroad in 1939 to visit clubs and missions (such as Bermondsey) which, Darling informed him, had profoundly altered so many men's lives. Second, Darling's idea of a larger community centre was in limbo until the completion of a Faculty of Commerce survey, undertaken (at Giblin's instigation) in February by E. Ward from the faculty (and engaged for twelve months on a stipend of £150 as the secretary to the APS headmasters' settlement sub-committee). Ward's job was to 'carry on research into the social services of Melbourne' and report on the merits of sites, although Darling's instructions were disarmingly vague: 'go and see each of the people to whom I recommend you, and embody the results of your conversations in a report to us'. By June, Ward was still dragging his feet, but the warden had begun tentatively by firing a volley of questions to Darling regarding policy, future expansion, charity grants and sponsorship. The warden addressed the

Public Affairs Society at Corio, and a tour that he arranged in May for Nield's public affairs form went well and the eighty boys at the club enjoyed themselves.[14]

The third problem was that Toc H was contemplating a centre of its own, and the heads had to decide whether to go it alone or combine forces. Toc H (of which Gilray was a council member with Darling) wanted to improve the standard of its clubs and planned 'a Demonstration Club and Training Centre' on a leased site in Beaconsfield Parade, South Melbourne. On Toc H's behalf, George Nicholas had employed an Englishman, F.A. Bracey, Warden of the Christ Church (Oxford) United Clubs. Toc H was willing to cooperate, but the warden was thought to want his own show. He had convinced (a slightly alarmed) Hyslop of the virtues of Nott Street, at which expansion was possible in adjacent properties then for sale. With Darling and the headmasters in a quandary, in late July 1938 Toc H sponsored a conference on boys' clubs for interested groups (including the Victorian Council of Social Training, Apex, Legacy, the Constitutional Club and the public schools). This gathering endorsed Toc H's scheme. The heads' equivocation arising from Darling's and Gilray's conflicting APS–Toc H membership loyalties was resolved in August when they agreed that Bracey should assume control over the warden and offered Toc H £60 towards the former's salary. They were even prepared for Bracey to open a club on a site for a community centre. Ward was asked to report on locations in South Melbourne and Port Melbourne as the heads had reservations about Beaconsfield Parade. Although Darling thought that it was 'admirable', the warden complained that in the summer 'large crowds of people congregate there, thus creating a bad atmosphere around the building'. If the headmasters located a better site, then Toc H would still cooperate but it was committed to securing Bracey. If the situation wasn't already messy enough, Barnett (vice-chairman of the new Housing Commission of Victoria) had been approached about a grant of land at Fisherman's Bend.[15]

Added to these internecine differences over recognition and lines of control, was the problem of identity: what kind of centre should it be (because lack of clarity delayed the selection and development of a permanent site)? Darling thought of a community centre in early 1938, because community implied a geographical unit rather than sectional sponsorship (as in 'Public Schools' centre'). He discarded social settlement because other groups (such as the Playgrounds Association) were lobbying the Melbourne City Council. A centre, he told R.G. Baxter (Toc H's secretary) was:

> a place where eventually the people of some suburb can come together for all those social, educational and recreational activities which are necessary for the building up of an active intelligent social life in a community.

Most agencies acted in splendid isolation, he thought, and were not linked on the basis of locality, whereas a centre's core work could potentially incorporate a host of services: antenatal work, a baby health centre, nursery schools, kindergartens, boys' and girls' clubs, recreational activities, all kinds of hobbies, acting, music, art, a library, adult education and clubs for older people, a gymnasium, a playground, a 'poorman's lawyer', probation work, and possibly a dispensary. Moreover, a centre could provide a residential hostel for young people undertaking social work in their spare time or as part of formal training. In late 1938, the Port Melbourne Settlement warden replaced Ward as sub-committee secretary and continued searching for sites. Although properties in and adjacent to Nott Street came onto the market, they could not be acquired by the headmasters. Hyslop suggested that Darling resolve matters by approaching the Housing Commission. Late in November, Darling sought a deputation of headmasters and urged that 'no large housing scheme today would be complete without a Community Centre'. On 29 November, the *Argus* reported that the deputation wanted a long-term lease at a peppercorn rental on 6 hectares of Port Melbourne land. The APS would provide about £2000 annually (sourced from Head of the River regatta and chapel funds, and old boys' contributions) to maintain its centre and they were praised for 'a definite civic gesture': a practical contribution to community service that accorded with the commission's scheme for a model village. Darling then outlined the centre proposal on speech day, and endorsed it as one of those opportunities 'which we all here enjoy for getting the best out of ourselves' that would be provided for 'people less privileged', where they might learn 'the obligations and the satisfaction of social responsibility'.[16]

Barely four months before Darling departed for England (and with Bracey about to arrive), however, there were snags. First, after a year's 'barely adequate' work (insufficient for special consideration), the Port Melbourne Settlement's warden failed two university subjects and, despite having 'done well' in practical work, could not complete the diploma in two years. Second, while Darling had been driving the scheme from the outset, his headmaster peers suddenly reneged. With few wealthy old collegians but a school greatly in need of their money, Rolland confessed that he was 'a little diffident'. J.R. Sutcliffe (Stacey Colman's successor at Melbourne Grammar) was also worried about the scheme's financial underwriting. As he really had to 'do something to put this place in order' his first call on the old boys would be for new buildings, with 'little support' available for the centre. More positively, Darling was being strongly encouraged by groups such as the Victorian Federation of Mothers' Clubs, the Victorian Baby Health Centres Association and the Australian Association for Pre-School Child Development. Gilray, Darling and Father Hackett (rector, Xavier College) met the Commission on 6 December but received 'no definite answer'—although Barnett described their discussions as a 'marked success'. Provided that the government 'grants us a fair slice of Fishermen's [sic] Bend', he said, 'I feel there is no doubt whatever that a Community Center project will go over'. Shortly afterwards, the warden sailed for England. Although the scheme was in abeyance, there was still considerable interest at Corio (thanks to Darling and Nield), particularly after the Port Melbourne Settlement members visited and performed their review, 'Broadcast of 1938'. But progress was inhibited by Darling's isolation in Corio: he was too far away to oversee the idea's implementation, and his Melbourne-based peers were half-hearted. He advised Bracey that as 'the only one who can keep the others up to the mark', Xavier's Father Hackett was the man with whom to work.[17]

At the Schools Board, Darling ran into vested interests against reform and, as with the Port Melbourne Settlement, he was frustrated by its machinations. He built alliances with fellow members whenever and wherever he could while banking on the public reception of his speeches and Corio reforms to help him erode board opposition, but it was stony ground. When he joined in March 1932, the Schools Board had existed for about two decades. The statute of the council of the University of Melbourne that established it created a membership comprising, in addition to the vice-chancellor, the president of the Professorial Board and (from 1919) the Professor of Education (its chairman), eight Professorial Board nominees, eight Minister of Public Instruction appointees, eight Incorporated Association of Registered Teachers of Victoria (IARTV) appointees and two registered schools members appointed by the chancellor. With his fellow APS heads, Franklin and Adamson, Darling was an IARTV nominee. The board made recommendations to the Professorial Board on matriculation and the admission of students, and prescribed the details of Intermediate and Leaving Certificate subjects and their examination. Its resolutions were transmitted to the council and the Professorial Board. On the board's behalf, subject standing committees exercised oversight of the secondary curriculum. The statute also empowered the board to recommend its own examiners and inspectors for appointment by the council, with Education Department inspectors acting (since 1914) on the board's behalf. It had also established a dual system of A and B class schools to manage the contentious issue of inspection. 'Approved' or accredited status (consequent upon a satisfactory inspection) entitled class A Intermediate and Leaving Certificate schools to exemption from public examination requirements, with internal school assessment deemed by the university to have been satisfied upon the production of a headmaster's certificate attesting to attainment of the requisite standard. Class B schools were not inspected and their candidates presented for public examination. GGS was a B-class school, because Darling thought that inspection constrained his freedom to experiment: it was excessively bureaucratic and (notwithstanding Kandel's 1937 report) public examination success provided 'no basis for argument about the result'.[18]

In Darling's view, the Schools Board was too large, its members' attendance erratic (with ratified items susceptible to subsequent rescission), and its standing committees fought (blindly) to preserve their subjects' place in the curriculum and maintain parity of status by making their subjects difficult. The 'constant negotiations' over the two certificates and the dual A and B system (with the discussions becoming 'increasingly scientific') began in the mid-1930s. Until then,

Darling's main effort was to reduce the length of the Intermediate examination, before jettisoning it at Corio. When GGS boys were taking ten subjects, he told Wrigley, the prospect of having to sit for two three-hour external papers in one day was simply 'too much for a boy'. Wrigley (who supported the Intermediate's abolition) urged him to seek a reduction in duration, but at only his fourth board meeting Darling's resolution to that effect was rejected. At this early stage, he dismissed the board as 'futile', not because he couldn't get his own way, but because of its factionalism and the pursuit of self-interest. The 'three parties' were the A and B schools, and the university, with 'practicing [sic] schoolmasters' the worst of all, he complained to Carslaw, because they 'never got out of their head how a proposed change will affect their own schools'. For the time being he stayed his hand on the Intermediate and focused on secondary education generally. Convinced of the injustice of a system dominated by university requirements, he began saying so publicly. His clearest exposition was in Sydney in January 1933 to the first conference of the Federated State School Teachers of Australia. He was honoured by the invitation, which Manifold recognised as 'quite an astonishing tribute & olive branch from an unexpected quarter'.[19]

Darling worked for hours over Christmas on the text of 'Education to meet the need of modern state'. In it he said that 'we must depart from the habit of educating all boys as though they were going to take advanced university courses'. It was ridiculous for matriculation requirements to dictate the structure of secondary schooling when three-quarters of the pupils never attended a university—an argument that was received sympathetically. His sister Margaret (in Hobart after a week's camping with her friend Margaret Maxwell and Masterman) was elated when she met two Sydney lawyers at the house of the artist John Eldershaw, both of whom had heard the speech '& had been very much impressed by it & by him'. W.A. Osborne (Professor of Physiology, University of Melbourne) endorsed Darling's remarks and related a mildly apocryphal story about the consequences of the university's demands:

> Not long ago Physiology was crammed into Scotch College boys to such a degree that the unfortunate youths memorized textbooks used in 3rd year medicine! I determined to smash this thing and with Agar [Professor of Zoology]'s help got a course going which gave a good biological ground work & and killed Scotch College pot-hunting.

Darling criticised the Intermediate examination's duration in March 1934 in a long letter to Browne (Wrigley's successor and board chairman). Three hours had never been justified. To defend it was pure expediency, because it was way too difficult to properly invigilate 1000 candidates, to vary the times for finishing scripts and the duration enabled the university 'to make an indecent amount of money out of the examinations' (a point that weighed heavily on Priestley). If these examination-related deficiencies were not enough, Darling told Browne, then the line taken on subject texts was even more exasperating: to require boys to read only prescribed textbooks was anathema and additional evidence of the board's constricted mentality. Gerry Dicker remembered a classics standing committee meeting in 1934 that discussed the next year's texts. Primed by Masterman to 'try and get something other than the usual fare', each of his suggestions was rejected by Professor Scutt (classics, University of Melbourne) as 'too difficult'. Small wonder, then, that on the eve of his departure for England Darling had concluded 'yours in wrath and anger'.[20]

During his absence, Franklin took up the cudgels. The year before he had argued that the board's standard was way 'too high' and Darling's information on the previous five years of GGS Intermediate results had borne out Melbourne Grammar's trends: low pass rates hovering precipitously around 50 per cent or just below. Franklin was adamant that his school had been 'thoroughly well organised for 10 years now, and in addition to that we do not let boys go into the Intermediate form unless we feel they are at that standard'. Franklin then sought the abolition of the February supplementary examination. It was in this slightly more receptive climate that Darling returned for his assault on the Intermediate, although board resistance to modifications was strong. Indeed, Priestley recorded the heated tenor of the meeting that adopted new supplementary examination regulations as 'highly controversial'. In July 1935 there was a small victory when the board adopted Darling's motion (eleven–seven) to reduce the Intermediate examination's duration. When Professor T.G.B. Osborn (Dean of the Faculty of Science, University of Sydney) addressed the Headmasters' Conference of Australia in 1933, opinion was divided over his criticism of university dominance of secondary education. Darling and Browne sought to satisfy the university while also permitting schools to offer a senior secondary education uncontaminated by its demands. Browne had detected a breakthrough in October 1934 with the appointment of a Professorial Board committee (himself and Professors Wadham, W.A. Osborne, Laby, Bailey and Cherry) to investigate 'alleged weaknesses' in the matriculation, which was 'prepared to make some strong recommendations if necessary', but his optimism was short lived. Four years later the situation was still 'a little depressing', and he and Darling were only marginally closer to a compromise.[21]

In Darling's view, the fault lay with Seitz (McRae's successor as Director of Education), the Catholic board members (opposed to changes) and the Professorial Board (resistant to altered matriculation requirements). This tedious wrangle resumed at the Schools Board in August 1936 after the adoption of a resolution by the Headmasters' Conference. In New South Wales, the council of the University of Sydney and the Parliament had stolen the march in reform by acceding to the headmasters' wishes and creating new certificates. Darling had been concerned about moving 'prematurely' but, after conferring with Copland, Browne assured him that he would submit the Headmasters' Conference resolution to the Professorial Board. Following Robson's paper ('External

examinations'), the headmasters agreed that secondary education should comprise two stages. The first would provide 'a sufficient general education in a fairly
wide range of subjects' and culminate at about ages sixteen or seventeen with
a certificate certifying 'sufficient evidence of a general education for matriculation purposes'. A board on which schoolmasters (not the universities) had effective control would oversee this award. The second stage should be a certificate
awarded after two years study and attainment of 'the required standard in English
and at least four other subjects from an approved list'. This proposal was then
considered by a School's Board examinations sub-committee (Darling, Browne,
Seitz and four others), which by September had reached broad agreement on the
proposed first stage, although agreement evaporated when a full board meeting
discussed the second stage. The sub-committee tried to combine the best features
of the class A and B system 'to serve the purposes of the great body of pupils
not proceeding to the University'. For each candidate, it proposed an external
examination (after five years' secondary schooling) in English expression and two
subjects (chosen from mathematics, a language and a science), supplemented by a
headmaster's certificate endorsing satisfactory completion of other subjects. The
standard would be higher than the Intermediate but 'considerably lower' than the
Leaving. If the two existing certificates were to be replaced, then it was hoped
that the university would make it 'a definite part of its entrance requirements' to
its pass degrees, with its honours degrees requiring another year.[22]

There was a brief but welcome respite for Darling amid all this wrangling
when, in October 1936, Margaret gave birth to their first child, a daughter,
Margaret Jane, known as Jane. When he returned to board politicking, Darling
did so with optimism, because Browne had won agreement on the sub-committee.
Two days before the November board meeting he briefed Priestley and Wadham
with a more detailed outline. Unfortunately, when the board met, Darling let
the side down with 'a very inadequate defence' at 'so difficult' a meeting. Despite
Seitz' 'unalterable' opposition, and convinced that his own scheme was a genuine
advance, Darling redrafted it and pushed ahead in the belief that the changes
need only be compulsory for class-B schools such as his own. Although Wadham
was sympathetic to a major examination overhaul, when he saw what was recommended he cautioned Darling that only 'the most cogent of arguments and
an extremely well-expressed memorandum' would secure Professorial Board
agreement. Debate resumed in March (1937). Proceedings polarised irreparably.
Seitz wanted the class-A system extended and argued that 'the ultimate solution' was the university's acceptance of 'the word of any approved school that
such and such a student is fit to proceed', an arrangement that would work, provided that the inspectors were officials of the university although responsible
to the Board. Seitz repeated this position in April when he presided over his
first meeting of the Council of Public Education (which Darling was shortly
to join) and argued that a Leaving Certificate of possibly lower standard along
with a headmaster's recommendation would be more appropriate for university

entry. Darling, however, wanted an improved class-B system: an external examination after five years supplemented by a headmaster's certificate to mark the completion of a general education (as originally agreed by the sub-committee). With additional not 'over-exacting' work this modification should satisfy the university's matriculation requirements. Seitz, however, was unhappy with his statement of his own case and foreshadowed another. It came in August and was endorsed as a well-considered attempt to head off the Professorial Board's misgivings about approvals.[23]

Two April 1937 meetings of the Schools Board (the first of which Priestley recorded as 'interesting' and tolerable only because he was sitting next to Darling) yielded few real changes. The board's temporary paralysis was neatly symbolised in the minuting of 'adopted tentatively' after a resolution moved by Seitz and seconded by Darling. In May, the sub-committee's suggestion of a senior school certificate (as evidence of five years general education) was adopted. This certificate retained the class-A system and, with the completion of an additional year's school work and a headmaster's recommendation, was sufficient to satisfy the matriculation requirements. Wadham's Professorial Board committee, however was 'in doubt' about the subjects for which a headmaster's certificate would be sufficient and requested further 'definition'. In July, the board's sub-committee spelt out the procedures for inclusion in a list of class-A schools. In October, Professor Cherry's comparison of the first-year performance of undergraduates from class-A and -B schools was tabled. It found 'negligible grounds for criticism' of approved schools. Unconvinced by Seitz' rebuttal and stung by Cherry's claim that the Schools Board was a 'mere cipher' in the approval process, the Professorial Board extended approval to matriculation, 'provided the University has adequate control of the machinery of administration and inspection'. Darling was now hopeful that, unless the Intermediate were to be a certificate issued solely by the Education Department, the board would shortly be rid of it. 'We have abolished it as a preliminary to the Leaving certificate', he informed Roff in Launceston 'and are substituting a slightly lower standard secondary school certificate for the latter with matriculation a year later in two special subjects suitable to a proposed university course'. For his sins, he was 'not a very popular figure in the department just now'. He was convinced that GGS's abandonment of the Intermediate had given him a freer hand, and that 'a very large number' of boys had attained Leaving standard earlier than they might have done. He told Kandel, who had addressed the board a fortnight beforehand, that a further liberalised class-A system might put the attainment of the Leaving within the grasp of 'the non-academic type' boy.[24]

When the standing committee of the Headmasters' Conference met just before Christmas 1937, Darling reported on the progress of the headmasters' resolutions, but his euphoria was premature. By insisting on supervision of inspection (as its price for conceding curriculum control to the schools) the Professorial Board rendered the reformers' victory pyrrhic. No departmental official, least of all Seitz—likeable, friendly to the university (yet because of his 'rather more Teutonic mentality and outlook', perhaps unimaginative, thought Priestley)—would take this rebuff lying down. And no Catholic schoolmaster, for whom his pupils' examination success provided a guarantee of public service entry (and social mobility for working-class Catholic families) would watch the Intermediate disappear. With debate adjourned until March 1938, in December Priestley noted that (predictably) the Catholic schools were 'up in arms' at the Intermediate's possible abolition and that Seitz was 'very prickly about the Inspectorate'. Darling must have sensed as much: Priestley recorded him as having confided that the dispute on the Board 'has dragged on for several years and he anticipates that the "last three years of the war will be the worst"'. Amid mounting disquiet, discussion recommenced on the proposed 3+2+1 structure: a first certificate examination after three years for fourteen- to fifteen-year-olds (instead of the Intermediate), a secondary school certificate after five years and a university entrance examination one year later. Although schools were informed of the proposals in November, few had commented. Now, however, the Catholic Teachers' Association wanted to retain the existing examinations, and in July the IARTV (Darling's own constituency) objected to the increased number of examinations and sought retention of the Intermediate. Then the Professorial Board declared that, without the mandatory study of mathematics and a language other than English and science, the secondary school certificate 'falls definitely short of providing the kind of general education which would be required of matriculants'.[25]

If he was powerless to determine the outcome of these protracted machinations, then Darling had genuine cause for celebration on the domestic front because in May 1938 he became a father for the second time. Jane now had a younger sister: Margaret had given birth to another daughter, Elizabeth Mary. The following month, in a last ditch attempt to try to reconcile their 'divergent views', the sub-committees of both boards met jointly (at Seitz' suggestion) in November 1938. They met in vain. In December, Browne described the position as 'very complicated'. Enthusiasm 'seems to have waned', he lamented, 'and the schools are tired of waiting for definite developments'. Darling was also despondent although not bitter. 'The whole scheme has been upset as usual by the attempt to satisfy everyone', he told Browne:

> If the P[rofessorial]. B[oard]. won't accept our competence to decide on that [a satisfactory basis of general education], I don't feel that there is much hope for reform. It seems to have forgotten that our aim was to get better education in the schools, not to get more people into the Unvi [sic].

Resigned to the inevitable, Darling's final word on the eve of his departure for England was that, without the two 'monsters' of organised sport and an unreformed Leaving Certificate, Victoria might just have some good schools.

Failing that, perhaps 'if we walk around the walls of Jericho the seventh time they may collapse'. Mastery of this unappealing intractable politics of educational reform had eluded him and the Schools Board reinforced his dislike of committees in which contending interests squabbled in set-piece ways. Less obdurate structures with biddable members were more his cup of tea. On this score, the (mostly male) fraternity of the Council of the University of Melbourne was more congenial. Here (as a member for thirty-eight years) Darling moved effortlessly within a freemasonry of friends, part of a dominion elite emanating from his own Anglophile caste, that exuded an assured gentlemanly Establishment style. That, at least was the implicit assumption, except that when the council skirmished (as it did twice in the space of five years over the appointment of successive salaried vice-chancellors), the grubby realities of power upset this cosiness.[26]

Darling barely made it as a council member. He was elected by Convocation in 1933 to a vacancy (following Littlejohn's death) by just one vote on the third ballot. In 1934, D.K. Picken (master, Ormond College) pressed him for an opinion on two Australian candidates for vice-chancellor, but as Darling knew neither of them well, he sounded out Professor Osborn (a GGS parent). Darling preferred a man of affairs who was efficient, a fighter and committed to the university as a seat of learning rather than as a credential-dispensing agency. Apart from their merits, he asked Osborn (because for gentlemen a positive answer counted) whether either man had 'adequate wives?' Giblin later noted 'a lot of sparring' over the position '& possibly some intrigue', as initially Priestley declined the council's offer which then went to David Rivett (chief executive officer, Council for Scientific and Industrial Research—CSIR). Rivett equivocated. When pressed by the Commonwealth government he agreed to remain at CSIR. After 'a fight', a renewed offer went to Priestley, with Giblin believing that a personal appeal (quite possibly Darling's—because he and Priestley were at Lord's during the Oxford–Cambridge cricket match and dined later at Clare College) coupled with strong University of Melbourne staff endorsement persuaded him to accept. Priestley stuck it out for three years until, thwarted within council and by government parsimony, he resigned. An unedifying succession struggle then ensued, during which the conduct of senior Establishment figures (Darling included) was by their own standards untidy, not to say indecent. Priestley had tried to elevate the university's public profile. He obtained £7500 from the Carnegie Corporation to survey universities in English-speaking countries to assist with planning, and he enriched student life by raising money to build a union house and appointing a New Zealander, Dr W. Bryden, as warden of the union in 1936. The aftermath of an acrimonious student debate over the Spanish Civil War in March 1937 earned the censure of Sir James Barrett, the ageing chancellor. The *Argus* had given advance publicity to the rowdy meeting, which was attended by numerous outsiders and was the subject of detailed press comment. Priestley believed (as was subsequently confirmed) that Latham (deputy chancellor) and another council member, Mr Justice Lowe, connived to have Barrett demand a

report from Priestley. He refused, because to accede would have relegated the
vice-chancellor to 'a man of straw'.[27]

Barrett denied any insistence or direction. He claimed that Priestley
viewed the chancellor's position as 'purely honorific' and against the spirit of
the *University Act*, and yet a council sub-committee (which included Darling)
found that the vice-chancellor was solely responsible to council and that the
chancellor had no executive functions. While Priestley anxiously awaited the
sub-committee's report, Barrett (for unrelated reasons) forwarded a small donation for the university. Darling made light of this gesture during the reception
at Bishopscourt for Stacey Colman. 'With his customary audacity', recorded
Priestley, Darling suggested 'that I had missed an opportunity. He said I should
have given the Chancellor's donation to the Labour [sic] Club. Truly apoplexy
might have forced a resignation if I had.' There had been a series of destabilis-
ing incidents by Barrett and subversion by the erratic Professor Laby (natural
philosophy), but the real straw that broke Priestley's back was the Dunstan government's refusal to grant an additional £25,000. Without 'better prospects' of
external support Priestley felt that 'the responsibility is more than I can carry'.
At the New Education Fellowship conference he conferred with Darling on
'a personal matter', and then Darling, Giblin, Wadham and Copland (four of
his strongest supporters) all read his draft letter of resignation. Wadham was
horrified and 'so sick about Priestley's departure'. Rumours about a successor
circulated. Priestley's advice to Herbert Brookes, a prominent businessman and
chairman of the council's finance committee, was to go flat out to secure Rivett,
but Giblin believed (correctly) that Rivett would decline. Next, over lunch at
the Melbourne Club, Priestley reported that another businessman, Russell
Grimwade, was anxious to head off Copland's possible candidature and had suggested Darling as his successor. Then, Priestley noted, Copland suggested Bruce,
Darling had mentioned Gilray and Brookes was pushing for Grimwade. Giblin
dismissed such speculative jockeying as unproductive.[28]

In late February 1938, events took a new turn when Grimwade canvassed
Medley. Darling thought that his friend's candidature might break the impasse,
but Brookes was determined to weaken the grip on council of Barrett and his
Melbourne Club associates and, as Copland's chief backer, sought Medley's
withdrawal. A complication was that Parkinson had resigned from King's,
Parramatta, on 31 January and Medley's name was in the frame. Gripped by
uncertainty, he sought Darling's advice:

> is it your opinion (in view of the fact that a first rate man has abandoned it in
> despair and disgust) that the difficulties of the job are surmountable a. by any
> ordinary human being and b. by me[?]

Copland also wanted the appointment, and Priestley backed him but was
surprised by the vehemence of some opposition (particularly in the Faculty of

Medicine). At the Melbourne Club, Darling was informed by Sir Brudenell White (retired Chief of the General Staff) that he did not think much of either candidate, and that the headmaster should try to persuade Priestley to stay on. By mid-March, however, there were only two candidates: the chairman of the Professorial Board (1935–37 and acting vice-chancellor, 1936–37) and the head of Tudor House preparatory school. Priestley advised those who consulted him to support Copland, but he worried that the latter was talking about the appointment far too much in public.[29]

Decision day (21 March) arrived. The sub-committee recommended a vote between the two candidates. It divided six–four in favour of Copland and, over lunch that day with Bailey (Professor of Law and Copland's successor as Professorial Board chairman) Priestley had said that he expected that the entire council vote would be a forgone conclusion (about nineteen–ten for Copland), but he miscalculated badly. Copland's offer to address the council meeting was declined as unnecessary, although Medley was invited to speak. As he was suffering from influenza he was not called on, and instead was taken initially to Copland's house and then to Grimwade's. After endorsing his candidate at great length (too long Priestley thought) Brookes moved that Copland be offered the vice-chancellorship. A second motion to appoint Medley was also debated and, after about three hours of argument, there was a secret ballot on the two motions with the second carried fifteen–fourteen. Priestley was flabbergasted. After further discussion, Latham moved (with Darling seconding) that Medley be invited to accept the position. This motion was carried seventeen–eleven. The outcome was announced next morning. Priestley was dejected about the likely effect of the choice of Medley. Both Brookes and Wadham had made uncomplimentary remarks about him, and Darling and Grimwade had also reacted in the heat of debate. Priestley was convinced that university staff would see the decision as a Melbourne Club victory: 'it is all a terrible tangle at the moment owing to the passions that have been aroused'.[30]

The expected recriminations followed. Barrett told Darling that due to his and Grimwade's references to Brookes, the latter could not open the vice-chancellor's house (for which, along with George Nicholas, he was a benefactor) on commencement day in April. Both Darling and Grimwade had accused Brookes of stupidity and rudeness. 'In each case the chair [Latham] failed to intervene until Brookes appealed and in each case the man concerned made a crestfallen withdrawal.' Barrett implored Darling to smooth Brookes' ruffled feathers. Brookes didn't believe that Medley's personal record qualified him 'for this really staggering job', given that the 'capable and practical idealist' Priestley had resigned, and he was more suited as an aide-de-camp to the governor or even Melbourne Club secretary. Giblin (at King's College, Cambridge) described the outcome as 'devastating'. After all, he told his wife, Medley was a writer of incomprehensible political satire in verse. Bruce agreed with Giblin. Having been convinced by Wadham that Copland was home and hosed, Giblin assumed that Barrett had sprung a snap vote: there was no other explanation. Priestley worried that Copland might make a public protest. Moreover, Brookes would be 'irreconcilable' after one of his most bitter defeats in public life. The tightness of the decision for Medley conveyed an impression of deep division and might prejudice a potential £15,000 benefaction. Medley, meanwhile, was grateful to Darling:

> Well, dear James, what I must do is to secrete an unlimited supply of the faith that will move mountains. I am so fortunate in my friends that there must be something in me, I think.

At the 4 April council meeting, Darling made an impassioned plea for Medley to be given a fair go. 'Your timely appeal to common sense & gentlemanly conduct was just what was wanted', Barrett complimented him. Copland was bitter, but came to terms with the outcome:

> Molly [Medley's wife] travelled up with Copland the other day and made great friends with him. He poured out his little heart to her and wept on her bosom. He came here next day, dined and caught the train at night. All very affecting.

A month later, he was still bristling and sought out Darling to try to set the record straight. His supporters continued baying for blood and, in March 1939, they engineered Barrett's removal. In September, Copland became Commonwealth Prices Commissioner and, by the beginning of the new year, Brookes reported to Priestley that 'Copland and Medley appear to be completely reconciled'.[31]

Away from the limelight of university politics, Darling contributed to religious observance in the City of Melbourne by establishing the Fellowship of St John in late 1936. As head of a Christian school, he took seriously Norwood's claim in *The English Tradition of Education* that religion was 'the first and the most important element ... the foundation for all the rest'. The Reverend J.H. (Joey) Allen was GGS's chaplain, but Darling prepared candidates for confirmation, preached regularly and took infinite pains with his sermons. 'I always write the beastly thing out in full', he told his mother, but 'try not to read it'. He was critical of his own efforts. There was nothing worse than 'a frost' of a sermon. The only good that he did was 'reading the lessons intelligently'. He was particularly concerned about the old boys. The Fellowship would provide:

> services of the same sort as are provided in school chapels and stimulating preaching which would hold in the church the young men and women who, at present, seem to drift away from it during the period of their lives when they might most be of some use.

When Baldwin's seven years as Toc H padre concluded he became the fellowship's first chaplain. The new congregation met in St John's church, near the *Argus* building and comprised mostly recent school-leavers. Baldwin's stipend and a payment to Board of the Mission of St James and St John for the use of the church were to be covered by the weekly offering. Curthoys chaired the fellowship committee. Of one Sunday night service he told Darling that the singing 'simply baffles description', but that the post-service meeting was excellent. 'We must go along steadily in the spirit of faith and hope for the best.' He wanted a self-supporting fellowship, but soon it was 'broke', and he was reduced to writing begging letters. Darling sympathised, sent him two cheques and reflected (in a familiar vein) that 'it is a weary life pushing people up hills they do not want to go. Is it Australia, or youth, or the age, or the Anglo-Saxon race?' By the end of April 1937, a steady stream of donations was received (from businessmen such as Essington Lewis, Kingsley Henderson and Robert Knox) although these could not dispel Curthoys' periodic synthetic rage at the committee's 'half-heartedness and tepidity'. He also tried persuading Darling to join the council of the diocese (to help iron out problems that it had created for the Fellowship). At Head's urging Darling filled a casual vacancy.[32]

Another satisfying public sphere was the Geelong Free Library and Museum. Darling believed (like many others) that Australia was poorly served by its libraries. In two talks, each entitled 'On reading', he spoke about the importance of good books. Although as a boy he had loathed his father's choice of literature for him (for example, *Lorna Doone*), he admitted to occasional trifling 'with transitory trash' and confessed that at Repton he began reading from priggish motives to 'appear more clever than I was'. His delight for books went back to childhood and being read to aloud. Reading enlarged an otherwise circumscribed life and prepared one for new situations. A good novelist explained processes of mind and heart that people were not aware of and taught readers a moral. Really good books were the works of fiction. Geelong's Free Library, he told Cunningham in 1934, was in 'so sad a state'—so sad that the *Geelong Advertiser* criticised it for its appallingly deficient book stock (due mainly to insufficient purchase funds). An appeal was launched to wipe off the overdraft and provide new book money. Darling learnt of the Children's Library and Crafts Club in Surry Hills, Sydney, and that became his model of improvement. He joined the Geelong Free Library's general committee, but attended irregularly (Bull substituted for him). Cunningham reassured Darling that Geelong's situation was not an isolated case but endemic, as became embarrassingly clear in an ACER national survey. Keppel's visit to the Geelong Library in 1935 had shamed it into eventually buying books, Darling thought, and the 'untiring persistence' of E.J. Fairnie (the library's vice president) was changing things for the better.[33]

Australian Libraries—a Survey of Conditions and Suggestions for their Improvement was the ACER-commissioned survey completed in eight weeks in 1934 under the auspices of the Carnegie Corporation by Ralph Munn (director,

Carnegie Library, Pittsburgh) and Ernest Pitt (chief librarian, Public Library of Victoria). Known as the Munn–Pitt Report, it was a damning indictment of the woeful state of Australian free libraries:

> As a whole, Australia was better provided with local libraries in 1880 than it is today. Almost every city and large town now contains a decadent institute or school of arts, many of which give evidence of having had a former period of real usefulness.

Geelong's Free Library was condemned as 'one of the poorest' in Victoria although the city's Mechanics Institute was 'somewhat above the average'. When making the blanket claim that Australian libraries 'are a disgrace to a civilized people', Darling had not distinguished between free and subscription libraries. He paid for his sins in 1939 when the Mechanics Institute politely pointed out that it had no record of him ever visiting it. 'Perhaps I should have said the "free" library system', he replied sheepishly. The Free Library Movement commenced life at a public meeting in response to the Munn–Pitt report in Chatswood, Sydney, in June 1935, with a young Sydney solicitor, G.C. Remington, as inaugural chairman. It was intended as a nation-wide movement to awaken public consciousness to the condition of Australian libraries, and 'create a clamant demand for this essential service' in the form of rate-supported municipal lending libraries. Early in 1937, Remington informed Darling that Tate and Cunningham were keen to get the Free Library Movement under way in Victoria and, two months later, a meeting was held at the home of the industrialist, Sir Herbert Gepp. Priestley noted that it was a large gathering, chaired by Latham, and attended by Tate, Cunningham and Croll among others. An official launch at the Melbourne Town Hall followed in May. Darling (along with Sir Keith Murdoch, Priestley, Seitz and Barrett) was a vice president. He focused on Geelong where following renovations the Free Library had reopened in March. After a deputation led by Fairnie to the City Council (in which Darling made a rather high-minded appeal to councillors to think of themselves as being responsible not just for the municipality, but for civilisation as well) £500 was granted to buy books. In June 1938, the long-awaited children's or junior library opened, and many of the 800 books donated were from GGS boys, who also built the bookshelves and remodelled the library furniture.[34]

Part of Darling's public engagement was speech-making and publishing. Early 1930s efforts included one in which he waxed lyrical about Bridges' *Testament of Beauty*, while in another he teased a Melbourne audience in his preamble to 'Some Poet Laureates' about the plural form of the title (either 'poet-laureates', 'poets laureate', or simply 'poet laureates'), then followed 'Vergil [sic] in the middle ages' and 'The transition from imperial Rome to mediaeval Europe' for the Classical Association. Increasingly, his energies were devoted to social and educational issues. In 'The good schoolmaster' (echoing his spat with Hansen about educated and trained men), his claim that if compulsory teacher registration served the profession in Australia, then it failed to provide well-educated and inspiring teachers for the schools, drew a sharp rebuke from A.A. (Tosh) Phillips, a Wesley College master. In 'The better schoolmaster', Phillips replied that while his own experience of the 'breadth and fine restraint of the English tradition of culture left [him] humbled and envious' of English schooling, the corresponding 'wastefulness of the English tradition of "muddle-through" restored some of my colonial uppishness'. In 'Public school education' (1931), Darling defended English public schools as valuable for a new society. Those founded in the tradition of Arnold and Thring were religious enterprises, he said, and had provided the empire with governors. The ruling classes at Home and in the empire might have been snobbish, narrow, stereotyped, uneducated, unimaginative and so on, but they were not lazy, corrupt, lacking in a sense of duty or moral cowards. Any deficiencies were not 'inherent in the system', he claimed, although 'the virtues' were'.[35]

By the mid-1930s, the stand-out theme in Darling's publications was education for citizenship in a democracy. Apart from the inherently religious nature of education and the importance of character formation, Darling had no compulsion to defend public school traditions. Education's role in a representative democracy was elaborated in 'Post-primary education' (1935). While criticising democratic leaders for a lack of clear educational policy directions or sense of educational purpose, he tackled what might be accomplished by free secondary education for the mass of people. He was certain that an extension of existing secondary schooling (as preparation for university entrance and a professional career) would be disastrous—while agreeing that it was the best form of education for those able to benefit from it. It was pointless expecting that a society's need for professionals was greater than its need for clerks and manual labourers. Hence, an alternative model was the East Suffolk area school, where the education of children of twelve to fifteen years of age had a practical basis that enabled them to serve their communities. Unfortunately, no Victorian political party laid claim to anything like a genuine educational policy: they were not prepared to take education seriously. There was a 'cheeseparing, niggardly, unwilling granting of supplies, an interference in trifling matters, and no leadership in matters of policy', yet:

> I can conceive a civilisation in which all received education up to the age of 18 or even of 22, but it would not be secondary and university education as we understand the terms. There must, for these boys, be education of the man, not of the specialist. Present secondary education in many ways unfits men to take pleasure in their work, and certainly does not fully develop what we may call public spirit and intelligence.

The four essential policy elements were: discrimination between different types of secondary education, a means of ensuring that universities trained the best minds, a guarantee that schools enabled people to fit into 'the life that they are going to lead', and a means of guaranteeing that teachers developed the whole man—'his ideals, his standards, and his conduct, his loyalty, and his willingness to serve'.[36]

Why the lack of decent policies? The public was to blame because governments followed rather than led public opinion, as Darling emphasised again in 1938 when addressing the Conference on Education for a Progressive Democratic Australia in Sydney, the Victorian Teachers' Union and a huge public meeting held in Melbourne to establish the Education Reform Association. Although education was crucial in forming public opinion, everywhere there was apathy: a product of complacency, ignorance, lack of imagination, lack of faith in the country, a tendency to count the costs of everything and the divisiveness of sectional interests. In successful democracies there was usually a strong local feeling and commitment to education, whereas Australia's typical reliance on centralised public utilities eroded local responsibility. He counterposed an ideal of democracy with a school and a community centre in each locality 'in which the individual learns to work together with other individuals, learning the habit and the art of co-operation and respecting as he does so the development of every other individual'. What was really needed, he told Apexians, was a planned ideal towards which to work, the building up by careful comparison with previous ages and the examples of other countries of a model of 'a new heaven and a new earth'.[37]

In Darling's mental universe, the true end of education was to fashion a heavenly city as a civilisation based on wisdom, for which education and religion were 'inseparable'. The aim, he maintained in 'Things to come':

> is the cultivation of the will, by which I do not mean the development of will-power, though that possibly comes into it, but rather the nurturing in the individual of those intentions which lead towards the good of the world.

Fostering such ideals in young people made teaching a high calling. 'Real education' had to equip people with insight; if mankind was to get the world right again, then it 'must be able to see clearly the working of the moral law in the universe, and to accept the implications which such clearness of vision imposes upon them as individuals'. The supreme object of a Christian education, therefore, was altruistic he told the ANZAAS audience in his 1939 presidential address entitled 'Growing up'. To achieve active serenity of soul, education had to aim at 'the building up of men and women to the fullness of the stature of Christ' or, in everyday terms, 'the teaching of men and women to find the best in themselves and to make the best of themselves'. He was adamant that, despite the effects on boys of heredity and 'bad breeding', an appropriately framed educational community could mitigate such effects and accomplish what he wanted. Tucked away in an obscure set of his notes, 'Books which have altered the world' was a middle-way conundrum facing 1930s reformers: how to reconcile planning and individuality? Planning was expressed most completely in Communist states; individuality, through a fusion of the Bible and Greek ideas, was central to Western civilisation and democracies founded on natural rights:

> Those two ideas have got to be fused into one idea somehow, and as yet, though you get the problem stated in one way or another in almost every book you read,—as yet, I think, no prophet has arisen to resolve it.

Darling's solution was brotherly love or fraternity. While he thought that they were sadly deficient in it, the French revolutionaries had been right in emphasising fraternity, because 'the truly Christian quality' and solvent of all earthly incompatibilities, was 'the only way to combine liberty with equality', or 'the just claims of the individual with those of a planned society'. In this the final year of his first decade as headmaster, Darling turned forty. In four decades he had journeyed a long way in his development, but in his positioning of fraternity as a social reform goal, faint echoes were discernible of his own growing up as a little boy in a big house in England.[38]

PRIDE COMES BEFORE A FALL

1938–1940

Denmark's a prison ... O God! I could be bounded in a nutshell, and count myself a king of infinite space; were it not that I have bad dreams.

William Shakespeare, *Hamlet*, II, ii.

After nine years as headmaster, Darling took an extended break. Council agreed in August 1938 to his request to go to England in March and to return in the new year. His leave was carefully timed: the last trip home was in 1934, Margaret was yet to meet his family, he was keen to see his mother (as Austen had recently died) and their two daughters, Jane and Elizabeth, were old enough to cope with the voyage. During a lengthy period straddling his absence (early 1938 to late 1940) he engaged in extensive soul-searching. Fast-forward fifty years or so and contemporary language might describe this as a mid-life crisis. He was not at one with himself: he knew it and so did his circle of intimates. When the family departed there was mounting speculation about whether they would return. Rather than nip it in the bud, Darling let it run—indeed, some people even thought that he fuelled it. Combine such speculation with procrastination about his future plans, add swiftly emerging negative (and unanticipated) reactions to his reforms and the outcome was near fatal: distrust, accusations of treachery, recriminations, flights of talent, abandonment of cherished plans, and erratic behaviour and sulkiness by the architect of the venture. In its barest essentials, that is the tale of this period.[1]

For some time, Darling had been mulling over English appointments. In mid-1932, when Fisher resigned from Repton for the bishopric of Chester he mused: 'I wonder who will get it[?]' Had he stayed in England, he might have stood a chance though he didn't know that he wanted it. A former acquaintance asked him whether he was a permanent fixture where he was or did he have 'an eye on the home market' because the competition for recent appointments was 'not very keen'. As for Australia, it ought to be able to produce its own headmasters, Darling told his mother. Felsted had snared Bickersteth but with nothing in prospect for him, he was resigned to being 'set here for life'. Suddenly, there was a feast of English vacancies: Haileybury, Uppingham and Sherborne. In August 1933, Frank Fletcher wrote that if he was thinking of returning, then 'Sherborne wd. be a good place to try for, & you wd. be good for them', but then dashed his hopes: there was 'no reason whatever to suppose that they wd. wait for someone so far away whom they cd. not interview', but he would contact Sherborne if it would help. There was Darling's dilemma: marketable, and yet far away and (unlike local talent) hidden from view. Little wonder when he returned in 1934 that he confessed to Dicker that there was no sign of anyone trying to get him back permanently.[2]

In 1936 there was a minor scare when Manifold informed Wadham that, were he to be asked, the headmaster might consider being Director of Education. 'The thought appals me!', said Wadham. 'The machine can never be reformed from within ... I have watched the way things go & when Hansen was alive he told me quite a lot.' Darling reassured Wadham that he was speaking hypothetically although (keeping the door ajar) it might have 'some sort of moral claim on me'. The possibility was unlikely and, in any case, he would 'hesitate a great deal'. Having mentioned the departmental succession, Priestley recorded that:

> He [Darling] surprised me by replying, when I suggested that he should become Director of Education when MacRae [sic] goes, that it was by no means entirely outside the sphere of practical politics.

While he saw little likelihood of Darling being appointed, Priestley was 'always afraid that he will go home to a headmastership, and I fear that the chance of this is greater since his marriage'. Any hope of Fletcher being the bearer of glad tidings when he visited in 1936 proved groundless. Returning to England in June on the SS *Cathay*, Fletcher remarked upon the ubiquitous evidence of Darling's successful work and 'the appreciation' that he had won: 'Australia may be exile, but it is a country where a man's reputation can be widespread'. His sting in the tail said: 'For the present I am sure you can exercise an influence & do work in Australia such as England cd. not offer you'. Undeterred, Darling continued thinking about English headships. The kind of school that he fancied was a well-endowed smallish school like Tonbridge. The following year, during Lord Somers' visit, he asked for the former state governor's advice only to be told that his duty was in Australia.[3]

In February 1938, there was a genuine possibility. Once more (as in 1929) the messenger was Bickersteth—who, within three months of his own return to England, had exhorted Darling '[not] to be in such a hurry to give up Geelong & take an English School!' as he longed for Adelaide and the smell of gum trees. English schoolboys were 'very far off and sticky', and the dark winters depressed him:

I have this week heard from the National Advisory Council and Grants Committee for Physical Training and Recreation that they have approached you with a view to your considering a job as Principal and Organiser of the new Training Centre for boys and young men in England. I do not know how you are placed now as regards Geelong and it would be very hard on Geelong if you were to leave, but cannot help feeling that this particular job is going to be one of the most creative and interesting jobs in the whole of England during the next few years.

Here was a tantalising prospect. The appointee would have a free hand and money to prepare future leaders of physical training. Darling's indifferent sporting ability would not be an impediment because spiritual and moral considerations were to complement the physical side. Bickersteth was promoting Darling to the National Advisory Council and urged him to think seriously as it was 'undoubtedly creative work of the highest order'.[4]

After the March school council meeting Darling informed the chairman (Fairbairn) about the English offer. Fairbairn requested him to alert Manifold and Turnbull. In a lengthy letter to Turnbull, Darling confessed to uneasiness during the meeting because of 'something on my conscience' with a direct bearing on GGS's finances. He wrestled with his motives and prioritised the conflicting considerations weighing on him. Obligations and personal desires were to be considered in regard to what the countries of his birth and adoption were asking of him. There was the school's heavy financial burden arising from his reforms and, because the council had been 'so consistently decent to me during the last eight years', it would be 'almost impossible to do anything which you regarded as shabby'. Had he completed what he set out to do? He wasn't sure. Was he essential to the future of the school? Again he had no idea. What was certain, however, was that 'if I turn this down it is very likely that it means deciding definitely to remain here for the rest of my working life, another 20 years or more'. As yet, there was no official offer and so the proposal was merely 'an opportunity to start life anew in a new job'. He was 'very fond' of Corio and he wanted to stay. He was attracted by Australia as 'a rising sun' and yet he also felt the pull of 'all the old interests' at home. If Turnbull and the council were adamant that he should clear the school's debt—reasoning that seemed to be inviting them to decide for him—then there was no question that he would stay. He and Margaret had spent a tortured weekend, but he sensed a 'real call'. He had 'always gone on the principle of accepting a challenge if it seemed to be offered' and this opportunity seemed to be clearer than 'the rather hazy chance of headmasterships which I have been studiously disregarding during the last few years, or even the vice-chancellorship'.[5]

Darling swore Priestley to secrecy with the 'promise to tell no one and so I had not even mentioned it in my diary'. The British Government White Paper, which was the spur for the *Physical Training and Recreation Act*, tempered

Whiskard's initial reaction (to forget it). Later he thought it wasn't 'a 'fancy' job' at all, but of 'very real importance & possibilities'. McKie (about to depart for Magdalen, Oxford, as its new organist) said, after five drafts of a reply letter, that there would be 'terrible shock' and 'absolute consternation' among Darling's friends if he accepted an offer. He was under no obligation to GGS and 'they can hardly expect you to stay until all the borrowed money has been repaid!' As for the argument that he was spiritually exhausted, McKie thought that that was 'pure blah—you are only just starting'. Curthoys, when told, was completely torn:

> You know how I feel about Geelong Grammar—that under your leadership it is almost the last hope of a revulsion from the gross self-seeking, the vulgarity and the mental inertia about the things that matter which characterise those who are called the best people in this country.

Piling on the flattery, he wondered whether Darling's first priority was to save Australia or the mother country. 'I incline to think that every month in the immediate future the forces of decency in England will need every accretion of strength they can muster' and, because the post afforded scope for his friend's widespread influence, that 'it seems to me, must be the determining consideration'. Having heard nothing official, Darling cabled Bickersteth (4 April): 'No official letter. Is suggestion off?' The latter replied despondently (15 April) and enclosed a missive from Captain L.F. Ellis (secretary, National Fitness Council), explaining that a letter had not been forwarded to Darling and that 'the matter and a good many questions connected with it have gone back into the melting pot'. Ellis assured him, Bickersteth said, 'that he was approaching you', and apologised for raising false hopes. There was relief all round. Fairbairn urged Darling to 'consolidate and safeguard' his Corio achievements. He and Hawker were aware of a 'possible period of marking time' in Darling's life and sympathised. Archbishop Head wrote that 'for the next five years I believe that God's call to you is here. I lean on you rather a lot.'[6]

But that was not all. In early May, Priestley contacted his friend: 'I saw in the Argus a couple of days ago that the Physical Training news had got out. These things will'. The headline read 'Tribute to Master. Recognition in England' and the article suggested that Darling 'might be prepared to take charge of a new welfare organisation for the physical training of youths proposed to be established in England'. It then mentioned a 'hitch' and an indefinite delay of the launch. Were it to be revived, 'further overtures may be made to Mr. Darling'. Fairbairn was quoted as saying 'emphatically' that the headmaster 'was definitely not resigning'. A furious Darling had already demanded a retraction from Staniforth Ricketson and remonstrated with the editor:

> I should be grateful if you could make it clear that there was no authority of any sort for such a statement. No communication of an official sort has

been received by me and I have no detailed information concerning the alleged proposals.

A newspaper report could not fail to be damaging and he wanted an explicit denial. (Darling had mentioned the offer earlier to Ricketson who insisted that he maintained confidence.) The source was Canberra 'where apparently it was a topic of conversation', said Ricketson. What was done was done: 'in matters of this kind if they are being commonly discussed it is inevitable that the press reporters will get hold of them'. Sure enough, the news spread. At a dinner in late May with Aubrey Burstall (Professor of Engineering at the university, and a GGS parent), Priestley noted his anxiety about Darling's prospects and recorded that many 'friends and admirers out here must have been worried by the recent disclosure of the offer'. On his final visit to Corio in late June, Priestley had a long talk with the Darlings about the proposed college, and agreed to speak to Sir Will Spens (master, Corpus Christi, Cambridge) and the chairman of the Grants Committee for the government's Physical Recreation Scheme.[7]

Physical Training and Recreation (the 1937 White Paper) outlined the government's proposed measures to supplement existing extensive local authority and voluntary agency programs to improve the 'national physique'. It focused only on training (nutrition was dealt with separately). A 'measure of central co-ordination' was needed (through financial grants) to instil the attitude 'that physical fitness has a vital part to play in promoting a healthy mind and human happiness'. A college would prepare leaders to organise recreation and training, and undertake research into the physiology of physical training. Teacher training was not the college's main purpose and it would train men only. The *Physical Training and Recreation Act* was passed by Parliament in July 1937. Section 7 said that:

> The Board [of Education] may provide, maintain and aid a National College
> of Physical Training for England and Wales, or more than one such College,
> and may make such provision with respect to the management thereof as they
> think proper.

Ellis' National Advisory Council saw this section as 'one of the most important' because if public awareness of training and recreation was to be increased, amenities provided and programs initiated then trained leaders and instructors were vital. The council believed that the board had already acquired a site for the National College of Physical Training and that buildings were planned. (Bickersteth described the location as 'magnificent' in 'glorious country' in Surrey.) On 28 May *The Times* quoted Lindsay (since 1937, parliamentary secretary of the Board of Education) announcing the acquisition of 90 hectares at Merstham (27 kilometres from London). *The Times* displayed an aerial photograph. The National College of Physical Training was to be a residential college for

200 students. Costs were likely to be a stumbling block: the parliamentary vote of £2.4 million for capital grants and construction was revised upwards in late 1938 to £4 million, yet by December (1938) the land purchase was not finalised and Ellis was informed (in August 1939) that if war was declared the work of the National Fitness Council and allied bodies such as the advisory council would be 'suspended'.[8]

If financial stringency threatened the National College of Physical Training, austerity (on the eve of Darling's departure) was biting at Corio. *Richly Rewarding* says that belt tightening was a bolt out of the blue in 1939: 'up to the end of 1938 it had seemed to be roses all the way', with a possible financial loss in 1938 and council calling in Price Waterhouse (actually, the accountants, Flack & Flack). The danger signals, however, had been obvious to everyone (Darling included) from late 1937 when council appointed a special sub-committee (of Fairbairn, Turnbull and Bell) to review the finances. It eventually met during June–August 1938, after which council agreed on the bank overdraft and day-to-day economies. Darling wanted to use Whittingham estate income to pay off the two loans, but he agreed to trawl through the accounts with Thewlis to make savings. He found £2000 worth that council endorsed along with other measures. The bank overdraft, as Max Bell reported, had been increased by £6000 to £41,000. In December, Darling reported that expected enrolments in first term 1939 would rise from 419 to 441 and, in February, Buchan, Laird & Buchan were instructed to prepare designs and cost estimates for alterations both to the headmaster's house and Manifold House—with the intention of providing for a married housemaster and estimates for the erection of a new boarding house. Then in March 1939 (two days before Darling's departure) council decided (on its sub-committee's advice) to ask AMP to consolidate all existing loans and extend the repayment period. Crucially, Phillips (of Flack & Flack), did not report until 8 May when Darling was in England. Phillips noted expenditure growth and a sizeable bank overdraft increase, and recommended reducing capital expenditure to an absolute minimum 'until such time as funds may become available from a source other than borrowing'. The council then committed itself to a 'rigid economy of expenditure' (twelve measures in all): no capital expenditure, scrutiny of the accounts by the works and finance committee, abandonment of all building and rebuilding plans, and reduced non-teaching staff.[9]

On 7 March, the Darlings sailed on the *Ulysses*. Previously, in 1938, the headmaster's views had been sought on a successor to Parkinson at King's, Parramatta—Denys Hake was eventually appointed. In desperation, King's council had even approached Darling (in July). He declined. 'Only a very strong call of conscience to a job with a much larger scope than this one would really justify me in leaving.' When F.B. Malim retired in the summer of 1937, Wellington College in England might have been another possibility, but Darling was not approached. The strongest indication that he might be in with a chance came from McKie. Marlborough was vacant and Fletcher might put Darling's name forward, although Fletcher had other things in mind:

> he has already discussed the business with [George] Turner, and mentioned your name; but he himself thinks Marlborough would not suit you as well as some other places, eg. Clifton, which will be vacant at the end of this term.

In Cape Town, the Darlings lunched with the Sir Patrick Duncan (governor-general and a member of Viscount Milner's famous kindergarten) and Lady Duncan. News arrived of Neville Chamberlain's unconditional guarantee to Poland. So, far, Darling told Curthoys, the voyage was unpleasant and the girls had not travelled well. A political crisis was looming in Australia, Curthoys wrote back. 'Exciting and disgusting times' had followed Joe Lyons' death on Good Friday, 7 April, with the United Australia Party (UAP) divided over the succession:

> Your Melbourne Club friends in the National Union, and their opposite numbers in the Union Club in Sydney, aided and abetted by Page, who not unnaturally hates Menzies for the devastating stories Menzies so openly and so tactlessly spreads about Page's leadership of the trade delegation in London; and by Casey, who, in the opinion of most people, comes out of the whole business very badly, made a dead set on Menzies.

Bruce (back from London) imposed impossible terms if he was to be party leader and by supporting Page to persuade Bruce to return, Casey ended his own prospects: '[Bruce] wd return if he cd refrain from belonging to any party, could choose his own team and cd have the support of Labour [sic]'. Casey then got cold feet and persuaded Lyons in late March to reject Bruce's terms. In the event, Menzies won by four votes from the aged Hughes, with Casey a humiliating third. Curthoys was sceptical about Menzies—'it is inconceivable that he will not soon become [a] megalomaniac'—but he chuckled at 'all the gentry who had done their damnedest to keep him out assembled to greet him at Spencer st [railway station] the other day'.[10]

The Darlings arrived in England late in April. For about the next eight months, two men thought by Darling to be loyal supporters, C.A. Cameron and Ned Austin, became the key people at Corio. When it granted Darling leave, the council stipulated that he would be absent 'under the same conditions' as in 1934, which meant that as acting headmaster Cameron would provide the advice which he 'thought I would have given' rather than his own advice. To assist Cameron, Darling insisted that, as council secretary, Austin should live in the headmaster's house and entertain guests—a decision that he would regret. Austin was a member of a well-known pastoral family with longstanding GGS connections, a bachelor, a devout Anglican and a council member for more than thirty years. For three years until 1935 he had been a UAP MLA for Geelong. One of Dr Brown's sons later described him as a 'conscientious steward'. Comfortably ensconced in 'your mansion' and experiencing all 'the interruptions and distractions' that went with occupancy of the headmaster's house, Austin observed day-to-day operations firsthand. The experience transformed his view of the school. By contrast, Cameron was rough-hewn, self-made, terse, blunt and practical. He and Darling were opposites: contrasting styles, outlooks and backgrounds, and different in age and temperament, yet they hit it off. Was second master the limit of Cameron's ambitions? His son Ross thought so. His father believed that serving in heaven was better than reigning in hell. And while the effect of substituting for Darling for four days at the Headmasters' Conference of Australia in May (where he was appreciative of attending and enjoyed 'the remarkable good fellowship') is a matter for speculation, from 19,000 kilometres away in England Darling began to sense betrayal.[11]

The first inkling of something amiss was a stiffly worded letter from Austin (11 May) that contrasted with his twittering epistle about a week earlier. The second letter arrived just as Darling was invited to apply for the headship of Bradfield. (He declined.) On reading it, and the enclosed Flack & Flack report and council minute (that said 'in view of the adverse financial position every effort must be made to stay Capital Expenditure'), he might have wondered whether he had done the right thing in returning to England. Perhaps he really was the 'prize' that, he had been assured, Bradfield had missed out on. Taken aback, Darling talked with Wadham (also in England) on 2 June:

> The most obvious thing would be to go back and fight them but this means leaving my family and all opportunity of getting another job over here: and I feel that I have to consider my own future a bit.

Wadham wrote to Turnbull, and said that Darling felt that the Corio correspondence had been rather 'official' and was 'hurt' by it. Darling wondered whether council 'would be glad if he resigned' and was concerned about its 'defeatist sort of attitude of retrenchment' rather than expansion, particularly when everything else was educationally sound. Wadham could hardly see why a firm of auditors had been appointed to advise on school matters. He didn't think Darling was looking for an English appointment, and there was no bombshell in store for the council, although the recent resolutions, the lack of any consolatory letters to him and, especially, 'the lack of a progressive <u>financial</u> outlook by the Council' had produced 'awkward reactions'.[12]

Wadham assured Darling that he had written an honest account for Turnbull of what they had talked about. He advised him to be mild and focus on the council's resolutions when replying to Austin. Darling protested that its decisions meant postponement of some of his 'cherished plans' and suggested that it have a rethink when he had returned, but thanked Wadham for reading his letter draft and left him to decide whether to mail it. After cabling Cameron he talked with Bickersteth. 'The truth is that Australia cannot understand anything except money: and people who have other ideas are better out of it', he despaired. A week later the Darlings stayed with the Priestleys in Birmingham during which they all motored over to Repton and toured the school. After the Darlings left for London, Priestley recorded that his friend wanted an English school in about three years' time, and that King Edward's School in Birmingham and Christ's Hospital 'were both mentioned'. Next, Darling wrote to Cameron—with a turn of phrase that would be misinterpreted:

> Do try to protect the masters and their wives from all the irritating economies which cause trouble without saving much money. The maintenance of good-will between the teaching staff and the Council is one of the most important duties of a Headmaster and it cannot be preserved if the Council is allowed its hand entirely in this economy racket.

He dropped plans for the new boarding house and said in passing that 'we might be able to take over Masterman's house at a pinch and let Gordon go into ours', but this proposed accommodation solution merely exacerbated matters. The impossibility of addressing policy decisions across vast distances was now obvious: with letters crisscrossing the globe, dates of dispatch and receipt, and transmission times were assuming a disproportionate importance. The time gap between a letter mailed in a distant part of the empire and the receipt of a promptly mailed reply could be up to six weeks. Likewise, letters between widely separated correspondents would cross in transit. If events had moved on by receipt of replies, then the sending or arrival of other letters relevant to the contents merely compounded this timing misalignment. With wording assuming significance, such circumstances were ripe for confusion, especially when the headmaster's prevarication increased.[13]

Before the arrival of further dispiriting news, the National College of Physical Training emerged again. Building operations were scheduled to commence that summer and to be completed within three or four years. Having got wind from Bickersteth of Darling's visit, Ellis and Darling lunched at the Athenaeum Club, after which Darling said that he quite understood that 'as regards myself everything is entirely unofficial'. His letter to Ellis highlighted personal concerns, while acknowledging his various obligations, but despite an ill-disguised sense of guilt he was keeping his options open:

> it was made clear to me that members of the [school] council individually would regard it as dishonourable for me to consider another position while I was home. I do not myself altogether subscribe to that view but have been so generously treated by them and am so much concerned with the welfare of Geelong Grammar School that I do not wish to let them down.

Then, with a tidy piece of rationalisation, out popped the reason that he was so intent on redirecting his career:

> The difficulty for me lies in the fact that having received the appointment to the headmastership of Geelong at 30 I am in danger of staying there until I am 60 or 65, which will be neither good for me [n]or the school. I do not feel particularly attracted by the possibility of moving to any other school, but a job, such as the one you have outlined to me, seems a different matter.

Darling's father had once said of his son's career that it had 'up to the present [1929] been so wonderfully mapped out for you': perhaps his luck was holding after all, despite a decade's remoteness from what he took for granted as the centre of things.[14]

It was the end of June and war was still about eight weeks away. On the day of his letter to Ellis, Darling wrote to Cameron, agitated at having heard nothing and intimating that he felt 'a little neglected'. The news took three weeks to arrive. Frustration and impatience surfaced. Colin Gordon kicked off with a few bombshells. After assuring his chief (and friend) that Cameron was doing fine, he revealed 'a certain section of discontent' centred on Bull, 'who moans that "in your absence, under a barrage of financial stringency, your whole policy was being ruined"'. Gordon tried to play down this grumbling as Bull venting dislike of Cameron. Russel Ward resented Cameron's 'resistance to some left wing propaganda in the P.A. [public affairs form]'; other masters had been niggled by Thewlis' economies and there had been a couple of staff dismissals. Gordon then asked Darling the question that was paralysing his friend: 'Are you coming back?':

> I see they've got a man for Tonbridge. I tell everyone valiantly that you are coming back & on the whole I think there's a shade of odds on it, but only a shade.

After a line or two about his forthcoming marriage, Gordon then revealed that he was 'thinking of writing to Hake at T.K.S. [King's] & seeing if he's got anything for me', adding blithely that the change of school would be good experience 'with a view to a future headmastership, wouldn't it. Incidentally do you know anything of openings there. Any more news of St. Peter's?' This grumbling in the ranks threatened the break-up of Darling's inner circle of intimates and disciples but, short of returning to Australia immediately, he could do little to prevent council austerity measures fuelling masters' inclinations to seek greener pastures. Eighteen months earlier he had been on the defensive when he was pushing P. Fletcher's candidature for King's: Frank Fletcher had 'strongly recommended' Gordon (then on leave in England). Relieved to be told that King's council felt that Gordon might be a little 'immature' and that 'youth and unorthodoxy were against him', Darling had quickly put up the shutters when King's also tried to snatch Bull. 'Bull not anyone's to be considered', his reply telegram snapped.[15]

Eventually, Darling received a whopping 21-page handwritten letter from Cameron. It was his first and arrived in mid-July about a week after Gordon's. Having ignored Darling's cabled directive (9 June) to await his next letter, Cameron admitted to acting against his better judgement and was muddled: 'I have so many items to write about that it will be well to abandon all idea of continuity'. There was little joy to be had with staffing, as a number of men had resigned and he had dispensed with a junior schoolmaster. Unless modifications were made to Manifold House to accommodate Gordon and his bride, he too was likely to leave. Further, Gordon's new wife (Pat) would probably work in a capital city. To deepen the gloom, he and Miss Moden had analysed the likely admissions for 1940, and 'the definite impression is that numbers will NOT be maintained'—as Austin separately confirmed. At page 16, the tone of Cameron's letter changed abruptly to umbrage. Headmaster or not, Cameron told Darling (fourteen years his junior) that he had a cheek reminding him about the baleful effects of council austerity:

> I did not take at all kindly to your reference in the last letter to the lack of support to the masters and their wives in various irritating details where it was suggested the School Council wished to economize. I am not one scrap concerned to know the source of this inaccurate or rather warped information and know that I have tried to act fairly and consistently. I am quite conscious of the bones of contention on the part of some men and you can take it that those who were and possibly still are angry include those men who in the past have had the greatest measure of consideration from you and the School Council.

He continued slugging it out by quoting Darling's earlier amazement that Cameron and Thewlis had been so supine with the council. (Darling had said: 'you must do all in your power to have rescinded the resolutions passed at the Council Meeting of May 8th'.) That was all very well, except that if Darling had not qualified his insistence in his cable, Cameron would have cabled back and advised:

> your return to deal with this matter in person. There was no sudden develop-ment in the position—you had noted the trend of affairs on the financial side during the earlier months and probably anticipated the nature of the expert report.

He had hit the nail on the head.[16]

Darling was prepared for Gordon to obtain a headship at King's (or even at Southport) but was unwilling to release him to an assistant mastership elsewhere, especially if the sticking point was married quarters in Manifold. Furious with

Cameron, but aware that he could ill afford to alienate him he pondered whether to return home by November. Again he undertook to arrange Masterman's exchange so that all three could swap living arrangements. He also wrote (18 July) to Manifold, sounding off at Cameron's 'complacency' and warning him of Gordon's imminent departure. His letter arrived (7 August) in time for that month's council meeting, but made no difference: council was adamant that the headmaster's shuffling of the accommodation was 'quite impracticable'. The likelihood of Gordon's departure increased because he had a definite offer from Hake. As a stopgap, Cameron offered him a choice of residences on the school site yet, Gordon complained to Darling, 'my whole idea of running the house is to be on top of it all the time', for which there was no alternative but to live in it. 'A non resident housemaster is nearly a contradiction in terms, isn't it?'[17]

Meanwhile, in the headmaster's house, Ned Austin had been entertaining masters and had held six dinner parties. The last thing that Darling needed was a rebuke, except that he got one. Any likelihood of making alterations to the residence had long since passed, but that did not stop Austin from querying Darling's original reasoning. 'I am at a loss to know what you find wrong with the kitchen or the serving pantry', he said. What was more, Thewlis (of whom Gordon had said he 'advances to a still higher degree of odium': 'sack him') had costed Darling's proposed alterations at a minimum of £420. The tone of Austin's opinion that 'you would be wise at this juncture to put up with any little inconvenience and be satisfied with existing conditions', however, came across as a tad too admonitory. Clearly, glimpsing the 'affairs of state' had altered Austin's views:

> the financial position of the School is as bad as it well nigh can be and it is the bounden duty of the Council to put 'our house in order', and I sincerely hope that to that end you will not ask for any more capital expenditure but will give the Council your faithful co-operation.

Furthermore, Austin was glad to see the back of Russel Ward who 'speaks with the voice of authority on certain matters, especially Communism':

> The hold this ugly thing has in certain directions here has shocked me. In preparing boys for Confirmation it has been revealed to me how very little some boys know about the vital truths of the Christian Religion, and the revelation has made me a sad man. It is appalling to know that in a Church School in a Christian Land one has to combat Communism as if it were quite the equal of Christianity.

Communism was 'the negation of all that Christian men hold dear in life'.[18]

Austin's letter gave the impression of a full-frontal attack on Darling's liberalism. After two years in the junior school, Ward had taken over from Nield in 1938 when the latter resigned to commence his own school at Warrandyte, near Melbourne. Not only had the public affairs form 'flourished remarkably under the leadership of Mr. J.C. Nield', said the *Corian*, but so too had the Public Affairs Society. It had stimulated engagement in matters of public interest in the remainder of the school and had been active in social service. As Nield explained to the 1936 conference of the Australian Institute of Political Science, the form operated on a self-governing basis in which 'we attempt to make people sufficiently alert and enthusiastic to run a democracy'. W. Macmahon Ball (senior lecturer in political philosophy, University of Melbourne) who had given several talks at GGS extolled its unique approach to political education. 'To me', he wrote:

> it is one of the most encouraging things I know, that this deliberate effort is being made to develop in boys, still in their teens, some sense of their responsibility in the community.

Small comfort for Darling, then, that another asset (Ward) was departing.[19]

With Austin and Cameron closing ranks with the council, and Darling's misgivings being fanned by his closest associates' letters, it is easy to see why he sensed plotting. An additional factor exacerbating a worsening relationship with Cameron, Austin and the council was the prolonged absence or erratic attendance of his key supporters. Darling had fought to persuade Wadham from resigning in 1937 but he was now, like Darling, a long way away from Corio. John Turnbull had requested leave of absence in June (due to illness) and was in the United States. Max Bell sought leave in August and, after his elevation to Menzies' Cabinet, Jim Fairbairn was frequently unavailable. An unanticipated consequence of this membership discontinuity (as Austin admitted) was that the finance committee 'have so far done nothing' other than maintaining a watching brief. This combination of factors made the task of Manifold (acting chairman in Fairbairn's absence) impossible in stemming the austerity tide: he had little choice but to support the acting headmaster and to uphold council policy. No wonder that Austin had become so prim and that Gordon could observe: 'poor Cameron—he is having a hell of a time'. And yet, if Darling read his words carefully he would have noticed that his sentence about Cameron also said 'complete loyalty to both you & the Council'.[20]

Reform, liberalism and expansion, if not threatened, were on hold. (Reaction, P. Fletcher had told Darling, was perfectly normal in schools after about four or five years of new broom upheaval.) Darling geared himself: if there was to be rigid economy, then so be it. He proposed a 20 per cent cut in his salary (£500) and offered to return before the end of the year. Leading with his trump card, he said to Manifold that it was impossible to simply chop here and there; rather, the entire system would need recasting, something for which GGS would pay a heavy price: 'we may very easily lose our position of predominance if we become a school just like all the others and not so good as St. Peter's'. Fairbairn told him to forget curtailing his leave. Four further letters were dispatched to Darling just after the August council meeting. In two of them, Cameron's and Austin's pessimism about enrolments persisted: the prolonged drought of 1938–39 was not helping nor was the drift to war. Once again Austin lectured Darling about the council's sincerity in its economising. He had no idea why Darling had said that he was dreading returning, whereas Gordon tried to reassure his boss that, all things considered, the school was going along 'very well', but the significance of one sentence in his letter may have eluded Darling (he didn't comment on it): 'If I had been offered Masterman's house I'd have taken that'. It would not necessarily have been easier being the Manifold housemaster from there but cheaper, as Masterman's house was furnished.[21]

Cameron cast himself as an honest council servant and was careful not to offend Darling when enquiring about his return date. As Darling had signalled his willingness to restructure the entire program, it was advisable that he 'should be here by the middle of January'. Cameron cited council's minute that Darling should: 'return to the school as late as possible consistent with existing conditions'. Next, Manifold, a past master in dispelling Darling's pessimism and buoying him up, weighed in (with a seven-page letter):

> I know from my own experience that once you get away from a job it is very easy to believe, on the slightest grounds, that the people left in charge are acting like fools or madmen or both. In this case you have certainly had more than slight grounds for thinking something of the sort. But this real financial stress seems to have fallen upon us most suddenly; and if in your first bitterness you had any idea (which in my opinion would be quite natural) that Council was just taking advantage of your absence to swing its weight about, put it right out of your head.

A badly depleted council was performing admirably. As for Gordon, he should give Cameron's offer a try, but the truth of the matter, Manifold surmised, was that Gordon was fed up with running Manifold House and 'he is attracted by the idea of a complete change'. Bear with Cameron, he exhorted his friend, because being in an acting capacity for so long and in such circumstances was invidious. His competence was not in question and his tendency to see the world in black-and-white terms stemmed from his honesty and single-mindedness in dealing with the facts. Nonetheless, 'I suppose bland complacency is his real trouble added to a complete lack of any sensibility'. Map out plans for the restructuring of the school, Manifold pleaded, and then leave Cameron to deal with the details for 1940. He was emphatic: 'there is no need to alter your arrangements about returning in any way'. On the eve of war, then, there was no question of not wanting the headmaster and no question of anyone reversing the previous decade's work: the council had made a different financial judgement from Darling, and it may well have been incorrect, but that was it. Despite his qualms, Darling agreed to fall into line with the council. The only unresolved item was his return date. 'You might also incidentally drown Ned', Darling said facetiously.[22]

Two factors might upset this applecart: evidence contrary to the rosiness that all was well and a declaration of war. The first came in an alarmist letter from Giblin. After visiting Corio early in August, he painted a disarmingly frank picture of plotting and scheming:

> Your deputy, the Bursar, & the Works Committee of the Council seem to be instinctively or deliberately throwing their weight against any kind of Liberal move. It is shown in a number of petty ways … but more generally in making difficulties & putting up obstacles to your National Service Scheme. I wish Wadham was not away too.

Full of praise for Bull, Giblin said:

> I hope you are coming back. If you don't, I'm afraid there is a danger of a bad slide: it looks to me as if these tendencies I thought I had evidence of, were part of a move,—perhaps half-conscious,—of the Old Guard (including Old Boys generally) to prepare for a reversal of policy, if you don't return; with financial considerations as an excuse or a blind. It would be rather tragic. The blessed old international situation has its part in all this,—coupled with the delayed reactions against your original renaissance,—a second wave. I expect the question of masters will be a problem. As you know, they are physically disintegrating this year,—morally it has been going on a good while, & has inevitably gone further in your absence. (There is probably some tendency but in the weaker members to trim their sails to the present trend of authority).— But I do think you will have to take time from other things to build up again the apostolic touch of the earlier years,—which of course you can do with one hand.—But I've said that before.

To whom had Giblin spoken? Darling had no way of knowing. A month later a departing master also pleaded with Darling 'not to desert Geelong: they will need you there more than ever'. Then Vi Moden wrote and said that 'so many other people have expressed the same hope to me', namely that her boss would return sooner than expected. When these two letters arrived, however, the second factor was in play: war had been declared.[23]

Vi Moden's loyalty to Darling caused her to break her silence. Normally she kept her opinions to herself, but 'lots of things are happening of which you would not approve'. The council was obsessed with finance, but why make restrictions right now? What was more, 'you were right when you said that Mr. Thewlis would be excluded from the confidence of Mr. Cameron and Mr. Austin'—an observation not quite squaring with those of Giblin and Gordon. Most unsettling was the rumour that the headmaster was not intending to return:

[This was] due perhaps to the fact that the offer you had some time ago reached the press [i.e., the National Council of Physical Training position]. Several people quite outside the school have mentioned it to me.

An earlier Giblin letter had mentioned a different rumour: 'the story is you have refused Marlborough,—so I hope you are going to finish the job here'. (Wadham had told Giblin in late September that he had even heard rumours in England of Darling's possible resignation.) If for any reason McKie's letter (mailed mid-January) about the Marlborough vacancy had arrived after the Darlings sailed, then Cameron (or Moden) might have read its contents, in which case the alleged story may have come from him. Darling had also alerted his deputy (after Giblin's visit) that he was going to Marlborough in mid-August to interview Phil Le Couteur about a possible job at Corio. In his letter to P.R. Le Couteur (the young man's father) Cameron had said:

> Very confidentially I can tell you that things are chaotic here at the moment and staff readjustment—I think staff reduction—is essential. We have been working on an extravagant basis during the past several years.

So uncomfortable at what she was observing was Moden that she pleaded with her boss to return:

> really Mr. Darling there is no need for me to say that this would make a difference to the school because you are the school and have done so much for it that you have a definite following as possibly all Headmasters have. But you know this.[24]

At about the time when Molotov and Ribbentrop were thrashing out their infamous agreement, Mabel and Ralph hurried south from Durham to Trimley. Ralph wrote in his diary that when he 'came down to breakfast next morning [23 August] Jim handed me *The Times* with "that's done it", & I saw that the German–Soviet Pact had been signed'. (Ralph's son Morris still recalls the look of 'absolute horror' on his uncle's face as he read *The Times*.) With the realisation that war was probably inevitable, Darling's brother-in-law recalled that:

> A feeling of unreality pursued us all day. I remember the scene at the Felixstowe Yacht Yard [?], groups studying papers, anxious faces & children exasperatingly unmoved and exacting so it seemed.

On the morning of 25 August, RAF searchlight officers arrived and requisitioned the Old Rectory. The le Flemings returned hastily to Durham. With the cares of Corio a world away, Darling's new job on 30 August was to organise the billeting at Felixstowe of 13,000 evacuees as part of the government evacuation scheme. He worked with officials and volunteers. It was a 'colossal task', he told Manifold. With 48 hours advance warning and only 24 hours' definite notice, he had thrown himself into the work. He personally met about 360 disembarking boat parties, most comprising school groups and young mothers. He then handled their reception, followed by their transport to, and billeting in, schools, halls and vacant houses. When required he arranged medical inspections. He was assisted by his wife and sister, and some OGGs. At his request, massive amounts of food had been ordered by the Felixstowe Urban District Council. The extent of the patriotic stirrings unleashed can be gauged from an early 1940 address to a Pleasant Sunday Afternoon service at Wesley Church in Melbourne. At no time in its history, Darling said, had England been 'more at one' and unquestionably the cause was right.[25]

It was the 'phoney war' period—formal declarations, but no hostilities. Any hope of the National College of Physical Training evaporated. Bernays (parliamentary secretary, Ministry of Transport) had been informed that for the time being the Board of Education had no way of 'making use' of Darling. But his return to Corio was not a forgone conclusion, he informed Manifold, because 'everything is of course changed by the war'. He was eligible for military service and, as the council should not hang on indefinitely, he decided to resign. Cables crisscrossed the globe for a fortnight. Darling's first was met with: 'Your true duty Empire return immediately feasible'. He replied: 'Return before next year impossible would you prefer resignation', whereupon Manifold said: 'Primary object our cable to help ease your problems emphatically refute resignation idea' and Fairbairn amplified by saying (9 October) that Darling could fly back for the start of the new school year, get it underway and then leave Cameron in charge. In his letter to Manifold, Darling was uneasy and unable to make up his mind:

> I am a little annoyed by the whole business and the difficulty of knowing what is right to do; but as I am here it doesn't seem possible to go back without offering my services. Of course, if nobody wants me the case will be altered.

Once again the door was left open for someone else to decide for him. There was another unexpected turn: courtesy of a friend (Tommy Wood, author of *Cobbers*), Darling landed himself a job in the (ill-fated) Ministry of Information. This new milieu gave him (six weeks) firsthand experience of state bureaucracy.[26]

The new ministry commenced in grand style on 1 September, but as a bloated edifice it was doomed. Under a director-general and a deputy there were no fewer than fourteen divisions and more than 1000 staff. On 15 September, Darling was a temporary appointee: salaried officer Grade 1 on a salary of £1000 in Division 5, empire publicity, the director of which was H.V. Hodson (editor of the *Round Table* and who visited Corio in 1934) and the deputy-director V.T. Harlow (Beit Professor of Colonial History, Oxford). Darling worked in the Dominions section housed at the University of London. Initially the work seemed worthwhile, but he harboured doubts. So vehement was the parliamentary criticism that the ministry was reorganised and scaled back, and Darling was an early casualty. With empire publicity 'greatly reduced', he was given a month's notice, with termination effective from the end of November. His objections and those of Hodson were to no avail because, as his Oxford chum MacDonald (Colonial Secretary) pointed out to Lord MacMillan, there was duplication in the information flow between Colonial Office staff and sections of empire publicity. Hodson thanked him for his valuable work and said that Darling's personal qualities had kept relations between the Dominions section and Dominions Office 'co-operative and friendly'. Wadham wrote to say that his real place was at GGS and, even before leaving the ministry, Darling told Manifold that Australia seemed 'desperately desirable' and hinted at his return. In no mood for equivocation, Manifold's ultimatum said: 'I think that what we most want from you as soon as may be is the statement that you intend to come back. Nothing really matters besides that.' He thought that the headmaster was deliberately keeping everyone dangling. 'Behind what you wrote I thought I could read an unexpressed hope that you were <u>not</u> coming back.' Then, sugar-coating stiffness with flattery, he said:

> Personally, I am not able to face the possibility that you may not return. I have
> no slightest doubt but that you are our greatest asset—our only asset in fact.
> Should you fade out—well, in my opinion, the School fades out also.

His ploy worked. On receipt of his letter (and an anxious one from Bull) Darling finally got a grip and cabled: 'definitely returning February—full of fight'.[27]

A letter arrived from Cameron about staffing. Gordon was off to King's, Dart had applied for a post in Armidale, Ponder was joining up in England and Fraser was leaving. With Ward also gone, the entire staffing establishment was crumbling. In a seven-page reply he laid out his plans, and warned Cameron (and Manifold) that he would not roll over and accept the new measures. Manifold replied testily:

> You say that a letter from me and one from Bull were the decisive factors in
> your decision to return ['the final push in that direction', Darling had said].
> Most definitely that by itself is not a good enough reason for your return, and
> on my part I simply cannot allow myself to be held responsible even to that
> extent for your decision.

He was fed up:

> There is a full-time job waiting to be done at the School—the School you
> have made! If your enthusiasm for your own handiwork has waned so much,
> and you are coming back to it with reluctance and with the intention of giving

it only part of your time and thought and energy, you are being fair to nobody
… your great work and most effective contribution to the general good lies
here: your true duty is still to get back to your own job as quickly as possible
and to do it better than ever before. All the other things you talk about as
being important are, in my opinion, just fal-lals in comparison.

The chairman had not minced words because he had taken Darling to imply that
council was being financially mischievous behind his back. Not so: there was a
very real possibility of bankruptcy.[28]

Despite the fact that sailing home was extremely dangerous and unwise—
the *Athenia* had recently been sunk in the Atlantic with many lives lost—the
Darlings took the risk. With Nanny Murray and Nurse Johnson, Darling and
Margaret and their daughters left England on Boxing Day 1939, on a nerve-
wracking trip. Because of the fear of sea mines in the English Channel they
arranged to fly to Paris and take a train to Naples, but fog put paid to flying.
Instead, they were five or six hours crossing the Channel from Newhaven to
Dieppe on a ghastly overcrowded and blacked-out ferry with neither lifeboats
nor life jackets. Wrung out emotionally when they reached Paris, they were
amazed to find house and streetlights on at night, and normal life. With a
party of fellow Australians, they waited for days in Naples idly frittering the
time away, their money desperately low and with no prospect of credit, until at
6.30 am one morning they received word that their boat had berthed. Theirs
was the first voyage through the Mediterranean since the declaration of war.
When they boarded, they were dismayed that personal effects were missing from
their suitcases. At Suez, Darling contracted a raging fever and an illness defying
accurate diagnosis but affecting his lungs until their ship was in the Indian
Ocean. Approaching Australia the drama continued: their ship diverted a long
way south of Fremantle to avoid possible submarine attacks. You 'poor old thing',
an English acquaintance wrote, 'you <u>did</u> have a rotten leave over here, & having
to cut it short & go back under such very difficult conditions must have been a
nightmare'.[29]

In December, Gordon assured Darling that his return was:

generally awaited in a spirit that is flattering to you but rather depressing
otherwise I think—a sort of feeling that only you can avert some intangible
doom which would otherwise engulf the school.

Cameron had had a hell of a year '& did extremely well to get them through it
without a collapse, but that he naturally failed to give the feeling of leadership
that we are used to …' Darling, however, did not feel welcome and fell out with
Cameron: "'I consider you have been disloyal to me while I've been away'".
Cameron is supposed to have stood his ground and answered back: "'I don't
agree with you at all'". Darling thought that Cameron should have defended his

policies to council, despite the weight of opinion favouring austerity restrictions, but because (Darling claimed to Manifold) Cameron was 'so wrapped up in his own conceit', he didn't. Cameron's defence was that his task was difficult enough with masters fleeing the coop without also having to endure Darling's continued equivocation. But Cameron and Austin might have been in cahoots against the headmaster because Austin was thought to be meddling in the business of the common room. Darling's position had not been helped by rumours of possible English appointments and the gossip that he was not returning. Damaging speculation had spread quickly in the small, isolated and closed community. With his anti-English prejudices and his view that Darling played favourites with certain staff members, the last thing Cameron would do was to stand in the way of departing masters such as Gordon and Bull. Their departure may have been indirectly encouraged by not making their lives any easier. He and Bull had never seen eye to eye. As Cameron told the Headmasters' Conference of Australia when presenting Darling's and Bull's reports on national service: 'I find it necessary at the beginning to state a point of difference in the make-up of these two men and myself', because 'we view the relative value of some items of practical work from different angles'.[30]

Darling's first council meeting on 12 February was tense. He had a guilty conscience about the English job offers:

> a man who goes home should not be bound to refuse consideration of all possibility of promotion to other spheres. If Council does not accept this it does in effect tie them to an English master or Headmaster until his death ... I wish to record my opinion which is supported by other eminent Headmasters in England whose advice I sought.

He voiced his 'strongest opposition' to the council's recent measures, but accepted that he was bound by them. Unable to come to terms with his changed circumstances, Darling sulked. Peter Westcott, Bull's successor, copped its full force on the day of his arrival:

> I went to the tower, to the study, and the door was open. I saw a person sitting on the chair. I said: 'I'm Westcott, and I have been appointed to the staff'. The person sitting there turned out to be [Barney] Hutton. A head came round the corner and said: 'I'm the headmaster'. So I said: 'I have been appointed to the staff', and he said: 'Not by me'. So I said: 'No by Mr. Cameron, the acting headmaster, I presume on your behalf'. 'Not on my behalf', he said, 'and you'll have to make yourself indispensable if you are going to stay'.

Every now and then when pessimism got the better of him, Darling grizzled in small asides in his correspondence. The council simply refused to see things as he did, he told Robson, and was obsessed with 'temporary expedients' so that things 'are not at all happy between us'. Whiskard and Head were doing their best to keep his spirits up, he told Bishop Booth, but it was difficult to steer a course between despair and extravagance and, he moaned to Brian Hone (before Hone left England to be head of Cranbrook in Sydney) that he wished he could have been at Marlborough.[31]

Slowly, Darling clawed his way back. He took Bull's appointment to the Australian Broadcasting Commission very badly. Desperately but unsuccessfully (and as late as June 1940), Darling tried inducing him to return. Bull had stuck his neck out on the *Corian* committee by signalling that things were amiss in 1939. He inserted Darling's photograph at the front of the May and December editions of the *Corian* with the caption beneath: 'Returning to Australia January, 1940'. Darling's report to the February council meeting hadn't really cleared the air, as Fairbairn had expected it might, and Darling was convinced that his opposition to stringency was being borne out. In self-vindication, he rubbed it in to Manifold:

> The economies are at the expense of just those activities which have given distinction to the school and the restriction of which when other schools have copied them will be the worst possible thing for advertisement.

A long list followed of (what he thought were) appalling expenditure reductions for the library, sporting equipment and buildings. How could the works committee, in ignorance of the worth of the activities concerned, have possibly decided on the merits of such cuts? 'Cameron, of course, doesn't believe that the out of school activities are valuable and so of course he agreed to everything. But', he asked Manifold bluntly, 'do you want to revert to 1929 standards and methods?' To give up without a fight would destroy goodwill and the school would go downhill, yet if he opposed austerity he would have to resign. He foresaw a general postwar lowering of income and 'socialization' with which the school would be ill equipped to deal:

> That I can see my way to facing if we are not bankrupt before it comes or myself dead of a broken heart, with Ned Austin and C.A. Cameron written on either of the broken halves—or should it be C.R. Bull?[32]

Darling's difficulties were not helped by disruption on council. There was a spate of vacancies in 1940: Ned Austin died of a stroke in May and in August, Jim Fairbairn was killed along with two other UAP Cabinet members, Gullett and Geoffrey Street, and Brudenell White, when their RAAF Hudson crashed near Canberra. The tragedy provided an opportunity for more sympathetic appointments but his attempt backfired and relations were further strained. Once more Manifold poured oil on troubled waters:

> I am forced to admit there is some truth in their [Turnbull's and E.T.H. Richardson's] contention that the Headmaster is not guiltless himself in the use of a stand & deliver attitude'.

Darling tried to secure Curthoys' nomination to replace Austin. For a while it looked as if he might succeed, because Manifold had told him that both the archbishop and Wadham approved and would back his appointment. Curthoys' ideas were 'sound', Wadham thought, although what was really needed was an educationist who would not be 'panic stricken by financial data of an awkward kind' but who also would not be 'recklessly extravagant'. Manifold believed that Curthoys' appointment would achieve 'a proper balance' and 'restore a better perspective', but John Turnbull disagreed. Curthoys himself was uneasy and asked Darling to withdraw his name 'unless there is a prospect of my being elected with some semblance of unanimity':

> My hide is not thick enough for me to allow myself to be muscled into the council over substantial opposition from those who have vested interests in the school that I can never acquire.

When Max Bell resigned in October, Darling managed to secure G.S. Colman (previously approached but opposed by Turnbull) to replace him.[33]

As well as seeking new blood, Darling tried two other ploys. First, he went over council's head and lobbied the OGGs about the school's financial plight, which was a masterstroke (for they were marginalised from the business of the school). Second, he sought an upper age limit for councillors. Was such a limit 'wise or possible', Manifold queried him. One OGG, Roger Webb-Ware, reassured Darling that there was 'a decided opinion' among OGGs in favour of an age reduction, that they were aware of the financial situation and were keen to raise money (through, say, a group war-savings certificate scheme). An OGG district representative, Edward White, thought that what Webb-Ware said was 'staggering'. Many more OGGs would support Darling's case if they knew more about the effect of council's 'ponderous' financial policy. In fact, continued Webb-Ware, the 'very unfortunate impression that the Old Boys' advice or help was definitely not wanted' was down to Ned Austin. By the end of the year, White reassured Darling that this situation had changed and that there was a lot of old boy support for him and his view of the school's future.[34]

At forty-one, Darling was at a crossroads. The spirit that visited Hamlet was his father's ghost, but Darling was haunted by possible lifelong self-exile in the far-flung Antipodes. Death preoccupied him. With masters and OGGs flocking to the colours, there would be casualties and his beloved England faced possible subjugation by the German Reich. Yet here he was, isolated at the other end of the world. 'I feel a worm being out here safe and well-fed', he told Ralph. He had, he insisted, returned 'reluctantly and on the highest moral grounds, according to my lights and being here one must I suppose carry on'. He confessed to his brother-in-law that, in his heart of hearts, he still hankered for the glittering prize that England had offered and then denied him: the National College of Physical Training. Corio was his Denmark. He had built his reputation there, but now it was conspiring to cut him down. Indications of reassertion crept into his letters soon after the declaration of war, but they were jumbled up with bleakness and sentiments of doom, sure signs of an uncertain state of mind. Some of his allusions, however, were scarcely comprehensible: Manifold was dumbfounded when he read (in a 28 September letter) that 'Australia is magnificent and really has supplied the great thrill of the whole beastly business'. The general public would be 'staggered by your remark', said Manifold. And then when committed to returning to Corio, he thought that the war might have a salutary purgative effect and, in a flight of fancy (on 7 November) wrote about a new 'sort of Federal Order in the world' and how 'the war with its forced community of interests does provide a great opportunity for developing along these lines'. Again, when rethinking the school's and his own future in mid-1940, he declared to Ralph that he looked forward 'to a great period of good government by a strong [British] Labour Government under [Herbert] Morrison and the repairing of the ravages made by the devil'. He was all over the place.[35]

A few days after Jim Fairbairn's death, Darling thought of standing as a candidate in the forthcoming federal elections. Casey had left for Washington in February and at the Corio by-election Labor's John Dedman won the seat from the UAP. Casey had cautioned him that 'it is not a fool-proof seat by any means'. Three years earlier, when he had raised with Gullett the possibility of entering Parliament he was told that 'the rise of a Radical wing to the U.A.P. may be very close ahead' and to put an end to any thoughts of the need for a new political party. 'It may be that Casey will not go on', Gullett had written. 'Corio would suit you well.' But Darling had said that 'the politics idea is very much in the distance'. This time he sounded out R.F. Sanderson (Chamber of Manufactures) who informed him of support in Melbourne for independent candidates and a national government. Corio might be won provided that a UAP candidate 'would be free if elected to go his own way to a degree'. Despite Darling's UAP connections, the idea of independent candidacy suddenly assumed importance. As he told Ian Potter (the stockbroker), this was because of 'the impossibility of attaching oneself to either of the parties which are in existence'. Potter had invited Darling to a meeting with Gepp to discuss 'the immediate political situation' because Gepp was considering standing for Corio. Manifold persuaded Darling against nominating, whereupon Darling confessed to Sanderson that 'it is really cowardice on my part' and that there was probably little that he could have done 'towards saving the nation' had he won the seat. Perhaps the state Parliament was a more appropriate arena because then he could retain his connection with GGS. At any event, he was reluctant to 'launch out into a completely new life'.

Sanderson described Darling's current work as of 'incalculable' national value, as did Dr Evatt (whose son Peter was enrolled at GGS) and Latham (Chief Justice of the High Court) to whom Darling had also pleaded cowardice:

> The job here is more or less what I am trained to do. After all nobody but myself has thought of me as a likely candidate and I have received no clear call.[36]

Hope of salvation came in November 1940. The headship of King Edward's School, Birmingham, would soon be vacant (Darling and Priestley had previously canvassed it). Priestley (now vice-chancellor, University of Birmingham) said that:

> I have had a talk with one or two of the other Governors about the succession ... [King Edward's bailiff] came to me himself and asked me if I could find out what you would be likely to say if you were by any chance invited to come.

Was this a call and what was Darling to do? 'Forgive me for being so long winded, but I am thinking it out, as I go along', he wrote. There were distinct possibilities at King Edward's and an offer would be tempting, except that 'I am best with second or third rate material' and the National College of Physical Training was more attractive. In either case, Margaret and the children would have to stay behind during the war, although he was prepared to return to England if necessary. 'What a prig!', he tut-tutted, 'but one can't preach as much as I do without becoming tainted. God help us.' After ten days of equivocation, he mailed an affirmative answer and a short postscript confirming his interest. He was concerned about having to leave his family in Australia and said to his mother:

> The need for such a decision may come sooner than we think: and I think that it would help if you prayed for proper guidance in the choice. I seem awfully bad and distant from prayer at the moment—though I don't quite know why.

King Edward's headship became vacant in the new year when the incumbent resigned due to ill health. Priestley's diary noted that he 'should very much like to see Darling appointed but we are going to advertise the vacancy I think'. He asked for Darling's curriculum vitae, which was duly dispatched. Over the summer, he lobbied hard for his friend. GGS's headmaster outshone the three short-listed candidates, but it was 'hopeless to try and make the governors see that' especially as he couldn't be sure that 'under present conditions he would accept an invitation'. Priestley's efforts were fruitless and the governors chose an Oxford don, C.J. (later Lord) Morris of Balliol College.[37]

For Darling, the past two years or so had marked another transition period. War had transformed him from a callow youth into a man, New Zealand forced him to sort out his conflicting allegiances and a decade later he was being pulled in different directions. If his grip on the educational edifice that he had built up had slipped, then this was largely because he had lost focus. In the career stakes, he was not well served by the gentlemanly approach of his own schooling. As it was vulgar to thrust oneself forward when opportunities opened up, his strategy had been to rely on the support and promotion of eminent backers: to be advantageously positioned if a vacancy came his way, with any moral claim or call in some measure being an artefact of the number and strength of his cheer squad. Making himself available to serve when others wanted him to was his way of checking ambition and vanity. Up until 1939 this strategy had worked, but not at this time, when the appointment that he wanted eventually eluded him. The only realistic option now seemed to be to do as Temple and Fisher had done: run a boarding school in wartime. Indeed, he told Ralph that he now felt much more sympathy for Fisher than he had as a pupil. But what had happened at Repton was about to happen at Corio. With Ward gone, Ned Austin's thought that his departure marked the end of GGS liberalism was premature, because, in third term 1940, a bright young Australian just down from Oxford named Charles Manning Hope Clark was appointed history master. On New Year's Eve, Manifold told Darling that:

> Peggy Fairbairn [widow of Jim Fairbairn] ... took the opportunity to complain to me in reasonable terms about the views of Manning Clarke [sic] as portrayed to her by [her son] Geoffrey. Her thesis was that in peace time it is probably good to emphasize the futility of war; but to continue to do it when we are fighting [for] our lives is just plain defeatism which should not be tolerated.

Little did he know it, but Darling was to about to play the headmaster to Clark's Gollancz and Somervell.[38]

13

SOMETHING LIKE STAGNATION

1940–1945

It is the logic of our times,
No subject for immortal verse—
That we who lived by honest dreams
Defend the bad against the worse.

C. Day Lewis, 'Where Are the War Poets?'

At the outbreak of war, Prime Minister Menzies impressed upon Australians the need for 'Business as Usual', an unfortunate phrase 'quoted against him ever afterwards'. Shortly after the humiliating Allied evacuation from Dunkirk, the *Corian* deemed Menzies' words inappropriate as the need for national defence accelerated, and yet it endorsed them as 'a very worthy motto' for schools and schoolboys. It was unnecessary for GGS to become 'a school for war' or a nursery for the fighting services, when its job was to perform 'even more energetically' its peacetime activities. Darling was appalled: carrying on as if nothing was happening was the antithesis of the need to mobilise the school and nation. In England the declaration of war had created a new spirit of community, so robust a sentiment that infringements of jealously guarded liberties (such as opposition to compulsory billeting of soldiers, as had just occurred at Trimley, and conscription) were being tolerated without a whimper. Central to this near-national unanimity was the idea that 'somehow out of this war at least we would win some chance of building a better world'. Darling, of course, was pontificating from an inaccessible vantage point for Australians (including Menzies until he went to England in 1941): firsthand experience of a belligerent nation facing the prospect of invasion.[1]

From his Puckapunyal army billet, Jo Gullett noted much the same thing and fumed about the tardiness in enlisting of 'our lovely wealthy Australians'. In his despondency, Darling told Brian Hone that he couldn't reconcile himself to being in Australia 'where the real seriousness of the world situation has not penetrated'. And, to Kandel, who had said that most Americans regarded the war as a battle between two versions of imperialism, he claimed to be optimistic about 'the new England which is being formed out of this ordeal', although he scarcely felt as assured about Australia. Worse still, the nation's laxity heightened his family anxieties. On his forty-first birthday (three days after the Nazis occupied Paris) Darling cabled Ralph to evacuate his mother and the le Fleming children (Rachel, Morris and Susan) to Australia. A week later, with sea passages provisionally booked, after 'a day of agony' Ralph and Mabel decided that the trip was too dangerous. Jane Darling's steely resolve was to sit tight. When Churchill replaced Chamberlain as prime minister, she referred favourably to the change and said that 'the more we go on as usual among the people who know us, the calmer we can all keep'. An exasperated Ralph told his brother-in-law that he and Mabel could not even dislodge her from Trimley for Durham, let alone the other side of the world. Undeterred, her son persisted with suggestions about safe evacuation areas but she resisted. 'Everything confirms me in the conviction that "staying put" was, at least, my wisest plan!' Eventually, after the death of Tizzie (wife of her elder brother, Alec) she relocated to Westbank in Falkirk where she spent most of the war alone or in company with her sister Peg. She clung steadfastly to her simple Christianity and with dogged Scottish persistence maintained correspondence with her scattered offspring and relatives.[2]

In September 1940, Jean Darling was killed. A year earlier, she had received a sadly prescient letter from Eaton in India: 'I picture you [in London] running from one rabbit hole to another with gas masks at the ready, and a hell of a noise all the time'. His sister's life was cruelly snuffed out in Chelsea during the Blitz. A bomb exploded on the shelter in which (as an ARP warden) she was huddling. Jean and forty-six Beaufort Street housing tenants were killed instantly. She was thirty-four. She was not disfigured, although a normally composed Margaret had had to gird herself to identify her sister's body before winding up her affairs. About 120 mourners attended her funeral service. Recently Jean had fallen in love and, since the fall of Paris, had written airily to her mother about her new friend, an older man, Kay (W. Bertram Kennett)—a solicitor, chairman of the Connaught Club and a fellow warden. After leaving Norwich in 1932, Jean had been a housing inspector, an assistant housing estate manager and, since 1934, a housing estate manager in Chelsea. She was also secretary of the 600-strong Association of Women Housing Managers. Jean was the best of all her children, Jane told her son, because of her nearly perfectly formed character: 'I feel God wanted her for something better where she is now'. Scores of condolence letters poured into Corio and Darling was a long time coming to terms with her loss. 'I am trying not [to] be angry with the Germans nor to get depressed as I know that I shouldn't.' He dedicated his ABC radio talk 'Tradition', delivered shortly after her death, to her. Two months later her death was still hanging like a cloud over his thoughts of Home.[3]

There were many reasons for Darling's despondency, although much of it was self-inflicted. Despite the wound licking and equivocation after the National College of Physical Training had slipped away, Colin Gordon urged him to think about 'just how damn good Corio is' and that if he were to go to any other job then that would be 'very selfish and crooked thinking'. Like it or not, said Alistair Stephen (a Sydney OGG), the impression afoot was 'that the school has been extravagant in its expenditure & lavish in its comforts, and that boys acquire expensive tastes & hobbies'. And, if Darling thought that Cameron had been scheming, and that council had connived in his treachery, then Manifold laid that ghost to rest: 'there is no antagonism to you either by individual councillors or by the body as a whole'. Moreover:

> Another myth that I have dispelled from my own mind (& therefore if it is
> in yours it should go from there also) is that some members thought that if
> you threw in the towel Cameron would be a satisfactory headmaster. You can
> accept my word for it that there is not a grain of truth in this idea.

Despite these assurances, Darling's relations with council remained sticky. They would improve slowly but turn sour again in 1945. Why, then, had the council been difficult to deal with? Manifold reasoned that its members had become a bit like Max Bell when he retired: their brains 'more inelastic'. If his friend thought about it they were 'never really elastic in the imaginative cultural sense' from the start, and there had never been 'any real common ground between you (or me, for that matter) & the present day Council personnel'. Manifold neatly distanced himself from the reactionaries—indeed, lectured them (or '"kept them in"'), following the September meeting, about improving relations with the headmaster—and again displayed his talent for not shirking the truth with his friend.[4]

The war brought with it anticipated and unanticipated consequences that impacted unpredictably on the headmaster, the school and Australian society. Unlike the previous decade, the circumstances were no longer running Darling's way and, by the time that the conflict was over, the wider society and culture had been reshaped extensively. He was constrained from initiating further reforms and innovations by scarce domestic resources (financial and human) and restricted externally by rationing and impositions on free movement. For the duration of the war, he and the school marked time. He could mostly only react rather than create and seize opportunities to take a lead. In this shifting wartime context, Corio's semi-rural location was a mixed blessing. It precluded the need for the school to evacuate or relocate, so that unlike the central Melbourne schools, GGS was not disrupted by military occupation. Moreover (to Darling's delight), the war played havoc with APS sporting fixtures and competitions were frequently abandoned. But isolation also required Corio's little community to rely increasingly on its own resources. Location and transport problems also made public criticism difficult to deflect (in late 1944). In addition, the school's pupil profile was modified inadvertently (from 1940–41) by a steady influx of boys from the Far East. Parents based in Asia (merchants, planters and bankers) who normally dispatched children to English boarding schools were prevented by threats to shipping and so enrolled their sons in Australian schools. The likely flood of applications necessitated coordination otherwise, Robson urged Darling, a rather undignified scramble for numbers would result. Negotiations on the headmasters' behalf were coordinated in India by Roy Gollan (Australian National Travel Association, 1937, and Australian government trade commissioner, 1942), and the schools forwarded prospectuses. At Corio, nearly one in every ten boys admitted was an evacuee, with such a flood of them in 1941 that more than a quarter of that year's 117 admissions were from overseas. Their arrival helped return a handsome profit in 1940 (making council far more amenable—'silly mugs', Darling could not resist gloating to his mother), but special arrangements during vacations (when boarders went home) had to be made, and the balance of the school risked being upset after the war when the evacuees withdrew.[5]

The two big wartime success stories were Darling's national service scheme and the Exhibition of October 1942. With Bull now at the ABC, Barney Hutton looked after national service until he enlisted and was succeeded by E.H. Montgomery in 1941. The aims were unchanged: 'to make us fit and pre-pared to stand up to the demands that are doubtless going to be made on us by an uncertain future', the *Corian* reported, so that 'a great lesson in co-operation is being learnt by all'. As a consequence of fires the boys' national service skills were stringently tested. One night in August 1941, GGS's carpentry and mechan-ics shop was razed to the ground. After the fire, about forty more boys than were needed volunteered to rebuild the 45-by-9-metre wood and fibro-cement building during the school holidays. In just five days, 'at a speed which seemed almost incredible', sixty boys in gangs under a boy foreman and a school work-man erected the new shop. The *Corian* patted everyone on the back. To boys in receipt of a traditional public school education, particularly scholars and athletes (most boys fitted neither category):

> a piece of work such as this may well stand as the symbol of the new "balanced" education which Geelong Grammar School has perhaps done more than any other school during the past decade to establish in this country.

It would never have happened at Winchester, Gerry Dicker told Darling. Bill Kellaway (son of Charles, Director, Walter and Eliza Hall Institute), for one, enjoyed the work 'greatly'. It had been 'a thoroughly exciting little experience', said Darling to the entrepreneur Sir Walter Massy-Greene and the truly amazing thing was 'the marvellous spirit of co-operation between the men and the boys'. Milton Thewlis (bursar and Austin's replacement as council secretary) had set a precedent back in April when he organised a group of boys to build the school's new yacht club premises that were finished in a mere twelve hours and saved £100. The following year, another team built a large carpentry shop at Bostock House and in January 1943, the school erected a house at Carrum Downs for the Brotherhood of St Lawrence—'go on giving Australia such lads and we can look forward to the future undismayed', wrote an exceptionally grateful Reverend G.K. Tucker. But the most impressive achievement was in 1944 in the tiny rural hamlet of Mount Duneed (near Geelong) where, after devastating bushfires, GGS boys rebuilt cowsheds, erected kilometres of fencing, and then designed and reconstructed St Wilfred's church.[6]

Boy labour made sense: it saved the school money, was educationally beneficial, provided invaluable service and it also fostered a sense of community. Darling also claimed (dubiously) that it helped free up labour to fight the war. For some time beyond Corio similar manpower considerations had been the basis of the boys' schools' participation in forestry camps, harvesting and fruit-picking during summer vacations. But when Darling sought the other schools' collaboration in assisting fire-ravaged areas he drew a blank. The response of MacNeil at Wesley (previously Knox Grammar School and from 1941 Stewart's successor), for example, was that boys were merely cheap and exploitable labour, and he saw no virtue in 'regarding our schools as mobile labour units to be turned on to difficult situations as they arise'. But Darling was determined to capitalise on the propaganda value of boy labour, so that when Archbishop Booth asked whether Corio boys could rebuild St Wilfred's, he stipulated two conditions: GGS would do it provided that Booth consecrated it and if the school had a free hand in its design, rather than reproducing a timber version of 'conventional pseudo Gothic'. When finished and landscaped, the church's garden (planned by Darling) included a life-size clay sundial designed by the new art master, Hirschfeld-Mack. Booth dedicated the new church on 6 August before a congregation of 600 people. This work gave GGS 'a reputation for effective help-fulness in a crisis', Darling said, and (drawing a long bow) may have also set 'something of a standard for country churches'. Boy labour would have been used if the school had had to evacuate—provisionally scheduled for 1941 and 1942 on two properties near Beaufort, but by 1943 the need had passed—and the timber planned for dispatch was used by the boys to build houses for GGS masters. On the day that Japanese aircraft bombed Pearl Harbor, elaborately floored, lined and roofed 2-metre trenches were dug in the school grounds, and connected by telephone in readiness for air attack or invasion.[7]

A GGS new master, Dr Edmund Parnes, commented very favourably on national service. The elderly Parnes was a member of the Polish Diplomatic Service who had fled Vienna, Warsaw, Romania and then Japan before ending up in Australia. Darling brought him to Corio in June 1941 to teach Russian. (In the latter part of the war another aristocratic Pole, an army general, was billeted at Westbank with his mother and Aunt Peg.) In his impressions of the school, Parnes was conscious of the collapse of European grammar school education and the corruption of education generally by Nazism and fascism, and the need 'to bring about the new human kind' after the war. Parnes saw much at GGS that was valuable (although he was not uncritical) and was 'spellbound' by the national service scheme. He called it 'the practical solution of the tormenting problem of the European future'. Indispensable to its worth was the great care being bestowed on manual labour at the school. 'Never and nowhere' had Parnes seen anything like it: the 'finishing touch'. 'I have found here all the preliminary conditions suitable for creating a post-war human being.' In particular, the razing of the mechanics shop was 'a holy fire', and the rebuilding of it 'a work of reconstruction'.[8]

Darling's interest in postwar reconstruction was influenced by people like Gepp who forwarded him articles and, particularly, an accountant Justin Hancock (a GGS parent and brother of Keith, the historian). Early in the war, Hancock established an informal group of prominent heads of industry, commerce and the professions (including Darling) who met to discuss the future of Australia. He also supported schoolboy work in clubs, camps and on farms. In 1940, on what would be the final speech day until 1945, Darling told the parents that:

> We are not fighting this great war to preserve with all its injustices and false standards the world which we have known and—let us be honest—enjoyed for the last twenty years. We hope that there is awakening in the community, as a result of the strain which is being put upon it, a clearer realisation of the weaknesses and injustices of the structure ... We must try to build a society based upon justice and equity, and we must develop a respect for duty at least equal to our respect for rights. We must make more real than it has been in the past the elevation of service as the criterion of success.

Would a possible outcome of the war be a better sense of values, he wondered, in which happiness and satisfaction would be found in the best possible way: 'in the forgetfulness of self?' That had been 'the lesson of the last six months at home'. Only late in 1942 when the uncertainties consequent upon Japan's entry into the war had passed could Darling begin feeling optimistic. Because he thought that the war could be won in a year or so, he said to Hancock, he was contemplating a large-scale exhibition on postwar planning. The aim was to give boys and the general public 'an idea of the particular things which we have got to aim at by some other means if we are to have a decent country' or, as he put it to F.B. Malim (at Haileybury College, England), 'getting our particular boys and girls interested in the actual work which will have to be done afterwards'. His mother was thrilled and wrote to Temple (Archbishop of Canterbury) that her son was stirring up the dry bones. Entitled 'Today and Tomorrow', the exhibition was organised in conjunction with the Hermitage. It was held on the last weekend in October 1942 (when the Allied cause hung on the outcome of the battles of Stalingrad and El Alamein) and was opened by Menzies (leader of the Opposition).[9]

The inspiration for the exhibition was Eric Linklater's *The Cornerstones*, a dialogue over the ends and purposes of government among Lenin, Abraham Lincoln, Confucius and Arden, a young English airman. It was re-enacted before a large Saturday evening audience. The *Corian* suggested that the exhibition's real value was the team spirit developed on 'a school-wide scale'. The boys acquired an understanding of the problems of the nations that they had investigated when preparing the exhibits—the accomplishments of the USA, the USSR, China, Britain and Australia—in the central quadrangle classrooms. The Chinese consulate offered assistance with China and a model of Red Square was constructed, supervised by Newman (who had visited Russian schools in 1932). Menzies was recalled as giving this particular display 'very short shrift'. Despite the shortage of senior Hermitage girls, Darling was assured by Miss Krome (the headmistress) that staff and girls were 'putting a great deal of work into it and are doing their best'. The exhibition was well attended and Menzies commended the students' efforts as 'a wonderful outlet for expression by the youthful mind on problems that were engaging world-wide attention'. (Giblin was unimpressed by Menzies' address and told him so.) A scale model of the Hagley Farm School, Tasmania, was included. Hagley was one of the Tasmanian Education Department's new area schools (whose young head teachers had 'considerable freedom in planning and developing their schools') championed by Browne during a visit in 1941. Browne teased Darling that Hagley's cottage accommodation was 'better than in your dormitories—that is saying a good deal', and introduced his friend to J.S. Maslin, the young Hagley headmaster, who visited Corio in December. Maslin told Darling that he was thrilled 'to find that someone working on along entirely different lines and under entirely different conditions, has come to the same conclusions upon the root matters of education as oneself'. 'Today and Tomorrow' won widespread praise, including an article by Keith Murdoch in the *Herald*.[10]

The contrast was strong between this sense of community and the circumstances endured by Darling's brother Eaton, who had disappeared on active service earlier in the year. Eaton had been grief-stricken by Jean's death. (He was the sole beneficiary of her will.) Like his mother, he thought that his sister was the best of the five siblings and in 1941 on the anniversary of Jean's death he composed 'Love', a free-verse poem. After his visit to Corio and New Zealand in 1932, Eaton taught for two years at Trinity College, Kandy. There was the possibility of permanent work at Borstal, but in Ceylon he had taken up the cause of the Anglo-Indian (or Eurasian) community. Inspired by the efforts of a courageous evangelical Anglo-Indian clergyman, the Reverend Arnold Paynter—'the vaguest man alive' and physically wrecked by war wounds—Eaton was assistant superintendent of the India Christian Mission, at Champawat, in the Himalayan foothills near Nepal. As an English sahib in the twilight of the Raj, he said that he laboured incessantly for more than six years battling poverty in an exacting climate, debilitating sickness, insect plagues, marauding wild beasts, infuriating Indian Civil Service paternalism and an intolerably slow, but calculatingly deferential, Indian temperament, to realise his vision of landed communal self-sufficiency for Anglo-Indian children. He and his brother were chalk and cheese. Whereas Eaton was introspective, quick-tempered, irritable, hapless, perverse, ill at ease in others' company, although witty, and lived in self-imposed exile, his elder brother was likeable, convivial and engaging, good humoured and respectable, and duchessed by a bunyip ruling class. British imperialism alienated Eaton utterly: he could only see evidence of its brutality and indignity. On another level, both brothers were conscience-driven idealists, each dedicated to the service and uplift of their fellows, and easily depressed by the state of the world. The gap in age between them and their different experiences of life meant that they were never close, although their relations were amicable and they corresponded irregularly. In early 1939, Darling had tried to have the Victorian Public Schools Party to India (thirty-six GGS, Melbourne Grammar and Scotch boys, two chaplains, an OGG and R.L. Curthoys) go to Champawat, but this had proved impossible. Eaton was disappointed, but when a vast amount of tools and equipment arrived from Corio in February, he was delighted by his brother's thoughtfulness and said to their mother: 'you must tell Jim when you see him what all this means to us'. Eaton was a romantic who took aim at his generation for its deficiencies. His sister Margaret despaired of him. 'Oh, dear, why will he so exasperatingly make difficulties for himself when he need not?'—after learning that Eaton had become a teetotaller and that this decision was a barrier to his social intercourse in the Indian Army officers' mess.[11]

In April 1941 Eaton married Eva, the sister of Arnold Paynter. They honeymooned at the colony and planned the house that they would build after the war, before he returned to the 1st/19th Hyderabad Regiment as a company commander. Armies, he said dismissively, comprised merely the 'hired assassins of other hired assassins'. After a couple of days in Madras in May prior to his embarkation for Malaya, they never saw each other again. The only way that Eaton could justify his involvement in this 'vile business', he told Eva, was with C. Day Lewis' line: 'Defend the bad against the worse'. With Japan about to enter the war, Eaton, armed with his rifle, Bible and copy of Thucydides, was ready to fight and reconciled to his fate. The last recorded sighting of him was in January 1942, but this information had not become immediately available and his family prayed that 'missing' would not be confirmed as 'killed in action'. Sadly, he disappeared and was presumed dead, his mother all the while trusting implicitly in the Creator's providence: 'God seems to give me a wonderful serenity on the whole & I take it as from Him & and am thankful'. As late as 1944 Margaret still raised with her brother the slim possibility that Eaton might just have survived (although personally she was dubious) as sketchy details of his whereabouts dribbled in. Determinedly, she and her mother kept up correspondence with Eva who (though neither had met her), Margaret felt, seemed 'vaguely reminiscent of Hilda [Wharton]'.[12]

Back at the Corio community, the gloss was taken off 'Today and Tomorrow' when a dispute erupted in December: the edition of the *Corian* that reported on the exhibition invoked its spirit but also criticised the public schools. An editorial written by J.A.C. Mackie, a prefect, triggered angry protests in early 1943 and the strongest reaction so far to Darling's liberalism. A South Australian OGG was perturbed by what he read because its spirit was 'far from parallel with the teachings and traditions of the school'. Why belittle the public schools in the middle of an international crisis? Darling said in reply that while he was also upset, he did not think that the boy 'meant any harm' and had given 'almost the opposite interpretation to what he wanted to say'. Part of the difficulty was timing: the editorial coincided with the return of the AIF's 9th Division from the Middle East, when a number of the boys came under the spell of Manning Clark (senior history master 1941–44). Like the headmaster, Clark was an inspirational teacher. Mackie spent two years in the VIth form and was taught by both men. Whereas Darling's discussions ranged far and wide, Clark's pattern was the lecture, tutorial and library approach of the universities. Although he later claimed that he did not set out to create a following, Clark widened the horizons of a small circle of highly intelligent and thoughtful boys who included Mackie, Stephen Murray-Smith, Donald Baker, Geoffrey Fairbairn, David Chipp and Frank Kellaway, all of whom turned to him for answers to troubling questions. Clark also influenced the Public Affairs Society and the History and Philosophical Society that, with Masterman, he organised from the beginning of 1942; his influence also extended to the cricket nets. When Clark (an able cricketer) coached the 1st XI, its performance improved significantly.[13]

During the next few months an antipodean version of Repton 1917–18 played itself out. So far at Corio, Darling had never quite managed to shrug off suggestions that, if he wasn't pink or slightly suspect, then his impact on the boys was. The council discussed Mackie's editorial in February 1943 and left the matter to the headmaster, but Manifold (acting chairman) was livid, although he backed his friend. From within their framework of mutual understanding he spoke freely. The editorial served no useful purpose. The boy could only have written it to please his headmaster and 'the really strange fact to me is that you are pretending that it does please you'. A flabbergasted Manifold could not understand why Darling seemed bent on playing into the hands of public school critics by allowing the publication of destructive comments. 'If there is anything in your thought that some may be thinking that you are becoming too socialistic, it is—in my view—being promulgated by this attitude I am stressing.' Darling's liberalism occasionally rubbed people up the wrong way. Allan Campbell had certainly been 'deeply hurt' in 1942 by Darling's criticism of the New Guard (founded by his father, Eric)—although Campbell's mother, sceptical at first, was grateful in the end for Darling's influence on her son's spiritual outlook. But Professor G.A. Currie (vice-chancellor, University of Western Australia) thought that Darling was less progressive—at least in argumentative terms—than Bishop

Burgmann. Darling certainly liked to style himself as leftward inclined. In late 1942, the distressed Toorak mother of an old boy wrote to voice concern about the influence of a publication (she said *Left Wing News*) on her son, a student at the University of Melbourne. Her lad was irritable and unhappy. He was being fed on 'the worries of the world' and, with her husband away, she appealed to the boy's former headmaster for advice. Darling replied that if her son really was to become a thinking person then he had no alternative but to be worried:

> In the past we did not worry nearly enough, and our present troubles are partially at least the result of that failure. At his age, it is almost inevitable that if he worries he will tend to the Left Wing. I certainly was so regarded at his age and so regard myself now, though the Left Wing probably regards me as a reactionary.

Momentarily confusing the publication with the Left Book Club, he reassured her that it was the creation of Gollancz, 'the publisher under whose influence I myself came very strongly when I was at school', and that although it tended to be a doctrinaire group, it was a useful counter influence to conservative opinion. Any young man 'interested at all in setting right the injustices of the world, must inevitably be a socialist in one form or another, and it would not be natural if he was anything else'.[14]

Darling's severest OGG critic of the editorial was Hubert Black (later a member of the council and a staunch Darling supporter). He was also worried about the headmaster's alleged socialism when, in the first of three letters, he referred to 'too much talk, often of Parlor [sic] Pink hue' at the school. Black was just back from the Middle East and his wife had recently died. The editorial was (for him) ill timed and symptomatic of something that had been wrong with Corio since the headmaster's arrival. Darling's numerous press criticisms of the public schools were well known and this latest incident raised 'doubts as to your consistency, even sincerity in your job'. The sentence in Mackie's editorial that had got up the noses of Manifold, Black and other critics said:

> At the moment, the Public Schools are a drag on the war effort: they produce too many boys with a distorted view of life, and they are costly in labour and money.

How, asked Manifold, could any boy have had the hide to be so certain that his own view of life ('this cry of undiluted stinking fish') was not distorted? If boys did leave the school with a distorted view of life, Black had suggested, then perhaps 'it is high time for a change of headmaster'. And, as for the boy's use of the adjective costly, fee levels had indeed been a matter of concern to the OGGs but the blame for the increased expenses that necessitated them and had produced a 'Hobby Hobby Curriculum' lay entirely with the headmaster—the very point to which Alistair Stephen had alerted him. While Darling might not have authored the editorial, Black was adamant that the responsibility for its publication was his. By condoning the contentious words, Darling's views were being expressed. Black said that, of about 1700 OGGs, there were nearly 1100 voluntarily serving Australia in the war, of whom fifty had already given their lives. Did they have a distorted view of life, he asked. 'No Mr Darling.' The editorial had been read as far afield as Milne Bay (at the eastern tip of Papua) where it had been the subject of heated army discussion. Black invited Darling to search his soul. Talk of sacrifice and service had to be exemplified by people like himself in top positions. Finally, the editorial was politically inexpedient—as Manifold had implied and Darling was aware, for he had just said as much in his annual report, and because the Headmasters' Conference of Australia was deliberating at this time on the future of boys' schools. The editorial's sentiments played right into the hands of opponents in the federal Labor government who delighted in attacks on the sector.[15]

In their rush to put pen to paper, Darling's critics had overlooked the sentence preceding the one at which they had taken umbrage. Mackie acknowledged that the public school system was threatened, and said that 'if it is to survive', justify its existence and strengthen itself financially, then it had to change. (This was the same argument made twenty-five years earlier at Repton by Gollancz and Somervell.) Medley twigged straightaway to what Mackie was on about. 'I have heard from two or three sources that you are incurring violent criticism', he wrote to Darling with characteristic wittiness:

> I cannot resist telling you that I agree most emphatically with every word of [the editorial]. The continued existence of what is good in the Public School idea depends entirely on the capacity for realism of those entrusted with its tradition—in the literal sense of that word—and I am dismayed to my heart that an approach to the problem of so admirably realistic a nature should have aroused unfavourable comment.

'Most profoundly' he hoped that 'the ideas contained in that article will not incur any kind of official condemnation'. Medley would be disappointed. Mackie had argued that the public schools, especially boarding schools, were expensive and wasteful, mainly because of the army of tradesmen, groundsmen, matrons and maids needed to maintain their institutional fabric. Waste also resulted from a wrongheaded emphasis on sport (one of Lytton Strachey's two charges levelled at Dr Arnold) and success in examinations—the same two evils that his headmaster had been relentlessly banging on about. Finally, Mackie's injunction to 'get more balance in our work' and to 'play games by all means—play as hard as you can— but the desire to win must not overcome the objects of the game—exercise, enjoyment and relaxation' was little more than a restatement of the English public school adage about playing up and playing the game.[16]

Salvation lay in national service, Mackie believed, and he drew attention to the 'stronger spirit of service' symbolised by the exhibition:

> Co-operation and unselfishness are obvious pre-requisites. In any community which is trying to make do on a little, it is only by working together and putting individual advantage after the general need that success can be achieved.

Such an emphasis would contribute to the war effort and rejuvenate the schools. Darling began a lengthy reply to Black but tore it up. In early April at the Old Geelong Grammarians Association AGM, Black moved the following resolution (forwarded to the council):

> It considers that the Article in question is unwarranted and not in accordance with the facts and further that its publication has damaged the reputation of the School.

> It instructs the Committee to inform the School Council that in the opinion of the Old Boys, either the Corian Editorials be discontinued or they be so controlled, in future, that a recurrence of the type of Article in question shall not be possible.

Darling's brief response to Black was that the school's future 'really is doubtful' and urged him to 'not allow your feelings on this matter or about me to influence you and through you other people in any way which will harm the school'. Black calmed down and apologised for his 'somewhat (perhaps excessively) downright' initial tone. Darling's admission that the editorial should not have been published 'in that form' perhaps did the trick. Black's information was that, when the editorial was mentioned to him, Darling 'had brushed it aside and had been rather flippant about it'. Masterman, the master in charge of the *Corian* editorial committee, regretted the offending views in Mackie's text and in his defence said that it was written during a hectic time of year when a normally hard-working senior prefect was preparing for his final examinations. The deadline for copy had been tight and there was no time for the wholesale redrafting 'which seemed to be called for'. Normally the editor would have consulted with the headmaster, but committee members 'were not aware that this had not been done on this occasion'.[17]

As at Repton, a follow-up editorial was used to counteract the alleged excesses of a liberal faction. Thus, Masterman suggested that it should be devoted to the special role of public schools. Darling was grateful for this face-saving assurance as it would 'strengthen my hand' if the matter was to go any further. He regretted that so 'large a storm should have arisen in so small a teacup' but he did not want to interfere. A hands-off approach had always been his way of doing things, he told council, 'because I want the Editorial to be the expression of the boys' opinion rather than my own'. Personally, he objected to the wording of the text—it ought to have been censored—but Mackie, he insisted, had not intended any malice. Darling also drew a line: under no circumstances could the council direct him in this matter 'without expressing want of confidence in the Headmaster'. Steps to dispel the editorial's detrimental impact would be taken and the master in charge would retain veto and censorship rights. The May 1943 *Corian* editorial (written by a new editor) defended the public schools against 'ardent reformers' who were products of that very system and yet simultaneously its failures. A common argument warranting rebuttal was that 'the Public School caters only for the rich, cultivates snobbishness, and strengthens class barriers'. The editorial apologia claimed that the schools were receptive to reform and acutely conscious of their national contribution. The editor cited the recent Headmasters' Conference resolutions framed in Sydney, the exhibition with its 'education both for those who created it and for those who came to see it', the national service scheme and GGS's proud record of enlistments. As to privilege (not part of Mackie's criticism), surely 'it would be best to increase the number admitted to the elite, rather than debar all from opportunities of this kind'. An acerbic closing note said that if class barriers were to be broken down by the public schools, then this would tend to 'raise the standard of the less well-to-do, rather than lower the standard of those better off, as would the extension of the State School system to the exclusion of all others'.[18]

Manning Clark played no direct part in *l'affaire Corian* and his memoirs do not refer to it. (Nor do two recent Clark biographies mention the incident.) Casting himself later as Mr Passion, Clark's reflections on his Corio years were that he scandalised (what he thought was) its rather straitlaced conformism. Why he subsequently ridiculed common room opinions, and the life of the masters and their families in Biddlecombe Avenue to the extent that he did in *The Quest for Grace* is unclear, particularly when he and his family—some of his children were born while at Corio—were remembered by his contemporaries as having been contented. Clark was sufficiently positive at GGS to provide an annual prize for a quality social inquiry by a boy and, after his departure, he tried to find staff for Darling at a time when there was a desperate shortage of competent masters. (Mark McKenna's recent biography, however, paints a picture of a deeply frustrated and unhappy man.) As a teacher, Clark's capacious mind brought an invigorating diet to a glittering array of talented young men in their formative years. This comprised much of the Western civilisation canon and included key figures of history, philosophy, literature, art and music. As Mackie confessed in his obituary to Clark, it was a heady experience and one never to be forgotten, except that he regretted that Mr Passion's account of his Corio days was 'so negative', and that all the good that he had done boys seemed to have been 'filtered out of his memory in old age'.[19]

Darling thought that Clark was a restless man who was unable to make up his mind about his future. In early 1945, he told Michael Thwaites (in England) that there were definitely good things happening at the school, although it lacked intellectual leadership:

> Manning Clark was a disastrous experiment leading vigorously and successfully in all directions but the right one. Nevertheless he has left something of a vacuum, which we tired old men inadequately fill.

With so many masters enlisting, Darling's perennial wartime complaint was his desperate shortage of quality teaching staff. But when sounding off to Thwaites, he neglected the one genuine jewel in his depleted pedagogical crown: Ludwig Hirschfeld-Mack. A painter and printmaker, Hirschfeld-Mack was a product of the Bauhaus in Weimar, Germany, who had immigrated to England. There he was interned and transported as an enemy alien aboard the *Dunera* to Australia where yet again he was interned, this time at Tatura. Darling first heard of him in late 1941 and told council that he 'was one of the best known art instructors on the Continent'. Bracey had visited Hirschfeld-Mack and interceded with the military authorities on Darling's behalf to arrange for his employment at Corio. He arrived in first term 1942. Darling said that he was 'first class'. While most Continental people were usually 'too highly educated on the academic side and insufficiently developed as men', and were therefore of little use, Hirschfeld-Mack 'would be exceptional anywhere'.[20]

Mr Passion, as Clark styled himself, dismissed GGS as a citadel of antipodean bourgeois wealth and power. The factual basis of his repudiation is irrefutable: the school's socioeconomically exclusive market profile remained unchanged in 1940–45. GGS was still overwhelmingly boarding, Anglican and Victorian (mostly Geelong and Melbourne), even though it recruited nationally. Slightly fewer boys than in the 1930s were from Yarraside suburbs (the stamping ground of Mr Passion's beastly bourgeoisie). Overall numbers rose during the war: there were 634 admissions (106 annually compared with 88 in the 1930s), in the range 84 (low) in 1940 to 134 (peak) in 1945. As previously, 70 per cent of boys were admitted from another registered school, and the sons of professional, business and landed families still dominated the profile, with the fathers of three-quarters of boys admitted during 1940–45 in business (35 per cent) or the professions (41 per cent). Darling sensed that the wider mood was shifting and he was increasingly glum about the future of the public schools: higher taxation to finance the war would diminish parents' fee-paying capacity (as he believed had occurred in England)—a fear that was magnified in July 1942 when the High Court acknowledged the constitutional validity of federal uniform taxation legislation. In this defensive climate, the council's austerity policy would prejudice GGS's competitive edge. Unless dispelled quickly, the allegation that schools like GGS were the exclusive preserve of the rich would stick. 'I can assure you that this is not so', he wrote to OGGs in 1941. The 'over-rich' had never had much of a run, he continued and, while there was no denying the presence of rich boys, he was 'absolutely sure that they do not throw their weight about on account of their wealth any more than they have ever done'. After all, he argued, a school was a democracy in which people were accepted for their own worth, and nobody needed to fear that boys were acquiring false monetary standards. (If it was any consolation, Gordon said that the boys' sense of responsibility at King's, unlike at Corio, was purely superficial.)[21]

GGS's social exclusiveness threatened to be Darling's worst public relations nightmare in late 1944, when isolation and wartime regulations ignited a debate about privilege. Asked in July 1944 why pupils were not permitted to travel interstate during the August holidays, E.J. (Eddie) Ward (Minister for Transport) informed the House of Representatives that children attending schools interstate were restricted to rail travel to and from home once a year at Christmas. When he learnt of this regulation in 1942, Darling was concerned about its effects on admissions, but urged parents to 'make no drastic decision' to withdraw their sons. Parents' travel fears were genuine. Neville Fraser told Darling about the recent experience at Albury of his twelve-year-old son Malcolm (the future prime minister): 'He arrived in the Spirit [of Progress] at 10.20 pm & left in the *3rd* division at 1.15 am, having put in 3 hours on the platform in the middle of a perishing night. [A] train was not available for him to go to bed earlier.' Three months after Ward's answer, the Sydney *Sun* reported that 'Geelong Boys Can't Get Back' and then, according to the *Sydney Morning Herald*, twenty-one boys were stranded in Sydney for a fortnight because their aeroplane had broken down. The next day in the House 'several' GGS boys were said to have been intercepted by transport officers at Albury and detained pending inquiries regarding their rail priority rights. Newspaper references to an aeroplane prompted a Labor backbencher to ask Ward whether or not Australian National Airways (ANA) had provided 'a special aeroplane' to convey the boys. Had the travel priority system been waived, would the minister ensure that the lads would not 'border-hop' and would he take action against ANA if a 'special privilege' had been extended? Four days later, the Minister for Air and Civil Aviation informed the House that in August ANA had flown eighteen boys half-fare 'austerity style' to Sydney in a 22-seater DC5. They had booked 'a long time ahead' and were flown only after being granted the lowest priority (no. 9, which precluded regular airline travel). For the next fortnight, an unsavoury spat raged back and forth in both the Parliament and the press. Ward made accusations that were denied, but he refused to withdraw. The result was parliamentary unruliness, intervention by Curtin (the prime minister) and Menzies, humiliation of the Speaker and two suspensions from the House.[22]

There was confusion about the boys' return and a week later Ward's department refused requests for rail permits. He named two of the applicants as David Loder (son of Lord Wakehurst, Governor of New South Wales) and the son of Captain Holyman (a director of ANA), and alleged that Holyman had arranged the original flight. He then named four other GGS boys as purchasing rail tickets at Albury and against whom 'prosecutions are being authorized' for border-hopping, and then three more who had obtained a ticket or booked a return passage by boat, including Loder and the son of Colonel Wynne (Lord Wakehurst's secretary). There was more confusion on 27 September when Holyman (in the parliamentary gallery during Ward's allegations) claimed that his son had not been in Sydney for some time. The same day, Dr Evatt (attorney-general and a GGS parent) announced that decisions about prosecutions would be made by him alone. Holyman's denial prompted demands for 'a dignified withdrawal' by Ward. In his protracted reply, Ward explained that when Holyman had been contacted by the assistant director of rail transport (after advice from a *Sun* reporter) he would neither confirm nor deny that his son was on the aeroplane and that the official's efforts to seek Darling's confirmation were to no avail. Despite Holyman's disavowal and the Minister for Air's earlier statement, Ward insisted that 'it was a special plane for a special purpose' and refused to withdraw. That evening, on the advice of the solicitor-general, Evatt announced that there would be no prosecutions. Ward was at odds with his senior ministerial colleague and became the press's whipping-boy. The *Sydney Morning Herald* (its Fairfax proprietors had close GGS connections) lambasted him with 'Mr Ward's Boy-hunt'. The minister's behaviour was 'an incredible self-revelation of pettiness' because numerous other stranded passengers had previously been granted rail permits. Ward persisted with claims of special travel facilities for the sons of the privileged few, and refused to back down even when the passenger list for the 23 August Melbourne flight was tabled. Holyman's son (hospitalised in Melbourne) was not among the eighteen GGS boys' names read out. To wrong-foot Ward, his parliamentary opponents cited instances of his own recent interstate travel. 'Behold how great a matter a little fire kindleth', intoned the *Sydney Morning Herald* (in one of three editorials) as the public took sides in letters to the editor. The *Sydney Morning Herald*'s Ross Gollan chastised Ward for having nearly brought the government into 'complete disrepute', with only Evatt's promptness saving it. The boys were blameless and merely vehicles for Ward to work off his political bias against their fathers. Ward, meanwhile, continued his attack in a radio broadcast.[23]

Darling's overriding concern was that the returning boys may have committed an offence. Transport regulations posed a problem for interstate boys with fathers serving in the forces, particularly farm boys, for their mothers were then left to manage alone. (The logic justifying restrictions was also frustrating. Why should 'jockeys, pugilists and third rate vaudeville artists', asked a parent, go 'to and fro throughout the Commonwealth—generally with sleepers and a priority second only to that accorded politicians, whilst schoolboys cannot legally see their homes and parents three times a year'?) Some lads played cat-and-mouse games with officialdom by contriving ingenious schemes using service cars and overnight stops at borders before purchasing rail tickets, and hoping that they would not have to produce travel permits. Boys from socially prominent families were singled out, as one New South Wales boy, Peter Henderson (future son-in-law of Menzies), recalled:

> Once on Albury platform the police were up and down. They knew we were all border-hopping but they were trying to catch the son of the Governor of New South Wales. They kept saying to us each in turn: 'Are you the Honourable Loder? Are you the Honourable Loder?'

On 15 September, a frantic Darling drafted three telegrams to Colonel Wynne. In one he advised 'Only course open plead guilty'. In another he said: 'clear we have no case' and then in the third he said: 'agitation about transport creating most undesirable publicity'. Thanks to the mounting backlash against Ward, his fears were groundless but he mentioned the incident in his annual report. He sympathised with the Department of Transport rather than with the boys, while regretting the minister's method of expression. The day after the story broke (14 September), Lord Wakehurst assured him (after criticising the press for its meanness) that 'David has broken no regulation that I know of either coming home or returning'. He feared that the press would have a field day but that the public would be more lenient '& look upon the whole thing as a schoolboy escapade, & that if anyone pushes the matter too far they will only make themselves ridiculous'. At the *Herald*, Keith Murdoch (another GGS parent) agreed. Suppression of such news would only have fuelled claims 'that rich men's sons were allowed to do things in secret that other men's sons cannot do', although the school would not suffer because the public would side with the boys. He was right. With Ward isolated and unrepentant, Darling apologised to Holyman. He was critical of 'our imbecile parliament' and grateful for Holyman's 'helpfulness to us':

> Some wretched boy must have first used the phrase 'special plane' which was picked up by an infernal newspaper man in Sydney and seized on with delight by an unpleasant Mr. Ward. The whole business seems to have been entirely political and to have annoyed the transport authorities themselves, who have tried to be decent in the matter, as much as it has annoyed me and probably you.

Such goings-on were incredible: 'Parliamentary privilege is a great thing when in the hands of irresponsible people and there seems nothing which the ordinary citizen can do about it'. Holyman regretted that he was unable to get the boys back to Melbourne. One of them must have said 'special plane', but it was pure coincidence 'that a large number of boys did travel in the one machine'. He thought that Ward attacked ANA because he wanted air travel placed under the Transport Board's control but this move had been 'strenuously opposed by the Department'.[24]

If public attitudes to the schools were shifting, as Darling thought, then so too was his attitude to educational reform. His 'strongest belief' about such reform was that there was 'no hope or sense in an education divorced from religion'. As he said to one correspondent, he could not see 'how a boy can be taught to live without some assumption on the part of those who teach him, as to what the purpose of living is'. Moreover, the quality of that teacher–taught relationship was central to the development of a boy's character. Blanket reform of education no longer had his unqualified support: reform and religion had to be in harness. He now advocated joint action by the Christian denominations, and believed that it was imperative to have Catholics and Protestants speaking with one voice. In *The End of Economic Man* (published in 1939—read by Ralph and sent out to his brother-in-law, who began mentioning it in speeches in 1941) the Austrian author Peter Drucker observed that, when confronted by totalitarianism, 'the one important fact is that the political and social activities of the forces of religion appear generally either as outright reactionaries or as meaningless fancies'. While scores of European intellectuals had jettisoned the security of various '-isms', ironically their newly chosen refuge the Christian church was incapable of formulating 'the new constructive concept of society which they pretend to have'. In this connection, in December 1941 Temple (then Archbishop of York), with three other English Christian clergy, had co-signed a letter to *The Times* headed 'Foundations of Peace. A Christian Basis—Agreement among the Churches'. This document prompted an important conference on religion and life sponsored by the Diocese of Newcastle, New South Wales, in mid-1942—'the first attempt to bring together representatives of the leading Christian denominations, including the Roman Catholic Church, in a religious effort'. Six broadcast talks soon followed over the ABC on the theme 'The Christian Challenge to the Modern World'. Darling delivered the first, 'Religion and education'.[25]

Just prior to being enthroned in 1942 as Archbishop of Canterbury, Temple reassured Darling that he would respond to his earlier plea to 'show such courage as I have ever had—(not much; it's chiefly lack of imagination)'. Darling's sister Margaret mused that Temple's contribution might well be 'a really Socialist England by the time you come back. I wonder—a labour Archbishop is certainly a step on the way', but his mother saw Temple's genius (or 'courage') quite differently. She believed that in his public utterances he was emphasising only those things that the various denominational bodies could agree on, in which case 'their differences just fade into the background'. Temple's Holy Week talks had been 'really grand, & I don't think he is letting the grass grow under his feet but keeps rubbing in everywhere his ideas of unity and the dealing with unemployment etc after the war is over'. People were definitely turning to him for a lead, she told her son, and—'you would have been thrilled to the marrow'—he had even quoted in his New Year sermon a long passage from Michael Thwaites' poem 'The Jervis Bay': 'a very searching sermon absolutely straight from the shoulder'. Tragically, Temple died of pulmonary embolism on 26 October 1944.

In Sydney, on the following Sunday evening Darling delivered a panegyric on ABC radio and shortly afterwards wrote to Temple's widow. He could not reconcile himself to his death:

> While he was active one felt that there was hope that even out of all this chaos some clear and good leadership might hold together the decencies and the better hopes of life.

There had never been a greater Archbishop of Canterbury, never anyone 'more fitted to unite all classes and types and denominations of Christian people' and never any time at which such unity was more necessary. Temple's death was devastating. 'I loved him personally and owed so great a debt to him that I cannot express myself decently.' Darling then recounted his various contacts with Temple, and the kindness of herself and her husband when he was at Liverpool and they were in Manchester:

> You cannot possibly imagine what those weekends meant to me and how enormously I enjoyed them and how indecently proud I have always been of being able to say that I knew him, and how much I have valued the occasional letters which he found time to write in his own hand and the encouragement which they have been to me.

Her husband's death must have been unbearable for her, but he trusted that she would manage. 'I shall always be proud of his kindness to me, prouder and more thankful than any other piece of good fortune in my life', he concluded, 'and I have had very much. Nor can I ever forget all that he did for me and meant to me.'[26]

'Religion and education' got Darling into hot water. Taking Temple's ecumenicalism as his starting point, he articulated a model of Christian education based on two principles: first, God as creator and planner of all things; second, human brotherhood and obligations to one's neighbours. In claiming that 'our duty towards God is the sanction of our duty towards our neighbour' and that 'Life properly lived can only be considered in relation to these obligations', Darling had paraphrased two biblical commandments. There was no more succinct summary of the core values by which he justified his public actions than these prophetic claims. What followed logically was that character training and the development of virtue were the prime objectives of education, except that if Australia was ever to be a Christian nation then its secular education had to be changed. For this there were only two alternatives: either the church schools (Catholic and non-Catholic) became part of the state system and receive aid, or the state schools had to become 'genuinely religious'. This second (and to him better) option would only occur if the churches adopted a common basis for common religious services within the schools, although not so watery (as he said later) as to surrender any resemblance to Christian teaching. Following his broadcast, Darling read a speech by Maslin, passed on to him by Dr Justin Simmonds (Catholic Archbishop of Hobart) whose sentiments mirrored his. Darling urged him to break through the religious 'tangle':

> There is no hope of solving the present stale mate while we each jockey for position. There is no hope while the Education Department and the politicians can play us off against each other. There is a long history of suspicion and dislike between us and we do not trust each other. We are probably quite right in not doing so.

The only outcome of continued division, he asserted, was a slow but perniciously increasing paganism. Somebody on either side had to be prepared to speak bluntly, he insisted, so that 'the real hidden doubts which divide us may be brought to the surface and discussed'. It was pointless trying to devise a compromise if there was a lack of honesty and an explicit statement of each party's fears. Darling's Protestant critics saw his attempted denominational alliance as playing into Rome's hands. The Anglican Bishop of North Queensland could not see Catholics agreeing on a common form of religious education, nor were all Christians likely to agree on state aid for all religious schools. At Brisbane Grammar, W.P.F. Morris said he would refuse state aid point blank if it were also given to Catholics.[27]

As to his alternatives, Darling didn't want church schools abolished but sought to make them more widely accessible. He made the point forcibly in 'Religion and education' that some parents were already being charged twice over for educational expenses by paying fees (and easing the state's financial burden) while underwriting public provision through their taxes. The problem was to ascertain how to embody them into a wider and varied national system, because 'in education more than anything else variety is essential and uniformity death'. A number of the themes in his thinking (eradication of secularity and snobbishness, a diverse national system, state aid, common religious worship and instruction, and the administrative and pedagogical implications of a 'specifically and dogmatically Christian' schooling) were articulated in another speech in Bendigo in August 1943. In 'Education and the future' Darling displayed remarkable prescience, in light of the path taken some three decades later in Australian educational policy. He sketched the kernel of a scheme that no politician would advocate until an expert committee advised the Labor leader (and future prime minister) E.G. Whitlam to implement a similar idea as the basis for the Australian Schools' Commission. 'Let the best schools in the Commonwealth', state or public, Darling urged, 'be the standard in buildings, equipment, and staff salaries to which all schools should be brought, and you will remove any causes of jealousy which exist'. The machinery for oversight ought to be a 'Commonwealth Board of Education', the function of which was to grant money to 'equalize the opportunities of service which the different schools can offer'. Curiously, just as quickly as he articulated this idea, he put it aside and never developed it.[28]

As institutions justifying their existence by Christian precepts the broad mission of church schools was the moral development of the young. To reform society, however, first the schools had to get their own houses in order, a theme that dominated Darling's annual reports for 1943 and 1944. He attacked Australian society as decadent, aimless and drifting. Its character was soft and shapeless, and Australians were way too ready to forgive every action in the name of broad-mindedness. The alliance of school, home and church had failed to curb the widespread desire for selfish gain and the schools had not instilled the necessary courage, loyalty, self-sacrifice, initiative and perseverance. Whatever bred the 'sort of woolly tolerance of evil' that he detected among the old boys and at Corio, it had to be eradicated. 'When disciplined by good government or even by circumstances', the Australian was as fine a man as any in the world and possibly better, for he preserved a certain independence of judgement and free-dom of initiative even while submitting. But without discipline, habits of obedi-ence, thoroughness and that sense of mutual dependence that was the authority for discipline, Australians quickly degenerated into 'a self-seeking, contumacious and jealous rabble'. His stirring rhetoric struck a chord with Gordon, Colman, Professor Portus and Sir Frederick Mann (Chief Justice of the Supreme Court), but reveals a headmaster who was frustrated (as previously) with the easygoing nature of the country. Australia had only woken up to itself in 1942 when faced with possible invasion, he told Ralph, 'but we are all lulled to sleep again now'. Isolated in Corio, he tried to influence the reporting of the war. He chastised the *Age* editor, H.A.M. (Ham) Campbell, for the detrimental effects on public morale of a gloomy article on 'Gibraltar's Danger' and he lectured his former Ministry of Information colleague Vincent Harlow when he thought that the BBC was overdoing its reporting of the part being played by Australian troops. Doubly annoyed at not being able to develop the school, his powerlessness was a bit like 'suspending one's efforts in the middle of a fire in order to discuss the better construction of fireproof houses'.[29]

'Do I say <u>our</u> country to you now?' William McKie inquired from the Bahamas in 1944 (where there were some Australians whom he felt were a good advertisement for the nation). He had been going to say '<u>my</u> country'. But McKie's friend and former employer was still feeling and behaving like an Englishman abroad. In his struggles to get to grips with the Australian mentality Darling mentioned to D.A. Warren (a friend of Jo Gullett) that it was 'a queer country':

> I think that it affects a sleepiness and unawareness which is more apparent
> than real, like the sort of Englishman who considers it very bad form to show
> enthusiasm about anything. I do not think that it is a good quality at all, but
> it does mean that more goes on under the surface than may be apparent, and
> there are often reserves of strength which the foreigner does not suspect.

It was so hard in Australia to find anyone wanting to be educated in the best possible way according to their talents, for there was an almost universal desire in Australia to be a doctor or an engineer. His growing frustration with the war and the country readily spilled over into exasperation with the simple mechanics of his job, which every now and then he let get to him. After a long rambling soliloquy on Australia's future to Ralph, the handwriting and tone changed abruptly when he interposed:

> My God—Who would be a Headmaster? Have just had to pacify an irate music master three filthy little boys having shoved orange peel into one of the pianos. Who cares anyhow? I suppose they may tomorrow, but it certainly takes me off the high horse of international affairs.

Once again, the explanation for his ambivalence was that Darling could not make up his mind where he wanted to be and, even had he been able to, he couldn't have done anything about it. He still hoped that Australia was his temporary abode. But would he have taken an English job if offered one? Would he have really allowed ambition and self-interest to override domestic bliss, particularly such events as the birth of a third child, Caroline (Coodles), in 1941—'increased by a daughter', teased Humphrey Grose Hodge from Bedford School when he saw the birth notice in *The Times*—as well as being kept abreast of the other two girls' daily doings that were so faithfully recounted by Margaret during her confinement in Melbourne? Rejected for military service and surplus to Ministry of Information requirements, Darling tried promoting Jennings' idea (known as the Geelong Grammar School Scholarship Scheme) that aimed to educate orphaned English boys in Australia. (Sutcliffe told him that Melbourne Grammar had something similar in mind.) Funded in Australia and administered from England, the sole British government responsibility would be to subsidise the cost of fares. Darling assembled a committee of supportive notables in England (McKie, Priestley, Bickersteth, Lady Huntingfield and F.L. McDougall—S.M. Bruce's former agent), but because of the disruption of shipping the plan was delayed, which was yet another source of frustration.[30]

Darling's irrepressible urge to be Home became such a talking point in 1945 that he was hosing down rumours and speculation on speech day. 'Can I stick this place much longer ...?' he had asked Gordon back in April. The school was better than in 1944 except that it was 'impossible to produce anything but intermittent efficiency and the place suffers'. Inwardly, he had 'come to the sober conclusion that I ought to get out' and yet there was nothing else on offer. Persistent reports of his appointment to an English headship ('the boss is leaving', an old boy, Jim Cranswick had told his father) were false, he reassured his audience:

> I cannot, of course, with definiteness deny this, but if it is so, it is wholly without my knowledge, and I rather imagine that someone should have told

me about it if it had been true. There is also the undoubted fact that the headmasters of the schools mentioned are still alive and flourishing, and have expressed no intention to resign; in fact, I think that all the evidence points in the opposite direction, and the story may be safely discounted.

If being trapped on a foreign shore was not frustrating enough for Darling, there was another battle royal with council shortly before speech day, which added to his woes. Once again he offered to resign. Use of boy labour instead of domestics and inflated admission numbers (thanks to the Asian evacuees) had kept expenses down but, with increased taxation and living costs rising, the consequence was a false economy. Only in 1944 had Darling felt that he could plan seriously for the school's future, after he and Thewlis had tried in 1942 but had given up. Apart from minor cutting and pruning, such as reducing Darling's own salary (which he did, voluntarily, twice: in 1943, and then again in 1945, by £1000 a year), the council was unable to devise a long-term debt-reduction strategy. A fee increase would require a submission to the prices commissioner, and a Victorian Assistant Masters' Association campaign for salary increases was looming. In July 1944, Darling compiled an eleven-page report that Manifold thought was 'a masterly document' and, on the basis of it, with the assistance of the Old Geelong Grammarians Association, council planned a financial appeal for early in 1945. But by the middle of the year, Darling was moaning to Colman that he was in 'a state verging on despair of getting any real good out of council meetings'. Then, in October, a crisis erupted. The council's finance committee convened and, at Turnbull's insistence, broke with precedent by debarring Darling from its meeting. Turnbull's 'dogmatic utterance' and 'seeming reputation for infallibility' was all very well, Manifold told Richardson as (yet again) he played the peace-maker. While Manifold was fully cognisant of the financial situation (debt repayment, interest on a substantial overdraft and a loss of £4000 in 1944), when compared to the possible loss of the headmaster, 'I regard the former as definitely the lesser problem'. Both matters were so interlocked with the school's greatest asset (its goodwill) 'that his loss at this juncture could not fail to be less than calamatous [sic]'. Of course, economies were essential:

> But where economy militates against the standard, live[li]ness or efficiency of the School, I think you will agree that it must be ruled out … The Headmaster is the only one who can advise on such points.

Thewlis and Darling simply had to be parties to the finance committee's delib-erations and every effort made to get the headmaster's agreement.[31]

Darling next lectured Richardson about good governance: a council com-mittee or the council should not meet without the headmaster. Suppose that he strongly disapproved of the committee's decisions: he would have to oppose them, and council would have to decide between its committee and its executive head, in which case 'it can hardly do so without offending one or the other'. Did that mean that his exclusion was a vote of no confidence?

> I am conscious that a feeling exists to the effect that this administration has been extravagant and it is responsible for our present financial difficulties. It may be that the Council would prefer to have as Headmaster someone who had less ambitious ideas about what the school should be.

The gauntlet was dropped at Richardson's feet while Darling gave himself wriggle room:

> I am not sure that I have not been here too long and have already discussed this with the acting chairman. If it is a fact that the Council and I are out of sympathy with each other this obviously has a bearing on the problem which cannot be overlooked. If on the other hand it was not the desire of the Finance Committee to raise this issue then I am prepared to continue to serve unless something turns up which it seems to me to be clearly my duty to accept.

Six years of 'something like stagnation in the school' made a positive policy and renewed cooperation between council and headmaster imperative. Manifold brought everyone back from the brink by commending Darling on an incisive but restrained letter and telling him that Richardson regretted meeting without the headmaster. He was now ready 'to do everything possible to set matters straight'. But the incident left a nasty taste, and ensured that the war years ended as they had begun: Darling uncertain about what he wanted, not sure whether the council wanted him and unable to do much either way. Again he had to rebuild relationships. The war had left its mark on the school: standards had slipped in a number of respects he admitted on speech day ('The miracle is that things have not been worse', he told Alistair Davies, an old boy). He undertook to return them to what parents had a right to expect, but the school could hold its head high because it had done its bit during the war: 1272 old boys had enlisted and 124 (10 per cent) had died. This figure compared very favourably with the 419 enlistments in 1914–18 of whom 88 had died. (Subsequent analysis showed that 143 OGGs died compared with 87 in 1914–18.) Many of the dead were 'the best of their generation', said Darling. Only he and Mr Cook (the Old Geelong Grammarians Association secretary) could fully realise how great that the relief from anxiety was in knowing that more than 1000 old boys were coming home— because Cook prepared the casualty lists, and he read them out every Sunday evening, with an image of every boy's face coming to him as he pronounced the names. If ever anyone was tempted to despair about the future, he urged his audience, then think about those who would never be returning.[32]

A QUESTION OF PRIORITIES

1940–1945

*Every art and every investigation, and similarly every action and pursuit,
is considered to aim at some good.*

Aristotle, *The Ethics*

Darling's wartime commitments beyond GGS followed a not dissimilar holding
pattern, but with the difference that his public profile broadened. Two constraints
on him were time and travel. The tyranny of the school timetable dictated the
diurnal rhythm and made time scarce. Most external engagements required travel
to Melbourne. With Corio 65 kilometres south-west of the city centre, 10 kilometres north of Geelong and GGS about a couple of kilometres from the closest
railway station, Darling's self-chosen travel regime ate into the working day. His
prewar estimate was that he drove about 22,500 kilometres annually, or just over
430 kilometres weekly and about 65 kilometres daily. He went to Melbourne four
times each month and 'usually at least twice that number'. If so, then he was a
very mobile headmaster who spent a significant proportion of his waking hours
in railway carriages or at a steering wheel. Two wartime restrictions disrupted this
regularity: revised railway timetables and fuel rationing. Not someone to submit
meekly to clerks in a faraway government department, Darling had to accept
that the luck of the travel draw went with the territory of being a Corio-based
headmaster. Equally, he and the school were at the mercy of APS interschool
sporting arrangements. The normal expectation was lesson interruption due to
match fixtures and railway timetables, so that whenever, in such finely tuned
time-and-travel circumstances, the Victorian Railways amended its timetables,
frustration boiled over. Darling protested at the disruptive impact of reschedul-
ing and pleaded (without luck) to be consulted about proposed alterations—
not unreasonable, given the extent and regularity of the school's custom over
many years. Reductions in his monthly wartime petrol allocation made him even
more reliant on rail travel and meant extended absences from school. Perversely,

however, wartime travel restrictions played into his hands: with his disdain for interschool sport, he relished avoiding rescheduled matches.[1]

Such statistics bear recounting because the external duties competing for Darling's time increased. In addition to his family and school responsibilities, and the roll call of existing memberships (not to mention his speech-making to schools and community groups, often in far-flung parts of Victoria), there were added (in 1940) the Council of Public Education and (in late 1942) the newly created Universities Commission. The Council of Public Education entailed more travel to Melbourne and the Universities Commission necessitated an overnight return rail journey to Sydney. Yet again Margaret resigned herself to prolonged absences (but refused point blank to let him fly). These responsibilities helped rescue her husband from his isolation. He enjoyed the (mostly male) company; attendance ensured that he remained in the educational loop and committee meetings were arenas for influence. The council indulged his absences, with the trade-off that his involvement elevated GGS's public profile.[2]

The first membership body tested by the war was the APS. In early 1940, the six schools reviewed their war efforts and reassessed the cherished tradition of interschool sport. (Australians called them sports, the English term was games, but the rationale was the same: be fair and play the game.) Darling regarded sport as an Achilles heel because of its potential to corrupt educational values. The boys who benefited most from sport, Darling explained (in 1938), were those who were 'not good at it', because playing sport helped them to overcome their physical fears or assisted them in acquiring a sense of coordination. But for proficient boys, there was no virtue in sporting contests because these developed 'a wrong standard of values', so that the emphasis on winning representative matches and giving preference to the training of 1st teams was 'bad'. Yet Darling was equally emphatic that competitive games should be played hard to the limits of one's capacity and with every intention of winning, otherwise there was no point. When a match was over 'it should not matter in the least whether you have won or not', yet this belief 'cuts against the whole league system'. Rowing was the only sport of 'real educative value', because those who were no good at it tired equally with, or more than, those who were proficient. Unfortunately, Victoria had 'to have a boat race in order to make people try', with its 'particularly obnoxious form' of overemphasis on the winning of crews. His alternative was GGS's version of Saturday rowing which he regarded as 'one of the best things in the school'.[3]

Darling preferred 'unofficial' sport—competitiveness without 'elaborate machinery' and interschool cups. But to a tribally minded public school diehard, the most charitable interpretation of these remarks would have been effete, and the least charitable perverse, because they reduced sport to a pastime. The bullish Sutcliffe regarded 'unofficial' as farcical—such was his reaction in 1942 when it was positioned before 'premiership' on the plinth of the Argus & Australasian Cup for the combined sports. The apologia for current APS practice was summarised some years later in a penetrating analysis by Sutcliffe's successor Hone (then four years into a battle with Melbourne Grammar sports tyranny). The 'Adamson tradition' was a product of Adamson's late nineteenth-century heroic-age games experiences at Rugby. Six assumptions were the foundation of Victoria's public school sporting edifice (Darling used games and sport interchangeably, Hone preferred games). The list of orthodox verities was familiar: school games are the battle of life, to perform well meant performing well in life, games heroes become school heroes and then heroes in life, school games moulded character ('courage, endurance, self-sacrifice, unselfishness, loyalty, co-operation, leadership [and] chivalrous ideals'), such character was 'transferable' to serving community and country, and games developed physique, physical fitness and bodily skills. Hone (once an accomplished South Australian Sheffield Shield cricketer) then identified the troubling by-products of this Adamsonian doctrine: schools were judged good or not so good according to the success of crews and teams, schools unable to compete satisfactorily were deemed inferior, as a corollary the strong temptation was to allow older boys to return solely to play games and to represent their schools, games prowess was the all-important prerequisite and model for leadership, competition was the overriding justification for contests except that competitiveness bred exclusiveness and excessive games publicity, winning (and, as a corollary, coaching) became paramount and team results were occasions for triumphant self-glorification in victory or personal failure in defeat.[4]

In 1930, Darling had been horrified to discover the dominance of APS sport, which was nowhere more evident than in the tangled connections between sporting fixtures, charity funds generated by interschool matches and APS service initiatives. Forewarned by John Nimmo, he knew the difficulties in trying to reform sporting contests, especially the Head of the River, an annual regatta that had begun in 1868. Custom dictated that each school exercised 'choice of water' in strict rotation—the effect of which was that for two consecutive years the race was rowed on the Yarra in Melbourne and every third year in Geelong on the Barwon. In 1926, E. Glanville-Hicks (secretary, Melbourne Lord Mayor's Fund for Metropolitan Hospitals and Charities) suggested to Adamson that the fund could 'control the financial side of the Head of the River Races' (previously commercial firms had sold race programs). The fund's aim was to secure official program status and advertising to defray the costs of printing, and to obtain a net return from sales for the schools' fund to be dispersed to charities nominated by their charity committee. After the other heads endorsed this deal, the Yarra's south bank was enclosed for spectators (followed later by the north bank) to which admission was by program only (at a cost of 1/-) during the race heats and final. For thirteen years until Darling's departure for England in 1939—by which time he had persuaded his fellow heads to direct most of the proceeds to the proposed community centre at Fisherman's Bend (about £2000 annually)— the charity committee had forwarded more than £10,000 to the fund (or about £800 annually). In return, the enclosing of spectator areas, staffing of ticket boxes and gates, canvassing for advertisements, counting and auditing of admission receipts, and mailing of cheques to the recipient charities was undertaken by the fund 'as an example of civic service' and entirely free of charge. The adoption of Darling's Fisherman's Bend initiative, however, scuttled this cosy charity–cash nexus, upset the balance of civic and old boy sporting interests, and put some noses out of joint, including the sporting editor of the *Argus and Australasian* (Old Boy—or R.W.E. Wilmot, an Old Melburnian and a high-profile figure in Victorian amateur sport), the APS Sports Committee (or delegates' committee) that devised the annual fixtures and some Melbourne City councillors, including the lord mayor, the redoubtable A.W. Coles.[5]

Shortly after the 1939 Head of the River (when the Darlings were in England), Old Boy attacked the decision of the Headmasters' Association—the six heads who met twice annually on Boatrace Day and combined sports day at the school of the chairman:

> No-one can object to any organisation which is destined to uplift the young
> men of the community [i.e., the proposed centre], but not at the expense of
> the charities. I understand that the delegates were not in favour of diverting
> the charity fund but were ordered to do so by the headmasters.

After the 1940 Head of the River, with Darling's ardour for a centre cooling, the Headmasters' Association rescinded its offer of money even though at Fisherman's Bend contracts for dwelling construction had been let, roads completed and sewerage installed, and Barnett was banking on the centre proceeding. When Darling and Gilray informed him of the heads' decision, he was disappointed but determined to press ahead. The heads offered to run the Port Melbourne Settlement in conjunction with a Fisherman's Bend boys' club if Barnett could provide a building. Meanwhile, pressure mounted to restore the former arrangement between the Headmasters' Association and the fund. Coles told the delegates that the fund's support had been withdrawn as he could scarcely justify his office assisting a 'venture from which the L. M. Fund received no benefit'. The delegates (already peeved by an association decision to disallow printing of junior regatta results in the Head of the River program) tried to force the heads' hand by suggesting that all annual charity monies should go to the fund 'which shall set aside the amount necessary for the Port Melbourne Settlement, and distribute the remainder to nominated Children's Institutions'.[6]

With awareness growing in Australia of a disastrous turn of events in Europe—withdrawal of British forces from Norway, the fall of Chamberlain's government, the Nazi entry into Paris and a French–German armistice—it was high time to grasp the sport nettle. Having raised with MacNeil (the Headmasters' Association secretary) the possible Head of the River suspension for 1941, Darling sent him a newspaper clipping from Robson that reported that Sydney's Greater Public Schools sporting competitions had been abandoned, with its chairman saying that it was 'indefensible to compete for premierships at such a time'. When the Headmasters' Association met on 22 June, it resolved for 1940 that 'the Football and Athletic Premierships shall not be held', although schools would be 'at liberty' to hold matches with one another to leave them free 'for the exertion of their own maximum war effort'. MacNeil's press statement admitted to embarrassment about premiership competitions 'in times like the present' and highlighted the cessation of the 'inevitable clamour' associated with school games. (Rolland could not understand what the fuss was about: 'No one comes to see our football matches'.) As to the delegates, the heads agreed that the Port Melbourne Settlement commitment precluded changing the administration of funds. Darling (absent from the meeting) regarded the cancellation decision and reduced publicity as laudable, except that only some of his objections had been addressed. Later (when still fighting for a reduced emphasis on sport) he characterised his two decades of effort as the equivalent of gaining a mere 'few yards'. It is not hard to see why.[7]

In his skirmishes with Adamson in 1930–31 (in private correspondence and in the *Argus*), the young pup tried (in vain) to convince the old dog of the odiousness of sporting publicity. Their differences illustrated how two Englishmen constructed themselves as Austral-Britons: one indulged his adopted culture while the other condemned it. By endorsing interschool sporting rivalry, Adamson pandered to the nascent aspirations of society keen since colonial days to construct its self-image by reference to sporting prowess and success, whereas Darling tried to temper what he viewed as sporting mania. To an onlooker, there was a stark contrast between pragmatism and idealism in the careers of the two longest serving and most influential headmasters (their combined tenure stretching over six decades). In the cloistered small world of the Headmasters' Association, the reconciliation of these different world views reduced itself to making decisions about such mundane matters as choice of competition venues (school grounds or public ovals?), fixture dates (school days or weekends?) and the adjudication of requests (alcohol on Boatrace river barges?). Darling's problem was that alteration of existing arrangements risked unleashing passionate hostilities (especially among APS old boys) or foundering on the association's bizarre governing conventions—all decisions had to be unanimous, but while a single dissentient was bound by this consensus, a minority of two could thwart the majority. There were other vested interests in the schools: antiquated privileges for sporting heroes (special diets, release from classroom work for training) that over time had become sacrosanct beneath a carapace of tradition. At GGS pre-Darling, for example, the 1st VIII was released from the last afternoon period to go to the Barwon to train and the 1st XI 'were cheered off in a hansom cab to go to Corio station on a Thursday afternoon and return[ed] to school on Saturday evening after a two-day match, [and] some even returned on a Sunday'.[8]

To complicate matters, new and less predictable ingredients were added to the mix during Darling's absence in England. The Headermasters Association's

new membership had altered the balance of headmasterly power when Father
Costelloe succeeded Hackett at Xavier and MacNeil came to Wesley. (In late
1940 Rolland was temporarily absent overseas on Australian government
business.) At forty, Darling was still comparatively youthful (the second
youngest head after Costelloe) although apart from Rolland (the chairman) he
was the longest-serving incumbent. Costelloe was an unknown quantity and
Neil Harcourt MacNeil seemed like a natural ally (he and Darling had much
in common about values and service). He was an Old Scotch Collegian with
an impeccable public school pedigree: Rhodes Scholar for Victoria (1914) and
an Oxford history BA (Balliol). When it came to sport, however, MacNeil was
muscular. For most of his Wesley headship (tragically cut short by a fatal heart
attack in 1946) he coached the 1st VIII. It was not long before the heads' initial
agreement to suspend competitions began to fray, and Darling and MacNeil
were sparring. The latter suggested that the delegates make 'the ordinary
arrangements' for 1941, which could be cancelled if necessary. While Sutcliffe
concurred, Darling believed that the wording committed the schools to 'carrying
on as before' and, because he loathed the existing arrangements, he was opposed.
MacNeil was his own man and not deferential to Darling. He assumed that
1941 would be a 'normal' year (which Darling considered 'queer') and his view
prevailed. By their September meeting, any possibility of further dampening of
sporting publicity had evaporated. The 'usual premierships' were to go ahead in
1941 with all matches played on school grounds (four schools preferred Saturday
home matches and two others weekdays). As to the Head of the River, there
were more hopeful signs: it was timetabled for the last Thursday and Friday of
first term—which suited Darling as weekdays were more convenient for GGS
parents. The heads agreed to inspect the lower Yarra (to the west of Princes
Bridge) to relocate the regatta (MacNeil's preference) and toyed with moving it
to Lake Wendouree in Ballarat. In the end nothing changed: the Harbour Trust
commissioners vetoed the lower Yarra option and the attraction of all six crews
rowing abreast on one day (thus saving a day lost to the heats) was thwarted
by the difficulties of transporting boys as spectators and the irksome chore of
maintaining discipline on trains to and from Ballarat.[9]

With the unfinished business of charity money disbursement hanging fire, support for the APS community centre was fracturing. MacNeil and
Sutcliffe supported the Port Melbourne Settlement but wanted to revisit the
APS–fund relationship and, with the 'usual conditions' varied, councillors and
Town Hall officers were confused about the heads' position. At the request of
the Headmasters' Association, MacNeil met Glanville-Hicks in April 1941, just
as some children's charities were inquiring about the restoration of previously
received monies. The delegates upped the ante by recommending that the regatta
profits be divided equally between the Red Cross and the Lord Mayor's Fund,
and by requesting a public announcement to this effect before the Boatrace.
MacNeil's view was that fund officials 'could make things awkward for us' unless

kept on side, in which case while continuing his support for the Port Melbourne Settlement, he favoured forwarding the fund a substantial grant. Darling objected and emphasised the association's prior legal obligation to support its warden's employment—it had agreed in June to pay him £400 per annum until the end of 1942—part of Darling's argument being that his 'positive reconstruction work' was 'very much better' than what the delegates had in mind.[10]

With the heads' unity fracturing, Costelloe and Sutcliffe supported MacNeil's compromise: pay the warden's salary and forward the remaining money to the approved children's charities. Gilray (Darling's staunch supporter) was 'not keen' to return to the original agreement with the fund, but he was wobbling. He agreed that the heads 'might well this year' support the children's charities as these were 'likely to be ill-supported at this time'. Finally, with a rather prickly 'all right' to MacNeil—who had told Darling that by preventing the fund from collecting Boatrace income he was (effectively) cutting off his nose to spite his face—Darling yielded on the amended agreement. In May, Glanville-Hicks advised the fund that there was about £520 from the Head of the River for distribution with the combined sports takings to come. The Port Melbourne Settlement's future was assured, but the implications for the Fisherman's Bend community centre were unclear. Following the warden's overseas visits to centres, settlements, clubs and associated ventures, he prepared an eighteen-page report. He was still keen to secure the agreement of the heads and Port Melbourne Settlement trustees to a Nott Street centre. He and Darling canvassed various options, including the lease of properties and purchases of residences (despite the earlier rejection of such possibilities), for which the estimated cost was about £4000. At same time he kept in communication with Barnett who, true to his promise to Darling and Gilray, had set aside two adjoining estate houses for their community centre—one for a baby health centre and a kindergarten, the other for boys' and girls' clubs, and adult work. But conflicting local interests were jockeying for the attention of Barnett and the commission. The estate officer's survey (indicating that the residents' priority was for boys' and girls' clubs) strengthened the warden's arm and he was confident that he had Bracey's support. Darling praised him for performing 'a really good job', confessing personally that he was now over a 'personal trough of despond'.[11]

Without warning the warden's personal life imploded and he severed all contact with the heads. Bracey recounted that the young man had been apprehended, charged by the police and bailed to appear in court. Three days later Bracey located the warden who for some time had been wrestling with acute personal problems and was under strain (working long hours seven days a week). While also trying to raise money for the Port Melbourne Settlement, he felt as though he was under the surveillance of, and being thwarted by, the housing commissioners. He was in financial trouble as well. On medical advice he did not appear in court and he was moved to a private nursing home. The Port Melbourne Settlement boys were informed of the warden's 'temporary illness' and Bracey assumed responsibility for the Fisherman's Bend centre. The warden's debts and expenses (£300) had to be repaid and Darling took most of the responsibility. Employment was found for the warden along with a financial guarantor for his debts. Reminiscent of the same kind of compassionate disposition when aiding a fellow Strattonite at Repton in 1917 (caught up in not dissimilar circumstances), Darling said that 'we are right in remembering in spite of everything the good pioneering work that [the warden] has done in the past'.[12]

Sutcliffe's attitude to the Port Melbourne Settlement had stiffened. Despite being 'more than ever convinced' after a visit in April of the need to support it from the Boatrace receipts, he now claimed that a 'loose and unbusiness-like arrangement' characterised a charity scheme that had been unnecessarily superimposed on well-established and deserving charities: 'we should cut the cable and withdraw from an unsavoury situation'. Sutcliffe's 'recalcitrant attitude', as MacNeil characterised it to Gilray, highlighted the need for a tighter governance mechanism, but he told Sutcliffe that there was nothing to be embarrassed about in the history of the settlement. The year before, the Headmasters' Association had put the onus on the warden to secure public school representation on the governing body but he had dragged his feet. The settlement had building trustees and a governing council. The council of six (with the warden as secretary) included Angus (later Sir Angus) Mitchell—a public-spirited Melbourne Rotarian who, prior to the warden's appointment in 1938, had established the original settlement in 1932, along with another Rotarian and the mayor of Port Melbourne. The warden wanted a larger representative body and had been building school support (by visits and talks) among old boys and service clubs. The council was now overseeing a sizeable settlement: five clubs for the 200 boys who used its facilities, a girls' club, a recreation club for about twenty–thirty mothers, a play centre, monthly fathers' and mothers' evenings, dances and sporting teams, and educational classes for youth staffed by volunteers. It also provided placements for social work students. A coordinating committee would appoint a replacement warden (a Geelong Apexian), and control and pay his salary rather than drawing it from the charity fund as previously. In September, with the headmasters committed to their continued support of the settlement, Gilray became the Headmasters' Association representative on the reconstituted governing council. Despite pressure by new lord mayor of Melbourne, Frank (in 1942, Sir Frank) Beaurepaire, to assist the schools' previously supported charities—now suffering to a 'lamentable extent' due to diversion of public generosity in patriotic appeals—the Headmasters' Association distributed 80 per cent of its money to the fund and Red Cross (half each), and the remainder to the Port Melbourne Settlement.[13]

By year's end, relations between the fund and the Headmasters' Association had been smoothed over, and Glanville-Hicks reassured MacNeil that the association's policy regarding its allocations would be honoured. In addition, the delegates' correspondence with the headmasters became much more conciliatory.

Finally, with the Port Melbourne Settlement seemingly back on a more even keel, Bracey and Darling were planning the wider cause of centres. Progress at Port Melbourne, however, was short lived when early in the new year (1942) the newly appointed warden was called up for military duties. An appeal for his exemption to the Minister for War Organization of Industry in the new Labor government, John Dedman (Casey's successor as Corio MHR) fell on deaf ears. To add insult to injury, the Port Melbourne City Council requisitioned the Port Melbourne Settlement building for an ARP warden and evacuation depot. Much to Gilray's chagrin, the settlement was forced to suspend operations. Four years of collective social service effort had been halted by a couple of abrupt decisions: there was little to show for the heads' work and they still had to wrestle with interschool sport. By now the military authorities were occupying more than sixty schools in the five mainland states. GGS was not one of them, but its capacity to play sport in any meaningful way, Darling complained, was limited. The usual fixtures would be impossible because of a dearth of masters capable of training teams and crews, the playing fields were in nowhere near their normal condition, senior boy numbers were thin on the ground and transport difficulties made travel hazardous. For these reasons, he did not want GGS to participate in 'any more than a very limited amount' of interschool sport in first term. He could not believe that it would be 'wrong' for boys to be made to realise 'the full urgency of the national situation'. In all truth, 'this crisis' was in some ways 'an opportunity for the public schools to take a lead in the community in this respect'.[14]

Darling won himself half a loaf: the combined sports were held at Scotch College and the Head of the River was abandoned (although there was some interschool rowing on the Barwon). The next year (1943) saw the temporary cessation of formal premierships and, after protracted argument between the headmasters and delegates about practicalities, there was another make-do rowing arrangement: Wesley agreed to a race on the Barwon with the winning crew from the two Geelong schools. The problem with MacNeil's offer was that GGS could only borrow a practice rowing shell, and would be significantly disadvantaged against a racing VIII. An irritated Darling complained about 'confounded rowing' as he struggled to equalise conditions for a race that he asserted would be 'entirely informal and no question of spectators or cost will arise'. 'Perhaps it would be unkind' to remind him, MacNeil said, that it was he, Darling, 'who has confounded it'. MacNeil was equally unimpressed by Darling's response to the need for a possible Headmasters' Association meeting to consider the delegates' suggestion to dissolve the APS Sports Committee. Darling's claim that to travel to Melbourne for this purpose meant that he and Rolland would have to forgo an entire day got him nowhere: 'unfortunately the world won't wait for us, and there are certain things that have to be done', said MacNeil dismissively. Appreciative of Wesley's offer to row in Geelong, Darling was still twitchy. In response to the fifth of five queries from the delegates (about the form of the 'Saturday Rowing Regatta' and its connection with the junior regatta) Darling replied tersely to

MacNeil: 'Nothing to do with me'. He also persisted with his familiar refrain that the Wesley race should generate 'as little publicity as possible' and could in no way be deemed a Head of the River 'substitute'. Under continued pressure from the delegates to dissolve the Sports Committee, the heads agreed in March 1943. Henceforth, an honorary secretary would be assisted by committees of school representatives (appointed by their respective heads) for each of the four sports (football, cricket, rowing and athletics) to give effect to the policy of the Headmasters' Association. E.A. Wells (Wesley), honorary secretary since 1930, declined to continue, as it would be too much work for one person and (as an indication of the simmering tensions between the masters and heads) because he no longer saw it as 'a real "job of service"'. He also refused the heads' offer of an honorarium for the previous year's work because to accept it was tantamount to 'robbing the children'. Wells was replaced by E.M. Davidson (Scotch). By late 1944 after the combined athletics sports, children's charity disbursements were resumed and £420 was distributed.[15]

Away from APS and Port Melbourne Settlement bickering, two other potential external priorities for Darling were national fitness and youth. In the late 1930s, the mounting imperial belief was that the fitness of the young lagged behind that of the central and eastern European dictatorships. The physical condition of youth became a policy focus in England (as the National College of Physical Training indicated) and Australia where, in January 1939, on the advice of the National Health and Medical Research Council, the Minister for Health convened the forerunner of the National Fitness Council. His action culminated in a public campaign that climaxed in 1937–38. Legislation in 1941 facilitated the creation of state councils and the provision of financial grants to fund state organisers. Victoria's organiser was Dr Alexander Scholes (a Scotch College chemistry teacher). Previously, voluntary groups and charitable agencies in welfare and among the churches had assisted underprivileged youth. Now, a specific focus on adolescents emerged in the public consciousness over the next two decades or so with increased media attention given to teenagers. Adolescence was difficult terrain because 'at no point in the 1940s and 1950s was there any consensus either on ways of defining youth-related problems or possible solutions and strategies'. If young people were experiencing personal difficulties, had got into trouble or if their elders believed that they were wasting their talents in frivolous pursuits and antisocial behaviour, where lay the blame for such indiscretions: with the individuals themselves, or were families and neighbourhoods partly culpable? And where did social background fit into the explanation? Finally, to what extent was the antidote for a misspent youth simply a matter of offering young people a mix of opportunities and social supports? To do the right thing by the young depended on whether one interpreted their behaviour as evidence of deviance or an indication of poor socialisation and maladjustment. Darling's view was that responsibility for youth development rested on the young themselves and the society of which they were members.[16]

Darling's most forthright statement was 'Youth' (an address to the Federal Institute of Chartered Accountants in November 1945) in which he posed two questions asked by the Hungarian-born sociologist Karl Mannheim (who, in 1933, had fled Germany for England): 'What do we expect from Youth?' and 'What therefore do we owe to Youth?' (Mannheim's actual wording was slightly different.) Darling defined youth (very loosely) as puberty to about 30–35 years. He then painted a picture of youthfulness as a remedy to social sclerosis. After mentioning youth's wartime sacrifice (four of ten GGS senior prefects for 1930–39 had been killed) and the nation's debt to them, he extolled young people's virtues of faith, courage, enterprise and idealism as 'what we need'. And yet too often caution, greed, fear and cynicism supressed them. 'There is no greater sin than the disillusionment of the young—and today no greater folly.' With the old structural basis of society destroyed by three decades of war and revolutions, democracy had to be made to work. Young people might just be able to revitalise society, provided that they had opportunities for education and to 'take control'. Denial of educational opportunity by 'our whole set up' highlighted the need for leadership as 'those qualities of mind and character which give poise and sureness to the possessor', and which 'free him from the inhibitions and fears too often at present as much the characteristic of youth as are their opposites'. He had in mind honesty of mind, clarity of judgement, sense of responsibility and courage of decision, which required reforms to extend the school-leaving age, elevate the teaching vocation, stimulate planning vision and develop the talents of all. As for opportunities for youths to prove themselves and take control, they were invariably barred by 'the bogey of seniority'.[17]

National fitness played a back-seat role in Darling's view of youth. Unlike Curthoys and Medley, he was not a state council member (more potential travel to Melbourne), although he did a broadcast on youth and national fitness for Scholes who was impressed with GGS's national service scheme. Fitness, Darling said, was not an end but 'a means' that applied to mind and personality as well as body. His perspective presupposed a society that cooperated in the pursuit of national ends and in war: 'an A1 nation' that worked hard and for long hours, and extended training to as many capacities as possible. 'Usefulness' ought to substitute for fitness, with people shown how to be useful because modern living had eroded their personal independence. Useful people were happier in themselves and better citizens:

> we want to re-capture the power to do things for ourselves, and to depend upon ourselves, we want to re-discover the joy of making things, the joy of moving about in preference to being carried, the greater pleasure of entertaining ourselves rather than being entertained.

Fitness 'of the whole man', able to use his natural endowments 'for the satisfaction of his own soul and the service of his fellowmen' was what was required. Professor

Boyce Gibson (chair of the Board of Social Studies) thought that Darling may have galvanised public opinion and his efforts were a 'real tonic' for the 'lethargy, complacence & sedition' to which recently he had had to listen. Darling also played a part in the formation of peak bodies devoted to work with young men, such as the Victorian Association of Boys' Clubs, and led a training day in April 1940 at Anglesea.[18]

The Victorian Association of Boys' Clubs was to work in tandem with the Exhibition Youth Centre at the Melbourne Exhibition Building. It would 'promote the physical, mental and social well-being of boys, especially those in poor circumstances', direct attention to the need for youth facilities, and promote cooperation between voluntary youth organisations, statutory bodies and individuals to further these objectives through a central headquarters, club cooperation, leadership training and various outdoor activities such as camps. G.S. Colman (chairman of the advisory committee), Scholes, Bracey and Darling were among the eighty or so in attendance on the Sunday afternoon when Darling led a discussion on the education of youth 'in the present Circumstances'. Boys' clubs were training grounds for democratic citizenship (in which boys 'rubbed shoulders with others') and they had to provide debates, crafts and drama to counter idleness and boredom. Subsequently he attended a three-day conference of youth organisations at Merton Hall, but he was really a late arrival in an area already well populated by stalwarts. Apart from his argumentative weight and influence, Darling was useful in the youth area for his network of connections. In 1940, Bracey's strategy for thrusting national service into the public gaze was to establish a council of elders with Darling heading his list of 'BIG GUNS'. This group (which included Medley, Colman and Browne) 'should meet purely as an unofficial social club at dinner every two months', receive reports on youth labour camps, schemes and activities, and make representations to the press, high-level public servants and politicians. Bracey also proposed a reserve set of 'LITTLE GUNS', including Bull. (In his overall gun battery, there were two women: the sole one with a public profile was Dorothy Ross, headmistress of Merton Hall). Instead of a talkfest, Darling preferred boot camps: 'go straight out for a campaign in favour of compulsory work camps for all boys'. The states should organise such a scheme for fourteen- to nineteen-year-olds while the Commonwealth paid for it—two months' mandatory work in camps for reafforestation, soil erosion, drainage and youth hostels. If this scheme was 'more or less the same as the German labour camps', then that could not be helped, because discipline was 'what we need as a nation more than anything else'. On reflection, Bracey backed away from compulsion and thought that voluntary camps might attract wider application. Darling saw merit in Bracey's suggestion, but justified his momentary lurch into high-handedness by claiming that Evatt (elected three weeks earlier as MHR for Barton) 'admitted to me yesterday that something of the sort would be necessary and would have to be compulsory'.[19]

Darling's more familiar home turf of the Unemployed Boys' Club generated a slightly different angle of insight into the possibilities of boy labour. When McPhillimy (the owner of the Geelong West property) died he bequeathed the Centre £1000, with which the committee purchased the site and buildings. A new trust deed was drafted and new trustees (including Darling) appointed. By September 1941, the number of Centre attendees available for ongoing and casual employment fell due to the wartime demand for labour. With the unemployed youth problem 'more or less non-existent', there was an opportunity to rethink the Centre's identity and role. Darling wanted to renovate the building, provide more occupations, cater for more boys (in anticipation of increased post-war demand) and expand the recreation side. He sounded out Bracey, 'the dispenser in chief of government money', who sympathised and agreed not to insist on the affiliation of the Unemployed Boys' Club with the Victorian Association of Boys' Clubs in return for a grant. Darling did not often visit the Centre (GGS boys and Montgomery were his key information sources), but intended to speak about community centres. The week before at the Prahran Library, he had said that community centres 'grow organically out of men's minds', rather than large buildings. They also helped redeem the debt owed to those shouldering the war effort by planning for the cessation of hostilities. Community centres were crucial for a democracy, which meant more than political representation—as he impressed upon Ham Campbell when urging him to begin an *Age* campaign for centres. In fact, a system was democratic when there was 'the willing working of the whole people', because they were so bound together by common interests 'that each feels a responsibility for the whole'. Such holism was antithetical to sectionalism. 'Mammoth industrial corporations' and the like, which viewed labour solely in economic rather than human terms (a 'denial of the facts of God and Nature'), had created the gap between the ideal and reality of a community, so much so that material economic considerations dominated 'all others in our own time'. A community centre was an antidote to sectionalism because it was an organically growing place, rather than formed ready-made, in which 'people join together to get those social amenities which individually they cannot afford to buy' and because a centre should be 'the creation, the property and the concern of the people whom it serves'. When assembled in one location, shared services (educational, medical, recreational, arts and crafts, and advisory) helped preserve the family unit. Such an arrangement was much more economical than competition between organisations and provided a 'focus for the social life of the community'. What was required to kick-start community centres were sympathetic municipalities and good wardens with imagination.[20]

Darling's 'impassioned speech' to the Unemployed Boys' Club committee and trustees, he told Bracey, had convinced them to approve plans to improve the Centre and there was 'every chance of being able to build up a really good unit' centred on the employment problem. An application for £150 was submitted to the Victorian Association of Boys' Clubs, with the plan being for an employment bureau, a vocational training centre and a recreational club (with the Victorian Association of Boys' Clubs providing funding for the recreational component). More than fifty boys aged from fourteen to eighteen were attending daily and in the evenings. A refit of the Centre had commenced, using the voluntary labour of current and former Centre boys, and those from Corio (although the unavailability of trains after 6 pm precluded more frequent attendance). In its less than ten-year life, over £1600 of the £3000 outlaid on the Centre had been raised privately, £1000 of it by GGS boys. In May 1942, however, work was suspended and the Centre went the way of the Port Melbourne Settlement. With the Boys' Employment Movement prohibited in wartime from engaging in the employment of boys, Tullis (the daily organiser) was transferred under manpower regulations to Geelong. Even though the Centre had dealt with 2345 boys over a decade and had found employment for most of them, Darling's appeal to be treated as an exception failed.[21]

Bracey returned to England and in his absence, Darling and Judge Stretton handled Unemployed Boys' Club–Victorian Association of Boys' Clubs relations. As mutual confidants, they debated approaches to youth. Stretton claimed that Bracey discounted 'assisting people to advancement in material things' and was incapable of seeing that 'idealism could not flourish amongst people who were hungry & insecure'. Stretton doubted whether the 'present order' should be maintained, and yet 'our institutions are so good in essence' that he would be loath to see them go. They had to be made to work better, yet he wondered whether the real purpose of justifying boys' clubs was to make people satisfied with 'their little & the other fellows [sic] "lot"'. Darling invoked social class: 'damn it, there are classes, so why be afraid of using the word?'. Bracey's problem was his 'terrible distrust of the "bourgeoisie"', a common fault of all social workers, he said, which diverted him from the real target. If, like Bracey, one concentrated on people who have had the least chance in the world, then:

> you may lift the level slightly of them, and you may get an occasional leader from amongst them, but you will not, I think get a movement which grows from the initiative of its own members. The people who need to be made socially conscious are neither the very rich nor the very poor, but the despised bourgeoisie, particularly the respectable clerk, workman and shopkeeper.

At the same time as Darling thought that such people constituted the mass of society and were worthy of rescue, he rounded on his middle-class peers as 'rather selfish, self-satisfied and unimaginative':

> To some extent it is true that they make up the biggest numbers of church members, but there must be thousands who are untouched. Boys' Clubs can help them, provided that they are made to run them for themselves, and encouraged to extend their activities beyond their own circle.

The very poor, by contrast, had had 'such a rotten spin' as to be 'almost unclubbable and give a much smaller return for the effort spent on them'. One could not really 'save their lives for them', except by altering the circumstances that had created their conditions: adult and juvenile unemployment.[22]

In this curtain-raiser to subsequent postwar exchanges about social class and the welfare state, Darling was being open but patronising. Continuing in his airy way, he said that boys' clubs were exclusive—in fact 'the lower classes are worse snobs than the upper'—and failed because their purposes were pleasure, recreation and keeping boys off the streets. As palliatives, clubs were of little more than superficial usefulness, except that if a boys' club operated as a juvenile employment bureau (Darling was preparing the ground for Stretton's visit to the Unemployed Boys' Club) then there were added advantages. An employment-focused club had a definite place in the social structure: it had a constructive purpose, catered to all classes, boys could run their club, and a club's information and statistics enabled it to tackle problems at their roots. Stretton described Darling's letter as 'penetrating' and expressing precisely what he had tried to impress on Bracey: that 'you can't grow ideals or social doctrine on empty bellies'. Stretton visited the Centre, regarded it as a 'fine show' and liked Tullis 'immensely'. He would seek to have the Centre's grant reinstated and to have Tullis reinstalled at Spring Street (although Pillow and Tullis were reluctant)—with his friends in Labor politics (including Albert Monk, the ACTU president) and the ALP propping up the minority (and vulnerable) Dunstan government, it was worth a try, but Darling was reluctant to offend Pillow (with his 'fine Presbyterian independence' and distrust of government). He was preoccupied with educational reconstruction, he told Stretton, and was reading *The Socialist Sixth of the World* by Hewlett Johnson (known as the Red Dean of Canterbury), which highlighted for him the 'impossibility of planning any educational system in a completely unplanned economic system'. The 'un-organised competitive profit-seeking system of society' made impracticable an educational curriculum for children up until about fifteen, followed by subsequent provision for students and their families while they were training, and the possibility of part-time employment coupled with continued education. There might be something to be said for 'communist planning', except that he didn't know how to avoid the 'dead hand of inefficient civil servants'. Without a planned economy, an education system 'must be haphazard also'. Darling also confessed that it was 'a minor trouble to me that I can really see no justification for a school like this' although his instinct convinced him that 'it is not altogether bad'.[23]

The first of Darling's two new wartime memberships, the Council of Public Education, further crystallised his thinking about youth and their education, and enabled him to make a significant policy contribution. The council was a creature of the *Education Act* (1910). There were twenty governor-in-council appointees: four for the Education Department (including the director), four for registered schools, three for technical education, one for education in music, five representing industrial interests and three from the University of Melbourne. As Darling was aware, the council was also responsible for teacher registration. Along with Browne and Medley (from early 1942), Darling formed a three-man university contingent. Appointed from the beginning of 1939 (although he did not attend until the following year), he was a member until 1963. With the director (Seitz) as its president, the council was a committee of advice to the Minister of Public Instruction and reported annually to Parliament. It could provide information about methods of education and developments in other countries, advice on secondary teacher registration terms and conditions, and on ministerial matters referred to it. In addition, it reported on 'questions relating to the development and general administration of public education in Victoria' and the 'co-ordination of all branches of public education'. Its president and the registrar (the council's sole employee) were civil servants (subject to ministerial control and public service regulations) and the remaining members were honorary and part-time. This difference was an in-built structural deficiency that was ill conducive to 'long-term independence of action', such that by the end of the 1930s, the council had lapsed into torpor, with its proceedings 'reduced to the level of farce'.[24]

Because the Council of Public Education was visiting educational organisations when Darling joined, he invited it to Corio in April 1940 (to show off the national service scheme). Darling and Browne were already well rehearsed in manoeuvring with Seitz on the Schools Board (Darling shortly ceased to be a member), but with the arrival of Medley in 1942 they, not the president, dictated the council's priorities. After Medley's memorandum on the advancement of education in Victoria was tabled (July 1942), this three-man cabal gave the council a makeover, with discussion of this memorandum culminating in 1945 in a 42-page Report on Educational Reform and Development in Victoria. The report filled a vacuum: the utter failure of the political process to articulate an educational policy. A glimmer of support among UAP Legislative Council members for a higher priority for education prompted Browne to persuade Darling to write to the premier (A.A. Dunstan): endorsing points made during upper house debates 'might be very helpful'. Darling duly wrote, but Dunstan was unmoved. Browne's concern was that Dr John Harris (Minister of Public Instruction, 1935–42) had never once consulted the council, while being responsible for the government's 'failure to repair the damage inflicted on the state system of education by the drastic economies of the Depression budgets'. Darling was in a quandary about how to push for reform: pressure on state parliamentarians or a campaign for a Commonwealth takeover of education? For the June 1943 state elections, the council prepared a nine-page report for the then minister (A.E. Lind) but with the return of the Dunstan government, the straw that broke the camel's back was Dunstan's failure to include education reform in the governor's speech. The council, Darling told Browne, should pass a resolution lamenting this omission: 'If this does not produce any concrete result from him within a month, then I think that all non-Departmental members of the Council should resign as a protest'. It was 'quite useless' to keep on passing pious resolutions and getting nowhere.[25]

In July 1943, Darling sought postponement of business for consideration of his motion on the government's attitude to educational reform. Seitz ruled that suspension of standing orders required seven days' notice. Browne then moved to that effect. The president objected. The normally anodyne minutes then record how:

> Mr. Darling protested that this ruling was at variance with the general wish of the Council. He asserted that adequate evidence had been given of the Council's desire to consider the proposed motion and notwithstanding The Standing Orders he felt that opportunity should be afforded to members to discuss the matter. Mr. Seitz replied that he was not disposed to allow the proposed motion to be discussed without notice. He would, however, be willing to give the Council an opportunity of considering the matter under the chairmanship of the Vice-President. He therefore vacated the chair which was then occupied by the Vice-President (Professor Browne).

With a showdown likely at a special meeting a week later, Browne was delighted by Darling's initiative, and wanted press attendance at future meetings (university council practice) and press publicity. Darling's motion (seconded by Medley) read:

> THAT the Council of Public Education is concerned at the omission from the Governor's Speech of any programme of educational reform. It asks the Minister of Public Instruction to seek from the Government an assurance that educational reform at an early date is the definite intention of the Government.

This motion (and a second to make it available to the press) was carried. Embarrassing the government for inertia had now morphed into shaming it into action. The rebels paused. The trouble, moaned Browne, was that 'those who have vision do not appear to have any power, and those who have power do not appear to have any vision'. What was next? Politics, answered Darling. If the premier staved off defeat on the floor of the Assembly and remained in power and 'there should be deputations to all three parties' (although Darling was 'not much in favour' of deputations) to highlight the urgency of the problems and to request a public commitment. If they failed to match promise with practice, then 'we could have [a go?] at them publicly'.[26]

Still the council waited. In September, the Dunstan ministry was defeated in the Assembly. A new Labor ministry headed by John Cain (Snr) was sworn in. It lasted a mere week. A Country Party–UAP ministry led by Dunstan then took office with T.T. Hollway as the new Minister of Public Instruction. Darling was part of a combined delegation from the Educational Reform Association and the Headmasters' Conference of Australia to Hollway in October, following which (March 1944) the reformers flushed out the minister: he agreed to attend the Council of Public Education. Before he addressed the meeting, Darling and Browne supported a closer working relationship between the council and the minister, and the 'necessity of some reform that would result in the Council's being more independent and effective in its statutory functions'. Darling also queried the 'wisdom and propriety' of the director being the council's president. In reply, Hollway said that he agreed with about 80 per cent of the council's suggestions in its last two annual reports and disclosed that an education amendment Bill was in preparation. Patience was running out in the reform camp. The minister was pressed to attend for a third time (he was present in July) in order to reiterate their views to him regarding the council and 'the desirability of formulating a definite scheme of educational development to extend over a period of years'. Again Hollway obliged, this time in April 1945, at which meeting Seitz tabled the draft of the council's report. When expressing his thanks, Hollway claimed that the more he thought about the council, 'the more impressed he became regarding its usefulness'. He could even imagine the council becoming a board of education, a possibility to which Darling and Browne attached importance—although this idea had been raised previously by Hansen in 1927 (during the Hogan Labor government's term) and rejected by the council.[27]

The report was released in July 1945. As Seitz' foreword indicated, the government was taking action already on some of the matters canvassed (such as raising the school-leaving age—although only to fifteen, not sixteen as the council wanted). The recommendations were couched in a commitment to an 'enlightened democracy' in which there should be 'genuine equality of educational opportunity for all citizens'. The changes proposed were intended to realise seven aims (health, character development, participation in family life, knowledge of learning, vocational preparation, democratic citizenship and use of leisure). A quarter of the report was devoted to technical education. Some of its more noteworthy aspirations included the 'urgent necessity' of a thorough reorganisation of post-primary education, establishment of a 'central Institute of Technology' affiliated with the university, provision of systematic adult education under the direction of the University Extension Board (five pages on this topic), a review of rural education (another five pages), continuation of payment of fees beyond the compulsory age and the need to be able to train and recruit teachers with 'personality, ability and enthusiasm' (nine pages)—because in the absence of a teaching service possessing these attributes none of the proposed reforms could be implemented effectively. Areas downplayed (or where the council equivocated) were sex education classes in schools ('no good purpose could be served' by so 'dangerous' a procedure) and religion, where a majority voted in favour of deletion from existing legislation of the provision for secular instruction in schools. A start on reform had been made.[28]

Darling's other new educational forum, the Universities Commission, was more to his liking. It commenced life with a clean slate, and its deliberations and decisions were directly connected with the national war effort. In late 1942, he accepted Dedman's invitation to become one of three part-time members of this new Commonwealth agency. Because Dedman had been keen (and sufficiently intelligent) to avoid inviting as members those with interests in the state education departments and the universities, and public servants generally, he appointed Dr Lloyd Ross (Research Officer, Australian Railways Union) and F.P. Baker (MHR for Maranoa). R.C. Mills (Professor of Economics, University of Sydney) was chairman. Darling now occupied an Australia-wide platform that catapulted him out of the independent sector, gave him a firsthand national understanding of education and invaluable experience of a government agency. The commission consulted with the major peak bodies (university vice-chancellors, state directors of education, and the students' and teachers' unions), it received deputations from a range of examining boards for professional courses and it considered the needs of particular sectors (technical colleges, army education and adult education). Not only did Darling acquire a firmer understanding of the connection between schooling and manpower, and education and the economy, but also an accurate mental map of the key individuals and groups in a federal system. The economy's wartime manpower needs after the Japanese attack in 1942 had prompted the commission's establishment. University students admitted to quotas in courses reserved from military call-up (medicine, dentistry, engineering, veterinary science, science and agriculture) were provided with financial assistance to cover fees and living allowances on a means-tested basis. The universities decided the criteria for admission to quotas, while the commission's job was to administer the scheme, revise quotas, supervise selection, modify classes of students reserved, and mediate between universities and government. The commission's creation marked the entry of the Commonwealth into the (states') sphere of education; acceptance of Dedman's offer positioned Darling at the heart of the Commonwealth's developing relations with the university sector (the commission became permanent in 1945) for a decade and freed him from the numbing constraints of war. A friend wished him well and hoped that his appointment would have a 'suitable cathartic effect on the universities'. The commission was headquartered in Sydney (although occasionally it met in Melbourne) and during meetings there Robson put him up at Shore. The commission was a ways-and-means body that gave effect to policy and was also concerned with policy aims. Unlike the 'three Rs' that schools were said to be concerned with, it focused on four Rs: manpower reservation, redeployment, reconstruction and rehabilitation (although not a fifth R: repatriation). This remit afforded Darling access to documents and high-level submissions, including university annual reports, statistical analyses, international combatants' plans for reconstruction, papers on student selection problems at universities, ACER's reports

on testing and speeches delivered on education by notable international identities. Dedman had done him a big favour.[29]

Because of his domestic situation, Darling's Universities Commission meeting attendance was irregular: he and Margaret had difficulties obtaining home
help, she occasionally fell ill and he was reluctant to leave her with the children, or
members of staff were ill and he could not get away. He wrote cryptically worded
letters of apology to Mills and twice (1944 and 1945) he offered to resign, his
complaint being that 'as usual' he had 'taken on more than I can properly cope
with'. He was responsible for reviewing student appeals for inclusion in faculty
quotas but, with his extensive educational contacts (Headmasters' Conference of
Australia schools, state education and University of Melbourne), his real value
was to act as Mills' eyes and ears. Once at Spencer Street station (now Southern
Cross station) he was beset upon by a science and engineering faculty delegation, and was 'frequently attacked' at the university. After a returned servicemen's dinner he was alerted to the problems created by manpower officers who,
when finding employment for discharged servicemen, were inclined to adopt a
hole-plugging approach. As a consequence, in the absence of a training scheme
the men concerned would lose their positions at the end of the war and had no
opportunity of 'really rehabilitating themselves before the rush [for jobs] begins'.
Darling acted as an occasional spotter of training anomalies: what about widows
of soldiers, he asked, shouldn't they be able to benefit from reconstruction training schemes as well? He also fended off aggrieved parents, such as a 'tearful and
irritating and persistent' mother whose son, having failed his Leaving Certificate
(after Darling assured her that he would pass) was precluded by changed examination requirements from matriculating in three Leaving subjects.[30]

Darling enjoyed the work and the cases interested him. His correspondence
with Mills and Jock Weeden (the commission's secretary) is full of his usual
mirthfulness—600 school reports to write, he panted, with 'something relevant'
for each one: 'Monstrous task'—and the meetings were an opportunity to talk his
head off about education (and to quote Mannheim). He and Ross also discussed
community centres and, on receipt of a memorandum on Geelong West's Boys'
Employment Movement prepared by GGS boys, Ross forwarded it to colleagues
in Ministry of Post-War Reconstruction who were compiling a report on
centres. At this news, Darling scrawled a note to Montgomery to '"plug" the
idea everywhere we can. Menzies[,] Chifley, Ryan etc.' In late 1944, however,
Canberra considered the Boys' Employment Movement in a different light. A
letter from Chifley to Dedman indicated that its premises might be acquired for
lease by the Commonwealth as an annexe to the Gordon Institute of Technology
in Geelong for reconstruction training. A less-than-impressed Darling thought
that the Centre would have to meet the needs of boys 'who have been put into
dead-end jobs during the war and will be discarded as soon as it is over'. If the
Centre was not open in the daytime the 'evil results' of casual employment would
be visited on yet another generation of 'messed up' young people.[31]

Occasionally, the Universities Commission ran into difficulties when placating the professions. In 1944, after a Melbourne Club conversation, Darling's friend, the surgeon Alan Newton, contacted him on behalf of the wartime Central Medical Co-ordination Committee (CMCC), which was alarmed by the commission's activities. In a silly outburst of prejudice, Newton claimed that medical course recruits were 'mainly Jews & Irish peasants (or should I say descendents of Irish peasants)', with the result that future doctors will be 'Yids or Micks'. Character, he insisted, was as important as cleverness. This disquiet (and that of six other correspondents' letters that Newton gave Darling) was about the unintended consequences of quotas. One worry was that servicemen suitably qualified to enter a reserved faculty ought to be able to enrol (and but for their wish to do their bit might have enrolled) after (say) two or three years' service. Another concern was that previously enrolled students who may have failed their examinations were precluded from repeating their year and were uncertain about their future status upon release from service. Others who had not been allowed to enrol (due to being employed in protected industries) faced stiff competition from returning ex-servicemen for the limited places permitted by quotas. There was also a strong whiff of social exclusivity in Newton's outburst: the commission's subsidy would enable students from families otherwise unable to afford it to be admitted, but would the subsidy facilitate admission of those qualified by 'all the standards desirable in members of the [medical] profession'? The commission, Darling replied, was alert to the need to recognise war service and would do so by treating ex-servicemen applicants as 'extra to the quota'. But the men themselves had to apply for release after which the services had to release them. He smoothed Newton's feathers by assuring him that, while there were 'some odd names' among financial assistance applicants they were 'not unduly prominent'. Moreover, there was no evidence of religion. There might also have been a 'worse type' at university in the period prior to informing boys that they ought to enter reserved courses and surely the real concern was the professoriate's failure to put before boys the ideals of the professions that they were seeking to enter.[32]

Two aspects of the commission's work particularly interested Darling. The first was shortened university courses for ex-servicemen, for which he drafted a memorandum in November 1944 that was distributed to vice-chancellors in the following year. He asserted the principle that the universities:

> should be asked to realise the very great sacrifice made by men who will have served four, five and six years, who will have gained so much in maturity by so doing, but who will have lost contact with academic work.

Possibly he had his Oxford days in mind when he claimed there was much to be said for two years at university after war service, although he thought that men were unlikely to want to do three even if they received reconstruction training benefits. The second matter was adult education (on which the Universities

Commission was preparing a report). Darling told Mills (as a way of sparking Dedman's interest) that his recent suggestion at the Council of Public Education that the Commonwealth take responsibility for adult education (and libraries, education for fifteen- to eighteen-year-olds and universities) had been favourably received by Hollway. Then, in a letter (now missing) to Dedman, he pressed him on the educational role of the commission and the Commonwealth. Dedman's lengthy response suggests that Darling had discoursed vigorously on political representation, party differences and the imperfections of democracy, with Dedman replying point by point and assuring him that Cabinet was considering his ministerial submission on the commission. He answered Darling's impatience at delays in decisions on education policy by expressing his own frustration with the electorate for failing (in the 1944 referendum) to augment the Commonwealth's constitutional powers. If democracy in a federation was to work, one needed 'the heart of a lion, the strength of an ox, the patience of Job, the wisdom of Solomon and many other attributes'.[33]

Darling's wartime work-in-progress, evident in his exchanges with Stretton (and his jottings and speeches), was about the nature of a reconstructed society. Mannheim's 'third way' idea was useful, because rather than a stark choice between laissez faire and planning for conformity, Mannheim championed 'planning for freedom and variety'. With laissez-faire liberalism leaving too much to chance and self-equilibration, and bureaucratic militarism having spawned dictatorships in Germany, Italy and Russia, Mannheim hoped for a militant democracy united around a framework of civilised values inherited from antiquity, 'and even more from Christianity', which left the more complicated values 'open to creed, individual choice or free experimentation'. In his speeches, Darling quoted Mannheim as a way of bridging the gulf between individualism and collectivism, and forging a link between religion and education. The divorce of education from religion in a democratic community of Christian ideals, he wrote, was a 'root defect' and an education without religion was 'a farce or a crime'. Nineteenth-century competitive laissez-faire ideas and the principle of equality of opportunity were not ends in themselves, and it was fallacious to regard economics as the measure of everything (as Drucker conclusively demonstrated in *The End of Economic Man*). Moreover, to preach equality of opportunity on its own begged the question: opportunity for what? The rightward and leftward drift towards collectivism had to be acknowledged but the choice was not between a planned economy and free enterprise: rather, there had to be a compromise that depended on a method of control other than state ownership and on the 'means adopted to secure at the head of the state those best fitted to govern'—'a planned society without the betrayal of liberty':

> in which the objective is clear[:] that is the freedom to practice [sic] the higher
> spiritual virtues and to develop the individual excellence of the individual
> in the various higher spheres of which he is capable, but we cannot do this

haphazardly—it will not come of itself—Decisions will have to be made [as?]
to the proper scope and degree of planning and the amount of liberty which
will have to be sacrificed in order that opportunity for the higher liberty may
be secured.

The robust prescription for compromise between 'necessary collectivism and our
inherent individualism' was a 'new birth of liberty UNDER GOD'. Darling's
Christian version of the third way was 'the way of planned liberty based on our
traditional ethics'.[34]

Darling's means of anchoring this cosmology was an organically emergent
human brotherhood. Rather than being restricted to the anticipated kingdom
of God, this had to be an immediately realisable order. Two examples inspired
him. The first was nationalistic. Despite all the hardship and tragedy being experienced in England, Darling had been struck in letters received since the Blitz
by the 'note of happiness and satisfaction prevalent in that country'—almost all
his correspondents had been united in saying that 'they would not have missed
the experience for anything'. This may have been true for 1941 perhaps, when
he wrote these words, but was wishful thinking for a postwar world. Here was a
vision of what a community could, and ought to, be: people rising to the occasion, experiencing the sense of being useful and valuing their deeds. In this connection, he also highlighted a difference between 'organic and unselfconscious'
English practice and a German tendency to be 'deliberate and theoretical'. His
second example was unashamedly self-justificatory. A school was a community
within a community, he asserted, in the very way that GGS had become with its
national service scheme, the mechanics shop rebuilding, pageant plays, and its
Boys' Employment Movement work and forestry camps. In these examples, a
sense of purpose emanated from God and a sense of usefulness came from love of
one's neighbour. Creative crafts were needed in schools as outlets for 'the creative
instinct', one of the 'strongest things in man and [which] has been killed by large
scale production' in how people earn their living and in the provision of negative
pleasures. These instances of unity contrasted with a self-satisfied Australia; the
latter was a society 'criss-crossed by divisions and jealousies' of religions, classes
and states, and by the self-seeking interests of daily life. There were also vices of
money standards and frivolity to be fought 'wholeheartedly'.[35]

With this reasoning Darling was groping towards saying that, because crises
(national or local in scale) brought out the best in people, such behaviour ought
to be the basis of a third way. But was it reasonable to expect mass populations to
live as if in a constant state of crisis and willing to be mobilised perpetually on
that basis? Liberty had to be restrained by moral law and a sense of brotherly
love, and because he regarded schools as 'societies in microcosm' it was up to
them (regardless of whether they were residential, area or community schools)
to teach what it meant to lead a good life. An implication was that character
development was prioritised ahead of knowledge acquisition, which in turn

entailed the teaching of individual tastes and talents, and the interdependence
of the members of a society. All of this was a prelude to the question of whether
or not it was possible 'to create by education a society in which self-interest is
not the criterion'. An educational plan for social renewal was needed to outline
the essential elements of democratic citizenship: literacy, health and physical
fitness, honesty, independence of judgement, willingness to cooperate, sense of
service and understanding of institutions. As to the framing of a plan or policy
embodying such elements, Darling was mildly optimistic: Victoria may have had
a government (in 1941) 'which on the whole has done more for education than
most governments', but the fact that it hadn't done more was the general public's
fault and all the more reason for better educating a government's political masters.
But his assumptions—that religion was the basis of education that was in turn
a means of democratic renewal—were tricky to reconcile in practice. To support
lifting the school-leaving age was definitely consistent with obtaining a better-
informed electorate, but to insist on a spiritual basis for schooling, regardless
of type, entailed removing 'secular' from state legislation (as he argued at the
Council of Public Education). Until that happened (and there was no sign that
it would), when addressing state school speech nights (as at Castlemaine High
School in 1941), he was left publicly exposed: to mention God and prayer in such
a venue may not have been 'tactful' for a guest like himself.[36]

The comfort obtained from England's response to the Blitz introduced the
final theme in Darling's pantheon of priorities: empire. For the moment it was
intellectually embryonic. His brief Ministry of Information sojourn breathed
life into his imperial pride, but the trigger for his thoughts of Home in his
Castlemaine High School speech was an accident of timing: 18 December 1941,
ten days after Australia's declaration of war on Japan. Conscious of his and of the
audience's pride in their 'British stock and British character', with 'the blood of
the races mixed in your veins and mine', the sinking of the *Repulse* and the *Prince
of Wales* (a week earlier) had shaken everyone's false sense of security. His pride in
being English was second to no-one's but, he conceded, the British people had a
weaker side: their individualism made them unwilling to submit to organisation
and war preparation, their refusal to be defeated meant that they wouldn't even
countenance the possibility of it, unruffled calm bred complacency and self-
satisfaction, and they distrusted brains and capacity among leaders. To be 'the
greatest nation in the world', however, and for Australia to 'endure as a free
nation at all', required confronting such defects. The full import of his reasoning
might have gone over the heads of this Australian audience, but his sentiments
resonated with his brother-in-law. After the humiliating retreat from Europe the
year before, Ralph groaned that 'The Dunkirk show does make one proud to be
English'. But why, on the other hand, 'do we always have to get in a jam, & then
show our best qualities in escaping from disasters instead of winning victories!'[37]

A page and a half of patriotic indulgence in a speech to a country high
school may not have signalled a shift in a world view, but it revealed a stirring.

Equally, a graphic if slightly overdone running commentary on the pomp and circumstance of Home, juxtaposed with mundane imagery of the fatalism and drudgery to which ordinary Englishmen and women had been reduced, may have tugged at the heartstrings (and reinforced his feelings of isolation). Such a description arrived in late 1945 in a six-page letter from Lady Wakehurst. She and her husband had recently returned to England, and she had attended the opening of the new Parliament (the day after the Japanese surrender):

> The morning was dull and showery but the crowds collected all along the route, they are so quiet & patient and uncomplaining[,] some had umbrellas, most of the women wore those 3 cornered scarfs on their heads tied under their chins or done up in some fancy way ... We were all shown our allotted seats, ladies segregated from the gentlemen, but all in the same kind of seats—the ladies in the front 4 rows gentlemen at the back 2 crossways all down the centre—the thrones are at one end and I had a very good view. The King and Queen are a wonderful pair—she looked so charming (but definitely too plump,) the King led her up to her seat with such a charming gesture like people dancing a minuet their hands held high & clasped—the Queen & her ladies wore long dresses & hats, all the rest of us short ones.

Next:

> The King read his speech in a strong non hesitant voice. The Commons crowded up to the bar at the far end—and I saw Winston, & Eden, Attlee and Bevin, and many of the others whom I did not know. Bevin stood out, I thought, he has an arresting face, with that rock like feeling which the great have to have. Winston was rather hidden, he is very well but does not look too good a colour or too bright eyed, but I was far away and he is so small so I could not say much about him ... The atmosphere of the gathering was one of relief and yet great solemnity.

Sadly, she only spotted the new archbishop (Fisher) in the distance. Her impression was that people were 'so exhausted & so pale', and their constant waiting for everything had induced a passive resistance 'which is not good'. Things seemed 'incredibly old-fashioned': compared with the USA the 'drabness of London is dreadful' and, even though bombed-out buildings (with grass growing in them) communicated a sense of a departed life, 'people keep wanting to go back to where they were'. Although she could detect 'very little feeling of lets [sic] get together & see how we can make a brighter future', beneath it all there was a 'great deal of vitality still'. After eight years in New South Wales, she was adjusting to a different tempo of life, which was not easy. She and her husband had mingled with the crowds on VJ Day, surrounded by much whistling, blowing of kisses and paper hat–wearing. From the Buckingham Palace balcony, the king and the queen had waved to milling crowds amid the cheering, which 'brought a lump to your throat' and 'such a feeling that these two tiny figures on a faraway balcony belonged to them personally, one vast family'. This mixed picture suggested that Darling was better off (and lucky to be) where he was, away from it all. At any event, unlike the Wakehursts, another three years had to pass before he could obtain a firsthand sense of what she was recounting. By then, it would be fourteen years since his first return voyage, during which time he would have returned to England just once. Things English were becoming remoter and things Australian familiar, with that familiarity breeding just a shade less contempt.[38]

GRAND PANJANDRUM

1946–1948

So, still within this life,
Though lifted o'er its strife,
Let me discern, compare, pronounce at last,
'This rage was right i' the main,
That acquiescence vain:
The Future I may face now I have proved the Past'.

Robert Browning, 'Rabbi Ben Ezra'

December 1945 was the midpoint of Darling's GGS incumbency. There were sixteen years behind him and he was forty-six. What did the return to peace hold for him? Normality, perhaps, but did normal make sense any more and when was normal? Dismal economic realities soon came into play. The bottom line, as his council reports said (invariably the first item), was numbers. These posed difficult choices. The aggregate of boys actually and potentially enrolled determined GGS's income. Tuition fee income in turn dictated the size of the staffing establishment, the level of masters' current and projected remuneration, and pension entitlements. Periodic across-the-board basic wage awards and the effects of upwardly revised salary scales for state school teachers, along with increases in the cost of living, threw some large spanners into these calculations. And while higher enrolments might yield replenished financial coffers, they also altered the ratio of masters to boys, and exerted pressure on classrooms and boarding space. In that event, the employment of additional masters facilitated by enrolment growth disrupted accommodation and (especially if they were married) necessitated shuffling residential occupancy or the construction of new dwellings. This was the supply side, but demand management was equally hazardous. To refuse applicants admission might make little long-term sense if it pushed families into the arms of rivals and it was not a good look: a fee increase intended to cover costs helped sustain the pecking order of cachet among the church schools, but unless carefully computed it could put GGS out of the reach of aspiring families and strengthen perceptions of it as a snob school. Another enrolment growth consequence might be to increase the school's size and complexity to such an extent that it approached a machine-like threshold—indeed, as the school grew, 'machine' was exactly how Darling referred to it. These were the grim economic parameters that defined the council's (and the headmaster's) postwar dilemma: how was GGS to become a marketable educational commodity again?

The headmaster himself was also a marketable commodity, and his and the school's marketability were inextricably connected. The answer to the question of who needed whom the most was that school councils were hostages to the fortunes of their heads. The logic was compelling. Heads of Darling's calibre and profile were selling points for schools. Given the magnitude of their authority and status, and the weight of expectations that was evidenced by their every action, the destiny of a school was tied to that of its head. Provided that a headmaster possessed a highly regarded profile, then this worked to a school's advantage. The other side of the marketability coin, however, was the awareness that the more successful that schools and their heads became, the greater the likelihood that they might move on—star heads were much sought after, open to better offers and tempted (if ambitious) to seek greener pastures. As the events of 1939–40 showed, these ingredients had all the hallmarks of a morality play. On that occasion a full-scale institutional and personal disaster had been narrowly averted, but was there any guarantee of future avoidance? Darling knew his market value—at least in Australia, although England was another story. It was three years before he took Home leave again (1948), and on that occasion his handling of the council was very different.

Aside from the big 1939 hiccup, all of the differently composed school councils since his arrival had given Darling his head. Both sides kept their part of the bargain: as it was not councillors' function to 'interfere with the internal working of the school', they accorded him unfettered right of appointment and dismissal, and it was his duty 'to report to the Council anything which may happen in the school which is to its detriment'. A footnote to this tacit understanding was that 'if councillors wish to criticize internal things then this is done in the form of a question to the Headmaster or Secretary', with the answer being 'read and approved by the Secretary'. While this was not a high-wire relationship, councillors were by no means supine—as Darling's recent burning at the hands of Turnbull, Richardson and the finance committee showed. The year 1946 was welcome for the headmaster because it ushered in membership changes more to his liking. After thirteen years, Wadham resigned at the end of 1945 and was replaced by Jack Lindon (chairman of the Old Geelong Grammarians Association). Herbert Austin also resigned (early 1946) after thirty-seven years' membership. Then, after thirty-five years as a member, W.F. Volum departed. There were also three deaths: John Turnbull (a councillor since 1914) died in March (replaced by Holyman), the Reverend R.D. Peatt (member 1942–46) and

A.G. White aged seventy-seven (a member since 1908). Balcombe Griffiths, another OGG, joined in May 1946 and John McKie (Bishop of Geelong and brother of William) followed in August. In December, Lindon became council chairman. Thanks to these changes, Darling was less cramped. Publicly he reasserted himself, although in different circumstances from the 1930s: the chorus of competing educational reform voices was louder and the political terrain for the conduct of reform debates had shifted leftward. Darling engaged publicly in two main ways: first (at face value trifling, although actually very successful), he used Corio as a conference venue; second, he advanced the interests of church schools by cementing connections with politicians of all persuasions. He assumed that the future of church schools was much more precarious than prewar (due to heightened state school competition) and that tuition-fee income was not enough to guarantee their survival—about which, he told Hake, he was 'increasingly glum'. In company with Headmasters' Conference of Australia colleagues, Darling actively courted state largesse to ease fee-paying parents' financial plight.[1]

On the home front, normality for the headmaster and his family had a new meaning because health considerations punctuated their domestic rhythm. While 1946 had begun on a high note with the birth of a son, in this and the following year his and Margaret's lives came unstuck when she was weighed down with a nervous disorder. Both 1946 and 1947 were each an *annus horribilis*. Late in February 1946, on a stormy day of thunder and lightning, Margaret gave birth to their fourth child in the Mercy Hospital: John Austin Campbell Darling. She was well, she said, except that 'my tummy feels as though it has been through a mangle'. Wittily worded epistles soon arrived from friends. Colin Gordon (now headmaster of St Peter's) pictured the proud father watching intently to see which of the infant's hands first grasped his rattle 'and whether the grip is that of a tearaway [fast bowler] or a spinner'. Gerry Dicker hoped for a left arm bowler like the youngster's father, while Hackett suggested that his friend should 'make sure of a good education' and enrol the boy at Xavier. At Westbank, his mother was elated and Mabel was 'thrilled to the marrow!' The four children delighted their parents. Jane and Elizabeth boarded at Toorak College and, under Caroline's attentive and adoring eye, the sisters' baby brother made steady progress. 'Glad to hear that John is ruling the family benevolently', quipped Robson, his godfather.[2]

Darling was in Canberra when his son was born. 'Pity you can't be here—can't be helped', Margaret wrote the day before the birth. Not long after John's arrival, her husband was away again. 'This [Universities] Commission seems to be taking up more and more of your time', she grumbled. Barely a fortnight after John's arrival, Margaret was depressed. It seems to 'hang over me all the time', she complained from Purrumbete (with the Manifolds). She couldn't bear it. Moreover, she had begun 'smoking like a chimney again'. By April, a household routine was emerging and Darling reported to his sister Margaret that 'John flourishes and we have a cook as well as a nurse. Bankrupt, therefore, but luxurious is the note.' To complicate matters, Darling's eyes were troubling him throughout Margaret's postnatal recovery and for the first time in his life he wore spectacles. In the following month (May), he headed north for a respite after the council gave him temporary release. During his nearly four-week absence, Margaret kept him abreast of developments in the small bayside community, which had become a big nursery: the Masterman, Fraser, Cartwright, Howard and Tunbridge families were all raising young children. Margaret felt like 'a rudderless ship', 'which shows how very much I depend on you for Everything & nothing seems worthwhile till you come back again'. There was some compensation in being able to refuse 'various speeches for you'. She urged him to have plenty of early nights, late risings and to play lots of golf, which he did: 'Brisbane was grand', he told J.O. McEwin (at the Unemployed Boys' Club), and 'my golf dramatic, (good, I mean)'. He also caught up with old boys in Queensland and New South Wales, and visited schools.[3]

There seemed to be no end to their afflictions. By July, Darling was moaning about 'a despairing few days with everybody in the household sick', and then in December he and Margaret contracted a debilitating stomach bug. In early 1947, she was still recuperating from depression. Because there had been no relief from her mother's incessant questioning while staying with her, Margaret had decamped to Dueran, the Lesters' property near Mansfield. In one letter, her husband mentioned possible job appointments in England (but gave her few details) and triggered her latent anxieties:

> I do know there is a lot against going home, but this country seems so awful at the moment & I am sure the Communists have a stronger hold here than they have in England. I really get quite frightened sometimes when I think of the future of Australia.

Still in 'considerable confusion because of my domestic situation' was how he summarised his life. The doctor described Margaret's experiences as like the tide coming in and out: she would feel better but then a small incident would make her 'rattled or mentally tired'. She knew that she was not yet recovered and that she could not be hurried, as everyone had been telling her husband, 'so please believe it'. After briefly improving, she relapsed in August. The news from Britain was scarcely more cheerful. 'We are not a very happy nation at the moment', said Ralph. Politically and industrially it was all 'pretty chaotic', wrote Gerry Dicker. An old boy, David Darling (no relation), described London as 'filthy and battered', with women everywhere queuing outside food shops, and the food itself starchy, although not in the West End hotels where the choice was abundant. These privations were exacerbated by the shocking winter weather, which, Darling's older sister said, 'has really been the limit'. Keep the family in Australia, she cautioned, as 'we look a pretty fair mess here economically & politically':

The Labour Party will have to curtail their program. Already rates have gone up all over the country & now the Govt: are looking for new sources of taxation to balance the Budget partly on account of this disastrous stoppage of industry. I think the rank & file are beginning to realise that there is not much left in the kitty and I imagine it is a very good thing it is a Labour Government that have got to tell the unpalatable truth. I don't think Churchill [Leader of the Opposition] is behaving in a way that makes one want him as a peace time leader but I think Shinwell [Minister of Fuel and Power] must have been dangerously improvident.

Their mother was reporting by the end of the month that there were floods right up to the railway sleepers and a continuing coal crisis, but she said that this should not prevent her son from coming home and that to get his wife well again they should make the trip. 'I'd just be off my head with joy if I could have the chance of seeing you both again.'[4]

In May 1947, the Darlings took a break. Margaret's return to Corio from her recuperation was conditional (said her doctor) on the employment of a cook, but Darling could not secure a suitable person. Equally frustrated by being unable to take leave in England, for which he was due, he suggested that his mother and sister come out to Corio, but his sister would have none of it. For six years she and their mother had lived in other people's houses '& are enjoying being on our own again'. Moreover, they had an excellent maid and tenants, and could not afford to lose them; she was a school governor, and 'Mother would, I think, inevitably find living in your busy house exhausting—she can't do with more than about a fortnight of Poole House [the le Flemings in Durham]'. By September, a worried Jane Darling was advising her son to think about a new line of work that would not entail her daughter-in-law having to manage the entertaining. Mabel had just experienced a similar breakdown to Margaret's: maybe 'the thought of your life work should not deter you from making a change' if it would be for her benefit. He had to be sure that 'a perhaps too conscientious thought of the work God has called you to do in the world' wasn't blinding him to his responsibilities nearer home: 'the care of your wife & children which after all is God given work also'. Perhaps that sphere 'should come first for a bit anyhow'. She had not wanted to annoy him, 'but I just felt I must somehow'. In desperation—because 'my wife doesn't seem to be getting much better and is very anxious that she should be with me'—Darling requested further release from his duties, so that the two of them could be at Barwon Heads. For a couple of months his mother (to her annoyance) was completely in the dark about Margaret's progress and, towards the end of October, with a 'scolding' she insisted on 'a letter at once'. By December, the news from Down Under was that Margaret was 'really feeling better' and able to travel. They would go to England in 1948.[5]

To compound Darling's domestic instability, day-to-day GGS normality was being disrupted by the supply-and-demand equation. To be tackled successfully, he needed a fit-for-purpose administrative apparatus, but it eluded him. The problem was structural and personal. GGS's inherent weakness, he mused, was that it was akin to 'a very old-fashioned family business'. Unlike impersonal bureaucracy, the hallmark of the state, GGS's strength and weakness was that 'it is a compound of loyalties, to the place and to each other'. Loyal colleagues who served it and made that service 'a life's work' should not expect to be 'treated as employees and sacked even though they become inefficient'. But in early 1948, Darling told Jack Lindon that, in regard to Milton Thewlis, he was in 'a very awkward position'. The bursar was devoted to the school and Darling felt strong bonds of personal loyalty to him for sticking by him 'in the very difficult years of 1939–40 especially', but also in 'all the difficulties with what was for a time a very difficult council'. And yet Thewlis was 'clearly inefficient': behind in his work, tied to the past and loyal to '<u>his</u>' own inefficient staff, and 'the situation has got beyond his control'. Employed at Corio for more than thirty years, Thewlis oversaw the business and domestic sides of the school with the assistance of an accountant (A.D.H. Stephens) and three women. Darling had his own secretary—June Morrish, much slower than Vi Moden (now married to a master, Rolf Baldwin) had been, he moaned to his sister—as did Doug Fraser (master of junior school). Between all six of these people, Darling had explained to Gordon, 'the work of the school is done, including the Bostock House accounts'. As bursar, Thewlis micro-managed 'everything' because he deemed no-one else reliable enough to attend to the accounts, yet 'in a place of this size the Bursar should do almost nothing else except inspect and organize'. His strength was that he was an 'extremely practical person capable of understanding and controlling the staff in a way that an ordinary man would not'.[6]

To achieve administrative economies, council appointed Stephens (from the catering section of Holyman's airline) in 1946—or rather (said Darling) had 'allowed itself to be stampeded' into appointing Holyman's nominee. Thewlis was not consulted, felt slighted and, to make matters worse, the new man, thinking that he was to be bursar, had never tried to win Thewlis over (with the latter adamant that he was not to be won over). The following year, Thewlis fell ill and was granted leave. His relationship with the council had soured when the school piggery lost money. In Thewlis' absence, council considered sacking Stephens, but hesitated in the belief that after a year's experience he might prove useful. Darling tried to reassure Thewlis:

> I don't want to urge you to any expression of faith in this direction until after you have returned from your holiday, but if later on you would find it in your heart really to accept this and be determined to make it work I am sure that it would be in the best interests of the school and of happy relations all round.

Thewlis was unconvinced and, Darling believed, terrified 'of letting anything get out of his control during his absence, with the result that when he comes back, he has to accept a situation of which he doesn't approve'. For his own part, Darling was reconciled to working with 'three parallel heads' (Stephens, Thewlis and his recent appointee as maintenance manager) although council thought that the arrangement was untenable. Thewlis was bitter about changes in what he thought of as his exclusive bailiwick and felt let down by Darling. Eventually in early 1948, council subdivided his portfolio and appointed P.O.L. Owen to be responsible to Darling for the housekeeping and general school upkeep. Accounts and finance stayed with Thewlis and Stephens (relieved of his duties later in the year). Getting things sorted hadn't been easy. The nub of the problem (Lindon said) was to try to persuade Thewlis to delegate and to have a team 'rather than a one man band'. Darling's patience had also worn thin and a recent finance committee meeting had been messy. On the making of the new appointment, Thewlis 'as usual, more or less dissolved into tears', the chairman lost control of the meeting, an embarrassed few moments ensued and 'we were left exactly as we were with the decision that Stephens was to go but that nobody knew what we were going to do next'. Since that meeting, Darling had had another painful interview with Thewlis and exclaimed that 'I'm damned if I know either'. Truth to tell, 'the whole affair has been badly handled throughout and everyone is to blame'.[7]

During these difficulties Darling was appointed as an educational consultant to St Catherine's School in inner Melbourne, and then later to its council's education sub-committee. The St Catherine's council (chaired by Bishop McKie) controlled the school from May 1947 when ownership passed from the Langley family to an association of parents. K.F. Cox (the council secretary) sought Darling's advice on the respective duties of bursar and headmistress to forestall any likely friction and felt that 'the same relationship as exists between yourself and the Bursar at Geelong Grammar would be most satisfactory'. The irony cannot have been lost on Darling, who replied with a two-and-a-half-page report (with most of which Thewlis agreed) that included the gratuitous remark that 'between two women it is impossible to make sure that no friction will arise. Rather the contrary.' He also said that 'no absolute delineation of frontiers is possible'. The head–bursar relationship could only work with 'co-operation and mutual support'. Above all, the headmistress is 'in the last resort' responsible for running the school, so that the bursar 'must be loyal to the Headmistress'. The bursar was subservient in all matters affecting the school's wellbeing, while the headmistress should devolve as much responsibility as possible for the material side of the school and 'feel able to trust her discretion absolutely in such matters'. He was emphatic that council's finance committee 'clearly understand the impossibility of trying to use the Bursar in order to curb the extravagances of the Headmistress'. Such economy could only be carried out 'with the full co-operation of the Headmistress', provided that she saw the need for it.[8]

Darling's role was short lived. Quite apart from his asinine view of two women's relationship, there was another sensitive matter: he was a man invited by another man into the domain of a woman. Would the reverse situation have been tolerated and on his patch? And did he know much about girls' education? To his credit, after conferring with Cox he stipulated that Sophie Borland (the headmistress) should not feel that he was undermining her, that he was not bound to attend meetings and he was not constrained from advising other girls' schools. But if Darling, Cox and Borland were sanguine, the Headmistresses' Association was anything but and conveyed two resolutions to the St Catherine's council:

> The HMA puts on record its opinion that the appointment by a School Council of an Educational Adviser & Consultant who is not the H.M. is a grave threat to the profession.

And, crucially:

> If a School Co[uncil] appoint such an advisor & consultant then the so-called Headmistress of that school is not eligible for election to the H.M.A. since she is not in fact in complete control of her staff …

With his continued engagement prejudicing Miss Borland's association membership, Darling resigned in late 1948 (although he remained a life governor of the school). Dorothy Wardle (headmistress, Toorak College), whom Darling had contacted about the consultancy, informed him of the resolutions, which upset her. 'The whole thing has arisen from [a] misunderstanding', which she tried to correct with the association, but got into a wrangle with Bishop McKie. He had:

> tried to brand all concerted action as communism. An unfair weapon at the moment but he does believe it. He is doughty & straight, but implacable. Such a help in any affairs!

At the same time, St Catherine's was divided by reactions to Borland's liberalism (again communism was alleged) and this triggered her departure. 'She looks a wreck', Wardle informed Darling. Her resignation had come within days of her mother's death and, Wardle claimed, a member of the school community had behaved in a highly unprincipled manner by hoodwinking the school council. Wardle admired Bishop McKie for 'hitting out & shouldering everything', except that his doing so 'makes one hit back'.[9]

Another postwar development with economic impact and potential complications for GGS's administrative impasse was the council's acquisition of Glamorgan, a privately owned school in Toorak. On the positive side, Glamorgan's incorporation consolidated GGS's Melbourne recruitment base by promising a feed-line of future admissions. But acquisition came at a price: GGS increased from two existing sites (Bostock and Corio) to three. In 1947, with the inclusion of Glamorgan's 28 boarders and 137 day boys the total school enrolment was more than 800. As Darling admitted to his sister Margaret, the purchase 'doesn't ease the load on me at all'. Andrew Lemon's *The Pride of Miss McComas* recounts the full story but the GGS council's view during 1946 was that the outcome was touch and go. Two years after the property in Douglas Street had been compulsorily requisitioned (1942) the Australian Women's Army Service vacated the premises, whereupon the Commonwealth valued the school at £20,000. Isabel McComas (its owner) was eighty and anxious to secure Glamorgan's future. In October 1946, following the collapse of a proposal for joint control in conjunction with Toorak College, McComas' wish that her school become part of GGS was realised. When the contract of sale was signed, Darling wrote to Jennings' sister: 'wouldn't Reginald have been pleased'. The following February (1947), with H.R. McWilliam as housemaster, Glamorgan commenced as a GGS preparatory school.[10]

After his brief northern sojourn (June 1946), Darling began tackling the thicket of problems that had grown more tangled during the war—most caused by an ongoing shortage of money. Inadequate masters' salaries and superannuation were exacerbated by increased taxes and rising living costs. Attention to the deteriorating state of the school fabric (after wartime neglect of repairs and maintenance) was well overdue. Most masters, he told Gordon, were 'grossly underpaid and suffering in efficiency in consequence'. Their plight was offset by a few perquisites (provision of a nursery school, a baby health centre and free education for their sons), but the critical element was the absence of 'a really adequate superannuation fund'—a point emphasised later by the common room association. The postwar departure of temporary assistants, delays in demobilising returning masters, insufficient married living quarters and the attraction of better salaries in rival schools created a staffing headache for the headmaster. In April 1946, the prices commissioner agreed to a fee increase (£165 to £201), but until the effects on admissions of this 22 per cent increase were clearer to the finance committee, Darling's hands were tied when trying to improve remuneration. This problem persisted until after his return from leave in England. The Victorian Assistant Masters' Association had been pressuring the Headmasters' Conference of Australia about its salary grievances since 1944. Darling's mention of an unpredictable future creating difficulties for the headmasters cut no ice with the Victorian association's secretary, W.D. Kennedy. For twenty-five years, it had campaigned for a 'definite salary schedule' but the moment was always 'an unfortunate one': when the times are bad 'nothing can be done' and when schools are full and prospering 'such prosperity may prove illusory'. Nothing if not forthright, Kennedy mentioned some successes but mostly 'it has been a case of trying to wring blood out of a stone'. The Victorian Assistant Masters' Association sought protection for its members, especially those struggling financially and wanted an 'absolutely binding scale of minimum salaries'. At the same time as the association was disappointed that so little of substance had come from the headmasters, it reposed 'complete trust' in them to 'put the teaching profession on a proper professional basis'. For this reason it resisted pressure to create a wages board. The masters kept up their pressure during 1945–46. Darling was sympathetic, but the situation was 'one of considerable delicacy'. In the pursuit of better salaries he said that the heads had no status beyond being colleagues of the masters, because the real targets were the individual school councils. He was content for a masters' delegation to meet with the Victorian heads who, if there was agreement on a minimum salary scheme, might influence the councils.[11]

The meeting was at Scotch in November. The association's priorities, in addition to the salary schedule, were to seek the heads' approval to submit to their councils 'the principle' of a pension scheme for long-serving retired masters, recognition of sixty-five as the retiring age and combined action with the heads to seek taxation rebates for school fees. At GGS, the 1947 salary increase had not stilled the common room clamour for more generous remuneration and in April 1948 another masters' deputation complained about difficulties in making ends meet. In August (Darling was in England) the masters sought another rise, but council treated their submission as 'ungracious' (because it exaggerated the depreciated monetary value of their salaries), although they were compensated for costs of living rises with a general increase of £60. The common room association regretted being thought of as ungracious and it would still be pressing in 1949 for a revised salary scheme. This time Darling presented the request to council, but refused to support it despite the increasing inadequacy of the school's salary scales compared to those recommended by the Headmasters' Conference, those sought by the Victorian Assistant Masters' Association and, especially, those of Education Department teachers—by early 1950, GGS masters were £189 to £289 annually worse off than their departmental counterparts at equivalent incremental levels. As for superannuation, GGS was similarly placed to other schools. There were 'grave difficulties' in financing the scheme, which was a work in progress with two components. First, there was an insurance endowment entitling a master to £2500 at age sixty retirement (after teaching for thirty years). It included death cover, and the school and masters each contributed half. Second, there was the 'quite inadequate' superannuation fund itself, the interest from which council used to fund allowances for retiring masters. Council was trying to improve matters by establishing a £200 annual retiring allowance, additional to the lump sum contributed by each master. The allowance was to be non-contributory (and so masters leaving before the retiring age had no equity in it). Darling hoped that in about a decade 'the fund will be sufficiently established to give [the masters] at any rate a minimum guarantee'.[12]

Such was GGS's financial position in December 1946 that (with increased costs, and shortages of labour and materials) the council was unable to underwrite superannuation, and undertake necessary repairs and maintenance, let alone finance new developments, without sizeable capital. Apart from tuition fees, occasional gifts and bequests, GGS's only other income was £1500 annually from the Whittingham estate. Fees and enrolments were insufficient (even though from 1948 the annual fees were £216). A financial appeal had raised only £8700 and so council decided in March 1948 to clear its bank overdraft and apply for an AMP loan of £80,000 for twelve years at 4 per cent per annum. In November AMP increased the loan to £100,000. On speech day, Darling told the parents that there was much of which the school could be proud, except that there was also 'so much which makes me ashamed when I go round, so much shabbiness and so much lacking'. He loathed devoting time to financial stringency, because a headmaster's real job was education 'as a theoretical problem' and individual boys in particular. Following financial advice the council agreed to launch yet another appeal, this time for £100,000. 'We must succeed', Darling told Lindon, and 'there can be no half-measures once we are committed'. In a statement drafted at council's request, Darling said that half this amount would help reduce the school's debt (of about £140,000) while the other half would be a reserve for capital needs. One-third of the debt was to be reduced by the centenary year of 1957. 'The school is full even beyond its proper capacity and a long way beyond what is desirable', yet it was not possible to increase fees:

> while taxation on larger incomes remains so high, without risking a fall in numbers or at least without excluding from the school many boys whom we would be very sorry to keep out.[13]

Money worries had not dampened Darling's reconstruction zeal and he commenced a program to influence the old boys' postwar thinking, the first of two types of conferences inaugurated. After incubating the idea for some time (probably with Newmarket 1919 in mind), he hatched it with council and OGGs late in 1944 in an appeal for a sense of responsibility for the country's political and economic life. His idea was a summer school–style forum to discuss social and international problems, about which he had been encouraged 'by the opinion of a few of you whom I have met recently'. 'After the last war', he said on speech day 1945, 'there was plenty of good will, but not much direction of it. We cannot afford to make the same mistake again.' The conference would consider problems facing the nation, because men absent from civilian life for five or six years had lost touch with developments. Australia needed 'fresh blood in its leadership' of politics, industry, local affairs and education, but leadership would be 'valueless without knowledge', the pursuit of which had to be the first step. A society was an organism, in which 'only by the working together of little people in small ways will anything ever get done'; there would be no life as a whole if there was no life in its parts, and there would no life in the parts (or not a lively one) if responsibility was 'left in the hands of old and tired men'. The young should take control of the parts first, and then the country as a whole. The following April, forty-five OGGs—including a future state premier, R.J. (Dick) Hamer, and a future prime minister, J.G. Gorton, determined to be there rather than be a 'bucolic rustic'— attended the conference in Perry House. For five days they listened to speakers, asked questions, had general discussion and debated resolutions on soil erosion and land utilisation, industrial relations, socialism, housing, immigration, the constitution and relations with South-East Asia. The organisers (principally Montgomery) assembled an impressive array of speakers who included Wadham, Gepp, C.E. Sayers (journalist), Dr E.G. Coppel (barrister), E.C. Laird (school architect) and A.G.L. Shaw (historian). Having read the list of old boys killed in the war, Darling was conscious of 'how many of the very best have gone' and he felt 'some pardonable pride at the quality of the boys who turned up'. Overall, the weekend pleased him and he was struck by how every discussion returned to the need for more, better and relevant education. 'It is queer', he confessed to Fred Thomas of the Victorian Teachers' Union, how intelligent people seemed to agree on the matter and 'yet so little gets done'.[14]

Darling hoped for a permanent social service group to emerge from the Old Geelong Grammarians Association, to inform the younger old boys of how they could help, but such a group savoured 'of patronage', said David Hay. Hamer concurred: 'OGG's should have some kind of public conscience, and a desire for social service' but it was better that they fit into the community's offerings 'rather than form some exclusive cell of their own'. Darling also hoped that the conference would be annual. After initial inertia, at Hamer's instigation a second conference was held in September 1947 and thirty OGGs attended. Two members of the state parliament, A.G. (later Sir Arthur) Warner (Liberal) and Frank Crean (Labor) discussed the case for and against socialism, an International Harvester Company group dealt with workplace industrial relations, Hay (Department of External Affairs) spoke on the United Nations, G.W. Leeper led a discussion on soil erosion, John Buchan considered decentralisation and regional planning, and J. Cannon (for Francis Field, the Minister for Public Instruction) reviewed Victoria's educational planning. Darling was sufficiently impressed with the OGGs present to remark to Casey that while 'my swans are but geese really' his friend 'would find some leaders for the future amongst them', particularly Hamer. Thereafter, the old boys' conference became an annual event.[15]

The other Corio conference was in 1948 when sixty delegates from five states accepted the invitation from the Headmasters' Conference of Australia to attend the four-day meeting (20–23 January) as guests of the GGS council. The attendees included the heads of independent and government schools, Professors Browne and Mills, Dr C.E.W. Bean (historian) and Bull. They were welcomed by Kent Hughes (Field's successor as minister) and the Bishop of Geelong, and addressed by Mills and Sir Edmund Herring (Chief Justice, Supreme Court of Victoria). Although such luminaries testified to the pulling power of Darling and the school, and gave this first-ever joint conference an easily-done-deal appearance, there had been considerable paddling below the waterline. Sensitivities had abounded. Victoria (twenty-seven attendees) and New South Wales (nineteen) were disproportionately represented, there were no Queensland attendees and the Catholic schools were glaringly under-represented (neither

Hackett nor Costelloe could attend). The initiative had largely been Darling's at the Headmasters' Conference meeting in September 1946, where the tensions had tested his persuasive powers. Ralph's letter (recounting a Durham address by Lindsay, at which teachers complained about petty state interference) reminded him that he was treading on eggshells. As public servants, state headmasters were unable to self-select (directors or ministers might even nominate inspectors, he feared), let alone self-fund: there were no school councils to underwrite their travel costs, particularly remotely located heads, and his attempts to obtain travel subsidies for them from the Commonwealth Office of Education, state rail authorities and Holyman's airline had mostly drawn a blank. It was not an option for GGS to pay the attendees' expenses, either, because to do so (he admitted to Gordon) would look 'either like a tip from the wealthy to the poor relation or like a bribe to the increasingly powerful Government Departments'. Nonetheless, he said, 'I refuse to be beaten'. Another option was for independent school heads to forgo their subsidies to help defray their state peers' expenses.[16]

There was no difficulty securing conference endorsement from Field (Minister until Labor lost office in November 1947). Darling cited the Headmasters' Conference's concern about problems arising from the education system's dual nature and how the heads saw virtue in increased cross-sector contact. 'I am most anxious to have your support and approval.' Field assured him that 'what you are doing in this instance is only one of many things which you have done to build up good relations between State and public schools'. (At GGS an unknown hand saw the obvious publicity value of these words and scrawled on a note in the file with Field's letter: 'USE!') So long as he was consulted about the selection of the Victorian heads to attend, Field was content. But what had threatened to derail the initiative was the New South Wales heads' intransigence, especially Robson. At a 'fiery debate' at the May 1947 Headmasters' Conference standing committee meeting, Darling (chairman) threatened that if conference reneged on sponsoring the proposed gathering then he would convene it under GGS's auspices. In the following months, he sensed that the 'Sydney members' were still grumbling, a suspicion confirmed by Hone. A few Sydney heads were 'somewhat disturbed' about the enthusiasm of the state heads, and were 'hanging off waiting to see if the whole thing will fall through' because of lack of travel expenditure reimbursement for their state counterparts. At best this kind of thinking was foot-dragging and at worst wilful subversion. Apart from grizzling about his own expenses, Robson thought that there would be insufficient material to discuss, could foresee no positive benefits of a joint meeting and complained about a lack of information. No wonder there were waverers, given that 'we are all too busy to tackle it. I'm just as busy as I can stick.'[17]

Darling's persistence paid off. After six months' slog in sorting out the travel costs, the conference went ahead with a lofty focus on 'The needs of the nation'. Six headmasters addressed the gathering, including (in addition to Darling) Gordon and Hone. Darling's 'Wisdom and understanding', however, was not one of his best efforts as he later admitted to Hackett. It was an awkward combination of gloom, hyperbole—within ten years 'it will be true, with no exaggeration, that civilization may vanish from the earth'—and the mundane: the twin themes of genuine wisdom and understanding were at the mercy of 'the sordid facts of curriculum and timetable'. It was not the schools' job to produce scholars or to train pupils for their future vocations; rather, their mandate was to cultivate habits of mind (such as logical reasoning from observed data) and to provide mental training. But his gloom was mingled with half-heartedness and lack of conviction: his speculations about the relative merits of curriculum subjects, for example, were sprinkled with hesitations ('I confess that I am out of my depth here') and his conclusion about timetabled periods for particular subjects was rather aimless. (After later checking the proofs of the text of the speeches for a 63-page Headmasters' Conference of Australia booklet, he told Hone that he no longer felt 'apologetic' and could not understand why 'it fell so flat'.) At the conference's conclusion, the headmasters agreed unanimously on a four-paragraph statement. In his opening remarks, Herring threw down a rather high-minded gauntlet: 'all of you' had to bridge the divide between the two school systems in the interests of national unity, and develop the nation's 'corporate moral conscience' by instilling the highest moral standards in young people. His speech was peppered with a familiar litany of antidotes to social ills (courage, sacrifice and responsibility, strengthened moral fibre). The heads' statement adopted a similar moralising tone of reverential urgency, although its impact was weakened by the choice of anodyne phraseology bemoaning the nation's inability to meet adequately the challenges confronting it. They urged young people to think of a career in teaching, deplored national divisions, emphasised character development, and prodded agencies of community influence (for example, home, press, cinema, radio) 'to be conscious of their responsibilities in these critical days'.[18]

Rhetoric so strong on pious exhortation risked dismissal as platitudinous (or as moral panic), and yet it was part and parcel of headmastering's public face. Realistically, were there any tangible outcomes? What was the conference's significance? The deliberations revealed strong commonality of views and a depth of goodwill. In their eight-page report, three South Australian delegates specified the benefits of an exchange of ideas, the opportunity to see and meet other schools and headmasters, informal discussion, 'odd conversations', 'rubbing shoulders' and 'the absence of any attempt to shape and lay down a definite policy'. Echoing this enthusiasm, Gordon was adamant that the conference had done 'a lot to prevent any possible rifts' between the sectors and heal existing ones. Similarly, Paul Radford saw the likelihood of round-table talks with the Tasmanian Ministry of Education on relations between the sectors (and held out hope of a possible agreement on state aid). Darling's own view was that the conference had fostered the building of friendships and provided mutual assurance about common principles. The way to break down barriers, he told Herring, was 'to make personal contacts' and his own close friendship with Major-General Alan Ramsay (head, Melbourne Boys' High School) had been instrumental in winning the backing of key Victorian state heads for the conference. (He filed away a valuable tactical lesson for the founding of the Australian College of Education a decade later.) An exchange of masters between the two systems was a valuable next step. Even allowing for the usual cheer-squad tone of the accolades received, the conference was a personal triumph for Darling. The cameo provided by the three South Australians is instructive: GGS's headmaster was 'full of mental vitality' and his chairing of the conference was 'admirable'. He had that 'rare quality of continued freshness of mind; he is enthusiastic; and because of his dissatisfaction with what has been accomplished he shows a great willingness to experiment'. He was ready to admit criticism and acknowledge failure. Hone said:

> When I think back over the past 18 months and recollect the various depres-
> sions and the way that you had to lift the whole business out of a depression
> on several occasions and see it all through, my admiration is unbounded and
> you should realise, I think, that your Chairmanship made the whole difference
> to the success of the Conference itself. I thought also, if you do not mind my
> saying so, that you and the school put the whole show on extraordinarily well.
> I have never been to one which was better catered for and better produced.

Hake also congratulated his friend for having thought of the idea, for getting his way without friction and for 'making such admirable arrangements'. On behalf of the conference delegates, Mills presented Darling with a small tobacco pipe.[19]

Darling was saddened during the conference planning by the departure of Francis Field (minister for two years and fellow member of the council of the university), and he went on the public record in a letter to the *Age* (a gesture that Field appreciated):

> It will, I think, be the general opinion of those interested in education that the
> recent elections, whatever their other advantages, have removed from office,
> at a very important crisis [?], a Minister for Public Instruction, who has won
> great commendation from all sections of the educational world.

Was it too much to hope that the incoming government would recognise the 'essentially non-party nature of educational reform' and would as much as possible carry on Field's plans, to the preparation of which he had devoted so much time? Credit where credit was due: Darling thought that Field was the first minister to take education seriously. Browne had had two long conversations with Field's successor and assured Darling that Kent Hughes was 'anxious to have a progressive policy continuous with the one initiated by Mr. Field'. As a military man, he would run the Department of Education 'in a flexible way as though

he were the General of a Division carefully advised by staff officers'. He wanted
Browne and Darling to 'write him an "appreciation" of the educational position'—in effect, to tell him what he ought to be thinking. He expected something
concise and thorough, strengths and weaknesses, and 'forward movements that
should be continued and new movements that should be considered'. He liked
his departmental officers, but thought that they were 'limited in outlook and he
finds it difficult to get information from them'. He was also keen on Field's idea
of a board, but was ignorant that the Council of Public Education could advise
him (and that Seitz was due to retire). Browne would compose thoughts on the
departmental schools if Darling tackled the registered (or independent) schools.
Having done something similar for Hollway, Darling was 'flattered and pleased'
to be asked.[20]

The outcome of the pre-Christmas exchange of the professor and the
headmaster was a dossier for the ex-Olympian, Old Melburnian and recently
appointed minister. Browne drafted fourteen pages and Darling four. It was a
month before the heads' joint conference, and Darling's comments about the
school sectors are enlightening. He tried grafting on to Victorian education attributes gleaned from the two systems that he knew firsthand: the Headmasters'
Conference schools and English schooling. Victoria's lack of direction in education and absence of 'spiritual significance' had produced administrative centralisation, economy, statistics and uniformity, defective teacher recruitment and
training, and secularism had resulted in a valueless religious education and divorce
between the sectors. The consequences were jealousy, snobbery and community
division. Regardless of sector, however, education had to be taken as a whole and
directed by a board with a relationship to the director paralleling that between
headmaster and council, and giving it direct ministerial access. It should devise
a ten-year plan for training in democratic citizenship, development (through to
adult education) of individual qualities and provision of equal opportunity in
vocational training. Schools would be reclassified as primary or post-primary
(academic, agricultural and technical), but with the rub that 'more use should be
made of non-state schools for academic purposes', and the state 'should do what
private enterprise in Schools cannot do' and (residualising the state's role) provide
for special needs: (in the language of the day) 'defective and subnormal children,
children with maladjusted personalities, cripples, etc.'[21]

Darling also wanted more individuality for schools (which centralised
control precluded by denying heads the selection of teachers), because this
was required to foster school spirit in more than a handful of the best schools.
Improved status and salaries for teachers were equally essential. Teachers, in turn,
should be encouraged to engage in local affairs, and to be in touch with town
councillors and parents. Headmasters' houses ought to be built in the grounds of
schools, and school buildings and grounds should be centres for the educational
and social life of districts. Much of this reasoning exuded high-minded unreality, but when he tackled the 'fusion without undue sacrifice of independence' of

the two systems he was more pragmatic. With independent schools financially stretched, the state had two options: kill off the sector (and alienate Catholics and create a financial burden) or, 'if you like by bribery', bring them into the system and use them for the preliminary training of teachers. Other reasons for fusion were a gradual abatement of bitter sectarianism, general acceptance of the importance of spirituality in education and the inadequacy of religious education provided by 'visiting parsons'. Get rid of 'secular' in the educational legislation, he also urged, subsidise church schools to half the cost of educating state school students, require church schools to enrol 'any' students whom the state wishes to send them (not just its 'best', as he said separately to Radford) 'on some agreed basis of payment', encourage interchange of teaching staff and recruit higher state officials from non-state schools, introduce religious education into state schools based on an agreed syllabus and reduce overall class sizes: a very tall order.[22]

It is not clear whether Kent Hughes responded. Shortly after the joint conference, when Margaret was again afflicted with headaches and depression (and sequestered with the Ritchies at Delatite), she reported to her husband (in Sydney for a Universities Commission meeting) that she had met Kent Hughes' wife and daughter. The latter suggested that, while her father held two state ministerial portfolios, transport as well as education, he really only wanted the former. The revelation that education 'was wished on him as well' got Sylvia Ritchie 'very hot under the collar'. It was 'an absolute disgrace that there weren't about ten people wishing to take on education'. Also of interest was what a *Geelong Advertiser* journalist at the joint conference told Darling when it concluded. 'Someone said to me', he claimed, that:

> 'Darling is too big for one school. What a great thing it would be if someone had the foresight to appoint him Director of Education in place of Seitz (?) who retires at the end of this year'.

Margaret had been lost for words at her friend's outburst because she knew that Kent Hughes was considering her husband as the new director. Although she was worried about him taking it on, her worries were groundless because the wish of the journalist's informant was not to be. Ramsay got the nod, although her husband was close to being made an offer. (Two years previously, in debate on the Teaching Service Bill in the Legislative Assembly, the possibility of Darling as director had been mentioned in an exchange between Field and Hollway.) Kent Hughes explained that he:

> felt that your position was a somewhat delicate one, so I discussed the proposition with Cabinet in a very general way in the first instance—mentioning several names in order to sound out reactions—but not on the basis of candidates or applicants.

He erred on the side of caution: 'After thinking it over very carefully and taking all the various factors into consideration I decided that it would be wiser to make the appointment from within the service'. He hoped that a sound decision had been made. If for no other reason than that minister and director shared military backgrounds, then this seemed likely, and Ramsay assured Darling that he and his new boss seemed 'to be agreed on the main things'.[23]

Along with making public pronouncements and offering free advice, Darling was honing his lobbying skills. The Headmasters' Conference of Australia wanted taxation relief. They waged a long (and successful) campaign. Their initial foray occurred while federal Labor was in office, and the main game (after Darling's return from England) followed the 1949 election. The heads' efforts went back to 1944 and the campaign gathered a head of steam in 1946. Wartime price controls imposed a moratorium on fee increases. With controls lifted, the schools adjusted fee levels to realistically reflect their actual costs. The problem, as Darling said repeatedly, was that tuition fee income (even with endowments) was not sufficient. Church schools (although the view was 'not generally shared') 'could and should be subsidized by the State', without subsidies compromising independence. The higher the subsidy, the lower the fees 'or the more scholars we could take'. Either way, 'you would do something to modify the present class division on the basis of income alone'. As he and his fellow heads saw it, the solution was to try to secure income taxation relief for fee-paying parents by convincing the Commonwealth to permit tuition fee deductions from parents' taxable incomes. To this end, members of the Headmasters' Conference of Australia wrote letters and sought ministerial deputations. The difficulty for their schools was that, for taxation purposes, they were deemed public educational bodies and did not enjoy the concession rebates applying to charities.[24]

There was a big mountain to climb, although the introduction of wartime uniform taxation simplified the task of the Headmasters' Conference (the heads no longer had to lobby on separate state fronts), but concentration on one target still required the mobilisation of all heads and councils. The parents' and old boys' associations also had to be in the loop, and then go public with their arguments in the media. All the while, advice had to be sought from accountants and lawyers with expertise in taxation law. This required time and money. Pressing the case for exemption with the politicians fell to Darling and Gilray. The ace in their deck, they believed, was that fee-paying parents were penalised by paying twice for education—once for their sons and also for children in state schools that their sons did not use. When, in an *Age* article in 1946 Darling called for a taxation rebate, Dedman (the acting treasurer) intimated that, if requested to provide one, the government would consider it. Later that year, Darling and Gilray met the former prime minister, Scullin (on behalf of Chifley, prime minister and treasurer), who sympathised with their cause (inability to charge maximum fees for fear of 'overstraining the parent'). But Scullin's view was that the concession sought was regressive, because it would benefit richer parents more than poorer ones. This point was 'difficult to answer', Darling conceded, and he came away feeling outfoxed. Later, Chifley informed him that the government would extend the application of the general taxation rebate from eighteen- to nineteen-year-old students 'in accordance with your representations' and increase its value from £75 to £100 annually. Pre-1950, then, the heads won some crumbs, but nowhere near the loaf that they were after.[25]

After the headmasters' conference, Darling's thoughts turned to England. With the decision to take leave made, he was 'not very keen on the idea' (he confided to Gordon) although warming to it. 'Lucky man', said Sutcliffe. At this point his different strategy with council became clear. Thewlis' future was still unresolved, but perhaps his absence would enable council to make a clean sweep of every administrative position including his own, he said to Lindon. Fed up with 'this continual struggle about money' and, while not seeking another posting in England, there was always the possibility of something turning up 'which I should feel it wrong to refuse anyhow, but I don't think this is at all likely'. Then he offered to resign. With its present difficulties, the council might decide to be rid of him. If it did, 'I shall not take it amiss'. (Had his offer been accepted, Darling would have forgone an annual salary of £2500, paid domestic service, council reimbursement of his expenses, and recompense for fuel, light, laundry and entertainment, not to mention a roof over his family's head.) He had made 'some' contribution to GGS, but with him out of the way 'you might find it easier to deal with the other problem [of Thewlis and Stephens], and I therefore give you the freedom to accept this offer of resignation'. Finally, while the future of schools 'such as this' was at the mercy of the wider political process, standards had to be maintained in the meantime and there was no way that he could happily go to England:

> if the same kind of thing is going to happen again as it did in 1939 and I come back to find all the hard won ground lost as I did then.[26]

This was not an ultimatum but a signal that Darling's options were open. Did it indicate a mood change, given that less than a year earlier he insisted that being a headmaster was 'a job worth while and with far more compensations than difficulties', after being at it for nearly eighteen years? True to form, the headmaster had been sniffing the wind. In late 1946, his name was bandied about in relation to two Australian university vice-chancellorships (Adelaide and Sydney). After a stay at Corio, Ward from Prince Alfred College wrote Darling a long letter on the respective merits of coming to Adelaide as vice-chancellor or staying put at Corio. Darling's inclination had been against an occupational change:

> I am not at all certain that I would do a new job at all well, but I have not been able to make up my mind and am merely hoping that the situation will not arise which will force me to do so.

Darling's response ran true to type: toy with the possibility among his circle of intimates. Priestley (in discussion at Oxford with Marcus Oliphant, Sir Howard Florey and Keith Hancock about the new university in Canberra) also raised with him a vice-chancellor appointment. Darling demurred, because such an appointment was 'not in my line' and university council meetings with professors 'irritate me more than they should'. There was still much to do in Australia, he said, and if he could 'find some way of making myself free to do it', then 'I should probably be satisfied to remain'.[27]

Then, in March 1947 his sister Margaret wrote to say that the Felsted and Charterhouse headships were vacant. (The Felsted head had been killed in a motorcycle accident and Birley—Charterhouse—was directing postwar educational reconstruction in Germany.) 'Had you realised this? & does it interest you at all?' The lure of the positions aside, she acknowledged the lack of incentives to return amid postwar disruption, although 'it would be very nice to have you and family at Felstead [sic]'. Nothing came of either possibility, but in Birmingham Priestley was still touting on his friend's behalf. In July 1948 (when the Darlings were in England) he floated three further possibilities. First, he had given Darling's name to Bristol University as a vice-chancellorship candidate (although 'it has to be admitted that absence is a handicap'). Second, King Edward's School might still be an option if Morris moved on:

> He has a tough job with well-entrenched middle aged staff & you know what that means ... the whole educational world here is on the move at the moment & is likely to be more so in the immediate future. I wanted you last time & although Morris has been a good as well as an adventurous appointment, I would return to the chair if he went & if you would care to try out such a post ... I am, however, at the moment very short of ammunition when I am trying to put your claims.

The third possibility was the University of Birmingham itself, for it was proposing to create a teacher training institute in the Midlands. Priestley believed that its head should be paid £2000 a year '& be an administrator rather than a scholar, with a second Professor of Education at his elbow'. Other views might prevail, but if Priestley's were to succeed, then he would 'like someone like you'.[28]

The voyage home commenced on 1 June 1948 when Darling, Margaret, Nurse Gammon, and Caroline and John sailed for England on the RMS *Stratheden*. During his absence, E.W.H. (Joe) Pinner was acting headmaster: Darling expressed 'the most absolute confidence both in your prowess and in your loyalty'. The travellers arrived in early July after 'a rotten voyage as far as weather went'. Letters updating them on domestic news awaited them at Aden—including a witty one from Roger Day (an orphaned English boy who lived with them at Corio) reporting that he had 'just received one of Elizabeth's short (very short) and snappy letters, requesting that she be informed about the state of John Gubbins' leg as his sister wants to know'. After barely a week, Darling told Pinner—surprisingly in view of the advance warnings from correspondents about industrial stoppages, food shortages, increased rates, appalling weather and the like—that England did not seem to 'have changed at all in any of the ways that really matter'. Later that month, Doug Fraser reassured him that at Corio 'all is going quite smoothly'. Darling then received from Pinner an 'interesting though concise letter'. Was its tone a hint, perhaps, of the previous problems with Cameron? Following Darling's reply, in his next letter Pinner displayed the kind of subtlety and mirth of which Cameron had been incapable. He apologised for his conciseness and then ever so gently chided him:

> but you surely know that even I am capable of appreciating how skilful you are in reading between the lines. It was, indeed, an unkind reprimand from one who invariably leaves out most of the subordinate clauses when he gives advice or instruction.

Sadly, Pinner continued, the headmaster's 'implicit trust in the intelligence and "nouse" [sic] of other people' had not made 'the task of managing your managers' any simpler. (A reference to the new administrative arrangements: Thewlis as secretary and bursar, and Owen as manager.) It had not been easy, Pinner said, to 'bring your two "Prussians" into complete harmony, but, after opening safety valves on a couple of occasions, the atmosphere cleared' and the two men were now 'combining quite well'.[29]

The tone of successive letters indicated that Pinner relished his responsibilities, although Spear, his assistant, was swamped by the huge number of letters that he had to write. At the end of October, 120 of Professor Browne's students were due to arrive at Corio, but without the headmaster there to outline the purpose of the school, Pinner mused about what he might say: 'Anyhow, where are we heading? Probably the time has arrived for real experiment', he teased. Later he reported that the new prefects and sub-prefects for 1949 had been appointed, none of whom 'embarrasses you for next year'. Later still he said that everyone was looking forward to Darling's return, as 'the value of your trip will be most apparent after you get back', for 'it is then that the ideas & brain waves will be precipitated'. In his final letter, Pinner reported that, as a Liberal Party by-election candidate for the Assembly seat of Geelong, Montgomery had won by just over 800 votes, and that his resulting absence would leave 'rather a gap, especially in out-of-school activities'. Pinner's nerve failed him with speech day (Darling had said that he was expected to deliver the address), and he bobbed and weaved: 'We are expecting something fresh & inspiring, and I am sure you are the last one to wish a draught-horse to be functioning when there are thoroughbreds about'. Having handballed this chore back to the boss, he suggested that Darling 'give them something new instead of the usual Headmaster's report'.[30]

If Priestley's earlier speculations about appointments were straws in the wind, then there were two other possibilities: Stowe—where Darling had considered teaching in the 1920s—and Shrewsbury. J.F. Roxburgh (Stowe's first headmaster) would retire in 1949, the chair of the governors informed Darling and:

> it has been suggested to me that it is a position which you might be glad to consider, and that you might authorize me to tell the Governors this, if it should be so. It is a fine school and Roxburgh's work for twenty-five years there has been magnificent.

Darling met the chairman at the Athenaeum Club and was reassured that Stowe had turned the corner following a couple of difficult years. The planning of the work and salaries needed a 'fresh and experienced eye' and a bit more 'normal and systematic discipline'. He urged Darling to visit the school (which he and Margaret did, several times, in mid-October). Roxburgh (known by Darling at Oxford) also contacted him about his plans, and then they met in late September when Darling addressed the Headmasters' Conference in England. Unlike in 1939, Darling tried to choreograph the information flow and warned Pinner about rumours:

> It is true that I have been asked by two schools to allow my name to be put forward for appointment, but that is as far as anything has gone or probably will, but there are arguments on the other side which make it difficult to make a positive denial. This for your own ear primarily, but to use if necessary.

Pinner had heard nothing. Then, as of old, Darling began rehearsing his future. Again his Corio supporters indulged him and again Manifold brought him to his senses. After receiving a letter from Darling, Lindon spoke to Manifold and reiterated 'what I told you last March [when Darling had offered to resign]', namely, that council would regret his departure from GGS. Any criticism received had not come from council but 'ill-informed or un-informed persons'. Having done all that he had for the school, Darling was likely to receive criticism in some quarters but not from people 'who have the School's welfare most at heart'. As for his conscience and desires:

> Council have no right to expect you to stay at the School if you feel yourself that you can do better work elsewhere, and that is entirely a matter for you.

A week beforehand Manifold confirmed Lindon's words earlier in the year:

> If I said more I would only be repeating what I have said on several similar occasions previously. If the rather nebulous, & I suppose exceptional job really did present itself I suppose it is such that you would feel bound to accept it.

In the meantime, 'here is your job & never more important than it is today!'[31]

Stowe's chair of governors was keen to snaffle Darling and sought permission to confer with the governors: 'If you are still ready to consider the matter, we must have another talk before you go [back to Australia]'. Darling then told Pinner that he had heard from the chairman but was:

> rather dithering with the fear that I may get stale or bored with another twelve years at Corio. I shall value your advice when I get back and know that I can rely on you to be honest.

After equivocating, Darling decided (for reasons that are not entirely clear) that he was no longer a serious candidate. 'It merely put on paper what you had already told me by word of mouth', Roxburgh said, 'but I could not help reading it with a certain note of disappointment none the less'. At this point, Darling confessed to Pinner: 'I have had great temptations, and I am hating to leave my mother'. Nonetheless, 'as you say, there must be other fish in the sea and I shall set about trying to land one'. A plum appointment eluded Darling, but he was not entirely empty-handed. On 31 July, Oxford University conferred on him an honorary doctorate of civil law while he was attending the Empire Universities Conference as a representative of the University of Melbourne. Edith Head (wife of the former Archbishop of Melbourne) said that she had had a visitor from Oxford who:

> saw Hon: Degrees, & a tall man, a Schoolmaster from Australia, had one.— His head was dark, & he stood looking as if amused to find himself there, but prepared to play his part.

One of the many congratulations that he received probably brought memories flooding back: the Whartons had arrived from Trinidad, although their paths had not crossed. 'Isn't it fun to be successful?' Hilda wrote. 'I love Louis' [success?] & in spite of his poor wan body his spirit still sparkles & life is by no means heart aching all of the time'. Corio received the news of the doctorate with effusiveness, according to Michael Thwaites, for when Pinner described the headmaster as 'one of the foremost educators of our time' at an Old Geelong Grammarians Association dinner, he received 'rounds of spontaneous and warm applause'.[32]

As for Shrewsbury, Darling was probably never in the hunt and didn't really want it. Again his sister Margaret was his scout. Earlier in the year she alerted him that J.F. Wolfenden, Shrewsbury's headmaster, had resigned to take a university appointment. When he knew of Darling's interest, Bickersteth lobbied on his behalf as did Fisher (after Bickersteth's prompting). Even though by mid-October the Shrewsbury governors had still not made an appointment, Fisher explained that there was little that he could do for him. Don't leave Corio, he advised him, 'unless it is to go to something better'. With his 'very great reputation' the 'happiest solution' would be an Australian vice-chancellorship. To return to England to the kind of appointment that was deserving of him wouldn't be easy. George Turner (Fletcher's protégé) had returned in 1947 (aged fifty-six) after eight or so years in Uganda as Principal of Makerere College and 'we were able to put [him] to Charter House [sic]', because younger men had not been through the war and lacked experience, which meant that 'a gap was created'. (Did Darling wonder why his erstwhile headmaster had not made an exception for him as well?) Fisher sugar-coated the pill by assuring his former pupil that 'if I see any chance of putting you into a job at home of the right kind I would take it'.[33]

A month later, Wolfenden informed Darling that interviews would be held in December. The chairman of governors had had 'more than one conversation with me about your letter' and 'I can with complete honesty say that he and his colleagues on the Selection Committee have given it very full and careful consideration'. Once again (as Fisher implied) Darling's nearly twenty-year Australian sojourn had marginalised him in the English headship market, because the Shrewsbury governors 'felt bound' to 'look for a headmaster nearer home; and they have asked me to write and let you know of this decision'. At this stage in the school's history they needed somebody 'familiar with developments in this country at the present time, and somebody who could be expected to have twelve or fifteen years in the job'. Wolfenden sensed that Darling would be disappointed and feel that 'this is a poor reward for spending so many of the best years of your life in the Dominions'. (Another factor was that, as the headmaster, he would have been required to teach the VIth as a classical scholar and this may have defeated him.) It was highly likely, Darling told Charles Kellaway, that he would remain in Australia for the rest of his life. Tosh Phillips tried to buoy him up in his disappointment, by saying that Australia could ill afford to lose him as an educationalist and that England 'would probably have taken no notice of you (apart from whatever midden you hoped to be cock of); & in our lumbering and grudging way, we do really'. Phillips considered Darling's work to be 'sounder' now than a decade earlier for, 'judging by the odd whiffs which reach an outsider's nose, G.G.S. smells healthier now than it did in the late thirties'. And Darling could also take comfort from the fact that 'when one enters the Common Room, one is no longer immediately aware of the rival cliques arching their backs and preparing to spit'. Nor did the boys seem 'so laboriously listless as they used to be'.[34]

While the Darlings toured England, his mother spent time with her grandchildren. 'All goes smoothly here', she reported in September. John was 'in tremendous form, full of chat & merriness, & very good', and 'such a reasonable creature'. Sadly, much of the 1948 summer was wet—to add insult to injury, while they were returning home in November, his sister said that the weather was 'gorgeous'. They had set sail for Melbourne on 28 October, but not before catching up with many friends. Ralph was sad to see them go, and Darling's sister

Margaret tried to be buoyant about national recovery. The returning travellers met Eaton's widow, Eva, briefly in Colombo and the weather on the return journey was kinder than on the voyage across. They arrived back just in time for the wedding of Margaret's sister Alison. As she had done two decades earlier, his mother counselled him:

> I quite understand your feelings about the Australians & can see that maybe the work you can do out there is more important than any you could do here for it's a young country & good guiding is very important but I won't altogether despair of something tempting you to come back to the old Country some day, for one never knows! So don't worry about me & my feelings.

Darling said on speech day that he and Margaret were grateful for the way in which they had been 'received back into the fold'. He had left Pinner in charge 'without the slightest qualm' and quite honestly felt 'that in many ways I have found the School better on my return than when I left', at which listeners with memories of 1940 must have breathed sighs of relief.[35]

UNCOMFORTABLE PLATEAU

1946–1951

Life is increasingly specialized and complex. Each specialization, financial, economic, scientific or administrative, has developed its own language and symbols. Every measure of national or international organization begets, for example, a wilderness of committees, known by initial letters, whose powers, whose composition and whose very names are forgotten by those whose lives they affect.

Charles Morgan, *Liberties of the Mind*

In 1950, Darling gave a speech entitled 'Specialization—Good or bad?' to the conference of the South Australian Teachers' Union, in which he said:

> Between the revolutionary certainty of youth and the reactionary certainty of old age there lies an uncomfortable plateau of cynicism, during which a man wonders whether it is really worth fighting either for or against these causes which he once thought so important. If one has for twenty years been concerned with framing time-tables for schools, sitting on examination boards and university councils, then one is even more firmly convinced that there is really nothing fresh to say about Education and no real solution to the eternal conflict.

The lives of leaders generally are known to include periods when they go off the boil, experience staleness or feel stuck. Darling's choice of 'uncomfortable plateau' in his address was his way of alluding to this. The impact of plateauing leaders on institutions and people ebbs, and they tend to wait for, rather than create their own, opportunities. GGS's leader thought that he may have stalled or even peaked. An antidote for Darling's malaise during this period was Charles Morgan's book *Liberties of the Mind*, which he read soon after it was published in 1951. The book influenced him deeply. Morgan's two themes chimed with his preoccupations: complexity with respect to GGS's future specifically and specialisation in relation to education generally. During his indecision about Stowe, Darling had voiced his self-doubts to Pinner, but his speech to the teachers' union was their first public outing. Clive Fitts (his surgeon), however, dismissed his complaints. After gall bladder X-rays, he gave him the all clear and was reminded of the year before (1949) when Darling asked him: 'Why am I so tired at fifty?' The truth, Fitts had said, was that his friend was more fortunate than most people in not having had to 'face the lassitude both physical & mental, that is part of an awareness of a lack of achievement in middle life'. 'Perhaps the journey to your present position has left you unscathed', Fitts speculated, or 'perhaps you have equanimity. I do not know.'[1]

Darling was between two career phases: having set the schooling world ablaze in the 1930s, it would take Timbertop, the College of Education and Marcus Oldham College in the 1950s for his flickering flame to renew its spark. The postwar years consolidated his profile as a worthy, rather than a vital, public figure, with sporadic panjandrum-like exertions giving him prominence. He had become a creature of committees, rather than a man of action, and while these forums were useful and necessary, in claiming his time, energy, expertise, name and reputation they were not of game-changing significance. In respect of them, Darling's attendance was patchy. Despite wartime travel restrictions, he had been a dutiful university council member (and in 1940–45 had attended half its meetings), but in 1946–51 his attendance fell away (partly due to being in the UK in 1948). In two of his few minuted contributions he combined forces with Gilray to oppose the crowding out of humane studies in the Leaving Certificate by a curriculum emphasis on mathematics and science (1946) and expressed concern about the new matriculation structure (1950). His only notable contribution was in the choice of the new vice-chancellor, but by comparison with the prewar shoe-horning into office of Medley, the politicking this time was child's play. After Medley gave notice of retirement (effective from June 1951) and discussion of his successor was 'already well-ventilated', Darling threw his weight behind George Whitecross Paton, Professor (since 1931) of Jurisprudence (dean of law, and chairman of the Professorial Board). His support for Paton was not unequivocal and, had Eric Ashby been available, Darling would have endorsed him—but having departed Sydney in 1946 for a chair in Manchester, his friend was already spoken for (vice-chancellor, Queen's University, Belfast, from 1950). A letter to Medley (headed cryptically 'Private and Confidential, though either the Chancellor and/or Paten [sic] may see it, if you think wise') reveals Darling to have been hard at work. He was one of ten councillors on a sub-committee considering the terms of appointment, which was split on a point of procedure: whether or not to advertise the vacancy. Darling was baffled by university staff opposition to advertising (evidence that they had already made up their minds). Paton may have been the best man available, but (as in Copland's case) he was a member of staff and it was a 'very rare man indeed' who could come from within and 'lead a show of any sort'. If Paton was to get the nod, then other possibilities had to be considered and be judged as less well suited. Eventually, in July 1950, the division of opinion was resolved, and without causing Paton to think twice.[2]

Within the Headmasters' Association, Darling's attendance was more regular. In the absence of big ticket items, the heads attended to housekeeping stuff: the utility of forestry and cadet camps, joint appeals to have rail concessions restored for student travel to Geelong (initially rejected by the railways commissioners and then reinstated) and finalisation of sporting contests. There was the usual ritual deprecation of Head of the River press publicity, protests at proposed festivities such as a 'Boatrace Eve Dance' and concern about the potential obstruction of spectators' race viewing at the Henley staging (due to the construction of the new Swan Street bridge), but nothing anywhere on the scale of the earlier charity funds disbursement wrangle. Despite Darling's antipathy to sport, privately he was as buoyed up or let down as anyone by GGS's fluctuating results. The year 1949 (when losing ground in preventing boys from returning to school solely to row in the Boat Race) was particularly disheartening because three teams (cricket, rowing and football) should have achieved 'what was clearly within their grasp'. Even though GGS 'should win more than we do' and these underperforming teams had betrayed 'some sort of weakness', he wasn't prepared to 'concentrate very whole heartedly in the achieving of results in this direction'. He took some comfort from the 'unexpected victory' in the 1950 Head of the River and was also grateful for the offer of help with coaching from the Old Geelong Grammarians Association committee—but because professional coaching was against the APS rules, this posed a potentially sticky situation.[3]

Darling's attendance pattern at the Universities Commission was also choppy: regular in 1946–47, interrupted in 1948 and then, due to impeded travel caused by the mid-year coal strike and domestic constraints, irregular in 1949. In 1950, when his attendance fell away he signalled the likelihood of non-reappointment because he felt that he contributed little more than 'warmish air'. His attendance also slackened off in 1951. As he told Mills, running GGS was 'very exacting' and made him 'very depressed', and he:

> could not quite determine whether the value of the lift which I get from meeting different people and the pleasures which I get from being associated with the larger world in this way sufficiently compensates for the physical tiredness involved and the difficulties caused by my absence.

Following the legislative reconstitution of the Universities Commission by the Commonwealth in 1945, Darling was reappointed (in 1946 and 1949) for two more terms. Prior to 1945, he was engaged in an unpaid capacity, but from 1946 he was paid £100 annually (along with daily meeting and travel allowances). He was content to contribute voluntarily and, because his absences from Corio impeded his 'efficiency as Headmaster', have his income go to the school council. (As this arrangement necessitated circumvention of his income taxation obligations, the commission refused.) After 1945, the commission met monthly, mostly in Sydney, with its work now including the Commonwealth Reconstruction Training Scheme and the Financial Assistance Scheme (subsequently the Commonwealth Scholarships Scheme), a regular February conference with the vice-chancellors, university admission of sponsored (or private) Asian students, research training and the needs of the Commonwealth public service for research workers, professional training generally, and liaison with directors of technical education and the heads of technical colleges.[4]

In Geelong, the Unemployed Boys' Club reopened in May 1946. As a trustee, Darling had an arm's-length relationship with it and, while formally a Centre committee member, he continued to rely on Montgomery as his point of contact. In the postwar years—when there were 'more positions available in industry than there are boys to fill them'—the Centre redefined its role. Its new challenge was placement suitability: that is, ascertaining 'the right employment so that individual boys can find positions in which their own special talents can be used to most advantage and developed to their own satisfaction'. Now in its sixteenth year, the Centre was a Darling success story. In 1947, it placed 232 of 240 boys registered with it for employment, and businessmen visited the premises regularly and praised its work. Moreover, the Centre had consolidated its political connections (on both sides of the aisle), so much so that its visitors comprised a succession of politicians (both state and municipal), including on two occasions P.J. Clarey (state Minister of Labour). Casey (no longer a trustee) retained a continuing interest and, despite his insistence that there was 'no politics in this project' for it was 'equally enthusiastically supported by all political parties', on the minister's second visit Montgomery could not resist scoring a political point at Clarey's expense. To the latter's announcement in July 1947 (coinciding with an appeal for funds to renovate the Spring Street building) that the government's annual grant to the UBC had been increased from £250 to £350, Montgomery dismissed Clarey's offer as merely '(The Sop!)'. The remainder of the committee was 'captivated' by the minister, but Montgomery and the mayor of Geelong (J.J. Young) had refused to be taken in: Clarey 'oozed sympathy & from my point of view little else (Mr. Young was of the same opinion)'.[5]

Darling continued trumpeting the Centre as a community development model. One evening he buttonholed Menzies on centres, and then afterwards wrote and mentioned both Clarey's interest and the state government's financial assistance. He extolled what he and Montgomery believed was the Centre's virtue: a 'comparatively simple and [inexpensive?] social measure' with sixteen years of facts and figures to back it up. 'Our solution', he told Menzies, was quintessentially English: 'government finance with local and voluntary administration' that guaranteed the possible employment of individuals by individuals, rather than the creation of numbers in a card index. The Unemployed Boys' Club was the 'natural nucleus' for youth and community centres. Possible employment was the raison d'être and discipline for boys' clubs, and without it these were often 'short-lived and valueless'. On the basis of a running cost of £2000 annually for a centre to serve a population of about 50,000 (Geelong), Darling insisted that 100 such centres could be set up nation-wide at a total cost of about £200,000 annually, with about £15,000 in capital costs set aside for each centre. If he saw merit in the idea, would the leader of the Opposition talk with Tullis and Montgomery? (Tullis had tried unsuccessfully to get Dedman, the Minister for Post-War Reconstruction, to visit the Centre the year before.) Menzies met the two men, although nothing came of it. The statist temper of the times was ill conducive to Darling's volunteerism: in 1946, the government had created Commonwealth Employment Service offices for the guidance and placement of juveniles, 'staffed by specially trained officers and psychologists'.[6]

In the postwar years, three over-arching ideas cohered in Darling's thinking: cultural lament, empire and religion, with each employed (separately or together) to transcend social and political divisions. Lamentation characterised his regret at the fading of elements of a civilised society, at the root of which was money because (in his view) it had become an end in itself, not merely a medium of exchange. Wherever he looked, evidence abounded of this baleful perversion: enterprises 'of lasting value to society' were strapped for cash and constantly seeking funds to survive—universities, research, music, schools, libraries, youth clubs, churches, orphanages, institutes and hospitals. By contrast, 'frivolous and wasteful expenditure' was ubiquitous in gambling, drinking and entertainment. The 'heyday of the great middle class' and the influence of responsible editors, preachers and popular novelists was long since gone, with newspapers, 'cheap' libraries, football arenas and racecourses all at the mercy of commercial interests. In virtually every instance these popular outlets were 'irresponsibly controlled' and set their standards to 'catch the largest possible number by catering for the lowest possible intelligence and taste'. Considered alongside the increased demand for specialised learning (acknowledged by an antipathetic Darling as required in 'a complicated world') the results were disastrous: basic studies of language, history, literature, philosophy and religion—in short, 'a concentration which really produces the best men' and an appreciation of which was the hallmark of a civilised community—were increasingly excluded due to their 'very little market value'. The educational battle of adolescence was for 'citizens and souls' and, to produce an educated citizenry, specialisation had to be delayed as long as possible.[7]

With regard to empire, there were disparate influences on Darling's thinking: experience of two antipodean dominions in 1929 (and since), friendship with leading scholars of empire in the Ministry of Information in 1939 and occasional meetings with imperial promoters—such as Lionel Curtis (Fellow of All Souls, Oxford, and member of Milner's kindergarten) at Gilbulla where he and Margaret had stayed after the 1939 ANZAAS conference. In the immediate aftermath of hostilities in Europe and the Pacific, when 'the Empire' was a renewed source of loyalty across the party political spectrum, Darling became an avowed apologist for it. But this terrain was tricky, because national and imperial sentiments jostled with each other. On speech day in 1946, he noted how the British empire stood poised 'rather precariously, like the donkey between the two heaps of hay': Russian Communism and American individualism. But unlike Buridan's ass, each conception was 'not equally delectable' although 'equally poisonous, because equally materialistic'. Here, again, was a third-way opportunity:

> The British group of nations has to justify its continuance not by allying itself either diplomatically or spiritually with either of these conflicting theories, but by finding a middle way for the world which preserves liberty and justice.

The trigger for these remarks was probably the Corio visit of the governor-general and his wife, the Duke and Duchess of Gloucester, on an inclement day in November 1946. Although it rained, the day went well. Jane presented a posy to the Duchess, except that during the planning her father had discovered that he was 'far more ignorant about the proper way to behave' than he thought: What flag should the school fly? How much of 'God save the King' was to be played as a royal salute? What would their royal highnesses prefer to eat and drink? How many chauffeurs and policemen would be present for lunch? These were some of the questions rattled off to the duke's aide-de-camp.[8]

Darling's most articulate exposition of imperial rebirth was 'The English record', an address in March 1946 to the Royal Empire Society. He talked about one nation, England, to an audience whose members (unless like him they were English-born) probably thought of themselves as dual nationalists: Australian and British—British subjects, British by outlook and tradition, and British-speaking (as Curtin and Chifley said). But he also talked about an empire that was British (not English), albeit in his capacity as an Englishman (by upbringing, although with Scottish and English parentage he was as much British as English). In short, Great Britain comprised four nations and the empire was multinational. What was distinctive about the British empire was not its size or sense of being 'Top Nation', or greed for land or markets, but a 'capacity to elicit willing allegiance'. No single nation could dominate the world, and all made a contribution to 'civilization'. That civilisation was European. He then reeled off two pages of names of great national (and overwhelmingly male and English) religious figures, poets, writers, scientists, inventors and protagonists of social betterment who had contributed significantly to civilisation. Only when citing examples of explorers did he catch himself out with 'The English, or should I say the British'. The genius of the English, however, was in the 'art, the theory and the practice of government'. In addition to mathematical democratic representation, the British Parliament also pioneered a mechanism for the removal of governments in which voters lost confidence. Responsible and representative government had been diffused to different degrees across the empire. With the 'growing interdependence' of the empire's parts, 'bound together by a common sentiment and common principles', Darling proposed a model of a commonwealth of nations with reciprocal relations between the parts, and which was simultaneously heterogeneous and hierarchical, because the nations and colonies comprising its parts were at different stages of development and civilisation. Gilding the lily (in his idealised view), GGS's headmaster insisted that the empire's function was to educate, not oppress (although historically there had been 'blots') and to perpetuate itself by reproduction instead of force. The most glorious hour of the English record had been 'only yesterday' and it was 'unthinkable that there is not more to come'.[9]

Darling's resurgent imperial thinking was expressed practically in his membership of another committee-based group: the British Memorial Fund, brainchild in 1947 of an empire enthusiast, H.J. MacLean—two years before, the British Labour government, in 'almost the last flourish of imperial enthusiasm', engineered the conversion of the older idea of empire into the Commonwealth of Nations. MacLean had been inspired by the British people's endurance during sustained German assault after May 1940. As a 'memorial to the valour of those days', the British Memorial Fund planned to facilitate imperial interchange by visits of British people to Australia so that they could 'know at first hand the extent of and importance of their influence among us' and enable Australians to 'profit from their experience, their advice and their example'. The British Memorial Fund paralleled the British Council's work, except that the visits to Australia of people and groups in the arts that it facilitated—such as the Boyd Neel Orchestra—were funded by the British taxpayer. The British Memorial Fund wanted Australians to provide the financial underwriting, while also extending the number and breadth of visits.[10]

Louis Boyd Neel (a trained doctor) led a string orchestra that toured the Antipodes in 1947. After hearing a radio performance, Darling had moved heaven and earth (principally through the OGG Brian Jones at the British High Commission) to bring Boyd Neel to Corio. (In 1949, Darling also arranged for the English stage producer Tyrone Guthrie to visit GGS.) Darling rated the orchestra's concert at Corio in June as 'superb'. After Boyd Neel's short sojourn in New Zealand, he was persuaded by Darling to adjudicate the house music competition. According to Curthoys, Boyd Neel's orchestra was highly likely (on the cessation of its subsidy) to need finance. Knowing the mind of his friend, Curthoys tugged at Darling's imperial heartstrings by invoking the latter's well-to-do connections. 'Would it not help to bridge the yawning gap between words and deeds in this country', he wrote, if such well-off people who were always beating the drum about Australians 'not doing enough about the Old Country' could help the likes of Boyd Neel who, thanks to British government financial largesse, had given Australians 'such rare pleasure'? Precisely, his friend replied. In this connection, Darling explained, the British Memorial Fund hoped to raise £1 million to generate £30,000 annually with his role being 'to suggest means of spending it'. The entire point of encouraging an imperial interchange of people and ideas, Darling told Casey, was better understanding and integration 'particularly in the lower levels [of society?]', to preserve cultural activities in England as assets that were imperial (rather than exclusively English) and to complement the British Council's current 'one-sided activities'. Curthoys' view about digging deep was borne out by Darling's friend (and fellow fund member) Sylvia Ritchie: she told her friend that a potential donor on her list was a Toorak matron from whom she said receipt of a donation would amount to 'making use of the mammon of unrighteousness'—especially as the donor's husband owned fifteen hotels and who, because no-one called on either of them any more at their mansion, simply 'backs horses & buys hats' to while away the hours.[11]

The British Memorial Fund was Victorian, rather than Australian, in origin and composition. Notables among the star-studded array of public identities associated with it in 1951–52 (by which time Darling was ceasing to be active) included: the state governor, Sir Dallas Brooks (patron), Sir Edmund and Lady Herring, Gladys Lewis (the wife of Essington Lewis), Professor Joseph Burke (inaugural 1946 appointee to the *Herald*-endowed chair of fine arts), Sir Thomas Blamey, Casey, the lord mayor, Zelman Cowen, Myra Roper (Sinologist and principal of University Women's College), Sir Keith Murdoch and Sir Charles Lowe. The fund's 'gesture of loyalty, gratitude and affection to the Motherland' was, first, to create eight memorial fellowships tenable in Australia by citizens of the British Isles (each worth £7000, available every five years); second, to produce an autographed memorial book to coincide with the visit of King George and Queen Elizabeth in late 1948 (postponed due to the king's ill health), with subscribers paying £1 to sign it. For the first initiative, there was a London-based advisory and selection committee (which included Wakehurst, Keith Hancock and J.B. Priestley) and part of Darling's responsibility in 1948 was to publicise in England the fund's work. For the latter initiative, the memorial book repository was the British Museum.[12]

Progress on the capital fund was slow. Darling said that he was 'obsessed with the importance of people in this country understanding the present phase in imperial development', although frustrated with speech-making for the British Memorial Fund. 'I don't do it at all well and I am not sure why', he confessed—his wife Margaret thought that he was way 'too high brow'. Brandishing quotations from Hodson's recently published *Twentieth Century Empire*, Darling recycled neo-imperial thinking that was currently being reworked around the 'Commonwealth' ideal. Australia was part of the 'third British Empire', with a fourth in prospect (quintessential Hodson, but also articulated in 1943 by John Curtin)—along with the possibility that this may have been the 'nucleus of a new League of Nations'—while simultaneously being a member of a third international power bloc (the Commonwealth). In an exposition that was a tad too ethereal for his audiences, Darling tried lacing it with some colourful imagery. As in 'The English Record', he said that the empire (or British Commonwealth—he embraced both descriptions) consisted of a whole and Australia a part. On its own no component part could 'count for anything'— 'not even the U.K. Certainly not Australia.' The dominions were completely independent of Britain, but if the Commonwealth functioned properly as a network then they each had to merge that independence 'for the greater good of the whole'. Australia was merely a limb of a global body politic, with the heart and 'much of the brain' residing in the 'Old Country' that (in an over-the-top assertion) he claimed was home to 'probably the most sensible and decent civilization yet evolved by the world'. Its 50 million people were highly civilised, intelligent and imbued with tradition, and still looked to for spiritual and intellectual leadership. Although Darling's model of empire was an association of free and (consistent with the 1926 Balfour definition) equal peoples, his muscular civilising mission envisaged for this postwar imperium was mostly one-way traffic. The British Memorial Fund's role in relation to distant imperial outposts was to facilitate the passage of English men and women who 'will come out to see us, to meet us, to advize [sic] us and to learn from us' and return with a 'wider conception of the infinite potential for good' of the empire for the world.[13]

Two ways in which Darling cemented imperial ties at GGS were the Jennings scheme—for which in 1947 Roger Day was the initial beneficiary— and an exchange scheme for masters that (after wartime desuetude) he revived in 1949. But for all of his passionate promotion of England, there were small signs of Darling's identification with his adopted country. While his speech-day address following his return in 1948 contained yet another paean to the land of his birth—the most beautiful country, 'the only really civilised country' in the world (in respect of the things of the spirit and the mind), where one lived 'decently with one's neighbours and courteously with everyone', its people politically more adult, honest and intelligent than any other democracy—he held out hopes for Australia. In late 1946, he remarked to an Englishman who had returned home that 'there is something to be said for this country, especially if one has young children'. To another correspondent his opinion was that 'this could be, not a great, but certainly a much better country than it is, and education is of prime importance for the attainment of the best here'. Perhaps the most telling indication of viewing the world through Australian eyes came when he had tried to arrange with the British High Commission for an officer to address the first Easter conference of old boys on English social legislation. At the last minute 'one of his superiors got cold feet, and argued that it would be most dangerous for him to take part in any such conference'. This was 'idiocy': the Dominions Office seems to treat us 'with even more delicacy than they would a foreign country'. If the Office could not take 'our membership of the British family for granted', for fear of treading on the toes of a faction, it would 'never get anywhere' and would 'only succeed in exasperating that part of the country which desires to remain loyal to the Empire'.[14]

As for the religious element in Darling's postwar outlook, the core of it was the importance of Christian belief and doctrine. While he extolled Christianity in the public arena as a virtue, he self-consciously lacked success on the home front. In 1946, J.G. Campbell (an OGG at Trinity College), whose recent spiritual home was the Student Christian Movement, described religion at Corio as 'pretty dead'. Darling could have taken the bait, but held back. 'Some pious souls serve at the altar', Campbell said, 'and in chapel a slightly larger number listen to your discourses from the pulpit'. And because there were not many hard-core atheists at GGS, Christians were tolerated as 'quite harmless' while being thought of as narrow-minded although at heart probably decent. This was scarcely a ringing endorsement, and yet it aligned closely with Darling's own wartime assessment of GGS religion as 'totally inadequate' and of his efforts in shouldering chapel responsibilities as 'deplorable'. He confessed to Booth (while complaining of difficulties in obtaining chapel services dedicated to the worship of God minus 'what some people might call trappings') that the religious side of the school was 'failing you'. Booth had no business being satisfied with GGS 'until we have found a way to do better'. There was plenty of willingness to perform good works, Darling continued, but much of it was 'not sufficiently rooted in religion', and it withered easily. One correspondent reported how an acquaintance spotted the Scotch College–GGS difference in boys building a swimming pool at a Blacks Spur youth hostel:

> The Geelong boys worked well, but it seemed to the observers, rather consciously doing 'good works', whereas the Scotch boys [led by Hugh Stretton, son of Darling's friend, the judge] set to & appeared to do the work with zeal & enjoyment for its own sake.

Three years after his admission of failure, Darling still complained (this time to the Reverend D.A. Garnsey) of 'a permanently desperate situation about the religious life' at Corio. By 1951 he was more optimistic about boys interested in taking holy orders, but even then his enthusiasm was tempered: 'we are not yet getting the best to go the whole way'. The best-fitted boys held back, he said, while those with less to offer were pushing themselves forward. Was God 'choosing the weak things of the world to confound the strong'?[15]

The culprit, he thought, was worship. (As if to confirm his verdict, weekend chapel attendance became compulsory on every third Sunday in 1947 rather than each Sunday.) Darling relied on an array of clergymen to conduct GGS worship except that their quality was variable. In chapel, he tried to model himself on Frank Fletcher, while in the planning of chapel services he depended on Allen as chaplain. Ideally, he told Gordon, a chaplain should be a man 'who has had experience outside schools', rather than 'a teacher with ecclesiastical leanings'. At Melbourne Grammar, Sutcliffe (then wrestling with the problem of 'useless chaplains') was convinced that chapel worship problems were caused by the Church of England system of dual authority chaplaincy appointments, the justification for which was chaplains' parallel functions. In reply to the bishop of Ballarat's query (in 1944) about the taking of confessions by boys, Darling (with the help of Allen—who, after twenty-nine years as chaplain, retired the following year) summarised the GGS situation. A chaplain was a schoolmaster, and for that reason was appointed and controlled by the headmaster, but as an officiating priest he was licensed by the archbishop. (When Allen gave notice of his resignation, Darling assured the school council that he would consult Booth and would not appoint anyone 'with whom he is not well satisfied'.) Once appointed, a chaplain's relationship with the headmaster was like that of a vicar and church wardens: with the headmaster representing the council and school—although in practice both head and chaplain jointly ordered the chapel. If there were disagreements, then the court of appeal was the archbishop (who, in GGS's case, was none other than the council president). Darling also maintained that a headmaster should be consulted about chaplain appointments—the last thing that he wanted was an Anglo-Catholic–evangelical split between head and chaplain. As for inviting boys to take confession (as had happened in Ballarat— where in that diocese the chaplain had been appointed by the school council, not the bishop), Darling could not condone such action, although if a boy felt obliged to confess he would not forbid him. In any case, he couldn't (as the headmaster *in loco parentis*) prevent him unless specifically requested by parents. If a headmaster deemed a chaplain to be satisfactory, then the dual authority system worked well. Where this was not the case, however, a headmaster had difficulty engineering the removal of an unsatisfactory appointee.[16]

Beyond Corio in speeches and the forums of which he was a member, Darling continued (as in wartime) promoting religion in education in four ways: he pushed (again) for the removal of the secular clause in Victoria's education legislation, he pressed for the teaching of religion in schools, he continued championing state aid to the church schools and (influenced by Morgan's book) he promoted the formation of conscience by church schools as a bulwark in defence of the 'fortress of the mind'. On the first two points, Darling remained vocal in the Council of Public Education. Before leaving for England in 1948, he supported a council motion to omit the word 'secular' from the *Education Act*—although carried thirteen–three, nothing came of it. It was also 'wrong to ban the name of Christ from the classroom'. During 1949 and 1950, the council indulged him (as its vice president) by discussing a four-page report, 'A blue-print for education', in which Darling saw religious instruction as part of two proposed primary and general education stages. On state aid, Darling again argued that the patronage of church schools lessened considerably the state's financial burden, and then proposed an extensive battery of measures, including taxation relief for fee-paying parents, a prolonged payment period for child endowment, maintenance provision for students forced to reside away from home, transport allowances, an increased value of scholarships and parental educational allowances, low-interest state loans to schools and the inclusion of registered school teachers in the state's superannuation scheme. His council colleagues responded by affirming the continued existence of the church schools and (in agreeing to some form of state aid) acknowledged that their financial problems rendered doubtful their continued existence. Thanks largely to the efforts of Darling (and Father Conquest), by 1951 the possibility of tax deductions for tuition fees, loans to independent schools for capital works and even per capita grants as a proportion of the cost of state schooling were Council of Public Education agenda items. Beyond the council, he claimed that fees alone were insufficient to maintain church schools, the existence of which offered the 'variety and competition' that was the essence of British democracy. Financial aid ought to be based on principle, not political practicability, in which case if the Protestant churches renounced aid on the grounds that Catholic schools stood to gain, then there were two key objections. To forgo aid was to deny parents a Christian education for their children, simply because of their inability to afford tuition fees. The greater benefit of aid to the Catholic Church was a matter of 'great honour to it', for which the proper Protestant response was to compete with the Catholic system by reducing fees. More significant than sectarianism was the need to defend Christian conscience ('imbued with a sense of the divine ordering of the world') from the threat of materialism and collectivism to individual liberty of the mind.[17]

Postwar developments at Corio underscored Darling's line on state aid. Apart from the unresolved streamlining of the school's administration, his discretion was constrained by a cat-and-mouse game between fees and admissions arising from escalating costs. In May 1947, total enrolments following the acquisition of Glamorgan were 816 (on three sites): 531 at Corio (338 senior boarders, 45 day boys and 4 school associates; 141 junior boarders and 3 school associates), 121 at Bostock House (42 boarders) and 164 at Glamorgan (24 boarders). A year to the month later, council (on his recommendation) agreed to accept boys in order of receipt of applications to a level of 80 per cent of the anticipated vacancies, with the remainder placed on a waiting list. The final 20 per cent were to be selected according to application date, and special claims or abilities, with parents being informed of the category. When (in July) 80 per cent was reached, the parents of acceptances had to confirm their applications, produce from their son's previous school a certificate indicating prior academic standard and pay a £25 entrance fee, following which the remaining 20 per cent of applications were processed. In September 1948, the absent headmaster's assistant warned him that the senior school would be 'very full next year'. There was 'a mild panic' as 1949 projections were similar to those for the past two years.[18]

Postwar and into the early 1950s, tuition fees rose inexorably. The 1948 fee of £216 increased by 11 per cent to £240 in 1949, for the reason (given by Darling) that 'repairs and renewing goods after the ravages of the war years' were needed. Such was the extent of overcrowding in the boarding houses in early 1949 that prospective admissions were being turned away, although a slight mid-year income dip (due to a handful of sudden departures and enrolment miscalculations) necessitated a staff reduction of two. The fee increase meant that the headmaster was fielding parental complaints. There was another fee hike in 1950, agreed to despite the archbishop's opposition and 'a strong division of opinion within the Council on this question'. Darling saw it as the lesser of two evils. Schools 'of this sort and this school especially' could be killed, he told Booth, by making the fees so high 'that people cannot pay them' or by failing to appoint a staff who could 'properly carry the very heavy responsibilities imposed upon masters in a boarding school'. Corio masters were in a more precarious financial position than prewar and yet there was no slackening of demand for places. Moreover, increased fees levied by rival schools showed that these amounts were not beyond the reach of parents. The forces hostile to GGS and schools like it lay elsewhere:

> Continued Labour [sic] governments will endeavour to equalize society in such a way that the class which uses this school will be eliminated completely; but, before this happens, the actual physical difficulty of carrying on a boarding establishment in a society in which no-one is prepared to do domestic work for anyone else may well have caused our collapse.

In these circumstances, GGS had to be as good as possible 'and our goodness depends upon the quality of the staff, especially the new ones, whom we can recruit'. Reluctantly, but 'in order to provide some safeguard for the future', the council agreed to another fee increase to £285 annually effective from second term 1950.[19]

Other schools were in a similar pickle. In February 1951, Gilray moaned to Darling that he was 'getting sick of all this' increasing of fees. Two months earlier, Darling informed the parents on speech day of yet another increase, this time to £300. Such was the pressure for admissions by the end of 1950, he said, that there was a waiting list for every year through to 1956. A candidly worded two-page background document was distributed. When reporting on the new figure, Darling elevated the matter 'into the realm of the whole social future of this country'. He appealed for endowments, with statism in his sights:

> We are living in an age of transition between that of private enterprise and State monopoly. Politically, I think most of us object to the idea of State monopoly and would not like to live in a society in which everything was run by the State and paid for out of national revenue. If we mean that, then we must see that there are preserved into the future those institutions which stand on their own feet and continue to support themselves by their own activities. Of these none are more important than the independent schools.

At the mercy of spiralling costs, but lacking access to substantial endowments with which to liquidate debt, the council, he said, had before it three alternatives: a minimal tuition fee increase to balance the budget, high fees that would have dampened enrolments, and a reduction in standards in the interests of economy (which would have prejudiced GGS's reputation). The new fee of £300 represented an 82 per cent increase in a decade. Seven months later (July 1951) fees rose again: to £360—a total, Darling confided to Gordon, that was about the sustainable limit. To cushion the financial blow for hard-pressed parents, council provided bursaries (from a £7000 fund). For some students (for example, the sons of clergy) up to £240 worth of bursary support could be obtained. A possible fee-containment solution, Darling told Black, particularly if the federal government stood by its promise to make gifts to schools free of income tax, was a fees assistance fund to sustain the quality of the boys admitted while supporting the less well-off old boys.[20]

In 1950, enrolments spurted yet again. With the four senior boarding houses laden to the gunnels, Corio was under huge pressure. All up, the combined senior and junior school enrolment was 585, or (discounting 48 Geelong House day boys) 17 more than the budgeted figure of 520 boarders. In 1951, when there were 589 boys at Corio (545 boarders), Darling reported that 'almost every square inch in the school is occupied' and lamented that such pressure made the running of the school 'very difficult'. His estimate for 1952 was 613: 558 boarders and 55 day boys. Apart from the financial drain created by the maintenance backlog—'the domestic and physical side of the School is quite frightful', Darling admitted to Lindon—the other priority (he intimated to Booth) was to provide the masters with decent pension entitlements and attractive stipends. After considerable effort and actuarial advice, an effective superannuation scheme was in place for 1951. The pension drew on the capital of the superannuation fund and ensured that masters retiring at sixty-two after three decades' service received a lifelong annuity of £300 yearly. Rather than a lump-sum payment, Darling thought that a pension was appropriate for masters retiring early—due to ill health or when requested by council at age sixty—with their pension equivalent in value to their entitlement had they remained until sixty-two. The superannuation component had a twofold purpose. Darling wanted to support the widows and families of men who died due to war service, and to assist masters moving to other school appointments. Improved masters' salaries directly impinged on admission numbers and fee levels: fee increases covered the new salary scales, and salary levels (and employment conditions) had to be sufficiently attractive to recruit more masters to teach the increased admissions. In March 1950, in the lead-up to the £285 and £300 fees, Darling informed council that a 'very serious crisis' had been reached in respect of salaries. His hand had been forced by a recent Teachers' Tribunal award for state secondary teachers: a generous bursary now enabled prospective teachers to have paid in full the cost of their university degree and diploma of education on the condition that they taught for three years. Any aspiring teacher, he said, 'would be a fool not to take this opportunity' as it was offered regardless of private means and he estimated its worth as £1000. A huge labour-market headache resulted for GGS: a £239 disparity between what a GGS master and a state bursary-recruited teacher would be earning after the mandatory three-year period: £525 and £764 respectively. The only alternative was equivalent salaries.[21]

During this rapid growth, Darling added a new string to his bow: dispensing of patronage in the headmaster stakes. At times his advice was disarmingly frank. Although in one instance he knew very little about the (Sydney) college in question, it had experienced difficulties with the previous-but-one incumbent who 'was delightful but inconsequential and left the place in a pretty fair mess'. This particular head, however, had not been helped by his council that, he believed, had 'treated him personally rather badly', and then the health of the succeeding incumbent, who commenced with considerable promise, collapsed prematurely. The difficulty for any man who headed this denominational institution was that it was governed by an entire state-wide church, in which case a headmaster risked having to 'stand up against nearly every parson in Sydney'. Occasionally, as with the appointment of H.L. Tonkin's successor at Camberwell Grammar School, the advice-seeker was an educational layman, in this instance (1949) the school council secretary, L.G. Robinson (a reputed political reactionary). 'Knowing the English field, we thought you might have an Englishman in mind', he had written. By April, a large field of applicants had been reduced to six, with the former GGS pupil and master Peter Thwaites (brother of Michael) 'easily first': he was impeccably qualified, but were his politics suspect? 'We will have no Communist, Socialist or pink blooded H.M.' Thwaites was 'cautious and you have no fear of his blotting his copy-book that way', Darling reassured him, before listing the headmasterly virtues:

> There is no such animal as a good headmaster, and it is becoming increasingly difficult for anyone to get even near to the definition. A man now needs to be not only an inspiration to boys, capable of stimulating them intellectually, as of understanding them sympathetically, a wise and fair judge, an acute detective, a firm disciplinarian, a loving father and an olympian figure imperturbable, serene and strong—all these qualities have always been required together with the capacity to speak in public, at least to the School as a whole and to assemblies of parents, he must also be able to deal with men and women, to unite an underpaid and worried staff in the spirit of service unstintingly given to boys who are the sons of parents palpably unworthy of such devotion and for the most part unappreciative, indeed unaware of the huge surplus of care which their sons receive over and above what they pay for: he must know something about Education with a big E in order that in the process of routine organization he shall not lose sight of the main purposes; he must be aware of modern experiment and able to select and use it within the limited financial means at his disposal.

For good measure he added an accountant, an architect and a handyman, a boarding-house keeper and a 'successful cadger without losing his dignity'. After commenting on those of the six with whom he was familiar, Darling advised Robinson that it was up to the council to decide what it wanted. Given that he had made 'too many mistakes' in the past, he did not put his own judgement 'at "a pin's fee" nowadays'.[22]

Headmaster-making was fraught and an applicant's pedigree was no guarantee of success. One of Camberwell's six was an Englishman, Michael Searle, an assistant master at Maidstone Grammar School, Kent. A former Marlburian, Searle had been taught by Brian Hone, had been head prefect and his closest friend at Marlborough was Harry Fisher, son of the Primate of All England. Indeed, Fisher (who visited Corio in late 1950 during his tour of the Anglican Communion) told Darling that Searle, who was George Turner's protégé, 'ought to be very good'. Having selected him, Robinson's euphoria was boundless. Searle, he believed, would someday 'be one of Australia's leading educationalists'. But this pronouncement was the kiss of death and the council's love affair with the Englishman became progressively frostier. After five years, the relationship ended in bitter acrimony. Turner (who visited Camberwell Grammar twice while touring Australia in 1954) told Darling when Searle was appointed how he had explained to the council that he had had 'very little experience'. Darling had also cautioned the council to give Searle 'a fair spin'. Their advice was ignored. In June 1954, Searle resigned and left the school in December. When Gordon enquired about his departure (a St Peter's master was interested in the vacancy), Darling dismissed the episode as a case of small men and even smaller minds: Searle had wanted to 'turn the place into a real school', the council didn't know what that meant, was not prepared to back him and Darling was inclined to let them 'stew in their own juice'. Searle went to King's for two years and then taught for the rest of his working life at Sydney Grammar.[23]

During 1951, while the fee and enrolment developments were boiling away, Darling looked increasingly to GGS's future. In October, he told Turner that, after twenty-one years' absence from England, 'there was very little likelihood' of his ever returning. He had also written to Mills and gave notice of his resignation from the Universities Commission (the following February). The commission had been a success, he said, thanks largely to Mills' 'imperturbable sense of justice' and the humanity that he had displayed. Darling's working relationship and friendship with Mills had taught him that it was possible for government agencies to preserve such humanity in their dealings. More importantly (in light of the public sector appointments awaiting him), Darling drew the lesson that 'a better solution of the bureaucratic problem' was the principle of public administration by commission, instead of direct administration under ministerial control. While there had been no ministerial pressure on the Universities Commission, Darling thought that much of the community's time and money could be saved if there was less Treasury control of departments. There were two reasons for his departure: the usual domestic excuse of his constant difficulty in 'getting away' for meetings, and a slightly more enigmatic excuse. He was hatching 'an enterprise' that, if it came off 'will very greatly increase my duties'. His resignation marked the end of the first of three decades during which he performed prominent advisory or executive roles as part of the apparatus of state. Universities Commission membership had been a useful apprenticeship. At Menzies' request, Darling agreed in early 1952 to stay on as a commission member until the government reconstituted it after Mills' retirement in November. (Sadly, Mills died in September.) Darling agreed, knowing that his attendance would be irregular because he would be devoting himself to his enterprise (or 'mountain scheme'). But before being able to remove himself from the temporary tenancy of his mid-career plateau, there was other unfinished government business to attend to with his fellow heads of direct bearing on the GGS fee and enrolments battle. The heads' lobbying was mostly out of the public gaze, and coincided with an ugly and vituperative downturn in the substance and tone of national politics that, as Darling was to discover, tested the limits of his equanimity.[24]

MANDATED TRUTHS

1948–1954

For we wrestle not against flesh and blood, but against principalities, against powers, against the rulers of the darkness of this world, against spiritual wickedness in high places.

Ephesians (King James version)

At the election on Saturday 10 December 1949, the federal Labor government lost office. A week later a Liberal–Country Party Coalition led by Menzies was sworn in. After an electoral redistribution, the House had been enlarged from 75 to 121 representatives. Its composition was young and dominated by ex-servicemen, especially the Coalition: of its 48 new members, 34 had served in the recent war and the average age of 39 new Liberals was forty-three (with 12 under thirty). Eight Liberal MHRs and Senators were OGGs: J.B. Howse (Calare), D.E. Fairbairn (Farrar), A.R. Downer (Angas), R.S. Ryan (Flinders), Jo Gullett (Henty), G.W. Brown (McMillan), E.D. Mackinnon (Wannon) and John Gorton (Senate, Victoria), a result that 'must be very satisfying', Lindon remarked to Darling, as five had been pupils during his incumbency. Darling congratulated Gorton and prophesied that one day he might be prime minister, which Gorton brushed aside with 'at the moment I am not nearly ready for it', and suggested that the election results reflected credit on Darling and showed 'value from your work'. In the 1946 election (won by Labor) six OGGs had stood 'in the Liberal interest'—in the *Corian*'s quaint phrase. Three had been successful and a recently exited old boy wondered whether his headmaster would 'offer a Labor OGG candidate the same good wishes'. This time, Hay (back from the United Nations in New York) observed similarly: the number of new Liberals was 'remarkable', except that it 'mightn't be a bad idea if we could also produce a few members for the other side, too—or are the two lines of thought incompatible'? One of the eight (Downer) rejoiced 'at the prospect of 8 O.G.Gs. in the Federal Parliament' and, after enduring a 'welter of rubbish & misrepresentation' about the old school tie, it was 'grand to know that in 8 constituencies this derided piece of cloth has triumphed'.[1]

Continuous Coalition rule followed until 1972. It overlapped with the Cold War, a period when much of the ideological polarisation typical of international relations was directly mirrored in Australian political debates and alignments. Up until about 1951, the 'great debate' in Australian politics, notes the historian Geoffrey Bolton, was about objectives: 'Was Australia's first priority to seek security for all through government planning, or to create the best conditions for private enterprise to generate economic growth?' This debate was more apparent than real, he insists, given the broad agreement on the need to control and develop the economy. Bolton's dismissal of the mood of the times—'the shrill accusations of Communism and crypto-Fascism'—as a 'futile, noisy, and largely irrelevant side-show', might be right in hindsight, but for small 'l' liberals such as Darling, this stiffening of the political atmospherics during the 1950s was a testing time. Unlike his friend Hackett (up to his neck in fighting the cause of anti-communism), Darling was not a Cold War warrior, but his liberalism was tested because he became caught up in debates about reconstruction, Cold War entanglements and foreign policy realignment. When confronted by demands calculated to push him into the arms of either the Right or Left, how would he react? Would he refuse to be drawn in or, if alignment was unavoidable, how would he justify himself? (There were two instances in 1949 and in late 1953.) Second, suppose that he was positioned to arbitrate conflicts between the political extremes: would he find a way through and could these be reconciled in the interests of consensus and unity? Third, what if his own political soundness was queried (as previously and again in late 1950) or if others judged GGS and its old boys as suspect? Finally, with so many OGGs at the centre of national power, how would Darling respond to the siren call of Downer's much derided cloth? Would he, for example, exploit the potential for patronage that this new network opened up?[2]

A taste of what was in store came after his Headmasters' Conference of Australia address at St Peter's in January 1949, where, in a cogent and tightly argued analysis, he laid out an agenda of issues preoccupying his peers but that were diversions from their 'proper concerns' (the welfare and development of boys):

> We have at the moment the phenomenon of the combination of crowded schools and long waiting lists, with unsatisfactory balance sheets, in spite of considerably raised fees. With costs as they are, only a very brave school can dare to expand, and no-one in his senses would attempt to start a new school, however great the need. In the meanwhile, the councils of existing schools know that the fees are inadequate for the task of running them as they wish, but fear to raise them higher lest heavily-taxed parents may become unable to pay them. The teaching profession remains in most cases inadequately

paid, and there is some evidence that the supply of teachers is for this reason drying up.

His speech got up some noses, including that of the editor of the *Bulletin*. This fervently nationalistic magazine was less interested in Darling's hard-headed realism about the schools' plight than in his reasoning. Darling had mentioned an inevitable onward march of egalitarianism and creeping statism, but a *Bulletin* editorial (entitled 'Quality and equality') accused him of capitulation. 'We must accept it and endeavour to see how we can fit in', Darling had said, after explaining to the assembled heads that in the emerging social order mass justice meant the denial of privilege and that the masses were the new political masters. The *Bulletin* italicised 'We must accept it'. 'So', it screamed, 'the Australian character is sentenced to death, is it?' Darling was deluded in swallowing the poison that mass mediocrity was Australia's 'ineluctable fate'. Meek acceptance of the levelling-down of the herd was defeatist. He also incurred the wrath of a disgruntled Rockhampton Boys Grammar School master who had inferred that 'the flag of the Public Schools' had to be lowered in the face of Canberra policy and an increasingly hefty tax burden on parents. 'So far from lowering any flags', the master huffed and puffed, 'I intend spending some time this year in working for Mr Menzies's Party'. Darling's defence that the remarks reported were a very small part of his speech reassured this critic, who dismissed the Labor government with: 'we have had enough of the present gang'. Darling was also annoyed with the *Sydney Morning Herald* because, having been forwarded the entire text, its reproduced version cut it by a third. Actually, he was 'not in the least ready to abandon the struggle against tendencies of which I disapprove'.[3]

The *Bulletin* was offended by the idea that, while English democracy (after the 1832 *Reform Act*) had evolved into majority government based on universal suffrage, democracy had become equated with an egalitarian society. Of the famous tripartite French revolutionary slogan, Darling claimed that liberty had been largely discarded, fraternity had 'never been tried' and equality had supplanted both. Justice, then, had become the equivalent of the denial of privilege and the masses were the new masters. 'It was useless to deplore this, even if we have the courage to do so. We must accept it and endeavour to see how we can fit in.' But the next two sentences troubled Manning Clark when he read them in the *Age*:

> What is depressing about it is, of course, that you cannot combine justice for all on an egalitarian basis with the liberty of individuals to get what they as individuals want to get out of life for themselves and for their children. It is, as it seems, impossible to have liberty and equality.

In intermittent postwar correspondence Clark had tried to manoeuvre his former boss into taking a lead in various causes. When commending Darling on his support for the Save the Children Fund, for example, he asked: 'Do you remember how you inspired a whole generation of young men with the idea that something really worth while was occurring in their era—a renaissance[?]' But because he thought that Clark had left 'so very nasty a mark behind him' at Corio, Darling was wary and more positively inclined to the other sometime Corio master and historian, Russel Ward. He liked Ward's textbook for schools—based largely on ideas developed as a 'rather callow and bumptious' Junior House teacher, Ward confessed, thanks to the freedom that Darling gave him to devise his own syllabus.[4]

What saddened Clark was the alleged conflict between liberty and equality. Because Western Europeans no longer tolerated privilege, it was important to ensure that:

> in creating an egalitarian society we do not sacrifice 'participation', and the liberties of speech, dress, conscience, tastes and pursuits. I believe we can, though I am more impressed now than before with the great perversions which may rob us of the fruits of this work.

Clark's hopes were pinned on making the state (or 'Leviathan') more human and democratic. Darling refused to be drawn. The year before in England he had been distressed by the condition of England under socialism (even while conceding that 'quite possibly it is the hardening of the arteries in old age'). Voluntary effort was English democracy's lifeblood and yet liberals were excluded from the administration of the country. Moreover, class hatred was ubiquitous. He had no idea whether Australia could avoid a similar situation, but its stark choice was either 'liberty with injustice' or 'justice enforced by "Leviathan"'. As he had impressed on Lloyd Ross two years earlier, statism was his real concern. Then, Darling had responded to Ross's recent *Australian Quarterly* article in which he argued that even though the Bolshevik revolution had resulted in Stalinism, this was not proof that democratic social revolution would destroy freedom. Contrary to F.A. Hayek who, in *The Road to Serfdom*, had argued that increased state control threatened liberty and was the slippery slope to totalitarianism, Ross argued for democratic planning. Darling was 'vaguely uneasy', because his dislike of 'what seems to me progress towards totalitarianism' was throwing him 'more and more into company amongst those whom I feel equally uneasy'. His escape route was to distinguish state ownership from state control: 'You can't argue against the necessities being run in the interests of the whole people, but is nationalization the best way to ensure this?' In many cases he would eliminate private interests but he much preferred independent corporations to political control, regardless of who was in power.[5]

After the cessation of Korean hostilities (July 1953) and before the defection of the Petrovs (April 1954), these mild differences over statism, liberty and equality escalated into something more sinister. The Menzies government's legislation to ban the Communist Party of Australia had passed both houses of Parliament in September 1950 but in March the High Court struck down the *Communist Party Dissolution Act* as unconstitutional. Then, later in the year, following the double dissolution election of April 1951 (when the Coalition acquired a Senate majority), the referendum to give the Commonwealth power to ban the Communist Party was lost. The narrowing ugliness of the Cold War climate was encapsulated in an exchange of three letters about Clark: two from Senator Gorton and one in reply from his erstwhile headmaster. Gorton wanted to know when Clark (at Canberra University College) had taught at GGS and why he had departed:

> Mr. Manning Clark is now in a position where he has a great deal to do with selecting and training cadets for our diplomatic service and I would like you to let me know anything you know about him.

Such information would go only to Casey (Minister for External Affairs). Darling smelt a rat. Sensing that he might be dragged into a witch-hunt he exclaimed: 'Blast you! I am not Mr. Harry Truman.' He provided the relevant dates and Clark's desire for a university appointment:

> It would be easier but not honest to leave it at that. He was of course, very Left Wing and I got into a good deal of trouble with parents because of his influence upon the more intelligent boys in that direction. He always maintained that he was by no means Communist, and he certainly would be one of the first people to be strung up in any Communist regime, but he may not realize this. My reason for not being sorry to lose him was not that I disapproved of his political views. It is a nuisance to a headmaster when everybody does not think alike, but having been at Repton in 1916–17 with D.C. Somervell and Victor Gollancz as masters in a similar situation but on the other side I can still realize that it is right and even necessary that the opposition should be heard.

His objection to Clark was psychological. He was a 'silly ass and had no judgment'. Playing the amateur therapist, Darling thought that Clark's tendency towards epilepsy, his failure to win a Rhodes scholarship, and his inability to join the army and to compete on equal terms with other men had held him back psychologically. (While the assessment of a recent Clark biographer, Brian Matthews, is not quite as blunt, it is consistent with Darling's view.) Clark was heterodox on morality as well as politics, which made him a difficult member of staff. Now that he had joined 'the ranks of the higher bourgeoisie', however, he might have mellowed, although Darling would still be disinclined to 'entrust him with the care of a human soul' especially given that he was 'a wonderful teacher and capable of winning enthusiastic disciples'.[6]

'What the devil do you do now?' Darling asked. As respectable a person as Keith Hancock had also once been a nonconformist, he protested, and had had a similar effect on pupils as Clark on his, but surely the Department of External Affairs cadets were old enough and sufficiently well educated 'to make them capable of seeing through falseness and finding the truth for themselves'? He was glad to be free of having to make political decisions. He hated and feared the communist attitude to life and dreaded 'being driven into the necessary measure of protection against it' and 'the whole field of what is called "security" fills one with alarm'. By being honest with Gorton he had done his duty. The decision was now his. Was Clark a Christian? Clark thought so, said Darling, but he 'could never make out' whether he was, although he was certain that Clark believed in 'the sanctity of individual freedom'. As a 'maladjusted' person, however, Clark could not be a good influence on the young. Gorton apologised for shaking the foundations of Darling's 'ivory tower', but protective measures were 'necessary'. While preventing 'clots' like Clark from thinking and believing what they did was not the point, removing them from positions where they could do damage was very much the point. If he had anything to do with it, therefore, 'M.C will go'. 'Flabby' (not 'true') intellectuals were 'the enemies [sic] most useful allies'. At the end of 1953, Clark's services as a teacher of the diplomatic corps were no longer required. Clark thought that he was no longer wanted by 'the men in black'.[7]

Darling's letter may not have been important in de-frocking his former master—historian Alan Fewster claims that high costs, low cadet numbers and academically well-qualified intakes justified the ten-year-old program's closure. A potentially less malign instance of Left–Right entanglements that engaged Darling, albeit briefly, was the shaky future of *Current Affairs Bulletin*. This matter may have been small beer, but it went to the heart of Darling's mid-1951 argument with the prime minister—during the lobbying by the Headmasters' Conference of Australia for tax concessions—about a society's need to be able to safeguard Charles Morgan's 'liberties of the mind'. *CAB* (as it was known) was a government-funded publication emanating from the Commonwealth Office of Education. Over three and a half years, it had built up a circulation of about 50,000 and each (anonymously authored) edition discussed topics and issues of general interest. As well as the education service that it provided for the Australian community, it was an invaluable resource for senior secondary school humanities classes. Indeed, as the University of Sydney staff member said when he contacted Darling about the *CAB*'s threatened demise (as a result of foreshadowed public service cuts), the magazine had gone 'some way towards filling a gap in our public life' that, in Britain, was filled by 'the many weekly and monthly periodicals of responsible opinion'.[8]

Peter Westcott (senior English master) said that if the *CAB* folded it would be a 'great pity'. The cost to GGS was a trifling £10 annually for 100 fortnightly copies (one penny each). Ominously, Westcott added that 'some suspect it, as usual, of being Left' and 'there have been hostile questions at Canberra'. He was confident that senior colleagues would support their headmaster with signatures if he 'cared to protest'. Darling was predisposed to defend organs of opinion. He had been gleeful back in 1947 when the *Observer* appeared and Dedman had sent him the first issue. He had long agitated for a weekly newspaper after the style of the *New Statesman* or *Spectator*, he said, and always felt that in Australia 'a "left" paper of this sort was more necessary than even a more or less enlightened conservative paper'. The new organ of opinion should be 'progressive and even Labour [sic] in the narrower party sense', except that if it 'gave the impression that it was wholeheartedly and uncritically the supporter of any particular government' that would be a pity—one editorial had pictured the present ministers as 'a covey of archangels', a sin of which the *New Statesman* was never guilty as it approved of nobody and regarded it as a matter of principle not to. He hoped that the new venture would not give uncritical support:

> I feel so strongly that a government should be criticized intelligently from both sides and that one of the troubles in this country is that divisions of thought are always too much on party lines.

He was reluctant to press Menzies on the *CAB* while 'pressing him in the other direction on behalf of church schools', even though he 'very strongly' believed that it was worth preserving. He asked Geoffrey Brown 'to watch it'. Although *CAB*'s future was 'awaiting a decision by the P.M.' the University of Sydney would probably sponsor it. Darling's action (and that of others contacted) had been 'quite evidently very fruitful'.[9]

The concluding part of Darling's 1949 Conference speech kick-started the second phase of the bid for tax concessions. This was a story of persistence and incremental gains. He called on the other heads to 'co-operate with all other interested bodies, even to the extent of planning a political campaign', except that mobilising collective pressure on the government was not his cup of tea. Rather than direct involvement in the 1949 election campaign, the Headmasters' Conference encouraged school council and church representatives to coordinate state by state. Advice was also taken from taxation consultants. Following the Coalition victory, Hone and Robson wanted to strike while the iron was hot, and urged Darling and Gilray (the Headmasters' Conference of Australia secretary and chairman, respectively) to meet Canberra officials. Darling was reluctant: tax was tricky and after the Scullin meeting he did not want his fingers burnt again. They toyed with approaching Casey (MHR for Latrobe) but eventually Gilray drafted a two-page statement for Fadden (treasurer). Hope sprang eternal, because Labor was rumoured (Colman told Darling) to be supporting a policy to allow educational expenses as tax deductions: if Labor switched, then so might Fadden.[10]

As the respective chairmen of the Headmasters' Conference and the Headmasters' Association, Gilray and Darling coordinated during the lead-up to the budget (mid-October) when Darling activated the OGG backbench network, especially the two Victorian orchardists, Gorton and Brown, his 'spies'—who styled themselves, as 'more or less', the 'Old Geelong Grammarians Parliamentary Committee'. Their intelligence-gathering, he told Gilray, led him to believe that gifts to schools might soon become legitimate tax deductions. But when there was no joy in the budget for tax relief on fees or tax exemption for gifts, Gilray and Darling telegrammed their concern to Menzies. Schools had received a double financial whammy, Darling explained to Brown: no budget joy, but a basic wage award. Their combined effect would necessitate yet another fee hike, to the tune of about £20 per boy. Again Darling played the class card, by bemoaning the fact that the 'unfortunate middle class' would now have to organise itself to save itself (the treasurer had let it down badly), and he anticipated a leakage of 'lower middleclass' boys from church schools, especially the grammar schools.[11]

After speaking to Menzies, both Gorton and Brown reaffirmed that 'the matter is very dear to his heart'. Menzies was aware of, and in sympathy with, the arguments for tax relief, and did not want to leave office without meeting the heads' requests, but Fadden was a different proposition. He was less enthusiastic about tax deductions. Menzies had had to concede to a 'very over worked and nervy' treasurer on 'a few small money matters' during the budget's finalisation, yet Brown believed that Menzies would regulate for changes early in the new year—'notes to that effect were on his desk when we saw him' and he cautioned the heads to wait until after Parliament passed the budget. Darling accepted Gorton's suggestion to leave it to Menzies, but implored Brown to approach him again. With two major cost increases in two years amounting to £20,000—the basic wage rise and a new award for the Victorian Assistant Masters' Association— tax rebates would help to secure endowments, reduce debts and provide for a masters' annuity fund. An early public announcement would relieve the gloom, he urged, and would help schools to help themselves. After all, the schools were 'representatives of that diminishing group which habitually gives more than it is paid for [the middle class], and I think that we should be encouraged'. Robson's information differed. Senator Spooner (Minister for Social Services) had told him that the heads' proposal 'was most favourably considered' and had been dropped only at the last minute. Spooner urged persistence and claimed that there was 'an extremely good chance' of success in 1951 and that an estimate of the measures' cost to the government would help the heads' cause. Hone, Robson said, had been softening up Spender (Minister for External Affairs) but the advice was to not press him further. The Sydney diocesan synod had 'passed a motion opposing our plans' but, said Robson dismissively, 'no one will take any notice of them'. Brown and Gorton persisted with Menzies, with Brown confident especially if concessions were only applicable after a child had attained the state school–leaving age, but deductions on gifts presented difficulties. Obviously, 'we can't agree that some enormously rich wool grower shall give most of his taxes to the schools instead of the Treasury'. He had spoken to Chifley who had a similar view to Menzies.[12]

Had the Gilray–Darling telegram given the prime minister 'many sleepless nights', as Darling thought? Probably not. Menzies insisted that the budget's omission of tax relief was not evidence of lack of interest in education. Indeed, Labor's previous increase in the student child allowance to age nineteen had been lifted to twenty-one and the government was 'keenly aware' of the need for an adequate educational system. He assured them of two things mentioned in their telegram: both items were being considered by a committee examining the taxation laws, and the government would 'give serious consideration' to its recommendations. Brown reiterated that Menzies had had to make budget concessions to Country Party allies and stuck to the line that fee concessions would follow taxation law adjustments. Darling was grateful for Menzies' interest but pressed him on the schools' immediate difficulty that (with speech nights approaching) the heads were about to 'face our parents and tell them the rather gloomy news about the future'. In the months before the April 1951 election, pressure mounted for a concerted schools' campaign to influence local candidates to extract tax-deduction pledges. Darling trusted Menzies and urged caution because, as he told Hubert Black, 'if one wants the Liberal Country Party back in power, one should embarrass it as little as possible before the election'. Were the government to be returned, then 'I think that Menzies will stand by his promise given to Geoffrey Brown'.[13]

Two months after the Coalition's re-election in 1951, Darling again pressed Menzies in a lengthy letter. Rather than appealing narrowly to the schools' self-interest, he expounded the intellectual merits of their case by reference to Morgan's *Liberties of the Mind*: 'I earnestly beg you' to read it. Marginal annotations in Darling's copy suggest that Morgan's turns of phrase had resonated strongly. He was more convinced than ever of the need to preserve institutions that 'endeavour to keep alive the idea of the importance of individual thinking in the face of the prevailing threat of uniformity and mechanistic pressure'. Because it brought control with it, however, direct state aid to the schools was not the way to attain such an end. Instead, could it not be 'a cardinal point of policy' to encourage 'the rich to keep alive for the future those institutions which preserve the liberties of the mind or at least its variety?':

> You want independent schools to survive; you want churches to survive and to be more strong [sic]: surely it is logical and desirable that gifts to both should be exempt from income tax? that is that some of the money which the state would otherwise take shall be diverted for the task of doing in a better way the work which the state would otherwise have to do?

Annual gifts of £1 million to all the schools meant much more to them than the tax earned on such an amount by the state. But Fadden's estimate was a loss of up to £1.5 million in revenue if tax deductions on school fees were

introduced. This information and a forthcoming budget left the headmasters
in a quandary by July 1951. Should they concentrate on deductions on fees
or gifts and bequests? And what was the best way to make their case? Hake
saw little point in a meeting with Fadden and urged individual representations
to people known to have the ear of the treasurer or the prime minister—as
Robson had done with D.H. Drummond (MHR for New England and former
New South Wales Minister for Education). Gilray had written to Fadden,
but Darling was disinclined to be part of a deputation as this betrayed lack of
confidence in his 'agents' and Menzies' promise. His sense of powerlessness was
compounded by the knowledge (from Council of Public Education data) that in
1948 the independent schools had saved the Victorian government £15 million
expenditure for primary and secondary students. If preserving institutions vital to
the liberties of the mind was unconvincing, then claims about state money saved
by the existence of independent schools would not advance the argument either,
because the Commonwealth could claim (perfectly correctly) that schooling was
a state responsibility. Preservation of liberties of the mind was vital because 'we
are in danger of becoming a pretty utilitarian and uniform society'. Menzies
would try to read Morgan's book, but tax-deductible school gifts presented
'thorny problems' for the tax commissioner.[14]

Eventually, when the budget provided no tax relief Darling felt badly let
down, and 'a bit fed up' with the treasurer and prime minister. After purposely
holding back from showering parliamentarians with letters and telegrams, he
could not believe that concessions on fees and gifts made all that much difference
to the government. The only two plausible explanations for the refusal to meet
their demands were, first, the opposition of Treasury officials—probably unsympathetic due to their social origins and habits 'and because they are bureaucratic
egalitarians anyhow'—and, second, the Coalition's cynical betrayal of Liberal
philosophy:

> I can only assume that they [sic] Liberal–Country Party feels so sure of the
> support of the unfortunate middle class that it thinks that it can afford to
> neglect its interests and squeeze it out of existence as the socialist government
> in England has deliberately and successfully killed it, that is by forcing it with
> the socialist mould, making it use State Health services and hospitals, and
> now schools as well.

If this meant wearing 'the drab grey uniform of the Welfare State' then 'this
all-embracing machine which seeks to turn us all out according to a pattern'
should be fought to the last breath. Without encouragement from the Liberals
the middle class would lose all hope, and the nation would be the poorer for its
lost independence and individuality. He also poured out to Hake his disgust with
the treasurer. Behaving like gentlemen had been unwise and 'we might have got
further if we had done what everybody else does'. His line on the middle class,

and the fostering of individuality and independence by schools and churches had made no difference.[15]

Brown conveyed his bitter disappointment to Menzies after a party briefing on the budget. His defence that a decision on tax concessions was not necessarily a budgetary one and that something might be forthcoming within twelve months was small consolation. What probably killed any hope of concessional allowances was advice to Fadden from the Commonwealth Committee on Taxation. It was true that fee-paying parents saved state governments 'considerable expenditure', but income tax law was not the way to assist parents. Specification of a maximum fee concession was complex due to certain exclusions (for example, cost of board and maintenance) and, because the measure varied by income levels, some taxpayers would not benefit (which would not help needy schools). Strong cross-party support for changes, however, might win the day. Darling's fellow Council of Public Education and University of Melbourne council member, the Labor MHR, T.W. Andrews (Darebin), was interested in exemptions on gifts. Darling was grateful for the copy of the committee's report that Andrews forwarded him and his persistent questioning of the treasurer in the House. He did not think that the tax concession claim was 'a very good case', he told Andrews, and that the one for gifts was stronger. Meanwhile, the parliamentary OGGs discussed Darling's late September letter to Brown and Menzies was given a copy. Brown was confident of mustering a delegation of twenty or so (20 per cent of all Coalition MHRs and senators) to descend on Menzies' office. Fadden was 'very non-committal', but the door was still left slightly ajar: the Commissioner of Taxation asked the delegation for the meanings of the terms 'secondary schools' and 'secondary education'—to prevent the application of provisions to the likes of schools of elocution.[16]

By the new year—1952—there was a lull. Gorton mustered the back-benchers in May and reassured Darling that the fees campaign should proceed with 'unabated vigour'. By mid-year, Hubert Opperman (Dedman's successor as MHR for Corio) was actively lobbying, although Fadden continued stalling, and Andrews advised that Menzies was considering draft amendments. Then, in August, Opperman telegrammed: 'Glad to report my request for concession for educational expenses up to a maximum of £50 for each dependent child under 21 receiving full time education granted'. Darling viewed the new measure as 'the thin edge of the wedge', but was disappointed about the lack of concessions on gifts, which he regarded as more important. The heads' efforts had won them half a loaf. Opperman assured him that all that could be done would be done 'by quite a number of Members' to secure the measure on gifts. Menzies had also talked about this with Brown and Gorton. Two years later in 1954, when the heads received the other half of the loaf, Darling expressed his gratitude to Menzies and the treasurer for the tax concession on gifts. This provision, admittedly, would 'help the Roman Catholics more than it will us but that is because they take Education more seriously and are more generous'. It also meant that other denominations, provided that they had the courage, had help in building new schools. Doing so would help preserve the balance between church schools and state schools, 'a balance which seems to me of the greatest possible importance to the future of the country'.[17]

This entire episode indicated the ease of access to power facilitated by conservative connections, yet Darling had also cosied up previously to Labor politicians, including Evatt, Calwell, Dedman, Field and Crean. His strategy was to keep communication lines open, but was also evidence of the significance that he attached to friendship and personal relations in overriding political divisions. Even though he and Dedman (then his MHR and Minister for Defence) had disagreed about the appointment of W.J. McKell (the former Labor premier of New South Wales) to succeed the Duke of Gloucester as governor-general, for example, the two men hit it off: a man of integrity, intelligent and passionate for the underprivileged was how Darling later described Dedman. In 1946, when the school had applied to the prices commissioner for permission to increase the fees, Darling had sought him out. Later, he thanked Dedman for his help, but was keen to signal that 'I was not in anyway asking you to use your influence over the decision, which would have been most improper'; rather, 'we were seriously troubled by the delay in getting a decision at all, and your intervention has been a very great help in this matter'. Then, in 1948, he notified Dedman of his trip to England and of his availability to assist Calwell (Minister for Immigration) if required. (Darling knew the Labour peer and Atlee government minister, Lord Pakenham, from his Ministry of Information days.) Eligibility for immigration, he told Dedman, ought to include displaced and expelled persons from Germany, and he was 'almost obsessed with the idea of bringing out much larger quantities of orphan children to this country so as to develop it and build it'. He later thanked Dedman for arranging a meeting with Calwell and, urged him to 'let me know about his son who was so seriously ill at that time'. (Darling's concern mirrored that of Casey who, after frantically trying to locate doctors for the eleven-year-old dying of leukaemia, developed a close friendship with Calwell.)[18]

Friendship and personal relations also applied to religion, as illustrated by Darling's bond with Hackett. With his middle-class Kilkenny upbringing, in which the cultural values influencing him were both English and Irish, Father William Philip Hackett SJ was, like Darling, at 'ease in crossing the sectarian divide'. Among conservatives, Hackett befriended Lord Somers (Governor of Victoria, 1926–31) and Menzies, and he shared with Darling a loathing of competitive school sports. In his periodic urgings to Darling about the dangers of communism, Xavier's former 'maverick rector' (as his biographer labelled him), positioned as he was to Darling's right, was an intellectual counter-foil to Manning Clark. Hackett had founded and built up the Central Catholic Library, an access point to a young Catholic intellectual network anchored on the Campion Society and the *Catholic Worker*. He was the confidant and right-hand man of the formidable Daniel Mannix, a fellow Irishman and since 1913 the Catholic Archbishop of Melbourne. In 1951, Mannix appointed him as ecclesiastical assistant to the National Secretariat for Catholic Action. In this web of connections, Hackett was at the heart of the fight against communism, the leadership of which became associated with a public identity, B.A. (Bob) Santamaria. With unlimited access to Mannix, by the late 1940s Hackett was a person of considerable influence.[19]

Every so often Hackett would importune Darling—no doubt (with his well-known sense of humour) chuckling privately at the salutation 'My dear Darling'. In 1948, he impressed upon his friend the danger of the 'Red Menace', which he thought was worse than ever, and wondered whether Darling had read *I Chose Freedom*, by Victor Kravchenko (a Soviet defector). Shortly afterwards, he thought that 'Communist pressure is near or has reached its maximum'. Apologising for his inability to attend the Corio joint conference of headmasters (due to a bad heart), he said that:

> I wanted to talk you about the two movements engaged in controlling them. Now they (the Comms) can't go very far. They will meet with very definite opposition. Still our efforts are concentrating on wresting the unions from red control. This is a difficult and costly job. The bishops give us £6000 per annum—this is about half enough.

Could Australian youths of all classes, he asked, be made aware of the need to serve God loyally? In his somewhat eccentric way, Hackett poured into the short, sharp staccato-like sentences of his letters his current or even momentary preoccupations. Two years later (after the federal election) he was concerned about the public schools' future: wouldn't the elimination of religion from them lead in large degree to 'incipient anarchy'? Up to the present, he said, 'the State does not penalise the Comm's' so 'why should they penalise religious schools'? Another 'menace' was unlimited immigration: did Darling know 'anything of Communistic activity among the new arrivals'? All displaced persons and émigrés could easily become 'raw material for subversive propaganda'. 'Can this be countered?' he inquired. He supposed that 'your people' (Menzies' government?) were 'doing something' about it, but he did not wish to see 'Geelong Grammar School turned into an institution—run by the reds—for the diffusion of atheism'. For the time being, the other thoughts surging through his head would have to be 'put in celophane [sic] till we meet'. Later still, he wrote: 'despite your work at Corio and my work in Collins St. disaster closes in on all sides', and he wondered whether 'a spiritual awakening may stave off if not avoid the disaster', but would there be such an awakening?[20]

When Hackett died in 1954, Darling was shocked by the tragic circumstances. On a wet wintry night, Hackett was knocked down by a taxi when crossing a busy road in the Melbourne suburb of Kew. Described as a 'feckless jay-walker', the injuries to Hackett were horrendous (broken legs, pelvis and ribs). He lingered on for a week in semi-consciousness in St Vincent's Hospital before dying on 9 July. He was seventy-six. His death provided a rare occasion for Darling to communicate with Mannix. His touching note said:

> Please forgive me for writing to you without knowing you—but I cannot let my dear Father Hackett's death pass without telling someone how much I loved him and I know that you will be missing him greatly. When he was at Xavier he endeared himself to us all but I think that I knew him best and found him unfailingly stimulating and spiritually comforting. He had the kind of mind which I most appreciate and a bubbling sense of humour which made him a perfect companion. We were lucky to know two such people as him and Rolland and I have learned a lot and profited greatly from both of them.

If it isn't 'too blasphemous', he added, 'I like to think of him in Heaven', as there were not many people in the world 'who would feel at all at home in such an atmosphere, but certainly Father Hackett will be one who will'. Hackett's death was a personal loss for His Grace and the Catholic community that would be shared by 'many who are 'in a sense' outside it'.[21]

As for Hackett's wish that GGS not be run by 'Reds', there was a rumour to that effect doing the rounds. It was seven years or so since the *Corian* editorial and similar allegations, but this time the source was Sydney. In early 1950, John Dunlop (Margaret's cousin and an F.E. Brown old boy) dined with a company general manager (known to Darling) who remarked that GGS had changed a lot 'since your day, from what I hear'. Dunlop then jested about the amount of work demanded of pre-Darling boys and 'the many improvements instituted by you'. No, his companion had said, '"I was referring to the talk one hears as to left-wing bias" (that wasn't his phrase, I can't remember it exactly, but it meant that), "but no doubt you know more about it than I do"'. Dunlop replied that such talk was 'all balls', except that it was not new, he reminded Darling for, 'as you will know well, similar things have been said in Sydney for a couple of years— or rather, were said a couple of years ago', although he presumed that he and others had killed them off. (An allusion, perhaps, to Vincent Fairfax's mention in 1948 that 'a very small number of reactionaries some times indicate their fear of the present school boys being allowed to hold more liberal views than were held by them when they were at school'.) But there was more. Dunlop's wife had attended a social function with the wives of business friends (including that of her husband's dinner companion), and during the meal a woman 'apparently went somewhat to town in an attack on your political beliefs and "dangerous indoctrination" of the young', or words to that effect. Her husband was an OGG whose son, like himself and his father before him, had been intended for GGS, except that hearing the 'rumours' and having visited Corio he had come away 'horrified' and enrolled the boy at Cranbrook. The tittle-tattling was serious enough to be nipped in the bud. As fate had it, the horrified old boy was a

C.A. Cameron fan who had visited Corio in 1939 during his brief occupancy of the throne and enquired about Darling: 'What sort of a head is he?' 'I hear conflicting reports at times and they disturb me a bit for one should not hear bad reports from there.'[22]

While such criticism was not new, Darling said, the odd thing was that it was prevalent now 'when I am a hardened conservative of over 50 and not in my early days out here' when 'there might have been some justification for it'. He was baffled. The only explanation was that some boys 'in rather prominent social positions' must have reacted against their background and the school 'in such a way as to and largely in order to, draw attention to themselves'. If the worst that GGS boys did during adolescence was to hold some unacceptable political views, then 'I do not think that they disgrace the school'. In fact, 'those who have no social conscience at all and waste their lives in idle dissipation seem to me infinitely worse'. (This, as Darling had indicated previously to Casey, was his default position on boys from conservative backgrounds holding radical views during adolescence.) Wasn't the whole point of a school to 'encourage people to think for themselves and certainly not to indoctrinate them with political views wither [sic] Conservative or Socialist'? And if they thought for themselves 'they won't all think alike':

> I hate Communism myself with my whole soul and I view with profound distrust the tendencies of Socialist governments, who do not realize that the only logical conclusion of their argument is in fact very much akin to Communism. But that does not mean I regard them as criminals or even as dishonest, nor that I do not regard myself as satisfied with the existing social and economic system, nor have I met any man of intelligence in either party who is.

He could not detect a disinclination on the part of old boys to enrol their sons, but this gossip had hit him where it hurt. In reply he devoted a page to his acceptability in the eyes of others, in particular the offspring of prominent Victorian families currently enrolled and others from interstate (including the sons of the brother of the horrified OGG), along with Casey's son, eight Canberra Liberals, and a swag of Establishment figures in business, the law, politics and the vice-regal sphere, all of whom would vouch for him. 'No! really it is a lot of rot' yet, while it 'does undoubtedly do harm to the school', it was difficult to see what to do about it. A 'very Conservative Vice-Chancellor of Oxford', familiar for many years with the products of the school, would scarcely have awarded him a doctorate 'if I had been really dangerous', he said. New South Wales enrolments might have fallen off recently (with the rebirth of Cranbrook under Hone and the incorporation of Tudor House into King's) but he would stick to his guns: boys had to think for themselves and he certainly had 'no intention of trying to turn them all out to pattern'.[23]

Wild accusations of heading up a nursery for Leftish subversion were annoying, but Darling's support of the *Call* initiative ought to have given them the lie. In the face of Cold War threats to national unity in early 1950s Australia, there were various options available to public worthies in elite circles. A statutory stick in the form of the Menzies' suppression legislation was one and another was to paper over divisions with patriotic appeals to national consensus. A prominent example was *A Call to the People of Australia* in 1951, the jubilee year of Federation. The *Call* was a single-page document signed by twelve prominent men: four senior heads of Christian churches, Rabbi Danglow (senior Jewish Chaplain for the Commonwealth) and five chief justices of the state supreme courts (but not New South Wales). Latham (Chief Justice of the High Court) refused to sign. The text was broadcast nationally on the ABC and more than 100 commercial radio stations on Remembrance Day evening, Sunday, 11 November, and reproduced in the next day's newspapers. The moving spirits included Darling's friend Herring, a *Call* signatory. As Director-General of Recruiting promoting armed services recruitment throughout Australia, Herring was convinced that a 'kind of moral dry rot had taken hold'. Another promoter was Paul Maguire, a South Australian Catholic activist and writer (friend of Hackett and Menzies' adviser at the Commonwealth conference of prime ministers in January) and the third was Menzies himself. While in London, he and Maguire devised a national campaign for mobilising Australians amid deteriorating international developments. Maguire then drafted the *Call* and approached Herring to head the initiative. Coming two months after the failed referendum on the dissolution of the Communist Party, the *Call* expressed a diet of hortatory pieties and was later described as an exercise in ideology-making by 'those charged with high responsibilities'. There was 'danger' everywhere for Australia, the signatories alleged and, with 'mortal enemies of mankind' threatening to sap the will, darken understanding and 'breed evil dissensions', a 'restoration of moral order' was required as the true basis of society. Australians were members, 'one of another', of a community to which all owed loyalty and service. Following this preamble, there were four assertions of belief, six specific calls (headed by the need to advance moral standards) and a New Testament injunction ('Fear God, honour the King') positioned above the signatures.[24]

Darling attended an occasional *Call* meeting but, apart from drafting a 500-word statement of Christian conviction for the organisers in 1953, his direct involvement was minimal. He was useful to Herring by relaying to him (in 1952) one enthusiast's suggestion that, 'following in a way on "The Call"', something ought to be done to mark the forthcoming coronation. This proposal crystallised around the idea of a pledge to serve the new monarch (inspired by a comment of Darling's about Princess Elizabeth in response to a newspaper letter of Casey's) that was eventually taken up on Empire Youth Sunday in 1953. At the same time, Darling capitalised on lingering post-*Call* euphoria by referring to it (a month after the *Call* broadcast) in his speech-day address where he made his strongest appeal to the GGS community since his 1945 speech—about the donkey paralysed by indecision between the hay bales—to exercise moral leadership. Historically, GGS had been expected to produce 'the future leaders of Australia' and boys had thought of themselves as leaders by right. It wasn't a right, he urged on his hearers, but 'an obligation' because most boys in the school 'are privileged' relative to the rest of the community. To seek their own good would be selfish, mean and despicable, and selfishness destroyed a democratic society. In high gear, he then said:

> Now, more than ever, at a time in the history of Australia when it has been judged necessary by the responsible leaders of the community to issue a Call to the Nation to abandon its selfish and unmoral materialism, it lies upon us whose education makes us capable of understanding that call to be the first to respond to it, and to accept the leadership which such a response involves. For it is above all, moral leadership which is required; that is a refusal to accept the low judgment of the many in matters of right and wrong in conduct, of good and bad in taste, and in the willing recognition of national and social duty.

There was nothing undemocratic about such leadership: in fact, it was the only way in which democracy could survive. The real threat to 'our way of life' was not 'revolutionary Communism' but 'the spirit behind this Communism': a two-headed monster of materialism and intolerance proclaimed by Marxist philosophy or, in simpler terms, selfishness in personal ambitions and the refusal (or fear) of honest thinking. Such evils could only be conquered by their opposites. With this justification about leadership and morality, he would then go on to launch his special enterprise.[25]

Communism in the 1950s was cited as a symptom of social and cultural ills in a number of Darling's twenty-five or so surviving addresses and speakers' notes. In 1951, for example, in 'Crisis and Opportunity', he insisted (to Traralgon Apex) that, while communism's threat was an obvious feature of the public landscape, it was not the 'basic disease'. To the extent that Australians lost faith in themselves and their institutions, then Marxist doctrine might prosper. In Ballarat in mid-1952 (to a Home and Family Week function) he suggested that this particular '-ism' was merely the outward sign of something 'more subtle and serious': an 'attack on all individuality'. The authoritarian answer to the problems of the age was to force people to cooperate for the common good and hope that they would come to like it, whereas Christianity bestowed an inherent right to choose. He emphasised the overriding importance of mutual love, because love drew out love in response. The good family, this 'interdependence of independent souls bound together by love', was a microcosm of a society that taught its members to treat all people as God said that they ought to be treated. A good society was one in which liberty and order were possible. While conceding that communism may have been a geographical threat to Australia, he asserted (to Colac Rotary

Club) that its real threat was to standards and thinking. In 1954, he reiterated (to Apex) that the problem was not communism, but the disease underlying it: frivolity in standards of taste and leisure, contempt for things of the mind, dislike of the highbrow, apathy towards and failure to face up to the realities of the crisis confronting the nation, lack of national unity, and lack of organic life in cities and the country. What he termed the 'Each for himself interpretation of democratic liberty' was not a sufficient alternative to communism. In the same year (Horsham High School speech night) he insisted that more than anything the world needed men and women who 'are sensitive in conscience and yet have the courage to fight for what they believe to be right'. And finally, in 'Education for the crisis' (Hamilton, Education Week) he said that the heart of communism was materialistically based thought and that the danger it presented was the loss of 'our very liberty of thought, or rather the power to think at all'.[26]

To avoid even passing mention of the ideological controversies of the day was not easy when commenting on 1950s Australian democracy and society. This was as true, in Darling's case, of his addresses to learned societies as in his speeches to community groups. Towards the end of his Röntgen Oration ('On looking beneath the surface of things') to the College of Radiologists of Australasia in late 1954, for example, he said that contemporary society's aimlessness should be condemned. He focused on the dichotomy between scientific and religious thinking, and the 'multiplicity of fragmented specialization' of knowledge, for which his solution was the 'teleological conception of evolution'—an intriguing choice, because a book that popularised this idea, *The Phenomenon of Man* (by the Catholic palaeontologist, Father Pierre Teilhard de Chardin), was still a year from publication and four years from an English translation. Just as a boy 'goes wrong' when losing his sense of purpose, so too does 'a democratic society as a whole', he said, unlike 'our Communist opponents' who have the coherence and sense of direction 'almost wholly lacking in the western world':

> Consider England before and after Dunkirk and you cannot fail to realize the resolution which such purpose gives. The problem of discovering for our liberal democratic society with its heritage of *laissez-faire*, a purpose as clear and as compelling as Communism is indubitably one of the greatest needs of our time. Only in the light of such a discovered purpose can we lead Australia into an attitude of mind which is prepared for sacrifice and service.

Without discovery of such a purpose, Darling could see only disintegration of conflicting selfishness, and chaos stemming from individual greed and laziness, so that 'we shall not hold this country for long'. Donning a philosophical mantle, he once more addressed parts–whole relations that he tried to subsume within a Christian cosmology. Scientists might ask how and theologians why, but the wholeness of life demanded that both questions be asked and answered: it made no sense to divide man into parts and to make him whole by means of arithmetic computation. The story that was known as evolution on the one hand and as creation on the other had to be comprehended as one, including 'its end no less than its beginning'. St Paul had reconciled the two. The teleology of the creator was that mankind was whole and healthy only when it was Christ-like, while the purpose of evolution for mankind was to attain perfection by growing into the measure of the stature of Christ.[27]

Jostling for a place in Darling's mindset alongside teleological evolution was imperialism, particularly while striving to build links with Asia. A prominent element of this strand was race. The reasoning associated with this idea and its connection to empire and nation were tricky for him. Race was first mentioned publicly in his 1946 'English record' speech where he had attacked the 'sin of racial pride'. As for the English race, English made little sense as a unitary idea because it was a nationality comprising a 'strange amalgam' of thirteen 'crossbred strain[s]'—Celts, Teutons and Angles among others—so that it could claim 'no purity of stock'. But the notion of a non-white person was more complicated. In the 1949 elections, Darling's attitudes were put to the sword by the psychiatrist, missionary and Christian activist, Dr C.I. McLaren and he struggled. McLaren was a single-issue candidate standing against Calwell. His platform was uncompromising opposition to the 'Race & Colour Prejudice which informs the White Australia Policy' on the ground that it was 'quite un-Christian'. Would Darling chair his first public meeting? Emphatically no, Darling shot back. Why? Not because McLaren would not be a good member of parliament, or that Darling was critical of the his attack on the un-Christian basis of the policy, or that he was personally 'just a coward' and did not want to adopt a line of thinking that would get him into trouble, 'though that comes into it', but because he had enough on his plate already and because it wasn't sensible to chair a meeting:

> that is bound to take a lot of controversy and to identify myself, as I should have to, with a cause which I had not heard expounded and with which I might possibly not agree.

Ducking for cover, Darling said that opposition to the policy was not easy politically unless one was prepared to advocate racial intermarriage and 'the gradual merging of white and yellow into one race'. This was a view that he held 'so so tenuously and on the basis of so little scientific knowledge of the biological implications, that I am not prepared to propound it'. He was not sure whether he would like one of his daughters to marry 'an oriental, however cultured and Christian he might be' and he would prefer not to be tested. Finally, he was not a private person, so that 'whatever I do I almost have to do in the name of the School'. He knew that he was on the spot, he had questioned himself (and had even asked the VIth form for its advice) and he had experienced some unease.[28]

Race had practical import at Corio. In May 1946, when there were still forty-five boys at GGS from the wartime Asian influx, Darling considered it worthwhile to maintain this connection by appointing 'representatives in the East'. The two main categories of boys were the offspring of British families resident in Asia and indigenous Asians. With British boys, Darling was keen to maintain the link. With Asian lads, he was willing to admit them (as was the council), provided that it was permitted by Australian government policy. But he hesitated, due to the same problem experienced previously: the difficulties of guardianship during term holidays for all categories of overseas boys. He was also uncertain how happy Asian boys would be at Corio and whether or not they might be taken for granted by the other boys, except that somebody had to 'take the risk and make the experiment':

> I don't think that I have any prejudice against them as such, and I don't think that such prejudice would be found to exist. It is, however, unexplored country and I feel the need to be a little careful about it.

An added difficulty, he told Malcolm MacDonald (now governor-general of Malaya) was age. Two Chinese boys who expressed interest in enrolling in 1948 were in their twenties. (For age reasons, he also rejected a seventeen-year-old Thai prince.) Age fifteen had always been his preferred upper limit for admission and he was 'not in the least concerned' about race or nationality:

> Odd though it may sound, there is no racial feeling in Australia or very little, (the White Australia policy is economic in origin), and anyhow the good Chinese is usually so civilized that he can fit in anywhere.

In these comments to the boys' headmaster, Darling was making extraordinarily light of national attitudes on race, given that fourteen Malays and Indonesians were deported from Australia later in 1948 (fuelling Asian suspicions of diplomatic offers of scholarships for older students) and because a recent public opinion survey revealed deep-seated prejudice against non-English Europeans, let alone Asians.[29]

Officially, Far East boys at GGS were private overseas students. Until the drafting of Department of Immigration guidelines in 1950 there was no government policy. From that year private overseas students were eligible for initial entry to secondary school up until age nineteen. Thanks to the Australian consul general in Bangkok, there was soon a conveyor belt of Thai boys to Corio: two enrolled in 1949 and at least three others were in the pipeline. Darling said that 'we are really delighted with the boys' and would be 'very glad indeed to continue taking them', but language was a problem. It would be better, he advised the consul general, if more English language preparation occurred in Thailand. There was also a need for proficiency in Latin, a requirement for entry to the University of Cambridge (the Thais' favoured university). Latin exemption was possible for Far Eastern boys provided that they passed an examination in one of Arabic, Sanskrit, Chinese or Pali, languages which 'to the Siamese boys', said Darling wittily, were apparently 'equally Greek'. If these four were not realistic alternatives for them, then it had to be Latin, in which case they ought not come to Corio until they were sixteen and had already attempted to master it.[30]

At speech day on the Monday following the 1949 federal election, with Casey at his side (to present the prizes) Darling devoted part of his remarks to Asia. With characteristic apocalyptic urgency he described civilisation and the world as 'at a period of crisis'. As a Christian democracy 'pushed out into Asia', Australia's only chance of political survival was to 'so save ourselves by our exertions that we can save Asia by our example'. With South-East Asia likely to be the 'centre of the world crisis in the next twenty-five years', he envisaged Australia's response as:

> the sending of missionaries of every sort, not only preachers and priests but engineers, doctors, agriculturalists and schoolmasters, filled with the desire to tackle the most difficult problems wherever they are to be found, and winning by their services to Asia a respect and a gratitude for the Australian civilisation which produced them and sent them out.

Boys who responded were promised adventure, interest and a creative way of tackling the world's crisis and would be steered away from 'vulgar personal ambitions and greeds' to a realisation that they could play a part in history. The key word was 'missionaries'. Had the headmaster been requested to cite examples there were two. First, there was Eaton's work in Champawat, and second, the attempted rebuilding of the infrastructure of New Guinea Anglican missions destroyed during the war.[31]

GGS's New Guinea engagement was brief. Flushed with the local success of national service, Montgomery had contacted the Right Reverend Philip Strong (Bishop of New Guinea) with a view to exporting GGS's model to help rebuild 'some of the churches and stations lost during the war'. (Darling had first broached the idea with Strong in 1943.) Shortages of materials and experienced builders suggested that 'sending up to us a team of builders' would be welcome, but not for twelve months. Strong's enthusiasm was endorsed by his brother bishop, the Right Reverend G.H. Cranswick (chairman, Australian Board of Missions), who also urged Darling to bring to bear his influence on 'people in big places' to obtain materials. All over Papua there were buildings left by the departing armed forces, but no-one capable of relocating them. Strong floated the possibility of GGS preparing prefabricated sections of dwellings or schools and then sending them for assembly by teams of boys during school vacations. Sangara, he thought, might be the appropriate site because of the Anglicans martyred there in 1942. Despite intensive negotiations with Holyman during 1947, the high cost of air transport of boys (regular air service or charter) killed the proposal, and the school contributed financially to a reconstruction fund for the Martyrs' School.[32]

By 1951, Darling and the school were finally getting their act together. He had made a patchy speech-day attempt two years earlier to provide a manifesto for relations with Australia's northern neighbours. Darling had no strategy as such, but thought it out as he went along, groping for Christian imagery: 'a limb of Western Civilization pushed out into the middle of Asia' was one example of God's will for Australia; another was 'a white race in the middle of Asiatics' with a mission to provide technical aid. The two main focuses of interest became Malaya and Thailand. With Casey having replaced Spender (architect of the Colombo Plan) as Minister for External Affairs following the election in April, Darling got cracking. Delighted by his friend's appointment, he teased that he would be 'a continual worry to you from now onwards'. Speaking with his Universities Commission and university council hats on, he highlighted the urgent matter of providing hostels for Asian students to avoid them suffering the humiliation of 'being turned away over and over again by ignorant landladies, who refuse to house coloured peoples'. Having raised in university contexts this urgent need for student hostels, he was exasperated: 'in the good Australian way [this matter] is passed backwards and forwards because nobody will take the responsibility'. It was surely 'your responsibility and that of the Federal Government' to put a stop to this pass-the-parcel routine. (Few others could have traded on a friendship to speak so insistently with a senior member of the government.) Not only did Darling insist that all family applications from the Malay states be routed through the commissioner's office, but that the office had to 'extract from them, the relevant information which they often omit to tell, and also give me some estimate of the character and prospects of the applicants': age, educational standard, university intentions and their likelihood of achieving them, ability to pay the fees and possible holiday contacts in Australia.[33]

Of the two diplomatic agencies—Bangkok and Singapore—that Darling courted to play de facto roles in GGS's admissions process, the former was fertile ground, and the latter barren. A politely worded reply from the Singapore commissioner's office said that its business was not advice-giving but the processing of visa applications. In any case, when Malay boys came to the commission they were already armed with advice from students enrolled in Australia, so that GGS's interests would be better served by a background questionnaire for completion by the boys. Darling's badgering of Casey paid off, because he raised the issue of student accommodation and welfare as a matter of urgency with Menzies, while also alerting him that the Department of External Affairs had begun formalising the role of commissions and legations in the provision of advice about schools. In each instance, extracts from Darling's letter to Casey had been circulated. There were about 1100 students (primary, technical and university) paying for tuition in Australia, a figure well in excess of the number admitted under the newly created Colombo Plan. (There were some appalling examples of hardship being experienced.) For good measure, Casey also informed Menzies of his department's concern that difficulties experienced by students 'leave the way open to Communist influences' and there were 'already indications that this is happening'.[34]

In 1951, there was a South-East Asia exhibition at Corio. In the usual pattern, Darling decided and Montgomery provided. It opened on the first weekend in November, following which, thanks to the enthusiasm of General Ramsay, it was transported for a fortnight's viewing in December in the grounds of the Teachers' Training College. The five sections located in the classrooms included one devoted to the Colombo Plan. The aim was:

> to awaken interest in our neighbours, to show how they lived, how they were progressing, and in what ways, if any, we in Australia could play our part in assisting their progress

At the same time, the boys would be 'learning from them [the Asian countries] in quite a number of different ways'. Darling thought that if boys could focus their minds on the impoverished countries of Asia, then they 'might be spurred on to do something to help them'. By the end of the year, GGS had consolidated its Asia links: Geelong Grammar was the school of choice for Thai parents' sons, the Australian legation in Bangkok was advising Darling, and in the reputation stakes it believed that GGS was 'quite over-shadow[ing] those of all other Australian schools'. Yet there was a catch: while they were hearing GGS's message, Thai parents learnt of a dearth of vacancies at Corio. The problem was about to be solved, Darling advised the legation, because with an ambitious plan about to commence in 1953 senior school places would be available. There were 271 private primary and secondary Asian students in Australian schools at the beginning of 1952, about 230 from Malaya, Singapore, Brunei, Sarawak and Borneo, and another 22 from Thailand (8 at GGS later that year). A measure of the Commonwealth's ill preparedness for dealing with an Asian influx was the legation's request to Darling for advice about boarding alternatives to Corio, not merely for boys but also for girls. This information lacuna was also a commentary on the inadequacy of the schools' own preparation. Casey wanted to courier directly Darling's reports on Thai boys' scholastic progress (after rounding off 'anything that you have said so as not to cause worry in the parents' minds'). To do so afforded him some leverage, as a letter to 'these people now and again' has 'its political value', and it highlighted the welfare sensitivies of Asian boys resident in Australia. (The government of Thailand appointed an Australian-based student supervisor in 1952.) Darling's influence on overall developments is difficult to assess—Casey's three-page letter to Menzies indicated that Darling was not the only voice pleading the case for Asian students. Out of gratitude to his friend, Casey undertook on Darling's behalf (in 1953) to persuade the Commonwealth Relations Office in London to tackle the 'rather narrow-minded attitude of the people at Cambridge' concerning the language entry requirement that was a headache for Asian boys.[35]

If that is what it was, narrow-mindedness would have been unfortunate had it persisted as Darling maintained strong connections with a number of Oxbridge colleges. Such links were the capstone of his imperial mental edifice. Like Phelps at Oriel, although from the reverse geographical position of Antichthon (Cicero's 'southern zone' of Earth, as said at the conferring of Darling's DCL in 1948), he was at the hub of an imperial diaspora of OGG Oxbridge graduates, as he said in 1938:

> It seems to me of some importance from an imperial point of view that there should be the possibility of entrance from Australia into good Colleges at Oxford and Cambridge. It is also desirable, I think, that these boys should be split up amongst the Colleges and not congregated together, and for that reason I have tried to establish connections with different Colleges.

Darling made it his business to know personally a number of the Oxbridge masters, provosts and tutors, because headmasters' recommendations for admission to a college carried weight. At Oxford, for example, about ninety overseas students went up each year, a figure which, when spread across the twenty-two colleges for men at the end of the war, meant that the competition for admission from any one country, let alone from one within the imperial fold or even a single school, was very tough. Apart from an applicant's record, testimonials on character and ability were 'necessary credentials' for overseas applicants' admission to Oxford. The reputation of a headmaster, his school, and the track record of previous old boys' admissions were critical in such circumstances. In one instance, Darling described the relationship as 'an understanding' that the college in question would take up to two boys annually on the strength of his say-so. In another instance a college head jested that 'your flattering remarks about this College and about me carry weight!' When new connections had to be built up, reputably sourced opinions could usually be called on to attest to one's soundness:

> I think that if you cared to enquire about the school and me personally from the Provost of Oriel, the Principal of Brasenose or the President of Magdalen, they would give us reasonably honourable commendation.

Firsthand knowledge of GGS might help as well: 'Sir Henry Tizard, who has actually been to the school, would probably be the best of these [at Cambridge]'.[36]

A gentleman's word may still have been his bond, but bonds aside, these examples speak to the potential fragility of the college–school connection, although the relationship was not uni-directional (that is, Darling as a dominion supplicant), because college heads courted school heads as well. 'I shall always be glad to receive good candidates from Geelong, if you have any whom you would like to send us', wrote a new Oxford college head. Others said: 'As you know there are few things I value more than the connection between Brasenose and Geelong' and:

> I am always very happy to have Australians and I should like the Geelong–Clare connexion to start again. It is a great help to me to know that you will only urge me to take really good men and you may be sure that any men you strongly advise me to take I will always do so if I possibly can.

In postwar England these recruitment networks were upset by applications from repatriated servicemen: these inflated the potential admission numbers and put pressure on already scarce accommodation. (In 1948, one Oxford college head told Darling that he had rejected about 900 applications for October.) An added complication by the early 1950s, Darling thought, particularly for boys wanting to enter Oxbridge colleges directly from their schools, was the increased pressure on places due to the greater availability of county scholarships. But when all else failed, an appeal to a boy's good and the greater imperial good might just swing a decision his way. Some dominion boys, Darling admitted, might not be 'top draw[er]' and would not contribute a lot to the life of their college and university. But in the longer run 'they do bring back something' of significance for 'the formation of standards in this country', and for that reason it was important for England and Australia to continue keeping in step.[37]

While Darling was a man who had, by this time, consolidated power through networks that were also almost exclusively male and who sought to exercise influence by educating young men, it would in fact be a high-profile young woman in the early 1950s who would keep both countries in step. For loyalists at this time, the apotheosis of their aspirations and the most tangible expression of their imperial enthusiasm were captured by the coronation of a new monarch, the youthful Princess Elizabeth. In a service of glittering splendour at Westminster Abbey, the ceremony took place on 2 June 1953, a day of pouring rain. Not only had GGS been well represented in the new Parliament of 1950, but both GGS and its headmaster had a close, albeit indirect, connection with the grandeur of this day. Darling's former headmaster, the Archbishop of Canterbury, officiated and placed the crown on the young queen's head, and the same Geoffrey Fisher had chosen as director of music for the coronation service the man once appointed by his former pupil as director of music at Corio, the then organist of Westminster Abbey, William McKie. Six weeks before the great day, McKie told Darling that he was relishing his new responsibilities: 'It is fun here now, and I must say I am enjoying the Coronation immensely'. Earlier in 1950, during his world tour Fisher had observed firsthand the fruits of his former pupil's handiwork. Then, some seven or eight months after her coronation, the new monarch visited her far-flung Commonwealth, including Australia. If it is exaggerating slightly to suggest that these events were a sign for GGS's headmaster that God was in his heaven and all was well, then at least he was able not merely to toast a new queen, but he also had a government in power in Canberra that was to his liking, and that was headed by a leader who was even more to his liking. And just as some imperial apologists looked to her Britannic Majesty to inspire a new age of Elizabeth, hopes were harboured at Corio that a new idea of Darling's might revitalise GGS, although few people could have imagined that it would eventually result in closer ties between royalty and the school. This idea, Darling's enterprise, his ambitious plan, was Timbertop.[38]

A GREAT COMMON ENTERPRISE

1951–1961

'And that', put in the Director sententiously, 'that is the secret of happiness and virtue—liking what you've got to do. All conditioning aims at that: making people like their unescapable social destiny'.

Aldous Huxley, *Brave New World*

Character-training describes programs and activities designed to instil in young people varying combinations of moral rectitude and physical prowess. At Darling's instigation, GGS created its own customised character-training: the Sparta project, a Hellenic title with warrior overtones that was soon replaced by a blander southern hemisphere word, Timbertop—a mountain. The Timbertop initiative made the headmaster an undisputed educational innovator. Perversely, the word that embedded itself initially in the consciousness of overseas observers was Timbertops—in confusion with Treetops, the Kenyan tree-lodge visited by Princess Elizabeth and the Duke of Edinburgh on the day of her father's death in February 1952. Bland the name may have been, but the location was stunning and the concept's potential far-reaching. Within two months of Darling outlining his idea to council in June 1951, nine possible sites had been reduced to two near Mansfield, where Colman's Australian Estates agent (with the assistance of the Ritchies at nearby Delatite) had made discreet enquiries about land. These were the Timbertop Creek paddock (6 kilometres east of Merrijig and adjacent to the Mount Buller Road) and the Orchard Block (a site threatened by the imminent enlargement of the Eildon Weir). Darling preferred the former. With its eye on a speech-day announcement, council endorsed the new venture in October, approved the site, authorised land purchases and agreed on the name—decisions 'almost as important in the history of the school as the decision to move out to Corio'.[1]

The site was an inspired choice. It comprised 200 hectares (and a leasehold of another 485 hectares) 600 metres above sea level on the northern side of the Great Dividing Range—sunnier and with less rainfall than a south-facing position. This location was also within reach of Mansfield and its rail connection to Melbourne, which would facilitate transport to and from Corio. Timbertop Creek formed a natural site boundary on a north-west to south-east axis and supplied fresh water. Lightly wooded terrain rose gently from the creek and then more steeply on a forested slope up the face of Mount Timbertop, 1200 metres high at the summit. The surrounding ranges were the watershed of the Delatite and Howqua rivers to the north and south of Mount Timbertop respectively. To the immediate east was the Mount Buller alpine village, Victoria's premier skiing resort. It was a breathtakingly picturesque area comprising dense bushland and pristine forest with picture-postcard vistas in every direction from the surrounding peaks, which were snow-capped in winter. The virgin countryside provided mountaineering enthusiasts with numerous walking tracks in valleys and along craggy escarpments and, with its generously endowed native flora, was 'one of the most perfect areas possible in which to build our school'.[2]

There were a number of elements in the making of Timbertop. First, Darling had finally sorted out his personal priorities and ambitions:

> As one gets older I think one realizes more fully the truth that one 'can only light a little candle to the glory of God' and that adequate stewardship must probably be content with the sphere limited by one's personal contacts. While I may have had great ideas of being an influence in the educational and political life of the country I am now much more content to understand that the boys actually in the school at any given time are my main responsibility and opportunity.

Feeling 'very much older', however, and unable to work 'so quickly or recover so rapidly from crises', Darling thought that his grip on the school was loosening: 'organization and administration tend to crowd out the more valuable personal work' and it was 'very difficult to get out of the office'. He was tired of waging a 'continuous battle against the tentacles of the machine, with examinations, public school sport, out of school activities all the result of enfolding and cramping the boy himself'. A new peak might lift him from his uncomfortable plateau:

> Briefly [the idea] is to take a whole year of boys (14½–15½ probably), buy a property just under the mountains in the real bush and send them there to do a year of the[ir] education in harder but more natural surroundings outside the claims of the machine.

The purgative purpose of this 'epoch-making' idea was to strengthen boys' bodies and their wills, help them conquer their physical fears and satisfy their 'natural instinct for the earth'.[3]

Because it would also alleviate Corio's desperate shortage of space, Timbertop was an expedient initiative, which is why Darling later attributed it to 'practical difficulties of the school rather than as a result of any abstract educational theory'. The escalation of tuition fees in 1950 and 1951 precluded the dispersal of costs in a boarding school 'over large numbers of day boys'. Such were the pressures of being 'terribly full next term', Darling told Colman in December 1951, that a predicted excess enrolment of fifty-three boys would impose an intolerable accommodation strain. The new site was to be constructed by minimising expenses: no domestic service and ensuring that 'everything should be done' to eliminate work completed by paid labour. There would be no 'brick or stone or unalterable buildings which bind posterity'. The design and materials would suit the setting, and the self-contained nature of the mountain school would be operationally distinctive. Balcombe Griffiths (council chairman and an architect) explained to the Old Geelong Grammarians Association in 1952 that Timbertop's development was also an insurance policy: if on its present site the school felt 'pushed out' by encroaching industrial development, then the new venture 'might provide a future for it'. Apart from that, he said, the buildings were out of date, expensive and difficult to operate. The pay-off from the relief afforded an overcrowded Corio by Timbertop was compelling: Darling told council that the master:senior boy ratio in 1950 was 1:16.8, 1:17.9 in 1951 and 1:18.9 in 1952, but with Timbertop up and running it would fall to 1:14.75 and impose less pressure on housemasters.[4]

There were no Australian precedents on the proposed scale of Timbertop and few globally, apart from an Outward Bound mountain school (opened in 1950) at Eskdale, England (followed by a second at Ullswater in 1955 and another in 1956 at Baad, Austria). If there was a model, then it was probably Gordonstoun in Moray, Scotland. (Subsequent public awareness of Timbertop in and beyond Australia grew following the presence in 1966 of a famous Gordonstoun student: Charles, Prince of Wales.) Gordonstoun's founder was an expatriate German, Kurt Hahn, headmaster in 1939 when the Duke of Edinburgh was head boy. Hahn had fled the Nazis in 1933, and in an article in 1934 informed English-speaking educators of his earlier coeducational boarding school experiment at Salem (near Lake Constance, Baden). Barney Hutton had drawn Darling's attention to this article. Before Darling met Hahn in England in 1955, his key information source was a Gordonstoun housemaster, Colonel Freddie Spencer Chapman (adventurer, explorer, author and executive director of Outward Bound), whom he met while Chapman was in Australia as part of a commando-training mission (at Wilsons Promontory). Chapman visited Corio in mid-1941. (He also got to know Peggy Fairbairn, widow of Jim and, according to his biographer, nearly married her.) He was 'tremendously impressed by Geelong'—an assessment that Darling proudly confided to Browne—and noted how 'the boys resemble Gordonstoun boys far more closely than the products of other public schools at home. What a country for Moray Badge and Gordonstoun activities!'[5]

In April 1951, council had a hint of what to expect when Darling cited this passage from a recent Hahn BBC broadcast—'the most compelling reason' (he said later) for Timbertop:

> the so-called deformity of puberty had been considered by doctors and educators as unavoidable. I deny this. You can avoid these loutish years, that dim and cantankerous period when even the movements become awkward and sluggish; you can preserve a child's strength, the undefeatable spirit, the power of compassion, the eager curiosity, the joy of movement—on one condition: that you kindle on the threshold of puberty and subsequently sustain, the non-poisonous passions; the zest for building, the craving for great adventure, the joy of research, the love of painting, music or writing, the devotion to any skill demanding care and victorious patience.

Darling disclaimed originality when justifying Timbertop to the school community and aligned it with Hahn's Salem, Gordonstoun and Outward Bound. The novel part of the idea was described subsequently as an 'attempt to fit the project into the framework of a very orthodox traditional boarding-school'. Others begged to differ. George Turner knew Hahn well and detected a significant point of difference between the two men. Hahn's starting point was the doctrine of the so-called 'grande passion'—the alleged freeing of latent capacities from the 'emotional bondage' of adolescence. Even though Hahn's doctrine had been 'useful & stimulating', Turner was doubtful. Sometimes it provided a clue to understanding young men's developmental needs but not generally, whereas Darling's idea of 'the discovery of personal confidence', he reassured his friend, was 'truer'.[6]

The final justification for Timbertop was that it would better enable GGS to fulfil its self-proclaimed mission of moral leadership to and for the nation. On speech day 1951 (when promoting the *Call*), with his friend Russell Grimwade present, Darling unveiled his latest, most ambitious and far-reaching plan. He had devised a scheme that would give GGS a new edge—'something more than what we have already'—was in keeping with the school's tradition of outdoor pursuits and links with the natural world, and would also produce a cadre of national leaders. A pamphlet outlining Darling's proposal was distributed to parents and old boys. Timbertop would be as self-supporting as possible, emphasise the development of individual self-dependence and initiative, and foster a love of the land. The dispatch to the new site of about 100 middle dormitory boys would also alleviate 'in one glorious hit' the school's desperate overcrowding. The scheme illustrated how periodic adjustment renewed institutional vitality: GGS had to change if it was to continue to be 'an abiding influence in the life of Australia' and simultaneously preserve 'its true spirit and tradition'. In giving it his stamp of approval, Grimwade was right on message: in the forested Timbertop environment, every boy would have a better chance of development and those boys with qualities of leadership 'will show up better and sooner than they would in orthodox surroundings'.[7]

With the hearts-and-minds battle underway, Darling still had to find the capital—by end of 1952 the estimated cost had blown out to £115,000. When AMP refused to provide a loan, Darling moaned to Black that 'every progressive scheme for the last 21 years has been held up in this way by the necessity for haggling'. Either that or a scheme had been 'spoilt in the end' because the council had gone ahead without sufficient money 'to do it properly'. AMP's refusal was 'a great shock', he told Geoffrey Brown: whenever one did anything, one was always 'at the mercy of the rich and probably stupid people who control money'. In the depths of gloom, he was reminded by Sylvia Ritchie that when she had been feeling flat he quoted the C.S. Lewis antidote (in *The Screwtape Letters*): the law of undulations. In desperation, Darling approached Sir George Nicholas for a £60,000 loan to pay for the buildings and equipment but, without 'any money lying idle', the latter declined. Eventually, in late 1951 AMP (to which GGS's debt was already £129,000) agreed to lend £20,000 provided that the school raised £40,000 through endowments. There was no alternative to yet another financial appeal to the parents and OGGs.[8]

The disappointing initial response to the speech-day appeal was £3000 or so in gifts and promised donations, considerably less than Darling hoped for but, Black reassured him, 'irrespective of yesterday's result', he and Richardson were adamant that '<u>we go on</u>'. An initial trickle of donations soon became a steady stream. Some were remarkably generous: Black gave an interest-free loan of £350 for ten years and soon there was another interest-free offer of £1000—later in the year one donor committed a hefty £5000. By March, £24,000 was in the kitty; by May, £40,000 had been received or promised. Although accolades, wishes of success and promises of money from OGGs poured in early in 1952, the euphoria was not universal. On OGGA day in March, with 300 people present, Darling had had to hose down rumour-mongering about Timbertop while Black was conscious of an undercurrent of 'stupid criticisms' to be rebutted. 'Old Boy (Vintage 1924)' dealt with these parental and OGG anxieties in the May issue of the *Corian*—including suggestions that the entire school would eventually be relocated to Timbertop, there would be no sport, it would be like an army camp, the site was in 'hillbilly mountain country', the quality of education would suffer, and the council had rushed into a decision. His sentiments were endorsed by an appeal from Darling for unanimity.[9]

Site work commenced during Easter 1952. About sixty boys and masters (including the headmaster) were encamped at Timbertop by Maundy Thursday. Work gangs cleared the terrain, erected fences, built garages and cut wood. After a worship service on Good Friday morning, half the party climbed Mount Timbertop on a very hot afternoon and erected a cross at the summit. On Easter Day, Darling preached the sermon at St John's, Mansfield—which commenced a lasting association between the school and the parish. A second work camp in May was dogged by inclement weather (1952 was one of wettest years on record) and Darling pronounced it 'a real disaster'—'a Dunkirk when we needed an Alamein'. Contracts for building construction and an access road had been let but, although some work had commenced, overall progress was patchy. The plan was for two groups of boys to spend six months away from Corio, with the first in residence in February 1953, but Darling was still wondering whether to proceed. Despite a snowfall (deep enough for tobogganing) some construction work was completed during the August camp. Thereafter there were weekend working parties of boys and workmen, and another camp over Christmas. Further construction contracts had been let (for a kitchen, sanatorium, domestic quarters, garages and single masters' accommodation) and two quarters for married masters were nearing completion. The first unit had been lined, wired and plumbed, and two others were being built. Sewerage pipes were laid and a septic tank installed, although a water pipeline trench was still being dug, roads were incomplete and work on a diesel plant to generate electricity would not commence until the new year.[10]

February 1953 was the official start date. Who would be in charge? Montgomery, of course, although momentarily Darling had considered the footloose Chapman, who had just resigned as head of the King Alfred School in Plön, West Germany. The latter had enthused about Darling's 'exciting new experiment in the mountains' and wondered how it would turn out. He was tired of working in England because for 'this generation' the academic public school had run its race and he disdained comprehensive schooling. Darling's aerogram reply (not mailed) said that he had 'very nearly had the temerity to ask you to take on Timbertop yourself but [I] thought that you were completely tied'. Montgomery or Mont (Basher to the boys) was Darling's factotum 'when anything practical needed to be done'. Manifold thought that 'there is a good deal in Montgomery': intensely practical, 'a big chap, with a very domineering manner and a very straight way of talking', and a proven organiser and supervisor of boys' outdoor pursuits (national service, forestry camps, fruit-picking, school pageants and building construction). Until he retired in 1963, Montgomery was the founding housemaster (and master) of Timbertop. His job, after Darling is supposed to have said 'I want you to buy me a mountain', was to turn the idea into reality. They were chalk and cheese—a rough-hewn Australian larrikin and an English public school gentleman—and the succeeding decade bore witness again to their odd couple–style relationship, but on this occasion the stakes were higher when Montgomery exercised his delegated authority: the new venture's success depended substantially on him.[11]

Montgomery's job was to shape the boys' development beyond the strictures of 'the machine'—or, as the *Corian* said, Timbertop would neutralise the tendency for Corio boys to be 'levelled out with the mass'. Darling's four selling points to the parents were that the challenging natural environment would foster their sons' physical and moral development, the boys would be responsible for the operation of Timbertop (no domestic or other staff) and therefore more self-reliant than at Corio, the responsibility of looking after themselves would develop their capabilities, and the harsh physical conditions and challenges of the terrain should soon convince them that they were able to surmount difficulties, and 'overcome the weakness of their bodies'. They would also learn to be independent, Darling believed, which should 'give them the confidence derived from the knowledge that they can be so'—Turner's point about his departure from Hahn:

> It is believed that this self-confidence will be transferred into all departments
> of their lives, giving them courage in tackling difficulties in school work and,
> later, to take the responsibility of leadership in all sorts of public opinion.

Finally, living close to nature would free boys from the dominance of an urban environment, and enrich their lives by permitting them to experience the joys of fishing, birdwatching, mountain climbing and hiking. Montgomery's translation of these ideas into the fabric and pulse of a new school would not be easy, because building materials were in short supply and council was keeping a lid on expenses. The condition of the access roads and tracks was dreadful—mud, slush, potholes and ditches—such that as late as December 1952 (just prior to the first thirty-five boys' arrival), building materials had to brought in from the main road by tractor and trailer. Until the installation of a telephone line in 1953, communication with the outside world was difficult. Despite these obstacles, Darling insisted on speech day in 1952 that 'the back of it is broken and it is going to be a great success'. He was committed to opening on schedule and, while concerned about insufficient funding, remained quietly confident. Thanks to newspaper publicity and Timbertop's inclusion in new maps of the region, awareness of the school was growing. The project, Darling told Bickersteth, was 'a sort of holy madness', and a pilgrimage destination for parents, OGGs and Darling's own circle of intimates.[12]

The self-governing units were constructed by the boys from locally milled timber. Each unit accommodated twelve boys and consisted of a living room and fireplace, dormitory, pantry, boiler room, changing room, bathroom and lavatory. Montgomery said that the early signs justified Darling's optimism:

> The first term has shown that the method of allowing boys to 'run themselves'
> as much as possible is most successful. Two boys are elected each month
> from each Unit, and act as spokesmen for their Unit, and are responsible for
> organisation and general 'looking after' of their own interests. Much valuable
> information has been forthcoming in the form of suggestions and requests,
> all of which have gone towards the better working of the School … Because
> of this method of running, discipline, as such, is hardly apparent, and with
> the feeling that it is 'our' School and not 'the School', there is little necessity
> to suggest ways and means whereby boys should take more care of furniture,
> books, and a hundred and one things which are so often badly treated.

Timbertop traditions were also taking root, such as the weekend hike and camp in which three boys completed a 'comparatively ambitious' return journey of more about 50 kilometres. These were a variation on Corio's Saturday parties: bemoaned by the *Corian* in 1948 as a lapsed tradition (due to such popular pastimes as sun-bathing and listening to the radio, but mostly because of weekend sporting demands). Four months of congenial weather facilitated the genesis of civilisation by the end of first term 1953. The untiring assistance of the manager of a nearby sawmill (Harold Doughty) enabled the access road's completion, construction of a bridge over Timbertop Creek and a road around the site. Transportation to and from was a logistical exercise: each group of returning boys was assembled at Mansfield station at 7.40 am for the five-hour rail-motor trip to Melbourne and the final leg to Corio station. Incoming boys, however, had to be brought by a special rail service (the regular evening train arrived too late at Mansfield). In readiness for the second batch of seventy-two boys (July 1953), the main block of buildings was nearly finished, the units and houses were supplied with water, a 4.5-metre-deep dam had been dug, a septic tank was operational and electric light would be ready for second term. On the eve of the July changeover, Darling's report to council brimmed with glee: 'the news from Timbertop is good'. In company with Denys Hake and his wife, he and Margaret had just spent a few days on site. Hake was bowled over and some of the first batch of boys' parents were full of praise. 'Black Jnr. arrived home yesterday looking a picture of health. He is most enthusiastic about Timbertop', his father reported, and 'I am only sorry that he won't have a full year there—one half term has made a big difference to him'.[13]

Finance was still a major concern—Darling estimated that another £55,000 was needed—but on speech day 1953 he was adamant that it had been a good year and that Timbertop was 'the vindication of all our efforts':

> It is comparatively rare in life when one does anything for it to turn out very nearly as one expects that it will, but in this case, at least as far as our experience with the smaller numbers go, the results and the development of character, the confidence, the poise and the adult attitude to life have shown themselves at once and almost universally.

Timbertop simply had to rank 'amongst the bravest of educational ventures' because of the council's courage in committing GGS to the idea at a time of so many other difficulties. The headmaster's sentiments were echoed by Major-General Sir Kingsley Norris (Director-General, Medical Services of the Australian Military Forces) who had visited Timbertop in October. Conscious of the need to promote the scheme's virtues, Darling had sought an address from someone 'who can honestly speak enthusiastically' as well as being some-one 'whose opinion will be respected and valued'. When presenting the prizes, Norris extolled the site's beauty and the presence of so many ingredients for the promotion of manliness. 'There among those wooded slopes lies adventure', Norris said, 'the seeking for something new and good, something worthy awaiting the challenge'. With a swipe at the welfare state ('the Farewell State'), Norris described Timbertop as part of a pioneering community tradition, and pleaded for it to be viewed as a hard-won reward for self-reliance and sacrifice, rather than being taken for granted. Finally, he praised the service (rather than servility) that he had observed among the Timbertop boys.[14]

In 1954, routine and regularity at Timbertop began competing with the excitement of experimentation. Darling's rousing speech to the annual old boys' day in March, in which he thanked the council for its 'courage, pertinacity and enterprise' in supporting the scheme, waxed lyrical about his belated awareness of Australia as '*the* Dominion of the Commonwealth' which was poised to shape its future over the next two decades. He spent a week at Timbertop in September and continued to exude optimism. Curiously, he later judged Timbertop's second year as not 'very successful' and 1955 as the year that it 'got properly into its stride'. Thanks to the lack of 'proper classrooms', difficulties such as poor school work and ill discipline were surfacing. Darling and the council had tried to head off intermittent rumblings within the GGS community that classroom work would suffer neglect at Timbertop—his fear was that it 'might not get its due weight'. Both problems were attributed to a delay in the completion of the main classroom block in time for the new school year. To avoid spoiling the boys' living quarters (with their smart, newly polished floors) and unduly disrupting their amenities, he had the classes taught in marquees. But this temporary measure 'must have had a bad effect'—for which he took the blame. On the other hand, responsibility for poor discipline during homework time in the units lay with the masters. Even though Montgomery was 'never better when facing difficulties and [he] does succeed in passing on this spirit to the boys under him', Darling reported to council that Montgomery knew that Timbertop 'must be regarded as a failure in so far as in the handling of it we have relapse[d] to making it just an ordinary part of the school, governed in the same way'.[15]

The antidote for misbehaving boys was leadership rather than increased supervision and discipline, Darling reasoned, particularly the adventurous leadership of the masters who might have to be taught (in the way that he believed junior army officers were taught) 'how to get the right spirit into their particular command'. In speculative remarks betraying his anxiety, Darling thought that he could detect another weakness: perhaps the boys had been allowed to become too soft. They may well have reacted to the cold mountainous weather by shutting themselves up 'in rooms with closed windows', having 'too many hot showers' and not taking sufficient 'vigorous exercise'. Perhaps the monotony of the winter weather was also psychologically detrimental. In second term, boys had been caught smoking cigarettes in the units—a persistent disciplinary headache for Montgomery—and a particularly uncooperative young fellow was removed. A complicating factor in second term was a prolonged bout of illness—for which

Darling found it 'hard to account'. This included Montgomery's own struggle with severe pneumonia (he was relieved of duties to convalesce at Swan Hill). So concerned by this sickness was Darling that he dispatched Dr Renowden (the GGS doctor) to Timbertop for a weekend in August and arranged for Norris to undertake a week-long hygiene inspection in November 'to trace the cause of sporadic gastric disorders, and tinea troubles'. In 1956, there were cases of hepatitis and appendicitis, followed by influenza and hepatitis again in 1957. Despite these woes, there were positives: a play was staged in Mansfield and raised £80 for the hospital; the school attended the annual carol service at the end of term and in late September the Reverend Eric Barker (diocese of Newcastle) conducted the first of what became a series of annual missions.[16]

A source of comfort was the wave of positive publicity that Timbertop attracted. The *International Yearbook of Education, 1954* devoted a paragraph to it as an Australian educational innovation and Darling's own article 'Timbertop, an experiment' was published in the Commonwealth Office of Education's *Education News* (and reproduced in the Education Department's *Educational Magazine*). Medley wrote a congratulatory piece in the *Age* (and said privately that he wished he could have done something half as good) and a lengthy report (compiled with the help of Peter Westcott) appeared in *The Times Educational Supplement*. Acknowledging his debt to Hahn and others, recognising concerns about the quality of the boys' school work and hoping that their individualities would develop amid their shared responsibilities, Darling was frank about the basis of the school's appraisal:

> For various rather complicated administrative reasons, the establishment of Timbertop will help the main school, but it is upon its educational merit that it is to be judged, and the verdict on that question will depend upon the degree to which it succeeds in answering the problems posed in the first part of this article [i.e., growing up into self-confident independence, 'the core of the educational process']. So far it can be said at least that the results are promising.

The Times Educational Supplement drew liberally on Darling's article and, to differentiate (for an English readership) the scheme's Australian nature from a boarding-school regime, it expatiated on the unit discipline system. Unit leaders were 'speakers' elected monthly by secret ballot—whereas at the Aberdovy Outward Bound sea school in Wales the captains and vice-captains of 'watches' of ten–twelve boys were elected weekly:

> These 'speakers' form a sort of democratic assembly with whom the master in charge confers about such matters that arise, but they have no powers or privileges conferred by authority and are very much leaders among equals. There being no prefectorial hierarchy the whole community really runs on trust

and the essence of belief at Timbertop is that boys of this age can be trusted
to be responsible for themselves. If they cannot the whole experiment fails.

What seemed like an absence of organisation and routine to an unschooled eye,
said *The Times Educational Supplement*, was actually self-discipline.[17]

There were nine units by 1955. Schoolboy democracy, Montgomery reassured Darling about the 1957 group of leaders, was taken seriously and in return
they 'receive backing from their Units'. As an expression of adolescent self-
discipline (and simultaneous reliance on it) the unit model was underpinned by
the self-sufficiency ethos permeating not merely the educational side but the
entire operational basis. Self-sufficiency extended from the boys' production of
their classroom equipment (in 1955, for example, they built their own carpentry
benches) and responsibility for the chaperoning of site visitors, to their engagement in large-scale on-site clearance and construction work (the badminton
courts). The boys were also active in the carpentry shop (they made toboggans,
cupboards, tables and garden seats). Such self-sufficiency substituted for features
of the normal boarding-school apparatus. According to W.N. Jaffray (acting
headmaster during Darling's 1955 leave in England), what made Timbertop
unique was the absence of prefect control (as *The Times Educational Supplement*
noted) and competitive sport. All kinds of jobs replaced games, Jaffray explained:
'fencing, wood chopping, cutting out bracken, maintaining roads and drainage
gutters, growing vegetables [and] poultry farming', in addition to weekend
skiing and hiking. Reliance on boy labour was a distinctive feature of Darling's
headship, but if such reliance amounted to dependence or even exploitation, then
financially he had very little choice.[18]

There were hazards with self-sufficiency. Exposure to the gaze of visitors
was a potential risk. Nearly 400 turned up on open day in March 1955 but, apart
from such set-piece events, the trickle of occasional visitors increased as awareness
of the scheme spread. They included numerous Victorians (heads of schools,
Browne's Diploma of Education students, Father Tucker and the Brotherhood
of St Laurence, the Bishop of Wangaratta, and groups from Melbourne Boys'
High School and Swinburne Technical College) and overseas guests such as
Turner. Medley and Hone came with Turner—Montgomery dubbed them a
'pride of Headmasters'. Hone was ecstatic and Turner rated Timbertop as one
of his two most memorable experiences in Australia. On return to England, he
forwarded an article of Darling's on Timbertop to Hahn, who was so excited
that he telephoned Turner from Salem to arrange a more detailed discussion.
('Never met a man so fertile of ideas', Turner claimed.) Whenever Turner was at
Gordonstoun, he spotted similarities between the two schools. After eventually
meeting up with Darling at the Old Rectory in September 1955, Hahn said that
what he heard from him about Timbertop was like an antidote: 'a good wind
behind a tired runner'. To be able to do as Darling had done, Turner explained,
was entirely out of the question in England, where (quoting Sir Richard

Livingstone) the truth of something might be accepted but about three decades was required to translate it into reality. Other English correspondents were also full of praise. One from Marlborough reported that, having read *The Times Educational Supplement* article, a Salem exchange student commented on the similarities that he detected between his own school and Timbertop, and noted how 'from a boy's view, your ideas sounded more all-embracing and attractive'. Other important local visitors to Timbertop in 1954 were John Brookes (general manager, APM Forests, and an early Darling old boy) and Professor J.S. Turner (botany, University of Melbourne), both of whom advised on pine plantations. Brookes admitted that he had harboured doubts, but having seen Timbertop for himself was 'well on the way to being converted'.[19]

The royal tour to Australia was in 1954. Unfortunately, an eminent person whose presence at Timbertop would have been a genuine coup eluded Darling. Early in the year, Aunt Peg had written and wondered whether the Duke of Edinburgh might visit 'Timbertops' but, as this was not possible, the Timbertop boys came to Melbourne (and also to Benalla) to see the royal couple. With Prince Philip also due in Melbourne in late 1956 (for the Olympic Games), Darling tried to ensure that a Timbertop visit would be on his schedule. His letter to Buckingham Palace made a calculated appeal to the Hahn–Salem–Gordonstoun link and the prince's 'well known interest in this kind of education'. The duke's private secretary, an Old Xaverian, Commander Michael Parker (whom Darling had met some years earlier when, as Parker said, 'I was a very insignificant and very beastly schoolboy—still am!'), had already informed the prince about Timbertop (including details from Hahn) and assured Darling that it was 'high on our list' of possible visits and functions. Delighted at this news, Darling urged secrecy 'or it might be spoiled'. In September, the Victorian premier, H.E. Bolte, informed Darling of the prince's firm intention to visit Timbertop, but later that month Parker had 'some rather gloomy news for you', because the prince's Melbourne itinerary was simply 'too concentrated to include a visit—even by helicopter'. Darling was bitterly disappointed. The real reason, he suspected, was that 'the Premier's Secretary wouldn't allow it; blast him!'[20]

Just after Darling sailed for England in March 1955, Jaffray informed Montgomery that the headmaster was 'very pleased with his visit and the way things are going'. There were, however, areas for concern. One was bullying. During Darling's absence, Montgomery dealt with a spate of it in three of the units. Because the unit system was the heart and soul of the boys' community life (as Medley had told his *Age* readers), schoolboy government was simultaneously Timbertop's strength and its weakest link. There was more bullying in 1956. Shortly after his return from England in 1955, Darling confessed candidly to Montgomery that reports of it 'frightened' him. 'God knows I am in no position down here to throw any stones' yet, because Timbertop was the 'very apple' of his eye, 'anything which affects its reputation hits me very hard'. He was acutely conscious that 'we have staked our all' on the belief that the supervision and vigilance of masters could be dispensed with and exercised by the boys. Moreover, he confessed to being nagged by feelings of unease that he and Montgomery had been wrong to try to 'pass the responsibility round, with the inevitable result on occasions of having very weak leaders':

> Is it possible that we should try to achieve more continuity by holding back the twenty best boys of one year for a month or a term to introduce the new ones to the system, and how could we fit that into the school work programme?

In the first incident, a boy (A) had first informed the chaplain, the Reverend E.K. (Eckle) Leslie, that he had been daubed with shoe polish—although he later told Montgomery that Leslie had misunderstood him. 'On no occasion', Montgomery had reported to Jaffray 'was the offence done in any "Sexual Urge"', but out of a sense of horseplay and rough justice to boys 'not pulling their weight in the work of the unit'. Thankfully (from Darling's point of view), Montgomery was alerted to the bullying before Jaffray received reports of it from outside Timbertop.[21]

Before leaving for England Darling reinforced what Jaffray had reported to Montgomery: everything that he had witnessed on his recent short visit was absolutely 'first-class' and there was so much about which he felt 'greatly inspired and delighted'. But this bullying episode was just a taster. A's problem was that he was 'the 'cat that walked alone' type', a home-loving lad who annoyed and irritated the other boys and yet who dismissed most of them as rough and uncouth. A's parents visited Timbertop and, for an hour one Saturday evening, had subjected Montgomery to 'a diatribe—mainly nebulous' about the school being 'a sink of iniquity'. Offending words of a lavatory humour variety were alleged to have been uttered or written by the boys and the parents would go to Corio the next day to see the headmaster because, Montgomery wrote (paraphrasing them), 'the whole thing must go to Council and be exposed'. That evening he had mostly listened to their grievances but the next morning he counterattacked. Their son was by no means the only white sheep in an otherwise black flock. Whatever had occurred was mostly his own fault and A simply had to learn that 'what he gave so must he take'. His lack of a sense of humour and his refusal to cooperate had not helped his cause. The parents eventually calmed down, Montgomery assured Darling, and admitted that they had spoken hastily. A was still there at Timbertop and 'everything is in a stable position'. The parents expressed their confidence in Montgomery and departed. Montgomery then took the offending unit aside after chapel, gave them a 'fatherly & moral' talking-to and, unbeknown to the others, appointed one of them as A's guardian angel.[22]

Montgomery then told Darling that the episode had ruined his weekend and joked that to deal with any more such incidents justified an annual salary of about £10,000. The reason for taking fright at bullying, Darling replied, was not only because it was bad for GGS's reputation but because bullying 'seems to undermine all our faith in the theory upon which Timbertop is based'. Bullied boys, he impressed on Montgomery, nearly always asked for it and, when trying to get to the truth of what actually happened, the victim usually exaggerated and the bullies invariably minimised:

> If it is true, as it seems to be, that the victim is nearly always the boy who fails to do his share of the community's work, shouldn't we try to find a correct way of dealing with this problem? Are the masters on the spot enough? I mean, do they actually visit the units sufficiently at unexpected and dangerous times? [D]o they know the boys well enough to spot this sort of thing quickly enough? Thank Heavens that you have always been quicker on the mark than the complaint. That makes a very great difference in answering: but I am frightened nevertheless.

According to Darling, Timbertop now had 'a great reputation' in England. In July, accompanied by *The Times Educational Supplement* editor, he had given a radio broadcast about it on the BBC Home Service. And, so taken by Timbertop's progress was the Master of Marlborough, T.R. Garnett, that he tried to persuade his governing body to let him go to Australia to visit it firsthand. Moreover, the Outward Bound Trust knew of Timbertop through Chapman and other sources, except that the trust's description of it as 'your Tree Tops House at Geelong' highlighted the fog of ignorance still to be penetrated.[23]

The following year, 1956, Darling was notified of another father's complaint: unpleasant language and 'too much sexual talk'. This time Montgomery dealt with it by summoning the unit leaders and, when he visited each unit he had a general word about behaviour, how the boys should look after themselves and the bodily changes that they were experiencing. Leslie also tackled these matters in his confirmation classes. The very next day a telegram from a concerned parent (probably the complainant) to his son was dictated to Montgomery over the telephone by a Mansfield Post Office official: 'Stick to high ideals. Avoid boys of filthy conversation and you always win. Destroy this after reading.' The incident followed a bout of cigarette smoking in which (despite his 'adamantine façade') the offender admitted initially to 'moral cowardice' but then (after a subsequent transgression and suspected wilful destruction of school property) refused to confess fully. Having failed to obtain repentance from the boy after spending more than an hour with him, Montgomery was at his wit's end: 'I dressed him down hard but I might just as well have been talking to the Sphinx'. 'I am upset in that I feel I should have been able to do something with him.' Such blemishes did not constitute an epidemic, but so sensitive was Darling about Timbertop's reputation that he raised a bullying case with council. Further, these matters began to strain his relationship with Montgomery: 'I am a little afraid that the people up there are inclined to defend themselves and minimise the importance of such cases as are brought to their notice'. At least at Corio a bullied boy to some extent had the defence of the machine to fall back on, he argued to Montgomery. There had been similar trouble at Corio that year, he said, and preach and harangue, and chase prefects and housemasters as much as he might, he still felt insecure. Couldn't a Timbertop haven or sanctuary be set aside where a boy could rest secure in the knowledge that he was safe from his oppressors? Or, perhaps the composition of the units should be reshuffled? There was a balance to be struck somewhere between overprotection (and a consequent hopeless softness) and misery resulting from continual nagging to provide a guarantee of a safeguard.[24]

Another problem was the difficulty experienced by boys from Corio in transitioning to their new environment. One boy (B) had scarcely arrived at Timbertop before he informed Montgomery that he wanted to leave. He was a lad who was 'far too old in his conversation', Montgomery thought and, in any case, he disliked boys 'who talk to me of complexes & then quote psychology at me'. Darling insisted that B's trouble was that he talked too much for his own good. But B did walk out of Timbertop and, by the time that Leslie discovered that he was missing, he had hitchhiked to Mansfield to catch a bus back to Melbourne. B returned 'most penitent'. He was a strange boy, Montgomery thought, who 'sees slights and injuries everywhere & when there are none he imagines them'. Sensitive cases like this runaway highlighted another problem for Darling: boys who returned after their year away were 'not fitting [back] into the machine as well as they should'. He put this down to stories about the nature and demands of the experiences that they were likely to encounter being spread among pupils scheduled to go to Timbertop: 'I am annoyed at last year's boys talking to 3rd Form boys and putting them against Timbertop', Montgomery complained.[25]

Closely related to sensitive examples like the runaway boy were occasional lonely and homesick boys whose letters to their families, Montgomery believed, were weapons to have them taken away from Timbertop, and whose parents (especially mothers) were 'driven nearly crazy with them'. In lengthily written reports to Darling, he would outline the relevant details, provide his assessment and offer to come to Corio to meet the parents in person. In his reply Darling would apologise for the trouble to which Montgomery had been subjected, express confidence in the way that the matter was being handled and suggest additional courses of action. Every now and then, accusations about his mismanagement of Timbertop boys found their way back to Montgomery via a circuitous network of informants. In one instance the 'idle words of a prof'l [sic] man' threw him into a flat spin when '"unmercifully" treated' or a similar accusation was uttered at a dinner of Melbourne psychiatrists. 'Presumably medical ethics blew out with the Atom Bomb', Montgomery fumed. After an investigation, he assured Darling that no physical or psychological evidence had come to light to substantiate the claim. He put a stop to such teasing of the boy as was found to have occurred— the lad in question had refused to mix and 'had a real phobia about the place'.[26]

These cases were Montgomery's most difficult. As both he and Darling knew, if not properly dealt with, a handful of troublesome situations could prejudice the venture, but these instances were deviations from the norm. In 1957, Darling exposed GGS (and his reputation) to another potential risk by commissioning an independent external evaluation led by Professor W.F. (Bill) Connell of the Department of Education, of the University of Sydney. He was under no compulsion to seek this review, which (apart from school inspections) was rare at this time. Connell's team spent a week at Timbertop in early 1957. (Margaret Connell's desire to accompany her husband created a headache for Montgomery due to accommodation and ablution difficulties arising at short notice.) While Connell formed negative judgements of other features of GGS, Timbertop came up trumps. The mountain experiment had successfully fostered self-reliance, for example, and developed non-authoritarian personalities among the boys. Connell also conducted an extensive sociometric analysis and concluded that:

> there were very few isolates or rejectees, that 'getting along with other boys' was the developmental task which caused the least amount of worry, and that the friendliness of other boys and the happy relationship between boys and masters were such as to call for special comment from the boys.

Not only did this assessment confirm the success of Darling's self-governing units, but the four pages on Timbertop in Connell's bulky final report were a ringing endorsement. In contrast to the first blandly worded triennial inspection report conducted by the Education Department (1955)—'all the necessary equipment for effective work appears to be available'—Connell called Timbertop 'one of the best conceived and best executed developments in Australian education in recent years'. Its objects were 'wholly admirable' and were being implemented soundly. From an educational perspective, Connell's team judged Timbertop as 'the most exciting and provocative part of the School'.[27]

Connell's few caveats were those with which Darling and Montgomery were trying to get to grips. The first was classroom work. Connell was not convinced that 'a very good balance had been struck', because insufficient advantage was being taken of Timbertop's uniqueness by masters to have their subjects 'grow out of the local situation'. Whatever remedy was chosen, it was essential to retain continuity with the Corio curriculum. A former Timbertop master, P.J. McKeown, later concurred with this observation about the under-exploitation of Timbertop's unique opportunities—to McKeown's way of thinking, mainly because Montgomery was not 'an inspired educator'. Little was done in history and geography classes to make use of local material. There were sporadic attempts in English lessons but the one dimension of the curriculum that did benefit (as expected) was science. For Jeremy Pickett-Heaps (later a world-renowned botanist) his year at Timbertop (1954) was his most enjoyable at GGS. For the first time as a pupil he experienced 'real freedom to come and go and pursue things like birdwatching'. In 1956, the boys had launched *Timbertop Magazine*,

"THE HEADS" ON THE RIVER--By Wells

TOP Sportsday at Corio

ABOVE Free publicity for the headmasters' big event

TOP Doing what he did best
LEFT At Lake Louise, Alberta,
1934

Wedding, 21 August 1935

TOP Daughters Jane, Caroline and Liza
ABOVE With his mother, probably 1948
LEFT Family photograph, 1946

OPPOSITE TOP LEFT Father and son John
OPPOSITE TOP RIGHT Addressing the ball
OPPOSITE BOTTOM Family group, Kamarooka, 1950s
ABOVE At a Timbertop work camp

With Robert Menzies

a publication to record the 'interesting and worthwhile activities' pursued at the mountain school, particularly in natural history. Numerous accounts were published of journeys and noteworthy features of the surrounding terrain, along with photographs and articles on insects, birds and wildflowers. Darling was overjoyed about *Timbertop Magazine* and saw its main virtue as a means of enabling boys to ground their writing in new and genuine experiences: 'It doesn't interest me much to read words or stories which have no real basis of experience behind them'. Connell recommended use of the Winnetka Plan (division of subjects into a core work program supplemented by creative activities), which was implemented in 1958. Only in 1961, however, did Darling feel that he had persuaded the masters to allow boys to work at their own pace and to undertake extra work in weaker areas of performance. The *Corian* described the new system as fortnightly assignments in the afternoons and evenings, and formal teaching in the mornings, with possible early departures for weekend hikes late on Thursdays (instead of on Fridays) built in as incentives for early completion.[28]

Connell's second concern was the boys' readjustment to Corio after their return. The magnitude of the transition for returning boys was significant. To discipline them into 'an earlier pattern of behaviour' was 'quite wrongheaded' to Connell and 'a waste of much of the value and achievement' of the year away. Darling had been alert to this likely consequence: in 1955 he reported to Montgomery that the Manifold housemaster (W.J. Howard) had said (unprompted) 'how struck again he was with the keenness to work on their own shown by the Timbertop boys from last year' (in which case Darling 'may have done them an injustice'). Connell's solution was to adjust the house system at Corio to try to sustain personality developments from Timbertop. Campbell McKnight (Timbertop, 1956) thought that his year in the units was a deliberate (albeit a temporary) attempt to break with the boarding-house regime, because units comprised boys from different houses and the beds were allocated strictly alphabetically. A consequence of this measure was less contact with former house friends scattered across the other units. A negative effect of the year away may have been interruption of learning to play instruments as there was little opportunity for music in the mountains. Other boys managed to strike out in new directions after returning from Timbertop. Years after leaving school, Pickett-Heaps recalled a conversation in England with Darling in which he expressed disappointment that returning boys had not tried to 'change the system back at Corio'. Pickett-Heaps gently reminded him that, when he had returned to Corio in 1955 with the determination to take on weekend outdoor pursuits instead of rowing, he was told 'absolutely not'.[29]

Montgomery was confident that Connell's visit 'went off well' and that he had had the opportunity to 'see all & talk to everyone'. A feature of Timbertop that may have eluded Connell (or that he ignored) was another way of developing self-reliance and independence. By late 1955—by which time a substantial amount of the building work was completed—more than 2000 pine trees had

been planted and the area fenced for protection from rabbits and kangaroos.
There were also well-established vegetable gardens and increasing numbers of
livestock. Bags of potatoes had been dug, pigs bred (and sold in Mansfield), and
about 100 poultry were supplying the little mountain community with eggs. Much
of Montgomery's correspondence to Darling displayed a monotonous stock-
and-land style of reporting: progress on pigs, poultry, potatoes and pine trees.
Every now and then there would be a mishap. In 1957, cattle broke into the pine
nursery and destroyed about 1700 plants, which annoyed Montgomery, although
he was resigned to feeling that 'running this place is rather similar to True Love'.
Forty-four wet days and 445 millimetres of rain in first term 1956 played havoc
with the potato harvest, but the ground around each unit was terraced and lawn
was planted. Darling's policy—based on Professor Turner's recommendation—
was to try to maintain the Timbertop site in as natural a state as possible and to
resist the temptation to 'beautify' it. A custom was to exhibit Timbertop livestock
at the annual Mansfield Show (where prizes were occasionally won) that—with
the fortnightly organisation of a boys' club in Mansfield, the regular staging of
dramatic productions to aid the town hospital and Advent carol singing at St
John's church—expressed Darling's high priority for community service. Sylvia
Ritchie assured him that 'the general feeling in the district' was that Timbertop
'is a lovely thing to have in our midst'.[30]

Apart from risks, self-sufficiency had its costs. Soil erosion had to be prevented (in 1955 Professor Turner reported on its likelihood and consequences, but
his preventative measures were expensive). The soil was unlikely to erode, but the
location of numerous buildings on a steeply sloping site ensured that run-off water
flowed along unprotected routes. Barrel drains were needed to channel water to
the creek to ensure that pathways remained dry. Provision also had to be made for
drainage between the buildings. And, to prevent hillside deterioration into bare
mud, Turner recommended dry-wall installation at the rear of units. The previous
year (1954) had been a low rainfall year and Darling had been alerted to another
hazard: fire. If buildings caught fire, adequate arrangements were in place—
a power house burned down in January 1959—but his real worry was bushfire.
The *Corian* reassured parents periodically of evacuation to Mansfield in the event
of impending danger. The Forestry Commission of Victoria inspected the site
and provided advice on safety (and showed films and gave talks). Montgomery
introduced several measures, including land clearing, dugout construction, procurement of a water tank, installation of hydrants and fire hoses, and fire drills.
Another concern was snakebite, for which there was a regular supply of antive-
nene. The dam was also a worry; in 1960, tragedy struck on 10 February when,
within 24 hours of the arrival of a new group, a boy drowned. Darling notified
the school community, for which Hubert Black was grateful as 'it has been rather
difficult to face much questioning over the last few days'. Everything possible was
done to ascertain the event's cause and yet the tragedy was unaccountable. Black's
son recalled the extreme cold of the Timbertop dam below the surface, in which

case a bodily shock induced by the water temperature might have resulted in the drowning. 'Apart from all else I am truly sorry that we should have lost this boy in what is almost your last year [as headmaster]'.[31]

This death was one of a spate of incidents that made early 1960 'extremely miserable'. A week earlier a Corio boy died of cancer, there was a case of senior school hepatitis—a 'schoolmaster's nightmare nowadays'—a master was rushed to hospital for an emergency operation and another had had to have his appendix removed. In reply to Black, Darling discounted the water temperature as contributing to the boy's death, because of where the body had been found and because the doctor who went into the water at midnight remarked that it was not all that cold. In the absence of other explanations, Darling thought that 'the answer is in the Psychological field, which makes it rather worse'. By coming down to Corio and preaching on the Sunday after the drowning the Most Reverend Frank Woods (Booth's successor as archbishop) had helped the school to recover its equilibrium. Darling feared that the tragedy had 'broken [Montgomery] up badly', because while everyone was 'a bit knocked', the responsibility had been his and 'nothing can make it much better for him'. Weeks later, Darling told council that the lad's death was a mystery. He must have gone down 'in full view of the whole school and of two or three masters', but he reassured councillors that no 'real blame can be attached to anybody'. The water indeed had been cold, he said, but the dam bottom was still and the surface sufficiently dirty to prevent depth of visibility. The incident could just as easily have happened on 'any day at the school's baths', he continued, and he reassured Montgomery of the council's sympathy. Perhaps the boy had fainted 'or something like that'. A coroner's inquest followed. Montgomery was instructed to ensure in future that there were always two ropes stretched across the water and that to the outer of the two there was attached a floating raft with a lifebelt.[32]

On a positive note, Darling's crowning glory for Timbertop's first decade was the dedication by the archbishop on 6 December 1958 of the new chapel of St John the Baptist. The building was designed by Buchan, Laird & Buchan, and comprised an imposing A-framed structure thrusting outwards from the mountainside. Its design ensured that a worshiping congregation would be visually attentive not merely to the huge stone alter (built by Domenico Meneghini, one of the maintenance men) in front of the vast north-facing window and the external cross encompassed by the framing (the east window and wall), but also to the shafts of sunlight transporting their gaze upwards. Momentarily, the chapel's construction threatened to pose a 'difficult ecclesiastical problem'—and a potential rerun of Corio's dual authority arrangement. This time the hiccup resulted from Timbertop's location within the Diocese of Wangaratta. Booth had insisted that (because the site formed part of GGS) control resided with the (Melbourne) Diocesan Trust Corporation. Even though the Bishop of Wangaratta had conducted Timbertop confirmation services and was 'very friendlily disposed to the school', its chaplain was licensed to the Diocese of

Melbourne. Approval, however, lay with the archbishop who, having sighted a model of the chapel, and agreeing to the sketch plans and costs, issued the licence to build. The estimated cost of construction was about £13,000, of which £12,000 was the gift of Margaret McWhae. The boys were expected to complete 'a fair amount of the work'. Sporadic attempts were made (from early 1956) to clear the site and finally in March 1958 in what Montgomery described as the striking of the 'first real blow' towards 'the fulfilment of our dream', Harold Doughty's bulldozer levelled the platform of earth earmarked for the foundations, after which digging to support the concrete pillars commenced on 14 April.[33]

The building's dimensions were 10 metres × 24 metres, with an inverted-V roof 11.5 metres in height that sloped to 9 metres at the rear. The east window cross was 10 metres high with a 3-metre arm. All the material used was local except for the six imported oregon timber beams. Construction proceeded uneventfully until the dedication. After the service, Montgomery returned from quiet contemplation in the silence of the newly sanctified space and penned a quick note to his chief. On the previous evening 'we had a building tonight we have a chapel'. The change 'is a miracle'. The day was one of the most wonderful, 'if not the most wonderful' that he had ever had. Darling confessed to experiencing a similar sense of transformation and he found it 'hard during the service to keep myself under control':

> The building and dedication of the chapel seems to have been the culmination of so many plans and hopes and I was greatly moved when I saw the procession wind up the hill in the way that I had for so long visualized it doing.

According to Sylvia Ritchie, McWhae was heard on the day to murmur 'I never dreamt it could be so beautiful'. The archbishop said that he was 'thrilled'. After 'praying out of a "suitcase" for so many years', said the *Corian*, that practice would be a thing of the past. Much of the credit was due to Roy White, the school's maintenance manager, for whom it had been 'his last big job' before his death in 1959 after twenty-seven years' service to GGS.[34]

Another Timbertop achievement for Darling was the chaplaincy. After his patchy success at Corio, Darling hit the jackpot with the appointment of Ken Leslie. 'I thought I was fairly placid', Montgomery told Darling, but Leslie was 'completely imperturbable'. In July 1961, the headmaster said of Leslie (then Bishop of Bathurst) that 'what he did at Timbertop will prove in the end to have lasting results'. So capable was Leslie that, when he departed for Bathurst, Montgomery regarded his loss as a 'blow of the first magnitude'. With other staff members, however, Darling was unable to appoint many men of comparable quality, which frustrated him because (in 1960) he described staffing as 'the key to everything' at Timbertop. He could not quite understand why potential masters proved unwilling (he thought) to make the sacrifices required, such as forgoing the comforts of suburbia. As at Corio, the limited amount of Timbertop housing for married masters constrained his staffing flexibility. For Montgomery, the two stand-out masters, from their arrival in 1955 until their departure in 1957 and 1958 respectively, were J.M. Landy (OGG, Australian Olympic miler and later governor of Victoria)—a man renowned for his abilities as a naturalist—and McKeown (later headmaster, Canberra Grammar School)—who had taught at an Outward Bound school. Perhaps the delegated authority of the masters in charge of GGS's branches (the 'offshoots of the School') were making them too self-contained and divorced from school policy and, in the interests of 'more continuity', Darling needed to increase the staff interchange between them.[35]

Was Timbertop the one glorious hit for which he hoped? Mostly, yes. The scale of Darling's ambition for his innovation was evident in 1957 when an arrangement was under discussion with Melbourne Grammar for its boys' fortnightly vacation access. 'We have, I think', he remarked to Montgomery:

> set something going which is more important than ourselves and the more people that are caught up in it the better for the country in the long run, even if it involves us in trouble meanwhile and interferes with our own plans for the extension of the idea.

Jolted by this about-face ('doing something' in the Christmas holidays for under-privileged boys was the original idea), Montgomery's concerns were practical: eight weeks additional annual occupancy of Timbertop would stretch the site's recuperative capacities. While he might fantasise about the scheme's national impact, Darling was more selective when showcasing it. In 1959, when the television station GTV-9 wanted to make a film of the new school, he hesitated even though he was confident that Browne's involvement would ensure that the production was not 'too much of an advertisement for us'. Overall, he was pleased, as he reported to council in late 1959 after a visit:

> Whatever complaints there may be about Timbertop from time to time, the happiness and naturalness of the boys up there and the almost unbelievable physical feats which they perform must be good. Apart from that probably the lasting benefits may not be apparent for many years to come. Obviously some years are better than others but in total I don't think there can be any doubt about it.

When fully up and running Timbertop ought to have solved the overcrowding problem at Corio and, by facilitating increased pupil admissions, provided additional revenue. In turn, the pressure to increase fees should have eased. One consequence of GGS's growth in the 1950s was that if groups returning from Timbertop exceeded 100 (particularly when including former Bostock House day boys) there was an increased likelihood of overcrowding at the school's top end. There were 560 GGS borders in 1955; 587 in 1956 (with the senior school at maximum capacity); 635 in 1959 (349 in the senior school, 179 in the junior school and 107 at Timbertop); 630 in 1960 and 641 in 1961. As for costs, the initial 1952 estimate was £60,000, yet by July 1961 the actual expenditure was £170,000. With regard to quality of learning, Darling was unable (in 1961) to pinpoint evidence that his innovation had militated against the school's Leaving Certificate examination success—although there was a hint in his July report to council that he thought that it might have done.[36]

A simple measure of the distance travelled by Timbertop in a decade is a mundane statistic about one of its distinctive features: weekend walking trips. In first term 1961 there were 100, the *Corian* reported, mostly completed by boys unaccompanied by masters and in a mountainous area of more than 2500 square kilometres. In late 1955, one group trekked nearly 110 kilometres in a weekend. The boys' preparation for these outings included first aid, map reading and camping, on the assumption that 'a fifteen year-old boy has to prove things for himself'. Trudging through snow and fording unbridged flooded rivers were out-of-bounds activities but, despite the precautions, there were occasional difficulties. One trip went badly amiss in June 1956 when, caught in a blizzard on the Timbertop ridge en route to Mount Buller, four lads did not arrive on time at their destination. Eventually they turned up, although only after a public search (bringing undesired publicity—Melbourne press reports and an ABC radio news item). Montgomery took comfort from what was learnt from the mishap, yet his 'cross' was that he had had to request Darling to agree to the all-out search—'I must confess that I honestly felt at the time that we could not afford to wait longer'. Thankfully, during the search and the masters' absence the remaining boys had 'run the place unaided' for two days. 'On the whole', Darling reassured Booth, '[I] think the episode was fairly creditable to the boys and to the organization'. Yes, 'there were a few weaknesses which the episode will have helped to clear up' but, all things considered, 'I am not particularly worried about it'. The missing boys got into difficulty when they descended the lee side of a spur, tailed off and missed the track. 'It was intelligent enough to get on the lee side but they should have kept someone on the track to direct them. I am sorry to have subjected you to such a hectic couple of hours.' No harm had been done, Booth said, and after another month the only people recalling the event would be the lads, their parents, the other boys and the masters.[37]

When a boy went missing in 1960, however, Darling was 'rattled'. In desperation before the boy was found, he telephoned the chief commissioner of the Victoria Police and, between them they tried (in vain) to keep the story out of the press. It was unpleasant to be of 'news-value', but Darling reflected that he had no complaint: his distaste for newspaper reports always had to be balanced against the safeguarding 'of the rights of the individual and a protection against wrongful imprisonment' guaranteed by a free press. These incidents also underscored the significance of the *Corian*'s point that, while 'boys do have to cope with real emergencies during their journeys in the bush', it was only by 'meeting the challenge' that they gained the 'independence and character that Timbertop hopes to develop in them'. There were other occasions when Timbertop boys exemplified such traits, as in July 1956 when a group arrived at the Howqua River to discover that Fred Fry (local identity and friend of the school) lay gravely ill in his hut. Unable to chop wood for his fire, Fry had been indisposed for five days. The boys fed him, cared for him, and eventually saddled his horse and brought him to Timbertop, where he was diagnosed with pneumonia. Leslie then drove Fry to the Mansfield hospital from where, after a week's recuperation, he was discharged.[38]

Between 1953 and 1961, more than 1000 boys attended Timbertop. In 1961, 135 boys were in residence, the largest cohort so far. With nine units chock-full with fifteen boys each, the site was at 'absolute capacity'. Darling's earlier expressed hope (to the businessman, Sir Ernest Fisk) that GGS boys would complete their education for a year in the conditions of a mountain setting 'outside the institutional machine which this place, in spite of all my efforts has tended to become', had been realised. He anticipated a 'bit of a struggle' in starting out but had been 'fairly confident' that he and the school would achieve their goal, described in 1953 as 'a great common enterprise'. They did. In mid-July (by which time he was already performing his new role as Chairman of the ABC—see chapter 23), Darling paid a quick whistlestop visit to Timbertop and then on Friday, 4 August, he arrived for his final extended stay. On the next Sunday he read the lessons and preached at evensong. He conducted his final assembly, and thanked Montgomery for his 'great kindness' and 'wonderful thoughtfulness' in planning such a memorable weekend. He was sad that this was his last official visit, but he enjoyed it (and was back a week later with Garnett, his successor, in tow). For the time being, when feeling 'fairly near the end of his tether' and still to get through his remaining retirement speeches, his brief sojourn at the mountain settlement had provided a 'greatly needed respite'. With that, his partnership with Montgomery of two decades ended (although their friendship continued). Their mutual trust and implicit understanding had resulted in some highly productive outcomes for the boys and for the school. After the dedication of the chapel, Darling had told Montgomery that Timbertop 'could not have got going without you' and that he had shouldered a great responsibility. Their tag-teaming had brought mutual professional satisfaction and they had drawn from it considerable personal strength.[39]

NAKED EMPEROR?

1951–1961

> *This is the state of man; To-day he puts forth*
> *The tender leaves of hope, to-morrow blossoms,*
> *And bears his blushing honours thick upon him:*
> *The third day, comes a frost, a killing frost;*
> *And,—when he thinks, good easy man! full surely*
> *His greatness is a-ripening,—nips his root,*
> *And then he falls, as I do.*
>
> William Shakespeare, *King Henry VIII*

Apart from the triumph of Timbertop, Darling's achievement at GGS during his final decade there was mixed. On the credit side, there was the Highton project, the establishment of a nearby community centre and the GGS centenary events. On the debit side, two internal difficulties dogged the school. The first was Corio's continued malfunctioning administration, which, under enrolment growth pressures, was a problem until 1955. The second was the council's persistent financial worries, in which there were three phases: hand-to-mouth increases in fees to cover rising costs rather than financial planning, then (as part of the centenary) an endowment fund to free the school of debt (by capitalising on tax deductions for school gifts) and, finally, the raising of loans through unsecured notes. The school's plight was complicated by continued council indulgence of the headmaster's external responsibilities that entailed prolonged absences from Corio. Darling's characteristic response was a sense of guilt (and frequent admissions that he wasn't doing his job properly), periodic complaints about the school's increasing complexity and offers of resignation (three in all).

Darling's state of mind was evident in a confessional letter to Ralph shortly after the July 1951 council meeting that had increased the fees to £360. The situation was bleak. What was the poor devil of a headmaster expected to do:

when he discovers that more than half of his staff is decrepit, incompetent, lazy and in general unco-operative, not to say disloyal. I have striven to give them security of tenure, increments [?] cost of living and superannuation and the main result of all this damned security seems to have made them complacent and idle. I can't really sack many of them because they have been with me too long, but a new headmaster would have to.

As for himself:

I can't get out because I can't afford to, but I am sure that I really ought to, if I thought of the good of the school. The trouble is that there is very little room for young men and the old men are very common-roomish, not to say Persia [?] like to the younger ones and do not encourage much enthusiasm. Also the young ones aren't what we were when we were young, at least I don't think so, for they suffer poor things from the most devitalizing knowledge that there are five jobs around the corner if they like to leave this one. [But] not many people are really good enough to survive that knowledge.

Those whom he had in mind were probably worn out serving the school, and he simply had to put up with them. Australia was 'in full inflation for a variety of reasons, but very largely because of an unwillingness of anyone to work'. Rising prices triggered regular automatic wage increases, and there seemed little hope of preventing them. On top of non-cooperation between the various interests, the threatening world situation was calculated 'to make me believe in the inevitable and the ultimate inanity of another war'. He had 'tried to be good, within reason and it is a bit exasperating to be so depressed at this stage'. In his household, he reported, thankfully, that the situation was brighter.[1]

Darling was aware of GGS's false economy. The council had adjusted for rising costs by increasing fees but, as he saw it, the problem was that a 'tight budget' relied on overcrowding to increase the operating profit. Two negative consequences were overworked masters and, thanks to inflation (especially escalating materials prices), disposable income was grossly inadequate for repairs and the construction of masters' residences. After the March council meeting, Darling summarised the 'critical' financial decisions required. In respect of capital, the school's liabilities were £159,000 and its assets (exclusive of trust funds, property value, annuity fund and anticipated release from various repayments by 1957–58) were £471,000. The overdraft was £16,000. As for operations, expenditure was anticipated to increase by £39,000 for 1951; council could meet it by cutting costs or increasing fees (in one hit or stages). He was averse to cutting costs and chose the easy option: 'swallow the fact that we are a school for the rich' and raise the fees to £360. Neither a slump nor a boom period was the time for cuts, he said, but only when costs and money were 'stable enough' to make long-range planning 'effective'—but when was that? So low were his spirits in July 1952 that he drafted a resignation letter (his fourth offer since 1939). A year later he wrote another one—although he didn't submit either. The problem was council's continued dissatisfaction with the bursar and council secretary, and its refusal to tackle the issue. Darling's loyalty to Thewlis had prompted both his resignation letters, although other considerations included the effects of increased running costs (due mainly to the impact of rapidly rising inflation on costs of living), difficulties caused by the departure and illnesses of masters, shortcomings in his own financial expertise and state school competition. Council sensed that not all was well. In April a worried Black expressed unease to Griffiths about 'the drift down there' at Corio, following a 'substantial' financial loss in 1951, the 'alarming position' in the 1952 draft budget and a 'further slide' in first term. The headmaster usually came up trumps in difficult circumstances, but Black was concerned about the strain on Darling who, in desperation, appealed to Robson to inquire into 'our present distresses' in respect of the school program's costs. 'Are we, all things considered, being unduly extravagant? Are we over-staffed?' If a fee commensurate with 1938 standards was £495, not £360, was it any wonder that 'we are in strife?' Robson was not well, had his own problems at Shore and declined.[2]

In July 1952, Darling told Griffiths that to resign and be free from respon-sibility was 'so agreeable a prospect', that 'once the fatal words are spoken my heart leaps within me for joy'. The need to earn a living and the desire to launch Timbertop, however, militated against departure. If the 'financial side must dom-inate everything', then he was 'badly suited' to being headmaster and GGS's unhappy condition was his fault. Someone with business experience and youth was required. As for the bursar, no-one knew of his failings better than Darling did, but 'thinly veiled suggestions' circulating about alleged corruption and dis-honesty were 'quite fantastic' and, in view of Thewlis' service to the school, 'quite unworthy of this place'. The council would safeguard the school's best interests, but the importance of the finances was 'subordinate to the preservation of our own true self-respect'. Thewlis' previous refusal to take leave had been motivated by his sense of duty, and (quoting Hamlet's words to Polonius) he did not deserve to be treated 'after his desert', but with 'honour and dignity'. Ill again, Thewlis took four months' leave. Retirement on a pension would be his just reward. As for himself, Darling would stay until the end of 1953 (with the fee budgeted at £390). State school teachers' salary awards were making the appointment of masters very difficult and, when coupled with basic wage increases, lessened the likelihood of an operating profit. If the school was to be competitive, another £20,000 had to be expended (a fee increase to £430). The August *Corian* sum-marised the financial situation's gravity and the council's options. It called for administrative economy and, if embarking on Timbertop was thought to be exac-erbating the difficulties, then it should produce substantial long-term savings, ease the immediate financial situation and indicate how 'the School can eventu-ally be preserved'.[3]

Darling's nadir was 1952. To D.M. Bennett (an incoming councillor and OGGA president) he said that it was 'the worst year I can ever remember'. He told Gerry Dicker that the fees were 'terrifyingly high' and that running the school was 'quite fantastically difficult'. To the parents he spoke again about GGS as a complex community in which diverse educational provision and the interdependence of the component parts had to be reconciled. The value of money was falling (compared with ten years earlier), and the 'grim' financial story was that if GGS was to charge high fees, then it could not afford to let its standards fall. If the parents' and boys' expectations about the running of the school were to be met, then there was no alternative but to raise the fees 'considerably higher'. At the same time, 'growing evidence' suggested that the fees were already too high (especially for parents with several children to educate), and so they had to be at a level that families would deem worthy of the sacrifice entailed. Short of a bursary fund for those for whom high fees were unattainable, the only other family-support mechanism was the recent taxation concession. With projected enrolments for 1954 and 1955 still 'very pressing' the temptation to lose heart in such difficult circumstances was 'sometimes too much to resist'. He felt trapped. The auditors (Flack & Flack) conducted a review. They recommended siphoning off GGS's business management to the 'sole control' of a general manager, to free Darling to attend to the academic side, but he dismissed this idea as 'quite impossible'. When suggesting that the school's administrative capability and infrastructure were seriously wanting, Flack & Flack said that as 'a very big business' GGS had to be administered in a business-like manner. Yet, to their suggestion that fee levels were being set to 'meet expenditures' Darling noted: 'Lack of decision by Council and lack of capital'. The auditors could not detect clearly defined lines of responsibility or control, or policy-informed organisation to achieve cooperation and teamwork. Darling's (enigmatic) defence of the jumble of inefficiency was: 'This largely due to being in a state of suspended animation'. Finally, the auditors said that no GGS administrative staff were anywhere near the standard required of a general manager—which was a no-confidence vote in the bursar.[4]

From the receipt of this report until the restoration of stability in mid-1954 (following the appointment of P.C.L. Desborough), the headmaster, council and finance committee, various school officers and the auditors engaged in an undignified arm-wrestle to devise fit-for-purpose administrative structures and processes. Given the school's self-chosen market position, a new system had to be up to managing GGS's recent machine-like growth in size, scale, complexity and impersonality. But the speed of response was glacial and again Darling seriously contemplated his departure. In February 1953, council appointed as acting bursar a representative of the auditors (R. Eabry). The division of labour was that Eabry (with the school accountant's assistance) would control and institute 'new systems desired by the auditors', and prepare all council and finance committee budgets, while Thewlis continued as council secretary. In March, Darling complained that the school's main troubles were 'still numbers and money', and in May the *Corian* made a Canute-like appeal to parents and old boys that, when confronted by high fees, it would be helpful if they refrained from 'complaining more than is absolutely necessary to their peace of mind'. The first of two comprehensive Flack & Flack reports (22 pages) was submitted to the finance committee in late June. But, there was so little progress that Darling (yet to read the report) was very near to 'breaking point' about the financial administration. If Eabry was to be the 'last word' on control systems, then he had to be continually available otherwise it would be better 'to flounder along in our own way'. Flack & Flack estimated that Eabry could devote about 10 per cent of his time to designing the new office procedures. It was all very well to observe that business decisions were made by council members or the headmaster under the direction of a council minute, Darling said, because this pattern of decision-making resulted from 'the absence of Eabry when wanted'. Moreover, Flack & Flack's idea that in respect of business management and accounting matters Eabry had been called on increasingly (and that this illustrated further 'the present deficiencies in the available administrative personnel') was pure 'nonsense'. In reality, Eabry had simply been hired to 'alter the office routine'.[5]

Darling's second reconsideration of his future followed the council's resolve in July 1953 to retire the bursar (with effect from September), to appoint a general manager (on £2000 a year) and to request Flack & Flack to supply a finance manager for six months. Two years short of retirement, the bursar contested his severance package as a breach of an earlier (1941) council agreement. While Darling backed him, there was 'much' that was correct in the auditor's report: administrative development had not paralleled school growth and was not helped by the bursar's continued ill health. In fact, the 'administrative crisis' of the past six months was 'the worst that it has ever been': the pull of Eabry's other responsibilities constrained consultation with him and maintenance control was suffering due to Roy White's absence at Timbertop. The bursar's problem was his failure to adapt to changed conditions and his unwillingness to give new staff a chance. Darling foresaw a domino effect: Thewlis' departure would be followed by the accountant and (if the proposed general manager were to be appointed) Roy White, in which case (although his decision was personal and should not influence council) 'it is hard to see how a headmaster can honourably keep his own job in these circumstances'—if the 'underlings' were to be sacrificed, then honour dictated that he should go. 'Clearly', Darling said, the present system had got beyond him, but the work of headmaster 'could be adequately accomplished by someone with a better brain, more organising [ability]' and with 'less of a personal approach in all aspects of the job'. As for the proposed headmaster–general manager arrangement, this was a 'dangerous' dichotomy of two equal authorities with defined (and yet inseparable) spheres of action, because 'however much the Commander may do in a ship, he must still be subordinate to the Captain'. Either the general manager (who had to be someone of the stature of a Medley or a Fisk) was to be at the same level as the head's assistant (Hutton) or above the headmaster and all the satellite school heads, with himself as head in charge of the senior school, except that there were negative implications for Headmasters' Conference of Australia membership and future headmaster appointments. Apart from all that, and because he had 'given as much as I can to this school' he was not averse to resigning from the end of the year. He had no idea which course of action was the best, but he would risk the financial hardship entailed. The clear options were: the proposed plan, which 'will make it easy for me. I cannot accept it, and must resign', or a decent way of releasing the bursar.[6]

The council came to its senses: it deferred the appointment of a general manager and, at a special meeting in late July 1953, agreed to pay the bursar's salary until the end of the year, with an ex-gratia retirement allowance to follow. Thewlis' thirty-seven years as a school officer would conclude in December. This departure was 'not accomplished without bloodshed', said Darling, and Thewlis was 'very bitter'. While 'things have simmered down' in the office, he was still concerned to let the bursar down gently and to find sufficient clerical work to keep him occupied and feeling connected. Despite the auditors' insistence on the business side of the school being a department solely responsible for business matters, Darling was beginning to get his way. Flack & Flack's immediate priority was a system of centralised purchasing control and it viewed GGS's dependence on Eabry as confirming its dim view of the office staff's capability. Clearly, Darling mused to Griffiths in late November 1953, the auditors had calculated their best form of defence as being attack. In March, Darling's exasperation with Flack & Flack boiled over: he objected strongly to 'being run' by people in whom he had 'no confidence at all', who had extracted large amounts of money from the school, had left Eabry in charge and promptly loaded him up with other work which prevented him from doing what he was contracted to do. The council was also in Darling's sights, principally because he was firing its bullets—it was he who gave the accountant his marching orders (the first of three office resignations during June–August)—and it had not offered him any control of the school's business side (although he hadn't sought it and didn't want it). Darling's view was that during Thewlis' absence he had dealt directly with the accountant and Roy White, and that side of school worked smoothly. Council's problem was twofold: the new purchasing operations were 'most distasteful to swallow' and 'unfit for an institution of this sort' and, due to the irregularity or non-convening of sub-committee meetings and lack of accurate financial information (Darling's crunch point), council was 'not properly in control of the school'.[7]

Darling was right. With about 950 boys on four sites, GGS could not be run by remote control from Melbourne and by buying in part-time financial expertise. After conferring with Griffiths about Darling's letter, a sheepish Black confessed that:

> neither the Council, nor you, nor the admin. staff have had a 'fair go' for some
> years. I make no attempt to lay the blame for this, but it is true.

Black's excuses were his own inadequacies, geographical remoteness, lack of time
to commit and poor-quality financial details. Darling grabbed the whip hand
and pressed for the clarification of Eabry's status: if the new (office) system was
to go ahead, then a replacement accountant had to be appointed and answer
directly to Eabry, who would then have to work exclusively for the school for
three months (as an employee of either GGS or the auditors). Failing that, the
accountant should be retained (under the headmaster's control), Flack & Flack's
plans would be modified and new auditors appointed. Darling then gave Eabry
an 'ultimatum' of pressing expenditure priorities and was promised answers by
30 April. 'If Flack and Flack fail us in this', he told Griffiths, 'I shall have to shoot
somebody'. In this power struggle, Darling's hand was strengthened considerably
by the arrival in July of the new bursar, Peter Desborough who, within a couple
of days, had already appraised the school office and clarified the status of the
accounts. With Eabry increasingly surplus to requirements, hostility towards the
auditors was stiffening: they had misrepresented their assistance to the school
and the ultimatum-like tone of their communications grated. Their second (and
final) report on office systems (this time 36 pages plus exhibits) arrived in late
August. Its headline point was that streamlined procedures for cash receipts, cash
disbursement, stock control, inventories, invoicing, payrolls (for 300 employees),
wages payments (£160,000 per year), purchase and sale of items, record keeping,
cheque-signing and the like, and the preparation of accounts (for all four sites)
and budgets were not in place or had been let slip. Such was the magnitude of
the transactions that the Corio office handled money from about seventy school
clubs and societies, not to mention school farm and tuckshop income, cash for
meals for casual workers and even cash from bus drivers. Moreover, the annual
book-room sales amounted to 22,000 items, and every term there were more than
50,000 items to be recorded and then charged to parents. Finally, so complicated
for parents was the system of advance fee payment that 'every arrangement has to
be an individual contract and worked out as such'. Thankfully, Desborough was
shaping up as the man of the hour: Darling thought that he was a good choice
and Black was 'more firmly of the opinion than ever' that the council had made
the right appointment.[8]

Another development with potentially prejudicial implications for GGS's
financial viability and future was neighbouring Corio land usage. In June 1950,
Darling got wind of the likely construction of an explosives jetty and store less
than 5 kilometres to the school's north at Point Lillias. The effect, as Darling said
colourfully to Senator G. McLeay (Minister for Fuel, Shipping and Transport),
would have been to leave the school stranded between an ammunition jetty and
an oil refinery—'two targets which would in the event of war make propinquity to
them at least alarming to the more sensitive parents, if not really dangerous'. On

receipt of the news, the eight parliamentary OGGs descended on the minister. The departmental committee, which had already spent a decade searching for a site, was directed to look elsewhere. The worst-case scenario (relocation of the school at an estimated cost of £1 million), Geoffrey Brown assured Darling, 'has been stopped'; but three years or so later, to Darling's consternation, an ammunition dump and security area was being proposed for the You Yangs. 'I need hardly point out to you', he told Brown, that this area was 'about the last remaining amenity which this school possesses'. With this and other rumours he was seriously alarmed. Would Brown please see Opperman about 'this last loathsome project'? Brown's reply was not reassuring. Clearly, defence probably was 'more important than anything else', but wasn't there something odd, said Darling, about positioning everything in the one (vulnerable) place? If the Department of Defence dug its heels in, then a combination of defence activities and factory buildings would force relocation within the next two decades, otherwise GGS would be 'an isolated oasis in the middle of a factory area'.[9]

Formally, the GGS site was zoned agricultural—a classification sought deliberately to forestall enclosure by its neighbours. When Black floated the possibility (with an English fire insurance company) of mortgaging the school in return for a £250,000 loan, this classification was a potential impediment. For this reason, Black raised with Darling the possibility of rezoning. Aware that its southern neighbour (Shell Refining) had successfully thwarted GGS's attempts to secure land adjacent to the railway line (and acquired it for itself), Darling's concern was the spectre of compulsory land acquisition. He urged retention of the status quo, while attempting to improve relations with the school's industrial neighbour. He collaborated with Shell in anticipating the emerging needs of the nascent Victorian government housing estate in nearby Norlane. With the school cut off from the wider world during term time, he was keen for GGS boys to engage with the immediate neighbourhood. He sought from Shell a piece of land in the south-west corner of its site on which to construct a hall and smaller rooms for entertainments, debating, gymnastics, clubs, boy scouts and girl guides, a library and a cafeteria. He also envisaged a baby health centre, kindergarten and crèche. Shell gave him its 'fullest support' and, in November 1954, the company and the school combined to raise over £1700 for the project at a GGS fair. Eventually, the Housing Commission of Victoria (the estate developer) allocated 2.2 hectares for the centre, which was to be located adjacent to the Corio State School, owned by the Corio Shire Council and financed by Shell. GGS boys provided working parties during the estate's construction (for example, for shrub distribution to estate tenants).[10]

These attempts to secure the school crystallised support for an endowment fund. At the October 1954 council meeting, Darling outlined the extent of the maintenance and capital works required at Corio, and raised the possibility that 'the School could not continue to operate on its present site and under existing conditions'. For GGS's future, the council determined that 'it is essential to make good on this site' and it established an appeal fund with a target of 'at least' £200,000. Aside from the 'more obvious dilapidations', the basic infrastructure and building fabric at Corio needed urgent attention. With the adoption of the endowment fund, Timbertop's added significance as a possible relocation site began to recede. A week or so after the meeting, Darling thanked Black for his recent help as 'beyond all price'. He thought that the fund needed to be managed by a joint committee of councillors and OGGs, but as he was at the end of his tether (having been ill during the winter), 'useless in school' and 'intolerable to live with' he excluded himself as a member. He felt desperately tired and weighed down by the thought of speeches to be delivered, in the interests of 'advertisement purposes' (after a recent 'bad run' of speaking, which had been 'getting worse and worse'). He estimated that about £165,000 would cover immediate needs, capital requirements, maintenance, completion of Timbertop and various other 'around-the-back-reforms', while the added bonus of £300,000 would permit a reduction of the debt and fee levels. In November 1954, council established the Geelong Church of England Grammar School Centenary Building Restoration Fund and an appeal committee.[11]

A source of comfort for Darling was receipt of an OBE in the New Year honours for 1953. 'Richly deserved', wrote one correspondent and, with Timbertop about to kick off, very fitting timing too. Hone thought that the honour should have been 'a C.M.G. at least, or something really worthwhile'. There was additional satisfaction when, thanks to a 'splendid triple triumph', GGS crews scooped the pool at the Head of the River. For once, his sport misgivings were put aside and he was 'pathetically pleased'. Respite from financial gloom, however, was short lived: by the end of 1954, the fees had skyrocketed to £450—of which tuition comprised £103 (or 23 per cent), housekeeping and general service £216 (48 per cent); and maintenance, interest, transport, bursaries and administrative expenses the remaining £131 (29 per cent). A year later, after much debate and with Darling uncertain whether 'the market will stand it', the fees leapt further to £480. The decision to raise the masters' salaries by an annual average of £250 (a cost of £10,000) meant that a fee increase was the only option. His other preoccupation at this time was television. Council had granted him Home leave in 1955, but for two-and-a-half months beforehand he was almost exclusively run off his feet by participation in the Melbourne and Sydney television licence application hearings, following his appointment to the Australian Broadcasting Control Board in late 1954. A fortnight before sailing he said that he was in 'a hopeless condition' due to 'too much work, another bad cold & inoculations of every kind & colour'. On 14 March 1955, he and Margaret and Jane sailed on the *Orsova* for his fourth period of leave in twenty-five years.[12]

During the pre-Colombo leg of the trip, Darling had mostly 'sulked' and not met anyone, he confided to Hutton (who, with his wife Marion, was minding John), although after a lovely time as guests of a Colombo-based GGS family, he was getting into a shipboard routine with its 'customary plethora of drinks'.

He apologised for having been 'quite unbearable' at school. Margaret's Christmas letter for 1954 had urged her brother to have a 'real rest' on the voyage and not to have 'too many ploys on hand'. They were both becoming middle-aged, she reminded him, and he should work at 'an appropriate pace'. She also warned that she was more aged since his 1948 visit, more so than their mother who had changed little. Only her eyesight was a bother and at eighty-five she took longer to recuperate when feeling below par. (Actually, Ralph told him that she had slipped and fallen in the pantry at Easter, and had broken her left wrist.) After a brief stopover in Italy the Darlings arrived in England on 16 April. Released from his normal routine, he wondered at Trimley: 'Why on earth did one ever leave England?' The countryside was so 'unbelievably beautiful' that he fancied being quite happy staying there and doing nothing. Domestically, he was delighted about the recent apple harvest at Kamarooka (his recently acquired cottage at Beaconsfield, on the other side of Melbourne)—a source of bemusement to his mother who, thrilled about the acquisition of his 'wonderful estate', had never quite fancied him as an 'apple overlord', particularly since none of her children had cared much for apples.[13]

The headmaster's itinerary soon made a mockery of Margaret's plea about ploys. There were occasional Corio rumblings to attend to (dealt with in letters to Hutton or the finance committee): not all the masters were supportive of Desborough's efforts at economy, Black reported and, despite the operating deficit, Jaffray was pushing for salary increases. Black's August letter—detailing OGGA grizzles that were making his Melbourne Club lunches burdensome—prompted Darling to send two pages of reflections on GGS's future. Was the struggle to preserve church schools likely to succeed or even necessary? He argued (with some exaggeration) that state school buildings and facilities had 'outstripped' those of the church schools (teachers in newly built spartan urban-fringe schools would have disagreed). Moreover, church schools were being outbid in salaries and pensions, making balancing budgets imperative, and endowments, rising enrolments, increased fees and economies were the only available options. With no immediate likelihood of an annual endowment income of £1 million, GGS was thrown back on a combination of the three options. The logic was compelling: more admissions (council's stock response) and a decline in monetary value required fee increases to compensate. With fees beyond the reach of some prospective parents, bursaries had subsidised the admission of about sixty boys; but eliminate them and the loss of sixty would increase per capita fees by an additional £10. Economies could only be achieved through efficiency gains and/or reduced 'quality of article offered'. If the masters' salary request was acceded to, then an already precarious financial situation would be worsened, but to delay it increased the likelihood of disgruntled staff and turnover. From 19,000 kilometres away, he could make 'no positive recommendation' other than urging the masters to hold fire. Bennett (now a finance committee member) begged to differ: Darling was wrong to question the preservation of church schools; Timbertop was the real drain on finance and, as for the masters restraining their demands, the council could not afford 'not to pay adequate salaries'.[14]

Apart from seeing his family members (including the Auchinleck branch in county Omagh, Northern Ireland), Darling caught up with a succession of English friends and work-related acquaintances. These included Chapman, Bickersteth, Pentreath and McKie (ten years at Westminster Abbey, he said, was 'getting me down'), various OGGs (including Brian Harrison, a Conservative Party MP), numerous officials and former contacts at the BBC, Old Carthusians, Ministry of Information cronies (for example, Bob Fraser, now with the Independent Television Authority) and British Council contacts. He did a round of meet-and-greet visits to some Oxbridge college heads to shore up GGS's connections, and he also visited schools (at Rugby he preached in the chapel). Thanks to the Marconi Company, he and Margaret viewed British television (despite the poor transmission reception near Ipswich) and, in early September, there was a reception for them in the House of Commons. They were also invited to a royal garden party and he attended Ascot. In July, he gave a broadcast talk over the BBC Home Service on the work of the British Council in Australia, and then in September he was part of an on-air discussion of Timbertop and educational experiments generally. He also addressed the Headmasters' Conference. With such a list of commitments, it was little wonder that seeing everybody had been 'very strenuous'. But the stay at Trimley, he reassured his mother from somewhere out in the Red Sea, had been the most enjoyable. He was so fond of Suffolk and its simple life, despite being tempted by 'this other when it is put in my way'. He remained 'very much disposed' to retiring in England, which he had not felt previously.[15]

Darling and his family returned to Corio on 4 November. 'Don't be too long coming back to see us again', Mabel said, because his visit had made a big difference to Ralph and was a joy for her to see. A letter from Desborough soon provided a reality check: there had been a downhill financial slide, and there was an urgent need for economy and efficiency everywhere in the school. Readjustment after a lengthy release from duties proved difficult. Shortly after his return he was he complaining about a 'very strenuous and difficult time'. Despite Jaffray's admirable substitution for him, it was no use Darling's pretending that the school was 'not in a very bad shape' and that only 'a great deal of hard work' would put it right. He was despondent about maintaining standards of behaviour and belief 'in the face of their general abandonment' externally. Throughout the year his mood oscillated. At the August 1956 council meeting, his familiar complaint about the 'very complex machine' was playing on his mind again and he felt 'increasingly incapable' of performing his duties as he preferred to, so much so that he wondered whether the headmastership was bigger than one man. Perhaps there were two jobs: 'administration of the whole business' and head of the senior school at Corio. He assessed himself as 'patterned for the latter role', but 'circumstances' were eating up more of his time on the former. On the other hand, he was buoyed by being unable to recall such a comparatively good year ('unless it was 1934') when 'the boys at the top of the school were so good, or when there were so many of them'.[16]

The year 1956 was noteworthy for other reasons. Internationally, the XVIth Olympiad was held in Melbourne (22 November–8 December), in which ten OGGs, including John Landy, represented Australia. The Games had been preceded by the Suez crisis (following the nationalisation by Colonel Gamal Abdel Nasser on 26 July of the Suez Canal Company). Locally, there was another encroachment threat when Shell applied to have 30 hectares rezoned on the east side of the Geelong Road and to the school's north. This land was part of a green belt (between North Geelong and Lara), the basis of the school's 'whole future policy'. Retention of the belt and its current zoning were essential because, if the land were to be rezoned, Shell's proposed extension was a 'real threat' to be 'strongly resisted'. Throughout the year, the company's action 'weighed heavily' and consumed much of Darling's time. The council engaged legal counsel to fight the proposal and committed the school to the present site 'for as long as possible' (while preparing for a possible relocation). It was apprehensive about the attractiveness of the area to industries dependent on petroleum by-products. By the end of the year a legal showdown was averted when Shell withdrew its application (a 'generous action', the school said) and council purchased considerable acreage of land to the school's north. Darling had been urging this commitment because the alternative was to 'allow ourselves to be encircled and to be blamed by posterity for not having had the foresight to acquire the land', which might increase tenfold in value in two decades.[17]

With the possibility of a Corio departure hovering, Darling outlined a different conception of the school, but others got cold feet. Vincent Fairfax (a councillor) cautioned about a twofold effect of Darling's draft memorandum: council's adoption and public affirmation of an alternative model of GGS would 'destroy the morale of the school' (if it was unrealisable) and reduce the centenary appeal to a 'farce'. As for the Centenary Building Restoration Fund appeal (launched by an OGG, Colonel Allan Spowers, in June 1955), the total in hand by March 1956 was £70,000 (20 per cent of the target), which made Black think that momentum had 'stalled somewhat'. About £85,000 was needed for capital works, including a wartime maintenance backlog (repairs to brickwork and woodwork, electrical wiring, replacement of roofing, guttering and plumbing) and equipment modernisation. The remaining £265,000 was intended to liquidate GGS's loans and bank overdraft. With debts cleared, lower maintenance costs (due to repairs and reduced office expenses, thanks to Desborough's reorganisation and efficiency savings) the finances would be under control. Rather than donations, the appeal was for loans (at 4 per cent interest). If sourced from personal income, these counted as deductions for income tax assessment, the effect being to distribute indebtedness among old boys and friends of the school.

Reliance on loans for income was essential: fees were set at the maximum level that parents and prospective parents could meet.[18]

The year 1957 was equally noteworthy. Total enrolments reached 1045 (685 boarders and 360 day boys—mostly Bostock House and Glamorgan). Barely one month after a Soviet satellite completed the first space orbit of the planet, John Manifold died aged seventy. He was remembered as an immensely important and longstanding benefactor, servant of the school and council member for nearly forty years. Four months earlier, Jane Darling had died. She was eighty-seven. Sylvia Ritchie penned her friend a touching note. Of course her death would be a 'grievous blow' but, rather than suggesting that she had reached a great age and that 'we couldn't wish her to linger on', she said that:

> Your great consolation must be that no mother can have been given greater joy by the life of her son than yours, even though that life did take you so far away from her.

Some months later, Victor Gollancz contacted Darling—his 'My dear Jimmy' salutation echoing relations of forty years earlier. He and his wife were due in Melbourne the following April. Gollancz' former pupil was bowled over by the thought of the visit, but as the timing coincided with the Head of River, Darling didn't want the trip sullied by that 'abominable institution'. He sounded off about 1957 as one of the worst years that he could remember, because 'almost every known crime and vice seem to be luxuriantly flourishing'. On the other hand, he had enjoyed very much his 28-year stint in Australia and hoped that Gollancz might visit Timbertop. Sadly, Gollancz postponed. (Eventually they met in London in 1962 and dined at The Ivy.) The 'two jobs' idea of headship reared its head again in 1957. Having dismissed the auditors' dual authority headmaster–general manager arrangement, Darling broached with Black the idea of a provost and headmaster. Then, after offering at the August council meeting to resign—to resolve his difficulty in successfully juggling all of the responsibilities consuming his life—at the next (October) meeting he pressed to have his role reorganised. He could not do justice to the three core functions of headship: social and public relations; administration and financial planning; and contact with staff and boys. The meeting agreed that the first and last were essential, with Darling adamant that he least wanted to forgo the contact with staff and boys. Council was reluctant to direct him or propose solutions. There had to be 'one key man', said Fairfax (Robson confirmed for him that the personal contact role was paramount as a headmaster was always a schoolmaster), and the entire organisational design had to 'spring from him', so that a decision about a headmaster-in-chief and a headmaster of Corio 'rests with you'. The public relations and planning functions were easier to perform than the personal contact role, Turner believed, because of Australia's 'lack of sufficient good men at the top' (heads, professors and vice-chancellors): hence the general overemphasis in the country (he thought) on their importance. For the time being, the discussion went nowhere and was overtaken by the centenary finale.[19]

Commencing with an old boys' day in March, the organising committee (Griffiths, Darling, Desborough, Newman and two OGGs) had devised an impressive series of events culminating on speech day on 17 December: a garden party (5 April), Timbertop weekend (17–19 March), cathedral service and founders' centenary dinner (24 June), a ball (26 July) and three drama performances, each of which was overseen by a web of sub-committees. An added bonus was an April 1957 *Illustrated London News* edition that devoted six pages to GGS's centenary. As an aid to the appeal fund, 5000 copies were purchased and distributed among OGGs and donors. The garden party was a grand affair, commencing with afternoon tea on the Perry oval for 2000 expected guests. There were to be exhibitions by the various houses, forms and schools, a cricket match between GGS and King's, rowing on the Barwon, gymnastics and tennis. A memorial bay in the school library was to be dedicated to Charles Hawker, for which Darling invited the Australian historian Sir Keith Hancock (Institute of Commonwealth Studies) to speak at the garden party about his former friend. Darling wanted 'this centenary affair to mean something, if possible' and there was 'no-one with whom I would rather associate school ideals and traditions than Charles Hawker'. Grateful for the invitation, Hancock declined: he was not in the habit of making speeches, had never spoken to schoolboys or parents and was not inclined to do so. Anyway, by early April he would only have been back in the land of his birth about a month, and was hoping to become a part of a country and a community which were 'now strange to me'. He had only known Hawker intimately during 1926–33 and met him just twice more before his tragic death.[20]

The afternoon thanksgiving service in St Paul's Cathedral, Black claimed, 'could not have been bettered', and more than 400 people attended the Royale Ballroom gala dinner that followed. Darling agreed about the thanksgiving service although he didn't enjoy the dinner 'very much'. The official party included the lieutenant-governor and the premier—but not the prime minister (in London for the Commonwealth Prime Ministers' Conference)—along with Ramsay, Gilray, John McKie, Gorton, Spowers and the presidents of each of the APS old boy associations. One serious protocol slip-up was that nobody thought to invite the archbishop (and president of the school council) to preside—prodded by McKie, Darling confessed later that 'I never thought of it'. At the dinner, Griffiths announced that the centenary fund stood at £100,000 and Darling arranged for an old boy from 1930, Alan Brown (Worcester College, Oxford) to propose the toast—a 'brilliant piece of practised oratory', Spowers said later—following which the headmaster paid a moving tribute to Hawker. He spoke at length, he told Joey Allen, so as to 'fix him into the tradition of the School'. Allen confirmed for Darling what he had always suspected about Hawker: 'I remember Jim Fairbairn—who had just been made Minister for Air—saying to me at the funeral', Allen recalled, 'that the thing he regretted most of all [was] that he was not in Hawker's Cabinet, for he was destined to be Prime Minister if that great tragedy [the air crash] had not occurred'. Hawker had lost an eye at Ypres on the Western Front in 1915, following which he recuperated after numerous operations and returned to battle, only to be severely wounded. Paralysed from the waist down, Hawker taught himself to walk again and, until he died aged forty-four, his legs were permanently in irons. Spowers commended Darling for what he said about Hawker as he had 'never known of greater determination or what[']s commonly called guts' in anyone.[21]

A centenary highlight was the performance on the lawn of the Chapel of All Saints on 8–10 November of yet another pageant play, *Their Succeeding Race*, scripted by a young GGS master, Michael Persse. The ABC televised the production. The original idea for the play (said the *Corian*) had been the headmaster's. Hundreds of boys participated and between them they acted over 1500 parts in a story weaving together three strands or 'visions of three kingdoms': the school; Britain and Australia; and the Kingdom of Heaven. After the initial scenes in England, the remainder of the storyline wove between events in 1788 at Sydney Cove, 1957 at Corio and other key dates in GGS's and the nation's past. It was set at various Western District and Geelong locations, and sprinkled throughout with important GGS identities, including three early headmasters, J.L. Cuthbertson and Dr Brown. Cuthbertson's poems were quoted and the perspectives of Timbertop boys were juxtaposed with some of the experiences of earlier generations of GGS's outdoor tradition. One of the play's characters was Hawker:

> Some say Charles Hawker was the perfect type
> Of all Australians can both do and be.

Two pages of dialogue extolled his virtues with words from Hancock suggesting that, but for the air tragedy, Hawker may have been Australia's Churchill 'in our gravest hour'. Contemporary events (including Shell's attempted land incursion— although it assisted by erecting stands for the pageant) and the school's potential move formed part of the script. Darling figured in Scene 13 as The Boss: 'what the School now is is largely him', after which his view of the school appears as 'first a parish, then a sword'. John Manifold (W.T. Manifold, his father, was one of the characters) had not survived to witness the pageant, as he had died a few days before on 5 November.[22]

The other significant centenary event was the evaluation by Bill Connell, since 1955 a newly minted 41-year-old professor from Sydney. Darling rued his decision to have the school reviewed when presented with the evaluation team's whopping 375-page report in January 1958, as it was not happy reading. Like Manning Clark, Connell was a Melbourne Grammar scholarship boy— both had attended Mont Albert Central School, that 'scholarship shop for the aspiring middle class children of the eastern suburbs of Melbourne'. Darling later assessed his commissioning of the evaluation as equally the 'most honourable' and the 'most stupid' decision. Barry Connell had been a GGS master since 1951 and, when on Darling's behalf in late 1956 he sounded out his brother about heading up the review, his sibling fancied that this might be 'quite important for Australian education generally'. Before the council agreed (in October 1956) to the headmaster's recommendation, Darling was expressing his reservations to Connell: his feet were getting colder at the prospect because 'there is so much wrong with the place', about which he was aware and yet seemed 'unable to correct'. There was also much that he probably knew nothing about because the school had 'got very much out of hand recently'. Even if the council concluded that he was responsible for a negative evaluation outcome that was not a reason for Connell to 'hide the truth'. As the council had not laid down terms of reference, Darling said that Connell was to inspect and then report on 'how effectively [the school] seems to be carrying out the purpose of its existence'. If he wished, Connell could even write his own terms of reference. Struggling to contain his defensiveness, Darling's reasoning became obtuse and he could not stifle the theme of ossification. Connell's team would encounter 'mysteries' that would require 'a confidential explanation' from himself and, while financial information dominated 'the situation', the facts of the school's educational incompetence were all 'too obvious to need to be glossed over'. He also wanted Connell's help to extricate him from 'certain impasses' because he felt incapable of breaking out of his ways of thinking. Would Connell commence with 'a completely open mind' or would he prefer a 'more specific commission'? His findings would be confidential to the council. Connell forwarded Darling a 'rather formidable' list of requests for background information and he came to Corio during the Olympics. In their correspondence, Darling continued to feel his way, while acknowledging his and the school's shortcomings. As a multi-purpose institution GGS endeavoured to 'do the best it can with the material presented to it by parents'; by tradition it supported Western District grazier families while catering for boys of both very low and superior intelligence. For this reason, he wanted Connell to help him handle more effectively the realisation of 'such a variety of objectives'. He had appointed many staff during his 'salad days', but he and they were ageing and becoming conservative. A school in excess of 660 boys (that is, the senior school) was 'too much' for him to handle and he knew that he needed to decentralise further.[23]

From March and intermittently throughout 1957 a panel of six reviewers visited GGS for eight weeks at an all-up cost of £250. In return, Connell's group was permitted to 'invade and inspect the school with an entirely free hand'. In addition to Connell, the team comprised Dr W.J. Campbell, H. Philip, G. Howie, R.W. Stanhope and A. Cullen. About 250 pages of their report was devoted to the curriculum (including Timbertop), while most of the remainder concentrated on GGS's objectives, administration, teaching staff, testing and examinations,

and the boys. The report pulled no punches. It located GGS squarely within
an English prototype of service and playing the game. After criticising the
noblesse oblige ideal as conducive to patronage, a form of leadership based on
an excessively inward-looking loyalty and solidarity rather than cooperation,
the report itemised deficiencies arising from the school's commitment to its
objectives. There was little or no opportunity for 'common planning' by staff,
no rethinking of the service ideal in contemporary Australia, constriction of
boys' personal development (notwithstanding Timbertop's opportunities) and
introspection bred by GGS's 'semi-monastic' isolation. Having stormed the
ramparts, the report launched an assault on the administrative apparatus, which
was dismissed as not only 'authoritarian in character' and producing 'benevolent
autocracy', but as bestowing (consequent on the centralisation of authority in the
person of the headmaster) an unduly fragmented and disjointed character.[24]

If this was a trenchant broadside against the philosophical foundations
of Darling's headship, the teaching staff were also candidates for Connell's
blowtorch. While the masters possessed a 'high degree' of the knowledge and
attitudes required for co-curricular activities and relationship-building, they
did not cut the mustard in classroom teaching techniques. There was 'too much
in-breeding' (thirty-one of thirty-nine senior school masters were independent
school–educated; a third of that thirty-one were OGGs); more than 40 per cent
of the masters lacked a professional teaching qualification and few undertook
in-service education. Compared with their senior school colleagues, junior school
masters were better prepared professionally but distinctly inferior academically.
Connell's report despaired: successful professional work was 'inconceivable'
without preliminary training, and opportunities to accumulate knowledge and
technique concerned with education and adolescence. Equally, the absence of
any further training was 'little short of disastrous'. Staff exchanges with English
schools helped enrich the masters' experiences and broadened their horizons,
but were no substitute for regular and planned in-service education. Connell
saw little rhyme or reason in a staff selection policy based on roughly one-
third proportions of OGGs, other Australians and Englishmen. Finally, while
the housemasters were able and devoted, they had no psychological training
and experience to deal with maladjusted boys, and lacked the back-up support
of a second or junior housemaster. Few stones were left unturned. Beginning
with science and mathematics, the team's criticisms were often scathing—the
languages area was savagely mauled—but there were helpful suggestions for
nine curriculum areas, including recommendations for changes based on an
assessment of resources and observations of GGS classrooms. There was also
some good news. Religious education was at least on a par with, if not better
than, that of most Australian Anglican schools, even though this was not an area
in which GGS was 'conspicuously successful'. Timbertop was an innovation of
which to be genuinely proud, and the work of the art and music departments was
something else—their level of quality was 'first rate', could 'scarcely be matched

anywhere else in Australia', and both departments dripped with talented, devoted and sensitive masters.[25]

There was also much that was inadequate. For testing, guidance and record-keeping the report asserted that the school desperately needed a full-time educational psychologist, but Connell's killer punch was a toss-up between two measures of the school's negative impact on the boys: their comparatively poor examination performances or their acquisition of regressive social values. The intellectual building blocks were in place, but when the Leaving and matriculation results were compared with samples of other Victorian schools, GGS performed poorly. The other indication that three decades of Darling's chickens had come home to roost was a worrying tendency detected in senior boys' values. Their interest in religious and aesthetic values was low, which, given GGS's social and spiritual objects, Connell's panel found 'somewhat surprising'. The overall picture among senior boys was 'acceptance of authoritarian, almost anti-democratic, values in more than expected proportions'—although whether this trend reflected social backgrounds or was fostered by their schooling was 'not possible to decide'. Finally, the report found strong acceptance by third- and fifth-year boys of a need to achieve, a result usually due to the influence of male adults, and a propensity to evaluate situations in respect of material achievement of success or failure. The boys' coping strategies for failure were blame avoidance or the maintenance of self-esteem through withdrawal. Taken together, the findings were suggestive although incomplete, but there were worrying signs of low esteem.[26]

Connell's results were less than Darling was hoping for—not 'a feather left to fly with', he said immediately and again twenty years later. He had prepared himself for the worst by deliberately signalling to Connell that he was 'relying on the promise of advice'. To his annoyance—because he hoped to implement the findings in first term 1958—Connell overshot his late 1957 submission deadline. After wading through the extensive report Darling said that he was 'immensely grateful': it was shrewd and the team had fingered 'most of the many weaknesses', although he had a few quibbles. Connell did not appreciate the economic demands involved in running a very expensive school that was obliged to accept boys whose families could afford the fees. Darling also doubted whether Connell understood the difficulties in obtaining and maintaining an adequate staff (although Darling conceded that GGS's in-house superannuation scheme strongly constrained staff mobility). War service had played havoc with the age profile and the Education Department provided stiff competition in recruiting teachers. He accepted responsibility for the lack of staff consultation as he had overburdened himself 'with other things'. While the examination results were distressing, the parents ignored the school's advice and insisted on their sons sitting for them. Some suggestions had genuine merit (for example, incorporation of the third year into the junior school, creation of a preliminary language course) and yet Darling shrank from the implications: would it be better to 'hand [the report] over with the School to someone else'?[27]

Darling used Connell's document to 'beat the masters with', and wanted a 'prolonged open discussion' of it over dinner after a council meeting and a three-day staff seminar in the May 1958 vacation (with the Sydney-based reviewing team in attendance) to consider the findings. Distressing as these were, Darling told Griffiths that they had so stirred up the teaching staff that 'the place is buzzing with conferences and discussion'. Most staff who responded took Connell's criticisms on the chin. The common room association accepted the need for the rethink prompted by the recommendations, but asserted that the claim about the lack of confidence between itself and the headmaster was exaggerated. One young master thought that GGS's problem was not its geographic isolation but (echoing Darling's mention of Persia to Ralph) the mental isolation and experience of longer-serving colleagues who were quite 'unaware of the really important values of life, and how they operate in the "world outside"'. Theirs was a Morris Room world of 'stultifying' talk. Peter Westcott's view was that what was said was there to be said, except that there had been recent improvements (for example, school buildings) and Timbertop was 'a remarkable counterblast to any idea that we are moribund'. Furthermore (reiterating Darling's point), because it was the school's lot to educate the rich, 'we have to do the best we can with the sort of people we get' and, he added, 'we didn't do too badly'. Extensive council discussion of Darling's detailed response went ahead on 12 May. Staff seminars were productive and relations with Connell amicable. Darling assured him of the report's 'great practicable benefit', such that he and the masters had been forced to 'think in a way that we have not done for years'. The challenge was to resist backsliding.[28]

Salt was soon poured into the wound opened up by Westcott when GGS became the target of negative press coverage. In 'An anatomy of Australian snobbishness', published originally in the *Sydney Morning Herald*, the English journalist Malcolm Muggeridge (the newspaper's guest for three months while in Australia) well and truly sank the boot into Darling and GGS. The school was a perfect litmus test of the egalitarianism of which Australians were so boastfully proud, but egalitarianism was a sham: as the Eton of the Antipodes, GGS gave the idea the lie by being 'commonly regarded as a citadel of snobbishness' and the nursery for Australia's patrician families. Muggeridge's feeble attempt at lese-majesty was to sneer that Darling was 'affable and seasoned' enough, although a member of an outdated post–World War I–vintage generation. Moreover, his school was little more than a replica of the English public school model and, because it was merely a copy, could never be first-rate. One 'disgruntled, rebellious old boy' (to whom Muggeridge had spoken) insisted that he had loathed GGS, although its saving grace was that if one wanted a career in the Department of External Affairs then it might confer the necessary edge. But here again there were echoes of Home, the dismissive Muggeridge said cheekily, because the Foreign Office was one of the few remaining English upper-class enclosures, which explained why it had a record of 'almost unbroken failure'. Australia was just as class-ridden as England, although it was more fluid at the same time that it was cruder, brasher and a more openly brutal, but also a simpler, society.[29]

Clyde Packer now had a guilty conscience because he had requested his former headmaster to allow Muggeridge to visit Corio. When quizzed about GGS by Muggeridge, Packer had tried to persuade him 'that he was wrong' and hoped that 'if he saw the place, he might change his mind'. Packer apologised. He had no idea that the outcome would be an 'offensive and personal attack' on Darling and the school. Apart from the blow to his vanity, Darling's major concern (without having yet read the article) was the controversy that Muggeridge's piece might spark. (Exactly what Geoffrey Dutton wanted for *Australian Letters* when he invited his former headmaster to write on the 'urgent necessity of educating Australians to the subtleties of snobbery, and the dangers of a sense of humour'.) Darling blamed himself. 'Blast him! I don't really feel as detached as this about it.' With James Fairfax, on the other hand, Darling wondered whether he was still on speaking terms with anyone at all at the *Herald*: if it was incapable of preserving 'some decent etiquette in such matters', then heaven help the Australian press. Yes, Fairfax conceded, the *Herald* had let Darling down and he was sorry: while Muggeridge had not clarified whether he would write about GGS, 'we assumed that you knew' he would. The newspaper was not presuming on GGS's hospitality. Personally speaking, Fairfax said that the article had been 'very stupid and superficial and quite unworthy of the school'. For levity's sake, one old boy farmer's solution was to take to Muggeridge with a pair of burdizzos (a livestock castration device).[30]

Darling put on a brave face. The damage was his fault: 'I should have known better', he told council because, having agreed to entertain Muggeridge in the naive belief that no article would be written, he had let his guard drop. Leopards didn't change their spots, but '[was] Muggeridge right?', he pondered while wrestling with Connell's charge that GGS was stuck in a nineteenth-century mould and priced at the high end of the market. Muggeridge was merely round one, because in late 1960, a copy of Connell's report ended up with the *Nation* journalist Ken Gott. Alerted by Connell, Darling suspected that the culprit who leaked was a master, but he chose not to play detective and rode out the criticism. In Gott's far less caustic tone, Darling's invitation to a team to scrutinise the school was an 'enlightened initiative', although slightly more worrying was Gott's suggestion that Connell's report offered the headmaster's successor a 'quarry' of stimulation. Apart from praise of Timbertop, *Nation*'s readers were given liberal dollops of Connell's negative findings—relatively poor examinations results, inbred staffing profile, authoritarianism and unsuccessful religious education. Gott also highlighted the critical appraisal of Darling—as more a gentleman than a scholar—and the pressing need for a contemporary adaptation of *noblesse oblige*.[31]

Jamie Mackie visited Corio when Gott's article was published and after-wards wrote that Darling seemed 'so depressed about all you have done for the school & the country since you came to Corio'. Earlier, Jo Gullett said likewise after reading Darling's speech-day report of Connell's findings ('you were a bit cast down'). And, from Swarthmore College in Pennsylvania, USA, the young philosopher (and OGG) Michael Scriven said that, despite Connell's assessment, the school's merits were such that headmasterly depression should not be countenanced. But why had it come to this? A number of factors were working against GGS in the 1950s. First, the pull of Darling's external commitments, with their demands and absences meant that his mind was elsewhere (as he and the school knew). Second, GGS's market position had also changed. On its home turf in Victoria it was competing with an expanding state secondary sector (under the leadership of his friend Ramsay and, ironically, from 1956 under the ministerial oversight of an OGG, John Bloomfield). Among the APS schools the balance of influence had shifted compared with the 1930s when Darling had been the pacesetter. Rival schools had lifted their game under heads with high reputations, like Gilray and Hone, and intensified GGS's market pressures—as Darling admitted in his twenty-point response to Connell's report. Specifically, the comparative fortunes of the two Anglican schools, GGS and Melbourne Grammar, had changed. When the entry demand for Melbourne Grammar had been weaker (as during Melbourne's mid-1930s low ebb), GGS had prospered; but when GGS's St Kilda Road competitor was attractive, there was a double whammy for GGS. First, high boarding fees were a potential disincentive for prospective parents and the justification for boarding was less persuasive. Second, Glamorgan (unintentionally) may have been less of a GGS Trojan horse in its rival's hinterland and more of a de facto Melbourne Grammar preparatory school (mainly a day school) alongside Wadhurst and Grimwade.[32]

Early in 1958, Darling thought that the financial tide might be turning. Bostock, Glamorgan and the senior school returned an operating profit (for 1957) of about £19,000 and he expected the corresponding 1958 figure to be £25,000 (it was actually £33,000). As a result, GGS was less dependent on its overdraft and budgeting for depreciation on assets was easier. If the market held for three years, he told Ted Richardson, then 'we shall almost be out of the wood'. With the agreement of the archbishop-in-council, an act passed by synod enabled GGS to create a nominee company. Coupled with recent amendments to council's constitution—which had increased the non-diocesan appointees and put it out of reach of the 'vagaries of [the] ecclesiastical politics' afflicting Sydney diocesan schools—GGS had more flexibility to shape its future. The new company would hold the school's securities (reserves and endowments)—although the title deeds were still with AMP (as loan security). Such was the rosiness of the asset–liability balance at the beginning of 1959 that Darling was confident that £55,000 could be expended on vital priorities. He was also pushing to have the council think about financial policy and, because between them Corio and Timbertop were bursting with 635 boarders, to gear its collective mind to planning for future admissions—a key problem of growth being the need for an additional boarding house. Closely associated in councillors' thinking were the likely future educational needs of Geelong Anglicans and, with the growth in secondary education demand, the need for another Protestant school. Here, the Highton project was significant.[33]

Marcus Oldham, 'Gentleman deceased', died in 1939. In early 1957, Black alerted Darling to his estate, estimated to be worth £220,000. Oldham's will directed that, upon the death of his wife, the estate trustees (the Union Trustee Company of Australia: Black was a trustee) should establish a 'Training School for the maintenance and education in pastoral farming or agricultural pursuits' for the 'sons of Protestant parents'. The will stipulated that the school should be called the Marcus Oldham Farm, and that in respect of the new school the trustees should exercise 'absolute discretion' in their disbursement of estate capital and income, particularly with regard to the ages of the students, the duration of their education and the conduct of the school. Crucially, if twenty-one years after Oldham's death (1960) the estate income had not been expended, then the income and accumulated interest could be applied for 'such legal charitable purposes in such manner as my Trustees in their discretion shall think fit'. Various efforts to give effect to this clause in the will had been unsuccessful, said Black, and 'we really must do something about it'. He had conferred with John Larritt, the general manager of the Union Trustee Company (and a GGS parent), and they were aware that 'the Presbyterians are after us'. When Black sought Darling's views, his idea was to provide practical education for the sons of graziers—there were agricultural colleges at Longerenong and Dookie, and a horticultural college at Burnley. Boys wanting to be graziers, Darling believed, were inadequately educated at GGS because on leaving school they became jackeroos and returned home with very little grazing knowledge. Having been consulted by the trustees, Darling's task (as he said later) was to try to weld together 'the hopes and purposes of the various parties involved'.[34]

In early 1959, GGS's council purchased at £85 per acre a 116-hectare site at Highton, south-west of Geelong, to establish a new college to give effect to the will of the testator. Darling had conferred with Rolland's successor Dr Buntine (Geelong College was also unable to provide for graziers' sons) and both saw a need for another independent Geelong secondary school. When council purchased the land, Darling returned to his model for the future, this time with wider applicability in the form of 'an educational complex': education for both boys and girls, for adults and religious institutions, and playing fields shared with the community. This was 'the proper concept of the future', not the current prototype of clinging exclusively to 'possessions and its privileges'. Pragmatically, the idea made sense: he could sell Bostock House and relocate the boys, and the Hermitage also wanted to vacate its premises. Black's advice was that the Oldham component of the complex had to be a legally separate entity, although capable of integration with the other school elements (about 8 hectares). Early indications from Larritt (in London) and an on-site inspection of the land were favourable.

Darling pressed Black to purchase an adjoining block of about 46 hectares as its acquisition would strengthen GGS's negotiating hand. If the Union Trustee Company refused its endorsement, then 162 hectares would be of appreciable future investment value to GGS.[35]

Just prior to the expiry of the AMP loan (February 1960) and while awaiting the trustees' deliberations, Darling tried another way of financially securing the school: instead of the centenary fund, the issuing to parents and old boys of unsecured notes at 4 per cent interest. With the school still starved of capital, the fund had had limited success—the best guess in late 1957 was that it would recoup £120,000. This figure only enabled completion of the maintenance backlog and general reserves were being built up for future maintenance. A large number of people holding small amounts of capital (say, £1000 each) would spread the risk and lessen the negative impact of potential mass redemptions. Darling had in mind £350,000 (or 350 contributors) to cover the school's liabilities: liquidation of the AMP loan, repayment of the bank overdraft and debentures, and provision of a reserve for repayment demands and an investment sum through the school's new company (Geelong Grammar School Nominees). His proposal (belying his disclaimer about lack of financial capability) made sense: as Commonwealth state aid funding was still some years away and, unless generously endowed, independent schools were constantly searching for capital. With an eye on who might be the next headmaster, he also wanted the school to be financially sound. Despite Vincent Fairfax's best efforts to convince AMP by highlighting the commitment of old boys and parents as potential contributors, it was less than enthusiastic. Long-term reliance on parental loans at concessional rates would be 'unwise', AMP believed, because Darling had underestimated the rate of potential loan redemptions, especially in the case of deceased estates (which tended to call these up). Traditional routes to capital security (mortgage finance and endowments) offered sounder planning bases. The only other alternative, Fairfax believed, was to continue with the existing AMP loan and to use loans from parents to replace the bank overdraft, thereby going beyond the limit that the loan lender was willing to go, and try to have the bank underwrite the lenders. In the event, AMP extended by a further fifteen years the existing loan of £92,000 at 7 per cent interest (although the school had wanted £100,000).[36]

During the gestation of his Highton concept, Darling kept Archbishop Woods in the loop because he was keen to reserve part of the new site for 'church purposes' (1.6 hectares in GGS's purchase) and to ensure that a new school was Protestant rather than solely Anglican. Confident after a conference with the Oldham trustees in late 1959 that the project would proceed, Darling knew that he was committing his successor but he saw no alternative. By the following August, the Oldham trustees were attracted by the 'likelihood of the establishment of other educational institutions' at Highton. A meeting of the 'interested parties' (GGS, Bostock, the Hermitage and the trustees) convened on 9 November. As part of a scheme of cooperation, they established a project joint oversight committee (excluding the church: Woods inspected the site in 1959 but the diocese had no money) and agreed to share in the establishment costs, with GGS's share being 40 per cent. 'Common land' (in the name of Geelong Grammar School Nominees) was set aside for buildings for common use (for example, a chapel and hall). GGS paid half the costs, Oldham a third and the Hermitage a sixth. 'Generously though reluctantly', 8 hectares of unallocated land for the development of a secondary school and the Hermitage was set aside by the trustees. The anticipated sale of Bostock House would finance GGS's share. The new complex was scheduled to open in 1962. Site works commenced in May 1961 and tenders were called to construct the buildings.[37]

During these Oldham discussions, Darling contacted Griffiths shortly after his sixtieth birthday in 1959. 'I intend at the next Council meeting to inform you that I do not intend to ask you to continue my term of office beyond the end of 1961 which would be the normal date of my retirement.' With that, Darling's 32-year-long incumbency would be over. His decision triggered a succession—the transition period following a leading figure's departure. It needed careful handling. As high-ranking, visible, influential and socially prominent men, the appointment and departure of heads generated a mixture of hopes and weighty expectations. It was not unusual for incumbent heads to take part in their peers' successions because a tacit assumption was that the more senior of them were also headmaster-makers. Heads saw themselves as members of a quasi-priestly caste with firm views about suitability for admission to their ranks, for which reason they expected to be consulted about headmasters-in-waiting. They could make or break up-and-coming aspirants by either bestowing or withholding their stamp of approval. Such customary behaviour was not unreasonable, because long before it became standard practice to contract search firms (or headhunters) to locate and screen candidate successors, no-one else possessed overall knowledge of the talent pool—least of all part-time amateurs like councillors. Advice could come from serving or retired heads. Even the gentle Frank Rolland could not restrain himself when approached (in retirement). With the best of intentions he confessed to having 'poised himself far aloft from Geelong College affairs' for nearly fifteen years since he left in 1945, but with Dr Buntine shortly to depart the College (about when Darling gave notice), Rolland asked his friend's opinion about his likely replacement.[38]

Incumbent heads acted as sounding boards or advice-givers (and, therefore, prospective testimonial writers), as Darling had done in 1943 for Gordon (then in the Australian Army) when, after learning that Pentreath was returning to England, the latter asked him to confirm the information and to advise on whether he 'should have a go' at St Peter's. A typical feature of the grooming or coaching feedback provided was about readiness—as with Brian Hone (while a master at Marlborough in 1936) when George Turner (the head) advised him to obtain more teaching experience rather than to apply for the Melbourne Grammar post vacated by Stacey Colman. Occasionally, male heads

even intruded onto female ground when advising girls' schools about possible
headmistresses (the reverse process was probably unthinkable). In 1942, Isobel
Hamilton of Toorak College approached Darling about a successor to Winifred
Allen, the headmistress: he suggested possible candidates and limited himself to
such un-contentious banalities as a woman who was 'aware of the changing needs
of society and prepared with imagination to adjust herself and the school to these
needs'. The next level in the pecking order of advice-giving was intervention
in the internal machinations of the appointing school councils. With Michael
Searle, Darling had tutored the chairman about how to find an exemplary head.
But engagement beyond this level entailed anointment of a successor, which is
what Darling did in 1958 when Lieutenant Colonel Basil Holmes (Jika) Travers
succeeded Robson at Shore.[39]

Len Robson had thrown in the towel in November 1957. By March, one
of the names in the frame was Travers (headmaster, since 1953, of Launceston
Church Grammar School), for whom Darling (as the senior tribal elder among
Conference headmasters) wrote a reference. To not appoint a candidate when
it had from such an eminent man a poignant description that included such
glowing language as 'shrewd, capable of self-critical self-judgment, imaginative,
creative and courageous', called for a very brave school council. Letting people
down gently was also part of the heads' skill-set, so that when one aspirant (an
OGG) sounded out Darling about Shore, his politely worded advice (not in so
few words) was to forget it. Not only did Robson's successor need to be a 'big man
with a rather magnetic personality added to efficiency and scholarship', he said,
but (drawing on his own prewar experience) a key consideration was the legacy
that one left behind. In Darling's case, Lord Somers' advice was that:

> a Headmaster who had made something of a revolution in the character
> of a school should not leave until he had built up a sufficient body of old
> boy–parent support to prevent his work being undone by the reaction which
> might set in after he left. This was 1936 or thereabouts. In 1939 I went home
> to England and they thought I wasn't coming back. It was astonishing how
> quickly the reaction set in.

Moreover, Manifold had persuaded Darling that the satisfaction of having made
a really significant contribution to one school was 'better than having a career'.
It was when asked to amplify his remark that Travers was 'a man of real stature'
that Darling was drawn further in at Shore and when later requested to weigh
the 'relative merits' of the final two candidates—with his opinion being a 'kind of
yardstick to gauge the standing of the U.K. Candidates against the Australian'.[40]

This request upped the stakes significantly. Both men were thirty-eight:
Travers was a Shore old boy and his rival was P.M.C. Hare, a Rugby assistant
master who in 1949–50 had been on exchange at GGS and for whom Darling
was also a referee. (Previously Darling had alerted Robson to Hare as a 'really

first class person' and 'one of the best young Englishmen that I have had out here'.) With little choice but to comment further, Darling contrasted two sets of candidate dispositions, and yet because he was 'very fond of both men' who were 'entirely adequate people', he resisted choosing. He compiled two lists for the Shore council: 'Do you want a rather English Englishman or a rather Australian Australian?', and was pressed to be 'less cautious and circumspect'. Put himself in Shore's shoes, the council secretary urged; use his knowledge of the school and say what he would do had he been in its place. Darling relented. After comparing each man against six criteria, he plunged in with a five-page letter. The council had to decide 'what sort of man they want in a particular situation for a particular school at a particular time'. First, to replace an eminent headmaster after a long incumbency required an individual in his own right who was capable of extending his predecessor's contribution. Second, to meet the challenge posed by state schooling, Shore's best guarantee was someone likely to produce leaders for the Sydney community and who could link his vision to the 'more general problem'. Third, the 'critical situation' confronting Australia required a man imbued with Christianity. On all three counts, Travers was that man. Darling also said that Turner was delighted to hear that Travers was likely to go to Shore as there was no-one as good 'this end' and it was high time that Australian schools appointed Australian headmasters, 'so far as they can'. In short, it would be 'madness', Darling asserted, not to appoint a person of 'proved [sic] ability' about whom Shore already knew a great deal in the vain hope that a better outsider might turn up.[41]

Travers was chosen and grateful to Darling for his support. Robson was delighted. He had been pushing Shore's council to contact Darling. 'You can guess what is going on', he had written, 'the sensible ones are for him [Travers], I believe, but the few silly damn parsons are hesitant', although they could not 'see any better'. From his vantage point ('looking disgusted whenever my side plays badly'), Robson had been certain that Travers was right, but a few wiser men than him had sought a unanimous decision and were moving most patiently. With the decision made, Robson said (cryptically) that it had been a 'battle', about which 'one might write a book'. The nucleus of the council had brought the others to their senses, after drawn-out deliberations during which the 'most violent of the knights', bearing a 'lance (poison-tipped)' for the other side, had retired at a critical moment. As for the defeated candidate, the nub of the problem, Darling confided to Brian Hone, had probably been that he was suspected by the Sydney diocese of being high church.[42]

In his own case, Darling went one step further and chose the man who succeeded him. He knew when he was writing to Griffiths about the handover date as the end of second term 1961 that time was needed to 'plan for a successor' as well as finding one. He was sanguine about his decision and not regretful when breaking the news to Ralph. A year later, he quipped to Julian Bickersteth that the timing of his imminent visit might coincide with the public announcement, in which case 'having been at the birth so to speak, it would be fitting for you also to be at the death'. His mood, however, had shifted. To Robson, who had retired the previous December, and had peppered his friend with advice about what to do and what not to do in his retirement, Darling expressed doubts. In September 1959, he told him about one school crisis after another, so much so that he could not 'ever remember so distressing a year'—forgetting, possibly, that he had said the same about 1957. The attractiveness of beckoning retirement was also a 'prospect, which I fear'. Secure in the knowledge that he could forget all about 'mumps, or cooks or masters for 1960, or the clergy of the Sydney diocese', Robson sympathised but was nonchalant. When the news broke at Corio, people became resigned to Darling's departure. Archbishop Woods said that his friend's resignation letter was received with 'very great regret', Griffiths was equally regretful and Black said that it was 'rather a shock' to be shown his letter by Griffiths. Black thought that there was 'plenty of time now to consider the question' of who should succeed him and, when his letter was tabled at council, Darling took it upon himself to outline 'very briefly some of the steps that would have to be taken in securing a successor'.[43]

Was Darling playing with fire? Gordon's different rule of thumb had been to refrain from 'interfering with the choice of my successor'. Darling had been weighing up the available alternatives for some time. In 1954, there was a tantalisingly brief mention (in a letter from Turner) of another Englishman, P.C.W. Disney (Scotch College, Adelaide), which hinted that Darling had asked him to give Disney the once-over. 'I think you may very naturally think of Pat Disney as a possible successor', Turner had written from St Peter's, as:

> I greatly like what I have seen of him, both on his own ground & elsewhere. His present idea seems to be to do 10 years or so out here & then to go home; but no doubt he wd. reconsider this if a wider opportunity came his way in Australia.

As to himself Darling guessed that he still had 'about seven or eight years' left as head and that 'a lot may happen before then'. His preferred replacement was Thomas Ronald (Tommy) Garnett, Master of Marlborough College. When offered the headmastership in July 1960, Garnett was forty-five and sixteen years Darling's junior. (He had been a Charterhouse pupil during Darling's time there. Later, he had returned to teach classics.) He had been Master since 1952. He and Darling were moderately well acquainted. In 1933, Frank Fletcher had written about Garnett's dazzling brilliance with the willow (1023 runs in eleven innings for Charterhouse) and his various scholarly successes. Garnett and Darling had been in irregular correspondence since 1953, but particularly during Turner's Australian visit when Darling informed Garnett that John Landy (in London prior to the Commonwealth Games in Vancouver) was considering a brief teaching appointment in England. Turner was sanguine about the succession being settled 'satisfactorily to yourself'. Council authorised Darling to negotiate the handover date with Garnett who boarded a flight to Australia in August for a ten-day visit to GGS.[44]

When Garnett was appointed, Darling was pleased. He told Bishop Moyes (Diocese of Armidale) that he had known for a year about Garnett's willingness to come to GGS, for which reason he thought that it 'was almost dishonest of the Council to go on with the advertisement [for the vacancy], but they felt otherwise'. To his way of thinking, it had been 'fairly obvious that there was not likely to be any candidate from anywhere of [Garnett's] standing'. The relationship between head and successor seemed destined to get off on the right footing. The *Corian* provided an effusive two-page profile of the man that, among his many accomplishments, drew attention to his cricketing prowess, his rural upbringing in Cheshire and Suffolk, his love of the outdoor pursuits and noted his 'high-tone deafness'. (When it appointed him, council agreed that Garnett's 'slight deafness' could 'properly be disregarded'.) His wife, Penelope, was the niece of Darling's almost exact contemporary, Birley (Fletcher's successor as head of Charterhouse and later head of Eton). Darling extolled Garnett's virtues in his final speech-day report. Unlike the risk taken in appointing himself as an unknown quantity, this time council 'had taken no risk at all':

> It is a great thing for the School to have attracted so eminent a Headmaster of so great an English school. I have always felt that after me the School might be almost ready for a scholar and would need it; and, with apologies to the great rowing tradition of the School, I derive some satisfaction from having got a real cricketer.

Sadly, after Darling's departure his relations with Garnett turned frosty.[45]

For the time being the limelight was Darling's to monopolise. He was frank and indulgent in his final lengthy report to council. GGS was far better placed financially than 'at any other time in the past', with more than £680,000 being outlaid on buildings during his thirty-two years. Yes, the debt was £318,000 but the insured value of the assets (excluding land values at Corio and Toorak) was about £2.4 million. Total endowments were about £250,000. The expected cost of the Highton project was £100,000 of which the Bostock sale would return £75,000. There were now nearly 750 boys at Corio and Timbertop, and 49 masters compared with only 17 in 1926. While Connell's academic judgement had been right, three decades' results displayed a 'continued tendency towards improvement'. To assist Garnett to improve the Leaving Certificate results further (and to ease each Timbertop cohort's transition back to Corio), he agreed (after prolonged resistance) to seek A-school status—with inspection being the price for the curriculum flexibility facilitated by that classification. If these were the jewels of an extended litany of accomplishments there were also the pageants and plays, the tradition of community engagement that he had built up, and the successes of numerous old boys. Two areas of patchy success were skated over fairly quickly. First, the sporting results when graphed did not point to improvements (but they did not support old boys' accusations of decline). Second, success with religion was 'entirely unassessable', although an unassailable point was that while a GGS boy might drift, he could not (as he said on speech day) 'drift with a clear conscience'. As for his failures, he was unable during his final years to inspire the masters and improve the quality of teaching, there were pockets of persistent bullying, more stealing by boys, boys' dishonesty, overcrowded boarding houses and, finally, his recent inability (unlike in his early years) to appoint sufficient numbers of the 'right people'. When the reality of letting go the reins finally hit him, he was sad to be leaving after so many years. He wondered whether Christina Brown (retiring headmistress, Toorak College) was feeling similarly:

> No-one, I think, who has not done the job knows just how continuous and intense is the pressure of responsibility, and speaking of myself, the sense of inadequacy. It is a job in which one could never do enough to satisfy oneself, let alone anyone else and the rewards are very distant and perhaps inconclusive. I don't think, however, that this means that they are the less real. It is the great number of individual lives that one has touched that makes it all worth while and I am sure that you [also] feel happy about that. [46]

III

SETTLING IN
1954–1995

Hans Castorp had the daily schedule down pat, though it would perhaps be too much to say that he had now 'settled in,' as the expression goes.

Thomas Mann, *The Magic Mountain*

CIVILISING A CITIZENRY

1954–1961

There is no qualification for government, but virtue and wisdom, actual or presumptive. Wherever they are actually found, they have, in whatever state, condition, profession or trade, the passport of Heaven to human place and honour.

Edmund Burke, *Reflections on the Revolution in France*

In Adelaide in August 1960 Darling delivered the George Adlington Syme Oration to the Royal Australasian College of Surgeons. Composing it had been 'a ghastly sweat', he remarked to Colin Gordon. His text was populated with themes similar to those in his earlier Röntgen Oration such as specialisation and professionalism, except that this time beneath his grand mandate-dispensing title, 'The education of a civilized man', Darling varied his line on specialisation. As a surgeon, Syme's life showed that a specialist could embody civilised 'wholeness of manhood'. Moreover, specialised practice was here to stay. The two cultures of specialisation were the scientific and the humane, which, given their likely divergence, had to be reconciled. A classical education was not the way to achieve this and, while Teilhard de Chardin's suggestion of evolution was one possibility—*The Phenomenon of Man* was now available in English— Darling's preferred alternative was 'the cultivation of a more general sensitivity and awareness as the objects and criteria of a full education'. Burke had said of 'the true lawgiver' that he 'ought to have an heart full of sensibility', but Darling claimed that a civilised man was distinguished by 'sensitivity, or sensibility or sensitiveness'. The ingredient that made a human being sensitive was a living and growing conscience, for which the cultivating instrument was a liberal education for 'the development of the whole man'. His exemplars were such religiously anchored men as St Francis or Dr Schweitzer or, closer to home Louis Wharton ('the paragon of his age, endowed with every talent') and Charles Hawker (to whom it was 'a privilege to pay tribute'). Civilised men might have to specialise, but they should not despise the specialities of others. Moreover, no activity was too lofty or too humble to engage civilised men, or beneath their dignity.[1]

Written and delivered near to his retirement, this oration was a near-definitive statement of the moral foundations of Darling's three decades of educational and public endeavours. In 1950s Australia, there were numerous ways in which a sensitive man (like GGS's headmaster) could be virtuous. Locally, there was communal self-help, and for about five years from 1953 Darling worked with the Geelong and District Community Chest Association. In April 1954, at the Geelong City Hall, he was elected chairman and a foundation director (later, president) of the new community chest—a donation-based funding idea (originating in the USA) designed to coordinate money-raising by an annual appeal for subsequent dispersal to charitable and welfare groups. In Geelong, the moving spirit behind the adoption of the community-chest idea had been Apex, which had approached him for assistance in 1953. Darling willingly supported the community chest because it drew 'into a sense of responsibility for their fellows all or as many as possible of the citizens of a whole district', who then supported all the necessary social services 'through the willing contributions of a maximum rather than a minimum of people'. This was a way, in short, of citizens transcending their isolated individual status and lack of any common bond, and achieving a sense of organic wholeness. The community chest's success varied. Initially, there was 'considerable opposition' to it in Geelong, partly because the notion of a chest was thought to be 'an un-English method' and there was also a shadow of class about it: the hospital finances, Darling said, were 'a very sore point, particularly with the working class who feel that they have been swindled'. By 1958–59 nearly £64,000 had been raised for the Geelong and District Hospital, although in respect of its annual appeal targets, the community chest's reach often exceeded its grasp.[2]

Darling's other local commitment was the Unemployed Boys' Club. Until he resigned as a trustee in October 1960, his engagement in the life of the Centre, like that of his fellow trustees (C. Murray, after the death in the mid-1950s of J.O. McEwan, and Dr Pillow until his death in late 1960), continued to be arm's length. Whenever he was asked for advice about centres, clubs or adult education Darling's departure point was a twofold philosophical conviction. First, he maintained that such work needed to be centred on 'something that the boys themselves can recognize as useful'—for which purpose employment was the 'obvious thing'. Second, activities for boys had to be handled 'in this difficult age' as much as possible by 'people of their own kind and, if I may risk the word, class'. The problem could not be properly understood by people from different backgrounds. The fostering of community bonds as exemplified by the community chest and the Centre provided a foundation for a civilised society. Another building block, Darling claimed in his Syme Oration, was a nation's culture, which, if it was to attain the requisite quality of expression, depended on 'the quality of the men and women which it produces'. As a product of education, a civilised man was not only sensitive, but also 'wide in his interests, tolerant and yet courageous, intellectual and strong in principle'. Character-building was important in the production of civilised men and, in late 1953, Darling was alerted to another appealing possibility.[3]

Keith Officer (then Australia's ambassador in Paris) mentioned to Darling a proposal for a dominions sailing ship, brainchild of Sir William Garthwaite, a British ship owner in the Bahamas. Garthwaite envisaged a ship for training fourteen- to sixteen-year-olds, in the belief that sailing 'toughens their characters and gives them a feeling for the winds and weather that no other form of training can give'. He envisaged a ship with a crew comprising between 50 and 150 boys who were 'the pick and elite of the Dominions, a floating symbol of the Empire at sea!' Darling quickly contacted Commodore H.J. Buchanan (chief of naval personnel for the Naval Board) and said that the idea tied up with 'a magnificent conception which I once had of a peripatetic Empire Youth ship'. Unlike the earlier School Empire-Tour Committee tours, vessels would not sail merely to one country but 'continuously around the world', picking up and setting down in each dominion visited a quota of boys from that dominion. The outcome would be a 'continual mixing of the boys of the Empire and an opportunity for each group to see something of the other parts'. While he admitted that he had 'never thought of the possibility of doing this in sail', he supposed that this wind-powered option made the idea more practicable, less expensive 'and probably an even more magnificent conception'. If Buchanan would talk to his superiors, then he would try to contact the prime minister.[4]

Few public figures make every post a winner. Darling secured some support for his proposal but was trumped by an idea with wider appeal and more powerful backing. Sanguine about the outcome, he threw his weight behind the alternative scheme: Outward Bound. A sail-training ship in the 1950s was always going to be a hard sell (even with the grandiose title of *Golden Hind*). To have captured the imagination of Buchanan was one thing, but the weight of Australian naval opinion was not interested. The two men tag-teamed the proposal through various political and vice-regal networks in Australia and Britain (including Buckingham Palace) but to no avail. The Minister for the Navy (W. McMahon) helped kill the idea stone dead by informing Casey (Minister for External Affairs) that sail training was not a priority of the Royal Australian Navy. A new niche in the character-training market was also hard to find and Kurt Hahn's Outward Bound Aberdovey Sea School in Wales already had two training ships operating, the *Warspite* and *The Golden Valley*. (There was another, *Prince Louis*, at the Moray Sea School.) Aberdovey's underlying philosophy, where the duration of the residential course for boys aged sixteen to nineteen was 26 days, was based on a 'challenging course that had been used to stiffen the vitality of merchant navy lads who had been apt to lose their lives in conditions of protracted emergency'.[5]

On the home front, Darling had more luck with a different water-borne vessel, the rowing shell. When Brian Hone became headmaster of Melbourne

Grammar, Darling finally acquired a rock-solid ally in his protracted battle with that aquatic demon of APS incivility: the Boatrace. In the early 1950s, there were already differences of opinion in the Headmasters' Association concerning cricket. Viewed from the perspective of amateurism, Darling considered that preparatory cricket matches to spy out the opposition were 'repulsive', and the distinction between practice and real matches 'untenable'. The key battleground, however, was the Head of the River. Even though publicity had diminished following the regatta's relocation to the Barwon during construction of the Swan Street bridge (nearing completion in 1952) and the heads were resigned to the Barwon as the event's 'permanent home', sporadic ugly incidents were upsetting otherwise containable interschool tribalism. Despite pre-race agreements between the respective schools' prefects, contests for occupation of the key vantage point for spectator viewing known as 'the hill' (or 'perch', as Darling said) created a 'danger of elimination' of small boys and the theft of rivals' caps. Down on the bank, as Frederick told Darling after the 1951 regatta, there were also instances of mud-throwing and 'other forms of crude nonsense'. Such 'silly rows' aside, Darling's disgust at the Boatrace persisted, because it was generally 'deplorable that we should countenance so monstrously false a standard of values', particularly when 'this country is so lamentably fiddling itself into destruction'.[6]

In April 1954, the heads grasped the nettle by decreeing that ten weeks was sufficient for pre-regatta training, and they frowned upon crew selection and training in the final term of the preceding year. Then, at a special meeting at Melbourne Grammar in July, convened to remove 'objectionable features' from interschool games, Hone (supported by Darling) led a debate on the future of games and sport, in which he posed some blunt questions. Compared with the priority of school subjects, how could all the time, energy and money expended on games be justified? And, 'why are we organised into a tight and exclusive group of six schools for the purposes of playing competitive games, as in fact, we are?' Surely 1st team matches were no more important than others and, in any case, what was the APS trying to achieve with games? Were the aims merely to secure the schools' reputations and satisfy the clamour of old boys 'suffering maladjustments from adolescent fixations'? Although Hone put himself out on a limb, he felt that the meeting was 'extraordinarily amicable' and at the same time one of 'the most revolutionary' Headmasters' Association meetings. The heads agreed to no boating before February, football played on Saturdays (with a reduction in the duration of quarters), the scrapping of cricket premierships, and individual schools to determine the number of two-day matches and choice of opponents. Ironically, Darling tried (in a memorandum to Vic Tunbridge) to salvage some of the system's more positive features: in a country dominated by professional sport, at least the APS competitions offered examples of high-standard amateurism, 'real fellowship' arose out of the common bond of competition and, even in the case of rowing, the training provided was 'character-forming'. Portentously, however, in the pantheon of civilised virtues, courage (in tackling an APS tradition) yielded to prudence, because Darling also thought that the 'most desirable improvement' would be to enlarge the fellowship 'by taking in other schools'.[7]

To Hone, three problems demanded resolution: boys' loss of lesson time due to games, cultivation of a proper sense of values and sense of proportion, and 'To do something as subtly and as skilfully as we can' about breaking down 'the powerful asset of exclusiveness of the "Great Six"', an exclusiveness deriving from a games organisation that was restricting the growth of independent schools. If there were six APS schools in 1910, then on wealth and education grounds in 1960 there ought to be about sixteen. If this figure was an avowed aim, then schools had to be confident that they could stand on their own, not only 'without the bolster of this exclusiveness' but also the 'spectator crowds and games gladiators' who were regarded by the heads' predecessors as the chief defence against competition from the high schools. But for the departure over the past five years of sporting diehards among the masters, Hone admitted, the Melbourne Grammar common room would have carried on as normal, except that now it was on his side. The heads' thinking was moving quickly. By the next special meeting on the eve of the combined athletics sports (15 October), the dampening down of sporting premierships had morphed into a concern with schooling exclusiveness. This time, Darling drafted a statement, which indicated that he favoured a full-frontal attack on a system that was 'to a grave extent responsible for the childish standard of values prevalent in our community' and calculated to destroy it. The heads kept their newly defined position under wraps. Even though the exclusiveness of the premiership system acted against the interests of schools 'not included within the select circle', some means of enlarging of the scope of the combined sports and the Head of the River might be 'possible at a later date'.[8]

Darling was sceptical about the other heads' endorsement of the way forward as they saw nothing wrong with the present set-up (Geelong College refused to accept that 'the picture [was] as black as has been painted') and their nerve was likely to fail them when standing up to their assistant masters. Because GGS was in such 'a bad way' and he should have been 'doing more about it', Darling's hoped-for 'direct and honest attack' had to wait. He and Hone were both absent on leave for much of 1955. When they returned, they were appalled to find that the mice had played: the APS had slipped back into a five-match two-day cricket routine and the Boatrace was back in Melbourne. 'Distressed' by this recidivism, Darling could no longer 'still' his conscience. In yet another memorandum, his number one objection to the current interschool set-up (ahead of lost study time and the perversion of values because of the emphasis on winning) was 'the unwarrantable social prestige' resulting from the restriction of membership to a mere six schools. This situation was not in the interests of the independent sector, because it militated against the success of newly established church schools 'either in existence or contemplated'. But the situation was delicate: Frederick was about to leave Wesley (in 1957) to succeed Browne as Professor of Education and his successor (Dr T.H. Coates) was an unknown quantity. Also, Hone felt that he didn't yet have the measure of Gilray's successor at Scotch (R. Selby Smith). He could see 'no hope' of a change of heart at Xavier or Geelong College and, in any case, the products of the gung-ho 1920s sporting generation were now entrenched as APS parents. Never mind, 'once again into the breach' he urged his friend.[9]

When the heads met at Corio on Boatrace day in April 1956, Darling circulated his memorandum. He was appalled by the GGS boys' behaviour that day and depressed that the contest and the social side that he loathed had been transferred with such ease back to the Yarra. In October, at his request the heads rescinded their earlier decision to allow individual schools to make choice of water. A year later, with Coates in post at Wesley, the weight of support favoured the Darling–Hone changes. Five special meetings between August and November 1957 completely transformed the membership of the APS. On 8 August, the heads resolved unanimously to invite Caulfield Grammar School, Brighton Grammar School, Haileybury College, Carey Grammar School and 'one of the Roman Catholic Schools (choice yet to be decided)' to join the APS. In October, after 'vigorous, frank and sometimes spirited discussion', and a reconsideration sought by Father Boylen (Xavier), the heads reaffirmed their invitation. The four Protestant schools 'picked themselves out as the necessary recipients' and Boylen was requested to recommend a Catholic school. At that point progress stalled because Boylen and Xavier believed that membership extension would dissolve the APS. After encountering more Catholic community support than anticipated, however, Boylen agreed (reluctantly) to submit a name in November. There was a complication for Catholics. Which religious orders ought to be approached? The Marist Brothers declined an offer and so the final choice was between De La Salle College, Malvern, or St Kevin's Christian Brothers' College, Toorak. As the latter was 'ready in all respects' the heads agreed that St Kevin's would be the fifth school to be approached. An unintended consequence of Hone's blistering attack on the 'Adamson Tradition' was an expansion of the APS's membership.[10]

All five schools accepted their offers. Following a dinner, the new head-masters were admitted to the second part of the Headmasters' Association meeting, at which Darling (as chairman) outlined the 'queer conventions of this archaic body'. A public statement was issued some days later. Darling explained that the previous association of schools had been 'unrealistic, slightly offensive and bad for the independent schools as a whole'. With the resurgence of state schooling, measures to prevent the balance tipping in its favour ought to be enacted. Moreover, because education without religion was 'a lie' the heads did not want the state schools to play a completely dominant role. Fallout followed. The Associated Grammar Schools (AGS) lost members but was compensated by an infusion of new schools. Four years later, a head of one of the AGS schools (Tom Timpson, Searle's successor at Camberwell Grammar) thought that the APS expansion 'did not cause as big a stir as it was expected to do' and that the remaining AGS schools had kicked on after an initial 'bad effect' through loss of status. Darling identified a perverse consequence for the APS, however, because the emphasis on sport was exacerbated, not diminished. How, he asked an irritated Hone, could the new schools be anything but worse than the old, when Scotch, Melbourne Grammar and Xavier set the standards of performance so high? Surely if the smaller and newer schools were to hold their own, then it was impossible to expect them to take sport in their stride.[11]

In the wider sphere of education, Darling's engagement in the 1950s continued as previously. He remained sceptical of the worth of the Council of Public Education, although his loyalties were pulled in different directions—he was honoured to be deputy president to his friend Ramsay, but regarded the council's activities as 'perfunctory' and its influence 'negligible'. Having done his best to breathe life into it he accepted that 'it doesn't seem to do much good', so much so that after a lapsed attendance period of nearly twenty months, he marked his return to council meetings in April 1953 by calling into question the need for its existence. What useful purpose did it serve and why couldn't it adopt 'a more aggressive attitude' to educational problems? As chairman during Ramsay's absence for that year, the Council of Public Education reaffirmed its utility as a talking shop at best. Darling then absented himself again for all of 1954 and 1955. When he returned in April 1956, the council was discussing *Assumptions Underlying Australian Education*—a report on Australian education authored by Professor R.F. Butts, a Fulbright scholar (Columbia University, New York) attached to ACER during 1954. Darling pounced on one target of criticism in Butts' short book—the centralised provision of public schooling—to shift the council's discussion focus to school decentralisation more generally understood and thence to the virtues of the registered schools. (Darling was personally committed to decentralisation; W.G.L. Cartwright at Bostock and McWilliam at Glamorgan exercised considerable autonomy.) Henceforward until 1961, Darling intervened only sporadically during council meetings on matters mainly to do with the needs of adolescents: juvenile delinquency, the success of the Unemployed Boys' Club in Geelong, the irregular college attendance of Asian students admitted to Australia by the Department of Immigration, Commonwealth secondary scholarships, the quality of general teacher training and the specific training provided by Mercer House. He also summarised progress with the Australian College of Education and promoted Highton.[12]

At the council of the University of Melbourne, Darling's meeting attendance pattern reflected that of the previous decade: of 144 meetings for 1952–61, Darling attended about half (or seventy-one). The pattern of his (officially minuted) contributions was imprecise, although a common element was the precarious state of the university's finances. After the fire in January 1952 that razed Wilson Hall to the ground, the council debated the respective merits of restoration of the original construction or its replacement by a new design. Although sceptical about the estimated cost difference of almost a quarter of a million pounds (in favour of the latter), Darling expressed himself as 'converted' and took the majority view in favour of a new hall. Here he was endorsing the idea of paying for what could be afforded, but (in 1953) in respect of university staff salaries, he thought that 'the right course' was to determine the scale of remuneration that ought to be paid, as such a demonstration of self-help might persuade the state government to honour a request for financial aid. He thought that the time was ripe to prepare for both state and federal governments a comprehensive statement of the needs of universities. On the other hand, he was ambivalent about university self-help, particularly when the council launched a public appeal for £1 million in 1954. As he confessed to Sir Ian Clunies Ross (appeal deputy chair), GGS was about to launch its own appeal for £300,000 and charity had to begin at home:

> Strictly between ourselves, I am perhaps not so sympathetic to the University Appeal as I ought to be. If Geelong Grammar School doesn't get money from outside, it dies—public charity is our only source of supply. The University, on the other hand, is unique in the State and is clearly the responsibility of the Government. In the end whether or not the appeal is successful, the Government cannot let it fail. It really is an evasion of its responsibilities to try to pass off its financial obligations to the public. I might not feel this so strongly were it not for our own really desperate plight.

Darling's Council of Public Education frustrations with wasted energy and time were matched by university council frustrations with impecuniosity. Leslie Martin (Professor of Physics) hoped that he would 'go on being exasperated, impatient and complaining' during meetings, and Paton (whom he had championed to succeed Medley) said that Darling's genuine value as a councillor was that he could 'say all the things I would long to say, but for obvious reasons cannot'. He too was fed up with 'scrounging for every penny' and by stories spread by the staff association to the effect that the previous premier (John Cain Snr) had offered £300,000 for better salaries, except that as vice-chancellor he was said to be opposed to retaining staff. The only antidote to such inaccuracies was to 'roar with laughter, even if occasionally it feels a little hollow'.[13]

Beyond education, Darling branched out in the 1950s into an entirely new sphere of public life: immigration. Most likely on the recommendation of Geoffrey Brown, in 1952 he was appointed to the Commonwealth Immigration Advisory Council, chaired by Brown. Darling's only prerequisites for his appointment were his own personal experiences as an immigrant, GGS's employment of a handful of European workmen and its enrolment of the steady trickle of South-East Asian boys, particularly from Thailand. Apart from that, his ten years with the Universities Commission had acquainted him with the wiles of Australian civil servants and something of the rhythms of the corridors of power. Established in 1947 by the Chifley Labor government, the Immigration

Advisory Council's function was to advise the Minister for Immigration (H.E. Holt) on a range of immigration-related matters: 'day-to-day administrative as well as legislative and sociological'. The council's size ranged from twelve (1951) to twenty-seven (1974), with its members chosen from a cross-section of interests and groups, including employers, farmers, trade unionists, returned servicemen, the YMCA, the National Council of Women, local government and members of Parliament (both government and opposition). The Department of Immigration provided secretarial support, and departmental officers attended meetings of the Immigration Advisory Council and its sub-committees. Membership of the council entitled Darling to a daily sitting fee of seven guineas, for which the price tag, of course, was additional absences from Corio and, as with the Universities Commission (of which he had ceased to be a member the year before), interstate travel.[14]

Darling's first job in 1953 had been to chair a committee to consider an advanced English course as part of the Adult Migrant Education Scheme. Darling was mindful of the need to bridge the gap between the Commonwealth government's courses and the standard of English required of immigrants intending to enter educational institutions, not to mention their introduction to English literature. Expansion of existing provision, however, was opposed by the Immigration Advisory Council, as language knowledge and literature were seen as state responsibilities. Darling was vocal in 1954 on the maximum age (twenty-one years) for admitting Asian students to Australia for matriculation study by insisting that the students' real problem was uncertainty about what they would do following their courses. The GGS Thai matriculation boys had struggled with English Expression and he had tackled the registrar of the university on the case of one boy who passed four matriculation subjects (including English literature) and yet because he failed English Expression failed his entire examination. He cautioned the Immigration Advisory Council that (in his experience) Asian boys were often older than they claimed to be and that a number of those who failed because of English difficulties would return to their countries feeling (justifiably) aggrieved and experiencing ill will. To have to spend twelve months in a coaching college was not a genuine solution for them. What was needed were the proper provision of student accommodation (about which he had been bending Casey's ear), and cooperation between schools and the universities in teaching English.[15]

While Darling was in England in 1955, Tasman (Tas) Heyes (Secretary, Department of Immigration) asked him to provide 'impressions of the prospects of recruiting immigrants' in England and Europe, and comments on 'the immigration machinery'. After lengthy talks with officials in Italy and in London, Darling's assessment was that the 'people at this end' were 'very much hamstrung by the regulations imposed to meet Australian requirements'. Generally speaking, if Australia was seeking to capitalise on the 'miraculous achievement' of its large-scale postwar immigration program then it could not do so without some 'pai[n] and grief'. He believed that the Italian government was reluctant to encourage 'its best people' to depart and for this reason imposed obstacles, whereas in England R.E. Armstrong (Chief Migration Officer) said that the names of 200,000 Britons were on file for three years, but he was unable to help them because 'they don't fit into the right categories and have no-one to nominate them'. The prolonged delay and frustration experienced by potential immigrants was bound to impact negatively on the program, Darling asserted, and make official propaganda for the preferred categories 'look ridiculous'. Housing shortages and trade union 'stickiness' were domestic stumbling blocks, but in his view Australia could no longer pick and choose its immigrants as previously. He cited Trieste where there were thousands of potential immigrants, except that, in that 'dead or dying' city, people had no hope of fulfilling the two-year certificate of employment requirement after having been unemployed for so long. One group was the police force from Venezia-Giulia, 'trained by the British—English speaking and already hand-picked'. Surely Australian police forces would be interested in them?[16]

Darling's implied plea for liberalisation put Heyes on the back foot. While 'we' must have due regard for humanitarian objectives, he explained to Brown, the immigration program could not be entirely subject to fulfilling such considerations. The department had to obtain the 'best settlers' within the government's annual target and available funding. Consequently, many 'highly desirable' migrants would not be assisted as there were 'even more desirable migrants offering'. Prospective UK immigrant numbers were also affected by a lack of available shipping berths. Moreover, the priority accorded Australian residents' nominees and state government nominations on behalf of employers able to provide guaranteed employment and accommodation ensured that of about 8000 Commonwealth government nominees (allowing for family dependants) there were only 2000 nominated workers, all with vital national development skills. At four times the cost of a non-British immigrant's passage, British migration was the most expensive to the public purse. As for Trieste, most recruitment during 1955 had been from this area, including the policemen mentioned by Darling—2000 were in the process of selection (most of whom were recently employed police and had qualifications and backgrounds in different trades). There were also Iron Curtain–refugees whom he had not mentioned. Finally, he insisted, Darling was wrong about the need for elastic and adaptable schemes because these attributes needed to be related to Australian (not European) conditions. 'Hard realism' was the priority, not sentiment.[17]

Brown forwarded Heyes' letter to Darling and reassured him that what he (Darling) had written had also been raised elsewhere. (While Darling was in England, Brown died in October 1955 after collapsing in June in the House of Representatives.) The following year (1956), Darling was appointed to a committee to consider suggestions made by delegates to the annual citizenship conventions—by which the Commonwealth promoted new immigrants' citizenship. Until the 1956 convention, the theme of assimilation had been 'exhaustively dealt with'. From that year presentation papers were prepared by acknowledged experts (for example, Copland) and circulated to delegates prior to the convention. For some years, Darling played a lead role in successive conventions: planning, attending, presenting occasionally (1958) and synthesising deliberations, for which he was thanked for the 'acceptable and efficient leadership essential to their success'. Darling was also a departmental conduit for numerous personal inquiries about citizenship. In 1956, he reiterated to the Immigration Advisory Council his concern about Trieste voiced privately to Heyes, as well as the need to assist the many thousands of English residents wishing to emigrate but lacking nominators. He had returned from overseas 'somewhat depressed' at the 'lack of long distance thinking' by UK authorities on that country's future and migration generally.[18]

Darling's approach to immigration was consistent with his other public engagements: familiarise himself with the task, get to know the key people (Mills, Ramsay and Heyes among others), befriend them ('Dear Tas', 'Dear Jim'), engage with the issues and, where necessary, ask tough questions. Heyes soon learnt that Darling meant business. In his pencilled marginalia on a fifteen-page paper presented to an Immigration Advisory Council meeting ('What immigration means to Australia') he queried the value for money of financial grants to states, and the validity of official statistics on the impact of immigrant child enrolments on school building costs. He drew a three-page (defensive) response from Heyes. Darling was also willing to promote official policy publicly, as in 1958 when he addressed the Roman Catholic Institute for Social Order—using documentation disclosing new measures (assisted passages for non-nominated immigrants and a preference for Britons ahead of Europeans) that he personally favoured and for which he had been pressing. Darling even took the unusual step of directly obtaining information on migrant ship conditions by returning (with Margaret) after the Headmasters' Conference Association conference in Perth on the *Fairsky*, an immigrant ship, to see 'how they really treat them [immigrants] and what sort of people they really are'. Finally, as part of an Immigration Advisory Council policy, in which members (instead of officials of the Department of Immigration) tackled newspapers on misleading reporting, Darling communicated with the press on a range of issues. These included cautioning James Fairfax (politely) about pre-publication checking of facts and interceding in a dispute between the department and the Melbourne *Herald* editor about the veracity of articles concerning the procurement of young women for espresso bar vice rackets run (allegedly) by southern European immigrants.[19]

These activities were interesting, he confessed to Ralph, but they were taking him away from school more than they should have done. He knew it, the school council knew it, but they were complicit in letting the situation drift. Immigration advice-giving had one other important consequence: it forced Darling to weigh up the merits of the circumstances and policies of the two countries to which he owed allegiance, with the result that he became less censorious about Australian culture (given his previous view of its vacuity) and more open to what the nation had to offer. Thus, if there was still an overall lack of 'stimulating intellectual life' in Australia, he told one English correspondent (whose daughter was about to venture out) in 1959, 'she will probably be able to find it in a small way anywhere'. To Putt Nimmo, he had said during the Olympic Games that Australia 'seems a much better place to be than England in these days': if only the British government would realise this and be 'more co-operative about immigration'. These comments hinted at an attitudinal shift during the mid-1950s that was particularly evident during the Suez crisis, especially in correspondence with the Australian-born Conservative Party MP (and OGG) Brian Harrison. The timing of Suez positioned Harrison and Darling in their respective adopted countries at opposite ends of the world. On the day that the Foreign Secretary, Selwyn Lloyd, withdrew all British forces from Egypt (3 December)—dispatched as part of the military operation hatched with France (following adoption of the infamous Sèvres plan)—a distressed Harrison wrote from the House of Commons to tell his former headmaster that he could not recall a more worrying time or when distinguishing between right and wrong had been so difficult. He needed to talk with him. He recalled Darling saying to the VIth form immediately following the Munich Crisis in 1938 that GGS must work for the Save the Children Fund. Harrison thought that British military action in Egypt was justified (as it would have prevented world war and Arab attacks on Israel) and he rejected suggestions circulating about collusion with Israel to contrive an excuse for Anglo-French intervention (which, essentially, was what had happened). Yet, he was torn between trying to support 'with moral justification' leaders who had blundered badly, and withdrawing his support of the government and resigning, in full knowledge of the consequences.[20]

Darling replied that Britain and France had been right to act militarily, or at least had had 'good grounds', except that the United Nations had ruined their case. He then vented his 'fury' at the British government for failing to tackle the postwar 'Re-distribution of Empire resources and population'. The result was that Britain was now 'hopelessly vulnerable' to atomic warfare and the economic pressure of American oil interests, and had become 'the expendable front line of American policy'. He foresaw 'overwhelming unemployment' in England within twelve months and increasing pressure for emigration, which, had a carefully planned joint British-Australian program been in place, could have been tackled. Yet, 'the chance has been missed and it is not Australia's fault'. He lurched on, with his judgement of Suez 'clouded by all sorts of angers and frustrations'. Whether action was right or wrong depended on the question asked:

> For a Christian it is hard not to believe that the use of force is <u>always</u> wrong, particularly if it is in furtherance of national aims. Must, or can one order one's affairs as though the world was already God-ruled, when it clearly isn't? On this level it is perhaps the curse of Adam that there can be no absolutely right

answer on the moral level in the field of Politics, national or international. That kind of answer would only be possible if one could go back and remove the impurities of the system, which in fact are the cause[s] of the dilemma.

It was difficult to know what to advise because Britain was no longer clear about what it was trying to do. In the next few sentences, an English Australian then lectured an Australian Englishman on Britain's dilemma: 'You have not faced up to the fact that without the rest of the Commonwealth [of nations] you are no longer able to be a first-class power'. The root of the problem was 'the attempt by the U.K. to maintain a false position, both as a great nation, and in the maintaining of an artificially high standard of living'. One or the other alternative may have been possible, but both only by 'selling your freedom to the U.S. for financial assistance—and this is what has happened. Hinc illar lacrymae [sic—hence these tears]'.[21]

It was too late for Britain to return to empire, but from out on that former empire's periphery, Darling let other sentiments surface:

—incidentally, why are visiting Englishmen such bloody fools? The British Olympic visitors have been for the most part deplorable and have created a very bad impression—(my authority the most reasonable and friendly of people—John Landy and of course others.)

Returning to the main point, he insisted that as Britain's population increased over the next two decades it would be left with the following choice: 'Freedom + Poverty and Meekness' or 'an appearance of prosperity and greatness with subservience to the whims of American policy'. Britain could not possibly combine both. In these circumstances the likelihood was a Bevan government—a 'horrid thought'—but 'the Upper Class Englishman is incorrigible and certainly unteachable about the Empire'. This was because he 'clings to his own divine right of superiority and transposes that into an assertion of England's divine right long after the time for that is past'. From that attitude's unreality the 'rest follows'. In these ramblings an antipodean Englishman was struggling to come to terms with bitter home truths about his country of birth and its faded global supremacy. Don't resign; keep faith with those who voted for you, he urged his erstwhile pupil. The curse of earthly living was that 'it has to be a compromise between the absolutely good—as it would be if the Kingdom of God had come on earth—and the expedient'. The only escape was a monastery or the killing of one's conscience. Don't quit. Take the strain and give others also under strain credit for having arrived equally as honestly as he had at a different conclusion. As far as earthly life goes, 'the Devil has us on his two-pronged fork'.[22]

Invited some eighteen months later to comment on the British Council's report of its Australian activities, Darling expressed similar sentiments to Sir Paul Sinker, the Council's Director-General (since 1954). In 1955 Sinker had complained to Darling about his difficulties in securing teachers of English in Asian countries. Darling had then lobbied Casey, his departmental head Sir Allan Watt, and the OGG and diplomat Peter Henderson. This time, Darling focused on the British Commonwealth. He summarised what he regarded as a general but nonetheless correct view. Australians and New Zealanders were 'becoming extremely upset' that nobody in positions of importance in England cared much about the Commonwealth's future. Their support (evident during Suez, 'rightly or wrongly') was taken for granted. But if these dominions followed their own lines there would be surprise and annoyance, '—as Churchill was annoyed, I think wrongly, over the refusal to allow the [Australian] Sixth and Seventh Divisions to go to Burma':

> there is an increasing feeling amongst us who have left England and come out to work here, and a fortiori amongst second and third generation Australians, that Britain is not interested in us officially, that it is on the whole opposed to [e]migration from England to Australia, and that Australia and New Zealand are so far off and South East Asia so dangerous that they are an embarrassment to British policy.

As a corollary, Australia looked increasingly to, and had integrated itself with, the strategic, military and policy thinking of the USA. Was the official view at Home that Britain had nothing more to offer these dominions? More and more Americans were visiting Australia, but he could see few attempts to sustain cultural affinity with Britain, nor to retain its intellectual, cultural and spiritual leadership of the Commonwealth. Home links were being broken—it was becoming harder to get boys into Oxford and Cambridge. Was his letter an instance of Australian touchiness? No. He wrote as an Englishman who 'came out here primarily and expressly' because he 'believed in the English way of looking at things and considered it of world importance that Britain should retain its influence in the world for at least another fifty years'. Perhaps people at Home had lost their confidence? He hadn't, but he was losing belief in the capacity of British leaders to 'see policy as it might affect history'. If Sinker needed confirmation of these views, then he could contact Wakehurst, Ashby, Pentreath and Bickersteth. (There was a parallel lament about Australia being taken for granted by 'people at home' in a letter to James Pitman.)[23]

Sinker protested about the limited spread of British Council resources and its need to prioritise the field of English teaching in Asia, but these fuelled Darling's anxieties about political developments in that region and Australia's 'distressing isolation'. He conceded that while Australians might fall back on the easy assurance of reliance on the United States, they might also rise to the occasion and show South-East Asian nations 'what a good democratic country can be like'. In spite of 'all its faults', Britain still had more to offer Australia inspiration-wise and intellectually than the USA. He urged a rethink of British

Council policy to facilitate more of the kinds of influential visits undertaken by such people as George Turner and Richard Livingstone. As for Australian cultural accomplishments, these surfaced in correspondence with Nevil Shute Norway (whose novels appeared under his first two names)—an Englishman who had emigrated in 1950. Norway was preparing a paper for a citizenship convention and was interested in whether Australians were punching above their weight by achieving success disproportionate to the country's population, particularly in sport. If so, why, and did such success extend to other spheres? Rather than sport, Darling cited better than expected Australian international success (for a small country) in research, administration, newspapers and 'even' the arts—although he gave no examples. Despite an education system 'which nobody could call excellent', and in spite of (or was it because of?) less specialisation, GGS boys going Home, for instance, seemed to do 'extraordinarily well'. Maybe stored-up energy from the sun found release in a cold climate, or the absence of intellectual stimulus made overseas stimulus so exciting? Whatever the answer, the 'very great virtue' of Australians when absent from Australia was their lack of inhibition, their refusal to accept tradition as making something right and their willingness to have a crack at solving problems. In his own case, he had been astonished to discover during his few months in the Ministry of Information just 'how Australian I was myself'. Not even Menzies was immune to Darling's outpouring of sentiment. The year before (1957), prior to departing for the Commonwealth Prime Ministers' Conference, Menzies was urged by Darling:

> [to] do something with 'those English' whom, English though I still am, I am
> beginning to find peculiarly exasperating in their attitude, as far as one can
> judge it, towards the Commonwealth in general and Australia in particular.

Nor, just for good measure, he continued with Menzies, could he pinpoint the origins of a 'persistent attack' on the Department of Immigration, which was undeserved and probably anti–Roman Catholicism disguised as loyalty.[24]

More localised attitudes found expression in Darling's continued public speaking. As previously, the groups to which he spoke varied in status and type. For 1956, speaker's notes survive for (among other topics) 'Advice on choosing a career', 'Work means this to me' (an ABC broadcast talk), an Empire Youth Sunday address, 'Prep school masters' and 'On leaving school'. One contentious area was sex education. On speech day in 1954, he touched on the question of boy–girl relations and earned himself a supportive letter from F.G. Phillips (retired headmaster, Sydney Grammar School) who read the address in the *Sydney Morning Herald*. Revised arrangements for the school dance had prompted Darling to highlight the pursuit of pleasure, fashion and a 'precocious and in many cases a forced pre-occupation' with girls on the part of boys in the closed atmosphere of school. Darling had then commented on the manners and behaviour appropriate to gentlemen: they did not discuss their love affairs with 'all and sundry' and they certainly treated women of every age and class with 'respect'. Far from being a matter of old-world courtesy, he insisted that this was because of 'deep and definite physiological and psychological truths about the sexes'. Neglect respect and you destroy good family life, which 'is the secret of health in a society'. As he explained to Phillips, what he could not abide was 'this American promiscuity'. In 'my day', Darling said, it was not done to be interested in girls, let alone to talk about them and, while this meant that Englishmen of 'our class' were supposed to be very bad husbands, at least they tended to keep the same wife for longer than most people. 'Some principles of sex education, so-called', drafted for a course in health education for school medical officers in September 1956, continued this theme. The word 'so-called' betrayed his scepticism and signalled uncertainty. If part of the object of sex education was to increase the possibility of a healthy home life, then more than a little knowledge was a dangerous thing, particularly when he distrusted the drawing of firm conclusions and the treatment of sex as a special subject might be 'the basic cause of the trouble'—instruction-based information might arouse curiosity 'before it arises itself'. Social health necessitated a moral code. Yet this created taboos, and in turn produced aberrations and then perversions (of deed and desire). Here, the commercialising of sex (and its artificial stimulation of desire) was a real offence to society. Rather than instruction, then, education should develop the personality. Puberty, of course (quoting Hahn), was the time for 'the cultivation of the non-poisonous passions' in the case of boys, while for girls emotional needs had to be satisfied in a 'protective sense rather than a predatory' one—whatever that meant. Later, when the headmaster of Mount Scopus Memorial College (A. Feiglin) sought advice on sex education, Darling said that removal of the veil of ignorance and getting boys to talk to adults about sex was the extent of his ambitions as a head. The key thing was timing: tackle the subject too early, 'as was the case I am sure with my own boy [John]', and boys would become bored by the subject and have no idea what one was talking about.[25]

As earlier in the 1950s, Cold War controversy was difficult to avoid, only this time Darling encountered it out of the public gaze and in the person of Dr Frederick Charles Schwarz (a Queensland-born general practitioner and psychiatrist, Baptist lay preacher and founder of the Christian Anti-Communism Crusade). Ned Herring (a Schwarz enthusiast) alerted Darling to his activities. In July 1959, at a dinner hosted by Herring's fellow Victorian Supreme Court judge, Reginald Sholl, Darling met (or, as he said to Casey, he was 'subjected to') Schwarz. Afterwards, reeling from a crusading diatribe, Darling felt that he was 'reduced to pulp':

> Is it all true [he enquired of Casey about what Schwarz had said]? and, if true, what does one do? I cannot see my responsibility in terms of trusting everyone until they have been checked by security. Who checks security?

In fact, he reported to Ralph, this 'damned professional Anti-Communist' had made his flesh creep. Darling 'passed on the gloom' to which Schwarz had adverted to the VIth form, he told Sholl, although he assessed this group of boys as a 'soft generation impregnated with the base philosophy that nothing matters except one's immediate personal comfort', for which reason he could not see much hope 'in them or for them'. Even if it was agreed that the expressed aims of communism should be taught at school and 'the fallacies of its theories exposed', there was (quoting Harold Laski) far less point in persecuting those who worshipped the new faith and more virtue in people being able to scan an alternative horizon no less compelling in its demand for allegiance. The answer to the lie of communism, then, was the faith of Christ and so his response to it would be theological rather than political. Sholl—another Schwarz enthusiast— wanted Darling to spearhead the creation of a 'confidential vigilance committee of some sort' to act on behalf of all church and independent schools. Couldn't he also try to prevail on Ramsay? Sholl rejected the idea that attacks on communism served little point because if foolish people were being offered toadstools rather than mushrooms, then there was no reason that 'one should not warn urgently of the evils of toadstools with appropriate explanations, without necessarily waiting to buy a lot of mushrooms & offer them @ the same time'.[26]

Casey had also had a 'session with Schwarz'—at a gathering of about a dozen men organised by Sholl. On top of that the anti-communist crusader had spent an hour in Casey's office in the company of an ASIO official, during which time Casey had had 'the greatest difficulty getting a word in edgeways'. Schwarz (an 'evangelist' on his subject) had resorted to 'headlines' and 'flamboyant terms'. Even though he may have been a bore who talked in clichés, if his friend was asking him whether Schwarz' claim was true, then the answer was: 'Yes, I think it is'. And at this point the Minister for External Affairs—not a Christian, let alone religious—parted company with his friend the headmaster:

> You speak about materialism and the press and all that. Of course, we're sur-
> rounded with materialism. Private enterprise and capitalism—and democra-
> cy—are materialistic—the reflection of the fact that every human being wants
> to do as well for himself, in a material way, as he can. It may horrify you for
> me to say it—but what's the matter with that?

In a competitive world, then, materialism was inevitable regardless of whether that world was communistic or founded on private enterprise. The pity of it all—and this, he insisted, was one of Schwarz' arguments that was very true— was that the Protestant churches simply had to stop fighting Catholicism and fight communism instead. Rome was the one bulwark against communism and, in the battle with it, the sole contribution of the Protestant churches had been to 'help propagate the silly argument that it's a toss-up which is the worst menace, Moscow or Rome'. This was 'rot'. Moscow had enslaved a billion people over the last two decades or so. Protestantism needed to be militant in the fight against communism, because if the latter won there would be no churches at all, Protestant 'and' Catholic.[27]

In 1958, Herring had also tried to persuade his friend to join the General Committee for the Billy Graham Crusade. Darling demurred. Even though he had not heard Graham preach, he was 'old-fashioned or perhaps only timid about religious matters'. The reason may have been (as the archbishop said) that he was 'incurably public school' or that he shunned en masse–style evangelism due to his mother's Presbyterian influence. Religion-wise, the 1950s was a decade of 'confidence and expansion' as the membership of the Australian Protestant churches grew. It was also a time of large-scale open-air crusades. One of Graham's Sydney rallies in May 1959 attracted 150,000 people and in 1953 the crowd at a Catholic Family Rosary in Melbourne's Botanic Gardens was of comparable size. Darling continued trying to find common ground with Catholic divines, including sporadic joint attempts to secure state aid. In 1958, he (and Hone) met with Brother P.B. Murphy (principal, St Bernard's, Essendon) to plan a campaign, and in 1959 he arranged a meeting with Archbishop Woods and his Jesuit friend Philip Gleeson (rector, Newman College). He wanted Gleeson to preach at a GGS ecumenical initiative. 'There is a problem with the chapel', said Gleeson, for which reason in October 1960 Darling invited him to address the boys in the school hall, thereby breaking with GGS tradition: Gleeson was the first Jesuit ever to address the school. (Darling had spoken at Xavier during Hackett's time at the latter's invitation.) Gleeson outlined Catholic doctrine and spoke about the Society of Jesus. Darling wanted to invite the clergy of all denominations for, as the *Corian* reported, 'only by a clear, informed and objective mutual understanding can we ever achieve any sort of Christian unity or common front'.[28]

Darling congratulated Gleeson on his 'admirable' exposition, while being depressed that 'your church should be so logical'. There was no way out of their 'tragic divisions' if everyone adopted an assumed position. 'Isn't there something in the Bible applied to the Holy Spirit about the wind blowing where it listeth?' he enquired. As it had to be God's will that his church should be one body, it was 'our job' to achieve this. The talks had awakened 'a lot of genuine interest amongst the boys' and young people generally were more intolerant of the existing situation than 'us older people'. In their brief correspondence during 1960–61, the two men were concerned about secularism and how to respond to it. 'I tremble at the thought', said Gleeson, of the education of youngsters of his and Darling's 'persuasion' in (secular) state high schools. (This possibility was increasingly real: in March 1958 Ramsay summarised for the Council of Public Education some key statistics on Victorian state education: 73,000 students were enrolled in 117 high schools—an increase of more than 7500 students in twelve months; an increase of 2400 students in 55 technical schools for the same period; about 18,000 teachers in training in 1957, an increase of nearly 4000 since 1954.) Later, when Gleeson sent him a review (by a fellow Jesuit) of *The Phenomenon of Man*, Darling got more than he bargained for on the point about logic. Wasn't it possible in respect of particularities in philosophical and theological speculation that Catholicism 'may conceivably have got it all wrong'? While faith and morals taught by Christ through the church could not be wrong, replied Gleeson, censorship by the church in the speculative realm was necessary to ensure that truth was not undermined. Far from being a denial of freedom, censorship was no different from a chemist using a label such as 'Poison, Not To be Taken'. Such labelling was a source of 'joy & relief' to the intellectuals among Catholic converts, and by no means the 'tethering' about which Darling had expressed 'some wonder'.[29]

Toadstools and mushrooms, and labels, poisons and bulwarks: all a far cry from the cosy confines of Darling's Melbourne Anglicanism. With Booth's retirement as archbishop imminent in December 1956, Darling took a more active part in diocesan politics, particularly in the search for his successor. The first appointment of an Australian-born archbishop was still a decade away (Marcus Loane, Sydney, 1966) and the Australian Church of England's episcopal bench was dominated by Englishmen: in 1957, all Australian metropolitan dioceses had only ever consecrated English bishops and, in 1956, bishops in nine of twenty-five dioceses were Englishmen. When Darling's Oxford contemporary T.S.R. Boase (President, Magdalen College) visited Corio during his twelve-week British Memorial Fund–sponsored visit, the two men had had a 'long conversation about the episcopal position in Australia'. Later, when back in the UK, Boase (with the Bishop of Bristol) sounded out possible candidates. Darling acted immediately on Boase's advice, but the diocesan Board of Electors (chaired by John McKie), he reported, was 'still desperately worried about finding the right man'. Darling then communicated with Fisher (during his leave in England)—but was not the only one to exert pressure on Fisher, who received more than sixty letters about the appointment. A 'great man' was required, because there had not been such a man since Charles Perry's successor, James Moorhouse (1877–86). Darling cast the significance of the appointment as the provision for leadership for the entire Church of England in Australia, not merely the Province of Victoria, let alone the Diocese of Melbourne. With his customary air of urgent gravitas, capaciousness of message and sweeping rhetorical flourish, Darling justified his claim by suggesting that national church leadership could only come from one of the two major centres of population, but with Sydney hopelessly in thrall to the evangelical cause, the mantle fell by default to Melbourne. Booth (administrator of the diocese during the interregnum) had been an earnest and humble prelate, but for scholarship or preaching one had had to look solely to the Presbyterians. By sheer 'dead weight' of numbers, however, and by offering the only genuine point of contact with Roman Catholicism, the Church of England commended itself as the 'obvious leader of Protestant thought'.[30]

But how did Melbourne stack up against comparable English jobs? If Darling had remained in England and become the head of 'some intermediate standard school', then he could not have had 'so wide an influence and it must be admitted', Darling wrote, 'that I have had (forgive me—Not I—but—)'. How much greater influence, then, could a man 'who was really first class have had!' In Australia it was possible to '<u>act</u>', and 'much more quickly and with less appeasement than at home', because the soil was 'nearer to its virgin state, and the return for effort spent accordingly greater'. In sum: 'We do quite desperately need leadership'. In the battle between God and materialism, Australia would not turn to communism ('far from it'), but it was in danger of surrendering to the materialist philosophy of 'pursuit of comfort and gain without responsibility', with only the church to save it. England might well be in the same boat, although he doubted it; even so, 'we are, I think, in the final analysis of History more important and in the greater need'. Australia's possible destiny was to become the torchbearer of 'the British tradition, and the Christian religion'. For these reasons and because the job was more important than even the highest jobs at Home, England simply had to send 'its very best man'. 'I do beg you to do your utmost to persuade some really great man to come to us'—great in old-fashioned scholarly terms and also in spiritual (rather than administrative) qualities. Ever hopeful, after hearing that the electors' unanimous offer had been accepted by the Suffragan Bishop of Middleton, the Right Reverend Frank Woods, Darling informed Boase that the new archbishop 'sounds just exactly what we want'.[31]

If some are born great and others have greatness thrust upon them, then Woods was probably in the latter category. Fisher's estimate of his chances of episcopal preferment seemed to suggest (at least initially) that Darling's hopes may have been dashed—although Woods' biographer insists that by the end of his incumbency (1977) these had been realised. With the news of his acceptance known, Darling wasted no time in wishing him well. As earlier with Fisher, he went over the top: many people felt that 'this is perhaps the most important ecclesiastical position in the Empire'; even if it wasn't, it was still 'the position of greatest opportunity in Australia'. Moreover, people ('us all') were 'most ready to follow your lead wherever you wish to take us'. He assured Woods that, while as archbishop he had a formal role to play as president of GGS's council, he should make use of the school (like Priestley and Head) as a periodic 'relief from your labours'. Because he thought that GGS had not produced anywhere near sufficient candidates for holy orders, he appealed specifically to Woods to find him a chaplain (as 'we have never had a real chaplain at the school'). He wrote in the capacity of a self-styled fox that had irredeemably lost his tail, for he 'strongly recommended the step' that the archbishop-elect had taken in deciding to come to Australia. Woods (eight years Darling's junior) replied that he was 'overwhelmed' by his appointment, which was far and away 'the most astonishing thing that has ever happened to me', even though the prospect now and then filled him with fear and trembling. GGS, he assured Darling, was not alone in religious failure because the same situation applied in its English counterpart schools. He and his wife Jean (and their children) would arrive in mid-December. These two letters commenced a 35-year friendship and working partnership until Woods' death in 1992. About nine months after his arrival, Darling sang the new archbishop's praises to Fisher. The latter had read his former pupil's letter with 'profound thanksgiving', if only because in what was thought to have been 'some moment of aberration', Archbishop Mowll (of Sydney and Primate) had told Woods (before he had accepted the archbishopric) that 'it was not worth his coming'—Melbourne was not important and that he would be better off remaining in England.[32]

Anglican cosiness may have been a misnomer. A few months after his arrival, the new archbishop was thrust into the public limelight by a rebellion of senior mistresses at Merton Hall (the sister school of Melbourne Grammar) that exposed deep fissures within Establishment Melbourne. At the height of the fracas (October–November 1958) Darling became an important confidant for his new friend. As in 1917 at Repton, at GGS in 1942, at St Catherine's in the late 1940s and on the occasions of finger-pointing at the headmaster himself in respect of alleged pinkness, a broadly all-too-familiar script played out at Merton Hall: a whiff of liberalism diffuses within a tight-knit community and, when its aroma is deemed on the nose, self-appointed school community mind-guards or thought police swoop to remove an unendurable stench. Thus it was when Dorothy J. Ross (eight years Darling's senior, a co-founder with him of the College of Education and known by her intimates as DJ) retired in 1955 after sixteen years as the headmistress. She was an 'anti-authoritarian liberal', and to that extent she and Darling were birds of a feather. Bill Connell (her principal academic champion) regarded her as a genuine pedagogical progressive for whom a school was a 'co-operative democratic community'. In addition to Ross' liberalism, some of her staff were known to have left-wing inclinations. (Sholl told Darling that one of the mistresses sacked by Ross's successor had been a former official of the British Communist Party.) In 1957, after a five-term interregnum, an Englishwoman, Edith Mountain, was appointed to succeed Ross. An anti-liberal reaction set in. As with Garnett at GGS, Mountain arrived at the school with the endorsement of her predecessor but, after four terms of her incumbency (October 1958), fifteen senior women—firm in their belief that the educational principles that brought the school renown during Ross' time were being eroded—resigned en masse. Merton Hall was also haemorrhaging enrolments and, by speech night later that year, the staff exodus had climbed to thirty-eight (with five at most accounted for by 'natural attrition'). Woods had not appointed Ross' successor but as council chairman it was his mess to clean up.[33]

The trigger for the crisis had been a 'loyalty letter' written to Woods by Mountain's supporters and circulated on 8 October—the day of the fifteen resignations. A fortnight later (after the council expressed its confidence in Mountain),

the new archbishop told Darling that after 'endless comings & goings' about the
school he had no idea of the likely outcome and that the parents of the senior
girls were 'very restive'. To find a *modus vivendi*, he was set to meet 'the recalci-
trants (now 17 out of a teaching staff of 65)'. Acting on Hone's advice and on his
father's behalf, Theo Woods had urged Ian Sabey (of Australian Public Relations
Services), an adviser utilised during the crisis, to consult Darling—'as someone
closer to Far [father]'—for advice. Here was a small group of men pronouncing
on the destiny of a woman caught in a crossfire between rival groups of strongly
opinionated women. Sabey detected a split on council, he told Darling, and the
tide of parental opinion was moving against the new headmistress—who, on
the school's open day had (apparently) made herself unavailable. The council
ought to have held an inquiry, Sabey asserted, instead of which it had supported
her. An inquiry could still be convened (an idea supported by the fifteen senior
mistresses) and, Sabey thought, Brigadier Langley (retired head of Melbourne
High School) ought to conduct it and report within ten days—if not Langley
alone, then Myra Roper and Sir John Medley in conjunction with him. Bishop
McKie, on the other hand, said that 'no self-respecting School Council' ought
to be expected to convene an inquiry independent of itself. There was still time
for mediation between those at loggerheads and (despite unanswered questions
concerned with the taking of evidence under oath and the role of legal counsel)
the council ought to conduct its own inquiry.[34]

From the sidelines, Darling scribbled himself two pages of questions and
in a three-page memorandum gave Sabey his more candid opinion. For someone
as measured as himself, he gave all the parties an unusually blunt serve. He was
witnessing an instance of men and women behaving at less than their civilised
best. With his second point, Darling may have put his finger on the cause of the
school's problem: the prolonged interregnum (of more than two-and-a-half years
until Mountain's arrival) had been 'fatal'. The school had been run democratically
under Ross' strong personality, but after her departure it had been 'virtually run
by the assistant mistresses'. He also drew attention to the fact that, aside from
Mountain, no other woman had wanted the job (or had been deemed to be worthy
of it). While the new headmistress might also have failed early on to have won
over the older staff members, he doubted whether she had been encouraged to
do so. Indeed, the council chairman had known unofficially about the unrest for
'some months before the storm broke' and, because he had done nothing, it was
his 'failure'. (John McKie was probably in his sights, as he was acting chairman
while Woods attended the Lambeth Conference between June and September.)
Darling's memorandum was communicated on the day (29 October) when more
than 1000 people attended a heated evening meeting (convened by the parents'
association and chaired by Woods) that ended chaotically and generated negative
press coverage. The council, Darling told Sabey, was culpable for failing to head
off the rumblings prior to the loyalty letter's publication and refusing to meet the
disaffected mistresses who had orchestrated an attempt to force the headmistress's

own resignation. This was 'unpardonable' and left the council with no option but to back Mountain. She should have prevented the loyalty letter from becoming public. With remarkable lack of insight, those involved had allowed the situation to 'fester': in short, virtually everyone had 'blundered' badly. The time for an inquiry was long gone and no sensible purpose could be served. A fortnight later, after a seven-hour council meeting, Woods informed Darling that the occasion had been 'a personal triumph for Miss Mountain'. The council had been 'rocked', he wrote, '& so was I'.[35]

At a personal level, two notable events in the late 1950s impacted on Darling. The first was the death of Colin Gordon—intimate friend, his best man, former colleague and fellow headmaster—in August 1960 following a drawn-out battle with cancer. He was fifty-two. Cancer was a 'foul business', Darling told Ralph, and one's response was a mixture of a feeling of sympathy and hope that the afflicted person would not suffer for long. Darling's letters to Gordon's wife Pat (who, after her husband's operation, was feeling 'very lost') had provided her with great comfort. The day after Darling had been involved in a significant meeting for what would become yet another outside engagement (the Australian College of Education), Pat Disney informed Darling that his friend was fading fast:

> I dropped in on Colin this afternoon to let him know how well things had gone … He was talking about going home this week-end. The recovery from the op. is going very well: he was full of praise for the surgeon's job, and the consequent 'reasonableness' of the after-effects, but he went out of his way to make it clear that he knew the sands were running out. (I imagine not many know that.)

Cheerily, under the circumstances, Gordon cabled Darling the next day: 'Well done old man [on the founding of the new organisation]' and 'hope now golfing'. In a *Carthusian* obituary, Darling described his friend as all that a headmaster could have asked for in an assistant master, in addition to which, as a headmaster, Gordon had the great gifts of organisation and control, and sense of relevance and direction in policy. He was fun to be with on the cricket field, the golf course, the bridge table or in conversation—some of the marks of a civilised man, he may have thought.[36]

On the brighter side, in June 1958 a letter arrived from London informing Darling that, in the Birthday Honours, the queen had appointed him CMG— Companion of the Most Distinguished Order of Saint Michael and Saint George. In excess of 300 letters, cards and telegrams of congratulation arrived from well-wishers, hot on the heels of what one correspondent described as Malcolm Muggeridge's 'abusive' article on GGS and his insufferable mention of 'affable'. For once, Fisher was mildly glowing in congratulating his former pupil, as the honour was 'splendid recognition of the glorious work that you have done for education in Australia'. There were too many people, Fisher then intoned, who went out to serve good causes in the Commonwealth and yet got tired after a while of being away from England and hankered to return. But then either Fisher's memory failed him or he let his recollections pass: 'Whether you have ever hankered', he did not know, but having remained where he was Darling had undertaken work that would not otherwise have been done. At any event, if he had had charge of the honours distribution lists he would have inserted a K at the front of CMG. Philip Gleeson also expressed his delight. Despite the regret with which he viewed 'a certain heretical establishment', Gleeson's devotion to truth made him pay tribute to its 'Presiding Genius!'[37]

The Syme Oration was delivered six days before Gordon died. It was Darling's summa (or apologia) because sensitivity was what he had 'always half-consciously believed to be the main job of a school' and for that reason he had always tried to make it possible. The prospect of having to deliver an oration on this theme, however, he told Ralph, was terrifying him, simply because it was a very swagger affair and 'out of my class altogether'. A curious feature of the text of his address is that, while referring favourably to Teilhard de Chardin's view of evolution, he made only indirect mention of Canon C.E. Raven (Regius Professor of Divinity, University of Cambridge) and yet, as he said to Michael Scriven, it was Raven who had crystallised his thinking. Like Teilhard de Chardin, Raven had looked to evolution when arguing persuasively (in 1943) for the need for the domains of science and religion to be in dialogue. Indeed, Darling's argument was based on Raven's observation in his book *Science, Religion and the Future*, that:

> survival value does not belong to the predatory or the insensitive ... but to the adaptable and the sensitive, to those who live dangerously and gain a high vitality and quickness of response.

The other curious feature about Raven's book—especially given that this particular passage had had such a marked impact on him—was that whenever Darling mentioned it directly (as to Scriven) or indirectly (as in the address itself and in a speech back in 1954 on the Geelong community chest) he invariably used 'immune' rather than 'insensitive'. Maybe this omission was forgetfulness. The volume of Darling's public engagements highlights how this particular civilised man was being pulled increasingly from schooling and Corio. Whereas he had been endeavouring—both through his own influence and that of the masters appointed by him—to produce generations of young men with civilised sensibilities, the scope of his influence was broadening. This was not direct influence on the wider Australian population, but on the work of the institutions that were shaping the consciousness and behaviour of Australians. The most obvious arena in which this had already begun to happen for him, and in which for the foreseeable future he would have to come to terms with Raven's predatory and insensitive notion, learn to live a little dangerously himself and which would certainly demand of him a quickness of response (and even some immunity) was broadcasting. This was an area of responsibility that overlapped for seven years with his headship, and to which he would devote himself for thirteen years overall. At the same time as he was doing that, however, there was a college that he had to establish.[38]

FILLING A GAP

1958–1961

... we are brothers in something, and not brothers in isolation. It is not by contributions to a pool that fraternity is ensured. Fraternity is the creation of sacrifice alone. It is the creation of the gift made to a thing greater than ourselves.

Antoine de Saint-Exupéry, *Flight to Arras*

The college in question was created over a weekend, beginning on Friday, 15 May 1959, when about eighty men and women from all over Australia assembled at Corio. About seventy were in residence for four days as guests of the school council. The college was for educators, the gathering was the founders' convention and the outcome was the Australian College of Education. This event was the third founding educational forum at GGS following the inaugural Headmasters' Conference of Australia meeting in December 1931, and the conference of heads of schools in January 1948. After months of preliminary work, the convention was 'something of a triumph', Darling told Ralph. The founders had 'got off to a good start on an all-Australian basis and with all branches of the teaching profession included'. It was early days for the new infant, but so far the Australian College of Education had gone 'tremendously smoothly'. It was 'a big thing' to have the state education departments involved, he insisted, although with their 'usual arrogance' the universities had not been easy to win over. There had been a drafting committee, a provisional council and then the Corio gathering. Darling had chaired all three bodies, and he was also appointed the inaugural president. He aimed to curb the 'general materialistic influences' that he believed were ruining education and to plead the importance of spirituality 'as defined by Gollancz in the Devil's Repertoire'. Darling was also elected to the first Australian College of Education fellowship, 'an honour not only for him but also for the school', although in the circumstances, as he told councillors, 'it was hardly possible for them to avoid electing me as the first fellow and President of the College'. While the council had generously underwritten the event (to the tune of about £1500), Darling believed (with an eye on publicity value yet again) that the 'invisible gain to the school' could 'hardly be over-estimated'.[1]

After Timbertop and Marcus Oldham, the college was Darling's third major project in the 1950s. There had been a number of attempts to establish a college, the first in 1946 at ANZAAS in Adelaide where MacNeil (in a paper read posthumously by Darling and quoted at the founders' convention to the delight of his widow) had noted the lack of community recognition of teaching. His solution was that the profession 'must take matters into its own hands and become the architect of its own fortunes'. He suggested a guild of teachers along the lines of the Educational Institute of Scotland, which was founded in 1847 and granted a Royal Charter in 1851. His idea was light on detail other than that a guild ought to 'speak with authority in all matters affecting the profession itself' and it should not be a 'glorified trade union'. It would provide a 'common pool' from which both church and state school teachers from across Australia 'might move, when necessity requires', and which might also provide a 'high-grade professional organization'. The sting in the tail of MacNeil's proposal was that 'the world takes institutions, as it takes people, very largely on their own estimate of themselves'.[2]

Another attempt had been made in May 1951 when, at the annual conference of professors of education at the University of Melbourne (and after earlier consideration at ACER) there was discussion of 'an educational association of national scope'. Cunningham had contacted twenty-one sets of interested parties (one of which was 'Certain heads of independent schools', including Darling) to test the water. Browne, T.L. Robertson (Director of Education, Western Australia, but then at the Commonwealth Office of Education) and Cunningham explored the matter further. The view was that an association ought to 'stand entirely on its own feet', not be sponsored by existing organisations and be limited to 'those who earn their living in the study and practice of education'. With no existing organisation fitting this bill, the formation of a professional body would be a 'common meeting ground' for teachers, administrators and researchers, like the National Education Association in the USA, and which might help 'raise the standing of the profession in the community'. Cunningham's letter (to which Darling replied) had been met with a 'very dampening' reception. After lying dormant until the triennial meeting of the Headmasters' Conference of Australia at Corio in May 1957, Hone referred to MacNeil's speech and claimed that the profession needed a body equivalent to to the royal colleges of surgeons or physicians (with their fellowships), or the institutes of engineering (with their advanced standing qualifications), or passed staff college (as it was referred to) for the military and 'all that that meant for future promotion in the Army'. As to how to bring it to fruition he had no idea; nor did he know whether the Conference schools might share such a body with the state education departments.[3]

The creation of the Australian College of Education was a testament to patience and persistence. For Darling, the grind of meetings and committees was leavened by the heads' sense of fellowship. The support of two big teacher unions and the presence at the founders' convention of two key unionists helped: J.G. Baker (Department of Education, Victoria, and past president of the Victorian Teachers' Union) and Bessie Mitchell (headmistress, Cheltenham Girls' High School and past president of the New South Wales Teachers' Federation). Darling was more fortunate than he knew as Mitchell had been telephoned by a departmental officer and asked whether she was interested in attending the Corio gathering. Darling also capitalised on friendships built across the educational divides, such as Alan Ramsay and Dr H.S. Wyndham (Director of Education, New South Wales)—known to him through Gordon (with whom Wyndham had worked in the RAAF during the war). As to models for the college, Darling did not replicate a specific precedent, although he was aware of the newly founded (1954) Australian Academy of Science, and he and his peers were not flying entirely blind because they could call on Professor Moorhouse's invaluable experience of the engineering profession. The Australian College of Education was a landmark educational development in a country in which, as late as 1962, Tosh Phillips could claim that 'one of the notable features of Australian education' was that there was 'no such thing', largely because of its imitative nature and variations in practice between the states.[4]

There were three phases in the emergence of the Australian College of Education: first, a twelve-month gestation period following Hone's speech; second, the founders' convention itself; third, the weaning of the new infant and the formation of its early identity. Hugh Philp recalled Darling talking about the possibility of a college during the evaluation of GGS in 1957, but it was Timpson who nudged events forward early in 1958 during discussion of the needs of the teaching profession at the Victorian section of the Headmasters' Conference of Australia. Key meetings followed over the next three months (6 June, 27 June and 1 August) that culminated in the establishment of a provisional council. The Headmasters' Conference heads established a sub-committee comprising Dr T.H. Coates, Timpson as secretary and Darling as chairman. Immediately, Coates notified the Victorian High School Headmasters' Association of the Headmasters' Conference heads' plans and invited its president, L.J. Millar, to nominate high school headmasters to attend the first June dinner meeting at Wesley. He asked Paton to nominate professors. Fourteen high school headteachers, fourteen independent school heads and three professors attended the Wesley meeting chaired by G.F.J. Dart (Ballarat Grammar School) with the assistance of R.E. Chapman (University High School). Hone led the discussion. For surgeons a college may have been of 'definite material advantage', but the key question for education was: 'what advantages could be gained from [college] membership'? As for a college's (or institute's) aims, Darling thought that the key object was not to raise the status of the teachers because 'this would be incidental as the quality of the teaching profession was improved'. His priorities were in-service training, the bringing together of different parts of the profession and finding ways of raising professional quality. There was uncertainty about how to proceed, but eventually a sub-committee of nine (including Darling), along with four coopted members, was established to draw up aims and objectives, and to appoint a provisional council. During the drive home from Wesley, Darling thought about the first draft of the constitution, which he committed to paper the next morning. His 'Notes' covered eight areas: name (with 'Victorian' in the working title), membership, objects, governance, fellowship elections, fees, activities and preliminary steps. Crucially, his number one priority was the maintenance and raising of professional standards through the appointment of 100 fellows as a 'higher grade of membership'—with a lower membership grade ('Associates') established later on if 'thought desirable'. Fee levels needed to be 'considerable', given that 'people are inclined to value more what they have to pay for' and because 'if any dignity in the proceedings is to be achieved' then there needed to be funds to underwrite it. He also foreshadowed an annual lecture (perhaps named after Tate or Littlejohn) and possible college incorporation through a royal charter.[5]

Three weeks later, the sub-committee reconvened at Wesley. Darling was elected chairman and his college prototype provided the basis of the deliberations. He was delighted about 'much more progress than one would have thought possible', although this time his trip home had been a 'trifle troublesome', due to poor visibility caused by fog and having to play good Samaritan for two inebriated young drivers who had run their car off the road. He had been wondering whether to invite an assistant master to the August meeting. Nothing came of it, but his brief rumination was as close as any of the founding heavyweights came to engaging classroom teachers to help shape the nascent college. (He had had in mind Vic Tunbridge who later, with Doug Fraser, helped to organise and attended the convention.) He and Timpson were feeling their way tentatively during this early period. Should they consult the state Minister of Education about a royal charter? What about the other states? Should Gordon (chairman, Headmasters' Conference of Australia) be informed of progress because there was 'some danger that we may go on faster than would suit the Conference as a whole'? So far, the embryonic college was entirely Victorian. Professor Hunt (Classics) advised keeping it that way for the time being—Darling may have had in mind the negativity of New South Wales heads towards the 1948 joint conference. Gordon (when updated on developments) agreed with Hunt, and was even more adamant about an initial one-state identity and focus if a college was to become an 'effective organism with a definite character'. Another concern was how the college would occupy the landscape alongside bodies such as the New Education Fellowship or the Victorian Institute for Educational Research.[6]

In preparation for the 1 August meeting a wider membership net was cast. Notification of the discussions in progress went to the Director of Education, the

Director of Catholic Education, the high school headmistresses, the technical college principals, the Association of Headmistresses and the Kindergarten Training College, along with invitations to representatives of most of these key organisations and groups, and others (including the Victorian Institute for Educational Research, with which Frederick and Coates were closely associated, but of which Darling seemed to be oblivious). At this point in time (late July 1958), word of what was afoot had percolated beyond Victoria. Colin Healey (Sydney Grammar School) had been alerted by Hone to developments and, because 'we know nothing of what you are doing' was keen for information. Darling promised that Timpson would keep him in the loop—with the latter contriving the lame excuse for Healey's ignorance as avoiding people getting the wrong ideas and 'discussing them in the kind of atmosphere which would hinder the development of the whole scheme'. Two significant features of these early developments were that the emerging entity was an entirely male affair and, as news of its gestation disseminated, Darling's name became closely associated with the proposed college. Professor Colsell Sanders (Dean of Education, University of Western Australia) who had campaigned for something like a college—he claimed to have been 'preaching the same idea' (anchored on 'the pillars of scholarship, intellectual integrity and freedom') but with little response—hoped that this renewed effort would be fruitful and was reassured that Darling was 'behind the move'.[7]

The 1 August Wesley meeting was a working session. 'A statement of aims and organisation for an institute of education ...' (drafted by Darling's sub-committee) was adopted. The invitees in attendance (thirty-three of forty-six) then debated it clause by clause and (two-and-a-half hours later) adopted an amended version. The draft statement (with the inclusion of the proposed provisional council's membership) was based substantially on Darling's initial notes, although there were two significant changes: deletion of his mention of professional standards, and inclusion of the purpose as the creation of a fellowship of teachers to foster educational thought and the ethics of professional responsibility. The embryo was christened 'The College of Education', the number of its fellows was set at 100–150 and the provisional council's composition was endorsed. In addition to Darling, this body comprised his circle of educational associates (D.J. Ross, Ramsay, Coates, Selby Smith, Gleeson and Moorhouse), along with Chapman, Alice Hoy (foundation principal, Secondary Teachers' College), Dr W.C. Radford (Cunningham's successor at ACER) and A. Tylee (principal of Swinburne College). Darling's strategy was clear: lock in the support of the relevant interests in one state, and then win over parallel interests and groups across the country. So far, so good: 'it is astonishing how well things have turned out', he confided to Timpson. Robson gave the idea his blessing. In contrast to his 1948 recalcitrance, he pronounced the college idea as 'good'. He had certain objections, 'which one naturally feels' should be 'overruled by common sense', to wit the need to avoid 'a closed corporation within a barbed-wire fence with a very narrow gate which is opened only with difficulty', which he believed was true of the surgeons' and physicians' colleges. He was at a loss to suggest names of fellows; some unsuitables would be hard to exclude, while other suitables would be difficult to include. He cautioned his friend on the need to be 'very much more clear what sort of person you want' and to hasten slowly. Hone reported that the New South Wales Department of Education was 'enthusiastic!!'—a good result in light of Darling's confession that he wished that he had 'a rather clearer idea of what we are aiming at'. Two distractions threatened to impede progress: the lure of a royal charter and the possible elevation of provisional councillors to fellow status. Darling pursued the royal charter idea with Sir Kenneth Bailey (the solicitor-general) and deputed Radford to press the case further in Canberra. As for fellow status, the question was whether to issue immediate invitations to the twelve councillors or to hold fire. Darling thought that acceptance of provisional council membership implied readiness to become a fellow, and the letters of invitation to join the council reflected that assumption.[8]

During third term of 1958, the provisional council met three times (successively at Scotch, Wesley and Melbourne Grammar). By the second and third meetings the nascent college became an interstate body. It had been agreed in September that other states 'be invited to sit with' the council, but Victoria's two neighbours had different concerns. Gordon in South Australia was keen to confine the college membership to Victoria: fix its quota of fellows at about a third of a projected 200, top up this target with fellows from the other states to 100 overall, and only allow them to increase their quotas when state branches had been formed. To bolster this Victoria-first strategy, all kinds of limp excuses were contrived to keep the others at arm's length. Because the preliminary work needed to be done by people 'who can easily keep in touch with each other', for example, most of it had to be completed in Victoria in cooperation with New South Wales members, and only then with the help of other states' representatives. The provisional council had sought close consultation with New South Wales regarding the selection of original fellows, and it wanted a Headmasters' Conference of Australia member from that state to attend its meetings. Gethyn Hewan (head, Cranbrook), on behalf of a New South Wales committee of educators, believed that the main players in the school sectors (for example, departmental officers) were sanguine about the provisional council's broad approach and were content with liaison rather than membership. Their main concern was with fellowship status: the need to minimise the number of foundation fellows elected by the council (no more than twenty), with the general rule to be that fellowships should only be bestowed on those who 'had made a very marked contribution to education'. Hewan foresaw the danger of prospective members regarding the college as 'additional kudos for eminent people in the Community who already have their standing', so that fellowships should be based on performance rather than positions held.[9]

Advice from the Department of the Prime Minister in October ended thoughts of affixing royal to the college title. (The two alternatives, for which approval would be protracted, were grant of the right to use the prefix or incorporation under royal charter.) Attention turned to fellows and members. As for two classes of election, the provisional council agreed on the need for them, although the basis of the difference between them and the relationship of both were to be determined by the first elected council. The criterion endorsed for a foundation fellow was 'distinction in education'—except that the meaning was not spelt out. Here, the need to placate a range of interests (people 'acceptable to all interested parties') assumed more importance than definitions of accomplishment. In retrospect, in a precipitate (not to mention, presumptuous) move, twelve of the thirteen members of the provisional council then voted themselves as fellows and also elevated to fellowships six professors of education, six state directors, the Director of the Commonwealth Office of Education and one head of an education faculty. Finally, they approved as fellows thirty-nine state and non-state officials, heads of schools, academics, principals of training colleges, amongst others (most of them Victorians), with the expectation of other forthcoming nominations (following consultations) from both South Australia and New South Wales. Hewan, however, was adamant that New South Wales' cross-sectoral educational group did not see itself as competent (and did not want) to submit the names of possible fellows to the provisional council. Subsequently (November) this decision was revised: to ensure that the first council was elected by a representative group of fellows, the provisional body would choose no fewer than 100 from all states (with up to sixty being non-Victorian).[10]

Having pushed the council on the question of fellows, Darling thought that he had miscalculated. Juggling lists of possible fellows' names was 'invidious and difficult' and, in relation to Hewan's concern, he was anxious that the provisional council did not acquire the status of a 'self-regarding clique'. He was persuaded by Timpson's view that the basic composition of the college was its membership, except for his insistence that 'technically' a college was a self-governing college of fellows even if (compared with the members) their merit may have been the 'comparative imminence of their departure from the earthly sphere'. When Timpson returned from a New South Wales group meeting in early December, he made it clear that its members were strongly against the initial appointment of 100–150 fellows. Bill Connell, for instance, was emphatic that 'we had to decide just what kind of body this [college] was to be': academic, professional or an association of interest. Likewise, a departmental official harboured 'considerable doubts about how we have set about organising the College': he objected to it being an examining body enabling placement of initials after peoples' names, when it ought to be a meeting ground for people from different fields of education. For these reasons and despite the provisional council's authorisation, Timpson urged Darling to refrain from offering people fellowships. With letters ready to be mailed, a frustrated Darling complained that this was 'exactly what happens when one tries to do a thing in Australia on a Federal basis'.[11]

By early 1959, with the convention just over three months away, the state of play was as follows. Spearheaded by Darling, the proposed college was a creature of the Victorian Headmasters' Conference of Australia heads, for which virtually all of the major education interests and groupings in that state were on side. For the other states (particularly New South Wales), however, the proposal was far from done and dusted. In more ways than one, Darling's college model was displaying its true elitist colours: the credentials of the first batch of fellows had not been examined (despite examination being the hurdle requirement for admission to a fellowship); there was not one practising teacher's name among those canvassed during the previous year and the breadth of the appeal of Darling's baby to the broad mass of teachers would be limited until the fellowship–membership relationship was properly worked out. Now that Timpson was again playing a go-between role for a second meeting at the University of Sydney in February, these deficiencies became bones of contention. His notes summarised the familiar ring of the Sydney meeting's key points (a number of which were at cross-purposes). In status terms, would the college be an academy (or learned society), something similar to a medical college or the equivalent of the National Education Association in the USA? Shouldn't the fellows' numbers be kept small, and wasn't it undesirable to fill a college with fellows and present this 'as a fait accompli to assistant masters and mistresses'? One official was still strongly opposed to fellowships, membership and examination for admission to fellow status. Just as the 1948 Corio conference was a forum for educators to confer, the college ought to act as a similar kind of meeting ground for heads and teachers, 'although not necessarily together'. (This response differed from that of Ramsay in Victoria.) There was also disagreement about whether the status of teachers needed elevating and, if not, whether a college was even required. Despite its twists and turns, the Sydney meeting was disposed to be positive. Its unanimously agreed-to motion approved 'the idea of the College of Education', which 'should be supported'.[12]

To ensure that firm proposals would be ready for the founders' convention, the provisional council met on three occasions in early 1959. In late February, it considered Timpson's Sydney meeting report (which Darling thought made 'irritating reading'). Armed with a firmer grip on the sensitivities, the council rescinded its earlier decision to create 100 fellows. In a stroke of genius, the word 'founders' was substituted for 'fellows', a switch, Hogg commented to Robson, that had 'apparently arisen out of meditations in Melbourne upon suggestions made in Sydney!' A more credible explanation for this change than Sydney sensitivities was (as Sanders pointed out) that if everyone associated with the college's formation became fellows, rather than foundation members, then the awarding of future membership would be 'extremely difficult'. Moreover, the Western Australian view was that 'the motives of the founders would be suspect'. In a closely associated move, the council reduced the previous thirty-nine approved names by one and requested New South Wales to nominate thirty founders. In early April, the council met for the last time to finalise the May convention program. Darling's draft was the starting point. Additional names of founders had trickled in. These were endorsed and another thirteen were added. But the founder–fellow distinction still left unresolved the preferred number of fellows. It was 'generally agreed' that there would be about 500 'eventually'. Some provisional council members wanted a form of membership other than fellows, and a procedure to facilitate the attainment of fellowship. A working document circulated pre-meeting noted a 'considerable divergence of opinion' concerning college membership, and even a 'contrary view' that the college ought to comprise primarily members, with a 'much restricted body of Fellows of special distinction'. The founder title had been agreed to because of this division of opinion, with the form of the 'ultimate organisation' to be determined at the convention. Tension between the democratic notion of membership and the exclusivity of fellowship was still unresolved, but everything else was in readiness as the delegates assembled at Corio.[13]

Darling was pleased with himself. The outcome of the April meeting was that he had won everyone over to his way of thinking, he told Gordon (by then battling cancer), although it had taken him until 11.30 pm to do so. The New South Wales response was 'staggering' as 'almost all the big boys from there are coming'. The only state in doubt was Queensland, which, 'characteristically', had not even replied to invitations. He was confident that a 'proper' college would commence with fellows, and that the other categories would be sorted out later. Acceptances of the provisional council's invitation to found a college tallied 114. Perusal of the names suggests that it was a gathering of the good and great of education, although thirty of them could not be present. Twenty (or about a quarter) of those who attended were women. Alan Cash's detailed three-page checklist reveals that no organisational stones had been left unturned in preparing for success: a South Australian founder, Dr A.W. (Alby) Jones, recalled that there were '[GGS] prefects at the ready to help guests even to [the extent of] cleaning their boots & shoes'—although there was no hot water in the bathrooms, Timpson later complained. When the invitees arrived, they were handed a conference folder, the cover of which displayed an adaptation of John Tenniel's illustration from *Through the Looking Glass*, in which Alice meets the two little fat boys, Tweedledee and Tweedledum, in the forest. This was an enigmatic choice, although in light of the contentious lead-up period it conveyed an intended irony. The accompanying inscription read: "'I was thinking," Alice said very politely, "which is the best way out of this wood."' Sanders (unable to attend) explained to Timpson the failure of ACER's earlier attempt to create something similar. Although not personally involved in the earlier initiative, he had taken a strong lead in promoting a college idea in various professional conferences and publications on the ground of a need for an Australian association of educationalists concerned with 'the problems of education and not with its politics'. Nothing had come of ACER's attempt because its conception had been 'too broadly based'; it 'collapsed through lack of interest in some influential quarters and sectional interests in others'. When the Headmasters' Conference of Australia heads had been canvassing the college idea, Sanders had promoted it at ANZAAS in Adelaide, where Gordon had alerted him to the developments in Victoria. Generously, given that his own efforts had so little to show for them (although they probably helped produce a receptive climate), Sanders gave the Victorian initiative his 'whole-hearted support' and wished it every success.[14]

The delegates were welcomed at the convention dinner by the archbishop. As convention chairman, Darling then declared the proceedings open and conferred the provisional council's honorary fellowship on Rolland. Typically, the two friends indulged themselves: Darling said of Rolland that he was 'harmless as a dove, wise as a serpent, on the tennis court lively as a gazelle' and with 'presumably the constitution of an ox', while Rolland, with his well-known self-deprecation, claimed that he had never heard 'so charming a speech about so ordinary a person!' and that he was 'glad to hear how extraordinary I have been'. Darling then introduced Dr David Russell (a University of California academic with expertise in children's reading and writing) who gave the opening address: 'A profession and a college of education'. The next two days were to be given over to business meetings, followed by ratification of the college's constitution on the Sunday evening, and concluding with lunch after a final meeting on the Monday morning that would appoint officers, fix fees and plan the future.[15]

It is not known who invited Russell to take the podium or why. Darling made no written commentary on the speech, but it was not his cup of tea—he would have been in sympathy with Russell's view of teaching as an art, but Russell made no mention of religious values, and his constant references to research, knowledge, training and correlation would have been discordant to anyone schooled in liberal humanism and character formation. (The convention proceedings recorded the address as 'inspiring and useful'.) A four-page extract on the evolution of the professions by the philosopher A.N. Whitehead was circulated by Moorhouse and is more likely to have been to Darling's taste. Russell urged the need for a profession and the leadership that only it could provide in developing education as a discipline, a 'body of knowledge with more intellectual bite than it has today'. Education was still becoming a profession and, in developmental terms, it had progressed to about where the natural sciences had been a century earlier and the social sciences forty years before. For Russell, a profession exhibited the 'marks of a high calling', of which there were six: ideals of high service to society, comprehensive knowledge enriched by continuing research, selection of members according to standards, integrated preparation and training through in-service (and pre-service) measures, determination and administration of a profession's own standards, and self-evaluation of members' performance. Then, as part of an 'action-program', Russell threw his audience a series of challenges (for, having perused the agenda papers, he could not find much on what the proposed college would do). These included, once again, the need to assist with research and its dissemination, the problem of ascertaining a desirable balance between liberal and professional education, the provision of specialist leadership training for the various categories of educators (heads, teachers, inspectors, and so on), and finally ways of preventing the college from becoming little more than a 'superior trade union sufficient unto itself instead of getting all the parts of the profession working together'.[16]

The following morning in the music school the proceedings proper commenced. In what (he had warned Rolland) would be a 'portentously solemn' address, Darling moved that 'the Founders here present agree to form a college of Education'. He gave three reasons. First, the college had to unify the activities of numerous educational organisations and 'bring together the leaders of all branches of the profession'. Second, in arguing for the importance of teaching and its community value, he quoted the Whitehead extract in support of his view that institutions founded on professional qualifications prevented the state 'from imposing its authority outside its lawful limits'. Then, invoking the example of the Academy of Science (a body that 'might be consulted' by governments) he said that the proposed college should 'think out and stand for', not merely opinions about education, but (because all educators had personal and moral responsibilities for those whom they taught):

> certain standards and principles upon which all who are concerned with the passing on and building up of the world's culture must be agreed. This is done by honesty of mind, integrity, scholarship, and, in its truest sense, spirituality of outlook.

Third, the college would help raise the status of the teaching profession, not only in its own eyes but in those of the general public, by claiming for it 'a dignity not less than has been achieved' by other professions. College membership or fellowship, therefore, had to be regarded as 'an honour to be sought after and valued'. Fourteen other people spoke, following which the motion (seconded by Ramsay) was carried unanimously. Selby Smith and Wyndham were then elected as the drafting committee, and thenceforward the convention resorted to the parliamentary procedure of debate in committee.[17]

Despite the circulation of Whitehead's observations, the question of what counted as the profession of education was never really debated at Corio. The assumption seemed to be that the Australian College of Education would be the voice of the profession in Australia, but with the notion of profession restricted mainly to teachers, and with teachers understood primarily as schoolteachers rather than (say) university teachers. Yet, the Australian College of Education was proclaimed as a college of education not merely a college of teachers (as in England since the granting of a royal charter in 1849 to a body christened the College of Preceptors). Education generally then (as now) meant something wider than teachers or teaching. A related point was whether education included or subsumed the idea of training and those engaged in training—certainly not in the view of Richard Livingstone whose 1943 book *Education for a World Adrift* was cited by some of the founders. If training was not synonymous with education, then what was the basis of their differentiation, given that both ideas entailed learning? These definitional problems existed because some institutions had a direct interest in teaching and learning—traditionally the core business of schools, colleges and faculties of education—although not a monopoly interest. Others who presumed to be, or were acknowledged as, authorities in these matters included professors from faculties other than education (such as Moorhouse), heads of educational agencies that fulfilled semi-credentialling functions (for example, Copland at the Administrative Staff College) and vice-chancellors (for example, Medley). As Moorhouse observed, all professional bodies, 'concerned as they are with the qualifications of their members', were 'inherently interested in education'. In his notes for his opening address, Darling had acknowledged these difficulties associated with the concept of education, as well as sectional or state-based allegiances, sectoral divisions between state and independent schools, differences in the education of boys and girls, and various types of educational activities, except that he did not try to resolve the tensions between them.[18]

After agreeing to establish a college, discussion of the draft constitution proceeded without a glitch until consideration of the contentious issue of the examination of fellows and members. Three of the following aims of the college were agreed to unanimously:

a. to provide a meeting ground for leading members of the profession in its various fields
b. to protect from external pressures the intellectual freedom and integrity of the profession
c. to uphold within the profession and to promote in the community a belief in the higher values of education

In the discussion of aim (d.), the chairman exercised his prerogative and ruled out a proposed amendment:

d. to encourage and where necessary provide for advanced specialised professional training
e. to recognise outstanding contributions to educational practice
f. to co-operate with the Universities and other bodies in the furtherance of these aims
g. to sponsor visits from leaders of educational thought from overseas

On aim (d.), Dr I.S. Turner (principal, Sydney Teachers' College) wanted the college to establish an 'adequate minimum standard of admission' to teaching. Darling's view was that this was a 'matter of policy' rather than an aim, which might 'come later' when the college gained government recognition. Had Tosh Phillips been present, his worst fears about his recently originated idea of Australia's cultural cringe might have been confirmed. By including 'from overseas' in aim (g.), Australia's educators were signalling a comparatively low estimate of themselves and homegrown practice—which hearkened back to MacNeil's point in 1946. (Subsequent documentation disseminated to the newly formed state chapters revised the wording to 'visiting speakers either from overseas or inter-state'.)[19]

Aims (h.)—'to hold regular meetings for hearing papers and for discussion'—and (i.) —'to provide for the publication of learned papers'—were adopted with little comment. Aim (j.), however, was a different story. While the provisional council's innocuous wording said: 'to hold examinations and elect new members and fellows', this turned out to be (as Darling told the delegates) 'the most controversial subject that had been discussed'. The question of how the college was to be constituted and its ongoing life were 'the most difficult of all the problems that had to be faced at the Convention'. Darling was in a quandary. The advice from Oliphant (founding president of the Australian Academy of Science) was that the college should be small and select, except that (unlike the academy which had been inaugurated by twelve Australian Royal Society Fellows) if the new college was too restrictive to begin with then it might fail to persist (thanks to conceit or inbreeding). On the other hand, if admission was broad there might be 'no distinction' in being a member. This latter possibility was compounded by the existence of so many other 'educational self-help institutions and groups', Darling believed, that there was 'no particular point' in adding another one. He did not regard the proposed dual grade of membership (fellow and member) as a solution to the problem. His bottom line was both chronological and legal: fellows had to comprise the college from the outset, for they alone could own and control its resources and property. Subsequently, a lower grade of membership was a possibility. The alternative of establishing a large membership to then select fellows from among themselves was 'undesirable'. To cap it all, the means of election and methods of government were still to be decided. With Medley seconding him, he proposed an upper limit of 500 fellows throughout the country but his motion lapsed.[20]

Discussion adjourned until the Saturday evening. For nearly three hours after its resumption, deliberations threatened to unravel as delegates argued about grades and types of membership, incorporation and articles of association, and numbers of fellows (and there were even attempts to revisit the previously ratified aims). Eventually, Selby Smith and Wyndham moved to declare as foundation college members those present and invitees unable to be present. Darling's attempt to defer discussion was defeated. After the rejection of two attempted amendments the motion was carried. Crucially, Selby Smith's second motion (that the foundation members present should elect the first council) was also carried. The meeting then adjourned. Fancy footwork was required before the morning and it came during a late night meeting of the provisional council's executive and the drafting committee. The next morning, the contrast between the extent of the ground covered then and the previous evening's faffing over membership could not have been starker. Darling called on Wyndham who sponsored successively proposals concerned with a council, officers, membership, election and powers, and the constitution of state chapters. These were agreed to. Darling's and Wyndham's motion to create two grades of membership (fellows and members) was carried unanimously, along with Darling's and Robson's motion that the council (as the college governing body) appoint fellows and members. Selby Smith then outlined three membership criteria (unusual skill as a teacher, long and successful service and special contributions to thought or practice), with the council to be responsible for electing members. Similar criteria applied to fellows, along with completion of a thesis or an examination—although there was cloudiness about whether a person self-nominated to be a member or was invited. Finally, there was agreement on fees and subscriptions.[21]

By the Sunday evening, then, the founders had got their act together. They rattled through possible activities for the college (for example, paper presentations, discussions, attempts to solve educational problems, production of authoritative reports) after which Darling's motion that the constitution be ratified was carried unanimously. The next item was the election of office-bearers. Darling was the sole nomination for president, a fact of which he made light:

> [He] thought it naturally rather difficult for the Provisional Council with himself in the chair to suggest that he should vacate it and he should hate to be left in it because of any weakness of moral character in the Provisional Council.

Wyndham and Moorhouse were nominated as vice-presidents, Timpson as secretary and Radford as treasurer, but the convention hit a snag with the composition of the remaining council membership. During the rehearsal of potential college activities, the founders prefaced their suggestions with 'Australian' yet they were incapable of constituting a council from among those present that was genuinely national—there was only one invitee from Tasmania and Queensland (each was an apology), and the ACT, and no-one from the Northern Territory. Darling cautioned against the election of a preponderance of Victorians and independent school heads. Eventually it was agreed to elect thirteen councillors from a composite list of twenty-eight provisional council and member nominations. After that there was some minor tidying up, including re-ratification of the constitution after ironing out some small anomalies. It was agreed to notify the newspapers about the founders' deliberations and then Hone and Wyndham moved a vote of thanks to Darling and the school council. Because he felt so deeply touched by what had been achieved, Wyndham was effusive, particularly about the school's hospitality, but also because of the atmosphere provided by the venue: it was 'good to have been here, to have met together, to have lived together, in conditions that Dr. Darling, his staff and the boys had made possible'. Darling replied and was 'remarkably moved' by the way the motion was put and the fact that it was carried with acclamation. But there was more. On the Monday morning, after attending to some general business (including suggested arrangements for a visit of an 'international authority in education' in 1960 and a recommendation that the new council consider the establishment of minimum standards for the profession), Robson had asked from the floor that the convention 'instruct' the new council to elect Darling as the first Australian College of Education fellow. Again, this was carried with acclamation. Darling then thanked the gathering, announced the results of the council poll, and with that they were done.[22]

No wonder Darling had been so pleased with himself when he had reported developments to Ralph. The publicity was positive and there were reports or editorials on the new college in most capital city newspapers. After returning to earth from the rarified hothouse convention atmosphere, however, Darling had mixed feelings about some of the decisions. With people like Ross (who fell ill and missed the second half of the weekend) he was circumspect. 'I am rather indecently gratified by the whole business', he told her, but there were some misgivings. The constitution, for example, had not turned out according to his 'line of thought' and he felt that, as chairman, he had been 'outmanoeuvred at every point'. Furthermore, he was grumpy about the adoption of what he thought was a 'silly' election system, if only because it had deprived Coates of a spot on the council—although Gleeson thought that '11 of the Machiavellian 12' had been elected. The election outcome might have been different, Darling thought, if he and his provisional council cronies had had their 'way'. What was more, he complained to Ramsay, there were far too many headmasters on the council. Hone also griped about the council's composition, and was scathing that 'none of those first rate high-school headmasters who really set the thing on its feet that night at Wesley' had been elected (although he had overlooked Chapman and a technical college head, Tylee, both of whom were councillors).[23]

There was unfinished business. Not all states and territories were on board, and the hearts and minds of the new state chapters were still to be won— Robertson was quick to arrange for Darling to speak to a group of Western Australians about his 'hopes and aspirations' for the college after the September meeting of the Headmasters' Conference of Australia conference in Perth. There was also the question of donations and gifts, and whether for taxation purposes these might qualify as tax exemptions. (They didn't.) There was some creative light relief while consolidating the infrastructure of the new college when Darling and Tylee pooled their talents for the design of a college badge and motto. They toyed with a single-line passage from 1 Corinthians 12: 11–12 (about many members, but one body)—which was a reading for the Sunday morning convention chapel service. Finally, there were the teachers' unions. Despite the presence of Baker and Mitchell, one of the biggest unions yet to be persuaded about the college's legitimacy was the Australian Teachers' Federation. Its president complained that he knew 'nothing' about the college apart from what he had read in the newspapers. Despite what the founders may have thought, the Australian Teachers' Federation was not just concerned with teachers' salaries and conditions of employment but also with the theory and practice of education. He hoped for relations of 'friendly co-operation'. So too did Darling. The basis of college participation was individual, rather than organisational, he explained, while conceding that it had to earn the confidence and respect of teachers represented by the Australian Teachers' Federation, as well securing the federation's support, but without granting it ex-officio election to membership or fellowship. This, he conceded, was a 'real problem'.[24]

But what about fellows and members? The founders had appointed themselves members. At its first meeting in Melbourne on 26 June, the new council resolved that in future it would elect such people: prospective members could apply for admission, they could be nominated or a combination of both entry modes was possible. Membership enlargement after the convention would be by invitation and there was to be an initial overall ceiling of 700 (with the chapter targets set roughly in proportion to each state's population). The mechanism for initial enlargement was that the foundation members in the respective states would issue invitations to be forwarded to the council. To be selected, a prospective member would need to satisfy two criteria: a minimum of five years' experience in education and an 'outstanding contribution over and above basic needs' (for example, present a distinguished paper, or provide evidence of a special contribution or an unusual skill). Unlike members, fellows were a different matter. At its first meeting, the new council conferred fellowships on Medley, Hoy and Robson. This group, along with Darling, was charged with making recommendations about future fellows from lists of names submitted by the state chapters. To be elected the nominees had to have made a 'really notable' contribution or provided 'exceptional service' to education in Australia. Darling foresaw the difficulties in identifying very many worthy people and asked Medley: 'Which of us [had made such a contribution?]'[25]

Jockeying for preferment began. As to who might be nominated during the three months before the next council meeting in October, Robson confessed to being 'stumped'. He thought that the first of two nominees was 'ordinary & undistinguished' while other people were 'lukewarm' about the second. Calculations of merit were colliding with the need for balanced state representation. Darling did not rate one suggested nominee as especially 'remarkable', but as nominations in that state were low, and this person had been 'extremely helpful', the name should probably go forward. As for teachers, Hewan had exercised his headmasterly prerogative to nominate about half-a-dozen heads of department as members and Darling's comment to Timpson on the Victorian chapter's recommendations was that there were insufficient assistant masters and mistresses. An immediate headache had been whether to award fellowships to Ramsay or Wyndham or both. Ramsay was not elected to the council (he withdrew in favour of Wyndham and Robertson) but, as Radford pointed out to Darling, he was the 'doyen' of the state directors and was less than a year from retirement. Radford's concern was that while Wyndham had first claim (as three of the four fellows were Victorians) Ramsay was probably more deserving as he exercised a 'great deal of quiet influence in the ways the college wants to go'. Likewise, he was the 'most human' of all the directors and should not be overlooked. Maybe the gang of four should become five, Darling wondered; but to write follow-up letters to councillors or arrange a telephone ring-around to rectify an oversight by appointing Ramsay would merely cement Victorian dominance.[26]

Despite Gordon's advice against elevating Ramsay (or to simultaneously elevate Wyndham) Darling prepared a lengthy and persuasive case on his behalf ('the outstanding Director of Education in Victoria with the exception of Mr. Tait [sic]') and sought council's agreement to appoint Ramsay as a fellow. He got his way. Wyndham did not mind waiting until the next round. The question raised by Darling's intervention was whether similar action would be tolerated as the gift of presidents or, having put his stamp on the college, did his action mean that it was still seen as his baby? He knew that he was a looming shadow because he stepped back from involvement in the Victorian chapter, although when Boylen read newspaper reports of Darling's impending retirement, he 'tremble[d] to think what could happen if your guiding hand were withdrawn'. Whether Boylen was exaggerating the extent of dependence on GGS's headmaster, the college still needed his pulling power before he became an *éminence grise* in the wings. An immediate benefit, out of the blue, was the promise of £1000 from the press baron, Frank Packer—who had had a recent exchange of views with Darling at the television licence hearings. Why he gave the money to 'a louse such as you', Packer didn't know (it was explained to Darling by Jika Travers) except that in a recent conversation the businessman had made 'very "Packerish" remarks about your influence on his life' and felt that GGS 'had done a great deal for his two sons'. Back in house, the new council (with its executive of five, mostly Victorians) had met on three occasions to attend to housekeeping and machinery matters: draft articles of association, aims and activities, admission procedures for members and fellows, and state chapters (including the building of cooperative relations with teachers' unions). A visit to the states by the president helped to kick-start the chapters—but for him that meant even more travel and absence from GGS. Another early priority was wider legitimacy for the Australian College of Education. After the convention, Darling informed the prime minister about the new educational infant and assured him that he did not want any money for it (yet). If, however, Menzies wanted undertaken 'any particular job in connection with education', then he might approach the college.[27]

In May 1960, Darling delivered the presidential address at the second annual Australian College of Education conference at the University of Sydney: 'Educational values in a democracy'. After his speech and a vote of thanks by the governor-general (Viscount Dunrossil)—who declared the college inaugurated— there were five other addresses, each elucidating in more detail his central theme. Composing his address and delivering it 'nearly finished me', Darling later confessed. No wonder. He tried cracking possibly the hardest educational nut of all: the provision of education, and its relationship to equality and merit. The new college was significant, he said, because it bridged the 'crevasses' of the Australian educational world, both vertical (between the state, Catholic and independent sectors) and horizontal (the stages from kindergarten to university), and provided a 'common meeting ground' rather than previous 'occasional battlegrounds' on which educators met to 'tilt with their opponents, either for the glory of the fight or occasionally *à l'outrance* [to the bitter end] for very life'. If in respect of its purpose the college was to speak for and on behalf of the education profession, and if the profession's dignity rested on whether or not it was seen to be meeting society's needs, then the critical question was: 'What has a society, allegedly free, democratic and literate, the right to ask from its educational leaders'? The key word here was leaders. The essence of a free society was the power of choice and the purpose of education in a free society was to make right judgements, yet schools could do little to alter the values of a free society, because 'the world is too much with us, getting and spending, for us to pursue for long untrammelled the good and the beautiful and the true'. Powerless, although swept along on a tide of materialism, schools were easy targets for radicals, and yet they had to improve, as well as preserve, culture. The particular problem that school systems had failed to solve—which, as a result, made arrival at 'any' general philosophy of education exceedingly difficult (a point reiterated shortly afterwards in his Syme Oration)—was how to provide simultaneously for gifted and not-so-gifted individuals. In this connection, 'as needs we must', educational equality had been accepted as a corollary of democracy, except that 'we have never made up our minds clearly as to what we mean by this education for all'.[28]

Darling then argued for democratic elitism: education for a stratified meritocracy. Although education for all was an admirable idea, to disguise from pupils as part of educational equality the fact that they were not all equally gifted (or gifted in the same way) diminished recognition of the need for an educated elite 'upon whom must lie the responsibility of leadership in all the various fields of life'. As a result, scholarly qualities of intellect, logic, precision and style in reasoning (marks of 'a true culture') had been lost. To fail to train the leadership of the collective mind of the body politic in intellectual quality and moral courage was to end up with the 'cowardly and servile state' depicted in Orwell's *1984*. Hierarchically positioned below the gifted were two types of pupils: the 'ordinary student'—an 'anxious group of aspirants for the hand of Athene', no less—who, under pressure to succeed, tended to contrive by all manner of short cuts and expedients to excel like their gifted peers, and those (many) who were staying on at secondary school because of a growing recognition that 'this is a good thing to do'. Other than discriminating between the three groups from within a common philosophy that could be 'applicable in different ways to suit the different needs of each', he saw 'no complete solution'. If the first (elite) group were to develop fine scholarship then it required 'leisure'. This was a poor choice of word (with, by 1960, its old-fashioned gentlemanly overtones) that he declined to define, and that may or may not have resonated with his audience. What he seemed to be after was sufficient scope for his leadership elite to be able to follow its own inclinations beyond the narrow demands of a syllabus. The second group would comprise the rank and file of the specialist professions, the preparation for which required time. The remaining 'mass' needed subjects related as closely as possible to their lives and ambitions: 'the stimulus of tangibles'. Essentially, then, Darling's way of reconciling equality and education entailed different educational treatments based on different identified abilities that, when stripped to its barest essentials, was little more than an updated version of his 1935 justification for GGS curriculum reform. This was not an education geared to each individual's needs (for that was 'pious nonsense') but geared instead to the 'educational type to which he [sic] belongs'. Boys and girls in all three groups needed, first, to be fitted for adulthood, life and labour in 'that state into which it has pleased God to call them'; second, trained to preserve and enhance the principles and culture of the body politic; third, enabled 'so to know God on earth that they shall enjoy him forever in eternity'. To a critic, these outcomes looked suspiciously like education for one's place, democratic duty and godliness.[29]

In the week after the conference a *Nation* columnist quoted an allegedly 'sceptical' delegate, according to whom the Australian College of Education served two purposes: the conferring of educational status on masters in the great public schools who were light-on intellectually and social status on state school teachers who were correspondingly light-on socially. This 'pretty fair exchange'—an ounce of snobbery for an ounce of pedagogy—might enable the college to 'do quite well'. 'Damn all newspapers and journalists', Darling cursed. During July, he went to Queensland, accompanied by Timpson, to assist in forming the state chapter. He and Timpson were a working duo (as previously with Montgomery). Although he could probably have got by without him in Brisbane, he told Timpson, his time there 'would have been much less successful and much less efficient'. In fact, a reward of being associated with the college was that 'I should have found your friendship'. Eight months later (March 1961), Darling was confident that the Queensland developments were working out 'admirably', but there was still much work to do federally if the college were to become the 'authoritative body' in education and it was crucial that each year's annual meeting was a success. To that end, he continued actively courting Menzies. Would the prime minister address the college about Australia in the next twenty years, he enquired in late 1960, and about what he expected of its teachers? He had tried previously (without luck) to secure Menzies to open the annual meeting in Sydney and (again without luck) to meet him earlier in the year to impress on him the college's representative status, to secure its recognition as an organisation for which gifts counted as legitimate deductions for income tax purposes and to keep open the possibility of a royal charter. While there was no joy on the income tax and the charter, the college president landed his big fish: the prime minister addressed the Australian College of Education conference in Adelaide in 1961 with a speech entitled 'The challenge to democracy' (sprinkled liberally, as Darling would have been pleased to note, with excerpts from Morgan's *Liberties of the Mind*) and judged to be an 'excellent and valuable' contribution.[30]

Throughout 1960, the college council continued wrestling with an acceptable means of fellowship elections and membership though nomination (rather than application). Darling was concerned with the lack of interest taken in the college by university teachers and lack of progress in establishing a Tasmanian chapter. For him, the key college purposes continued to be: first, to override the divisions between all branches and levels of education to create a fellowship of teachers; and second, to raise the status of teaching through a professional body in which the members have 'some distinction'. 'Just exactly what the College might do apart from its Annual Meeting', he confided to Browne, 'I don't think anybody can yet say'. Within the privacy of relations with those who shared his view of the inextricable link between education and religion, however, such as the Jesuit Father Michael Scott (Aquinas College, North Adelaide), Darling insisted that the teaching profession genuinely required a spiritual revival ('preferably religious, but not necessarily so'). After all, teaching was a vocation that entailed a sense of duty to those for whom teachers were responsible, rather than improved technical efficiency. Teaching, as he reminded Frederick, was an art rather than a science. In 1961, with the pre-retirement 'prospect of repeated dinners', packing up, and counting down the days when he could work in the garden at Kamarooka, Darling sought to step aside from the presidency. The college, he told Wyndham, was a 'bit too associated with me' and to be more widely accepted there had to be a change at the top. Wyndham, he believed, was just the man to succeed him, but he had to wait two more years before the presidency changed hands.[31]

Why did Darling and his peers succeeded when they did? In 1960, the historian R.M. Crawford asked when Australia came of age as a nation and suggested the 1930s. For education, the case is stronger for the late 1950s or 1960s. By 1959 there were a number of peak agency voices claiming to speak nationally on behalf of the sector or parts of it. With the formation of the conference of directors of education following an inaugural meeting in 1916, and a national council of state education ministers in 1936—the Australian Education Council—ministerial decisions were being made by the states, but at least with an eye on what the others were up to. (In truth, the Australian Education Council limped sporadically until its revival in 1958 and, as late as the end of the 1960s, state ministers were still striving for a nationally uniform mode of statistically reporting schooling data.) As for educational research, since 1930 the sector had benefitted (thanks to Carnegie money) from its own exclusive research agency, the ACER, and a year later the Headmasters' Conference of Australia had begun life as a forum for independent boys' school headmasters—until there were members from all states, it (like the Australian College of Education) was an interstate body before being fully national. The Australian Vice-Chancellors' Committee had been speaking on the universities' behalf since 1920 and in 1942 the Universities Commission was the first federal education agency. The fore-runner of the present day Australian Education Union, the Australian Teachers' Federation, had been established in 1937 and, in the same year, the National Union of Australian University Students began speaking for students. In 1959, the Australian Universities Commission was established, followed by the Australian Schools Commission fifteen years later in 1974. When the found-ers had met at Corio, then, they can have been under no illusions about the magnitude of their task in trying to establish a nation-wide agency to speak for education. The above examples confirm Tosh Phillips' view that 'Australian' was a tenuous description of the sector. The time turned out to be ripe to try to have one Australian professional voice for educationalists and, thanks in large measure to the efforts of an expatriate Englishman, the country got one. Moreover, with more than half of his earthly life now behind him and with the majority of his working life spent in Australia, his admirers might well have seen the formation of the college as that Englishman's finest hour. Darling lamented to the chairman of the GGS school council (who, due to illness, had not attended the convention) that, while the weekend had been a 'most memorable' one, he had landed himself yet another job. 'I wish I could sometimes avoid going into everything with both feet.' But it was because another body had been added to the growing pantheon of national Australian education forums that Dorothy Ross said that he was jus-tified in feeling pleased about the convention. It 'was an achievement', she said, because 'a gap has been filled'.[32]

NEW TOY

1954–1961

But culture indefatigably tries, not to make what each raw person may like,
the rule by which he fashions himself; but to draw ever nearer to a sense of
what is indeed beautiful, graceful, and becoming, and to get the raw person
to like that.

Matthew Arnold, *Culture and Anarchy*

Indications of what might be termed the Australian-isation of James Darling were clear by the mid- to late 1950s. There was no abrupt time line between being English initially and then Australian but a gradual transition. This shift had been evident in education and public life, and in the creation of the Australian College of Education and was about to become evident in broadcasting. Far from abandoning his Englishness, then, Darling's allegiances were divided. Dual-country allegiance was not uncommon. Another Englishman in Australia—the Reverend Dr John Nurser (Warden, St Mark's Library, Canberra)—recalled a conversation with Margaret in which, instancing her husband, she said that one could 'never really be happy either in England or Australia after you've lived in both'. By the late 1950s, Darling had lived nearly as much of his life outside of England as in it. Three factors were nurturing his Australian-ness. First, his immediate family members were Australian-born, Australians by identity and, despite their affections for England and their forebears' British roots, Australia was home. Second, vestigial hopes of employment in England had evaporated—although as late as the mid-1970s Darling was fantasising about spending his final years in England and being buried at Eyke. Third, his increased national-level responsibilities were broadening his knowledge of the country and deepening his affection for it. Darling's work in broadcasting and television consolidated his emerging sense of Australian-ness.[1]

Just before Christmas 1954, Darling had informed the school council that, with the chairman's permission, he had accepted the prime minister's offer to become a part-time member of the Australian Broadcasting Control Board (ABCB), for which he would be paid about £600 annually. Back in 1949, after heated debate and amid allegations that the Chifley government was antagonistic to commercial television development, Parliament had established the ABCB as the regulator of broadcasting and television. Its authority derived from Part 2 of the *Broadcasting and Television Act*. Board members were appointed by the governor-general for up to seven years, and its regulatory responsibilities were confined to commercial broadcasting and television. In 1954, following the recent Royal Commission on Television, the ABCB was reconstituted to include, in addition to the chairman, R.G. (Bob) Osborne, and two full-time members, R.B. (Bruce) Mair and R.A. Yeo, two part-time members, R.M. White and Darling, who were expected to advise on program standards. The ABCB met roughly fortnightly in Melbourne. Subject to the approval of the minister (the postmaster-general) who, as noted by the Royal Commission, was the licensing authority, the ABCB's responsibility was to ensure that commercial broadcasting and television services accorded with its plans, stations' operations and technical equipment met its standards, and programs were 'adequate and comprehensive' to 'serve the best interests of the general public'. Legislative amendments (in 1956) revised the ABCB–postmaster-general relationship. The ABCB became subject to ministerial direction concerning the operating power of stations and their band frequencies, it could determine station transmission hours and advertising conditions, and the postmaster-general was obliged to refer applications for licences to the ABCB for its recommendation, prior to which the ABCB conducted inquiries. Licensees had to transmit programs in accordance with standards determined by the ABCB.[2]

To this role of communications regulator Darling brought with him a level of ignorance of television in the early 1950s shared by many Australians. He was scarcely a devotee of sound transmission, let alone visual imagery. At the same time, he was not unfamiliar with mass communications media and had delivered occasional radio talks. During World War II, he had been appointed to the ABC's Broadcasting Advisory Committee—a recommendation of the Joint Parliamentary Committee on Broadcasting (the Gibson Committee) in 1942 was to establish state-based advisory committees. After rejoining the Victorian committee, he was a member from 1953 to 1957. As a sounding board on program feedback for the ABC's commissioners, the Victorian committee included, among others, Colin Badger, Myra Roper, Dr Eric Cunningham Dax (chairman, Mental Health Authority), Dr Zelman Cowen and Professor Joseph Burke. Darling's view of the committee's purpose, expressed (somewhat dismissively) in 1945, was 'to guard the morals of the people'. At that time he had had very little faith in it, largely because of the commercial radio broadcasters' low view of the public's taste. Given their commitment to offering a listening audience what they thought that it wanted, the most that anyone desirous of improving public standards could hope for, Darling thought, was to keep the commercial operators 'just on the safe side of actual obscenity'. His later ABCB experiences confirmed his pessimism about the baleful impact of commercialism. In the meantime, when the advisory committee met with Medley (the commissioner for Victoria), Darling dutifully tabled his views about such programs as the ABC's news commentaries and was forthright about its religious broadcasting policy.[3]

Television arrived relatively late in Australia. BBC transmission had commenced in 1936 and, after wartime suspension, resumed in mid–1946. The Canadian Broadcasting Corporation began telecasting in 1952 (in Montreal and Toronto) and, after the resumption of television's prewar start-up, by 1953 there more than 300 stations in the USA. During World War II, Australian commercial interests had spotted television's potential and by war's end twenty to thirty applications for licences had already been received by the postmaster-general. Both party groupings dragged their feet, and there were divisions within each about approaches to provision. Following the change of government in 1949, there was another spate of licence applications and pressure from newspaper interests to establish commercial television. Labor had wanted a public television monopoly (as in Britain), but the new Coalition was committed broadly to a dual (commercial and national) arrangement, although its enthusiasm for television was less than wholehearted. Cost was a key concern along with the diversion of resources from other more pressing national economic priorities. For three years Menzies' Cabinet dithered. In this policy vacuum swirled the vocal claims of interest groups, especially those concerned with television's social effects. Darling's friend, the chairman of the ABC, Sir Richard (Dick) Boyer— supporter of an ABC television monopoly—authored a 25-page report on the new medium's unique visual attributes, which Darling absorbed 'carefully and with great interest', at about the time of the Royal Commission hearings (March 1953). His enthusiasm for television was a long time coming. He tossed up whether or not to give evidence, particularly if invited to—which he wasn't. On the other hand, unlike Wadham and Medley (supporters of the economic case for deferment), Darling did not oppose its introduction. In 1951, during lobbying for the introduction of television, Colin Gordon had been urged (by A.P. Rowe, Vice-Chancellor, University of Adelaide) to try to 'stir up some agitation' among his fellow heads but his efforts to engage his former boss fell on stony ground. Surely television was 'just another of those "things" with which the adolescent will have to contend in the old way by forming tastes and standards for himself', Darling had written. Shortly before the Olympic Games in Melbourne, Darling was still dismissing television as a fad: just another 'of the useless ways of frittering away time'. While conceding that its dangers may have been overrated, he thought that one of its insidious effects was that it was 'difficult to turn off'. Even in 1957—when ABCB members and staff had been allocated 21-inch (53 cm) television sets made by STC—he was still proclaiming (to Boyer) his lack of enthusiasm for it. He did not watch 'the wretched thing as much as he ought' and, while there may have been nothing offensive telecast, there was also 'almost nothing' worth looking at.[4]

As part of the Coalition's adoption of the findings of the Royal Commission (chaired by Paton and with Osborne a member), commercial television licences were to be issued in both Sydney and Melbourne. No sooner had Darling been appointed than in early January 1955 the minister (C. Davidson) referred twelve applications for commercial television licences to the ABCB: four applications for two licences in Melbourne and eight for two in Sydney. The Melbourne hearings were scheduled for later in the month and Sydney's in early February. At the February school council meeting, councillors experienced a sample of what they (and the school) were in for after acceding to Menzies' offer. The headmaster had had to apologise for being poorly prepared as he had been 'desperately tied up with television during the last month' in Sydney. During the Melbourne hearings he grumbled to Casey that television was taking up much more of his time than he (and Osborne) had anticipated. By 1957, he was so exercised by his frequent absences from Corio that he doubted whether he was performing any of his commitments satisfactorily, and at about the time of Connell's evaluation he absented himself from the final three ABCB meetings for that year. The demands imposed by his ABCB membership during the three rounds of the national television rollout during the years 1955–60 are evident in the following figures. Apart from the Melbourne and Sydney hearings (completed prior to telecasting the Olympic Games), there was a second round of television transmission licence hearings in Brisbane, Adelaide, Perth and Hobart listed for 1958, and a third in 1959–60 for thirteen eastern Australian regional centres. During these rounds, the ABCB took 142 days (exclusive of weekends) to obtain evidence from applicants. The hearing transcripts prepared by the ABCB staff tallied well over 10,500 pages. Darling sat through about half of the ABCB's deliberations—or sixty-nine days—the equivalent of 14 five-day working weeks. During his final six years or so at Corio, then, he was absent for more than a third of an entire school year on ABCB business alone.[5]

The hearings were an endurance test because the transcripts reveal how quickly the proceedings became a lawyers' picnic. The Melbourne and Sydney hearing transcripts (a mere 1000 pages of the total) highlight the adversarial pattern of cross-examination of witnesses (as the applicants and their representatives were referred to), established by the conclusion of the Melbourne hearings. At the Sydney hearings (and thereafter), a rugby scrum of judicial counsel from among the good and great of the Australian legal fraternity jostled for air space to champion their clients' bona fides while seeking to discredit their rivals' bids. In his notes, at the top of his pencilled diagram of the Sydney hearings, Darling scribbled the surnames of the attending senior and junior counsel. Read from left to right the list was a legal *Who's Who*: (Clive) Evatt, Bridge, Redapple, Asprey, Newton, Shand, Larkins, (Dr) Evatt, Barwick and Else Mitchell. The initial exchanges between counsel in Melbourne (Douglas Menzies and Keith

Aickin—both later justices of the High Court of Australia) were gentlemanly enough, but the subsequent Brisbane hearings showed how the proceedings could descend into an unsavoury slanging match, despite Osborne's best efforts:

> MR. TAYLOR: Before I commence, Mr Chairman—
> THE CHAIRMAN: Are you going to say anything at all in reply to Mr. Kelly?
> MR. TAYLOR: This is obviously something which Mr. Kelly has been put up to by Mr. Larkins during the weekend, and it should be treated with the contempt it deserves.
> MR. KELLY: That is an unworthy comment.
> THE CHAIRMAN: It is indeed.
> MR. LARKINS: I wish to say that that is an absolutely false statement. I have not seen Mr. Kelly nor been in communication with him since we left this Board.
> MR. TAYLOR: Let us get on with the Inquiry!
> MR. LARKINS: Now my friend descends from false accusations to vulgarity! I ask the Board to examine what he has to say in the light of that. He is ready to make a false accusation at the drop of a hat.

The ABCB was to blame for this quasi-judicial hijacking of its hearings, because the presence of counsel to represent and cross-examine applicants and their legal representatives lay entirely within its discretionary gift (as provided for by the Act). The Sydney hearings, Darling told Boyer, were a 'cat and dog fight'.[6]

At the outset, Osborne indicated that licence applications would be considered in the order of receipt by the ABCB, and that applicants and persons with an interest could make observations or call witnesses with respect to any application. All witnesses were to provide sworn evidence. There were procedural hiccups. Dr Evatt (leader of the Opposition, and an applicant with Tom Dougherty of the Australian Workers' Union for licences in both cities) claimed that as Parliament had not laid down principles of procedure for the hearings, this matter required consideration, as important principles would be argued prior to dealing with particular cases. Would the ABCB countenance a public interest argument? Take the supposed case, he said, of 'a great corporation with tremendous control of mass communication in relation to the Press extending its field to radio broadcasting': would such a corporation in the public interest be entitled to a television licence? Osborne's curt response was that this matter was not something about which the ABCB wanted an argument. Evatt also queried what he took to be the hasty conduct of hearings in January. 'Was it because Dr. Darling was going back to school next month?', he speculated. There was another difficulty regarding the availability of applicants' exhibits—correspondence, company articles of association, annual reports, detailed listings of share registers or holdings, financial statements and balance sheets, and documents concerned with the equipment and technical capacity of actual or proposed applicant companies.

The ABCB alone had access to this material yet, Evatt asserted, if there was to be cross-questioning of submissions then such documentation had to be available (as the chairman realised in Sydney) to other applicants and counsel.[7]

The bulk of the hearings comprised penetrating counsel questioning of applicants about the intricacies of company ownership and control, cross-company share transactions, connections with other communication media, profit motivation, business experience and acumen, company capacity to transmit television programs, actual and potential links with overseas investors, motivations for entering the television market and personal character (and by implication their fitness to be put in charge of a television station). There were few if any holds barred in the lawyers' probing, as in Brisbane when (shortly after the previous exchange) Mr Taylor said that:

> In Queensland, Herald and Weekly Times and C.W.L. of course are doing now what Sir Keith Murdoch and the late John Wren did for very many years, they are running and controlling the papers and radio stations of Queensland. They did recently let the public in to some extent but, as was said by Mr. Sherman, the way they are being run is a continuation of the way they were run when Sir Keith Murdoch and the late John Wren regarded that as their empire in Queensland.

Darling's priorities were different. In the early ABCB meetings, he focused on production-related issues, particularly the potential licensees' engagement of people with 'proper qualifications', and the quality and distribution of broadcast programs for children. As part of the ABCB's division of interrogation labour, Darling's questions were about what the applicants (if successful) proposed to do with their licences: What did they understand by program quality and standards? How would they maintain quality and standards if these conflicted with commercial imperatives when building and sustaining a viewing audience? And were the applicants willing to make provision for children's programs to the extent of utilising specialist expertise? He also asked about religious programs, suspension of transmission hours and film material. Unlike his fellow ABCB members, Darling was in a slightly unusual (and somewhat privileged) position arising from his prior knowledge of, and enduring personal links with, a number of the publicly prominent applicants—although not such as to constitute a conflict of interest. Evatt had been a GGS parent and so too had Frank Packer. The Fairfax family, whose interests formed part of the bid by Amalgamated Television Services (ATS), was also very closely associated with GGS. Another applicant in 1958, the then 27-year-old Rupert Murdoch, was an OGG. Moreover, Murdoch's father (until his death) had been, and his mother and his aunt continued to be, Darling family friends. Finally, in 1959 when the quasi-inquisitorial character of the hearings was deeply entrenched—such that its own members' questioning of the applicants almost exactly replicated counsel in tone and substance—the

ABCB decided to employ its own legal adviser. The advocate whom it engaged was John (later Sir John) Young, who was also an OGG.[8]

A priority close to Darling's heart was quality, which quickly became apparent in the Melbourne hearing during his questioning of V.G.H. Harrison (appearing on behalf of General Television Corporation—GTC):

> I notice in the report of the Royal Commission a rather distressing unanimity
> of opinion from commercial interests that the standard of programmes can be
> best regulated by public opinion. Would you agree with that opinion expressed
> there or would you say that, owing to the novelty of television, there would be
> a great opportunity for people responsible for television to set standards which
> might be a bit higher than the public would expect?

Darling was also preoccupied with 'the main danger of television', about which he closely interrogated Sir John Williams (appearing for the Herald & Weekly Times—HWT): the risk that everyone in the home 'may see things that were intended for an older audience'. Was it practical from a commercial point of view, therefore, to cease telecasting after the children's session (as was the BBC's practice)? What did Williams regard as the points for and against such a measure, 'because obviously from an educational point of view it is highly desirable'? Williams replied that, in order to develop and build up an audience, and get it viewing, only to have to tell it to come back in an hour or so before shutting down transmission, would fly in the face of this general principle. Darling thought that this was 'a little unrealistic'. Surely all that he was proposing was the manner in which Williams himself behaved as a viewer?[9]

Gold Logie–worthy performances were given by the silks and their juniors at the Sydney hearings. The tone was set on the very first day by the leading Sydney barrister, Sir Garfield Barwick (soon to be attorney-general and then Minister for External Affairs, in Menzies' Cabinet) who, armed with a copy of the Royal Commission report and the Melbourne hearing transcripts, lectured the ABCB imperiously and at length on how, in light of the *Broadcasting and Television Act*, he thought that it should arrive at a recommendation. In short, he presumed to tell the ABCB what it ought to be thinking. Not only that, but he also tackled the same elephant in the room that had been bothering Evatt in Melbourne—the question of whether or not those persons with the resources and previous experience in the written and spoken mass media were worthy of being awarded television licences. Barwick differed from Evatt and maintained that, provided such people exercised discretion and judgement, and possessed a sense of responsibility, then they were:

> more likely to use this instrument as it ought to be used than somebody
> who is completely new to the exercise of such a power and the practice of
> making those compromises between personal gain and public interest which

you unquestionably have in this field, and which have to be made from time
to time.

Throughout the cross-examination of the ATS witness, Barwick sparred with his
fellow jurist (and Fort Street Boys' High School alumnus) Evatt. Then, in seven
pages of transcript, Darling pursued this same witness assiduously about his
company's plans for children's programs and quality. Next came consideration of
the Television Corporation (TC) bid, an application submitted by Consolidated
Press. Testimony was given on its behalf by Douglas Frank Hewson Packer
himself. For the next 148 pages of transcript, until such time as he exited the
hearing (held in the No. 1 Court of the Workers Compensation Commission),
counsel questioned Packer closely.[10]

The newspaperman was also subjected to close interrogation (about six transcript pages) by the headmaster of his two sons. Their exchange was candid and
civilised, and Packer gave his Corio interlocutor as good as he got. Both men
agreed on the importance of television as a leisure-time medium for Australian
families and both accepted, due to the large numbers of people exposed to television viewing, that the new medium would play a defining role in shaping the
nation's character. But, asked the headmaster, did the witness favour this important educational influence being shared by commercial interests? Yes. If so, then,
no doubt the witness would agree that his company would be accepting a very
serious educational responsibility? 'And a trust', came the reply. Was this more
likely to occur with television than with other forms of news dissemination and
other kinds of recreation? 'At least equal with them, and probably more.' A short
while later, Darling switched tack when he inquired about popular programming.
Didn't the notion of popular mean 'what is regarded as popular', and wasn't the
popular standard lower in fact than it could be—a tendency that he personally
was 'exercised in endeavouring to prevent'? Packer answered his questions with
another question: wouldn't Darling agree with him, if he looked back over twenty-
five or thirty years, that what may be regarded as popular in 1955 would have been
regarded as high-brow all that time ago? Take, for example, the number of young
people listening to music and having an interest in art: in each instance the numbers were much higher than three decades earlier. Indeed, Darling conceded, there
'had been considerable development', although standards in many other activities
had been permitted to fall. Trying to counter with another example, he enquired
of the witness whether he believed that little books of comics were beneficial.
(Earlier, when asked by Shand about the comic-strip character Joe Palooka, and
whether it was in keeping with the Australian spirit, Packer had replied: 'I would
say Joe Palooka is the greatest example of goodness, worthiness, and wholesome-
ness that has ever existed in the world'.) Surely, said Darling, the witness was not
claiming that comics had helped to improve the Australian character? They were
not entirely bad, Packer replied and, regardless of what Darling may have thought
about them, it was invariably the case that:

every comic and every script that is published in Australia carries one theme, and that is that the villain always loses and the hero is always a clean type; in other words, crime does not pay. That is going on every day in every newspaper throughout the world and throughout Australia.

This response prompted Shand to interrupt: 'You play with a double-headed penny', to which Packer's retort was: 'It must have some effect'. Finally, Darling tried to obtain an undertaking from the press magnate:

> You will promise us that in the case of such a state of affairs arising [advance purchasing of programs which turned out to be commercial duds] you would regard it as your duty to the public to supply them with good material, as above that of your duty to your shareholders to get their money's worth for what they have spent?

'I think the two go hand in hand', came Packer's deftly worded response.[11]

Three years later in Adelaide, Packer was again questioned by Darling. By then (1958) ABCB members had become increasingly preoccupied with program networking between stations and whether these arrangements were likely to result in improved quality material for the viewing public. Darling tackled Packer on this matter:

> I am really, honestly giving you the opportunity to prove it. It seems to me a very important point. The point is that the most important thing is that programmes offered in the City of Adelaide should be comprehensive and appealing to people of different tastes and not all therefore necessarily high rating programmes of the type we have come to know as high rating programmes. It is the object of the Board, I should think, to try to ensure that you would get this comprehensive range of programme[s] and I want to give you the opportunity of proving or convincing me that this tie-up with a station in another State is going to make that easier rather than harder.

Packer's response was that whichever applicant was awarded a licence was likely to link up with licensees in each of the other states otherwise they would not earn the estimated revenue. Not necessarily, Darling insisted; rather, wouldn't the stations be inclined to play one off against the other? They might, except that if they did such action would result in a deterioration of programs in Melbourne and Sydney. In a rare show of defensiveness, Packer continued:

> Well, I really believe, Dr. Darling, that you will get in Adelaide programmes that are comparable in every way to the general programme that is put over in Sydney and Melbourne. Now if you say that you are dissatisfied with the standard of programme in Sydney and Melbourne, I cannot assure you that

Adelaide is going to do better. As a matter of fact, we are very proud of the
standard of the programme we put on in Sydney, and we are very proud of
what we have achieved in the establishment of live shows.

But did this reply mean that the witness was admitting to having compromised
his highest ideals? Packer did not know whether it ought to be thought of as a
compromise, because:

I have never thought it my function to say, if it is an ordinary, good, clean,
exciting programme, you must not look [at] it, it is bad for you. I think the
people who pay the licence fee, their wishes ought to be considered somewhat.

In regard to the 'better' programs that Darling had in mind, and with which the
witness agreed, it was only possible to increase gradually that type of program.
At such time as stations had built up more financial reserves, then the additional
money would be spent producing programs. These might not have mass appeal
yet they were likely to be popular with certain sections of the community, and
to have a general educational and uplifting value. But the production of better-
quality programs had to be undertaken 'within the bounds of reality', the witness
insisted. 'We have done a lot of it. We cannot do as much as we would like until
we are strong enough financially.'[12]

     This was the first time during the Adelaide hearings that Darling tried
to tame the ambition of a powerful man by extracting a public affirmation that
he would behave honourably. He did it again, this time with a much younger
man who, when he was cross-examined, was a far less-seasoned newspaper
proprietor than he was to become: his former pupil, Rupert Murdoch. Darling
inquired whether the witness regarded television as an instrument of power in
the community. Yes, of responsibility and power. And did he realise that power is
exercised indirectly by the raising or lowering of standards? Very much so. Well,
then, was it a television licensee's duty:

[to] take the rating as given by the surveys, which are looked at by the
advertisers, as being the main guide as to whether or not they put on or do not
put on a programme?

No. 'Are you sure that this is not something to which you will be forced?' The
witness: It would depend on the comparative situation. But, Darling insisted,
given that the licensee company to be formed by the applicant would be a subsidiary of News Limited, the question was whether Mr Murdoch would control
it. 'Yes, subject to my advisors.' His erstwhile headmaster then intoned weight-
ily: 'That is a very great personal power and responsibility?' Yes. 'Coupled with
a fairly considerable personal interest in the results?' 'Yes, Sir.' In that case, had
the witness taken steps to guard against having to bear all that responsibility:

for example, 'why haven't you asked in some other directors who do not come under your influence and are not subservient to you?' Ouch. 'My directors are not subservient to me', the young proprietor shot back. Realising that he had pushed the wrong button, Darling apologised. His intended meaning was: not associated with the witness in his other ventures. He then continued:

> if television was such a great responsibility and regarded as an opportunity to
> educate the public, shouldn't there be people involved who will view it from
> that perspective rather than with profit in mind?

The applicant claimed that he was very conscious of all these considerations, so much so that he had even provided for the appointment of extra directors and had set up his own advisory committee on which there would be represented a cross-section of people interested in programs. Like all of the witnesses who had had access to the transcripts of the hearings and could rehearse their responses, Murdoch may have anticipated Darling's questions—and, equally, may have been playing deliberately to the latter's high expectations of him. Next, as if seeking to extract a vow, Darling asked Murdoch: 'Will you guarantee to back Miss Priest [his specialist children's program adviser] up even if it costs you money?' Miss Priest would indeed cost money. But, 'you will continue to back her up?' 'Yes.' Then, could he take it that 'you will try to take the licence as a responsibility and as an educational force in the community rather than as mere entertainment?' Yes, 'completely'. Presumably, then, the applicant would not regard this 'highly suspicious survey and rating as being the ultimate guide' to his policy? 'Certainly not', replied the witness.[13]

Throughout these proceedings Darling cast himself as safeguarding Arnoldian virtues. But it was not only in such extended exchanges that he staked out a moral claim—by (in effect) inviting potential licensees to clamber up to join him on the high ground or to show cause why they were unwilling to do so. His nobility of purpose was also apparent in his brief comments. Again when questioning V.G.H. Harrison in Melbourne, for example, he brushed aside the latter's assurance that GTC would be assisted in its programming by an advisory committee, by objecting that its members would 'probably be just as ignorant as everyone else on the subject', by dismissing Harrison's anticipated use of the term 'sermonette' as a means of presenting religious programs as a 'distressing' choice of word and by exclaiming 'that rather relieves me', when told that a proposed 90-minute Saturday evening sporting timeslot would comprise afternoon highlights and telecast night sports (and not daytime re-runs). One legal counsel (Douglas Menzies) commented that Darling was asking 'searching' questions, although most of the lawyers during the hearings appealed to a version of standards (if only to pay lip service to them). Evatt, for example, out of a self-proclaimed concern for political democracy, was on a mission to expose ownership concentration in relatively few hands along with the reactionary political leanings of newspaper proprietors (as prospective licence-holders) also adopted occasional high-mindedness. There were other times when Darling's manner of interrogation bordered on the quixotic, such as when he queried Sir John Williams about possible links between the HWT and the London *Daily Mail*, and whether the potential influence of the *Mail* on HWT would be 'in the highest interests of humanity'. On the other hand, there were also instances when Darling used his appeal to moral reasoning to productive effect (particularly in Sydney). Whereas Evatt equated the public interest in television licensing with something other than an arrangement that was calculated to secure a monopoly by the press barons, and Barwick (at one point) reduced 'public' to the idea of a member of the general public being able to raise objections to an application, Darling pressed those applicants who claimed that they would safeguard the public interest in their programming to specify whether they meant the good of the public or simply what the viewing public happened to be interested in. As he was aware, there was a world of difference between the pursuit of mass appetite and an Aristotelian sense of something that was for the good of all.[14]

For Darling, then, the public good was secured by moral uplift and high standards of programming taste. He was also aware, however, that there were limits to the extent to which standards could be legislated (through, say, control or censorship measures). And while proprietors such as Packer may have been adamant that the solution to the problem of the maintenance of standards lay with the imperatives of the market ('competition makes you get better programmes', he had urged in Adelaide in 1958), Darling was unimpressed. He viewed competition as a commercial battle for higher ratings (and audience reach) that could just as easily be obtained by the transmission of lower-quality programs (and, indeed, was more likely to be). It was one thing to extract from licensees by the exertion of moral pressure in a public hearing their guarantees of full cooperation with the ABCB in securing the good of the public, by having them utter, hand on heart, 'yes, sir', and quite another to enforce such promises. Appeal to moral pressure was a rather limp sanction. (Osborne once confided to the postmaster-general that, while Darling was liked and respected by all of the industry people with whom the ABCB dealt, some of them were 'also frightened by him'.) Apart from law, markets and morality, the only other basis of enforcement was character. The occasion on which Darling resorted enthusiastically to it (the quality of a medium of communication 'depends on the personal character, quality and taste of the person who is running it') was in Sydney when he cross-examined J.W. Gallery, the manager of *Truth and Sportsman*. Darling played the character card negatively. Did Gallery honestly feel, given that people in the questioner's 'position' like himself, such as clergymen and schoolmasters, found the justification for the existence of the *Truth* (its shorthand name)—with its reputation for salaciousness and scandal-mongering—difficult to comprehend, that the paper was fulfilling a public duty, sufficient to earn its backers a television licence, because the standards for television had to be different?[15]

Of course, the problem with having 'the right people trying to do the right thing in television', as Darling asserted when concluding his cross-examination of Gallery, was that questions were left begging. What counted as right? And who would make that decision? Early in March 1955, just before Darling's departure for England, the ABCB recommended the granting of licences for three years in Melbourne to GTC and HWT, and in Sydney to ATS and TC. In effect, if the postmaster-general agreed, then applicants with newspaper interests would scoop the pool. They did. Moreover, their vice-like grip on commercial television was entrenched when the Menzies government extended the licence period to five years before seeking renewal. What had happened, in light of these outcomes, to the idea of getting commercial television into the hands of the so-called right people? This, Darling confessed to John Casson (son of Dame Sybil Thorndike and Sir Lewis Casson) some years later, 'we have abysmally failed to do'. Why?

> Answer: because none of the right people applied. The amount of capital
> involved in starting a television station meant that only those who could lay
> their hands on large sums were available and the only ones interested at all
> were the newspapers. Newspapers nowadays, more or less by definition, have
> no sense of responsibility and, whether they admit it or not, subscribe to the
> Daily Mirror theory that you must give the public what they want. In the face
> of such an attitude, you can prescribe standards which will prevent them from
> being positively obscene and sadistic, but you can't educate them in such a
> way that they take responsibility as being one of the educative influences in
> the community.

The ABCB may have fought a losing battle but, given his view of the imagination and sense of responsibility exhibited by English production companies, Darling was willing to put his faith in (the character of) program-makers in Australia:

> The only way in which the situation could be improved would be the build
> up of television production with some kind of professional standards so that
> at least people who are actually doing the job fight against their revolting
> superiors.

Halfway through the Sydney hearings Darling had intimated to Osborne that the outcome was a forgone conclusion. Indeed, Evatt's worst fears (of concentrated media ownership) would be realised, augmented audience reach would debase standards and the intrusion through share ownership of the English *Daily Mail* and *Daily Mirror* interests into the newspaper bids was disquieting because they would be 'largely impervious to local pressure'. Darling even wondered whether the ABCB should refrain from making recommendations. If the government was incapable of influencing the appointment of 'responsible people' at the top of the successful licensee companies, then the ABCB fall-back options would be to limit television transmission hours, tightly control children's programs, require close down after the children's hour and restrict the use of imported films.[16]

By mid-1955, then, with the Melbourne and Sydney licences allocated, there were few grounds for the ABCB being the 'ferocious watch-dog' that one of Darling's correspondents thought was required. A fundamental flaw at the heart of the regulatory framework made this highly unlikely, as Darling recognised later. With seeming indifference (or ignorance?) the Royal Commission had skated over the question of the ownership of the television transmitters. In a brief paragraph in their report, the commissioners (with the exception of Osborne, who dissented) had endorsed transmitter ownership by the licensees, although the sole justification given was an enigmatic appeal to 'practical considerations'. The government never challenged this position. Yet, as the historian Ann Curthoys pointed out, due to the huge financial investment required by commercial operators to construct transmitters, the effect of licensees owning the infrastructure was to minimise any likelihood of a licence non-renewal by the postmaster-general, no matter what the ABCB might recommend. For reasons of financial loss, not to mention political risk, revocation 'would be an extreme step'. The potentially threatening big stick of ABCB oversight was actually a damp squib. Nonetheless, Osborne remained optimistic because he felt that the licensees had trusted the ABCB and yet they could not depend on the present membership of the ABCB continuing in office indefinitely. For his part, by contrast, prior to the official announcement of the successful applicants, and while awaiting the accompanying public 'inevitable explosion', Bruce Mair had jested whether he might be better off wearing a suit of armour. As for Darling, his absence in England during the wash-up period after the hearings had spared him the agony of the residual squabbling between the ABCB, the minister and the licensees over the final *i*-dotting and *t*-crossing of the licence conditions (including what Osborne described as the licensees' rather '"lofty" stand' against any form of control).[17]

Until the headmaster's return the ABCB deferred detailed consideration of some related telecasting matters, such as audience research (on which Darling obtained advice while in England), the standards framework for programming, advertising and film censorship, and discussions of these with the licensees and other Commonwealth agencies (Department of Trade and Customs, the ABC, the Film Censorship Board). Deliberations on these matters continued during 1956, when ABCB members (including Darling) inspected broadcasting facilities in rural Victoria and New South Wales. At ABCB meetings in 1957, Darling was vocal about the ABCB's licence renewal procedure, he was apprehensive about applications from commercial telecasters for increased hours of service, he was critical (in an early display of concern about Australian content) of the government's decision to relax restrictions on the import of overseas programs and films (Hector Crawford of Crawford Productions was lobbying him at this time about the dumping of US viewing material at prices below the cost of production) and he attended all ABCB hearings into the use of VHF band frequency modulation. Finally, interspersed among these discussions were the ABCB's deliberations over its Television Programme Standards. Although Darling contributed to their finalisation, he is unlikely to have been solely responsible for the drafting (as claimed by the historian Cameron Hazlehurst). Here, the ABCB took advice from its children's programming advisory committee and, particularly during 1956, the draft standards became the focus of intense negotiations with the licensees.[18]

In April and May 1958, the Brisbane and Adelaide television licence hearings commenced in these two cities and, when the venue for the cross-examination of witnesses was transferred to Melbourne late in May, Darling was able to attend regularly. His cross-examining of Adelaide witnesses demonstrated a shrewd understanding of the interplay of profits and programming. When the possible licensing of two stations was still to be confirmed, for example, he obtained from J.R. Humphrey, federal director of the Australian Association of Advertising Agencies, the (qualified) admission that the existence of two stations might drive down the price of advertising. Agreement was also forthcoming that, in the event of advertisers being willing to pay less money for access to viewing audiences, there might be less profit for stations to spend on programs, although audience size and the cost of a feature or program were two other factors that affected price. Similarly, in reply to Sir Lloyd Dumas, managing editor of the *Advertiser*, Darling queried whether or not his view—that the Adelaide viewing public's interests would be better served by having one licensee rather than two—was affected by the desire to maximise his ratings (on the assumption that program ratings would fare less well with two stations). And, when pressed by Darling on whether higher program standards would result from the existence of two competing stations, Dumas said that this would depend on who was in charge of each and the standards that they set themselves. Likewise in Brisbane, where, having probed closely on whether program standards would be raised or lowered by the existence of one or more stations, Darling's incisive line of questioning reduced one witness (J.H.M. Oswin of ATS) to helpless confusion.[19]

In June 1958, prior to the submission of its report and in the face of the government's reluctance to specify the number of licences to be allocated, the ABCB nailed its colours to the mast by adopting a series of principles. It was under no illusions about the intentions of the Melbourne and Sydney licensees to try to dominate commercial television in Brisbane and Adelaide (by shareholding or networking), and it tried to forestall such an outcome by guaranteeing the presence of independent stations in both metropolitan centres. Moreover, as it regarded the issuing of two licences in each state capital as detrimental to this end (because securing local capital would be difficult for an independent licensee), the ABCB believed that one television station would be sufficient in each instance. For this purpose, it tried limiting the extent of newspaper share ownership by calling for fresh licence applications. It highlighted 'evils' accruing in the USA, for example, whenever existing licensees sought program outlets in other American cities, and it wanted priority to go to licence applications from residents and businesses in South Australia and Queensland, with such groups to be precluded from entering program arrangements with existing commercial stations. With this declaration, communications between the postmaster-general and the ABCB entered delicate terrain. In July, the minister sought an interim report. The ABCB refused to provide it. When the minister insisted on receipt of a report prior to the ABCB's assessment of applications in Perth (in July) and Hobart (in August), the ABCB relented a week before the commencement of the Perth hearings and, on 25 July, forwarded its report. Darling had absented himself from the hearings in these cities—Margaret was having a 'recrudescence of her foolish fears' (as he termed them), which by his absence he was unwilling to aggravate, and he was overwhelmed by his responsibilities and 'more than usually tried [tired?]'.[20]

On 15 September, the ABCB was informed that, in rejecting its report of 25 July, Cabinet had stipulated that there must be two commercial licences issued in each state capital and that the ABCB should recommend to that effect. Darling believed that this intervention had compromised the ABCB's standing and he tendered his resignation to Menzies. While the government may have been perfectly within its rights to reject the ABCB's recommendations, it was equally legitimate for a part-time ABCB member, he told Menzies, to query whether such a rejection meant that there was any point in continuing to serve. How could he possibly do so honourably 'in the face of so clear a condemnation by the Government of a principle as strongly held as I hold and am known to hold as this one'? That principle was the ABCB thinking, for which it was confident that it had the government's support, of 'how dangerous it would be to allow Television to fall completely into the hands of the powerful newspaper interests':

> We believe that it cannot be in the best interests of Australia that the Television Empire should be split up between the present holders of licences in Melbourne and Sydney. The Government's decision seems to hand us over, bound, to a group upon whom we have fairly obviously declared war. We are in the position of David, if he had missed with his first stone and are at the mercy of Goliath. It looks as though we were foolish to have thrown it, without being more certain of our aim.

In effect (although they had not admitted as much), Darling and the ABCB had arrived at the same conclusion as Evatt. Having hurled a pebble that had fallen shy of its target, in Darling's view the ABCB had forfeited any likelihood of control of the commercial sector. Henceforward it would merely play a pretend game, because dismissal of its recommendation by the government was a clear expression of lack of confidence in the ABCB and that was how the licensees would interpret its action. As to the effect of his departure, some good may have come from it, he told Osborne, because while not to resign might 'look very funny', to do so, on the other hand, might just 'really strengthen your hands in the future'.[21]

After a while Darling dismounted from his high horse and (as he said later) 'stayed'. In reply to his mini-tutorial in good governance, Menzies had said: 'I have for a long time hoped that this would not be your last piece of public service in Australia', and urged him to 'shrug your shoulders and remain'. Darling might have read these words as a promise or signal of glittering prizes lying in store for him, or he may have taken them as light-touch advice to avoid cutting off his nose to spite his face. In Cabinet the issue boiled down to whether the newspapers' interests would be advanced further by the grant of two licences rather than one. The allocation of two licences, Menzies claimed, would at least ensure a measure of competition. For his part, Darling told the prime minister that, in arriving at his final decision, he had had difficulty in distinguishing between personal vanity and a matter of honour. Osborne may have had a hand in Darling remaining because, as he (Darling) also said to Menzies, 'It would be very hard for the Chairman of the Board to be without me'. At its twenty-fifth meeting for the year in late September (with Darling in attendance), the ABCB applied the same standards by which it had judged the earlier licence applicants back in 1955—good character and high reputation, appreciation of responsibilities and willingness to comply with the licence conditions, 'genuine intention' to commence with high standards, financial stability, 'good record' in allied fields and 'ability to provide a satisfactory service'—and, in accordance with the wishes of the government, duly recommended that licences be granted to two of the three applicants in both Brisbane and Adelaide. For Perth and Hobart, the ABCB recommended the allocation of one licence for each city. After another couple of months of tidying up some shareholding details, the government adopted the ABCB's recommendations, and with that state capital commercial television licences were done and dusted.[22]

Having lost face (through no fault of its own), the ABCB now had its work cut out. Since 1954 the three key features of the government's television policy had been dual-system transmission (parallel national and commercial stations), assignment of all stations to the VHF band and gradualism (or phased introduction of transmission). But so popular was television that by January 1959 there were already an estimated 500,000 television receivers in Melbourne and Sydney. The duration of station transmission in those cities averaged about 70 hours per week, and transmission time extensions into the afternoons and mornings were being mooted by the major telecasters. Furthermore, the capital city commercial licensees were poised to tighten their grip on regional transmission via microwave links through networked relay (or satellite) stations. The ABCB regarded this expansion of metropolitan influence as a 'serious disadvantage'. In the year or so prior to the commencement of the regional hearings (November 1959) it retrieved some lost ground by securing a change in the rules applying to the regional television rollout: the postmaster-general and the Cabinet endorsed a policy of local station control. Thanks largely to Osborne's shrewdness, the ABCB had exploited an inconsistency in the government's decision to award two commercial licences to each of the four larger state capitals, but only one each to Perth and Hobart. This numerical disparity strengthened the possibility that two potential regional operators might be licensed, provided that they could demonstrate their capability to transmit (as had been evident when the ABCB was overridden). To clarify matters, the ABCB prepared two reports (a longer one for the postmaster-general, and an abridged version for Cabinet) in which it sought policy guidance on television provision for the regions and country towns (of populations of more than 5000). After all, it argued successfully, ownership and control of more than two television stations was precluded by section 91 of the *Broadcasting and Television Act*, a section intended in the public interest to prevent commercial ownership concentration.[23]

The supremacy of local companies at the expense of the city stations, however, was complicated by the question of whether one commercial and one national station would be sufficient in all regional areas or whether, due to their larger population size, some locations (for example Newcastle, New South Wales) could sustain two commercial licensees. If a decision went in favour of the latter possibility, then an additional complication was that there was unlikely to be sufficient available channel space on the VHF band. The government's decision to prioritise licence allocations to local independent companies was announced in Parliament by the postmaster-general on 30 April 1959. The other way in which the ABCB sought to bolster its authority was by stiffening program standards. At Darling's insistence it informed commercial station managers that, in respect of children's programming, it expected a 'great improvement' in production quality. Here Darling maintained that when applying for licences all of the eventual licensees had undertaken to rely on suitably qualified people, in which case they should be reminded of their promise. To this end, he wanted them to employ an 'expert' with the requisite training in teaching children and in child psychology. (The parallel on which he drew here was the prescribing of teacher registration qualifications—precisely the obstacle that in his early days at Corio he had tried to circumvent when employing masters.)[24]

The final set of hearings was for licences in thirteen rural regions (that is, thirteen separate inquiries) commencing in early November 1959 until late May 1960. The choice of the South Melbourne Town Hall as the venue made Darling's attendance easier, although by mid-January he was looking for ways to streamline the remaining inquiries. Indeed Sir John Young recalled that his former headmaster was 'very troubled' by the protracted hearings. As in previous rounds, this municipal setting was similar: a big room with 'an array of half a dozen lawyers, sitting round, and four members of the [Board]', the lawyers mostly from New South Wales. Young outlined on behalf of the ABCB the procedure to be followed. The first licence was for Canberra. Once again

Darling sparred with Oswin. Unlike in Adelaide, this time they skirted around the relationship between commercial station numbers and programming quality. 'I think you know my views', said Darling, to which Oswin retorted: 'Yes, Sir, and I think you know mine, too'. Instead, they focused on issues affecting local station viability, principally the impact of a capital city relay station. The mood was testy. Darling pressed the point that if there were to be two commercial stations in Canberra then one could not be a genuinely local station, because it would be unable to compete if the other was closely associated with a city station that relayed programs. The result, surely, was that both stations would have to be linked to the two Sydney stations. Did the witness consider that this pattern of association was for the good of television all over Australia? Oswin: 'All over the world'. But surely such a pattern would result in almost all Australian television stations taking their lead and control from existing city stations in either Melbourne or Sydney? Yes, Oswin conceded. Well, then, Darling queried, was this a good thing? And, what about the power of television to mould opinion, and set standards and tastes in 'developing national spirit'? Oswin contested these queries. Rephrasing his question, Darling asked whether the witness would deny the very considerable influence of television, and the power of those who control it. Oswin's reply was that it would happen only to the extent that 'the powers who control them' would allow it. And who were the powers that control them, Darling inquired?

> Well, I hope, Sir, your good selves.
> DARLING: Oh, Mr. Oswin! You know, and you have admitted, have you not, that the standards that the Board sets are minimum standards?

Didn't the only real control and power rest with 'the integrity' of the managers of the boards of television stations, Darling continued, and wasn't the only real way to keep standards high and raised 'by the type of people who run them'? 'You have admitted that', said Darling, 'so don't throw it back on us'. In these circumstances, the ABCB played a rather negative hand, Darling claimed, but what the witness was really advocating was control of television by comparatively few powerful interests, wasn't he? No, insisted Oswin. Then would the witness regard this form of control by such interests as a bad thing or as a good thing? Oswin replied that, provided they were responsible, then it could be good.[25]

Despite Darling's frustrations as an ABCB member, there was a lighter social side to the life of a regulator. Throughout his membership, relations among his fellow ABCB members were entirely amicable, and no-one ever had to 'abandon or compromise' on any point about which they felt strongly. With his characteristic gift for friendship and ignoring sectarianism, Darling hit it off with Board staff, particularly Jo O'Kelly, the ABCB's secretary and a devout Catholic, whose habit when he passed by a church was to remove his hat. Once, he wrote to Darling to say that:

If you have not seen Coles (Bourke St) effort to put Christ into Christmas [in its pre- Christmas window display], <u>you must do so</u>. It is magnificent. So pleased was I that I sent them a letter to tell them of my pleasure.

During his ABCB membership, Darling also maintained intermittent correspondence with Boyer at the ABC, and they also dined at the Melbourne Club. Both men had similar priorities in respect of television: concerns about standards, the spread of transmission hours and the need for an evening break, and the genuine problem (in the face of press dominance of the medium) of being able to find publicity outlets for television criticism. For Darling's 1955 trip to England, Boyer had helped smooth his friend's path with introductions to the BBC. More generally, Darling would vent his periodic despair about the future of democracy, while Boyer (after six weeks spent in England) would bemoan the Suez crisis. They did not, however, always see eye to eye. So fiercely protective of the Commission's independence was Boyer that his stubbornness in relation to the censoring of films proposed for ABC telecast threatened to derail ABC–ABCB relations. He preferred the ABC to 'have the last word in the matter on what is suitable', whereas Darling sought to rely on a mixture of existing censorship machinery and mutual agreement between the two instrumentalities. Privately, Darling's view was that, compared with the speed at which the commercial stations had been preparing for television, the ABC had been rather 'dilatory'.[26]

For over six years Darling had fought the good fight with the moguls of the press and, thanks to his efforts, within the arrangements recommended by the Royal Commission and endorsed by the government he had served the interests of the Australian taxpayer as well as anticipated. It was the royal commissioners who had described the medium of television as a 'new toy'. And it was because of the added burden of responsibilities that they believed it would impose on the ABCB that they had recommended the appointment of two part-time members. The profile of the persons whom they had in mind did not include the representation of sectional interests, but the exercise of 'special responsibilities' in relation to programs. The commissioners had been preoccupied with aspects of programming—in 80 of the 499 paragraphs in their report they wrestled with the merits of claims and counter-claims about the possible positive and negative social impacts of the new medium. Moreover, given that reporting on standards and the public interest comprised one of the commissioners' five terms of reference, it is little wonder that they devoted another 62 paragraphs specifically to program standards. They were particularly concerned for the special interests of children and religion, but also more generally with the telecasting of quality programs through commercial outlets. These kinds of issues had given Darling his mandate. From his point of view, the only way to get to grips with the novelty of television was to evaluate it in respect of taste and what (if anything) it added by way of cultural value. His time as an ABCB member indicates that this was the mandate to which he adhered and that it was also a mandate that he more than fulfilled.

Considered in this light, in relation to broadcasting and telecasting 'adequate and comprehensive' may have been a curious choice of wording to enshrine in the statute books. Ironically, though, if he harboured reservations about them then Darling never once took issue with them (at least on paper). While he was unlikely to have quibbled with programming that was 'comprehensive', 'adequate', on the other hand, could mean that to only a minimal extent was an offering fit for purpose. This description signalled in relation to standards of taste what may have been necessary, but not what may have been sufficient, such as an incentive to excel. More ironically still was that, having spent so much time adjudicating the merits of the efforts of investors, owners and managers in living up to these stipulations, Darling himself was about to be held to account in relation to them, because in June 1961 he was appointed to succeed Boyer as the new chairman of the ABC and these same two words formed part of the legislative charter of the national broadcaster. It was clear at that point in time that his ABCB membership had served as an apprenticeship and that for the foreseeable future he would be evaluated once again in respect of whether or not he had furthered the interests of the taxpaying public.[27]

HORNETS' NEST

1961–1964

The first duty imposed on those who direct society is to educate democracy; to put, if possible, new life into its beliefs; to purify its mores; to control its actions; gradually to substitute understanding of statecraft for present inexperience and knowledge of its true interests for blind instincts; to adapt government to the needs of time and space; and to modify it as men and circumstances require.

Alexis de Tocqueville, *Democracy in America*

After sixteen years as chairman of the ABC, Boyer died on 5 June 1961. A couple of days later, following a swan-song OGGA retirement dinner for Darling, at which he had given 'his usual accomplished talk', Tas Drysdale and Geoffrey Dutton wondered what the headmaster might do next 'for he seems to have too much energy to sit back'. Drysdale reported speculation that he might replace Boyer. He was correct. In the line of chairmanship succession, a Methodist grazier would be followed by an Anglican independent school headmaster. Darling's hat had been in the ring since February when, with his own retirement looming, Boyer had wanted to recommend his friend. Characteristically, Darling had tempered gnawing ambition with an appeal to duty:

> This all boils down to the fact that I am flattered that you should be considering me, that I should feel bound very seriously to consider it, if they wanted me, but that I do not seek it and would in some ways be much relieved if they could find someone else. This doesn't mean that my vanity would not suffer, if they did, but that wouldn't do me any harm.

As his rule of thumb with 'my boys' was to importune them to 'never say No! to an opportunity or to a responsibility', he could not decline Boyer's support. With little warning and amid a host of farewell dinners, and while a desperate struggle had been raging between his 'real but not apparent' humility and 'easily blown up' conceit, he told Ralph, the postmaster-general had offered him the chairmanship. Other names were mooted and he had not expected the job 'on a platter', barely 10 minutes before the Cabinet meeting that made the decision.[1]

By 1961, the ABC had existed for almost the duration of Darling's time in Australia. Its forerunner was the Australian Broadcasting Company, a national body that in 1929–30 had taken over some A-class licensee companies upon the expiration of their broadcasting licences. In May 1932, the Lyons government legislated to establish the ABC in a form similar to that proposed by the previous Scullin government. Despite his ABCB experience, the choice of a headmaster to chair a national broadcasting service may have seemed odd. (Darling's opposite number on the BBC Board of Governors, Arthur fforde, had also been a headmaster: of Rugby.) Two factors probably influenced Menzies. The first was the strong mutual respect that Darling and Bob Osborne had built up: with ABCB–commission (the ABC's governing body) relations known to be 'acrid', Darling believed that he could rebuild them. The second was confidence in Darling's ability to re-establish trust between the commissioners and the long-serving General Manager, Sir Charles Moses—seven months Darling's junior, and grammar school and Sandhurst-educated rather than public school and Oxford. Due to his club connections (particularly Medley who, until December 1960, had been an ABC commissioner for nineteen years), Darling was aware of Moses' dominance of the ABC. His tenure as general manager was approaching three decades. In 1958, Professor Moorhouse had been bitter about the 'short hymn of hate' at the ABC and was nonplussed by Moses' response to his suggested creation of a science advisory committee that it would present 'organisational difficulties'. Shortly after his appointment, Darling told Osborne that commissioner–general manager relations 'could not be more deplorable' and that 'the hornet's nest into which I have put my head is worse than I had thought'. All that he had conceded to the prime minister was that there was 'a good deal to be done' unspectacularly behind the scenes with an organisation that has 'grown up so rapidly'. He would need Menzies' 'sympathetic understanding and support'.[2]

There were seven part-time commissioners including the chairman and vice-chairman. (At least one from each state by customary practice rather than legal requirement.) To speak as chairman on its behalf, Darling had to be able to hold the commission together internally (if there were votes, the pattern was generally three–three, with Jock Reid, Victoria, the one to be won over), while having to keep onside Moses and his acolyte-like secretary, Betty Cook (both of whom attended most commission meetings). With respect to 'adequate and comprehensive' programming, the public broadcaster was required—by section 59(1) of the *Broadcasting and Television Act*—to 'take in the interests of the community all such measures' as in its opinion 'are conducive to the full development of suitable broadcasting and television programmes'. This was not straightforward. Nor, in pursuit of its mandate, was the independence of the ABC, because the legislation vested considerable discretionary power in the minister (the postmaster-general). The commission had to submit annual financial estimates to the minister for Parliament's approval, and section 64 permitted the minister to direct the commission (in writing) to broadcast or televise matter deemed to be in the 'national interest'. Section 77 authorised him or her (again in writing) to prohibit any matter from being transmitted. The commission furnished Parliament with an annual report, in which the commissioners were required to cite instances of ministerial intervention under section 77, and examples of ministerial direction or prohibition. (In 1967 the minister was required to provide a written explanation to the Parliament for actions taken under sections 64 and 77.) Apart from clauses in part of the *Act* concerned with the definition and transmission of political, controversial and objectionable items (for example, section 116), that was about it. The chairmanship was ill defined and the minister–chairman relationship unspecified. The result, thought Darling, was that because of ministerial susceptibility to external sensitivities and pressures, constant parliamentary scrutiny, and with the newspapers ready to pounce at the merest hint of an infringement of the ABC's charter, the role of favourite whipping boy defaulted to the chairman. As the head of a statutory corporation, Darling was not a departmental Sir Humphrey required to advise the postmaster-general and he was reluctant to offer personal advice, particularly if it put him at odds with his fellow commissioners and isolated him should the minister take that advice.[3]

Whereas Darling's GGS job had been the equivalent of a chief executive, he was now in a role requiring a different skill-set and public profile. Moreover, because the mission of a taxpayer-funded national service (let alone the words 'adequate' and 'comprehensive') was open to wide interpretation, there was bound to be controversy. In these circumstances, part 3 of the *Act* demanded acute political navigational skills (or, as Darling later reflected, patient subtlety). Darling was chairman for two three-year terms, during which three priorities emerged. First, his overriding aim was to maintain the ABC's independence. Second, he sought to establish an internal working environment in which staff exercised autonomy and took responsibility for their actions. Third, in his second term he tried to put the senior management of the ABC on a sound footing after Moses retired in late 1964. In this regard, he inherited (he said later) an organisation in which the commission and general manager were 'completely at loggerheads, neither trusting the other'. Moses was an autocrat who had built up the ABC by 'using fear and favour as his weapons'. This approach had worked when the ABC employed 500 people (most of whom Moses knew and had appointed), but for an organisation many times larger it was dysfunctional. Populated as the ABC was with 'prima donnas and other oddities', managerial directives and threats were pointless. Darling's three closest allies were Talbot (later Sir Talbot) Duckmanton, Moses' successor with whom he developed a particularly strong working relationship, Clement Semmler (assistant general manager, Programmes, and later deputy general manager) and Wally Hamilton (controller of news and then assistant general manager, Administration). Despite Darling's abiding suspicion of newspaper journalists, his strongest external ally was the editor of the *Anglican*, the inimitable Francis James (whose elder boy was enrolled at GGS under Garnett). The son of an Anglican priest and, since their schooldays at Canberra Grammar School, a lifelong friend of Gough Whitlam, James had acquired notoriety in Sydney. Well known for his flamboyant and eccentric behaviour, he dressed in a wide-brimmed hat and black cloak and, when he was a journalist for the *Sydney Morning Herald*, had used the back seat of his 1936 Rolls-Royce as a mobile office.[4]

After his appointment was made public, Darling received about 340 congratulatory letters and telegrams from Australia and overseas (*The Times* reported the news). A recurring word in his replies to well-wishers was complexity. His proposed writing of a life of Hawker was put on hold. Unfortunately, there was not a smooth start. Day-to-day ABC management was mostly conducted in Sydney, but Darling made his appointment conditional on working in Melbourne—in an office in Majella, the ABC's Victorian headquarters in St Kilda Road. In addition to attending commission meetings in the state capitals, this decision resulted in frequent travel to Sydney and the ABC's provision of rental accommodation. The result was a kind of Melbourne–Sydney chairman–management duopoly. An added difficulty, owing to the timing of Boyer's death, was that Darling took over earlier than expected: his appointment was effective from 1 July 1961 but the formal GGS handover to Garnett was not until the end of August. As a result, Darling performed two jobs simultaneously. A further complication was that on 17 September he was operated on for a hernia in the Freemasons' Hospital, Melbourne. Although the operation was successful, he contracted pleurisy. Hospitalisation and recuperation laid him low for two months—a period that overlapped with the federal election campaign when the ABC was under close external scrutiny. For the conduct of commission business during his recovery, the ABC installed a second telephone line (to minimise domestic disruption) at his new residence in Maple Grove, Toorak. Francis James commiserated. He could not understand why he had to be 'hard at it', when surely the 'whole object of the exercise' was for the chairman to be 'leisured, dignified, unhurried, with plenty of time to meet friends and influence people?' Boyer may not have carried the job off quite like that, 'but you should if you want to live long'.[5]

Despite these hiccups, Darling scored a significant early victory. He commenced detoxifying staff attitudes to the commissioners by building a strong understanding with E.E. (Ted) Lawrence, federal secretary of the 2500-strong ABC Staff Association. His feet were barely under the table when in a six-page letter Lawrence provided chapter and verse on issues that, during the previous three years, had 'virtually destroyed the confidence of the staff in the administration of the Commission', and embroiled no less than senior management, the commission, the minister, the public service arbitrator and both houses of Parliament. There had been industrial relations duplicity, bad faith, engagement in charade-like consultation, and an aloof and dictatorial attitude—for which, said Lawrence, Boyer, the commissioners and senior management were all culpable. From Corio, the chairman pleaded for Lawrence's indulgence: after taking on the job with little warning and with six weeks until his retirement, he needed time. He wanted to hear the other side of the arguments and meet with Lawrence to get 'the facts behind the facts'. Assured by his even-handedness, Lawrence said that there was 'tremendous support' for the chairman (and the commission) not feeling inhibited in getting to know the staff and ascertaining their views. Public-sector industrial relations was new territory for Darling. But this was merely round one. The following May (1962) round two commenced when Lawrence (this time in a seven-page letter) told him that, while evidence of a more reasonable attitude to the association on the part of commission representatives was yet to materialise, the association had been 'very heartened indeed' by the new chairman's willingness to meet and talk with staff, and to see for himself. What stuck in the Staff Association's craw was the commission's system of staff reports. Press articles prompted him to contact Darling again after his return from England in September 1962. The system (revised in January 1962 and implemented during Darling's absence) aimed to identify shortcomings in the capabilities of individual staff members with a view to improvement through guidance and training, except that the staff could not view their reports. Moreover, the senior officers conducting the assessments were permitted to inquire into an employee's outside interests (including domestic and financial matters). But, asked the association, why the secrecy? Where was the guarantee that information in employees' reports was accurate and would not be used against them? And why was it necessary to pry into an officer's private business? Management's view was that viewing of ABC staff reports might prejudice the honesty of the appraisals. Another grievance was the association's belief that if senior officers made judgements about their colleagues' training needs, then they ought to be trained to make such assessments.[6]

The commissioners discussed the reporting system in September 1962, following Darling's meeting with Lawrence and an assistant general manager. Darling regretted press interference and then lectured the association: in future, communication and negotiation were to be with management, with the chairman to arbitrate in the event of lack of agreement. He agreed on the need for training, reworded the question on outside interests and agreed that ABC officers should see their reports. His gamble in committing the commission in advance to the removal of the association's grievances worked, because it resolved that:

> in order to establish confidence within the staff it is agreed that any member who wishes to do so, may be allowed to see and initial as seen, the whole or any part of the report.

The next day, Darling informed Lawrence. Darling was to be congratulated, the *Daily Mirror* editorialised, as secret dossiers were 'repugnant to our democratic principles'. Duckmanton had had carriage of the reporting scheme but, while overruled by the commissioners, he bore the chairman no ill will. Such was the positive reception of the commission's decision, said Lawrence, that Darling had succeeded 'with one typically generous and idealistic gesture' in putting relations between staff, management, commission and association 'on a footing of mutual trust and respect'.[7]

Darling was also in good standing with the Senior Officers' Association (SOA), although only after an initial misunderstanding (thanks to a Moses sleight of hand). The position of the ABC's overseas representative was to be reclassified. Although the general manager had given an undertaking that the SOA could put its case to the commission prior to a reclassification, in June 1962 Moses informed it that the matter was finalised. Darling (in England) assured the SOA president, Robin Wood, that, while the commission's decision was correct, the SOA had not been given a proper explanation. Come and see him when he returned to Australia, Darling said: 'We must somehow restore confidence between the Senior Staff and the Commission. This can only be done by open dealings between us.' The SOA appreciated Darling's intervention on the staff reports and Wood applauded the chairman, commission and management on an outcome that facilitated improved management–staff relations. Moreover, Duckmanton's helpful approach with Lawrence had boosted sagging morale. 'If the present atmosphere can continue', Woods said, 'and there can be plain speaking on all points of serious disagreement, tempered with reasonableness & consideration for each side's viewpoint', then success was assured. But because he had allowed the SOA to go over Moses' head, Darling risked alienating the general manager, who protested that the SOA had always approached the commission through him. To do otherwise would 'drive a wedge between the Commission and Management'. As with Lawrence, Darling advised Wood of Moses' wishes and, while endorsing them, left the direct-access door slightly ajar by saying that henceforward it would be improper for the chairman to meet him, except in the presence of a member of management.[8]

The big ticket item and Darling's first test of ABC independence during these negotiations was Intertel (the International Television Federation), the brainchild of John McMillan, an expatriate Australian working in Britain with Associated Rediffusion. Apart from the ABC and Rediffusion, the other consortium members were the Canadian Broadcasting Corporation (CBC), the Westinghouse Broadcasting Company and the National Educational Television and Radio Centre in the USA. Shared ideas, facilities, resources and expertise promised a win–win outcome for all members, with viewers benefiting from program production and exchange. ABC participation was vital because it provided the four northern hemisphere members with a link to South-East Asia. A wrangle over Intertel between the ABC and the government had been simmering since

March, despite Davidson's assurance to Darling that it was resolved. There was
also a bad odour about Intertel: the psychological and emotional burden of dealing with the dispute was thought to have hastened Boyer's death. Commission–
government differences over Intertel quickly reached boiling point and, because
these challenged the commissioners' authority, Darling stared momentarily into
the abyss of resignation. Barely one month into the job, he told Gorton (Minister
for the Navy):

> It seems to me, with what justice I don't know, that the A.B.C. has been so
> concerned with its independence that it has plunged into things without prop-
> erly preparing the ground and without acknowledging where it is legitimate
> for the government to have a point of view. While equally determined not to
> become a government instrumentality I hope I am not doctrinaire about it and
> realize where previous consultation is necessary.

He would return to Intertel because he doubted whether anyone had 'handled it
very intelligently up to now'.[9]

Threats to the ABC's independence came from a number of directions. The
first was government interference. To ensure objectivity in production, Intertel
members decided not to make programs about their own countries. As agreed in
1960 at an Intertel meeting in Vancouver, there were twelve programs, with the
ABC responsible for a documentary entitled *United States–Canada Relations—
Living with a Giant*. There was intense interest in both countries in this topic
and the CBC was keen for the ABC to adopt 'a probing, clinical and frank
approach', but this was precisely what the Menzies government didn't want and
it was even less enthralled by the likely involvement of the journalist Rohan
Rivett in its production. Some Cabinet members took a dim view of the ABC's
Intertel membership. When Boyer had advised the postmaster-general about the
agreement in December 1960, the objectivity arrangement was mentioned in a
press release yet no-one had informed the government, let alone the Overseas
Travel Committee—the body that approved overseas visits undertaken at public
expense by civil servants and officials—about *Living with a Giant*. The red flag
went up in early March 1961 when the travel committee said to Duckmanton—
then assistant general manager (Administration)—that it was 'seriously
concerned'. The committee also told the general manager that the prime minister
was 'troubled'. Boyer countered by expressing the commission's concern to the
postmaster-general and then in May, following Cabinet discussion, Davidson
informed Boyer that, while the government was 'acutely conscious' of the need
not to interfere in the ABC's decisions, it refused to approve the making of the
program or the ABC team's North American visit. With Boyer ill, Intertel was
left to his deputy, Edgar Dawes. The ABC had no alternative but to withdraw
from Intertel, Dawes told the postmaster-general, because the government's
decision 'must inevitably restrict our freedom and ability to fulfill [sic] our role

as a member'. Davidson retorted that such definitive action was not required as a result of the Cabinet's decision.[10]

Enter Darling. For nearly two years the Intertel controversy dogged him. It flared in three phases: the lead-up to the 1961 federal election (9 December), early 1962 and a year later. By Darling's very first commission meeting (July 1961, chaired at his invitation by Dawes), Intertel and Davidson had been informed of the commission's intended membership withdrawal. The meeting confirmed Dawes' action and resolved to include a statement in the commission's annual report. Then, McMillan indicated that he would come to Australia to persuade Menzies to bless the ABC's continued Intertel membership—small wonder, Duckmanton thought, that 'the whole thing is getting a little out of hand'. In August, largely thanks to Darling (after talking with McMillan and the postmaster-general), the commission resolved to retain ABC membership without sacrificing independence of programming judgement. Dawes wanted pressure kept on the government, but the deferral of the next Intertel meeting in New York bought Darling time. To strengthen his hand with his fellow commissioners, he sought two things from Davidson. The first was a note to the effect that the door was not 'irremediably closed'. He did not want Intertel mentioned in the commission's annual report, and was keen to retain the ABC's Intertel membership and to make a program on a different subject. His other idea was to apply to ABC international television ventures the existing consultative process between the Department of External Affairs and Radio Australia (which facilitated ABC access to helpful confidential information when making radio programs for foreign audiences). After communicating with the postmaster-general in August and September, there was a lull: Moses could not meet the secretary of the External Affairs department (Sir Arthur Tange) as, like Darling, he fell ill.[11]

Apart from Department of External Affairs–ABC consultation, there were two other reasons for the government's resolve over Intertel. First, it was concerned about the subject matter, because it dealt with the delicate relations between the USA and Canada, and passions aroused in two recent Canadian elections. Second (in Dawes' view), there were consequences arising from the ABC's Intertel membership: the government risked embarrassment if other consortium members reciprocated with documentaries on controversial Australian subjects, such as the relationship between white Australia and Indigenous Australians, or Australia's trusteeship of Papua New Guinea. Complicating these considerations was the possibility that the ABC was identified internationally as too close to the Australian government and seen as its master's voice. And yet if the ABC withdrew from Intertel there was nothing to prevent a commercial licensee joining it and making similar controversial programs. While the commission continued to press its case with the minister during the chairman's absence, from his sickbed Darling assured Davidson that before arguing the commission's case further he would wait until after the election and his return to work. He also wanted to postpone the ABC's notice of withdrawal from Intertel pending a 'discussion of the principles involved'.[12]

One principle was commission independence. Twice during his chairmanship Darling publicly and systematically articulated his views on this theme. The first was in early 1962 in 'The ABC and the Australian community'—a conference address delivered in at the University of New England in Armidale in rural New South Wales. With Intertel still unresolved, Darling was circumspect about his speech's possible reception. To cover himself, he forwarded advance copies to politicians (Menzies, Calwell, Davidson) and the media (Osborne— who opened the conference—Clyde Packer, Sir Lloyd Dumas, Rupert Murdoch and Keith Sinclair among others). He explained to Menzies that to have consulted him in advance about his thinking would have been wrong but, in the interests of accuracy, he ensured that the prime minister had the text. Likewise with Davidson: there was no prior consultation because that would have been seen to invite approval or endorsement. With Murdoch, however, he wanted a serious and responsible report of his address and avoidance of unnecessary controversy. He inquired plaintively of the then-youthful media proprietor: 'Is it reasonable for me to ask you so to treat it?' Darling's lecture claimed that Australians had to be able to regard the ABC as a 'fair, disinterested communicator of factual news and balanced comment'—a reputation earned by 'consistent avoidance of sensationalism, partisanship and prejudice'. The ABC was responsible to all sections of the community, including minorities, and to 'Truth', the criterion 'by which all programming should be judged'. Governments were obliged to regard the ABC as sacrosanct and free from arbitrary interference, and were fully responsible for its freedom. But independence was constrained as the ABC depended on the public and Parliament for its funding, and the commission's estimates for parliamentary appropriation were included in those for the postmaster-general's department. The ABC was answerable to Parliament, although not directly through the minister (who could be blamed for the ABC's actions). Moreover, ABC staff were subject to Public Service Commission regulations. Finally, while ABC decision-making might cut across government policy, the ABC could be seen as the voice of Australia and the government's mouthpiece (especially in countries in receipt of Radio Australia broadcasts). Therefore, 'close and friendly contact' between chairman and minister, he said, was his way of achieving 'some sort of understanding' between commission and government.[13]

With regard to the ABC's mission, Darling asked a series of questions, particularly in respect of television—which continue to be debated half a century on: did service to the community entail satisfaction of its 'wants' or education and elevation of taste 'at the expense of audience ratings', and was the ABC (as part of a dual national and commercial system) to compete with or complement the commercial networks? To appeal only to a minority was to draw fire for expecting and expending too much public money, whereas to pursue popular appeal risked ABC complicity in lowered standards. Not unexpectedly, Darling was uncompromisingly Arnoldian and de Tocquevillian:

> [Complementarity] does not mean that [the ABC] should be 'highbrow' in such a way as to have the result that nobody looks at its programmes at all; but it does mean that it should not try too hard in fields in which it cannot successfully compete with the main advertising programmes of the commercial stations. It should in all that it does concentrate on quality of production, it should set standards higher than those that are, to some extent, imposed upon the commercial stations, and it should aim at satisfying the best taste of the community and raising it [in television] in the same way that it has done in broadcasting.

Ratings of 5 to 10 per cent still translated into respectable viewer and listener numbers. Service to this proportion of the community was useful and, rather than embodying dullness, respectability and an exclusive educational focus (although there were clear responsibilities in this realm), ABC programming had to be 'adventurous, experimental and aim at high quality'. Risk aversion (and intolerance of occasional failures) was a prescription for the ABC not fulfilling its adequate and comprehensive charter. Criticism from both sides of the aisle meant that the ABC was succeeding in being fair, but it also had to be a voice to and for minorities, especially those without parliamentary representation. As democracy entailed variety and a fair chance for all, minority opinions could only be confronted if they were heard. Education had to elevate public taste, but not 'too fast'.[14]

Close and friendly contact between minister and chairman, however, could not save *Living with a Giant*. When, shortly after Darling's speech, Intertel flared again all hope of making the program had vanished. The commission now tried to convince the government to retain its Intertel membership. In January 1962, Darling complained about feeling 'weighed down with the responsibilities of this office' because there were so many things that he could do little about. He met Menzies and informed him that, provided the ABC remained an Intertel partner, it would make programs on Tahiti and Antarctica. Neither presented difficulties for Department of External Affairs officers. In February, the commission deferred notice of its intention to withdraw from Intertel. Later in the month, after toing and froing between the ABC and External Affairs over wording, the commission adopted a seven-point protocol, three of which were key points for Intertel productions. First, in consultation with the consortium, the ABC would choose its subject matter, although only after ensuring that it would 'not embarrass the Australian Government in its international relationship'. Second, subjects deemed suitable would be discussed with Department of External Affairs officers prior to Intertel meetings. Third, the ABC would arrange for a Department of External Affairs briefing during the planning of films and would be guided 'by whatever background information concerning the selected topic' that the department made available. To remain in Intertel, then, the ABC made itself hostage to External Affairs.[15]

In March, Davidson briefed Cabinet. He sought approval for the ABC's continued membership of Intertel on the basis of a series of advantages: exchanges between members' news services of high international interest and high-quality documentaries, increased ABC standing with sister organisations and the viewing public, and provision of an overseas market for local productions. Cabinet was unconvinced and directed Davidson to confer again with the chairman who, after considerable thought, said that if the government exerted its powers under section 77, then:

> Such a decision, following on the conversation which I had with you and the Prime Minister, would inevitably give rise to a quite critical issue between the Government and the Commission, and I have no doubt that you, yourself, are fully conscious of this fact.

This was a statement of the obvious. 'Please believe', he implored, that:

> I write this with the greatest reluctance and with a full sense of responsibility only in order to make it clear into what a critical situation I believe that we may be moving.

Having gone to the precipice, it was not clear whether the government would pull back as the commission had earlier. The matter was also hotting up in Parliament, where Whitlam (deputy leader of the Opposition) asked Davidson whether honourable members might view the Intertel programs and decide for themselves the merit of the ABC's membership. Moreover, the newspapers were feeding off leaks from the ABC. In these circumstances, Darling saw no alternative but resignation. On 6 April he drafted a memorandum:

> Saw Mr Opperman [Minister for Immigration] and explained position to him and my reluctance to put anything on paper which might make conciliation impossible. At the same time anxious to ensure that the Minister and the Government realized before my meeting with him on the 11th that matters were moving towards a head-on collision (his phrase).

If the government vetoed the ABC's membership, then there were only three options, all with undesirable consequences. First, accept the decision—although relations with colleagues would be 'impossible' and the government would conclude that 'I was prepared to accept direction'. Second, point out that he would have to resign, in the hope of changing the government's mind, although that would end hopes of its support for his plans for the ABC. Third, resign and give the government its way, but at the risk of adverse public discussion and reaction (although life for his successor might be a bit easier). It was difficult to escape option three 'as the most honest resolution of the problem'.[16]

On 1 May, Davidson said that Cabinet had given the green light to continued ABC membership of Intertel and denied ever requiring its withdrawal from the consortium. Further discussion ensued in both houses of Parliament. In *Inside Politics*, in 'Darling gambles his job', The Whip claimed that the ABC had won 'a public brawl' with the government: 'I'm told that in this case someone had to put his [i.e., Darling's] head on the block before the Government saw sense'. 'Why had the Government capitulated, especially after such adamant opposition?': 'It is strongly reported in Canberra that Mr. Menzies had the choice of giving up or of accepting the resignation of the new chairman, Dr. Darling'. While Darling was described as resolute, The Whip thought that the ABC would tread carefully in its future choice of Intertel subjects. Darling's actions also found favour with Ted Lawrence: no-one in Canberra could have been left in any doubt that the chairman exhibited 'complete determination to play his hand right out whenever he decided that there was a vital principle at stake'. If Darling had lost the first round, he had scored a minor triumph in the second, after which the sting went out of Intertel until flickering briefly again a year later. Rediffusion made *Living with a Giant* and later in May it was telecast in Melbourne and Sydney. Some years later, Darling informed Duckmanton (by then the general manager) that the former public servant responsible for the Overseas Travel Committee had said that this committee was 'intended as a restraint which would operate only because of its existence', with the expectation that almost all requests were automatically approved. This same official was 'horrified' that it had been invoked to deal with Intertel. Darling thought that he had had to clarify his position on Intertel to the government, the commission and the general public. He did so 'as inoffensively as I could' so as 'not to queer my own pitch before I began', although perhaps he was 'a bit equivocal in not telling all the truth'. To be part of the establishment, as he said he had made clear at the Armidale conference, was 'not all beer and skittles'.[17]

After a ten-week visit to Australia, J.D.F. Green (controller of talks, BBC) compiled for Sir Hugh Carleton Greene (the BBC's director-general) a report in which he said that Intertel illustrated 'the kind of tactical brawling in which Australian Governments become involved'. Green regarded Menzies' veto of the ABC in making *Living with a Giant* as arbitrary and his earlier refusal to see Boyer about Intertel as sheer arrogance. Despite the government's 'high-handed act' of interference and the constitutional crisis that this had created for the commission, the ABC's relationship with both the major political parties was better than that of their opposite numbers and the CBC in Canada. Even so, in March 1963 the postmaster-general intervened to forbid another telecast. This time the threat to ABC independence came from the attempted muzzling of Georges-Augustin Bidault, exiled former prime minister of France, quasi-fascist and opponent of President de Gaulle's policy of Algerian independence. The BBC's interview of Bidault was scheduled for telecast on Sunday, 10 March. Instead it was withdrawn, ostensibly because of poor technical quality. After being notified on 6 March by the *Age* that the French government had requested the ABC or the Australian government to not use the film, Darling got in touch with Moses. The next day, the Commonwealth censor and Sir Garfield Barwick (Minister for External Affairs) viewed the interview and raised no objections. On the evening of 8 March, Margaret Darling received the postmaster-general's telegram that directed the ABC (in accordance with section 77 of the *Act*) to not telecast the interview. In her husband's absence (in South Australia) she contacted Moses. Menzies had directed Davidson to telegram the chairman. Unaware that Barwick had seen the film, Davidson's request to view it delayed the telecast. With the newspapers circling for more information, two days later Duckmanton had driven to Canberra for a special screening in Parliament House for the prime minister, the deputy prime minister, the postmaster-general and the his press secretary. Menzies dismissed the film as 'boring' (Barwick called it 'innocuous'), although Bidault appeared 'smug and very pleased with himself', and said that it should not be telecast. The other Cabinet members present concurred—to telecast it would offend a friendly nation and ally. Despite his point about press publicity, that Bidault appeared to be a 'somewhat pathetic figure' and that, while boring, it was precisely as Barwick had described it, Duckmanton's protestations fell on deaf ears. The postmaster-general would direct the commission by writing to Darling and, if necessary, would similarly direct the commercial networks. The next evening (having been secretly given a copy of the film by Moses) TCN-9 telecast the interview in Sydney and it was later screened by HSV-7 in Melbourne. On 17 March the ban was lifted and it was aired on the ABC.[18]

Francis James thought that Darling and the commission were on the side of the angels. 'You've been first class over this Bidault affair', he said. 'Anyone who can get even the secular Press so thoroughly pro-ABC is a wizard!' But had he been first class? In its relations with the government the commission was unwilling and unable to capitalise on this official Bidault backdown, thanks to Intertel. At the Department of External Affairs, Tange had got wind of an Intertel film on Malaysia proposed by ABC staff (1963 was the height of Indonesia's 'confrontation' with the new federation) and said that production should cease. With no desire to 'rub the Government's noses in Bidault or Malaysia', Darling believed that the latter highlighted 'more clearly and effectively' than previously 'the true problem' of ABC independence. As he was keen to avoid legalistic arguments about interpretations of the Act (in particular about the relationship between sections 77 and 116, on which the Crown Solicitor's Office was being consulted) he toyed with a possible 'new charter' with the government by modifying the Moses–Tange agreement. Continued clashes were a 'hellish waste of time' and instilled excessive caution in ABC staff. Davidson had been alerted to the Malaysia film when he met some of the commissioners at their April meeting in Sydney, but before formally approaching the postmaster-general about his plans, Darling had sought Casey's advice. Casey's instinct was to defer the film on Malaysia for a while as the subject was 'so prickly'. He thought that while External Affairs could ask the ABC 'not to do something', it could not 'make you do something'.[19]

For the Malaysia production, Wally Hamilton (controller of news) had prepared a comprehensive nine-page memorandum. His program overview included a strong emphasis on local cultures, the new nation's racial composition and achievement of multiracial unity, and postwar political developments among the former colonies that had culminated in nationhood. Darling foresaw problems. So ambitious was the proposal's scope, he told Moses and the commissioners, that the coverage was bound to be superficial. The subject matter was so important, however, that it demanded genuinely serious treatment, although this probably could not be done within the ABC's resources. The need for seriousness was all the more pressing because contact with the Department of External Affairs was required prior to an ABC commitment. He was convinced that 'it is our duty to do this film and to do it, while it remains a live issue', except that this was surely a case in which the government 'must be allowed a strong voice' and 'encouraged to intervene if it wishes to do so, at an early rather than a later stage'. About a fortnight later, Darling told Davidson that the justification for an independent commission rested on the democratic idea that dissemination of news and views ought to be 'beyond the power of any government to control', in which case while the government and External Affairs might have qualms about the impact in Indonesia of a program about Malaysia, the commission's view was that the ABC's duty was to inform the general public of the points at issue between the two countries. To be prevented from making the film would require the ABC to leave Intertel (for not having fulfilled its obligations) and would indicate the government's 'unwillingness to regard the Commission as a responsible and independent body'. Late in April, the Melbourne *Herald* reported (slightly confusingly) that Barwick had 'vetoed' an ABC proposal to send a film crew to 'Malaya' to make an Intertel program and that this would now be made by the BBC. The next morning, the *Sun* and *Age* carried denials from both Darling and Barwick of a government ban on the making of the film on Malaysia, but exactly when the film would be shown depended 'largely on the international situation', Darling had said.[20]

The delay in protesting to Davidson about Bidault divided the commission. Initially, Arthur Lowndes (New South Wales) felt that for once it was in a position of strength in its relations with the government. He was aggravated by Darling's slowness in communicating with Davidson and because the draft 'seemed weak': the critical question was whether or not the commission stood by the position, 'unquestioned before Intertel', that it was independent of government in handling news and commentary. Had simultaneous consideration of Bidault and Intertel weakened its position? After meeting Dawes and Moses,

Darling was aware that several commissioners 'felt strongly' in favour of writing and that, even though he and another commissioner had had second thoughts, they had given way to 'what seemed to be a majority view'. The commission was 'seriously disturbed' by the postmaster-general's direction and thought that it was wrong to invoke section 77 because of the responsibility conferred by section 116. (These two points were the essence of what was to be included in the commission's annual report.) Menzies' statement at the time of the withdrawal of the prohibition—that the Bidault incident made clear that the ABC was not an organ of government—was welcome. With that letter dispatched and the Malaysia film not to proceed, Darling thought that little purpose was served by a longer statement to Davidson on commission rights and responsibilities. (In 1966, he assured Boyer's biographer that after Bidault the government had 'fully accepted the autonomy for which Sir Richard contended'.)[21]

There were other threats to independence, sometimes from within the ABC itself. In late April 1962, Professor Leicester Webb (Political Science, Australian National University) informed Darling that a recent telephone call from Semmler was the third personal appeal from top levels of the ABC to refrain from speaking about commercial television licensing (during *Notes on the News*). Assured that the topic was not banned, Webb said that he would only comply if told unequivocally that his talk would not be accepted. His concern with personal persuasion, rather than a straight-out prohibition, was that it created a 'preference for commentators who can be relied on to be "reasonable"'. Webb's letter, Darling said, was 'unanswerable' and he ought to do the commentary as he wished, although preferably not 'in the middle of our delicate negotiations with the Government'—presumably over Bidault and Malaysia. Why? Because knowing that they had made a mistake over television licences in Brisbane and Adelaide, some government members were caught like 'rats in a trap' trying to escape from the consequences of their decision and were 'preternaturally sensitive'. Darling believed that the postmaster-general had been 'on the side of enlightenment' and was trying to do the right thing, in which case deal with him gently, he enjoined Webb, as he is 'not really to blame'. Having recently gone to Canberra himself, full of anger and threats, he had come away 'sorry for the poor blighters'. He also sought Webb's understanding in respect of the ABC's previous actions: when trying to act on principle tempered by discretion, it was difficult, even in one's own eyes, to preserve 'any true integrity'. Webb broadcast on 15 May by which time Darling and Margaret were en route to the UK.[22]

The Darlings had sailed just after Davidson's announcement, but the chairman's respite from pressure was only brief, as an old adversary, Eddie Ward, was asking parliamentary questions about the financing of his trip. On 12 April, Ward had enquired of the postmaster-general whether Darling's 'overseas mission' was undertaken on the 'recommendation of the Commission'. Yes, was the answer—although this was not strictly correct (as Davidson knew) because, when Darling accepted the chairmanship, he gave advance warning of his intention to travel in 1962. Ward also asked for the list of countries that Darling would visit (there were seven) and the purpose of the trip: private, said the minister, although the chairman would attend conferences, and undertake work for the government in educational television and road safety. Moreover, Davidson had replied, the Darlings were not travelling at public expense. But Ward was gunning for the new chairman. He kept up the pressure, on and off, throughout May, July (when he directed queries to Menzies) and October. Dawes was perturbed about the first ministerial answer to Ward, and Moses was unclear about how to draft a reply about the financing of the trip. In desperation he forwarded to the chairman the Hansard extract with Ward's later questions. Darling responded. Immediately prior to his departure, he had covered his back by providing a reply for the minister to Ward's initial inquiries and had formally sought Davidson's permission to take leave. (His travel bill was mostly paid by the British Commonwealth International News Agency and himself—he was embarrassed about the generous working expenses while acting on the ABC's behalf.)[23]

The Darlings sailed on the SS *Orcades* and on 14 June they arrived in London to be met by their three daughters. En route, their father had prepared for Moses a short résumé on the ABC's office in Singapore. In Bombay (Mumbai), he gave a radio broadcast. In Europe, apart from time in Brussels in mid-June for a meeting of the European Broadcasting Union General Assembly (accompanied by T.W. Bearup, the ABC's London representative), he visited television studios in Paris, Rome and Milan. He and Margaret were in England during June and July, and then Scotland in August. After Brussels, there were lunches and dinners in London in the company of new contacts and former cronies from the major television and news-gathering agencies (such as Reuters, Rank, BBC and Independent Television Authority). Darling consulted on television with numerous scientific and technological experts—including the Polish-British polymath Jacob Bronowski, the physicist Lawrence Bragg, the biochemist Lord Todd, and the father–son activist and science writer combination, Baron Ritchie-Calder and Nigel Calder. (Casey was also in London and peppered the chairman with suggestions.) Darling travelled on his own to North America, following which he arrived in Sydney on 18 September, while Liza accompanied her mother on the return sea voyage. While in Canada, Darling stayed with David Hay (then High Commissioner for Australia). His main mission in the USA was to learn more about the possibilities of educational television (for John Bloomfield). His North American odyssey commenced in New York, where he met the state commissioner of education, school system officials and broadcasters, Harkness Fellowship people (he was a member of Victoria's selection committee) and the World Council of Churches. From there he headed to Boston, Chicago, Madison, Seattle and San Francisco (where he stayed with Sam McCulloch).[24]

Darling's experiences at the BBC were highly instructive. When recapitulating them to Moses, there were more indications of his fading

Englishness. He had warmed to Carleton Greene—although 'his brain is a bit powerful for me'—and also to the BBC's head of finance. Try as he may, however, he got nowhere when trying to dig and delve on program purchasing policy (the ABC had first right of refusal on BBC programs): 'They are all friendliness and helpfulness until one makes any specific suggestion and they then become as hard as flint'. The English were also adept at having things both ways. His tersely worded summary to Moses, in which he suggested (rather airily) that the ABC may have erred in haggling over prices, was taken as a mild rebuke because Moses replied with an extraordinarily detailed summary of ABC–BBC commercial negotiations. This confirmed Darling's view that the BBC wanted the best of both worlds—high financial returns for on-selling its programs and low outlays for purchases of ABC material. To Casey he confided that, while the BBC people had been extremely kind to him, they 'do not give much away, do they?' Experience of the BBC had convinced him of one thing: the ABC could make a much better fist than its British counterpart of programming in South-East Asia where its people were providing advice on technical matters, schools and agricultural broadcasting in Malaya and Singapore, and where the ABC was about to become a member of the Asian Broadcasting Union. Darling believed that educational television and radio might bridge the gulf between the desire of countries in the region for enlarged educational opportunities and the lack of trained teachers—which he had discussed with the Ford Foundation in New York and the Nuffield Foundation in London. Here there was considerable scope for cooperation between old and new Commonwealth countries.[25]

Back from overseas, Darling dealt immediately with complaints about programs. The bulk of these re-ran the Cold War disputation that he had been drawn into sporadically in the 1950s, although this time there was more of it, and it was intense and persistent. There were other complaints about the ABC's coverage of moral and religious issues. The main focus was communism and the two overriding criticisms were alleged ABC imbalance and bias. Sometimes the accusations about each were separately expressed; on others they were interwoven. Charges of imbalance were twofold: questions about the status of broadcast points of view and the significance accorded to them (for example, amount of program time, reputation of speakers). Bias concerned the extent to which personal values and particular allegiances were over-represented among ABC staff, and whether these dictated the treatment of controversial program topics. During his absence, the Returned Sailors' Soldiers' and Airmen's Imperial League of Australia (about to change its name to the Returned Services League—RSL) had complained about *The Candidates*. Inspired by BBC and ITV coverage of a recent UK general election, the ABC had telecast this program initially in late 1961 during the federal election campaign. As Darling had told Davidson at the time, because there was a risk of '"fringe" type individuals nominating' and expounding their particular panaceas with the ABC's help, advance program advice would not be aired. The following April, the RSL tackled Davidson about viewing time allocated to communist candidates (when three minutes was given to every candidate, state by state, in alphabetical order of electorates). With *The Candidates* due to screen in 1962 during three state elections, A.G.W. Keys (RSL national secretary) asked Davidson why, when the object of the Communist Party of Australia was to 'overthrow Democratic government in Australia and install a dictatorship in keeping with the Communist doctrine', Australians should be expected (courtesy of the national broadcaster) to pay for its publicity. The RSL demanded a review of the commission's decision and prevention of a recurrence.[26]

Davidson sought Darling's advice. Instead of drafting a reply, Darling insisted that the minister had to decide on matters of principle in respect of ministerial intervention. The commission had acted with its eyes open when deciding that, as communists were legal candidates, the electorate ought to be able to see them on television:

> The decision turns on whether the recognized knowledge that it is the objective of the Communist party to destroy the free society in whose privileges it shares, places it automatically outside the law and beyond the reach of consideration which a statutory commission concerned with mass communication clearly ought to accord to minorities. The Australian people, rightly or wrongly, refused to make the Communist Party illegal. For the Commission to place an absolute ban upon it would be to act beyond the law as it exists and arrogate the powers of censorship which have not been granted to it. But beyond all this there remains the true liberal doctrine that everyone has a right to be heard, and that it is the duty of the majority to ensure that the minorities enjoy equal rights. To act otherwise is to swallow the Communist one-party system to which we so strongly object.

Darling also emphasised the value of public exposure by asserting (optimistically and naively) that if, during the Hungarian uprising of 1957, Australian communist leaders had been given an opportunity to justify Soviet repression, then they were likely to have declined. In that case 'we should have fixed communism for good and all'. He also assured the postmaster-general that, as he knew A.J. Lee (RSL national president)—they were both members of the Commonwealth Immigration Advisory Council—he was confident that by dealing with him directly they could 'fairly satisfactorily straighten out the matter'. Even though he hated and feared communism as much as the RSL did, he and the commission had to be 'allowed to decide for ourselves what our duty is'. While Darling was returning to Australia, Davidson replied to Keys and quoted extensively from the chairman's letter (including the above extract). But Darling's appeal to liberal virtues cut no ice with Keys for whom opposition to communism was in the national interest and above party politics (which justified the RSL in treating communists differently from other party candidates). Keys thought that the commission had erred gravely. By adopting what the RSL regarded as a doctrinaire posture, the ABC had given the 'enemies of democracy full opportunity for propaganda' and viewer indoctrination. People wanting access to communists were free to go to listen to them during election campaigns. So-called rights, Keys asserted, amounted to the commission giving candidates access to a viewing audience about ten times the size of the electorate that they might eventually represent. As for exposing the leader of the 'enemy' to scrutiny that would be fine except that communists did not have a leader as such.[27]

Darling assured the postmaster-general that his views about communism's iniquities replicated those of the RSL, except that to exclude a party that was not illegal was to interfere with 'basic democratic rights' and establish a dangerous precedent. He reiterated his argument that communists could not be excluded from the program and the importance of disclosure: it was better to have 'the enemy' seen and heard, particularly given that 'many great movements' had begun as minorities that sometimes had proved subsequently to be right. The two principles at stake, then, were the rights of minorities, even communists, to be heard ('blast them!') and the commission's right to determine its own programs undeterred by the pressure and opinions of others. Although on reflection Darling was sceptical about the value of *The Candidates* and concerned about the 'invidious position' in which it had put the ABC, the issues that it raised were of wider importance. The prospect of freely available broadcasting time at public expense during elections was highly prized by political parties, especially if numerically small in size, adherents and appeal. Who, then, was to be allocated program space, on what basis and for what amount of time? The commission's policy was based on the parties' electoral performance: significant prior public support (that is, election of an MP or 5 per cent of votes cast) and forthcoming contesting of 5 per cent of seats. When in early 1963 for *The Candidates* Moses sought to rework this formula (20 per cent of lower-house seats contested, a full Senate team and 5 per cent of votes cast in either chamber), Darling objected: 'It too deliberately rules out minority voices, and, is designed in particular to rule out the Communists'. In principle, minorities had to be heard, although he was 'damned' if he knew the answer. Based on the previous election results, Moses' proposal would have let one party in and excluded another. Was this the 'right way to determine a point of principle?' Moreover, the change would mean surrendering to the Liberal Party's objection to the original program and would be a public admission that the ABC had been wrong. Far better, he said in exasperation (much as he disliked quarrels with the government and because he regarded such quarrelling as only moderately important) to concentrate the ABC's energies on the 99 per cent of areas where it was unrestrained.[28]

With more than 500 topical news broadcasts annually, there was ample opportunity for viewers and listeners to take offence. The hosing down of their criticisms required time, considerable internal fact-checking by program staff (to whom Darling forwarded letters of complaint before replying), communication among commissioners, and even consultation with government members (often at their behest). An illustrative case was the Cuban missile crisis in October 1962 when Dr Peter Russo (an academic) and Dr John Burton (secretary of the Department of External Affairs when Evatt was the minister) commented. On 4 December, Darling was interviewed by Menzies and the postmaster-general about the 'wretched Russo case'. Russo had been invited to speak by Allan Ashbolt (Federal Talks supervisor—Topical) and had accused the Americans and the Russians of mendacity during the crisis. Following complaints from the US government, Ashbolt's office was raided by Commonwealth police. A cabinet was broken and Russo's script (already publicly available) seized. In light of Menzies' 'serious view' of Russo's commentary, Lowndes told Darling that, while he agreed that the Americans had lied, he was also confident that the ABC's overall coverage was not anti-American. He urged firmness with the government on the ABC's policy that it did not take responsibility for the views expressed by its commentators, because to capitulate (by censoring talks, which was 'apparently expected of us') would be disastrous after measures taken to strengthen the Talks Department's morale. Darling's response to a listener aggrieved by Burton was frank but firm. His views may have been 'a long way away' from his own, he said, but Burton was not a communist. Indeed, as a recent Rockefeller Foundation grant recipient, the Americans clearly did not regard him as 'so very dangerous a character'. Apart from all that, it 'must be the duty' of the ABC to give a hearing to views other than those of the government or the commission, 'or even the majority of the people'. Equally, the ABC had to ensure that opposite points of view were aired and Professor Zelman Cowen had put a 'quite different standpoint' on Cuba on 26 October.[29]

Speaking slots on ABC news commentary programs such as *Notes on the News* were much sought after, although the use of speakers' panels was fraught. Commentators' estimates of their worth, for example, could be higher than those deciding whether or not to invite them. In 1964, Rohan Rivett—who had had a regular stream of ABC work in 1961–62 until he left for UPI in Zurich, and whose self-image was of someone articulating 'certain uncomfortable facts and truths' that precluded him from permanent newspaper employment—wrote a 'slightly injured' letter (Semmler said to Darling) complaining about his lack of recent engagements. Other potential speakers objected to being overlooked for commentaries, such as the medical practitioner Sir Raphael Cilento. He noted Darling's defence of Russo and how 'No commentator was ever, or would be, censored cried Dr. D', but in his view the well-meaning chairman had been duped. Probably, he surmised, Darling relied on his heads of section for advice on speakers and then approved them, but the problem was that this 'inner circle' was 'stiff with leftists, racists, homos., and other close knit scum'. What he regarded as the sourer half of the ABC, therefore, would regard Darling's claim about censorship as a joke, while the other half would regard the sentence as unfinished and would complete it with 'as long as they are recognizably leftist!' Darling's censorship response had confirmed for his admirers (Cilento claimed to be one) that the chairman's field was semantics, rather than political jugglery. Was Darling aware of this? Because of his defence of Russo, 'the Commos' regarded him as the supreme answer to their prayer (if that was an appropriate word) because they wanted a man who was 'popularly esteemed & guileless, approachable by flattery, cautious on controversial issues and, therefore, an ideal front for their hidden hand & hidden activities'. Twice he had tried unsuccessfully to secure an interview with Darling.[30]

These attacks about balance and institutionalised bias were incessant. They emanated from supporters and representatives of both sides of politics and were targeted at people identified (or presumed to be identified) with both sides. Letters of complaint were directed mostly to the chairman or to MPs and the minister (and the prime minister) who forwarded them to the chairman for a reply. Sometimes Darling drafted his own replies; at other times staff prepared replies for him and he added a personal note. Having said to Arthur Calwell that he was attacked on the grounds that 'the A.B.C. is riddled with extreme "Left Wing" bias', he believed that the ABC really did try to be 'fair, though cautious'. And, when defending another commentary by Burton—criticised by a Queensland MP on the grounds that he was assisting the communist cause— Darling's reply tried to reassure Davidson in mid-1963 that a formal assessment had been undertaken of the Left–Right 'problem'. 'We were all rather surprised' at the outcome, he said: there was a high proportion of 'what might be termed orthodox, or detached or establishment speakers' and only a few who were 'critical of the status-quo'. (Even the Communist Party of Australia complained to Darling in one instance about the 'shopworn propaganda' of alleged communist brainwashing in the telecast of *The Prisoner*, a play inspired by the story of Cardinal Mindszenty.) Surprised or not, the ABC chairman was damned if he did and damned if he didn't. The explanation was to be found in the preamble to a nondescript two-page document: 'Commission's directive—Policy concerning talks programmes' (or the Talks directive). The commission, it said, believed that its charter entailed a responsibility for 'aiding citizenship', which meant:

> not the diffusion of any particular point of view, but the stimulating of inde-
> pendent judgments on the problems of life—social, political, philosophic—
> and of independent appreciation of cultural values. It is the ABC's function
> to interest the public in current issues; to provide factual information; and to
> broadcast a variety of viewpoints with the aim of assisting listeners and view-
> ers to reach their own opinions.

Straightforward? Not necessarily if talks were contentious, because the 'Balance of viewpoints' part of the directive stipulated that an immediate counter was unnecessary, 'provided that over a reasonable period' there was adequate provision for alternative views.[31]

Talks was the one ABC programming area calculated to create problems for an ABC chairman. Immediately after Bidault and Malaysia, it mired the commission in controversy that precipitated a redrafting of the directive (only to be altered a year later and then again in 1966). Complaints about two Talks programs aired in May 1963, *Any Questions* and *Four Corners*, prompted Darling to require the commission to consider, in the former case, where responsibility lay for the selection of questions and, in the latter, who authorised the choice of material. He expressed 'considerable concern' at questions asked on *Any Questions* (chosen by Talks from advance written audience suggestions). Then Senator Spooner (Minister for National Development)—who was invited to appear on *Four Corners* but declined—claimed that the government's position had not been represented in that program's report on housing problems. When he was given space to make a specially prepared statement in a future edition of *Four Corners*, Whitlam asked to present the Opposition's view, but was refused. In June, Alan Carmichael (Director of Talks) met the Commission. Quizzed on why, when he agreed that some of the *Any Questions* material had been inappropriate, he had not edited it out, Carmichael claimed that he was forbidden by the directive. He was asked to revise the wording. In doing so he claimed that television, particularly because of the probing interview technique that it facilitated, had changed the rules of the game: radio's taboos on subjects and their treatments were gone, and the success with which protagonists might defend their views could not really be known until they were in front of a camera. 'Reasonable period', therefore, should be jettisoned in favour of a new time limit–free criterion: 'a balanced picture on matters of contention over its [the ABC's] total output'. Duckmanton objected. 'Over its total output' wouldn't do because these words avoided the problem that prompted the amendment: that is, removal of a program segment (and therefore opinions) thought by the commission not to be in (say) good taste. In short, the redraft gave Talks staff inadequate guidance about what to omit. The commission abandoned the directive for the time being for a summary of policy that had evolved and was common to the BBC and CBC, for which purposes Moses drafted a single-page statement. The key wording now read:

> Opposing points of view on controversial issues will normally be presented in
> the same programme but, where this cannot be done, the Commission expects
> its officers to achieve the necessary balance as soon as possible in the same
> type of session and at an equally favourable time.

Carmichael was insistent that there would still be practical difficulties, given the wide variety of situations addressed by the programs.[32]

As for *Any Questions*, from the telecasts that he had watched, Darling regarded it as benign although, as he told Moses, 'it would be rather better if they did not try so laboriously to be clever'. Some viewers thought differently and a flood of complaints poured in during May and June 1963. First, there were objections to questions asked. Offence had been taken at a discussion about the recent royal visit. A segment about the queen had been cut when she was in Perth except that, Darling reassured Davidson, there had been 'no instruction about censorship'. Then, two questions ('Are virgins obsolete?' and 'Are homosexuals treated too harshly?') prompted Sir Wilfrid Kent Hughes (MHR, Chisholm), to query their suitability for the national broadcaster, particularly when most of the panel belittled Christian standards. He also complained about a subsequent program in which a question from a 'seedy-looking, long-haired teenager' was met with roars of laughter: 'Should young couples [be required to] live together for [a period of say] three months before marriage?' While this may have been debated in a soldier's mess, it was not appropriate for the ABC and should have been labelled as not suitable for children. Darling regretted the asking of such a question, although Talks staff had cleared it and no audience member had complained about it or the subsequent discussion. Second, there were objections to the composition of panels. In a Christian community there simply had to be Christian representation, the Right Reverend Monsignor Moran (Vicar General of the Catholic Archdiocese of Melbourne) impressed on Darling. Ten South Australian clergymen also complained about a question on the incidence of schoolgirl pregnancies, particularly when 'the christian point of view' was not adequately represented on an *Any Questions* panel. Moreover, this panel had been 'cynical and flippant' about contraception, abortion and the inevitability of such pregnancies. Chastity, purity and self-control were given scant attention, and the broadcast ought to have been scheduled when children were unlikely to have been watching.[33]

Darling's friend Alick Downer (Minister for Immigration) said that a deputation of the South Australian clergymen had objected to the telecast, and there was disquiet at the program and uneasiness in Adelaide—which was not helped by publicity about the recent Profumo case in England. The situation had become 'mildly explosive'. Not merely once, but four or five times weekly in Sydney and Melbourne, Darling replied, there had been questions and answers that offended 'many' viewers, and he 'rather agreed' that these were not unconnected with the collapse of moral standards that resulted in the Profumo scandal. Sexual relations among the young needed to be tackled seriously at another time, as 'all is far from well', but it was quite wrong, 'even disgraceful' to deal with it superficially and flippantly in the 7.30 pm timeslot. ABC officers thought that to have removed the offending excerpt from the pre-recording would have been a 'limitation on free speech', except that the commission viewed freedom of speech as entailing responsibilities. On the other hand—in a reflection encapsulating the unenviable position in which he was placed as chairman—the mail for one day contained so many letters of objection that cancelled each other out that 'I wonder very much whether we have been wrong at all'. Nonetheless, the ABC's error was that the wrong people had talked about the matter in the wrong way at the wrong time. Not surprisingly, Darling claimed later in the year that the

Any Questions program gave him more trouble than 'the rest of the A.B.C. put together'.[34]

As for *Four Corners*, on Saturday evening, 31 August (and on the following Sunday afternoon) it included a 30-minute report on the RSL. The timing was fresh on the heels of comments by the governor-general (Viscount de L'Isle) at the opening of the RSL's Canberra headquarters (and an *Age* editorial), urging its members not to allow 'their prejudices to harden with their arteries'. The announcer was Gerald Lyons. The reporter was Ashbolt. Although it was unusual for a producer to be a program reporter, there had been two recent high-profile staff departures from *Four Corners* and, as an ex-serviceman himself, Ashbolt claimed to possess specialist knowledge. The film was shot at the Caulfield RSL branch—with which Ashbolt had had 'past associations' (a part of Melbourne in which he had grown up). His program was intended as a 'critical questioning' of the pressure group's 'special relationship to government, its peculiar influence in shaping the national ethos and its claim to stand outside and above party politics'. Following the telecast there was turmoil in sections of the ABC. Although Moses called the report 'not balanced' and 'terribly one-sided', after Darling viewed it he was reported later in *Nation* as having said to Margaret: 'Thank heaven the documentary was quite balanced' and that he saw 'nothing unfair or really critical' about it (which he confirmed to Francis James). While the RSL's national reaction was initially mild, its state and sub-branches protested vehemently. About a week later, Menzies received complaints from the RSL (although none with official status), by which time Neil Hutchison (acting federal director, General Programmes) had sought an explanation from Ashbolt about program editorialising and censorship, and the RSL's view that it had been 'conned'. Ashbolt's final commentary had said:

> If, then, the R.S.L. is ready to become involved in Party politics on one issue, it would probably be prepared to go in on other issues. This would lead to a basic change in its philosophy, its function and its power structure within the Australian community. An important question facing the R.S.L. is whether the rank and file of members would accept such a change. But more important still is the question of whether the Australian people as a whole would accept it.

Yes, explained Ashbolt, film segments of RSL spokesmen had been cut, although only in the interests of 'thematic unity', and RSL officials were omitted (to avoid repetitive comments and also because after lunch on filming day one RSL member had not been 'very coherent'). Finally, some anti-RSL commentators had been dropped, although one communist critic was interviewed.[35]

At this point, the ABC fumbled badly. Ashbolt stuck by his story but was 'exiled' from *Four Corners*—only to return as executive producer in 1964 (although, bizarrely, with his name omitted from the weekly credit list) and then barred again. Given its 'rather uneasy' feelings, and while contemplating disciplinary action, the commission had instructed Darling to seek a meeting with RSL representatives. No matter which way their explanations for what had happened were looked at, senior ABC staff ducked for cover. Lyons dissociated himself from the telecast. Moses felt that the effect on program staff of further action would be unfortunate. He echoed Semmler, who urged no further action, because any 'suspicion of a witch-hunt' would induce staff to 'play it safe'. Carmichael thought that the program's analysis was 'penetrating', but he agreed that Ashbolt's final statement 'should have been cut', and that in the interests of 'balance' a small segment on another aspect of RSL work should have been inserted. Why, therefore, hadn't he (Carmichael) been much more closely in touch with the development of the program's content? With a rumour circulating internally that he had succumbed to over-cautiousness, Carmichael judged it desirable for the production team to operate without any 'undue sense of inhibition'. After his initial three-page defence of himself, Ashbolt refused to provide a further report to the commission because to do so (he claimed) might have prejudiced his legal action against a senior RSL official (as to whether an accusation reported in the Brisbane *Courier Mail* that ABC staff included communists was a reference to him). Quite apart from the rights and wrongs of Ashbolt's actions, the problem for Darling and the commissioners created by disciplining him was an impression of knee-jerk capitulation to external pressure. This was exactly the point made in newspaper coverage and triggered a 19-signature staff petition protesting about Ashbolt's treatment (and which had been leaked to the Sydney press). Just how much conviction was carried by Moses' explanation to these staff for Ashbolt's removal from *Four Corners*—his work for it was always 'intended to be temporary' and this program had diverted him from his 'normal work'—is guesswork. (Later, Moses fingered Semmler for the removal decision, while claiming that he had wanted Ashbolt to remain as compere.) Indeed, when Moses told the commission that no public criticism of Ashbolt had been intended and that as general manager his public support of staff had been previously forthcoming on several occasions, Darling's disquiet was evident in his marginal note: 'a bit equivocal'—although he confessed later to Francis James (a close friend of Ashbolt) that he was 'as much responsible' as anyone for the way that the program had been dealt with.[36]

After eulogising the ABC in June as 'a great national asset', in a seven-page letter in September James summarised for Darling the inside dope to which he had been privy. Of his nineteen points, Darling considered two to be critical. In relation to the first (James' fourth point, which was that because information provided by Ashbolt in a memorandum had not been made known to Darling when Moses had brought it with him to Melbourne, could the chairman not send for it?) Darling refused point blank. 'No! I don't think so. A pretence of confidence and loyalty must be preserved.' The second point was that a teleprinter message had been sent by Carmichael to supplement that memorandum. The Talks director thought that part of what Ashbolt had said was a bit blunt and advised him to indicate two things: first, that he (Ashbolt) held and had put into effect a view on how *Four Corners* material should be presented; second, that if the commission didn't like that view and wanted a different form of presentation, then as a loyal commission servant he would do this 'as they wanted it'. Moreover, Ashbolt 'is' a loyal commission servant, James insisted. 'Please have no doubt about this.' 'Yes', said Darling about Ashbolt's loyalty, 'I agree'. On the question of Carmichael's advice, Darling said that:

> There is a real point of disagreement which cannot be resolved by directive but only by argument and consultation. Is it more important to be fair than to be interesting? Are these qualities compatible[?] Personally, I believe that the A.B.C. has no and must have no editorial policy, and that this applies to programmes except news commentaries, which are specifically the views of one person, and in the planning of which it is our responsibility to present a variety of views. In a programme of the sort of 'Four Corners', this balance must be presented within the programme. I don't think that the Talks people agree with this view.

In the end, Darling said, the commission had to decide this matter. Its failure so far, however, which was a basic failure, was that it had been unable to find 'the machinery of getting them [the staff] to agree with us'. James was adamant that Darling had to look after his own personal welfare. Why should he take the rap and be the villain in the public's mind? 'Must you remain the bunny?' He was hanged if he could see why. To have to take responsibility when one lacked power was not really on.[37]

Earlier James had arranged a meeting with *Nation*'s editor, Tom Fitzgerald. The outcome was that Fitzgerald—who thought that Darling was an idealist— now knew that the chairman was 'dinkum' and from that point onwards would not permit anything to be written 'ex parte about the A.B.C.' But Fitzgerald also thought that as chairman Darling was ignorant of what went on inside the ABC, was not in touch with the feelings of some sections of the staff and underestimated the importance of public relations—which was partly what James' meeting was intended to address. On the other hand, said James, Fitzgerald was equally aware that Darling was acting out of innocence, rather than laziness, and that he was moved by principle, not cowardice. Continuing in this vein of brutal honesty, and adopting an almost campaign manager–like tone, James then said 'I do hope we can build on this' because Fitzgerald was such an important person who was selfless and universally trusted. Ominously, he thought that 'we're only at the beginning of this latest row [over the RSL]' and he was willing to dampen the flames. For all of his friend's astuteness, Darling believed that James (along with other people whom he had mentioned) was overlooking one basic fact: the ABC was approaching the end of an era and until a change at the top could be made it was futile to expect any radical alteration. Having to 'possess my soul in patience' before that could occur was 'frustrating and exasperating'. He had tried to sow the seeds for a better future for the ABC and had avoided doing anything likely to invalidate hopes for better times. Darling also said that he knew that he had been unsuccessful. Living in Sydney may have helped matters, although possibly not. As the heir apparent to Moses, Duckmanton was in an even worse position. All that one could do, then, was to hang on and 'do one's best in the circumstances as they are' and hope that it would not be too difficult later on to put together 'the bits'. He was sorry, but it was simply too late now to do anything about James' point four. 'Do try to persuade people to give me time', he exhorted his friend. He confessed to being not 'as innocent as you all think me or as I pretend to be'.[38]

Fifty-two telegrams to the ABC objected to actions taken in respect of the *Four Corners* RSL segment and Ashbolt's removal. James' *Anglican* tore into the RSL for its lack of democracy and claimed that its entry into politics was engineered by 'racketeers who have insinuated their way into the top strata of the movement'. The federal election (30 November) followed this tumult. The campaign period was mostly pain-free for the ABC and its chairman—apart from Lowndes' isolated bleat about a *Four Corners* program the week before polling day for which a 'terrible castigation' was deserved. 'The whole Talks situation is clearly a horrible muddle with internal politics not unimportant', he complained to Darling. Menzies' Coalition government returned to office (with an increased majority). Davidson retired and was succeeded as postmaster-general by Alan Hulme (Liberal MHR, Petrie). A week before the election the world was stunned by the assassination of the youthful thirty-fifth President of the USA, John Fitzgerald Kennedy, in a motorcade in Dallas, Texas. The next day, Darling struggled to come to terms with the tragedy and penned a three-page reflection. 'Disbelief, horror, anger, fear, compassion': these were the successive waves of emotion engulfing him. 'Our generation', he wrote, had lived through hard times when the world seemed to return to a barbarous past and the veneer of civilisation was exposed as skin deep. Thankfully, however, 'the English' had been mostly free of assassinations. Apart from his recall of a couple of remote historical instances, the worst recent example was the 'saintly Gandhi'. The Western world had come to believe that such an event could not happen, so that in these circumstances anger was a natural-enough reaction: it was always 'infuriating' to witness the 'constructive efforts of great and good men nullified by the destructive forces of those whose motives seem to be exclusively based on hatred'. Anger, however, was the wrong response, for it was of the Devil, the product of fear and the father of hatred. A better response was evident in God's revelation of himself in Christ. Evil could not be overcome with evil, but only with good through compassion. God grant 'us', he wrote prayerfully, 'the power to enlarge our compassion beyond those for whom it was easy to have a fellow-feeling even to those who persecute us'.[39]

Despite the assurances at the meeting organised by James, Darling became locked into a brief epistolary feud with Fitzgerald about the Kennedy assassination when, in January 1964, *Nation* reported comments alleged to have been made to ABC staff by Darling. The columnist Acrux claimed that:

> While satisfied with the television presentation of most aspects of the tragedy, he [the chairman] indicated that there was one conspicuous omission. He regretted that there had been no treatment of the theological aspect. When asked to explain himself more precisely, Dr Darling told the television men that the question they had failed to consider was, Why had God allowed it to happen?

When he read it, Darling flared. He was riled at being misquoted and thought that this was yet another ABC leak. While he did not blame *Nation* for being gossipy, the lack of loyalty within the ABC that it revealed was 'distressing'. If he could not talk to ABC staff about programs or principles without the risk of conversations being passed on to journalists then he couldn't talk to them at all. Did the columnist really think him 'such a boob' to have uttered the words attributed to him? What he had said was that some people's understanding was such that they were bound to ask how contemporary religious thinking might interpret political and international events. There was an opportunity for a religious leader to put them right or interpret such an event (as, he said, his friend Archbishop Woods had done). There was a theological side to such events, so that if the ABC had a duty to report all sides of an issue, then such reporting included religion. Next time, therefore, before a person in public life was likely to be reported as 'having said something palpably childish', would the publication check whether he had actually said it? The source had not been the ABC, Fitzgerald replied. Again he said that he respected and admired Darling's ideals but, while he claimed to have some 'faint idea' of the complexity of the chairman's job, he also had very different view of the ABC's role. The national broadcaster's problem was that it suffered from 'other worldliness and a great attention to moral niceties'. Francis James thought that Darling's protest letter had been justified. According to his ABC sources, the view was that 'you aren't nearly schoolmasterish enough—and they don't catch on', although interestingly, he thought, 'Ashbolt <u>does</u> catch on'. As for loyalty in 'your bludy [sic] ABC' there wasn't any. Loyalty was reciprocal, but there was little loyalty from the top of the ABC to the staff, and almost no human understanding or sympathy, with the result that staff (certainly in Sydney) continued to be 'disgruntled, unhappy, disloyal, inefficient and a lot more'. Furthermore, established ABC staff enjoyed a parson's freehold, which was crazy because this left the commission in a 'hopeless and helpless position'. 'You mugs! You all carry the can—and especially J.R.D. as Chairman—for things you cannot control.'[40]

As for Ashbolt, perhaps James was right. The journalist (and ex-ABC staff member) Mungo McCallum claimed in the same edition of *Nation* that, since the RSL program, *Four Corners* had 'lost distinction' to such an extent that nothing in its subject matter would make 'great-grandmother falter for an instant in her knitting'. But *Any Questions* continued to give the chairman grief. In a program telecast the following month, it pointed to a concern about increased numbers of teenage pregnancies and had asked: 'In light of these figures, do you [the panel] consider that chaperons should be reintroduced?' Ashbolt smelt a rat, he told Semmler, because the question had been put 'partly as a "test" of our willingness to allow it to be broadcast'. The climate in which the Talks department had been working over the previous six months had to be borne in mind. 'Those of us' concerned to defend the ABC's reputation for integrity and objectivity, Ashbolt said—the chairman, commissioners and senior officers, Talks staff—had had 'a rather worrying time'. There had been a lot of negative newspaper reporting and even *TV Times* (the ABC's in-house journal) was writing openly of a 'ban on controversy' in *Four Corners*. As far as he knew, there was no such ban. During the past few weeks he had quashed several projected press stories on it that had been leaked from across the ABC, not Talks. In a hint that he may indeed have been catching on, Ashbolt supposed that 'barring, perhaps, the Chairman and the G.M., who as figureheads have to suffer a great deal', he was probably more sensitive than anyone in the ABC to misrepresentation and trouble caused by the press. Yet such sensitivity in deciding about the *Any Questions* program had probably not influenced him, because he saw the choice as a press row or 'the possibility that a very few listeners (not the majority) might be offended'.[41]

Notwithstanding McCallum's view that *Four Corners* may have lost its edge, Darling was still defending it (in mid-1964) against complaints to the minister. A debate between opposing politicians had got out of hand, thanks to the 'incompetence' of the interviewer. An exposé of a Nazi group in Sydney was by no means an advertisement for Nazism but had made the group appear 'ludicrous and contemptible' (about which the security service, when contacted, was satisfied). And Sir Raphael Cilento (now on the speakers panel)—'just as much a red rag to a bull' to some people as was Senator Cohen of the ALP—was being called on sparingly and then only to comment on matters for which he was qualified to speak. Once again, Darling explained to Hulme, with 'balance' being maintained over a series of commentaries, the difficulty was that if people heard merely what they heard and disagreed with it, then they would conclude that this was the sole point of view. In Left–Right terms, more complaint letters came from the Right about Left bias than the reverse, except that 'when we studied' the commentators' list, the scales were weighted in the other direction. Were people on the Right less tolerant than those on the other side, then? As for allegations of communism and institutionalised bias in the ABC, the Communist Party was not illegal and even if commission staff were communists, they could not be dismissed or penalised. The ABC's 'only safeguard is Security'—with which it was in fairly close touch. Were there 'innocent sentimentalists' and 'near-travellers' of communists in the ABC? He had no idea, but it was 'sheer nonsense' to pretend that the ABC was dominated by such people or even that it was 'predominantly

Left-wing'. Possibly journalists tended to be more left of centre than rightward, as was true of newspapers owned by 'the most fervid conservatives', and it was such types whom the commission inevitably recruited. But, he asked rhetorically, was this situation avoidable and could 'any sort of conscience-test' be imposed by a public institution? To create a truly professional spirit required the prevention of personal opinions being indulged in programs. Building such a spirit would take time, short of which attempted control was the main interim measure. This was bad, however, because shelving personal responsibility worked against the mutual confidence that was the hallmark of a profession, and instead created grievance and insecurity. He could not, he reiterated, detect Left-wing bias and, 'certainly Messrs. Calwell and Whitlam' continually accused the ABC of the exact opposite. In fact there were 'too few' ABC commentators of a leftward inclination. The problem with 'Conservatives' was that they did not 'really believe in the Liberal doctrine of free speech', because they disliked criticism of their beliefs and habits. If Hulme was seeking consolation, then, there was none to be had: it was certain that the ABC's attempt to preserve the rights of all, 'Left, Centre and Right', would continue, said Darling, to 'land us—and you—in trouble'. 'Your Government won't like it, nor will the Prime Minister', but at least he would understand the point and 'would not really wish it to be otherwise', although the entire matter was 'devilishly difficult'.[42]

It was early days in his relationship with the new minister and Darling's difficulty in being so forthright was that he had no guarantee that this was what Hulme wanted to hear. Hulme (and the government) had been delivered a problem: complaints about the ABC. Would such a bald statement of the obvious be seen as a solution or as exacerbating it? Moreover, was Darling serving his own cause well? Menzies would indeed have understood his point and swallowed the truth, however unpalatable and, while Darling could not simply be dismissed as Menzies' man, what would happen when Menzies was no longer there to back him? To try to satisfy others, Darling thought, doomed one to 'disappointment'. Instead, one had to use one's judgement and 'try to be honest to that'. In the case of replies by ministers to criticisms aired by Opposition members, the ABC's policy was not to contact ministers because most preferred to answer at a time of their own choosing. With disgruntled or angry viewers, by contrast, Darling's tactic in his correspondence was to agree with them or to sympathise where possible, and to cite the results of the Left–Right check. The twofold risk here was prolonging of the correspondence and fuelling complainants with additional grounds for their grievances or, in the face of a refusal to accept the evidence (without him knowing in advance), expending mental energy in an exercise in futility. For the time being, Darling's explanation mollified Hulme. The *Four Corners* debate that had got out of hand—Senator Cohen and Dr MacKay, his Liberal opponent, had been discussing the influence of Croatian groups in Australia and anti-Semitism, and Cohen had dominated proceedings—illustrated how easily, for both minister and chairman, these considerations could be compounded by political malfeasance. Thus, Hulme thought that the complaints received were less about the Cohen–MacKay debate per se and more to do with newspaper reports of MacKay's objections to a leftward bias within the ABC. He had raised this accusation in a party room meeting and sadly it 'was not kept within the four walls of the party room as it should have been'.[43]

ABC religious programming (about which Acrux had pilloried the chairman) raised different issues. Following a Sunday afternoon telecast of the British philosopher Bertrand Russell, Darling's former ABCB colleague Randal White—'a good man in every sense' and strongly committed to Moral Re-armament—protested that such a program destroyed Christian faith and moral standards. As an atheist, Russell's potential for harm was genuine, 'silly old man' that he was, said Darling, not only because he thought that he knew everything but because he convinced others that he did. Atheists could not be denied expression of their views and they had to be heard to be answered. Was Australia a Christian country, Darling asked, and was it up to the ABC to maintain 'the' Christian standpoint? 'I am far from sure about this', he confessed. And who was to interpret what Christian truth was anyway? He was less concerned about Russell than the cumulative 'steady drip effect' of murders, crime and vice—such as the 'beastly' *Maigret* detective program, which had cost the ABC a financial packet and was acquired in the belief that it might maximise audiences. Fitzgerald's criticism of the ABC's otherworldliness and its obsession with moral niceties armed him with a counterbalance to White. Apart from its alleged subversion of Christianity, the ABC was also attacked for how it conveyed Christian truths. Darling replied to Calwell's criticism of a contemporary dramatic production of the *Passion of Christ* by sympathising, and saying that with the failure of conventional religious approaches in attracting the younger generation, part of the duty of religious broadcasting was to reaching them in new ways. The play in question was 'not blasphemous'.[44]

On 25 June 1964, Darling was reappointed as chairman. His private feelings (expressed to Rivett) that the government was hesitating were ill founded. Continuing doubt about the renewal of himself and Edgar Dawes was a key factor—along with the Coalition's knife-edge one-seat majority—in inducing decision-making paralysis on the commission's part midway through the previous year, and Darling had told (a then ill) Lowndes, that he wished that he was 'not more persona grata with the P.M.' With the election over and the government back in office, speculation during early 1964 about termination or reappointment had continued right up until the last minute. Dawes (deputy chairman since 1945) had thought that Darling was a certainty, whereas he and Harrie Halvorsen (Western Australian commissioner since 1956) were vulnerable. When all three were reappointed, Darling thanked Hulme and said that he was under no illusion as to the worth of his contribution so far. His three years' work had been a mere 'holding operation'. Now, however, with Duckmanton as general manager–designate to succeed Sir Charles Moses, another three years of 'really hard constructive work' could begin. Having secured Duckmanton's succession, there was still the 'problem of Miss Cook' to be solved, of course, which had to be done, preferably without tears 'but more likely with plenty of them'. The magnitude of the commission's challenge was forcefully evident in a *Nation* journalist's description of the ABC, two days after Darling's reappointment, as a 'network of fear and suspicion', headed by a man with a reputation for dictatorship and ruthlessness (Moses), and assisted by a frail, pleasant-looking and grey-haired woman (Cook), described as 'the most feared individual' in the organisation, with the commission itself depicted as 'autocratic and uncompromising'. In his retirement, Davidson was delighted at the news of Darling's second term: 'I am very glad even though I know I persuaded you into a tough assignment'.[45]

AN IRRITATING YEN FOR PRINCIPLE

1964–1967

No longer is the framework within which a man lives fixed by traditional institutions. Mass communications replace tradition as a framework of life. Being thus afloat, the metropolitan man finds a new anchorage in the spectator sports, the idols of the mass media, and other machineries of amusement.

C. Wright Mills, *White Collar*

In March 1964, Talbot Duckmanton was appointed deputy general manager. In June, the commission made him general manager–designate, although it got into a pickle with the wording. Moses had not attended the meeting (and Betty Cook, his secretary, was absent for this item). The intention was that he would retire on his sixty-fifth birthday, with the date confirmed as no later than 26 February 1965. Not only would Duckmanton then 'take over', but he would be acting general manager in Moses' absence. At its August meeting the commission rescinded its decision and now said (confusingly) that Moses would retire on 21 January 1965 except that, because his Asian Broadcasting Union work required him until 4 December 1964, he would take his remaining accumulated recreation leave until 26 February. By its pre-Christmas meeting, however, Moses had given notice of intention to cease duty from 25 November, take his pre-retirement leave and then vacate the general manager's Broadcast House suite no later than 18 December. After Moses' departure (to Asian Broadcasting Union–rented rooms in the Lowes Building) the commission would sell the general manager's suite's furnishings to the Asian Broadcasting Union and Cook's services would be available to the Asian Broadcasting Union secretariat. To anyone not in the know, and yet who might have noticed in June that Cook had not spoken to Duckmanton and had seen Lady Moses 'cut him publicly at a party', the question was: What was going on?[1]

Apart from a reluctance to let go of the reins, Sir Charles Joseph Alfred Moses (general manager since 1935) had refused to implement commission policy. To Darling, he was as a law unto himself. Boyer's predecessor (W.J. Cleary) had resigned because of Moses' feral behaviour, Boyer had told Darling about it repeatedly, Medley had advised him not to accept the chairmanship because of it, Dawes had also warned him about it when Darling became chairman and so too had Jock Reid. Once in office, he had trusted the general manager, but to no avail:

> Not only did he [Moses] refuse to take me into his confidence, he was several times extremely rude positively to me and I have little doubt that he intrigued against the Commission behind my back in the attempt to get his term of office prolonged. I have had evidence of this from England and from Canberra.

Moses' directives and rebukes had destroyed the trust of ABC senior officers and program staff. Darling identified three difficulties: first, Moses was never available to staff during working hours; second, he depended on Cook 'who is generally hated'; third, he and Cook were autocrats who had failed to adjust to the changed conditions of the ABC arising from its increased growth and size. The commission had first broached with Moses in January 1963 the date of his sixty-fifth birthday and retirement, and signalled its intention not to extend his term, after which Moses absented himself by taking accrued leave (Europe and the USA in 1963, the Asian Broadcasting Union and then Nigeria with UNESCO in 1964). Duckmanton was made deputy general manager to clarify who was in charge during these prolonged absences. (The intention was also to end the 'growing volume of gossip and speculation about the future' that was widening the gulf between staff and management.) Despite this decision, Duckmanton had informed Darling that 'Miss Cook remains in charge of the mail' and 'that she keeps in continual touch with the G.M. and does not seem to recognize his [Duckmanton's] position'. Such wilfulness was making matters 'virtually unworkable'. Eventually, Darling went to the minister before the commission's June 1964 meeting. Armed with the knowledge (from Hulme) that commission reappointments were confirmed, it was then that Darling (after a private prior meeting with Duckmanton) had requested the commission to appoint the deputy general manager as general manager–designate. But the commission had gone further and fixed the February date—which Darling did not consider 'wise' or 'decent' in Moses' absence, although the general manager was unlikely to be back for the July commission meeting, and possibly not for August.[2]

In fact, Moses had not even bothered to inform Darling about his leave. The latter had tried to do the right thing and telegrammed the commission's decision to him (in Vienna), although he thought that Moses' retirement was unlikely to be achieved with 'dignity or decency'. Moses retaliated. While accepting the commission's right to decide who was to be the general manager and agreeing with Duckmanton's appointment as the general manager–designate, he claimed that the announcement less than a week after his heading overseas

was 'rather puzzling', especially in light of the commission's earlier decision
to appoint Duckmanton deputy general manager. He insisted that after the
announcement there had been negative reactions to his successor within the
ABC and beyond. Long before the commission finalised its position, Darling
had speculated privately about Moses' successor. He canvassed Duckmanton,
Semmler and A.N. (Huck) Findlay (assistant general manager). Initially, he
had inclined towards Findlay (although at sixty in 1963, age was not on his
side) and suspected that Semmler (a 'not impossible' appointment) would be
endorsed by Lowndes and Rhoda Felgate (commissioner from Queensland),
on the grounds that an ABC head ought to come from the programming area
and because they were unlikely wholly to trust Duckmanton (Moses' choice).
Someone who combined the strengths of Semmler and Duckmanton would be
ideal, Darling thought, but 'quite unequivocally' the latter had to be appointed.
In the absence of an ideal person, therefore, 'the machinery must be created
in such a way as to enable them to work as a pair or team'. Top-level management, he concluded, should be: Duckmanton (general manager), Semmler
(deputy general manager, Programmes) and Findlay (deputy general manager,
States and Regions). This was to be regarded as a 'Trinity in the theological sense
and not three persons'. Between them the director (Radio Programmes), director (Television Programmes) and head of the Programmes division would then
take on Semmler's detailed work. Proceeding downwards from 'this conception
of hierarchy' would ensure that any separation at the top between programs and
administration was unlikely, and that the necessary machinery would be 'evolved
for policy to be passed down and understood'. Semmler warmed to the comple-
mentary general manager–deputy general manager arrangement as 'more practicable and less cumbersome than a Triumvirate'—as this might be 'creating too
many Generals'. Moreover, because he would serve the ABC more effectively
than currently, Semmler told Darling, 'I really <u>want</u> that second prize because I
believe I could do the job better than anyone else'.[3]

There was a broadly rational–romantic contrast between the respective
temperaments of Duckmanton (the crown prince) and Semmler (the prodigal
sibling). On the one hand (according to the historian of the ABC), Duckmanton
was 'calm, judicious, flawlessly competent, rich in understanding of the organisation, middle-brow, and detached from the ferment of program-making', whereas
Semmler (seven years his senior) was 'impulsive, head-strong, impatient of
bureaucracy, highbrow and lowbrow in tastes, and dedicated to the making of fine
programmes'. In 1958, as the president of the SOA, Semmler had conducted the
arbitration case for increased salaries for senior officers. Moses (on the commission's behalf) had opposed the claim in court. For Semmler, the experience had
been an unremitting slog. There were 'agonies of spirit' that no-one else could
ever have known, he told Darling, 'day after day for 6 months, having to face
the G.M. in all his might across the table'. It had been a painful experience for
the ABC, but the public service arbitrator noted that every senior officer, 'under

painful cross-examination and under some provocation', had 'behaved with the greatest of dignity'. A handwritten note of Darling's indicates that during 1963 Moses had contemplated sacking Semmler or at least making his position 'intolerable' and he sought an assurance that this was not his intention. There was no surprise, then, when Semmler thanked Darling at Christmas for having made that year 'better for me than it might have been largely for your understanding & help'. Perhaps there was even less surprise late in the following year at Semmler's schadenfreude-like description of the soon-to-depart Moses—the pathetic image of 'our late General Manager's sulkiness and silliness' in commuting backwards and forwards between Lowes and Broadcast House in the ABC car that he had arranged for himself, 'grey witch in tow, a remnant of former glories'. With his appointment, Semmler was 'exhilarated to be named as Tal's no. 2'.[4]

This long-running succession saga was over and done with in March 1965, when the commission recorded its recognition of Moses' contribution. Darling was determined to make the transition as dignified as possible. He added a personal note to the commission minute and thanked Moses for building up and developing the national broadcasting and television service. (Some months later he chastised Duckmanton for a note on Moses as 'disgracefully ungenerous, and [which] must be improved upon'.) At the same time, because of what the retiring general manager might interpret as 'liberal terms' during his leave, the commission stood firm. He was informed that he ceased to be general manager on 26 November and that in the new relationship between the ABC and the Asian Broadcasting Union there would be no continuation of public service conditions. There was no way that a retiring general manager could embarrass his successor by persisting in claiming 'privileges that only accrue to the active Head of the Department'. Nor would the commission tolerate Moses' equally embarrassing assertion that he remained a commission employee: ABC dispatch staff were neither authorised to collect him from Lowes by car, nor to park the vehicle and then return it to him as he required. Dawes, especially, was hyper-vigilant in ensuring that a statement to Moses carried no 'inference of apology', because the commissioners had none to make. Right to the bitter end, then, the commission ensured that the dog was wagging the tail, and not the reverse.[5]

In anticipation of a post-Moses era, Lowndes said to Darling in early 1964 that a 'colossal job' lay ahead in 'rehabilitating morale and renewing enthusiasm'. He was not wrong. 'Our calm period' (following the Cohen–MacKay exchange on *Four Corners* in June of that year) ended in late August with a curtain-raiser to the main event—yet another brawl over this program. In a news commentary, the Melbourne *Herald* journalist, Denis Warner, criticised Australian foreign policy. A minor delay in retrieving his transcript (when the postmaster-general requested a copy) put Darling on the back foot, but raised a key point of principle. Apart from the administrative hassle in giving Hulme 'automatically' a copy of every ABC talk (about 500 annually), to be required to do so was tantamount to the minister being 'personally responsible for political matters put over the A.B.C.' Darling (gently) tutored Hulme on the political implications entailed. The commission would 'contest this admission' (of Hulme's presumed responsibility) and the newspapers 'would play it up', which, surely, would be 'disastrous'. If and when he required a script, therefore, Hulme should simply contact the general manager who would dispatch it by express delivery, thereby avoiding misinterpretation of an 'entirely innocent and justifiable request' as an attempt to 'muzzle' the ABC. If there was potential government embarrassment in news commentaries generally, then that could be dealt with by extending the existing Radio Australia arrangement across the wider foreign policy field. Apart from that, 'an essential of democratic government' was exposure to criticism of the policies of the government of the day (including foreign policy). To be criticised over 'what you regard as your own system' might well be irritating for the postmaster-general, but the ABC's receipt of government finance did not make it a government instrumentality because the broadcaster's money originated from licence fees paid by the users of television sets, a fact which the Treasury 'when it suits them' conveniently slides over.[6]

The *Four Corners* saga was as ugly as it was protracted (October–December 1964). Once more Ashbolt's name was in the frame and again the chairman was in the spotlight. Apart from the blip of a program on pensions, which Darling thought was a 'very superficial performance', he confided to Semmler that *Four Corners* was 'improving and doing quite well'. Then late in October, Ashbolt sent a young reporter, John Penlington, to Perth to prepare a story on capital punishment and the impending execution of a convicted murderer, Eric Edgar Cooke, with the expectation of a *Four Corners* report being aired on the preceding Saturday night (24 October). But in answer to a question in state Parliament (20 October) on whether he approved of the ABC's 'gruesome commercialisation' of capital punishment and, if he didn't, would he investigate with a view to preventing the telecast, the premier, David Brand, agreed to raise the matter with the ABC. After news broke of the film crew's presence in Perth, Semmler's press statement (21 October) said that the ABC was gathering material for three special stories about Western Australian locations (Exmouth Gulf, Ord River and Esperance) and that, while a program on capital punishment as 'a national issue' was being planned, the crew's appearance in Perth, albeit with the hanging imminent (Monday, 26 October), was 'a mere coincidence'. Moreover, such a telecast would be in 'poor taste' and smacked of sensationalism. No matter what had been alleged in Parliament, Semmler insisted, the ABC's decision had nothing to do with that discussion. Two days later on Friday, the *Australian's* editorial ('The Four Corners mirage') quoted Semmler and a direct denial by Ashbolt: yes, his crew had been filming public reactions to the hanging and the film had arrived in Sydney. Not only that, but if what Semmler was reported to have said was true then this reflected negatively on Penlington's ability and integrity. The *West Australian* editorialised that it had no objection to a film on capital punishment and its sole concern was timing (on the eve of the execution), although there would not have been embarrassment if the ABC had kept a tighter rein on *Four Corners*. Finally, the Melbourne *Herald* claimed that the commission had capitulated to Brand's pressure and, in doing so (on the back of the federal government's foolishness over Bidault the year before) had rendered 'rather fragile' the ABC's political independence.[7]

Behind closed doors, Semmler intimated that coincidence was a furphy, and that when he prevented the screening of the hanging program, his overriding considerations were poor taste and sensationalism. Darling endorsed Semmler's point about poor taste, although in offering to give the assistant general manager 'executive level' support, he was aware that such action 'may merely be rubbing salt into wounds of the 4 Corners team and Mr. Ashbolt' and could be construed as attacking them. With Whitlam breathing down his neck (had Brand complained to the prime minister, the postmaster-general or the ABC's general manager, the deputy leader of the Opposition had asked the chairman—by telegram), Darling insisted that no complaint had been received (although representations had been made to an acting manager) and the decision not to telecast was taken prior to 'notice of any complaint received'. Despite press perceptions, Semmler (and the ABC) had not buckled under political pressure. As for sensationalism, Semmler cited complaints against the camera crew over three incidents in Perth (unauthorised filming of a suburban residence, and filming of the scene outside the jail on the day of the hanging and of a clergyman in attendance). The situation became even messier when, instead of telecasting the Cooke item, John Power (*Four Corners*' producer) substituted an interview with Rohan Rivett on the right of journalists to not disclose their sources. A case apposite to this particular issue was being heard in the New South Wales Supreme Court. When it was alluded to in the *Four Corners* introduction (although not discussed during the program itself), the presiding judge attacked the ABC and said that he would refer the matter to the state's chief justice and attorney-general. Prior legal advice had been taken by the ABC, according to the Director of Talks (Carmichael), except that Power had misunderstood it. Moses said that the program's association with the court case was an 'error of judgment'. Semmler agreed and fingered Ashbolt and Penlington for making 'unauthorised statements' to the press. He reprimanded Ashbolt (any more unauthorised newspaper statements and he would be 'immediately suspended'), returned Penlington to Talks and Power to general production work, and removed responsibility for *Four Corners* from Talks. Reports about *Four Corners* in two Sydney newspapers provoked Ashbolt to accuse the *Sun* of 'vicious distortion' of his actions and Semmler to dismiss as a 'lying report' the *Daily Mirror*'s claim that two Talks officers had resigned.[8]

With the ABC tearing itself apart and the press having a field day, the chairman was fighting on two fronts (public and internal)—possibly confirming as he did so the *Nation* editor's estimate of him as idealist prey adrift in a sea of encircling media sharks. He told the commission on 12–13 November that four matters were disturbing him: sections of the press could get away with lying and be believed, and yet no-one believed in the ABC's integrity; staff were disloyal in feeding the press with material 'so continuously'; high-level disagreements could not be conducted in private; and, the state of ABC public relations was 'deplorable'—even though he and Duckmanton had maintained daily contact and spoken publicly about *Four Corners* only with the other's permission, this practice had not been universal and ABC staff were even obtaining their information from the press. The commission wanted Darling to summarise its position in a *Four Corners* interview but when Lowndes queried the suggestion's advisability, it agreed to hold fire on the interview in the hope that the controversy died. It didn't and, as the war of words intensified, alleged ABC capitulation to political interference became the focus of public comment, a charge to which, in its post-meeting press release, Darling said the commission took 'strong exception'. As a public instrumentality the commission expected criticism, he said, and the ABC was not faultless, but the current criticism in the absence of evidence had reflected on the motives of senior executives and sown public suspicion. Management had to be able to manage, and in doing so it would not make 'internal issues' (about ABC rules, discipline and management) the subject of public debate. Repeated attacks fuelled unhealthy 'discord and disquiet'. The ABC's responsibility, like that of its critics, was to seek the truth, 'for honesty and fair play' and, in particular, 'not to mirror evil where none existed'.[9]

Darling's discomfort was exacerbated when correspondents wrong-footed him. The day before the commission's meeting, Semmler berated the SOA secretary, Harold Hort (Duckmanton's brother-in-law as it happened), about a statement quoted in the *Australian* that attacked Darling and claimed that fifty senior officers had strongly condemned him. Semmler accused Hort of disloyalty to the chairman. A week later, Darling's letter in response to an official of the Australian Council of Salaried and Professional Associations was found to have been passed on to the two ABC staff associations (both affiliates of the council)—despite his precaution in marking the letter 'PERSONAL NOT FOR PUBLICATION'. Although the council thought that the ABC had made 'very bad' decisions about some of its members and that Darling's letter had reinforced its view, the chairman regarded as odd its discourtesy in not informing him about passing on his letter. 'The way things have happened does not encourage me to answer letters in the future in any other than a completely non-committal way.' A succession of correspondence, press editorials and leading articles then escalated the *Four Corners* wrangle into an argument about free speech. Invidious comparisons were made between the ABC and the BBC. Darling received a press clipping headed 'An open letter to Dr Darling … from a land where free speech is a way of life', authored by Peter Grose. He took issue with the chairman's claim (in a letter) that programs about a controversy should not go to air when emotions were running high (that is, *Four Corners*). A festering wound was salted further when Grose cited a counter-example from the BBC in which Michael Charlton (the ABC's interviewer when *Four Corners* first aired in 1961) had probed instant studio reactions to the chancellor of the exchequer's budget speech (on which emotions were running high) and then by reporting his own conversation with 'one of your brightest young men'. The upshot of the latter, 'doctor', Grose sneered, was that 'your repeated denials of outside interference are a joke amongst your staff'. He wondered whether the chairman's conscience was clear on free speech denial. Darling did not disagree with much that Grose had written, but he questioned whether the BBC was right to mock England's institutions, particularly when that country was 'suffering more from a lack of confidence than anything else'.[10]

But Darling had some supporters. Judge Stretton's son Hugh (University of Adelaide) was one. There was no way that the ABC interview with Rohan Rivett could be deemed in contempt of court, Stretton insisted, and Darling's critics were being unfair because 'their rosy picture of the liberties taken by the BBC' was 'very much overdrawn'. That said, 'we' still needed to achieve the 'very moderate and restrained range of debate' that the ABC's sister broadcaster allowed. The reason that so many people had been contacting Darling, Stretton explained, was because as chairman he was the one person who was both 'within the ABC, but somewhat free of it' and because Darling's 'own distinguished history of courageous public utterance encourages us, too'. The hope was that the ABC, like the universities and too few newspapers, might become a responsible vehicle for public criticism of Australian society and values. Darling and Stretton differed about the role of *Four Corners*, while agreeing that it ought to be a 'respectable political weekly'. Darling wanted the program to have the necessary freedom, except that those entrusted with freedom had to accept its inherent responsibilities. But what 'really breaks my heart', he said, was the damage done to morale: 'We start a long way behind scratch now, and it is not our fault'. He had no idea how to rebuild that morale, he told a senior staff member, while reassuring another correspondent that there was no intention to alter *Four Corners'* style or content. With another he pulled no punches: allegations of political interference in the ABC were 'absolute nonsense'. Hearkening back to Bidault, Darling said that the government had not disagreed with the commission's statement on this matter in its recent Annual Report and, in fact, the minister had since 'taken exactly the line we asked him to take'. Maybe the ABC was oversensitive to criticism, but it had to tackle problems (even if it offended sections of the community) and its readiness to do so depended on the training, professional capacity and responsibility of its staff.[11]

Shortly after the Cooke hanging, there appeared 'Headmaster in a hot seat', a feature article by Craig McGregor, who provided a detailed assessment of the chairman's public persona and Establishment pedigree. McGregor piled on the flattery with such epithets as 'extraordinary vivacity, forthrightness and sense of humour', a rare human being combining a 'fine intellect with great personal charm' and a 'truly charismatic personality who attracts others to him without effort'. The chairman's moods were said to oscillate—between buoyancy and depression—and McGregor detailed an arsenal of distinctive mannerisms: displays of frequent clapping of hands to his stomach, pipe between his teeth while talking and striding the room or 'feet planted well apart, arms akimbo, coat thrust back'. Darling was the quintessence of the 'English governing class' who, with his blend of Christianity and humanism, could 'afford to be non-conformist'. Despite his critics, McGregor continued, Darling had not been a weak ABC chairman (as he had forced the government's hand over Bidault), and he brought intellectuality and breadth of vision to a commission that was a vehicle for state and sectional pressures. As for the prime minister, Darling was 'a match for Menzies intellectually', although 'not politically'. McGregor cast Darling as a paternalistic figure—excited by the 'quality of the good young men' in the ABC, eager to 'make sure they aren't killed' and yet not allowed to go 'too far', and keen that the ABC should set the pace in public taste, although it 'shouldn't get too far in front'. In this vein, Darling was said to have asserted that the ABC should not try to be another BBC because Australians were not ready for it—although McGregor did not quote him directly and Darling may well have been alluding to the BBC satire, *That Was the Week That Was*, first telecast two years earlier, which lampooned the British political Establishment. Darling stood for impartiality, McGregor claimed, but he did not comprehend the pluralism of the ABC and society, and misunderstood producers' needs for programs to have an edge (and, therefore, abrasiveness), despite his commitment to *Four Corners* sticking its neck out. The last three years as chairman, Darling told McGregor, had been 'hell'. The chairman, this journalist concluded, was someone who was limited by 'his own completeness': a perfectly balanced individual, but in that respect a bit like a spinning top that was 'moving nowhere'.[12]

One of Darling's so-called good young men was upset and sought (and obtained) an audience with him. John Penlington was one of two officers to whom Darling had referred in a letter as publicly contradicting their senior officer, flouting instructions and acting against 'all decent practice'. It was because of their 'lack of the responsibility necessary' to conduct a program of the *Four Corners*-type that they had been returned to their previous positions. Penlington took umbrage and insisted that he had been sent to Perth to do a story on the Cooke hanging. The chairman backed off. He was pleased to have met Penlington and appreciated hearing about his difficulties in the Perth assignment. Darling still thought that he was wrong to disobey instructions and speak to the press, but he respected 'the integrity of your intentions and therefore feel that I should apologize and withdraw the two phrases "against all decent practices" and "lack of responsibility"'. Once the headmaster, however, always the headmaster:

> At the same time as I do this I hope that you may have been able to get something out of the rest of our conversation of yesterday morning, and that it may have helped you to a better understanding not only of your responsibility but of ours.

As an earnest of his willingness to make amends, Darling would write to Brand and all other recipients of his letter. Some seven months later (July 1965), headmasterly rebuke was counterbalanced by headmasterly protectiveness. When a returned serviceman complained to Hulme that while soldiers were being killed in Vietnam *Four Corners* was being used by the ABC as 'blatant Communist propaganda', and that in two programs Penlington had mouthed undiluted propaganda, Darling came out swinging. The letter, he told the postmaster-general, had libelled and defamed Penlington (and the ABC), and its additional claim about Penlington's reinstatement under pressure was 'ridiculously untrue'. Moreover, his verdict after he had viewed both programs, was that suggestions of communist propaganda were nonsense.[13]

Meanwhile, the *Four Corners* controversy refused to die. Such was the damage that Darling felt that his personal reputation had sustained, 'even for honesty', that in late November he drafted a note of resignation to Hulme with effect from 31 December. Dawes ought to replace him for the next two-and-a-half years. Despite looking forward to working with Duckmanton and Semmler, Darling said that he could 'no longer be of any help to the organization', and to continue as chairman would only make Duckmanton's task more difficult. As with Intertel, however, he did not submit his note. About a week later in the Senate election campaign, the flames of controversy were stoked once more, this time by Bill Hartley, a Victorian Labor candidate. Semmler telephoned Darling (in Canberra) to alert him to Hartley's incendiary pre-recorded election broadcast script on radio station 3LO: not only was it deemed to contravene the spirit of the conditions governing such broadcasts, but it also contained 'a mass of falsehoods', Darling noted, along with some 'very libellous statements' about the commission and himself. Worse still, the commission's hand was drawn because Hartley had given the script to the newspapers. A flurry of telephoning ensued between Semmler, Darling and Cyril Wyndham (general secretary, ALP federal executive), along with conversations between Darling, Sir Owen Dixon and Sir Dallas Brookes (both also in Canberra), and indecision about whether or not to consult Calwell and Whitlam (kept informed by the ABC throughout the *Four Corners* controversy). Then, on the cusp of Christmas 1964, Dawes was interviewed on Adelaide's Channel 7 where two *Meet the Press* journalists grilled him relentlessly on the ABC's alleged 'timidity': 'Why were Ashbolt, Pennlington [sic] and Parr [Power] dismissed from the 'Four Corners' session?' After this first question, they raked over every recent controversy (when these were introduced by Dawes)—the Cooke hanging, the RSL documentary, Russo, Senator Spooner and housing, along with Bidault, Hartley, Denis Warner and the ABC–BBC comparison.[14]

Eventually, the *Four Corners* fracas fizzled out. The timing marked a transition in the issues claiming Darling's attention. In February 1965 (by which time Duckmanton was general manager), Professor Jock Marshall (zoology and comparative physiology, Monash University) castigated the commissioners in an

Australian article as 'inept and inexperienced old wives'. Within the commission itself, an anonymously authored two-page document speculated that Darling may even have connived in its publication. This 'dastardly suggestion' by the document's author (Lowndes?) arose because in respect of possible commission membership changes, the chairman's demeanour and desire were claimed to coincide with the appearance of Marshall's article. When tackled, Darling said that he had not read it, he didn't intend reading it and that 'members of his Club thought there was no need to answer it'. The document's author regarded this refusal to engage as 'an indictment', given that Darling would normally have responded promptly to such attacks with 'dignity and determination'. A number of considerations were thought to lend weight to the author's claim. First, Darling was known to have wanted to recruit three additional commissioners of 'such status and prestige' so as to position the commission 'beyond challenge in matters of controversy, political issues, etc.', except that it had rejected this idea. Nonetheless, Darling had made the suggestion to a Senate committee and, when challenged at a commission meeting, was supposed to have responded dismissively: 'Oh, did I?' Next (the author claimed to have been told by Duckmanton), the chairman had written to congratulate Rupert Murdoch on two *Australian* articles on *Four Corners*, had then travelled from Canberra with him and had had a 'very friendly discussion' in the hope of an improved climate of relations with the ABC. At the commission's March 1965 meeting in Hobart, this commissioner had had to remind the chairman that he was merely one of a membership of seven, with no more power than any of the others, because he had tried to jump the gun on a possible extension to the ABC's Victorian premises at Ripponlea in Melbourne, following receipt in February of a favourable High Court judgement. In short, by behaving as a 'chairman apart', Darling was presuming to run his own race.[15]

There was some validity to the accusation that the chairman was keen to get cracking on the commission—understandable, perhaps, with the ABC finally delivered of Moses and a new broom in place. Ripponlea, however, was another story. This property in Elsternwick in Melbourne was built in the late 1860s by the Victorian clothing and drapery merchant, and politician Sir Frederick Sargood. It comprised a mansion, ornamental gardens and a lake. It had been reduced by subdivision from its original 27 hectares to a roughly rectangular plot of just under 6 hectares. Ripponlea was owned by Louisa Jones, who inherited it from her father in 1935. The ABC's interest dated from 1954 when it purchased a triangular wedge of about a hectare at the southern end. The commission declined an offer of an additional land parcel in 1958–59 and in 1963 the Commonwealth had (compulsorily) acquired for the ABC an additional 2 hectares (including the lake and part of the garden). Over £2 million of taxpayers' money had been expended on the site and Darling was keen for an agreement on price with Jones' family because without it plans for the ABC in Victoria were on hold: expanded television facilities and consolidation of Victorian operations in a large multistorey building. Some residents (supported by the municipality) opposed the siting of the building frontage in an area defined for planning purposes as open space. While the Jones family could not sell the property for housing, the municipality was unlikely to take over Ripponlea as a park and the National Trust lacked the necessary finance. Moreover, an ABC access road had already been approved by the planning authority (the Melbourne Metropolitan Board of Works). In 1965 Darling counted fourteen groups or individuals 'to be got on side before a satisfactory solution is reached'. After two High Court appeal hearings, Darling assured the prime minister (Holt), that he wanted a resolution 'without any more spilling of blood'. He aimed to fulfil the ABC's charter obligations while keeping those 'beautiful gardens intact'. Jones (who lived at Ripponlea) and her family resisted acquisition. She died in 1972 and bequeathed Ripponlea to the National Trust (acquired in 1974) and the Commonwealth transferred its holding to the Trust. Darling's efforts at a resolution, according to the Trust's chairman (Rodney Davidson), had helped to preserve the estate.[16]

Allegations about the chairman's machinations regarding the commission were correct. Its quality and composition ranked in importance (for him) with the ABC's independence, and were tied in with it. The Senate inquiry referred to by his anonymous critic was the Committee on the Encouragement of Australian Productions for Television (the Vincent committee, chaired by Senator Victor Vincent). Prior to the publication of Marshall's article, the commission discussed the committee's recommendations (November 1964). Its view (dispatched to Hulme the following February) was unequivocal about Vincent's recommended increase in commissioners with the additional three being 'representative of the cultural life of Australia': men or women of 'the highest reputation and experience in this field'. The claim that this composition would assist in 'matters of political and public controversy on topical issues' was a 'naive belief'; whatever their personal reputations such people would still be part of a collective entity (the commission) and would be viewed in that way. Moreover:

> In the Australian community, it is unjustifiable optimism to hope that there are any three men or women who, because of their status, would be accepted without question in everything they did on the Australian Broadcasting Commission.

In short, if the Vincent committee's aim was to superimpose on the commission a cultural coterie of three wise men (or women) then the commission's reaction killed it.[17]

Despite this official commission position, Darling wanted a membership model in which the ABC would not be hostage to federation-related pressures, an idea that he pursued vigorously from mid-1965. If the aim was to retain 'the Reithian [after the first director of the BBC] concept of independence', he wrote, then the two key questions were: was a 'system of control suitable for a monopolistic Radio system in the twenties' still fit for purpose (that is, for a complex national broadcasting system)? If yes, then what was the composition of its governing body to be? If Reith was correct that mass communications were so powerful that they should not become the political instruments of a government, then the commission's composition and the quality of its chairman were vital. Commissioners could not be:

> a group of ordinary men or women of good will representative only of the way ordinary men and women may be expected to think. True that they must not be so academically remote from the common man that they fail to understand him altogether, but in addition to this they need to be capable of understanding the implications of their decisions in the building of the nation of the future, and they must have critical judgment political and aesthetic as well.

Such lofty meritocratic elitism required commissioners to be 'representative of the whole spectrum of national life' and not creatures of particular interests. The problem with the current membership of seven was that the filling of vacancies evoked 'state partisanship' and a belief that in one's own state the commissioner was a 'state commissioner', along with the temptation to interfere in ABC management at that level. The interests of 'good policy', however, dictated the need for compromises between the demands of states and, above all, responsibility for the task necessitated 'freedom to choose the best people, wherever they are to be found'. Factors influencing the attraction of such people included emoluments (commissioners were paid £500 annually, the vice-chairman £750 and the chairman £2000—with the first two shortly to be increased by £250 and the chairman by £500), travel time and the burden of criticism of the ABC borne by the chairman, who possessed 'no specific powers', although possibly influence, and whose tenure should be longer than the others (ideally, two five-year terms). In essence, then, appointees required common sense, the 'capacity for political, moral and artistic judgment' and a realisation of the role that the national broadcaster played in 'the development of the nation's thinking'. And who did Darling think fitted the bill as commissioners? Why, none other than (men of) the likes of Zelman Cowen, A.G.L. Shaw and Lloyd Ross (and later Alec Ramsay—general manager, South Australian Housing Trust), but not retiring vice-chancellors such as Paton and Robert (later Sir Robert) Madgwick (five years Darling's junior) who were 'too old'.[18]

But wasn't the fact that the ABC operated in a democracy at odds with his model of collective leadership by cultural experts? In preparation for a discussion with Menzies in 1965, Darling thought that the commissioners should be 'representative of the community': they had to 'understand its tastes rather than impose its own upon them', they could not have axes to grind, and their interests and contacts needed to be spread over a wide field. He also noted (patronisingly) the political desirability of the commission having 'at least one member with Labour [sic] sympathies' and religiously 'at least one Roman Catholic'—confirmation, if one needed it, of Craig McGregor's Establishment typecasting of him. Above everything, however, the commission had to comprise people capable of understanding 'the philosophy of Broadcasting', its potential in 'the creating of a nation' and, therefore, political, religious and aesthetic 'common sense'. As for the chairman's autonomy, in his own case Darling reflected some years later— appointed as he was, like his successor Madgwick, from outside the commission, unlike Boyer who had come from within—that 'it was always made abundantly clear to me' that 'I was only the Chairman' and could speak only 'on behalf of the Commission'. This was reasonable on matters of genuine political significance, he believed, and in between commission meetings he had tried to keep his fellow commissioners informed and to obtain their comments before issuing public statements. One thing led to another. To govern the ABC by a commission that was responsible to Parliament was to leave the minister hanging fire: exposed through parliamentary questioning and reliant on the chairman—an intolerable situation in which both were 'poised between the Scylla of alleged government interference and the Charybdis of irresponsibility', and which demanded great forbearance by the minister and integrity by the chairman. If the structure of the relationship was to work, then it depended on the character of the individuals concerned and the 'existence of natural confidence between them'.[19]

But the minister's dependence on the chairman for advice was difficult if the latter was little more than a mere commission mouthpiece, particularly when consulted about commission appointments and reappointments. Political sensitivity, therefore, was an understandable requirement of a chairman. Other key ingredients, Darling thought, included intellectual integrity, moral honesty and mental capacity. In addition, he (Darling did not consider the possibility of a woman holding the role) needed to be interested in the performing arts, and capable of understanding the educational function of broadcasting and television. And because the media world in which the chairman moved was a tough one, it called for the 'qualities required in a man of affairs'. Finally, a chairman needed to be articulate, and known to and trusted by ABC staff. Lord Reith had sought wisdom in a chairman rather than enthusiasm, and certainly had not wanted someone who would 'mould the organisation to his own heart's desire' and he had been right, Darling believed. The chairman was the 'front man' of the ABC, Darling told Judy La Marsh (Secretary of State for Canada, who visited Melbourne in mid-1966), and the only alternative to the current arrangement would be to extend the chairman's tenure (to up to seven years) to give him greater security, and to increase his financial compensation. In his memorandum to her (and forwarded to Hulme) he said that while it was undesirable to make the position so attractive that the chairmanship could be used as a reward for political services, it was equally undesirable that it should be 'so large' an office as to affect the incumbent's integrity. The rewards had to be such as to attract a man of about fifty-five and to hold him for up to two seven-year periods, either as part-time or partly remunerated. In that way, an 'enlightened businessman of

status', a vice-chancellor or a lawyer might be selected. 'It is not good enough to
have to wait for an older man and to have him only for a short period.'[20]

So much for Darling's prototypical Reithian chairman, but what about the
Reithian enterprise itself and its civilizing mission? (In 1962, Darling had confided
to Reith that there were 'countless ways' in which he drew on his experience and
principles to do his job 'better than I otherwise would have been capable'.) The
sheer scale of the ABC, as Darling said (in a 1966 address), was evident in some
key statistics: 5000 staff (an increase of 3200 alone during a decade of television),
an annual operating budget of $34 million—after the February 1966 transition
to decimal currency—83,000 news bulletins annually (including 16,000
transmitted in seven languages by Radio Australia), 700 annual public concerts,
support of six symphony orchestras and a choir, televised screening of the works
of forty-six Australian playwrights, more than 1200 kilometres of 16 mm film
for twenty-eight films; direct broadcast instruction programs to 3000 schools,
and overseas staff and offices in eight major cities around the world. Add to
all of that in-house production facilities and engineering training and, by any
measure, this public instrumentality was a very big beast. What was more, all
of this activity was undertaken within significant financial constraints and its
employment of personnel was subject to public service rules. While authorised
to acquire property, for instance, the ABC could not be revenue-producing;
neither could it borrow money nor carry over unspent monies. And yet for all the
publicity generated by its political and public affairs, Darling emphasised, this
area constituted a mere 1 per cent of the entirety. Unlike the BBC, the ABC was
not a broadcasting monopoly. Financially dependent on Parliament, the ABC
was in the unique position of (in effect) biting the hand that fed it: 'it is hard for
a Government to have its policies criticized over what is regarded as the national
station'. Equally, if it was not the ABC's function to support that government,
then the dilemma of its independence boiled down to this question: to what
extent could principles be identified on which 'the vast majority of the nation'
agreed and that it would be 'improper to allow to be attacked' on a national
system, and what were the limits of such principles?[21]

Parliamentary democracy may have been one such principle, and the ideals
of a Christian society and the monarchy were two others, except that if these were
to be immune, where did that leave minorities such as communists, rationalists
and republicans, and their right to be heard? Was this democracy 'as we understand it' and who was to decide? Darling confessed that he didn't know, even
though the commission and ABC officers were charged with this responsibility,
and could only exercise it 'empirically as each occasion arises'. But what about
treason: surely a national organisation should not lend itself to that? Yet, there was
another but: what counted as a treasonable practice? Was it treason, for example,
to oppose a war in which a country's troops were involved? If it was, then 'the
Opposition would be in gaol', and so where did 'this' begin and end? Such were
the challenges of independence, the flipside of which was responsibility. There

were times when the exercise of responsibility required 'control' by the commission and senior officers over what might be said. The idea that such intervention amounted to censorship—any more than the actions of a newspaper editor in screening newsprint content so as to avoid transgressions against libel or obscenity laws counted as censorship—was 'nonsense'. Such responsibility was about integrity of purpose, and intellectual capacity and competence in the weighing up of evidence. He despaired, therefore, of complaints in his daily mail from the defenders of sundry sacred cows who disliked any criticism of their democracy, and departure from its standards and beliefs. If he at his age—'deeply embedded as I am in the Establishment', and grounded in his British past and Christian upbringing—felt this way, then what must it be like for young and enthusiastic people who joined the ABC, and wanted to better enlighten and reform society? While the ABC should not be a vehicle for its employees' causes and crusades, at the same time it was not a means solely for the expression of orthodoxy and the notion that the majority was always right. The ABC's duty was to stimulate thought, allow minority views to be heard and to 'admit the existence' of diverse community opinion. The questions, then, of what was true and of good report, and who should decide, were up to the 'collective wisdom of the Commission'. The dilemma was that such collective wisdom 'may tend towards conservatism' in defining what counted as adequate and comprehensive, and 'suitable and in the interests of the community'. Oh, what a heavy charge for seven ordinary men and women: 'Who then can be saved?'[22]

In practice, if it were to elevate taste effectively, then the ABC's television programming had to instil the habit of watching, which could be done only by 'making some concessions at certain times'. For commercial sector colleagues, by contrast, questions about taste were cut and dried: unlike commission staff, their existence depended on popularity and commercial outlets had no choice but to pursue it. Moreover, there was nothing 'disreputable' for those who sold time in order to give the public what it wanted—however oddly this imperative may have sat with the 'high principles' expressed during the ABCB licence hearings. With the ABC's revenue drawn from all Australians, public money had to be expended in the public interest, although this did not necessarily mean that the ABC should exit the light entertainment field. Rather, the ABC could show 'how well such programmes can be done and without giving any just cause for offence'. Over the years through its radio service and contribution to 'good music' it had built up a rather 'select and small clientele of its own', although there were still many people who rarely listened to or looked at the ABC's programs. Towards the conclusion of his address, he returned to the matter of overriding principles. In a passage that may have been difficult for him to articulate publicly, realism was allowed to triumph over sentiment. Were Christian ethics to be the ABC's standard? Even assuming that one could be sure about such ethics anymore in 'a shifting world', Darling doubted whether (beyond its voice being heard in a 'largely secular' world) Christianity could be proclaimed much further as it was a creed 'which is no longer universally accepted'. Not even democratic principles, representative government and parliamentary systems were 'sacrosanct'. In a liberal democracy there was 'no body of opinion' that a national organisation 'should unequivocally support, except perhaps the doctrine that no doctrine is so sacrosanct that it must never be questioned'—words that suggested (despite Craig McGregor's opinion) that Darling had come to terms with social pluralism. That said, ordinary people still wanted decency and standards that made life worth living. Portrayals of needless infliction of cruelty, habituation to criminality and sexual perversions, for example, he did not see as conducive to a healthy society, healthy homes and families—and 'the family' was a 'nearly absolute good and should not be undermined'. At the end of the day his only guideposts were intellectual honesty and good taste (itself largely a 'matter of manners'). If the gentleman, that 'old-fashioned and despised type', could be described as a man who was 'never unintentionally offensive', then the same had to be true of programs.[23]

The *Four Corners* controversy and the accompanying anguish for the chairman eased in early 1965. Soon, however, Darling was forced to defend his antipodean Reithianism again (out of the public gaze) in relation to Radio Australia's role in Papua and New Guinea (PNG—then an Australian-administered territory). Darling was aware when he was appointed that Radio Australia was the ABC's pride and joy. His early conversations with Hasluck (then Minister for Territories) had got off on the right foot, but in late 1962 the relationship soured. When Hasluck was invited by Darling to attend the opening of a radio station in Rabaul, not only did he decline but he alleged also that there was a 'good deal of disappointment both on my own part and on the part of many people working in PNG at the failure to make better use of the wireless set as an instrument for advancement'. Two years passed before their next communication. Mindful of funding pressures, Darling informed Hulme (in March 1965) of a significant shift in the ABC's PNG programming to meet the needs of indigenous peoples with broadcasts in Pidgin, Motu, Tolai and simple English. As the PNG administration planned to establish its own radio transmission (twenty-two stations), the provision of two separate 'broadcasting complexes' called for a reconsideration of responsibilities and expenditure.[24]

In response to the views of Hasluck (who became Minister for External Affairs in April 1964) about the control of Radio Australia, the commission said that if the government wanted it to be its policy arm—or, in Darling's words, an 'instrument of propaganda in the furtherance of Australia's interests among its neighbours'—then responsibility for it ought to be vested in another authority. But such a move would be unwise, Darling cautioned, as there was fifteen years' solid evidence of Radio Australia's effectiveness and liaison with the Department of External Affairs had been mutually satisfactory. There would be reputational damage for Radio Australia in this shift of control as it was the most popular and successful overseas service, and it was known regionally for freedom from government interference. There were discussions between the ABC and External Affairs in 1965 about strengthened liaison between the department and Radio Australia but, just before Christmas, Hasluck returned from Asia and put a spanner in the works when forwarding to Hulme the results of his inquiries into the effectiveness of Radio Australia broadcasts. He had sought impromptu answers to three questions from a Bangkok conference of thirteen Australian ambassadors stationed in Asian cities: Was the Radio Australia reception 'good'? Was the listening audience large or small? What was the quality of the news broadcasts and news commentaries? Hulme passed the results to Darling who (after consulting Duckmanton) responded in early 1966. The dual radio broadcasting situation in PNG required clarification and he urged Hulme to 'let sleeping dogs lie' in respect of Radio Australia. Hasluck was wrong to want Radio Australia to become a propaganda service, he said, and if it did there would be significant repercussions in Parliament and the press. He also systematically refuted Hasluck's accusations and the ambassadors' claims. First, their answers were imprecise. Second, they were the wrong people to ask (as other mission officers were better informed). Third (and this was the clincher), for nearly all the thirteen diplomatic postings there were 'many thousands' of letters received by Radio Australia's Melbourne headquarters and overseas officers, mailed by people for whom the cost of an air stamp was a sacrifice (equivalent in price to that of a meal). These letters commended programs or requested program guides. Darling's sting in the tail was that Radio Australia's impact was out of all proportion to 'the comparatively small expenditure it entails'.[25]

These exchanges occurred during a period in which Darling compiled a diary (for about a month from 1 January 1966 and then a year later). Fortuitously, the timing coincided with the mounting speculation about Menzies' retirement and a pause in Darling's exchanges with Hasluck. On 16 January, Darling drove to Canberra for a Citizenship Convention. He stayed in the same hotel as a number of the politicians and he recorded the febrile atmosphere. Among those who addressed the convention, Darling noted that Casey's was a 'good' speech, Holt's 'not so good' and that while Whitlam's attack on the White Australia Policy was 'courageous', 'right and well-timed', he found him 'hard to admire wholeheartedly'. At a Parliament House garden party, he observed parliamentarians in 'significant huddles'. On the morning of the Liberal Party leadership ballot (20 January), he met with Hulme, who was 'a bit glum over his [ministerial] prospects'. No wonder, Darling noted, as his ambitions had nosedived:

Saw P.M. arrive, Hulme very strong against McMahon. Result of voting however Holt unopposed. McMahon defeated Hasluck [for deputy leader of the Liberal Party] by small margin. This probably means Hulme not promoted. Hence his gloom later on. Rang up Tal [Duckmanton] to report.

Later that same day he spotted Menzies, who beckoned him over to his Bentley. He commiserated with the former prime minister and 'pressed him to become Chancellor of [Melbourne] University'. (The following month, Menzies replied: 'You know my decision about the University—Yes'.) Later, he also saw Holt and congratulated him on becoming prime minister and the next morning at breakfast he did likewise with McMahon (although he 'felt rather a cad'). On Australia Day, the new Cabinet was announced. With ministerial appointments settled, Hasluck finally responded to Darling's defence of Radio Australia. Determined to have the last word, he told Hulme that the chairman's self-justification was 'a pity'. The ambassadors had spoken honestly and in good faith. As for the numbers game, the ambassadors' reports had been confirmed by ABC listeners' mail. About 224,000 cards and letters had arrived in 1965, nearly 211,000 from Indonesia. The remainder were from a population of 800 million (excluding the People's Republic of China), or the annual equivalent of about 200 cards and letters from the entire Australian population. Conclusion? 'The clear fact' was this, said Hasluck: the Indonesian Radio Australia audience was very large but small elsewhere in Asia. It was May 1966 before this numerical stand-off was broken when Duckmanton contacted Darling and quoted a letter from Tony Eggleton, the new prime minister's press secretary. 'The Prime Minister was very impressed with Radio Australia's standing in the Asian countries we visited and we were regular listeners to the R.A. news bulletins.' 'Ha Ha! So sucks to Mr. Hasluck!', said Darling's marginalia: game, set and match to the chairman (although despite commission pressure, competition and overlap between the two PNG-based radio services persisted).[26]

Compared to Radio Australia, the ABC's visual medium was not, as Darling said to Hulme, the 'brightest jewel in your crown'. The advent of educational television might have given it some momentary lustre, except that it became ensnared in inter–broadcasting agency politics and Commonwealth–state relations. While overseas in 1962, Darling had extensively investigated the educational use of television and his later mention of its potential had prompted a senator to ask the minister representing the postmaster-general whether the ABC would establish a dedicated educational television channel. When contacted by Davidson, Darling hesitated initially: wasn't the decision a matter for the ABCB? Further, if the proposed fifth television channel for Sydney and Melbourne was for educational television, would the ABC operate it in consultation with educational bodies, or would a committee of the latter operate it (and make the dual system tripartite)? Darling put the commission on the front foot by early 1963 when he argued that, with its skilled staff and facilities, the ABC ought to operate such a service, even though the ABCB recommended on channel allocations. Two pilot studies (in cooperation with the state education departments and other authorities) were planned for 1964: televised instruction in secondary school science and mathematics; and school–university bridging courses to assist with tertiary readiness. Direct televised instruction, he told Hulme, could make up for a shortage of qualified science and mathematics teachers, while the ABC's existing telecasts to schools would aid classroom teachers. Likewise, telecasts might assist students inadequately prepared for tertiary education. As part of this envisaged partnership arrangement, the education authorities would supply the expert teachers and student audiences, and the ABC the technical expertise. Some additional rehearsal and production costs were anticipated, along with extra staff required for production work, but the overall cost implications would be low, he reassured Hulme, particularly in comparison with the resulting value for the community.[27]

Delay in resolving the future of educational television resulted from the establishment of the Advisory Committee on Educational Television Services, chaired by W.J. (Jock) Weeden (now director, Commonwealth Office of Education), whom Darling knew from his Universities Commission work. The advisory committee had been appointed by the ABCB in January 1964 and reported thirteen months later. Even though the board did not believe that the ABC should assume responsibility for educational television, the commission was already effectively undertaking pilot educational television work (as the Weeden committee pointed out): there had been weekday kindergarten programs in Sydney and Melbourne since 1957, experimental programs for secondary schools since 1958, primary school programs since 1960 and two evening telecasts per week of the University of the Air, which was planned for extension in 1965 by transmission of the teaching of Asian languages in a Sunday morning timeslot. The Weeden committee saw no role for the ABC in instructional programming. It wanted a new educational broadcasting authority and a VHF channel for instructional television, an outcome to which Darling was resigned.[28]

To cover his back politically, Hulme requested Osborne, Darling and Frank O'Grady (director general, Posts & Telegraphs) in September 1965 to advise him on the report's implications. Having been invited (in effect) to scuttle the report, the three vested interests duly did so. They fuelled doubts about a number of issues that lacked clarity. In the absence of a plan for allocating frequencies, capitulation to pressures to obtain frequencies to experiment with educational television had to be avoided. It was also unclear whether the responsibility for educational television was state or federal: the Post Office would provide transmission facilities but a state-level body might choose to operate independently. It was uncertain whether the integration of instructional television and education was best achieved by a new authority or at state level. The three men were divided over the ABC's role and its relationship to a new authority, particularly because of the educational technology resource burden and disruption to be shouldered by the ABC while the new authority was scaling up, and then the ABC's subsequent withdrawal when it commenced. The commission, Darling told Osborne, was 'to say the least of it, divided' over whether it had a role in educational television and personally 'I do not really know what I think'. At best he was half-hearted, while believing that the ABC could do what Weeden's committee wanted better, more cheaply and with 'less constitutional and administrative muddle' than a new body.

The long-run solution, he told Arthur Calwell, might be to open up the UHF band to educational authorities. The other potential virtue of this educational television experiment (but which no-one else seemed to be interested in), he told the leader of the Opposition, was its application by Australia as a way of lending its expertise to meet a rapid need for education among emerging South-East Asian nations.[29]

The three wise men's report went to Hulme in November 1965. Early in the following February Darling's diary noted that educational television was 'still in the air because the government cannot make up its mind'. In March, Cabinet considered the two reports. Gorton (Minister in charge of Commonwealth Activities in Education) recommended that the government should neither reserve nor allocate the remaining VHF channel (pending further study); not commit to Weeden's estimated combined capital and operating costs for the new authority (of $17.5 million), but fund the capital cost of one studio (if, after consultation with the states, this was a high priority); and provide the recurrent costs of such a studio, with the states to fund production costs and establish the new authority if there was a demand for it. Hulme released the Weeden committee report to the House of Representatives in May 1966. He told the House that the government acknowledged the significance of educational television, but that it was a state responsibility. The Commonwealth would consult the states, offer additional resources if requested and assist in the 'provision of coordinated activities', such as facilities for the production and transmission of instructional materials. The ABC could continue to provide instructional-type programs in consultation with the states, with existing provision representing a significant educational investment by the Commonwealth. With that, Hulme (and Gorton) had effectively kicked the topic into the long grass. Small wonder, then, that educational television enthusiasts were outraged, and felt that the government had backed away in a 'patently dishonest' manner and by resorting to reasoning that insulted one's intelligence—the Weeden report had been supported in principle by the government, but wholly rejected by it in practice.[30]

The timing of the death throes and obsequies of the Weeden committee coincided with yet another round of public affairs controversy that simmered throughout 1966. Again the key figures were Russo and Ashbolt. A telecast interview with President Ho Chi Minh (Democratic Republic of Vietnam) in early 1966 was an entrée to the main event. 'Trouble brewing', Darling noted cryptically on 4 January, after being informed of developments by Duckmanton: 'Kent Hughes [Liberal MHR, Chisholm] and others on the warpath'. The ABC was correct in telecasting the program Darling thought and, while preparing himself to face the commission, he also noted that of the many people to whom he had mentioned the matter he had not found 'anyone who disapproves'. Did this mean that the government was 'out of touch or merely being illiberal?', he wondered. 'Or perhaps that it knows more!' The pity of it all was that politicians mostly judged the ABC 'on minuscular bricks and not on its total effort'. There was no negative reaction on the commission. Cabinet had objected to the interview, but Dawes flicked this criticism away. Had Cabinet been consistent, it would have demanded prior to this program, for example, that 'we never show anything on television relating to [the President of Indonesia] Soekarno or his Cabinet'. In early February the commission viewed the film. It was unanimous that there was nothing in it to support critics' objections (such as Kent Hughes' view that the ABC was siding with the enemy in the Vietnam War) and that it had not breached its obligation to act in the public interest. The commission endorsed the programming actions of ABC officers.[31]

In this same month, an ABC radio listener had contacted J.M. (Malcolm) Fraser (Minister for the Army) to object to 'destructive and vicious propaganda' voiced by Russo on the *Australia Looks at the World* program, as calculated to undermine national morale while young men were sacrificing their lives in Vietnam. Fraser wrote to Hulme, Hulme wrote to the chairman, and Duckmanton asked Darling to confirm that invitees with views differing markedly from government policy should continue to commentate. Duckmanton was prompted by a recent escalation in Australia's Vietnam commitment and the sending of national servicemen (conscripts) to fight in a war in which a formal declaration had not been made. The effect of this latter point, said Duckmanton, was that the ABC was reporting events for which none of the usual wartime censorship machinery was in place. Should speakers with views different from the government be invited to the microphone, therefore, and if the answer was yes, then how was the ABC to respond to criticism? Darling's view (expounded the year before to Wally Hamilton) was that the community was best served by a broad range of comments. (Try to avoid extremists on either side, he had advised Hamilton, and have commentators eschew emotional language and expressions of opinion calculated to foment animosity between different sections of the community.) Because the commission's attitude on controversial matters was 'completely impartial' it was wrong to tell commentators what they should say, in which case its role was to ensure 'overall, a fair balance of opinion'. Russo, he said, was one of more than thirty regular speakers and other speakers' views differed from his. Furthermore, his experience of South-East Asia was extensive and, in any case, his comments had been balanced a week later by airing those of the US Vice President Hubert Humphrey, who defended the sending of troops to Vietnam. Darling had taken the exact same line with another Liberal backbencher, W.C. Wentworth: the country was 'deeply divided' about the Vietnam War and Australia's participation in it, and the commission's responsibility was to those who believed in its participation and those who did not. Probably, the ABC gave 'much more voice to the former' and yet 'you and your friends complain about any expression on the other side'. Only the government could declare what was admissible or inadmissible in respect of public utterance and, no matter what his personal opinions might have been about the war, 'I certainly will not', he affirmed. Also at issue, however, was not merely what was said (or not said), but the ways in which things were said—or not said: one frustrated correspondent pointed out how technical programming expertise could be used to communicate a viewpoint, but without that viewpoint ever being expressed verbally.[32]

End of round one. Round two commenced almost simultaneously with a speech by Ashbolt on 3 March 1966 to the Sydney University Socialist Club, in which he accused the ABC of being run by a network of old boys. External speakers and controversy (in particular, Vietnam) were one thing, but the ABC's own employees, especially if they had an emerging public profile and influence, were a different matter. Aged in his early forties, and having spent three years for the ABC in the USA until 1961, Ashbolt was a controversialist and a rising journalistic star. By the early 1970s, according to the ABC's historian, he was assembling about him a 'kindergarten' of young, highly intelligent and creative program-makers whom he fostered and protected. For the time being, he flexed his wings and, throughout 1966–67, Darling, the commission and the general manager struggled to get his measure. Darling was under no illusions about what he was dealing with. In early 1967 he discussed with Duckmanton the UK Independent Television Authority's guidelines for the editing of interviews, which he said did not cover cases of producers with preconceived ideas of what they wanted programs to say, as 'Ashbolt did in the R.S.L. programme, and … is still very frequently done'. And why, he asked, when reflecting shortly afterwards to Francis James on his battles to instil a sense of responsibility among ABC staff, 'would Ashbolt in the literary field put on 6 Communists out of 10 into a programme?' Ashbolt and the chairman were located nearly 1000 kilometres apart in separate cities. Nevertheless, Darling tried (with some success) to engage with him personally. Following publication in the *Australian* of Ashbolt's article on the churches, for example, Darling said, in September 1966, 'I agree with you, as would most Christians who are concerned seriously', and he would be happy to talk with him when convenient. Was Ashbolt aware that there were 'explosive things' occurring among theologians and the Christian laity, to which the Australian Frontier Commission (of which he was the chairman) was 'striving to give expression in this country'? Ashbolt (who said in reply that his wife was working to encourage wider lay participation in the Catholic Church) did not think that he was all that far away from Darling's viewpoint, 'except, of course, that I don't accept Christ in the way that Christians do'.[33]

Ashbolt was reported to have said (as SOA president) that there was no direct censorship of ABC programming. Rather, through rules learnt and attitudes acquired, one was 'supposed to know' what to put to air and what not to. In any case, a politician objecting to the airing of a program was always only a telephone call away from having something done about it. While in his own case (his earlier RSL report) it could not be claimed that the prime minister had picked up the phone, there were 'forces at work'. As an ABC employee, therefore, one learnt to be discreet (but this was a mask for fear) at the risk of being labelled 'immature'. As for his claim about old boys, Duckmanton asked Ashbolt two questions:

had he in fact made the statements attributed to him (reported in the *Australian*); second, had he sought permission from his senior officers to address the meeting? To the first question Ashbolt said that in his address (on the topic of free speech) he had answered an audience question 'rather flippantly', and that he had complained in a letter to the *Australian*'s editor (published on 9 March) because the news item focused on a mere 2 minutes out of a total of 75–90 minutes. Dissatisfied as he was with the text of this letter, Duckmanton pressed Ashbolt again. The first question, Ashbolt replied, had been dealt with adequately in his letter and, as to the second, as SOA president he had not seen any need to obtain prior permission to speak. Duckmanton let the second answer pass, but tackled him further on the first—in the knowledge that the *Australian* report had prompted a parliamentary question (to Hulme) that demanded Ashbolt name the politicians who used the alleged network or publicly retract his claim. Here the general manager was in two minds. Charge Ashbolt with misconduct and he was likely to go to the Disciplinary Appeals Board, with the risk of 'considerable publicity' for the ABC and a possible upholding of his appeal—an untenable outcome. Duckmanton's own personal view was that, at the same time that he was a 'difficult person to understand', Ashbolt was also an able man who would 'very much wish to be made a martyr'. The general manager relieved Ashbolt from involvement in controversial programs and current affairs, and would speak to him about embarrassment to the ABC and the risk of his loyalty becoming 'seriously open to question', although he was not overly hopeful of the outcome.[34]

Despite Darling's defence of impartiality in respect of Vietnam, the ABC continued to be attacked for alleged leftist thinking. Try as Darling may, his response to such criticism—as in the case of J.F. Dredge (general secretary, Country Party, New South Wales)—fell on deaf ears or was met with further accusations of bias and imbalance. Late in 1966, Ashbolt created still more headaches for the commission during the federal election campaign. In the wake of the Ho Chi Minh interview, the ABC became self-absorbed about its management of controversy. In August, the commission revisited the Talks directive. Apprehensive about some clauses in the directive's annex as open to 'misinterpretation and distortion, especially if taken out of context', Darling was concerned to restrict its circulation (three pages of guidance). Then, in September, Carmichael tried to revisit the removal (two years earlier) of *Four Corners* from Talks. Next, in November (without Darling's or the commission's knowledge), *Four Corners* was suspended during the election campaign. The commission thought that this decision was 'an error of judgement'. Finally, to cap it all, while Carmichael was on a fortnight's leave, Ashbolt was removed as acting director of Talks. When this information was leaked to the press, senior management and the commission were again wrong-footed. Telegrams and letters of protest were directed to Darling and the SOA sought a meeting. Duckmanton said that the reason he and Semmler took action against Ashbolt was because of potential conflict between his program responsibilities and his decision to speak publicly in favour of certain election candidates (which he was not precluded from doing). Ashbolt responded by foreshadowing industrial action. The SOA asserted that his removal portended a possible loss of civil liberties and a threat to individual rights. The general manager and deputy general manager quizzed all SOA members (individually) about the leak. All denied responsibility. The SOA regarded this managerial inquisition as 'intimidating', which Duckmanton rejected, and on 1 December Duckmanton met with the SOA executive as a whole. He said that he trusted Ashbolt but, Ashbolt having committed himself publicly to certain causes, people would have difficulty accepting the ABC's claim to impartiality were he to have continued as acting director. The ABC's difficulties in managing its creative talent were expressed by a correspondent who wondered whether 'to have campaigned for orthodoxy would have limited Mr. Ashbolt's usefulness to the A.B.C.' The merit of the point was obvious to Darling who impressed upon Duckmanton the need for a 'reasoned answer', except that he wasn't going to draft it, 'for fear of giving too much away as is my habit'.[35]

In early December, barely a week after the election (in which the ALP was routed), Ashbolt gave another address ('National broadcasting as a profession'), this time to the staff association of the University of New South Wales. Events took yet another turn, because Ashbolt could not resist mentioning (albeit indirectly) his own recent predicament and the alarm generated in the ABC by the very idea that 'somebody' with declared political beliefs (those of the 'perfectly respectable Opposition party') should act as director of Talks, even though that very same somebody had carried out these duties many times before. The main target of his address, however, was the deadening effect (in the SOA's view) of the Public Service Board in depressing professional broadcasting standards: because the board's approval of staffing-related matters brought the ABC 'too much under the shadow of the Government of the day'. Although forced to deal with it in industrial matters, the SOA refused to recognise the board as a respondent in this area. In regard to the determination of professional standards, the risk was that the board might force senior management to impose a philosophy on staff that was antithetical to the inherently creative nature of broadcasting. It was a moot point, said Darling, whether or not by virtue of his office of president of the SOA Ashbolt was immune from the staff rule that prohibited officers from public comment on the ABC, without prior permission. While he thought that Ashbolt was permitted to speak publicly about industrial matters, as the rule currently stood he was in breach. What was the appropriate disciplinary action and what would be the effect of this action? Possibly the extraction of an 'unequivocal promise' not to break it in future (on pain of a charge and dismissal) might suffice, except that Darling doubted the 'ultimate wisdom' of the rule if it militated against the building of professional responsibility among senior officers. Moreover, if they were to be a profession, shouldn't officers contribute to public discussion on professional matters? And, finally, if they were not the appropriate group to influence public opinion on broadcasting philosophy and policy 'with whom does the right lie?' Eventually, after being reminded by the general manager that he was bound by the declaration of secrecy and the staff rule, Ashbolt agreed (following publicity given to yet another speech, in March 1967, this time calling for peace in Vietnam) to advise Duckmanton in advance of his future speaking intentions, whether or not about ABC activities. What Ashbolt did not see, said the general manager, was that he was a 'headline' figure who, solely by virtue of his ABC position, was 'news'. Again he moved Ashbolt sideways, this time to head up Special Projects.[36]

The final issue involving Darling as chairman was the ABC's relationship with the (then still-to-be-completed) Sydney Opera House. A change in the government (from Labor to Coalition) after the New South Wales elections of May 1965 dramatically altered the Opera House's fortunes. Following differences with the new government headed by the premier, R.W. Askin—mainly over the refusal of the Minister for Public Works, Davis Hughes, to pay his fees—the award-winning Danish architect Jørn Utzon resigned in February 1966. At about that time, while modifications to the interior design were being made by a replacement team of architects, ABC officers became aware of problems created by the proposed new layout. The ABC was committed to the Opera House as the permanent home for its Sydney Symphony Orchestra (SSO)—rather than its current headquarters, the Sydney Town Hall (where it paid no rental)—and to its use for orchestral concerts, recitals, rehearsals, recording and studio broadcasts. Faced with likely steep hiring charges, however, the ABC's commitment was thrown into doubt, with the knock-on effect, now that the intentions of the ABC (as the principal user of the Opera House) were on hold, of a delay in the building's completion. An added difficulty for the ABC was inadequate seating in catering for its nearly 9900 Sydney concert subscribers (plus waiting list), as the seating in the Opera House main hall was unlikely to be larger than that of the Town Hall (2200), whereas the ABC had hoped (as per the original specifications for the Opera House Design Competition) for 3000–3500 (and with symphony concerts given the highest priority). There were also uncertainties about acoustics and the lack of a permanent organ in the main hall. Finally, the possibility of providing choral concerts with an orchestra had also taken a hit, and problems with external noise were thought likely to inhibit direct broadcasts of concerts (a legal requirement of the ABC whenever it charged admission). All things considered, Askin was informed by Duckmanton—who was representing the ABC—that he could see 'little advantage' in the broadcaster relocating its concert venue. Negotiations continued throughout 1966, with the number of interests to be accommodated or conciliated being fewer than at Ripponlea although weightier. These included, in addition to the state government and the commission, the New South Wales Department of Public Works, the Opera House Trust, the Australian Elizabethan Theatre Trust, the architects, the SSO, SSO subscribers and (potentially) the Musicians' Union. It was not until January 1967 that Darling intervened more directly, particularly in discussions with

Dr H.C. (Nugget) Coombs, the current chairman of the Australian Elizabethan Theatre Trust (of which Darling was a vice-president).[37]

Coombs held out a compromise. Instead of establishing its own orchestra, the Australian Elizabethan Theatre Trust would financially underwrite the creation of an ABC studio orchestra separate from the SSO. This would enable the latter to meet its subscription series demands (and increase these from five to six), relieve it of Opera House work and facilitate the reduction in the main hall seating. The proviso was that ABC make available its symphony orchestras in all states for the Elizabethan Theatre Trust's opera and ballet seasons. Darling replied that this was unacceptable. For a start, additional subscription concerts, and increased opera and ballet work for the Elizabethan Theatre Trust would increase the SSO's overall workload, whereas the ABC wanted to reduce it. There was also the potential loss of key musicians and Musicians' Union opposition, not to mention increased costs. Moreover, a studio orchestra (of a mere forty-five members) was not an acceptable SSO substitute. Coombs revised his offer. As a trade-off for reduced seating, the main hall acoustics would be improved. The ABC could reduce the number of SSO series concerts, use the new studio orchestra to lessen its SSO workload and seek additional government money for a second theatre orchestra based in Melbourne (to relieve the pressures on the Melbourne Symphony Orchestra). Once again, in what cannot have been music to the minister's ears (seven or so pages of tightly argued objections), Darling said no. Use of the main hall as a dual-purpose facility, he informed Hughes, would result in what one consultant described graphically as Sydney 'being saddled with a third rate concert hall in a first rate envelope'. On the other hand, if the rentals were reasonable, and because the panel of architects' Review of Programme 'would meet our requirements', the SSO might be based at the Opera House for some performances. But a slight sticking point was that the Opera House Trust had recently convened discussions about the use of the main hall, although without ABC participation. In effect, consultants were recommending on technical- and performance-related matters in ignorance of the details of the ABC's scheduling and commitments for its concert season. There was still a fundamental disagreement about seating capacity: the ABC calculated that only 1900 seats were available for orchestral concerts and 1750 for opera and ballet—capacity that would prevent the staging of Berlioz's *Requiem*, for example, which the ABC had already performed in the Sydney Town Hall.[38]

The ABC and the Elizabethan Theatre Trust were deadlocked over a single- or multi-purpose facility. Thanks mainly to a media campaign to soften up and shame the commission into shifting ground by backing it into a corner, developments turned nasty. Coombs was disappointed at Darling's rejection of his second offer. Having agreed to participate in a joint study of alternatives, he claimed, the ABC had arrived at its current position without any consultation. Moreover, he told Hughes, the cost to the community of orchestral concert exclusivity in the main hall would be 'unduly high': wasted resources, under-usage, denial of adequate provision for grand opera and full-scale ballet, inability to attract high-level overseas companies, and so on. What did the ABC's subscribers think? Were its acoustic judgements backed by the experts? Were the interests of performing-arts lovers being sacrificed to the prejudices of those responsible for concert-going? Without consensus, the argument (then circulating) that it would be impossible for the architectural team to give effect to Utzon's original conception would be reinforced. Darling was convinced that a highly placed Elizabethan Theatre Trust source was passing information to the press. He tackled Coombs. The sole purpose served by publication in the *Australian* of Coombs' letter to Hughes (he presumed with the permission of the former) was to exacerbate 'an already bitter situation'. He had not publicly stated (without the postmaster-general's permission) the ABC's case, he said, and had not criticised the Elizabethan Theatre Trust. Nor had the ABC urged Hughes to decide in its favour. He resented 'the accusation' that the broadcaster had refused to join a working party, because the minister had never invited it. Neither was cooperation possible if discussions were to take place in public; however, he would proceed 'in this hope' of helping each other in their respective difficulties. (As an indication of the pressure on him, he quipped to David Hay: 'I think, speak and dream of nothing but the damned Sydney Opera House'.) Hughes then sought a conference (on 28 February) between the two bodies, and urged Darling to talk to Sir Ian Potter (the president of the Elizabethan Theatre Trust). Lowndes objected, and claimed that Darling had not consulted the commission prior to agreeing to take part, by dint of which he had 'inevitably and seriously jeopardised the Commission's interest', embarrassed Duckmanton and fuelled the public acrimony.[39]

Darling corrected Lowndes. Potter had requested the meeting (via Hughes), not him. He had agreed to attend (in company with Lowndes and Duckmanton) knowing full well that 'if I had not agreed, a "victory" was in sight for the ABC' and that the minister was likely to decide in favour of the ABC's wish for a concert hall and because he did not want 'this affair' to be viewed as a contest with just one side victorious. Instead:

> it was a matter of such importance that responsible people should endeavour both to be reasonable and to appear to be reasonable, in so far as they could do so without betraying their duty to their own organization.

In fact, Darling told the commission, the Australian Elizabethan Theatre Trust had been 'quite reasonable', unlike the Opera House Trust, which had been inflexible in its demands for a multi-purpose hall. The meeting adjourned until 14 March, pending receipt of further architectural advice on the practicality of a demountable roof shell. A week later, the state government announced that the major hall would be a concert hall with seating for 2800 people, and the minor hall would be an opera hall for an audience of 1500, the coda to which (not surprisingly) was recrimination. Darling knew that he was very unpopular in

Sydney and blamed for the outcome while he was convinced that he was 'the only person who genuinely strove for a compromise'. Lowndes was not at all happy and Darling believed that he was intriguing with the treasurer (McMahon) to replace him as chairman. In the belief that the commission had never properly appreciated the full significance and implications of the Opera House, Lowndes blamed Moses for having put 'us' in an indefensible position, and 'we are most culpable for never having controlled him'. Not once, he told Duckmanton, had the former general manager reported to the commission on this matter, he was never nominated by the commission for Opera House Trust membership and he had always sidestepped any questioning about it. There was bad blood between the ABC and the Elizabethan Theatre Trust, thanks to the latter's press release, which Darling read with 'some dismay'. To insist that 'the fundamental issue was how far the A.B.C. was prepared to compromise' oversimplified matters because the commission's responsibility was to adhere to its minimum requirements for a first-class concert hall. The only point served by the Elizabethan Theatre Trust's 'selective impressions' of the lengthy negotiations was to throw 'out of perspective' and blur in the public mind the 'positive results' of the state Cabinet's decision. Potter stuck to his guns. While acknowledging Darling's role in trying to initiate discussion between the parties, from that point onwards he saw 'little indication' of ABC compromise.[40]

If there were winners and losers in this commission–Australian Elizabethan Theatre Trust stand-off, then Darling was not among the winners, as Hulme gave him his marching orders on 25 May. In a business-like letter, the minister expressed his 'sincere appreciation' for six years' work, but his appointment would not be renewed. Darling was surprised. He had informed the postmaster-general on 1 March of his willingness to serve another term (and confirmed Dawes' and Halvorson's availability for reappointment), and that he could provide 'some comments on the difficulties of the Chairman's position'. Hulme ignored his offer and the government kept him dangling until 20 May, when he was 'confidentially informed' (confirmed in a subsequent newspaper report) that he would be succeeded on 1 July by his friend Madgwick (recently retired Australian Vice-Chancellors' Committee chairman). Darling wrote to his successor to say that, although disappointed at not being allowed to continue, he was glad about his appointment. The government, he said, had been entirely graceless in not letting him know about Madgwick and he was 'infuriated by the discourtesy' of its treatment in not informing him of his non-renewal until the last minute and allowing rumours about his departure to circulate unchecked for more than three months. If Madgwick needed any assistance then he was available. This offer was welcome, said Madgwick, and it would be helpful to Darling to know 'the truth of the matter'. The new chairman reassured his friend that he had been approached very late in the piece and only accepted the government's offer on 26 May—after being informed (according to Semmler) that Darling had not wanted reappointment. (Two days before Hulme's letter, Duckmanton had

had no 'further "grapevine" information about the future'.) To have heard from Madgwick, replied Darling, made 'all the difference' to himself and Margaret, because he was feeling that 'they' had begun to denigrate him to Madgwick and that Madgwick had been forbidden to have any contact with him. He was hurt by that misperception because he did not consider that he had been 'as much of a failure as that'. Once bitten, twice shy: having made such 'a mess' of his GGS retirement by cutting himself off completely from both GGS and Garnett—resulting in a 'most unpleasant situation of divorce and dislike between my successor and me'—he wondered whether it would be a good idea before he departed 'for us to be seen kissing each other in public'.[41]

The first intimation of something amiss had come in January. Darling thought that Lowndes wanted to be chairman, expected it and had informed Dawes (who, after twenty-one years on the commission, would also have liked to be chairman). Darling had hoped for one more term and, with the government wanting to appoint two new commissioners, he had suggested Zelman Cowen and Keith Sinclair—with the latter positioned to succeed him, willing to 'carry on all that I have tried to start' and to be 'a help to Tal'. A distressed Casey (now governor-general) telephoned to put paid to such imaginings by confirming that his doubts were justified and that the government would not reappoint him. In his diary, Darling reproached himself for not having responded to this non-reappointment news with the proper ordering of priorities—such that he felt like a sick animal withdrawing to a corner where he would not be noticed—when really he ought to have been grateful for having had so few setbacks in life and that Margaret ('who had never really liked the ABC job') would be happier. The financial consequences would be severe—withdrawal from all government work would entail an annual income reduction of $7000. By February, he was reconciled to the likelihood of not being reappointed. The postmaster-general probably didn't want to get rid of him but was being pushed, Darling suspected, by McMahon and John McEwen (deputy prime minister). Lowndes ticked a number of the chairmanship boxes (but not all): age, Sydney, educationally qualified, time on his side and ten–eleven years' commission experience, except that internal ABC reaction was unlikely to be uniformly positive.[42]

When he heard about the appointment of Madgwick (an 'old mate'), Francis James fumed at Darling's mistreatment. 'He is an excellent <u>executive</u>, is Bert. Efficient, clear headed, prompt', although not in Darling's class. Madgwick was original and creative-minded and would get on well with Duckmanton, except that 'Tal is going to miss that irritating Darling yen for principle', which was a pity, as 'Tal needs someone more like you to inspire him'. The rumours referred to had come to a head back in April with a report by the *Inside Canberra* journalist Don Whitington that Darling's appointment might not be renewed. His suggested replacement was said to be Sir Howard Beale (until 1964, Australian ambassador in Washington), which was denied. Darling canvassed a number of explanations for his likely non-reappointment. As he was seen to have blotted his copybook in the Sydney Opera House negotiations, the bottom line of the jockeying was probably a Sydney push to install the New South Wales-based commissioner. Shocked, James assured Darling that no other man in Australia could match his contribution and he had been hearing all morning the horrified reactions of ABC staff in Sydney 'who are now right on your side'. Morale in the ABC, he assured his friend, was higher than for a good many years. Darling alerted Duckmanton that the newspapers 'have had a field day' about the chairmanship. He and Dawes had tried to reassure the minister and had dissociated themselves from any campaign. The Staff Association, however, made a 'rather foolish statement', the *Daily Telegraph* supported Lowndes as the new chairman and 'this highly unsatisfactory (by all accounts) program, This Day-To-night [sic], or whatever they call it' (which had first gone to air just two days beforehand) had devoted ten minutes to the topic. 'If this was a deliberate intention to put the last nail in my coffin it could not have been more successful and I rather believe it was so intended.' If not, then because they had given the program their approval, the judgement and sense of responsibility of two men who had Duckmanton's ear— Neil Hutchison and Ken Watts (Director of Programmes for Television)—were seriously at fault:

> It is intolerable to be put in the position of giving people responsibility and being continually let down, with the added humiliation that there is absolutely nothing that one can do about it.

It was hard copping such treatment from inside the ABC while 'everyone outside is also attacking me'. Darling was fairly certain that, while Hulme had publicly disavowed 'more political control' of the ABC, 'some Cabinet members' wanted a change.[43]

James' letter, Darling said, was balm from Gilead. If there was to be some scheming to secure him another term of office, then external pressure was unlikely to do much good: there was no way with its huge parliamentary majority that the government would be stampeded. He had refrained from saying anything other than that 'my term runs out in June 1967 and that the Government has the right either to re-appoint me or not, as it sees fit', in the belief that this implied his unavailability, albeit with a growing reluctance on his part. He had known for some weeks about a move in 'some quarters of the Cabinet' to be rid of him for someone 'more amenable'—which he took as a compliment. Hulme's excuse for the delay was the prime minister's unavailability. Darling did not think that Hulme conspired against him, because he had been 'admirable' in abiding by the 'independence theme'; he had not resorted to any economic weapon and had never made life difficult. To its credit the government had also behaved correctly since the earlier battles but, all the same, they probably weren't particularly enamoured of the current situation. The 'personal attacks on me by the Murdoch Press' (that he had failed and that ABC staff opposed him) provided fuel for his opponents. Any defence of him to the contrary would be interpreted not only as pressure on the government but as pressure on his own behalf. The reason that, despite 'this racket', he wanted another term was because, as an 'old-fashioned liberal', he remained committed to building a sense of responsibility down the ABC spine: the 'only' thing' that accounted for the ABC's timidity and held it back from being more adventurous than the BBC or the CBC was the problem of getting staff to accept the 'responsibility of freedom'. This was a long-term job and responsibility was a two-way street: if people let one down, then there had to be discipline, whereas some staff wanted it both ways: no controls at the top and no responsibility at the bottom—in effect a prescription for the return of management to its bad old ways.[44]

On James' balance sheet of Darling's supporters and opponents, the chairman seemed to be at odds with some of his old boys—what with the ABCB licence hearings and now the ABC chairmanship it had been difficult to be free of them. Apart from Murdoch's 'chaps', James also thought that 'young Packer' (Clyde) was offside, although he would 'shove a dose of conscience' into him. He was aware that Lowndes had been talking to the *Telegraph* and that at one stage he had ambitions not only to succeed Darling but Moses as well. As to the views of Cabinet members, he did not think that McMahon was a Darling supporter, but neither was he a fan of Hulme. As for the ABC itself, Dawes was onside, while Darling would be 'really and truly astonished' at the extent of support for him below the assistant general manager level. At the same time, James thought that his friend was impatient about devolution of responsibility: this was not something that people could be taught; instead they had to learn it for themselves and all that he could do was watch them and hold his breath. James would try to find out (through 'chaps who were at school with me') Holt's thinking, although as prime minister he wasn't as easy to read as Menzies had been. When the axe had finally fallen, James said that 'they put the acid on Bert [Madgwick] last week' and had told him to make up his mind and 'let 'em know one way or the other by Friday' (26 May). James assured him that when he had seen Madgwick in Armidale prior to the decision he had had no interest in the chairmanship. McMahon had been cagey when questioned by James, who was certain that Madgwick had not been his first choice. He then rounded on the Cabinet: 'My God. What a lousy, miserable, gutless ruddy mob they are. Outsiders all. I do know they were all in it. All the senior ministers, anyway.' Darling, he thought, was better off out if it: he had played it straight and had emerged with an enhanced reputation. Rather than playing the politician, like everyone else, the fact that he hadn't added to 'the Darling mystique'.[45]

Among the remaining letters in the inch-high pile of resignation correspondence was one from a sympathetic politician: Calwell. Darling had a number of friends, he was assured, and 'I am one of them'. He should have been reappointed as chairman and those friends regretted the government's decision. Another condolence epistle came from Osborne, who hoped that Darling was satisfied with the changes for the better during his time at the ABC, particularly the transformation at the top since the easing out of Moses. Manning Clark's letter to his former boss painted his removal in apocalyptic terms. No man with Darling's 'great fit of heart and head' could be the servant of 'those who had taken charge of our country' during this 'ominous silence' between its days of dependence on Europe and its future. Darling's work lay in the fashioning of minds steeped in the rich creative civilisation of Europe: a mixture of Hellenism, Judaism, Catholicism, Protestantism and Enlightenment that is forever 'the European spirit'. The 'best of those who were influenced by you' must have sensed the anomaly of the situation, and so Darling should not despair about those persons in the twilight of an era who had no eyes for 'a man who stood for something'. That was your glory, said Clark, and 'no-one could take it from you'. Darling thanked him, particularly for the work that he was doing at the ANU for his son, John. He was in no mood at the moment to reply in Clark's terms, but would talk to him sometime. He was prompted to write a book that would show how 'one's capacity to be oneself in any way completely' in any walk of life was eroded by the various loyalties with which one cluttered one's life: employer, class, club and even church. There was a point at which all such allegiances, while no bad things in themselves, went beyond merely inhibiting one's freedom and became a genuine problem.[46]

Thus it was that a significant contribution to Australian broadcasting spanning more than thirteen years ended. Back at Broadcast House, there were already signs of a different regime. Semmler said that it was clear from the first month or so after Madgwick's arrival that there would be little chance of any friendship or relationship developing between chairman and management. In fact, he had seen Madgwick for barely twenty minutes since his arrival. He seemed to be a 'reasonable sort of person', said Semmler, but not capable of 'noticeable flexing of the imagination', although well-disposed. For his part, Darling told Duckmanton that, on looking back through the files, he marvelled at 'how many crises' there had been, and yet how 'silly' the wisdom now seemed that he had tried to distil into his many memoranda. One 'malicious pleasure' was that the seat of Corio had fallen to the ALP in the recent by-election (after Opperman's retirement), which was a 'slosh in the eye' for the government. He thought that he had failed with Hulme (but to have 'more assiduously' licked his boots would have put him offside with the commission) and that after Casey, Menzies, Barwick, Downer and Opperman had left government, he 'had no real friends in power'. But he did have friends in the SOA and the Staff Association, both of which (in April, when his days were numbered) had wanted to take the fight to the press on his behalf. He had dissuaded them. The SOA's estimate of him (in its press release), Ashbolt told Duckmanton, was that Darling represented a 'fine liberal humanist tradition in an age increasingly dominated by technocratic and bureaucratic ways of thinking'. His liberalising influence had been felt throughout the ABC. Even though the SOA differed from him at times, it respected his 'honesty of thought, generosity of spirit and concern for fundamental democratic values'. For his part, Ted Lawrence, on behalf of the Staff Association, said that he was embarrassed that the government had not renewed his appointment. Speaking personally, he had the 'highest respect and warmest regard' for him, and said that Darling had restored for him his faith in the two qualities that previously had taken the 'worst beating' in the ABC: courtesy and integrity. The credit for moving the association from its original posture of 'defensive belligerence and suspicion' was entirely down to the former chairman: 'Well done, Dr. Darling—a first rate job in very much more difficult circumstances than is likely to be acknowledged'.[47]

25

EASYGOING

1961–1973

But suppose the whole notion of 'a God' who visits the earth in the person of 'his Son' is as mythical as the prince in the fairy story? Suppose there is no realm 'out there' from which the 'Man from heaven' arrives? Suppose the Christmas myth (the invasion of 'this side' by 'the other side')—as opposed to the Christmas history (the birth of the man Jesus of Nazareth)—has to go? Are we prepared for that?

John Robinson, *Honest to God*

The events described in this and the preceding two chapters occurred during a period of cultural upheaval. One year—1968 (when Darling was knighted)—symbolises what is seen as good or not so good about the 1960s and early 1970s: dewy-eyed nostalgic fondness for liberals or dismissive contempt bordering on horror for conservatives. A noteworthy feature of Australia in this period was the combination of economic prosperity—apart from the 1960–61 credit squeeze engineered by an 'over-complacent' government—and the political ascendancy and legacy of Robert Menzies. The fruits of this second half of the postwar long boom included social stability, material comfort and a sense of insularity, which prompted Australians, as noted by Donald Horne (in *The Lucky Country*, where he poured scorn on Menzies and his generation) and Robin Boyd (in *The Australian Ugliness*), to think of themselves as 'easy-going'. Another feature was cultural thawing. The juicy program content of the ABC's *This Day Tonight* (*TDT*)—which had reported that Darling would not be reappointed as chairman was an illustration—as was the (at times) irreverent tone of this new program, as in the prank perpetrated on *TDT*'s 'awful' first evening. The reporters (Sam Lipski and Allan Martin) had contrived 'a "spoof" telegram' (said to be authored by Darling) that was read aloud by the compere Bill Peach. Did the chairman have a sense of humour, they had asked Ken Watts. 'KW said he thought he had.' Other signs of the new mood were campaigns for censorship liberalisation, demonstrations against conscription and Australia's Vietnam involvement, a growing awareness (and acceptance) of new definitions of public taste (such as modes of speech, fashion and dress codes, trendy hairstyles, and forms of popular and avant-garde music), and the appearance of previously taboo topics on stage (for example, homosexuality) and in screen images (for example, nudity). Even theologians, as part of the Death of God debate in the wake of John Robinson's *Honest to God*, were questioning the very existence of a Christian godhead. (Free from jargon, but 'not theologically watertight' was Darling's view of this influential book.)[1]

For Darling and his contemporaries, then, this period was the twilight of cultural certainty. Previous self-evident ways of thinking and taken-for-granted social values were being scrutinised, challenged, refuted and even ridiculed, and increasingly their apologists were on the defensive. In such circumstances, there was a temptation for a public figure in his seventh decade to remain stuck as a frozen Edwardian relic. Darling, however, moved sufficiently with the times (although not uncritically) to embrace some of the core currents of the day. By 1970, for example, in a speech entitled 'The Whole Environment' in which he championed the theme of participation and focused on the proper use of earthly resources for 'the good life', social pluralism had become his departure point. He also spoke about the speed of social changes and their magnitude, and explicitly acknowledged (rather than bemoaned, as he had since the early 1950s) the 'ever-increasing complexity of society' (and its diversification and fragmentation) with the consequence of 'a more and more divided specialisation'. Moreover, if such a pluralist world was to be conducive to a good life pursued in the public interest, there had to be a recognition beyond the clash of competing individual interests that it was also an interdependent social world. But the absence of social unity had resulted in 'disenchantment', particularly of youth, which accounted for the 'prevalence of protest'. One response to disenchantment was the cult of technology. Another was to rebel against being educated to be a mere 'cog in a machine'. The 'passionate claim for participation' was a reaction to pluralising trends. The assertion of the right to participate in the forming of policy by those who previously had been 'mere victims of it' was 'essentially right', Darling said, because it was 'an extension of true democratic principles' lost since the days of the Greek city-states.[2]

While there were glimpses of these themes in Darling's outlook in his ABC work, they are also evident in two other areas recounted in this chapter: road safety and student unrest at the University of Melbourne. But the sphere in which he particularly got to grips with 1960s cultural developments was the Australian Frontier Commission. This was an initiative with which the Christian churches tried to confront religious drift and indifference by connecting with some of the new cultural currents. Frontier led a rather charmed life due to the lack of a viable infrastructure and resource base, and as an expression of volunteerism built on hope and possibility it would experience all of the wavering commitments that bedevil voluntary bodies. Frontier's precariousness was exacerbated by

its offspring: a bold attempt to create a national agency, the Institute for the
Study of Man and Society, which ended in tears. The gestation of the institute
gave Frontier a dual-track identity and was quite unlike other schemes that
its chairman had previously inaugurated. Darling tried with Frontier to adopt
a facilitative approach to social problem-solving by mobilising networks of
talented Australians (committed Christians, lay people and ordinary citizens,
and occasional arrays of academics, consultants, public officials, politicians and
businessmen). Throughout his association with it (1962–73) and beyond, three
factors prevented Frontier from realising its full potential: first, the vagueness of
its mission; second, a constant battle to keep its head above water financially; and,
third, an inability to capture the public imagination in respect of the Institute for
the Study of Man and Society. (There were times when Darling's work on behalf
of both entities so overlapped as to be indistinguishable.)

In September 1961, the Ecumenical Institute Advisory Committee of the
Australian Council of Churches planned a commission to develop Australian
Frontier 'as an independent yet related organization'. In December, the Australian
Council of Churches executive appointed five honorary Frontier commissioners,
all with education connections: Darling as chairman, Bill Connell (deputy chairman), the Reverend J.A. Garrett (warden, Camden Theological College), Merrilie
Roberts (headmistress, Ascham School, Sydney) and Dr J.W. Staines (senior
lecturer, psychology, Newcastle University College). The Reverend Alan Watson
(moderator general, Presbyterian Church of Australia) told Darling that those
who 'can properly be called the leaders of the Churches in Australia' were unanimous that he should be its first chairman. A Presbyterian clergyman, the Reverend
Frank Engel, was Frontier's honorary secretary, and the theological and sociological brains behind the outfit. He had helped shape Frontier's identity and purpose, and the prior thinking of both the Australian Council of Churches and the
Ecumenical Institute Advisory Committee. The commissioners met at Darling's
residence in January 1962 and in Sydney on seven occasions during the year for 'full
and free discussion' over a meal. They were to appoint additional commissioners.
The Ecumenical Institute Advisory Committee itself was established following
a national conference of Australian Christians at the University of Melbourne in
February 1960 attended by 430 representatives of eighteen Christian denominations and ten other organisations. It was during a series of capital city and regional
meetings convened by the advisory committee that the idea of Australian Frontier
took hold rather than an ecumenical institute. The word 'frontier' (and much of the
underpinning theology) derived from Europe, in particular the Christian Frontier
Council founded in England in 1939 by J.H. Oldham (a Ministry of Information
colleague of Darling's), which paralleled Oldham's other important forum the
Moot—an intellectual group (1939–47) that included Darling's much-favoured
author Karl Mannheim and studied his ideas for postwar planning.[3]

Frontier's purpose coalesced gradually around the ideas of catalyst and consultation. It came to see its mission as offering a non-partisan facilitative means

of resolving social problems. A consultation was Frontier's vehicle for achieving this mission. There were seventy-five consultations from 1964 to 1982. As Darling explained in 'The Whole Environment':

> A social problem having been raised ... the method is to do some preliminary inquiry and research, and, this completed, to bring together those immediately concerned to hear each other speak, to confront each other's points of view, and, if not immediately to find an answer, at least to understand more clearly what is involved. At the lowest, this develops awareness and increases mutual respect; at a higher level it opens up a vision of what might be, awakens and intensifies a sense of responsibility and points the way in which interested individuals can exercise it.

These ideas had taken shape during the Ecumenical Institute Advisory Committee consultations. In a country as large and as sparsely populated as Australia, Frontier had to be a '"mobile" operation'. With Australian society fragmenting and diversifying there were frontiers or 'lines of division that ran through the community' across which there needed to be 'real meeting', including denominational divisions, church and non-church, faith and non-faith, management and labour. Christians (initially Protestants) had to listen to others, discover ways of expressing the faith 'which convey its meaning in modern terms' and learn the implications for belief, daily work and action in contemporary society. By seeking to serve both church and nation, it was hoped that Frontier would promote unity and wellbeing, and establish ways of helping men and women to 'better understand the meaning and relevance of their faith', and its application in their work and relationships. Engel envisaged Frontier as a body that was constantly betwixt and between—church-related, but not so close as to frighten off those already at arm's length from the churches; worldly, but not so far away as to prevent churchly connection with the un-churched. He called this 'bridging the gap'. As Engel acknowledged later, this 'neither fish nor fowl' status was Frontier's simultaneous strength and weakness: it lacked the appeal of a charitable agency serving the needs of identifiable groups and did not have the loyalty of conventional organisational membership on which to draw. Its supporters were widely dispersed and came together temporarily for consultations, and it appealed altruistically to individuals and groups concerned to improve contemporary society. Somehow Darling and the commissioners had to clothe this inchoate entity in an institutional membrane. Previously from the pulpit of All Saints, Darling had inveighed against worldly ills, but Frontier called for an approach in which a Christian did not 'seek to impose his views on society', and to learn not teach, confer not pronounce and research rather than preach.[4]

In 1962 David Scott (Brotherhood of St Laurence), Frank Crean (Labor MHR, Melbourne Ports) and Arthur McCutchan (Queensland Irrigation and Water Supply Commission) joined Frontier. Darling also tried (through

Archbishop Eris O'Brien) to have a Catholic Church representative appointed (either Robert Jackson, an Australian administrator with the United Nations or his then wife, the journalist, lecturer and broadcaster Barbara Ward) but to no avail. In February 1963, the much sought-after vacancy for the position of full-time director (there were thirty-eight applications) was filled by the appointment of Peter Mathews, a 45-year-old South Australian. During 1948–57, Mathews had been the director of Congregational Youth in Australia and New Zealand, while for the previous five years he had been working in (what was then known as) Northern Rhodesia (Zambia) where, with the Mindolo Ecumenical Foundation, he had provided leadership training for lay Africans. Darling soon learnt that the director's energy level functioned at one speed only: breakneck. (As he noted in 1967: 'I don't direct [Frontier], but rather hang on to Peter Mathews' coat tails to prevent him from taking to the air'.) In his first four months, Mathews addressed thirty-nine gatherings across the country and made two television appearances. His role was to set up state councils and constitute advisory panels of about a dozen people in key urban centres that brought together specialists in town planning, architecture, housing and social work, and clergy. Panels convened for consultations to tackle problems associated with community development. Theologically, the bringing together of people engaged in social problems—with each party potentially jealous and ignorant of the others—was justified as 'the work of reconciliation' that was 'basic to the teaching of Christ'.[5]

An anonymous gift of £4000 and an annual income of £1500 to kick-start Frontier's operations signalled that a sound start had been made, although at least £7000 was required to employ Mathews. The receipt of an anonymous donation of shares worth £19,000 confirmed the impression of a sound start, and yet this manna from heaven heralded what was to become a problematic financial relationship. The donor had died on ship while travelling to England and, even though Frontier was not mentioned specifically in his will, the deceased man's family was committed to carrying out his wishes. The donor had been a businessman, V.E. Hancock, the part-owner of a Queensland family firm in Ipswich, Hanbro (manufacturers of laminated woods and plywoods), who had gifted Frontier £7000 and then an additional £4000 as an advance against the income to be realised from his shares. The hope of Hancock and his widow had been that Frontier 'would be a means of bridging the gap between the Church and the Man in the Street'. Mathews had assured Mrs Hancock that contact would be maintained, but by early 1964 she had heard nothing. Her solicitor said that if Frontier came to nought, then she would be bitterly disappointed, particularly if the money was dissipated 'without any real fruits'. As the matter was 'serious' and required 'urgent action', Darling swung into damage control. Mrs Hancock's solicitor's letter had caused him 'grave concerns', he said, but with the family's wish for donor anonymity, her husband's death and her own absence overseas, the commissioners had been uncertain about her exact wishes. Indeed, only recently had he been informed of the donor's name. Frontier had been dilatory and wrong to rely financially on her and her husband, except that 'it was inherent in the project that until we had some money it was impossible to have anything to show and until we had something to show it was impossible to get any money'.[6]

Darling's defensive reply to Mrs Hancock's solicitor dispelled the idea of a sound start and his excuse-making may have unwittingly conveyed the impression of a slightly ramshackle outfit. The appointment of the full-time director had 'occupied the whole of the first year' and there was little organisational machinery. (Legally, Frontier was an association incorporated under an ACT ordinance.) The letter reveals both Frontier and chairman gingerly feeling their way. Because of Frontier's inherent nature, Darling explained, 'the producing of results in such a field must be slow'. As chairman he was 'unhappy' about the lack of progress and the 'whole proposition remains very amorphous and difficult to explain'. A delay in the printing of a brochure had held up an appeal for funds, even though much thinking and talking had occurred, and a number of projects had been undertaken. Tellingly, he appealed to intangibility as a virtue:

> It is as I have previously said, more or less inherent in the idea that [Frontier's] results will not be visible, because they will be so largely in the minds of individual men and women and the improvement in the way in which they make their contribution to the building of a more responsible society.

Darling urged patience. Frontier appreciated the Hancocks' generosity and support, but it was not content to rely on this when wider support was needed. He voiced his insecurity to the solicitor:

> if you can show me how to do this peculiarly difficult job better than we are doing it, I wish that you would because I do feel truly anxious about it, and more than usually ineffective.

If the letter's tone had annoyed the director then its content had rattled the chairman, so much so that Mathews was urged to go to Brisbane to meet the solicitor and give him an analysis of Frontier's accounts. Darling suggested that he express gratitude for the help in giving Frontier its start, accept any further financial support offered, but indicate that it could not be dependent solely on Mrs Hancock's husband's generosity. If people did not want to give money, then Frontier was better off not having it. 'I wish I could take a trick somewhere', Darling mused, 'but "tis not in mortals to command success" and it's even harder to keep on trying all the time'. Fortunately, a cordial meeting between Mathews and Mrs Hancock in Canberra in January 1964 mended fences.[7]

In May 1965, the Hancock family made another donation to Frontier. Mathews recalled Vivian (son of V.E.) Hancock counselling him to avoid being on the move all the time and suggesting that he should locate permanently in one place. (Mathews worked from premises in Canberra but co-location alongside the chairman in Melbourne would have been more sensible—it occurred in 1969 as a cost-saving measure—and removed the need for regular long-distance telephone conversations and visits.) For this reason, the family was willing to fund the construction of a college in Canberra. Mathews recommended this course of action to Frontier and it agreed. Fontier's commissioners, Mathews told the Hancock brothers, could scarcely believe their good fortune:

> Dr. Darling is usually very moderate in his speech and rarely if ever stuck for words. On this occasion he was dumbfounded. Having recovered from the initial shock he said that gratitude for such generosity and such a gift could never be fully expressed in words of thanks but only in 'praise of God and determination to serve him more faithfully'. News of this development is going to reverberate nationally. It is a real breakthrough for the thinking Christian community.

The offer came during a period of financial difficulty. Although there were more than 300 Friends of Frontier, its financial appeal was attracting mainly small donations and its application for tax concessions on gifts had stalled. It desperately needed a regular income stream. Darling confided to Frank Crean: Frontier's annual budget was £12,000, but little of this could come from funds earmarked for tax concessions (as such monies would be used to extend Frontier's work). On the other hand, to have part of its appeal money made tax deductible would mean drying up Frontier's sources of discretionary funds. In addition, £20,000 was needed for research and £10,000 for ordinary expenses. To make matters worse, Connell resigned (due to university commitments) and was replaced by Engel. The consultations, however, were working well: in the first half of 1964 there were three (on town planning, the social needs of a new housing estate and training for youth leadership). Darling was comforted by the fact that Frontier was bringing people together on joint committees to tackle problems. He could 'never have believed that this state of affairs [that is, people's previous inability to work together] existed had not so many of them told us'. Moreover, because they had genuine vested interests, the churches could not have succeeded, whereas 'Frontier, if it can keep itself pure, can do it'.[8]

The Hancocks' promised gift of £300,000 would provide some of the capital for what Engel termed Frontier's 'great dream'. For the next decade, much of Frontier's energies were devoted to giving shape to the college and its location. No wonder Darling and his fellow commissioners had been gobsmacked by the Hancocks' generosity. Their gift would contribute significantly to a building that included offices, a hall, lecture theatre and conference rooms, a warden's residence, living accommodation, dining hall and kitchen, recreation room and bedrooms for 120 people. The preferred site was land adjacent to St Mark's Anglican National Memorial Library on the southern side of Lake Burley Griffin in the Canberra suburb of Barton. Had the dream been realised, the new college might have become part of the 'great obsession' of another man—Bishop Burgmann who, when he founded the St Mark's Library in 1957, envisaged a theological research centre for postgraduate students. Subject to the agreement of the Diocese of Canberra–Goulburn and the National Capital Development Commission, would St Mark's agree to lease a bit over a hectare of its land? Because the college site would provide a base for Frontier's research activities ('on the sociological and Theological front') co-location made a lot of sense. The purposes of Frontier and St Mark's 'overlap so much as to appear almost identical': the library itself and the planned accommodation could be a shared facility, and there was scope for cost sharing. But there was a debit as well as a credit side. The St Mark's site was isolated from the city centre and the Australian National University in Acton— an important consideration in respect of Frontier's proposed research function (Connell chaired its research committee, established in 1966). Furthermore, Frontier was an ecumenical initiative and yet it would be aligned with a church under diocesan control. In June 1965, however, the diocese made the site available and, having met with representatives of St Mark's in September, Frontier's site sub-committee (of which Darling was a member) agreed to build.[9]

For the next two years the idea morphed from a Frontier-specific college into the much more grandiose Institute for the Study of Man and Society (and discarded an explicit connection with Christianity) that would promote understanding of the nature of society, and the roles and responsibilities of mankind in society, advance the study of issues of living and working together, bring people together to exchange ideas and views, provide instruction, study and research, and foster an understanding of Australian society's responsibility to the world community, especially in the Asia–Pacific region. In 1968 Frontier's Institute Committee (Mathews, Connell, Engel, Basil Hetzel—Professor of Social and Preventative Medicine at Monash University—and Darling, who was mostly absent in England) undertook the planning of the institute. By mid-year, an interim council was constituted and an architectural model of the institute was on public display. A twenty-member council was appointed and included, in addition to Darling, Connell, Hetzel, Mathews, Engel, V.M. Hancock (donor), Ross Hohnen (registrar of the Australian National University), Laurie Short (general secretary, Ironworkers Federation of Australia), two academics (Professor Cecil Gibb and Dr Chris Duke both from the Australian National University) and two federal parliamentarians (Tony Street, Liberal MHR, Corangamite, and Manfred Cross, ALP MHR, Wide Bay). In December 1968, an ordinance of incorporation for the institute was gazetted, a tender was let for the erection of the first phase of construction and, in February 1969, the new council held its first meeting in Canberra. Henceforward, as chairman of the institute's council and of Frontier, Darling would be battling on two fronts, although developments and activities in each domain were not always synchronised. During 1969–70, for example, Frontier's commissioners were divided about whether to prioritise

Frontier's work or the institute. In 1965 taxation deductibility had been secured for gifts of £1 or more to the institute (but not for its endowment fund), and yet this arrangement did not apply to Frontier. In England in 1968, Darling had tried to secure charitable trust funding, but without luck. Whenever he was wearing his Frontier hat, then, Darling appealed to people to take an interest in its activities and to stump up money. As with the abortive Empire Youth Ship scheme, he even tried to secure the endorsement of Buckingham Palace by meeting the Duke of Edinburgh at Windsor and to have the duke (when he was in Melbourne) talk to Hetzel and Mathews about Frontier's work. To convince the duke of the virtue of Frontier and the proposed institute, Darling styled the latter as an agency that was attempting to:

> provide a mechanism by which people come together as much as may be freed from their prejudices and vested interests, in order to discuss the needs of our society in an age of revolution, probably more acute than that of the Renaissance, but which shares with that period the fact that the structures of society, political, religious, educational, medical, etc. are no longer capable of coping with the new situation.

Hetzel and the duke met without a hitch, but that was all.[10]

Throughout his chairmanship of Frontier, Darling was wracked by self-doubt. Part of this concerned the lack of ready-made solutions to institutional religious difficulties and where Frontier fitted. He had said to James Fairfax in 1964 that he wasn't 'quite sure myself' what Frontier was attempting to do, except that something like it had to be done because the churches were increasingly introverted and unable to restate the gospel in a way that appealed to ordinary Australians. And, when pursuing a gospel-related point with Madgwick, he speculated whether high-profile identities were needed to revitalise Australian Anglicanism, such as another Burgmann or someone like Archbishop George Appleton of Perth who could express the idea of the Trinity in language acceptable to modern minds. Maybe the solution was structural: someone had to be courageous enough to examine the Church of England and its parochial system and (in a rare, for Darling, lurch into brutalism) 'smash it up in favour of an organism more suitable to present day conditions'. Two years later he reported to an English correspondent that Frontier was an idea that was 'difficult to explain to the uninitiated' but that it 'stumbles on'. Unlike Francis James, who was sceptical about it from the start, Darling stuck with the Australian Frontier Commission, insistent that it was 'doing useful work' despite being 'bankrupt and desperate', and in one heat-of-the-moment remark he said that he would 'devote the rest of my life' to Frontier once he had got over 'sulking about [his non-reappointment to] the A.B.C.' An added frustration was his inability to allay disapproval of Frontier 'in some quarters' of the Australian Council of Churches. (Hetzel was blunt: 'the churches have never supported us'.) Perhaps the way to deal with Frontier's financial woes, Darling told Mathews in mid-1969, was to stay small and not grow: maybe 'we should train ourselves to be content with the lighting of little candles to the glory of God at this stage'. It was so difficult to 'stir an affluent and smug society, however much it needs to be stirred'; a crisis was needed to prod people of British stock into action. Public image was also a concern. John Dunlop (now a Frontier counsellor) was asked, following a Sydney forum on student protest: 'Isn't FRONTIER a bit pink?' Committed as he was to reconciliation through consultation, Darling was 'alarmed' that, despite its disavowals, Frontier had acquired an 'only partly deserved' reputation of being 'a basically revolutionary agency, anti-establishment, and not least anti-established church; and particularly anti- the parochial church'.[11]

Financially, Frontier continued to limp. John Poolman, an OGG, provided the funding for the office and as a result Frontier employed a secretary for Darling. 'I really cannot afford to alter this unsatisfactory situation', he lamented. By the end of 1968, Frontier's operating debt was $22,000, a figure that had nearly doubled in 1969 and rose by April 1970 to $67,000. The situation was fast approaching dire. Darling's attempted fund-raising with some OGGs and business contacts had borne little fruit. Economies in late 1969 (a reduction in office staff and a relocation to Melbourne) helped to reduce the deficit, which was eventually cleared by early 1971 thanks to generous donations from the Hancocks (who had earlier helped to bail out Frontier's research fund) and a Melbourne businessman (and Church of Christ layman), Rowley Morris. After coming within a whisker of shutting down altogether in 1970, Frontier's situation had improved by 1973 to a point where it was surviving on the back of small annual donations (from about 500 individuals and 150 companies), and income from eight foundations and trusts, although it was still heavily reliant on voluntary labour. Until 1970, the bulk of the fund-raising had fallen to Darling, Morris and Mathews—with the perverse consequence of diverting their energies from the main game of realising Frontier's objects (its 'real cause'). It was (mostly) because of his qualms about the executive's recommended budget strategy in 1970 that in December Darling gave Hetzel notice of resignation as a 'not wholehearted' chairman. As Darling had given it his best shot for the past nine years, Merrilie Roberts reassured him that his conscience had 'no reason other than [to] be clear'.[12]

In his self-doubt, Darling turned on himself as the weak link financially: 'Saw Peter Mathews in afternoon and wrote together report for A.C.C. [Australian Council of Churches]', said a cryptic diary note. Despite being overworked and worried about finance, Mathews:

> remains full of faith and enthusiasm. I wish that I was as good as he is, but he still [insists] that I am not letting them down. I doubt it.

Urging Darling to remain with Frontier rather than resign, the executive created the figurehead role of president for him—he accepted it, he explained to Hetzel, as a way of conveying the appearance of change without revolution. The executive also wanted to give its inaugural chairman a proper send-off. Darling, on the other hand, partly because the well-intentioned 'wake' when he departed the ABC had been such a 'horrible occasion', simply wanted to 'slide out unobtrusively'. Unable to extricate himself immediately, because the chairman of Frontier was also ex-officio chairman of the Institute for the Study of Man and Society, and because he thought it unreasonable to expect someone else to take on that role, he agreed to hang on until April 1971. Frontier's problem was that it had become a victim of a dilemma that Jock Reid (a Frontier donor and ABC commissioner) had pinpointed in late 1967: 'the whole operation is getting too big for its financial safety'. To expand, Reid cautioned, would impact negatively on donors of small sums of money during Frontier's first five years. And, the likelihood of Frontier losing its way spiritually as a consequence of increased size was genuine. Echoing Darling's late 1940s concerns about an expanding GGS, Reid was worried about the build-up of 'machinery'. At the same time, Frontier's very intangibility made it a 'valuable concept', and the fact that it was becoming less intangible may be 'a danger'.[13]

As for 'the "house" in Canberra' (as Darling said to Francis James), the Institute for the Study of Man and Society proceeded at slower than glacial speed. Because construction on the Barton site had not commenced, an official in the Department of the Interior sought confirmation from Darling in April 1972 of the institute's council's intention to build. Frontier's answer was still no clearer a year or so later when (in August of 1973) Darling explained to the Minister for the Capital Territory (K.E. Enderby) that funds had not yet become available, but that Frontier had amalgamated with the institute and had become a division of it. Submissions for financial support were being prepared by the council's executive and a clearer sense of its intentions and funding arrangements was shortly expected. He hoped for a delay until September 1974 before informing the minister of those intentions. For about five years, a number of factors had conspired to thwart the institute's progress. The major one was an inability to finance it. Eventually the Hancocks ran out of patience: 'Any vision splendid we all may have had, in our case has vanished', they told Darling in late 1970. But it had not been for want of trying. A capital fund of at least $1 million was required to generate sufficient interest to cover annual operating costs before commencing construction. One way to obtain it (John Hancock's suggestion) was to begin the institute by using existing facilities in Canberra and creating an income stream. Another (Darling's suggestion) was to establish an endowment fund. But that needed donors and not even a Darling charm offensive (with some Adelaide OGGs) could prise open their pockets—although Ted Cleary (the Adelaide Frontier panel chair) was agog at the 'reality of the Geelong Grammar "thing"':

> It is indeed impressive to see at first hand the devotion shown publicly by
> the business leaders of our community, to their old school master. It says a

great deal for the type of education that you imparted to them and for the relationship that you fostered at that time and since.

A government grant might have been another possibility. During 1970, Darling worked through Andrew Peacock (Minister assisting the Prime Minister), Robert Southey (OGG and president, Liberal Party) and Tony Street in an effort to meet with Prime Minister Gorton to spark his interest in the institute. 'If it is not rude of me to say so', he told Street:

> he [Gorton] might also improve his own reputation by recapturing something of the appearance of a man with vision for the future, which I once thought he had but which the struggle for [prime ministerial] survival seems rather to have destroyed.

Gorton displayed no interest.[14]

There was the possibility of a major donation in June 1970 when Darling was a fellow speaker with an English businessman, Sir Mark Turner (deputy chairman, RTZ), at the annual Conference of the Institute of Directors, at which he had delivered 'The Whole Environment' and Darling was also confident of securing financial backing (for Frontier) from CRA (RTZ's Australian subsidiary). With Turner due to return to Australia in November, Darling pulled out all stops and in an extended letter trumpeted Frontier as a solution to many current social ills. Everywhere one cared to look, there was evidence of an alarming 'polarization of Right and Left'. Moreover, it was increasingly difficult for 'the middle, sane and liberal-minded people to remain without taking sides':

> It ought to be the function of the church to hold this middle position, but it has lost the capacity. Frontier is doing exactly this, and providing the place where Right and Left can meet without spitting in each other's eyes.

Trouble was obvious in numerous spheres around the world, such as in:

> Belfast, in the race question, Black Power v Powellites, in the Universities, S.D.S. [Students for a Democratic Society] versus the administration, in industrial matters and many other places. On my University Committees to deal with Student Participation I have become very much aware of this hardening on both sides and the tendency even on my own part to get exasperated. The S.D.S. boys really want this polarization and not a solution, because they really believe in Anarchy and Revolution; but, if you answer this with a return to Authority you either give them what they want with an increased chance of an unworkable system, such as the U.S. seems to have grown into or you encourage the return to the Police State which is equally a denial of all that we believe in.

By late 1970, with little progress having been made on the Endowment Fund, the Hancocks wanted to divert their donation for other purposes (if this was legally possible). Darling pleaded for a stay of execution while waiting for RTZ in England. He was in an invidious go-between role, constantly shuttling backwards and forwards between the increasingly frosty Hancocks, and other interests and parties. If that was not enough, St Mark's was cooling about an affiliation and so in desperation Darling turned to the Australian National University's Centre for Continuing Education as both a potential new partner and venue for the Institute for the Study of Man and Society. This redirection raised the Hancocks' eyebrows (given the Centre for Continuing Education's focus on adult education). They were aggrieved that their money had not been used to good effect and felt that it was 'morally wrong' for it to lie idle for so long. No wonder, then, that Darling moaned to Ross Hohnen in December that the Institute was 'about the most intractable exercise that I have ever been engaged on'.[15]

By early 1971, Darling's last hurrah was a hoped-for favourable outcome of a study into the institute's feasibility. CRA had been prepared to underwrite the cost ($10,000) but withdrew its offer when alerted to the Hancocks' legal challenge and because the scheme was 'too woolly'. The legal challenge raised moral issues for the institute's council. Assuming that the money could be real-located, should it try to forestall that possibility? Or, having received money in trust for a certain purpose, could it 'actually say that it is not proceeding with that purpose, particularly when it remains very anxious to do so'? And wasn't there an overriding moral constraint anyway, that it 'hardly seemed decent to go on using the Hancock money when they do not want us to do so'? W.D. Scott & Co. conducted the feasibility study in May. The complicated and confusing relationship between Frontier and the institute was reflected in the inquiry's terms of reference: the Institute for the Study of Man and Society would only come into being when Frontier was better established. The inquiry would assess community attitudes and likely responses to the development of the institute 'by inference from the work of Frontier'. Assuming that these were favourable, it would then consider the institute's proposed programs and activities, its capital and operating costs, various methods of financing it and then the marketing of it with a view to encouraging public support. In November its 98-page report gave the institute a big thumbs-down. The points of concern to Darling (evidenced in his margina-lia) were that the cost of building the institute and funding its operation was esti-mated at $1.2 million, its proposed residential conference facilities were contrary to its original establishment terms, it would strain Frontier's already overtaxed management resources, there were questions about the scope of its research con-sultations and association with a church body might prejudice its neutrality. Scott & Co. recommended deferral of plans for the institute, its merger with Frontier, and the conversion of the building fund into a research foundation.[16]

With that, the great dream was as good as dead. Darling's pencilled doodle on an agenda paper some six months later said as much: a grave and headstone with 'RIP Inst' below a $ sign where the horizontal axis intersects with the vertical on a cross. Scott & Co.'s report raised a number of issues. First, its rejection of possible research consultations in South-East Asia did not chime well with a rather late-onset enthusiasm that Darling had developed for Japan (that probably arose from an Asian Broadcasting Union tour in late 1965 and a meeting with the former Japanese prime minister, Shigeru Yoshida). Second, was Darling's dogged pursuit of the institute a vanity project, even though the decision to pursue the vision was a collective one? Persistence in the face of setbacks and obstacles is one thing, but cutting one's losses when unable to realise a plan is quite different. Maybe the delay was nothing more than hope springing eternal in the pursuit of a cause, and yet this intention was open to misinterpretation (by the donors) as dithering and drift. From another angle, the entire Frontier-institute episode may have been an indication (despite Cleary's observation of the so-called Geelong mystique) of the ebbing of Darling's persuasive powers, and to have jettisoned the project might have been an admission to that effect.[17]

Gracious in defeat, but with his tail between his legs, Darling told John Hancock that he had been right all along: the institute was 'not a practicable proposition' (although qualifying this admission with 'at least in the immediate future'). Responsibility for some of the institute's failure was down to himself as chairman. The Hancocks agreed that construction of the institute should not proceed, but what was not clear was whether Frontier would continue to operate. Darling had said (in 1970) that there was no indication that Frontier had 'so impressed itself upon the community, church, public or industrial magnates, that any of them would be in a state of despair if it did not continue to exist'. A year later potential funders were still not persuaded to support it because they believed that there was insufficient to show for its efforts, with the result that it was left in the 'damnably awkward position of knowing that they must be right until we get an adequate staff', except that there could not be adequate staff until there was more money, 'and round and round we go'. Darling queried Turner on CRA's coolness and whether this was evidence that the Australian financial and industrial sectors still wished, by and large, 'to keep themselves insulated from the social consequences of their activities'. If the answer was yes, then he was 'driven to despair' and it was enough to persuade him to 'join Mr Mao's boys immediately'.[18]

In March 1973, the Hancocks finally walked away. Attempts made during 1972 to explore means of utilising the interest on their donation had come to nothing. The family was now satisfied that the proposed Institute of Educational and Social Research (to be attached to the School of Australian Environmental Studies at the newly established Griffith University) was similar in concept to the original idea of the Institute for the Study of Man and Society and worthy of their money. (Intriguingly, in 1970 Darling had thought that, with a donation in mind, the family was being primed by the vice-chancellor of the University of Queensland, Zelman Cowen.) Acknowledgement of Darling's contribution to Frontier had been bestowed on him at the April 1971 meeting of the commissioners, at which point he had ceased to be chairman. At that meeting Engel had paid tribute to the inspiration and strength of Darling's leadership, which had been 'outstanding'. At a personal level, Engel also said, a number of commissioners had benefitted from the chairman's 'flashes of insight' into the nature of society and the gospel, his wide interests that ranged from cricket to religious poetry and, more generally, 'the stimulus of his comments'. Darling was said to have been courageous and tenacious in a crisis, and was a person who would hang on and find ways through various difficulties encountered. There was also his wisdom with respect to Frontier's policy and his moral integrity in dealing with its finances and his intellectual leadership, especially as evidenced by his 'Whole environment' address. Darling replied by affirming that he had benefited from his association with Frontier. He urged everyone present to remember that this organisation was a Christian exercise and to 'not lose sight of the fact that it was started in this faith and was an attempt to co-operate with God in the building of His Kingdom'. (Three years before in See—the Melbourne diocese newspaper—he had said that Frontier's link with the churches 'seems to have been lost', even though Frontier's activities were completely in line with what had been proclaimed at the meeting of the World Council of Churches at Uppsala, Sweden, which he had attended in 1968.) Frank Crean spoke next and endorsed Darling's remarks. Darling remained as president of Frontier until 1974, at which point he was succeeded (yet again) by Madgwick.[19]

Simultaneously with Frontier, Darling was working in road safety. In April 1961, just three months before his ABC appointment (and still in harness at Corio), he attended his first meeting (in Hobart) of the Australian Road Safety Council (ARSC). Originally established in 1947, the ARSC's membership and remit were revamped in 1960, following which Darling was appointed as chairman. Road safety catapulted him into the unpredictable and volatile cauldron of Commonwealth–state relations. Consistent with the Australian pattern of federalism, transport had at its apex a ministerial council, the membership of which comprised federal and state ministers: the Australian Transport Advisory Council, of which the ARSC was a sub-committee. The states regarded safety as their responsibility, said Hubert Opperman (Minister for Shipping and Transport) at the first ARSC meeting, but following the report of the Senate Select Committee on Road Safety (September 1960) the states wanted the ARSC's objectives, program and operation reorganised to better reflect their autonomy, to enable it to take account of the views of ministers, and more closely integrate the states' road safety campaigns and activities. Apart from Darling and the executive director (T.G. Paterson), the ARSC comprised sixteen representatives of the states, Commonwealth, private motorists, commercial motorists, the motor vehicle manufacturing and retail sectors, and the Transport Workers' Union. Of a total annual Commonwealth grant of £150,000 for public education in road safety, £50,000 was earmarked for the states and the Commonwealth would spend £100,000 on road accident prevention. The main function of the newly reconstituted ARSC was to 'co-ordinate, in a balanced programme, the Commonwealth and State Public Education campaigns, and to integrate, with these campaigns, the support accorded by non-governmental bodies and the general public'. This function was to be realised through the machinery of continuous public education to improve road users' understanding and behaviour, encourage motorists to observe traffic laws, stimulate increased interest in road accident prevention, make available educational and informative data on road accidents and advise the Australian Transport Advisory Council on matters that it referred to the ARSC.[20]

During the 1960s and 1970s, the automobile became the nation's 'central emblem of adulthood'. It was no longer merely a vehicle for leisure (Sunday outings, holidays and shopping) but increasingly the main means of access to and from the workplace ('which had once been the preserve of public transport'). As the quintessence of easygoing affluence, there was no better symbol of a property-owning, possessive individualist democracy than the motor car. For this reason, the importance of the ARSC's work is evident in national trends in vehicle registrations, licensed drivers, and injuries and mortalities due to road traffic accidents. Taking 1947 as a baseline, by 1961 motor car registrations had almost quadrupled (550,000 to 2,126,000) and then nearly doubled again by 1971 (4,057,000). There was a twofold increase in licensed driver numbers from 1,500,000 in 1947 to 3,198,000 in 1961, and a nearly two-thirds increase by 1971 (to 5,001,000). In 1947 deaths and injuries attributable to road traffic accidents were 1346 and 24,062 respectively. By 1961, these figures had leapt to 2542 and 60,749, and during Darling's chairmanship they had trended upwards by 1971 to 3590 and 91,036. In the 1970s, deaths hovered annually between about 3500 and 3800, and thereafter fell to around 3300, while injuries remained in the high 80,000s or low 90,000s. As Darling discovered, the entire road safety portfolio was statistically saturated and the ARSC's obligations in respect of data—'collect, collate, publish and distribute' said the first meeting agenda—introduced him to a new decision-making calculus (illustrative of the 'governing by numbers' idea fashionable with later generations of social scientists). At GGS, Darling's reliance on numbers was confined to pupil enrolments, fees and budgeting, with everything else justified by argumentative appeal to logic or principle. His ARSC experiences completely changed that and eroded his previous disdain for specialisation, because this was also an area replete with specialists. The problems of road deaths, injuries and their costs were multi-causal, and statistical reduction and representation (trend lines, estimates, percentages, graphs, annual achievement targets and pie charts) provided the weaponry with which to justify initiatives and political solutions.[21]

Darling set the tone in Hobart by drawing attention to the tension between the states' responsibility for the problem of safety and the general public's expectation that the ARSC would deal with it effectively. Only 'continuous co-operation between all concerned', therefore, would reconcile these imperatives and ensure the ARSC's success. There had to be a willingness to listen, he urged, with due weight accorded others' experiences. Unless a newly constituted group of sixteen people could act as one, it would degenerate into a factionalised arena for the articulation of set-piece position statements. He was quick to assert, therefore, that when the ARSC was in session its members 'virtually ceased to represent the Commonwealth or States etc., and became members of a national body'. The corollary, of course, was that those members must also 'necessarily share their knowledge and experiences and take back to their representative bodies, for implementation at their level, the decisions arrived at by the A.R.S.C.' Barely two months later Boyer died and Darling was simultaneously juggling his GGS, ABC and ARSC responsibilities, with the result that he was 'even more remiss about Road Safety than I might have been'. His late 1961 illness and absence overseas during 1962 were not conducive to moulding the ARSC as a unit and it limped along until early 1963. There was sporadic discussion of potential safety initiatives (such as mandatory motor vehicle inspections, a road-safety school curriculum, driver training in schools, and installation of seatbelt fittings and tinted windscreens) but the ARSC's focus in this two-year period was the recommendations of the report of the Senate Select Committee on Road Safety. At the sixth meeting of the ARSC (in April 1963) Darling began championing the importance of research evidence, both overseas and local (by bodies such as the Australian Road Research Board and the National Health and Medical Research Council), in the form of road accident statistics, and the psychological and sociological aspects of road accidents, as the bases for improved and effective public education campaigns.[22]

By the July 1963 ARSC meeting in Brisbane Darling's overall strategy was clear. Imbued with education's potential to change antisocial thoroughfare behaviour, there was to be a plan entailing collaboration between the three key groupings: states, Commonwealth and non-government bodies with interests in road safety. Darling had signalled the ARSC's commitment to such a programme when addressing the ministers at the Australian Transport Advisory Council in June. To persuade them of ARSC's intention and that collaboration between levels of government was do-able (in a comprehensive approach to road accident prevention), he cited tuberculosis and highlighted how previously governments had collaborated successfully to tackle this Australia-wide public health problem. He argued that in 90 per cent of cases the key cause of road accident death was human failure, with weather conditions and vehicle defects being the other contributing factors. The road toll was equivalent in order of magnitude to an armed forces national catastrophe: the loss of one in three army battalions of killed and wounded (or 60,000 men). The ARSC's task, then, was to educate all classes of road users to 'so adapt themselves to present day traffic conditions that they did the right thing instinctively'. What mattered was not so much the passing of road tests by drivers as the 'benefits derived from the process of learning'. Darling cited annual road death and injury statistics, and quoted the results of a 1962 Roy Morgan poll: 89 per cent of 1047 Australians interviewed thought that road-safety campaigns were worthwhile and 70 per cent said that road safety publicity sensitised them to road dangers. Moreover, having consulted state directors of education in Perth, Darling said that there was considerable potential in road safety for the school curriculum, either as a stand-alone subject or on an integrated basis. The five elements of the plan were identification of road users responsible for accidents, an education campaign, measurement of the plan's effectiveness, commercial and community support, and annual targets. It was agreed to adopt a publicity protocol as part of which, in order to sustain joint agreement, at the conclusion of each meeting the chairman would designate which items were to remain confidential. The direction of travel was clear.[23]

At face value, the provision by a small advisory group of high-level advice on the safety of a nation's roads seems unremarkable. But the ARSC soon developed its own peculiar brand of internal politics as a result of which Darling had to call on all his accumulated management skills and experience. It slowly dawned on him during 1963 that, as constituted, the ARSC was not fit for purpose. Not only that, but its purpose had to be grander than mere public education. Apart from the need to convince his fellow councillors on this score, his proposed structure for the pursuit of this larger purpose was unlikely to be universally acceptable. Not surprisingly, his model was a commission, à la the Universities Commission with Mills and Lloyd Ross: a small body of friendly and highly committed experts freed of partisan politics and departmental strictures who could be trusted to get on with the business in hand. At the next ARSC meeting (in Melbourne) political obstacles emerged and Darling's vision began to unravel. Having reminded the ARSC that the program was intended to reduce road accident vehicle fatalities to a figure comparable to the world's lowest (Australia then ranked seventh-lowest), Darling had to go into reverse gear. He and Paterson, on behalf of a standing committee of the ARSC, had proposed a national coordinating body—a national road safety commission (or committee: both terms were used)—of eleven members chosen on the basis of function (for example, traffic engineering, research, health and policing) who would not be appointed by governments but by the relevant safety agencies. This new body would not report to the Australian Transport Advisory Council but directly to the Premiers' Conference (the annual meeting of state premiers and the prime minister). It was a bold idea that threatened to bypass the states and for which, if agreed to, Darling would seek ministerial endorsement. The scheme hinged on the argument that to reduce the vehicle fatality rate from 8 per 10,000 vehicles to less than 5, then anything less than an 'ambitious project of this magnitude' with a 'beneficial psychological effect on the community' was no more than a holding operation.[24]

The 27-page report that Darling and Paterson prepared for the ARSC suggested that, based on an anticipated increase in vehicles over the succeeding four years (until 1968–69), a fatality reduction from 8.0 to 5.5 per 10,000 vehicles would save 3060 lives. Because during 1957–62 the annual fatality rate ranged between 8.0 and 9.2, a view of the 'whole problem' necessitated 'unified planning, covering all aspects'. All contributing factors had to be considered, singly and as they interrelated, and a program devised that was 'basic and comprehensive, soundly developed, specific in its objectives, and geared to the breadth and depth of the problem', to secure official agency cooperation. This strategy ensured a 'more rational selection of the resources to be marshalled against accidents'. Darling was appealing for road-accident prevention rather than public education. The new commission would develop 'a Master Plan for a National Road Safety Programme':

> a balanced and comprehensive scheme in keeping with the political, adminis-
> trative, social and economic realities of our national life. It would incorporate
> measures believed to be in the best interests of the entire nation, based on the
> viewpoint of all of the [relevant] agencies, and also direct attention to those
> aspects considered inimical to the public welfare.

'The Five Year Plan'—words redolent of USSR-speak—would ensure comple-mentarity of agency efforts, and remove overlapping activities, conflicting simul-taneous messages to the general public, and timing disparities among agency initiatives. Everything proposed added up to an 'enlightened public opinion'. This was a bold and rational plan for mobilisation. It was bound to get up noses and it did, because the plan reduced the status of the eleven agencies cur-rently represented on the ARSC to implementation bodies. Instead of shaping national policy they would be directed to where and how they should deploy their resources. Darling also left himself open to the charge of touting for a new job, because the head of the proposed commission would be a prime ministe-rial appointee, endorsed by the Premiers' Conference and, because the ARSC had initiated the plan, 'it would be anticipated that the current Chairman of the A.R.S.C.' would be appointed as the new agency head. No sooner had argument commenced over this new machinery, than Darling had to defer further consid-eration (until April 1964).[25]

The campaign's military-style approach was unmistakable: 'The Plan dif-fers from previous programmes in that it involves OFFICIAL ACTION, the bringing to bear of all the forces which Governments can muster, and doing this simultaneously'. This rhetorical flourish was also evident in the adoption of 'Operation Impact' as the slogan intended to engage the nation, because people's imagination and interest in road safety had to be captured and sustained for the long haul. While the bulk of the plan's framing, structuring and reasoning are likely to have been driven by Paterson, Darling put the weight of his office and authority behind it. The April ARSC meeting did not go well, although the New South Wales representative thanked the chairman for his 'control of such a difficult meeting and congratulated him on the manner in which he had done everything possible to achieve success'. A vote of thanks to Darling was proposed and carried by acclamation. He replied by commenting how distressing it was 'when we cannot get full agreement', except that if all members 'pay respect to other points of view there is hope for the future'. The ARSC, he said, 'had a long way to go in its battle against road accidents but he hoped that it would reach ultimate success'. The meeting had been difficult because Darling—experiencing 'considerable anxiety', while insisting that he had the Australian Transport Advisory Council's and ministerial endorsement for widening the ARSC's brief—had delivered an ultimatum on the ARSC's future if it disagreed with the plan. The four options to tackle road safety were public education (but without the ARSC), Commonwealth involvement without the states, Commonwealth cooperation with those states willing to work with it or Commonwealth withdrawal. The motion to adopt the plan was eventually carried thirteen–three. On one side were the majority of members who agreed with the creation of the proposed Australian Road Accident Prevention Advisory Committee (or the compromise of a strengthened ARSC with additional members) with some dissenting state representatives on the other.[26]

Sadly, this vote counted for nothing. Not only did the ARSC meet (in March 1965) when there was a 'fairly alarming deterioration in recent road casualty figures' but 'under the shadow of rejection' of the plan and the proposed new committee by the state ministers (two were in favour and four against). Darling thought that the ARSC was right and the dissenting ministers 'wrong'; there was unlikely to be a genuine solution to the road-accident problem until more was known about the causes of accidents 'as a result of much more penetrating enquiry and analysis of the relevant data'. As the victims of uncooperative federalism, Darling and the ARSC pressed on during the 1960s to fulfil the ARSC's existing public education brief. Doggedly, in the face of setback over the plan, Darling continued scheduling road engineers and other specialists (for example, on drink driving) to address ARSC meetings, to liaise with state safety councils and to work with ARSC and Australian Transport Advisory Council sub-committees, the Australian Road Research Board and the National Health and Medical Research Council on various aspects of road safety. Opperman's departure as minister in December 1963 meant that much of Darling's road-accident prevention strategising occurred under the new Minister for Shipping and Transport, Gordon Freeth, who did not provide the ministerial support for which he had been hoping. After more than three years of working with him, Darling noted that it was still 'very difficult to get Freeth on to the mark', although the new departmental official was 'likely to be more helpful than anyone we have previously had'. (By mid-1966 he was feeling optimistic about road safety, he told the prime minister, although without saying why.) A draft note for Freeth (not sent) reveals his frustrations. The minister, he wrote, had to decide whether to take the Commonwealth's concern for road safety seriously by providing the ARSC with a continuing secretariat and a statistical research fund, or exit the field and rely on publicity generated by Paterson. If the latter course was preferred, then there was no point in him being chairman. On the other hand, if Freeth wanted to enlarge the ARSC, he would stay on until such time as the right person was located. He was unclear in his own mind whether the Commonwealth's job was to collect, examine and evaluate information and leave the states to take action.[27]

Darling was still pessimistic at the end of 1967, writing in his diary that road safety 'does not make much progress'. Occasionally as chairman he was contacted by road users. When one woman wrote to allege that her husband suffered a cerebral haemorrhage as result of wearing a seatbelt, he followed up by contacting a surgeon for her. His own experience as a motorist back and forwards to Canberra also coalesced his experiences in three jobs: citizenship conventions for immigration, the ABC (for which he affirmed its radio programming quality as 'pretty good') and (with firsthand observations of poor driving) road safety:

> always young men usually in Holdens driving too fast for crowded road and type of car. Not enough police ... but driven again to the conclusion that N.Z. plan of Traffic officers, not ordinary police must be the solution. Can the Commonwealth government move in on this level? Everything else a mere palliative. A most frustrating assignment.

Darling's release from interminable meetings was occasional drollery. When the new Minister for Shipping and Transport (Ian Sinclair) increased his annual remuneration to $1950 in late 1969, Darling was grateful for the increase, except that: 'If it is to be based on results, it is excessive: if, on the other hand, upon effort, attendance at innumerable committees and general exasperation, it is inadequate'. In for a penny, in for a pound: he then queried the ARSC's raison d'être as coordinator of publicity material generated by the state-level councils. If that could be done twice annually at a state transport secretaries' meeting chaired either by himself or by a departmental officer, then the ARSC was redundant. But if the road problem was to be tackled nationally, then the best mechanism was a statutory commission. Darling informed Sinclair that he would soldier on until the end of 1971 if required, after which 'I really must give myself a rest I think'. His advocacy of a statutory body paid off. When he completed his term as chairman in August 1970, Sinclair wound up the ARSC and replaced it with the Commonwealth Expert Group on Road Safety with Darling as its inaugural chairman. Sinclair conceded that Darling's ARSC role must have been 'a fairly unrewarding job'.[28]

After nearly a decade in road safety, Darling told the Australian Transport Advisory Council that no government could be expected to take drastic and unpopular steps unless the need was proved beyond reasonable doubt:

TOP The chairman concentrating on the interviewer
ABOVE Doing what a chairman does, 1966

TOP With Liza, T.W. Bearup (the ABC's London representative) and Mrs Bearup, 1962
ABOVE Looking avuncular at Sydney airport

TOP Arise Sir James
ABOVE With Charles Davidson (PMG) and Archbishop Eris O'Brien, Canberra, 1962

TOP James Darling House, Australian College of Education
ABOVE With Sir Zelman Cowen, 1991
OPPOSITE TOP In the study at Myamyn Street
OPPOSITE BOTTOM Immediate family

25 12'93

TOP With fellow Marcus Oldham trustees
ABOVE Dr Darling yet again, Deakin, 1989

TOP In the backyard, Myamyn Street
ABOVE Seven grandchildren. L to R: James Sutherland, Michael Gray, Charles Sutherland,
Timothy Shearer, Peter Gray, Andrew Shearer, Nicholas Sutherland

Probably the final photograph

This cannot be true in most cases without further investigation, statistical survey and research. The resources for such measures do not as yet exist. If they were provided they would still require the willing co-operation of the Transport authorities in the States.

One of his final duties was to help prepare a national symposium in 1972. He advised a state minister that dealing with road safety without attending to urban mobility was a 'merely remedial exercise'. At best road-safety measures were a second-line defence 'or even further back'. Urban mobility ought to be the conference theme and that would entail engaging experts in demography, town planning, public transport, and road and railway engineering. If one wanted an example of the 'best basic material', then go no further than Tokyo, he said; for 'the most horrid example of failure', then look at Djakarta. When after twelve months he relinquished his chairmanship of the expert group, Sinclair's successor (Peter Nixon) paid tribute to Darling's advocacy of the need for road-safety research. So too did Professor J.S. Robertson (Department of Pathology, University of Adelaide). The cause of road safety 'owes a great deal to you', he said, envious of Darling's forthcoming relief from 'the administrative rigmarole & drudgery that seems to bedevil this field more than most': 'Lives saved per word spoken or written probably equal about 0.0000001', Robertson continued, 'but we will fight on of course'. And therein lay the rub. Darling's efforts, however, had been vindicated. A public servant member of the ARSC congratulated him on his appointment as chair of Sinclair's new group. 'I was also pleased', he wrote, 'to see that the old Australian Road Safety Council had folded up and passed into limbo!' The Commonwealth's decision reminded him of the ARSC's discussions and the suggestions advanced, 'unsuccessfully of course', between 1963 and 1965. The decision showed what was possible when the right kind of minister and permanent head were in place. 'I'm afraid we were too far ahead of our time in those days and prophets unhonoured in our own country.' The new arrangement was belatedly correct and the former chairman was largely instrumental in bringing it about.[29]

In respect of road safety, Darling was on the right side of history. But what about student politics: was there a right side and who would be on it? In 1961, the English cultural Marxist Raymond Williams had said of British youth that 'the most useful service already performed by the new generation is its challenge to the society to compare its ideals and its practices'. By the end of the decade, during which an 'unusually able group of student politicians' (of both Left and Right persuasions) enrolled at the University of Melbourne, and student activism—increasingly evident from the late 1950s—had escalated on the Parkville campus. In its more openly rebellious 1960s version, Victorian student activism was more prominent at Monash University. If comparison of ideals and practices at its Clayton campus was mostly associated in the public

mind with a student named Albert Langer, then by mid-1969 the public face
of Melbourne's emergent activism was increasingly personified by Harry Van
Moorst. In September, Darling chaired the first meeting of the 'Committee
on Matters concerning Student Members of the University'. The reasons for
this rather anodyne choice of title are evident in the committee's brief. Two
student meetings in June and August had sought to establish a body comprising
students, staff and university council members to 'examine the nature and
structure of the University'. But, after meeting the President of the Students'
Representative Council (SRC), Brian Burdekin, Professor David Derham (the
vice-chancellor) proposed to council the formation of a committee 'to receive and
consider submissions from students', channelled through the SRC and from joint
student and staff committees, to initiate staff and student discussion of 'matters'
affecting student members, and to examine the constitution of the council. The
presence, in addition to Darling, of Derham and Burdekin, two professors, two
judges and a leading member of the state Labor Opposition gave the committee
weighty eminence. An OGG, K.G. Armstrong (Department of Politics) was a
non-professorial member. By December, with only two submissions received, the
committee agreed not to adjudicate on grievances but to survey opportunities for
student participation and possible means of their improvement. Early in the new
year it was sceptical about the adequacy of faculty-level communications channels
for students and began discussion of council's composition (while intoning that it
did not accept that 'numerical representation of interests on Council had any real
significance'). Eventually, in June 1970, Van Moorst met the committee. Having
read and circulated his document entitled 'Inscape', Darling invited suggestions
from its author. These and the interview that followed were summarised in a
58-page transcript.[30]

During his interrogation, Van Moorst used 'the university' in several different ways and kept his interlocutors guessing. Sometimes he had in mind the very
idea of the university as an institution, at others universities generally and at still
others the University of Melbourne specifically. At the outset of his remarks Van
Moorst evoked the themes of alienation and depersonalisation by highlighting
a lack of staff–student contact and the pressure-packed examination-oriented
courses typical of mass universities. A closely related point of culpability was
the turning of universities to industry for money and for research (for which he
instanced the MBA degree). A key concern for him was 'the succumbing of the
University to technology and its desires' down to the level of specific course subjects where he asserted that modes of thinking were indicative of a technological
society creeping into the university. He also drew attention to compartmental-
ised knowledge. Oscillating between generic observations and criticisms aimed
at Melbourne, Van Moorst signalled his concern with the hierarchical nature of
the university academically and administratively, because this structure created
problems for student participation. While he was also interested in the aims of
education, his main initial point seemed to be technology. Next, taking aim at

the University of Melbourne, he said that it was worthy of full investigation, especially its direction and relationship to the wider society. Such an inquiry should proceed by open hearings, meetings and seminars with experts brought in to speak. Proposals for change ought to be based on the principle of education for 'the growth and development of the individual to his fullest desires or abilities', and other aims 'subordinated to this principle'. Van Moorst wanted the university to be integral to society and not a mere ivory tower. Darling's query about what he meant by integral was met with a lengthy shopping list of claims: relaxation of quotas on student places, access not confined to an elite few, a focus on solving social problems (to be facilitated by course restructuring), community self-management, staff–student control and changes in department and faculty structures, with hierarchy to be jettisoned in preference to a circular structure with the council at the centre, surrounded by interrelated departments, and with no semblance of a ladder. Van Moorst also proposed to abolish the Professorial Board, replace faculties with vocational boards linked to vocational training, reconstitute the council (with a majority of directly elected staff and students, and officers elected on a rotating basis), make departments independent, require open council meetings and make policy by referendum.[31]

To anyone familiar with northern hemisphere student rebellion in North America and Europe, Van Moorst's thinking would have struck a familiar chord: full-on participatory democracy rather than conventional representation. After Darling interrupted to ask for an example of referendum-based policy-making, Van Moorst's demands resumed: meeting transcripts available to staff and students, staff and student control of departments with the latter operating by discussion, reason and consensus, and not run by those whom he styled as dictators. Van Moorst was asked whether he was familiar with the current process for electing deans. Perhaps such elections were restricted, said Darling, and the electorate should be widened? Yes, the student replied. Darling thanked him for his submission. He commented that the young man's proposals would shift the university in 'the democratic direction, in inverted commas', which amounted to the kind of 'comprehensive assault which could be used probably on any institution that exists anywhere, and probably any institution that ever has existed anywhere, ever'. He detected some sense in what had been said although in the absence of more specific suggestions the submission could not be properly rebutted. Darling viewed the meeting as concerned with the following problem ('I have been making speeches about it all over the place'):

> [the] desire on the part of the people who are in all kinds of walks of life to revolt against the idea of being pushed around by [other] people even in their own interests. And this is called the demand for participation, actually to play some share in determining their own future.

If so, then the committee's job was to listen, establish in respect of this demand 'how on earth you do it' and do it in such a way that avoided 'getting a complete hotch-potch of an organisation which will just not function'. Darling foresaw the inevitability of compromise, but he wanted to extract specific points from those that Van Moorst had proposed, 'many of which in principle I very much sympathise with'. He drew the line at referenda, because even though he was 'probably stupid' he just could not see how every decision made in a pluralistic university and a pluralistic society would work if these were to be referred to students.[32]

What about the practicality of referenda-derived decisions on submissions to the Australian Universities Commission, given the limited time available to students, their likely loss of valuable study time and their need to process vast amounts of paper? Darling then summed up Van Moorst's contention as being that there was too much emphasis on the economic benefits derived from a university education, and too little based on individual grounds and growth. Derham called it too much stress on materialism and too little of a spiritual emphasis, to which Darling added intellectual benefits. If this was Van Moorst's contention, then he accepted it, except that the young man had underestimated 'the honesty, integrity, decency, devotion and dedication and all of the rest of it of the people who are actually engaged'. Darling wanted to be able to recommend a couple of positive possibilities. The first was for students to realise that people were concerned about them and their opinions, 'because I think this is more important than that they actually control': even though actual control was physically and politically impossible, students had to feel that they were being listened to. The second was the need for lower-level mechanisms to allow their voices to be heard. The committee would not get far unless it could devise specific ways for Van Moorst to be confident that this might occur. (Student membership of faculty and departmental bodies might be a step in the right direction, Van Moorst had conceded, even though he was querying the representative principle.) Discussion then turned to issues associated with open access to meeting information (such as confidentiality, protection of reputations and inhibition of free discussion). Darling next queried whether there might still have been an argument in favour of the 'aristocracy' of the Professorial Board, and then fingered Van Moorst for trying to change the University of Melbourne into something that, in the ordinary sense of the word, was not a university. Van Moorst saw this as the perfect opening: but the traditional sense of the university had disappeared, he protested. Summing up, Darling hoped that 'we have not been impolite' and said that, while he did not agree with some of what the student had claimed, he accepted the contention about opportunities for participation, and the 'consideration that in these days we have got to give to the victims of the system'.[33]

After Van Moorst had departed, Darling asked for any further consideration to 'Mr. Van Moorst's outpourings'. He then suggested that he and Armstrong work on a couple of specific proposals, given that 'we have operated together in the past [at GGS]'. 'Surely not on the basis of equality', replied Armstrong, in an attempt at post-meeting levity, to which Darling quipped that he never presumed to that extent and then jested with his former student: 'Well you do the work and I will correct it. The same basis as before.' The day after the committee meeting (16 June), Van Moorst and about thirty students laid siege to a meeting of the Professorial Board—a calculated act, presumably, rather than a knee-jerk response to Darling's offhand remark the day before to the effect that if he had an axe to grind, then the last place that he would want to grind it would be the Professorial Board. A rash of picketings of meetings and attempted stormings of buildings continued until October (the examination period) and erupted again in early 1971. In light of these developments, particularly Derham's lament that its work was not more widely known, Darling's committee was a quiet achiever. Its view of itself was that it had justified its existence, 'even if only in showing that there was not a large body of dissatisfied student opinion'. Two university historians have described the pace of Darling's committee as 'slow' and its work 'little known', but they viewed it as an invaluable clearing house for including student representatives on university bodies. In this respect, in July 1970 it approved in principle the idea of open council meetings—an endorsement that put it at odds with Derham who was perturbed by the implications of openness for the maintenance of confidentiality in relation to individual staff, students and the university's external dealings. Among his other caveats about openness, Derham insisted that it was not 'a step towards participatory democracy' and, in any case, a so-called 'right' to participation in the day-to-day governance of an 'organization larger than a small tribe' was merely a prescription for bringing government and administration to a standstill. In addition to openness, Darling's committee was committed to the representation of undergraduate and postgraduate students on faculty bodies, and student representation on curriculum committees. It deliberated until late 1971, by which time, following a lock-in of university staff by students in May, Council's agreement to an inquiry into university government had subsumed the focus of its work.[34]

Darling's 'prolonged association' with students at the university, the impact on him of a television program about the trial of the Chicago Eight (who in August 1968 had demonstrated outside the US Democratic Party National Convention) and, closer to home, John's impending return during the middle of his 'Oxford Experience' prompted him to record an extended diary reflection in October 1971 (his first for nearly four years). This entry was a moment of truth. Dr Ainslie Meares, the Melbourne psychiatrist (eleven years his junior), had recently said that:

> we of my generation will never grasp the situation unless we realize that there is a real and deep gulf between those who were born before the last war (1939–45) and those who have been born since.

This was not a mere generation gap—common to all ages, Darling noted—
but 'something special, a gap between two almost completely different ways
of looking at things'. To get to grips with the magnitude of the difference, he
reflected on what being radical had entailed for him:

> In my day this meant being a socialist, voting Labour, sympathizing with the
> General Strike and in my case at any rate having a perhaps over-developed sense
> of social responsibility, and a rather optimistic belief in the beneficial results
> which would follow as a result of greater educational opportunities for everyone.
> While in retrospect it must be admitted that there wasn't much else that I could
> have done after Oxford with limited capacity and no money in the post-war job
> shortage situation I may perhaps claim that I became a schoolmaster without
> reluctance because of the above basic beliefs. Schoolmastering was the only way
> in which I could do anything at all to make a contribution towards leaving this
> world in any way the better for my having lived in it.

He cited the familiar influences on him as Gollancz, Shelley and the War Office
School of Education, and his schoolmaster father ('a son has some bias either
for or against his father's occupation, just because he knows a bit more about it
than about other professions'). There had also been the war, and the experience
of those having grown up during it and seeing so many of their contemporaries
killed that kindled a sense of obligation in them 'to do our best to fill the gap
which they had left'.[35]

Darling's generation had been different in accepting much which 'seems
repulsive' to the present generation: British empire, white man's burden ('which
was, I suppose, a form of Racism'), parliamentary government, class society
('though in a patronizing way we wanted to make it less unfair'), elitism, paternalism, nationalism ('though we paid half-hearted support to the League of
Nations'), and Christian doctrine and morals ('as the basis of all that was best
in society'). His generation had begun to question 'the 'precedent to precedent'
theory of progress', but tellingly 'we did not question the whole structure of society'. For sure, there were questioning figures like Lord Tennyson and George
Bernard Shaw, who ('as he would have liked to think') was 'the Voltaire of the
present revolution, but we didn't really accept him as such or take him to that
degree seriously', even though Shaw laughed at the family, moral values, capitalist society, the services tradition, physical courage and the empire:

> We laughed with him in the same way as did the French enlightened aris-
> tocrats of the XVIIIth Century, but we did not really take him seriously any
> more than did they take seriously Voltaire.

Nonetheless, Darling's generation had genuinely desired reform: more justice,
'even' more equality, a steady movement of the colonies to dominion status and

less exploitation of the weak, but again tellingly, all of this 'was to be within the basic structure which we had inherited and which we believed to be capable of an evolutionary improvement'. Here, then, was the fundamental break with the modern young radical who had ceased to believe that 'evolution will work':

> Disappointed with Russia he looks to Cuba and China as the hope of the new world which he wants to create. There is no hope for the Capitalist society activated by the Profit motive and centred on nationalistic objectives. Only a clean sweep and a new beginning seem worthwhile. Even if he has no concept other than the simplistic idea of the commune and if his destruction involves him in anarchical and nihilistic conclusions, this seems to him better than our half-hearted and to his mind hypocritical efforts at reform.

No wonder, then, that the elderly, who thought (perhaps foolishly) that they had tried their best to make the world a better place, 'find this hard to take' and 'take it personally and with a resentment, which is partly personal vanity'.[36]

The real question was whether the current generation of radicals 'may not be right'. There was no doubting their sincerity: it was impossible to hear the speeches of the Chicago Eight or to talk with the university's students:

> without being impressed by their deep convictions about the atrociousness of the Vietnam War, about the racial discrimination in the U.S. or in South Africa, or about the inequalities of education in our own country.

Added to this was their 'complete distrust of the integrity of our judicial and political institutions, and of the deep seated wickedness of those who control finance and industry', so much so that to them 'the whole "establishment" is corrupt'. They also believed that society was 'bent on self-destruction by the pollution, physically and morally of the environment'. In this belief the current generation was supported by many people who were not revolutionaries: conservationists, ecologists and psychologists. Contemporary radicals believed that:

> the whole society must be destroyed, if it is to have a chance of survival, and they proceed by the only means open to them to make this society unworkable, by protest, by violence, by abuse and by mockery so as to bring into contempt the institutional framework which we have erected and on which we think that we depend.

To that extent, radicals were impervious to the lesson of history that 'revolution has always ended in dictatorship of one sort or the other, Napoleonic or Stalinist'. But they did not mind and indeed welcomed 'the polarization of opposites which their conduct creates'; they viewed the 'hardening of opposition in the name of "Law and Order" both as justification of their own views as a necessary preliminary to their revolution which they desire'. They dismissed the old-fashioned nineteenth-century liberal as anachronistic, hypocritical and a stumbling block. Kerensky, for example, had been more dangerous than the Tsar and deserved equally of annihilation. Naturally enough, such thinking brought revolutionary youth into direct conflict with their parents' generation: indeed, to have an affection for, and a sense of obligation to, them 'makes things the more difficult for them'. The effect was to force them into 'libertarian attitudes which are not really germane to their problem', such as contempt for sexual continence, marriage vows, regularity of behaviour, punctuality, tidiness and commitment, all of which restrained their 'unlimited freedom to be themselves'.[37]

And what ought to be the response of an older generation to the redemptive nostrums of this new-found fanatical true belief or to such neo-puritanical angel-making? All that these outward manifestations of revolt achieved, said Darling, was to 'infuriate the old even more than do their more basic opinions because they are more easily seen and are more immediately irritating'. To argue that the young would achieve more by outward conformity and acceptance (or apparent acceptance) of the rules of the game was way too easy. The young's reply was likely to be that that would be dishonest ('in exactly the way that the society which they wish to change is dishonest') and that it was only by violent protest anyway that they could make themselves heard. 'Oppressed by the weight of the system which surrounds them', then, such 'violent and disagreeable protest is their only weapon, and it has found its self [to be] effective'. As examples, they could point to the suffragette movement and the building up of the opposition to the Vietnam War in the USA 'which would not have happened without their initiative'. Because 'negroes' had 'remained oppressed for a hundred years since slavery was abolished', it was only when 'the blacks became militant' that anything had been done about their condition. 'Unfortunately there is more truth in this argument.' Indeed, Darling conceded, 'if little has been won for the world by Revolution, nothing at all would have been done for it without it'. The conclusion for the elderly who cannot go along with them, therefore, 'and whom indeed the young do not want', was simply to 'try to understand them', as he had done with Van Moorst:

> to be determined not to be polarized ourselves in opposition, to try perhaps as much as we are allowed to help them to put their case more reasonably and so with greater hope of success, to modify them a little and to help them to clarify their thinking, and above all then to accept the integrity of their intentions and to try to persuade our own contemporaries to do the same as much as they are capable by nature of so doing.

Success in being acceptable to the young was unlikely, though, and such an attempt risked being labelled as 'traitors' by one's own generation. It was an uneasy role to play, but the only alternative was 'to incite the head-on collision and all its consequences'.[38]

Perhaps what persuaded Darling to put pen to paper was closer to home. The day before his diary entry he had received a letter from Josie Adler, his former secretary (now secretary to the vice-chancellor of Flinders University). So far, she said, in respect of students' requests for participation on various committees, the membership places were sometimes difficult to fill and there had been no student sit-ins at Flinders. Whatever the diary entry trigger, it is not surprising that Darling was so attentive to what the students had been saying. Since easing himself out of the exclusive hold on him of the small world of Corio, he had been listening and responding to numerous people: complainants to the ABC, community members during Frontier consultations, and experts on the reduction of road carnage. As for his point to Van Moorst of having been making speeches 'all over the place' about concerns similar to those bugging the young man, there was some validity. Although Darling could not have been described as a voice or champion of the dispossessed—because (since his arrival in Australia) he had served the interests of the rich and powerful—a shift in emphasis was discernible. The bulk of his new responsibilities had required him to appraise from the perspectives of ordinary people—viewers, listeners, readers, motorists, pedestrians, city-dwellers, immigrants, students, religious faithful and the doubtful—the quality of (mostly publicly funded) services. In some instances he had had to speak on behalf of these service recipients—not in the sense of having consulted them directly, but in advocating on their behalf in the corridors of power and other key arenas (and to that extent still talking above their heads). Thus, while mulling over his future and considering his options for gainful employment in public life, at the point at which he had confirmation of the non-renewal of his ABC chairmanship, he had noted in his diary (May 1967) that 'the right thing to do, of course, is to try to serve God in the best way possible'. Such service probably entailed a continued concentration on Frontier and the completion of odd jobs for the Archbishop of Melbourne. He had speculated:

> This might mean trying to write a book on the present religious changes that we are undergoing and endeavouring to express the new theology without jargon and in a way which ordinary men and women can understand.

But the period when this sentiment was written was a trough in his life. Articulation and possible rebuttal of the thinking of the likes of John Robinson and his contemporaries would have to wait, because there was still much to do in public life, particularly in education and immigration.[39]

LOTUS-LAND

1961–1973

Australia today [1968] is in a state of flux: indeed the key to comprehending the nation and its people is to understand that this is a society in transition, in which the old patterns of living and thinking and acting have broken up and the new ones are still evolving … It is a complex, pluralist, dynamic country in which conflict, uncertainty and contradiction are far more characteristic than the old certain certainties. There is a sense of change and experiment which would have seemed impossible twenty-five years ago when the country was stuck fast in its Antipodean isolation, a cultural and economic backwater of the Western world whose only function seemed to be to provide the more advanced nations of the world with wool, cricketers and shock troops.

Craig McGregor, *Profile of Australia*

The impression in respect of transition conveyed by the relative uneventfulness of Darling's accession to his new ABC, Frontier and road-safety responsibilities was one of plain sailing. Transition into something is but one side of the adjustment coin; the other is transitioning out—divesting, relinquishing or, in plain speak, letting go—an experience that induces withdrawal pangs. In late 1972, Alan Cash (Darling's special assistant, 1956–61, and then headmaster of the Armidale School) wrote to his former boss about the post-Garnett succession at GGS. Garnett was due to retire in 1973 (to be succeeded by Charles Fisher, son of Archbishop Fisher). Cash had not applied for the vacancy, partly because he thought that the 'era of charismatic Headmasters' had passed. While its eclipse was due to a number of factors, he speculated, including 'lack of talent' and 'the downgrading of authority', heads had to work a lot harder at 'explanations, guidance, "nurture of the faculty" at the level of the "first among equals" to get what we hope to achieve'. Apropos changed circumstances, Darling had written in a like vein a few years earlier: 'The day of dignity and a corresponding awe seem largely to have passed, but I am not sure that it is for the better'. He also mentioned something similar to an English correspondent when explaining his limited success in marrying humanism and faith at GGS. By the 1960s, material competition in academic standards was dominant in contemporary Australian schools and probably also in English ones, 'largely undoing everything that we [his headmaster peers] thought important'. Such a turn of the wheel meant that GGS was 'certainly back where I started'. This observation about the driving force of educational competition resonates with Craig McGregor's analysis of the emerging 'ethic of materialism' in the postwar Australian middle class's pursuit of status. And, while Darling's remark may not have been intended as direct criticism of his successor, it was indicative of the new environment that Garnett had to navigate, captured neatly in a GGS history in a chapter title on his incumbency: '"More madness"—Education for democracy 1961–1973'.[1]

In respect of his successor, the one blot on Darling's otherwise blemish-free escutcheon during his post-GGS retirement years was the aftershock of regime change at Corio. In the decade or so following his departure, Thomas Ronald Garnett kept drifting back sporadically onto his radar. The situation of dislike and divorce between the two headmasters that Darling had described to Madgwick in mid-1967 was an unequivocal expression of *mea culpa*: despite the free hand that he had been given by the council and the attention that he had lavished on Garnett until his arrival, he made a mess of the transition between them. In fairness, the breakdown in relations at Corio was not entirely Darling's fault. Anyone with firsthand experience of succession between executive heads and leaders, or who is familiar with the (extensive) research evidence in this area, knows that there is no sure-fire recipe for avoiding bad blood—as testified by the Searle and Travers transitions. The hope is usually to mitigate a potentially detrimental impact. With hindsight, two things should have happened at GGS in 1960–61. First, someone ought to have taken Darling aside and quietly impressed on him the need for an explicit handover strategy. Had he lived, John Manifold was the obvious person. But there was no-one else of comparable stature, wisdom and knowledge of the headmaster's moods—in particular his pride and touchiness, and his predilection to threaten resignation or to sulk when he couldn't get his own way—who could have belled this cat. (Frank Woods is the only possibility that comes to mind.) Second, Darling probably should have done what he did with F.E. Brown—remain in touch and make himself useful to Garnett if required. Why he chose not to is a mystery. Instead, he cut himself adrift from Corio. Not only that, but in 1978 he castigated Garnett publicly for allegedly circulating a school novel (G.F. Bradby's *The Lanchester Tradition*) as the latter's means of asserting his autonomy and signalling his intentions. But this recounting is evidence that (in seeking to salvage his *amour propre*) Darling had missed the real point: for anyone anticipating the dynamics likely to play out following Garnett's arrival, the script was already there in Daphne du Maurier's novel *Rebecca* (1938).[2]

The problem seems to have been that no-one bothered to see matters from the point of view of the new chum—that is, an inability (or unwillingness) to appraise the situation that the new headmaster saw himself walking into. In *Rebecca*, the new Mrs de Winter was consumed by the shadow of the much-loved first Mrs de Winter; she knew that she could never replace her and she lived in constant fear of failing to measure up. Did it not occur to anyone at GGS, therefore—particularly if they were familiar with the plot of this novel—to obtain a sense of the situation that Garnett would encounter? George Turner had warned Darling that while GGS's 'particular clientele' would appreciate Garnett, he would not be 'the kind of leader on the wider front of education that you have been & are'. Expectations of Garnett had been (understandably) high: he was regarded as a prize catch and described as a 'knock-out candidate'; small wonder, given his Malburian pedigree and sporting record. When he got wind of Garnett's appointment in 1960, Darling's former Charterhouse colleague A.L. Irvine said that 'Geelong and indeed Australia are very fortunate', particularly when he assumed that Garnett had been destined for career advancement in Canada. And Darling had reported to Eric (by then Lord) Hacking (a 1929 New Zealand tour party member) that 'we are very excited' to have secured him. Garnett was taking over from a man who—despite his battering at the hands of Connell's evaluation team—was regarded at GGS after thirty-two years as a legend in his own lifetime; a towering figure in Australian education (doyen of the headmasters and the Australian College of Education) and beyond, who had founded Timbertop, the educational innovation that had put the school on the map globally. In appointing Garnett, was the GGS community seriously expecting a dose of more-of-the-same and that his mission was to keep the Darling heritage ticking over? Did anybody think to ask whether the new broom might have contemplated altering the old broom's arrangements, and with what consequences? It is not difficult to imagine that Garnett must have felt trapped because, no matter where he looked, Darling's supporters and acolytes were watching his every move with reproachful eyes like Mrs Danvers, nemesis of the second Mrs de Winter.[3]

But the complication was that these people didn't merely watch. They poured out their grievances to their former chief who, while he had decamped up the Geelong Road to Melbourne, was still within earshot. Initially, relations had got off on the right foot. Garnett's wife, Penny, had been delighted in August 1961 when Margaret Darling had arranged a party for her to meet 'all the wives'. She even urged Margaret to return as a parent to Corio (where John was enrolled in senior school). And yet, barely ten months later while the Darlings were in England—a gap in time in which (to be fair to Darling) he had not only been ill but had taken on new jobs that were dragging him all over the nation—Frank Woods wrote to his friend to say that, with a 'fateful Council meeting' scheduled for the next day, he was 'gloomy indeed about TRG & all that'. Woods had spent hours talking with Garnett and the second master, Vic Tunbridge, and, despite urging Garnett to 'have it out informally with the housemasters', both Tunbridge and the headmaster expected 'a blow up a la Merton Hall'. Garnett's appointment, then, had soured quickly. Indeed, the development of the situation at GGS, as Robert Southey (chairman of the council) told Darling, was such that to be perceived as a supporter of Tommy implied opposition to Jim. The reverse situation applied equally, said Southey, which was why his former headmaster had become the 'focus of opposition to Tommy'—and which, he said, was the opinion of 'many people'. If, therefore, Darling continued to sup with his friends among the staff and, no matter how wise or temperate he might have been when his 'old lieutenants poured out their woes to you', they would report to their GGS cronies that 'I said such and such to Jim about Tommy'. After the inevitable whispering campaign in the Corio common room, such sentiments would transpose into: 'Jim said such and such about Tommy'. Like it or not, then, Southey concluded, Darling's stature and influence made him a focus for opposition.[4]

Notwithstanding Southey's acuity, was he seriously expecting his former headmaster to have cut himself off completely from all former colleagues? To do so would have been entirely out of character. But the real difficulty with Southey's letter was that he wrote it in 1966: five years after the changeover, by which time it was probably way too late to begin mending fences. Back in 1961, then, much had been left to chance and the festering of wounds had been compounded by Darling's strategy of avoidance. Early on he had rejected Garnett's hand when it had been extended, despite his successor's pleas:

> Can you and Margaret yet bear to return to the Headmaster's house at Corio[?] There are so many things that I should dearly like to talk over with you: but we are both so busy (at least whenever I do see you, you note [?] how much busier you are now!) that there doesn't seem to be time.

When informed later that Darling and Montgomery were co-authoring a book on Timbertop, Garnett was delighted, offered access to the documentary sources and exhorted him once more: 'I still hope you will come down and see us one day. The invitation, of course, remains open.' As to his beloved Timbertop, Darling was bound to have known that changes were on the cards because Sylvia Ritchie was likely to have relayed the gist of correspondence with Garnett about three months after his arrival. She feared in response to the latter's comment that he perceived a 'too great apartness' of three sections of the school (Corio, Bostock and Glamorgan) that Garnett may have been contemplating sending junior school boys directly to the mountain school, when in her view (while acknowledging her lack of expertise) they 'came here [Timbertop] at the right age'. Indeed, Garnett had concurred about the transition age ('That is what I believe too') except that he claimed that he was under pressure to alter this arrangement. In fact, he was minded to transfer the third form from the senior school to the top of a newly named middle school, where the boys would be prepared for their year away from

Corio. (He had announced something similar, although after no debate, to a shocked school assembly about three weeks earlier.) He undertook to talk further about it with her when he was next at Timbertop.[5]

Darling, then, became a letterbox for complaints. Joey Allen, for example, reported that Hutton had wailed to him that he was 'fed up with things at Corio where he says there is no leadership and no discipline' and that he 'would be glad to get out of it'. Francis James was concerned that under Garnett's regime his son didn't seem to be doing any work at all. At one point Darling was girding his loins to intervene and David Hay (himself mulling over his two sons' education under Garnett) urged 'caution' in the face of his friend's 'acute anxiety & worry'. Eventually, the unthinkable happened. Darling could no longer contain himself when he learned in 1964 that Vic Tunbridge (aged sixty) was soon to be dispensed with (no offer of retention until age sixty-five and required to take leave during 1966). Apart from the inherent unfairness to Tunbridge himself, Darling told Griffiths that the council had underestimated the negative impact of his departure on GGS's 'already declining reputation'. No old boy from the past two decades would stand for Tunbridge's ejection and the staff's sense of security would be 'destroyed' by knowing that he had been 'pushed out before he wants to go'. Much that had happened in the past four years had been 'quite daft', Darling asserted, and was in some ways worse but he had quite deliberately kept his mouth shut. Duty to Tunbridge as a continuing staff member and 'a loyal personal friend', and the school, however, had stung him into action. Two years earlier when alerted to the school council's intentions, he was 'so angry' that he 'nearly exploded'. To back a council appointee was one thing except that it 'must be within reason', because a headmaster could not be allowed to do 'irreparable damage to the very life of the school'. However much Garnett might dislike Tunbridge and see in him 'the continuity that he wants to destroy', by such action he would only end up destroying himself and the school. Having misunderstood the assurances given to the council that Tunbridge was content with his retirement arrangements, only to discover from Darling that Tunbridge was 'so distressed over the whole business', George Laird (a councillor) confided that if he 'institute[d] any move to put the matter in order' then his 'small influence will be exerted in the direction of fair play'.[6]

Belatedly, then, Darling switched tactics and had intervened. But it was to no avail because the council stuck by its man. The realisation had also dawned on Darling that he was a victim of his own disengagement. As he told Eaton's friend, Sir Desmond Lee (then headmaster, Winchester College), in June 1964:

> Things at Geelong Grammar School do not seem to improve substantially.
> He [Garnett] has collected enormous sums of money out of the Old Boys
> and parents, and seems to me to spend it most extravagantly. The masters, all
> but a very few and those not the best, seem quite irreconcilably opposed on
> the grounds basically that they cannot trust him. This is probably unfair, but

arises from the fact that he still seems like a rat in a trap making inconsequent dashes in different directions. But I know little about it and would like to know less. Fortunately we don't have to meet, and I try to see as little as possible of anyone connected with the school. This is a bit hard as Johnny is still there and Elizabeth has married one of the masters, but I do not think that it can be helped.

The year before, Darling had wanted to attend Montgomery's farewell dinner (following his retirement from Timbertop), but said to his friend 'I have not been asked' and that, in any case, to have attended 'would not be very satisfactory'. Montgomery would be departing Corio to become the Registrar of the Diocese of Rockhampton. Apparently, in response to what he had assumed to be Montgomery's 'troubles', Garnett had persuaded the council to second him to Rockhampton on full salary until 1968 (when he would retire) to enable him to retain his annuity. Despite Garnett's generosity, Montgomery could not help surmising that he was 'the first of the (perhaps) nonconformists that is being paid off'. (There was additional evidence of generosity in 1974 when 'as a result of a request from Tommy Garnett, the Executive Committee of the School Council has decided to increase your [Darling's] pension from the School by $1,000 p.a. as from January 1st'.) In May 1967, Darling's diary note read: 'six years watching destroyed what one had tried to do at G.G.S. over 32 years'. Garnett could not take a trick: even in 1973, with his retirement imminent, some old boys were still divided over his merits. A.B. Brown, for example, confided to Darling how he hoped that when his former headmaster compiled his memoirs he would 'reveal (as the media say) just how the School Council came to choose Garnett!' He was also aware that 'Bob Southey has convinced himself that my consciousness of Garnett's shortcomings is a bit of sour grapes'.[7]

The school council, if Bill Manifold's view (expressed just prior to his resignation from it in 1965) is to be believed, urged Darling to communicate with Garnett. Manifold's quirkily worded letter tried to reassure Darling that Garnett had been acquiring more of a sense of his 'proper relationship' with the council and the school. (Bear in mind that he was describing a headmaster who was a third of the way into his incumbency.) Manifold thought that the 'gulf' between the two men was 'quite absurd'. There was no way that the council would get rid of Garnett—most councillors were ignorant of how much in four years he had altered GGS; they felt that 'the worst is now over' and that the school was on a 'sound basis'. As for Darling, the council could see the reasons for an 'undercurrent of feeling' of staff dissatisfaction and their sense that he had been 'unapproachable' before departing in 1961, and the overcrowding problem to which he had pointed. Darling's 'continuing opposition', however, could only harm him and the school. By all means tell Garnett that 'he is a louse and that his methods are hopeless' but 'TO HIS FACE'. Tell him also about finance and scholarships, Manifold urged, but be prepared for a man who could 'keep his end up too'. Moreover, for someone who was thought to lack understanding, Garnett was proving to be 'extraordinarily open to suggestion'. Perhaps his deafness gave him the benefit of the doubt:

> i.e. difficulty in receiving data, leading to [his] mind pretending it has assembled all the facts when it has only half of them. But when other facts are presented later, [the] right decision is taken.

If Manifold was right, then to have left Garnett alone at the start of his headmastership to sort everything out for himself, precisely when he needed all the facts to be gathered for him, had been a 'terrible thing'. If Garnett had had only half the facts then Darling's view that he seemed incapable of sorting things out was clearly wrong. With the redefining of Tunbridge's role as deputy headmaster (following a consultant's report) and the appointment of A.J. Spear as assistant to the headmaster, Garnett would no longer be in a vacuum. Manifold then urged Darling 'for everyone's good' to 'please take the first opportunity of meeting TRG even if it is only to discuss the weather', because he would find him 'very ready to listen to your views even though he won't ask for them'. (Manifold's tune had changed by Christmas 1965, at which point it was known that the Prince of Wales would attend Timbertop. Garnett-educated boys were at the top of the school, Tunbridge was no longer around, the boys had a lot of free time to do their own thing and he seriously questioned Garnett's competence.)[8]

After being so closely identified with the school for so long, Darling deemed that the new GGS regime was not his cup of tea. Unable to forgive his successor, he could not seem to forget him either. 'Doug [Fraser] and Barney [Hutton] came in before dinner—very nice and sympathetic. No talk about the school, thank God!' and 'Another pleasant evening with Mont[gomery]. Very little talk of school, thank God!' said two diary entries in early 1966. His negative view of Garnett was also being reinforced by others. Colin Healey, for example, queried what he regarded as Garnett's odd way of handling his GGS staff, 'as if they were pawns'. On one of the few occasions in which Darling lapsed into undignified name-calling (in his diary), he likened someone whom he had met recently as being 'after the pattern of T.R.G. a self-righteous Puritan who can never be wrong'. (Peter Westcott thought that Garnett was the headmaster that GGS 'absolutely needed' for the 1960s and to that extent admired him, but he also told Darling that he still found him hard to like because 'he would NOT "instinctively" do the compassionate thing'.) Perhaps Darling's attitude was partly coloured by his awareness that Garnett had contemplated (in 1962) selling off the school and relocating it, and even shutting down Timbertop (in 1968). Garnett aside, Darling knew that departure from office entailed not only psychological and emotional adjustment, but also the loss of the trappings. When he first got wind of Madgwick's appointment to the ABC, he noted that his own value for Frontier would be diminished compared with when 'I had a public position and the use of contacts, not to mention free travelling'. Exit from office also required the shedding of affiliations: no more GGS meant (by default) no more Headmasters' Conference of Australia and no more APS. The eleventh triennial meeting of the Headmasters' Conference in Perth had been his last (after having been honorary secretary from its inception in 1931 until 1948, at which point he had become chairman for 1948–49 and a standing committee member until 1954). At Darling's final APS meeting in April 1961, the heads minuted 'with enthusiasm' the association's debt to him, in particular his many years of 'wise guidance' as chairman, and the 'determination and consistency' with which he had set before them the highest ideals and professional standards to which the APS schools ought to aspire.[9]

Post-1961, then, Darling was in an after-glow world. His eminence educationally no longer derived from the authority of headmasterly office, but was entirely reliant on his reputation-based esteem. The Australian College of Education was his main educational anchorage, but only until 1963 when he ceased to be president. He also resigned from the Council of Public Education. The best that the council could do to recognise his twenty-four years of council membership was a scantily worded minute highlighting how his 'penetrating and worthwhile point of view' had 'usually provoked discussion'. So much for discontinuation of affiliations; as to continuation, the other educational body with which he maintained membership until December 1971 (after serving for thirty-eight years) was the council of the University of Melbourne. While his attendance fell away to just over a third of council meetings for the 1960s, he was active on its sub-committees. After securing Menzies' willingness to be chancellor (March 1967), Darling offered to stand aside if a legislative amendment was required to appoint the ex-prime minister (who was not already a council member). He had second thoughts, given that his resignation would have necessitated an election by convocation and 'would not necessarily be safe'. But the body on which Darling had the most significant impact was the Library Committee, of which he became a member (with his friend and surgeon, Sir Clive Fitts) in early 1969 and then chairman in March 1970. With his Free Library Movement and Geelong Free Library experiences on which to draw, Darling was no stranger to the problems confronting libraries and education. Here, he developed a close working relationship with the librarian, K.A. Lodewycks (brother-in-law of Manning Clark).[10]

In the 1950s and 1960s, the university library—known as the Baillieu Library (after the opening of the Baillieu building in 1959, made possible by generous W.L. Baillieu Trust funding)—experienced extreme financial stringency. Such was the extent of its neglect that an entry line for 'library' in the index of a university history is '1960s poverty'. Arising out of what Lodewycks characterised as its 'schizophrenic predisposition' in tolerating an uncoordinated dual system of book acquisition and provision—simultaneous central and departmental monograph allocations—the library had endured a litany of indignities: book stock shortages,

staffing shortages, parsimonious funding and deeply embarrassing performance
levels on a range of measures when compared with other Australian universities'
libraries. The root cause (according to Lodewycks) was the humiliating intrusion
of Professorial Board into the library's business. The nub of the problem entailed
the according of executive authority to the Library Committee rather than the
librarian, who was reduced in status to an administrative factotum. Somewhat
opaquely, two university historians note that the low priority accorded the case
for the library was 'never sufficiently persuasive to achieve major action' in a professionally and scientifically dominated university, and that relations with the
vice-chancellor were 'soured' as a result of a dispute over the statutory rights
and responsibilities of the librarian. In these less than satisfactory circumstances,
Lodewycks welcomed Darling's appointment as chairman (for two years) as a
godsend. 'Throughout my association with him', he recalled:

> I experienced nothing from him but the manners and insights of a gentleman
> and a complete absence of presumption, by which men of lesser calibre seek to
> compensate for their shortcomings.

High praise indeed. With the depth of Darling's experience in education and
public life, Lodewycks felt that he could hardly have hoped for 'a better qualified'
chairman. Such was Darling's willingness to accord the librarian the status that
he deserved that (in February 1970) there was a reformulation on the committee
of executive–head relations and authority over policy. Their mutual confidence
was also expressed in their coordination of strategy in the committee's relations
with the Professorial Board, and in such necessary housekeeping matters as the
joint drafting of the committee agendas and minutes during regular meetings at
Darling's residence.[11]

After resigning from council, Darling was admitted to the honorary degree
of Doctor of Laws. Although an earlier diary entry said that he was 'not much
use' as a member, on this occasion he appreciated the gesture as he regarded this
particular degree as having been:

> awarded by people who did have close contact with me for a considerable
> number of years. I had rather begun to feel that I was more trouble to the
> University than I was worth.

The vice-chancellor's citation noted how in university circles Darling had acquired
elder statesman status and was turned to 'for wise opinion and for disinterested
and always imaginative if sometimes unpredictable advice'. He combined long
experience with 'a remarkable freshness of mind', 'lack of prejudice' and 'transpar-
ent integrity' that meant that 'he was listened to and trusted by people across the
whole spectrum of opinion'. Those with whom Darling worked at close quarters
regarded him 'not only with respect but with affection'. In his March 1973 speech

to the graduates Darling talked about faith. What made the current historical era different from all other ages, he said, was 'its disillusionment, disenchantment [and] disbelief'. Amid this disintegration the whole armour of God and the shield of faith were required. Quoting Hebrews, he emphasised two key aspects of faith. The first was a sense of confidence based on knowledge, competence and experience. This quality was what set apart professionals like lawyers, surgeons or engineers. 'Woe betide you', he intoned, 'if ever, through idleness, or conceit, or ignorance you fail to justify this confidence in yourselves or that which others will put in you and your professional judgement'. And yet faith was also something more personal and concerned with decisions about the basis on which people would live their lives, such that it gave 'substance to our hopes, and makes us certain of realities we do not see'. While to some people such faith entailed religious faith, the decision of others unable to accept this understanding would be equally a decision of faith. Either way, he could countenance no excuse for (in effect) lotus eating: 'The one unpardonable sin is frivolousness, sloth, accidie, disengagement, the refusal to become involved. The most damnable phrase in common use to-day is "couldn't care less".' With their opportunities and forthcoming responsibilities in such a prosperous country, graduates should not treat those responsibilities lightly: 'To be young and to be cynical is to be damned before you start'. (A decade earlier he had urged Newman College students to revolt if that is what they felt like doing, but only revolt against society's weaknesses, rather than the things that 'though they may appear stuffy, you really know to be good'.)[12]

But this was merely one speech and there was little let-up in his post-Corio speech-making. For the period 1961 to 1973, the texts of about seventy addresses survive in his papers (along with a handful of undated others probably from this same period). These cover a wide range of subject matter and equally diverse audiences, including old boy associations, school prize-giving nights (independent, Catholic and state), Children's Book Week, library conferences, teachers' subject associations, art and craft exhibitions and prizes and festivals, weddings and diamond jubilees, the National Council of Women, service clubs, the Melbourne Club (where, as chairman in 1968, he welcomed the former British prime minister, Harold Macmillan), the Australian Student Christian Movement, professional societies, the Victoria League, the Boobooks Club, the Australian Asian Society, the Australian Chemical Industry Council and the Administrative Staff College. There were three learned society orations: the W.D. Chapman Memorial Lecture (1962) to the Institute of Engineers, an address to the Congress of the Asia-Pacific Academy of Ophthalmology (1964) and the Buntine Oration (1972) to the College of Education. A number of these addresses display shifts in his outlook. His tone also changes, and his wording often conveys urgency, and a sense of time running out in his invoking of arbitrary date lines and time frames. There is also (as in his address to the Melbourne graduates) some preachifying and borderline shrillness. The feature in respect of self-identity that stands out in them is his increasing public affirmation and projection of himself as an Australian. In an otherwise unremarkable and, by his standards, rather dreary speech to the ophthalmologists, he signalled this new incarnation with:

> What I have to say will have to be said from the point of view of an Australian—I think that I may call myself that, though I was born in England ...

Not only that, but Darling also presumed in the 1960s to speak about the country and its destiny—an unmistakeable shift in temperament. He was optimistic about Australia, which was 'not doubtful about its future' and 'not depressed about life'. In fact, it was 'full of confidence in its own future, whether rightly so or not I do not know', although that didn't really matter: 'as a nation or as a people we are an optimistic, forward-looking self-confident people'.[13]

Australian identity was one theme. Leadership was another. Apart from periodic exhortations to GGS schoolboys to exercise moral leadership and *noblesse oblige*, he had had little to say about it. In the 1960s, however, leadership began to preoccupy him. In sporadic work for the Staff College at Mount Eliza in 1966 and 1971 he noted in one address (presciently, in light of subsequent psychological work in this field) that leadership was not about what one is but 'what other people think that one is'. Leaders displayed devotion to and enthusiasm for a cause, competence (including thoroughness, attention to detail and preparation), foresight, courage (physical and moral, even to the point of hardness), strength in dealing with superior opponents and critics, consideration for other people (particularly a leader's team members), along with a willingness to take the blame for the failure of subordinates and to share or even give away praise. If dignity and awe were features of a bygone era, their eclipse did not deter him when assessing the work of the Staff College's syndicate (or study) groups from devising 'some common standards in the assessment of greatness'. Tongue in cheek, perhaps (for he claimed that it was an 'Age of Arithmetical Absurdity' marked by a 'contempt for value judgments'), he scored each biographical figure nominated by the students out of ten on criteria such as intellect and industry (both 'sine qua non'), integrity, imagination, judgement, charm and opportunity.[14]

Another theme was greatness, which Darling often merged with leadership. In the Chapman lecture ('The anatomy of greatness'), Darling was meant to speak about the education of engineers, but he abandoned the brief early on to adopt the persona of a reader of history, biography and 'even novels' interested in the analysis of the word 'great'. If exactitude of measurement was essential in the engineering profession, then the bases for assessing human greatness were entirely inexact and fraught. The lecture was an opportunity to bestow accolades on a few of his favourites, including three greats whom he had met personally: Temple, Lord Bryce (the British Liberal politician and jurist) and Sir John Monash, while conceding that closer inspection of people admired at a distance was likely to reveal feet of clay (although not in these three instances).

Specification of an order of precedence of greatness, he said, was virtually impossible. Likewise, to define a yardstick for comparing greatness across diverse fields was equally difficult, particularly in domains susceptible to the 'vagaries of fashion and taste' (such as the arts). Moreover, in respect of great stature there had to be recognition of individuals while they were alive as well as after death. (Darling allowed for greatness among women, while focusing on men.) At the same time, however, acknowledgement of a man's greatness might lapse upon his death. A great man stood out in his field and beyond it during his lifetime as well as in his field after death, but to be able to stand out in some fields was harder than in others. There was also the potential in discussions of greatness for confusion between the contribution of a man and the pedestal on which his reputation rested, such that the position that he occupied might be (incorrectly) taken as the source of his greatness. Darling was also aware of a chicken-and-egg problem: which came first in the circumstantial fit between a particular individual and a moment of time? Was it a case of the person who was right, or the person being in the right place at the right time? Which made which?[15]

Judgements about greatness should be made on the basis of 'an enduring contribution to the world', Darling claimed, while acknowledging that such a yardstick left the question begging of whether such a contribution had to be solely constructive (so as to eliminate consideration of historically destructive individuals). He was also adamant that 'creative imagination' had to be part of the estimate of a person to assess evidence of breaking with past social and cultural patterns, and striking out anew. He then turned momentarily to the engineering profession and Isambard Kingdom Brunel (1806–59): a genius who (like Sir Isaac Newton), he reckoned, was 'one of the giants upon whose shoulders other people stand'. Poets and artists were continually striving for original contributions rather than repeating past successes. Great generals, by some 'imaginative gift', were those able to add something to the art of war. The twofold genius of statesmen was to be in tune with their own times while manipulating present circumstances in anticipation of the future. The source of a leader's power was insight and far-sightedness—'this genius of the imagination sees answers to questions that seem unanswerable, and solves problems that seem insoluble'—and bestowed the necessary faith in himself and his abilities, without which leadership was impossible. The gifts of leadership, then, were faith, enthusiasm, courage and power—'the power to attract other men to follow you'. Both Caesar and Napoleon exemplified this influence that was exercised 'hypnotically' over others. But he wondered whether personality was the source of this attribute along with certainty, sureness of touch and confidence. At this point, Darling took another swipe at specialisation: if leadership required an understanding of men, then an education built around specialisation was detrimental because it served merely to separate 'a man from other men'. Bryce, Monash and Temple, with their humility and ability to draw the best out of the person to whom they were talking, had all given him this feeling of understanding.[16]

To query specialisation with specialist professionals—engineers—was to skate on thin ice. Darling took his leadership cue from the Scottish writer and essayist, Thomas Carlyle (author of the Victorian-era paean *On Heroes, Hero-Worship and the Heroic in History*) to try to specify properties that his hearers' common-sense reasoning could make real. In addition to what he had already said, he proposed sincerity, single-mindedness (or pureness of purpose) and serenity. If such lofty sentiments almost elevated leadership into saintliness, he acknowledged a dark side to greatness: the temptations of vanity (really 'an amiable human weakness'), pride ('those whom the gods wish to destroy they first make proud' perhaps) and hubris breeding self-destruction ('Almost the worst thing' was that a man 'should get the idea that he is a man of destiny'). After musing about when great men make their mark (such as Caesar, Napoleon, the Duke of Wellington and Abraham Lincoln), Darling then speculated whether beyond destiny lay the fate of a great man's mission 'to fulfil God's Will'—as in the cases of John Knox, Oliver Cromwell and Martin Luther. With the latter's mission being conscience-based, he concluded that a great man had to be 'in tune' with God's will, a rule of thumb applying equally to himself and aligning him with the angels: 'But I also, in my small way', he remarked, 'can do no other in what I write and say than what my conscience tells me'. The moral order of the world made a clear distinction between good (which, he acknowledged, he had not defined) and bad; there was also a purpose to life, and evolution (thought of in Teilhard de Chardin–like terms) was a movement 'towards something higher'. A man could not be great, then, 'unless he is on the side of the good', and unless he was contributing to that slow movement towards order out of chaos. Great men were able to see into the processes of evolution, the laws governing nature and the universe, and glimpse 'the Mind of God'. Anything less was a relapse into mere taste.[17]

The Chapman lecture was Darling's most systematic attempt to spell out greatness. But why choose it and why at this point in his life? With Garnett's redirection of GGS playing on his mind, he was probably concerned about his 32-year legacy and verdicts on his own greatness. In that case, what better way to assess one's own league-table ranking than by sublimating anxiety about it into speculations about the comparative claims of others? Greatness bobbed up again in 1966 during the prime ministerial transition between Menzies and Holt. Was the departing prime minister a great man? Darling noted in his diary that Menzies could 'hardly be called great, I think', except that he was 'so large by comparison with the others [among politicians?] that he bestrides the world like a colossus'. In 1963 Darling also touched on greatness in an address to the Newington Old Boys Association on the need for morality in public life and the mission of schools to try to produce good people. Again, he fused leadership, greatness and goodness. At least passing mention of John Wesley and the Wesleyan heritage was *de rigueur* at Newington, and the Victorian age of piety (with its hypocrisy) would not have been possible, Darling observed, without the likes of Wesley,

William Wilberforce, Lord Shaftesbury and Florence Nightingale, and 'all the other great figures' of the nineteenth century. Likewise, in boys' schooling Arnold and Thring had been great headmasters, as among Newington old boys were Boyer, Clunies Ross and (the former state premier) Sir Thomas Bavin. Elsewhere in notes on Thring, Darling said that greatness was the capacity for attention to detail added to principle, imagination and vision. The irony in his adulation of Thring, the 'bewhiskered martinet' who thought of himself as God's instrument and whose success was limited by 'the asperity he brought to his task', was his prescription for schooling. Darling thought that Thring's 'Machinery, machinery, machinery' (arrangements for sleeping, living, leisure, eating, ablutions and sickness, classrooms, playing fields, and opportunities for friendship outside houses, the school hall, chapel and spiritual life) ought to be the motto for every school—and yet 'the machine' had been the aggravating pebble in his shoe during his final decade at Corio.[18]

Greatness was also in the spotlight in mid-1964 when Darling opened the Dobell Retrospective Exhibition at the Art Gallery of New South Wales. Here he was concerned with the contribution of greatness to national (or what he called indigenous) culture, and William Dobell (thrice winner of the Archibald Prize) was, Darling proclaimed without hint of equivocation, the 'greatest Australian painter, past or present'. For a retrospective to be held in an artist's own lifetime was 'a rare distinction'. And as a painter Dobell was distinctively Australian, he asserted, just as Raphael and Rembrandt had been distinctively Italian and Dutch. A thriving national culture arose from the virility of a society and from 'the distinction of a few great men' born at a time of receptiveness to their influence. What, then, he enquired of his audience, did greatness amount to? This time he emphasised stature, originality and humility. If these attributes were true of Dobell ('and you all know that they are') then 'he is great'. But if Dobell was great, Australia was 'bedevilled by conformity and dominated by fashion'. Nowhere was this truer than in art. Between the bank crashes of the 1890s and the outbreak of World War II, he asserted, there had been way too much dependence on British standards and insufficient belief that Australia had anything to show off. Perhaps, as he proclaimed in 1967 at a school prize-giving in Burnie, Australia's opportunity was to create a new culture that blended two traditions, East and West. Or maybe, as he speculated at All Saints' College in Bathurst, Australia's moment in history had arrived. If so, then there was about a decade to become a truly independent country in mind and morals, and in finance and material goods. (But why a decade—or any deadline?) Returning to the same venue four years later to address a development appeal dinner, he stretched the 'decade' to ten to twenty years: Australia had to discover an identity for itself and, while not breaking with tradition, should avoid derivation and imitation. As a geographic outpost spiritually dependent on somebody else's past and strategically vulnerable while simultaneously economically booming, however, the temptation to be imitative was a real and present danger. Education amid prosperity might help to shun conformity and enable people with trained minds to think for themselves.[19]

Darling's most explicit post-retirement statement on education was 'Responsibility', his Buntine Oration. Apart from elaborating his diagnosis of student protest, it was noteworthy for two reasons: his revised view of second-ary education and repudiation of views articulated twelve years earlier in his Australian College of Education presidential address. He saw much for students to protest about. In Europe and small-town religious America there were still countervailing standards to monetary values, whereas:

> People here are classed by income, the prestige of occupations by the financial returns which they offer, success by the motor cars and boats which a man can own. This money standard turns upside down any proper sense of values and it is not surprising that the sensitive and intelligent young revolt against it, and especially so when the educational process seems to accept, even to encourage it.

It was educationally responsible to try to combat such circumstances, but university students had dismissed the education system as an ineffective instrument of social change. They complained about the 'very affluence' of their lives compared with earlier generations—an annual increase in the gross national product did not strike them as a worthwhile objective (a view for which he had some sympathy). They also reacted to technological sophistication and the elevation of efficiency as the 'supreme object of devotion', but responded by blatantly attempting 'to live irregularly, to make no plans, to accept no commitments in such a way as in fact to involve themselves in a quite intolerable lack of consideration for other people' (for which he had no sympathy). Finally, young people objected to their elders' hypocrisy in not living up to their stated ideals (for which he had a modicum of sympathy). Articulate, powerful and increasingly numerically preponderate, the young were a source of fear among the elderly, a fear that was exacerbated by the speed of change, 'universality of experience', 'extreme mobility' and 'threats of global cataclysm'. Growing up was difficult enough in a stable world and it was satisfying to buck the Establishment when that Establishment 'really was established authority', but when it became 'so very unsure of itself', growing up and trying to buck it were 'harder and less satisfying'.[20]

Secondary schooling was important in the management of a society's demand for, and supply of, talent. On the supply side, Darling dismissed previous models of talent production and claimed that 'adjustment for life' was required to meet the needs of contemporary technological society. The school should fit men and women 'as happily as may be to live in the world and age in which at no request of their own they have been born'. Secondary schooling also had to assist with the capacity to earn a living and help to discover ways of being happy 'which do not demand monetary resources'. This role did not necessitate curriculum relevance, so much as 'conscious training of the intellectual and moral qualities which are the marks in all ages of the civilized man'. He then proposed a new educational ladder and a way of breaking down the state–independent sector schism: sub-primary education provided by local government, the churches and (possibly, as in Japan) industry, followed by a ten-year period (ages six–sixteen) fusing primary and secondary education (with the state and independent systems operating side by side), then three-year fee-paying US-style selective junior colleges (administered by the states, funded by the Commonwealth and enrolling state and independent students) offering diplomas or lower degrees as both preparation for university entry and more general (and terminal) education. Beyond that, the universities would be left free to 'do their real work', released of the burden of students entering them with no prospect of completing their courses. Darling's characterisation of the six-to-sixteen schooling experience was a significant rowing-back from the democratic elitist vision that he had outlined in 'Educational values in a democracy'. To insist that education should attend to 'the real needs of the child and to his interests and thus away from the demands either of university or future employer', and to claim in 1972 that this was what many of his listeners had been trying to do, was correct in one sense. In another sense, however, mention of children's real needs and interests in respect of curriculum was symptomatic of an increasing disdain for elitism in educational circles. There was an unresolved tension in his speech between an inherited elitist legacy and more a child-centred approach to learning, a tension (with which numerous educators were then grappling) that he left up in the air: 'This is not the place for—nor am I capable of—defining further what I mean by this'. Finally, to meet the needs of the 'disenchanted young', his new structural pathway had to be complemented by an attitudinal shift on the part of teachers. Because teaching was akin to watering a growing plant, teachers had to provide 'the frame' in which pupils would grow until they were older, by which time the need for it had passed. Such framing was inherently risky and teaching was a 'hazardous and dangerous profession': to stand for, or appear to stand for, nothing was a denial of 'the essence of the job', simply because this in turn denied the personal relationship that teaching and learning inevitably involved for the participants.[21]

As for the Australian College of Education itself, it had not entirely fulfilled Darling's hopes for it and the report card on its first decade or so for others in Darling's circle was mixed. He had insisted to Francis James in 1967 that the college had so far 'proved worth while' and that he was still winning accolades for his speeches, but after listening to the next year's oration, Vic Tunbridge wondered whether 'we forget to put in the articles inspiring as well as learned papers'. Peter Moyes rated the 1968 conference a mixture of good, very good '& some poor stuff', except for the 'technical jargon of the worst kind & verbosity' in some social science papers, and he had 'never seen so many people sleep' during one address. After the 1970 conference, K.C. Masterman complained to his former boss about the 'unutterably dreary stuff we have heard and read again & again from the old stagers who don't seem interested in education—only in organization'. There were, he said, complaints 'from many quarters'. Darling had been consistent about what the college stood for, as he explained to Viscount Dunrossil (while priming him for the appropriate delivery pitch in 1960):

> our main need at the moment is recognition as the representative of all-Australian, all-stages Education, something which no-one has, we think, ever succeeded in achieving. With recognition, either before or after, should come a prestige, that is a realization of the importance of Education and therefore of those to whom it is entrusted.

As a Scot, said Darling, Dunrossil would have understood that 'it wasn't Education as a means to profit which inspired your forbears, but something much higher in conception, the highest prize being the Ministry [of the church]'. Moreover, as he impressed on another correspondent, he had not attempted merely to privilege a liberal education, because the technical ('or should it be technological?') aspect was also part of what he was after. Any idea that 'the joy of craftsmanship went out with the Middle ages or with the introduction of Machine Tools' was silly, and yet academic educators had not sufficiently acknowledged technical college education, even though it 'so often gives a boy a more real love of learning than the School'.[22]

As Darling summarised them in 'Educating for tomorrow' (his final presidential address in Perth, 1963)—where again he touched on greatness—the college's three aims had been to create a society in which educational leaders could meet; enhance the profession's view of itself and elevate that of the public; and undertake work of a national character. Success could not be asserted 'categorically', but with more than 1000 members and eighty fellows the college had 'made more progress than seemed likely' when it began. Darling's problem in these early years of the college was that his other post-retirement commitments competed for his time and precluded extensive involvement. He said to Tom Timpson in late 1961 that he ought to have been doing more about the college, except that he was reluctant to take on 'anything extra if it can be avoided'. During his recent illness, Professor Moorhouse had held the fort. Darling's disconnectedness during 1961–62 was evident in his patchy attendance at college council and executive meetings. As with the ARSC, he could not find a rhythm until 1963, the year that he relinquished the college presidency to Wyndham and the end of his office-holding. His final presidential address in Perth, he said, was 'a last farewell to the educational world'. He maintained contact during 1964 with parallel college bodies in Canada and New Zealand and in 1966 he opposed proposals by Moorhouse (then president) that were calculated to 'substantially and fatally alter' the college's character, and destroy two of his original aims for it: a fellowship for teachers and enhanced prestige for the profession. Attempts to broaden the membership base (as was proposed) would mean that 'when everyone is somebody, then no-one's anybody'. Invited to intervene, he had put pen to paper reluctantly because it was better that the college develop 'according to its own wishes', rather than in a way that it may have originally planned for itself. Thereafter, his attendance at executive and council was sporadic. He was a member of the former until 1969 and the latter until May 1973, at which point the then president (W.N. Oats) proclaimed the 'end of a "Darling era"' in the college's life.[23]

Throughout the 1960s, Darling remained a member of the Commonwealth Immigration Advisory Council. From 1961, then, with the ABC, ARSC and the council, he was shaping or implementing institutional policy and practice in three substantial Commonwealth portfolios. In a number of respects, immigration had been the great Australian success story. Postwar conditions (a population of a mere 7 millions, a numerically declining workforce and loss of the Depression generation's 'unborn') meant that Australia had been ripe for immigration, particularly with many Britons and Europeans keen to rebuild their lives after years of carnage and devastation. In the 1950s, a succession of agreements had been signed with European countries and, as a member (since 1947) of the International Refugee Organization, Australia had actively supported the work of the UN High Commissioner for Refugees. By 1962, 265,000 postwar refugees had entered Australia, a figure unequalled by any other country (excluding Israel) and second numerically to the USA. In aggregate, 1.8 million people migrated to Australia during 1945–62 (about half from Britain) of whom 920,000 had been assisted immigrants (again, half from Britain) and 600,000 children had been born to immigrant parents. As a result, the Department of Immigration saw Australia making good on its Great Depression and war losses, and entering a 'period of development unparalleled in its history'. In addition to this economic contribution, it was 'truly remarkable' that the newcomers had been integrated 'with so little disturbance' to the community's mores. Socially, thanks to immigration, the nation was 'very much a British community but with a different flavour'. Finally, the rate of immigrant attrition had been low: 94 of every 100 immigrants arriving since 1945 were still in the country five years later. This was the positive policy legacy of the 1940s and 1950s, except that cracks were opening up in the broad immigration policy consensus.[24]

Considered in this context, the Commonwealth Immigration Advisory Council was more than a forum for well-meaning worthies. Although there was regular membership turnover, in the early 1960s it comprised (in addition to interest group nominees) a handful of well-connected and liberal-minded citizens immersed in public service, including (in addition to Darling) Boyer; (from 1976, Dame) Ada Norris (prominent in United Nations circles and women's rights), Justice Dovey (of the Supreme Court of New South Wales and father-in-law of Gough Whitlam) and Gertrude Kumm (of, inter alia, the YWCA and the National Council of Women). While providing advice on matters referred to it by the minister, the council mostly worked hand-in-glove with Sir Tasman Heyes—yet another senior civil servant for whom Darling had an abiding affection. ('He was a past master at handling a diverse group of people and almost always getting the result which he wanted'; his way of working was 'public administration at its very best'.) The council reviewed a multitude of disparate migration program-related issues, including: the incidence of immigrant mental illness, child custody and passports, opportunities for immigrant language study at school and university, immigrant immunisation, naturalisation, the citizenship rights of alien (or non-British) spouses of Australians, foreign language broadcasting, publicity (encompassing migration offices in Europe and provision of country-of-destination films on immigrant ships), employment exploitation of immigrants, the balance of the sexes in immigrant intakes, disturbances at migrant hostels and citizenship conventions. The council members had access to departmental statistical data on migration flows, commissioned reports, migration survey results and transcripts of the proceedings of conferences addressed by leading migration scholars, and they were regularly alerted to (and canvassed for advice on) potential shifts in policy. The council and the department relied on members' eyewitness accounts of Australian offshore migration offices and facilities (especially in Europe and Asia) during or following overseas visits made for personal or professional purposes. The council members' links with external groups were also fundamental to its success.[25]

The Commonwealth Immigration Advisory Council's deliberations provide a window into emerging immigration tensions. Darling was particularly involved with periodic media discrediting of immigrants as culturally deviant recent arrivals and non-European immigration. On the first matter, a council committee (the Conduct of Migrants Committee, chaired by Dovey) was formed in 1951 following adverse publicity about migrant criminality. It had reported periodically and then disbanded. In December 1960, press reports quoted senior Victoria Police vice squad officers about the procurement in Melbourne espresso bars of teenage girls for 'immoral purposes'—prostitution—and the men living off their earnings (although the allegations went beyond Victoria). With nearly all of the forty or so men charged said by the police to be immigrants, there followed a farrago of claim and counter-claim about the factual accuracy and inaccuracy of the reporting, and the numbers of people involved. One alleged participant, Jill, had already been interviewed by television station HSV-7. Had media interest escalated, then an association in the public mind between immigration and the nurturing of vice rings might have been strengthened, with the default law enforcement solution seen as migrant deportation. Unless dealt with promptly, this story would run and damage the immigration program's public image. Equally, because this case entailed deportation (orders had been issued already against four men), the Minister for Immigration (the OGG Alick Downer) was keen for the council to have the full picture. Deportation was a big stick and the case involved some powerful agencies: the police, the Immigration department, the newspapers and television. Darling said (enigmatically) that this problem was evidence of something new: 'blatancy to vice generally' and suggested that Dovey's committee make further enquiries. Caught on the back foot, the council improvised a containment strategy (at Darling's suggestion) of approaching the newspapers to explain the 'true position'.[26]

Darling thought that council members' private representations to media people would be 'much more effective than the issue of any Minister's statements', which would be regarded as suspect by the press. He tackled the Melbourne *Herald's* editor-in-chief, A.K. Thomas. His impression after speaking with Thomas was that the evidence base for the story was thin and Jill was a 'not very reliable witness'. He gave Thomas the department's tabled paper on the vice allegations. Still three months off retirement at GGS, he was not convinced that Thomas had come clean with him 'and I fear may have led me a bit by the nose'. He hoped for more media cautiousness in future, but the damage was done; false statements could not be recalled once published, and the really sad part was that the *Herald* journalist who broke the story must have known that he was exaggerating, and that he was being aided and abetted by a police officer with prejudices against Italians. Darling viewed this deception as the 'most serious aspect of the matter', and believed that the prime minister ought to complain formally to the Victorian premier. The *Herald* refused to take the department's paper lying down, for which reason it conducted an in-house analysis of its own material. Determined to have the last word, the outcome of the newspaper's examination of its library files of sources and attributed statements cleared it, Thomas believed, of having grossly exaggerated the incidence of vice. Suitably reassured, he told Darling that while Heyes was a 'good bloke', and was 'one of the best public servants and helpful to us', the police on the beat rubbing shoulders with the people in question were far better placed than 'the policy boys in Canberra' to know the full facts (although his newspaper could not vouch for the accuracy of the statements of the police and state ministers). Nor, Thomas reassured Heyes, was the *Herald* attacking immigration policy even though the department's document was 'loaded' against the paper, which had simply acted as a vehicle for reporting what it had been told. What was new about the 'racket', said Thomas, was the youthfulness of some of the girls (as young as thirteen), plus the fact that unpublished police material indicated that only the 'fringe' of the alleged racket had been revealed. Dispatch a 'good man from Canberra' to talk to the police, he advised, to obtain the full picture for the department.[27]

The other issue that involved Darling was 'Established policy towards non-Europeans'—bureaucratic-speak for a legacy of entrenched attitudes and practices known popularly as the 'White Australia Policy'. In September 1960, the Immigration Advisory Council chairman K.C. Wilson (South Australian Liberal MHR for Sturt) mentioned at a council meeting a 'recent tendency in some quarters' to advocate policy changes in respect of non-Europeans. Did the emerging criticisms need to be answered? If yes, then how? Both the Australian

Council of Churches and the Presbyterian Church were instanced as critics. Darling argued that 'the way of stating the basic policy required changing'—which was the line slowly crystallising as the council's likely default response. Attitudes to non-European immigration had shifted, Darling claimed, as evident on the council itself. (In 1963, he confessed during his Australian College of Education speech in Perth to being 'astonished and ashamed' in respect of racial and colour tensions when he looked back to the narrow-minded and primitive conceptions of society with which he had been brought up.) The 'official viewpoint' (in a tabled agenda paper) did not finger the churches but a pamphlet entitled *Control or Colour Bar?* emanating from a group at the University of Melbourne. This influential publication was the bête noire of criticism for the department because it contained six pages of errors (summarised in a circular to the Immigration Advisory Council). There was no discounting the reformers' motives—'to foster goodwill with our Asian neighbours'—but they had ignored how existing policy was no longer rigidly exclusionist. There was approved temporary entry for 'special' work (for example, business, training or study), for which 8000 Asians had been admitted, non-restricted admission of spouses and minors of Australian permanent residents, admission for indefinite stays of 'distinguished or highly qualified Asians', 'special circumstance' admissions (such as the non-enforced departure of 800 wartime refugees and extension of permits to potential deportees to Communist China), and the removal (in 1957) of the bar of racial origin that enabled naturalisation of Asian spouses and holders of fifteen-year temporary permits. In the 1954 census, there were 27,000 non-Europeans in Australia, with Asians comprising a mere 0.28 per cent of the population. There were also more than 17,000 reported as being 'Chinese', of whom 5000 had been born in Australia.[28]

Throughout 1961, the council ummed and ahhed about responding to criticism that it regarded as ill founded, but its awareness of a veil of ignorance about Australian immigration policy in parts of Asia lent weight to the need for clarification. In October 1962, for example, one council member reported the surprise of her hosts on learning during her recent visit to India how, after a requisite period, foreign-born spouses of Australian nationals were permitted to live permanently. Despite her best efforts to explain a policy that she claimed was based not on skin colour but on living standards and economic differences, Australians were regarded as 'selfish and prejudiced, and I had some difficult moments'. So was it time for an 'authoritative statement', given that the official position until recently was one of denial? The view of the Department for External Affairs (according to a tabled paper) was that 'it was undesirable to draw attention to the subject even by informative publicity'. But that thinking had changed, partly because *Control or Colour Bar?* had significantly raised the stakes. Darling (then under the surgeon's knife for his hernia) was in a quandary. He had the distinct impression after talking with Thomas that the *Herald* would be sticky about immigration, but 'for my own part', he told Heyes:

I am quite certain that something should be done fairly quickly about this and the re-statement of this policy more in accordance with the facts. I don't think that I under-estimate the difficulties of this but believe that public opinion has swung very strongly in the direction of loosening the restrictions and that the opposition from the old guard, though it may be vocal, does not get much of a general response.

As he confessed to Downer, the issue kept eating away at him:

my conscience is still giving me twinges of pain about our failure to re-state the White Australia policy—I use the phrase because I cannot find and neither have you yet found, an alternative suitable name for it. It seems to me of real importance that we should do so.

An added discomfort was that the convenor of the Immigration Reform Group, which was responsible for *Control or Colour Bar?*, was none other than Jamie Mackie—the same Jamie Mackie whose *Corian* editorial had given him grief in 1942. He therefore urged one old boy (Downer) to confer with another old boy (Mackie), because the latter was 'a bit of an expert on Indonesia', and also 'a person of real integrity, intelligence and good judgement, even though we may not agree with him'.[29]

The Immigration Reform Group's reformist case for non-European immigration steered a middle course between unlimited entry and an outright entry bar. It rejected the idea that Australia only had to better explain the current policy (the lifeline to which the Immigration Advisory Council was clinging), because non-Europeans resented rigid exclusion as a 'gross insult'. The Immigration Reform Group gave four reasons for a policy change. First, a colour bar was inherently immoral (even though Calwell, for example, asserted that 'people with skins of different pigmentation cannot, as yet, live side by side within the same community or geographical unit'). Second, the inability of so few Asians to put down Australian roots created a 'needless barrier' that inhibited the building of understanding and precluded the country from benefiting from 'the richer experience of diverse cultures'. That is, the current policy punished Australia. Third, exclusion prevented non-Europeans from fulfilling their needs (for example, to extricate themselves from poverty) and to have that opportunity by coming to Australia. In this instance, the policy punished non-Europeans. Finally, there was reputational damage: by insulting non-Europeans (with the current policy), Australia's attempts to be constructive in global interracial councils were 'seriously impaired'. The group's argument for an immigration entry policy that better served Australia's interests hinged on the criterion of absorptive capacity—or the ability of a community to 'absorb migrants without undue [economic and social] stress'. Instead of imposing entry quotas for different nationalities (as favoured by the Methodist Church and practised in the USA but discredited, the

Immigration Advisory Council believed), the Immigration Reform Group urged the Commonwealth to enter into bilateral immigration agreements (as it had in Europe) with friendly Asian neighbours (as proposed in 1959 by the Australian Council of Churches). The way forward, then, was controlled extension of non-European immigration, with the recent experience of Asians in Australia suggesting that the annual non-European intake target could about 1500 'without strain'. But before any changes, the Commonwealth had to declare publicly that the White Australia Policy was at an end.[30]

Darling's increasing discomfort was exacerbated by Downer's creation in 1963 of a third advice pipeline: the Commonwealth Immigration Publicity Council. This had been recommended at the 1961 citizenship convention, but Boyer's death had delayed a decision until October. When Downer asked Darling to be the ABC's representative and Immigration Publicity Council inaugural chairman, he could hardly say no. To assist him with immigration publicity, Darling was given a team of a dozen media people from metropolitan and provincial newspaper associations, foreign language newspapers, the ABC (represented by Semmler), federations speaking on behalf of commercial television and broadcasting stations, and the Sydney Morning Herald Group. The new Commonwealth Immigration Publicity Council first met in May 1962, and then three times annually, with one meeting deliberately coinciding with the January citizenship conventions. It was responsible for all public relations: publicity to attract immigrants and to assist their integration, and the provision of information to the Australian public about immigration policy, programs and procedures. Before long, the Immigration Publicity Council's work cut across the Commonwealth Immigration Advisory Council and established policy on non-European immigration, with Darling caught in the crossfire. With the advisory council's opinion firming on the need for a review of existing non-European policy, he reported to it that the publicity council wanted to hold its horses: no publicity ought to be issued pending removal of the anomalies that had exposed the policy to criticism, and open discussion of the policy at the next citizenship convention was thought inadvisable.[31]

There was a lot riding on what the Commonwealth Immigration Advisory Council would eventually decide, because as Downer was widely reported to have said: 'on this cardinal matter Government and Opposition are as one'. But the council risked being spooked by non-European immigration. In October 1961 it set up the Committee on Established Policy to 'investigate the question fully', the prototype for three other standing committees introduced in November 1962 to facilitate 'detailed investigations': Migrant Women, Naturalization and Social Patterns (of which Darling was a member)—Dovey's Conduct of Migrants Committee reincarnated. Five departmental officers attended the initial meeting of the Committee on Established Policy (April 1962)—a measure of the seriousness attached to its non-European agenda. The minutes disclose just how little wriggle room the council was giving itself. For a start, if the object of the exercise (said the chairman) was 'not to alter the existing policy' but to make it better known, then the council had one hand tied behind its back. Department of Immigration officials (and community supporters of the current policy) disavowed 'White Australia'—because the provisions of the *Migration Act, 1958* were claimed to apply equally to all nationalities—and yet these words were still used in the constitution of the RSL and the platform of the ALP, both of which were represented on the council. But so long as this practice persisted 'it was difficult to argue successfully the case for the existing policy'. Moreover, despite the department's disavowal, the reality was that race was fudged and arbitrarily interpreted. In an admission that confirmed the Immigration Reform Group's claim—that White Australia had no statutory existence but was 'imposed administratively within a legal framework which is unobjectionable'— the working rules ensured that 'basically evidence of a predominantly European appearance, upbringing, manner and outlook was a pre-requisite for permanent admission', with the minister permitted to exercise discretion in individual cases. An additional difficulty was that the Immigration Reform Group had lifted its game with a revised pamphlet republished as a book: *Immigration: Control or Colour Bar?* Heyes' successor as secretary, P.R. (later Sir Peter) Heydon— 'different [from Heyes]', Darling considered, 'but no less competent'—described this version as a 'decided improvement', despite a few exaggerations, and as 'an honest attempt' to present the policy and criticisms of it. With rebuttal of a more plausible reform case now all the more difficult, one council member responded by burying her head in the sand: the book's authors had 'closed minds', because anything short of radical policy surgery was unsatisfactory. Forget them, she urged, and concentrate on the 'open minded'.[32]

If public opinion was moving in the direction of 'progressive liberallisation [sic]', then the Commonwealth Immigration Advisory Council and its Committee on Established Policy were increasingly on a hiding to nothing. Heydon said that the committee was on its own defending the non-European policy and that, while the time for 'free and frank discussions' in the wider community had probably arrived, these should occur without any departmental guidance. Eventually the council agreed to prepare the case for established policy for wider publicity (for 1963 convention discussion), to secure three speakers of varying views and open discussion to follow, to request Darling's Commonwealth Immigration Publicity Council to enlist Australian press support, and to be vigilant with suitable replies to all relevant letters to the press and statements in other outlets. With that its work was done and Wilson conveyed this defensive arsenal to Downer in October 1962. After the re-election of Menzies' coalition, Downer was replaced as minister by Opperman, who in 1964 eased the rules governing the entry of mixed descent persons. A year later the ALP finally deleted from its platform any reference to white Australia. Darling thanked Whitlam for informing him of the party conference decision, and said that it 'certainly goes some way towards a better definition of Immigration policy and I congratulate you on it'. After hearing Whitlam speak at the 1966 convention, Darling noted in his diary that 'Whitlam made a courageous, I think, attack on White Australia Policy. Most people disappointed but I think that it was right and well-timed, though it may have had political undertones.' (A few weeks later to Heydon he was less enthusiastic: Whitlam's convention speech had comprised 'vague remarks'.) Darling may well have been right about Whitlam's timing, because seven weeks later in March, Opperman introduced two further changes. The eligibility period for resident status and citizenship for non-Europeans was reduced from fifteen to five years and, in a loosening of the previous stipulation 'well-qualified people' wishing to settle (after five years' stay on temporary permits) would be considered 'on the basis of their suitability as settlers', ability to 'integrate readily' and the possession of qualifications useful to Australia, and on first arrival they would be able to bring their immediate families with them.[33]

Two days before Opperman's parliamentary announcement, Darling contacted Heydon. He was very exercised. With a generous use of 'we', he articulated his sense of the collective fears holding back the nation—and himself. He had lots of questions but few answers. Notwithstanding Opperman's measures, the real question had been avoided. Was it not time, he asked, to face up to the issue of restricted immigration? 'As I see it, the real grievance remains and cannot be altered.' Australia claimed that it was under-populated and needed immigrants and yet, while it was prepared to 'scrape very near the bottom of the barrel' for the likes of Greeks, Cypriots, Italians and Maltese, it was unwilling to let in 'similar types' from Africa or Asia. But 'why not'? The answer was that 'we do not believe that such people would mix up and inter-marry and become Australians', while 'we' had evidence that Greeks and others did. What about the original Chinese in Australia: 'Are they not assimilated by now?' He didn't know. 'The truth is that we believe'—and, as an indication that he was being pulled in opposing directions—'and I think on the whole rightly believe' that non-Europeans would form 'indigestible pockets of population', work for lower wages, 'create impoverished conditions by over-breeding' and accentuate racial animosities. But was this true? Was there any contrary evidence? Honolulu, perhaps? (The Immigration Reform Group had cited Hawaii as an example of a relatively successful multiracial society.) And, was it fair to lump together 'all those who have not [got] a white [sic] skin'? Did Japanese, Malayans, Chinese and Indians come into this category? The problems, he considered, were 'different in each case'. Did Christianity make 'any' difference to the overall problem and, if it did, how in any case was a Christian defined? The idea that a possible solution was to introduce quotas or admit highly skilled professionals was '[s]heer hypocrisy'. 'We should do' the latter, but ought to 'cover ourselves' by emphasising that such people had worked in their countries for x number of years and that they had 'a clearance' to emigrate from their country of origin. As for the fifteen-year discrimination provision, that had to go. The minister's two measures solved little and were a retreat from what the Commonwealth Immigration Publicity Council had advised him 'some years back'. Honesty was called for, because the measures would not absolve 'us' from responsibility for the real policy, for which it was believed that Africans and Asians if admitted slowly would not be assimilated.[34]

In 1967, Darling agreed to chair a Commonwealth Immigration Advisory Council committee on citizenship conventions. Although he had won early praise for providing 'the acceptable and efficient leadership essential to their success', he was increasingly sceptical about the utility of conventions. He valued the group discussion component of convention programs, and yet for the January 1966 convention his diary noted that these were 'not very inspiring'. In that same year Opperman rescheduled citizenship conventions every eighteen months, rather than annually, but B.M. Sneddon (his successor from December 1966) countermanded this decision and delayed the next one until January 1968. In October 1967, Dovey's committee produced its 67-page final report, *The Departure of Settlers from Australia* (with the drafting being undertaken by Dovey, Darling and two departmental officers), which affirmed in more detail its earlier conclusions. The minister considered that the committee's contribution marked a coming-of-age moment and he directed that the focus of the 1968 convention would be a review of twenty-one years of migration. Sneddon was grateful for Darling's six years work on the Commonwealth Immigration Publicity Council. He then reconstituted all three immigration councils, but did not renew Darling's or Dovey's membership. Severance of Darling's advisory council work was financially costly. With non-renewal of his ABC role confirmed, he was unlikely to continue chairing the publicity council (worth a daily sitting fee of $30). 'I am not enamoured of the present Government', he said to Heydon. Why continue working for it when it had treated him 'so impolitely, not to say crudely', he reasoned in his diary. On receipt of a non-committal reply about his future in immigration from a colleague of Heydon's, his mood stiffened: 'let them sack me if they want to'. It was twelve months before Sneddon brought the guillotine down, although he wanted Darling to remain for a further three years as chairman of the Commonwealth Immigration Publicity Council.[35]

Money continued to be a worry for Darling throughout 1967, due principally to decreased income from less government work (there were Johnny's university fees to pay and his own Melbourne Club presidency expenses), although his financial concerns were alleviated by the boom in mining shares that enabled him to pay off the bulk of his bank overdraft. Another worry was health. He travelled to Melbourne by train and, when walking to and from the railway station and in the city, noticed that he was tiring more in one of his legs than the other. He consulted Fitts. 'The diagnosis and prognosis are not very pleasant', for he had a 'considerable clot' in an artery that was denying blood flow to the leg, but there was no immediate need to operate. Darling put this condition down to his smoking, for which there was only one remedy: 'to give that up'. Pressing on when tired was not a good idea, but that meant 'no more golf' and very little walking. The leg was unlikely to improve and, indeed, would probably worsen, although how soon or how badly he didn't know. He wondered whether he would be crippled in old age. 'It may be worse if I don't find a way of being sensible, and the spectre of my father's affliction naturally worries me.' (In 1971, without any mention of these circulation difficulties, Fitts gave him the thumbs-up: heart and lungs were good, but abdominal girth was large for his height and he ought to have been fitter.) Despite these misgivings, Darling could still travel. In 1968, after Frank Woods' inability to secure his appointment by the General Synod as a member of the Australian Church of England's delegation to the Assembly of the World Council of Churches in Uppsala, Sweden, the World Council of Churches agreed to Darling's attendance as an adviser. At about that time, he turned down Francis James' offer (which Woods had urged him to accept) to take over the 'Church and Nation' column in the *Anglican*. Ironically, given his wariness of (and sensitivity about) the print media, Darling joined their ranks temporarily when the *Age* editor, Graham Perkin, commissioned him to file reports on the proceedings of the World Council of Churches. He also did about ten days' work for Heydon (for an income of $300), in providing forthright comments on the work of Australian officials and querying the benefit of films about Australia—produced by the Commonwealth Film Unit—unless they were tailored to particular course needs in schools. As to immigration publicity, he had detected 'great ignorance, and lack of interest' in Europe. Apart from kangaroos (a 'blessed gimmick in a thirsty world') the image of Australia abroad was sport: although it might have been wise to cash in on this, he confessed, 'I blush to suggest it'.[36]

While touring Europe in the northern hemisphere summer, it occurred to him that during the long winter bits and pieces about Australian sun and climate could be 'infiltrated' into publicity, although to be effective publicity had to be carefully targeted. Take Sweden. 'Why', he asked Heydon, 'would a Swede leave so well-ordered and comfortable a social system?' 'I think just for that reason', he replied—which might have confounded the thinking of Australians for whom 1960s Sweden was the quintessence of social democracy:

> My rather superficial observation is that Sweden is a curious amalgam of the traditional and the progressive socialist state. Both create a static rather than a dynamic society and although it is a comfortable life for most people it is not very exciting. This may account for some of their psychoses. Australia does offer the challenge of a dynamic society and the possibility of lifting oneself out of that state of life into which it has pleased God to call one. Freedom—enterprise—mere [or more?] size and the unstratified society would make the appeal, I think, to those who would make the best settlers.

He was 'agreeably surprised' about the potential for increased Scandinavian immigration to Australia. Because Norway and Finland were 'very poor' countries offering little scope for ambitious people, and Sweden was a 'very constricted

and rather smug' society, Australia would have definite appeal. His private mus-
ings to Heydon were echoed in an eight-page report. (He typed it himself and
said rather gleefully: 'I have only just taught myself to do it at all'.) In total,
Darling visited six Continental countries (before setting off to provincial centres
in England), and spoke with fourteen departmental and ambassadorial staff. The
situation in the other European countries that he visited (Norway, Denmark,
West Germany, Belgium and Holland) was 'roughly similar' to Sweden. Programs
(and publicity) to attract immigrants had to be specifically tailored: the simple
line that 'we want more of you and that you ought to want to come will cut no
ice'. Norwegians willing to come would resent having to deal with the Stockholm
office as they did not love the Swedes. For their part the Swedes were a 'difficult
people', and 'anti-English, self-satisfied, not to say smug'. (His view of the Danes
was 'a most delightful people, happy, himorous [sic] and superficially cynical'.)
Unemployment in Finland (although he hadn't visited it) might trigger an interest in immigration. He saw no prospects in West Germany (with its prosperity)
and little promise in Belgium. Overcrowded Holland, however, with 'standing
room only' expected for its population by 1980, would continue to be a steady
source of supply.[37]

Overall, potential immigrants would have to be wooed except that staffing
'on the Publicity side' was presently 'quite inadequate'. From an educational point
of view, in addition to the need for films to be made by educationalists rather than
publicity experts, those responsible for education in the ABC should engage in
this work and he detected an untapped opportunity for adult education. With
the local activity available in Swedish communities and the folk high schools
of Denmark during the long winter evenings, there was considerable scope
to further the 'cause of international understanding' by acquainting people so
engaged (through documentary films rather than travelogues) with some of
Australia's more serious political, social and cultural problems—such as states'
rights, local government, mineral development, urbanisation, droughts, New
Guinea, the Pacific, 'even the Restricted Migration policy' and 'Aborigines'.
Canada had stolen the march on Australia with the 'great pull' of the Canadian
Film Board's first-class material, and it 'might be worth while to point this out
to the Government'. As for the available advice booklets, these were 'not entirely
satisfactory'—a judgement that was endorsed by the Commonwealth Migration
Officer in London—for which the Immigration Publicity Council had to accept
the blame. Because these booklets tried simultaneously to provide information,
not mislead people and yet attract them, they succeeded admirably with the
second aim but failed completely with the first and third. Darling said that he
had arrived at a solution close to that rejected earlier by the publicity council:
supplement a version of the existing booklet in a reduced 'strictly factual' form
with a tourist-friendly booklet using the 'tricks of visual presentation'. He also
recommended that the Public Service Board should be mindful of the need for
the inclusion of language skills in the employment awards for stenographers and

clerks, and, as an indication of the thoroughness with which that he was taking his publicity responsibilities, he even commented on the quality of immigration window displays. On the whole, these had been 'good'.[38]

In 1971, when yet another new Coalition Minister for Immigration, this time Dr A.J. Forbes, changed the membership of the immigration councils, Darling was asked to stand down from the Commonwealth Immigration Publicity Council. Forbes thanked him for his service as its chairman ('a source of inspiration to your members') and appointed Semmler to succeed him. With that, Darling's formal contribution to Australian immigration ended. In all probability after nearly nineteen years as an adviser to governments, there was little that he was unaware of or that he did not know. But in 1966, just after Opperman's announcement of his reform measures, a new angle on the immigrant experience had impressed itself on him. John Sumner, a fellow expatriate Englishman, and director of the Union Theatre Repertory Company, invited him to the dramatisation of *The Young Wife*, by the Hungarian-born Australian author David Martin—himself an immigrant in 1950. Martin's novel recounts the encounter of two cultures, Australian and Greek, through the tragic story of the lives of Annoula (Anna) Christofidou, a young Cypriot girl who arrives in Melbourne for her arranged marriage, and Yannis Joannides, her greengrocer husband. Darling was deeply touched by what he witnessed. It was a 'good play', he told Sumner, 'at least for orthodox chaps like me'. He thought that *The Young Wife* had been superbly well acted, or superbly well cast, 'or both', and his sister Margaret, who was in Melbourne, thought that it 'ought to go to London'. One aspect of the story-line had alarmed him, and he wanted his fellow advisory council members to see the play:

> We [on the Commonwealth Immigration Advisory Council] talk very glibly about assimilation and integration, but I fear that we very gravely under-estimate the difficulty of adjustment and the pressures created by the struggle to make good in a totally strange environment. From this point of view also the play is a valuable social document, and I shall write to Peter Heydon of the Immigration Department telling him that he ought to see it. The atmosphere and characterization was extremely convincing.

An added bonus had been to observe one of his OGGs, Michael Duffield, playing a lead role. Sumner said that for all its 'utter simplicity', *The Young Wife* had been one of the most difficult scripts that he had worked on. Starting with Ray Lawler's *Summer of the Seventeenth Doll*, this had been his eleventh original production. It was always 'difficult to make Australians believe in original scripts', whereas if one arrived in printed form from elsewhere then it would be accepted. If scripts had to be altered, though, as was 'very much the case' with *The Young Wife*, then 'artists suspect the play enormously'. On this reckoning, there was still some way to go in winning the acceptance of homegrown productions in

Lotus-land. The Union Theatre was part of the University of Melbourne and associated with the Australian Elizabethan Theatre Trust. It was because of Darling's close association with the theatre trust that, following his road-safety, broadcasting and immigration work, his next major contribution to Australian life was to be in the performing arts.[39]

SEDULOUS

1973–1982

In a fallen world the bourgeois life is not perfect. But it's better than any available alternative.

Deirdre McCloskey, *The Bourgeois Virtues*

After more than forty years in education in two countries Darling was asked in 1966 to spell out his view of it, but the request 'completely defeated' him. He had 'never been an intellectual or an academic' and never had 'much in the way of theories'. Certainly, he had read books and borrowed other people's ideas in a 'quite unprincipled way', whereupon having passed these through the crucible of his mind he tended to think of them as 'my own' and ceased to recall their provenance. Despite thirty-two years as a headmaster, his wider engagements in the later years probably accounted for his failure to keep abreast of modern educational thinking. In reply to his correspondent, Darling said that both Professor Mills and Jock Weeden used to say that he was 'capable of persuading myself of anything', which was 'fair criticism', but that no-one had ever considered him capable of 'Thought', and on that score they were 'quite right':

> I have therefore always been a school master rather than an educationist, a pragmatic rather than a theoretical chap, and in consequence if I have done anything it is likely to be found in the influence on individuals, perhaps masters as well as boys, rather than in the contribution of any body of ideas.

As for his 'sort of philosophy', there were three tenets to it: a school existed for boys, not the reverse, and an individual was more important than the organisation and had to be provided for in 'the way best suited to him'; the whole man had to be developed, which required provision for music, art and poetry as well as mathematics, science and languages; and, a school had to be integrated with the community of which it was a part. If this amounted to being a Christian humanist, then he supposed that 'this is what I tried to be'. There wasn't very much 'philosophy or theory about me', he cautioned. In fact, he had never really considered himself to be 'anything other than a "sedulous ape"', although he supposed that even an ape 'has to make some sort of personal selection'.[1]

To invoke Robert Louis Stevenson's verdict on his literary style as sedulously aping others was a curious way to make light of a reputation. Was Darling's self-deprecation warranted? Personal influence on others was part of the story, but not the whole of it: sedulous in the way that he approached his commitments, but hardly ape-like in imitation. Was a similar verdict warranted in the arts, in particular the Australian Elizabethan Theatre Trust? Founded in 1854, the trust had, in its memorandum of incorporation, specified its objects as the promotion of drama, opera, ballet and theatre art; the writing of plays, operas, ballets and other theatrical works; and, the producers of plays, musicians, singers, dancers and other theatrical personnel. The trust would assist the presentation of drama, opera, ballet and any other theatre art by lending or giving money or by acting as a surety, by appealing for funds (mainly donations or annual subscriptions). There were to be 5000 members and forty initial directors, the most prominent of whom was Nugget Coombs. Other notable directors included a sprinkling of the country's great and the good: Professor Fred Alexander (history, University of Western Australia), Warwick Fairfax, Charles Moses, Myra Roper and Professor F.J. Schonell (education, University of Queensland). The first president was Sir John Latham (recently retired as chief justice of the High Court) and the first vice presidents were Dame Enid Lyons (former MHR for Braddon and an ABC commissioner), Sir Arthur (Lum) Rymill (lawyer, politician and Lord Mayor of Adelaide) and Boyer.[2]

In 1962, Darling joined the Australian Elizabethan Theatre Trust Board of Governors because as ABC chairman he was automatically a trust vice president. He confessed to Colin Badger (director, Council for Adult Education), who had helped secure premises for Sumner's Union Theatre, that he was a 'very uninstructed member' and knew 'very little' about trust policy. Badger regarded the trust as a 'very great nuisance' because it failed to 'do anything significant'. (He felt similarly about the ABC; as he said in 1964 to Semmler, his University of Adelaide undergraduate chum: 'I have long held the view that the A.B.C. represents a monument to wasted opportunity'.) The trust had lost the goodwill of 'most of the people who count in the Arts in this country', Badger claimed, and its only genuine success had been to extract money from governments—no wonder with Coombs as its chairman. Badger preferred a body like the Arts Council in Britain or its Canadian equivalent. The principle at stake was the proper use of public money and responsibility to Parliament:

> The present method of financing the Arts is mischievous, is bound to lead to trouble, it creates fears and jealousies and suspicions, and, worst of all, encourages those who are the fortunate recipients of the Government's favour

to adopt an attitude that they deserved this by their merit rather than achieved
it by their manipulative skill.

Darling replied that there were 'rifts' within the trust and 'a good deal of
confusion' about policy and he knew of its 'running feud' with the National
Theatre Movement (with which Badger was connected). It was better to keep
out of a situation that he did not properly understand and could do little about.
He preferred a 'single concentrated body' supported by the government and by
private gifts that could be 'a source of supply' to the various arts bodies, although
administering it would be 'an unenviable task'.[3]

In 1983, Coombs reflected that it was difficult in retrospect to realise 'how
poverty stricken' theatrical life in Australia had been with 'no indigenous professional theatre'. Four decades earlier, a succession of economists (Coombs, Giblin
and Copland) had pressed for government stimulation of the arts. Darling had
even played a small advocacy role in April 1944 in a speech ('The Importance
of the Drama in National Life') at the Melbourne Public Library, in which he
argued that a vigorous stage life was indicative of a vigorous nation. He also
called for reform through local dramatic societies, the playing of relevant and
serious plays, the creation of demand for drama, encouragement and appreciation of good acting and, if necessary, 'the subsidizing of a national theatre'. There
were three dominant arts organisations in the 1940s. The Australian National
Theatre in Melbourne (the National Theatre Movement's successor), presided
over by the opera singer Gertrude Johnson, and committed to the development
of theatre, drama, ballet and opera. In Sydney there was Clarice Lorenz' National
Opera of Australia. Both groups received state government subsidies and private backing. There was also J.C. Williamson Ltd (founded by the expatriate
American actor and entrepreneur, James Cassius Williamson), which imported
overseas productions, companies and performers. The theatre's lifeblood, however, was capital city-based 'enthusiastic amateur and semi-professional repertory groups' (the Independent, Metropolitan and New Theatre in Sydney, and
the Little Theatre and Union Theatre in Melbourne). At the same time as
Australian actors (Peter Finch, Leo McKern and Keith Michell, and the singer
Joan Hammond) were trying to build their reputations in London, high-profile
English thespians were touring Down Under (thanks to the British Council):
Laurence Olivier and Vivien Leigh with the Old Vic Company in 1948, and
the English Shakespearean theatre director, Tyrone Guthrie. In 1949, Chifley
commissioned Guthrie to report on a possible Australian national theatre. While
his report 'occasioned controversy' in arts circles, Guthrie's proposals for a trust-
controlled theatre were endorsed by Cabinet in October, only to be shelved by
Menzies' government.[4]

The trigger for the Australian Elizabethan Theatre Trust was the 1953 visit of
the Shakespeare Memorial Theatre Company, directed by Anthony Quayle, who
had toured in 1950. With his 'enthusiasm for things Australian', Quayle strongly

advocated an arts body independent of government and other sources of funding. Simultaneously, Boyer, Ernest Burbidge (the Sydney-based British Council representative, 1952–57) and O.D. Bisset (a Sydney businessman) proposed a national theatre, with Burbidge suggesting a link with the forthcoming royal visit. In company with Charles Moses, J.D. Pringle (another Englishman and *Sydney Morning Herald* editor) and Ian Potter (the Melbourne financier and arts patron), Coombs resurrected the national theatre trust idea, 'took over' Burbidge's suggestion and, armed with pledges of corporate financial support, approached Menzies, who was 'more sympathetic' than anticipated. The deal hammered out was that the new trust would launch an appeal for funds with the government matching £1 for every £3 raised. This arrangement yielded an initial capital fund of £120,000. After this 'flying start', the Australian Elizabethan Theatre Trust quickly 'grew in influence and authority in the Australian theatre scene'. While historian Geoffrey Serle conceded that, thanks largely to the trust, the amount of serious theatre in Australia in 1964 was 'far greater' than in 1954, the trust's first decade was judged as mixed. With the ABC providing for the state symphony orchestras, the trust established national opera and ballet companies, but not a national theatre (or drama) company. Instead of working with the little amateur theatres, from 1961 the trust assembled touring companies that served up drama and opera 'as commodities to be consumed by widely dispersed audiences' with capricious tastes. It suffered heavy financial losses, was not building audiences, training or maintaining artists, and 'only randomly serving the theatre arts', although Pringle thought that its achievements under the directorship of Hugh Hunt, former director of the Old Vic, were 'remarkable'. In 1963, Potter (at Coombs' instigation) succeeded Latham as president. The new strategy was to support regional theatre groups to assist the organic growth of a theatre culture.[5]

In 1966, the trust 'directed' Coombs to discuss a revised trust–government relationship and a possible new statutory arts body. Coombs thought that the trust's capacity was 'overstrained', its decision-making over-centralised and arts agencies needed greater autonomy. His fifteen-page memorandum to Harold Holt was crucial in redesigning Australia's arts administration and in redefining the Australian Elizabethan Theatre Trust. He recommended an interim council for the performing arts to advise on funding support administered in accordance with government policy. The trust should transfer its theatrical production responsibilities to its eleven affiliated enterprises, each with its board of management, staffing, income sources and capital city headquarters. Two of the trust's largest financial commitments were to ballet—through co-sponsorship with J.C. Williamson of the Australian Ballet—and opera: originally through its Opera Board, succeeded (after wrangling with the National Theatre Movement) by the Trust Opera Company and renamed the Australian Opera (1970). Coombs said that the trust should be a federal body coordinating these affiliated enterprises, and provide services while being an entrepreneur for interstate and overseas tours. In 1968 Prime Minister Gorton created a permanent body, the Australian

Council for the Arts, chaired by Coombs, to cooperate with the trust and govern-ment bodies responsible for music, painting and literature.[6]

Darling probably had minimal influence on Coombs' thinking. An enig-matic diary entry (about the 1966 citizenship convention—the day before the Holt–Menzies transition) records his difference with Coombs:

> Group discussions in morning—not very inspiring. Lunch at G.H. [Government House] …—afternoon discussions in groups again—[I] spoke about the need in Australia for an Arts Foundation, initially subsidized by government and also for Australia to realize its function as a fusing point for Western and Eastern Culture. Apparently misunderstood as Coombs attacked me later at the general assembly. As I didn't hear it I didn't answer and wasn't hurt, though I spoke to him about it later—went to office and telephoned.

Darling knew about progress of the Australian Council for the Arts from Masterman, in mid-1968:

> Yesterday we had the 2nd meeting of the Aust. Council & the personalities are beginning to sort themselves out. Barry Jones [a lawyer, proponent of the arts and later a federal ALP minister] voluble in pushing for vigorous action on film and T.V., the rest rather quiet except for me, who had at first to do nearly all the talking that Coombs didn't do; but now Geoff Dutton [OGG] is speaking up well. The women are rather quiet, but Betty Archdale [Headmistress, Abbottsleigh Girls School] and one from W.A. are abroad till next month. We are tackling drama first, then film & T.V. & I can see it's going to be hard to wean Coombs from his love for the spectacular—prestige opera, ballet & now drama—enough to get something for [the] country, the young people & minor arts, all of which I'm trying to push as a counterpoise.

The consequence of the creation of the Australian Council for the Arts (given effect by the new prime minister, John Gorton, after his predecessor's death in December 1967) was that the Australian Elizabethan Theatre Trust now played second fiddle. Such was the state of play when Darling presided over the trust.[7]

Aubrey Gibson—a Melbourne businessman, art collector, arts patron, and founding director and then (1968–71) president of the Trust—lured Darling into an active trust role and then in June 1973 (on his seventy-fourth birthday) Potter persuaded him be president. He held office until October 1982. Why Darling agreed is unclear. (His sister Margaret chided him the year before with her typical elder-sister bluntness that if retirement really was 'so boring' then he ought to find a local committee job or play bridge.) No rest for the wicked: Darling occupied yet another hot seat. He had to fight a rearguard action to reconstruct the Australian Elizabethan Theatre Trust as something more than a mere shadow of its former self. There was a legacy of consequences arising from recommendations by the Australian Council for the Arts to the prime minister (Whitlam) who, in January 1973, requested it to review its operations and those of its affiliated boards in light of his government's arts policy. Darling also had to ride out criticisms by the Australia Council (the 1975 successor to the Australian Council for the Arts), the Industries Assistance Commission, hostile consultants and the media. Due to internal differences, the trust also threatened to implode but survived in a modified form. There were about 9000 trust members (in 1973) and their annual fees secured them preferential performance bookings, especially for opera and ballet. They elected state representatives to the Board of Governors, which met four times annually and was answerable to them. The trust received financial subsidies from state and municipal governments and the Australian Council for the Arts, and private donations. Its 'strength and influence' derived from recognition of its independence and 'community effort'. It claimed to have operated 'continuously, efficiently and economically' while maintaining contact with community developments in the performing arts. It also cast itself as 'the link' between the Australian Council for the Arts and state governments, and 'the trusted adviser of both'. Moreover, it channelled gifts directed in conformity with donors' wishes—a more appealing feature (it thought) than payments to a government instrumentality. Finally, it bore significant financial risk on behalf of arts companies.[8]

None of this activity cut much ice with the Department for Services and Property, which dismissed the trust's response to the Australian Council for the Arts recommendations as a compendium of past actions, and 'far too long, tedious and diffuse'. It had overstated its role and conveyed an impression of 'slavish adherence' to the council's wishes. Thrown off-guard by the tone and substance of the department's missive, Darling conceded that the trust's dependence on the council for a 'significant source of supply' created an impression of subservience. The Australian Council for the Arts, he noted, 'pays the piper and therefore to a large extent must call the tune', not a situation that he relished although he recognised that 'in a semi socialist world it has to be accepted'. An added difficulty was that the trust blurred the line between public and private: individuals from both sectors had been board members, and it received public and private finance, but there was a lack of public accountability (Badger's point). During 1975, Coopers & Lybrand were commissioned by the Australia Council to report on the trust's future. Darling accepted some of their recommendations (for example, to divest control of the trust's two Sydney- and Melbourne-based orchestras and relinquish its subscription department unless it was self-supporting without the opera), which were received during the dying days of the Whitlam government, but otherwise dug his heels in. Within the trust, he argued that the trust had to decide whether to place its entrepreneurial and membership functions under the new Australia Council's direction and depend on it for grants or carry on alone. He objected to a proposed name change, and alteration of the trust's board and management because he feared a membership loss. If it was to survive, then the Australia Council had to be 'openly and determinedly resisted, by every possible means: if we lose, as we probably will, we should accept the position of trying to carry on these functions without any grant'. Receipt of a directly allocated Treasury subsidy, however, might guarantee survival—far better than 'putting our trust again in a body [the Australian Council for the Arts] which has consistently robbed us, deceived us and frustrated us in the past and is likely to do so again'. Better still might be a dollar-for-dollar subsidy mechanism to keep the trust 'as it ought to be and originally was' connected to 'its democratic base', an arrangement that redefined the issue as a choice between submission to 'centralised inefficient and dishonest bureaucracy' and a 'truly Federal and democratic approach'.[9]

In early 1977, the journalist Brian Hoad described Coopers & Lybrand's report as 'largely damning' and a 'rather hard slap in the face' to the trust, which he dismissed as the plaything of Australia's 'ruling elite', founded in a 1954 'fit of imperial enthusiasm'. The trust 'huffed and puffed', and succeeded in having the report withdrawn temporarily for the Australia Council's legal reassessment. The year before the trust had streamlined its structure. Control by a large Board of Governors had been cumbersome when the trust was entrepreneurial in ballet, opera and drama, and board meetings were reduced to rubber-stamping decisions by the chairman and the executive director. With ballet and opera hived off, the division of labour on the trust executive was for individual members to exercise specialist oversight of activities—in Darling's case, orchestras. The new board of twelve directors (chaired by Potter) would meet monthly and there were four committees (finance, orchestras, marionettes and entrepreneurial), with a Council of Governors responsible for representing members' views to the board, increasing the membership and fostering trust activities. Darling was president of the governors and the trust, in which capacities he attended board meetings (as did Moses). As president, Darling revived his acquaintance with Lloyd Ross (vice president, New South Wales governors). Financial subsidies sufficient for trust operations until the end of 1976 were guaranteed by the Australia Council. Trust membership produced $70,000 annual income (mostly expended on disseminating trust news) and the Australia Council's entrepreneurial grant was $44,000. To breathe life into the new arrangements and revive the trust, Darling emphasised its democratic base. Notwithstanding Hoad's frustration that the trust's 'demolition' was a 'painful exercise', Darling assured state governors in 1976 that their roles were meaningful (amid uncertainty about their importance). He saw the Council of Governors as akin to a legislative upper house: to keep an eye on the trust's activities and to try to increase membership.[10]

Prior to the restructure, Potter and Darling (especially) had chafed under what the latter termed 'the growing policy of domination of everything by Canberra' during 1974–75, a centralised system in which the Australian Council for the Arts (and then the Australia Council) had the final say in the allocation of arts expenditure by the selection and appointment of those to do the work and take responsibility. But the money belonged to taxpayers not public servants. Darling bristled:

> Those who have to spend the money are responsible to these taxpayers not to a Federal Government which sees itself as carrying out a 'mandate' given to it from little over half the electorate. This is in my opinion a wrong concept of British Democracy and of representative government.

For all its weaknesses, the trust was better qualified for this role than Canberra and its 'multiplicity of incompetent and toad-eating committees'. The trust, however, was on the back foot due to difficult-to-answer criticisms that it was clumsy and expensive, a 'self-perpetuating gerontocracy of men and women who may once have been of some use but no longer are', and that it was out of touch, especially with youthful musical and theatrical artists. Potter did not demur at these criticisms, but couldn't see any other way of relating to taxpayers and giving account to the chosen instruments of duly elected governments. All that could be hoped for was a substantial degree of independent decision-making about trust activities. When communicating with trust members, Darling tried bolstering support for its restructure: coming of age in 1975, he wrote, was inextricable from the 'almost unbelievable growth of Australia herself under the impact of a phenomenal number of stimuli' (such as an increase in numbers of people, educational developments, greater prosperity and the 'emergence in many fields of a distinct Australian culture'). The Australian Elizabethan Theatre Trust had responded flexibly and modified its operations. Opera and ballet had been given their autonomy, and as an entrepreneur the trust would service and cooperate with Australia's now-flourishing theatrical activities. Structural streamlining was needed to better protect the members' interests. Despite Darling's rehearsal with members and directors of the arguments for revised organisational machinery, the trust turned inward on itself.[11]

After twenty-one years as a director Fred Alexander felt compelled out of self-respect and other obligations to terminate his association with the Australian Elizabethan Theatre Trust. He saw no point in continuing if he could not shape policy or serve as a board member. Darling sympathised, but persuaded him to stay for twelve months. There was no reason to change the trust's role, but if the Australia Council and the government wanted it then, Darling told him, it was 'wisest to go quietly, preserving as much continuity as we can', musing that this was the 'realist's—or the coward's—answer!' In 1976, Darling told Potter that there was a 'growing division of opinion' between those viewing the trust as a 'tight and limited, but economical, organisation centred upon and operating largely within Sydney' and those seeing it as it originally was: 'a National, almost an educational, enterprise entrusted with the responsibility for furthering the development of dramatic art' across the nation. These views were not entirely at odds, although the latter was adopted and expressed in the constitution newly ratified by the membership. The governors could now advise the directors on policy, even though some directors didn't understand this or refused to accept it, although Darling thought that the arguments to support the governors were compelling. First, the governor role conformed to the principle of the trust's foundation and underlying philosophy. Second, with the states now concerned to develop the arts it was vital that the trust persist with a state-level presence. Third, wide and increased membership would enhance the trust's importance in obtaining more Commonwealth money and also afford it opportunities for ascertaining what the public wanted or would accept. Finally, Darling claimed, only the Australian Elizabethan Theatre Trust could coordinate Australia-wide activities cooperatively with the new state arts centres and festivals. State-level success implied a strong membership base in as many states as possible; to try to restrict the trust to Sydney-based commercial enterprise was ineffective and unconstitutional.[12]

The other problem for Darling and Potter was the financial difficulty faced by the two Elizabethan orchestras. A $30,000 deficit for 1974 threatened to balloon out by $170,000 in 1975. Between them, the orchestras (one each in Melbourne and Sydney) employed 136 musicians and were subsidised to the tune of $1.58 million. Much hinged on the trust's capacity to become more entrepreneurial—Coopers & Lybrand had recommended that the Australia Council reshape the trust as the National Arts Corporation with a remit to cultivate links with commercial sponsors. Entrepreneurialism (for example, arranging national tours by international and national companies), however, was not universally endorsed. Lloyd Ross was concerned that the Australian Elizabethan Theatre Trust Board and staff had been seduced by entrepreneurialism as the trust's salvation, and that small projects were a waste of time and unable to fill the gap left by opera and ballet. Contrary to what Hoad thought was in the arts' best interests, the trust outlived both the consultant's recommendations and the (November 1976) report of the Industries Assistance Commission. As the successor to the Tariff Board, the Industries Assistance Commission had taken evidence from about 200 witnesses, including the Australian Elizabethan Theatre Trust. Consistent with its hardline rational economic approach to resource allocation, and its view of the performing arts as a private (not a public) good, it wanted government financial support redirected towards improved community capacity to interact with the arts rather than underwriting arts providers: that is, demand-side support, not supply-side. Federal arts assistance had 'risen dramatically' (approximately doubling) in the three years to 1974–75, and the commission utterly rejected the 'flagship philosophy' of selective and generous subvention of a handful of high-end arts companies pursuing excellence. Instead, it endorsed the principle of demonstrable community benefit, with financial assistance directed to educating Australians in the qualities of the performing arts, assisting with innovation, and supporting arts dissemination to build awareness and appreciation. There was 'little firm evidence' to support current federal assistance and no 'coherent justification'. Evidence of community benefit was meagre and rested on witnesses' 'unsupported assertions'; to its beneficiaries, community support of the arts of their choice was 'an unquestioned article of faith'.[13]

The Industries Assistance Commission foreshadowed the phasing out over eight years of all government financial patronage of the performing arts (including the ABC's symphony orchestra funding, and provision of radio and television drama), and the reallocation of the total arts subvention in one-third proportions to education and innovation in, and dissemination of, the performing arts. Although it did not directly mention the Australian Elizabethan Theatre Trust, the Industries Assistance Commission was strongly against subsidies to performing companies that were intended to aid their dissemination by lowering ticket prices and enabling patrons to be entertained at less than real cost. On the Australian Elizabethan Theatre Trust specifically, it bracketed the trust's two orchestras with the Australian Opera and the Australian Ballet, and projected the total assistance required in 1980 by these four bodies as in excess of $11 million, an amount equal to all federal funding of the arts in 1975. It saw no valid reason for not attaching the Sydney Elizabethan Orchestra to the Australian Opera, and the Melbourne Elizabethan Orchestra to the Australian Ballet, despite the trust's objections. More generally, in respect of tracking direct links to activities supported by federal and state funding routed through the trust's Theatre Services division, the commission believed that the trust's annual reports were opaque. Invited to respond to the commission's draft report, the trust had done so. Privately, Darling dismissed the draft report as 'nonsense', while in more measured tones he re-ran by way of objection the same elevation of cultural taste claims that he had used previously at the ABCB and the ABC. He attacked the Industries Assistance Commission's 'arithmetical concept of Democracy' on two grounds. First, taste could not be elevated if there was no provision for opportunities to enjoy it (by driving ticket prices down with public subsidies, thereby putting access within the reach of more people) because this view had preserved the lowest standards in commercial broadcasting. Second, the commission had ignored the (equally valid) argument that the state's role in a pluralistic society was to support the interest, tastes and wishes of minorities. He also dismissed the commission's claim that because performances took place in the states it was up to them to provide subsidies. Uniform income taxation had made this view untenable, but if it was accepted then withdrawal of federal support from numerous other activities would follow logically. In the event, the Australian Elizabethan Theatre Trust needn't have worried because the commission's economic rationalism bit the dust when Fraser's Coalition government junked its recommended eight-year phase-out.[14]

For the remainder of his presidency, Darling played a difficult middle-man role: on the board, he was an upward conduit for the members' concerns and grievances, while having also to justify downwards to those same governors and members the board's policies and decisions. Keeping the membership happy was not easy when trying to gauge the potential audiences for plays. The elderly, for example, needed considerable enthusiasm to attend the theatre, thanks to ticket costs, availability of suitable transport or car parking, and insufficiency of time to arrive home from work (if still employed), travel and the skipping of a meal. There was more entertainment available than fifty years earlier, but pre-television there was more enthusiasm to attend the theatre. European Australians were interested in concerts, opera and ballet, whereas plays presented language problems for them. And Melburnians subscribing to both the Melbourne Theatre Company and the performances of other companies found such a level of commitment 'as much as their enthusiasm will carry' and were unlikely to attend dramas 'unless they are extremely well presented and performed'. His confidence in governor–board relations oscillated and state-level practice varied. In Sydney, for example, where Lloyd Ross maintained a watching brief for him, the governors had difficulty getting going because the Sydney Ladies Committee was doing most of their work, which prompted Ross to quip:

> Well—we must be patient—but I feel that the present generation of the Trust leadership needs a few ideas—but so does the ALP! We at least are on the right track'.

In 1982, there was a changing of the guard. Darling resigned as president and Potter stepped down after fifteen years as chairman to replace him.[15]

During the early part of Darling's trust presidency a political crisis brewing in Canberra reached boiling point in October–November 1975. For the first time in four years, Darling composed two lengthy diary entries, which captured his thoughts about Australian character and institutions. Having obtained a double dissolution and re-election with a slightly reduced majority in the House of Representatives in May 1974, but lacking a Senate majority, the Labor government experienced a succession of crises during 1974–75. These included an inability to contain soaring inflation and unemployment, devaluation of the Australian dollar, the sacking and reshuffling of ministers, controversy resulting from the appointment of Senator Lionel Murphy (attorney-general) to a High Court vacancy, swirling sexual innuendo about a ministerial staff member, resignation of the Speaker and the Loans Affair—unauthorised borrowings through a foreign money-trader by a Cabinet minister. The temperature rose further in mid-October after a High Court ruling upheld the validity of legislation extending Senate representation to the Northern Territory and the ACT, as a result of which there was a possibility of a Labor majority at the next half-Senate election. When the Senate deferred a vote on the government's budget (16 October 1975), thus blocking supply but not denying it outright, federal politics entered new territory. No-one quite knew what might happen next, or whether and how this political stalemate might be resolved. Darling's initial instinct was to take the high ground in defence of democracy and to declare a pox on both the political parties' houses, but imperfect human beings were involved and that put questions of character centre stage.[16]

In an increasingly febrile political atmosphere, Darling condemned the Opposition and its leader Malcolm Fraser. Having unseated Sneddon as leader of the Opposition back in March, Fraser (Darling noted) had then stated 'almost unequivocally' that a party with a majority in the House should be allowed to run its full term. He viewed Fraser's tactic of withholding or delaying supply, therefore, as a lever intended to force Whitlam to call an election, except that his preparedness to yield to the 'reactionary elements' in his own party 'only makes things worse'. 'I had thought that he [Fraser] was a man of real strength of character', Darling noted, 'even though perhaps unduly ambitious and unduly sure of his own right to rule' and (slightly misquoting Macbeth) 'Vaulting ambition which doth oer'r leap itself and fall on t'other'. The question to be asked about Fraser was akin to that asked about the execution of King Charles I. Transposed from whether the king's execution was 'morally justifiable, constitutionally indefensible and politically disastrous', Darling's verdict on Fraser was that his action 'has been moral[ly] questionable, constitutionally legitimate but politically disastrous'. Next he turned his wrath on Whitlam. Here was a man who, although commanding a democratically elected majority and confronted by a hostile upper chamber acting with dubious constitutional validity and suspect morality (given that two state governments had defied conventional practice when filling occasional Senate vacancies), could take his stand 'with a self-righteousness' that 'regard having been given to his consistent past behaviour, is quite revolting'. It was difficult not to believe that 'he has quite deliberately cast the fly over Mr. Fraser, who has taken it like a foolish fish'. And yet two wrongs did not make a right: it was not enough to claim that Whitlam's government had 'already flouted all moral justification' in trying to engineer a Senate majority (by elevating Murphy and enticing another senator to accept a diplomatic posting) and that there was a case for its reprehensibility. If both government and prime minister had acted incompetently and forfeited the electorate's confidence, in the face of 'scandal after scandal', did it follow as Fraser claimed that the Opposition's duty was to take 'any steps open to it to force the government to meet the electorate'? It was hard to prove that the state of the country was entirely a result of government maladministration to justify extreme measures, and 'the P.M's contention that the Liberals cannot adapt themselves to rule by anyone but themselves is difficult to counter'.[17]

Here were two political titans at loggerheads: the one with his 'abominable smugness' goading the other, who started from 'high principles' and then fell foul of party diehards, each believing as part of the '"game" of politics' in his right to rule, 'and neither side caring tuppence about the country'. Having surrendered the moral ground, Fraser had 'handed it over to the P.M.' and put himself politically 'in a hopeless position' that, 'if he persists in it', may well 'strengthen the hand of the P.M. by giving him a case, of which he was desperately in need'. The result was a divided country experiencing class polarisation, its politicians discredited, and unable to find any consensus and readiness to work together for the common good. With the likelihood of trade union militancy increasing and conservatives resorting to the language of 'using force to meet force', Darling speculated about possible civil war—justifiable, perhaps 'in a country in real distress', although 'absurd as well as tragic in a country essentially so prosperous and comfortable as this one'. Darling's second lengthy soliloquy was dated Tuesday, 11 November—Remembrance Day, the day on which the governor-general (Sir John Kerr) sacked Whitlam and installed Fraser as caretaker prime minister. This shorter entry was no less despairing. Defeated on the floor of the House, Fraser was granted a double dissolution. With an election set for 13 December, two possibilities alarmed Darling. If the ALP secured a majority in both chambers, then Whitlam would 'press on with the movement to Presidential government and leaving the Queen and the Commonwealth'. If, however, the Liberals won a majority in both chambers, then the country would be 'utterly divided and the unions unmanageable'. Was any solace to be had? While 'in any other country this would bring us near civil war', Australians were probably 'too lazy for that'. Darling's dilemma was that 'the Labour [sic] government has done some good things and was needed', yet it had also been both incompetent and corrupt, and its ministerial dismissals had simply shored up its leader's 'own unquestioned power'. The Liberals by contrast, had had an unanswerable case four weeks earlier (because of Labor's litany of deficiencies), and yet the Senate had consistently resisted the government's legislative measures and the country's business interests had 'sulked'.[18]

Confronted by intransigence, the governor-general 'could do nothing other than what he did', although Whitlam may have deliberately manoeuvred Kerr into intervening in order to profit from the unpopularity of his decision, Darling speculated, to invoke 'the old appeal to the people against THEM'. Certainly, the former prime minister was 'profiting now and glorying in his righteous indignation and mud slinging at the G.G. and Fraser'. To such a low pitch had matters fallen that 'we can expect the foulest of all elections and even bloodshed'. So far the backlash against Kerr had played in Whitlam's favour, but that might well boomerang out of a fear of what Whitlam might do if he obtained 'real power'. The Liberals were likely to win, except that having got power they would be unlikely to enjoy it, 'and the country will become increasingly divided. God help us all!' Darling was frustrated at being unable to influence the outcome. 'It is one of the worst hazards of old age to see things in a detached way and to be utterly impotent to do anything about them', said the concluding sentence of his first entry. The election campaign dominated the collective consciousness of Australians for the next month or so. It intruded into Darling's Australian Elizabethan Theatre Trust circle when, on the day before Kerr's intervention, he exchanged views about the political stand-off in Canberra during a flight home with Fred Alexander who, two days after the dismissal, put a slightly different spin on the ageing process:

> What an interesting time it is for old codgers like you and me to be able to live in and watch the antics of others with a greater degree of detachment than we might have had twenty years ago!

Alexander thought that the odds on a Labor victory might be shortening. 'I believe there is at least a 50:50 chance that Gough will end up by thanking the G-G for another lucky break in his tempestuous political career'. Between them, said Alexander, Kerr and Fraser 'have given Labour [sic] and its Leader not less than a really good fighting chance' provided, of course, that the trade unions did not 'evoke an anti-violence backlash'.[19]

Darling continued to obsess about Whitlam. Alexander tried to quell his worst fears: 'I appreciate your point about EGW but I doubt whether one should allow dislike of the man to determine one's judgment of his potential role as a political leader'. For his own part, he simply could not see 'Malcolm F as an effective P.M.' Alexander lightened the mood by saying of democracy that he had:

> never recovered from reading [Alfred] Zimmern & discovering that the vaunted democracy of Athens was that of a slave state. I also have [?] sympathy with a friend of my undergraduate days who said he'd believe in democracy if it weren't for the bloody democrats!

Post-election fallout followed. An aggrieved section of the electorate vilified the governor-general. Alan Brown told Darling that attacks on Kerr were reported in the English press in 1976 and, barely a month after the Fraser-led Coalition's triumph, Lloyd Ross touched on this nerve when updating Darling on a Sydney development 'before my friend Kerr made most of my other friends republicans'. He added that Kerr 'should remain a friend, if one can be friendly with a G.G. without being suspected of ulterior motives!' Several months earlier, two days after Frank Crean had been appointed as deputy prime minister (2 July), Darling wrote to his friend (although the first page says 'Never sent. Met him at a party'; in August Crean thanked him for his note—possibly a different one):

> How much I feel for you and a number like you who have dedicated your whole lives to the concept of democratic socialism, have waited for the opportunity, and are now seeing, or at least seeming to see, it thrown away, as a result of what? I am not quite sure.

Despite the government's afflictions, Darling reassured him that a banker friend had claimed that if Crean had been allowed to have his way with his 1974 budget (Whitlam sacked Crean in December of that year) then 'none of this [the government's woes] need have happened'. Perhaps Crean should have resigned—'there is room for an essay on "reasonable loyalty"'—but because he judged his friend as one for whom there were 'no shades' in loyalty or honesty, it must be harder for him to witness the results of so many years of struggle thrown 'wantonly' away:

> I believe that there were injustices to be corrected and your government has done much that is good and cannot be undone, and the others certainly haven't much to be proud of, though I think that Malcolm Fraser may make some sort of a grade.

What saddened him was the 'plain bloody stupidity' of some government members bringing down others who were 'good and wise and compassionate men' (but not 'the P.M'). He doubted whether it could recover, and saw many years in the political wilderness awaiting the ALP. Most of all, however, he assured Crean of 'my friendship and confidence in you personally' and also to express his sympathy 'in what must be a galling experience'.[20]

So much for character in politics; with the publication of *Richly Rewarding* in 1978 Darling's own character was in the spotlight. *Richly Rewarding* was a decade-long project after Darling had finally grasped the nettle in December 1967—he had promised himself to write a 'lot of other things' yet, as he could not quite bring himself to do so, this task might 'make the harder ones easier'. Why record his life? Principally for his grandchildren because no matter how ordinary a life was, when looked back on after a century and if discovered in (say) the middle of the twenty-first century, such a life might just be of interest. He acknowledged the 'monstrous presumption' in composing an autobiography unless one was a capable writer or, unless having made 'so great a contribution to life' others might be interested in seeing how the author thought that he had done it. While also recognising the difficulties in being honest and the strength of the temptation to make the best of oneself in retrospect, he intended the book to be 'a mere record of memory'. Semmler's review positively glowed. Both his review and Ashbolt's settled old scores: Semmler with the politicians, Ashbolt with Moses. Both criticised Darling for the superficiality and paucity of detail in his account of his ABC years, but for different reasons: Ashbolt because he thought that his former boss was bruised by the experience and because his loyalty to the ruling class dictated the need for confidentiality; Semmler because Darling had been the Christian gentleman in not giving chapter and verse. Darling, said Semmler, had been the best of the six ABC chairmen under whom he had worked, principally because of his 'dignity, integrity and especially intellect'. There was no valid reason for not appointing him to a third term and, in the 'sordid' world of internal and external ABC politics Darling had been 'shabbily and rudely treated' in not being properly informed of his non-renewal and thanked for his work until reading about it in the press, and because

Madgwick had been given to understand that he resigned. Semmler said that few public men displayed 'so splendidly' the virtues of humility and integrity as Darling.[21]

Character and institutions were intertwined themes in Ashbolt's review, which built on his SOA press release a decade earlier. Regardless of what Darling thought of himself, he had underrated the impact of his personality at the ABC. Ashbolt was scathing about Moses. He had been 'ruthless' and 'monarchical', and made decisions based on 'whimsy, caprice or self-protection'. The ABC's creative morale had slipped to a 'cheerless level', so that Darling entered an 'atmosphere of despondency'. By contrast with the former general manager, the new chairman had been a man 'jovially, optimistically brimming over with good fellowship and generous thoughts', said Ashbolt. The most admirable of Darling's traits was that 'he had no appetite for power', and yet this same disdain for power was a source of weakness: 'chaps' with a creative bent were not expected to be so relentlessly competitive or compulsively ambitious, and Darling had been quite unprepared for Moses' toughness, bluntness and rudeness. What was important about Darling, then, was what he was rather than what he did. Ashbolt revisited the *Four Corners* incident of 1964. When he had met the commissioners he refused to be a party to what he regarded as a lie—Semmler's press statement that Penlington's presence in Perth at the time of the Cooke hanging was a coincidence (when Ashbolt had explicitly sent him there). Darling was discomfited at that meeting, Ashbolt recalled, and when he explained in respect of his setting straight the record by publicly contradicting Semmler that he was 'burdened with a Methodist conscience', Darling had retorted 'Yes, but anglicans can have a conscience too'. And that, said Ashbolt, was what Darling brought to the ABC: conscience and moral judgement, which to that point in time had been missing from an instrumentality overwhelmed by cutthroat careerism.[22]

But there was more. Of all the chairmen of the past twenty-five years, Darling had been 'the most approachable and affable, the least guarded, weary or defensive, the most anxious to foster artistic and political courage' and 'the least accustomed to manoeuvring in a bureaucratic maze or pursuing a consistent strategy'. A key weakness, however, had been indecisiveness: if sufficient pressure was exercised by a combination of politicians, pressure groups and commissioners, said Ashbolt, then Darling's inclination was 'to retreat'. He cited the *Four Corners* RSL program, after which having been reported as saying publicly that it was 'quite balanced', Darling agreed to Ashbolt's removal from editorial control ultimately because Darling deemed him to be lacking in discipline and loyalty, the two attributes that outside the love of God (long since abandoned by Ashbolt) that he felt Darling prized. Then (his Marxist slip showing), Ashbolt said that as a member of the ruling class Darling had an unquestioning faith in hierarchy and one's place, and that he had said to Ashbolt when he (Darling) departed the ABC that while he thought he was loyal to his own beliefs, he still had to learn how to be loyal to institutions—those institutions that, according to Ashbolt, 'underpin a capitalist social formation'. Darling was party to the idea of the loyalty of 'key institutional functionaries', a loyalty ensuring that institutions remained closed to scrutiny, so that the interests of an open and egalitarian society were of secondary import. And yet, said Ashbolt, Menzies' successors had judged the chairman as too lax, liberal and tolerant, and that he had to go. Paradoxically, even when he suggested to Darling that he ought to have asked Menzies to 'intervene with the new boys' Darling had refused to plead on his own behalf. 'By far', Darling had been the most interesting chairman in the ABC's history, particularly because he kept critical inquiry alive 'at a time when dissent was almost equated with treason'. Notwithstanding Darling's approach in *Richly Rewarding*—written as though he was the 'last imperial Englishman', with a 'lulling edwardian rhetoric' infused with nostalgia and moralism—Ashbolt could think of no other public figure 'able to arouse such widespread affection, despite and even for his faults'.[23]

Manning Clark's review of *Richly Rewarding* publicly repaid a debt that he owed his former boss—which he had described some three years earlier as 'quite a large one'. He was well aware that Darling had given him a long leash during his wartime Corio sojourn. Back in 1968, when John Darling had completed his Australian National University course, Clark wrote to Darling (in England) to discuss with him whether his son's powers lay more in 'grubbing around in the works of Mr. Dry-as-Dust' or in the pursuit of a vocation of the heart rather than the head, and then said that:

> Those days at Geelong Grammar have helped me here. That was one of the times in my life when I found to my delight and surprise, that I had something to say. I am eternally grateful to you for giving me the chance. At the moment there is a great dryness, where four years ago there was a springing well. One must live in Australia to feel the full force of that remark about turning the first flint stone into a springing well.

Back in 1971, when communicating about John (this time in relation to Clark's advice about a possible academic career), Darling had said: 'It seems a very different world from the one in which I grew up and I fear that I am unable to adjust my ideas to it'. Clark is likely to have been intrigued by another Darling letter in early 1978 (had it been posted) to thank Clark for the copy of his 1976 Boyer Lectures. Following Clark's public denunciation of the governor-general's sacking of Whitlam, there was vehement Coalition criticism in Parliament of his appointment as Boyer Lecturer. The response of an ABC executive, Keith Mackriell (an OGG and former student of Clark at Corio), in trying initially to vet Clark's text before its delivery, had made the public broadcaster appear supine.[24]

Darling regarded the lectures as 'extremely interesting'. Sidelined from physical activity for some months following a serious fall when in the UK, he had been thinking that:

> people like myself with an orthodox Christian upbringing expected life to
> be, so to speak, in straight lines: Cause leading to effect, baddies and goodies,
> black and white—whereas in fact it is all so complicated that it is more like a
> book made up of crocheted bits of different coloured string all somehow tied
> together inside and inaccessible but presenting a certain shape on the outside
> with traces of the different strings visible.

As to himself, it was 'virtually impossible', he wrote, 'to access in myself the
innumerable influences which have all through one's life played a part', though
he supposed that some strings were 'more dominant than others'. This was even
more likely to be the case when analysing the growth of a nation, he imagined,
'particularly because no one nation is a place by itself; it is part of a world and
of an era'. If the entire Western world had suffered from the adoption of, and a
preoccupation with, material acquisitiveness, then Australia had suffered more,
partly because the opportunity to indulge in acquisitiveness had been 'so great'
and because 'we have lacked the counter action of, the all be it [sic] paternalistic,
concept of responsibility and service'. The almost complete absence of this idea
and its practice when he arrived in 1930 had shocked him the most. His efforts,
he concluded, 'now look of course very old fashioned as they were perhaps
even then'.[25]

Clark's review served up more character, although less emphasis on institutions. Darling's book should be read by anyone worried about the future of
civilisation in Australia, he wrote, because its author had lived long enough to
see that 'all he believed in' was up for review—the teachings of Christ and a less
materialistic style of life—and 'threatened with being swept into the dustbin of
history'. In his first decade as headmaster, when imbued with compassion for
a suffering humanity after the 'holocaust of 1918', Darling came to Corio and
stamped the young men who departed GGS as 'men of the middle ground' (the
likes of Gorton, Hamer and Southey), who had fought for their headmaster's
view of life 'against the "boss-sherrifs"' in their own political party'. The 1939–40
reaction against him, however, meant that Darling went the way of those who
sought to reform 'the existing order in Australia': conservative power simply could
not be shaken by his vision of what he stood for. From then on, when trying to
rebuild what had been weakened by his opponents, Darling was like a man with
'a harpoon in his back'. At the ABC, Darling again discovered that 'the forces
of history' were moving against him and he was bewildered by the gap between
his high-minded sense of impartiality and the 'behaviour of the "men in black"'
in Canberra's political bear pit. He had had to watch the world that he stood for
crumble before his eyes. Dunstan, Clark's former GGS history pupil, also told a
tale of character and described an institution in action. Did this 'sometimes bril-
liantly imaginative, often absurd, often maddening, frequently inspiring, occasionally laughable' headmaster really know 'some of the things' that Manning
Clark, with his radical views on religion and politics, had been saying in his

history classes during the war, Dunstan asked. 'We used to wonder... how on earth did the man survive?' 'The Boss' or 'Ralphie'—this 'walking conscience'— had had a headmasterly aura about him. He had worn down sport at Corio, especially rowing until it had become 'a nothing affair on the outcast Barwon', and had devised schemes such as national service to ensure that GGS's sporting record became even worse. Manning Clark had been Darling's Gollancz. His battle, not realised at the time, had been no less easy than Fisher's at Repton before him. To his credit, however, Darling had not sent Clark packing, as Fisher had Gollancz—although (controversy aside) Dunstan might not have realised that with so many masters in wartime service, Darling could have ill afforded to lose him.[26]

   Richly Rewarding was also the focus of a brief flurry of correspondence between Darling and Geoffrey Fairbairn (then Reader in History, Australian National University). Fairbairn had sent him K.C. Masterman's review, and it prompted Darling to think that there may have been too much 'mock modesty' at the end of the book. He hadn't been 'a complete failure' in his last jobs, thought Darling, 'but they weren't jobs in which there was much chance of any visible result'. Fairbairn judged *Richly Rewarding* as '"lovely", as nice Australians used to say in a happier age', although it was 'all so ludicrously ... self-effacing' that a biography was called for. Attention then turned to Manning Clark (who had taught Fairbairn at GGS) and his influence. Darling could not explain the then public antipathy to Clark and ascribed it to jealousy 'due to the way in which in recent years he has been publicised as the only reputable Australian historian'. Some ill feeling arose because Clark had done less than full justice to the heroes of historians such as M.H. Ellis. While Ellis was right, Clark was being accused of not being the 'sort of historian that he has never tried to be'. Darling put Clark in the 'greater' tradition of historians (like Gibbon, Froude and Macauley) who 'care more for their theme and the philosophy of life than about recording'. Maybe Clark 'has a hang-up about religion', said Darling, and 'he might not be happy until he resolves it'. Whether or not he resolved it in this life or the next, 'I am sure that he is an acceptable man to the Lord, because he is full of a true compassion and that is the basic criterion'. Two years later (1980), Fairbairn wrote from London and quoted an 'exceedingly interesting & important' extract from Jamie Mackie:

> 'at the age of seventeen I found the tension between Manning's vision of the brotherhood of man and JRD's a marvellously challenging educational experience, such that even now I'd be hard put to say which one I found the more appealing or the more influential for me ...'

Surely that did 'honour to all three of you', Fairbairn wrote, because Darling had named Stephen Murray-Smith, Mackie and Fairbairn in *Richly Rewarding* as three people who owed a great debt to Clark, 'which we certainly did'.[27]

Thanks to another key player in the October–November 1975 events, Sir Garfield Barwick (Chief Justice of the High Court), Darling became involved in a new educational venture that engaged him into his nineties: the United World Colleges. In August 1971, Barwick said that he had been contacted by Lord Mountbatten (Chairman, International Council of the Atlantic Colleges). 'One ought really to be born without goodwill', said Barwick, pompously:

> Such men seem to get by and save themselves a great deal of time and effort. I've now paid the price or at any rate the major part of the price of yielding to Mountbatten's importunity. I have done as promised and assembled a Committee. You will be receiving a letter from me which will tell the story … there will not be a great deal to be done but from time to time good counsel would be valuable.

This initiative renewed Darling's contact with the legacy of Kurt Hahn (who died in 1974). In 1962, Hahn and Sir Lawrance Darvall (retired air marshall and one-time commandant of the NATO Staff Training College) had founded Atlantic College on the south coast of Wales 32 kilometres from Cardiff at St Donat's, a medieval castle once owned by the newspaper baron, William Randolph Hearst. It promoted international understanding as a way of breaking down national barriers to ensure that education worked for unity among nations rather than division. This thinking was reinforced by Darvall's NATO experience in transcending narrow nationalism through postwar inter-country defence collaboration. He also believed in 'the advantage of continuous consultation and cooperation, the superiority of discussion over argument, and the conviction that resort to force is childish, useless and unworthy'. Coupled with Hahn's emphasis on the outdoors (coastal rescue services), a socially mixed admissions profile, a broadly based and academically demanding curriculum (the International Baccalaureate was adopted eventually) and community-based social service, the plan (in 1970) was to disseminate the model worldwide as the United World Colleges Project.[28]

Earlier, as the Empire Ship scheme fizzled out, Darling had lent his name to two new Outward Bound–style initiatives: patron of the proposed Arkaba Mountain and Sea Schools Trust in South Australia, for which he wrote an introduction for a brochure that linked the new venture to Hahn and Outward Bound. He also joined the new council of the Australian Outward Bound Memorial Foundation (along with Healey, Frank Woods, P.J. McKeown, Betty Archdale, Vincent Fairfax and Potter), the patron of which (from 1966) was to be Prince Phillip; the president was to be Casey. In 1970, then, when (with Casey's connivance) he was alerted by Lord Hankey that a global network of United World College schools was in the wind, Barwick's letter would not have come as a complete surprise. Hankey said that the aim was to collect young people of both sexes aged from sixteen to eighteen from different countries, 'put them through a two-year pre-university course and to teach them to understand and co-operate with other young people of different races, colours, religion and social origins'. There was a United World College in Singapore (at the former British military forces school for children), although as yet 'the idea has not clicked officially'. The attitude of Australian government ministers was unknown, except that it had to be known because 'we need government support'. This was where Darling would play a part, and by the late 1970s he was chairing the United World College's Victorian committee and lobbying the state government (with some success) for funds.[29]

The United World Colleges (Australia) Trust was established in 1972, the year that Darling initiated the Victorian scheme. The Singapore International School had opened in 1971 (from 1975, it became the United World College South East Asia) and the first Victorian student enrolled in 1973. Over the next decade, fifteen Victorians attended United World College schools in Singapore, Wales, Canada and Italy. From 1974, the Victorian government provided $6000 annually to support two scholarships for students (increased to $14,000 in 1980–81). At this time (1973), Darling's circumstances precluded more extensive national United World Colleges involvement—the cost of interstate travel for meetings was prohibitive and those organisations that had previously paid for his travel 'had all learned to dispense with my services'. As he also had no secretarial support, at his request the Sydney-based national committee arranged to have typed copies made of his letters of importance that were dispatched back by return mail. Darling believed that an endowment fund was essential to support prospective students, a purpose that required 'one very rich man'. He was confident that the prime minister (Whitlam) would be 'on our side', and he estimated that about $40,000 annually was required to maintain twelve students in Singapore. More generally, commerce and industry might provide scholarship funding, and international trading firms should be encouraged to fund Asian students. Later on (1979), while remarking to Sir Mark Turner (of CRA) that having just turned eighty he did not 'seem very different in consequence', he changed tack on fund-raising when the United World Colleges Australian national committee could not secure taxation relief for donations. He hated fund-raising organisations, he confided to the national committee chairman, Sir Charles Cutler, and had 'always been a complete failure in raising money'. As with Frontier, the options were big (or even huge) gifts or numerous small ones. In 1978, Sir Ian Gourlay (director-general, United World Colleges) discussed with Fraser (Whitlam's successor) and the governor-general (Cowen) the founding of an Australian United World College named after Menzies (who had died in May). This effort came to nothing. To have Menzies' name in the title might have been a tax-deduction inducement, Darling surmised, but he doubted whether the idea 'really married well with Menzies himself'. As a general rule, fund-raising required a paid organiser, and a small committee of interested and 'very rich men' who would give a lead and try to 'fleece their colleagues and competitors'.[30]

By the end of the decade an OGG was heading the United World Colleges, as Prince Charles agreed in 1978 to be president of the international council. The membership of Darling's state committee was a moveable feast, but included (in 1982) Chris Leschinski, Peter Gebhardt (principal, Geelong College), Dorothy Pizzey (headmistress, St Catherine's) and Robin Chapman (Department of Education). At this time the United World Colleges project was hamstrung in four ways: the Australian national headquarters' inefficiency and poor links with London, insufficient funding, alleged elitism (competitive college entry was based on academic ability, personal qualities and a commitment to furthering the international aims), and a looming conflict with the Victorian Department of Education. The national committee, Darling complained to London, met 'sporadically' but never bothered with advance notice of its meetings, thus excluding the two Victorian members. Gebhardt attended the 1982 annual meeting and called it a 'most unsatisfactory affair' that quickly degenerated into a social discussion group, interrupted only by a man 'extolling the virtues of History' and a retired army officer 'criticizing the youths chosen for their failure to contribute to the generation of a better Australia'. As Sydney paid no dues to London, it was hardly surprising that its service was 'inadequate'. Because New South Wales was so dominant about the issues and even 'gerontocratic', Victoria should try to go its own way. As for funding, Darling confessed to being 'so defeatist' about securing the Australian government's agreement to tax deductibility for scholarships—'Everyone', he told a contact at the international office, 'including H.R.H. has tried but to no avail'. The international council rubbed salt into the wound by appealing directly to the Australian Italian community to finance students to attend the new United World College of the Adriatic (in Duino, Italy) in 1982. Two scholarships were provided by *Il Globo*, the Australian Italian-language newspaper, and the Italian government, on whose behalf Darling's committee selected the students (while occasionally choosing the one funded by the Commonwealth).[31]

Fund-raising success did eventuate, but for the time being lack of tax deductibility and lack of money put paid to the idea of an Australian United World College. The OGG Rod Carnegie (of CRA) confirmed that even with the Menzies moniker the idea was a non-starter, because after six months' investigation Sir William Vines (of the Sir Robert Menzies Memorial Trust—later the Menzies Foundation) concluded that an estimated capital cost of $6 million made the venture impractical. The likelihood of federal funding for recurrent purposes was also minimal and, even if a college were not named after Menzies, a future Labor government was thought unlikely to support it 'because of its elitist character'. Equally, said Carnegie, while he had seen firsthand the project's Lester Pearson College on Vancouver Island in Canada, no corporate support would be forthcoming because in CRA's case its guidelines precluded gifts for purposes or institutions outside of Australia. There was even more salt in the wound when Sir Mark Turner informed Darling that he and Carnegie had secured from CRA's

UK subsidiary a gift of £25,000 for St Donat's, as part of an RTZ trust fund that memorialised Val Duncan (who died in 1975). This was a doubly galling situation, because Darling had hoped for a $75,000 donation from this source. If there were to be an Australian-based United World College, Darling's personal preference was for it to be focused on Australia and the islands of the South Pacific and biased towards an agricultural curriculum. Three potential locations were considered: St Leonard's College in the Melbourne suburb of Brighton had a site of well over 40 hectares suitable for expansion, a Western Australian scheme (had it taken off) might have drawn on resources from the Fairbridge Farm, and Marcus Oldham College was a possibility: its buildings and facilities were then under-utilised and its principal was receptive to the idea. Despite Darling's discussions with Turner and the Labour peer Lord Shackleton (a former Wilson government minister) these possibilities came to nothing.[32]

Patron, trustee, fund-raiser, loyal correspondent, lobbyist, committee member and chairman—all honorary and honourable, sedulously performed to a fault and exemplifying Deirdre McCloskey's bourgeois civic virtuosity. Other elements in Darling's post-GGS years were educational consultant, promoter, planner and adviser, and these roles came to the fore in December 1970 when the Caseys signalled release of a parcel of their Berwick property to the federal and state governments. Victorian independent schools had expanded incrementally in number in the 1960s. Darling had endorsed the efforts of the promoters of the Peninsula School, which had opened at Mount Eliza on the Mornington Peninsula in 1961 and, in August 1964, he helped launch the proposed new Yarra Valley School, which opened in 1966. Yarra Valley, he said later, was a school located on a 'wonderful site' (on the north-eastern perimeter of suburban Melbourne) in 'a good area where there is a strong and growing demand'. Its backers were 'a first class group of people' with 'the right ideas of how a school should be administered and the humility to be prepared to take advice'. Darling's prototype for greenfield-site new schools was Oldham and articulated further in his Buntine Oration. The essence of what he had in mind (he told a 1975 Old Geelong Grammarians Association dinner) was that for political and economic reasons the future lay in 'educational complexes, with consequential savings in overheads and mutual benefits through contacts' between their component parts. These were the outcome of cooperation, not competition. They had to provide for both sexes, all age groups and denominations, and adult communities. The difficulty in the 1970–71 Berwick discussions was that the Caseys had other plans. Darling became aware of their intended gift during discussions about the future development of St Margaret's, Berwick (he was a school council member). He was also a member of the 'Reid committee'—sponsored (from April 1970) by Len Reid (Liberal MHR, Holt)—a body investigating the feasibility of a boys' school for Berwick. Casey had been alerted to this development by Reid and also to its potential name as the Casey boys' school. Discussions between St Margaret's and Reid's committee commenced in early 1971, with Darling a joint steering committee member. It was tasked with trying to establish a coeducational school in Berwick and approaching Casey about making available 28 hectares of his land. At that point, Darling drafted his educational complex proposal.[33]

Darling's model came to nothing in Berwick. But what of Oldham? Since his departure from Corio, Darling did not think that Marcus Oldham Farm Management College had been travelling well. (He did not become active until after Garnett's retirement.) Darling's gripe with Oldham was its betrayal of his original vision. The bone of contention was the purpose and usage of 1.6 hectares set aside as common land in the north-eastern corner of the 161-hectare estate. Development of the Highton site had proceeded slowly. The dust experienced during the first two months of 1962 had been 'frightful', said Bill Cartwright (of Bostock), although later (May) there had been a four-day battle with mud of 'a peculiarly affectionate variety'. Yet the transformation witnessed in the first few months of the school year, particularly of the woolshed's conversion into an art–craft centre, Cartwright thought, was testimony to the fact that 'we have not entirely lost the spirit which made possible efforts like Mt Duneed Church, the re-building of the Mechanics and Carpentry Shop, the early stages of Timbertop etc.' At this point GGS Highton (as it was known) comprised the six primary forms of Bostock and the boarding house, and the first three forms of the secondary component known as Highton House. (The Hermitage's middle-school involvement commenced in 1963 but only in 1970 was there a staged move of the entire school to Highton from its Newtown site.) In-common sharing of facilities had been underpinned by the principles of cooperation and cost sharing, as originally proposed by Darling to the Highton Joint Committee. Potential in-common facilities in 1960 included a sanatorium, entrance roads, gas, electricity and water provided as part of a shared understanding and funded in the following proportions: GGS 40 per cent, Oldham Trust 40 per cent and Hermitage 20 per cent. These facilities were separate from those owned by any of the institutions on their land (for example, ovals) but accessible to the others. Darling's idea was a 'multi-level educational complex grouped around a common cultural centre'—although the details were not spelt out. Because of legal difficulties in creating a joint trust to control common lands and buildings, Hubert Black's advice in 1960 was that GGS own the common land (to mitigate its overall investment risk) and build with money lent by the other parties.[34]

It was in 1968 when Cartwright's successor Graeme Renney made contact that Darling may have heard the first faint ring of alarm bells. Renney had persuaded the joint committee to begin construction of the in-common facilities and by October a swimming pool (funded by the Oldham trustees and the Bostock parents) had been built near the shared sanatorium—at a capital cost for both facilities of $25,000 (although the sanatorium closed in 1971 and, at GGS's initiative, was converted into a staff residence). Rather than contribute capital funding, the Hermitage had opted to pay rent for the use of the swimming pool and to contribute to its annual maintenance. In 1976—the first year of

GGS coeducation—Darling met with Ivo Dean (the Marcus Oldham Farm Management College principal) and David Turnbull (of the solicitors Blake & Riggall and an Oldham trustee) to formalise the previous gentlemen's agreement and to ensure continuation of the cooperative spirit at Highton. In the new agreement between GGS and the trustees, GGS granted to Marcus Oldham Farm Management College and its students the right to 'use the Common Land and all buildings and other improvements erected thereon'. The Marcus Oldham Farm Management College council accepted the draft document, but in May 1977 GGS's council 'rejected it as a statement of the position'. In the interregnum following the death of GGS's headmaster Charles Fisher in December 1978 (prior to the arrival from Eton of John Lewis), the chief executive officer was Robin Ritchie and the council chairman, Rod Carnegie—both previously Darling-appointed prefects. There was a simultaneous changing of the guard at Oldham, as its council searched for Dean's successor. On a couple of occasions Ritchie had tried to pay out Oldham for its original contributions (half the cost of the sanatorium and a third of the pool cost), but this gesture was rejected. The offer made no allowance for the improved value of the assets but, in any case, Oldham regarded its investment in the facilities as a tangible commitment to the future of the common land ideal. There was a stand-off. A lunch with Ritchie and Carnegie to ascertain whether there was still interest in Darling's original idea failed to break the deadlock. GGS would not commit to an agreement if it tied the new headmaster's hands.[35]

Darling was steaming. In September 1980, he wrote a letter of resignation (another addition to his 'not sent' collection). 'All right! I withdraw', he said. The common land idea was much more than an 'untidy bit of finance' and something on the plate of the 'new man': it was the 'abandonment of an almost visionary concept' of a complex that ought to be a future model for independent schools. A shared community facility was the way forward, he insisted, not 'an independent school which clings exclusively to its possessions and privileges'. If a younger headmaster saw virtue in it, then it might mean the 'hiving off of Highton' as a third secondary school in the district—an idea which he, Buntine and Gebhardt all believed to be necessary. Ritchie, however, labelled him a conservative, a charge that was not entirely water off a duck's back:

> Having been called in my day Socialist, Liberal and even Communist and having done more in the way of innovation in education than most people, I suppose it is fitting that I should end up by being damned as a hide-bound conservative. This rankles, but is, I suppose true.

Darling was abandoning the struggle and regretfully withdrew his opposition. By all means play them on the money issue, he counselled the Marcus Oldham Farm Management College council, 'and get as much out of them as you can'. He would not accept another three-year term on the farm college's council, and it was better to get out 'before I become more of a bloody nuisance than I am already'. And, as his main purpose in being a member was to pursue the community idea, there seemed to be little point in remaining. But remain he did, for another three terms until 1989 when he was ninety. He may have judged humble-pie eating as better than being dismissed as a curmudgeon in high dudgeon. Eventually (early 1984), the GGS council paid out its share of the residence on the common land and in 1981, the Marcus Oldham Farm Management College council named a new building in his honour: the Sir James Darling Resource Centre. The episode had been akin to a falling out among family members, but it also illustrated how the fruit of learning comes back later to bite in unpredictable ways: encourage independence of mind in the character development of young men and they might exercise it later on maturity, although in ways of their own choosing.[36]

By the end of the 1970s, three themes about life and living had crystallised in Darling's mind: the implications of pluralisation and his realisation (as voiced to Manning Clark) that one could no longer live life in straight lines, his fear that Australian democracy was ill served by polarised political partisanship and, especially, his conviction that antipodean adaptations of English public schooling were things of the past. Compared with Oldham, his other educational ventures were calmer. In 1968, he joined the council of Ridley College, an Anglican training college for clergy, where he remained a member until 1981 and in 1982 chaired its development appeal. Then, in 1976, Braemar College opened as a low-fee ($70 per term) secondary ecumenical community school on the Mount Macedon property vacated by Clyde (after amalgamating with GGS). Darling was its patron and he helped select the first principal, Graham Farley, a man keen to harness Darling's 'inspirational abilities'. To realise Braemar's mission entailed swimming against the tide of 'social habits and educational fallacies', Darling said, something easier to do three decades earlier when society 'seemed reasonably stable'. Now, however, almost every force for social stability was threatened: faith, patriotism, empire, monarchy, democratic government, the family, morals, manners and financial security. People were doing their own thing 'regardless of responsibility to anyone else', which made for disintegration bordering on anarchy. Schools were subject to the push and pull of social needs, conflicting forces, economic demands and parental ambitions for children. With some people committed to freedom from the indoctrination of principles and others desiring children's moral and intellectual discipline, schools strove for a balance. Braemar, he said, was seeking to be a minority group in a world that 'has for the most part abandoned even the pretence of being Christian', which made its life both easy (it knew what it stood for) and difficult (worldly standards impinged). Because Braemar's community emphasis entailed participation—'possibly the only new idea which this generation has produced'—everyone in the school had to sacrifice for the common good: individuals could state their views but then had to think about the 'larger concept of the whole' and leave decision-making to those with 'ultimate responsibility'.[37]

This reasoning tapped into two countervailing 1970s trends. Diffusing plural values were vitiating moral absolutism, while entrenched divisions between denominations were softening as their beleaguered adherents sought common cause. At the inauguration service in 1974 for another Christian ecumenical school in Maryborough, housed in former Brigidine Convent buildings, Darling was delighted about the 'extraordinary change' that he was witnessing among the churches: cooperation, not competition, was the way to preserve a Christian influence in education amid liberalised morals and manners. But he struggled to get to grips with changing social trends. W.B. Yeats might be right, he told Trinity Grammar School boys (in 1980): maybe the centre wasn't holding and things were falling apart. He asked whether the current era was one of decadence or renaissance. And to what extent, he added, could the boys' contemporaries mould the forces of history or did they have to submit to them? While there didn't seem to be much to be proud of in the twentieth century (thanks to war, Depression, the atom bomb, destruction of the environment, population and poverty, Nazi genocide and communist imperialism), there was unequalled change and even progress (in technological and scientific discovery, communication, recognition of the rights of man, the end of empires, the birth of new nations, creation of a welfare society not based in slavery, revolt against hypocrisy and double standards, and participation). At Brisbane Grammar School (in November 1975), he again bemoaned the extreme divide between the political parties and the public's perception of them as liars, bad and unnecessary. To the Xavier College Staff Association, the year before, he had expressed hope that these polarities might be moderated and cited the opinion of Bob Hawke (then the president of the ALP) that a movement away from capitalist democracy to a modified democratic socialism was likely. Darling asked: if he was right, then what did that mean for independent schools?[38]

In 1978, Ranald Macdonald (OGG and chairman of the *Age*) sought Darling's advice about commemorating the newspaper's 125th anniversary. At his suggestion, Macdonald and Evan Walker (chairman of Frontier, and soon a minister in the state Cain Labor government) planned a conference with him on 'the wide questions of Australian identity (perish the word!)', with Frontier to make the arrangements. One potential conference outcome might be a centre, 'as envisaged by me for Frontier many years ago', he told John Dunlop, along the lines of the Ditchley Foundation or Political and Economic Planning (PEP— later the Policy Studies Institute) for the pursuit of ideas and the education of the public towards 'more sophisticated thinking'. This future focus expressed Darling's concern about Australia's lack of a common national purpose, and reflected a wider contemporary interest in long-term developmental trends as part of futurology. A key thinker whose writings shaped this academic field was Herman Kahn (Director, Hudson Institute, New York), who had embarked in early 1978 on the 'Future of Australian society' in collaboration with the Australian consultants, P.G. Pak-Poy & Associates. Darling was not a futurology disciple, but had read Alvin Toffler's *Future Shock*. He hoped to target about 120 attendees in the thirty to forty-five age-group with responsibility for Australia over the next two to three decades. They could confer anywhere in the country that they liked, he thought, provided they didn't choose Canberra (as this city was 'dominated by political and bureaucratic thinking' and remote from ordinary community activities). If an ongoing entity was formed after the conference, then he hoped for Frontier-style reports comprising 'unbiased facts' and records of discussion to avoid the 'polarisation of opinion which at present hinders the provision of national solutions'. Darling was troubled about a divided Australia:

> if democratic government, and more particularly, the Westminster system of two-party democracy, is to last, it can only do so if there are more points of agreement than of disagreement: objectives must be similar even if methods of reaching them are different. A total diversity of objectives and values will drive the country into a conflict resulting in total victory of one side over the other, a dictatorship of one side or the other. This will happen unless we can find out the points on which we agree and develop a patriotism based on this agreement. There is very little of this understanding today because, as a new nation, we do not know what is our place in the world.

Darling proposed the following conference topics: the mechanics of representative government, external relationships, participatory democracy, energy, resources and conservation ('I am out of my depth here and don't really know what I am talking about'), moral values, and economic problems ('beyond my powers to consider in any detail'). The moral values area was 'the most important subject of all' and the most difficult.[39]

After lead-up workshops and a preliminary conference in Sydney in 1979, Frontier's public conference ('Future Directions') convened at La Trobe University, Melbourne. Darling was pleasantly surprised by its air of optimism. He was happy with the preparation, although worried that 'we might have bitten off more than we can chew'. He could not resist a pot shot at academics (especially sociologists) who 'tend to express themselves in language which they have made up for their own purposes'. He returned to his anxieties about the future of the country in 'Patriotism, identity and purpose' (1982). The prediction some months earlier by James Wolfensohn, the Australian international merchant banker, of imminent 'fundamental changes' in the world's financial system was his departure point. Darling asked: hadn't his generation experienced enough of such changes 'from the world of our boyhood'? There was a lack of confidence in the 'power of the system to right itself', leaders were not trusted to find a way out of conditions that 'look like destroying us' and 'we' (his readership) were afraid of change to a way of life derived from 'our civilisation' and accepted as unalterable. What could be held onto by way of continuity while not resisting 'too irrationally the inevitable movements of history'? As a geographically remote offshoot of Western capitalism, Australia had been historically culturally dependent on its European origins. The Fraser government was struggling to get to grips with a severe economic downturn while he was putting pen to paper, and with Australia 'stuck with' free enterprise capitalism, like it or not, he could see no salvation if the laws of supply and demand were left to their own devices. Symptomatic of the 'prevailing disease' was the common ground between those who prioritised the control of inflation ahead of reducing unemployment, and their opponents who reversed these priorities. Another symptom was the gulf of ignorance between manipulators of the monetary system and its victims. There were moral problems with the international world of finance: when capital pursued the highest interest rates what hope was there for poorer countries (he instanced Uganda and Ethiopia)? 'Horror of horrors! Could Marx have been right when he argued that exploitation was the inevitable result of capitalism?'[40]

From the perspective of the 'old-time economists'—who, though?—the production process was meant to satisfy human needs, except that these now played second fiddle to profit-making. The world would be improved if every occupation was thought of ('as it should be') as a service and every trade a vocation. And yet instead of job satisfaction, he detected greed among employers and trade unions. Revival required social unity: no matter how diverse it was, a society had to be 'at one in its basic beliefs', for which a sense of purpose (an attribute of character) was the only answer. Such purpose acknowledged a driving force 'more powerful than oneself' and was recognisable in all men with a claim to greatness (and women: he cited Florence Nightingale and Caroline Chisholm). What was true of individuals was true of nations. Here he worked his way through phases of European history and empire to locate a model for Australia, possibly Holland, Sweden, Switzerland and a couple of the eastern European countries. As for the idea of Australia as a lucky country, in which 'everybody is more equal than anybody else and everyone can have everything that the richest can have', this was not a reasonable identity because it was contrary to nature, impossible anyway and not good enough. Australia's ambition should be about quality of life and the force of example rather than power. 'We should aim to be a good country rather than a great one.' Again he saw Australia as a bridge between East and West (and 'protector and developer of the Pacific Islands'), but didn't spell out what he had in mind. In this disturbed period, 'between one era and the next', the imminent age would be one of unity and universality, to which each person would contribute according to their means and talents. Here, Australia was peculiarly well adapted. With this rather lame finale, Darling's discussion ended by defending (in effect) the nation's postwar multiculturalism.[41]

Darling was now eighty-three. Unlike their brother, neither of his two sisters attained their ninth decades. Margaret had died in 1975, aged seventy-eight, and Mabel in 1980. Margaret had lived with Aunt Peg (until her death in 1965) in St Andrews, Scotland, but due to failing health (having contracted Parkinson's disease) by the early 1970s she relocated to Cirencester, in Gloucestershire, not far from Mabel's cottage in Fairford, where (from 1969) she had been living following Ralph's death. Margaret's health had deteriorated rapidly. In early 1971, she had written to her brother to say that, with the family having badgered her to get some home help, a young woman was coming for another two days a week 'so that I don't do any housework & just the minimum of cooking'. Her 'Parkinson tremor', she wrote stoically, was 'quite unaccountable in its attack & makes writing rather wearisome'. It was also 'rather bad for my spelling': 'I get into the middle of a word & it looks so odd that I can't think how to finish it off!' In a steady stream of correspondence to her brother in Melbourne, Mabel described their sister as muddled and frail, and then bored and unhappy at being on her own. In late 1973, Margaret had been found wandering in the town at 2 am, 'thinking she was going shopping', although defiant about carrying on alone. In June 1974, she had been admitted to a nursing home in Cheltenham. Six months later she fell and broke her hip. When she died the following March, a still-grieving Mabel had written to lament that neither she nor her brother had really appreciated her as they should have done. She herself had never really been close to her elder sister Margaret, who 'seemed to need the support of the family to give her confidence & was yet unable to inspire real affection'. Margaret had adored her younger brother and her nephew John, Mabel said, 'but neither of you needed her love'. While none of the family members had ever begrudged him going to Australia, and they had all taken pride in his success and basked in his glory, there remained a lingering bit of hurt, because on one of his trips home he had not taken more interest in his elder sister and in Ralph. On the other hand, the weeks that he and Margaret (his wife) had spent at St Andrews on their last visit (1968) had been a source of great pleasure to their sister Margaret. The final fortnight of their sister's life had been 'dreadfully sad' but, thankfully, she had been well cared for by the doctors and nursing staff. For her own part, Mabel had visited her brother in 1970 and again in 1979, as a surprise for his eightieth birthday. This time she travelled by air rather than ship. The flight home she described as safe and easy 'but a considerable test of endurance', nonetheless, before having been met at Heathrow by her son Morris. She died not long after of a heart attack, aged seventy-six.[42]

Darling had a painful (and humiliating) intimation of his own mortality in between the deaths of his two sisters that was sufficient for him to write an eleven-page diary reflection on death and dying. The incident occurred in 1977 while he and Margaret were in the UK. After attempting one evening to retrieve his pipe from the kitchen of the Edinburgh flat of his cousin, Helen Nimmo, he mistook in the darkness a stairwell door for the kitchen door and fell backwards down a flight of stairs. Although there were no bones broken, it was a near-run thing. When his cries for help were finally answered, something of a comedy of errors ensued, as Helen promptly fainted and cut her head and Margaret tripped over and ended up sitting on him. An ambulance ride to the Royal Infirmary followed by X-rays had preceded six days of being watched over by nurses who, he thought later, had seemed unaccountably resentful towards him, and had rebuked him whenever he tried to remove his oxygen mask. Under sedation with painkillers and hardly able to walk, he was confined to a wheelchair. (The boot was on the other foot, he reflected: accustomed to being responsible for himself and to giving orders to others, he was now on the receiving end.) He was then moved to a private nursing home, where he had not felt like eating and was reluctant to get out of bed. He supposed, as a result of the shock and the drugs administered to ease his pain that he was 'not really very much in this world': 'I had always been afraid, not of death itself (which is either nothing or an intensely interesting adventure) but of the inevitable process of dying'. In this metaphysical vein, he also remembered, 'to my shame, feeling that I was deserted by God'. Throughout his life he had 'clung to' a text in 1 Corinthians: 'God is faithful, and he will not let you be tested beyond your strength ...' At one stage during his incapacity he had felt as though this was not the case and that 'I <u>was</u> being tried beyond my capacity to endure', and yet he had come through his time of despair 'and God is still here'. When eventually he would encounter the process of dying, he thought that the memory of this unfortunate event would assist him. Still in excruciating pain, he was flown to Gatwick airport. During the flight he believed that he had experienced a miracle—'the result of someone's intense prayers on my behalf and God's response': with the effect of the drugs having worn off while airborne, he reported all his pain as having disappeared and feeling suddenly comfortable. Mabel, when he informed her of this, had been 'rather ashamed' of him for feeling this way and for speaking of it, but he insisted that it was a real and vivid experience that had been difficult to explain. The conclusion that he drew was that on this occasion God had indeed been faithful and, when reflecting on the entire episode, despite its dampening impact on his and Margaret's trip, he considered that the kindness of the doctors and their friends was sufficient for him to wrap up his diary entry by affirming that 'God moves in a mysterious way'.[43]

ONCE AN ENGLISHMAN

1980–1995

Unless a man bends his every effort to advance in his spirituality, then other things being equal it must grow feebler: progressively so (unless something specific should occur to arrest the decline), in that his materialism is always there on the look-out in him, eager to profit by the freer play that his spiritual enfeeblement has given it, and so still further to increase this enfeeblement.

Victor Gollancz, *The Devil's Repertoire*

Following the incident in Edinburgh, Darling was preoccupied by death. 'Is it unreasonable or morbid to think about death as much I seem to do?', his diary recorded in 1985. When he was ninety, he returned to this theme (twice). He knew that at his age when people met him they remarked that he didn't seem old, and asked out of courtesy how he felt. He thought that he was old 'by any standard', and wanted to know how he was faring: 'I have never been old before. It is a new experience, hard to accept and it follows that I don't know how well I ought to feel. Certainly not 100%.' After all—with Jaques' speech about the seven ages of man from Shakespeare's *As You Like It* in mind—there were capacities that he was 'sans [without]'. He gave a self-diagnosis of organs and abilities: teeth, eyes (he'd always been afraid of blindness, because at eighty-six his mother had almost totally lost her sight), short-term memory ('pretty bad'), things long past ('I generally astonish myself and others with the recall'), his mind (superficial and quick, as 'always', and fairly good at problem analysis) and physically he'd been very lucky, although without deserving to be. He smoked (a pipe) way too much and 'cough[ed] the rest of the time'. His circulation was bad and he was kept alive, he said, by warfarin and monthly blood tests, and yet his heart and blood pressure always seemed to satisfy his doctor when he checked them. His feet (due to the circulation difficulties) were able to carry him but not move him, and deprived him of exercise. He guessed that he could probably still walk a kilometre and a half without a rest, but to play bowls was out of the question—although he had been playing in 1980. Golf and his annual Boxing Day fishing jaunts with medicos and other male friends at Waterfall Farm, Khancoban, en route to citizenship conventions, were things of the past.[1]

Age, then, was wearying him. There were times, he had told Mabel some years earlier, when he resented having to do more than one thing in a day. It was a case of accidie, he said, something to which 'I have always been somewhat prone'. He was trying not to let age get to him and, away from the privacy of these introspective diary ruminations and family letters he still wanted to be listened to on the public issues of the day. One way was to exploit his status as an elder. Other elders were on the same wavelength. In 1982, Sir Barton Pope (a South Australian industrialist), and the eminent Australian scientists, Sir Mark Oliphant and Sir Macfarlane Burnet, founded the Challenge to Australia Committee and then Pope created the Australian Advisory Council of Elders. This body comprised seventy notable septuagenarians (the age threshold was later lowered to sixty to include those not in paid employment). For a short while Darling was a member of the council's Education Committee. The council saw itself as a think-tank that 'put forward ideas based upon the insights, training and long years of experience of its members' and it aimed 'to inspire and encourage other people with more resources to become involved in matters important to Australia'. In April 1984, Darling attended a meeting in Melbourne convened by Sir Cecil Looker (a businessman partner of Sir Ian Potter and, like Potter, once the private secretary of Casey and Menzies). Among the more well-known public figures who attended were Burnet and Lady Burnet, the retired army surgeon Sir Edward (Weary) Dunlop, the businessmen Sir Albert Jennings and Sir Charles McGrath, the philanthropist Dame Elisabeth Murdoch, the foundation director of the Institute for Public Affairs (C.D. Kemp) and the chemist L.W. Weickhardt. After the gathering Darling commented to Alby Jones (a South Australian College of Education and council contact) that the attendees didn't appear to be a 'very influential collection when assembled in bulk', although 'the ladies were better than the men'. It wasn't easy to get anything 'to go all over' Australia at the same time—although the Australian College of Education had been an exception—and there was the added problem that 'we old chaps' were 'a trifle transitory'.[2]

Darling's involvement with Australian Advisory Council of Elders was brief. He was sceptical about the potential effectiveness of the council's public pronouncements and, given his Australian College of Education experience, even whether it would be listened to and consulted by governments. He provided some feedback to Jones on a council document, 'Challenge to Australia and its Education', except that reading it made him feel 'quite deplorably ignorant, muddle-headed and futile'. Perhaps it was silly for old people to attempt to say anything at all, he told him, as it was unlikely that anyone would listen. Having suggested some amendments to the draft document, Darling then confessed that, as a believer in the fall of man, one could only be saved by the grace of

God. What this meant educationally was that one could only do one's best with humane education, but that it wouldn't work without God's help. In his own case at GGS, he attributed himself with some success in 'altering the attitudes of a segment', and a 'fairly important segment' of Victorian society at that, whereas Melbourne Grammar, which was a 'better school in many ways', had not succeeded in doing so. He was presumptuous enough to think that his 'moderate success' had resulted from a combination of teaching boys to think honestly and the religious influence of chapel worship, particularly Bible reading and 'even' sermons: a consecrated building such as a chapel forced one to speak *sub specie aeternitatis* (from the perspective of the eternal), which was a salutary, although risky, experience for both speakers and hearers.[3]

Another way to be listened to was as a committee member, but sometimes this frustrated Darling. At an Oldham council meeting in 1988, he scribbled on an agenda paper a note that spoke volumes: beneath 'Oldham' he wrote 'John of Gaunt' and 'Feeling that I have outlived my usefulness. Out of tune with modern ways of thought; but have difficulty in keeping quiet.' This scribbling was triggered by his antipathy to the council's establishment of a computer centre and a riding school, a decision lacking in merit for a number of reasons, he admitted, including 'some prejudice and a fair amount of ignorance'. He disliked putting money into facilities for which he could see no direct return and was opposed to spending money unless he had to. A riding school might be necessary if horse courses were a permanent curriculum fixture, but there was a deal with Deakin University in the offing. And why was a brand new building needed for computers? The bigger issue was Oldham's precarious finances. It was Australia's sole fee-paying agricultural education college and there were no other comparable international private colleges, yet its independence was costly. At $7900 annually for residential students and $6600 for non-residential students, its fees were about $5000 above those charged by Glenormiston Agricultural College and Orange Agricultural College, its government-funded rivals. If it was to be viable, the college had to accept all applicants. It had been fully enrolled in only one year (1982), when about ten students could easily have been rejected as unsuitable. The principal viewed this situation as prejudicial to Oldham's public image, educationally unacceptable and morally dubious. Fee-paying courses for low-income students were out of the question and yet about a quarter of students (in 1983) required support or financial assistance.[4]

Until the creation of Glenormiston and Orange in the 1970s (both based on the Oldham model) Marcus Oldham Farm Management College had been the only one of its type in Australia. It trained young men and women to deal with the complexities of modern farming, and to be able to adapt to agriculture's developing technological and economic conditions. It offered the sole three-year Associate Diploma in Farm Management in Australia, with farm-based practical training included in the second year. About one-quarter of the course was devoted to farm management and the remaining three-quarters to technical skills. The qualification was accredited by the Victorian Post Secondary Education Commission and there was a cross-crediting arrangement with Deakin University's Bachelor of Commerce degree. Prospective students needed to have satisfactorily completed a Year 12 certificate and worked on a farm for at least a year. The college recruited sixty to seventy students annually, mostly nationally and from independent school backgrounds. The average age of admission was twenty-one. The seven full-time staff members (and some part-timers) utilised a form of 'participative teaching' that included such elements as case studies (derived from the Harvard Business School's approach), integrated problem-solving, study tours and team teaching. There was also a one-year certificate in horse management for prospective horse industry employees. A variety of short courses were also available for rural-sector people (farmers, bank managers and stock agents), and a suite of self-paced, self-instruction kits and external studies courses.[5]

Yet another way for an elder to exercise influence, as Darling discovered, was to be a moral guardian. In 1985–86, he was asked by the council chairman to intervene in a matter that touched on principal–council relations. This was a relationship that he had written on some four years before (in 'The Governing Body & the Headmaster') in which he had said that it was part of a headmaster's life to 'expect criticism' from a council and to 'endure it in good cause without taking offence'. As a result of Darling's intervention, relations were restored. He was determined to be heard on other college matters. One was to urge (without success), as a solution to the problem of college recruitment, financial assistance to students and the offer of places to overseas students (including farmers from China). Another was governance. Darling was part of a group that reviewed the operation of council and its committees (1985). Here he took a different line from John Lewis (an Oldham council member) on the GGS council's practice: a membership of sixteen, four meetings annually to which he reported, and an executive of six who met monthly. Darling thought that the Oldham council was a 'very large sledgehammer to crack a very small nut', but the executive committee idea was not attractive—Lewis conceded that non-executive members might feel excluded from GGS council business—because it would reduce Oldham's council to a rubber stamp, make the overriding of executive decisions difficult, render the full council meaningless and deprive it of the expert advice 'so painstakingly collected'. An added difficulty was the two trustees: would either (or both) want to be proposed as executive members? If they didn't, the trustees and council risked disagreement. The way forward, then, was to increase the finance committee's powers but refrain from going down the executive committee route. Likewise, the number of council meetings and the membership should be reduced. The future of Oldham's finances came to a head in 1988–89 after the creation of a new trust and the Marcus Oldham Farm Management College Foundation (launched in May 1989). The Union Fidelity Trustee Company (rebadged as the Trust Company of Australia) notified Oldham that from November 1989 it wished to be relieved of its responsibility for the trusteeship of Marcus Oldham Farm Management College. Darling helped to define the new trust's role and composition, and then ceased after twenty-seven years to be an Oldham trustee and councillor.[6]

With the United World Colleges, however, he continued until he was ninety-two. As the national committee in Sydney was in 'disarray', Sir Ian Gourlay contacted Darling about a replacement for the retiring chairman Sir Charles Cutler. A chairman was expected to work with state and federal governments of opposing political sympathies, and so Gourlay was wary of the risks with political appointees. To allay his anxieties, after Sir John Atwill (president, Liberal Party) was appointed, Darling initially suggested Jill Wran (wife of the New South Wales Labor premier) or the unionist Laurie Short as a possible deputy or co-chair, but with Atwill in post and getting 'the machinery in order', he was less concerned now that the Hawke Labor government was in office. 'Oddly enough', Hawke might be 'a bit more susceptible' to the Prince of Wales than his prime ministerial predecessor, he said, because Hawke was 'after all a Rhodes Scholar, and he has imagination', whereas 'Fraser always had money and certainly has very little imagination'. But the real task was still to find someone with lots of money for education and a commitment to opportunities for young people:

> Some of these people are now so rich that tax-deductibility is not as important as it might once have been, and [$]30,000 [two years funding for a United World College student] doesn't sound a lot of money to a man worth 300 million.

To assist Atwill to get the national office back on track (there was unpaid money owed to the United World Colleges in the UK) Darling wanted Gourlay to be in Australia during the prince's forthcoming visit, so that he and Atwill could confer with them. Private sector interest might be secured by bringing together Prince Charles, United World Colleges ex-students and 'rich men'. Such a gathering (in Melbourne) would be better than a dinner, because one dissentient at dinners was enough to give others present an excuse to not get involved. The presence of the premier and the Minister for Education would be an added bonus. Darling's other priority was to try to secure money from Australian companies with UK operations (where they might obtain tax deductibility) to earmark funds for Australian students. Another possibility (he was aware that he was a 'lone voice') was to create one-year post–Year 12 scholarships to enable students to complete secondary schooling, secure university admission, and then support themselves while travelling before attending a United World College institution prior to university. A third option was for parents to pay part of the cost of their offspring's attendance at a United World College institution.[7]

Darling's eighth and final trip to England in 1987 provided a respite from a United World College concerns. He and Margaret went primarily for the conferral of the honorary fellowship awarded him by Oriel where his friend Sir Zelman Cowen was provost. The trip gave him a new lease of life. He was 'more active in the last two months', he told one correspondent, and had 'done more in them than in the last five years in Australia' and he felt better, even though being 'occasionally tired and needing R[est]. & R[ecreation].' Receipt of a complimentary letter from Kensington Palace following his eighty-eighth birthday also put a spring in his step. The Prince of Wales thanked him for his 'admirable leadership' of Victoria's United World Colleges committee. Darling was determined to find 'one very rich man who will be lured into giving us major support'. Gourlay thought that his idea of appealing to a man's 'vanity and his yearning for immortality' was 'excellent'. The escalating cost in the 1980s of two-year scholarships for students to attend the colleges made Darling's committee reliant on an annual state government grant (although well short of a two-yearly cost estimate of $30,000). In trying to achieve consistent scholarship and support the Victorian committee was thwarted by the fluctuating value of the Australian dollar (floated by the Hawke government). Persistence eventually paid off. In July 1988 the chartered accountants Peat Marwick Hungerfords notified Darling that, 'in response to your very sound representations', James Fairfax was 'pleased to donate some $375,000 to endow a scholarship at the United World Colleges'. Thanks to Fairfax's generosity, for the first time in 1989 there would be a privately endowed United World Colleges scholarship (112 had been awarded since 1972), with the recipient alternating annually between New South Wales and Victoria. Fairfax's gift was not sufficient to remove the need for government support, and so Darling appealed in early 1989 to the Victorian treasurer, Rob Jolly, to increase the state's annual grant to $20,000. It was 'rather humiliating', he wrote, to be reliant on a Canadian college's generosity in assisting an occasional Australian scholar—Lester Pearson College in British Columbia funded a free scholarship for Australia, provided that it could fund one for itself—and he encouraged Jolly to meet some of the ex-students and then judge their quality.[8]

Darling's request was forwarded by Evan Walker (Minister for the Arts),' who was persuaded by the United World Colleges program's merit and importance 'for the personal development of some of our future leaders'. Darling secured a grant increase to $15,000 annually. This success highlights how the state-based United World Colleges committees had unintentionally drifted away from their original focus on scholarship applicant selection towards fund-raising, with the labour of ex–United World Colleges students for the latter purpose called on for such activities as art sales and concerts. Over the seven years to 1984, the number of scholarships awarded ranged from six to nine annually (occasionally supplemented by Victoria's Italian community—although with conditions). The increasing cost of scholarships and simultaneous reliance on government funding (the availability of which tightened in the mid-1980s) resulted in constant financial precariousness, so that in 1985–86 no scholarships were awarded. The 1990–91 target was eight scholarships, estimated to require an annual income of about $220,000 from a capital fund of $1.77 million (invested at 12.5 per cent interest)—about five times the value of the yet-to-be-established James Fairfax Scholarship Fund. With Victoria accepting responsibility for two scholarships, its estimated share of such a capital fund would be about $442,000. These calculations signalled a formidable future challenge but, from February 1991, the point at which Darling resigned the committee chairmanship to become its patron, that task ceased to be his problem. No more meetings, then, in the cosiness of 'that famous study with the thick pipe smoke and the cracking fires in winter' in Myamyn Street, Armadale. A Darling poem captured two decades' ups and downs:

There was a man. We'll call him HE.
Caught in the web of U. World. C.
Ensconced by several noble lords
With many re-assuring words.
Thinking it might be rather fine
To raise himself above the line.
And fellow-work with famous men
He preened himself a little bit—But then
The noble lords went to their rest
Their souls inexorably bless'd
Their works enshrined in massive tomes
Their faults interre'd with their bones.
And HE was caught within the trap.
He found himself a lonely chap.

Things turned out harder than he'd thought
When he discovered what he'd bought.
With quick deceit he moved to ask
Others to help him in the task
Deluding them with expectation
To ease his own exasperation.
At last there came the long-sought break
From one who gave for us to take.
The finger stroked the only string,
Allowed Hope's lute at last to sing.
Thus momentarily bless'd
HE grasped the opportunity to rest.
Like noble lords before him gone.
He handed over work—and throne.

The moral of this simple tale:
Determine that you will not fail

Even when others tend to mock
Cling like a limpet to the rock.[9]

Darling's final public engagement was to be an elder turned prophet. Relatively few public figures experience the luxury of their own dedicated newspaper column or a television or radio timeslot with which to give voice to their views, apart from newspaper editorialists, seasoned reporters and radio shock-jocks. In the esteem and celebrity stakes, even fewer people are granted the privilege in their ninth decade, so that when Darling was invited in 1980 by the Melbourne *Age* editor, Michael Davie (an Englishman and acquaintance of his friend Sir Mark Turner) to write a set of reflections ('a sort of brief weekly sermon') he was in unique company. From August 1980, Darling's 319 600-word reflections were published (mostly fortnightly from April 1984) until his ninety-fifth birthday in 1994; each expressed (mostly) Christian virtue-rhetoric and was initialled J.R.D. An edited selection was published in 1991 in *Reflections for* The Age and then the complete set was published posthumously in 2006 in *Reflections for An Age*. Darling was eighty-one when he commenced with the *Age*. As he told his nephew he remained 'astonishingly well' despite his great age, although 'time's chariot is hurrying by'. There were still books to be written, but unlikely to be because of his daily rhythm: bed at 10 pm, up at 9 am, sleep after lunch, and television from 7 pm to 9.45 pm. In between time, he was 'puzzling over my accounts' with a view to finding money to pay his and Margaret's income tax. There were 'occasional meeting commitments, and speechifying and considerable correspondence', which meant that there was 'not much time for creative effort'. Politically Darling's reflections commenced before the Fraser Coalition government's third term, encompassed the four Hawke Labor governments and ended during the Keating government. During this period (documented by Paul Kelly in *The End of Certainty*) the nation experienced economic changes paralleling in magnitude the cultural upheavals of the 1960s and 1970s, with free market liberalism and entrepreneurialism ascendant. Globally, the Berlin Wall was breached in 1989 and the break-up of the USSR followed.[10]

Darling's enthusiasm for or misgivings about what he was witnessing and experiencing intruded into his commentaries. But for whom was he speaking? Who read his column and how wide was his audience reach? Was it largely small 'L' liberal Victoria—or merely small 'L' liberal Melbourne?—because the *Age* was not a national circulation newspaper and Darling's thoughts were not reproduced in the other leading Fairfax stable broadsheet the *Sydney Morning Herald*. (Apart from the *Age*, Darling read the English *Observer* and *Sunday Times*. With its 'querulous objections to everyone and everything', he could not abide the *New Statesman* and, as a gift from his nephew and sister, he began reading the *Guardian*. As nothing in it made his hackles rise, surely he was not 'so desperately conservative and re-actionary', he pleaded, as Mabel thought that he was.) Answers to questions about audience reach cannot be known—in his papers about a dozen letters contain correspondents' reactions to what he had written. His reflection-writing followed an earlier publishing venture for the *Age*. When Ranald Macdonald heard of his likely replacement at the ABC by Madgwick, he offered him a column, but in the let-down period following his non-renewal as chairman, Darling opted for the quiet life. 'I am (a) too lazy (b) too diffident. I don't want to set myself up as an arbiter of everything and to be in continual trouble because of what I write', he recorded in his diary. Two years earlier (May 1965), under the pseudonym 'R.J. Lingard', he had written thirteen book reviews for the literary section of the *Age*. Most books that he discussed were biographical or historical (for example, accounts of English political figures; a life of Julius Caesar). While he had been keen to undertake the reviewing, Darling said to Stuart Sayers (the then editor) that he was reluctant to 'draw down upon my head the wrath of real historians'.[11]

For fourteen years, then, Darling occupied a perch on the *Age*'s Saturday editorial page that, until 1988, earned him a weekly fee of $120 and from 1989 $150. He was given a free hand in what and how he wrote, as Creighton Burns, Davie's successor (from 1981), made clear. Probably in response to receiving Darling's 'The Pope in Canterbury Cathedral' (5 June 1982), Burns reassured him that he had 'no "terrible Protestant prejudice" which you are likely to offend'. Later he told Darling not to hesitate on any topic because he thought that he might conflict with the paper's policy. The security breach at Buckingham Palace in July 1982 (when an intruder entered the queen's bedroom) provided an early test. The Australian commentator, journalist and leading republican Philip Adams penned an *Age* article that had offended Darling's monarchist sensibilities. Tempted to write about the monarchy, Darling refrained so as not to be at odds with (what he thought was) the *Age*'s anti-monarchist position. (Later he wrote 'Monarchy', 30 November 1991 and 'Flags and Monarchs', 15 August 1992.) Short, punchy reflection-writing for such a sustained period was different from anything that he had done previously. Press reports of speech-day remarks and occasional addresses were one thing, but to write regularly for an unknown readership with a diverse profile and pet prejudices was quite different. Grouped thematically, the 319 reflections fall into one of thirteen categories (albeit with occasional overlap): Christianity (80), virtues (56), social customs (43), leadership (39), vices (18), social problems (17), education and national issues (14 each), international events (11), science (9), and evils, history and elections (each 6). An analysis of these reflections reveals evidence of continuity and discontinuity in Darling's thinking. While realistic in acknowledging that change was 'inevitable and with change some abandonment of values which we once deemed immutable' ('Long Term Concepts', 7 January 1984), he occasionally struggled to get to grips with new ideas and practices. Certainly, 'each age and generation must work out for itself what it wishes to preserve and what it can safely discard', but his difficulty was not always being able to detect the 'principle behind these decisions'.[12]

Darling's reflections on Christianity (a quarter of the total) ranged across significant events in the church's seasonal calendar (particularly Advent, Christmas, Epiphany, Easter and Pentecost), doctrine ('The Holy Trinity', 4 June 1983), behaviour ('Repentance', 3 March 1990; 'Forgiveness', 5 December 1987), along with vocation and calling ('Obedience to God', 3 October 1987) and various admonitions ('Right Enjoyment', 19 August 1989). He knew about the changed climate of religious opinion during which he wrote because, despite affirmation of a belief in God by about 80 per cent of Australians, he noted how regular church attendance had dwindled to 'almost an idiosyncrasy' by the early to mid-1980s. Few people understood the point of regular public church worship any longer and its critics claimed that God could be worshipped (and adored) anywhere and whenever. Moreover, he conceded ('Regularity in Church Going', 31 March 1985) that the churches were not helping themselves as not all services were necessarily conducive to a sense of worship. The other battle for Christians was religious redundancy: 'modern man' not only 'endeavours to comprehend everything within the bounds of his own reason' but 'finds it hard to accept a God at all whose existence cannot be proved' ('An All-loving God', 1 May 1982). And yet, Christendom was getting its house in order. In 1982, Darling marvelled how after more than 400 years of division a historic meeting had occurred in England between the Pope and the Archbishop of Canterbury ('two good men') who, watched by a worldwide television audience, had knelt and prayed on the same cathedral stones on which hundreds of years earlier the blood of Thomas à Beckett had been shed ('The Pope in Canterbury Cathedral'). In a less receptive social climate, Darling mostly eschewed preaching or moralising and avoided making his editorial-page platform a religious call-to-arms. Instead, his light-touch didacticism comprised basic faith education for uninitiated readers, correction of common misconceptions about faith and assertions about the Christian basis of Western civilisation, interspersed with regret at the passing of much that was religiously worthwhile.[13]

Darling was prepared to attack institutional religion while anticipating the criticisms of potential non-believers. He chided the church for 'shockingly' neglecting the Old Testament while conceding that it contained 'some awful stuff which offends the delicate sensibilities of the young'. He brought to life Old Testament narratives, particularly stories of the prophets, by exercising licence about their moods: 'When Elijah obeyed [the injunction to 'Go forth and stand upon the mount!'], the Lord said to him, it may be thought a little ungenerously, "What doest thou here, Elijah?"' ('The Justification of Faith', 6 July 1985). He also passed judgement on biblical characters, such as Caesar Augustus 'that cold-blooded fish' and the 'abominable Herod' ('Christmas', 21 December 1985). Darling drew on hymns, poetry, plays, prose and aphorisms as well as scripture, and mostly avoided repetition of content. Christianity's core beliefs entailed acceptance of miraculous events, but Darling's line was that it was 'a mistake, surely, to try to bring everything in life within the bounds of our present reason'. He cited as instances love, beauty and 'even Truth' ('An Easter Reflection 1986', 29 March 1986). One miraculous event (marking the birth of the Christian church) was Whitsunday. Enthusiasm was the appropriate feast day feeling for believers, except that the 'established, organized, respectable' Western church was largely incapable of such an emotion, in contrast to modern Pentecostalism and the African churches that 'may have got it better than we have' and were 'almost certainly nearer to the experience of the first disciples' ('Pentecost', 18 May 1991). At other times Darling reached out to believers and non-believers alike. For those searching for salvation or something akin to it, he offered reassurance (or consolation): 'The sins of most of us are not scarlet, more a dingy grey. Many of us do not commit murder, or even adultery, or, except circuitously, steal' ('Salvation', 19 October 1987). For ordinary people redemption lay not in imitating the lives of Mother Teresa or St Francis ('Mother Theresa', 17 January 1987) but in doing what duty called them to do and pursuing this caringly when serving others.[14]

If, indeed, it was a 'tolerant, indeed apathetic age' ('Obedience to God', 3 October 1987), as Darling claimed, then maybe the *Age*'s readership was willing to indulge his liberal religiosity. The decade or so following his death witnessed growing hostility to Christianity in public debates about belief and non-belief (from Christopher Hitchens and Richard Dawkins). The furthest that Darling ventured into such terrain was to claim that the atheistic certainty of 'rationalists' denying God's existence was as much an act of faith as Christian adherence ('God's True Believers', 16 October 1993). His posing of conundrums for his own faith may have appealed to readers as evidence of his honesty, as in 'Prayer' (21 January 1989)—where he conceded for non-religious people who gave priority to meditation that this practice was 'all right too'. Given that the God of the Christians was omniscient, then that raised the question of whether there was any point to prayers of supplication:

> If God is all-knowing and all-loving, he will surely do what is best for us without any prompting from us? There can be no need for us to jog his memory and to remind him of our need. In the end, probably not but perhaps he is restricted by his own nature. Perhaps he needs our reliance on him in order to release his comfort, and perhaps reliance needs expression.

Theologically inclined readers might have objected to such speculative assertions. Earlier in 'Prayer through Jesus Christ' (2 July 1988) he said that prayer was not a list of wants, as God was already aware of these but 'the expression of our desire to live according to his will'. Finally, although Darling was not nostalgic, he once expressed what readers brought up as church-going Edwardian English children may have experienced as a warm inner glow. In fact, 'Going to Church' (15 November 1986) evoked the image of his Tonbridge childhood:

At a precise time, according to the distance from the church, families emerged from their front doors in due processionary style, father in top hat and frock coat, mother in her seal-skin coat in winter and the group of slightly subdued children, faces shining from the application of Pears soap, hands and even nails clean. Religious observance had taken over.

At matins, families sat in the pews for which they had paid rent and in country churches the squire might even attend in his 'little room at the front under the pulpit', complete with a fireplace, chairs and table. Sunday family dinner followed devotion: roast beef, Yorkshire pudding and then apple pie (although 'no cream'). Nine decades on, such a cameo of ordered predictability probably no longer resonated.[15]

A porous line demarcates Darling's Christianity and virtue reflections. Some virtues had figured prominently in his 1960 Syme Oration, but in the *Age* he concentrated on hope ('Christian Hope', 3 January 1981 and 'Hope', 6 June 1981) and touched on the remaining cardinal virtues in other reflections. He also ranged across forms of behaviour generally recognised as virtuous, such as 'Giving' (2 May 1981), 'Taxation and Giving' (18 August 1984) and 'Giving to Charities' (15 April 1989), 'Integrity' (6 August 1983), 'Service' (20 October 1984), 'Honour' (7 March 1987) and 'On My Word of Honour' (4 December 1993), and 'Humility' (6 August 1988). One surprise was 'Tolerance' (3 September 1988 and 'Tolerance and Dogmatism', 2 February 1991), which Darling regarded as the 'prevailing virtue of our age'. While tolerance might make for an easier and happier world it also meant 'anything goes and must not be checked'. Society's apathy in the absence of 'any guiding and necessary principle' was neither good (morally) nor good enough (acceptable). A healthy society required 'some assertion about the nature of health' and efforts to control what was unhealthy; if that entailed restraint or even censorship then 'so be it'. The other surprise was conscience. In 'Tolerance', Darling had said that when making judgements a politician's conscience or prejudices lacked the authority grounded in reasoned belief. His wariness was evident in two reflections—'Conscience' (21 July 1984) and 'Morals and Conscience' (19 October 1985)—in which he quoted an unnamed source's suggestion that conscience might be little more than a bundle of acquired prejudices derived from experience. Here Darling got himself in a tangle, because later (15 July 1989) in 'Conscience and Principle', where he gave an example of reasoned belief, in this instance Christianity's principle of the sanctity of human life, he claimed that historically that principle had not prevented Christians from killing one another, nor from killing a heretic's body to save his soul. Small wonder, then, that later he also said that 'a man's conscience is no clear guide to goodness' ('Conscience and Goodness', 16 December 1993).[16]

Switching tack slightly, Darling discoursed for the first time on the role of women. Although brought up in a household and extended family with a numerically strong female presence, professional dealings with women were infrequent during his working life: mothers of his GGS students, boarding house staff, masters' wives, headmistresses, or occasionally on the Schools' Board and the University of Melbourne council. His working world (like his club) was a world of men defined by an unquestioned (male) belief about a fixed division of labour between the sexes. In this regard, Darling was akin to an Edwardian preserved in aspic, except that his thinking loosened up in some *Age* reflections. His difficulty was that ascribing or attributing characteristics on the basis of membership of social categories was no longer uncontested in the 1980s, so that what it meant to be male or female was questioned. *Age* readers in the early 1980s may have brushed off his remark that 'women do seem a bit more ready than men to say what they really think' ('Christian Charity', 5 May 1984). But, in 'Feminine Virtues' (23 June 1984), in which he described a recent call for the cultivation of such virtues ahead of masculine ones as tantamount to 'a piece of masculine assertiveness from a dedicated feminist', Darling may have raised a few eyebrows. While he insisted that such a call had 'some sense' to it, the male–female contrast should not be 'exaggerated'. Either because of biology or the expected roles that women played in family and society, he claimed, virtues designated as feminine had arisen. And yet the female–male contrast—between capacity for affection, unselfishness, love of peace, humility, lack of self-assertion, and aesthetic and artistic taste, on the one hand, and strength, courage, endurance, fortitude and enterprise to the point of aggression, on the other—should not be overdrawn, he felt, simply because few men were ever wholly masculine and few women lacked some of the qualities expected in males. In reality each person was 'an individual, a compound of virtues and vices entirely of our own and drawn from both lists'. He retained the female–male contrast when criticising the 1980s emphasis on increased economic competitiveness that he was witnessing for crowding out the 'more civilized and feminine virtues'. Consistent with Darling's elevation of feminine virtues was his attempted salvaging of gentlemanly chivalry ('The Gentleman', 6 November 1982). Chivalry's day was done, he acknowledged, if only because 'the women themselves have decided to have none of it and it is difficult to go against their wishes, even by offering them a seat in a tram', except that it didn't follow that other admirable gentlemanly qualities (courtesy, manners and honour) ought also to be jettisoned. The distasteful social superiority implied by the gentlemanly idea might be anachronistic, but not the more acceptable features of gentlemanly conduct.[17]

Awareness about overdrawn male–female differences did not prevent Darling from airing his prejudices. As Christmas shoppers, women were 'probably more discriminating' than men and seemed to 'enjoy the amount of time involved' ('Giving at Christmas', 15 December 1990). Women were also 'more prone to criticism than men' ('Criticism', 31 August 1991). If such remarks didn't yield allegations of gender blindness then his comments on domesticity ('Family Quarrels', 1 October 1983) were bound to have done, given his advice on motherhood, fatherhood, marital and de facto relations, and divorce. Shifting

Australian social mores meant that the context shaping his sentiments was a far cry from the settled cosiness of his 1950s Home and Family talks. In respect of family specific roles, he even championed Mrs Beeton, the Englishwoman celebrated for her cooking recipes and home-help remedies, but he was disdainful of her omission from the *Dictionary of National Biography* ('At Mother's Knee', 21 March 1992). At the same time, however, he extolled the traditional family role of mothers. Indeed, much (by way of skills and standards), he said, was learnt 'at our mother's knee', so that when the family fails 'there is grave danger to the whole society'. As for historically notable Australian women, he acknowledged women in general rather than specific individuals. In 'Taste' (6 March 1988) he claimed that early colonial women in New South Wales had preserved gentility, perhaps a reminder that 'women are always the arbiters of taste, certainly in the rules of social behaviour'. Likewise ('Bicentenary Year', 31 December 1988), he asserted that 'no country in the world has ever owed so much to its women' as Australia for having reared the nation's children in a state of decency, in the worst of conditions on an untamed continent. Occasionally, Darling was able to rise above conventional assumptions, as in his sensitive discussion ('Keeping the Home Fires', 16 May 1992) of the Canadian film then screening called *Company of Strangers*, about a group of marooned women, and in 'Aunts' (16 December 1989) where he referred to the 'long overdue liberation of women from the captivity of home and the drudgery of domestic duties'. And yet here he bemoaned (what he saw as) a downside of such liberation: discouragement of marriage and the bearing of children, and a concentration on self-expression and self-interest at the expense of the (nuclear) family and community.[18]

A stark sub-theme in Darling's reflections in respect of virtues or customs was lamentation: much that was worthwhile in life was fading fast. 'We', he wrote ('Prophecy', 20 September 1986)—which implied, presumably, Australians generally and people of Judeo-Christian heritage—needed prophets of the ilk of Moses, Joshua, Elijah, Elisha and Jeremiah, but especially Isaiah, to call us back to our true vocation except that 'we don't seem to produce prophets among us' (and for that matter didn't believe any more in 'our vocation'). Were there to be a modern prophet, then a prophetic script for sinful admonition might include:

> Woe to the rich who make a necessity of luxuries! Woe to the people of commerce who prefer profit to quality! Woe to the leaders of trade unions who put their own good above that of their members and wages for the fortunate above the needs of the unemployed! Woe to those who avoid paying their due taxes at the expense of the honest, and to those who cheat the welfare system and make things worse for those in need! Woe to the whole lot of us who are greedy for ourselves and neglectful of the needs of others.

'Old values' were being rejected by people refusing to be bound by 'previously accepted concepts', a rejection putting egoism and altruism at odds. Post–World

War II conditions had fuelled resentment against authority and a post-Freudian philosophy of the realisation of personality freed of restraints—although some people were genuinely committed to causes (nuclear disarmament, Greenpeace and ecology, women's equality and 'some rather strange manifestations of religion'). The freedom sought might well prove illusory, Darling thought, because democracies survived with the continued devotion and sacrifice of their citizens, undertakings not forthcoming solely in wartime ('Commitment', 21 September 1985). The adjusting of moral behaviour to momentary circumstances was another cause for concern, but worse still was the older generation's acceptance of standards of conduct in young people that once were deemed 'shocking'. His example was 'living in sin', which nowadays scarcely even raised an eyebrow. Lest he be dismissed as a complete reactionary, Darling reassured readers that he didn't want a return to penitence stools in churches or branding the foreheads of sinners; he was merely highlighting dangers in the 'charitable reasonableness of today's alternative'. All manner of things, big and not so big (lying and stealing, for example, and not just outwitting the taxman), required the maintenance of social standards if there were to be trust ('Situation Ethics', 29 June 1985).[19]

Other things to be lamented were vanishing previously desirable modes of behaviour, including honour, good manners, courtesy and consideration ('Style in Living', 3 June 1989). Likewise, smallness in scale, personal contacts and amateurism had been largely eradicated from Australian life—to be viable, everything had to be big; no amount of 'the "you're-welcomes-and-have-a-good-days" in the supermarket' could compensate for the across-the-counter shopping friendships of former times. Games used to be played for enjoyment, but not any more ('The Personal Factor', 7 December 1991). Writing letters, one of the 'decencies of life', was being killed by the telephone—although in 'The Demise of the Letter' (30 August 1986), when networked computing was becoming more common, Darling could be forgiven for ignoring emailing (even though it was possibly a poor substitute for the lost social etiquette that he favoured). Later still ('Letter Writing', 15 September 1990), the fax was cited as causing the diminution of this activity to 'a pleasant frivolity of the past'. And then there was the Sabbath: 'something precious' was being let go by the recent scheduling of football matches and Test cricket on Sundays ('Sunday Observance', 6 June 1984). (Three decades or so later this issue still rankles in Christian circles. Darling claimed in the Sabbath's defence that 'circuses every day of the week are a bore', but an Anglican clergyman's opposition in the *Guardian* in 2015 to a legislative extension of UK Sunday shop-trading hours, in 'Money is the only god Tories want us to worship on Sunday', was to trumpet Sunday as the day 'when we are not forced to worship the market'.) The danger for the West of a lack of clarity about its beliefs was that 'If you don't stand for something' then there was a risk that that world might 'fall for anything' ('What Do You Stand For?', 19 February 1994). The one belief that Darling (in his last reflection: 'The Business of Humanity', 18 June 1994) thought that the world was clear about was economic management, 'the catch-cry of the times', although this had veered out of business proper and into professional life. What he perceived as the intrusion of business principles into medicine, education and the law was something about which to be 'seriously alarmed'. What was at stake in these domains, business or professional, was not a transactional exchange to satisfy a buyer by making a seller rich, but a relationship that was 'only incidentally financial', an understanding that 'raises every or almost every transaction to the dignity and satisfaction of service'.[20]

Australian life was the other big theme in Darling's customs and virtues reflection categories. Instances of Australian achievers and national narratives were prominent departure points for what he wanted to say: such as Essington Lewis and John Monash (when offering advice about success to young people in 'Choice of Profession', 3 December 1988), along with mention of the television adaptation of George Johnson's *My Brother Jack*, when considering the life of lower- and middle-income families ('A Proper Frugality', 18 February 1989). With 'No worries' (3 July 1982), at the commencement of a discussion of everyday worldly concerns, he ventured into the Australian idiom, as he also did with 'wowser' ('Puritans', 7 July 1984) and 'too true' ('All Sorts', 18 July 1992). In fact, Australian English, he believed ('The English Language', 21 September 1991), would be all the richer after it had 'properly absorbed' the ways of speaking of post-1950 immigrants from Europe, Asia and the Pacific. A feature of Australian life that he particularly warmed to was the increased incidence of Australians taking up painting as a hobby ('The Artist', 21 March 1987) because their eyes were being opened: people now had opportunities to form their own tastes and judgement, and there was joy for so many more people in 'really looking at things'. As for the natural environment, Darling commented occasionally on the consequences of its harshness ('Ash Wednesday Fires', 5 March 1983), and he regularly marked commemorative national events ('ANZAC Day', 23 April 1988, and 'War, Sacrifice and Service', 7 May 1994). Patsy Adam-Smith, herself a historian of the Anzacs, complimented him on an 'apt' reflection that 'carefully balanced the myriad conflicts in the minds of many of us' and, while signalling her aversion for Sir Thomas Blamey (Australia's sole field marshal), encouraged him to write another reflection on battle leaders—who were 'often followers!', she said—which he did. In the first of two reflections on the 1988 Bicentenary ('The Bicentenary Year', 2 January 1988), he urged the nation that 'once prided itself on being at the forefront of the world in its attempt to create a society in which freedom and justice existed together', to be the first to achieve 'some equality in the good things of the world', because no society had yet done so—but his 'distressing conclusion' (as in his debate with Manning Clark) had been that freedom and equality were 'incompatible ideals'.[21]

Darling was critical of other Australian characteristics. Pride in improvisation may have been good for meeting immediate needs but was not a 'satisfactory solution' to genuine problems ('Common Sense', 7 May 1983). Nor could

Australians be accused of excessive good manners ('Our National Manners', 17 October 1992). The tough, outspoken, inconsiderate, rough-diamond stereotype with the heart of gold beneath was all very well, but people could no longer pretend that they were responding to harsh bush conditions: society was overwhelmingly urban, and the nation needed to learn from its new (and 'generally less aggressive') arrivals from Asia. And then there was sport. Following the Eagles' loss at the hands of Hawthorn in the 1991 AFL Grand Final ('The Culture of Sport', 5 October 1991), he noted (slightly tongue in cheek) 'what ill-mannered victors we Australians are'. The country's saving grace in such 'annual exhibitions of idiocy' was that, while it was not a perfect society, there was nothing on anything like the scale of disadvantage elsewhere in the world. If it was a pity that 'we as a nation' did not habitually seek the higher life, and were 'stupid enough to let greedy people make fools of us', then at least we 'should be thankful to have got as far as we have' and were able to 'seek our pleasure as we see it without doing anyone else any damage'. That said, he turned the thumbscrews on himself ('The Skills of the Artisan', 23 January 1988), because when arriving almost sixty years earlier, he confessed:

> I was young, English and, I suppose, rather brash. I was certainly prejudiced, although I had already had some contact with this part of the world [in 1929]. There were differences between life here and in Europe, some of which I did not like, the ugliness for instance of the haphazard architecture of the country towns and the suburbs and the apparent lack of so-called cultural activities— theatre, libraries and music. I also resented the habit of thought which was content to believe that everything good of that sort could only be found in the old world.

But he had encountered one rare quality among tradesmen that set this group off as 'some of the most adult, sensible, genuine and kind people in the world': their pride and satisfaction in doing a good job. They were adaptable and, yes, they could also improvise; they were cooperative although unwilling to do anything that they deemed silly and they trusted one another. Their training in practical skills had given them 'confidence without conceit, assurance without assertion, [and] satisfaction free from jealousy', traits still in evidence.[22]

Darling also commented on Indigenous Australia. Over time, he had revised his inherited imperialism and its racial baggage, although not without some pain, as he had confessed to Mabel in 1979. So many people of their generation 'really thought that they were doing a great service to the world' and still 'were'. The Thai boys at Corio, his encounters with Asian students generally, and his exchanges of views with Casey had helped shift his attitudes, and by the mid-1960s he had been in tune with the direction that Opperman took the country on non-European entry. More baggage was off-loaded in 'The Change from Era to Era' (3 August 1985) and especially in 'All Part of the Main' (30 October

1993) where he described racial snobbery as 'the worst' of all snobberies, and acknowledged that the use of racially based terms was 'as unsafe now as it always was morally and socially objectionable'. With respect to religion, Darling had communicated with Catholics and championed their educational interests in the face of entrenched Protestant prejudice. Likewise, he had made special provision (against intransigence) for the worship needs of (the few) Catholic and Jewish boys at Corio. He had also befriended a number of Jews, particularly Zelman Cowen, and the most prominent formative intellectual influence on him, of course, was Gollancz. The Melbourne Club had a reputation for blackballing candidates of Jewish descent (the OGGs Ken and Bails Myer suffered in 1953 and 1970 respectively), and when asked about temporary Jewish Melbourne Club membership in 1959, Darling said that it was high time 'the aforesaid club grew up anyhow'. In 'Morals and conscience' he acknowledged the Jewish people as those 'to whom Western society owes a great deal', but in early 1985 there was a hiccup. An OGG, John Bennett, had sought the endorsement of Darling (and other public figures and institutions) for his *Your Rights 1984*. Darling said:

> While not always in agreement with the views expressed in *'Your Rights, 1984'*
> I consider the publication a valuable, even necessary watchdog of citizens'
> rights which, without vigilance, may easily be eroded.

Bennett, a civil libertarian, was accused of anti-Semitism by the Anti-Defamation Board of the Australian Council of Jewry (Holocaust denier was a phrase not yet in common currency) and it thought that Darling's words lent weight of reputation to Bennett's views. (Darling's handwritten first draft had said, very guardedly: 'While frequently not in agreement ...', with 'frequently' struck through with red.) The Board wanted Darling to dissociate himself from Bennett and his book and requested a meeting (after taking nearly three months to get back to him) which Darling had offered (his envelope was marked not sent) and there the matter ended inconclusively.[23]

When Darling reflected that conscience might mean little more than a repository for social prejudices, he mentioned the volatility and unreliability of the consciences of public men, as illustrated by nineteenth-century slavery, children employed in mines for twelve hours a day and 'the signing of bogus contracts with uncomprehending Aboriginals for the purchase of their land in exchange for goods of little real value'. On Indigenous Australia, he commented in his second reflection ('Noonkanbah and the Aborigines', 6 September 1980) on a dispute arising from the Western Australian government's decision to authorise oil exploration at Noonkanbah, sacred Indigenous land in the state's north-west on which there was a pastoral lease. Most white Australians, he said, were 'obsessed' by guilt for the crimes of their forebears against Aboriginal people who 'quite rightly' resented the settlers who had misused them. He appealed for 'magnanimity' on both sides and compromise, and left open the possibility of a treaty. We are 'fellow Australians, and fellow human beings whose fate is to live together', despite having different views of life as it ought to be. Unlike 'the white man' who had upset the natural environmental balance on arrival on the continent, Aboriginal Australia understood what this meant and maintained it ('The Balance of Nature', 1 March 1986). Moreover, when commenting on violence in contemporary Australia ('The Futility of Anger', 5 March 1994), he asserted that prior to being 'infected' by Western civilisation, Aboriginal people 'knew better and were the least prone to this sin'. So far did he push his general view of how national or racial superiority had resulted in the destruction of cultures by 'invaders' ('A Culture for Everyone', 29 January 1994)—W.K. Hancock's word in his celebrated *Australia* in 1930—that Indigenous Australia was his main illustrative case. British settlers had seen only 'savages' against whom they retaliated violently to defend their sheep and cattle, but more disastrous still, and 'often with the best of intentions', those same settlers forced on Indigenous Australians 'their own idea of the way to live'. They failed utterly to recognise that 'the old inhabitants' had their own culture 'which they observed strictly and which had ensured their survival for thousands of years', including a relationship with their environment necessary for that purpose.[24]

When Darling turned to leadership, a number of his thirty-nine reflections reconnected him with themes on which he had discoursed in the 1960s. One was greatness. As R.J. Lingard, he had reviewed *Julius Caesar—Man, Soldier and Tyrant* for the *Age*:

> Great men retain a curious fascination for mankind without their claim to greatness ever being seriously questioned. The length of time required for the establishment of the title depends partly on their compatability [sic] with the tastes and opinions of their immediate successors. In this regard Julius Caesar was fortunate, because it suited Augustus to treat him with honour. Napoleon had to work harder for his legend.

In the early 1980s, he thought that there were still some good men as leaders. Thus far, Robert Mugabe was shaping up as a responsible statesman in the new Zimbabwe, he said to Mabel, and the good men whom he mentioned to her son Morris were Lord Carrington (UK foreign secretary) and Willy Brandt (former German chancellor), while François Mitterrand (President of France) was 'probably' another, as possibly was the US president, Ronald Reagan. Three months into the first Hawke government and he was holding out hopes for the new prime minister, but to be in England and confronted by the prospect of having to vote for either Mrs Thatcher or the Labour Party was 'impossible' in the former case and 'even more impossible' in the latter. A decade or so later and Darling was still wrestling with greatness ('The Making of Greatness', 1 May 1993), but was more willing to question it. Australians were not particularly good at being led, he said in 'Leadership' (28 May 1988), which was probably why so few of their leaders commanded respect or devotion. He now thought leadership was an art with a bit of science thrown in. The leaders whom he cited were all men, the 'most spectacular' of whom had been conquering men of war. If leadership were to work, there had to be loyalty and loyalty came from trust. Darling had a fascination for Napoleon Bonaparte, often mentioned in tandem with Julius Caesar (as in the Lingard book review and in his Chapman lecture), in no fewer than eleven reflections. Napoleon, the subject of Thomas Hardy's *The Dynasts*, Corio's 1933 pageant play, was considered by Darling to be 'the most unlovable of rulers' ('Management through Care', 3 December 1983) who used people for his own interests ('Leadership', 28 May 1988), except that he had 'the first indispensable attribute of greatness': a mind like 'the best computer in which every memory was stored and easily accessible'. Where the French emperor had erred was in his failure of political judgement, underestimation of the strength of resentment against him among conquered peoples and his vaulting ambition, when what he really needed was a dose of humility ('The Risk in Greatness', 5 April 1986). In leadership, Darling looked constantly for signs of hope. While there were none in the sad case of Harold Macmillan ('Clash of loyalties', 21 October 1989), there was some comfort in the godly example of Michael Ramsey ('Archbishop Michael Ramsey', 4 August 1990) and Churchill, where the man and the hour had been 'perfectly matched' ('Churchill', 4 July 1992). As for the future, hope was in the hands of three contemporaries: Mandela, de Klerk and Gorbachev.[25]

In the first of two reflections ('Mandela and de Klerk', 17 November 1990), shortly after Nelson Mandela's visit to Australia following his prison release in February 1990, Darling extolled him for a speech to a Sydney ecumenical service that was:

> without blemish; free from vanity or pride, unspoilt by malice, resentment or anger, full of faith and hope and charity, the speech of a good man who had suffered much and had achieved serenity.

His words had 'asserted the possible dignity of humanity'. But the forgotten man who had secured Mandela's freedom, stood up to his friends' and colleagues' values, and admitted that he had been wrong and that a new course of direction was needed was F.W. de Klerk. He had displayed genuine courage and deserved 'sympathy and acclaim and prayers'. Nearly four years later ('Saga of Two Men of Faith', 21 May 1994), with the formal ending of apartheid, Darling complimented both men for having made a start in the regeneration of their country. People's faith in 'the power of a few individuals to achieve the impossible' had increased as a result. It was tempting after the break-up of empires for the West to watch with despair and to think that colonial disengagement was too quick. Yet, with twenty centuries of civilisation behind it, Europe could not be said to have done much better than some former colonies. Two terrible wars and the deaths of millions, the rise and fall of the communist experiment, the attempted 'elimination of the Jews' and the chaos of the Balkans should have been sufficient to dissuade anyone from throwing stones at Africa. Darling wrote three reflections on Mikhail Gorbachev (general secretary, Communist Party of the Soviet Union, 1985–91)—'Mr Gorbachev's Chance' (16 March 1985), followed by 'New Hope—Gorbachev' (18 June 1988) and 'Hopes and Fears after Gorbachev' (30 December 1989). In the first, Darling willed the new man to succeed single-handedly in reforming the Soviet Union. As an atheist, the general secretary was in no position to pray for himself and yet, Darling thought, as a human being 'called upon to carry on his shoulders, not totally but ultimately, the whole future of mankind', yet lacking an external reference point for action, Gorbachev needed God to be with him. Readers should pray for this solitary figure. The later televised image of the Reagans and Gorbachevs walking in Red Square gave Darling added hope of a thaw in the great power mistrust—the last thing needed at such moments was an assassin's bullet.[26]

Fast forward eighteen months to 1989 and the 200th anniversary of the storming of the Bastille, and the Soviet's Eastern European empire was collapsing. One after the other, in 'a mixture of popular protest and élite negotiation', wrote the English journalist and academic Timothy Garton Ash, having witnessed firsthand many of the events of that year, 'prisoners became prime ministers and prime ministers became prisoners'. It was an illusion for the West to claim a great victory after the Soviet Union's collapse, Darling told his readers. The newly independent former Soviet satellites had not discovered the beauty of capitalism but that their loss of personal liberty had been 'too heavy a price to pay for any social ideal, however grand' (see also 'The Pursuit of Happiness', 9 December 1989). The West had little to be proud of as the sum total of the current 'unbridled liberalization and privatization' unleashed in Western economies amounted to:

> excessive debts and the collapse of wildcat entrepreneurs, excessive and unreal fluctuations on the stock exchange and in currency, [and] bankruptcy and insecurity for honest workers. Above all, an unprecedented failure to solve the problems of the Third World and, in general, a hectic and futile tendency to abandon responsibility in the gambler's desire at all costs to 'get rich quick'.

The great powers had to turn swords into ploughshares and spears into pruning hooks, he urged; the rising generation had 'the call' and responsibility for an attainable objective. But leadership had a dark side: abuse of power, dictatorial relapse and consequent democratic fragility. Darling was struck by the televised image of the Romanian tyrant, Nicolae Ceausescu, without hope, resigned to his fate and anxious, and his wife 'angry and spiteful, unrepentant' ('Dictators', 20 January 1990). Years earlier, there had been the Shah of Iran and Ferdinand Marcos. The tragedies of dictators were of Shakespearean proportions: 'so very few men potentially great know when to stop'. Even the global summits of great power leaders 'backed by monstrous bureaucracies and a welter of advisers' played into this theme. If concentrated and absolute power was not necessarily corrupting, it imposed strains ('Public Opinion', 30 November 1985). Belief in God and subjection to his will was no safeguard either—witness Oliver Cromwell.[27]

Events in June 1989 in China—the military crackdown on demonstrations in Tiananmen Square, Beijing—were yet another instance of the abuse of power and convinced Darling that the threat to the world 'is not communism at all, but dictatorship' ('Democratic Government', 1 July 1989). If, 200 years after the storming of the Bastille the French Revolution had achieved nothing else, dictatorial government had been put on notice as a result of 'the power of the people', that there are limits beyond which it dare not go. Moreover, he asserted— with a tad of wishful thinking—had fraternity not been lost sight of 'The Terror need not have happened'; although as a religious concept denoting godly fatherhood and human brotherhood, fraternity and revolution did not go together well ('Revolution', 29 July 1989). As he thought further about the momentousness of the events of 1989–90, particularly about countries contemplating democratic government for the first time after prolonged authoritarianism, he wondered what their peoples' expectations were. In Australia, where the frequency of elections had become a bore for many people, there was deep-seated cynicism; the danger of such cynicism and frustration in new democratic countries was that they ignited a demand for strong men and, without democratic constraints, 'strong men become dictators' ('Responsibility in Democracy', 17 March 1990). Dictators were also sought in times of crisis ('Wisdom and the Will', 4 April 1992), and disciplined but docile societies were fertile ground for them as well ('Discipline and the Middle Way', 20 July 1991). A genuine danger for newly freed peoples everywhere was the expectation of doing 'in decades' what had taken Europe centuries. This might turn out to be 'one of the worst results of imperialism'—the imposition of an imperial power's ideas and its abdication of authority were not enough to build the national unity necessary for democracy in former colonies. Intoxication with new-found freedom might be the danger faced by Eastern Europe ('Impatience of the Freed', 5 May 1990).[28]

In respect of vices, Darling chose not to occupy the high moral ground to pontificate about human weaknesses, but reassured his readership ('When Virtue Turns to Vice', 19 June 1993) that what were known 'somehow and some time' as the seven deadly sins were only 'exaggerations of what most of us regard as virtues'. The two that he discussed directly were 'Pride' (21 November 1992) and 'Avarice' (February 1981). (Sloth and envy had been Corio sermons in the 1950s.) Sins were thoughts, words and deeds that separated humans from their creator ('Sins and Crimes', 2 October 1982, and 'Sin', 29 April 1989), but not necessarily crimes, although they counted as offences if they disadvantaged a fellow human being. Darling singled out gambling, to which Australians 'seem particularly prone' ('Gambling', 31 October 1987). He included as examples stock exchange risk-taking behaviour as well as conventional horserace betting and lotteries. (He was taken to task by one reader on the grounds that life itself was a gamble and that the courage to take a gamble enabled human advance.) Gambling, Darling also said, was part of the Australian nature and derived partly 'from our origins' ('Our Vices', 1 August 1992), although he was dubious about poker machines and a cash-strapped government's line that, as a popular pastime, poker-machine gaming contributed to the general good through state income. These machines drew money away from other spending opportunities as gamblers were encouraged to outlay money in 'this doubtfully profitable way'. Vice was one thing, but evil was something else and had to be 'resisted on the larger scale', Darling said: if a society did something that 'we know to be wrong' then its members had 'a duty to resist, by protest and even by force if necessary' ('Resistance to Evil', 4 June 1988). Evil fed on itself until it was 'finally destroyed by its own excess' ('The Fight against Evil', 5 January 1985). The fanatical hatred of an assassin was one example—was there any instance in history in which assassins' bullets had yielded good results, even to the perpetrators ('Assassinations', 17 November 1984)?—and terrorism was another that, if it invited retribution, merely stoked the flames and was a 'victory for the devil' when we reacted similarly ('Terrorism', 5 November 1988: one of three on this topic).[29]

Among the international events to which he devoted eleven reflections, Darling also detected evidence of global-scale evil. In a 'tragic cycle in the affairs of men', he wrote ('The Crisis in Lebanon', 4 September 1982), 'injustice begets envy, envy fear, fear resentment, resentment anger, anger cruelty and cruelty hatred and injustice'. Breaking the cycle would require a 'supreme act of sacrifice' on someone's part. Earlier in comments on the Soviet occupation of Afghanistan ('World Despair', 6 December 1980), he fingered greed as the culprit for much of the world's ills. Perhaps having realised that his reasoning might have been simplistic and that his limited word space could not do justice to the complexity of the issues, it was nine years before he commented on another crisis, in this instance 'The Gulf War' (19 January 1991). Both sides were at fault: Saddam Hussein for his invasion of Kuwait and invocation of a holy war, and the UN Security Council coalition ranged against him for its greed, ambition, pride and oil demands. Shortly after ('Destruction of War', 16 March 1991) he drew attention to the humiliating Gulf War defeat and the Iraqi forces' retreat, and took another swipe at dictators and the 'insanity' that had prompted Hussein, 'supreme in his own absolute power', to try to challenge the world 'and to sacrifice his own people on the altar of his own vanity'. He wondered whether, having defeated him, the example of a united world sinking its minor jealousies and fears, and asserting that such usurpation was no longer to be tolerated, could be made to last.[30]

In his reflections on social problems, the chord that Darling tried to strike concerned the desperate economic and social plight of many young people. He focused on street rioting in English cities ('The Young Unemployed', 5 September

1981) by expressing sympathy for the police, who were 'not responsible for the evil', rehearsing causes of the riots in depressed areas and highlighting the youths' violence. The young had nothing to do, nothing to lose and had 'no inherent moral restraints to their actions'. He communicated a strong sense that while he wanted to try to understand the actions of youth, he would not condone them. Darling asked whether the restraints imposed by a stronger application of law and order make any difference. These might be necessary but 'the disease' had to be healed from within. And the disease, so-called, did not become evident until he wrote about yet another evil (as he called it), 'Alienation' (2 February 1985), at which point he claimed that 'too many of today's [Australian] young have been forced into this state of despair', principally due to youth unemployment. GGS's efforts at the former West Geelong confectionery factory in the early 1930s might have been in his mind as he wrote (he mentioned the Unemployed Boys' Club in another reflection), but it was up to employers, governments and trade unions to try to seek agreement to rectify the situation, because 'for the future of our nation nothing can be more important'. The words 'forced into' and 'enforced' (cited elsewhere in the reflection) provide clues to his bogeyman, because the alienated young were 'the victims of the economics of our time':

> The most damnable of consequences is the feeling of not being wanted, let alone needed, by a society in which they have not asked to be born. They see around them all the signs of prosperity, even of luxury, a prosperity in which they have no share. They are excluded from its benefits through no fault of theirs and, to add insult to injury, are even accused of preferring idleness to work.

From this angle, resentment, anger, resort to vandalism and 'the false haven' of drugs were foreseeable. Everyone had a duty to help, whatever the cost to themselves. While not waving a banner on behalf of victimhood, Darling's diagnostic reasoning expressed empathy and moral outrage. In a similar vein ('The Good Samaritan on the Road', 29 November 1986), he said of the '[unspecified] derelicts of our society' in streets and suburbs that they should be put in touch with help, and could feel that they were someone's concern. One could never be sure, but in the person of the derelict, one could be entertaining an angel or Christ himself.[31]

In respect of the realisation of the kingdom of heaven on earth ('Progress', 30 July 1988), Darling thought that human beings may have been getting somewhere in achieving fair treatment for all, but there were still pockets of poverty and exploitation in Australia, and starvation, famine and disease elsewhere in the world. He was deeply offended by homelessness in Australia ('Homeless Children', 10 November 1988). He asked: how could anyone 'not entirely devoid of conscience' have read a recent newspaper series on homeless children and not felt a sense of horror and shame? Despite the work of the

Salvation Army, the Brotherhood of St Laurence, the Mission of St James and St John, and the Society of St Vincent de Paul, and whatever the causes might have been, there were:

> thousands of children who hate everyone and the society which they feel has deserted them, and they are like this because they have received no love from anyone, and distrust and reject it when it is offered.

There could be nothing worse, he claimed ('Homeless Children', 17 August 1991), than boys and girls 'destroying themselves before they have even had a chance' in life. This time he speculated as to causes. Trouble usually arose in the home, Darling claimed, where there were single and deserted mothers, unsympathetic stepfathers and stepmothers, tyrannical and even sadistic fathers, always a 'lack of understanding or the time and patience which understanding demands', and in some cases children deliberately making themselves very difficult to get on with. Sadly (in another expression of lament), society badly lacked the back-up support of extended families, which meant that schools, churches and local communities had to provide assistance. He was dead-set against any encouragement in the young themselves of a sense of deprivation and alienation. Resolution of the problem of homelessness lay primarily not with governments and bureaucracies, because 'only human solutions have a chance': teach people how to help and appeal to the young to help themselves. First respect yourself if you wish to be respected by the world from which you feel alienated was his message, and 'the rest of us will help you when you ask us'.[32]

To argue convincingly that the alienated young were victims of 1980s Australia's ordering of its economy, as Darling had insisted, required demonstration of a direct causal link between these two factors. The economy's new ground rules had certainly facilitated the unbridled liberalisation and privatisation to which he had also drawn attention and precious little of it was to his liking, as his reflections (mainly in the national issues category) indicate. The possession of wealth was when the 'real nastiness' of snobbery was on display. He could see little excuse for rich looking down on the poor, 'who neither have had the opportunity nor perhaps the desire to make money' ('Snobbery', 1 June 1985). The rash of 1980s corporate takeovers (such as the 'brouhaha' about BHP) was nothing more than a 'vulgar and disreputable struggle for power and money' between persons who already had enough power and 'more than enough money for their own or anybody else's good'. Moreover, if a 'healthy and prosperous society' was the ideal, then the purpose of 'all trade, industry and finance' had to be to provide services for the community, and equitably satisfy its needs for products, with the making of profit being merely a by-product, otherwise the whole exercise was 'deranged' ('Priorities in Finance', 19 April 1986). (Elsewhere, 'Principles and Pragmatism', 29 August 1987, Darling acknowledged that a perfect society rested on the perfectibility of those composing it and yet 'most of us are made of very common clay'.) Apposite here is what he intended telling James Fairfax, about eighteen months prior to the latter's generous United World Colleges donation. Just as the bidding war among the media magnates (a number of whom were Darling's old boys) to take over the Herald & Weekly Times was climaxing (January 1987), he expressed his condolences to Fairfax on the recent death of his father, Warwick. But then having just heard on the lunch-time radio news of the Fairfax bid of $2.5 billion for the Herald & Weekly Times—the 'largest ever cash bid in Australia's history'—Darling exclaimed in a PS: 'Are you all raving mad?' If the Fairfax company could put its hands on that kind of money, couldn't he find a 'miserable million' for the United World Colleges?—although this letter was another for his 'not sent' pile. Takeovers were built on credit, and living on credit was dangerous because at the same time that it discouraged thrift this practice encouraged people to live beyond their means. Unlike small shareholders outlaying cash earned from share transactions on a car or a mortgage reduction, the man with a million or more shares increased his credit (in anticipation of interest and loan repayments) and huge amounts of 'what is called money' were fed into the economy, except that when the 'great wheel' ceased revolving the whole business could be seen for what it was: 'a monstrous pyramid standing precariously on its point' ('The Credit System', 20 December 1986).[33]

To his nephew Morris, Darling had also said that, globally, 'we [human beings?]' were 'forever looking for a half way house, between force and appeasement, between full socialism and free-enterprise. The extremes obviously don't work, nor does the compromise.' With similar frustration, in one further unsent letter addressed this time (mid-1986) to Senator John Button (Minister for Industry, Technology and Commerce)—in which he referred to himself as 'a "disappointed socialist" but that is unimportant'—Darling wailed about Commonwealth–state relations and the 'muddle' of Australia's reliance on the public and private sectors. Also in a PS he added:

> Really! Can nothing be done to destroy, or at least check, the dinosaurs of the financial systems and their damnable irresponsibility? No single individual should have so great a power of disruption.

Part of what he was driving at became apparent later ('The Responsibilities of Privatization', 6 December 1986). If the argument then gaining traction was that the state's provision of services (hospitals and schools) was inadequate, so that after additional privatisation the state abdicated from its responsibility for welfare, then the 'obvious corollary' was that those profiting from reduced government and taxation 'must take up the responsibility themselves', on top of which they had to 'give with greater generosity than at present to the voluntary welfare organizations'. When, eventually, the economy turned sour ('The Economic Depression', 5 December 1992), it was with no sense of schadenfreude that every section of society earned a spray:

We all share in the blame: the greed of entrepreneurs who built up huge fortunes
most of which have collapsed; the banks which helped them, the public who
supported them in their greed for quick profit; the unions which saw nothing
but preserving and improving the standard of living of their section; all those
who have rorted the welfare system; the doctors and the lawyers who have
looked for personal rewards rather than the giving of professional service; the
teachers who have lost sight of their over-riding professional responsibilities;
the rich who have made fortunes by evading tax so that those on wages and
salaries have to carry more than their share; and all the rest of us who have
given up and hoped to preserve our little patch of comfort untouched.

A pox, then, on everyone. If Darling thought that there were educational
solutions to this economic mess, then there was no suggestion of it in any of his
fourteen education reflections, where he confined himself to such orthodoxies as
'Examinations' (4 February 1984), 'The Difficulties of Selection' (21 November
1987) and 'Grammar' (29 June 1991). Elsewhere there were hints. In
'Responsibility in Decision' (7 March 1981), he cautioned his readers that 'a self-
regarding action' no longer made any sense, because 'everything that any of us do
has repercussions in places far distant and removed from its immediate effects'.
In 'Esprit de Corps' (30 April 1988) he built on this idea of interdependence and
its Pauline theological assumptions (all believers were members of the one body
in Christ) by saying that in crises:

> the strength of the body and the strength of the individual parts depend upon
> the confidence of each that he can depend on his fellows, and the strength of
> each is enhanced by the determination not to let the others down.[34]

Detectable here is Darling's attachment to a fraternal social order, which
was not the same as saying that the interests of the society's members should
be sacrificed in the interests of the whole, and that the state should facilitate
such a development. To think that way was to position the state as dominating
individuals' consciences—which was 'what the conflict between East and West
is about' ('Evolution', 7 April 1984). If Darling's education reflections hadn't
suggested solutions to the country's economic woes, then neither did the
handful written on science and history, save for the reassurance of knowing that,
throughout history, 'from all times of disaster, the world has painfully recovered'.
Like the humble gum tree, he said, man's capacity for regeneration was 'infinite'.
Signs of progress had been positive during his lifetime, although World War II
with its 'most appalling, deliberate and seemingly successful manifestation of
evil' had been shattering for religious faith—so difficult had it been to reconcile
that manifestation with a God-ordered world that there would be very little
comfort for the sufferers in such a reconciliation anyway ('Disasters', 31 March
1990). The other insight revealed by history was its lesson, 'over and over', that

human weakness had thwarted mankind's attempts to bring justice and peace to the world. Generations of people looked back on so-called golden ages, but such periods had usually been short in duration because greed, jealousy and overwhelming ambition had taken over. 'Sadly it seems that mankind shows its best qualities in adversity and its worst in prosperity.' Certainly, history had been lit, and the cause of humanity advanced, by personal qualities (of imagination, sympathy and courage) in the 'bright flashes of the lives of great and good men and women'. For all these reasons, history ought to be a prerequisite study for those seeking or gaining power and economics was 'not a substitute' ('The Study of History', 29 December 1990). Finally, Darling's few reflections on Australian election campaigns provided additional avenues for lament: the minimal emphasis on the 'general good' ('General Election', 4 October 1980), the descent into point scoring and a blurring of the line between Parliament's executive and legislative functions ('Selection of Politicians', 1 October 1988), the tendency to choose candidates whom most electors least disliked ('Responsibility in Elections', 30 June 1990) and televised leadership debates in which the 'contestants' are 'so anxious not to drop a brick' that such bricks as they did throw, and with only slight vigour, ended up falling 'a little short' ('The Great Debate', 3 October 1992).[35]

The conclusion of Darling's reflection writing in 1994 marked the end of over six decades of public impact in his adopted country. As the topics, content and tone of his reflections demonstrated, he had advanced his own spirituality, as enjoined by his former teacher Victor Gollancz, and he had tried to combat (what he saw as) the spiritual enfeeblement of his fellow Australians amid the ubiquitous lure of materialism. And they were his fellow Australians in the 1990s, because by then he was 'once an Englishman'. In 'Brilliant creatures: Germaine, Clive, Barry and Bob', a two-part BBC documentary telecast in July 2014, the English novelist Howard Jacobson focused on four noteworthy Australian cultural figures: Germaine Greer, Clive James, Barry Humphries and Robert Hughes. (Curiously, Jacobson did not acknowledge the historian Ian Britain's comparative study of the global meanderings of these four expatriates, *Once an Australian*, published in 1997.) The gist of Jacobson's interviews with three of his subjects (Hughes had died in 2012) and the recollections of a selection of their contemporaries indicated how departure from country of birth can be a pre-condition for the construction of identities and reputations. A similar rule of thumb applied in Jacobson's own case, although the initial step up the career ladder for him entailed emigration from England to the very same country on which his four celebrities had turned their backs, a move that had given him a kick-start academically. This noteworthy 'gang of four' (as they were referred to by the Australian journalist, Phillip Knightley—whose own journalistic reputation was cemented during an extended English sojourn) were part of a twentieth-century diaspora of Australian expatriates making regular cultural pilgrimage to London and

Home. By 1931, for example, a year after Darling's arrival, there were more than 28,000 Australian-born people living in England and Wales, a figure that, on the back of expanding tourism, travel and employment relocation, had increased by the mid-1960s to more than 62,000. While in the case of Knightley's gang of four England made them, for James Darling it was Australia that made him. At the same time as it did so, Darling contributed significantly to the making of twentieth-century Australia.[36]

Sixteen months or so after his contract with the *Age* ended, Darling died on All Saints' Day, Wednesday, 1 November 1995. At home on the preceding Saturday, he had a bad fall that was fatal for his kidneys. One of his OGGs, Dr Richard Smallwood, had him admitted to the Avenue Hospital in the Melbourne suburb of Windsor. After lingering for four days, he slipped away peacefully on the Wednesday. Shortly after hearing news of his death on an ABC radio bulletin, my academic colleague and former school chum, Robert Manne, then the editor of *Quadrant*, telephoned to ask me for a short article on Darling for the next number of the journal. There were two reasons for my title, 'A Very Superior Man'. First, Edward Thring had used 'very superior men' to describe the founders of the Headmasters' Conference in England, and my slight adaptation linked Darling to the nineteenth-century figure with whom he most closely identified as a head. Second, I intended the words to reflect the wider recognition of Darling as an educator. They were as far as I was prepared to go in the direction of the epithet of 'great'—any reader familiar with my leadership writings will know of my reluctance to get into the greatness game. At the end of the day, the estimate of exceptionality or grandiosity in Thring's phrase has to be measured against the reality of a person's life and work. As for self-hood, there were various times in his life that Darling wrote about it and cited the advice of Polonius to his son Laertes in *Hamlet*: 'to thine own self be true' (in an *Age* reflection of that title, on 19 October 1991, and in two others). Indeed, his most pithily expressed statement about self, mentioned in the Preface, is captured in the Darling family motto *Esto quod esse videris* ('Be what you seem to be'):

> To be or not to be
> This does not worry me,
> Rather to see if I can see
> Which of these me's is me.
>
> Be what I seem to be.
> Fear not lest others see
> What I aspire to be,
> Lest that becomes the real me.

These stanzas capture one way in which Darling expressed what he thought was entailed in being authentic, and being seen as authentic, and so my choice of

Charlotte Elliott's 'just as I am' as this book's title is a testimony to his attempt to be his real me (or self).[37]

Darling earned and deserved his public recognition: OBE, CMG, knighthood, Oxford doctorate, other degrees and, especially, the honorary fellowship bestowed by Oriel. Of all of these, the fellowship was probably the one that he most treasured. But the accolades continued and, in the following year as part of the 1988 bicentenary, Australia formally acknowledged its adopted son in its own unique way, along with 199 others, as having helped make the nation great. Darling was one of only eight people recognised in the category 'In the halls of learning', and the sole person who had had an extended school connection. Those people with whom Darling had dealings throughout his life may have thought of him as great, although few if any write about him in such terms. Rather, they tend to affirm his influence on them as persons, his wonderful gift for friendship and his delightful personality. E.C. Marchant, the Malburian master at GGS when Darling arrived in 1930, summed up these qualities as well as anyone. In early 1971, from somewhere in outback New South Wales, after having met up again with his former boss, Marchant wrote to say that:

> You had no little influence on me in those days of my impressionable and very callow youth. I responded immediately to your deep sympathy for the inmost feelings of other people & your care not to bruise those feelings as far as the interests of the body politic would allow—& generally to prefer the human being to the body politic. It is surprising how few people, these days, retain those qualities.

Many years before, in 1949, about two months after his fiftieth birthday, in reply to a correspondent from the Shanghai Banking Corporation, Darling expressed his thoughts about his link with Home. His correspondent had just returned from a visit to England, his first in thirteen years, and reported that the countryside was as delightful as ever, but that the outlook of the people betrayed resignation and a lack of pride, and there had been a collapse in standards of honesty. For all of England's shortcomings, his correspondent still wanted to go back when his 'time out here [East Asia] comes to an end'. Darling replied that he felt similarly about the land of his birth: he too had been depressed on his visit there the year before, 'particularly by the poverty of one's friends'. Like his correspondent, he had come to the realisation that 'there was no place I should like to retire except England', although whether that would occur 'will not I suppose, really depend on me, but on my family'. Indeed, it did and he stayed.

A funeral service for Darling was held at his parish church, Holy Advent, Armadale, on 3 November, where the opening prayer was by William Temple and the first hymn was 'Just as I am'. His priest, Father Jim Minchin, described Darling as 'the most complete public and private person I've ever met'. On 30 November there was a memorial service at St Paul's Cathedral, Melbourne, where Sir Zelman Cowen read the first lesson to the hundreds of mourners in attendance. Shortly afterwards there was another service at Corio. Subsequently, Darling's ashes (and later those of Margaret) were interred in a garden plot beside the chapel that bears the name of the day on which he died, All Saints, at the main campus of GGS, on the flat windswept land adjacent to Corio Bay. The chapel wall plaque reads:

Here rest

JAMES RALPH DARLING

1899–1995

Headmaster of the School 1930–1961

and

MARGARET DUNLOP DARLING

1915–2008

constant companions for 60 years

'I will lift up mine eyes unto the hills'

Nearly seven decades after his arrival Ozymandias had come home.[38]

NOTES

Acronyms and abbreviations
These are used in the following notes and in the Bibliography.

AACE	Australian Advisory Council of Elders	CAEMP	Committee on Australia's Established Migration Policy
ABC	Australian Broadcasting Commission	CCF	Cunningham Closed File
ABCB	Australian Broadcasting Control Board	CIAC	Commonwealth Immigration Advisory Council
ACE	Australian College of Education	ClP	Clark Papers
ACEA	Australian College of Educators Archives	CMCSMU	Committee on Matters Concerning Student Members of the University
ACERA	Australian Council for Educational Research Archives	Cmd	Command Paper
		CP	Cabinet Papers
		CPD	*Commonwealth Parliamentary Debates*
ACFTA	Australian Council for the Arts	CPE	Council of Public Education
ADB	*Australian Dictionary of Biography*	CSA	Charterhouse School Archives
		CSP	Committee on Social Patterns
AETT	Australian Elizabethan Theatre Trust	Diary	Diary of New Zealand Tour 1929 and subsequently
AFC	Australian Frontier Commission	DiP	Dicker Papers
AP	Andrew Papers	*DNB*	*Dictionary of National Biography*
APS	Associated Public Schools	DO	Dominions Office
APSLW	*A Public School Looks at the World*	DP	Darling Papers
		DuP	Dutton Papers
AHISAA	Association of Heads of Independent Schools of Australia Archives	*ECM*	*The Education of a Civilized Man*
ARSC	Australian Road Safety Council	FLM	Free Library Movement
		GCR	Godalming Corporation Records
BCM	Boys' Club Movement		
BEM	Boys' Employment Movement	GGSA	Geelong Grammar School Archives
BEMR	Boys' Employment Movement Records	GGSC	Geelong Grammar School Council
BLO	Bodleian Library, Oxford	GGSCF	Geelong Grammar School Centenary File
BMF	British Memorial Fund		

GP	Giblin Papers	RCSA	Royal Colonial Services Archive
HC	House of Commons		
H–GP	Headley–Gullett Papers	*RR*	*Richly Rewarding*
HMA	Headmasters' Association	RSA	Repton School Archives
HMC	Headmasters' Conference	RSDS	Repton School Debating Society
HMCA	Headmasters' Conference of Australia		
		SB	Schools Board
HMCR	Headmasters' Conference Records	SE-TC	School Empire-Tour Committee
HP	Harford Papers	SP	Stephens Papers
HSA	Highfield School Archives	*SW*	*The School and the World*
IAC	Industries Assistance Commission	TC	Timbertop Committee
		TH	Toc H
INF	Ministry of Information	THR	Toc H Records
ISMS	Institute for the Study of Man and Society	*Tour*	*Tour to New Zealand*, unpublished draft for *Richly Rewarding*
leFP	le Fleming Papers		
LMF	Lord Mayor's Fund	TP	Temple Papers
LMFA	Lord Mayor's Fund Archives	*TT*	*Timbertop: An Innovation in Australian Education*
LP	Latham Papers		
LPA	Lambeth Palace Archives	UBA	University of Birmingham Archives
MGSA	Melbourne Grammar School Archives		
		UBC	Unemployed Boys' Club
MOFMC	Marcus Oldham Farm Management College	UMA	University of Melbourne Archives
MP	Mackinnon Papers	UMC	University of Melbourne Council
MTS	Merchant Taylors' School		
MTSA	Merchant Taylors' School Archives	UWA	United World Colleges Australia
NA	National Archives (UK)	UWC	United World Colleges
NAA	National Archives of Australia	VABC	Victorian Association of Boys' Clubs
NAC	National Advisory Council	VPRO	Victorian Public Record Office
NLA	National Library of Australia		
OGGA	Old Geelong Grammarians Association	VPRS	Victorian Public Research Series
OP	Officer Papers	WCA	Wesley College Archives
OS	Oversea Settlement	WeP	Weston Papers
OSC	Oversea Settlement Committee	WO	War Office
		WP	Wadham Papers
PP	Phelps Papers		
PSEB	Public Schools' Employment Bureau		

1 Victorian family, Edwardian boyhood

1 *Falkirk Mail*, 8 February 1896; Nimmo to M.E. Darling, 30 March 1896, DP.

2 Laski (1964), pp. 141–2; Laslett (1962), pp. 14–15; *RR*, p. 13; le Fleming (2007), pp. 55–6; 'Administration of the estate of Mary Emily Darling deceased 23 December 1913', DP; Sir James Darling to the author, 18 September 1992.

3 Woolf (1966), p. 12; Sir James Darling to the author, 14 November 1986.

4 *RR*, p. 4; Greene (1971), p. 69; J.B. Darling to M.E. Darling, 11 February 1911, DP; le Fleming (2007), p. 1.

5 le Fleming (2007), pp. 13–18, 23; R. Darling to M.E. Darling, ? May 1854; le Fleming 'The Darlings' (typescript), 1983, pp. 9–10; Hornby to J.G. Darling, 13 December 1855; Howard to Cambermere, 2 June 1853; Derby to J.G. Darling, 18 April 1855, 1 November 1856, all DP.

6 'The Darlings', pp. 13, 12; M.E. Darling, Diary, 1862; Hornby to J.G. Darling, 3 May 1855; J.G. Darling, Diary, 1854, 1866, all DP.

7 M.E. Darling to the Lord Bishop (Diocese of Bury St Edmonds?), undated; 'The Darlings', p. 12; 'Rules of Eyke Primary School, 1857'; 'A village clergyman's tribute' (newspaper clipping, source unknown, 11 May 1891); M.R. Darling to J.R. Darling, 6 September 1942, all DP.

8 Nimmo (undated), pp. 11, 12, 17, 21, 29–30, 40, 41, DP; le Fleming (2007), p. 59.

9 le Fleming (2007), pp. 66–67, 79, 85–6; Nimmo (1907), part 2, pp. 56, 77, 64; Kemp (undated), pp. 1–2, both DP; Sir James Darling to the author, 18 September 1987; Sir James Darling, 'Recollections of my father' (undated), pp. 3, 4; M.E. Darling to Nimmo, 23 July 1895; Ray to Nimmo, 28 July 1895, all DP.

10 Neve (1933), p. 347; M.R. Darling to J.R. Darling, 6 September 1942, DP; *RR*, pp. 8–9; 'Recollections of my father', p. 3, DP.

11 le Fleming (2007), p. 42, 27–8; J.G. Darling, *Diary*, 1870; 'Recollections of my father', pp. 1, 3, 8, 9; 'The review of the public school corps by Her Majesty the Queen, in Windsor Park' (29 June 1897), all DP; Robertson to Phelps, 22 May 1896, PP; *RR*, p. 8; Crompton (undated), pp. 3–4; *Kelly's Directory of Tunbridge Wells, Southborough, Tonbridge and Villages in the Neighbourhood, for 1907* (London, 1907), p. 273; *Mate's Illustrated Tonbridge* (Bournemouth, 1906), p. 1.

12 Leinster-Mackay (1984), pp. 121, 149, 330, 133, 135; Chapman (1976), pp. 75, 82–4; *Census of England and Wales, 1901* (63 Vict., C4. County of Kent. Area, Houses and Population), Cmd. 1,711 (London, 1902), Table 24, p. 67 and Table 35A, pp. 90–1; J. Hickman to the author, 18 January 1984; T. Darling to the author, 17 January 1984; *RR*, p. 6.

13 'Recollections of my father', pp. 4–5, DP; *RR*, pp. 8–9; T. Darling to the author, 17 January 1984; School reports, 5 November–20 December 1904; 6 November–19 December 1905, both DP.

14 School reports, 23 September–4 November 1905; 4 May–18 June 1906; 22 September–3 November 1906; Dictation, 1905; School reports, 20 September–2 November 1907; 4 November–16 December 1907; 4 May–15 June 1907; 25 September–5 November 1909, all DP.

15 School reports, 18 January–1 April 1908; 2 May–15 June 1908; 21 January–25 March 1910; 20 January–2 April 1912; 17 June–29 July 1912, all DP.

16 Sir James Darling to the author, 7 December 1984, 1 June 1984; 'Recollections of my father', p. 5, DP; T. Darling to the author, 17 January 1984.

17 *RR*, pp. 4, 10; Nimmo to M.E. Darling, 30 March 1896, DP; J. Hickman to the author, 18 January 1984; Laski (1964), p. 164; M. le Fleming to the author, 10 January 1984; J.B. Darling to M.E. Darling, 18 February 1911, DP.

18 Gathorne-Hardy (1985), p. 126; Sir James Darling to the author, 18 May 1984; J.B. Darling to M.E. Darling, 18 February 1911, DP.

19 Sir James Darling to the author, 18 May 1984, 19 October 1984; *RR*, pp. 15, 12–13; Whitby to Darling, 20 December 1929, DP.

20 M.R. Darling to J.B. Darling, September 1901; J.B. Darling to M.E. Darling, 18 February 1911, both DP; S. le Fleming to the author, 18 January 1984; M. Darling to M.R. Darling, 18 October 1914; J.R. Darling to M.R. Darling, 15 July 1919; A.E. Darling to M.R. Darling, 25 June 1914, 13 December 1914; M. le Fleming, 'Life and impressions of my uncle [Eaton] gained from his letters to his mother and sister Jean (1934–41) and other material' (undated), pp. 2, 14 ('*Addendum* by his brother Sir James Darling on seeing the foregoing—1982'), all DP; Isherwood (1938), pp. 41–2; Sir James Darling to the author, 14 November 1986.

21 Sir James Darling to the author, 3 August 1984; *RR*, p. 7; N. Darling to the author, 17 January 1984.

22 Hattersley (2004), pp. vii, 30, 74: Woolf (1966), p. 142; *RR*, pp. 4, 10, 17–18.

2 Highfield and Repton

1 *RR*, pp. 5–6; Leinster-Mackay (1984), pp. 141–2; R. Orr to the author, 18 April 1988; Sir James Darling to the author, 14 November 1986; *Highfield School Magazine*, 1912 (Christmas), p. 4, HSA; J.R. Darling to J.B. Darling, 2 March 1913, DP; *RR*, p. 18.

2 *Highfield School Magazine*, 1913 (Lent), pp. 6, 10, 11; (Summer) p. 4, (Christmas), pp. 5, 8–9, HSA; *RR*, p. 6; Temple to Darling, 27 May 1913, DP; Sir James Darling to the author, 20 May 1983, 14 November 1986; Mills to Darling, 27 November 1917, DP.

3 James (1981), p. 268; de Honey (1977), p. 319; *DNB, Supplement, 1901–11*, pp. 491–2; *DNB, 1941–50*, p. 870; Temple to Abney, 17 May 1914, RSA; *Reptonian*, 1914 (June), p. 135.

4 *RR*, pp. 36, 20, 21; *Repton School Lists*, 1913 (Christmas), pp. 7–13, RSA; Thomas (1957), pp. 119, 163, ch. 1.

5 Thomas (1957), chs 2–4; de Honey (1977), p. 119.

6 Half-term report, 13 June 1914; terminal report, 12 December 1914, both DP; Rathbone to Darling, 29 September 1960, GGSA; Thomas (1957), p. 87; J.R. Darling to J.B. Darling, 13 February 1915, DP.

7 Terminal reports, 12 December 1914, 30 March 1915, 19 July 1915; half-term reports, 6 November 1914, 26 February 1915; J.R. Darling to J.B. Darling, 13 February 1915, all DP; Sir James Darling to the author, 15 June 1984.

8 Sir James Darling to the author, 15 June 1984, 29 June 1984; half-term report, 6 November 1915; terminal report, 22 December 1915, both DP.

9 Gathorne-Hardy (1979), p. 156; Sir James Darling to the author, 29 June 1984; J.M. Coldham to the author, 27 October 1983.

10 Sir James Darling to the author, 29 June 1984; Sir James Harford to the author, 3 November 1983; Isherwood (1938), pp. 42–3; Hughes (1981), pp. 145–6; Vachell (1905), p. 16; Waugh (1972), p. 92.

11 *RR*, p. 19; Lewis (1986), p. 73; J.M. Coldham to the author, 27 October 1983; D.C. Somervell, 'Myself' (undated), p. 164, SP; Sir James Darling to the author, 29 June 1984.

12 Sir James Darling to the author, 15 June 1984; RSDS, Minutes, 1915, p. 111, RSA; *Reptonian*, 1917 (February), pp. 106–7; RSDS, Minutes, 1917, p. 169, RSA; *Reptonian*, 1915 (December), p. 47; 1916 (March), pp. 102, 104.

13 *Reptonian*, 1915 (December), pp. 47, 48, 49; 1917 (March), p. 128.

14 *Reptonian*, 1916 (November), p. 53 (December), pp. 83–4; J.M. Coldham to the author, 27 October 1983; *Reptonian*, 1915 (June), p. 170; 1914 (June), p. 151; 1917 (July), pp. 216–17, 211–12; 1914 (October), p. 222.

15 *Reptonian*, 1915 (December), p. 30; 1916 (February), p. 87, (April), p. 141; 1917 (February), pp. 107–8; 1914 (February), p. 82, (March), p. 111, (May), pp. 129–30.

16 *Reptonian*, 1915 (May), pp. 137–9; 1916 (November), p. 68, (December), p. 87; J.R. Darling to J.B. Darling, 13 February 1915, DP; Sir James Harford to the author, 3 November 1983.

17 Sir James Darling to the author, 14 November 1986, 1 June 1984; Distinction card, Summer term, 1914, Christmas term, 1914; terminal report, 3 April 1916; half-term report, 16 June 1917; Stratton, note, undated, all DP.

18 *Reptonian*, 1917 (February), p. 114, (March), pp. 138, 137.

19 *Reptonian*, 1917 (July), pp. 224, 223–4, 222–3, (May), pp. 169–170.

3   Some systematic teaching on questions of the day

1   Musgrave (1978), p. 43; Holdsworth to Darling, 27 November 1917, DP.

2   Gollancz (1953), pp. 177–8.

3   *Ibid.*, pp. 177–8, 221–3, 226, 240; *Reptonian*, 1917 (February), p. 92; Gollancz and Somervell (1918), pp. 59, 66–7.

4   Gollancz and Somervell (1918), pp. 62, 65–6; 'Myself', p. 173, SP; Edwards (1987), pp. 81, 84, 89, 93–4; Sir James Harford, Memoirs (undated), p. 16, HP; *RR*, p. 31.

5   Harford, Memoirs, pp. 15, 14, HP; Edwards (1987), p. 97; Gollancz (1953), p. 184; 'Myself', p. 174.

6   Gollancz and Somervell (1918), pp. 2, 6, 7–9, 10, 11, 12, 13, 15.

7   Gollancz (1953), p. 226; J.R. Darling, Repton notebook (undated), DP.

8   Gollancz (1953), pp. 262, 264–5; *APSLW*, 1(1), p. 4; 1(5), p. 9; 1(4), pp. 9, 7–8, DP; Darling (1917), DP; Gollancz (1953), pp. 181–2.

9   Terminal report (1 August 1916); Half-term report (3 November 1916); Phelps to Darling, 13 December 1916, 3 December 1916; Terminal report (April 1917), (July 1917); A.M. Darling to J.R. Darling, 7 September 1917, all DP; *Reptonian*, 1917 (October), p. 2.

10 *Reptonian*, 1917 (October), pp. 13, 2, (November), pp. 43–4; Thomas (1957), p. 106; Holdsworth to Darling, 7 October 1917; Harford to Darling, 8 October 1917, 12 November 1917; McLeod Innes to Darling, 4 August 1917, 2 October 1917; A.M. Darling to J.R. Darling, 7 September 1917; Balmforth to Darling, 15 September 1917, all DP.

11 Holdsworth to Darling, 27 November 1917; Manoukian to Darling, 29 December 1917, both DP; Z.M. 'Idealism and Education', *APSLW*, 1(3), p. 5; Harford to Darling, 12 November 1917, DP; Edwards (1987), p. 98; Gollancz (1953), pp. 278–9, 279–81, 281–3.

12 *Reptonian*, 1917 (October), pp. 33, 2; Gollancz (1953), p. 275, 284–7; *SW*, pp. 7–8; *Reptonian*, 1917 (November), p. 61; *APSLW*, 1(4), pp. 4, 9.

13 Gollancz (1953), pp. 253, 297; Snape to Darling, 2 November 1917, DP; RSDS, Minutes (1917–18), pp. 195, 199–200, 203, RSA; Gollancz (1953), pp. 261–2, 290–1; 'Myself', p. 186, SP; P.J.C. 'Repton personalities—2: Victor Gollancz', *Reptonian*, 1975 (Michaelmas), p. 24.

14 Harford, Memoirs, p. 23, HP; Gollancz to Darling, undated, DP; Gollancz (1953), pp. 300, 222.

15 'Jenny Wren' to J.R. Darling, 4 October 1917; M.R. Darling to J.R. Darling, 30 November 1917; Phelps to Darling, 13 December 1917; McLeod Innes to Darling, 4 August 1917; Cattley to Darling, 4 October 1917, all DP; *Highfield School Magazine*, 1917 (Christmas), p. 8, HSA; Holdsworth to Darling, 27 November 1917; Gollancz to Darling, 2 August 1917; Martin to Darling, 11 December 1917, all DP.

16 Phelps to Darling, 21 December 1917; Gollancz to Darling, undated; Holdsworth to Darling, 6 January 1918; A.M. Darling to J.R. Darling, 11 December 1917; Manoukian to Darling, 29 December 1917, all DP.

17 Martin to Darling, 14 December 1917, DP.

18 Phelps to Darling, 21 December 1917, DP; Gollancz (1952), pp. 29–30; Sir James Darling to the author, 29 October 1986; McLeod Innes to Darling, 16 December 1916; Somervell to Darling, 10 August 1917, both DP; Weatherby (1983), p. 16: Abrahams to Darling, 21 September 1917; Colley to Darling, 7 December 1917, both DP; Sir James Darling to the author, 31 October 1986; Abrahams to Darling, 17 September 1917, DP.

19 McLean to Darling, undated; Eames to Darling, 20 November 1917; Orr to Darling, 28 August 1917; A.M. Darling to J.R. Darling, 7 September 1917; Simpson to Darling (undated), all DP; 'Myself', pp. 169, 170, SP; Sir James Harford to the author, 3 November 1983; Gorringe to Darling, 27 January 1918, DP.

4 Baptism of fire

1 *Interim Report of the War Office Committee on the Provision of Officers* (1907), Cmd 3294, secs, 25, 13, 18, 23; *Reptonian*, 1914 (May), pp. 116–17, 115; 1916 (February), p. 75; Sir James Darling to the author, 26 July 1984; *Reptonian*, 1915 (February), pp. 33, 34, 81.

2 *Reptonian*, 1914 (October), p. 215; 1915 (March), p. 84; 1916 (April), p. 143, (May), p. 161, (November), p. 61; 1917 (May), p. 169, (June), p. 184, (November), p. 51; *Interim Report*, sec 22.

3 Gathorne-Hardy (1979), p. 218; Parker (1987), pp. 281–4; *Reptonian*, 1917 (May), p. 17; 1914 (December), p. 6; 1915 (March), p. 67.

4 *Reptonian*, 1915 (October), p. 231; 1916 (February), p. 77; 1915 (July), p. 183, (February), p. 39, (March), p. 65; 1916 (April), p. 134; 1915 (July), p. 180, (November), p. 2; 1916 (April), p. 121.

5 *Reptonian*, 1915 (February), p. 33; C. Smyth (1973), The boss and Repton: 1916–1921, Repton School Terminal Letter, 242: 4, RSA.

6 Dixon (1983), p. 222; Certificate of Discharge, 25 July 1918, DP; *RR*, pp. 39, 41; Army book, p. 13, DP.

7 *RR*, pp. 40, 42; Sir James Darling to the author, 26 July 1984; Sidey to Darling, undated; Darling to Harford, 30 April 1918; Notebook, Weedon; Certificate of Discharge, 25 July 1918; Army Book, p. 5, all DP; *RR*, pp. 43–5.

8 J.R. Darling to M.R. Darling, ? September 1918, DP; WO95/1991, 17th Div., 78th Bde, vol. 39, sheet 74, NA; *Diary*, pp. 20–1, DP.

9 Edmunds (1947), frontispiece, p. 509; Crutwell (1936), pp. 568, 569, 578; WO95/ 1991, 17th Div., 78th Bde., vol. 40, sheets 75, 76, NA; Atteridge (1929), pp. 422, 425.

10 Sir James Darling to the author, 5 February 1988, 26 July 1984; J.R. Darling to M.R. Darling, 3 November 1918, DP; WO95/1991, 17th Div., 78th Bde, vol. 40, sheet 78, NA; Atteridge (1929), pp. 451, 458; *RR*, p. 52; Notebook, Weedon, DP.

11 J.R. Darling to M.R. Darling, 3 November 1918, DP; Sir James Darling to the author, 26 July 1988, 5 February 1988; *RR*, pp. 49–50, 51–4; Darling to Phelps, 19 December 1918, 5 January 191[9], both PP.

12 Darling to Phelps, 5 January 191[9], PP; J.R. Darling to M.R. Darling, 5 February 1918, DP; Ministry of Reconstruction, Adult Education Committee, *Final Report* (1919), Cmd 321, p. 119; Army, *Report on Educational Training in the British Army* (1920), Cmd 568, sec 6; *RR*, p. 54.

13 *Report on Educational Training*, secs 13, 7, 12; J.R. Darling to M.R. Darling, 18 May 1919, DP; Darling to Phelps, 5 January 191[8], PP; Army Book, p. 5; J.R. Darling to J.B. Darling, 14 June 1919, both DP; *RR*, pp. 54–7; Sir James Darling to the author, 26 July 1984.

14 *RR*, pp. 57–8; *Report on Educational Training*, sec 7; War Office School of Education Certificate, DP; *Who Was Who, 1961–1970*, p. 1025; Protection Certificate (Officer); Cubitt to Darling, 6 December 1919, both DP.

15 *RR*, pp. 46–8; J.R. Darling to J.B. Darling, 14 June 1919, DP; Sir James Darling to the author, 26 July 1984; *RR*, p. 49; Weedon Notebook; Cleland to Darling, 16 December [1919], both DP.

16 Darling to Phelps, 12 January 1919, PP; Higher Certificate Examination certificate, DP; Sir James Darling to the author, 3 August 1984; Phelps to Darling, 21 December 1917; McLeod Innes to Darling, 4 August 1917, both DP.

5 A pleasant oasis

1 Rowse (1985), pp. 85, 49, 172; Sir James Harford to the author, 3 November 1983; Symons (1986), p. 3.

2 M.R. Darling to J.R. Darling, 20 July 1917, 31 October 1917, 30 November 1917; Holdsworth to Darling, 7 October 1917, 27 November 1917, all DP.

3 *RR*, p. 59; Rowse (1985), p. 223; Sir James Darling to the author, 3 August 1984; *Oriel Record* (1987), p. 7, quoted in Symonds (1986), p. 180.

4 Rowse (1985), pp. 237, 239; Olim Co Prae (1920) Oxford in 1920, *Oxford Magazine*, 38(9): 170–1.

5 'Oxford political clubs', *Isis*, 1921 (11 May), pp. 1–2.

6   J.R. Darling to J.B. Darling, 14 February 1915; McLeod Innes to Darling, 16 December 1916, both DP; Aristotle (1984), pp. 259, 288, 273, 294; Lewis (1986), p. 85; Emerson (1907), p. 135.

7   Goldstein (1982), p. 181; Sofer (1987), p. 102; Slee (1987), p. 936; Sir James Darling to the author, 3 August 1984.

8   Sir James Darling to the author, 3 August 1984; Nichols (1939), p. 62; *RR*, p. 61.

9   Sir James Darling to the author, 17 February 1988, 3 August 1984; Temple to Darling, 1 March 1921, DP; Hilda Wharton to the author, 30 April 1988; *Isis*, 1921 (15 June), p. 3.

10   *Isis*, 1921 (2 March), p. 11; Hilda Wharton to the author, 30 April 1988; *Oxford Magazine*, 1920 (7 May), (11 June), p. 391; 1921 (26 May), p. 348; *Isis*, 1921 (25 May), p. 4.

11   Hollis (1976); *Oxford Magazine*, 1921 (4 March), pp. 237, 236; M.J.M. (1921) Labour club notes, *The New Oxford*, 7:17, BLO; *RR*, pp. 63–4; Phelps, Testimonial, 25 February 1921, DP; *Oxford Magazine*, 1920 (12 November), p. 76; 1921 (25 February), p. 227, (16 June), pp. 404–5.

12   Sir James Darling to the author, 3 August 1984; Photographs, Hypocrites Club, BLO; *RR*, pp. 66–7, 68–9; J.R. Darling, notebook, undated; photograph album, both DP.

13   J.R.D. & A.F.G.A. Untitled, March 1920?; 'The great circus of Olympia', 1 March 1920?; 'German counter-revolution. March 1920', 14 March 1920; 'Grovely Wood', August 1920; Untitled, undated; 'The art of swearing', undated, all DP.

14   Lindsay (1972), p. 29; *RR*, p. 66; Clark, Testimonial, undated; Fisher, Testimonials, 31 May 1920 and 15 March 1921, all DP; Sir James Darling to the author, 3 August 1984; Cradock-Watson to Darling, 4 July 1921; J.R. Darling to M.R. Darling, 5 February 1919, both DP.

6   Public-spirited pedagogue

1   Luff (1970), pp. 21, 208, 225, 234–5, 238.

2   Fletcher (1936), p. 14; MTS, Staff Register (1908–), p. 81; Board of Governors, Minutes, 22 July 1921, 27 October 1921, 10 November 1921; Roll Book, all MTSA; Sir James Darling to the author, 19 October 1984; Black Book, 29 October 1921, MTSA; Darling to Phelps, 26 December 1921, PP.

3   'To those about to teach', draft 1, undated, pp. 1, 2, 4; 'To those about to teach', draft 2, undated, p. 3; 'The pedagogue's pedestal', undated, p. 6, all DP.

4   'The appreciation of poetry', 16 December 1921, p. 6, DP; Darling to Phelps, 26 December 1921, PP; 'The dramatic art and modern playwrights', undated, pp. 15, 18; Wharton to Darling, 8 May 1922, both DP.

5   *Merchant Taylors' Review*, 1922 (May), pp. 35–7, MTSA; Darling to Phelps, 22 April 1922, 2 July 1922, both PP; *RR*, pp. 77–9; Luff (1970), p. 240; *Merchant Taylors' Review*, 1923 (April), p. 9, MTSA; Sir James Darling to the author, 10 August 1984; 28 September 1984.

6   Darling to Phelps, 2 July 1922; 15 October 1922, 15 December 1922, all PP; Sir James Darling to the author, 19 October 1984; Wharton to Phelps, 19 November 1922, PP; *RR*, p. 77; Cradock-Watson, Testimonial, 5 December 1922, DP; *Merchant Taylors' Review*, 1923 (April), p. 13, MTSA.

7   *RR*, p. 81; Darling to Phelps, 15 December 1922, 6 April 1923; A.M. Darling to Phelps, 25 March 1922, all PP.

8 *Merchant Taylors' Review*, 1923 (June), p. 24, (December), pp. 50, 41, 38, MTSA; Darling to Phelps, 6 April 1923; 27 October 1923; 21 December 1923, all PP; Sir James Darling to the author, 19 October 1984; *RR*, p. 73.

9 'Elephant tusks', undated, p. 4; 'The bashful elephant', 22 October 1922; 'The abdication of the Kaiser. Nov 1918', undated; 'The economical field marshal', undated, pp. 4, 6; three untitled pieces; 'Education', July 1923, pp. 7, 8; 'The novel', July 1923, pp. 5–6, all DP.

10 Notes for a play, undated, DP.

11 Phelps to A.M. Darling, 4 February 1924, DP; Darling to Phelps, 25 May 1924, 23 December 1923; A.M. Darling to Phelps, 10 July 1924, all PP; Temple to Darling, 4 June 1924, DP; *Merchant Taylors' Review*, 1924 (March), pp. 17–18, (June), p. 27; 1926 (February), p. 180, all MTSA; *RR*, pp. 79–80; Douglas to Darling, 22 October 1968, DP.

12 Darling to Phelps, 17 July 1924, 11 August 1924; Sellar to Phelps, 15 September 1924, all PP; Gathorne-Hardy (1979), pp. 149, 338–9; *Carthusian*, 1924 (October), p. 673; Fletcher (1937), pp. 148, 151.

13 Charterhouse school and house lists, CSA; Darling to Phelps, 1 October 1924, PP; Temple to J.R. Darling, 12 October 1924, DP.

14 Wharton to Darling, 24 September 1922, 8 May 1922, both DP; Lawrence Neal to the author, 17 April 1988; Hilda Wharton to the author, 30 April 1988.

15 Wharton to Phelps, 23 November 1924, PP; *Carthusian*, 1924 (November), p. 710; 1925 (March), p. 776; Darling to Phelps, 23 November 1924, PP; G.C.W. Dicker to the author, 21 December 1983; R.L. Arrowsmith to the author, 9 January 1984; Wilkinson to Gronn, 1 December 1983; Morris to Gronn, 22 January 1984; Law to Cowen, 13 October 1987, DP.

16 Charterhouse Library Committee, Minutes, 4 February 1926, p. 336; 6 December 1929, p. 376, both CSA; *Carthusian*, 1925 (June), p. 812; 1926 (December), p. 178; 1927 (June), p. 240; 1928 (March), p. 332, (July), p. 387; Renwick to Gronn, 28 November 1983; Keenlyside to Sir James Darling, July 1984, DP; Sir James Darling to the author, 21 September 1984; Irvine to Darling, 21 August 1935, DP; John Bowen to the author, 1 May 1988.

17 *Carthusian*, 1927 (February), p. 181; 1925 (November), p. 14; Keith to Darling, 17 September 1930, DP; Dickins to Gronn, 25 November 1983; Wilkinson to Gronn, 1 December 1983; Keenlyside to Sir James Darling, July 1984, DP.

18 Fletcher (1936), p. 253; Stork to Gronn, 16 January 1984; G.C.W. Dicker to the author, 21 December 1983; W.O. Dickins to Gronn, 25 November 1983; *Carthusian*, 1926 (May), p. 65; Sir James Darling to the author, 28 September 1984; Renshaw (1976) *passim*; *Surrey Advertiser and County Times*, 8 May 1926, p. 5.

19 *RR*, p. 96; J.R. Darling to J.B. Darling, 23 April 1919, DP; Fletcher (1936), pp. 247–8; Godalming Corporation, Minutes and Reports (1927–1929), GCR.

20 *Carthusian*, 1926 (October), pp. 149–50; 'Taxation and local government', 11 February 192[7?], pp. 7, 11; 'The reform of parliament', Oriel, undated; 'The meaning of democracy', 6 November 1925, pp. 2, 8, all DP; Cole (1920), pp. 13, 27–30, 59, 67; 'The completion of democracy', 20 November 1925, p. 6, DP.

21 'Taxation and local government', pp. 9, 1; 'Credit', 11 December 1925, p. 8, both DP; Bill Locke to the author, 29 April 1988.

22 A.M. Darling to Phelps, 30 December 1925; J.R. Darling to Phelps, 7 April 1925, both PP; G.C.W. Dicker to the author, 21 December 1983; 'Notes on colonial history for a course of classes at Pentonville prison', October 1925, DP; Gordon & White (1979), pp. 104–5; Darling to Phelps, 21 October 1925, PP; Kenneth Lindsay to the author, 17 April 1988; 'Notes on a course of classes on the masters of English literature', Toynbee Hall, 7 October 1925, DP; Sir James Darling to the author, 28 September 1984; *RR*, p. 98.

23 *RR*, p. 98; Untitled, undated, p. 1; 'The problem of collective security', 17 October 1927, pp. 14, 7; Untitled, undated, pp. 8, 10, all DP.

24 Darling to Phelps, 7 April 1925, PP; *RR*, p. 85; Charterhouse teaching notes, DP; Darling to Phelps, 4 May 1928, PP; Patrick Law to the author, 1 May 1988; John Bowen to the author, 1 May 1988; Keith to Darling, 4 April 1930, DP.

25 Darling to Phelps, 4 May 1928, PP; John Bowen to the author, 1 May 1988; Notes for a play, undated; 'The diary of John Bull from the wars of roses until today', undated; 'What did the man who was born blind mean when he said that scarlet was as the blare of a bugle?', December 1924; Keenlyside to Darling, undated; 'To J.R.D. an appreciation', undated, p. 5, all DP.

26 Sir James Darling to the author, 21 September 1984; Temple to Darling, 12 October 1924, DP; G.C.W. Dicker to the author, 21 December 1983; *RR*, pp. 92, 93; Sir Desmond Lee to the author, 10 January 1984; 'On reading', undated, p. 1, DP.

27 Temple to Darling 16 November 1924; 22 February 1927, both DP; Sir James Darling to the author, 21 September 1984; *RR*, p. 91; 'On Reading', p. 2; 'Charterhouse memorial chapel', 12 July 1926; Darling to Harris, 16 January 1962, all DP.

28 *RR*, p. 81; *DNB 1951–1960*, p. 367; R.L. Arrowsmith to the author, 19 January 1984; Sir James Darling to the author, 7 September 1984; Renshaw (1976), p. 200; Kenneth Lindsay to the author, 17 April 1988; *DNB, 1901–70*, pp. 409, 410.

29 *Carthusian*, 1927 (June), p. 247, (July), p. 267; J.R. Darling to Phelps, 6 October 1928; 1 January 1929, both PP.

7 Dominionist?

1 Hyam (2006), pp. 69–70; Darwin (1980), p. 662.

2 OSC, *Report* (1919), Cmd 573, pp. 3–14; *Report* (1924), Cmd 2383, p. 14; *Report* (1928), Cmd 3308, p. 5; *Report* (1920), Cmd 1134, p. 9; Drummond (1974), pp. 35–7.

3 13 George 5, sec. 1 (1)–(4); OSC, *Report* (1920), Cmd 1134, p. 6; *Report* (1921), Cmd 1580, p. 9; *Report* (1932), Cmd 2107, p. 10; Imperial Economic Conference, 1923, *Record of Proceedings and Documents*, Cmd 2009, pp. 92, 97; PSEB, *Bulletin*, 1925, no. 2, pp. 17–18, HMCR.

4 Harper (2004), pp. 57, 54; Firth (1954), pp. 189, 200, 214; HMC, *Bulletin*, 1927, no. 1, pp. 7, 27–8, HMCR.

5 SE-TC, Meeting 4 October 1928, Minutes, 1927–1934, p. 95; SE-TC, New Zealand sub-committee meeting, Minutes, 1927–1934, 30 November 1928, pp. 98, 100, both RCSA; *Times*, 5 January 1929; W.E. Lamaison to the author, 29 April 1988; J.M.H. Weston to the author, 30 April 1988.

6 Diary, pp. 8–10, DP; *Otago Daily Times*, 16 February 1929; *Times*, 5 January 1929.

7 Diary, pp. 11, 12, 17, 18–22, DP; Weston to Weston, 17 January 1929, WeP; James Darling to the author, 20 December 1985.

8 Diary, pp. 24–9, 29–33, 35, DP.

9 SE-TC, New Zealand sub-committee meeting, Minutes, 1927–1934, 28 February 1929, p. 106, RCSA; Weston to Weston, 17 January 1929, WeP; Diary, pp. 34–6, DP.

10 Diary, pp. 37–8, 39–41, DP; *Dominion*, 15 February 1929.

11 Diary, pp. 16, 18, 42–3, 43–5, 46, DP; Weston to Weston, 10 February 1929, WeP.

12 New Zealand (1929) *Official Yearbook, 1930* (Wellington), pp. 290, 302–3; Chapman & Malone (1969), p. 32.

13 *Yearbook, 1930*, pp. 75, 77, 88, 92, 96–8, 283–4, 289; OSC, *Report* (1923), Cmd 2107, p. 7; British Oversea Settlement Delegation to New Zealand, 1923, *Report* (1924), Cmd 2167, p. 7; Burdon (1965), p. 71; OSC, *Report* (1927), Cmd 3088, p. 7

14 Diary, pp. 48, 53–4, DP; *New Zealand Herald*, 15 February 1929; Weston, Diary, 15 February 1929, p. 26, WeP.

15 Diary, pp. 113, 84, 75, 105–6; Sir James Darling to the author, 20 December 1985.

16 Diary, pp. 59–63, 86–8, 97–100, DP.

17 *Ibid.*, pp. 104–7.

18 *New Zealand Herald*, 15 February 1929; *Dominion*, 15 February 1929; Diary, pp. 74, 81, 49, DP.

19 Diary, pp. 88, 73, 71, 89–90, 96, 55–6, 67, DP.

20 *Otago Daily Times*, 19 February 1929; Diary, pp. 67–8, 70, DP.

21 Diary, pp. 88, 74, 54, 79, DP; *Dominion*, 20 February 1929.

22 *New Zealand Herald*, 28 March 1929; Diary, p. 107, DP; *Lyttleton Times*, 25 February 1929; Watson (1989), p. 141.

23 *Dominion*, 19 March 1929; Diary, pp. 107–9, DP; Sir James Darling to the author, 20 December 1985, 10 August 1984.

24 Diary, pp. 11, 109, 110–11, DP; Metaxa to Harford, 13 March 1929, HP.

25 Diary, pp. 112–14, DP; *Lake Wakatip Mail*, 5 March 1929; Sir James Darling to the author, 20 December 1985; *Tour*, pp. 7/8–9, DP.

26 *Tour*, pp. 7/10–11, DP; Sir James Darling to the author, 20 December 1985; *Dominion*, 22 March 1929; *New Zealand Herald*, 28 March 1929.

27 *New Zealand Herald*, 30 March 1929; *Tour*, pp. 7/11–12, DP; *Argus*, 9 April 1929; Weston to Weston, 25 April 1929, WeP; Sir James Darling to the author, 20 December 1985.

28 Bickersteth to J.R. Darling, 23 April 1929; *Tour*, pp. 7/11–14, DP; Weston to Weston, 4 May 1929, WeP.

29 Diary, pp. 5–6, DP.

30 *Ibid.*, pp. 7–8; Wharton to Phelps, 30 July 1929, PP; Temple to Darling, 31 December 1928; 30 May 1929, both DP.

8 Transition

1 OS57/103/2162, SE-TC, pp. 599–600; SE-TC, Meeting, 23 May 1929, Minutes, 1927–1934, pp. 116–20, 132, RCSA; Jane, Lady Portal to Gronn, 1 March 1986; Smith-Dorrien to Darling, 5 October 1930, DP.

2   DO57/2162, Chief Director's Report, pp. 2, 6–7, 10, 14; Report of 'Second in Command', p. 2; Advance Representative's Report, p. 6, NA; SE-TC, Meeting, 13 February 1930, Minutes, 1927–1934, pp. 148–52, RCSA.

3   PSEB, *Bulletin* (1929) no. 3A, p. 12, HMCR; Abraham to Darling, 26 March 1930; Ardell to Darling, 15 November 1929; Darling to Abraham, 3 April 1930; GGSC, Meeting 13 May 1929, Minutes, pp. 122–3, 10 June 1929, p. 132, 11 November 1929, p. 163, all GGSA.

4   *RR*, pp. 103–7; Temple to Darling, 30 May 1929, 12 July 1929, 29 July 1929; Derry to Darling, undated, all DP; GGSC, Meeting, 12 August 1929, Minutes, p. 140, Meeting, 9 September 1929, Minutes, pp. 147–8; 'Qualifications and conditions in connection with the headmastership', Meeting, 11 November 1929, Minutes, insert between pp. 165–6; Fisher to Darling, 14 September 1929, all GGSA; Darling to Phelps, 11 September 1929, PP.

5   Rendall to Darling, 22 July 1930, GGSA; *RR*, pp. 106–7; Ainsworth to Darling, 17 September 1929; Temple to Darling, 17 September 1929, both DP; Darling to Phelps, 19 September 1929, PP.

6   le Fleming to Darling, 21 September 1929; Ainsworth to Darling, 20 September 1929; Fyfe to Darling, 11 October 1929; A.M. Darling to J.R. Darling, 20 September 1929, all DP.

7   GGSC, Meeting, 11 November 1929, Minutes, p. 163, 9 December 1929, p. 168, both GGSA; K. Mackinnon to D. Mackinnon, 31 October 1929, MP; *Argus*, 21 November 1929; Rendall to Darling, 12 November 1929; A.M. Darling to J.R. Darling, undated, both DP; Andrew, Diary, 19 November 1929, AP.

8   Fisher to Darling, 15 November 1929; Phelps to Darling, 14 November 1929; Fyfe to Darling, 14 November 1929, 26 November 1929; Bickersteth to Darling, 23 November 1929; Turner to Darling, 31 December 1929, all DP; *Carthusian*, 1930 (February), p. 146, CSA; *Surrey Weekly Press*, 11 October 1929, 22 November 1929; Galbraith (1963), p. 25; Schedvin (1970), pp. 117, 118, 128–9.

9   Renwick to Darling, 29 November 1929; Butler-Wright to Darling, 23 December 1929; M.R. Darling to J.R. Darling, 29 September 1930; Wharton to J.B. Darling, 10 January 1930; Forder to Darling, 29 January 1931, all DP; A.M. Darling to Phelps, 1 May 1930, PP.

10 J.R. Darling to J.B. Darling, 12 January 1930, 14 January 1930, 22 January 1930; Scott to Darling, 5 October 1929, 4 December 1929; Pilcher to Darling, 16 November 1929; Nimmo to Darling, 14 November 1929, all DP.

11 *RR*, p. 111; Sir James Darling to the author, 18 September 1992; J.R. Darling to J.B. Darling, 22 January 1930, 1 February 1930, 7 February 1930, all DP; Darling to Goyder, 24 May 1930, GGSA.

12 Darling (1969), pp. 1–2; J.R. Darling to J.B. Darling, 10 February 1930, DP; McInnes (1967), p. 67; Bean (1950), p. 95; Andrew, Diary, 20 September 1930, AP; Sellar to Phelps, 28 January 1930, PP.

13 J.R. Darling to J.B. Darling, 28 May 1930, 15 March 1930, 9 April 1930, 21 May 1930, all DP.

14 J.R. Darling to J.B. Darling, 24 March 1930, 1 May 1930, 25 June 1930; Hammond to J.B. Darling, 27 June 1930; J.R. Darling to J.B. Darling, 28 May 1930, 10 February 1930, 13 May 1930, 31 March 1930, 8 May 1930, 19 May 1930, undated, all DP.

15 Derry to Darling, 29 December 1929; J.R. Darling to J.B. Darling, 10 February
    1930, both DP; 'Staff 1930. Confidential', GGSA; Jennings to J.B. Darling, 24 April
    1930; J.B. Darling to J.R. Darling, 4 June 1930; J.R. Darling to J.B. Darling, 20
    February 1930, all DP; Sir James Darling to the author, 19 October 1984.

16 H.D. Steward, to the author, 20 March 1985; M. Thwaites to the author, 23 May
    1985; H.B. Gullett to the author, 24 May 1985; S. Baker to Gronn, 17 July 1985;
    J.R. Darling to J.B. Darling, 15 March 1930, 15 April 1930, both DP.

17 J.R. Darling to J.B. Darling, 15 April 1930, 24 March 1930, 10 June 1930, 1 May
    1930, 20 February 1930, 24 February 1930, 15 March 1930, 1 May 1930, all DP.

18 Croll to Darling, 3 March 1930, 5 April 1930; Seitz to Darling, 4 April 1930, all
    GGSA; Certificate of Registration, no. 11936, 29 April 1930, VPRO; Darling to
    Hansen, 24 March 1930; Croll to Hansen, undated, both GGSA.

19 Wrigley to Hansen, 10 April 1930; Hansen to Darling, 15 April 1930; Darling to
    Hansen, 2 May 1930, all GGSA.

20 Darling to Hansen, 2 May 1930; Hansen to Darling, 26 May 1930, 16 June 1930;
    Darling to Wrigley, 4 June 1930, all GGSA.

21 Stephen to Darling, 17 March 1930; Darling to Stephen, 20 March 1930, both
    GGSA.

22 Darling to Stephen, 20 March 1930, GGSA; J.R. Darling to J.B. Darling,
    20 February 1930, 24 February 1930, 4 March 1930, all DP; Jermyn to Gronn,
    14 April 1989; McCulloch to Darling, 2 July 1954, GGSA; J.R. Darling to J.B.
    Darling, 1 July 1930, 9 July 1930, both DP.

23 J.R. Darling to J.B. Darling, 12 January 1929, 20 February 1930; Darling to Wells,
    25 February 1930; Scott to Darling, 30 June 1930; J.R. Darling to J.B. Darling,
    25 June 1930; A.E. Darling to J.R. Darling, 30 June 1930; Wharton to Darling,
    29 October 1930; Fyfe to Darling, 14 November 1929; J.B. Darling to J.R. Darling,
    16 July 1930, all DP.

24 Kiddle (1961), pp. 480, 483; Best to Darling, 17 December 1929; Gullett to
    Darling, undated, both DP; H.B. Gullett to the author, 24 May 1985; K. Officer,
    Diary, 19 May 1931, OP, ms2629/2/13, NLA.

25 Sir James Darling to the author, 7 December 1984, 15 November 1984,
    20 December 1985; Marchant to Darling, 2 September 1930; Duffield to Darling,
    25 April 1930, both DP; Mackinnon to Austin, 7 January 1930, GGSA.

26 Love (1982), p. 274; Darling to Phelps, 8 September 1930, PP; Bernays to Darling,
    undated; Scott to Darling, 12 October 1931; Phelps to A.M. Darling, 25 June 1922,
    all DP.

27 J.R. Darling to J.B. Darling, 22 December 1930; Bernays to Darling, 27 May 1931;
    Scott to Darling, 7 July 1930; J.B. Darling to J.R. Darling, 18 February 1931,
    27 April 1931, 8 April 1931, all DP.

28 J.B. Darling to J.R. Darling, 4 March 1930, 4 June 1930, 17 December 1930,
    21 January 1931, 11 June 1930, 13 May 1931, all DP.

29 J.B. Darling to J.R. Darling, 4 June 1930, 17 December 1930, 19 November 1930;
    M.R. Darling to J.R. Darling, 29 September 1930; J.B. Darling to J.R. Darling,
    17 September 1930, all DP; Phelps to Darling, 3 April 1930, PP; Brown to Darling,
    2 October 1930, DP.

30 *RR*, pp. 111, 119, 120; Darling to Maudesley, 16 April 1930, GGSA; M. Thwaites
to the author, 23 May 1985; Darling to Bickersteth, 29 September 1930; Darling to
Casey, 5 November 1930; Casey to Darling, 15 November 1930, all GGSA.

31 Darling to Murdoch, 14 October 1930; Guthrie to Darling, 10 June 1930, both
GGSA.

32 Darling to Franklin, 10 November 1930, GGSA; C.M.H. Clark to the author,
23 May 1985; Franklin to Darling, 10 November 1930, GGSA.

33 Dicker to Darling, 1 September 1930; A.E. Darling to J.R. Darling, 7 January
1931[?]; A.M. Darling to J.R. Darling, undated; J.R. Darling to J.B. Darling,
22 December 1930; J.B. Darling to J.R. Darling, 11 February 1931, all DP; H.D.
Steward to the author, 20 March 1985; Headmaster's report, 18 February 1930,
GGSA; Mackinnon to Darling, 12 April 1930, 22 September 1930, 17 December
1930; Darling to Rendall, 17 December 1930, all DP.

9 Renaissance

1 *Corian*, 1932 (December), p. 164; Priestley, *Australian Diary*, vol. 2, 18 March 1935,
p. 77, UMA; calculations derived from GGS Admission Books, vols 7–9, GGSA.

2 Darling to Browne, 10 October 1934, GGSA; Darling to Cunningham, 12
December 1938, CCF, series 22, vol 10 (Mar 1938–Sept 1939), A–L, ACER;
Cunningham, Testimonial for J.R. Darling, 1939, DP; Kandel (1938), p. 77.

3 Darling to Curthoys, 23 March 1937, 11 February 1937; Curthoys to Darling,
8 August 1937, all GGSA.

4 Sir James Darling to the author, 7 December 1984; Franklin to Darling, 24 July
1936, GGSA; Gullett to Gullett, undated, H–GP, ms 3078, 5/676, NLA; McKie
to Darling, 20 December 1936; Darling to Whiskard, 10 November 1936; Buck to
Darling, 7 June 1937, all GGSA.

5 *Corian*, 1930 (December), pp. 183, 92, 93; Waddy (1981), p. 162; M.R. Darling
to J.B. Darling, 8 February 1933; Brown to Darling, 17 January 1934; Parkinson
to Darling, 24 March 1933; Fyfe to Darling, 30 October 1931, all DP; Darling to
Parkinson, 25 February 1934, GGSA.

6 M. Masterman to the author, 23 May 1985; Andrew, Diary, 20 September 1930,
AP; GGSC, Meeting, 13 May 1929, Minutes, p. 122, GGSA; Carolan (1974),
pp. 105, 33, 45, 65, 97–8; B. Jones 'An austere but saintly headmaster', *Corian*, 1974
(April), p. 286; M. Thwaites to the author, 23 March 1985.

7 J.R. Darling to J.B. Darling, 27 April 1931, DP; Carolan (1974), pp. 115, 122–7;
Masterman to Andrew, 28 January 1980, AP; Sir John Gorton to the author,
22 May 1985; R.R. Andrew to the author, 22 February 1989; B. Jones to the author,
31 October 1983; O.M. Connellen to the author, 14 March 1989.

8 *RR*, pp. 117, 129; Headmaster's report, 18 February 1930, GGSA; *Corian*, 1930
(December), pp. 187–8; Bull to Darling, 20 January 1931; Gorton to Darling,
undated, both DP; G.K. Smith to the author, 24 October 1984.

9 E. Laird to the author, 26 August 1988; GGSC, Meetings, 14 April 1930, 12 May
1930, 14 October 1930, 13 March 1931, Minutes, pp. 191, 197, 229, 249; all
GGSA; Darling to Wadham, 2 October 1930, GGS Box, correspondence 1936–46,
WP, UMA; *Corian*, 1930 (August), pp. 106, 111, 112; Carolan (1974), p. 260, ch. 6.

10 A.E. Darling to J.R. Darling, 1 January 1931, 8 November 1930, both DP; A.M.
Darling to Phelps, 14 March 1933, PP; M.R. Darling to J.B Darling, 13 December

1932, 28 December 1932; Lloyd to Darling, undated; Nimmo to Darling, 9 September 1931; M.R. Darling to J.B. Darling, 14 June 1933, all DP.

11 Darling (1969), pp. 1–2; GGSC, Meeting, 13 July 1931, Minutes, pp. 264, 268 (attachment), GGSA; Darling to Phelps, 23 July 1931, PP.

12 *Corian*, 1943 (May), p. 14; Fairbairn to Darling, 16 March 1931, DP; B.R.A. Coulter to the author, 28 November 1989; R.G. Jennings, 'Teaching what industry means', *Herald*, 27 June 1934; Ward (1985), p. 9; Sir Rupert Hamer to the author, 16 March 1989.

13 GGSC, Meetings, 10 August 1931, 21 September 1931, Austin to Cameron, 22 September 1931 (attachment), 'Salaries and wages', 8 December 1931; 2 February 1932, Minutes, pp. 271–2, 279, 278, 1, 58, 64; Darling to Mackinnon, 28 August 1931, 8 March 1932, all GGSA.

14 Darling to Mackinnon, 8 March 1932; Darling to Head, 12 April 1932, both GGSA.

15 Mackinnon to Darling, 12 March 1932; Darling to Mackinnon, 15 March 1932, both GGSA; Mackinnon to Darling, 17 March 1932, DP; GGSC, Meeting, 11 April 1932, Minutes, insert at p. 73, GGSA.

16 Darling to Mackinnon, 8 March 1932, GGSA; *Union Trustee Company of Australia v. Whittingham and Others*, (1933) *QSR*, pp. 267–76, 280, 276; GGSC, Meetings, 18 September 1933, 8 February 1937, Minutes, pp. 158–9, 326–7, GGSA; *Austin and Others v. Union Trustee Company of Australia Limited and Others* (1934), 51 *CLR*, pp. 325–6.

17 GGSC, Meetings, 2 May 1932, Minutes, p. 79; Manifold to Darling, 20 July 1932, both GGSA; Bell to Darling, 17 May 1932; Manifold to Darling, 16 March 1933, both DP; Darling to Manifold, 5 June 1932, 11 August 1932; GGSC, Meetings, 13 June 1932, 11 July 1932, Minutes, pp. 82, 88, all GGSA

18 Manifold to Darling, 13 August 1932, DP; Darling to Manifold, 12 August 1932; both GGSA.

19 Manifold to Darling, 13 August 1932, DP.

20 M.R. Darling to J.B. Darling, 24 August 1932, DP; Dicker to Darling, 30 October 1932, GGSA; Schedvin (1970), pp. 288, 291; Darling to Jennings, 4 October 1932; Darling to Fairbairn, 11 October 1932, both GGSA; M.R. Darling to J.B. Darling, 16 November 1932, DP; GGSC, Meeting, 14 November 1932, Minutes, p. 108; Manifold to Darling, 23 October 1932, both GGSA; Brown to Darling, 20 October 1932; Dicker to Darling, 12 December 1932, both DP.

21 Manifold to Darling, 1 October 1932; Darling to Manifold, 29 September 1932, 28 July 1932; Report to Geelong Church of England Preparatory School, 12 May 1930; GGSC, Meetings, 13 March 1933, 6 February 1933, Minutes, pp. 122, 119, all GGSA.

22 GGSC, Meeting, 3 March 1933, Minutes, p. 125; Darling to Manifold, 8 December 1932, both GGSA; Wharton to Phelps, 3 December 1932, PP; M.R. Darling to J.B. Darling, 26 January 1933, 8 February 1933, 24 August 1932, all DP; V.J.H. Tunbridge to the author, 25 February 1985; Landale to Darling, undated; Lloyd to Darling, 13 March 1934, both DP.

23 M.R. Darling to J.B. Darling, 8 February 1932, 9 May 1933, both DP; Manifold to Darling, 25 April 1933; Darling to Turnbull, 25 April 1933, 21 June 1933; GGSC,

Meetings, 8 May 1933, 5 June 1933, Minutes, pp. 135–6, 141; Pownall to Turnbull, 14 June 1933; Turnbull to Thewlis, 15 June 1933; all GGSA.

24　M.R. Darling to J.B. Darling, 21 June 1933, DP; Turnbull to Darling, 5 July 1933; Report to council, 28 June 1933; Darling to Austin, 11 July 1933; ? to the AMP Society, 18 July 1933, all GGSA.

25　Manifold to Darling, 20 July 1932; GGSC, Meetings, 24 July 1933, 14 August 1933, 18 September 1933, Minutes, pp. 151, 152 (attachment), 158–9; Circulated letter, August 1933, GGSA; R.H. Deasey to the author, 14 March 1989; Darling to Bickersteth, 24 August 1933; Bickersteth to Darling, 29 August 1933, both GGSA.

26　O.M. Connellen to the author, 14 March 1989; J.R. Darling to J.B. Darling, 11 October 1933; Brown to Darling, 17 January 1934, both DP; Parkin (1900), pp. 75–6, 70.

27　*Corian*, 1931 (May), p. 6, (December), p. 175; 1932 (August), pp. 94–5; Report to council, December 1931, p. 2; Franklin to Darling, 15 June 1933, both GGSA; *Corian*, 1933 (December), p. 193; 1934 (December), p. 189.

28　Parkin (1900), p. 73; *RR*, p. 121; Bernays to Darling, undated, DP; J.S. Guest to the author, 16 March 1989; Keith to Darling, 27 September 1930; Hughes to Darling, undated, DP; H.D. Steward to the author, 20 March 1985.

29　Parker to Darling, 22 December 1930; Stuart to Darling, 5 March 1931, 11 May 1931; Thwaites to Darling, 20 December 1933, all DP; M. Thwaites to the author, 23 May 1985; Gullett to Gullett, undated (two); Gullett to Gullett, undated, H–GP, ms 3078 5/702 (1st), 4/138 (2nd) and 4/87 (3rd), all NLA.

30　R.H. Deasey to the author, 14 March 1989; J.S. Guest to the author, 16 March 1989; M. Thwaites to the author, 23 May 1985; Gullett to Gullett, undated, H–GP, ms 3078/4/129, NLA; Lloyd to J.R. Darling, 19 May 1936, DP; Gullett to Gullett, 23 April [1933], 31 March 1933, H–GP, ms 3078 4/96 and 4/50–2, all NLA.

31　G.C.W. Dicker, Memoirs, undated, unnumbered, DiP; M. Thwaites to the author, 23 May 1985; H.D. Steward to the author, 20 March 1985; Darling to Manifold, 6 December 1933, 3 October 1933, both GGSA; Brown to Darling, undated; Lloyd to Darling, undated, both DP; Darling to Colman, 30 October 1932; Report to council, December 1931, p. 2, both GGSA.

32　Temple to Darling, 27 June 1931, DP; 'Bickersteth's notes', undated, GGSA; Darling to Dicker, 6 April 1932, DiP; Bull to Darling 3 February 1931, DP; Sir Rupert Hamer to the author, 16 March 1989; McKie to Darling, 14 September 1934, DP; Bull to Darling, 8 March 1934, GGSA; Dicker, Memoirs, DiP; Fletcher to Darling, undated, 8 August 1935; Marchant to Darling, 5 December [1933], all DP.

33　Keenlyside to Darling, undated; Keith to Darling, 6 May 1931; Brown to Darling, 16 June 1931; Parker to Darling, undated, all DP. *Corian*, 1931 (December), pp. 196–7; Report to council, December 1931, p. 2, GGSA; *Times Educational Supplement*, 27 February 1932, p. 71; M. Thwaites to the author, 23 May 1985; Brown to Darling, 2 December 1931, DP; Dicker, *Memoirs*, DiP.

34　Darling (1933b), pp. 8, 13; J.R. Darling to J.B. Darling, 11 October 1933 (attachment); Brown to Darling, 3 February 1931, both DP; Jones to Darling, 12 October 1933, GGSA; Darling (1931) p. 29; Lloyd to Darling, 19 May 1936, DP.

10 Paterfamilias of Corio

1 *Corian*, 1934 (May), pp. 36–9; Dicker, Memoirs, DiP; Crystal to Darling,
15 February 1934, DP; Sir James Darling to the author, 7 December 1984; J.R.
Darling to J.B. Darling, 6 March 1934; Macarthur-Onslow to J.B. Darling,
10 March 1934, both DP.

2 *RR*, p. 135; J.R. Darling to J.B. Darling, 6 March 1934; Thwaites to Darling,
20 August 1934, both DP; J. Manifold 'Stowe, Charterhouse & Oundle', undated,
p. 2, WP, UMA; Manifold to Darling, 7 December 1933, GGSA; Darling to
Dicker, 6 July 1934, DiP; Darling to Bloomfield, 22 December 1934, GGSA;
Lawrence Neal to the author, 17 April 1988; Leach to Darling, 28 April 1934,
20 July 1934; Hawden to Darling, 19 August 1934, all DP.

3 Leach to Darling, 6 May 1934, undated, 12 June 1934; Lloyd to Darling, 4 July
1934[?]; Thwaites to Darling, 20 August 1934; McKie to Darling, 14 September
1934; Dicker to Darling, 12 August 1934, all DP.

4 Manifold to Darling, 1 August 1934; J.R. Darling to J.B. Darling, 25 August 1934;
'Recollections of my father', p. 9; Bickersteth to J.B. Darling, 26 August 1934;
Thorndike to J.R. and M.D. Darling, 24 June 1970; Thorndike to Darling, undated,
all DP; Darling to Cunningham, 12 December 1934, GGSA.

5 J.R. Darling to J.B. Darling, 29 August 1934, 6 March 1934, 16 June 1932; Findlay
to J.B. Darling, 25 November [1934]; Lake to Darling, 31 December 1934;
Manifold to Darling, 1 October 1934, all DP.

6 Brett to Darling, 9 June 1932; Darling to Brett, 22 June 1932, both GGSA; M.R.
Darling to J.B. Darling, 21 June 1933, 2 May 1933; J.R. Darling to M.R. Darling,
25 August 1934; J.R. Darling to J.B. Darling, 25 October 1934, 17 October 1934;
J.R. Darling to M.R. Darling, 1 November 1934; Medley to Darling, 6 November
1934; Gullett to Darling, 1 November 1934; Fyfe to Darling, 12 January 1935;
Temple to Darling, 24 December 1934, all DP.

7 Darling to Dicker, 6 July 1934, DiP; Darling (1935a), pp. 324, 331, 336.

8 Darling (1934), pp. 42–3; *Corian*, 1934 (December), pp. 196, 199; 1935
(December), p. 219.

9 Whately to Darling, 18 December 1934; Fink to Darling, 18 December 1934;
Shann to Darling, 19 December 1934; Coutts to Darling, 17 December 1934;
Parkinson to Darling, 27 February 1935, all GGSA; Landale to Darling,
17 February 1935, DP; Browne to Darling, 27 February 1935, GGSA;
Cunningham (1936), p. 642; Kandel to Darling, 21 March 1935, GGSA.

10 Dicker to Darling, 13 December 1934, DP; Darling to Manifold, 6 February
1935; Morris to Darling, 10 February 1935, 23 February 1935; Darling to Morris,
17 February 1935, all GGSA.

11 Board of Education, Melbourne Diocese (1933) *A list of Schools under the aegis of
the Church of England in the Province of Victoria* (Melbourne), GGSA; *Census of
the Commonwealth of Australia* (30 June 1933), vol 2, part xxvii, Income, Table 1,
p. 1908; Admission books 7–9, GGSA; Gronn (1992); *Census* (1933), vol 2, part xvi,
Religion, Table 3, p. 1022; *Census* (1933), Statistician's Report, p. 153; Rubinstein
(1979), pp. 32, 35; M.R. Darling to J.B. Darling, 16 November 1932, DP.

12 Cowen to Darling, 30 August 1977, DP; Darling to Manifold, 14 February 1935,
21 February 1935; Manifold to Darling, 16 February 1935, 23 February 1935;

Darling to Head, 22 February 1935; GGSC, Meeting, 11 March 1935, Minutes, p. 229, all GGSA.

13   Browne to Darling, 27 October 1936; West to Darling, 13 October 1936, both GGSA; *Corian*, 1935 (December), pp. 215–16, 217–18; 1936 (December), pp. 198–201; Darling to Browne, 23 November 1936, GGSA.

14   Giblin to Giblin, 4 April 1935, GP, ms 366, 1/724, NLA; Leach to Darling, 12 June 1934, 6 July 1934, DP; A.J.M. Davies' Geelong Grammar School' and C.J. Horne 'Observations at Geelong Grammar School', enclosures in Browne to Cameron, 6 August 1934, GGSA.

15   Whately to Darling, 20 December 1935, 20 June 1938, both GGSA; Darling to Ritchie, 22 November 1932, both DP; Darling (1935a), pp. 325–26; GGSC, Meeting, 12 July 1937, Minutes, p. 346, GGSA; Whately (1937), p. 18; Letter to parents, 23 November 1938; H.St.J.M.B. Gullett, Record card, both GGSA.

16   Darling to Medley, 18 February 1935, GGSA; Andrew, Diary, 1 December 1929, AP; Medley to Darling, 23 February 1935; Darling to Medley, 7 March 1935, both GGSA.

17   J.R. Darling to J.B. Darling, 27 February 1935, DP; Darling to Manifold, 21 February 1935; Manifold to Darling, 23 February 1935, both GGSA; Leach to Darling, 11 March 1935; Kagawa to Darling, 30 September 1935; J.R. Darling to J.B. Darling, 8 May 1935, all DP; Priestley, Australian Diary, vol. 2, 30 April 1935, p. 181, UMA.

18   *Corian*, 1935 (August), pp. 103–6; GGSC, Meeting, 10 February 1936, Minutes, p. 276; 'Statement of proposed new expenditure' (5 March 1936), both GGSA; J.R. Darling to J.B. Darling, 19 February 1936, DP; GGSC, Meetings, 24 April 1936, 20 July 1936, Minutes, pp. 286, 297, both GGSA.

19   GGSC, Meetings, 20 July 1936, 8 March 1937, 10 May 1937, Minutes, pp. 296, 298, 335, 338, all GGSA; *Corian*, 1936 (December), pp. 208–9; 1937 (December), p. 196; 1938 (August), p. 136; Curthoys to Darling, 4 May 1937, GGSA; *Argus*, 8 May 1937; Bell to Fairbairn, 10 May 1937, GGSA.

20   Darling to Johnstone, 21 October 1937; Johnstone to Darling, 12 October 1937, both GGSA; Priestley, Australian Diary, vol. 10, 10 December 1937, p. 121; vol. 2, 2 March 1935, p. 20; vol. 9, 3 August 1937, p. 77, all UMA.

21   Memorandum to the council of Geelong Grammar School with reference to the future of day boys in the school, 1930, GGSA; Hawker to Darling, 12 September 1933, DP; Darling to Eldershaw, 21 September 1935; Admission books 7–9, GGSA; Gronn (1992); Bickersteth to Darling, 18 January 1937, DP; Giblin to Giblin, 2 October 1937, GP, ms366 1/864, NLA; Fletcher to Darling, 27 April 1937, DP; Priestley, Australian Diary, vol. 10, 28 October 1937, p. 82, UMA; Darling to Stephen, 10 June 1932; Darling to Hutchison, 26 February 1936, both GGSA.

22   Morris to Darling, 26 November 1930; Dickinson to Darling, 16 August 1935; Darling to Dickinson, 19 August 1935, all GGSA.

23   Darling (1938), pp. 79–80; Gronn (1992); *Corian*, 1931 (December), pp. 175, 176; 1932 (December), p. 162; Darling to Sanderson, 6 April 1933, GGSA; Encel (1955), p. 33; Caiden (1965), pp. 3, 25, 244, 245, 257, 258, 155.

24   Scarrow (1965), pp. 39–42, 135–6; J.R. Darling to J.B. Darling, 8 June 1932, DP; Hughes to Head, 21 May 1936; Head to Darling, 21 May 1936, 15 June 1936;

Darling to Head, 3 June 1936, 16 July 1936, all GGSA; Sir James Darling to the author, 14 July 1989; Act no. 38 of 1933, sec 2(2).

25 J.R. Darling to Kent Hughes, 26 June 1936; Browne to Darling, 13 July 1936; Darling to Browne, 14 July 1936, all GGSA; *Corian*, 1938 (December), p. 215; Copland to Darling, 15 November 1938; Darling to Copland, 18 November 1938, both GGSA; *RR*, p. 156; Wells (1939), pp. 49–50.

26 *Corian*, 1939 (December), p. 205; Darling to Jones, 13 August 1941, GGSA; Giblin to Darling, 6 August 1939, DP.

27 Curthoys to Darling, 6 March 1937, 13 March 1937, 22 March 1937; Darling to the Advertising Manager, *Sydney Mail*, 21 November 1934; Darling to Curthoys, 23 March 1937, all GGSA; 'Alpha and Omega—An Australian play', *Times Education Supplement*, 9 January 1937; *Corian*, 1937 (December), p. 199; O.M. Connellan to the author, 14 March 1989; *Corian*, 1938 (December), p. 239.

28 *Corian*, 1937 (December), p. 194; 1938 (May), pp. 20–5; Darling to Curthoys, 16 April 1937; Curthoys to Darling, 25 April 1937, 9 May 1938; Darling to Tate, 13 April 1938; all GGSA; Priestley, Australian Diary, vol. 9, 7–9 May 1938, UMA.

29 Priestley, Australian Diary, vol. 1, 4–6 May 1935, p. 2; vol. 3, 6–8 July 1935, p. 3; vol. 6, 21 November 1936, p. 96, all UMA; Giblin to Giblin, 17 July 1935, GP, ms 366, 1/799, NLA.

30 Carslaw to Darling, 26 May 1936; Pentreath to Darling, 13 July 1936; Archer to Darling, 15 November 1935; Roff to Darling, 29 October 1937; Collinson to Darling, 24 October 1934; Bailey to Darling, 5 February 1936, all GGSA.

31 Priestley, Australian Diary, vol. 3, 26 September 1935, UMA; Darling (1935b), p. 1, DP; *Corian*, 1936 (December), p. 201; Darling to Lansell Clarke, 19 October 1938; Darling to Hume, 13 April 1938; Darling to Gillespie, 7 December 1938, all GGSA; Ward (1985), p. 7.

32 Head to Darling, 25 January 1939, GGSA; *Argus*, 9 July 1938; Darling to Browning, 27 April 1937, GGSA; Darling (1935b), pp. 6, 11; W.F. Connell to the author, 27 April 1984.

33 Darling to Head, 26 April 1937; Manifold to Darling, 10 May 1937; Darling to Bloomfield, 2 November 1937; Gullett to Darling, undated, all GGSA; Wood to Darling, undated; Hamer to Darling, 24 November 1938; Lloyd to Darling, 12 September 1935, all DP.

34 Bernays to Darling, 29 May 1931; J.R. Darling to J.B. Darling, 25 October 1934, both DP; Sir Rupert Hamer to the author, 16 March 1989; Leach to Darling, 25 September 1935, GGSA; Sir James and Lady Darling to the author, 19 September 1992; 'Golden wedding', 21 August 1985, DP, ms 7826, s9, b24, f5, NLA.

35 M.D. Darling to J.B. Darling, 23 March 1937, DP; Darling to Cunningham, 10 September 1937, CCF vol. 92, s37, ACERA; Kandel (1938), p. 7; I.L. Kandel (1937) 'Report on Geelong Church of England Grammar School, Corio' (October), pp. 3–6, 7–9; Head to Darling, 12 November 1937, both GGSA.

11 Conscience of the comfortable classes

1 E. Laird to the author, 26 August 1988; Fidge to Darling, 6 December 1937, GGSA.

2 J.R. Darling to J.B. Darling, 22 June 1932, DP; *Corian*, 1930 (August), p. 109; Bickersteth to Darling, 16 April 1931, GGSA; Hogg (1986), pp. 7–10; HMCA, Meetings, 18 May 1933, 21–22 December 1931, 17 May 1933, Minutes, pp. 26,

6–11, 10; Standing committee meeting, 6–7 September 1932, Minutes, pp. 16–17, all AHISAA.

3   Altschwager (1985), pp. 6–7; TH, State executive committee meetings, 21 October 1930, 15 December 1934, Minutes, pp. 96, 296, THR; Darling to Fear, 24 October 1933; Baldwin to Darling, 30 April 1935; Darling to Baldwin, 8 May 1935, 20 August 1930, all GGSA; Holbrook (1987a), p. 185; Giles to Darling, 7 May 1931, GGSA.

4   UBC, 'Report on activities since inauguration', 21 December 1932; draft jubilee press release, undated; draft constitution, undated, all BEMR; M.R. Darling to J.B. Darling, 24 August 1932, 21 September 1932, 5 October 1932; Darling to Manifold, 29 September 1932, all DP; Holbrook (1987b) pp. 50–76; Darling to Murray, 23 April 1981, BEMR; *Corian*, 1932 (December), pp. 196, 161–2.

5   UBC, Sketch plan, undated, DP; Committee reports, 8 November 1932, 22 November 1932, 20 December 1932, 31 January 1933, 7 February 1933, 11 April 1933; 'Report of activities', 17 May 1933; Annual Report, September, 1932–September, 1933, p. 1, all BEMR; 'Geelong Boys' Employment Centre', 16 December 1943, p. 3, DP.

6   *Corian*, 1932 (December), pp. 2–3; Giles to Flinn, 18 November 1933; UBC, Business manager's report, 18 December 1933, p. 2; Annual Report, 15 September 1934, p. 2, all BEMR; 'Regarding Mr. R.W. Curtis', 2 August 1937, DP.

7   Eagar and Secretan (1925), pp. 65, 100, 105, 106.

8   UBC, Committee of management, 2 March 1936, 4 February 1935, 13 November 1933, 17 October 1935, 4 March 1935, Minutes, pp. 60, 39, 12, 53, 41, all BEMR; Casey to Darling, 26 January 1933, DP; Casey to Flinn, 11 February 1935; Second annual report, 15 September 1934, pp. 3 & 7, both BEMR; *Corian*, 1935 (August), p. 119; Giblin to Giblin, 17 July 1935, 31 July 1935, both GP, ms 366, 1/796 and 1/812–813, NLA; 'Geelong Boys' Employment Centre', undated, p. 3, DP; UBC, Superintendent's report, 4 July 1933, p .4; Business manager's report, 9 April 1934, p. 1, both BEMR; Curtis to Darling, 11 September 1937, GGSA; UBC, Annual Report, 30 September 1937, p. 5, BEMR; Darling to Ebbs, 11 August 1936, GGSA.

9   Alomes (1979); Darling to Menzies, 10 April 1947; 'Geelong Boys' Employment Centre', 16 December 1943, p. 2; Darling to Stretton, 25 May 1942, all DP; UBC, Committee of management, 6 June 1933, 4 February 1935, 21 February 1933, Minutes, pp. 3, 39, all BEMR; Day to Darling, 16 March 1933; Darling to Day, 21 March 1933, both GGSA; UBC, Business manager's report, 3 December 1934, BEMR.

10 Marwick (1964), p. 297; Darling to Brett, 22 June 1932, 29 May 1933, both GGSA; M.R. Darling to J.B. Darling, 28 September 1931; Darling to Rolland, 27 June 1933, Darling to Hyslop, 12 July 1935, Hyslop to Darling, 15 July 1935, 3 September 1936, all DP.

11 Darling to Curthoys, 30 April 1937, GGSA; Sir James Darling to the author, 16 October 1991; Darling to Burgmann, 27 November 1937; Darling to Anderson, 28 June 1933; Darling to Hammond, 9 November 1933, all GGSA; *ADB*, 11, p. 25; '1932 from Miss Brett', marginalia on Fitzroy University Social Settlement, pamphlet, 1924[?], GGSA.

12 Darling to Colman, 3 August 1937, 5 August 1937; Curthoys to Darling, 26 July 1937; Fairbairn to Darling, 6 February 1935, all GGSA; 'Our Task—Mr. Darling's View—Social Reform', *Argus*, 10 June 1937; Darling to Malan, 15 June 1937, GGSA.

13 Phillips (1988–89); U'Ren and Turnbull (1983) pp. 236, 246; Barnett to Darling, 27 July 1937, GGSA; *Corian*, 1936 (August), p. 112; Russell (1972), pp. 27–8.

14 Hyslop to Darling, 24 February 1938, 18 February 1938, both DP; Darling to Taylor, 27 June 1938, GGSA; Darling to Ward, 1 March 1938, DP; Darling to Stewart, 23 June 1938, GGSA; Taylor to Darling, 18 March 1938, Darling to Taylor, 23 March 1938, both DP; Taylor to Darling, 20 May 1938, GGSA.

15 Baxter to Darling, 20 July 1938 (and attachment: Bracey to Nicholas, 5 July 1938); Hyslop to Darling, 30 July 1938, both DP; APS, 'Notes of conference on boys' clubs', 28 July 1938; Meeting, 1 August 1938, Minutes; 'Report of the committee members on boys' clubs', 5 August 1938; Darling to Stewart, 25 July 1938; Hyslop to Darling, 2 August 1938, all DP.

16 Darling to Baxter, 19 July 1938, 22 July 1938; Taylor to Darling, 16 September 1938, 21 October 1938; Darling to Taylor, 25 October 1938; Hyslop to Darling, 7 November 1938; J.R. Darling to chairman of the Housing Commission, 25 November 1938, all DP; *Argus*, 29 November 1938; *Corian*, 1938 (December), p. 216.

17 Hyslop to Darling, 23 November 1938; Rolland to Darling, 29 November 1939; Sutcliffe to Darling, 5 December 1938; McNaughton to Darling, 30 November 1938; Officer to Darling, 2 December 1938; a'Beckett to Darling, 2 December 1938; Darling to McNaughton, 7 December 1938; Barnett to Darling, 9 December 1938; APS, 'Report for the headmasters on preliminary work in connection with proposed community centre', all DP; *Corian*, 1938 (December), p. 236; Darling to Bracey, 27 February 1939, DP.

18 Badcock (1964), pp. 184–7; *Melbourne University Calendar, 1932*, pp. 240–2; Darling (1969), pp. 6–7.

19 Darling (1969), pp. 5–7; Musgrave (1992), pp. 108–9; Darling to Wrigley, 18 April 1932; Wrigley to Darling, 20 April 1932, both GGSA; SB, Meeting, 21 July 1932, Minutes, p. 392, UMA; Darling to Carslaw, 3 August 1933; Darling to Manifold, 28 July 1932; Manifold to Darling, 1 August 1932, all GGSA.

20 Darling (1933a), pp. 13, 17; M.R. Darling to J.B. Darling, 14 January 1933, DP; Osborne to Darling, 31 January 1933; Darling to Browne, 16 March 1934, both GGSA; Priestley, Australian Diary, vol. 3, 6–8 July, 1935, UMA; Dicker, Memoirs, DiP.

21 SB, Meetings, 16 March 1933, 19 July 1934, Minutes, pp. 409, 466, both UMA; Franklin to Darling, 15 June 1933, GGSA; Priestley, Australian Diary, vol. 2, 1 May 1935, p. 185; SB, Meeting, 18 July 1935, Minutes, p. 13, UMA; HMCA, Meeting, 17 May 1933, Standing committee meeting, 21 December 1934, Minutes, pp. 17, 2, both AHISAA; Browne to Darling, 13 October 1934, 15 May 1938, both GGSA.

22 Wallace to Copland, 15 June, 1936; Darling to Copland, 22 June 1936, 12 June 1936; Browne to Darling, 19 June 1936, all GGSA; HMCA, Meeting, 20 May 1936, Minutes, pp. 14–26, AHISAA; SB, Meetings, 19 August 1936, 30 September 1936, 12 November 1936, Minutes, pp. 64, 68, 74–5, all UMA.

23 Darling to Browne, 10 November 1936, 12 November 1936; Darling to Wadham, 10 November 1936; Darling to Priestley, 10 November 1936; Wadham to Darling, 23 November 1936, all GGSA; SB, Meetings, 11 March 1937, 12 August 1937, Minutes, pp. 81–3, 119–23, both UMA; CPE, Meeting, 13 April 1937, Minutes, p. 351, EDV.

24 Priestley, Australian Diary, vol. 8, 1 April 1937, p. 1; SB, Meetings, 8 April 1937, 8 July 1937, 14 October 1937, Minutes, pp. 92, 110, 132, 133, 130; all UMA; Darling to Roff, 25 October 1937; Darling to Walker, 21 October 1937; Darling to Kandel, 27 October 1937, all GGSA.

25 HMCA, Standing committee, Meeting, 20 December 1937, Minutes, p. 5, AHISAA; Priestley, Australian Diary, vol. 4, 18 January 1936; vol. 10, 6–7 December 1937, p. 129a; SB, Meetings, 11 August 1938, 16 July 1938, Minutes, pp. 181, 188, 173, all UMA.

26 SB, Meeting, 8 December 1938, Minutes, p. 202, UMA; Darling to Browne, 8 December 1938, 1 March 1939, both GGSA.

27 Darling to Browne, 8 November 1935, GGSA; UMC, Meetings, 31 October 1933, 11 November 1935, 6 January 1936, 5 April 1937, Minutes, pp. 286, 84, 284, 368, 369, UMA; Picken to Darling, 23 February 1934; Darling to Picken, 25 February 1934; Darling to Osborn, 25 February 1934, all GGSA; Giblin to Giblin, 14 March 1935, GP, ms 366, 1/714-5, s1, b1, NLA; Priestley, Australian Diary, vol. 1, 17 February 1935, p. 247; vol. 8, 5 April 1937, p. 12, both UMA.

28 UMC, Meetings, 3 May 1937, 6 September 1937, Minutes, pp. 415, 494; Priestley, Australian Diary, vol. 8, 7 April 1935, p. 15; vol. 8, 24–25 August 1937, p. 126; vol. 9, 28 September 1937, p. 41; 29 October 1937, p. 84; 26 November 1937, p. 108, all UMA; Priestley to Darling, 8 July 1937, 8 September 1937, both GGSA; Wadham to Darling, 31 August 1937, WP, GGS box, corresp 1936–46, UMA; Giblin to Giblin, 29 September 1937, 1 November, GP, ms 366, 1/856 and 1/855, both s1, b1, NLA.

29 Priestley, Australian Diary, vol. 11, 26 February 1938, 7 March 1938, 11 March 1938, 12 March 1938, 17 March 1938, pp. 48, 71–2, 85, 86, 109, all UMA; Rivett (1965), p. 166; Medley to Darling, 22 February 1938, GGSA.

30 GGSC, Meeting, 21 March 1938, Minutes, pp. 220–1; Priestley, Australian Diary, vol. 11, 21 March 1938, pp. 111–15, UMA.

31 Barrett to Darling, 22 March 1938, 23 March 1938, 5 April 1938, all GGSA; Rivett (1965), pp. 167, 169; Brookes to Darling, 24 March 1938, GGSA; Priestley, Australian Diary, vol. 11, 22 March 1938, 26 March 1938, 29 March 1938, 4 April 1938, pp. 114, 120, 123, 139, all UMA; Giblin to Giblin, 24 March 1938, GP, ms 366 1/968, NLA; Medley to Darling, 26 March 1938, 23 April 1938; Copland to Darling, 20 May 1938, 27 May 1938, all GGSA; Priestley, Diaries, 3–6 January 1940, p. 126, UBA.

32 Norwood (1929), p. 21; J.R. Darling to J.B. Darling, 6 June 1930, 20 February 1930, 24 March 1930; all DP; Darling to Munro, 7 July 1954, GGSA; Cole (1969), pp. 34–5; Curthoys to Darling, 27 February 1937, 1 April 1937, 27 April 1937, 28 April 1937, 4 May 1937; Darling to Curthoys, 2 April 1937; Head to Darling, 23 April 1937; Darling to Head 26 April, all GGSA.

33 'On reading [1]', undated, pp. 3, 4, 7, 6, 15–16; 'On reading [2]', Four Square Club, Geelong, 5 August 1937, pp. 3 & 5, DP; Darling to Cunningham, 17 December

1934; Lockie to Darling, 25 October 1934; Darling to Lockie, 15 October 1937, all GGSA; Sir James Darling to the author, 30 September 1992; Darling to Keppel, 16 July 1936; Darling to Remington, 5 March 1937, both GGSA.

34 Munn and Pitt (1935), pp. 23, 57; Bechervaise to Darling, 11 February 1939; Darling to Bechervaise, 13 February 1939, both GGSA; *Constitution of the Free Library Movement* (Sydney, 1935), p. 4; FLM, *Free Public Libraries* (Melbourne, 1937), p. 6; Metcalfe (1962), p. 141; Remington to Darling, 14 January 1937, GGSA; Priestley, Australian Diary, vol. 7, 8 March 1937, p. 136, UMA; *Geelong Advertiser* cutting, undated; Lyall to Darling, 22 April 1937, 2 June 1937, both GGSA; 'Recent library developments in Victoria', undated, CCF, b154, It224, ACERA; *Age*, 24 June 1938.

35 'Robert Bridges', undated; 'Poet laureates', 17 June 1930, p. 2; 'Vergil in the Middle Ages', undated; 'The transition from Imperial Rome to Mediaeval Europe', 16 June 1931, all DP; Darling to Maynard, 14 September 1937, GGSA; Darling (1930), p. 9; Phillips (1931), p. 24; Darling (1931), p. 32.

36 Darling (1935c), pp. 56, 57–8; Darling (1936a).

37 Darling (1938), pp. 2–4; Address to the Victorian Teachers' Union, untitled, October 1938, DP; *Argus*, 20 October 1938; Draft article for Apex, February 1938, p. 3, DP; Darling (1936b), pp. 9, 11; Darling (1939), pp. 6–7.

38 Darling (1939), p. 5; 'Books which have altered the world', undated, p. 5, DP.

12 Pride comes before a fall

1 GGSC, Meetings, 9 May 1938, 8 August 1938, Minutes, pp. 58, 76, GGSA.

2 J.R. Darling to J.B. Darling, 29 June 1932, 16 June 1932; Francis to Darling, 29 May 1932; Fletcher to Darling, 12 August 1932, all DP; Darling to Dicker, 6 July 1934, DiP.

3 Wadham to Darling, 10 March 1936; Darling to Wadham, 11 March 1936, both GGSA; Priestley, Australian Diary, vol. 4, 4 February 1936 (unnumbered), UMA; Fletcher to Darling, 17 June 1936, DP; *RR*, p. 164; Priestley, Australian Diary, vol. 10, 23 October 1937, p. 69, UMA.

4 Bickersteth to Darling, 30 January 1934, DP; Bickersteth to Darling, 18 February 1938, GGSA.

5 Darling to Turnbull, 14 March 1938, GGSA.

6 Priestley, Australian Diary, vol. 11, 11 May 1938, p. 234, UMA; Whiskard to Darling, 17 March 1938; McKie to Darling, 25 March 1938; Curthoys to Darling, 22 March 1938; Darling to Bickersteth, 4 April 1938; Ellis to Bickersteth, 8 April 1938; Bickersteth to Darling, 15 April 1938; Fairbairn to Darling, 27 April 1938; Head to Darling, 27 April 1938, all GGSA.

7 Priestley to Darling, 13 May 1938, GGSA; *Argus*, 12 May 1938; Darling to the editor, *Argus*, 12 May 1938; Ricketson to Darling, 12 May 1938, GGSA; Priestley, Australian Diary, vol. 12, 25 May 1938, 27 June 1938, pp. 19, 91, UMA.

8 *Physical Training and Recreation* (January 1937) Cmd 5364, pp. 745–56; *Physical Training and Recreation Act*, 1937, sec 7; ED 113/85, NAC 39(3), pp. 8, 1, NA; Bickersteth to Darling, 18 February 1938, GGSA; *Times*, 28 May 1938; ED 113/25, De La Warr to Simon, 2 November 1938, p. 1; Cabinet, National fitness grants, CP 283(38), memorandum by the President of the Board of Trade, p. 2; CP 283 (38), MGH to Ellis, 29 August 1939, all NA.

9   *RR*, p.165; GGSC, Meetings, 9 May 1938, 8 August 1938 (incls special finance
    sub-committee, 21 June 1938, 11 July 1938, 2 August 1938), 12 December 1938,
    13 February 1939, 6 March 1939, 8 May 1939, Minutes, pp. 60, 69–70, 90, 99, 102,
    111–12, 113, all GGSA; Darling to Wadham, 21 July 1938, WP, GGS box, corresp
    1936–46, UMA; Darling to Turnbull, 15 July 1938; Darling to Manifold, 1 July
    1938; Turnbull to Darling, 20 July 1938, Flack & Flack to the Trustees of Geelong
    Church of England Grammar School, 14 April 1939, all GGSA.

10 Brodie to Darling, 6 July 1938; J.R. Darling to Brodie, 8 July 1938; McKie to
    Darling, 14 January 1939, all GGSA; *RR*, pp. 158–9; Curthoys to Darling, 24 April
    1939, DP.

11 GGSC, Meetings, 9 May 1938, 12 February 1940, 'Headmaster's report', Minutes,
    pp. 58, 151, both GGSA; *ADB*, vol. 7, p. 124; Austin to Darling, 4 May 1939,
    DP; *Corian*, 1976 (June), pp. 377, 378; HMCA, Meeting, 26 May 1939, Minutes,
    p. 106.

12 Austin to Darling, 11 May 1939, GGSA; Ramsey to Darling, 29 May 1939, DP;
    Wadham, Pocket diary 1939; Darling to Wadham, 29 May 1939, undated, Wadham
    to T[urnbull?] (undated), all WP, GGS box, corresp 1936–46, UMA.

13 Priestley, Diaries, 8–12 June 1939, p. 161, UBA; Wadham to Darling, 5 June 1939,
    9 June 1939, both WP, Letters outwards, 1928–39, UMA; Darling to Austin, 9 June
    1939; Darling to Bickersteth, undated; Darling to Cameron, 9 June 1939, all DP.

14 Ellis to Darling, 21 June 1939; Darling to Ellis, 29 June 1939; A.M. Darling to
    J.R. Darling, 20 September 1929, all DP.

15 Darling to Cameron, 29 June 1939; Gordon to Darling, 16 June 1939, both DP;
    Brodie to Darling, 28 March 1938; Baker to Darling, 1 July 1938; Darling to
    Brodie, 3 March 1938, all GGSA.

16 Cameron to Darling, 24 June 1939; Austin to Darling, 16 June 1939, both DP.

17 Darling to Manifold, 18 July 1939; Cameron to Darling, undated; Gordon to
    Darling, 24 June 1939, all DP.

18 Austin to Darling, 13 July 1939; Gordon to Darling, 16 July 1939, both DP.

19 *Corian*, 1935 (December), p. 230; Bailey and Duncan (1936), pp. 57, 175.

20 Austin to Darling, 13 July 1939; Gordon to Darling, 24 June 1939, both DP.

21 Fletcher to Darling, 8 May 1939; Darling to Manifold, 18 July 1939; Fairbairn to
    Darling, 19 July 1939; Cameron to Darling, 15 August 1939; Austin to Darling,
    21 August 1939; Gordon to Darling, 19 August 1939, all DP.

22 Cameron to Darling, 15 August 1939; Manifold to Darling, 16 August 1939;
    Darling to Manifold, 9 September 1939, all DP.

23 Giblin to J.R. Darling, 6 August 1939; Ryder to J.R. Darling, 14 September 1939;
    Moden to J.R. Darling, 13 September 1939, all DP.

24 Moden to Darling, 14 September 1939; Giblin to Darling, 9 August 1939, both
    DP; Wadham to Giblin, 26 September 1939, WP, Letters outward, 1928–39,
    UMA; Cameron to Le Couteur, 11 August 1939, GGSA.

25 Untitled autobiographical notes (undated); Morris le Fleming to the author,
    23 December 2012; Darling to Manifold, 9 September 1939; Darling to
    Greenwood, 'Evacuation Scheme' (undated); 'England in Wartime', 16 February
    1940, p. 6, all DP.

26 Elliot to Bernays, 15 September 1939; Bernays to Darling, 16 September 1939; Darling to Manifold, 9 September 1939, undated; Manifold to Darling, 18 September 1939, 26 September 1939; Fairbairn to Darling, 9 October 1939, all DP.

27 351 HC. Deb. 5s, 7 September 1939, pp. 573, 575; INF.1/28, 'Staff organization empire division', file. A108/5; Hodson to Stewart, 19 October 1939, MacDonald to MacMillan, 16 October 1939, all NA; Hodson to Darling, 22 December 1939, DP; Wadham to Darling, 19 October 1939, WP, Letters outward, 1928–39, UMA; Darling to Manifold, 28 September 1939; Manifold to Darling, 15 October 1939; Darling, undated, both DP.

28 Cameron to Darling, 18 October 1939; Darling to Cameron, 6 November 1939; Darling to Manifold, 7 November 1939, Manifold to Darling, 28 November 1939, all DP.

29 Sir James and Lady Darling to the author, 19 August 1988; Darling to Strachan, 21 February 1940, GGSA; Fisher to Darling, 4 July 1940, DP.

30 Gordon to Darling, 22 December 1939, GGSA; RR, p. 171; Sir James Darling to the author, 30 November 1984; Darling to Manifold, 27 February 1940, GGSA; V.J.H. Tunbridge to the author, 25 February 1985; HMCA, Meeting, 26 May 1939, Minutes, p. 106, AHISAA.

31 Report to council, 12 February 1940, p. 1, GGSA; P.J.C. Westcott to the author, 14 August 1991; Darling to Robson, 8 May 1940; Whiskard to Darling, 12 February 1940; Head to Darling, 13 May 1940; Darling to Booth, 22 May 1940; Darling to Hone, 8 April 1940, all GGSA.

32 Sir James Darling to the author, 30 November 1984; Fairbairn to Darling, 20 February 1940; Darling to Manifold, 27 February 1940, both GGSA.

33 Manifold to Darling, undated, 26 July 1940, both GGSA; Manifold to Wadham, 18 July 1940; Wadham to Manifold, 22 July 1940; Manifold to Wadham, 26 July 1940, all WP, GGS box, corresp 1936–46, UMA; Manifold to Darling, 26 July 1940; Curthoys to Darling, 15 August 1940, both GGSA.

34 Manifold to Darling, 21 July 1940; Webb-Ware to Darling, undated, 21 July 1940; White to Darling, 15 August 1940, 10 December 1940, all GGSA.

35 Darling to le Fleming, 15 June 1940, 17 July 1940; Darling to Manifold, undated, 28 September 1939, 7 November 1939; Manifold to Darling, 14 November 1939, all DP.

36 Casey to Darling, 16 January 1940, DP; Gullett to Darling, undated; Darling to Gullett, 9 August 1937; Sanderson to Darling, 16 August 1940; Darling to Potter, 27 August 1940; Potter to Darling, 26 August 1940, 9 September 1940; Darling to Sanderson, 19 August 1940; Sanderson to Darling, 20 August 1940; Evatt to Darling, 30 September 1940; Latham to Darling, 22 August 1940, all GGSA; Darling to Latham, 19 August 1940, LP, ms 1009 65/172–173, NLA.

37 Priestley to Darling, 25 September 1940; Darling to Priestley, 19 November 1940; J.R. Darling to J.B. Darling, 23 November 1940, all DP; Priestley, Diaries, 28 April–10 May 1941 (unnumbered), UBA; Priestley to Darling, 14 May 1941, DP; Priestley, Diaries, 2–6 August 1941, p. 42, UBA.

38 GGSC, Meeting, 16 September 1941, Minutes, p. 181; Manifold to Darling, 31 December 1940, both GGSA; Darling to le Fleming, 17 July 1940, DP.

13 Something like stagnation

1 Martin (1993), p. 295; *Corian*, 1940 (May), p. 10; 'England in wartime' (11 February 1940), DP.

2 Gullett to Darling, undated; Darling to Hone, 8 April 1940; Darling to Kandel, 5 September 1940, all GGSA; le Fleming, Notebook, 18, 26 June 1940, leFP; le Fleming to Darling, 1 July 1940; J.B. Darling to J.R. Darling, 23 May 1940, 23 July 1940, all DP.

3 A.E. Darling to J. Darling, 17 September 1939; M.R. Darling to J.B. Darling, 14 September 1940; J. Darling to J.B. Darling, 29 June 1940; J.B. Darling to J.R. Darling, 21 September 1940; J.R. Darling to J.B. Darling, 26 September 1940, 23 November 1940, all DP; Darling (1940b).

4 Gordon to Darling, 27 July 1940; Stephen to Darling, 6 October 1940; Manifold to Darling, 6 October 1940, all GGSA.

5 Robson to Darling, 13 March 1940; Gollan to Darling, 2 October 1942; Darling to McNamara, 12 November, 1941; Darling to Robson, 9 October 1940, 17 October 1940, all GGSA; Gronn (1991); J.R. Darling to J.B. Darling, 16 February 1941, DP.

6 *Corian*, 1940 (August), pp. 147, 148; 1941 (August), pp. 113–14, 116, (December), p. 189; Dicker to Darling, 3 April 1942, DP; Kellaway to Darling, 25 September 1941; Darling to Massy-Greene, 19 September 1941; Report to council, 21 April 1941; Tucker to Darling, 9 February 1943, all GGSA.

7 MacNeil to Darling, 28 January 1944; Booth to Darling, 7 March 1944; Darling to Booth, 8 March 1944, all GGSA; *Corian*, 1944 (August), p. 85, (December), p. 136; Sir James Darling to the author, 7 April 1995; J.S. Cook 'The School in Wartime', *Thirty-Two Years*, pp. 69, 71; Darling to Aldred, 9 February 1942, GGSA.

8 Sir James Darling to the author, 10 March 1995; E. Parnes 'Remarks on the Geelong Church of England Grammar School', 4 October 1941, GGSA.

9 Gepp to Darling, 7 March 1940; Hancock to Darling, 1 April 1940, both GGSA; Sir James Darling to the author, 7 April 1995; *Corian*, 1940 (December), pp. 220–2; Darling to Hancock, 3 July 1942; Darling to Malim, 9 August 1942, both GGSA; J.B. Darling to J.R. Darling, 20 December 1942, DP; Darling to Krome, 28 August 1942, GGSA.

10 *Corian*, 1942 (December), p. 146; Darling to the Chinese consulate, 8 July 1942, GGSA; F.N.B. Newman to the author, 12 July 1990; Krome to Darling, 10 September 1942, GGSA; *Argus*, 26 October 1942; Giblin to Darling, 9 October 1942, GGSA; Selth (1973) pp. 181, 186; Browne to Darling, 10 September 1941, GGSA; Maslin to Darling, 15 December 1941, DP; Report to council, 9 November 1942, GGSA.

11 A.E. Darling to J.R. Darling, 6 October 1940; E.L. Darling to M.D. Darling, 25 June 1985; A.E. Darling to J.B. Darling, 17 March 1936, 4 February 1939; M.R. Darling to J.R. Darling, 15 September 1940, all DP.

12 A.E. Darling to E.L. Darling, 21 August 1940; 16 July 1941; 19 December 1941; J.B. Darling to J.R. Darling, 22 March 1942, 22 October 1944; M.R. Darling to J.R. Darling, 2 January 1944, all DP.

13 Barker to Darling, 3 February 1943; Darling to Barker, 6 February 1943, both GGSA; *RR*, pp. 34–5, 175–6; J.A.C. Mackie to the author, 22 May 1985; C.M.H. Clark to the author, 23 May 1985; Holt (1982), pp. 66–7.

14 GGSC, Meeting, 1 February 1943, Minutes, pp. 54–5; Manifold to Darling, 11 February 1943; A.M. Campbell to J.R. Darling, 23 July 1943; N. Campbell to J.R. Darling, 15 July 1943, all GGSA; Currie to Darling, 12 November 1943, DP; Pugh to Darling, 24 November 1942; Darling to Pugh, 2 December 1942, both GGSA.

15 Black to Darling, 28 March 1943, GGSA; *Corian*, 1942 (December), p. 135; Manifold to Darling, 11 February 1943, GGSA.

16 Medley to Darling, 6 April 1943, GGSA; *Corian*, 1942 (December), p. 136.

17 *Corian* 1942 (December), p. 136; OGGA, Minute Book 4, 1939–1952, p. 198; Darling to Black, 21 April 1943; Black to Darling, 17 May 1943, 28 June 1943; Masterman to Darling, 2 March 1943, all GGSA.

18 Darling to Masterman, 8 March 1943; Memorandum to council, 4 March 1943, both GGSA; *Corian*, 1943 (May), pp. 7–8.

19 Matthews (2008); McKenna (2011); Clark (1990); V.J.H. Tunbridge to the author, 25 February 1985; GGSC, Meeting, 8 May 1944, Minutes, p. 94; Clark to Darling, 23 June 1944, GGSA; J. Mackie 'Obituary to Charles Manning Hope Clark', *Corian*, 1991 (July), p. 230.

20 Darling to Thwaites, 3 April 1945, DP; Report to council, 10 November 1941; Bracey to Darling, 21 January 1942; Darling to the Bishop of Riverina, 17 August 1942; Darling to Holmes, 12 August 1943, all GGSA.

21 Gronn (1991), pp. 56–7; J.R. Darling to Hake, 9 May 1940, GGSA; J.R. Darling to J.B. Darling, 30 December 1940, DP; *Corian*, 1941 (December), p. 173; Hasluck (1970), p. 321; Darling to Booth, 22 May 1940; Circular letter, March 1941, all GGSA; Gordon to Darling, 27 July 1940, DP.

22 *CPD*, vol. 179, pp. 188–9, 881, 960; Notice to parents, 26 June 1942; Circular to parents of interstate boys, 17 July 1942; Fraser to Darling, 21 July 1942, GGSA; *Sun*, 14 September 1944; *Sydney Morning Herald*, 15 September 1944, 16 September 1944.

23 *CPD*, vol. 179, p. 1382; vol. 180, pp. 1558, 1559, 1674, 1768–9; *Sydney Morning Herald*, 27 September 1944, 28 September 1944, 30 September 1944, 2 October 1944; *Herald*, 27 September 1944;

24 Angas to Darling, 30 May 1944, GGSA; P. Henderson to the author, 8 May 1990; Draft telegrams to Colonel Wynne, 15 September 1944, GGSA; *Corian*, 1944 (December), p. 137; Wakehurst to Darling, 15 September 1944; Murdoch to Darling, 15 September; Darling to Holyman, 2 October 1944; Holyman to Darling, 3 October 1944, all GGSA.

25 Darling to Thomas, 1 April 1943; Darling to Stroud, 12 November 1943; Darling to Grimwade, 26 February 1945, all GGSA; Drucker (1939), pp. 94, 95; Bishop of Newcastle to Darling, 1 August 1942, 21 September 1942, both GGSA; Darling (1942).

26 Temple to Darling, 29 April 1942; M.R. Darling to J.R. Darling, 29 March 1942; J.B. Darling to J.R. Darling, 20 December 1942, 3 May 1942, 27 December 1942, all DP; Darling (1944b); Darling to Temple, 6 November 1944, TP, v47, f389, LPA.

27 Darling (1942); Darling to Aird, 30 September 1943, GGSA; Darling to Simmonds, 28 September 1942, DP; Darling to Bishop of North Queensland,

5 November 1942; Bishop of North Queensland to Darling, 20 October 1942 (and enclosure); Morris to Darling, 20 December 1942, all GGSA.

28 Darling to Garvin, 11 August 1943, GGSA; 'Education and the future' (Lecture to the United Christian Witness meeting, Bendigo), 13 August 1943, pp. 5, 11, DP.

29 *Corian*, 1943 (December), p. 156; 1944 (December), p. 138; Darling to le Fleming, 19 October 1942, DP; Darling to Campbell, 28 June 1940, GGSA; Harlow to Darling, 30 December 1941, DP; *Corian*, 1940 (December), p. 216.

30 McKie to Darling, 29 October 1944, DP; Darling to Warren, 20 April 1943; Darling to Cowan, 16 May 1944, both GGSA; Darling to le Fleming, 19 October 1942; Hodge to Darling, 2 June 1941, both DP; Darling to Crutchley, 29 July 1940; Sutcliffe to Darling, 11 October 1940, both GGSA; Priestley to Darling, 14 May 1941, DP.

31 Darling to Gordon, 11 April 1945; Cranswick to Darling, 23 November 1945, both GGSA; *Corian*, 1945 (December), p. 143; Report to council, 9 November 1942; Darling to Copland, 20 August 1943; 'Report on the future of the school', July 1944; Manifold to Darling, 7 August 1944; Darling to Colman, 17 July 1945; Manifold to Richardson, 15 October 1945, all GGSA.

32 Darling to Richardson, 6 November 1945; Manifold to Darling, 8 November 1945, both GGSA; *Corian* 1945 (December), pp. 142–5; Darling to Davies, 12 December 1945; Hutton to Osborne, 17 April 1951, both GGSA; Sir James Darling to the author, 7 April 1985.

14 A question of priorities

1 Darling to Secretary, Liquid Fuel Control Board, 21 November 1941; Darling to Greene, 24 October 1952, 12 November 1952; Darling to Oldham, 9 August 1943, all GGSA.

2 *RR*, pp. 186–7.

3 Darling to Jenkins, 2 May 1938; Darling to Hone, 18 September 1951, both GGSA.

4 Darling to Gilray, 20 February 1951; Sutcliffe to MacNeil, 15 November 1944; B.W. Hone, 'Meeting of the A.P.S. Headmasters, Tuesday, 13th July [1954]', all GGSA; *ADB*, vol. 14, p. 482.

5 Gronn (1994), pp. 244–7; 'Head of the River Races—Brief Outline of History in relation to Charities', attachment to Glanville-Hicks to MacNeil, 9 April 1941, GGSA.

6 'Head of the River', *Australasian*, 20 May 1939; Darling to Ansells, 5 February 1940; Attachment to Taylor to Darling, 25 April 1940, both DP; Delegates' meeting, 8 June 1940, report; Wells to MacNeil, 8 June 1940, 9 March 1940, all GGSA.

7 Darling to MacNeil, 8 May 1940, 17 June 1940; HMA, Meeting, 22 June 1940, Minutes, p. 1; MacNeil to *Age* editor, 24 June 1940; Rolland to MacNeil, 17 June 1941; MacNeil to Wells, 24 June 1940; Wells to MacNeil, 6 July 1940, all GGSA.

8 Memo to the Public School Association, 22 March 1956, GGSA; Gronn (1994), pp. 248–50; Lemon (2004), pp. 186–7; Darling (1969), pp. 17–19; Baillie to Darling, 4 October, 1983, DP, 7826, s7, b15, f4, NLA.

9 *ADB*, vol. 10, pp. 351–2; Lemon (2004), pp. 255–6, 279; MacNeil to Darling, 28 June 1940, 2 August 1940, 21 October 1940; Sutcliffe to MacNeil, 31 July

1940; Darling to MacNeil, 1 August 1940, 5 August 1940; MacNeil to Wells, 4 September 1940; Coleman to Coles, 7 August 1940, attached to Coleman to Darling, 14 August 1940, all GGSA.

10   Sutcliffe to MacNeil, 28 October 1940; MacNeil to Sutcliffe, 29 October 1940; Glanville-Hicks to MacNeil, 9 April 1941; MacNeil to Darling, 16 April, 1941, all GGSA; LMF, Notes of discussion at executive committee meeting, 9 April 1941, LMFA; Wells to MacNeil, 19 April 41; MacNeil to Rolland, 21 April 1941; Darling to MacNeil, 23 April 1941, all GGSA.

11   Costelloe to MacNeil, 27 April, 1941; Sutcliffe to MacNeil, 23 April 1941; Gilray to MacNeil, 25 April 1941, all GGSA; LMF, Notes of discussion at executive committee meeting, 12 June 1941, LMFA; 'Report for the headmasters of investigations and experiences abroad of Mr. Graham Taylor', undated; Taylor to Darling, 25 April 1940, 8 July 1941; Darling to Taylor, 9 July 1941, all DP.

12   Darling to Anderson, 14 July 1941, GGSA; Bracey to Darling, 21 July 1941 (and attachment), 19 August 1941; Taylor to Darling, 8 July 1941; Darling to Bracey, 23 July 1941; Darling to Gilray, 8 October 1941; Darling to MacNeil, 19 November 1941; Darling to Henderson, 24 November 1941, all DP.

13   Sutcliffe to MacNeil, 11 August 1941; MacNeil to Gilray, 12 August 1941; MacNeil to Sutcliffe, 12 August 1941; MacNeil to Taylor, 4 September 1940; Taylor to MacNeil, 5 May 1940, 12 September 1940; Report for headmasters (10/9/1940), all GGSA; *ADB*, vol. 15, p. 381; MacNeil to Darling, 30 July 1941; Taylor to Darling, 14 February 1941; Mitchell to MacNeil, 16 September 1941; Beaurepaire to Wells, 12 August 1941; MacNeil to Beaurepaire, 28 October 1941, all GGSA.

14   Glanville-Hicks to MacNeil, 1 December 1941, GGSA; Bracey to Darling, 7 October 1941; Darling to Bracey, 8 October 1941; MacNeil to Wells, 19 February 1942; MacNeil to Dedman, 6 July 1942; Cameron to MacNeil, 10 September 1942; Gilray to MacNeil, 3 March 1942, all DP; Spaull (1982), pp. 17–19; Darling to HMA, 2 February 1942, GGSA.

15   *Corian*, 1942 (May), pp. 30–4, (August) pp. 100–2; Darling to MacNeil, 5 March, 1943, 30 April 1943; MacNeil to Darling, 10 March 1943, 28 April 1943; Wells to MacNeil, 28 February 1943, 14 March 1943; MacNeil to Wells, 10 March 1943; Davidson to MacNeil, 12 November 1944, all GGSA.

16   Maunders (1991), pp. 29–31; Irving, Maunders and Sherington (1995), pp. 21–2, 51–2, 13.

17   Darling (1945), pp. 2, 6, 8, 9, 12, DP; Mannheim (1943), p. 31.

18   Darling (1945), p. 14; Darling (1940a), DP; Gibson to Darling, 3 May 1940, GGSA.

19   BCM, circular letter, 4 July 1940, VABC; First Conference Report, 1940, pp. 7, 10, both DP; Provisional constitution, p. 1; Organiser's quarterly report, July–September 1940, p. 1; Bracey to Darling, 10 September 1940; Darling to Bracey, 24 September 1940, all DP; Bracey to Darling, 27 September 1940; Darling to Bracey, 10 October 1940, both GGSA.

20   Darling, Attachment to McEwin to the secretary of the UBC committee, 13 June 1941; BEM, Geelong Branch, Statistical report for the month of September 1941; Darling to Pillow, 10 October 1941; Bracey to Darling, 3 October 1941; 'The need

for community centres', 6 October 1941, all DP; Darling to Campbell, 30 September 1941, GGSA; 'Community centres. Why do we need them?', undated, DP.

21 Darling to Bracey, 16 October 1941, 9 December 1941, both DP; Bracey, 'Recommendations for conversion and re-conditioning of the above premises [Geelong Boys' Employment Centre] for use as a social centre for boys during the evening', undated, BEMR; Darling to Brownbill, 8 April 1942, Giles to Mackrell, 16 April 1942, both DP.

22 Stretton to Darling, 30 April 1942; Darling to Stretton, 1 May 1942, both DP.

23 Darling to Stretton, 1 May 1942, 25 May 1942; Stretton to Darling, 23 May 1942, all DP.

24 1 George V, No. 2301, Part 1; Dunbar (1976), pp. 167, 178.

25 CPE, Meetings, 5 March 1940, 14 July 1942, 'Draft report for presentation to the Minister of Education' (sic), 1 June 1943, Minutes, pp. 54, 99, 137–44, VPRO; Browne to Darling, 27 November 1942, 5 March 1943; Darling to Browne, 10 March 1943, 1 July 1943; Dunstan to Darling, 9 December 1942, all GGSA; *ADB*, vol. 9, p. 211; Darling to Thomas, 1 April 1943; Darling to Parsons, 1 July 1943, all GGSA.

26 CPE, Meeting, 6 July 1943, Minutes, pp. 160–1, VPRO; Browne to Darling, 8 July 1943, 6 August 1943; Darling to Browne, 9 August 1943, all GGSA.

27 CPE, Meetings, 28 March 1944, 5 December 1944, 12 April 1945, Minutes, pp. 195–6, 223, 225–6, all VPRO; Dunbar (1976), p. 171.

28 CPE (1945), *Report on Educational Reform and Development in Victoria* (Melbourne: Government Printer), pp. 5, 7, 9, 10, 24, 25, VPRO.

29 GGSC, Meeting, 4 December, 1942, Minutes, p. 90; Spaull (1998), pp. 64–6; Butlin and Schedvin (1977), pp. 37–9; Ashby to Darling, 23 November 1942, GGSA.

30 Darling to Mills, 21 June 1943, 17 March 1944, 24 February 1943, 12 August 1943, 8 December 1943, 4 December 1944, all series A1875, item 8/01 (2)/part 1, NAA.

31 Darling to Mills, 19 December 1944, series A1875, item 8/01 (2)/part 1, NAA; Darling to Ross, 26 November 1943; Ross to Darling, 7 December 1943; Chifley to Dedman, 17 November 1944; Pillow to Darling, 28 November 1944; Darling to Pillow, 29 November 1944, all GGSA.

32 Newton to Darling, 22 April 1944, 30 June 1944 (and attachment); Darling to Newton, 5 July 1944, all GGSA.

33 Darling 'Shortened and special courses at universities for returned servicemen' (undated), series A1875, item 8/01 (2)/part 1; Darling to Mills, 15 April 1945, series A1875, item 8/01 (2)/part 2, both NAA; Dedman to Darling, 13 June 1945, GGSA.

34 Mannheim (1943), pp. 4, 7; Broadcast, November 1941, p. 2; 'Future of education', March 1941, p. 2; 'Rotary Club', 22 July 1941, p. 7; Darling (1942), p. 2; 'The ideal of the amateur', undated, p. 5; 'A new birth of freedom', 18 May 1943, p. 2; 'Crisis and opportunity', undated, pp. 21, 5, all DP.

35 'Our duty to the community in which we live', 22 July 1941, pp. 4, 2; 'The part played by education in a planned society', undated; Educational reform' section, p. 2, 'schools for citizens' section, p. 2; 'Legacy club', 11 November 1941, p. 2, all DP.

36 'A new birth of freedom', May 1943, p. 3; 'The need for a Christian view of education', 9 August 1943, p. 2; 'The part played by education in a planned society', undated, p. 5; 'The children's new order. The school', 25 April 1945; 'Our duty to

the community in which we live', 22 July 1941, p. 3; 'Castlemaine High School', 18 December 1941, p. 5, all DP.

37 'Castlemaine High School', 18 December 1941, pp. 1–2; le Fleming to Darling, 3 June 1940, both DP

38 Wakehurst to Darling, 18 August 1945, GGSA.

15 Grand Panjandrum

1 Darling to Le Couteur, 3 December 1943; Darling to Lang, 14 May 1946; Darling to Hake, 29 May 1947, all GGSA.

2 M.D. Darling to J.R. Darling, 26 February 1946; Gordon to Darling, 1 March 1946; Dicker to Darling, 9 March 1946; Hackett to Darling, undated; J.B. Darling to J.R. Darling, 3 March 1946; M.D. Darling to J.R. Darling, 12 March 1946; Robson to Darling, 8 July 1946, all DP.

3 M.D. Darling to J.R. Darling, 25 February 1946, 11 March 1946, 12 March 1946, 15 May 1946, 20 May 1946, all DP; J.R. Darling to M.R. Darling, 8 April 1946; Report to council, June 1946, both GGSA; Sir James Darling to the author, 12 May 1995; Darling to McEwin, 12 June 1946, DP.

4 Darling to Colman, 24 July 1946, GGSA; J.R. Darling to M.R. Darling, 20 December 1946; M.R. Darling to J.R. Darling, 24 March 1947, and undated; le Fleming to Darling, 8 April 1947; Dicker to Darling, 9 March 1946; D. Darling to J.R. Darling, 21 February 1946; J.B. Darling to J.R. Darling, 23 March 1947, 29 March 1947; M.R. Darling to J.R. Darling, 9 March 1947, all DP.

5 Manifold to Darling, 16 June 1947, GGSA; M.R. Darling to J.R. Darling, 30 July 1947; J.B. Darling to J.R. Darling, 14 September 1947, 24 October 1947, all DP; Darling to Lindon, 17 September, 1947, GGSA.

6 Darling to Lindon, 26 February 1948, GGSA; J.R. Darling to M.R. Darling, 20 December 1946, DP; Darling to Gordon, 15 March 1946, GGSA.

7 Darling to Lindon, 26 February 1948, 19 June 1947; GGSC, Meetings, 9 December 1946, 8 March 1948, Minutes, pp. 216 (and insert), 264, all GGSA; Sir James Darling to the author, 24 February 1995; Darling to Thewlis, 10 June 1947, GGSA; J.R. Darling to M.R. Darling, 20 December 1946, DP; Lindon to Darling, 4 February 1948, GGSA.

8 Hansen and Hansen (1996), pp. 117, 120–5; Cox to Darling, 29 April 1947, 28 July 1947, 1 July 1947; Darling to Cox, 30 April 1947, all GGSA.

9 Darling to Cox, 27 December 1946; Wardle to Darling, 6 October 1948, both DP.

10 'Answers to [C.E.W. Bean's] Questionnaire', undated, 008-01, ACEA; J.R. Darling to M.R. Darling, 20 December 1946, DP; Lemon (1999), pp. 87–116; Darling to Jennings, 10 October 1946, GGSA.

11 Reports to council, 17 June 1946, 8 July 1946; Darling to Gordon, 24 April 1946; Masters' common room association, memorandum, 20 June 1946, all GGSA; Kennedy to Darling, 5 August 1944; Darling to Kennedy, 20 March 1946; Darling to Gilray, 20 March 1946, all 008-01, ACEA.

12 Report to council on masters' salaries, undated [1948]; Lindon to Pinner, 31 August 1948; Memorandum on masters' salaries, undated [1949]; Spear to the chairman of council, 10 April 1949; Report to council, 13 March 1950, p. 4; Darling to Lindon, 27 October 1949; Darling to Freeth, 13 August 1947, all GGSA.

13 *Corian*, 1946 (December), pp. 142–3; GGSC, Meetings, 10 March 1947,
    10 November 1947, 8 March 1948, Minutes, pp. 224, 251, 262, all GGSA; *Corian*,
    1947 (December), pp. 159–60; Darling to Lindon (and attachment), 23 March
    1948, GGSA.

14 *Corian*, 1944 (December), p. 185; 1945 (December), p. 146; 1946 (May), pp. 66–71;
    Gorton to Darling, 16 March 1946; Darling to Gordon, 24 April 1946; Darling to
    Thomas, 2 August 1946, all GGSA.

15 Darling to Hackett, 26 April 1946; Darling to Hamer, 3 March 1947; Hay to
    Darling, 25 April 1946; Hamer to Darling, 27 February, 1947; Darling to Casey,
    5 August 1947, all GGSA; *Corian*, 1947 (December), pp. 211–14.

16 Conference of headmasters, delegates list; Darling to Gordon, 5 June 1947, 10 June
    1947, 25 November 1947; Darling to Mills, 18 October 1946; Mills to Darling,
    13 October 1947, all 008-01, ACEA; Hogg (1986), p. 86; le Fleming to Darling,
    22 June 1946, DP.

17 Darling to Field, 24 July 1947, 2 October 1947; Field to Darling, 31 July 1947,
    22 September 1947, 2 October 1947, all 008-01, ACEA; Hogg (1986), p. 86;
    Darling to Gordon, 10 June 1947; Hone to Darling, 8 November 1947; Robson to
    Darling, 28 November 1947, all 009-01, ACEA.

18 Darling to Lindon, 17 September 1947, GGSA; Darling to Hackett, 1 March,
    1948; Darling to Hone, undated, both 008-01, ACEA; Darling (1948), pp. 19, 20,
    24, 25–6; *Corian*, 1948 (May), p. 12; *Speeches at a Conference of Headmasters*, undated
    (Sydney: HMCA), pp. 1–5, 63.

19 Report by A.E. Dinning, V. Symonds and D.H. David; Gordon to Darling,
    2 March 1948, both 008-01, ACEA; Radford to Darling, 13 April 1948, GGSA;
    Darling, Preface to *Speeches*, p. vi; Darling to Herring, 23 July 1947; Darling to
    Ramsay, 8 August 1947; Ramsay to Darling, 14 August 1947; Darling to Hone,
    2 February 1948; Hone to Darling, 29 January 1948; Hake to Darling, 6 February
    1948; Mills to Darling, 28 January 1948, all 008-01, ACEA.

20 Letter to the editor, *Age*, 13 November 1947; Sir James Darling to the author,
    14 May 1995; Browne to Darling, 22 November 1947; Darling to Browne,
    24 November 1947, both GGSA.

21 Darling to Browne, 17 December 1947; Browne to Darling, 23 December 1947,
    both GGSA.

22 Darling to Browne, 17 December 1947; Darling to Radford, 15 April 1948, both
    GGSA.

23 M.D. Darling to J.R. Darling, 17 March 1948, DP; Wild to Darling, 25 January
    1948, 008-01, ACEA; Victoria, *Hansard* (Assembly), 1946, p. 1344; Kent Hughes
    to Darling, undated; Ramsay to Darling, 6 April 1948, both GGSA.

24 HMCA, Standing committee, Meeting, 21 January 1946, Minutes, pp. 58–9,
    WCA; 'Answers to [C.E.W. Bean's] Questionnaire', undated, 008-01, ACEA.

25 Chifley to Darling, 7 March 1947, Appendix A to HMCA, Standing committee.
    Meeting, 20–21 July 1947, Minutes, p. 11, WCA.

26 Darling to Gordon, 2 March 1948, 008-01, ACEA; Sutcliffe to Darling, 19 April
    1948; Darling to Lindon, 26 February 1948; GGSC, Meeting, 9 June 1947,
    Minutes, p. 237, all GGSA.

27   Darling to Keen, 1 June 1947; Gordon to Darling, 5 November 1946; Darling
     to Lewis, 6 September 1946; Ward to Darling, 17 September 1946; Priestley to
     Darling, 5 November 1946; Darling to Priestley, 22 November 1946, all GGSA.
28   M.R. Darling to J.R. Darling, 9 March 1947; M.D. Darling to J.R. Darling,
     24 March 1947; Priestley to Darling, 14 July 1948, all DP.
29   Darling to Pinner, 7 June 1948, 6 August 1948, 14 July 1948; Day to J.R. &
     M.D. Darling, undated; Fraser to Darling, undated [28 July?]; Pinner to Darling,
     21 August 1948, all DP.
30   Spear to Darling, 26 July 1948; Pinner to Darling, 28 August 1948, 3 October
     1948, 11 October 1948, 16 November 1948, all DP.
31   Pickard-Cambridge to Darling, 1 September 1948, 8 September 1948, both DP;
     Sir James Darling to the author, 28 April 1995; Darling to Price, 23 March 1949;
     Roxburgh to Darling, 24 September 1948; Darling to Pinner, 16 September 1948;
     Pinner to Darling, 3 October 1948; Lindon to Darling, 13 October 1948; Manifold
     to Darling, 6 October 1948, all DP.
32   Pickard-Cambridge to Darling, 17 October 1948: Darling to Pinner, 21 October
     1948; Roxburgh to Darling, 30 October 1948, all DP; Darling to Pinner,
     27 October 1948, GGSA; *Corian*, 1948 (May), p. 84; Head to Darling, 22
     August 1948; Wharton to Darling, 28 Sept 1948, both DP; Thwaites to Darling,
     24 October 1948, GGSA.
33   Darling to Fisher, 20 June 1949; Fisher to Darling, 19 October 1949, both GGSA.
34   Wolfenden to Darling, 23 November 1949, GGSA; Sir James Darling to the
     author, 28 April 1995; Phillips to Darling, 5 December 1949, GGSA.
35   J.B. Darling to M.D. Darling, 12 September 1948; Dundas to M.D. Darling,
     8 October 1948; M.R. Darling to M.D. Darling, 21 November 1948; M.R. Darling to
     J.R. Darling, 5 November 1948; J.B. Darling to M.D. Darling, 12 December 1948, J.B.
     Darling to J.R. Darling, 14 November 1948, all DP; *Corian*, 1948 (December), p. 150.

16   Uncomfortable plateau

1   Darling to Moore, 1 March 1950, DP; Darling (1950), p. 9; Fitts to Darling,
     16 March 1950, 14 April [?] 1950, both DP.
2   APS, Meeting, 13 April 1946, Minutes (unnumbered), MGSA; Musgrave (1992),
     pp. 272–4; UMC, Meetings, 4 March 1946, 18 December 1950, Minutes, pp. 278,
     14, UMA; Darling to Ashby, 29 June 1950; Darling to Medley, 29 June 1950, 7 July
     1950, all GGSA.
3   APS, Meetings, 6 July 1946, 19 April 1947, 17 April 1948, Minutes (unnumbered),
     all MGSA; Darling to Long, 2 December 1949; Report to council, 8 August 1949;
     Darling to Lester, 30 April 1950; Darling to Black, all GGSA.
4   Darling to Hook, 13 August 1950, 11 June 1946; Darling to Mills, 25 August
     1950; Hook to Darling, 6 June 1946 (appended *Commonwealth Gazette* extract),
     26 September 1946, 4 October 1946, all series A1361, 1/9/3 part 1, NAA.
5   Tullis to J.R. Darling, 15 May 1946; BEM (Geelong), Annual Report, 1947; Casey
     to Young, 14 August 1947; Memorandum by Montgomery, 29 July 1947, all DP.
6   Darling to Menzies, 10 April 1947, GGSA; Tullis to Dedman, 19 November 1946;
     Dedman to Tullis, 26 November 1946, both DP; Menzies to Darling, 30 April
     1947; Department of Labour and National Service (Geelong) circular letter, 28
     August 1947, GGSA.

7 'Education', 1950; 'Standards and values in a living society', 13 September 1947; 'Some aspects of the educational problem', 31 January 1949; Darling (1950), pp. 11, 13; Notes for the junior school prize giving speech, the Hermitage, 11 December 1946, all DP.

8 Sir James Darling to the author, 24 March 1995; Meaney (2003); *Corian*, 1946 (December), pp. 147, 154; Darling to Hawkins, 27 September 1946, GGSA.

9 Darling (1946).

10 'British Memorial Fund' (undated), DP; Hyam (2006), p. 162.

11 Darling to Jones, 17 April 1947; Jones to Darling, 28 April 1947; Darling to Brown, 30 June 1947; Darling to Medley, 28 May 1947; Darling to Casey, 8 July 1947; Ritchie to Darling, undated; Darling to Boyd Neel, 7 July 1947; Curthoys to Darling, 18 June 1947; Darling to Curthoys, 19 June 1947, all GGSA.

12 Darling to Findley, 3 December 1954, GGSA; BMF, List of members, as at 31 March 1948; MacLean to Darling, 19 September 1952; 'British Memorial Fund' (undated); 'British Memorial Patriotic Fund, meeting of executive, 18 February 1946'; BMF, Executive Committee, Minutes, 23 December 1948; Notice of meeting to members, 4 May 1949, all DP.

13 Darling to Isaacson, 27 June 1949; 'Shepparton', 6 April 1949, both DP; Hasluck (1970), pp. 449, 476; 'Royal Empire Society annual dinner', 16 February 1949; 'The British empire in 1949' (undated), both DP.

14 *Corian*, 1948 (December), pp. 151–2; Darling to Burstall, 26 November 1946; to Yencken, 1 October 1946; Darling to Bankes Amery, 18 April 1946, all GGSA.

15 Campbell to Darling, 18 March 1946; Darling to Campbell, 22 March 1946; Darling to Wilson, 11 March 1941; Darling to Clarke, 15 November 1944; Darling to Booth, 21 October 1946; Fitzpatrick to Darling, 24 November 1946; Darling to Garnsey, 27 June 1949; Darling to Oddie, 5 April 1951, all GGSA.

16 *Corian*, 1947 (May), p. 14; Sir James Darling to the author, 24 February 1995; Darling to Gordon, 24 March 1949; Sutcliffe to Darling, 10 April 1946; Darling to the Bishop of Ballarat, 23 June 1944, 29 June 1944; Report to council, 8 October 1945, all GGSA.

17 Darling, 'The need for community centres', 22 June 1945; 'Sydney Kindergarten Union', 19 November 1945 and undated, all DP; Darling (1951); CPE, Meetings, 6 April 1948, 6 September 1949, 7 March 1950, 9 May 1950, 3 April 1951, 4 September 1951, Minutes, pp. 277, 300, 303, 305, 314, 317, VPRS, 11353/P0001, Unit 5, Minute Book, 1938–1956, VPRO.

18 *Corian*, 1947 (May), p. 10; GGSC, Meeting, 10 May 1948, Minutes, p. 268, GGSA; Spear to Darling, 16 September 1948, DP.

19 Darling to Topp, 15 December 1948, GGSA; GGSC, Meetings, 14 February 1949, 13 June 1949, Minutes, pp. 7, 23–4; Booth to Darling, 7 December 1949; Darling to Griffiths, 9 December 1949; Darling to Booth, 8 December 1949, all GGSA; *Corian*, 1950 (May), p. 16; GGSC, Meeting, 12 June 1950, Minutes, p. 60, GGSA; *Corian*, 1950 (December), p. 175.

20 Gilray to Darling, 1 February 1951, GGSA; *Corian*, 1950 (December), pp. 174, 175, 185–6; Darling to Gordon, 18 September 1951; Darling to Dickson, 30 July 1951; Darling to Black, 9 May 1951, all GGSA.

21 Reports to council, 13 February 1950, 19 February 1951, 12 November 1951; Black to Jamieson, 22 February 1951; Darling to Lindon, 13 May 1950; 'Summary',

28 June 1950, and 'Pension Scheme' 1st draft, 10 June 1950; Report to council, 13 March 1950, all GGSA.

22 Darling to Brown, 27 September 1951; Robinson to Darling, 8 January 1949, 29 April 1949; Darling to Robinson, 2 May 1949, all GGSA; Hansen (1986), p. 202.

23 Robinson to Darling, 22 June 1949; Fisher to Darling, 5 July 1949; Turner to Darling, 27 June 1949; Darling to Turner, 5 July 1949; Gordon to Darling, 27 July 1954; Darling to Gordon, 2 August 1954; Searle to Darling, 15 October 1954; 25 October 1954, all GGSA; Hansen (1986), pp. 244–5.

24 Darling to Turner, 9 October 1951, DP; Darling to Mills, 27 September 1951, 17 March 1952; Weeden to Darling, 21 May 1953, all series A1361, 1/9/3 part 1, NAA; Brown to Darling, 4 March 1952; Darling to Mills, both GGSA.

17 Mandated truths

1 Martin (1999), p. 125; Lindon to Darling, 15 December 1949, GGSA; *Corian*, 1946 (August), p. 128, (December), p. 197; Graham to Darling, 16 December 1946; Gorton to Darling, 22 January 1950; Hay to Darling, 5 January 1950; Downer to Darling, 28 December 1949, all GGSA.

2 Bolton (1974), pp. 459, 503; Niall (2009), pp. 215–54.

3 *Corian*, 1949 (May), pp. 10–14; 'Quality and equality', *Bulletin*, 26 January 1949; Johnston to Darling, 19 March 1949, 11 April 1949; Darling to Johnston, 25 March 1949; Darling to Truman, 10 February 1949, all GGSA.

4 Darling (1949), p. 21, WCA; Clark to Darling, 30 April 1946, 15 April 1946; Darling to Booth, 23 October 1945; Ward to Darling, 8 October 1952; Darling to Ward, 17 October 1952, all GGSA.

5 Clark to Darling, 8 February 1949, 30 January 1949; Darling to Clark, 4 February 1949; Darling to Ross, 25 November 1947, all GGSA; Ross (1947), p. 77.

6 Gorton to Darling, 16 November 1953; Darling to Gorton, 18 November 1953, both GGSA; Matthews (2008), chs 4, 5.

7 Darling to Gorton, 18 November 1953; Gorton to Darling, undated, both GGSA; Clark (1990), p. 204.

8 Fewster (2015); Wilson to Darling (and attached statement), 27 July 1951, GGSA.

9 Westcott to Darling, undated; Darling to Westcott, undated; Darling to Wilson, 14 August 1951; Darling to Dedman, 3 May 1947; Wilson to Darling, 4 September 1951, all GGSA.

10 Darling, 'Inaugural Address', HMCA, Triennial meeting, 17 January 1949, Minutes, pp. 24–5, 71–2; Standing committee meeting, 24 October 1949, Minutes, pp. 4–5, both WCA; Aitken to Darling, 6 July 1949; Darling to Gilray, 27 February 1950; Darling to Hone, 24 March 1950; Gilray to Fadden, 20 March 1950, all 008-01, ACEA; Colman to Darling, 16 July 1950, GGSA.

11 Darling to Gilray—pencilled note on Lansdown to Darling, 18 October 1950, GGSA; Brown to Darling, 21 November 1950; Gilray and Darling to Menzies, 13 October 1950; Darling to Brown, 13 October 1950, all 008-01, ACEA.

12 Gorton to Darling, 26[?] October 1950, GGSA; Brown to Darling, 26 October 1950, 23 November 1950, both 008-01, ACEA; Darling to Gorton, 30 October 1950; Darling to Brown, 15 November 1950, both GGSA; Robson to Darling, 23 November 1950, 008-01, ACEA.

13 Menzies to Gilray, 17 November 1950; Brown to Darling, 21 November 1950;
Darling to Menzies, 22 November 1950, all 008-01, ACEA; Black to Darling,
28 March 1951; Darling to Black, 29 March 1951, both GGSA.

14 Darling to Menzies, 25 June 1951, GGSA; Morgan (1951), pp. 65, 139; Fadden to
Spooner, 6 July 1951—attached to Hake to Darling, 6 July 1951; Darling to Hake,
9 July 1951; Menzies to Darling, 23 August 1951, all GGSA.

15 Darling to Brown, 27 September 1951; Darling to Hake, 27 September 1951, both
GGSA.

16 Brown to Darling, 2 October 1951, GGSA; Spooner to Fadden, 28 September
1951; Andrews to Darling, 2 November 1951, 12 November 1951; Darling to
Andrews, 30 October 1951, 13 November 1951; Brown to Darling, 11 October
1951, 4 December 1951; Gorton to Darling, 1 December 1951, all 008-01, ACEA.

17 Brown to Darling, 23 April 1952; Gorton to Darling, 7 May 1952; Fadden to
Opperman, 27 June 1952; Andrews to Darling, 25 July 1952, all 008-01, ACEA;
Opperman to Darling, 7 August 1952; Darling to Opperman, 7 August 1952, both
GGSA; Opperman to Darling, 18 August 1952; Menzies to Darling, 18 August
1952, both 008-01, ACEA; Darling to Menzies, 30 August 1954; Yeend to Darling,
3 September 1954, both GGSA.

18 *RR*, p. 186; Darling to Dedman, 23 April 1946, 24 April 1946, 18 March 1948,
13 April 1948; Dedman to Darling, 23 April 1948, all GGSA; Hudson (1986),
pp. 197–8.

19 Niall (2009), pp. 16, 164, 190, 237.

20 Hackett to Darling, undated, 008-01, ACEA; Hackett to Darling, undated,
23 April 1950, undated [1952?], all GGSA.

21 Niall (2009), pp. 267–9; *ADB*, vol. 9, p. 154; Darling to Mannix, 14 July 1954,
GGSA.

22 Dunlop to Darling, 7 February 1950; Fairfax to Darling, 8 April 1948; Whitney to
Cameron, 23 August 1939, all GGSA.

23 Darling to Dunlop, 10 February 1950; Darling to Casey, 26 February 1947, both
GGSA.

24 Alomes et al. (1986), pp. 8–12; Hilliard (1997), pp. 133–5; *ADB*, vol. 15, pp. 222–5;
Niall (2009), pp. 244–5; Wolfson (1964); copy of the *Call*, GGSA; Sayers (1980),
pp. 309, 310–11.

25 Darling to Guiness, 4 August 1953; Bush to Darling, 10 May 1952, Herring to
Darling, 5 July 1952; Bush to Darling, 7 February 1953, all GGSA; *Corian*, 1951
(December).

26 'Crisis and Opportunity', September 1951; 'Ballarat—Home and Family Week',
5 May 1952; 'Needs of Australian democracy', 25 September 1952; 'Apex
Convention' (undated); Address to Horsham High School speech night, 9
December 1954; 'Education for the crisis', 19 August 1954, all DP.

27 Darling (1955), p. 561.

28 Darling (1946), p. 10; McLaren to Darling, 14 November 1949; Darling to
McLaren, 16 November 1949, both GGSA.

29 Report to council, 13 May 1946; GGSC, Meeting, 12 May 1947, Minutes, p. 231;
Darling to Hime, 26 August 1947; Darling to Westerton, 2 April 1947; Darling to
Compton, 26 November 1947; Darling to MacDonald, 5 January 1948; Darling to

Hunter, 5 January 1948, Darling to Drake, 8 March 1948, all GGSA; Megarrity (2007), pp. 91–2.

30 Megarrity (2007), p. 97; Darling to Eastman, 28 June 1949; Darling to Navayudh, 17 October 1952, both GGSA.

31 *Corian*, 1949 (December), p. 166; Darling to Chambers, 25 March 1947, GGSA.

32 Strong to Darling, 15 February 1946; Cranswick to Darling, 29 April 1946; 5 February 1947 (and attachment), 20 February 1947; Darling to Holyman, 21 February 1947; Darling to Cranswick, 5 March 1947; Darling to Peters, 22 June 1951, all GGSA.

33 'Crisis and Opportunity', September 1951, DP; Darling to Casey, 14 May 1951; Darling to High Commissioner, Singapore, 14 May 1951, both GGSA.

34 Truscott to Darling, 4 July 1951; Darling to Casey, 10 July 1951; Jamieson to Darling, 13 August 1951; Casey to Menzies, 19 July 1951; Casey to Darling, 4 September 1951 (and enclosure), all GGSA.

35 *Corian*, 1951 (August), pp. 87, 97, (December), p. 167; Hamilton to Darling, 1 April 1952, 14 May 1952; Casey to Darling, 14 March 1951, 9 May 1952, 24 August 1953; Darling to Hamilton, 17 April 1953, all GGSA.

36 *Corian*, 1948 (August), p. 84; Darling to Fisher, 9 August 1938; Oxford University, 'Note on the admission of overseas students'; Darling to Brown, 12 October 1945; Masterman to Darling, 19 July 1949; Darling to Miles, 1 July 1946, all GGSA.

37 Howard to Darling, 28 May 1948; Stallybrass to Darling, 12 November 1943; Thirkill to Darling, 11 February 1946; Masterman to Darling, 22 March 1948; Darling to Cherry, 17 July 1953; Darling to Trevelyan, 15 May 1949; Evennett to Darling, 13 June 1949, all GGSA.

38 McKie to Darling, 17 April 1953, GGSA.

18 A great common enterprise

1 James to Darling, 3 June 1955; GGSC, Meetings, 11 June 1951, 8 October 1951, Minutes, pp. 92, 97–8; Minutes of meeting in the headmaster's house, 9 June 1951, p. 2; Darling to Colman, 26 July 1951, all GGSA; *TT*, pp. 26–7; Darling to Black, 10 October 1951, GGSA.

2 Black to Darling, 19 December 1951, GGSA; *TT*, p. 28.

3 Darling to Gatenby, 30 May 1951, GGSA.

4 *TT*, p. 8; Darling to Dickson, 30 July 1951; Darling to Colman, 5 December 1951; Darling to Willington, 14 August 1952; Darling to Hake, 30 September 1954, all GGSA; *Corian*, 1952 (May), p. 68; Reports to council, 12 May 1952, 13 October 1952, both GGSA.

5 Hodgkin (1986); Hahn (1957), pp. 449–50; Hahn (1934); Barker (1975), pp. 182–4; Chapman to Darling, 13 July 1941, DP; Browne to Darling, 11 September 1941, GGSA.

6 Report to council, 9 April 1951, p. 2, GGSA; Hahn (1950), p. 527; Hahn (1957), p. 436; Darling (1954), p. 223; Turner to Darling, 26 August 1954, GGSA.

7 *Corian*, 1951 (December), pp. 149, 150, 151, 152, 154.

8 Darling to Black, 25 October 1951, GGSA; Darling to Brown, 25 October 1951, 008-01, ACEA; Ritchie to Darling, undated; Darling to Nicholas, 30 October 1951; Nicholas to Darling, 12 November 1951; Memorandum on financing Timbertop scheme, undated, all GGSA.

9   Black to Darling, 19 December 1951, 10 January 1952, 20 January 1952, 1 May
    1952; Darling to Luxton, 13 March 1952, all GGSA; *Corian*, 1952 (May), pp. 15,
    16, 67–9, 13–14.
10 *Corian*, 1951 (May), p. 16; Reports to council, 9 June 1952, p. 1, 14 July 1952, p. 2,
    both GGSA; *Corian*, 1952 (August), p. 91, 1952 (December), p. 171.
11 TC, Meeting, 15 July 1952, Minutes (unnumbered), GGSA; Chapman to Darling,
    14 September 1952; Darling to Chapman, 27 October 1952, both DP, ms 7826,
    s7, b15, f6, NLA; Darling (1987–88), Edward Hugh Montgomery, *Corian*, p. 15;
    TT, p. 19; Manifold to Darling, 6 October 1948, DP; Leslie (1985), p. 151; Gronn
    (1999).
12 *Corian*, 1953 (August), p. 103; 1951 (December), pp. 160–1; 1952 (December),
    p. 162; *TT*, pp. 29, 33, 38; Darling to Griffiths, 14 January 1953; Report to council,
    16 February 1953, p. 1; Broadbent to Darling, 12 February 1953; Darling to
    Bickersteth, 13 November 1953, all GGSA
13 *Corian*, 1953 (May), pp. 15, 17; 1948 (May), p. 9; A.E.M. Williams (1956)
    'Journeys from Timbertop', *Timbertop Magazine*, 1, p. 19; Greene to Darling,
    12 November 1953; Report to council, 13 July 1953, p. 2; Hake to Darling, 28 July
    1953; Black to Darling, 28 August 1953; Darling to Griffiths, 9 April 1952;
    Darling to Latrielle, 9 April 1952; Darling to Black, 9 April 1952, all GGSA.
14 Darling to Jackson, 6 July 1953, GGSA; *Corian*, 1953 (December), pp. 184–5,
    190–2; Darling to Norris, 15 October 1953, GGSA.
15 *Corian*, 1954 (May), p. 72; Reports to council, 18 October 1954, p. 1, 20 September
    1954, p. 1, 15 March 1954, p. 1; Darling to Mitchell, 13 October 1960, all GGSA.
16 Reports to council, 20 September 1954, p. 1, 21 June 1954, p. 1, 20 December 1954,
    p. 1, 16 August 1954, p. 1, 19 July 1954, p. 1; 'Hygiene inspection report' Geelong
    Grammar School, 'Timbertop', 15–18 November 1954; Montgomery to Darling,
    19 September 1956, all GGSA; *Corian*, 1954 (December), p. 181.
17 A.L. Moore 'Australia', *International Yearbook of Education, 1954*, p. 65; Darling
    (1954), pp. 223–5; J.D.G. Medley, 'School at Mt. Timbertop', *Age*, 24 April 1954;
    Medley to Darling, 22 April 1954, GGSA; 'Where men and mountains meet:
    Geelong's settlement in the bush', *Times Educational Supplement*, 15 October 1954,
    p. 964; Hahn (1957), p. 448.
18 Montgomery to Darling, 28 April 1957; Desborough to Montgomery, 21 January
    1955; Montgomery to Jaffray, 23 October 1955, all GGSA; *Corian*, 1957 (August),
    p. 137; Jaffray to Commerford, 4 July 1955, GGSA.
19 Montgomery to Jaffray, 23 March 1955; Report to council, 15 March 1954; Hone
    to Darling, 30 April 1954; Turner to Darling, 13 June 1954, 5 November 1954,
    6 December 1954, all GGSA; Hahn to Darling, 26 September 1955, DP; Mattingley
    to Darling, 3 November 1954; Brookes to Darling, 18 March 1954, both GGSA.
20 Nimmo to Darling, 18 February 1954, DP, ms 7826, s7, b20, f42, NLA; *Corian*,
    1954 (May), p. 12; Darling to Parker, 8 April 1954, 27 April 1956, 14 September
    1956; Parker to Darling, 19 April 1956, 26 September 1956; Darling to
    Montgomery, 29 October 1956, all GGSA.
21 *Corian*, 1955 (May), p. 13; Jaffray to Montgomery, 16 March 1955; Darling to
    Montgomery, 14 November 1955; Montgomery to Jaffray, 18 September 1955;
    Report to council, 7 November 1955, all GGSA.

22 Darling to Montgomery, 10 March 1955; Montgomery to Darling, 7 November 1955, both GGSA.

23 Montgomery to Darling, 7 November 1955; Darling to Montgomery, 14 November 1955; James to Darling, 3 June 1955, all GGSA.

24 Montgomery to Darling, 11 June 1956, 21 March 1956; Report to council, 8 October 1956, p. 2; Darling to Montgomery, 17 October 1956, all GGSA.

25 Montgomery to Darling, 28 March 1957, 6 October 1957, 15 February 1957, 3 March 1957, 24 October 1956; Darling to Montgomery, 20 February 1957; Report to council, 8 October 1956, all GGSA.

26 Montgomery to Darling, 9 March 1959, 3 May 1959, both GGSA.

27 Montgomery to Darling, 18 February 1957; Evaluation, pp. 282–3, 280; Victoria, Education Department, Inspector's Report Book, G.G.S. Timbertop, 1995, pp. 2–3, all GGSA.

28 Evaluation, pp. 280–1; P.J. McKeown to the author, 24 May 1985; J. Pickett-Heaps to the author, 20 May 1985; Anon (1956) 'Preamble', *Timbertop Magazine*, 1, pp. 4–5; Darling (1958) 'Foreword', *Timbertop Magazine*, 3, p. 5; Darling to Montgomery, 15 July 1958; Report to council, 13 March 1961, p. 2, all GGSA; *Corian*, 1961 (May), p. 31.

29 Evaluation, p. 283; Darling to Montgomery, 10 March 1955, both GGSA; C.C. McKnight to the author, 24 May 1985; J. Pickett-Heaps to the author, 20 May 1985.

30 Montgomery to Darling, 3 March 1957, 28 April 1957, both GGSA; *Corian*, 1955 (December), p. 193, 1956 (December), p. 187, 1957 (May), p. 21; Darling to Carnegie, 21 June 1954; Ritchie to Darling, 7 December 195[4?], both GGSA.

31 Darling to Montgomery, 22 February 1955; J.S. Turner & J.M. Stevens (1955) 'Preliminary report on "Timbertop" school grounds', 18 February; Report to council, 18 October 1954, p. 1, all GGSA; *Corian*, 1953 (December), p. 179; Desborough to Montgomery, 21 January 1955, GGSA; *Corian*, 1960 (May), pp. 18, 31; Black to Darling, 17 February 1960, GGSA.

32 Darling to Black, 18 February 1960; Report to council, 14 March 1960, pp. 2–3; Darling to Montgomery, 15 March 1960, all GGSA.

33 Clark (2003), p. 79; Darling to Woods, 18 February 1958, 7 March 1958; Darling to Montgomery, 21 February 1958, 25 February 1958; Report to council, 24 March 1958, all GGSA; *TT*, p. 111; Montgomery to Darling, 25 March 1958, 14 April, 1958, both GGSA.

34 Clipping, *Mansfield Courier*, undated; Montgomery to Darling, 6 December 1958; Darling to Montgomery, 9 December 1958; Ritchie to Darling, 8 December 1958; Woods to Darling, 8 December 1958, all GGSA; *Corian*, 1957 (December), p. 216, 1959 (May), p. 14, (August), p. 113; Report to council, 13 July 1959, p. 1, GGSA.

35 Montgomery to Darling, 21 March 1956, 10 November 1958, 13 February 1955; Reports to council, 10 July 1961, p. 7, 10 November 1958, p. 4; Darling to Montgomery, 13 October 1960, all GGSA.

36 Darling to Montgomery, 19 March 1957; Montgomery to Darling, 22 March 1957, 4 April 1957; Darling to Phillis, 10 December 1959; Reports to council, 4 December 1959, p. 1; 21 February 1955, p. 1; 12 March 1956, p. 1; 9 March 1959, p. 1; 10 October 1960, p. 1; 10 July 1961, p. 5, all GGSA.

37 *Corian*, 1961 (May), p. 32; Montgomery to Darling, 17 November 1955, 19 June
    1956, both GGSA; *Corian*, 1956 (August), p. 107; Leslie (1985), p. 148; Darling to
    Booth, 25 June 1956; Booth to Darling, 27 June 1956, all GGSA.
38 Darling to Montgomery, 7 October 1956; Montgomery to Darling, 13 July 1960,
    both GGSA; *Corian*, 1956 (August), p. 108.
39 Report to council, 13 March 1961, p. 1; Darling to Gordon, 30 April 1957; Darling
    to Fisk, 22 August 1951, all GGSA; *Corian*, 1953 (May), p. 18; 1961 (August),
    p. 158; Darling to Montgomery, 9 August 1961, GGSA.

19 Naked emperor?
1   Darling to le Fleming, 29 July 1951, DP.
2   Report to council, 19 March 1951, p. 2; Darling to Griffiths, 20 March 1951; Black
    to Griffiths, 8 April 1952; Darling to Robson, 9 April 1952; Robson to Darling,
    17 April, 1952, all GGSA.
3   GGSC, Meeting, 12 May 1952, Minutes, p. 110; Reports to council, 9 June 1952,
    11 August 1952, p. 3; Darling to Griffiths, 11 July 1952, all GGSA; *Corian*, 1952
    (August), p. 93.
4   Darling to Bennett, 28 July 1952; Darling to Dicker, 25 July 1952, both GGSA;
    Corian, 1952 (December), pp. 158–60; *Report on Survey of Business and Accounting
    Administration*, 25 June 1953, pp. 1, 4, 5 and 7, GGSA.
5   Minutes, extract on administrative arrangements (undated); Report to council,
    16 March 1953, p. 1, both GGSA; *Corian*, 1953 (May), p. 10; Darling to Griffiths,
    26 June 1953; *Report on Survey ...*, pp. 12, 19, both GGSA.
6   GGSC, Meeting, 13 July 1953, Minutes, p. 413; Thewlis to Griffiths, 16 July 1953;
    Memorandum on the report from the auditors, 2 July 1953, all GGSA.
7   GGSC, Meetings, 27 July 1953, 10 August 1953, Minutes, pp. 142, 10; Darling to
    Jackson, 23 February 1954; Darling to Griffiths, 22 October 1953; Flack & Flack
    to Griffiths, 16 November 1953; Darling to Griffiths, 26 November 1953, 1 March
    1954, all GGSA.
8   Black to Darling, 12 March 1954; Memorandum (Confidential), 11 April
    1954; Memorandum (Administration and Finance), 13 April 1954; Darling to
    Griffiths, 15 April 1954; Desborough to Darling, 28 July 1954, Flack & Flack to
    Griffiths, 11 August 1954; Memorandum on Accounting and Clerical Procedures
    for discussion with Finance Committee, 25 August 1954; Darling to Hewan,
    30 August 1954; Darling to Jackson, 13 July 1954; Black to Darling, 1 September
    1954, all GGSA.
9   Darling to McLeay, 9 June 1950; Brown to Darling, 21 June 1950, 27 October
    1953; Darling to Brown, 30 September 1953, 13 October 1953, all GGSA.
10 Black to Darling, 26 July 1954, 12 March 1954; Darling to Black, 28 July 1954;
    Darling to the Manager, Shell (Geelong), 2 July 1954; Crook to Darling, 26 August
    1954; Thomson to Darling, 12 July 1954, all GGSA; *Corian*, 1954 (December),
    p. 179; Jaffray, Report to council, 25 July 1955; Darling to Thomson, 14 July 1954,
    both GGSA.
11 Black to Griffiths, 20 August 1952; GGSC, Meeting, 18 October 1954, Minutes,
    p. 171, both GGSA; *Corian*, 1954 (December), p. 182; Darling to Black,
    27 October 1954; Darling to the Bishop of Wangaratta, 26 August 1954; GGSC,
    Meeting, 15 November 1954, Minutes, p. 172, all GGSA.

12   McDonald to Darling, 28 January 1953; Hone to Darling, 4 March 1953; Buntine
     to Darling, 20 April 1953; Darling to Buntine, 23 April 1953; Darling to McIndoe,
     18 November 1954; Darling to Montgomery, 14 November 1955; Darling to Lewis,
     25 February 1955, all GGSA.

13   Darling to Hutton, 28 March 1955, GGSA; M.R. Darling to J.R. Darling,
     13 December 1954; le Fleming to Darling, 24 April 1955, both DP, ms 7826, s7,
     b16 (1st) and b19 (2nd), NLA; Darling to Hutton, 2 May 1955, 7 May 1955, both
     GGSA; J.B. Darling to J.R. Darling, 15 May 1950, DP, ms 7826, s7, b16, NLA.

14   Black to Darling, 22 June 1955, 21 July 1955; 'Meditations on the future of the
     public schools and of Geelong Grammar School in particular', 8 August 1955;
     Bennett to Darling, 12 August 1955, all GGSA.

15   ? to Darling, 12 June 1955, DP, ms 7826, s7, b15, NLA; McKie to Darling,
     15 September 1955; Fraser to Darling, 6 September 1955; Hutton to Darling,
     9 May 1955; Darling to MacLean, 12 March 1955; Darling to fforde, 10 March
     1955; Kelsey to Darling, 5 April, 1955; BBC Talks Booking Manager to Darling
     12 July 1955; Weltman to Darling, 23 August 1955; Darling to Schonell, 6
     December 1955, all GGSA; J.R. Darling to J.B. Darling, 11 October 1955, DP.

16   M. Darling to J.R. Darling, 29 September 1955; Desborough to Darling,
     19 October 1955, both DP, ms 7826, s7, b18 (1st) and b16 (2nd), NLA; Reports to
     council, 12 December 1955, p. 1, 13 August 1956, p. 1, both GGSA.

17   *Corian*, 1956 (August), p. 105; GGSC, Meeting, 13 August 1956, Minutes,
     pp. 223–4, GGSA; *Corian*, 1956 (December), p. 191; Darling to Jackson, 27 June
     1956, GGSA.

18   Fairfax to Darling, 9 August 1956; Darling to Fairfax, 10 August 1956; Black to
     Darling, 13 March 1956; 'Memorandum regarding consolidated borrowing plan
     of Geelong Church of England Grammar School' (undated); 'Information for Old
     Geelong Grammarians' Committees and Agents-in-Chief, and reasons for the
     Centenary Building Restoration Fund' (undated), all GGSA.

19   Cash to Chisholm, 20 May 1957, GGSA; Ritchie to Darling, 1 August 1957;
     Gollancz to Darling, 29 November 1957, 10 December 1957; Darling to Gollancz,
     5 December 1957, all DP, ms 7826, s7, b21 f46 (1st) and b17, f19 (2nd–4th), NLA;
     RR, p. 137; Black to Darling, 29 April 1957; GGSC, Meetings, 12 August 1957,
     14 October 1957, Minutes, pp. 3, 1; Fairfax to Darling, 4 November 1957; Turner
     to Darling, 8 November 1957, all GGSA.

20   Darling to Scott, 2 April 1957; Darling to Hake, 23 April 1958; Darling to
     Hancock, 12 December 1956; Hancock to Darling, 19 December 1956, all GGSA.

21   Black to Darling, 26 June 1957; Darling to Fairfax, 28 June 1957; Darling to
     Griffiths, 11 December 1957; Spowers to Darling, 2 July 1957; all GGSA; *Corian*,
     1957 (August), pp. 128–32; Darling to Allen, 28 June 1957; Allen to Darling,
     27 June 1957, both GGSA; *ADB*, vol. 9, p. 231.

22   *Corian*, 1957 (December), pp. 224–6; Persse (1960), preface, pp. 87, 55, 93; Report
     to council, 11 November 1957, GGSA.

23   Connell (1984), p. 3; *RR*, p. 202; W.F. Connell to H.B. Connell, 17 September
     1956; Reports to council, 8 October 1956, 12 November 1956; Darling to Connell,
     25 September 1956, 9 October 1956, 2 November 1956, 13 November 1956;
     Connell to Darling, 8 November 1956, all GGSA.

24 Connell to Darling, 5 February 1957; Darling to Connell, 20 June 1957; *Evaluation of Geelong C. of E Grammar (Secondary) School—1957*, pp. iii, 5–6, 8–9, all GGSA.

25 *Evaluation*, pp. 19, 21, 23, 24, 25, 28, 29, 209, 275, GGSA.

26 *Ibid.*, pp. 314, 316–17, 318–19, 320, 321, 322, 328, 334, 338, 339, 352, 353, 354.

27 Darling to Richardson, 18 February 1958, GGSA; *RR*, p. 202; Darling to Connell, 14 February 1957, 28 June 1957, 28 January 1958; Report to council, 11 November 1957, all GGSA.

28 Darling to Black, 13 February, 27 February 1958; Darling to Griffiths, 30 April 1958; D. Fraser, memorandum (undated); K.J. Mappin, memorandum, 30 April 1958; Maynard to Darling, 17 April 1953; Westcott to Darling, 18 April 1953, all GGSA.

29 Muggeridge (1958).

30 Packer to Darling, 11 April 1958; Darling to Packer, 12 April 1958; Dutton to Darling, 6 May 1958; Darling to Fairfax, 23 April 1958; Fairfax to Darling, 28 April 1958; Jackson to Darling, 16 April 1958, all GGSA.

31 Report to council, 12 May 1958; Memorandum, 21 April 1958; Connell to Darling, 10 November 1960; Darling to Connell, 12 November 1960; Report to council, 14 November 1960, all GGSA; Gott (1960).

32 Mackie to Darling, 1 December 1960; Gullett to Darling, 17 February 1959; Scriven to Darling, 12 April 1959; 'Inspection of the school in 1957 by Professor W.F. Connell—Comments on his report', 21 April 1958; all GGSA.

33 Darling to Black, 13 February 1958; Darling to Richardson, 18 February 1958; Darling to Garner, 9 July 1958; Black to Darling, 31 March 1958; Darling to Fairfax, 27 February 1959 (includes Memorandum on Finance, 24 February 1959); GGSC, Meeting, 9 March 1959, Minutes, p. 283, all GGSA.

34 'Draft', 12 October 1976, DP, ms 7826, s15, b31, f2, NLA; Black to Darling, 10 April 1957 (extract of will attached), GGSA; *Corian*, 1959 (December), pp. 203–4, 1960 (December), p. 224; *RR*, pp. 204–5.

35 'Memorandum for finance committee—27 April 1959, GGSA; Darling to McArthur, 14 September 1980 (unsent), DP, ms 7826, s15, b31, f2, NLA; Black to Darling, 29 May 1959, 3 June 1959, 8 June 1959; Darling to Black, 31 May 1959, 18 June 1959, all GGSA.

36 *Corian*, 1957 (December), p. 218; Report to council, 21 September 1959; Darling, Handwritten notes and financial statement, C59/393 (undated); Fairfax to Buttfield, 18 November 1959; Buttfield to Fairfax, 25 November 1959; Fairfax to Darling, 1 December 1959; Ingoldby to Desborough, 18 February 1960; Desborough to Manager, AMP, 11 May 1960, all GGSA.

37 Darling to Woods, 11 June 1959, 19 November 1959; GGSC, Meetings, 8 August 1960, 14 November 1960 ('The Highton project (C60/515) Amended' appendix), 8 May 1961, Minutes, pp. 318, unnumbered, 14; Woods to Darling, 22 October 1959; Report to council, 13 March 1961, all GGSA.

38 Darling to Griffiths, 1 July 1959; Rolland to Darling, 23 January 1959, both GGSA.

39 Gordon to Darling, 4 November 1943, GGSA; *ADB*, vol. 14, p. 481; Hamilton to Darling, 23 September 1942, GGSA.

40 Dixon to Darling, undated; Testimonial, 7 March 1958; Darling to Moyes,
    16 March 1958; Darling to Ludowici, 4 July 1958; Ludowici to Darling, 22 July
    1958; all GGSA.
41 Darling to Robson, 25 September 1957; Darling to Ludowici, 24 July 1958,
    5 August 1958; 'Ideas for draft letter', undated, all GGSA.
42 Travers to Darling, 6 September 1958; Robson to Darling, 4 September 1958,
    6 July 1958, 13 November 1958; Darling to Hone, 9 October 1958, all GGSA.
43 Darling to Griffiths, 1 July 1959, GGSA; Darling to le Fleming, 4 August 1959,
    DP; Darling to Bickersteth, 29 February 1960, GGSA; Darling to Robson,
    18 September 1959, Robson to Darling, 23 September 1959, both ACEA 008-14;
    GGSC, Meeting, 13 July 1959, Minutes, p. 292; Black to Darling, 3 July 1959, both
    GGSA.
44 Gordon to Darling, 3 May 1960; Turner to Darling, 6 August 1954, 13 January
    1960; Darling to Turner 16 August 1954, all GGSA; Fletcher to Darling,
    12 August 1933, DP; GGSC, Meetings, 11 July 1960, 8 August 1960, Minutes,
    pp. 312–13, 318–19, both GGSA.
45 Darling to Moyes, 15 September 1960, GGSA; *Corian*, 1960 (August), pp. 115–16;
    GGSC, Meeting, 11 July 1960, Minutes, p. 312, GGSA; *Corian*, 1960 (December),
    p. 223.
46 Report to council, 10 July 1961, p. 1; Darling to Brown, 2 August 1961, both GGSA.

20 Civilising a citizenry

1   Darling to Gordon, 11 May 1960, GGSA; Burke (1986 [1790]), p. 281; Darling
    (1960), pp. 4, 5, 8, 11, 14, 15.
2   Darling (1953?), pp. 59; Darling to Cremean, 22 July 1954; Darling to Warner,
    4 July 1956; Annual Report of the Geelong and District Hospital (1958–9), all DP,
    ms 7826, s5, b9, NLA.
3   Darling to Brown, 19 August 1953; Tullis to Darling, 25 October 1960; Darling to
    Tullis, 26? October 1960, all GGSA; Darling (1960), p. 8.
4   Morgan to Waddams, 4 October 1953; Waddams to Officer, 5 October 1953;
    Officer to Darling, 12 November 1953; Darling to Buchanan, 25 November 1953,
    all GGSA.
5   Buchanan to Darling, 17 December 1953, 31 December 1953; Darling to
    Buchanan, 21 December 1953, 1 June 1954; Buchanan to Parker, 30 December
    1953, Report of the Council of the Outward Bound Trust, 1954, all GGSA.
6   Report to council, 12 August 1957, p. 3; Darling to the APS headmasters,
    28 October 1953, both GGSA; APS, Meeting, 19 April 1952, Minutes
    (unnumbered) MGSA; Darling to Frederick, 2 May 1951; Frederick to Darling,
    14 May 1951, both GGSA.
7   APS, Meeting, 10 April 1954, Minutes (unnumbered), MGSA; 'Meeting of A.P.S.
    headmasters, Tuesday, 13th July'; 'Proposals relating to the future conduct of Public
    Schools' games and Sports', undated; Hone to Darling, 14 July 1954; Darling to
    Tunbridge, 13 July 1954, all GGSA.
8   'Memo number two to headmasters of A.P.S.', undated; Darling to the APS
    headmasters, 18 October 1954, 27 October 1954, 10 November 1954, all GGSA.
9   Darling 'The public schools association', 22 March 1956; Hone to Darling,
    28 March 1956, both GGSA.

10 Darling to Smith, 18 April 1956, GGSA; APS, Meetings, 14 April 1956, 22 October 1956, 8 August 1957, 8 October 1957, 26 October 1957, 6 November 1957, Minutes (unnumbered), all MGSA.

11 APS, Meeting, 22 November 1957 (parts 1, 2), Minutes (unnumbered), MGSA; Timpson to Coates and Darling, 28 June 1961, 009-08, ACEA; Hone to Darling, 9 November 1959; Darling to Hone, 12 November 1959, both GGSA.

12 Darling to Ramsay, 31 May 1956; Darling to Hunt, 13 September 1958, 15 September 1958; all GGSA; CPE, Meetings, 14 April 1953, 7 July 1953, 10 April 1956, Minutes, pp. 326, 330, 359–60, all VPRS, 11353/P0001, Unit 5, Minute Book, 1938–1956, VPRO; Darling to Stevenson, 8 October 1958, GGSA; CPE, Meetings, 7 November 1956, 2 April 1957, 10 March 1959, 7 July 1959, 7 March 1961, Minutes, pp. 1, 2, 5, 10, 28, 31–5, 60, all VPRS 11353/P0001, Unit 6, Minute Book, 1956–1975, VPRO.

13 UMC, Minutes, 1952–1961 (books 44–53); Meetings, 17 October 1952, 2 March 1953, 4 May 1953, Minutes, pp. 281, 31, 102, all UMA; Poynter and Rasmussen (1996), p. 165; Darling to Clunies Ross, 20 January 1955; Martin to Darling, 7 January 1957; Paton to Darling, 11 February 1957, all GGSA.

14 CA 51/3, Agency registration sheet, 12 August 1980, NAA.

15 CIAC, 21st Meeting, 5–6 August, 1953, Minutes, min 475, p. 3; 23rd Meeting, 19 March, 1954, Minutes, min 532, p. 4, both A2169, NAA; Darling to Johnston, 6 March 1953, GGSA.

16 Heyes to Darling, 9 March 1955; Darling to Brown, 1 May 1955, both file 65/46066, NAA.

17 Heyes to Brown, 26 May 1955, GGSA.

18 Brown to Darling, 2 June 1955, GGSA; *Corian*, 1955 (December), pp. 252–3; CIAC, 29th Meeting, 5–6 April 1956, Minutes, min 726, p. 7 and agenda item 11, 'Citizenship convention 1956', A2169; Heyes to Darling, 16 January 1957, file 65/46066, both NAA; Massey to Darling, 4 February 1959, DP; CIAC, 30th Meeting, 26–27 July 1956, Minutes, min 763, p. 4, A2169, NAA.

19 'What immigration means to me' (undated); Heyes to Darling, 2 May 1957, 1 September 1958; Darling to Heyes, 20 June 1958, file 65/46066, all NAA; Darling to le Fleming, 4 August 1959, DP; Darling to Fairfax, 28 July 1958, GGSA; Darling to Heyes, 9 March 1961, 14 March 1961, both DP.

20 Darling to Scott, 3 July 1959; Darling to Nimmo, 7 December 1956; both GGSA; Martin (1989), pp. 176, 180–2; Harrison to Darling, 3 December 1956, DP, ms 7826, s7 b18, f22, NLA.

21 Darling to Harrison, 12 December 1956, DP, ms 7826, s7, b18, f22, NLA.

22 *Ibid.*

23 Darling to Henderson, 2 December 1955; Darling to Sinker, 2 May 1958; Darling to Pitman, 18 July 1958, all GGSA.

24 Sinker to Darling, 19 May 1958, 22 July 1958; Darling to Sinker, 17 June 1958; Norway to Darling, 26 September 1958, 16 October 1958; Darling to Norway, 13 October 1958; Darling to Menzies, 28 June 1957, all GGSA.

25 *Corian*, 1954 (December), p. 191; Phillips to Darling, 15 December 1954; Darling to Phillips, 25 February 1955, both GGSA; 'Some principles of sex education, so-called', 6 September 1956, DP; Darling to Feiglin, 16 September 1960, GGSA.

26   Fred Schwarz, *Wikipedia*, https://en.wikipedia.org/wiki/Fred_Schwarz (accessed, 25 November 2012); Herring to Darling, 16 April 1959; Darling to Casey, 23 July 1959, both GGSA; Darling to le Fleming, 4 August 1959, DP; Darling to Sholl, 23 July 1959; Sholl to Darling 26 July 1959, both GGSA.

27   Casey to Darling, 28 July 1959, GGSA.

28. Darling to Herring, 14 November 1958, GGSA; Hilliard (1997), p. 135; Hilliard (1991), p. 399; Darling to Murphy, 19 August 1958, 3 October 1958; Darling to Gleeson, 10 April 1959; Gleeson to Darling, 11 April 1959, all GGSA; *Corian*, 1960 (December), p. 218.

29   Darling to Gleeson, 10 November 1960, GGSA; Gleeson to Darling, 17 May 1960, 008-15, ACEA; Gleeson to Darling, 26 May 1960, 27 April 1961, 29 April 1961, all GGSA; CPE, Meeting, 4 March 1958, Minutes, p. 13, VPRS, 11353/P0001, Unit 6, Minute Book, 1956–1975, VPRO.

30   Porter (2007), pp. 15–16; Boase to Darling, 11 October 1956; Darling to Boase, 11 April 1957; Darling to Fisher, 11 April 1957, all GGSA.

31   Darling to Fisher, 11 April 1957; Darling to Boase, 15 October 1957, both GGSA.

32   Porter (2007), pp. 29–30; Darling to Woods, 23 September 1957; Woods to Darling, 1 October 1957, both GGSA; Fisher to Darling, 17 June 1958, DP.

33   Gardiner (1993), pp. 131, 128; Connell (1993), p. 104; Sholl to Darling, 26 July 1959, GGSA.

34   Woods to Darling, 21 October 1958, GGSA; Sabey to Darling, 28 October 1958; McKie, 'Memorandum on possible courses of action for the council', undated, both DP.

35   McKie to Darling, 9 July 1958, GGSA; Gardiner (1993), pp. 139–40; 'Memorandum on the Merton Hall crisis' (dictated over the telephone to Mr. Sabey, 29.10.58)', DP; Woods to Darling, 12 November 1958, GGSA.

36   Darling to le Fleming, 4 August 1960, DP; Gordon to Darling, 1 May 1959, GGSA; Disney to Darling, 19 May 1959; Gordon to Darling, 20 May 1959, both 007-09, ACEA; Darling to Arrowsmith, 20 September 1960; 'Colin S.E. Gordon', 19 September 1960, both DP.

37   Alexander to Darling, 12 June 1958; Austin to Darling, 20 June 1958; Gleeson to Darling, 13 June 1958, all DP.

38   Darling to le Fleming, 4 August 1960; Darling to Scriven, 21 April 1959, both DP; Raven (1943), p. 103; Darling (1960), p. 12.

21   Filling a gap

1   Hogg (1986), p. 142; Darling to le Fleming, 4 August 1959, DP; Report to council, July 1959, GGSA; Darling to Slim, 18 December 1959, 008-14, ACEA.

2   *RR*, p. 202; MacNeil to Darling, 11 May 1958, 008-12, ACEA.

3   Robertson to Timpson, 26 March 1959, 007-02, ACEA; Cunningham, circular letter, 15 May 1951, GGSA; HMCA, Triennial Meeting 1957, Minutes, pp. 11–12, 17, 008-11, ACEA.

4   'Beginnings' (1999), oral history interview with seven founders, ACEA; Phillips (1962), p. 105.

5   'Beginnings' (1999), ACEA; Timpson (1984), pp. 107–8; Coates to Sanders, 14 July 1958; Coates to Miller; 12 March 1958; Coates to Paton, 11 April 1958; 'Minutes of meeting held at Wesley College …' (6 June 1958); Darling, 'Notes on a proposal

to form a professional institute or college for the teaching profession', 9 June 1958, all 007-01, ACEA.

6 'Minutes of meeting of a special committee to make recommendations about the formation of an institute of education ...', 27 June 1958; Darling to Coates, 29 June 1958; Timpson to Darling, 9 July 1958, 15 July 1958; Darling to Timpson, 10 July 1958; Gordon to Timpson, 31 July 1958, 008-11 (2nd–5th) and 007-01 (1st & 6th), ACEA.

7 Darling to Timpson, 18 July 1958; Healey to Darling, 23 July 1958; Darling to Healey, 29 July 1958; Timpson to Healey, 18 August 1958, 30 July 1958; Sanders to Coates, 16 July 1958, 007-01 (1st, 2nd & 4th–6th) and 008-11 (3rd), ACEA.

8 'A statement of aims and organisation for an institute of education prepared by a special committee and presented to a meeting of interested people ...', 1 August 1958; 'Minutes of meeting ...', 1 August 1958; 'Aims and organisation of the college of education agreed to at a constituent meeting ...', 1 August 1958; Darling to Timpson, 4 August 1958; Robson to Darling, 18 September 1958; Darling to Selby Smith, 2 October 1958; Darling to Bailey, 25 September 1958; Timpson to Darling, 8 August 1958; Darling to Coates, 12 August 1958, 007-01 (1st–3rd & 9th) and 008-11 (4th–8th), ACEA.

9 'Minutes of meeting of the provisional council of the College of Education ...', 22 September 1958; Gordon to Darling, 22 October 1958; 'The College of Education', 28 November 1958; Timpson to Healey, 2 October 1958; Hewan to Timpson, 4 November 1958; Hewan to Darling, 21 October 1958, 007-02 (1st & 4th), 008-11 (2nd & 6th) and 007-01 (3rd & 5th), ACEA.

10 'Minutes of meeting of the provisional council of the College of Education ...', 20 October 1958; Hewan to Timpson, 4 November 1958; 'Minutes of meeting of the provisional council of the College of Education ...', 17 November 1958, 007-02 (1st & 3rd) and 008-11 (2nd), ACEA.

11 Darling to Timpson, 5 October 1958, 23 November 1958, 5 December 1958; Darling to Hewan, 24 October, 1958; Timpson to J.R. Darling, 4 December 1958, all 008-11, ACEA.

12 'Report of the secretary's visit to a special meeting ...', 6 February 1959, 007-02, ACEA.

13 Darling to Timpson, 5 February 1958; 'Minutes of meeting of the provisional council of the College of Education ...', 20 February 1959; Hogg to Robson, 10 March 1959; Sanders to Timpson, 7 May 1959; 'Minutes of meeting of the provisional council of the College of Education ...', 6 April 1959; 'The college of education' (undated), attachment to Timpson to council members, 6 March 1959, 008-12 (1st) and 007-02 (2nd–6th), ACEA.

14 Darling to Gordon, 8 April 1959; 'College of Education—Information and arrangements', 11 May 1959; Founders Convention, conference folder; 'Draft of interview—The founding of the Australian College of Education' (Dr A.W. Jones, 1998), p. 5; Sanders to Timpson, 15 May 1959, 008-12 (1st) and 007-03 (2nd–5th), ACEA.

15 'Proceedings and report of the founders' convention of the Australian College of Education, 15th to 18th May, 1959' (Third draft), pp. 9–10, 007-08, ACEA.

16 'Proceedings and report ...' (Third draft), footnote, p. 10; 'A profession and a college of education', 16 May 1959; 'The professions' (undated), 007-08 (1st) and (2nd & 3rd), ACEA.

17 Darling to Rolland, 12 May 1959; 'Proceedings and report ...', (Third draft), pp. 15–18; 'Proceedings and report ...', 26 June 1959 draft, pp. 4–5, 008-12 (1st) and 007-08 (2nd & 3rd), ACEA.

18 'Proceedings and report ...', 26 June 1959 draft, pp. 4–5; 'College of Education' (undated), pp. 15–18, (1st) and 007-04 (2nd), ACEA.

19 'Proceedings and report ...', 26 June 1959 draft, pp. 6–18, 007-06, ACEA; Phillips (1966), pp. 112–17; 'Australian College of Education' (undated), 007-04, ACEA.

20 Ibid., pp. 18–21, 007-08, ACEA.

21 Ibid., pp. 21–8.

22 Ibid., pp. 29–36.

23 Darling to Ross, 19 May 1959; Darling to Robertson, 19 May 1959; Darling to Coates, 19 May 1959; Gleeson to Darling, 20 May 1959; Darling to Ramsay, 19 May 1959; Hone to Darling, undated, 008-12 (1st–3rd), 007-09 (4th), 008-12 (5th) and 007-08 (6th), ACEA.

24 'Australian College of Education' (typescript of address to HMCA, 1959); Robertson to Darling, 22 July 1959; McGovern to Radford, 17 July 1959; Darling to Tylee, 19 May 1959; Tylee to Jordan, 28 May 1959; Golding to Darling, 18 June 1959; Darling to Golding, 23 June 1959, 007-06 (1st), 008-13 (2nd), 007-05 (3rd), 007-07 (4th & 5th) and 008-12 (6th & 7th), ACEA.

25 'Beginnings' (1999); 'Australian College of Education ...'; Timpson, memo to state chapter secretaries, 19 November 1959; Timpson to Darling, 28 July 1959; Darling to Timpson, 30 July 1959; Darling to Medley, 1 July 1959, 007-06 (1st–3rd) and 008-13 (4th–6th), ACEA.

26 Robson to Darling, 3 July 1959, 16 October 1959, 10 November 1959; Hewan to Travers, 29 June 1959; Darling to Timpson, 16 October 1959; Radford to Darling, 20 June 1959; Ramsay to Darling, 8 July 1959; Darling to Radford, 2 July 1959, 008-13 (1st, 6th–8th), 008-14 (2nd, 3rd & 5th) and 007-05 (4th), ACEA.

27 ACE, Meetings, 26 June 1959, 9–10 October 1959, 26 February 1959, Council Minutes (1959–1963) (unnumbered); Darling to Menzies, 6 August 1959; 009-14 (1st), 001-01 (2nd), ACEA.

28 ACE (undated), Educational Values in a Democracy (Melbourne: Cheshire), pp. 6, 9, 10, 11, box 101, ACEA.

29 Educational Values ..., op cit., pp. 11, 12, 13, 14, 15, 16, 17, 19; Darling to Bok, 29 February 1960, both 008-15, ACEA.

30 Melbourne Spy, 'Dr. Darling's two colleges', Nation, 21 May 1960; Darling to Tylee, 2 June 1960; Darling to Timpson, 17 July 1960; Darling to Basten, 18 March 1961; Darling to Menzies, 9 December 1960, 18 February 1960, 22 March 1960, 1 June 1961; Menzies to Darling, 16 March 1960, 4 August 1961; 'The challenge to education', 008-16 (1st & 2nd), 009-07 (3rd–9th), box 101 (10th), ACEA.

31 ACE, Council, Meetings, 13–14 May 1960, 28–29 July 1960, 20–21 October 1961, 24 March 1961, 14 July 1961, Minutes (1959–1963) (unnumbered); Darling to Browne, 1 March 1960; Darling to Scott, 3 June 1961; Darling to Frederick, 4 June 1961; Darling to Buntine, 24 April 1961; Darling to Wyndham, 18 March 1961; Darling to Timpson, 13 April 1961, 009-14 (1st) and 009-07 (2nd–7th), ACEA.

32 Crawford (1960); Spaull (1987), pp. 104–33; 'Notes on aim (f) of the proposed
    college of education', 007-04, ACEA; Darling to Griffiths, 31 May 1959, GGSA;
    Ross to Darling, 26 May 1959, 007-09, ACEA.

22 New toy

1 Nurser to Darling, 1 November 1969; J.R. Darling to C.B.A. Darling, 18 May 1974
   (not sent), both DP, ms 7826, s13, b28, f5 (1st) and s7, b16, f10 (2nd), NLA.
2 Report to council, 20 December 1954, GGSA; Curthoys (1986), pp. 127–32;
   Darling to le Fleming, 4 August 1959; Davidson to Darling, 28 October 1957, both
   DP; *Broadcasting and Television Act, 1942–1969*, secs 16, 83, 99.
3 Inglis (1983), pp. 105, 120; Ashley to Darling, 10 May 1943; Darling to Wilson,
   25 September 1945; Victorian State Advisory Committee, Meetings, 7 October
   1953, 28 September 1954, Minutes (unnumbered), all GGSA.
4 *Report of the Royal Commission on Television* (1954), pp. 11–19; Curthoys (1986),
   pp. 125, 133–42; R.J.F. Boyer, 'Television Report', 26 November 1951; Darling to
   Boyer, 12 March 1953, both GGSA; *Report of the Royal Commission on Television*
   (1954), pp. 51–2; Darling to Gordon, 15 October 1951, ACEA, 008-01; Darling
   to Hewan, 5 October 1956; Darling to Boyer, 18 April 1957, both GGSA; ABCB,
   Meeting, 22 February 1957, Minutes, min 34/1957, p. 894, C1993, item 9, NAA.
5 *Report of the Royal Commission on Television* (1954), rec 6, p. 102; ABCB,
   Meeting, 6 January 1955, min 2023, Minutes, pp. 689–90, C1993, item 7, NAA;
   Darling to Casey, 22 January 1955; Osborne to Griffiths, 15 March 1955, both
   DP; Report to council, 21 February 1955, GGSA; Darling to Osborne, 10 October
   1957, DP.
6 ABCB, handwritten notes accompanying exhibit 5A, B4489/1, box 1; *Public
   Hearing into Application for Television Licences in Brisbane, Transcript of Evidence*,
   1958, vol. 3, pp. 810–11, MP1233/4, box 2, both NAA; Darling to Boyer, 11 March
   1955, GGSA.
7 ABCB, *Public Hearing … Sydney & Melbourne Areas …*, 1955, vol. 1, pp. 4–7,
   MP1233/4, box 1; 'Discussions concerning procedure', pp. 1–2, exhib 10, B4489/1,
   box 2, both NAA.
8 ABCB, *Public Hearing … Brisbane …* 1958, vol. 3, p. 822, MP1233/4, box 2;
   Meetings, 14 January 1955, 18 January 1955, Minutes, pp. 692, 694; Notes
   accompanying exhibits 1–9 (undated), p. 6, B4489/1, box 1, exhib 5A, all NAA; *RR*,
   pp. 215–17.
9 ABCB, *Public Hearing… Sydney & Melbourne Areas…*, 1955, vol. 1, pp. 50A, 114,
   MP1233/4, box 1, NAA.
10 *Ibid.*, pp. 181, 186.
11 *Ibid.*, pp. 446–9, 380.
12 ABCB, *Public Hearing … Adelaide …* 1958, vol. 1, pp. 95–6, 108, MP1233/4, box 1
   NAA.
13 *Ibid.*, pp. 205–6.
14 ABCB, *Public Hearing … Sydney & Melbourne Areas …*, 1955, vol. 1, pp. 51–2, 113,
   138–41, 172, 282–3, MP1233/4, box 1, NAA.
15 ABCB, *Public Hearing … Adelaide …* 1958, vol. 1, p. 9, MP1233/4, box 1, NAA;
   Osborne to Davidson, 9 October 1957, DP; *Public Hearing … Sydney & Melbourne
   Areas …*, 1955, vol. 1, pp. 759–60, MP1233/4, box 1, NAA.

16 *Public Hearing ... Sydney & Melbourne Areas...*, 1955, vol. 1, p. 760, MP1223/4, box 1; ABCB, Meeting, 7 March 1955 (min 2078), Minutes, p. 714, C1993, item 7, both NAA; Darling to Casson, 16 July 1959, GGSA; Darling to Osborne, 8 February 1955 (including a 4-page memorandum), DP.

17 Williams to Darling, 2 March 1955, DP; *Report of the Royal Commission on Television* (1954), para 329 and p. 107; Curthoys (1986), pp. 147–8; Osborne to Darling, undated, 9 September 1955; Mair to Darling, 22 March, 18 March 1955, all DP.

18 ABCB, Meetings, 6 July 1955 (min 2156), 5 October 1955 (min 2246), 18–22 October 1956, 6 May 1957 (min 113/1957), 5 August 1957 (min 199/157), 19 August 1957 (min 222/1957), Minutes, pp. 747, 778, 854, 923, 949, 960, all C1993, item 7 (1st), item 8 (2nd) and item 9 (4th–6th), all NAA; Crawford to Darling, 9 October 1959, DP; Hazlehurst (1982–83), p. 118.

19 ABCB, *Public Hearing ... Adelaide ...* 1958, vol. 1, pp. 35–6, 308, series MP1233/4, box 1 and *Public Hearing ... Brisbane ...* 1958, vol. 2, p. 447, box 2, both NAA.

20 ABCB, Meetings, 17 June 1958 (min 200/1958), 7 July 1958 (min 220/1958), 21 July 1958 (min 227/1958), Minutes, pp. 1091–2, 1102, 1105, all C1993, item 10, NAA; J.R. Darling to Osborne, 12 August 1958, DP.

21 ABCB, Meeting, 15 September 1958 (min 283/1958), Minutes, p. 1128, C1993, item 10, NAA; Darling to Menzies, 15 September 1958; Darling to Osborne, 9 October 1958, both DP.

22 *RR*, p. 218; Menzies to Darling, 19 September 1958; Darling to Menzies, 30 September 1961, both DP; ABCB, Meeting, 26 September 1958 (mins 287/1958 and 288/1958), Minutes, pp. 1130–2, C1993, item 10, NAA.

23 ABCB, Meetings, 7 January 1959 (min 10/1059) (insert: 'Extension of television services—Report for the Postmaster General', pp. 8, 9, 12, 13), 2 February 1959 (min 26/1059) (insert: 'Extension of television services—Report for the Postmaster General', pp. 7, 8), Minutes, pp. 1172, 1179, both C1993, item 11, NAA.

24 ABCB, Meetings, 4 May 1959 (min 89/1059), 28 September 1959 (min 240/1959), Minutes, pp. 1212, 1272, both C1993, item 11, NAA.

25 Sir John Young to the author, 14 March 2005; ABCB, *Public Hearing ... Canberra Area ...* 1959, vol. 3, pp. 1005–8, MP1233/4, box 12, NAA.

26 J.R. Darling to Boyer, 11 March 1955, GGSA; Sir James Darling to the author, 24 February 1995; O'Kelly to Darling, 12 December 1957, DP; Darling to Boyer, 11 June 1956, 10 August 1956; Boyer to Darling, 15 April, 1957, 2 August 1956, 17 March 1955; Darling to Bearup, 13 March 1956, all GGSA.

27 *Report of the Royal Commission on Television* (1954), pp. 33, 104, 79, 80.

23 Hornets' nest

1 Drysdale to Dutton, 7 June 1961, DuP, ms 7285/2/30, b6; Darling to Boyer, 14 February 1961, DP, ms7826, s16, b33, f1, both NLA; Darling to le Fleming, 25 June 1961, DP.

2 Inglis (1983), pp. 5, 11–12, 17; Sir James Darling to the author, 24 February 1995; Moorhouse to Darling, 15 August 1958, 008-11, ACEA; Darling to Osborne, 5 July 1961, SP1849/1, box 5, ABC Control Board Correspondence file, NAA; Darling to Menzies, 13 July 1961, DP.

3 Sir James Darling to the author, 24 February 1995; *Broadcasting and Television Act, 1942–1969*, secs 31, 59(1), 64, 71, 77, 78, 116–18; *RR*, pp. 222–4.

4 Darling (1966), p. 3; *RR*, p. 222; Darling to Madgwick, 7 June 1967, DP, ms 7826, s16, b34, f11, NLA; 'Francis James', *Wikipedia*, https://en.wikipedia.org/wiki/Francis_James (accessed 30 December 2012).

5 Cockburn to Darling, 13 July 1961, DP; Winter to Moses, 22 August 1961; Griffiths to Moses, 6 November 1961; Moses to Davidson, 6 October 1961; Whitley to Sup. Eng. Vic, 24 October 1961, all C2327/1, 2/24, box 1, NAA; James to Darling, 24 November 1961, DP.

6 Lawrence to Darling, 14 July 1961, 4 August 1961, 10 May 1962, 8 September 1962; Darling to Lawrence, 18 July 1961, 22 July 1961, all SP1849/1, box 9, ABC–Staff Association–Lawrence file (1st–3rd, 5th–6th) and ABC Staff Association file (4th), NAA; *RR*, pp. 229–31.

7 ABC, Meeting 351, 20–21 September 1962, doc. 12934, Minutes, C1869/2, box 6; Darling to Lawrence, 21 September 1962; Lawrence to Darling, 9 November 1962, SP1849/1, box 9, ABC Staff Association file (1st) and ABC Staff General 1963–6 file (2nd), all NAA; *Daily Mirror*, 22 September 1962, in DP, ms 7826, s16, b34, f6, NLA.

8 Wood to Darling, 19 June 1962, 22 September 1962, 27 September 1962, 10 October 1962; Darling to Wood, 9 July 1962, 5 March 1963; Moses to Darling, 18 February 1963, all DP, ms 7826, s16, b34, f6 (1st–6th), b35, f15 (7th), NLA.

9 McMillan to Darling, 25 July 1961, SP1849/1, box 12, Intertel 1961–67 file; ABC, Meeting 342, 14–15 September 1961 (doc. 12537), Minutes, C1869/2, box 4, both NAA; Darling to Gorton, 1 August 1961, DP.

10 Intertel, 4 October 1960–14 April 1961 (undated); Davidson to Boyer, 23 May 1961; Dawes to Davidson, 31 May 1961; Davidson to Dawes, 2 June 1961, all SP1849/1, box 12, Intertel 1961–7 file, NAA.

11 ABC, Meetings 340, 6 July 1961 (docs 12470/1–4), 341, 10 August 1961 (doc. 12499), 342, 14–15 September 1961 (doc. 12541), Minutes, C1869/2, box 4, NAA; Duckmanton to Moses, 12 July 1961; Lowndes to Dawes, 20 July 1961; Dawes to Darling, 1 August 1961; Darling to Davidson, 4 August 1961, 8 September 1961, all SP1849/1, box 12, Intertel 1961–67 file, NAA.

12 Darling to Davidson, undated, 8 November 1961; Davidson to Boyer, 23 May 1961; Dawes to Davidson, undated draft, all SP1849/1, box 12, Intertel 1961–67 file, NAA.

13 Darling to Menzies, 20 January 1962; Darling to Davidson, 20 January 1962; Darling to Murdoch, 20 January 1962, all DP, ms7826, s16, b35, f12, NLA; Darling (1962b), pp. 9–14.

14 Darling (1962b), pp. 14–22.

15 Darling to Dickson, 4 January 1962, DP, ms7826, s16, b33, f1, NLA; Notes prepared for the chairman at his meeting with the Prime Minister, 19 January 1962; Darling to Davidson, 12 February 1962; both SP1849/1, box 12, Intertel 1961–67 file, NAA; ABC, Meetings 345, 1–2 February 1961 (docs 12657/1 & 3), 346, 20 February 1962 (doc. 12701), Minutes, both C1869/2, box 5, NAA.

16 'Australian Broadcasting Commission—Membership of Intertel', 8 March 1962; Cabinet min, doc. no. 128, 27 March 1962; Darling to Davidson, 6 April 1962; Telegram to the chairman, 3 April 1962; 'Intertel' (undated); Memo, 6 April 1962, all SP1849/1, box 12, Intertel 1961–67 file, NAA.

17 Postmaster General statement concerning ABC membership of Intertel, 1 May
    1962; 'Inside politics' (unsourced, undated); Lawrence to Darling, 11 May 1962,
    all SP1849/1, box 12, Intertel 1961–67 file, NAA; Darling to Duckmanton, 5 May
    1966; Darling to Wilson, 8 February 1962, both DP, ms 7826, s16, b33, f3 (1st) and
    b35, f12 (2nd), NLA; Darling (1962b).
18 Untitled, 1962, J.D.F. Green to the Director General, SP1849/1, box 8, BBC
    file; ABC, Meeting 357, 4–5 April 1963, docs 13151/4 and 13151/5, Minutes,
    C1869/2, box 7, all NAA; Inglis (1983), pp. 252–3.
19 James to Darling, 19 March 1963, DP, ms 7826, s16, b33, f1, NLA; Matters for
    discussion with General Manager and Vice-Chairman, 30 April 1963; Notes by
    Casey (undated), in Darling to Davidson, 9 April 1963; both SP1849/1, box 5,
    Status and function of the ABC and its commissioners file, NAA.
20 Hamilton, 'Malaysia—Film treatment', 28 February 1963; Darling to Moses,
    20 March 1963, with clippings (*Herald*, 26 April 1963, *Sun*, 27 April 1963, *Age*,
    27 April 1963); Darling to Davidson, 9 April 1963, all SP1849/1, box 11, ABC
    Films—1963/64–1967 file (1st & 2nd) and b5, Status and function of the ABC and
    its commissioners file (3rd), all NAA.
21 Lowndes to Darling, 18 April 1961, 28 April 1963; Darling to Commissioners,
    3 May 1963; Darling to Davidson, undated, all SP1849/1, box 10, Chairman's file:
    Wollongong WIN4 proposal (1st) and b5, Status and function of the ABC and its
    commissioners file (2nd–4th); ABC, Meeting 358, 8–9 May 1963 (doc. 13207),
    Minutes, C1860/2, box 7, NAA; Darling to Bolton, 8 August 1966, DP, ms 7826,
    s16, b33, f2, NLA.
22 ABC, Meeting 348, 2–4 May 1962 (doc. 12778), Minutes, C1869/2, box 5; Darling
    to Webb, 8 May 1962, SP1849/1, box 10, Talks file, both NAA.
23 File note, 'Australian Broadcasting Commission', 12 April 1961; Notice paper 29,
    House of Representatives, 17 May 1961; Moses to Dawes, 22 May 1961; Dawes
    to Moses, 24 May 1961; Moses to Darling, 17 July 1962; Darling to Davidson
    31 March 1962, 11 May 1962, all SP1849/1, box 13, Personal file, NAA.
24 Darling to Moses, 22 May 1962, SP1849/1, box 9, ABC General Manager
    correspondence, 1963–6 file, NAA; Darling to Davidson, 4 September 1962
    (marked 'Never sent'), DP, ms 7826, s16, b35, f13, NLA; Casey to Darling, 11 July
    1962; Darling to Hay, 27 June 1962, both DP.
25 Darling to Moses, 6 July 1962; Moses to Darling, 23 July 1962, both SP1849/1,
    box 9, ABC General Manager correspondence, 1963–6 file, NAA; Darling to
    Casey, 9 July 1962, DP; Darling to Casey, 17 September 1962, M1146/1, NAA.
26 Darling to Davidson, 9 November 1961; Keys to Davidson, 9 March 1962, both
    SP1849/1, box 13, ABC—Elections 1961/1962 file, NAA.
27 Darling to Davidson, 9 November 1961, 4 April 1962; Davidson to Keyes, 28 May
    1962, including the quoted extract from Darling to Davidson; Keys to Davidson,
    26 June 1962; all SP1849/1, box 13, ABC–Elections 1961–2 file (1st, 2nd & 4th)
    and 4 Corners file (3rd), NAA.
28 Darling to Davidson, 15 October 1962; Darling to Moses, 24 October 1962
    (attached to Munro memorandum), 19 April 1963, all SP1849/1, box 13, ABC–
    Elections 1961–2 file (1st), box 10, Talks directives and programmes file (2nd) and
    box 8, ABC Elections, 1963/1967 file (3rd), NAA.

29 Darling to Hulme, 23 June 1964, SP1849/1, box 10, Chairman's file: Talks;
    ABC, Meeting 354, 5–6 December 1962 (doc. 13015), Minutes, C1869/2, box
    6; Bowman (2005); Lowndes to Darling, 4 December 1962; Darling to Renouf,
    15 November 1962, both SP1849/1, box 10, News commentaries file, NAA.

30 Rivett to Darling, 12 August 1963; Semmler to Darling, 7 April 1964; Cilento to
    Bill (?), 20 February 1963, 1 March 1963, all DP, ms 7826, s16, b35, f15 (1st), and
    b33, f1 (2nd–4th), NLA.

31 Darling to Calwell, 24 June 1964; Darling to Davidson, 8 August 1963; Brown to
    Darling, 3 May 1963, all SP1849/1, box 10, Talks file (1st & 2nd) and box 11, ABC
    Films—1963/64–1967 file (3rd); ABC, Meeting 361, 22–23 August 1963 (doc.
    13357/4), Minutes, C1869/2, box 7, all NAA.

32 ABC, Meeting 361, 22–23 August 1963 (doc. 13357/1), Minutes, C1869/2, box 7,
    NAA; Semmler (1981), p. 24; ABC, Meetings 359, 13–14 June 1963 (doc. 13253),
    361, 22–23 August 1963 (docs 13357/3 & 13357/1), 362, 3–4 October 1963 (docs
    13417/2 & 13417/3), all C1869/2, box 7, NAA.

33 Darling to Moses, undated; Darling to Davidson, 13 May 1963, 17 June 1963;
    Davidson to Darling, 23 May 1963 (attached note); Kent Hughes to Davidson,
    31 May 1963; Whitely, memorandum, 7 June 1963; Moran to Darling, 16 June
    1963; South Australian churches' statement (undated), all SP1849/1, box 10, Talks
    file (1st) and box 12 (2nd–7th), Any questions file, all NAA.

34 Downer to Darling, 13 June 1963; Darling to Downer, 18 June 1963; Darling to
    McMaster, 20 June 1963; Darling to Ilott, 26 June 1963; Darling to Crawford,
    10 July 1963; Darling to Winter, 30 December 1963, all SP1849/1, box 12, Any
    questions file, NAA.

35 Carmichael, memorandum, 30 October 1963, SP1849/1, box 13, 4 Corners file,
    NAA; Inglis (1983), pp. 219–22; Ashbolt (1987), p. 375; Ajala (1964), pp 12–13;
    Darling to James, 2 July 1964, DP; Kristianson (1964); Ashbolt to Carmichael:
    'Four Corners'—R.S.L. Story', 4 September 1963, SP1849/1, box 13, 4 Corners
    file, NAA.

36 Ashbolt (1987), p. 375; Kristianson (1964), p. 24; Moses, 'Four Corners',
    7 November 1963; Semmler '"Four Corners" programme on R.S.L.', 4 November
    1963; Carmichael, '"Four Corners" Programme on R.S.L.', 30 October 1963;
    Ashbolt, '"Four Corners"—Programme on R.S.L.', 21 October 1963; Moses, 'Four
    Corners', 17 September 1963, all SP1849/1, box 13, 4 Corners file, NAA; Ajala
    (1964), p. 11; Darling to James, 2 July 1964, DP.

37 *Anglican*, 8 February 1963; James to Darling, 11 September 1963; Darling to James,
    13 September 1963, both DP, ms 7826, s16, b35, f15, NLA.

38 James to Darling; Darling to James, both DP, ms 7826, s16, b35, f15, NLA.

39 Kristianson (1964), p. 24; Lowndes to Darling, 24 November 1963, DP, ms
    7826, s16, b33, f1, NLA; 'Thoughts on the Assassination of President Kennedy',
    23 November 1963, DP.

40 *Nation*, 11 January 1964, p. 10; Darling to Fitzgerald, 13 January 1964; Fitzgerald to
    Darling, 22 January 1964, both SP1849/1, box 11, Various letters replied to by JRD
    file, NAA; James to Darling, 16 January 1964, DP, ms 7826, s16, b33, f1, NLA.

41 MacCallum (1964), p. 18; Ashbolt, Memorandum to AGM(P), 19 March 1964,
    SP1849/1, box 7, Clement Semmler file, NAA.

42 Darling to Hulme, 12 June 1964, 24 June 1964, both SP1849/1, box 10, Programmes file, NAA

43 Darling to Matthews, 13 July 1964, DP; Darling to Moses, 14 April 1962; Hulme to Darling, 26 June 1964, both SP1849/1, box 10, News file (1st) and various letters replied to by JRD file (2nd), both NAA.

44 *RR*, p. 211; White to Darling, 5 January 1964, 21 January 1964; Darling to White, 14 January 1964, 29 January 1964; Darling to Davidson, 14 April 1962, all SP1849/1, box 19, Religious broadcasts file (1st–4th) and News file (5th), NAA.

45 Rivett to Darling, 26 June 1964, DP; Darling to Lowndes, 13 March 1963; Dawes to Darling, 29 April 1964; Darling to Hulme, 26 June 1964, DP, ms 7826, s16, b33, f1 (1st & 3rd) and b35, f13 (2nd), NLA; Ajala (1964), p. 12; Davidson to Darling, 29 June 1964, DP.

24 An irritating yen for principle

1 ABC, Meetings 369, 18–19 June 1964 (docs 13766, 13767), 371, 20–21 August 1964, p. 1, 375, 10–11 December 1964 (doc. 13972, p. 5), Minutes, all C1869/2, box 10, NAA; 'Notes on the retirement of the General Manager' (24–25 June 1964), DP, ms 7826, s16, b35, f13, NLA.

2 'Notes on …', (24–25 June 1964), DP, ms 7826, s16, b35, f13, NLA.

3 *Ibid.*; Moses to the commissioners, 31 July 1964, SP1849/1, box 7, C.J.A. Moses file, NAA; 'Entirely confidential. (The only copy)' (undated); Semmler to Darling, undated, both DP, ms 7826, s16, b34, f8, NLA; Inglis (1983), pp. 254–5.

4 Inglis (1983), pp. 254–5; Semmler to Darling, 27 September 1962, 24 December 1963, 24 December 1964, all DP, ms 7826, s16, b35, f15 (1st) and b34, f10 (2nd & 3rd), NLA; Handwritten note (undated), SP1849/1, box 8, General Manager file, NAA.

5 ABC, Meeting 377, 4–5 March 1965 (doc. 14029), Minutes, C1869/2, box 11; Darling to Moses, 27 April 1965; Dawes to Darling, 8 January 1965; Darling to Duckmanton, 2 August 1965; annual reports 1964/1965 and 1965/1966 including correspondence file, all SP1949/1, box 7, C.J.A. Moses file (1st & 2nd); box 5 (3rd & 4th), NAA.

6 Lowndes to Darling, 29 April 1964, DP, ms 7826, s16, b35, f13, NLA; Darling to Hulme, undated, 1 September 1964; Senate Committee Report, all SP1849/1, box 10, Chairman's file: Talks, NAA.

7 Darling to Semmler, 19 August 1964, DP, ms 7826, s16, b33, f1, NLA; Brand to Naylor, 21 October 1964; 'Statement to press' (undated); *Australian*, 23 October 1963; *West Australian*, 23 October 1964; *Herald*, 23 October 1964, all SP1849/1, box 13, Chairman's file: 4 Corners—Viewers' letters, NAA.

8 Semmler, draft note, undated; Darling, draft note, undated; Whitlam to Darling, 26 October 1964; Darling to Whitlam, undated; Darling, press release, undated, all SP1849/1, box 13, Chairman's file: 4 Corners—Viewers' letters, NAA; ABC, Meeting 374, 12–13 November 1964 (docs 13940/2, 13940/1, 13940/3, 13040/4 and 13040/9), Minutes, C1869/2, box 10, NAA; Inglis (1983), pp. 222–3.

9 '4 Corners crisis', undated; draft press release, undated, both SP1849/1, box 13, Chairman's file: 4 Corners—Viewers' letters; ABC, Meeting 374, 12–13 November 1964 (doc. 13490, pp. 6–7), Minutes, series C1869/2, box 10, NAA.

10 Darling to Baker, 18 November 1964; Darling to Burgess, 27 November 1964, both SP1849/1, box 13, Chairman's file: 4 Corners—Viewers' letters, NAA; Semmler to Hort, 11 November 1964, DP, ms 7826, s16, b34, f10, NLA.

11 Stretton to Darling 13 November 1964; Darling to Stretton, 17 November 1964; Darling to Thompson, 4 December 1964; Darling to Henshall, 25 November 1964; Darling to Miles, 18 December 1964, all SP1849/1, box 13, Chairman's file: 4 Corners—Viewers' letters, NAA.

12 Cutting, SP1849/1, box 13, Chairman's file: 4 Corners—Viewers' letters, NAA.

13 'Dr. Darling's statement ...', 4 November 1964; Darling to Penlington, 4 December 1964, both SP1849/1, box 13, Chairman's file: 4 Corners—Viewers' letters, NAA; Inglis (1983), p. 253; Savage to Hulme, 14 July 1965; Darling to Hulme, 28 July 1965, both DP, ms7826, s16, b33, f3, NLA.

14 Darling to Hulme, Draft resignation, 25 November 1964?, DP, ms7826, s16, b35, f13, NLA; Darling, memo, 30 November 1964; 'Meet the Press', 20 December 1964, (transcript), both SP1849/1, box 9, Chairman's file: Press clippings—Matters related to the Commission, NAA.

15 J. Marshall, 'The old wives' ABC—Sweeping reforms needed for lively programmes'; Typescript (undated, unauthored), both SP1849/1, box 9, Chairman's file: Press clippings—Matters related to the Commission, NAA.

16 Darling to Meehan, 17 April 1963, DP, ms 7826, s16, b33, f1, NLA; 'The Ripponlea Affair'; 'The Ripponlea Estate', 7 April 1965, both SP1849/1, box 9, Chairman's file: Ripponlea, NAA; Darling to Holt, 15 June 1966; Darling to Anderson, 29 April 1965; Davidson to Darling, 30 January 1974, all DP, ms 7826, s16, b33, f2 (1st), f3 (2nd) and s7, b16, f10 (3rd), NLA.

17 Darling to Dawes, 10 November 1964; Darling to Hulme, 18 February 1965, both SP1849/1, box 12, Australian Production of TV Film file, NAA.

18 Darling, 'Memorandum on the composition of the Commission', 27 June 1965; Darling to Hulme, 17 August 1965, both DP, ms 7826, s16, b35, f13 (1st) and b33, f3 (2nd), NLA.

19 Darling to Duckmanton, 28 November 1966, SP1849/1, box 5, Chairman's file (G), NAA; Darling to Dawes, 2 February 1966; Darling, 'Discussion with P.M. on constitution of A.B.C. for Sept: 2: 1965'; 'Chairmanship of the A.B.C.' (1973?), all DP, ms 7826, s16, b33, f3 (1st) and b35, f13 (2nd & 3rd), NLA.

20 'Chairmanship of the A.B.C.', op cit.; 'Memorandum on the status and functions of the Australian Broadcasting Commission and its Chairman', 17 August 1965; Darling to Hulme, 22 August 1966, both SP1849/1, box 7, Chairman's File: Status and Function of the ABC and its Commissioners (1st) and box 13, Chairman's file: Personal (2nd), NAA.

21 Darling to Reith, 16 January 1962, DP; Darling (1966), pp. 4–6, 10–14.

22 Darling to Brown, 2 August 1965, DP, ms 7826, s16, b33, f3, NLA; Darling (1966), pp. 14–16.

23 Darling (1966), pp. 16–23.

24 Hasluck to Darling, 24 July 1961; Darling to Arrowsmith, undated, both DP; Hasluck to Darling, 23 November 1962, 11 March 1965, both SP1849/1, box 8, Chairman's file: ABC Regionals—Papua/New Guinea, NAA.

25 Darling to Hulme, 3 May 1965, SP1849/1, box 8, Chairman's file: Radio Australia Correspondence and General; ABC, Meeting 378, 13–14 April 1965 (doc. 14118), Minutes, C1869/2, box 11, NAA; Hasluck to Hulme, 21 December 1965; Darling to Hulme, 17 January 1966, both SP1849/1, box 8, Chairman's file: Radio Australia Correspondence and General, NAA; Darling to Hulme, 15 January 1966, DP, ms 7826, s16, b34, f18, NLA.

26 Diary, 12, 13, 18, 29 and 21 January 1966; Menzies to Darling, 23 February 1966, all DP; Hasluck to Hulme, 22 February 1966; Duckmanton to Darling, 13 May 1966, both SP1849/1, box 8, Chairman's file: Radio Australia Correspondence and General, NAA.

27 Darling to Hulme, 16 February 1966, DP, ms 7826, s16, b33, f3, NLA; Wilson to Darling, undated telegram; Darling to Davidson, 16 November 1962; press release, 23 December 1963; Darling to Hulme, 18 February 1964, all SP1849/1, box 12, Educational Television file (1st & 2nd) and ABC Education: Educational television 1964/66 file (3rd & 4th); ABC, Meeting 356, 20–21 February 1966, Minutes, C1869/2, box 7, all NAA.

28 Osborne to Darling, 11 October 1963 (and attached memorandum), DP, ms 7826, s16, b34, f6, NLA; ABC, Meetings 365, 29–30 January 1964 (doc. 13565) and 366, 10–11 March 1964 (doc. 13623), Minutes, C1869/2, box 9; Darling to Hulme, 23 January 1964 (with enclosure: 'Educational television'), 30 August 1965, SP1849/1, box 12, ABC Education: Educational television 1964/66 file, NAA; *Advisory Committee on Educational Television Services* (1964), paras 21–3, 1, 97–107, ACEA.

29 Hulme to Darling, 18 August 1965; Report on educational television services (undated), paras 6, 9, 11, 12, 15, 17–19, 20, 23, 26–7; Note by Darling (undated); Darling to Osborne, 5 October 1965, all SP1849/1, box 12, ABC Education: Educational television 1964/66 file, NAA; Darling to Calwell, 22 June 1965, DP, ms 7826, s16, b33, f3, NLA.

30 Diary, 2 February 1966, DP; 'Educational television', Cabinet submission, 2 March 1966; 'Educational television', Ministerial statement, 11 May 1966; 'Rejection of Weeden television report', *Age*, 19 May 1965; all SP1849/1, box 12, ABC Education: Educational television 1964/66 file, NAA.

31 ABC, Meetings 378, 13–14 April 1965 (doc. 14089), 379, 12–13 May 1965 (doc. 14128), 387, 17–18 March 1966 (doc. 14459), 390, 13–14 July 1966 (doc. 14584) Minutes; J.R. Darling to Hulme, 11 August 1965 (attachment to doc. 14296, meeting 383, 13–14 October 1965), all C1869/2, box 11, NAA; Diary, 4, 14 and 25 January 1966, DP; Dawes to Darling, 25 January 1966, DP, ms 7826, s16, b33, f3, NLA; ABC, Meeting 386, 10–11 February 1966 (doc. 14411), Minutes, C1869/2, box 13, NAA.

32 ABC, Meetings 388, 21–22 April 1966 (docs 14493/2, 14493/3 & 14493/1), 389, 9–10 June 1966 (docs 14529/1 & 14529/2), Minutes, both C1869/2, box 13, NAA; Darling, note (untitled, undated), DP, ms 7826, s16, b35, f14, NLA; Fairbairn to Darling, 21 July 1966, SP 1849/1, box 13, Chairman's file: 4 Corners—Viewers' letters, NAA.

33 Inglis (1983), p. 321; Darling to Duckmanton, 18 January 1967, SP1849/1, box 10, Chairman's file: Programmes, NAA; Darling to James, 13 April 1967; Darling

to Ashbolt, 6 September 1966; Ashbolt to Darling, 7 September 1966, all DP, ms 7826, s16, b33, f2, NLA.

34   ABC, Meeting 388, 21–22 April 1966 (doc. 14513/1), Minutes, C1869/2, box 13, NAA.

35   Darling to Dredge, 13 September 1965, SP1849/1, box 11, Chairman's file: Various letters replied to by JRD; ABC, Meetings 391, 11–12 August (doc. 14626), 392, 15–16 September 1966 (docs 14700 & 14700/4-6), 394, 10–11 November 1966 (doc. 14572), 395, 15–16 December 1966 (docs 14780 & 14780/2), all C1869/2, box 14, NAA; Darling to the SOA, 13 November 1966; SOA to Darling, 30 November 1966, DP, ms 7826, s16, b34, f6, NLA; Letter, 4 December 1966, SP1849/1, box 6, NAA.

36   Ashbolt, A. 'National broadcasting as a profession', 7 December 1966, pp. 4, 10, 11–12; 'Memorandum on Mr. Alan Ashbolt's speech', both SP1849/1, box 10, Chairman's file: Talks directive and programmes; ABC, Meetings 396, 1–2 February 1967 (doc. 14819), 397, 2–13 March 1967 (doc. 14862), 398, 6–7 April, 1967 (doc. 14909), Minutes, all C1869/2, box 15, NAA.

37   ABC, Meetings 387, 17–18 March 1966 (doc. 14463), 389, 9–10 June (docs 14528 & 14528/2), 391, 11–12 August 1966 (doc. 14635), 396, 1–2 February 1967 (doc. 14817), all C1869/2, box 13 (1st & 2nd), box 14 (3rd) and 15 (4th); Duckmanton to Askin, 6 May 1966, SP1849/1, box 7, ABC Concerts—Opera House Sydney 66-7 file, NAA.

38   Darling to Coombs, 27 January 1967; Darling to Hughes, 9 February 1967, 13 February 1967, all SP1849/1, box 7, ABC Concerts—Opera House Sydney 66-7 file, NAA.

39   Coombs to Hughes, 16 February 1967; Coombs to Duckmanton, 16 February 1967; Darling to Coombs (undated); Hughes to Darling 22 February; Lowndes to Darling, 21 February 1967, all SP1849/1, box 7, ABC Concerts—Opera House Sydney 66-7 file, NAA; Darling to Hay, 22 February 1967, DP, ms7826, s16, b33, f2, NLA; Diary, 16 April 1967, DP.

40   Darling to commissioners, 22 February 1967; Duckmanton to Darling, 21 March 1967; Lowndes to Duckmanton, 21 March 1967; Darling to Potter, 13 April 1967; Potter to Darling, 5 June 1967, all SP1849/1, box 7, ABC Concerts—Opera House Sydney 66-7 file; ABC, Meetings 397, 2–3 March 1967 (doc. 14860), 398, 6–7 April 1967 (doc. 14904), both C1869/2, box 15, NAA.

41   Hulme to Darling, 25 May 1967; Darling to Hulme, 1 March 1967, 27 May 1967, all DP, ms 7826, s16, b33, f2, NLA; Diary, 20 May 1967, DP; Darling to Madgwick, 27 May 1967; Darling to Freeth, undated, unsent; Madgwick to Darling, 4 June 1967, all DP, ms 7826, s16, b33, f2 (1st) and b34, f11 (2nd & 3rd), NLA; Semmler (1991), p. 97, Duckmanton to Darling, 23 May 1967; Darling to Madgwick, 7 June 1967, both DP, ms 7826, s16, b33, f3 (1st) and b34, f11 (2nd), NLA.

42   Diary, 15 January 1967, 30 January 1967, 8 February 1967, DP.

43   James to Darling, 1 June 1967, DP, ms 7826, s16, b34, f11, NLA; Diary, 16 April 1967, DP; James to Darling, 11 April 1967; Darling to Duckmanton, 12 April 1967; both DP, ms 7826, s16, b33, f2, NLA; Inglis (1983), pp. 257–9.

44   Darling to James, 13 April 1967, DP, ms 7826, s16, b33, f2, NLA.

45   James to Darling, 18 April 1967, 1 June 1967; both DP, ms 7826, s16, b34, f5 (1st) and f11 (2nd), NLA.

46 Calwell to Darling, 31 May 1967; Osborne to Darling, 30 May 1967; Clark to Darling, 9 June 1967; Darling to Clark, 21 June 1967, all DP, ms 7826, s16, b34, f11, NLA.

47 Semmler to Darling, 7 August 1967; Darling to Duckmanton, 24 July 1967; Ashbolt to Duckmanton, 5 June 1967; Lawrence to Darling, 23 June 1967, all DP, ms 7826, s16, b35, f15 (1st), b33, f2 (2nd), b34, f5 (3rd) and b34, f11 (4th), NLA.

25 Easygoing

1 Bolton (1990), p. 146; Horne (1964), p. 14; Boyd (1960), p. 75; Inglis (1983), p. 268; 'This Day Tonight. Telegram from Dr. Darling', undated, author unknown, DP, ms 7826, s16, b35, f14, NLA; Darling to Collins, 28 February 1966, DP.

2 Darling (1970), pp. 2, 3, 6, 9, DP, ms 7826, s12, b27, f1, NLA; Engel (1988), pp. 15–17.

3 Engel (1963) 'Australian Frontier: An account of the first year—1962'; Watson to Darling, 28 November 1961, both DP, ms 7826, s1, b1, f5 (1st) and b2, f9 (2nd), NLA.

4 Darling to Warren, 26 February 1962, DP; Engel (1988), pp. 15, 25–40, 197–9; Darling (1970), p. 13; Engel (undated) 'Report of the Ecumenical Institute Advisory Committee of the A.C.C.'; 'Crossing frontiers in Australia' (undated, author unknown); Engel (1961) 'Thinking about the church and the world—Some basic distinctions'; Darling to Engel, 5 March 1962 (Attachment 'Australian Frontier', undated), all DP, ms 7826, s1, b2, f9 (1st, 3rd–6th) and f1 (2nd), NLA.

5 Engel (1988), pp. 43, 53; Engel to Darling, 13 April 1962; Diary, 15 January 1967, DP; AFC, Meetings, 2 July 1962, 14 December 1963, Minutes; J.R. Darling, 'Australian Frontier', 6 October 1964; press release, undated, all DP, ms 7826, s1, b2, f1 (1st & 2nd), b2, f8 (3rd) and b1, f2 (4th), NLA; Engel (1988), pp. 48–9.

6 AFC, Meetings, 2–3 December 1962, 1 March 1963, 17 June 1963, 8–9 September 1963, Minutes; Fletcher to Darling, 10 January 1964; Darling to Fletcher, undated, all DP, ms 7826, s1, respectively b1, f1 (1st–4th) and b1, f5 (5th & 6th), NLA.

7 Darling to Fletcher, undated; Mathews to Darling, 4 January 1964, 13 January 1964, 31 January 1964; Darling to Mathews, 15 January 1964, all DP, ms 7826, s1, b1, f5 (1st) and f4 (2nd–5th), NLA.

8 Engel (1988), p. 57; Mathews to V. & J. Hancock, 10 June 1965; AFC, Meeting, 29 May 1965, Minutes, unnumbered; Darling to Crean, 6 May 1965; Darling to Taylor, 23 June 1964; Connell to Darling, 11 January 1965; Darling to Hall, 15 March 1965; all DP ms 7826, s1, b27, f4 (1st), b1, f3 (2nd), f4 (3rd, 5th & 6th) and f5 (4th), NLA.

9 Engel (1988), pp. 6, 57; *ADB*, vol. 13, p. 301; Darling to Kemsley, 15 June 1965; Darling 'Memorandum on the possibility of co-operation with St. Mark's library', undated; Two-page note (Diocesan Synod), June 1965; AFC, Meeting, 17 September 1965, Minutes, all DP, ms 7826, s1, b1, f3 (1st & 2nd) and b7, f3 (3rd & 4th), NLA.

10 Engel (1988), pp. 57–63; Lacey to Darling, 27 September 1968; Lanigan to Mathews, 27 May 1965; Woods to Darling, 27 March 1968; Darling to personal secretary, Duke of Edinburgh, 8 April 1968; Hetzel to Darling, 12 July 1968; DP, ms 7826, s1, b4, f19 (1st), f17 (2nd & 3rd), f22 (4th) and f20 (5th), NLA.

11 Darling to Fairfax, 11 September 1964, DP; Darling to Madgwick, 31 July 1964; Darling to Batten, 10 March 1966, both DP, ms 7826, s8, b23, f1 (1st) and f22

(2nd), NLA; Darling to James, 14 May 1962, ? May 1967, both DP; Darling to Neal, 1 March 1967, DP, ms 7826, s1, b4, f22, NLA; Hetzel to Darling, 22 December 1968, DP; Darling to Mathews, 21 June 1969; Dunlop to Darling, 22 July 1969, DP, ms 7826, s1, b4, f19 (1st) and f22 (2nd), NLA; *RR*, p. 262.

12 Diary, 18 November 1967, DP; Darling to Hetzel, 5 December 1970, DP ms 7826, s13, b27, f4, NLA; Roberts to Darling, 12 November 1970, DP.

13 Diary, 17 January 1966, DP; Engel (1988), p. 129; Darling to Hetzel, 2 November 1970; Darling to Mathews, 23 July 1970, DP ms 7826, s1, b2, f12 (1st) and b4, f22 (2nd), NLA; Reid to Darling, 9 December 1967, DP.

14 Darling to James, ? May 1967, DP; Corrigan to Darling, 30 April 1972; Darling to Enderby, 28 August 1973; V.E., V.M. & J.P. Hancock to Darling, 6 November 1970; Cleary to Darling, 12 July 1970; Darling to Street, 27 May 1970; 'Notes for the Prime Minister', undated; all DP, ms 7826, s13, b28, f6 (1st), b28, f12 (2nd), b27, f3 (3rd), b27, f4 (4th), b4, f22 (5th) and b22, f19 (6th), NLA.

15 Darling to Turner, 8 August 1970; 'Australian IMS', 3 December 1970; Hancock to Secretary, ISMS, 12 August 1970; Darling to Hancock, 17 August 1970; Nurser to Darling, 12 October 1970; Darling to Hancock, 29 September 1970; Darling to Hohnen, 8 December 1970, all DP ms 7826, s13, b27, f3 (1st, 3rd–5th) and s1, b2, f10 (2nd), b4, f22 (6th) and b4, f4 (7th), NLA.

16 Turner to Darling, 31 December 1970; Darling to Scott, 15 December 1970; Darling to Hohnen, 8 December 1970; Warburton to Darling, 19 February 1971; Darling to Hohnen, 25 February 1971; 'Proposed terms of reference for an assessment of community attitudes towards the Institute …'; Darling to Council members, 31 May 1971; 'Institute for the Study of Man and Society: Review of the projected operations of the Institute and their financial implications' (W.D. Scott); AFC, Executive Committee Meeting, 5 December 1971, Minutes, all DP, ms 7826, s13, b27, f4 (1st–3rd), s1, b2, f10 (4th–7th), f11 (8th) and f12 (9th), NLA.

17 AFC, Meeting, 26 May 1972 (agenda paper), DP, ms 7826, s1, b4, f17, NLA; Darling itinerary for Far East trip, 16 October to 17 November 1965, SP1849/1, box 13, Chairman's file: Personal, NAA; Darling to Stuart, 29 September 1966; Diary, 13 January 1966, both DP.

18 Darling to Hancock, 15 December 1971; Hancock to Darling, 29 January 1972; Darling to Porter, 7 October 1970; Darling to Cleary, 1 July 1970; Darling to Turner, 21 December 1971, all DP ms 7826, s13, b27, (1st), b28, f9 (2nd), b27, f1 (3rd), s1, b4, f22 (4th) and s13, b27, f2 (5th), NLA.

19 Hancock to Secretary, Australian Frontier, 5 March 1973; Darling to Hohnen, 14 August 1970; AFC, Meeting 3 April 1971; Draft of an article for *See*, May 1970, DP, ms 7826, s13, b28, f9 (1st), s1, b4, f22 (2nd & 4th) and s1, b2, f2 (3rd), NLA; Engel (1988), pp. 129–30.

20 ARSC, Meeting 5–6 December 1960, B16/0, b1, iR-1A/60, pp. 1–7, NAA.

21 Vamplew and McLean (1987), pp. 167, 171, 174.

22 ARSC, Meeting, 10–11 April 1961, Minutes, pp. 5, 13 (min 8), 11 (min 7), B16/0, box 1, item R-2C/61, NAA; J.R. Darling to Paterson, 13 July 1961, DP; ARSC, Meeting, 1–3 April 1963, Minutes, p. 26, B16/0, box 1, item R-6C/63, NAA.

23 ARSC, Meeting, 23–25 July 1963, Minutes, p. 4 (doc. B27/213), p. 1 (doc. B7/208), p. 7 (doc. B7/216), p. 30 (doc. B7/254), B16/0, box 1, item R-7C/63, NAA.

24　ARSC, Report of five year programme standing committee, 22 October 1963, pp. 2–10, 11–16, B16/0, box 2, item R-8A(1)/6, NAA.

25　*Ibid.*, pp. 17–27; ARSC, Meeting 26–28 November 1963, Minutes, p. 5 (doc. M8/262), p. 7 (doc. M8/264), B16/0, box 2, item R-8C/63, NAA.

26　ARSC, Australian road safety project second report, 24 October 1963, p. 15, B16/0 box 2, item R-8A(2)/63; Meeting, 23 April 1964, Minutes, p. 29 (doc. A9/322) and pp. 9–19b (doc. A9/305 which provides two sets of different minutes), B160, box 2, item R-9C/64, NAA.

27　ARSC, Meeting, 29 March 1965, Minutes, p. 2 (doc. M10/323), p. 7 (doc. M10/334), B16/0, box 2, item R-10C/65, NAA; Diary, 6 January 1966, DP; Darling to Holt, 15 June 1966; Darling to Freeth, undated, both DP, ms 7826, s16, b33, f2 (1st) and b34, f11 (2nd), NLA.

28　Diary, 18 November 1967, 14 January 1966, 2 January 1966, DP; Darling to Sinclair, 29 October 1969, 8 April 1970; Sinclair to Darling, 10 August 1970; all DP, ms 7826, s4, b8, f38 (1st & 2nd) and f37 (3rd), NLA.

29　'Notes for address to A.T.A.C.'; 'Notes on proposed road safety conference' (undated); News Release, 10 September 1971; Robertson to Darling, 2 September 1971, all DP, ms 7826, s4, b8, f38 (1st) and f37 (2nd, 3rd & 4th), NLA; Hodgetts to Darling, 19 August 1970, DP.

30　Williams (1961), p. 381; Poynter & Rasmussen (1996), p. 234; UMC, Meetings, 4 August 1969, 2 March 1970, 13 April 1970, Minutes, pp. 1495, 364, 699; CMCSMU, B99, 1-245-1, Meetings, 8 December 1969, 15 June 1970, Minutes, p. 2, all UMA.

31　CMCSMU, Transcript, pp. 2–11, UMA.

32　*Ibid.*, pp. 12–20.

33　*Ibid.*, pp. 21–55.

34　*Ibid.*, pp. 55–8; Poynter & Rasmussen (1996), pp. 399–405, 395, 393; CMCSMU, B99, 1-245-1, Meeting, 31 July 1970, Minutes, p. 2; UMC, Meetings, 31 August 1970, 7 September 1970, Minutes, pp. 2052 (includes a note by Darling, 28 August 1970), 2055, 2058, all UMA.

35　Diary, 21 October 1971, DP.

36　*Ibid.*

37　*Ibid.*

38　*Ibid.*

39　Adler to Darling, 20 October 1971, DP, ms 7824, s7, b15, f1, NLA; Diary, 18 May 1967, DP.

26　Lotus-land

1　Cash to Darling, 17 October 1972, DP, ms 7826, s7, b15, f6, NLA; Darling (1965), p. 70; Darling to Goodfield, 3 April 1967, DP; McGregor (1968), p. 117; Persse (1995).

2　*RR*, p. 117.

3　Turner to Darling, 28 June 1961, Irvine to Darling, 23 July 1960; Darling to Hacking, 15 August 1960, all DP.

4　Garnett to M.D. Darling, 13 August 1961, DP; Woods to Darling, 16 June 1962, Southey to Darling, 29 September 1966, both DP, ms 7826, s1, b1, f5 (1st) and s16, b34, f4 (2nd), NLA.

5 Garnett to Darling 1 February 1962[?], 18 February 1964[?], DP; Ritchie to Garnett, 4 November 1961; Garnett to Ritchie, 7 November 1961, GGSA.

6 Allen to Darling, 19 July 196?; James to Darling, 1 October 1962; Hay to Darling, 15 September 1962, all DP; Darling to Griffiths, 30 August 1965; Laird to Darling (undated), both DP, ms 7826, s8, b23, f2 (1st) and s8, b23, f3 (2nd), NLA.

7 Darling to Lee, 25 June 1964; Montgomery to Darling, 22 September 1964, both DP, ms 7826, s8, b23, f2, NLA; Darling to Montgomery, 4 July 1963; Diary, 20 May 1967, both DP; Ritchie to Darling, 2 June 1974; Brown to Darling, 14 June 1973; both DP, ms 7826, s7, b21, f46 (1st) and s7, b15, f3 (2nd), NLA.

8 Diary, 20 May 1967; Manifold to Darling, 15 June 1965[?], both DP; Manifold to Darling, 25 December 1965, DP, ms 7826, s16, b34, f4, NLA.

9 Diary, 6 January 1966, 12 January 1966, DP; Healey to Darling, 28 December 1971, DP, ms 7826, s7, b18, f22; Diary, 11 January 1966, DP; Westcott to Darling, 19 September 1983, 22 June 1975, 11 August 1981, s7, b22, f56 (1st & 3rd) and s7, b22, f55 (2nd), NLA; Thomson to Darling, 22 April 1968, DP; Hogg (1986), pp. 146–7, 294–5; APS, Minutes, 11 April 1961, p. 4, MGSA.

10 CPE, Meeting, 8 October 1963, Minutes, p. 101, VPRS, 11353/P0001, Unit 6, Minute Book from 7 November 1956, VPRO; UMC, Meetings, 6 April 1964, 4 May 1964, 6 July 1964, 17 December 1964, 7 June 1965, 7 March 1966, UMA; Diary, 1 February 1966, DP.

11 Poynter & Rasmussen (1996), pp. 229, 533, 238–9; Lodewycks (1982), pp. 341, 303, 304; Lodewycks to Darling, 5 February 1978, DP, ms 7826, s7, b19, f29, NLA.

12 Diary, 20 May 1967, DP; 'Sir James Darling honorary degree', UM267, 16-204-2, UMA; 'Students' dinner Newman College—Melbourne', 30 July 1963, DP, ms 7826, s9, b23, f2, NLA.

13 'Second congress of the Asia–Pacific Academy of Ophthalmologists', 6 April 1964, DP, ms 7826, s9, b23, f2, NLA.

14 'Manyung administration college', 10 August ?, DP, ms 7826, s9, b24, f3, NLA; Adams to Darling, 16 March 1971, DP.

15 Darling (1962c), pp. 1–6, DP, ms 7826, s9, b23, f1, NLA.

16 *Ibid.*, pp. 6–11.

17 *Ibid.*, pp. 12–17.

18 Diary, 22 January 1966, DP; 'Newington old boys dinner to celebrate centenary', 26 July 1963, DP, ms 7826, s9, b23, f1, NLA; Leinster-Mackay (1987), pp. 2, 12; 'Thring's almighty wall', 27 March 1962, DP, ms 7826, s9, b23, f2, NLA.

19 'The Dobell retrospective exhibition', 15 July 1964, DP, ms 7826, s9, b23, f1, 'Warrandyte arts exhibition', 9 November 1966; 'Festival of the arts—Sale', ? October 1963; 'Marist College—Burnie—prize giving', 25 November 1967; 'All Saints School Bathurst—prize giving', 7 December 1967; 'All Saints' College—Bathurst—Development appeal dinner', 5 May 1971; 'Scotch College—Adelaide', 16 September 1970, all DP, ms 7826, s9, b23, f1 (1st), s9, b23, f2 (2nd) and s9, b24, f3 (3rd–7th), NLA.

20 Darling (1972), pp. 5–9, DP.

21 *Ibid.*, pp. 10–16.

22 Darling to James, ? May 1967, DP; Turner to Darling, 30 May 1967; Thwaites to Darling, 2 June, 1967, both DP ms7826, s16, b34, f11, NLA; Tunbridge to Darling,

19 May 1968, Moyes to Darling, 7 September 1968; Masterman to Darling, 21 June 1970, all DP; Darling to Dunrossil, 7 May 1960; Darling to Leech, 29 February 1960, both 008-15, ACEA.

23 Darling (1963), pp. 1–3; Darling to Timpson, 14 December 1961; Timpson to Darling, 18 December 1961, box 101 (1st), 001-02 (2nd) and 008-17 (3rd), ACEA; 'On the future of the College of Education', 14 February 1966, DP; ACE, Council meeting, 12 May 1973, Minutes, p. 10, ACEA.

24 Nutt to Darling, 8 June 1962 (3-page enclosure), 65/46066; CIAC, 44th Meeting, 9 March 1962, Minutes, min. 1,192, p. 6, A2170, both NAA.

25 *RR*, p. 248.

26 CIAC, 42nd Meeting, 6 March 1961, Agenda, item 2 ('Melbourne vice charges'), pp. 2–3, Minutes, min. 1,150, pp. 3–4, sA2170, NAA.

27 Darling to Heyes, 9 March 1961, 14 March 1961, 17 May 1961; Heyes to Thomas, 13 March 1961; Heyes to Darling, 13 March 1961, 5 May 1961; McFarling to Edwards, 23 March 1961; Thomas to Darling, 4 April 1961; Thomas to Heyes, 4 April 1961, 11 April 1961, all DP; CIAC, 44th Meeting, 9 March 1962, Minutes, min. 1,191, p. 3, sA2170, NAA.

28 CIAC, 41st Meeting, 22 & 23 September 1960, Minutes, min. 1,140, pp. 9–10, Agenda, item 8, pp. 16–24, sA2170, NAA; Darling (1963), p. 6, Box 101, ACEA; Rivett (ed.) (1962), pp. 153, 130, 60.

29 CIAC, 44th Meeting, 27 October 1961, Agenda, items 2, p. 8, 5, p. 12, sA2170, NAA; Darling to Heyes, 9 March 1961; Darling to Downer, 27 February 1962, both DP.

30 Rivett (ed.) (1962), pp. 102, 87, 161, 88, 103, 121, 126, 104, 130, 135.

31 Downer to Darling, 18 October 1961, DP; CIAC, 44th Meeting, 27 October 1961, Agenda, item 10, pp. 21–2, 46th Meeting, 17 August 1962, Agenda, item 8/62-63, pp. 18–19, 47th Meeting, 30 November 1962, Minutes, min. 1,224, p. 8, sA2170, NAA.

32 Rivett (ed.) (1962), pp. 155, 141; CIAC, 44th Meeting, 27 October 1961, Minutes, min. 1,182, p. 5, 47th Meeting, 30 November 1962, Minutes, min. 1,226, pp. 12–16, min. 1,224, pp. 9–10; *RR*, p. 248; CAEMP, Meeting, 13 April 1962, Minutes, pp. 2–5, A2170, NAA.

33 CAEMP, Meeting, 13 April 1962, Minutes, pp. 2–7, A2170, NAA; Wilson to Downer, 2 October 1962, attachment to CIAC, 47th Meeting, 30 November 1962, Agenda, item 25/62-63, pp. 27–28, sA2170, NAA; Palfreeman (1967), pp. 163–6; Darling to Whitlam, 4 August 1965; Diary, 18 January 1966; Darling to Heydon, 7 March 1966, all DP.

34 Darling to Heydon, 7 March 1966, DP.

35 Massey to Darling, 4 February 1959; Diary, 19 January 1967; Darling to Heydon, 9 June 1967; Armstrong to Darling, 10 January, 1967; Darling to Armstrong, 22 June 1967, all DP; CSP, Report of the 8th Meeting, 26 July 1967, *The Departure of Settlers from Australia*, p. 21, sA2170; Sneddon to Darling, 17 June 1968, f65/46066, both NAA.

36 Diary, 30 January 1967, 20 May 1967, 18 November 1967; all DP; Fitts to Darling, 30 August 1971, DP, ms7826, s7, b17, f15, NLA; Woods to Darling, 2 August 1967, 13 November 1967; Perkin to Forell, 1 May 1968; Heydon to Darling,

29 May 1968; Darling to Heydon, 22 July 1968; Freedman to Waterman, 1 July 1968, all DP.

37 Darling to Heydon, 22 July 1968, 5 August 1969; 'Report on a visit to Northern Europe with special reference to the practice and use[?] of publicity in the field of immigration to Australia', all DP.

38 'Report on …', *op .cit.*; Kiddle to Heydon, 7 August 1968, both DP.

39 Forbes to Darling, 25 June 1971, DP; Minister for Immigration, press release 31 August 1971, DP, ms 7826, s18, b37, f4, NLA; Darling to Sumner, 4 May 1966; Sumner to Darling, 5 May 1966, both DP.

27 Sedulous

1 Darling to Quinn, 30 May 1966, DP.

2 'Memorandum and Articles of Association of the Australian Elizabethan Theatre Trust', DP, ms 7826, s2, b6, f31, NLA.

3 Kippax (1965), p. 199; Sir James Darling to the author, 24 March 1995; Darling to Badger, 29 July 1963; Badger to Darling, 19 July 1963, both DP; Badger to Semmler, DP, ms 7826, s16, b33, f1, NLA; Rowse (2002), pp. 193, 313.

4 Coombs (1983), pp. 236, 222; Rowse (2002), pp. 192–3; Darling (1944a), p. 8, DP; Serle (1987), p. 197.

5 Coombs (1983), pp. 236–8, 239, 241; Serle (1987), p. 201; Kippax (1965), pp. 200, 201; Pringle (1958), p. 129.

6 Coombs (1983), pp. 241, 242, 244; Rowse (2002), p. 296, 268–77; 'Organization and support for the performing arts' (24 May 1967), DP, ms 7826, s2, b6, f27, p. 4 and attachment 3, NLA.

7 Diary, 19 January 1966; Masterman to Darling, 12 June 1968, both DP.

8 AETT, Council of governors, Meeting, 6 October 1976, Minutes, p. 2, DP, ms 7826, s2, b6, f29, NLA; Yule (2006), p. 330; Kerrigan to Darling, 22 September 1982; M.R. Darling to J.R. Darling, 20 January 1972; Grace to Darling, 14 October 1982; ACFTA, Interim Report to the Prime Minister, undated: 'The future role of the Australian Elizabethan Theatre Trust under the new constitution for the Australian Council for the Arts' (December 1973) [incomplete], pp. 2–4, 8–9, all DP, ms 7826, s2, b6, f30 (1st), s7, b16, f10 (2nd), s17, b36, f8 (3rd) and s2, b6, f28 (4th), NLA.

9 Timbs to McCaffrey, 19 October 1973; 'Notes on the memorandum by M.C. Tymbs [sic]' (27 October 1973); 'Governors meeting', undated, all DP, ms 7826, s2, b6, f28 (1st & 2nd) and s2, b6, f29 (3rd), NLA; Rowse (2002), p. 360.

10 Hoad (1977), p. 31; AETT, Council of governors, Meeting, 6 October 1976, Minutes, pp. 2–7; Council of governors (NSW), Meeting, 19 December 1976?, Minutes, unnumbered, all DP, ms 7826, s2, b6, f27 (1st) and f29 (2nd & 3rd), NLA.

11 Darling to Potter, 10 December 1974; Potter to Darling, 23 December 1974; 'President's message' (1975), all DP, ms 7826, s2, b6, f31, NLA.

12 Alexander to Darling, 19 March 1975; J.R. Darling to Alexander, 2 April 1975; McCaffrey to Darling, 6 May 1975; Memorandum from the President to the Chairman (16 April 1974), all DP, ms 7826, s2, b6, f31, NLA.

13 Darling to Potter, 17 January 1975; Ross to Darling, 22 February 1977, both DP, ms 7826, s2, b6, f31 (1st) and b6, f26 (2nd) and f29 (3rd), NLA; Hoad (1977), p. 32; IAC, *Assistance to the Performing Arts*, pp. 2–12, sA12909, NAA.

14 IAC, *Assistance to the Performing Arts*, pp. 22–29, 60, 124, 128, 130, sA12909, NAA; Darling (to Waddy?), undated; Darling, two handwritten notes, undated; 'Orchestras', undated, all DP, ms 7826, s2, b7, f 32, NLA.

15 AETT, Council of governors, Annual meetings, 29 June 1981, 26 June 1978, Minutes, pp. 3–4 and unnumbered; Ross to Darling, 30 November 1976, all DP, ms 7826, s2, b7, f33 (1st) and b6, f29 (2nd & 3rd), NLA.

16 Walter (1980), pp. 256–62.

17 Diary, 18 October 1975, DP.

18 *Ibid.*, 11 November 1975.

19 *Ibid.*, 18 October 1975; Alexander to Darling, 13 November 1975, DP, ms 7826, s2, b6, f29, NLA.

20 Alexander to Darling, 24 November 1975; Brown to Darling, 12 June 1976; Ross to Darling, 19 January 1976; Darling to Crean, 4 July 1975; Crean to Darling, 21 August 1975; all DP, ms 7826, s2, b6, f29 (1st & 3rd), and s7, b15, f3 (2nd), b16, f10 (4th) and b15, f6 (5th), NLA.

21 Draft note (1 December 1967), DP, ms 7826, s11, b26, f4, NLA; Semmler (1978).

22 Ashbolt (1978).

23 *Ibid.*

24 Clark to Darling, 23 June 1975, DP, ms 7826, s7, b15, f6, NLA; Clark to Darling, 19 December 1968, DP; Darling to Clark, 18 August 1971, CIP, ms 7550/7/12, b38, fJan–Dec 1971(i); Darling to Clark, 9 January 1978, DP, ms 7826, s7, b19, f32, both NLA; Matthews (2008), pp. 369–72.

25 Darling to Clark, 9 January 1978, DP, ms 7826, s7, b19, f32, NLA.

26 Clark (1978); Dunstan (1978).

27 Darling to Fairbairn, 31 May 1978, 19 July 1978, FP, ms 9326, s1, b1, f1; Fairbairn to Darling, 24 July 1978, 4 July 1980, DP, ms 3826, s7, b17, f16, NLA; *RR*, p. 176.

28 Barwick to Darling, 23 August 1971, DP, ms 7826, s7, b15, f3, NLA; Sutcliffe (1991), pp. 27–8; Sutcliffe (2013), p. 199.

29 Simpson to Darling, 29 April 1963; Darling to Blackburne, 28 May 1963; Darling to Lewis, 29 May 1964; Darling to Harlow, 22 September 1965; Hankey to Darling, 15 July 1970, all DP, ms 7826, s5, b10, f50 (1st–4th) and s14, b29, f1 (5th), NLA; Hankey to J.R. Darling, 12 September 1970, DP.

30 Chapman to Fordham, 22 March 1983; Newspaper cutting, undated, unsourced; Thompson to Darling, 4 June 1980; Darling to Pelly, 8 February 1973; Pelly to Darling, 5 June 1974; Darling to Turner, 30 July 1979; Darling to Cutler, 3 February 1979; Gourlay to Cornish, 25 November 1982, all DP, ms 7826, s14, b29, f4 (1st) and f1 (3rd–8th), and b30, f11 (2nd), NLA.

31 Darling to Taylor, 18 November 1982; Gebhardt to Victorian committee members (undated); Darling to Bird, 6 July 1979; all DP, ms 7826, s14, b29, f1 (1st & 3rd) and f7 (2nd), NLA.

32 Carnegie to Darling, 2 December 1982, 5 May 1983; Turner to Darling, 27 September 1979; Darling memo 'United World Colleges, Australian Branch', 23 February 1979; Darling to Taylor, 18 November 1982; Darling to Cutler, 3 February 1979; Sutcliffe to Darling, 17 December 1982; McConnell to Darling, 8 January 1979, all DP, ms 7826, s14, b29, f6 (1st, 2nd & 4th) and f1 (3rd, 5th–7th), and s15, b31, f4 (8th), NLA.

33 Darling to Kent, 21 October 1964, DP; 'O.G.Gs Dinner 28.6.75'; Casey
    to Kilpatrick, 20 December 1971; Casey to Darling, 1 December 1970; 'St
    Margaret's—Reid committee joint discussions', 24 February 1971; Reid to Casey,
    11 November 1970; Reed committee meeting, 6 December 1970, all DP, ms 7826,
    s9, b24, f5 (1st) and s5, b9, f45 (2nd–6th), NLA.

34 Cartwright to Darling, 4 May 1962, 8 May 1962, both DP; Bate (1990), pp. 249,
    267–8; Highton Joint Committee, Meeting, 22 November 1967, Minutes,
    Appendix A, DP, ms 7826, s15, b31, f2, NLA.

35 Renney to Darling, 9 October 1968, DP; 'Draft' (12 October 1976); F.S. McArthur,
    'Marcus Oldham Farm Management Committee: Discussions between Sir
    James Darling and F.S. McArthur at the Melbourne Club, Friday, June 8th.
    1979'; Darling, 'Common Land—Marcus Oldham Farm Management College',
    15 October 1979; F.S. McArthur & J.R. Darling, 'Common Land—Marcus
    Oldham Farm Management College', April 1980, all DP, ms 7826, s15, b31, f2,
    NLA.

36 Darling to McArthur, 14 September 1980; MOFMC Council, Meeting, 9 April
    1981, Minutes, (unnumbered), both DP, ms 7826, s15, b31, f2 (1st) and f6 (2nd),
    NLA.

37 Upton to Darling, 5 July 1982; Tyler to Coates, 4 September 1975; Jackson to
    Darling, 22 September 1976; Farley to Darling, 6 October 1976; Darling, 'Braemar,
    12 December 1976', all DP, ms 7826, s3, b7, f35, (1st), and s5, b8, f41, (2nd–5th),
    NLA

38 Harris to J.R. & M.D. Darling, 5 March 1974; Darling, Notes for the service of
    inauguration (undated); '15 July 1980, Trinity Grammar School'; '27 November
    1975, Brisbane Church of England Grammar School'; '22 November 1974, Xavier
    Staff Association', all DP, ms 7826, s5, b8, f41 (1st & 2nd), and s9, b24, f3 (3rd–5th),
    NLA.

39 Darling to Dunlop, 23 February 1979; Darling, 'Conference 1979', 10 June 1978,
    both DP, ms 7826, s1, b3, f15 (1st) and f16 (2nd), NLA.

40 Henry to Darling, 3 September 1980; Darling, 'Memo on 1st phase conference
    1980', undated, DP, ms 7826, s7, b18, f24 (1st) and s1, b3, f14 (2nd), NLA; Darling
    (1982a), pp. 32–4; Bolton (1990), pp. 266–70.

41 Darling (1982a), pp. 34–6.

42 le Fleming (2007), pp. 113–14, 149; M.R. Darling to J.R. Darling, 17 January 1971,
    DP; M. le Fleming to Darling, 28 September 1971, 17 February 1973, 18 October
    1973, 16 June 1974, 15 January 1975, 20 March 1975; 24 February 1980, all DP, ms
    7826, s7, b19, f32 (1st–6th) and f31 (7th), NLA.

43 Diary, 4 January 1978, 1 May 1978, DP; 1 Corinthians 10:13 (New Revised
    Standard Version).

28 Once an Englishman

 1 Diary, 9 February 1985, 18 September 1989; Darling to le Fleming, 20 February
    1980, both DP; Jane Gray, Caroline Shearer and Liza Sutherland to the author,
    9 December 2010.

 2 Darling to le Fleming, 22 January 1979, 5 December 1979, both DP; *ADB*, vol. 18,
    p. 302; AACE, Meeting, 16 April 1984, Minutes (unnumbered); Darling to Jones,
    19 April 1984, both DP, ms 7826, s17, b36, f7, NLA.

3 Darling to Jones, 19 April 1984, 14 April 1984, 19 November 1984, all DP, ms 7826, s17, b36, f7, NLA.

4 Darling, handwritten note, 11 February 1988; MOFMC Council, Meetings, 11 February 1988, 7 April 1988, Minutes, unnumbered; G.R. McConnell, 'Discussion paper—Confidential' (10 February 1983), all DP, ms 7826, s15, b33, f19 (1st) and f18 (2nd & 3rd), and b31, f8 (4th), NLA.

5 Draft submission to the Victorian Department of Education and Youth Affairs (undated); Submission to the Victorian Department of Education and Youth Affairs (July 1984), both DP, ms 7826, s15, b32, f10 (1st) and b33, f20 (2nd), NLA.

6 Darling (1982b), p. 8; MOFMC Council, Meetings, 13 June 1985, 23 November 1984, 7 February 1985 and 11 July 1985, Minutes, unnumbered; Neilson to Darling, 6 September 1975; Lewis, 'M.O.F.M.C.', 11 September 1985; Darling to Neilson, undated; Financial statement, 31 January 1989; Untitled document, 28 January 1988; Darling, Memorandum, 26 November 1989, all DP, ms 7826, s15, b32, f11 (1st, 4th–6th), b31, f7 (2nd–3rd & 7th), b33, f18 (8th & 9th) and f17 (10th), NLA.

7 Gourlay to Darling, 22 May 1985, 1 August 1983; Darling to Gourlay, 10 August 1983 (marked 'not sent'), 15 June 1985, all DP, ms 7826, s14, b29, f2, NLA.

8 Darling to Tyler, 20 June 1987; Charles to Darling, 19 June 1987; Darling to Power, 30 August 1985; Gourlay to Darling, 23 September 1987; Robinson to Darling, 22 July 1988; UWC, General meeting (17 November 1989), chairman's report; Darling to Jolly, 21 February 1989; UWA Trust (Victoria), Minutes, 4 February 1989, all DP, ms 7826, s14, b29, f4 (1st, 2nd & 4th), f7 (3rd) and f3 (7th), b30, f11 (5th), f9 (6th) and f8 (8th), NLA.

9 Walker to Jolly, 29 May 1989; Jolly to Darling; Darling, Memorandum (13 March 1984); Tyler, Memorandum (24 April 1986); UWA Trust (Victoria), Meeting, 19 January 1991, Minutes, unnumbered, all DP, ms 7826, s15, b33, f17 (1st), b30, f8 (2nd & 3rd), f10 (4th) and f9 (5th), NLA.

10 *ADB*, vol. 10, p. 631; Davie (2000), p. 208; McCloskey (1994), p. 178; Kelly (1992); Darling to le Fleming, 24 October 1981, DP, ms 7826, s7, b19, f31, NLA.

11 Darling to le Fleming, 27 April 1980, 26 June 1980; Darling to le Fleming, 16 June 1982; Diary, 16 April 1967, 20 May 1967, 18 November 1967, all DP; Darling to Sayers, 6 May 1965, 26 May 1965, 16 August 1965, all DP, ms 7826, s5, b9, f43, NLA.

12 Burns to Darling, 2 June 1982, 4 August 1982; Darling to Burns, 26 July 1982 (marked 'Not sent'); Burns to Darling, 5 December 1988, all DP, ms 7826, s7, b15, f4 (1st, 2nd & 3rd) and f2 (3rd), NLA; Darling (2006), p. 45.

13 Darling (2006), pp. 73–4, 24–5, 25–6.

14 *Ibid.*, pp. 82, 94–5, 102, 242, 138.

15 *Ibid.*, pp. 138, 305, 178, 162, 194–5.

16 *Ibid.*, pp. 6, 13, 12, 58, 183, 39, 62, 130, 309, 164, 166–7, 57, 90, 191, 289.

17 *Ibid.*, pp. 51, 54, 55, 30, 31.

18 *Ibid.*, pp. 229, 250, 41–2, 267, 149, 176, 272, 202.

19 *Ibid.*, pp. 116–7, 87, 81.

20 *Ibid.*, pp. 187, 257, 115, 222, 62, 316, 323–4; Fraser (2015), p. 37.

21 Darling (2006), pp. 173, 179, 26–7, 55, 277, 251, 34–5, 131, 156–7, 146; Adam-
    Smith to Darling, 23 April 1988, 11 May 1988, both DP, ms 7826, s7, b15, f2,
    NLA; Darling (1982c), pp. 52–3, DP.
22 Darling (2006), pp. 37, 283, 252–3, 147–8.
23 Darling to le Fleming, 28 August 1979, DP; Darling (2006), pp. 84, 90, 306;
    Ebury (2008), pp. 428–30; Lester to Darling, 28 January 1959; Darling to Lester,
    2 February 1959, both GGSA; Bennett to Darling, 17 April 1983; Goldberg to
    Darling, 1 July 1985, 7 October 1985; Darling, handwritten note, undated; Darling
    to Goldberg, 21 October 1985 (marked 'not sent'), all DP, ms 7826, s7, b17, f4 (1st),
    f20 (2nd & 4th) and f21 (3rd & 5th), NLA.
24 Darling (2006), pp. 56–7, 2–3, 100, 317, 315.
25 Darling to Sayers, 3 September 1965; Darling to le Fleming, 24 October 1981,
    both DP, ms 7826, s5, b9, f43 (1st) and s7, b19, f31 (2nd), NLA; Darling (2006),
    pp. 296, 159, 44, 103, 198, 219, 276.
26 Darling (2006), pp. 227–8, 322–3, 72, 161.
27 Garton Ash (1993), p. 20; *ibid.*, pp. 203, 200–1, 204, 93.
28 Darling (2006), pp. 189, 191, 209, 268, 247, 212.
29 *Ibid.*, pp. 299, 285, 40, 8, 30, 184, 139, 278, 160, 65, 172; Handbury to Darling,
    31 October 1985, DP, ms 7826, s7, b18, f26, NLA.
30 Darling (2006), pp. 29, 6, 233, 237, 246.
31 *Ibid.*, pp. 17, 69–70, 121–2.
32 *Ibid.*, pp. 164, 172, 249–50.
33 *Ibid.*, pp. 79, 104–5, 134, 123; Fairfax (1992), p. 207; Darling to Fairfax, 21 January
    1987 (marked 'not sent'), DP, ms 7826, s7, b17, f16, NLA.
34 Darling to le Fleming, 24 October 1981; Darling to Button, 22 May 1986 (marked
    'not sent'), both DP, ms 7826, s7, b19, f31 (1st) and s7, b15, f31 (2nd), NLA;
    Darling (2006), pp. 122–3, 286, 45, 141, 245, 157.
35 Darling (2006), pp. 48, 210, 231–2, 3, 169, 217, 282.
36 Britain (1997); Knightley (2001), p. 237; Bridge, Crawford and Dunstan (2009),
    p. 10.
37 Jane Gray, Caroline Shearer and Liza Sutherland to the author, 9 December 2010;
    Darling (2006), pp. 39, 254, 130.
38 Marchant to Darling, 1 July 1971, DP; Hall to Darling, 1 August 1949; Darling
    to Hall, 11 August 1949, both GGSA; order of services and sermon text in the
    possession of the author.

BIBLIOGRAPHY

Manuscript Sources

Andrew Papers, family of Emeritus Professor R.R. Andrew, Melbourne
Boys Employment Movement (Geelong), Mrs V. Stott, Belmont, Victoria
Clark Papers, NLA
Darling Papers (i), family of Sir James Darling, Melbourne
Darling Papers (ii), NLA
Dicker Papers, family of G.C.W. Dicker, Winchester, England
Dutton Papers, NLA
Fairbairn Papers, NLA
Giblin Papers, NLA.
Harford Papers, family of Sir James Harford, Seaford, England
Headley-Gullett Papers, NLA
Latham Papers, NLA
le Fleming Papers, M. le Fleming, Wiltshire, England
Mackinnon Papers, Latrobe Library, Melbourne
Officer Papers, NLA
Phelps Papers, Oriel College Library, Oxford
Priestley Papers, University of Birmingham
Stephens Papers, L. Stephens, Eastbourne, England
Wadham Papers, UMA
Weston Papers, J.M.H. Weston, Ufford, England

Interviews

Interviews are cited in the notes with the phrase 'to the author'.

Emeritus Professor
  Rod Andrew
R.L. Arrowsmith
D.W. Baker
M. Bickmore
John Bowen
Professor Manning Clark
J.M. Coldham
Professor W.F. Connell
Mary Connellan
  (née Finnin)
B.R.A. Coulter
Sir James Darling
Norah Darling
Tom Darling

Roger Day
Reverend Randall Deasey
G.C.W. Dicker
Sir Talbot Duckmanton
Lady Fisher
John Gammell
Miss D. Gammon
Sir John Gorton
Jane Gray (née Darling)
James Guest
Jo Gullett
Sir Rupert Hamer
Sir James Harford
Sir David Hay
Peter Henderson

Joan Hickman
  (née Whitby)
Gilbert Hoole
Barney Hutton
Brian Jones
Dr Bruce Kent
Ewan Laird
W.E. Lamaison
Patrick Law
Sir Desmond Lee
Morris le Fleming
Susan le Fleming
Kenneth Lindsay
William Locke
Professor Sam McCulloch

Paul McKeown

Professor J.A.C. Mackie

Dr Campbell McKnight

Margaret Masterman
(née Maxwell)

Lawrence Neal

Nan Newman

Noel Newman

John Nurser

Barry Orchard

Ronald Orr

Professor Jeremy Pickett-
Heaps

Caroline Shearer
(née Darling)

Dr G.K. Smith

Henry Speagle

Dr H.D. Steward

Liza Sutherland
(née Darling)

Mrs F.G.A. Temple

Michael Thwaites

Vic Tunbridge

Tony Tyler

Peter Westcott

J.H.M. Weston

Hilda Wharton
(née Davies)

Sir John Young

Selected writings by Darling

The following selection comprises published articles, books, speeches, orations and newspaper articles cited in chapter endnotes. Also cited in chapter endnotes and available in the Darling Papers, either (i) or (ii), are numerous other unpublished prompt notes, typed notes, titled and untitled articles (dated and undated), and transcripts. Annual GGS speech-day addresses by Darling are available for each year, 1930–61, in the December edition of the *Corian*. Darling's speeches and addresses to the Headmasters' Conference of Australia and the Australian College of Education, if not cited in the text or itemised below, are available in the proceedings of those bodies.

(2006) *Reflections for an Age*, J. Bedggood and N. Clark (eds), (Melbourne: Robjon Partners).

(1991) *Reflections for the Age*, J. Minchin and B. Porter (eds), (Melbourne: Joint Board of Christian Education).

(1982a) Patriotism, Identity and Purpose, *Australian Director*, vol. 12, no. 6, pp. 32–6.

(1982b) The Governing Body & the Headmaster, *Independence*, vol. 6, no. 1, pp. 5–8.

(1982c) Freedom and Greed, *IPA Review*, 36, vol. 2, pp. 50–4.

(1978) *Richly Rewarding* (Melbourne: Hill of Content).

(1972) Responsibility (Buntine oration), Australian College of Education, 16 pp.

(1970) The Whole Environment, speech to the 3rd National Conference of the Institute of Directors, 10 June (Melbourne: Australian Frontier), pp. 1–14.

(1969) Educational Recollections of the Thirties, in R.J.W. Selleck (ed.), *Melbourne Studies in Education, 1968–1969* (Melbourne: Melbourne University Press), pp. 1–28.

(1967) (with E.H. Montgomery) *Timbertop: An Innovation in Australian Education* (Melbourne: Cheshire).

(1966) The Dilemmas of a National Broadcasting Authority (Address to graduates, University of Sydney, Standing Committee of Convocation), (Publisher unknown).

(1965) On Headmastering, in P.J. McKeown and B.W. Hone (eds), (1967) *The Independent School: Papers presented to the Headmasters Conference* (Melbourne: Oxford University Press), pp. 61–71.

(1963) Educating for Tomorrow, in Australian College of Education: *Educating for Tomorrow* (Melbourne: F.W. Cheshire), pp. 1–15.

(1962a) *The Education of a Civilized Man: A Selection of Speeches and Sermons*, M. Persse (ed.), (Melbourne: Cheshire).

(1962b) The ABC and the Australian Community (Media conference address at the University of New England).

(1962c) The Anatomy of Greatness—W.D. Chapman Memorial Lecture, Institute of Engineers, 20 November.

(1960) The Education of a Civilized Man (Royal Australasian College of Surgeons: George Adlington Syme Oration), pp. 1–15 and *ECM*, pp. 21–37.

(1955) On Looking beneath the Surface of Things, *Medical Journal of Australia*, vol. 1, no. 16, pp. 557–61 and *ECM*, pp. 60–76.

(1954) Timbertop, an Experiment, *Educational Magazine*, vol. 11, no. 5, pp. 223–5.

(1953?) Education for Community Service (typescript).

(1951) A Defence of Church Schools, *Church Standard*, 21 December.

(1950) Specialization—Good or Bad?, *South Australian Teachers' Journal*, vol. 36, no. 5, pp. 9–15.

(1949) Inaugural address (Sydney: Headmasters Conference of Australia), pp. 18–25.

(1948) Wisdom and Understanding, in *Speeches at a Conference of Headmasters* (Sydney: HMCA), pp. 19–26 and McKeown and Hone (1967), pp. 51–8.

(1946) The English Record (Address to the Royal Empire Society, Victorian branch, 14 March, and *Corian* 1946 (May), pp. 9–13 and *ECM*, pp. 127–136.

(1945) Youth (Melbourne: Federal Institute of Accountants).

(1944a) The Importance of Drama in National Life, address at the Melbourne Public Library (4 April).

(1944b) William Temple Archbishop of Canterbury, ABC broadcast (October), *ECM*, pp. 121–6.

(1942) Religion and Education, ABC broadcast (September).

(1940a) This Democracy and Its Future: What Shall We Do for Youth?, *Age*, 3 May.

(1940b) Tradition, ABC broadcast (November) and *ECM*, pp. 111–14.

(1939) Growing Up (Paper delivered to the Education Section of the Australian and New Zealand Association for the Advancement of Science, Canberra).

(1938) Geelong Church of Education Grammar School, *New Era*, vol. 19, no. 3, pp. 79–81.

(1936a) Public Education: Its Cost and Its Goal, *Argus*, 9 May.

(1936b) Things to Come, *Australian Educational Review*, vol. 8, no. 1, pp. 8–11.

(1935a) Current Problems in Secondary Education', in P.R. Cole (ed.), *The Education of the Adolescent in Australia* (Melbourne: Melbourne University Press), pp. 320–39.

(1935b) Education and Freedom. Eighth John Smyth Memorial Lecture.

(1935c) Post-primary Education, *Australian Quarterly*, vol. 25, pp. 55–60.

(1934) The Examination Problem, *Sydney Mail and Schools' Number*, vol. 12, pp. 42–3.

(1933a) Education To Meet the Need of the Modern State, *Australian Quarterly*, vol. 17, pp. 3–22.

(1933b) Renaissance, *Australian Quarterly*, 19: 5–17 and *ECM*, pp. 49–59.

(1931) Public School Education, *Australian Quarterly*, vol. 9, pp. 28–36.

(1930) The Good Schoolmaster, *Education Review*, vol. 6, no. 2, pp. 8–10.

(1917) Patriotism, *A Public School Looks at the World*, vol. 1, no. 3.

References

Ajala, O. (1964) Up and Down the ABC, *Nation*, 27 June.

Alomes, S. (1979) *'Reasonable Men': Middle Class Reformism in Australia, 1928–1939*, PhD thesis, Australian National University.

Alomes, S., Dober, M. and Hellier, D. (1986) The Social Context of Post-war
Conservatism, in A. Curthoys and J. Merritt (eds), *Better Dead than Red: Australia's
First Cold War, 1945–1959*, vol. 1 (Sydney: Allen & Unwin), pp. 1–28, 213–16.

Altschwager, L. (1985) *The First Sixty Years: A History of Toc H in Australia from 1925–
1985* (Adelaide: Lutheran Publishing House).

Aristotle, (1984) *The Ethics of Aristotle*, trans. J.A.K. Thompson (Harmondsworth, UK:
Penguin Books).

Arnold, M. (1869) *Culture and Anarchy: An Essay in Political and Social Criticism*
(Cambridge, UK: Cambridge University Press).

Ashbolt, A. (1978) Loyalty to the Institution, *Nation Review*, 18–24 May.

Ashbolt, A. (1987) Recollections: Alan Ashbolt, in A. Curthoys, A.W. Martin and
T. Rowse (eds) *Australians from 1939* (Sydney: Fairfax, Syme & Weldon), pp. 370–8.

Atteridge (1929) *History of the 17th (Northern) Division* (Glasgow: Robert Maclehose & Co).

Badcock, A.M. (1964) The Extension of State Control over Independent Schools in
Victoria, 1900–1925, in E.L. French (ed.), *Melbourne Studies in Education, 1964*
(Melbourne: Melbourne University Press), pp. 163–97.

Bailey, K. and Duncan, W.G.K. (1936) *Educating a Democracy* (Canberra: Australian
Institute of Political Science).

Barker, R. (1975) *One Man's Jungle: A Biography of F. Spencer Chapman* (London: Chatto
& Windus).

Bate, W. (1990) *Light Blue Down Under: A History of Geelong Grammar School*
(Melbourne: Oxford University Press).

Bean, C.E.W. (1950) *Here, My Son: An Account of the Independent and Other Corporate
Boys' Schools of Australia* (Sydney: Angus & Robertson).

Bolton, G.C. (1974) 1939–51, in F.K. Crowley (ed.), *A New History of Australia*
(Melbourne: William Heinemann), pp. 458–503.

Bolton, G.C. (1990) *The Oxford History of Australia*, vol. 5, *1942–1988* (Melbourne:
Oxford University Press).

Bowman, D. (2005) The Lion of the ABC, *Australian Policy Online*, 15 June, http://apo.
org.au/commentary/lion-abc (accessed 6 January 2013).

Boyd, R. (1960) *The Australian Ugliness*, 2nd rev. edn (Melbourne: Penguin Books).

Bradby, G.F. (1913) *The Lanchester Tradition* (London: Smith Elder).

Bridge, C., Crawford, R. and Dunstan, D. (2009) More Than Just Barry, Clive and
Germaine: An Overview of Australians in Britain, in C. Bridge, R. Crawford
and D. Dunstan (eds), *Australians in Britain: The Twentieth-Century Experience*
(Melbourne: Monash University epress), pp. 7–30.

Britain, I. (1997) *Once an Australian: Journeyings with Barry Humphries, Clive James,
Germaine Greer and Robert Hughes* (Melbourne: Oxford University Press).

Burdon, R.M. (1965) *The New Dominion: A Social and Political History of New Zealand,
1918–1939* (Wellington, New Zealand: A.H. & A.W. Reed).

Burke, E. (1986 [1790]) *Reflections on the Revolution in France* (Harmondsworth, UK:
Penguin Books).

Butlin, S.J. and Schedvin, C.B. (1977) *War Economy, 1942–1945* (Canberra: Australian
War Memorial).

Caiden, G.E. (1965) *Career Service: An Introduction to the History of Personnel
Administration in The Commonwealth Public Service of Australia, 1901–1961*
(Melbourne: Melbourne University Press).

Carolan, J.M. (1974) *A History of Geelong Grammar School, 1912–1929*, MA thesis, University of Melbourne.

Chapman, F. (1976) *The Book of Tonbridge: The Story of the Town's Past* (Chesham, Bucks: Barracuda Books).

Chapman, R.M. and Malone, E.P. (1969) *New Zealand in the Twenties: Social Change and Material Progress* (Auckland, New Zealand: Heinemann).

Clark, C.M.H. (1987) *A History of Australia*, vol VI (Melbourne: Melbourne University Press).

Clark, M. (1978) An Educationist Who Left His Mark, *Age*, 22 April.

Clark, M. (1990) *The Quest fort Grace* (Ringwood: Penguin Books).

Clark, M.R. (2003) *Geelong Grammar School Timbertop: Celebrating 50 Years* (Geelong, Victoria: Geelong Grammar School).

Cole, G.D.H. (1920) *Guild Socialism* (London: Fabian Society).

Cole, K. (1969) *Commissioned to Care: The Golden Jubilee History of the Mission of St. James and St. John, 1919–1969* (Melbourne: Ruskin Press).

Coombs, H.C. (1983) *Trial Balance: Issues of My Working Life* (Melbourne: Sun Books).

Connell, W.F. (1984) The Education of a Professor of Education, in I. Palmer (ed.), *Melbourne Studies in Education, 1984* (Melbourne: Melbourne University Press), pp. 1–30.

Connell, W.F. (1993) *Reshaping Australian Education 1960–1985* (Melbourne: ACER).

Crawford, R.M. (1960) *An Australian Perspective* (Madison, WI: University of Wisconsin).

Crompton, N.J. (undated) *Yardley Court, 1898–1973* (UK: Yardley Court School).

Crutwell, C.R.M.F. (1936) *A History of the Great War, 1914–1918*, 2nd edn (Oxford, UK: Clarendon Press).

Cunningham, K.S. (1936) A Critical Account of Australian Education, *Year Book of Education*, pp. 618–43.

Curthoys, A. (1986) The Getting of Australian Television: Dilemmas in Ownership, Control and Culture, 1941–56, in A. Curthoys and J. Merritt (eds), *Better Dead than Red: Australia's First Cold War, 1945–1959*, vol. 2 (Sydney: Allen & Unwin), pp. 123–54, 202–5.

Darwin, J. (1980) Imperialism in Decline?: Tendencies in British Imperial Policy between the Wars, *Historical Journal*, vol. 23, no. 3, pp. 657–79.

Davie, M. (2000) *Anglo-Australian Attitudes* (London: Secker & Warburg).

Davies, R. (1970) *Fifth Business* (Harmondsworth, UK: Penguin Books).

de Honey, J.R.S. (1977) *Tom Brown's Universe* (London: Millington Books).

de Saint-Exupéry, A. (1995) *Flight to Arras* (Harmondsworth, UK: Penguin Classics).

de Tocqueville, A. (1969 [1848]) *Democracy in America* (New York: Harper & Row).

Dixon, N.F (1983) *On the Psychology of Military Incompetence* (London: Futura).

Drucker, P. (1939) *The End of Economic Man: The Origins of Totalitarianism* (London: William Heinemann).

Drummond, I.M. (1974) *Imperial Economic Policy, 1917–1939: Studies in Expansion and Protection* (London: Allen & Unwin).

Du Maurier, D. (1938) *Rebecca*. (London: V. Gollancz).

Dunbar, A. (1976) The Council of Public Education in Victoria, in S. Murray-Smith (Ed.), *Melbourne Studies in Education, 1976* (Melbourne: Melbourne University Press), pp. 157–87.

Dunstan, K. (1978) A Read That's Richly Rewarding, *Bulletin*, 13 June.

Eagar W.McG. and Secretan, H.A. (1925) *Unemployment Among Boys* (London: Dent).

Ebury, S. (2008) *The Many Lives of Ken Myer* (Melbourne: Miegunyah Press).

Edmunds, Sir J. (1947) *Military Operations France and Belgium 1918*, vol. 4 (London: HMSO).

Edwards, R.D. (1987) *Victor Gollancz: A Biography* (London: Gollancz).

Emerson, R.W. (1907) Friendship, in *Essays and Other Writings* (London: Cassell).

Encel, S. (1955) The Commonwealth Public Service and Outside Recruitment, *Public Administration*, vol. 14, no. 1, pp. 28–43.

Engel, F. (1988) *21 Years of Australian Frontier: An Extraordinary Organization for Extraordinary Times, 1962–1983* (Melbourne: Australian Frontier).

Fairfax, J. (1992) *My Regards to Broadway* (Sydney: Angus & Robertson).

Fewster, A. (2015) Manning Clark and the Man in Black, *Inside Story*, http://insidestory.org.au/manning-clark-and-the-man-in-black (accessed 24 October 2016).

Firth, J.D'E. (1954) *Rendall of Winchester: The Life and Witness of a Teacher* (London: Oxford University Press).

Fletcher, F. (1936) *Brethren and Companions: Charterhouse Chapel Addresses* (London: R. Hale).

Fletcher, F. (1937) *After Many Days: A Schoolmaster's Memories* (London: R. Hale).

Fraser, G. (2015) Money Is the Only God Tories Want Us To Worship on Sunday, *Guardian*, 10 July.

Galbraith, J.K. (1963) *The Great Crash 1929* (Harmondsworth, UK: Penguin).

Gardiner, L. (1993) Back into Line, in R. McCarthy and M.J. Theobald (eds), *Melbourne Girls Grammar School: Centenary Essays, 1893–1993* (Melbourne: Hyland House), pp. 128–46.

Garton Ash, T. (1993) *The Magic Lantern: The Revolution of '89 Witnessed in Warsaw, Budapest, Berlin and Prague* (New York: Vintage Books).

Gathorne-Hardy, J. (1979) *The Public School Phenomenon, 597–1977* (London: Hodder & Stoughton).

Gathorne-Hardy, J. (1985) *The Rise and Fall of the British Nanny* (London: Weidenfeld & Nicholson).

Geelong Grammar School. (1961) *Thirty-Two Years* (Geelong, Victoria: privately published).

Goldstein, D.S. (1982) The Organizational Development of the British Historical Profession, 1884–1921, *Bulletin of the Institute of Historical Research*, vol. 55, no. 131, pp. 180–93.

Gollancz, V. (1952) *My Dear Timothy, An Autobiographical Letter to His Grandson* (London: Gollancz).

Gollancz, V. (1953) *More for Timothy, Being the Second Instalment of an Autobiographical Letter to His Grandson* (London: Gollancz).

Gollancz, V. (1958) *The Devil's Repertoire: Or, Nuclear Bombing and the Life of Man* (London: Gollancz).

Gollancz, V. and Somervell, D.C. (1918) *Political Education at a Public School* (London: W. Collins & Sons).

Gordon, P. and White, J. (1979) *Philosophers and Educational Reformers* (London: Routledge & Kegan Paul).

Gott, K.D. (1960) The Privileged Classroom: Geelong Grammar Searches Its Soul, *Nation*, vol. 56, pp. 8–9.

Greene, G. (1971) *A Sort of Life* (London: Bodley Head).

Gronn, P. (1991) 'A drag on the war effort': Geelong Grammar School, 1940–45, *Journal of the Royal Australian Historical Society*, vol. 77, no. 2, pp. 53–76.

Gronn, P. (1992) Schooling for Ruling: The Social Composition of Admissions to Geelong Grammar School, 1930–9, *Australian Historical Studies*, vol. 25, no. 98, pp. 72–89.

Gronn, P. (1994) 'Will anything ever be done?': Geelong Grammar School and the Associated Public Schools Head of the River in the 1930s, *Australian Historical Studies*, vol. 26, no. 103, pp. 242–61.

Gronn, P. (1999) Leadership from a Distance: Institutionalizing Values and Forming Character at Timbertop, 1951–61, in P.T. Begley and P.E. Leonard (eds), *The Values of Administration* (London: Falmer), pp. 140–67.

Hahn, K. (1934) A German public school, *The Listener*, vol. 11, no. 260, pp. 90–2.

Hahn, K. (1950) An Experiment in Education, *The Listener*, vol. 44, no. 1133, pp. 527–8.

Hahn, K. (1957) Outward Bound, in G.Z.F. Bereday and J.A. Lauwerys (eds), *The Year Book of Philosophy* (London: Evans Bros), pp. 436–62.

Hansen, D.E. and Hansen, I.V. (eds) (1996) *St Catherine's: A Centenary History* (Melbourne: Helicon Press).

Hansen, I. (1986) *By Their Deeds: A Centenary History of Camberwell Grammar School, 1886–1986* (Melbourne: Camberwell Grammar School).

Harper, M. (2004) 'Personal Contact Is Worth a Ton of Text-books': Educational Tours of the Empire, 1926–39, *Journal of Imperial and Commonwealth History*, vol. 32, no. 3, pp. 46–78.

Hasluck (1970) *The Government and the People, 1942–1945* (Canberra: Australian War Memorial).

Hattersley, R. (2004) *The Edwardians* (London: Little Brown).

Hazlehurst, C. (1982–3) The Advent Of Commercial Television, *Australian Cultural History*, vol. 2, pp. 104–19.

Hilliard, D. (1991) God in the Suburbs: The Religious Culture of Australian Cities in the 1950s, *Australian Historical Studies*, vol. 24, no. 97, pp. 399–419.

Hilliard, D. (1997) Church, Family and Sexuality in Australia in the 1950s, *Australian Historical Studies*, vol. 28, no. 109, pp. 133–46.

Hoad, B. (1977) Trust's Terminal Tryst, *Bulletin*, 29 January.

Hodgkin, R. (1986) Civilizing in the Wilds, *Times Educational Supplement*, 6 June.

Hodson, H.V. (1948) *Twentieth Century Empire* (London: Faber & Faber).

Hogg, J.W. (1986) *Our Proper Concerns, A History of the Headmasters' Conference of the Independent Schools of Australia* (Sydney: Macarthur Press).

Holbrook, A. (1987a) Slotting Them into the Right Niche: Adolescence and Vocational Guidance in Victoria, in B. Bessant (ed.), *Mother State and Her Little Ones* (Melbourne: La Trobe University, Centre for Youth and Community Studies), pp. 167–99.

Holbrook, A.P. (1987b) *Misfits and Idlers: Innocents and Victims—An Examination of the Responses to, and Dimensions of, Youth Unemployment in Victoria between the Wars*, PhD thesis, La Trobe University.

Hollis, C. (1976) *Oxford in the Twenties: Recollections of Five Friends* (London: Heinemann).

Holt, S. (1982) *Manning Clark and Australian History, 1915–1963* (Brisbane: University of Queensland Press).

Horne, D. (1964) *The Lucky Country: Australia in the Sixties* (Melbourne: Penguin Books).

Hudson, W.J. (1986) *Casey* (Melbourne: Oxford University Press).

Hughes, T. (1981) *Tom Brown's Schooldays* (New York: Oxford University Press).

Huxley, A. (1984) *Brave New World* (London: Chatto & Windus).

Hyam, R. (2006) *Britain's Declining Empire: The Road to Decolonisation, 1918–1968* (Cambridge, UK: Cambridge University Press).

Inglis, K.S. (1983) *This Is the ABC: The Australian Broadcasting Commission, 1932–1983* (Melbourne: Melbourne University Press).

Irving. T., Maunders, D. and Sherington, G. (1995) *Youth in Australia: Policy, Administration and Politics—A History since World War II* (Melbourne: Macmillan).

Isherwood, C. (1938) *Lions and Shadows: An Education in the Twenties* (London: Methuen).

James, W. (1981) *The Varieties of Religious Experience: A Study in Human Nature* (London: Collins).

Jennings, R.G. (1924) *The Human Pedagogue* (Melbourne: Australian Authors' Agency).

Judt, T. with T. Snyder (2012) *Thinking the Twentieth Century* (London: William Heinemann).

Kandel, I.F. (1938) *Impressions of Australian Education* (Melbourne: ACER).

Kelly, P. (1992) *The End of Certainty: The Story of the 1980s* (Sydney: Allen & Unwin).

Kiddle, M. (1961) *Men of Yesterday: A Social History of the Western District of Victoria* (Melbourne: Melbourne University Press).

Kipling, R. (1899) *Stalky and Co* (London: Macmillan).

Kippax, A. (1965) Drama, in A.F. Davies and S. Encel (eds), *Australian Society: A Sociological Introduction* (Melbourne: Cheshire), pp. 190–204.

Knightley, P. (2001) *Australia: Biography of a Nation* (London: Vintage Books).

Kristianson, G.L. (1964) The R.S.L. and 'Four Corners', *Australian Quarterly*, vol. 36, no. 1, pp. 20–30.

Laski, M. (1964) Domestic Life, in S. Nowell-Smith (ed.), *Edwardian England, 1901–1914* (London: Oxford University Press), pp. 141–212.

Laslett, P. (1962) The Solid Middle Class, *Listener*, vol. 57, no. 1710, pp. 13–15.

Lawrence, D.H. (1950) *Kangaroo* (London: Penguin).

le Fleming, M. (2007) *The Darlings of Eyke and the Nimmos of Falkirk* (Holt, Wiltshire: M. le Fleming).

Leinster-Mackay, D.P. (1984) *The Rise of the English Preparatory School* (London: Falmer Press).

Leinster-Mackay, D.P. (1987) *The Educational World of Edward Thring: A Centenary Study* (London: Falmer Press).

Lemon, A. (1999) *The Pride of Miss McComas: 111 Years of Preparatory Education at Geelong Grammar School* (Geelong: Geelong Grammar School).

Lemon, A. (2004) *A Great Australian School: Wesley College Examined* (Sydney: Helicon Press).

Leslie, S. (1985) *The Bishop Who Walked: A Biography of Ken Leslie (1911–)*, (Bathurst, New South Wales: S. Leslie and Robert Brown and Assocs).

Lewis, C.S. (1986) *Surprised by Joy* (London: Collins).

Lindsay, K. (1972) Post-war Oxford, 1918–1922, *Contemporary Review*, vol. 221, no. 1278.

Lodewycks, K.A. (1982) *The Funding of Wisdom: Revelations of a Library's Quarter Century* (Melbourne: Spectrum).

Love, P. (1982) Niemeyer's Australian Diary and Other English Records of His Mission, *Historical Studies of Australia and New Zealand*, vol. 20, no. 79, pp. 261–77.

Luff, H.M. (1970) *A History of Merchant Taylors' School, Crosby 1620–1970* (Liverpool, UK: Liverpool University Press).

MacCallum, M. (1964) Going Public, *Nation*, 11 January.

McCloskey, D.N. (1994) Bourgeois Virtue, *American Scholar*, vol. 63, no. 2, pp. 177–91.

McCloskey, D.N. (2006) *The Bourgeois Virtues: Ethics for an Age of Commerce* (Chicago, IL: University of Chicago Press).

McGregor, C. (1968) *Profile of Australia* (Melbourne: Penguin Books).

McInnes, G. (1967) *The Road to Gundagai* (Melbourne: Sun Books).

McKenna, M. (2011) *An Eye for Eternity: The Life of Manning Clark* (Melbourne: Miegunyah).

McKeown, P.J. and Hone, B.W. (1967) *The Independent School: Papers presented to the Headmasters' Conference* (Melbourne: Oxford University Press).

Mannheim, K. (1943) *Man and Society in the Age of Reconstruction* (London: Routledge).

Martin, A.W. (1989) R.G. Menzies and the Suez Crisis, *Australian Historical Studies*, vol. 23, no. 92, pp. 163–85.

Martin, A.W. (1993) *Robert Menzies: A Life*, vol. 1, *1894–1943* (Melbourne: Melbourne University Press).

Martin, A.W. (1999) *Robert Menzies: A Life*, vol. 2, *1944–1978* (Melbourne: Melbourne University Press).

Marwick, A. (1964) Middle Opinion in the Thirties: Planning, Progress and Political 'Agreement', *English Historical Review*, vol. 79, no. 2, pp. 285–98.

Matthews, B. (2008) *Manning Clark: A Life* (Sydney: Allen & Unwin).

Maunders, D. (1991) A Youth Service for Australia?: The Lobby for a National Youth Policy 1940–1960, *Journal of Australian Studies*, vol. 3, pp. 29–40.

Meaney, N. (2003) Britishness and Australia: Some Reflections, in C. Bridge and K. Fedorowich (eds), *The British World: Diaspora, Culture and Identity* (London: Frank Cass), pp. 121–35.

Megarrity, L. (2007) Regional Goodwill, Sensibly Priced: Commonwealth Policies towards Colombo Plan Scholars and Private Overseas Students, 1945–1972, *Australian Historical Studies*, vol. 38, no. 129, pp. 88–105.

Metcalfe, J. (1962) Ralph Munn and Australia, *Australian Library Journal*, vol. 23, April, pp. 96–102.

Morgan, C. (1951) *Liberties of the Mind* (London: Macmillan & Co).

Muggeridge, M. (1958) An Anatomy of Australian Snobbishness, *Sydney Moring Herald*, 10 May.

Munn, R. and Pitt, E.R. (1935) *Australian Libraries: A Survey of Conditions and Suggestions for Their Improvement* (Melbourne: ACER).

Musgrave, P.W. (1978) The Publication of the 'The Loom of Youth': A Moment in Public School History, *ANZHES Journal*, vol. 7, no. 2, pp. 43–54.

Musgrave, P.W. (1992) *From Humanity to Utility: Melbourne University and Public Examinations 1856–1964* (Melbourne: ACER).

Neve, A.H. (1933) *The Tonbridge of Yesterday* (Tonbridge, UK: Tonbridge Free Press).

Niall, B. (2009) *The Riddle of Father Hackett: A Life in Ireland and Australia* (Canberra: National Library of Australia).

Nichols, B. (1939) *Patchwork* (London: Chatto & Windus).

Norwood, C. (1929) *The English Tradition of Education* (London: John Murray).

Palfreeman, A.C. (1967) *The Administration of the White Australia Policy* (Melbourne: Melbourne University Press).

Parker, P. (1987) *The Old Lie: The Great War and the Public School Ethos* (London: Constable).

Parkin, G.R. (1900) *Edward Thring: Life, Diary and Letters* (London: Macmillan).

Persse, M. (1960) *Their Succeeding Race* (Melbourne: Cheshire).

Persse, M. (1995) *A Well-Ordered Liberty: A Portrait of Geelong Grammar School, 1855–1995* (Melbourne: Cliffe Books).

Phillips, A. (1988–89) Urban Reform and Local Response in Port Melbourne during the 1930s, *Melbourne Historical Journal*, vol. 19, pp. 58–75.

Phillips, A.A. (1931) The Better Schoolmaster, *Educational Review*, vol. 7, no. 1, pp. 24–6.

Phillips, A.A. (1962) The Schools, in P. Coleman (ed.) *Australian Civilization: A Symposium* (Melbourne: F.W. Cheshire), pp. 105–21.

Phillips, A.A. (1966) *The Australian Tradition: Studies in a Colonial Culture*, 2nd edn (Melbourne: Cheshire-Lansdowne).

Porter, B. (2007) *Frank Woods: Archbishop of Melbourne, 1957–1977* (Melbourne: Trinity College).

Poynter, J. and Rasmussen, C. (1996) *A Place Apart—The University of Melbourne: Decades of Challenge* (Melbourne: Melbourne University Press).

Pringle, J.M.D. (1958) *Australian Accent* (London: Chatto & Windus).

Raven, C.C. (1943) *Science, Religion and the Future* (Cambridge, UK: Cambridge University Press).

Remarque, E.M. (1996) *All Quiet on the Western Front* (London: Vintage Books).

Renshaw, P. (1976) *Nine Days That Shook Britain* (New York: Anchor Books).

Rivett, K. (ed.) (1962) *Control or Colour Bar? The Background to the White Australia Policy and a Proposal for Change* (Melbourne: Melbourne University Press).

Rivett, R. (1965) *Australian Citizen, Herbert Brookes 1867–1963* (Melbourne: Melbourne University Press).

Robinson, J.A.T. (1963) *Honest to God* (London: SCM Press).

Ross, L. (1947) A Socialist on Democracy, *Australian Quarterly*, vol. 19, no. 3, pp. 69–82.

Rowse, A.L. (1985) *Oxford in the History of the Nation* (London: Weidenfeld & Nicolson).

Rowse, T. (2002) *Nugget Coombs: A Reforming Life* (Cambridge, UK: Cambridge University Press).

Rubinstein, W.D. (1979) The Distribution of Personal Wealth in Victoria, 1860–1974, *Australian Economic History Review*, vol. 19, pp. 26–41.

Russell, E.W. (1972) *The Slum Abolition Movement in Victoria, 1933–7* (Melbourne: Hornet Publications).

Sayers, S. (1980) *Ned Herring: A Life of Sir Edmund Herring* (Melbourne: Hyland House).

Scarrow, H.A. (1965) *The Higher Public Service of the Commonwealth of Australia* (Cambridge, UK: Cambridge University Press).

Schedvin, C.B. (1970) *Australia and the Great Depression: A Study of Economic Development and Policy in the 1920s and 1930s* (Sydney: Sydney University Press).

Selth, D.V. (1973) Innovation by Stealth: Area Schools in Tasmania, in S. Murray-Smith (ed.), *Melbourne Studies in Education, 1973* (Melbourne: Melbourne University Press), pp. 175–91.

Semmler, C. (1978) Headmaster of the ABC, *Good Weekend*, 6 May.

Semmler, C. (1981) *The ABC: Aunt Sally and Sacred Cow* (Melbourne: Melbourne University Press).

Semmler, C. (1991) *Pictures on the Margin: Memoirs* (Brisbane: Queensland University Press).

Serle, G. (1987) *The Creative Spirit in Australia: A Cultural History* (Melbourne: William Heinemman).

Slee, P. (1987) Professor Sofer's 'History at Oxford', *Historical Journal*, vol. 30, no. 4, pp. 933–42.

Sofer, R. (1987) Nation, Duty, Character and Confidence: History at Oxford, 1850–1914, *Historical Journal*, vol. 30, no. 1, pp. 77–104.

Spaull, A.D. (1982) *Australian Education in the Second World War* (Brisbane: University of Queensland Press).

Spaull, A.D. (1987) *A History of the Australian Education Council, 1936–1986* (Sydney: Allen & Unwin).

Spaull, A.D. (1998) *John Dedman: A Most Unexpected Labour Man* (Melbourne: Hyland House).

Sutcliffe, D.B. (1991) The United World Colleges, in P.L. Jonietz and D. Harris (eds) *World Yearbook of Education 1991* (London: Kogan Page), pp. 25–37.

Sutcliffe, D.B. (2013) *Kurt Hahn and the United World Colleges with Other Founding Figures* (London: Butler, Tanner and Dennis).

Symons, R. (1986) *Oxford and Empire: The Last Lost Cause?* (London: Macmillan).

Teilhard de Chardin, P. (1959) *The Phenomenon of Man* (London: Collins).

Thomas, B. (ed.) (1957) *Repton, 1557–1957* (London: B.T. Batsford).

Timpson, T. (1984) A Registrar Remembers, *Unicorn*, vol. 10, no. 2, pp. 105–24.

U'Ren, N. and Turnbull, N. (1983) *A History of Port Melbourne* (Melbourne: Oxford University Press).

Vachell, H. (1905) *The Hill: A Romance of Friendship* (London: George Newnes).

Vamplew, W. and McLean, I. (1987) Transport and Communication, in W. Vamplew (ed.) *Australians: Historical Statistics* (Sydney: Fairfax, Syme & Weldon), pp. 166–82.

Waddy, L. (1981) *The King's School, 1831–1981: An Account* (Sydney: David Ell Press).

Walter, J. (1980) *The Leader: A Political Biography of Gough Whitlam* (Brisbane: University of Queensland Press).

Ward, R. (1985) Geelong at the Centre, *Overland*, vol. 101, pp. 7–12.

Watson, J. (1989) No mean city?: Christchurch's Labour city council during the depression, 1927–35, *New Zealand Journal of History*, vol. 23, no. 2, pp. 124–41.

Waugh, A. (1972) *The Loom of Youth* (London: Grant Richards).

Weatherby, W.J. (1983) *Chariots of Fire* (London: Collins).

Wells, H.G. (1939) *Travels of a Republican Radical in Search of Hot Water* (Harmondsworth, UK: Penguin).

Whately, R.K. (1937) The Measurement of Abilities, *Australian Educational Review*, vol. 9, no. 2, pp. 17–20.

Williams, R. (1961) *The Long Revolution* (Harmondsworth, UK: Penguin Books).

Wolfson, H. (1964) The Ideology Makers, *Dissent*, vol. 12, pp. 3–8.

Woolf, V. (1966) *Three Guineas* (New York: Harcourt Brace Jovanovich).

Wright Mills, C. (1951) *White Collar: The American Middle Classes* (New York: Galaxy Books).

Yule, P. (2006) *Ian Potter: A Biography* (Melbourne: Miegunyah Press).

INDEX

Throughout this index, James Ralph Darling is referred to as JRD; '*pl.*' indicates an illustration in one of the plates sections. Familial relationships in italic type describe the person's affiliation to JRD. Names in parentheses indicate a nickname or name by which the person was known.

JRD wrote and spoke extensively, and his publications are discussed throughout the book; this index lists the titles of specific publications mentioned in the text and their main topics. Unless otherwise stated, publications listed in inverted commas are by JRD.